A Diagnostic Approach to Organizational Behavior

Fourth Edition

Judith R. Gordon

Carroll School of Management
Boston College

ALLYN and BACON
Boston   London   Toronto   Sydney   Tokyo   Singapore

EDITOR-IN-CHIEF, BUSINESS AND ECONOMICS: Richard Wohl
SENIOR DEVELOPMENT EDITOR: Judith S. Fifer
ASSISTANT DEVELOPMENT EDITOR: Carol Alper
COVER ADMINISTRATOR: Linda Dickinson
COMPOSITION BUYER: Linda Cox
MANUFACTURING BUYER: Megan Cochran
COVER DESIGNER: Hemingway Design Assoc.
PRODUCTION ADMINISTRATOR: Deborah Brown
EDITORIAL-PRODUCTION SERVICE: P. M. Gordon Associates

Copyright © 1993, 1991, 1987, 1983 by Allyn and Bacon
A Division of Simon & Schuster, Inc.
160 Gould Street
Needham Heights, MA 02194

Library of Congress Cataloging-in-Publication Data

Gordon, Judith R.
    A diagnostic approach to organizational behavior / Judith R. Gordon.—4th ed.
       p.   cm.
    Includes bibliographical references and index.
    ISBN 0–205–14520–5
    1. Organizational behavior. I. Title.
HD58.7.G67 1993
658.3—dc20   92–16368
                                       CIP

To my family—near and far

PRINTED IN THE UNITED STATES OF AMERICA
10 9 8 7 6 5 4 3 2 1   97 96 95 94 93 92

Brief Contents

Contents

PART III   Diagnosing Group Behavior

Chapter 7   Developing Better Communication   *271*

Chapter 8   Evaluating Leadership and Leading Effectively   *327*

PART IV   Diagnosing Behavior at the Organizational Level

PART V   Implementing the Diagnostic Approach and Organizational Effectiveness

Preface

A Dual Emphasis

The fourth edition of *A Diagnostic Approach to Organizational Behavior* resembles previous editions in its dual emphasis. First, it focuses on *diagnosis:* describing, understanding, and explaining behavior in organizations. Second, it considers *action:* controlling, managing, or influencing behavior. This book includes text, readings, cases, exercises, and extensive examples of organizational situations. It draws from both the current and historical organizational behavior literature; therefore endnotes cite primarily research and thinking of the last decade but also include key earlier works.

The book is designed for students of organizational behavior at all levels. Undergraduate students, graduate students, and practitioners can study it to enrich their understanding of human behavior and subsequently improve their action effectiveness as organizational members.

New to This Edition

The fourth edition differs from earlier editions in its strong integration of issues associated with managing in a global economy and leading a multicultural work force. It also considers the ethical responsibilities of organizational members and leaders. This book incorporates the most current thinking in each area of organizational behavior; note particularly changes in the discussion of individual differences and work force diversity, group dynamics and teamwork, leadership, organizational design, and the management of technology.

The Diagnostic Approach

The diagnostic approach combines theory and practice by encouraging students to learn organizational theories, experience behavior in organizations, and then apply the theories to the analysis of these experiences. Taking this approach should stimulate effective employee performance, as well as facilitate effective managerial action.

Also new to this edition are edited CNN videos that provide the basis for some of the exercises; the videos feature current topics such as sexual harassment and intrapreneurship, or outstanding managers like Herb Kelleher of Southwest Airlines. They provide students with a real-life look at management in action.

The diagnostic approach encourages the application of diverse conceptual and theoretical frameworks to a situational analysis. The complexity of organizations and their environments makes it unlikely that any one theory will provide a definitive answer to all questions about how people in organizations act. Superleadership complements but differs from transformational leadership. Expectancy theories of motivation differ from needs theories. Various ways of classifying organizational structure—by means of coordination, type of specialization, or sets of alliances, for example—exist. Yet, the various theories can complement each other, and each can provide insight into individual, group, and organizational functioning and lead to more effective managerial behavior. Understanding theories of communication, group development, individual needs, conflict, leadership, and power, among others, improves the understanding of group problem-solving. Knowing theories of motivation, learning, and communication helps managers identify issues of work design. Focusing on diverse facets of behavior improves diagnosis and ultimately action. Students are also encouraged to carefully consider the implications for organizations of functioning in a multinational and multicultural environment.

The viewpoint of this book assumes that more than one perspective can be right. Thus understanding an organizational situation includes the ability to analyze it in a number of ways, rather than to assume that any one explanation is adequate. The use of *triangulation,* or taking a multi-perspective viewpoint, to more completely understand a situation and to reinforce the accuracy of the diagnosis is a significant feature of the diagnostic approach. Students are encouraged to utilize triangulation by viewing a situation from a variety of theoretical perspectives as a way of increasing their understanding of behavior and using this enriched understanding to improve action. The thorough internalization of new theories and concepts for regular use in observing and understanding behavior follows as a result of practice in diagnosis. More effective action can then occur since more effective action follows more accurate diagnosis. Of course, experienced managers do not try all approaches in each situation; they choose the tools that fit and help. As students become more practiced in using the diagnostic approach, they too become more adept in immediately selecting the appropriate frameworks to apply.

This book presents several processes for practicing diagnosis and action. First, students are asked to analyze a situation using various theoretical perspectives one at a time. Second, they are presented with an ambiguous case study and asked to identify diverse perspectives that help understand the events in the case; they analyze the situation from the various perspectives; and they suggest action on the basis of the perspectives. Finally, students are asked to observe their own and others' behavior in organizational simulations, analyze it from diverse perspectives, and consider the implications for action. The book encourages the use of a multifaceted pedagogy, where materials presented in text, cases, and exercises provide mutual reinforcement and practice in using the diagnostic approach.

Text Plus Readings, Cases, and Exercises

This book provides an integrated presentation of each topic, using text, readings, case analyses, and exercises to apply the diagnostic approach. The book is designed to be versatile in its use. Each chapter includes a presentation of key theories or concepts regarding a particular topic, and cases and exercises that allow the application of the theoretical perspectives to diverse situations; most also include a reading that examines a contemporary issue discussed in the chapter in greater depth. Each chapter includes a summary of the textual material as well as concluding comments intended to integrate the text and readings with the outcomes of the case discussions and exercises.

Readings are an integral part of the book because

they present the thinking of current writers and researchers in the field of organizational behavior. The readings have been selected to provide critical elaborations of core concepts and to consider organizational issues from diverse approaches. They include theoretical formulations, research reports, descriptions of organizational programs, and commentaries about organizational issues. Discussion questions following each reading highlight these concepts and their contribution to diagnosing organizational behavior and acting effectively in organizations.

Cases offer the unique advantage of allowing students to experience a real-life situation without leaving the classroom. As in real-life situations, the complexity of the human actions provides a significant challenge to the students' diagnostic skills. We can analyze the behavior that occurs and offer solutions for improving individual, group, and/or organizational effectiveness without suffering the consequences of inaccurate diagnosis or inappropriate recommendations. Students are encouraged first to list the facts of the case. They then identify the key managerial and behavioral issues in the situation. In problem situations they next specify the symptoms that indicate problems exist, as well as describe and show other evidence of the problems in the case. In all situations they then apply relevant theoretical models to diagnose the situation more thoroughly. They conclude by offering a prescription or plan for managerial action, directed at acting effectively or remedying a problem situation.

Finally, *exercises* give students practice in responding to situations similar to those they might experience as a member of an organization. The exercises may call for students to make certain decisions, redesign jobs, or plan ways to correct a dysfunctional situation. Students may be asked to participate in role plays, where they act the part of a character in a work situation; to complete self-assessment questionnaires or interviews; and to participate in other activities that encourage the description and diagnosis of their own and others' behavior followed by the prescription and implementation of effective action.

Organization and Content

The book begins with an introductory chapter which describes the diagnostic approach and illustrates it using numerous historical perspectives on organizational behavior. The book next discusses individual behavior. It then moves to an examination of interactions among individuals in group behavior and teamwork, which builds on knowledge of individual behavior and individual interactions. Finally, the book presents organizational issues; this discussion incorporates our knowledge of individuals and groups. Thus the organization of the book reflects a key feature of the diagnostic approach: viewing behavior from an increasing number of different but complementary, more complex but elaborating perspectives.

More specifically, in Part I, Chapter 1 sets the stage by defining the diagnostic approach. The first chapter also details various historical perspectives on behavior in organizations, concluding with a discussion of the contingency perspective that is the foundation of the diagnostic approach.

Chapter 2 begins Part II, which focuses on individual behavior, by describing perception, attribution, learning, and attitudes. Chapter 3 introduces perspectives related to individual personality differences, variations in personal development, role conflict, and stress experienced by individuals. Chapter 4 presents various theories of motivation.

Chapter 5, which begins Part III, discusses team performance and group dynamics. Chapter 6 examines decision making. Chapter 7 looks at communication. In Chapter 8, the role of leadership and management in dealing with groups is discussed. Chapter 9 considers the use of power in organizations and the process of negotiation. Chapter 10 concludes the discussion of group behavior and provides a transition to organizational issues by describing conflict management and intergroup behavior.

In Part IV, large-scale organizational issues are discussed and prescriptions for changing organizations are emphasized. Chapters 11 and 12 investigate the structures of organizations and the factors that influence their design. Chapter 13 considers the management of technology, innovation, and work design.

Part V concludes the book with Chapter 14, which discusses organizational change and organizational effectiveness. It also summarizes the role the diagnostic approach plays in increasing such effectiveness.

New Supplements Package

The supplements package that accompanies the text has been improved and expanded. *The Instructor's Manual,* by Robert Goddard of Appalachian State University, provides lecture outlines as well as teaching notes for the cases and activities. The *Manual* is available on computer disk, for instructors to add their own lecture notes or other information. The *Instructor's Manual* also includes CNN video notes and teaching suggestions prepared by Dr. Patrick Vann of the University of Colorado at Boulder.

The *Test Bank,* also by Robert Goddard, has been expanded, and is now available in a computerized format called the Allyn and Bacon Test Manager, for IBM-compatible PCs. Finally, a videotape containing actual edited CNN video programs is available; the CNN videos can be shown in conjunction with student exercises and activities in the text.

Acknowledgments

The development of this book has been influenced by the contributions of many individuals. First, I would like to thank adopters and reviewers of this and previous editions of *A Diagnostic Approach to Organizational Behavior:* Donald Baack, Pittsburg State University; Joanna Banthin, New Jersey Institute of Technology; James Daily, Wright State University; Cynthia Fukami, University of Denver; Robert Goddard, Appalachian State University; George Jacobs, Middle Tennessee State University; Dewey E. Johnson, California State University at Fresno; Bruce H. Kemelgor, University of Louisville; Vicki LaFarge, Bentley College; George Lyne, Appalachian State University; James McElroy, Iowa State University; Kris Mohandie, Woodbury University; Paula C. Morrow, Iowa State University; Elizabeth Ravlin, University of North Carolina; Richard Sebastian, St. Cloud State University; Kim A. Stewart, University of Denver; and Mary Anne Watson, University of Tampa.

I would also like to thank my colleagues at the Carroll School of Management at Boston College for their enthusiastic adoption of the book and their suggestions for its improvement. I also wish to thank the Dean of the School of Management, John J. Neuhauser III, for his support. I extend a special thank you to Susan Griffin who provided research and administrative assistance in the preparation of this revision. Thanks also to the professionals at Allyn and Bacon who worked on this edition: Rich Wohl, Editor-in-Chief, Business; Judith Fifer, Senior Development Editor; Carol Alper, Assistant Development Editor; and Deborah Brown, Production Editor.

My deepest thanks go to my extended family, whose support and enthusiasm have been greatly appreciated. Most of all, I would like to thank my husband and children, who create the chaos in which my work flourishes.

Chapter Outline

Setting the Stage

Learning Objectives

After completing the reading in Chapter 1, students will be able to

1. Cite three reasons why an understanding of organizational behavior is important to managers and other organizational members.

2. Discuss organizational behavior as a field of study.

3. Comment about the significance of a multicultural work force for organizational behavior.

4. Describe the impact of working for multinational organizations and in a global economy.

5. Describe the diagnostic approach.

6. Compare and contrast four methods of data collection and three types of research design.

7. Identify, compare, and contrast the major periods and perspectives in the history of organizational thought.

8. Illustrate the application of the diagnostic approach by using one or more historical perspectives to diagnose an organizational situation.

9. Comment on the way contingency theory addresses shortcomings of previous theories and meshes with the diagnostic approach.

Organizational Behavior in the Advertising Firm

Barker and Bolton, Inc., specializes in providing advertising and public relations services to high-technology clients in the electronics, communications, biotechnology, and computer fields. It is one of the largest agencies in the United States, having been formed by a merger of several medium-sized advertising firms. Many of its clients are multinational firms that do business in a wide range of European, Oriental, and South American countries. Barker and Bolton itself has staff members in a dozen countries, primarily in North America and Europe.

John Mercer, a certified public accountant, is the manager of the Accounting Department. He is responsible for ensuring the correct implementation of the company's policies both in the United States and abroad, interpreting new federal and international laws and regulations that apply to accounting practices in the firm, managing interactions with other department heads who must provide information for the accounting function, and supervising a staff of twenty managers, staff accountants, and clerical personnel.

Recently John has been experiencing some perplexing problems in performing his job. He has found that managers of other departments are increasingly asking his boss to approve practices that he has denied. Most recently, for example, the Creative Services Department under the leadership of Jennifer Wayne unilaterally changed its reporting of client hours in a way that does not mesh with the accounting system being used. For John, the most alarming part of the change was that Creative Services implemented it after John had specifically told them that in his opinion it was not the best way to report performance, would cause the Accounting Department significant delays in processing the information required to bill customers and pay vendors, was contrary to general accounting standards, and thus was not in the best interest of Barker and Bolton. Nevertheless, during a regular meeting, Jennifer Wayne convinced John's boss, Jack Ballantyne, whose title was vice president for administration, that the change was in the best interests of the department and the company and that John Mercer was being a bullheaded impediment to progress.

John had experienced a similar situation with the director of one of their European field offices. John had sent Marie Fabreau, the director of the Paris office, a directive about the schedule for reporting client billings. They had exchanged telephone calls and memos by fax about the matter. In the end, Marie seemed to ignore John's suggestions and created her own reporting schedule, again seemingly with the approval of John's boss. John has repeatedly tried to talk with his boss about these and other similar situations, but has had no success in preventing Jack Ballantyne from overruling him.

Even his own subordinates have been giving him a hard time recently. He learned from one of his friends in the Information Systems Department that several of his subordinates had complained to Jack Ballantyne about the disorganization in the Accounting Department and their feeling that John never listened to their concerns or suggestions; they also felt that John was "watching their every move." This complaint really surprised John because he felt that he gave his subordinates a great deal of autonomy and thought he had a good working relationship with them. He knew that it had taken him some time to learn to work with some of the newest hires. Their personal and professional experiences differed greatly from John's, and it took John a while to realize that they could do the work as well as the employees whose backgrounds were more like his. Still, he felt that a few "troublemakers" were giving him a bad reputation in the company.

Together these problems were having a significant effect on productivity in the department. They were also contributing to what John felt were some flawed corporate policy decisions.

● ● ● ● ● ● ● ● ● ● ● ● ● ● ● ● ● ●

*L*ike John Mercer, Jack Ballantyne, Marie Fabreau, Jennifer Wayne, and the members of the Accounting Department, we all belong to organizations. We work in organizations, are educated in organizations, and have our needs for such things as food, clothing, and recreation met by organizations. Often we find that our identity is tightly bound up with the organizations to which we belong. We are expected to act in an ethically responsible way in our role as organizational members. These organizations are composed of a diverse mix of employees, each of whom brings unique concerns, experiences, and aspirations to his or her job. Increasingly these organizations function in the global arena, multiplying the number and complexity of the issues and concerns that individual employees, managers, and top executives face.

THE IMPORTANCE OF ORGANIZATIONAL BEHAVIOR TO MANAGERS

As members of organizations, especially of work organizations, we are likely to face situations similar to the ones John, his boss, his coworkers, and his subordinates encountered. Managers must understand organizational behavior to ensure their own and others' performance and satisfaction. They must understand the way organizational behavior may change as a work force becomes more diverse and as organizations operate in a large number of countries and cultures. Good management enables organizations to be productive and effective. Why did Jennifer Wayne and Marie Fabreau go to John Mercer's boss to overrule decisions John was making? Why did his subordinates complain about his leadership? Why did productivity in the Accounting Department decrease? What can or should be done about the employees' attitudes toward John and the policies he suggests?

This case describes a situation neither new nor unique to Barker and Bolton, Inc. Many managers must deal with employees who do not produce in the way that the manager expects. Many bosses act in ways counter to their employees' hopes and desires. The director of Creative Services and the director of the Paris office, for example, "go over John's head" to his boss when they disagree with John's directives. John's boss overrules his decisions with no explanation to John. John's own work group, who initially supported his decisions, have become progressively more dissatisfied. John may be experiencing the difficulty of managing in an increasingly complex global environment with a multicultural work force. Clearly Barker and Bolton is experiencing leadership and management problems, which may ultimately affect the company's success.

How do situations such as these occur? Changes in the external environment of the work situation, such as the increased competition, requirements for new products, or increased pressures from customers for early delivery, may cause positive or negative reactions from workers. Changes in the arena in which a company does business, such as expansion into new international markets or acquisition of additional product lines or customers, may contribute to the need to change the way a company or department is managed. Changes in the resources available for a project, such as the alteration of the work force through hirings, layoffs, resignations, or terminations, the reduction of financial resources available for a project, or changes in scheduled due dates or completion schedules, may affect workers' satisfaction, involvement, performance, and attendance. Does the situation of the Accounting Department describe such changes? Or does it describe ineffective leadership, lack of employee motivation, ineffective communication, dysfunctional teamwork, or inappropriate organizational structure? The situation could result from any of these problems or, more likely, from several of them.

Insights from the field of organizational behavior help us to better understand the situation faced by John Mercer and the other employees at Barker and Bolton. These insights help us not only to describe organizational situations and problems, but also to diagnose them and determine reasons the situations exist as they do, to develop prescriptions for effective action, and to take action as appropriate to deal with the situations faced.

ORGANI-
ZATIONAL
BEHAVIOR
DEFINED AND
STUDIED

Organizational behavior is defined as the actions and attitudes of people in organizations. It is also a body of knowledge and a field of study about organizations and their members. Organizational behavior has its roots in the social-science disciplines of psychology, sociology, anthropology, economics, and political science, and it applies the models, or ways of thinking, of these areas to the study of people's behavior in organizations. For example, it addresses issues such as the following, which may be relevant to the case, and which are shown in Figure 1–1:

- What facilitates accurate perception and attribution?
- What influences individual, group, and organizational learning and the development of individual attitudes toward work?
- How do individual differences in personality, personal development, and career development affect individuals' behaviors and attitudes?
- What motivates people to work, and how does the organization's reward system influence worker behavior and attitudes?
- How do managers build effective teams?
- What contributes to effective decision making?
- What constitutes effective communication?
- What characterizes effective leadership?
- How can power be secured and used productively?
- What factors contribute to effective negotiations?
- How can conflict (between groups or between a manager and subordinates) be resolved or managed?
- How can jobs and organizations be effectively designed?
- How can managers help workers deal effectively with change?

Organizational behavior as a field of study represents more than a mere collection of separate theories and models. Rather, the field offers the opportunity to apply several different perspectives simultaneously to the understanding of specific, concrete events such as those faced by John Mercer and others at Barker and Bolton, Inc. Thus it offers the chance to understand some of the *complexity* of organizations and of organizational dilemmas and situations, and to understand that most organizational problems have several causes. Increasingly the study of organizational behavior also considers the factors that contribute to or hinder effective performance in the global arena; recognizing that significant differences exist between national companies, multinationals, and companies that function totally outside the United

Figure 1–1 **Potential Issues in Organizational Behavior at Barker and Bolton**

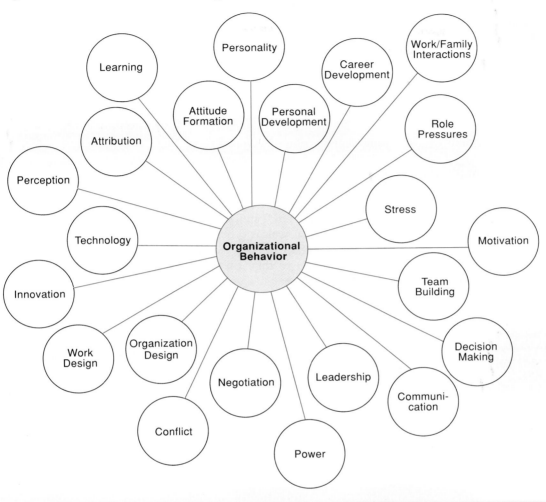

States is important for diagnosing the causes of functional and dysfunctional behaviors. The more fully we understand all the reasons for specific organizational events or problems, the more we can respond appropriately to them. The better John Mercer understands the reasons his decisions are being overruled and his subordinates are becoming disenchanted with his leadership, the more easily he can determine appropriate action for correcting the problems that cause this situation. Organizational-behavior principles play an essential role in determining organizational effectiveness, which is a central responsibility and focus for all managers.

The primary objective of this book is to make use of this capacity of organizational behavior: to develop the ability to *understand* organizational events as fully as possible and then to *act effectively* on the basis of this understanding. We are defining the application of knowledge and skill to a real situation as diagnosis. Accurate diagnosis forms the basis for effective action.

ORGANIZATIONAL BEHAVIOR AND THE MULTICULTURAL WORK FORCE

Complicating the management of organizations such as Barker and Bolton are the dramatic changes occurring in the composition of the work force. Managers such as John Mercer will supervise work teams with racial, gender, ethnic, and national diversity. For example, by the end of the 1990s, 33 percent of Americans will be nonwhite, and more than 33 percent will be 65 or older; 85 percent of new entrants into the work force will not be white males.[1] Managers are being asked or required to create a multicultural organization because increasing the diversity of the work force is seen as facilitating success in a multicultural world environment, as described in the next section.[2] As the director of international human resources at Weyerhaeuser Company noted, "Competing requires full utilization of all our resources that will provide critical leverage in a more competitive business environment. If we can't effectively recruit, train, and motivate, we will lose out; we won't be able to compete in the marketplace."[3] Managing diversity may include sensitivity and awareness training about cultural differences, addressing the relationship between individual supervisors and subordinates, and creating a culture that supports diversity.[4] It also requires a recognition that relationships, tasks, individual identity, social structure, communication, and time orientation, as well as other factors, differ in various cultures; for example, U.S. managers expect workers to maintain eye contact and be facially expressive, which may be counter to their own cultural expectations.[5] We highlight such differences throughout this book.

ORGANIZATIONAL BEHAVIOR AS A GLOBAL PHENOMENON

Multiculturalism extends beyond the borders of the United States. Companies are expanding into worldwide markets, and personnel are moving more freely across international borders as they conduct business. Barker and Bolton, described in the introductory scenario, has offices in the United States and abroad and thus must deal with a complex stream of laws, regulations, and personnel issues. Yet, "Americans have developed theories without being sufficiently aware of non-U.S. contexts, models, research, and values."[6] The cultural orientations of societies vary in terms of the nature and adaptability of people, the relationship of people to nature, the relationship of people to other people, the primary mode of activity, members' conception of space, and members' time orientation.[7] Only recently have researchers generated a significant body of literature about managing in a global environment.[8] This book emphasizes cross-cultural management and incorporates current research and thinking about international issues related to organizational behavior into the discussions.

THE DIAGNOSTIC APPROACH

What is the first step John Mercer and his boss should take to address the problems they face? They could just pick a quick solution: John could live with the situation as it exists now; he could fire his discontented staff and replace them with individuals more likely to be loyal to him; he could ask Jack Ballantyne to refuse to overrule him; he could take a leadership training course.

Will any of these actions be effective? Which would be the most effective? How do we know? Responding to a problem with the wrong solution may cause no improvement in the situation or may seriously magnify the existing problems. Before a person responds to or acts in a given situation, that person must first understand, as fully as possible, what is happening. John Mercer should *diagnose* the present situation. After a complete diagnosis, he can *act* by prescribing and implementing appropriate solutions.

We diagnose when we first describe a situation, behavior, or attitude, and then identify its components and causes. In examining the case of John Mercer and the Accounting Department, for example, we must first identify the key elements of the situation. John sees a change in his relationships with other department directors and his subordinates. He makes decisions that are overruled by his superior. He has difficulty in working with other managers both in the United States and abroad. His subordinates complain about his leadership style: they say that he does not give them enough autonomy, that he monitors their activities and progress too closely. We also know that several *symptoms* exist; symptoms are indicators that a problem situation exists. Here, for example, employee satisfaction and performance have declined.

Second, we can identify several problems or potential causes of these behaviors and attitudes. John uses an autocratic style of management that may not be appropriate for the situation. He also seems to be experiencing difficulty in communicating with his peers and his boss. John seems unable to motivate either his subordinates, his peers, or his boss to act in the way he expects and desires. In addition, John has been unsuccessful in negotiating with at least two of the directors about accounting procedures. Complete diagnosis would involve a full specification of all relevant aspects of a given situation. Often additional information must be collected, or the situation must be described more fully. Hypothesizing links between various facets of the situation may be required to complete the diagnosis; for example, testing the implications of leadership style for employees' behavior, the effect of organizational structure on management's actions, or the way in which sources of power affect subordinates' responses to management directives may be essential for John Mercer to diagnose the problems he is experiencing. Understanding the role of international issues, such as factors that uniquely affect his interactions with Marie Fabreau, is also essential. Finally, recognizing issues associated with managing a diverse work force is key. After identifying all possible causes of the situation, we can determine the likelihood that each of these potential causes affects the situation we have described. Ineffective leadership and faulty communication seem likely problems in the opening case; intergroup conflict between departments and faulty job design seem less likely. We can use the various theories presented in this book to help us evaluate the relevance of each potential cause to the situation.

Then we can prescribe and eventually implement a course of action for correcting the situation. Such a course of action, based on a strong diagnosis, should be more effective than action based on very little understanding of the problem. Correcting defective leadership calls for different strategies than does improving an inefficient organizational design; changing group norms calls for different approaches than does building new bases of power. Throughout this book you will be encouraged to understand organizational events or problems as fully as you can before deciding how you wish to respond to them; diagnosis precedes action. Even if no problem exists, applying the diagnostic approach allows a manager to anticipate potential difficulties and prevent their occurring by early effective action.

Diagnosis is a key skill for effective managers. Figure 1–2 shows the diagnostic approach proposed in this book for use by managers and other organizational members. This approach includes four phases: (1) description; (2) diagnosis; (3) prescription; (4) action.

DESCRIPTION Phase 1, *description*, is simply that: a reporting of concrete aspects of or events in a specific situation without any attempt to explain the reasons for the events, or to make inferences about a person's motives or purposes.

Figure 1–2 **The Diagnostic Approach**

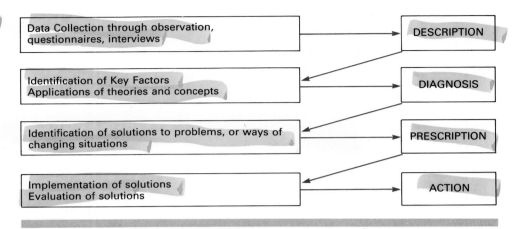

Data Collection through observation, questionnaires, interviews	→	DESCRIPTION
Identification of Key Factors Applications of theories and concepts	←	DIAGNOSIS
Identification of solutions to problems, or ways of changing situations	←	PRESCRIPTION
Implementation of solutions Evaluation of solutions	←	ACTION

The Process of Description

In the Accounting Department at Barker and Bolton, for example, we can describe a number of concrete and observable occurrences. John Mercer's decisions are being overturned. His subordinates complain frequently about his leadership style. Jack Ballantyne has not stopped overruling John's decisions. Employee satisfaction has decreased. In analyzing any situation, then, you can begin by listing the facts. In addition to the occurrences just described, we also know that John has asked his boss to stop overturning his decisions, that his employees feel that he monitors their behavior too closely, and that two directors have ignored his decisions and implemented ones they preferred. In analyzing this or other situations you might also specify any assumptions you are making about the events. For example, you might assume that the workers have a legitimate right to influence the way they are managed, that complaints signal the existence of a problem situation, or that effective managers respond to employees' complaints. As much as possible you should test these assumptions to identify any that can be added to the list of facts.

The process of simple description is much more difficult than it looks: sometimes it is not easy to separate facts from assumptions. Most of us have little practice in making such a separation. Yet, effective diagnosis and understanding of the situation depend on a valid and factual description of it. The better we can describe situations, the better we will understand them. So, throughout this book you will be given opportunities to describe what you have read or seen.

In the case of the Accounting Department at Barker and Bolton, we base our description primarily on the summary of the situation presented in the introduction to this chapter. This description is probably not complete; nuances of attitudes and seemingly insignificant behaviors may be excluded. Nor does description completely recount the views of the members of the Accounting Department, Jennifer Wayne, Marie Fabreau, Jack Ballantyne, or even John Mercer. In dealing with real organizational situations, we would attempt to secure a full description of the actual organizational events as they occur.

Methods of Data Collection

How can we obtain information that allows us to describe events, behaviors, and attitudes accurately? Managers and organizational researchers primarily use four methods for collecting data about situations they face or analyze: direct observation, questionnaires, interviews, and written documents. Each of these methods helps us to report events, not to diagnose their causes or effects. Together these methods help us validate our perceptions of the events, as described in greater detail in Chapter 2.

Direct Observation When as managers or organizational researchers we use direct observation, we describe concrete events that we see. We might, for example, spend some time attending staff meetings of the Accounting Department and then describe what we see happening, such as who talks most often, what topics they discuss, or how frequently John Mercer asks for his subordinates' views on a subject. We can construct formal instruments to use in collecting and tabulating our observations or we can rely on more informal commentaries. For example, we can watch the actions of the department members as they wait for an elevator, sit in the company lounge, or meet in the hallways. We can listen to their conversations and thereby learn their expressed attitudes toward their supervisor, job, or organization.

Questionnaires Rather than relying on our view of events, we can write questions designed to elicit organization members' opinions. We might develop a questionnaire that we distribute to all members of the Accounting Department to help determine their attitudes toward their jobs and their supervisor. Analyzing the responses to such a questionnaire at Barker and Bolton might help explicate the dissatisfaction of members of the Accounting Department. Repeated administration of such a questionnaire might indicate changes over time in their attitude toward the organization. Note that the use of questionnaires is quite common in the United States but less frequent in other countries.

Interviews We could also ask organization members a series of questions in person to explore in depth their attitudes and opinions. Managers often "interview" employees informally, chatting with them about their views of a particular situation. We might, for example, interview several department heads at Barker and Bolton to discuss their experiences with the Accounting Department and John Mercer. We might interview Jack Ballantyne to learn his rationale for overruling John Mercer's decisions. We would then describe their experiences and attitudes as part of the first step in the diagnostic approach.

Written Documents Finally, we could gather data about past performance, work team behavior, or other aspects of individual, group, and organizational functioning from the firm's records, including annual reports, departmental evaluations, memoranda, or nonconfidential personnel files. Then we can analyze the content of these documents. At Barker and Bolton, for example, an examination of accounting policy and its effect on profitability might suggest the existence and nature of a performance problem. A review of records, such as all internal memoranda or performance reviews, might further specify the nature of communication, the quality of supervision, or other possible reasons for the situation in the Accounting Department.

DIAGNOSIS The next phase, *diagnosis,* attempts to explain the reasons for, or causes of, the behaviors and attitudes described. This book will offer and describe a number of theories that people studying organizational behavior have developed to explain why events such as these occur. You can then use these theories to diagnose the situations or problems that exist. You can apply them in sequence and test whether they help you understand the situation better. Once you know and understand the theories you can choose the most appropriate ones to use in diagnosis. In the case of Barker and Bolton, for example, we might believe that John's leadership style is the major reason for the declining performance and increasing dissatisfaction; we might argue that John has failed to communicate effectively with his subordinates, peers, or superior.

Focusing on leadership as a problem at Barker and Bolton, for example, we might explore whether John's style fits with the requirements of the situation, whether he demonstrates transformational leadership, or whether his leadership behavior is reinforced. Alternatively, we might consider whether John fails to use two-way communication or has difficulty communicating with individuals who are different from himself; the multicultural work force at Barker and Bolton may create a barrier to communication both in the Accounting Department and with directors in other countries. Applying leadership and communication theories such as these, among others, helps us gain greater understanding of the reasons people such as John and his subordinates act as they do, and the reasons our behavior is more effective in some circumstances than in others.

Research Methods

Organizational researchers and occasionally other organizational members use systematic research methods to determine the causes of events, behaviors, or attitudes.[9] Laboratory experiments, field studies, or even simulations (often computerized) of organizational situations can assist in the diagnosis of the causes of certain behaviors and attitudes.

Laboratory Experiments

In laboratory experiments, researchers choose a phenomenon to study, such as obedience to authority, risk taking in decision making, or conflict in negotiations. They attempt to control all extraneous stimuli so that they can pinpoint the cause of certain behaviors. They simplify organizational phenomena under study to determine precisely the causes of behaviors or attitudes. Although such studies do not capture the complexity of organizational life, a set of these studies about a particular topic considered together may explain behavior outside the laboratory. No laboratory study acknowledges, for example, that risk behavior is a function of the interaction of such factors as individual personality, characteristics of the organization, and pressures exerted by group membership. Considering all laboratory studies about risk behavior together may result in identifying, without validating, a set of interactive causes. Still, the rigorous controls imposed to identify the "real cause" of the observed phenomenon often result in laboratory behavior that differs from the behavior obtained in real organizational situations. The type of risk individuals take in spending money in a laboratory may differ significantly from the risk they take when their own or their employer's resources are at stake.

Field Studies

To study behavior in more realistic settings and as it occurs naturally, researchers conduct field studies.[10] This approach differs from laboratory studies in the amount of control exerted over the behavior and the circumstances in which the behavior occurs. Here many factors can explain an observed phenomenon. Lowered performance might be attributed to changes in incentives, the personality of the subject, new organizational policies, or merely the weather. Thus, researchers can be more certain that they are obtaining "true" behavior but less certain of the correct explanations of the behavior or attitudes observed. Because field studies acknowledge the complexity of real-life situations, researchers are increasingly relying on this approach, rather than on more controlled laboratory testing.

Simulations Organizational simulations attempt to combine the advantages of laboratory and field studies. An organizational simulation is a computerized or noncomputerized facsimile of an organization that allows researchers to simultaneously study and control complex behavior. It prescribes the rules and regulations of the organization, specifies the actions and interactions of organization members, and defines the impact of various inputs and processes on the organization's functioning. Researchers manipulate the behavior or attitudes being studied as well as the circumstances in which they occur by providing diverse inputs and examining their effects. The challenge is modeling affective and behavioral responses, such as worker satisfaction and productivity, as accurately as organizational outcomes such as return on investment or market share. Because of the artificiality involved in manipulating the factors being studied, some argue that this research approach lacks realism and thus yields results of limited use. Using this method in conjunction with the other two or with the analyses described in the next sections may overcome some of its limitations.

The Steps in Diagnosis Although some managers and other organizational members rely on a more ad hoc, less controlled approach to diagnosis, applying the diagnostic approach enriches their diagnoses and ultimately improves their action. In this book, we take a specific approach to diagnosis: we assume that events, behaviors, and attitudes that occur in organizations typically have more than one cause, and that it is important to try to understand the causes as fully as possible. The more completely we understand the causes, the more appropriately we will act in organizational situations.

This approach develops diagnostic abilities in five steps, as shown in Figure 1–3. The first is to study a number of theories by themselves, without applying them to concrete situations. Students learn theories of motivation and leadership—models of effective communication and decision making, for example. The second is to indicate the ways in which the different theories help explain the reasons the situation exists as it does—how a particular theory of leadership, motivation, or

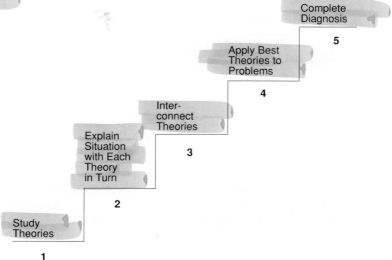

Figure 1–3 Steps in the Diagnosis Phase

organizational design, for example, might help to explain the situation faced by John Mercer or Jack Ballantyne. The third is to develop connections between the different theoretical perspectives, to see how motivation, leadership, and organizational design theories—as well as other areas addressed by the field of organizational behavior— complement each other and help to provide a richer description of organizational events. Throughout this phase it is important to be aware of the implications of managing in different cultures and with a diverse work force.

You should begin the diagnosis phase by specifying the problem or issues in the situation. To identify the problems, for example, you must first list the evidence that a problem exists. You might list, for example, the "symptoms" of increased complaints and decreased productivity in the Accounting Department. Then, reviewing these symptoms, together with the facts of the case and your assumptions, you should specify the problems in as much detail as possible. Where more than one problem exists, you should specify the relationships among the problems. For example, John Mercer's leadership style together with the Accounting Department's perception of loss of autonomy may contribute to the staff's declining performance and morale.

In the fourth step of the diagnostic approach you should apply the relevant theoretical models to the problems to increase the completeness and accuracy of your diagnosis. If, for example, the problem is ineffective leadership, you should apply several leadership theories in sequence to determine the precise deficiency in John's leadership: Does he choose the wrong style for this situation? Does he fail to perform the diverse roles of an effective manager? As you grow in experience and competence you will learn better which theories to use. Diagnosis concludes in step five when there is sufficient understanding for appropriate decision making and action. Diagnosis can also occur when the organization is not experiencing difficulties. Understanding and diagnosing the causes of functional behaviors and attitudes can facilitate continued personal and organizational performance and effectiveness.

Keep in mind that not all organizational problems and events can be understood by *all* organizational behavior models and theories. At best they only facilitate and enhance understanding—they do not produce it. The life-cycle theory of leadership described in Chapter 8 may help explain the situation faced by John Mercer and his subordinates, but the attribution theory of leadership may not. Looking at group norms may offer new insights into the situation, but looking at John's cognitive style may not. The ability to diagnose includes the ability to critically evaluate different perspectives and theories, and to determine whether they apply to each specific case. By examining the degree of fit between the theories and the key aspects of each situation, you will identify the most likely causes of specific behaviors and attitudes. You will also determine how well different perspectives apply. And, throughout the process of diagnosis, you will continually be encouraged to develop your own explanations for the events you describe.

PRESCRIPTION   Phase 3, *prescription,* involves identifying, reviewing, evaluating, and then deciding on a desired course of action for particular circumstances and based on the foregoing diagnosis. Prescription is the first part of translating diagnosis—or your understanding of a situation—into action. Managers and other organization members must *act* in problem situations and other organizational situations; they do not have the luxury of simply understanding them, although understanding alone can have value and relevance too. In the prescription phase the manager or other organizational member must propose ways of correcting the problems identified in the diagnosis phase. If, for example, you believe from your diagnosis that John Mercer is using an inappropriate leadership style, you might prescribe that John receive training in other leadership styles or obtain feedback about his performance to alter his style. If Jack Ballantyne should be communicating John's authority in decision making to his peers, then you might offer to act as a mediator in determining an appropriate decision-making process.

Most problem situations have no single correct response, in part because the problems are complex. Thus we should begin the prescription phase by proposing multiple solutions to diagnosed problems. We might recommend redesigning work, modifying the reward system, or ensuring direct communication as ways of addressing motivation problems. We might propose organizational restructuring, development of superordinate goals, or the introduction of new jobs as ways of dealing with conflict between work groups.

In this book you will be asked to suggest solutions to problems, to develop specific courses of action for different situations. You will then have the opportunity to evaluate the solutions proposed in terms of the models and theories discussed, and to test whether the recommended changes should result in the desired consequences. In the case of John Mercer, for example, you probably will prescribe a different leadership style. By comparing the style you choose to the style suggested by various leadership theories, you can predict the effectiveness of your prescription before it is implemented. Knowing what type of process the research about decision making would suggest, you can prescribe ways of ensuring that John's decisions are not inappropriately overruled.

You should consider as many reasonable, feasible, and practical alternative solutions to each problem or behavioral concern diagnosed as possible. Evaluate these alternatives and their effectiveness by using the relevant theoretical models to predict outcomes of various actions. Determine the costs and benefits of each alternative. Then select the alternative with the relatively lowest costs and highest benefits. For example, John Mercer can quantitatively or qualitatively assess the costs of training, recruitment, selection, or lost time associated with changing his leadership style or replacing many of his subordinates. He can similarly assess the likely benefits of each prescription in terms of increasing productivity. Such an assessment might indicate that in the situation faced by John Mercer, using a mediator to improve his communication with his boss and his peers may be the best alternative that has the relatively lowest costs and greatest benefits.

ACTION The final phase, *action,* is the implementation of the solutions you propose. Often we know the correct solution, but cannot apply it. We might know, for example, that John should find a way to improve communication with the other directors. But how does he actually do that? What pitfalls will he encounter in trying to translate solutions into behavior?

Action might involve testing the prescription in a limited part of the organization. Pilot programs are frequently used to implement change in organizations in measured, observable ways. Top management might introduce a bonus program or a new performance evaluation instrument. Or the executives may provide John with consultation or training about how to alter his leadership style. Experimentation might accompany effective action. Or we might simulate the action we propose using facsimiles of the organization.

Action involves a careful scrutiny of all individuals and other systems in the organization to plan for the impact of the changes. It means determining what resistances to change exist and planning strategies and activities to overcome them. Implementing staffing or policy changes might require the introduction of new education programs; new resources might be necessary to support the new programs. The effects of action may cascade through the organization.

In this book you will be given opportunities to test your ideas to see how they work in different problem situations. You can act as a manager would act in a given situation. You will then have the opportunity to evaluate these actions and consider ways of improving managerial action.

And so the cycle may start again. As part of the evaluation you will describe your own and others' behavior and attitudes. Then you can diagnose the reasons the behavior succeeded or failed, offer new prescriptions, and once more act. If John changes his leadership style, then we would expect that changes should occur in his subordinates' attitudes and productivity. We can assess whether such changes actually occurred and then act accordingly.

APPLYING THE DIAGNOSTIC APPROACH

Diagnosis is the cornerstone of effective behavior in organizations. If organizational members can understand the factors affecting themselves and others in a work situation, they have taken an important step toward effective behavior. Effective action complements quality diagnosis. Stopping at understanding a situation is insufficient. Good solutions must be prescribed and implemented.

What advantages does the diagnostic approach offer over others? It encourages managers and other organizational members to spend time on describing the situation in detail and completely diagnosing its problems as a way of understanding what is really occurring. It offers a means of applying diverse theoretical knowledge to organizational behavior and attitudes. It requires you to use and apply a range of theories to help understand in more depth a given situation or series of events. The diagnostic approach also fosters greater deliberation before jumping into prescriptions and implementing action. It encourages employers and employees to carefully evaluate the costs and benefits of various prescriptions for change. It requires them to assess the likely impact of proposed solutions and to test the fit between diagnosis and action.

Earlier viewpoints, philosophies, and schools of thought remain applicable and relevant today and can provide useful tools for description, diagnosis, prescription, and action. Tracing the history of organizational behavior provides a context for understanding the evolution of organizational behavior and effective management. By using these historical perspectives concurrently we can enrich our understanding of organizational situations because they both provide a backdrop for the development of current organizational thought and remain current and relevant to organizational diagnosis today. In the next section we briefly recount the history of organizational theory by presenting selected representative perspectives, as shown in the time line of Figure 1–4 and in Table 1–1.

Figure 1–4 **Time Line of Organizational Thought**

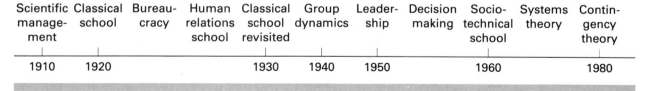

Scientific management	Classical school	Bureaucracy	Human relations school	Classical school revisited	Group dynamics	Leadership	Decision making	Socio-technical school	Systems theory	Contingency theory
1910	1920			1930	1940	1950		1960		1980

STRUCTURAL PERSPECTIVES

The earliest theorists focused on the structuring and design of work and organizations. Organizational theory prior to 1900, scientific management, classical theory, bureaucracy, and decision-making theory each addressed issues of structure in the organization.

Organizational Theory Prior to 1900

Prior to 1900, very little formal management or organizational theorizing occurred. In addition, few industrial organizations of the types we know today existed; the basic organizational models were the military and the Catholic Church. But the

Table 1–1 **Historical Schools of Thought and Their Components (by Decade)**

School	Decade	Perspective	Description
Organizational theory prior to 1900	Before 1900	Structural	Emphasized the division of labor and the importance of machinery to facilitate labor
Scientific management	1910s	Structural	Described management as a science, with employees having specific but different responsibilities; encouraged the scientific selection, training, and development of workers and the equal division of work between workers and management
Classical school	1920s	Structural	Listed the duties of a manager as planning, organizing, commanding employees, coordinating activities, and controlling performance; basic principles called for specialization of work, unity of command, scalar chain of command, and coordination of activities
Bureaucracy	1920s	Structural	Emphasized order, system, rationality, uniformity, and consistency in management; these attributes led to equitable treatment for all employees by management
Human relations	1920s	Behavioral	Focused on the importance of the attitudes and feelings of workers; informal roles and norms influenced performance
Classical school revisited	1930s	Structural	Reemphasis on the classical principles described above
Group dynamics	1940s	Behavioral	Encouraged individual participation in decision making; noted the impact of the work group on performance
Leadership	1950s	Behavioral	Stressed the importance of groups having both social and task leaders; differentiated between Theory X and Theory Y management
Decision making	1950s	Behavioral	Suggested that individuals "satisfice" when they make decisions
Sociotechnical school	1960s	Integrative	Called for considering technology and work groups when understanding a work system
Systems theory	1960s	Integrative	Represented an organization as an open system with inputs, transformations, output, and feedback; systems strive for equilibrium and experience equifinality
Contingency theory	1980s	Integrative	Emphasized the fit between organizational processes and characteristics of the situation; called for fitting the organization's structure to various contingencies

factory system had developed and was creating strong demands for theories of management.

In spite of the lack of formal theory, early economists such as Adam Smith provided the underpinnings of management theory. In his eighteenth-century book *An Inquiry into the Nature and Cause of the Wealth of Nations,* Smith included a chapter on the division of labor. In this chapter, which laid the groundwork for the later introduction of assembly-line processes, Smith spoke approvingly of a pin manufacturer that divided the work into a number of "branches," causing the separation of pin making into eighteen different operations.[11] The separation of operations radically increased the quantity of pins manufactured in a day because the workers had only to concentrate on one task. Smith also emphasized the importance of proper machinery to facilitate labor. Smith's perspective laid the foundation for later theories that were concerned with the structure of organizations and work.

Although Barker and Bolton could not have existed prior to 1900, does Adam Smith's perspective help us to understand the present situation in the Accounting Department and elsewhere in the firm? Perhaps the division of labor was not appropriate and contributed to the workers' declining performance and negative attitudes.

Scientific Management

In the early twentieth century, management emerged as a field of study with the theorizing of Frederick W. Taylor, a foreman at the Bethlehem Steel Works in Bethlehem, Pennsylvania. Taylor's observations at the turn of the century about industrial efficiency and *scientific management* focused management theory on manufacturing organizations, which had become more common after 1900, and offered prescriptions for the effective structure of organizations and design of management activities. He described management as a science with managers and employees having clearly specified yet different responsibilities. Taylor characterized a manager's responsibility in four ways:

> First. Managers develop a science for each element of a man's work, which replaces the old rule of thumb method. Second. Managers scientifically select and then train, teach, and develop the worker, whereas in the past he chose his own work and trained himself as best he could. Third. Managers heartily cooperate with the men so as to insure all of the work being done in accordance with the principles of the science which has been developed. Fourth. There is almost equal division of the work and the responsibility between the management and the workers. The management take over all the work for which they are better fitted than the workers, while in the past almost all of the work and the greater part of the responsibility were thrown upon the men.[12]

In his report of his classic experiment, Taylor showed that a pig-iron handler, who formerly loaded 12½ tons per day, loaded 47½ tons after application of the principles of scientific management.[13] Imagine, if you can, someone shoveling iron ore into a furnace. An observer, the equivalent of a modern-day industrial engineer, times how long it takes a worker to pick up a shovel, move it and the ore into a car, drop off the ore, and then prime the shovel for the next load. At the same time another observer records the precise physical movements the worker made, such as whether he picked up the shovel with his right hand or his left (no women handled iron ore at the Bethlehem Steel Works), whether he switched hands before moving it, how far apart he placed his feet, and so on. With these data, Taylor determined the physical positions that led to the fastest time for shoveling ore, and developed the "science" of shoveling. Taylor's principles had the greatest impact when applied to increasing productivity on a relatively simple task.

Classical School Henri Fayol was a French manager who wrote at about the same time as Taylor, though his works did not have a widely read English translation until 1949. Here we see the influence of management thinking abroad on the view of organizational behavior in the United States because, once translated, the principles described by Fayol became very popular in the United States. His comments typified the *classical* view of administration.[14] He listed the duties of a manager as planning, organizing, commanding employees, coordinating activities, and controlling performance, and he specified the fourteen principles of management shown in Figure 1–5.

Based on these structural elements and principles, organizational theories have identified four features of organizations.[15] First, organizations should *specialize*. That is, they should organize workers according to logical groupings, such as client, place of work, product, expertise, or functional area. At Barker and Bolton, for example, all staff are grouped either according to functional specialty or placed on a client team. Second, *unity of command* dictates that each organizational member should have exactly one direct supervisor; in the Accounting Department, for example, all staff report directly to John Mercer, who in turn reports only to Jack Ballantyne. Third, reporting relationships should be clearly defined within a formal organizational structure, beginning with the least skilled employee and extending to the chief administrator. The scalar *chain of command* at Barker and Bolton begins with the president of the agency and continues through the vice presidents to managers and ultimately to nonmanagerial employees. Fourth and finally, managers must *coordinate activities* through the use of mechanisms that ensure communication among specialized groups; this coordination seems to occur informally at Barker and Bolton, and it also seems to be a problem for John and the managers of other departments, such as Jennifer Wayne and Marie Fabreau.

Figure 1–5 **Fayol's Principles of Management**

1. Division of work—the specialization of work
2. Authority—"the right to give orders, and power to exact obedience"
3. Discipline—"obedience, application, energy, behavior, and outward marks of respect"
4. Unity of command—"an employee should receive orders from one superior only"
5. Unity of direction—"one head and one plan for a group of activities having the same objective"
6. Subordination of individual interests to the general interest—the interest of an individual or group should not supersede the organization's concerns
7. Remuneration—fair payment for services
8. Centralization—degree of consolidation of management functions
9. Scalar chain (line of authority)—"the chain of superiors ranging from the ultimate authority to the lower ranks"
10. Order—all materials and people should be in an appointed place
11. Equity—equality of (although not necessarily identical) treatment
12. Stability of tenure of personnel—limited turnover of personnel
13. Initiative—"thinking out a plan and ensuring its success"
14. Esprit de corps—"harmony, union among the personnel of a concern"

SOURCE: Adapted and excerpted from H. Fayol, *General and Industrial Management*, Trans. C. Storrs (London: Pitman, 1949).

Bureaucracy Max Weber, a German sociologist, addressed the issue of organizational administration in a somewhat different fashion.[16] Here, too, a global international influence on management permeates early thought. In the first part of the twentieth century, Weber studied European organizations and described what he considered to be a prototype form of organization—the *bureaucracy*. For many people bureaucracy conjures up an image of massive red tape and endless unneeded details. For Weber, however, the major asset of bureaucracy was its emphasis on order, system, rationality, uniformity, and consistency. These primary attributes in his view led to equitable treatment for all employees by management. To this end, bureaucratic organizations emphasize impersonality and strict rules. Weber defined bureaucracies as having characteristics that ensure this impersonality and fairness.[17] Although his principles were well known in the United States through spokespersons and interpreters, his writings were not translated into English until the 1940s.[18] Figure 1–6 summarizes Weber's principles of bureaucracy, which offered prescriptions for the best structure of an organization.

In bureaucracies, each employee has specified and official areas of responsibility that are assigned on the basis of competence and expertise. Managers use written documents extensively in managing employees. Rules and regulations not only exist, but also are translated into detailed employment manuals. Managers of offices or other work groups also receive extensive training in their job requirements. Finally, office management must use rules that are consistent and complete, and that can be learned.

Could we apply structural perspectives to diagnosing the situation at Barker and Bolton? Scientific management might suggest that the training of workers needs to be changed so that it more systematically prepares them for their jobs or that John Mercer needs to analyze the tasks being performed and change the work process to maximize performance. Applying classical principles might suggest that unity of command and a scalar chain of authority are violated in the decision-making process and that there are also problems with coordination, the division of work, discipline, and esprit de corps. In applying bureaucratic principles we can ask whether a lack of specified areas of responsibility, absence of a clearly ordered system of supervision, limited use of written documents, unavailability of expert training, lack of management dedication and devotion to the job, and failure to establish general rules could explain the problems experienced at Barker and Bolton. But are these explanations adequate?

BEHAVIORAL PERSPECTIVES

Although the scientific-management, classical, and bureaucratic perspectives emphasize issues related to the structure and design of organizations, which may contribute

---

Figure 1–6 **Weber's Principles of Bureaucracy**

- Specified and official areas of responsibility based on knowledge
- Orderly system of supervision and subordination
- Unity of command

- Extensive use of written documents
- Extensive training in job requirements
- Application of consistent and complete rules

SOURCE: Based on M. Weber, *Essays on Sociology,* trans. and ed. H. H. Gerth and C. W. Mills (New York: Oxford University Press, 1946).

to the problems at Barker and Bolton, they do not address worker dissatisfaction, the complaints about John Mercer's leadership, and dysfunctional interpersonal communication. Other researchers, including the human-relations, group-dynamics, decision-making, and leadership schools, have explicitly considered this *human* side of organizations.

Human Relations School

Beginning in 1924, the Western Electric Company, in conjunction with the National Academy of Sciences, performed five studies of various work groups at Western Electric's Hawthorne plant.[19] The first study looked at the effects of lighting on the productivity of workers in different departments of the company. In the tradition of scientific management, it considered whether certain illumination levels affected output positively or adversely. Essentially, the researchers first increased the lighting to an extreme brightness and then decreased the light until the work area was so dim that assembly material could hardly be seen. Do you think employee output increased, decreased, or remained at normal levels? Surprisingly to the researchers, the workers maintained or even exceeded their normal output whether researchers increased or decreased illumination.

Subsequent studies attempted to explain these results by introducing a variety of changes in the workplace.[20] The researchers examined the impact on output of rest pauses, shorter working days and weeks, wage incentives, and the nature of supervision. They also suggested that something other than the physical work environment (which scientific management would have suggested) or the organizational structure (which classical principles would have suggested) resulted in improved productivity among workers. In observing and interviewing the employees, the researchers discovered that during the experiments the employees felt that someone paid attention to them, so their morale improved and they produced more. This so-called *Hawthorne effect* offered the first dramatic indication that the attitudes and feelings of workers could significantly influence productivity.

Consequently, Western Electric instituted a program where interviewers questioned workers regarding their feelings about work. The interviewing program suggested even more strongly the close relationship between morale and the quality of supervision, and it resulted in the creation of a new training program for supervisors. In the final experiments of the Hawthorne series, the researchers identified one other human feature of organizations: the informal groups that workers develop among themselves, as described in Chapter 5.

Group Dynamics

Later in the century—during World War II—Kurt Lewin, a social psychologist at the University of Iowa, was asked to study methods of changing housewives' food habits away from meat consumption, because there was a shortage of meat.[21] He believed families, parents, and other housewives expected the housewives not to serve other kinds of food, and such expectations created a significant barrier to change. He and his associates conducted experiments that showed that participation in decision making broke down this barrier. Housewives who joined in group discussions were ten times more likely to change their food habits than were housewives who received lectures on the subject.[22]

Lewin's associates later extended these experiments to industrial settings. For example, Lester Coch and John R.P. French found that employees at the Harwood pajama plant in Marion, Virginia, were much more likely to learn new work methods if they had the opportunity to discuss the methods and have some influence on how to apply them in their jobs.[23] Studies such as these led to a greatly expanded awareness of the impact of the work group and spawned research on the relationship between organizational effectiveness and group formation, development, behavior, and attitudes.[24]

Decision-making Theory

In the 1950s, Herbert Simon and James March introduced a different decision-making framework for understanding organizational behavior.[25] Although they elaborated on the bureaucratic model by emphasizing that individuals work in rational organizations and thus behave rationally, their model (which eventually won Simon the Nobel Prize for economics) added a new dimension: the idea that a human being's rationality is limited. By offering a more realistic alternative to classical assumptions of rationality in decision making, this model supported the behavioral view of individual and organizational functioning. The model suggested that when individuals make decisions, they examine a limited set of possible alternatives rather than all available options. Individuals *satisfice;* that is, they accept satisfactory or "good enough" choices, rather than insist on optimal choices. They make choices that are good enough because they do not search until they find perfect solutions to problems.

Leadership

The 1950s saw the beginning of concentrated research in the area of leadership. Researchers and theorists in the 1950s discussed the roles of managers and leaders in organizations and initiated a stream of research in the area of leadership. One classification described groups as having both task and social leaders.[26] The task leader helps the group achieve its goals by clarifying and summarizing member comments and focusing on the group's tasks; the social leader maintains the group and helps it develop cohesiveness and collaboration by encouraging group members' involvement. A second classification distinguished between Theory X and Theory Y managers.[27] Those who believe Theory X assume that workers have an inherent dislike of work, that they must be controlled and threatened with punishment if they are to put forth adequate effort, and that they prefer to avoid responsibility. Managers who believe Theory Y, on the other hand, assume that people feel work is as natural as play or rest, that people will exercise self-direction toward the objectives to which they are committed (so they do not need strict control), and that the average human being can learn to seek responsibility. These assumptions that managers hold, then, affect the way they treat their employees and also affect the employees' productivity.

To diagnose the situation at Barker and Bolton using human perspectives, we can first examine whether the quality of supervision affected morale. The group-dynamics viewpoint might add that the workers were not sufficiently involved in decision making. We could also ask about the quality of the decision-making process. Finally, we can check whether the Accounting Department includes both task and social leaders and test John's assumptions about his subordinates. We can further diagnose whether his leadership style fits with various dimensions of the situation.

INTEGRATIVE PERSPECTIVES

In contrast to an emphasis primarily on structure or on the human side of organizations, organizational thought in the past few decades has emphasized the integration of these two perspectives, along with more specific consideration of environmental and other external influences. More recently, contingency theory has added an emphasis on fitting managerial and organizational features to the specific work situation. The contingency perspective is the foundation of the diagnostic approach presented in this book; that is, effective diagnosis is situational in nature.

Sociotechnical School   In the 1950s several theorists moved away from an emphasis on structure or behavior; they studied technology, which they viewed as a significant influence on structure, and emphasized its interaction with functioning work groups, an element of the human perspective. As members of the sociotechnical school, which studied organizations in England, India, and Norway, Trist and Bamforth described a change in technology in a British coal mine.[28] In the mine, workers were used to working independently in small self-contained units in which they organized the work themselves. But the technology for mining coal improved in a way that required management to increase job specialization and decrease the workers' participation in job assignments. This greater job specialization followed from the scientific management and classical management traditions, and was expected to increase productivity. But the coal miners hated the specialization. They much preferred working with each other and performing a variety of tasks.

Trist and Bamforth compared the performance of work groups whose jobs had become specialized when the new technology was introduced, causing a different social interaction, to that of work groups that retained the old pattern of social interactions. They found that absenteeism in the specialized groups was several times greater and productivity much lower than in the groups that had maintained their original interrelationships. After a number of studies such as these, the sociotechnical systems researchers concluded that technological changes must be made in conjunction with a strong social system: that both social and technical/structural aspects of jobs must be considered simultaneously.

How would these researchers assess the problems in the Accounting Department and elsewhere at Barker and Bolton? What effect did the work process have on performance and attitudes? How did the work process and constraints on it, such as time and human resources, influence the group's behavior? A manager who views the work situation as a technical system alone will likely have different concerns from a manager who views it more as a human system. Certainly a consideration of both structural and human issues should provide a more complete diagnosis of the situation.

Systems Theory   The general systems model, with roots in both the behavioral and natural sciences, represents an organization as an open system, one that interacts with environmental forces and factors, akin to physical systems such as the human body, a microscopic organism, or a cell.[29] First, this system comprises a number of interrelated, interdependent, and interacting subsystems. Second, the organization is open and dynamic. Third, it strives for equilibrium. And fourth, it has multiple purposes, objectives, and functions, some of which are in conflict.

The Accounting Department of Barker and Bolton is a subsystem of an organizational system; so is each of the other departments; so is each individual worker; so is the management of Barker and Bolton. Of course, each subsystem is a system itself, composed of other subsystems; each system is also a subsystem in a larger or superordinate system. Subsystems vary in size from a single cell in an organism to a major division of an organization. To trace subsystems in organizations, the observer generally specifies significant individuals and groups of organizations and examines

Figure 1-7 **The Systems Model**

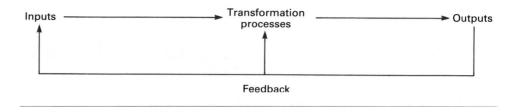

their interdependence. Typical subsystems of interest include individual employees, work teams, departments, and management groups. Pause for a moment and jot down as many subsystems at Barker and Bolton as you can think of. Now briefly describe ways each pair is interdependent and interrelated. Interactions such as these contribute to the complexity of organizations and make effective diagnosis and action more challenging.

An organization, as a system, is also open and dynamic; that is, it continually receives new energy. This energy may be added in the form of new resources (people, materials, and money), goals, or information (concerning strategy, environment, and history) from the environment, called *inputs.* The new energy can also affect the *transformation* of the inputs into new *outputs,* as shown in Figure 1–7. John Mercer's leadership or communication processes in the organization are transformation processes, as are others shown in Figure 1–8, that help employees become productive organizational members. The organization itself, composed of task characteristics, characteristics of individuals, the formal organizational arrangements, and the informal organization, transforms inputs into outputs.[30] *Task characteristics* include the degree of specialization, amount of feedback, and extent of autonomy involved in performing work activities. *Individual characteristics* include the needs, knowledge, expectations, and experiences of organizational members. *Formal organizational processes* encompass the organization's structure, job design, reward system, performance evaluation system, and other human resources management practices. Among the organizational arrangements are the rules and procedures of a company such as Barker and Bolton. The *informal elements* refer to leader behavior, group and intergroup relations, and power behavior outside the formal hierarchy. As a result of such transformation of inputs, changes in outputs such as performance, satisfaction, morale, turnover, and absenteeism may occur.

When organizations receive new inputs or experience certain transformations, they simultaneously seek stability, balance, or *equilibrium.* When organizations become unbalanced or experience disequilibrium, such as when changes in the environment or organizational practices make current resources inadequate, the organizations attempt to return to a steady state, which may mirror or significantly differ from the original state of equilibrium. They use information about their outputs, called *feedback* or exchange, to modify their inputs or transformations to result in more desirable outcomes and equilibrium. Let us assume, for example, as in the case of the Accounting Department, that worker performance has declined significantly. This information cues the organization to examine the nature of its inputs and transformations for a cause. The feedback may subsequently pinpoint changes needed in inputs such as employees' skills or in transformations such as a new leadership style or different communication processes.

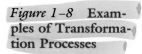

Figure 1–8 Examples of Transformation Processes

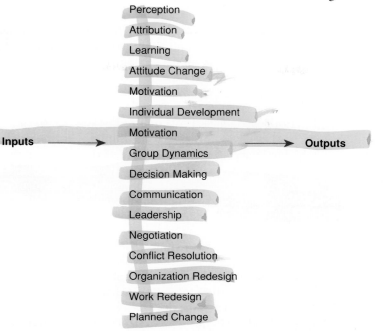

Perception
Attribution
Learning
Attitude Change
Motivation
Individual Development

Inputs → Motivation → **Outputs**

Group Dynamics
Decision Making
Communication
Leadership
Negotiation
Conflict Resolution
Organization Redesign
Work Redesign
Planned Change

Feedback may also indicate which subsystems have *similar goals* and which have different or even *conflicting goals*. Various parts of organizations—individuals, managers, work groups, departments, or divisions—have multiple purposes, functions, and objectives, some of which may conflict. For example, John Mercer might aim for consistency among the procedures for different departments, whereas other managers might want their unique needs addressed.

Finally, organizations as open systems demonstrate *equifinality,* which suggests that organizations may employ a variety of means to achieve their desired objectives. For example, McDonald's Restaurants achieves its objectives of growth and profitability by employing a highly specialized system for producing its hamburgers. Digital Equipment Corporation, on the other hand, employs a more flexible and adaptive operation to achieve growth and profitability. No single structure or other transformation processes result in a predetermined set of inputs, outputs, and transformations. Thus, to survive, organizations must *adapt* to changes with appropriate changes in the system. John Mercer must recognize, for example, that he is dealing in an international environment with a multicultural work force. This situation may call for a different managerial style or other adjustments. When organizations are unable to adapt or change, *entropy* may eventually occur, resulting in the system's decay and ultimate demise.

Contingency Theory   Like systems theory, contingency theory provides a more comprehensive view that calls for a *fit* between organizational processes and characteristics of the situation. Early contingency research looked at the fit between an organization's structure and its environment. One early study prescribed mechanistic (machinelike) and organic (living, human, and flexible) systems for stable and change environments, respectively.[31] Other research found that the type of structure the organization develops (and should develop) is influenced by the organization's technology: whether the technology is unit, mass production, or a continuous process.[32] A mechanistic type of organization fits best with a mass production technology (for example, producing pins, lifting pig iron, or manufacturing heavy equipment); a more organic form of organization responds best to a unit technology (craft) or a continuous-process technology (e.g., a gas refinery). Recent thinking in organization design has reemphasized the importance for organizational effectiveness of fitting organizational structure to various contingencies.[33] Contingency theory has also extended to leadership, group dynamics, power relations, and work design, as described later in this book. Its basic premise of fitting behavior to the situation underlies the diagnostic approach described here.

ORGANIZATION OF THIS BOOK

This book includes five parts. Each emphasizes one or more phases of the diagnostic approach. Part I sets the stage in this chapter and together with the first chapter of Part II examines in detail the descriptive phase of the diagnostic approach. Throughout Part II, diagnostic perspectives that focus on individual issues are introduced. Beginning with Chapter 2 and continuing through the rest of the book, prescriptions for increasing the effectiveness of organizations and approaches to managerial action are introduced. Part III emphasizes frameworks for dealing with group issues. Part IV emphasizes the use of organization-level theories. Part V concludes the book with a discussion of organizational change and effectiveness.

SUMMARY

Where do we find organizational behavior? What kinds of events should we seek to describe and understand? Clearly, organizational behavior does not occur only in profit-making, private-sector organizations like Barker and Bolton, Inc. It occurs in organizations around the world, both in ones that operate in a single country and in those that are multinational in scope. Governments, universities, hospitals, baseball teams, pet stores, and families are all organizations in which organizational behavior occurs. This book presents organizational behavior in diverse contexts. You will be encouraged to examine organizational behavior in *Fortune* 500 companies, as well as in situations you confront every day.

We have recounted several of the most influential historical perspectives used to explain organizational behavior during the twentieth century. At the same time, we have taken each perspective and used it to diagnose to some degree the situation at Barker and Bolton. The application of each perspective in this way has suggested that people taking different perspectives would ask radically different questions and would thus attempt to correct very different problems or create very different situations.

We must also recall that in some cases empirical data may question the validity of particular perspectives. For example, research studies have seriously questioned the validity of Taylor's pig-iron experiments and of the Hawthorne illumination experiments.[34] Must we ignore such perspectives and rule them out as invalid? Can we learn something by applying such perspectives while recognizing their limitations? In many situations, appropriate action depends on asking questions that come

Table 1–2 **Diagnostic Questions Using the Historical Perspectives**

- Is there an appropriate division of labor?
- Is work done efficiently, and are workers sufficiently trained to do their jobs?
- Do employees have specified areas of responsibility?
- Is the work defined effectively?
- Do work groups operate effectively?
- Do managers perform organizing roles and have an appropriate span of control?
- Does the group have effective task and social leadership?
- Does management work with the correct assumptions about employees?
- Is decision making effective?
- Is the interface of technology and individual workers effective?
- Does the organization's structure respond to the environmental contingencies?
- Is there a good fit between inputs and transformations?
- Are there good fits between individuals, tasks, organizational arrangements, and the informal organization?

from a number of different perspectives, because each perspective alone has a fairly narrow view and does not address the complexity of the behavior being considered. We can start our diagnosis by answering the questions in Table 1–2, but we must recognize that a comprehensive and accurate diagnosis and prescription require further questions and answers.

ENDNOTES

[1] W. H. Wagel and H. Z. Levine, HR '90: Challenges and opportunities, *Personnel* (June 1990): 18–42.

[2] See T. Cox, Jr., The multicultural organization, *Academy of Management Executive* 5(2) (1991): 34–47.

[3] E. Henderson, quoted in R. S. Schuler and J. W. Walker, Human resources strategy: Focusing on issues and actions, *Organizational Dynamics* 19 (Summer 1990): 4–19.

[4] S. Overman, Managing the diverse workforce, *HR Magazine* 36(4) (April 1991): 32–36.

[5] Wagel and Levine, HR '90.

[6] N. A. Boyacigiller and N. J. Adler, The parochial domain: Organizational science in a global context, *Academy of Management Review* 16(2) (1991): 262–290.

[7] See F. Kluckholn and F. C. Strodtbeck, *Variations in Value Orientations* (Evanston, Ill.: Row, Peterson, 1961), cited in N. J. Adler, *International Dimensions of Organizational Behavior,* 2nd ed. (Boston: PWS-Kent, 1991); and H. W. Lane and J. J. DiStefano, *International Management Behavior: From Policy to Practice* (Scarborough, Ontario: Nelson Canada, 1988).

[8] Adler, *International Dimensions.*

[9] Extensive writings exist regarding research methodology. Some good examples include A. Strauss, *Qualitative Analysis for Social Scientists* (New York: Cambridge University Press, 1987); W. B. Shaffir and R. A. Stebbins, eds., *Experiencing Fieldwork: An Inside View of Qualitative Research* (Newbury Park, Calif.: Sage, 1991); K. D. Broota, *Experimental Design in Behavioral Research* (New York: Wiley, 1989).

[10] T. R. Mitchell, an evaluation of the validity of correlation research conducted in organizations, *Academy of Management Review* 10 (1985): 192–205, discusses some of the drawbacks of correlational research as compared to experimental research; K. M. Borman, M. D. LeCompte, and J. P. Goetz, Ethnographic and qualitative research design and why it doesn't work, *American Behavioral Scientist* 30 (1986): 42–57, suggests ways of overcoming the limitations of qualitative research.

[11] Adam Smith, *An Inquiry into the Nature and Cause of the Wealth of Nations,* 1776.

[12] F. W. Taylor, *The Principles of Scientific Management* (New York: Harper and Brothers, 1911), pp. 36–37.

[13] E. A. Locke, The ideas of Frederick Taylor: An evaluation, *Academy of Management Review* 7 (1982): 14–24.

[14] H. Fayol, *General and Industrial Management*, trans. C. Storrs (London: Pitman, 1949).

[15] L. Gulick and L. Urwick, eds., *Papers on the Science of Administration* (New York: Columbia University Institute of Public Administration, 1937); and J. D. Mooney and A. C. Reiley, *Onward Industry* (New York: Harper, 1931) offered complementary views of management. F. B. Gilbreth and L. M. Gilbreth, *Applied Motion Study* (New York: Sturgis and Walton, 1917) earlier offered a similar view.

[16] M. Weber, *The Theory of Social and Economic Organization*, trans. and ed. A. M. Henderson and T. Parsons (New York: Oxford University Press, 1947).

[17] M. Weber, *Essays on Sociology*, trans. and ed. H. H. Gerth and C. W. Mills (New York: Oxford University Press, 1946), pp. 196–198.

[18] R. M. Weiss, Weber on bureaucracy: Management consultant or political theorist? *Academy of Management Review* 8 (1983): 242–248, argues that Weber was not concerned with prescribing the characteristics of an efficient organization but rather was solely offering political theory.

[19] C. E. Snow, A discussion of the relation of illumination intensity to productive efficiency, *The Tech Engineering News,* November 1927. Cited in E. J. Roethlisberger and W. J. Dickson, *Management and the Worker* (Cambridge, Mass.: Harvard University Press, 1939).

[20] Roethlisberger and Dickson, *Management and the Worker.*

[21] K. Lewin, Forces behind food habits and methods of change, *Bulletin of the National Research Council* 108 (1943): 35–65.

[22] M. Radke and D. Klisurich, Experiments in changing food habits, *Journal of the American Dietetics Association* 23 (1947): 403–409.

[23] L. Coch and J.R.P. French, Jr., Overcoming resistance to change, *Human Relations* 1 (1948): 512–533.

[24] See C. S. Bartlem and E. A. Locke, The Coch and French study: A critique and reinterpretation, *Human Relations* 34 (1981): 555–566, for another view of the significance of research on participation.

[25] H. Simon, *Administrative Behavior*, 2nd ed. (New York: Macmillan, 1957); and J. G. March and H. A. Simon, *Organizations* (New York: John Wiley, 1958).

[26] R. F. Bales, Task roles and social roles in problem-solving groups. In *Readings in Social Psychology,* 3rd ed., ed. E. Maccoby, T. M. Newcomb, and E. L. Hartley (New York: Holt, Rinehart, and Winston, 1958), pp. 437–447; D. McGregor, *The Human Side of Enterprise* (New York: McGraw-Hill, 1960).

[27] McGregor, D. *Human Side of Enterprise;* E. H. Schein, The Hawthorne group studies revisited: A defense of Theory Y (Cambridge, Mass.: MIT Sloan School of Management Working Paper 756–74, December 1974).

[28] E. K. Trist and K. W. Bamforth, Some social and psychological consequences of the long-wall method of coal getting, *Human Relations* 4 (1951): 3–38; other studies included A. K. Rice, *The Enterprise and Its Environment* (London: Tavistock, 1963), and F. E. Emery and I. L. Trist, Sociotechnical systems, *Management Science: Models and Techniques,* vol. 2 (London: Pergamon, 1960).

[29] D. Katz and R. L. Kahn, *The Social Psychology of Organizations,* 2nd ed. (New York: John Wiley & Sons, 1978).

[30] D. A. Nadler and M. L. Tushman, A diagnostic model for organizational behavior. In *Perspectives on Behavior in Organizations,* ed. J. R. Hackman, L. W. Porter, and E. E. Lawler III (New York: McGraw-Hill, 1977).

[31] T. Burns and G. M. Stalker, *The Management of Innovation* (London: Tavistock, 1961).

[32] J. Woodward, *Industrial Organization: Theory and Practice* (London: Oxford University Press, 1965); P. Lawrence and J. Lorsch, *Organization and Environment* (Boston: Harvard Business School Division of Research, 1967).

[33] H. Mintzberg, *Structure in Fives: Designing Effective Organizations* (Englewood Cliffs, N.J.: Prentice-Hall, 1983) summarizes the fit between structure and the contingencies of technology, environment, goals, work force, and age and size of organization.

[34] C. D. Wrege and A. G. Perroni, Taylor's pig-tale: A historical analysis of Frederick W. Taylor's pig-iron experiments, *Academy of Management Journal* 17 (1974): 6–17, shows that Taylor's story and the facts of the situation have little in common. R. H. Franke and J. D. Kaul, The Hawthorne experiments: First statistical interpretation, *American Sociological Review* 43 (1978): 623–643.

RECOMMENDED READINGS

Bryman, A., ed. *Doing Research in Organizations*. London: Routledge, 1988.

Duncan, W. J. *Great Ideas in Management: Lessons from the Founders and Foundations of Managerial Practice*. San Francisco: Jossey-Bass, 1989.

Marshall, C., and G. B. Rossman. *Designing Qualitative Research*. Newbury Park, Calif.: Sage, 1989.

Waring, S. P. *Taylorism Transformed: Scientific Management Theory Since 1945*. Chapel Hill: University of North Carolina Press, 1989.

Yin, R. K. *Case Study Research: Design and Methods*. Newbury Park, Calif.: Sage, 1989.

Chapter Outline

Explaining Perception, Attribution, Learning, and Attitude Formation

Learning Objectives

After completing the reading and activities in Chapter 2, students will be able to

1. Describe the process of perception and show how perceptual biases influence effective action.

2. Discuss perceptual variations in a multinational environment.

3. Describe the process of attribution and illustrate the way attributional biases influence effective action.

4. Comment about the variations in attributions in a multicultural work force.

5. Differentiate among and identify the key factors of three models of learning.

6. Describe the barriers to effective learning and the managerial issues involved in dealing with them.

7. Illustrate the process of attitude formation and cite two strategies for influencing attitudes.

8. Describe ways of assessing attitudes in organizations.

The Performance Problem at Rock Hill Savings Bank

Margaret Healey supervised a staff of ten loan officers responsible for residential lending at Rock Hill Savings Bank. In addition to making about 30 percent of the bank's loans, her department served as a training ground for employees wishing to move into the commercial loan area or into other executive positions in the bank. Margaret prided herself on her ability to work with any employee, often turning performance problems into success stories. But for the past few months she had been stymied in her dealings with Caroline Kraft. Kraft had entered the loan officer training program three years before, and she had earned rave reviews for her performance. Her first year in the residential department was also stellar, but in the past year her performance had really deteriorated. She made several bad loan decisions, was very sloppy in completing her regular paperwork, and for the first time had a significant number of absences from work. Margaret sent Caroline to several days of special training, hoping the experience would correct her performance problems.

When Margaret attempted to discuss Caroline's performance with her, Kraft said in effect that she was not having a performance problem. She commented that the bad economic climate was affecting everyone's loans. She admitted that she had made one or two mistakes in her paperwork, but felt they were just isolated incidents. She also expressed dissatisfaction with Margaret's actions; she said, for example, that the training program had been a total waste of time.

Margaret hated to have to fire Caroline, particularly knowing how difficult it would be for her to find another job. At the same time, she wondered whether it was possible to improve Caroline's performance, given her negative attitude toward Margaret and the job.

M argaret Healey and Caroline Kraft disagree about the cause and extent of Caroline's performance problems. Why did the perceptions of these women differ? What did each person perceive as the cause of Caroline's poor performance? How did the previous experiences of these two employees—their learned behaviors and attitudes—influence the events described here? What impact did Margaret's and Caroline's attitudes have on the situation? Questions such as these are fundamental to the diagnostic approach because they deal with the description of events and the reasons given for them. As the case suggests, different observers of an incident may describe and diagnose it very differently. Their actions in turn would be based on their different understandings of the situation.

In this chapter we explore areas of organizational behavior that deal with the way we perceive (and thus describe) events or other people, the way we understand (and thus analyze or diagnose) the events and people we perceive, the way our past experiences and acquisition of knowledge and information influence this description and diagnosis, and the way we form attitudes about the situations based on our perceptions, understanding, and experience. These four processes are referred to as *perception, attribution, learning,* and *attitude formation.* They comprise the basic processes that underlie the description and diagnosis of organizational behavior.

While these processes remain fairly constant, the context in which they occur may have significance for the outcome. For example, the process of perception is the same in the United States or in Japan, but the resulting observations of the same situation in the different cultures may differ. Diversity in the work force also will affect the outcomes of these processes because the characteristics of the observers will differ significantly.

THE PERCEPTION PROCESS

We begin our discussion by considering the situation at the Rock Hill Savings Bank. Let's view the performance problem from several different perspectives. First, think of yourself as Margaret Healey. What do you notice about the functioning of the residential loan department, and specifically about Caroline Kraft's performance? Which features of the situation stand out for you? You might notice the deterioration of Kraft's performance and the stable performance of the other loan officers. You might see Caroline complaining to other workers about the increased paperwork. You might recognize your increasing frustration with your inability to change Caroline's behaviors. You might notice the set of training programs being offered in the bank. Now think of yourself as Caroline Kraft. What features of the situation do you notice? You might experience Margaret's supervision as stifling. You might feel singled out for a few errors of judgment. You might feel stressed and pressured to produce more than you feel capable of doing. You might feel demeaned because your supervisor is watching your work attendance so closely. Now put yourself in the place of another member of the residential loan department. How would you experience this situation? You might echo Margaret's or Caroline's views, or feel instead that Margaret has singled Caroline out for special treatment by sending only her to training sessions.

When you put yourself in these different positions, you probably notice different features of the situation and think about the situation in the residential loan department in different ways. Even though objectively this situation was a single event, your experience of it—your perception—varies when you put yourself in the position of different observers of the event. You then act based on your perception.

Perception is the process by which each person senses reality and comes to a particular understanding or view. It is an active process[1] that results in different people having somewhat different, even contradictory, views or understandings of the same event or person. Rarely do different observers describe events or persons in exactly the same way. Often managers and their subordinates, coworkers, or supervisors see and describe the same situation differently. For this reason, presenting a clear, well-documented, agreed-upon description of a situation is the first step in the diagnostic approach. Because our perceptions have a strong impact on our descriptions, our diagnoses of events, and our subsequent behavior, it is important to examine the perceptual process and some of the factors that affect it.

A long-standing view of the perceptual process describes it as having two parts, as shown in Figure 2–1: (1) *attention* and (2) *organization*.[2] This view emphasizes both the physiological processes and the social context in which they occur. Social cognition researchers emphasize basic categorization processes as fundamental to the organization phase.[3]

Attention

In the situation at the Rock Hill Savings Bank, the members of the residential loan department *attend* to certain features of the situation. Quite possibly, because of their different concerns, perspectives, unconscious biases, and vantage points, they would pay attention to quite different features. For example, Margaret Healey might focus on the efficiency of her staff members, while other employees might emphasize the interference of the new filing requirements for loan processing. Margaret Healey said that Caroline Kraft's attendance has become problematic; Kraft disagreed.

Figure 2–1 **The Perceptual Process**

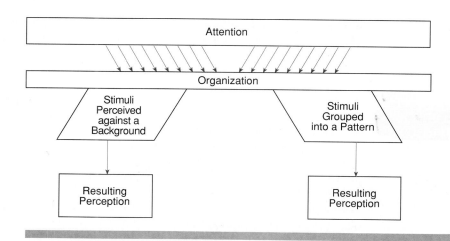

So many stimuli bombard us that we have difficulty taking full account of all of them. We continually face a mélange of sounds and sights. Different observers might select different sets of stimuli to pay attention to. We tend to attend to only some features present in any situation; we may pay attention to only certain workers' actions and conversations. We also attend to only some characteristics of the people we meet; we might be alert to a worker's experience with a particular piece of equipment or the worker's age or sex. This selection process helps us avoid dealing with information that seems to be irrelevant to us. It also helps us avoid information overload by focusing on the most relevant information in a particular situation. In some cases, however, individuals may overlook important stimuli. Caroline Kraft may not see the reduction in the number of bad loans resulting from the new filing requirements. Or her supervisors might overlook the pressure created by the increased demands.

Characteristics of the Stimuli Certain characteristics of the stimuli themselves influence what we attend to. We tend to select stimuli that are larger, more intense, in motion, repetitive, either novel or very familiar, or in contrast to their background.[4] We tend to overlook stimuli that are small, less intense, or stationary or those that blend with their background.

Consider, for example, an error in bookkeeping; a manager is more likely to see a large than a small error. Consider next a salesperson's response to a ringing telephone, a relatively intense stimulus; a salesperson frequently answers a phone before helping a customer waiting in person, because that individual—unless he or she is very vocal or demanding—offers a less intense stimulus. In another work situation, employees may not hear (or select) the voice of a supervisor who continually complains about the quality of their work; the voice may lack sufficient intensity, novelty, or contrast. Which characteristics of the stimuli in the case of Caroline Kraft's performance attracted the attention of her supervisor? Margaret Healey perceived her declining attendance, decreasing performance, and complaints about the amount of paperwork, perhaps because they are novel or in contrast to the previous situation in the loan department.

Characteristics of Selectors We also select stimuli according to our internal state and cultural experiences. Such states evolve from the individual's experiences, motivation, and personality. Figure 2–2 illustrates the role learning plays in our percep-

Figure 2–2 **Influence of Learning on Perception**

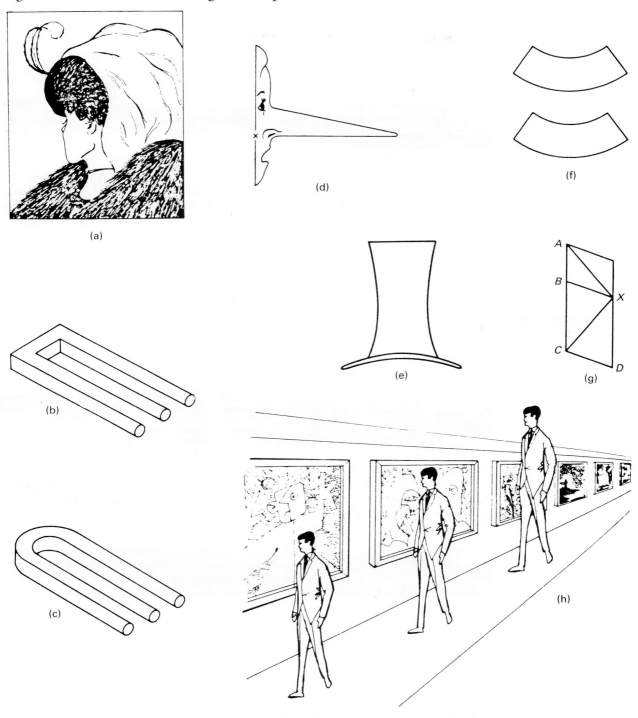

SOURCES: *a*, W. E. Hill, *Puck*, 6 November 1915; *d*, E. P. Johnson, *Student's Manual to Accompany Psychology*, 2nd ed. (Boston: Houghton Mifflin, 1951); *h*, F. Luthans, *Organizational Behavior*, 4th ed. (New York: McGraw Hill, 1985), p. 166. Reproduced by permission.

tions. In *a* you initially see an old lady or a young lady, based on your cultural experiences. Parts *b* and *c* are optical illusions. In *d, e, f,* and *g,* lengths you perceive to differ are in fact identical. In *h* all three men are the same height.

In organizations we might "see" an employee's tardiness, for example, in terms of our own education or experience in viewing key events—as a function of the person's social class, educational background, or job history. We might see it in terms of our own physiological requirements for sleep. Or we might see it in terms of our own personality, such as our aggressiveness, enthusiasm, or introversion. The more diverse the work force, the more likely individuals are to see events differently. In addition, as organizations become more global, the number of different views of the same situation increases.

Think of the situation that opened this chapter. Which stimuli in the situation in the loan department did Margaret Healey select? Which ones did Caroline Kraft select? Which ones did other members of the department likely select? Why did they select those? Why, for example, might the coworkers have seen Caroline's attending a training session as special treatment? Why might they have overlooked Caroline's attendance record? Both Caroline's supervisor and coworkers likely were influenced by their learning processes, motivation, and personality in selecting the stimuli to see or hear. Different experiences, needs, or personalities might have resulted in different perceptions of the situation. These different perceptions in turn result in different actions by various organizational members.

Organization   Once we have selected stimuli, we categorize and organize them so that the new material makes sense to us. If possible, we make the new stimuli fit with the ways we already understand and know the world. If we as managers, for example, see our current employees as being lazy, we likely will see new employees as lazy, too. We tend not to notice disconfirming evidence. We organize stimuli by placing them into categories.[5] Either we fit new stimuli into *prototypes* that represent the average, abstract attributes of a person or situation, or we match them to *exemplars,* which represent concrete examples or a sampling of circumstances.[6]

We might also organize stimuli in additional ways. First, we perceive stimuli as figures standing against a background.[7] We see stimuli within an environmental context, including the setting, work performed, and organizational culture.[8] A plant manager, for example, sees assembly line workers against a background of the plant's equipment, or sees the actions of one worker against the entire group of workers. The distinctions made between figure and background will influence the attitudes and behaviors on which the plant manager ultimately focuses.

Second, we group discrete stimuli into a pattern.[9] For example, we try to form a complete picture even when the data are incomplete for both physical and experiential stimuli. Figure 2–3 illustrates such *closure* for physical stimuli. Notice that you tend to complete the square and ignore the duplication of words in the three sayings. How does this principle apply to behavior in organizations? The supervisor who has thirty subordinates has a complete mental picture of each worker, generally based on just a few details. The workers have a mental picture of their coworkers' jobs, often based on a few tasks. Either may draw factual or erroneous conclusions about the other based on limited information.

Grouping of stimuli occurs when they are similar, near to other stimuli, form a continuous pattern, or create a completed pattern. For example, a vice president in an insurance firm may have difficulty distinguishing between the performance of two actuaries who have adjacent offices. An office manager may consider all the women as interchangeable and all the men as interchangeable. Such inaccuracies become

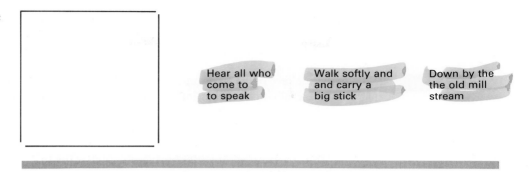

Figure 2–3 **Closure for Physical Stimuli**

more problematic in organizations that have a multicultural work force or that operate internationally. Such faulty grouping of stimuli underlies the interpretation of stimuli and contributes to the distortions of perceptions that are described in the next section.

Future Directions   More recent research about the structure and acquisition of knowledge links cognitive theory and perception.[10] Cognitive psychologists suggest that we store in our memories a description of the characteristic features of a person, situation, or thing. Then we categorize subsequent stimuli by matching them to the appropriate categories, known as schemata, prototypes, or exemplars, or by other names.[11] We aggregate these categorizations to develop a framework for processing information. This approach may ultimately supersede the more traditional view of perception we described earlier in this chapter.

PERCEPTUAL DISTORTIONS   In reality, both selection and organization generally suffer from inaccuracies or distortions. Although such biases are normal and human, they can have significant consequences when managers or other organizational members base action upon potentially invalid distortions. In this chapter we discuss stereotyping, the halo effect, projection, and the self-fulfilling prophecy as examples. Additional distortions include suppression, repression, denial, displacement, and rationalization.[12]

Stereotyping   Stereotyping occurs when an individual attributes behaviors or attitudes to a person on the basis of the group or category to which that person belongs. "Blondes have more fun" and "All managers are smart" illustrate stereotyping. We frequently stereotype members of ethnic groups, women, managers, white-collar workers, and blue-collar workers. What stereotypes do you think existed at the Rock Hill Savings Bank? Caroline might be stereotyped as young and flighty and Margaret as bossy and domineering. Though the stereotypes may be accurate, they often are not and result in uninformed action.

   Why does stereotyping occur? Often individuals do not gather sufficient data about others to describe their behaviors or attitudes accurately. They may look for shortcuts to describe certain phenomenon without spending the time to analyze them completely. Alternatively, some individuals have personal biases against certain groups of individuals. Historical attitudes toward certain cultural groups may result in stereotypes. Americans may have certain views of Europeans and different views of Japanese, based on their historical experiences with the two countries. Using stereotypes reduces the accuracy of our perceptions about these groups. The danger in some training in managing diversity is that understanding different cultures better might enhance stereotyping, rather than encourage managers to recognize individual differences *within* a cultural context.[13]

Halo Effect   The halo effect refers to an individual's letting one salient feature of a person dominate the evaluation of that individual. Working overtime, for example, can cause a supervisor to evaluate a person as highly cooperative and productive. A neat personal appearance can cause a person to be judged as precise in his or her work, reliable, and a good employee.

The halo effect frequently occurs in assessments of employee performance. Individuals may be judged on the basis of one trait—promptness, neatness, or enthusiasm, for example—rather than on a composite of traits over a period of time. In one study, a supervisor who had information suggesting identical performance from two female subordinates gave them different evaluations according to their personal attractiveness. Attractiveness increased the performance evaluations, pay raises, and promotions of women in nonmanagerial positions, but decreased these same outcomes for women in managerial positions.[14]

Projection   Have you ever heard someone say, "My boss is prejudiced; my boss doesn't like women; my boss doesn't like minority workers; my boss doesn't trust workers over 40"? These observations about the boss may be accurate, but they may also be a reflection of the worker's prejudices. Or consider a salesperson who hesitantly approaches a prospective customer feeling that the customer will consider the product to be shoddy. The salesperson may be seeing his or her own attitudes about the product in the customer's response, whether or not the customer feels that way.

Projection refers to an individual's attributing his or her own attitudes or feelings to another person. Individuals use projection as a defense mechanism, to transfer blame to another person, or to provide protection from their own unacceptable feelings. Individuals frequently attribute their own prejudices against minorities, managers, or employees, for example, to the other party. Hence, projection and its dysfunctional consequences can increase as the work force becomes more diverse; individuals who lack understanding or mistrust people who are different from themselves may project these insecurities onto others.

Projection involves an emotional biasing of perceptions. Fear, hatred, uncertainty, anger, love, deceit, or distrust may influence an individual's perceptions. In union-management relations, for example, each side attributes feelings of mistrust (its own) to the other side. Management might state that the union mistrusts them, when, in fact, it is management that mistrusts the union. They project their own feelings onto the other group, representing them as that group's feelings.

Self-Fulfilling Prophecy   In many situations, the participants expect certain behaviors from other participants. They then see these behaviors as occurring whether or not they actually do. Their expectations become self-fulfilling prophecies. They may expect workers to be lazy, bossy, or tardy; then they perceive they actually are lazy, bossy, or tardy. These expectations may be associated with stereotyping, the halo effect, or projection.

Assume you are a marketing manager with two subordinates. The first subordinate has demonstrated great creativity and productivity in the advertising campaigns she has developed. The second subordinate follows the directions given by the manager to the letter, but has demonstrated neither initiative nor enthusiasm for special projects. You have just found an innovative marketing plan on your desk. Which subordinate do you congratulate for the excellent work? If the self-fulfilling prophecy is operating, you would approach the first subordinate whom you expect to demonstrate creativity because she has in the past. Could you be in error? Of course, either subordinate could have developed the plan. Our expectations influence and bias our perceptions of others, reducing their accuracy; they have also been shown to influence the performance of those of whom we have expectations.

Dealing with Distortions

How can we reduce dysfunctional perceptual distortions in organizations? First, individuals must gather sufficient information about other people's behavior and attitudes to encourage more realistic perceptions. Managers, for example, must judge an individual's performance on his or her observed behavior, rather than on the behavior of a group to which the person belongs. Second, managers must check conclusions they draw to ensure their validity. Margaret Healey must check the true reasons for Caroline Kraft's absenteeism, for example. Third, they must differentiate between facts and assumptions in determining the basis of their perceptions. Margaret Healey may not know, for example, that the training session is not appropriate for Caroline Kraft. Fourth, managers must distinguish among various aspects of an individual's behavior, rather than grouping even superficially related aspects: They must separate appearance from performance, productivity from attendance, personality from creativity. Fifth, to eliminate or reduce projection, individuals must first identify their true feelings: Do they feel anger, uncertainty, distrust? After recognizing these feelings, managers or other organizational members must then repeatedly assess whether and how they are influencing their perceptions of others. Figure 2–4 highlights this advice.

PERCEPTION IN A GLOBAL ENVIRONMENT

Cultural differences exist in how individuals process information; they affect the cognitive map, or the content and structure of the schemata, used to understand the environment and influence behavior.[15] They affect the stimuli we select to perceive, the way we organize them, and how we interpret them. Our cultural background may cause us to distort our perceptions in predictable or unpredictable ways.

Consider how the situation at Rock Hill Savings Bank might be perceived differently if it occurred in Japan, in South Africa, in Peru, or in the United States (where it actually occurred). Certainly the interaction between manager and subordinate might be perceived differently by both parties as well as by outside observers. Cultural biases exist and affect perceptions and ultimately behavior and attitudes. Our cultural heritage, for example, may cause us to ignore certain stimuli and focus on others; an American may ignore certain gestures as part of normal conversation, whereas a Japanese business person might find them offensive. The cultural context in which a situation occurs may similarly affect our perception; we might "see" legs crossed at the ankles in certain countries and not perceive them in others.

Figure 2–4 Dealing with Perceptual Distortions

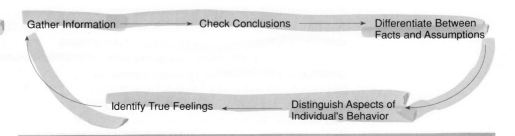

Gather Information → Check Conclusions → Differentiate Between Facts and Assumptions → Distinguish Aspects of Individual's Behavior → Identify True Feelings → (back to Gather Information)

Cross-cultural misperceptions occur for four reasons.[16] First, we have subconscious cultural blinders that cause us to interpret events in other countries as if they were occurring in our own. Second, we lack a complete understanding of our own culture and its influence on our behavior. Third, we assume people are more similar to us than they are. Finally, and in general, our parochialism and general lack of knowledge about other cultures contribute to our misperceptions. An awareness of these differences can help us consider and represent the perspectives of several different observers when we describe events or people. If we can incorporate many people's perceptions into an account of a person or event, our description should be more accurate than if we attend only to our own perceptions.

THE ATTRIBUTION PROCESS

Even if we objectify our perceptions as much as possible, is it sufficient simply to describe different events or people? Obviously, Margaret Healey or Caroline Kraft would not be content with a simple description of the performance problem. Most likely they would move to the next step, which involves determining the *cause* of the situation. In fact, as you read the case description, most likely you too pinpointed several potential causes of the problem.

The need to determine why events occur is a common one and is inherent in the diagnostic approach. Many of us, whether consciously or not, first ponder the reasons for many events and then decide why the events occurred. In this way, we attribute causes to the events. We move from *description* to *diagnosis*. As might be expected, different people often attribute different causes to the same event. In this book, we present a wide range of explanations for various phenomena so that individuals can attribute causes as *accurately* and *completely* as possible and then act on the basis of correct attributions.

When people try to understand reasons for behavior, however, they either focus on and even overestimate *personal* causes, such as habits, needs, abilities, or interests, or *situational* factors, such as increases in competition, poor supervision, shortages of resources, or the nature of the work itself. Think again of the situation at Rock Hill Savings Bank. How would Margaret, Caroline, or other members of the residential loan department explain the situation there? How would they explain the reasons for Caroline's performance problem? Margaret Healey might attribute it to Caroline's laziness or lack of skill or motivation; Caroline likely would attribute it to the plethora of new rules, regulations, and paperwork. Put yourself in the position of an observer of the situation. Why do you think Caroline's performance declined? Why would these reasons differ? How would the actions of members of the loan department likely differ given these attributions?

The Steps in Attribution

Attribution theorists and researchers have studied the process of determining the causes of specific events, the responsibility for particular outcomes, and the personal qualities of individuals participating in the situation.[17] One researcher has suggested that this process occurs in three stages, as shown in Figure 2–5.[18] First, a person observes or is told about another person's action, such as Caroline Kraft's performance problem. Second, having identified the action, we determine whether the observed behavior was intended or accidental. Did the change in performance occur on purpose, or did it just happen by accident? If we assume that the decline occurred accidentally, we attribute its causes to fate, luck, accident, or a similar uncontrollable phenomenon. If, however, we assume that the decline was intended or controllable, we then move to stage 3. Third, we question whether situational causes or personal

Figure 2–5 **The Attribution Process**

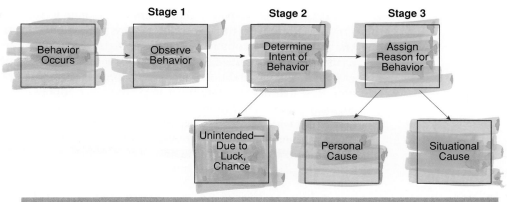

characteristics explain the behavior. We might consider, for example, that the new work regulations were the major explanation of the change in performance; if so, we will attribute the decline to situational factors. If, on the other hand, we feel that Caroline's personality—her laziness or ineptitude—influenced her performance, then we are likely to conclude that personal dispositions motivated the change. Although both situational and personal factors may have influenced the change in performance, we often simplify our understanding and attend primarily to only one cause.

The original research called for attributing the cause of behavior by determining how many others behaved in the same way (*consensus*), how unusual the behavior was (*distinctiveness*), and how consistent it was over time and situations (*consistency*).[19] Although the precise nature of the bias along these dimensions has not been consistently validated, research suggests that complex patterns of attributions occur.[20] Recognizing this tendency, this book encourages students to identify multiple possible causes of behaviors and attitudes. The diagnostic approach emphasizes the complexity of organizational situations and the value of using diverse theories and perspectives to understand them.

Cross-Cultural Attributions

In cross-cultural situations, behaviors similarly can be attributed to the situation—that is, the cultural differences—or to the personal characteristics of the individual, such as arrogance, laziness, or disrespect. To make accurate attributions in such situations it is essential that we be familiar with the culture in which the situation occurs. For example, managers of a multicultural work force must not equate poor grammar or mispronunciation with lack of ability because it often indicates use of a second language instead.[21]

ATTRIBUTIONAL BIASES

Attributions and attributional errors occur in predictable ways, based on a variety of factors. In this section we look at a subset of them.

An individual can participate in a situation as an *actor* or an *observer*. In looking at the Rock Hill situation, we can view Caroline Kraft, the loan officer, as an actor in the situation and Margaret Healey, her supervisor, as the observer, or the reverse. Whom we designate as the actor and observer depends on the behavior to which we are attributing causes. Research about such attributions indicates that an actor in a situation emphasizes the situational causes of a behavior and deemphasizes the personal factors to protect his or her self-image and ego; the observer does the reverse.[22] These biases may extend to ethical judgments through the moral evaluation of one's own or another's behavior.[23] For example, Caroline Kraft would emphasize the economic conditions or the institution of new regulations that affect her performance. Margaret Healey as observer would emphasize personal factors of the actor, such as Kraft's perceived laziness or stubbornness, and deemphasize situational factors, such as poor working conditions or unsatisfactory rewards, as explanations of the situation. Research has suggested that in performance appraisals in general, subordinates attribute performance more to situational causes, while managers attributed subordinate behavior to personal causes.[24] In addition, actors are less likely to assume moral responsibility for an action because they attribute it to external causes.[25] Recognizing this bias should alert individuals to possible inaccuracies in their attributions and diagnoses. These misattributions become particularly significant in the conduct of performance reviews.

The appropriateness of the behavior and the belief that the behavior was meant to affect the observer moderate the effect of point of view on attributions.[26] An observer who views a person acting in a way that is not considered socially desirable will attribute the actor's behavior to personality characteristics. If an assembly line worker was observed sabotaging the product, top management would attribute this action to the worker's personality. Similarly, an observer who believes that a person has acted in a way to specifically influence the observer will attribute the actor's behavior to his or her personality traits. If Margaret Healey felt that Caroline Kraft performed poorly to "get back at management," she likely would attribute the cause of Caroline's behavior to her personality.

The perceived success or failure of a behavior may also complicate the attribution of its cause, as shown in Table 2–1 and Figure 2–6. By successful behavior we mean actions that are viewed as effective and in line with the organization's goals. Increases in performance, efficiency, or following work rules are considered successful behaviors. Failures include increased turnover or absenteeism, declining productivity or morale, or more specific performance of unacceptable behaviors. Although the research results are somewhat mixed, the weight of evidence suggests that actors tend to attribute successes to personal factors and failures to situational factors, and observers do the reverse.[27]

In some cases, the tendency for a manager to make the easiest response causes different attributions.[28] A manager more easily assumes, for example, that a worker is responsible for a problem, rather than the situation. To determine the situational impact typically requires the manager to spend time investigating the situation in great detail. Correcting the situation is also more difficult than dealing with or removing the individual seen as responsible. A manager can more easily assume that a

Table 2–1 Summary of Attributions

Person Making Attributions	Behavior as Focus of Evaluation	Quality of Actions	
		Success	Failure
Actor	Actor's actions	Personal	Situational
	Observer's actions	Situational	Personal
Observer	Actor's actions	Situational	Personal
	Observer's actions	Personal	Situational

Figure 2–6 A Student Example of Attribution

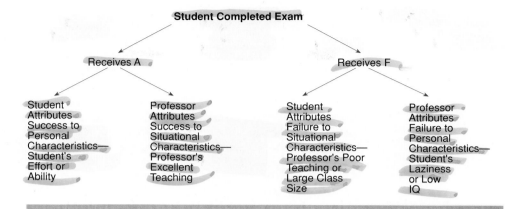

Student Completed Exam

Receives A

Receives F

Student Attributes Success to Personal Characteristics— Student's Effort or Ability

Professor Attributes Success to Situational Characteristics— Professor's Excellent Teaching

Student Attributes Failure to Situational Characteristics— Professor's Poor Teaching or Large Class Size

Professor Attributes Failure to Personal Characteristics— Student's Laziness or Low IQ

subordinate is responsible and might need to be replaced than he or she can alter organizational or environmental influences.

Maintaining one's self-concept also can modify perceptions and attributions. Managers may view their subordinates' behavior as a reflection of their own. To maintain their own self-esteem, then, the managers are more likely to attribute subordinates' successes to the manager's contributions (part of the situation) and failures to the subordinates' personalities.

Rectifying Attributional Problems

Testing the nature of attributions in a problem situation should be an early and recurring step of diagnosis. As much as possible, individuals should be involved in *actively* processing information about the situation.[29] By knowing the typical attributional biases, individuals can be alert to these biases in their own attributions and verify the accuracy of the causes they identify. They can then act on the basis of correct causal attributions. Although little research has been done about multicultural biases in attribution, managers should be alert to this possibility. Differences in assumed personal responsibility as opposed to situational responsibility may be a function of cultural attributes.

THE LEARNING PROCESS

In addition to perception and attribution, *learning,* which refers to the acquisition of skills, knowledge, ability, or attitudes, influences both description and diagnosis of organizational behavior. In this chapter we focus on the way individuals learn, beginning with three models of learning and concluding with the managerial implications of learning.

Behaviorist Approach

Behaviorists emphasize external influences and the power of rewards in learning. They emphasize the link between a given stimulus and response. Recall Pavlov's ground-breaking work with dogs, as presented in Figure 2–7.[30] He noted that, upon presentation of powdered meat blown through a tube (unconditioned stimulus) to a dog, the dog salivated (unconditioned response). The ringing of a bell (neutral stimulus) yielded no salivation responses. After pairing the ringing bell with the piece of meat several times, Pavlov then rang the bell without the meat, and the dog salivated (conditioned response). In classical conditioning, after repeated pairing of neutral and unconditioned stimuli, solitary presentation of the neutral stimulus led to a conditioned response, as illustrated in Figure 2–8. (1) The telephone rings and

Figure 2–7 **Pavlov's Conditioning Experiments**

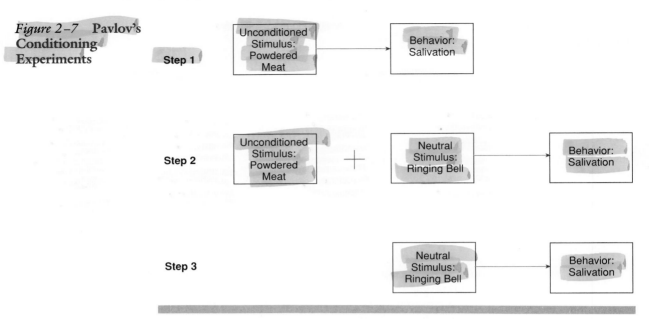

the salesclerk jumps. (2) Flashing the light when the telephone rings leads to the salesclerk jumping. (3) The light flashing alone leads to the salesclerk jumping.

Operant conditioning extends classical conditioning to focus on the consequences of a behavior, as shown in Figure 2–9.[31] While a stimulus can still cue a response behavior, the desired or undesired consequence that follows the behavior determines whether the behavior will recur. For example, an individual who receives a bonus (a positive consequence) after creative performance (behavior) on a work assignment (stimulus) is more likely to repeat the creative behavior than if his or her performance is ignored (a negative consequence). Continuation of Caroline Kraft's performance at the Rock Hill Savings Bank may depend on the consequences associated with it. She is more likely to continue her performance if she continues to receive pay increases and praise than if she is demoted or receives a warning. Chapter 4 examines the significance of operant conditioning for motivation in organizations.

Figure 2–8 **An Example of Classical Conditioning**

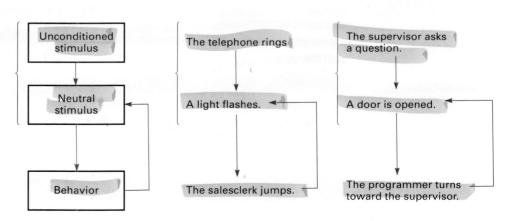

Figure 2–9 **An Example of Operant Conditioning**

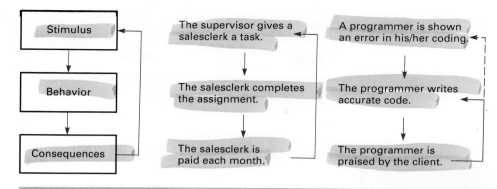

Cognitive Approach In contrast to the behavior-reinforcement links that are central to behaviorist theories, cognitive theorists emphasize the internal mental processes involved in gaining new insights. They view learning as occurring from the joining of various cues in the environment into a mental map. In early cognitive experiments, rats learned to run through a maze to reach a goal of food.[32] Repeated trials would cause a rat to develop and strengthen cognitive connections that identified the correct path to the goal.

Employees, too, can develop a cognitive map that shows the path to a specific goal, as illustrated in Figure 2–10; here the cognitive processes join (and act on) the stimulus to result in a given behavior. On-the-job training in a new work process should result in a new cognitive map of job performance for the members of the loan department. Cognitive learning theories have been integrated into expectancy and goal-setting theories as described in Chapter 4.

Social Learning Approach Extending beyond both behavioral and cognitive learning theories, social learning theory integrates the behaviorist and cognitive approaches with the idea of modeling or imitating behaviors.[33] Learners first watch others who act as models, next develop a mental picture of the behavior and its consequences, and finally try the behavior.[34]

Figure 2–10 **Cognitive Approach to Learning**

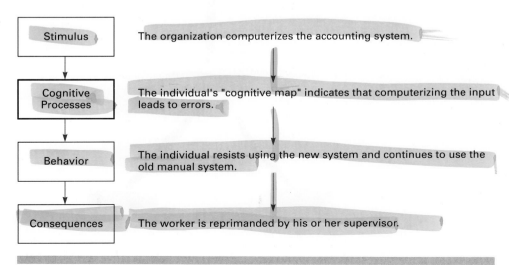

If positive consequences result, the learner repeats the behavior; if negative consequences occur, no repetition occurs. Figure 2–11 illustrates the social learning approach. The learning impact occurs when the subject tries the behavior and experiences a favorable result, as in the behaviorist approach. At the same time, the learner's development of a cognitive image of the situation incorporates a basic aspect of cognitive learning.

Figure 2–11 **Social Learning Approach to Learning**

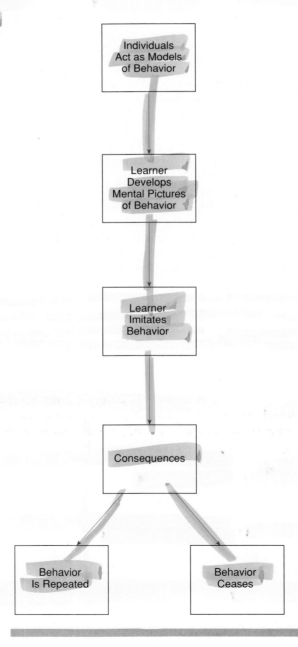

MANAGERIAL IMPLICATIONS OF LEARNING

How can managers encourage their own and others' learning in the workplace? They can ensure that appropriate conditions for learning exist; providing appropriate stimuli (e.g., complete and understandable information or material) should facilitate acquisition of skills, knowledge, or attitudes. Managers should reinforce desired learned behaviors. They should also provide environmental cues that encourage learning; structuring a context (e.g., a physical and emotional climate) that supports learning is essential.

Managers can also use the following modeling strategy, as shown in Figure 2–12. First, the manager should identify the goal or target behaviors that will lead to improved performance: For Caroline Kraft fewer errors will lead to better performance. Second, the manager must select the appropriate model and determine whether to present the model through a live demonstration, training film, videotape, or other media. Third, managers must make sure the employee is capable of meeting the technical skill requirements of the target behaviors: To ensure Caroline Kraft's skill level, Margaret Healey sent her to a training program. Fourth, the managers must structure a favorable and positive learning environment to increase the likelihood that workers will learn the new behaviors and act in the desired way. Fifth, management must model the target behavior and carry out supporting activities such as role playing. They must clearly demonstrate the positive consequences of engaging in the modeled target behaviors. Sixth, they must positively reinforce reproduction of the target behaviors both in training and back on the job. For example, Healey must make sure that the reward system fits the behaviors she desires from Caroline Kraft. Bonuses for greatly improved productivity or praise for a job well done clearly would encourage the desired behaviors. Once the target behaviors are reproduced, management must maintain and strengthen them through the continued use of appropriate rewards.

Finally, managers should provide individuals who can model desired behaviors. Reproduction of desired behaviors should be encouraged and reinforced. Reproduction of desired attitudes should also be stimulated. But the process of attitude formation is more complicated than can be explained by learning theory alone.

Learning by a Multicultural Work Force

Although the basic processes remain the same regardless of the type of worker or his or her cultural origins, the context in which learning occurs can significantly influence the outcomes. We know at a simplistic level that on-the-job training may have different outcomes than off-the-job training does. Consider the implications of conducting the training in an array of different countries that typically have significantly different approaches to learning: British universities, for example, emphasize tutorials, whereas schools in the United States more commonly use larger group learning experiences. In addition, different personal learning styles may be fostered by these various educational experiences. Japanese reasoning has been characterized

Figure 2–12 **A Modeling Strategy for Managers**

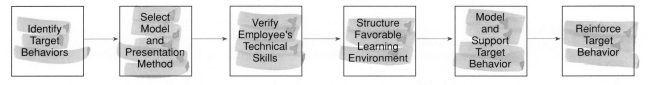

Identify Target Behaviors → Select Model and Presentation Method → Verify Employee's Technical Skills → Structure Favorable Learning Environment → Model and Support Target Behavior → Reinforce Target Behavior

as analytical, where the whole is broken into parts, and Western reasoning as comprehensive, where the parts are combined into the whole.[35] Diagnosing the nature of learning and constructing experiences that maximize it are essential for functioning in a global environment.

DEVELOPING PRODUCTIVE ATTITUDES

An *attitude* is a consistent predisposition to respond to various aspects of people, situations, or objects that we infer from a person's behavior or expressed attitude, as well as from other cognitive, affective, or conative responses, as shown in Table 2–2. Attitudes are pervasive and predict behavior toward their objects.[36] We might, for example, determine an individual's job satisfaction by inferring it from his or her general demeanor on the job or by asking the person to describe this attitude. We often use attitude surveys or other collections of attitude scales to assess individuals' attitudes toward their job, coworkers, supervisor, or the organization at large.[37] Identifying attitudes should be part of description in the diagnostic approach; determining their causes, part of diagnosis. How do attitudes form in organizations? What effect do they have on worker behaviors and organizational performance?

Components of Attitudes

Research has suggested that attitudes have three components, as shown in Table 2–3: cognitive, affective, and behavioral.[38] The *cognitive* component includes the beliefs an individual has about a certain person, object, or situation. These learned beliefs, such as "You need to work long hours to get ahead in this job," serve as an antecedent to specific attitudes. Although we have many beliefs, only some are important enough to lead to significant attitudes. The *affective* component refers to the person's *feeling* that results from his or her beliefs about a person, object, or situation. A person may feel anger or frustration because he or she believes hard work deserves promotion, and the person has worked hard but has not been promoted. The affective component becomes stronger as an individual has more often and directly experienced a focal object, person, or situation and as the feeling is expressed more often.[39] The *behavioral* component is the individual's behavior that occurs as a result of his or her feeling about the focal person, object, or situation. An individual may complain, request a transfer, or lower productivity because he or she feels dissatisfied with work.

The situation in the residential loan department at Rock Hill Savings Bank illustrates the three components of attitudes. Clearly the members of the department

Table 2–2 Responses Used to Infer Attitudes

Response Mode	Response Category		
	Cognition	Affect	Conation
Verbal	Expressions of beliefs about attitude object	Expressions of feelings toward attitude object	Expressions of behavioral intentions
Nonverbal	Perceptual reactions to attitude object	Physiological reactions to attitude object	Overt behaviors with respect to attitude object

SOURCE: Reprinted from I. Ajzen, Attitude structure and behavior. In A. R. Pratkanis, S. J. Breckler, and A. G. Greenwald, eds., *Attitude Structure and Function* (Hillsdale, N.J.: Erlbaum, 1989), p. 242. Reprinted with permission.

Table 2–3 **The Components of Attitudes**

Components	Definition	Example
Cognitive	Beliefs, knowledge, understanding	The workers' beliefs about performance standards and supervision
Affective	Favorable or unfavorable feelings	The workers' feelings about the new regulations
Behavioral	Human actions	The workers' performance

have a series of beliefs and values about performance standards, supervision, and the nature of appropriate loans. For Caroline Kraft, these result in negative feelings toward the new regulations and perhaps her job. These attitudes in turn result in the behavior of declining performance.

A more recent way of looking at attitudes takes a sociocognitive approach: It considers an attitude as a representation of an individual's interaction with his or her social environment.[40] The object of an attitude is represented as a member of a category in a person's memory. Then an individual uses the attitude to help evaluate an object, deciding, for example, whether it is good or bad, positive or negative, favored or not, and then determining the strategy to take toward it. Attitude-related information, then, helps process complex information. Applying this way of thinking about attitudes to the bank situation would suggest that Caroline's attitudinal strategies about her work may need to be altered, although they may be appropriate for other objects.

In addition, the accessibility of an attitude, or ease with which it is activated, affects its implementation.[41] Accessibility is increased by personal experience with the object and repeated expression of the attitude.[42] Thus the focus of change would be either on improving the fit between attitude and object or increasing the accessibility of attitudes about work that are not currently accessible.

But individuals may also experience cognitive dissonance, which will affect the relationship between their attitudes and behaviors. *Cognitive dissonance* describes the situation where items of knowledge, information, attitudes, or beliefs held by an individual are contradictory.[43] For example, Caroline Kraft might assess her own performance as excellent; this attitude might conflict with Margaret's communicated performance appraisals. To reduce the dissonance, Caroline might not "hear" Margaret's assessments, or she might hear them but devalue Margaret's position and hence the importance of her comments.

ATTITUDES IN A MULTICULTURAL WORK FORCE

The more diverse the work force the more likely it is that individuals will have an array of attitudes. Their beliefs, formed in large part from their socioeconomic background and other experiences, could vary significantly. Recent research suggests significant changes in attitudes toward various national and racial groups, as well as various gender roles.[44]

As the work force becomes multinational, diagnosing the basis of attitudes and predicting their consequent behaviors becomes more problematic. According to one researcher, national cultures have been described as differing, for example, on four dimensions, which he labels power distance, uncertainty avoidance, individualism, and masculinity.[45] *Power distance* is the extent to which a society accepts the fact that power in institutions and organizations is distributed unequally. *Uncertainty avoidance* refers to the extent to which a society responds to the potential occurrence of uncertain and ambiguous situations by providing career stability, establishing formal rules, not tolerating deviant ideas and behaviors, and believing in absolute truths and the attainment of expertise. *Individualism* implies a loosely knit social framework in which people are supposed to take care of themselves and their immediate families only. The opposite, *collectivism,* is characterized by a tight social framework in which people distinguish between in-groups (including relatives, clans, and employees to whom they feel they owe absolute loyalty) and out-groups. *Masculinity* is the extent to which the dominant values in society reflect traditionally masculine behaviors, such as assertiveness and the acquisition of money and things, and a lesser concern for relationships. As a result of variations on these dimensions, interpersonal processes, group behavior, and organizational structure vary in different cultures. How might these differences influence the management of a multinational work force?

Research about the relationship between attitudes and behaviors, for example, has been done primarily in the United States at work sites that function solely in the United States. Would the same attitudes occur in France, Germany, or Japan? Would the same behaviors result from the same attitudes? Because we can only conjecture about the specific correlation, we must be sure to describe and diagnose situations as accurately as possible.

MANAGERIAL IMPLICATIONS OF ATTITUDE FORMATION

In all countries managers should recognize the links between attitudes and behavior. Influencing an attitude requires altering both a belief and its related feelings. At the Rock Hill Savings Bank, for example, changing the attitude toward the new work procedures requires first altering the beliefs and values of the workers; Margaret Healey might need to show her subordinates that their belief that the new paperwork is superfluous is inaccurate. Dissemination of factual information may eventually change some beliefs, but more emotion-oriented persuasive techniques and longer term educational efforts may be needed to alter attitudes. In the United States, for example, training in managing a culturally diverse work force begins with awareness training, which focuses on changing attitudes toward various ethnic, racial, and national groups.[46]

Job Satisfaction

One of the most controversial issues for managers is the call for job satisfaction among workers. Satisfaction results when a job fulfills or facilitates the attainment of individual values and standards, and dissatisfaction occurs when the job is seen as blocking such attainment.[47] Although satisfaction was at one time believed to be the cause of improved job performance, recent research negates such a relationship. It suggests more complicated interactions between satisfaction, commitment, turnover, and productivity, for example.[48] Regardless of the current state of the controversy, job satisfaction likely is a desirable end in its own right and an attitude managers should encourage. Reading 2–1, "Organizational Psychology and the Pursuit of the Happy/Productive Worker," discusses the feasibility of having both satisfied and productive workers and how to facilitate such an outcome.

SUMMARY

In this chapter we focused on four basic individual processes: perception, attribution, learning, and attitude formation. Table 2–4 offers a set of diagnostic questions for them. Perception, or the selection and organization of stimuli, influences the way

Table 2–4 **Diagnostic Questions from the Perception, Attribution, Learning, and Attitude-Formation Perspectives**

- What factors influence the perceptions of organizational members?
- What distortions of perception occur?
- What factors influence the attributions of organizational members?
- What biases exist in these attributions?
- What behaviors are reinforced as part of the learning process?
- What cues encourage learning?
- What modeling strategies exist in the organization?
- How are these strategies supported in the organization?
- What beliefs and values do individuals hold?
- How do these beliefs and values influence the individuals' attitudes?
- What functional and dysfunctional behavioral intentions result from the individuals' attitudes?

we describe organizational situations. Because organizational phenomena are not totally objective, characteristics of the perceiver and the object being perceived influence what aspects become important and are incorporated into a description. Often, we distort perceptions through stereotyping, the halo effect, projection, expectancy, and other mechanisms, and cause inaccurate descriptions or diagnoses.

Just as we attend to and organize stimuli in predictable ways, we also attribute reasons for behavior in predictable ways. Individuals assign reasons according to whether they are actors or observers of the behavior, and also based upon the effectiveness of the behavior. Again, recognizing the biases is essential for accurate diagnosis.

We discussed the role of learning as another significant form of individual behavior. The behaviorists emphasize the links between behaviors and their consequences. Cognitive theories focus on attempts to understand and predict the functioning of the human mind. Social learning theorists encourage the development of a mental map of the situation and then build on it with the use of imitation in learning. Managers can develop protocols for learning that incorporate the principles of these approaches.

Finally, we discussed the nature of attitude formation in organizations. Attitudes have cognitive, affective, and behavioral components, the sequencing of which affects attitude formation and resulting behaviors. Individuals have certain beliefs and values that result in specific attitudes that in turn influence behaviors. Understanding attitude formation in a global environment poses major challenges for organizational leaders.

Reading 2–1

Organizational Psychology and the Pursuit of the Happy/Productive Worker
Barry Staw

What I am going to talk about in this article is an old and overworked topic, but one that remains very much a source of confusion and controversy. It is also a topic that continues to attract the attention of managers and academic researchers alike, frequently being the focus of both popular books and scholarly articles. The issue is how to manage an organization so that employees can be both happy and pro-

ductive—a situation where workers and managers are both satisfied with the outcomes.

The pursuit of the happy/productive worker could be viewed as an impossible dream from the Marxist perspective of inevitable worker–management conflict. Such a goal could also be seen as too simple or naive from the traditional industrial relations view of outcomes being a product of necessary bargaining and compromise. Yet, from the psychological perspective, the pursuit of the happy/productive worker has seemed a worthwhile though difficult endeavor, one that might be achieved if we greatly increase our knowledge of work attitudes and behavior. In this article, I will examine this psychological perspective and try to provide a realistic appraisal of where we now stand in the search for satisfaction and productivity in work settings.

APPROACHES TO THE HAPPY/ PRODUCTIVE WORKER

One of the earliest pursuits of the happy/productive worker involved the search for a relationship between satisfaction and productivity. The idea was that the world might be neatly divided into situations where workers are either happy and productive or unhappy and unproductive. If this were true, then it would be a simple matter to specify the differences between management styles present in the two sets of organizations and to come up with a list of prescriptions for improvement. Unfortunately, research has never supported such a clear relationship between individual satisfaction and productivity. For over thirty years, starting with Brayfield and Crockett's classic review of the job satisfaction-performance literature,[1] and again with Vroom's discussion of satisfaction-performance research,[2] organizational psychologists have had to contend with the fact that happiness and productivity may not necessarily go together. As a result, most organizational psychologists have come to accept the argument that satisfaction and performance may relate to two entirely different individual decisions—decisions to participate and to produce.[3]

Though psychologists have acknowledged the fact that satisfaction and performance are not tightly linked, this has not stopped them from pursuing the happy/productive worker. In fact, over the last thirty years, an enormous variety of theories have attempted to show how managers can reach the promised land of high satisfaction and productivity. The theories shown in Table 2–5 constitute only an abbreviated list of recent attempts to reach this positive state.

None of the theories in Table 2–5 has inherited the happy/productive worker hypothesis in the simple sense of believing that job satisfaction and performance generally co-vary in the world *as it now exists*. But, these models all make

Table 2–5 Paths to the Happy/Productive Worker

Worker Participation	The Pursuit of Excellence
Supportive Leadership	Socio-Technical Systems
9–9 Systems	Organizational Commitment
Job Enrichment	High Performing Systems
Behavior Modification	Theory Z
Goal Setting	Strong Culture

either indirect or direct assumptions that *it is possible* to achieve a world where both satisfaction and performance will be present. Some of the theories focus on ways to increase job satisfaction, with the implicit assumption that performance will necessarily follow; some strive to directly increase performance, with the assumption that satisfaction will result; and some note that satisfaction and performance will be a joint product of implementing certain changes in the organization.

Without going into the specifics of each of these routes to the happy/productive worker, I think it is fair to say that most of the theories in Table 2–5 have been oversold. Historically, they each burst on the scene with glowing and almost messianic predictions, with proponents tending to simplify the process of change, making it seem like a few easy tricks will guarantee benefits to workers and management alike. The problem, of course, is that as results have come in from both academic research and from wider practical application, the benefits no longer have appeared so strong nor widespread. Typically, the broader the application and the more well-documented the study (with experimental controls and measures of expected costs and benefits), the weaker have been the empirical results. Thus, in the end, both managers and researchers have often been left disillusioned, skeptical that any part of these theories are worth a damn and that behavioral science will ever make a contribution to management.

My goal with this article is to *lower our expectations*— to show why it is so difficult to make changes in both satisfaction and performance. My intention is not to paint such a pessimistic picture as to justify not making any changes at all, but to inoculate us against the frustrations of slow progress. My hope is to move us toward a reasoned but sustainable pursuit of the happy/productive worker— away from the alternating practice of fanfare and despair.

CHANGING JOB ATTITUDES

Although organizational psychologists have accepted the notion that job satisfaction and performance do not necessarily co-vary, they have still considered job attitudes as something quite permeable or subject to change. This "blank slate" approach to job attitudes comes from prevailing psychological views of the individual, where the person is seen as a creature who constantly appraises the work situation, evaluates the merits of the context, and formulates an attitude based on these conditions. As the work situation changes, individuals are thought to be sensitive to the shifts, adjusting their attitudes in a positive or negative direction. With such an approach to attitudes, it is easy to see why job satisfaction has been a common target of organizational change, and why attempts to redesign work have evolved as a principal mechanism for improving job satisfaction.

Currently, the major debate in the job design area concerns whether individuals are more sensitive to objective job conditions or social cues. In one camp are proponents of job redesign who propose that individuals are highly receptive to concrete efforts to improve working conditions. Hackman and Oldham, for example, argue that satisfaction can be increased by improving a job in terms of its variety (doing a wider number of things), identity (seeing how one's various tasks make a meaningful whole), responsibility (being in charge of one's own work and its quality), feedback (knowing when one has done a good job), and significance (the meaning or relative importance of one's contribution to the organization or society in general).[4] In the opposing camp are advocates of social information processing. These researchers argue that jobs are often ambiguous entities subject to multiple interpretations and perceptions.[5] Advocates of social information processing have noted that the positive or negative labeling of a task can greatly determine one's attitude toward the job, and that important determinants of this labeling are the opinions of co-workers who voice positive or negative views of the work. These researchers have shown that it may be as easy to persuade workers that their jobs are interesting by influencing the *perception* of a job as it is to make objective changes in the work role.

The debate between job design and social information processing has produced two recent shifts in the way we think about job attitudes. First, organizational psychology now places greater emphasis on the role of cognition and subjective evaluation in the way people respond to jobs. This is probably helpful, because even though we have generally measured job conditions with perceptual scales, we have tended to confuse these perceptions with objective job conditions. We need to be reminded that perceptions of job characteristics do not necessarily reflect reality, yet they can determine how we respond to that reality.

The second shift in thinking about job attitudes is a movement toward situationalism, stressing how even slight alterations in job context can influence one's perception of a job. It is now believed that people's job attitudes may be influenced not only by the objective properties of the work, but also by subtle cues given off by co-workers or supervisors that the job is dull or interesting. I think this new view is a mistake since it overstates the role of external influence in the determination of job attitudes. The reality may be that individuals are quite resistant to change efforts, with their attitudes coming more as a function of personal disposition than situational influence.

THE CONSISTENCY OF JOB ATTITUDES

Robert Kahn recently observed that, although our standard of living and working conditions have improved dramatically since World War II, reports of satisfaction on national surveys have not changed dramatically.[6] This implies that job satisfaction might be something of a "sticky variable," one that is not easily changed by outside influence. Some research on the consistency of job attitudes leads to the same conclusion. Schneider and Dachler, for example, found

very strong consistency in satisfaction scores over a 16-month longitudinal study (averaging .56 for managers and .58 for non-managers).[7] Pulakos and Schmitt also found that high school students' pre-employment expectations of satisfaction correlated significantly with ratings of their jobs several years later.[8] These findings, along with the fact that job satisfaction is generally intertwined with both life satisfaction and mental health, imply that there is some ongoing consistency in job attitudes, and that job satisfaction may be determined as much by dispositional properties of the individual as any changes in the situation.

A Berkeley colleague, Joseph Garbarino, has long captured this notion of a dispositional source of job attitudes with a humorous remark, "I always told my children at a young age that their most important decision in life would be whether they wanted to be happy or not; everything else is malleable enough to fit the answer to this question." What Garbarino implies is that job attitudes are fairly constant, and when reality changes for either the better or worse, we can easily distort that reality to fit our underlying disposition. Thus, individuals may think a great deal about the nature of their jobs, but satisfaction can result as much from the unique way a person views the world around him as from any social influence or objective job characteristics. That is, individuals predisposed to be happy may interpret their jobs in a much different way than those with more negative predispositions.

The Attitudinal Consistency Study

Recently, I have been involved with two studies attempting to test for dispositional sources of job attitudes. In the first study, Jerry Ross and I reanalyzed data from the National Longitudinal Survey, a study conducted by labor economists at Ohio State.[9] We used this survey to look at the stability of job attitudes over time and job situations. The survey's measures of attitudes were not very extensive but did provide one of the few available sources of data on objective job changes.

The National Longitudinal Survey data revealed an interesting pattern of results. We found that job satisfaction was fairly consistent over time, with significant relationships among job attitudes over three- and five-year time intervals. We also found that job satisfaction showed consistency *even when people changed jobs*. This later finding is especially important, since it directly contradicts the prevailing assumptions of job attitude research.

Most job design experiments and organizational interventions that strive to improve job attitudes change a small aspect of work, but look for major changes in job satisfaction. However, the National Longitudinal Survey data showed that when people changed their place of work (which would naturally include one's supervisor, working conditions, and procedures), there was still significant consistency in attitudes. One could, of course, argue that people leave one terrible job for another, and this is why such consistency in job attitude arises. Therefore, we checked for consistency across occupational changes. The National Longitudinal Survey showed consistency not only across occupational changes, but also when people changed *both* their employers and their occupations. This evidence of consistency tells us that people may not be as malleable as we would like to think they are, and that there may be some underlying tendency toward equilibrium in job attitudes. If you are dissatisfied in one job context, you are also likely to be dissatisfied in another (perhaps better) environment.

The Dispositional Study
The consistency data from the National Longitudinal Survey, while interesting, do not tell us what it is that may underlie a tendency to be satisfied or dissatisfied on the job. Therefore, Nancy Bell (a doctoral student at the Berkeley Business School), John Clausen (a developmental sociologist at Berkeley), and I undertook a study to find some of the dispositional sources of job satisfaction.[10] We sought to relate early personality characteristics to job attitudes later in life, using a very unusual longitudinal data source.

There are three longitudinal personality projects that have been running for over fifty years at Berkeley (the Berkeley Growth Study, the Oakland Growth Study, and the Guidance Study), and they have since been combined into what is now called the Intergenerational Study. Usually when psychologists speak of longitudinal studies, they mean data collected from one or two year intervals. These data span over 50 years. Usually, when psychologists refer to personality ratings, they mean self-reports derived from the administration of various questionnaires. Much of the Intergenerational Study data are clinical ratings derived from questionnaires, observation, and interview materials evaluated by a different set of raters for each period of the individual's life. Thus, these data are of unusual quality for psychological research.

Basically what we did with data from the Intergenerational Study was to construct an affective disposition scale that measured a very general positive-negative orientation of people. We then related this scale to measures of job attitudes at different periods in people's lives. The ratings used for our affective disposition scale included items such as "cheerful," "satisfied with self," and "irritable" (reverse coded), and we correlated this scale with measures of job and career satisfaction. The results were very provocative. We found that affective dispositions, from as early as the junior-high-school years, significantly predicted job attitudes during middle and late adulthood (ages 40–60). The magnitude of correlations was not enormous (in the .3 to .4 range). But, these results are about as strong as we usually see between two attitudes measured on the same questionnaire by the same person at the same time—yet, these data cut across different raters and over fifty years in time.

What are we to conclude from this personality research as well as our reanalyses of the National Longitudinal Survey? I think we can safely conclude that there is a fair amount of consistency in job attitudes and that there may be dispositional as well as situational sources of job satisfaction. Thus, it is possible that social information processing theorists have been on the right track in viewing jobs as ambiguous entities that necessitate interpretation by individuals. But, it is also likely that the interpretation of jobs (whether they are perceived as positive or negative) can come as much from internal, dispositional causes (e.g., happiness or depression) as external sources. Consequently, efforts to improve job satisfaction via changes in job conditions will need to contend with stable personal dispositions toward work—forces that may favor consistency or equilibrium in the way people view the world around them.

THE INTRANSIGENCE OF JOB PERFORMANCE
Although we have not conducted research on the consistency of performance or its resistance to change, I think there are some parallels between the problems of changing attitudes and performance. Just as job attitudes may be constrained by individual dispositions, there are many elements of both the individual and work situation that can make improvements in job performance difficult.[11]

Most of the prevailing theories of work performance are concerned with individual motivation. They prescribe various techniques intended to stimulate, reinforce, or lure people into working harder. Most of these theories have little to say about the individual's limits of task ability, predisposition for working hard, or the general energy or activity level of the person. Somewhat naively, our theories have maintained that performance is under the complete control of the individual. Even though there are major individual differences affecting the quantity or quality of work produced, we have assumed that *if the employee really wants to perform better, his or her performance will naturally go up*.

There already exist some rather strong data that refute these implicit assumptions about performance. A number of studies[12] have shown that mental and physical abilities can be reliable predictors of job performance, and it is likely that other dispositions (e.g., personality characteristics) will eventually be found to be associated with effective performance of certain work roles. Thus, influencing work effort may not be enough to cause wide swings in performance, unless job performance is somewhat independent of ability (e.g., in a low skill job). Many work roles may be so dependent on ability (such as those of a professional athlete, musician, inventor) that increases in effort may simply not cause large changes in the end product.

In addition to ability, there may also be other individual factors that contribute to the consistency of performance. People who work hard in one situation are likely to be the ones who exert high effort in a second situation. If, for example, the person's energy level (including need for sleep) is relatively constant over time, we should not expect wide changes in available effort. And, if personality dimensions such as dependability and self-confidence can predict one's achievement level over the lifecourse,[13] then a similar set of personal attributes may well constitute limitations to possible improvements in performance. Already, assessment centers have capitalized on this notion by using personality measures to predict performance in many corporate settings.

Performance may not be restricted just because of the individual's level of ability and effort, however. Jobs may *themselves* be designed so that performance is not under the control of the individual, regardless of ability or effort. Certainly we are aware of the fact that an assembly line worker's output is more a product of the speed of the line than any personal preference. In administrative jobs, too, what one does may be constrained by the work cycle or technical procedures. There may be many people with interlocking tasks so that an increase in the performance of one employee doesn't mean much if several tasks must be completed sequentially or simultaneously in order to improve productivity. Problems also arise in situations where doing one's job better may not be predicated upon a burst of energy or desire, but upon increases in materials, financial support, power, and resources. As noted by Kanter, the administrator must often negotiate, hoard, and form coalitions to get anything done on the job, since there are lots of actors vying for the attention and resources of the organization.[14] Thus, the nature of the organization, combined with the abilities and efforts of individuals to maneuver in the organization, may serve to constrain changes in individual performance.

ASSESSING THE DAMAGE

So far I have taken a somewhat dark or pessimistic view of the search for the happy/productive worker. I have noted that in terms of satisfaction and performance, it may not be easy to create perfect systems because both happiness and performance are constrained variables, affected by forces not easily altered by our most popular interventions and prescriptions for change. Should organizational psychologists therefore close up shop and go home? Should we move to a more descriptive study of behavior as opposed to searching for improvements in work attitudes and performance?

I think such conclusions are overly pessimistic. We need to interpret the stickiness of job attitudes and performance not as an invitation to complacency or defeat, but as a realistic assessment that it will take very strong treatments to move these entrenched variables. Guzzo, Jackson, and Katzell have recently made a similar point after a statistical examination (called meta-analysis) of organizational interventions designed to improve productivity.[15] They noted that the most effective changes are often *multiple treatments,* where several things are changed at once in a given organization. Thus, instead of idealistic and optimistic promises, we may literally need to throw the kitchen sink at the problem.

The problem of course is that we have more than one kitchen sink! As noted earlier, nearly every theory of organizational behavior has been devoted to predicting and potentially improving job attitudes and performance. And, simply aggregating these treatments is not likely to have the desired result, since many of these recommendations consist of conflicting prescriptions for change. Therefore, it would be wiser to look for compatible *systems* of variables that can possibly be manipulated in concert. Let us briefly consider three systems commonly used in organizational change efforts and then draw some conclusions about their alternative uses.

THREE SYSTEMS OF ORGANIZATIONAL CHANGE

The Individually-Oriented System

The first alternative is to build a strong individually-oriented system, based on the kind of traditional good management that organizational psychologists have been advocating for years. This system would emphasize a number of venerable features of Western business organizations such as:

- Tying extrinsic rewards (such as pay) to performance.
- Setting realistic and challenging goals.
- Evaluating employee performance accurately and providing feedback on performance.
- Promoting on the basis of skill and performance rather than personal characteristics, power, or connections.
- Building the skill level of the workforce through training and development.
- Enlarging and enriching jobs through increases in responsibility, variety, and significance.

All of the above techniques associated with the individually-oriented system are designed to promote both satisfaction and productivity. The major principle underlying each of these features is to structure the work and/or reward system so that high performance is either intrinsically or extrinsically rewarding to the individual, thus creating a situation where high performance contributes to job satisfaction.

In practice, there can be numerous bugs in using an individually-oriented system to achieve satisfaction and performance. For example, just saying that rewards should be based on performance is easier than knowing what the proper relationship should be or whether there should be discontinuities at the high or low end of that relationship. Should we, for instance, lavish rewards on the few highest performers, deprive the lowest performers, or establish a constant linkage between pay and performance? In terms of goal-setting, should goals be set by management, workers, or joint decision making, and what should the proper baseline be for measuring improvements? In terms of job design, what is the proper combination of positive social cues and actual job enrichment that will improve motivation and satisfaction?

These questions are important and need to be answered in order to "fine-tune" or fully understand an individually-oriented system. Yet, even without answers to these questions, we already know that a well-run organization using an individually-oriented system *can* be effective. The problem is we usually don't implement such a system, either completely or very well, in most organizations. Instead, we often compare poorly managed corporations using individually-oriented systems (e.g., those with rigid bureaucratic structures) with more effectively run firms using another motivational system (e.g., Japanese organizations), concluding that the individual model is wrong. The truth may be that the individual model may be just as correct as other approaches, but we simply don't implement it as well.

The Group-Oriented System

Individually-oriented systems are obviously not the only way to go. We can also have a group-oriented system, where satisfaction and performance are derived from group participation. In fact, much of organizational life could be designed around groups, if we wanted to capitalize fully on the power of groups to influence work attitudes and behavior.[16] The basic idea would be to make group participation so important that groups would be capable of controlling both satisfaction and performance. Some of the most common techniques would be:

- Organizing work around intact groups.
- Having groups charged with selection, training, and rewarding of members.
- Using groups to enforce strong norms for behavior, with group involvement in off-the-job as well as on-the-job behavior.
- Distributing resources on a group rather than individual basis.
- Allowing and perhaps even promoting intergroup rivalry so as to build within-group solidarity.

Group-oriented systems may be difficult for people at the top to control, but they can be very powerful and involving. We know from military research that soldiers can fight long and hard, not out of special patriotism, but from devotion and loyalty to their units. We know that participation in various high-tech project groups can be immensely involving, both in terms of one's attitudes and performance. We also know that people will serve long and hard hours to help build or preserve organizational divisions or departments, perhaps more out of loyalty and altruism than self-interest. Thus, because individuals will work to achieve group praise and adoration, a group-oriented system, effectively managed, can potentially contribute to high job performance and satisfaction.

The Organizationally-Oriented System

A third way of organizing work might be an organizationally-oriented system, using the principles of Ouchi's Theory Z and Lawler's recommendations for developing high-performing systems.[17] The basic goal would be to arrange working conditions so that individuals gain satisfaction from contributing to the entire organization's welfare. If individuals were to identify closely with the organization as a whole, then organizational performance would be intrinsically rewarding to the individual. On a less altruistic basis, individuals might also gain extrinsic rewards from association with a high-performing organization, since successful organizations may provide greater personal opportunities in terms of salary and promotion. Common features of an organizationally-oriented system would be:

- Socialization into the organization as a whole to foster identification with the entire business and not just a particular subunit.
- Job rotation around the company so that loyalty is not limited to one subunit.
- Long training period with the development of skills that are specific to the company and not transferable to other firms in the industry or profession, thus committing people to the employing organization.
- Long-term or protected employment to gain organizational loyalty, with concern for survival and welfare of the firm.
- Decentralized operations, with few departments or subunits to compete for the allegiance of members.
- Few status distinctions between employees so that dissension and separatism are not fostered.
- Economic education and sharing of organizational information about products, financial condition, and strategies of the firm.
- Tying individual rewards (at all levels in the firm) to organizational performance through various forms of profit sharing, stock options, and bonuses.

The Japanese have obviously been the major proponents of organizationally-oriented systems, although some of the features listed here (such as profit sharing) are very American in origin. The odd thing is that Americans have consistently followed an organizationally-oriented system for middle and upper management and for members of professional organizations such as law and accounting firms. For these high-level employees, loyalty may be as valued as immediate performance, with the firm expecting the individual to defend the organization, even if there does not seem to be any obvious self-interest involved. Such loyalty is rarely demanded or expected from the lower levels of traditional Western organizations.

EVALUATING THE THREE SYSTEMS

I started this article by noting that it may be very difficult to change job performance and satisfaction. Then I noted that recognition of this difficulty should not resign us to the present situation, but spur us to stronger and more systemic actions—in a sense, throwing more variables at the problem. As a result, I have tried to characterize three syndromes of actions that might be effective routes toward the happy/productive worker.

One could build a logical case for the use of any of the three motivational systems. Each has the potential for arousing individuals, steering their behavior in desired ways, and building satisfaction as a consequence of high performance. Individually-oriented systems work by tapping the desires and goals of individuals and by taking advantage of our cultural affinity for independence. Group-oriented systems work by taking advantage of our more social selves, using group pressures and loyalty as the means of enforcing desired behavior and dispensing praise for accomplishments. Finally, organizationally-oriented systems function by building intense attraction to the goals of an institution, where individual pleasure is derived from serving the collective welfare.

If we have three logical and defensible routes toward achieving the happy/productive worker, which is the best path? The answer to this question will obviously depend on how the question is phrased. If "best" means appropriate from a cultural point of view, we will get one answer. As Americans, although we respect organizational loyalty, we often become suspicious of near total institutions where behavior is closely monitored and strongly policed—places like the company town and religious cult. If we define "best" as meaning the highest level of current performance, we might get a different answer, since many of the Japanese-run plants are now outperforming the American variety. Still, if we phrase the question in terms of *potential* effectiveness, we may get a third answer. Cross-cultural comparisons, as I mentioned, often pit poorly managed individually-oriented systems (especially those with non-contingent rewards and a bureaucratic promotion system) against more smoothly running group or organizationally-oriented systems. Thus, we really do not know which system, managed to its potential, will lead to the greatest performance.

Mixing the Systems

If we accept the fact that individual, group, and organizationally-oriented systems may each do *something* right, would it be possible to take advantage of all three? That is, can we either combine all three systems into some suprasystem or attempt to build a hybrid system by using the best features of each?

I have trepidations about combining the three approaches. Instead of a stronger treatment, we may end up with either a conflicted or confused environment. Because the individually-oriented system tends to foster competition among individual employees, it would not, for example, be easily merged with group-oriented systems that promote intragroup solidarity. Likewise, organizationally-oriented systems that emphasize how people can serve a common goal may not blend well with group-oriented systems that foster intergroup rivalry. Finally, the use of either a group- or organizationally-oriented reward system may diminish individual motivation, since it becomes more difficult for

the person to associate his behavior with collective accomplishments and outcomes. Thus, by mixing the motivational approaches, we may end up with a watered-down treatment that does not fulfill the potential of *any* of the three systems.

In deciding which system to use, we need to face squarely the costs as well as benefits of the three approaches. For example, firms considering an individually-oriented system should assess not only the gains associated with increases in individual motivation, but also potential losses in collaboration that might result from interpersonal competition. Similarly, companies thinking of using a group-oriented system need to study the trade-offs of intergroup competition that can be a byproduct of increased intragroup solidarity. And, before thinking that an organizationally-oriented system will solve all the firm's problems, one needs to know whether motivation to achieve collective goals can be heightened to the point where it outweighs potential losses in motivation toward personal and group interests. These trade-offs are not trivial. They trigger considerations of human resource policy as well as more general philosophical issues of what the organization wants to be. They also involve technical problems for which current organizational research has few solutions, since scholars have tended to study treatments in isolation rather than the effect of larger systems of variables.

So far, all we can be sure of is that task structure plays a key role in formulating the proper motivational strategy. As an example, consider the following cases: a sales organization can be divided into discrete territories (where total performance is largely the sum of individual efforts), a research organization where several product groups are charged with making new developments (where aggregate performance is close to the sum of group efforts), and a high-technology company where success and failure is due to total collaboration and collective effort. In each of these three cases, the choice of the proper motivational system will be determined by whether one views individual, group, or collective effort as the most important element. Such a choice is also determined by the degree to which one is willing to sacrifice (or trade off) a degree of performance from other elements of the system, be they the behavior of individuals, groups, or the collective whole. Thus, the major point is that each motivational system has its relative strengths and weaknesses—that despite the claims of many of our theories of management, there is no simple or conflict-free road to the happy/productive worker.

CONCLUSION

Although this article started by noting that the search for the happy/productive worker has been a rather quixotic venture, I have tried to end the discussion with some guarded optimism. By using individual, group, and organizational systems, I have shown how it is *at least possible* to create changes than can overwhelm the forces for stability in both job attitudes and performance. None of these three approaches [is] a panacea that will solve all of an organization's problems, and no doubt some very hard choices must be made between them. Yet, caution need not preclude action. Therefore, rather than the usual academic's plea for further research or the consultant's claim for bountiful results, we need actions that are flexible enough to allow for mistakes and adjustments along the way.

REFERENCES

1. A. H. Brayfield and W. H. Crockett, "Employee Attitudes and Employee Performance," *Psychological Bulletin,* 51 (1955): 396–424.
2. Victor H. Vroom, *Work and Motivation* (New York, NY: Wiley, 1969).
3. James G. March and Herbert A. Simon, *Organizations* (New York, NY: Wiley, 1958).
4. Richard J. Hackman and Greg R. Oldham, *Work Redesign* (Reading, MA: Addison-Wesley, 1980).
5. E.G., Gerald R. Salancik and Jeffrey Pfeffer, "A Social Information Processing Approach to Job Attitudes and Task Design," *Administrative Science Quarterly,* 23 (1978): 224–253.
6. Robert Kahn, (1985).
7. Benjamin Schneider and Peter Dachler, "A Note on the Stability of the Job Description Index," *Journal of Applied Psychology,* 63 (1978): 650–653.
8. Elaine D. Pulakos and Neil Schmitt, "A Longitudinal Study of a Valance Model Approach for the Prediction of Job Satisfaction of New Employees," *Journal of Applied Psychology,* 68 (1983): 307–312.
9. Barry M. Staw and Jerry Ross, "Stability in the Midst of Change: A Dispositional Approach to Job Attitudes," *Journal of Applied Psychology,* 70 (1985): 469–480.
10. Barry M. Staw, Nancy E. Bell, and John A. Clausen, "The Dispositional Approach to Job Attitudes: A Lifetime Longitudinal Test," *Administrative Science Quarterly* (March 1986).
11. See, Lawrence H. Peters, Edward J. O'Connor, and Joe R. Eulberg, "Situational Constraints: Sources, Consequences, and Future Considerations," in Kendreth M. Rowland and Gerald R. Ferris, eds., *Research in Personnel and Human Resources Management,* Vol. 3 (Greenwich, CT: JAI Press, 1985).
12. For a review, see Marvin D. Dunnette, "Aptitudes, Abilities, and Skills" in Marvin D. Dunnette, ed., *Handbook of Industrial and Organizational Psychology* (Chicago, IL: Rand McNally, 1976).
13. As found by John Clausen, personal communications, 1986.
14. Rosabeth M. Kanter, *The Change Masters* (New York, NY: Simon & Schuster, 1983).
15. Richard A. Guzzo, Susan E. Jackson, and Raymond A. Katzell, "Meta-analysis Analysis," in Barry M. Staw and Larry L. Cummings, eds., *Research in Organizational Behavior,* Volume 9 (Greenwich, CT: JAI Press, 1987).
16. See, Harold J. Leavitt, "Suppose We Took Groups Seriously," in E. L. Cass and F. G. Zimmer, eds., *Man and Work in Society* (New York, NY: Van Nostrand, 1975).
17. William Ouchi, *Theory Z: How American Business Can Meet the Japanese Challenge* (Reading, MA: Addison-Wesley, 1981); Edward E. Lawler, III, "Increasing Worker Involvement to Enhance Organizational Effectiveness," in Paul Goodman, ed., *Change in Organizations* (San Francisco, CA: Jossey-Bass, 1982).

DISCUSSION QUESTIONS

1. What is the relationship between satisfaction and performance?
2. Is it possible to have a happy/productive worker?
3. Compare and contrast the three systems typically used to achieve such outcomes.

Activity 2–1   **Facts and Inferences**

Step 1: Carefully read the following report and the observations based on it. Indicate whether you think the observations are true, false, or doubtful on the basis of the information presented in the report. Circle **T** if the observation is definitely true, circle **F** if the observation is definitely false, and circle **?** if the observation may be either true or false. Judge each observation in order. Do not reread the observations after you have indicated your judgment, and do not change any of your answers.

A well-liked college teacher had just completed making up the final examinations and had turned off the lights in the office. Just then a tall, broad figure appeared and demanded the examination. The professor opened the drawer. Everything in the drawer was picked up and the individual ran down the corridor. The dean was notified immediately.

1. The thief was tall and broad.   T   F   ?
2. The professor turned off the lights.   T   F   ?
3. A tall figure demanded the examination.   T   F   ?
4. The examination was picked up by
   someone.   T   F   ?
5. The examination was picked up by the
   professor.   T   F   ?
6. A tall figure appeared after the
   professor turned off the lights in the
   office.   T   F   ?
7. The man who opened the drawer was
   the professor.   T   F   ?
8. The professor ran down the corridor.   T   F   ?
9. The drawer was never actually opened.   T   F   ?
10. In this report three persons are referred
    to.   **T   F   ?**

Step 2: In small groups, discuss your answers and then reach consensus about the answers. Write these answers in a separate place.

Step 3: The instructor will read the correct answers. Score the questions, once for you as an individual and again for your group.

Step 4: Discussion. Did your scores change? Why? Why do people answer these questions incorrectly?

───────────

This exercise is taken from Joseph A. Devito, *General Semantics: Guide and Workbook,* rev. ed. Deland, Fla.: Everett/Edwards, 1974, p. 55, and is reprinted with permission.

 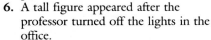

Activity 2–2 — A-Plus Aeronautics

Step 1: Read the following case. (Your instructor will distribute the performance charts to you.)

A-Plus Aeronautics is an electronics firm that manufactures components for instrument control panels used in commercial jets. The company operates as a large job shop, routing custom-ordered products through the work centers in three major shop areas: Fabrication, Assembly, and Testing. There are several work centers in each shop. The custom-ordered products are manufactured in lots of approximately 100 to 1,000, with each item flowing through at least thirty work centers on its way to completion.

Subcomponents such as circuit boards are assembled in the Assembly Shop, where there are fifteen different work centers dedicated to particular kinds of technologies and tasks. The 100 employees in this shop are highly skilled and most of them have been with the company for five or more years.

Hanna Yates is a first-line supervisor for the employees in Work Center 7 of the Assembly Shop. She was transferred to this position from Testing and has not previously held a strictly supervisory position. There are fifteen people reporting to her, ten of whom are on the day shift, and five of whom are on the night shift. The performance of day-shift employees is the easiest to monitor because it is possible for Hanna to observe them. Performance of night-shift employees is more difficult to monitor, however, and she relies heavily on daily performance charts generated by the company computer as a source of information about this group. Hanna has learned through informal channels that there may be a performance problem, having to do with declining output, during the night shift. She refers to her performance charts to see what the problem might be.

Step 2: Answer the following questions as if you were Hanna, using only the information available to you. Respond to each one by circling the number that best represents your assessment of the situation.

1. How would you rate the seriousness of Employee C's output decline?

1	2	3	4	5	6	7
not serious			moderately serious			extremely serious

2. What is the likelihood that the problem has something to do with Employee C him/herself (e.g., effort, ability, attitude)?

1	2	3	4	5	6	7
not likely			moderate likelihood			extremely likely

3. What is the likelihood that the problem has something to do with the work environment (e.g., task difficulty, materials, equipment, available information)?

1	2	3	4	5	6	7
not likely			moderate likelihood			extremely likely

Step 3: Your instructor will direct you in tallying the questionnaire results and displaying them.

Step 4: Discussion. In small groups, with the entire class, or in writing, as directed by your instructor, answer the following questions:

Description
1. How did the ratings of Group A and Group B differ?

Diagnosis
2. Would attribution theory have predicted these differences?

3. How do attributional biases influence supervisors' diagnostic judgments?

Prescription
4. How could we improve their judgments?

_____

This exercise was drawn from Karen Brown and Terence Mitchell, Teaching attribution theory with graphical displays of performance comparisons, *Organizational Behavior Teaching Journal* 8(3) (1983): 23–28.

Activity 2–3 **Carol Bevin**

Step 1: Read the Carol Bevin case.

In November 1990, Carol Bevin was manager of corporate administration at OptiCo, where she had worked for almost four years. Founded fourteen years earlier by Robert Johnson, who remained president, OptiCo was now a $40 million high tech company with 200 employees. After three years with the company, Bevin was uncertain of the future, and she recalled a meeting with Robert Johnson in February 1990 that had upset her greatly. About that meeting and what Johnson had said to her then, Bevin said:

> Reflecting back, I see that I was fooled by some elements of the culture: the president did not have a private office—hardly anyone did—and the culture was casual and informal. I still don't know what of real substance I did or said.

OptiCo designed and manufactured publishing systems that it sold to CD-ROM publishers in the information services industry. CD-ROM (Compact Disk Read-Only Memory) is a technology capable of storing huge quantities of data compactly. The publishers used the software and hardware that OptiCo sold to create large data bases, for example, of financial or bibliographical data. In January 1987, Bevin was hired as administrative manager of the company, which had about 125 employees at that time. She reported to Margaret Hanson, the director of finance and administration. Hanson had started at OptiCo ten years previously as a part-time secretary. At the beginning of 1987, hiring was on the increase at OptiCo and as far as Bevin knew, the company was doing well.

By the end of March 1987, however, OptiCo found itself in a downward spiral. As a result of rapid expansion, the company's costs were eroding the bottom line. Johnson created the position of chief financial officer (CFO) and hired Harold Levy to fill it. Levy's résumé consisted of two-year stints at floundering companies that he had successfully

turned around. In May and June, thirty people were let go from OptiCo in the first layoffs the company had ever experienced. Hanson had to submit a list of people she felt could be laid off—one of them was the facilities manager, a man in his late sixties. He left, and Bevin took over his job as part of hers.

In October 1987, Margaret Hanson decided to leave, and Bevin was promoted to manager of corporate administration, reporting to the CFO, Harold Levy. In addition to having a new boss, Bevin now managed facilities maintenance at OptiCo. Two maintenance assistants reported to her and looked after lights and power, heat, air conditioning, and cleaning. OptiCo leased a medium-sized suburban office building, and Bevin had previously been, and still was, responsible for subleasing space that OptiCo did not use. In addition, she managed the copy center, the mail room, all telecommunications needs, corporate travel, and property/liability insurance. She had a total of six people reporting to her.

In 1987, Harold Levy was in his early forties and, according to Bevin, he had a flamboyant and aggressive style that did not fit at OptiCo. Bevin recalled, however, that when he first came to OptiCo he was stern, demanding, and impatient. She thought that his true personality began to show itself only after he had been at OptiCo for several months:

> He was action-oriented and was able to make changes that no one else would have been able to. But also, he had a large ego, and one had the sense that he felt he was running the show. His behavior was loud. He would tell jokes and slap people on the back. He would say to the accounting manager, "So, Bill, how's tricks, and are you busy cooking the books?" and things like that. You had the sense that he was always on stage. He was also very flirtatious in relating to women.
>
> To understand why he didn't fit, you have to understand what it was like at OptiCo. There's not a lot of diversity—we have few minorities—it's mostly white

men. The floor plan is pretty open, and almost no one has a private office—in fact, it's viewed as undesirable to have a private office. The president, the vice presidents, everyone has workstations that are about chest height on an average person. There are no partitions. Everyone's on a first-name basis, and people often stand up and talk to each other over the top of their workstations.

Along with Carol Bevin, the manager of human resources and the accounting manager also reported to Harold Levy. Levy frequently disagreed with Robert Johnson, Bevin said, "and would go ahead and do what he felt was necessary." The three managers often felt uncomfortable about this tension, but as Bevin remembered it, Levy would say "*who* you work for is more important than the work you do. *I'm* your boss." The three managers had very little direct contact with Robert Johnson, who was often on the road and busy when he was in the office.

Bevin remembered a situation resulting from Levy and Johnson's dealings that was particularly uncomfortable for her. In 1988, several outages made it clear that the wiring of one of the building's main power panels was inadequate and, as one electrician who looked at it said, it was "a disaster waiting to happen." Bevin brought the situation to Harold Levy's attention. With his approval, she hired an electrical consulting firm to look at the wiring and give an estimate for replacement cost. She also spoke to the retired facilities manager about when the wiring had been worked on or replaced. The estimate for repair was $40,000—an unusually large facilities expenditure for OptiCo.

Levy spoke to Robert Johnson about the situation and told him the cost of the repair job. Johnson insisted that no work needed to be done. He said that he distinctly remembered that there was new wiring in the panel. Bevin recalled:

> Harold instructed me to continue with the process of contracting the work, and I did. On the day the work was going to start, I was called into Harold's office, where I found Harold and Robert. Robert gave what I would describe as a "lecture" about how new the wiring was, how unnecessary repair was, and so on. Harold's solution was to suggest that we all go out into the hallway and actually look at the wiring. I removed the panel, and we all peered into the space behind the wall, where we could see the old wiring covered with fraying cloth. Robert admitted that he was wrong about the new wiring and blamed various others in the organization for having misled him. Later, Harold congratulated me on having "beat Robert at his own game."

Though Bevin continued over time to find that Levy and Johnson disagreed on many points, she felt that she and Levy had developed a productive working relationship. Over the next eighteen months, the company started

to turn around. Levy successfully implemented a strategy of acquiring some small companies that could help OptiCo Systems improve its product. These acquisitions resulted in OptiCo's workforce doubling in size to 200. Levy was also working toward making OptiCo itself an attractive acquisition, a goal Bevin understood to be Johnson's wish. During 1989, there were negotiations with several companies who were interested in acquiring OptiCo, and in September 1989, one of the *Fortune* 50, a $25 billion company, acquired OptiCo. Bevin believed Robert Johnson and Harold Levy were both very pleased with the deal.

In February 1990, Levy unexpectedly announced that he would be leaving OptiCo. The announcement came as a surprise to Carol Bevin, and she remembered thinking that it did not seem to be Levy's decision. He was sarcastic at a going-away lunch given in his honor, commenting that he'd almost, but not quite, made it to three years at OptiCo. Before he left, Levy called a meeting with Bevin and David Mason, a senior budget analyst, to discuss how reporting relationships would work after he was gone. Bevin recalled that meeting:

> Harold was going to suggest to Robert Johnson that everyone who had been reporting to Harold would report to Robert, except for me, who would report to David Mason. This news came as a complete surprise, and I questioned it, saying that it didn't make sense to me. Harold said that David Mason would be "safe" for me and that Robert was "not pleased with me." I had always received high praise from Margaret Hanson and Harold Levy. I thought that I had a neutral to slightly positive relationship with Robert—he had always been cordial when I passed him in the hall.

After this meeting was over, Bevin asked to speak to Levy alone. She asked him what had given him the impression that Johnson "was not pleased" with her. Levy didn't really answer her question, and Bevin felt that he was holding something back. Believing that reporting to the senior budget analyst while her colleagues reported directly to the president would not, she said, "be in her best interest career-wise," Bevin asked for a meeting with Robert Johnson. He was very gracious, Bevin said, and named a time on the following day.

At the meeting [the] next day, Bevin told Johnson that the reason she had asked to speak to him was a remark that Levy had made, and she related the remark about Johnson being "not pleased." Johnson leaned back in his chair, looked at Bevin and said, "Quite frankly, I never thought we would have to have this conversation." He went on to tell Bevin that "the 'combination' of Levy and Bevin hadn't been a good one." Bevin was mystified—wondering what this had to do with the subject she'd brought up. She said:

> It seemed that Robert was associating Harold's work with me because we had worked so closely together. It was becoming clear that there had been more tension

between Harold and Robert than any of us had suspected. I was beginning to wonder if any negative impressions he had of Harold were attributed to me.

I asked Robert why he had the impression that the match between Harold and me was not good. He finally blurted out, "You're just controversial." I asked him what exactly that meant—in what ways he found me controversial. Again, he seemed unable to give me a direct answer.

Finally, Robert was able to relate a specific incident. What he said was, "Well, there was that time when you didn't change the light bulb."

Bevin knew immediately what Johnson was referring to. The incident had occurred in November 1989, a few months before Levy left OptiCo. Johnson and the eight-person board were scheduled to meet in a conference room. As manager of facilities, Bevin supervised a janitorial and maintenance staff, including a man named Jim. One of Jim's duties was to keep an eye out for any blown light bulbs and replace them as needed. The day of the board meeting, said Bevin:

I was walking down the hall and passed the conference room. The board was just gathering, and Robert happened to come out of the room just as I passed by. He said, "There's a light bulb out in here." I immediately blurted out, "Oh, I'm sorry. Jim's out today." Robert said, "Get a light bulb and I'll change it myself." I got one and came back and handed it to him.

Returning to her February 1990 meeting with Johnson, Bevin said:

Although I didn't realize it on the day of that board meeting, it was clear from what Robert said that we had very different interpretations of the light bulb incident. He told me, "I don't have the problem that you have." He obviously viewed me as someone who would not do things that were, as he said, "beneath my dignity." That was not what I wished to convey, but it was apparently what I had conveyed.

My interpretation was different. When he told me in the hallway that day that there was a light bulb out, my first thought had been, "I have to explain to him why the light bulb was out." I didn't want him to think that either Jim or I had been negligent in our responsibilities. It had not occurred to me that he would want me to step onto the conference room table in my skirt and heels, with board members seated all around, to replace the bulb.

Reflecting back, there was a much different way I could have responded. The message must have been that I was unwilling to help.

I was devastated. I'd been there almost four years and always had received high praise from Margaret Hanson and from Harold Levy. It had literally never occurred to me that Robert Johnson could have major problems with my performance. I was also frustrated, since he didn't seem able to give me anything concrete or anything that to my mind seemed substantial or problematic to the extent that might cause him to terminate my employment.

I broke down in tears and asked him if he really wanted me to leave. He recoiled slightly and said that he really hadn't thought it through. I told him the feedback I'd always received from all other departments was positive and it was my impression that I was doing good work. I was ready to resign at that point, but he didn't seem to feel that that was necessarily the best thing to do. I also suggested that I report directly to him.

I didn't leave OptiCo. He didn't fire me, and I did end up reporting to him—as did all the people who had been reporting to Harold. The disappointment was that none of us had much interaction with him. He traveled a lot. When he was around, his time was spent in high-level meetings and dealing with the VPs.

Eight months passed after Bevin's meeting with Johnson. During that period, there was no one who officially filled the CFO's role. The accounting manager and the senior budget analyst together filled in, giving Johnson reports as he requested them. Johnson was concentrating on marketing and was out of the office a good deal. Bevin recalled that in October 1990:

We were told that two new VPs were being hired—a VP of finance, who would also be treasurer and CFO, and a VP of operations. Both men were from our parent company, and they started at OptiCo on the same day. We assumed that we would all be reporting to the new CFO. An hour before the new CFO was going to meet with his new staff, Johnson called me to his office. He told me he'd been thinking, and he felt that my work fit better under operations and that I would be reporting to that new VP instead of the VP of finance.

Step 2: Prepare the case for class discussion.

Step 3: Answer each of the following questions, individually or in small groups, as directed by your instructor.

Description

1. What was Carol's perception of Levy and Johnson?
2. How did Carol's perceptions change during the case?
3. What were Levy's and Johnson's perceptions of Carol?
4. How did their perceptions change during the case?
5. How did Bevin's, Levy's, and Johnson's perceptions differ?

Diagnosis

6. What factors affected their perceptions?
7. What were Carol's perceptions of the light bulb incident? What were Johnson's?
8. What misattributions occurred?

Prescription

9. How could the situation have been improved?

Step 4: Discussion. In small groups, with the class as a whole, or in written form, share your answers to the questions above. Then answer the following questions:

1. What symptoms suggest a problem exists?
2. What problems exist in the case?
3. What theories and concepts help explain those problems?
4. How can the problems be corrected?
5. Are the actions likely to be effective?

This case was prepared by Cinny Little for the Institute for Case Development and Research, Simmons Graduate School of Management, Boston, MA. Copyright © 1991 by the President and Trustees of Simmons College. Reprinted with permission.

Activity 2–4

The Learning-Model Instrument

Step 1: For each statement choose the response that is more nearly true for you. Place an X on the blank that corresponds to that response.

1. When meeting people, I prefer
   _____ a. to think and speculate on what they are like.
   _____ b. to interact directly and to ask them questions.
2. When presented with a problem, I prefer
   _____ a. to jump right in and work on a solution.
   _____ b. to think through and evaluate possible ways to solve the problem.
3. I enjoy sports more when
   _____ a. I am watching a good game.
   _____ b. I am actively participating.
4. Before taking a vacation, I prefer
   _____ a. to rush at the last minute and give little thought beforehand to what I will do while on vacation.
   _____ b. to plan early and daydream about how I will spend my vacation.
5. When enrolled in courses, I prefer
   _____ a. to plan how to do my homework before actually attacking the assignment.
   _____ b. to immediately become involved in doing the assignment.
6. When I receive information that requires action, I prefer
   _____ a. to take action immediately.
   _____ b. to organize the information and determine what type of action would be most appropriate.
7. When presented with a number of alternatives for action, I prefer
   _____ a. to determine how the alternatives relate to one another and analyze the consequences of each.

_____ b. to select the one that looks best and implement it.
8. When I awake every morning, I prefer
   _____ a. to expect to accomplish some worthwhile work without considering what the individual tasks may entail.
   _____ b. to plan a schedule for the tasks I expect to do that day.
9. After a full day's work, I prefer
   _____ a. to reflect back on what I accomplished and think of how to make time the next day for unfinished tasks.
   _____ b. to relax with some type of recreation and not think about my job.
10. After choosing the above responses, I
   _____ a. prefer to continue and complete this instrument.
   _____ b. am curious about how my responses will be interpreted and prefer some feedback before continuing with the instrument.
11. When I learn something, I am usually
   _____ a. thinking about it.
   _____ b. right in the middle of doing it.
12. I learn best when
   _____ a. I am dealing with real-world issues.
   _____ b. concepts are clear and well organized.
13. In order to retain something I have learned, I must
   _____ a. periodically review it in my mind.
   _____ b. practice it or try to use the information.
14. In teaching others how to do something, I first
   _____ a. demonstrate the task.
   _____ b. explain the task.
15. My favorite way to learn to do something is
   _____ a. reading a book or instructions or enrolling in a class.

_____ b. trying to do it and learning from my mistakes.

16. When I become emotionally involved with something, I usually

_____ a. let my feelings take the lead and then decide what to do.

_____ b. control my feelings and try to analyze the situation.

17. If I were meeting jointly with several experts on a subject, I would prefer

_____ a. to ask each of them for his or her opinion.

_____ b. to interact with them and share our ideas and feelings.

18. When I am asked to relate information to a group of people, I prefer

_____ a. not to have an outline, but to interact with them and become involved in an extemporaneous conversation.

_____ b. to prepare notes and know exactly what I am going to say.

19. Experience is

_____ a. a guide for building theories.

_____ b. the best teacher.

20. People learn easier when they are

_____ a. doing work on the job.

_____ b. in a class taught by an expert.

Abstract/Concrete		Cognitive/Affective	
Column 1	Column 2	Column 3	Column 4
1. _____	2. _____	11. _____	12. _____
3. _____	4. _____	13. _____	14. _____
5. _____	6. _____	15. _____	16. _____
7. _____	8. _____	17. _____	18. _____
9. _____	10. _____	19. _____	20. _____

Total Circles _____ _____ _____ _____

Grand Totals _____ _____

Figure 2–13 The Learning Model for Managers

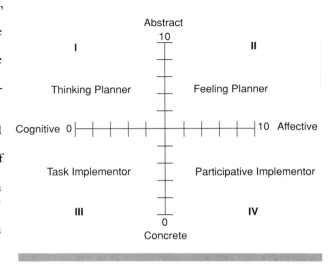

Now circle every *a* in Column 1 and Column 4. Then circle every *b* in Column 2 and in Column 3. Next, total the circles in each of the four columns. Then add the totals of Columns 1 and 2; plot this grand total on the vertical axis of the Learning Model for Managers [Figure 2–13] and draw a horizontal line through the point. Now add the totals of Columns 3 and 4; plot that grand total on the horizontal axis of the model and draw a vertical line through the point. The intersection of these two lines indicates the domain of your preferred learning style.

Step 3: Discussion. In small groups or with the class as a whole, answer the following questions:

Description

1. What was your score?
2. What type of learning style did it represent?
3. How does this result compare with the styles of others in the class?

Diagnosis

4. What are the implications of your style for learning in an organizational setting?

Activity 2–5

Assessing Attitudes toward Work

Step 1: Select two individuals who hold jobs. (You may select two classmates and have them use their jobs as students.)

Step 2: Ask each person to complete the following questionnaire.

Please indicate how satisfied you are with your work situation in each of the respects listed. For each item circle the number that most accurately describes your attitude.

	Very Dissatisfied	Dissatisfied	Neither Satisfied Nor Dissatisfied	Satisfied	Very Satisfied
1. Content of my work	1	2	3	4	5
2. Challenge provided by my work	1	2	3	4	5
3. Variety in my job	1	2	3	4	5
4. Autonomy in my job	1	2	3	4	5
5. Chance for advancement	1	2	3	4	5
6. Salary I receive	1	2	3	4	5
7. Opportunity for promotion	1	2	3	4	5
8. Opportunity for creativity	1	2	3	4	5
9. Opportunity for personal growth	1	2	3	4	5
10. Job security	1	2	3	4	5
11. Supervision I receive	1	2	3	4	5
12. My relationship to my coworkers	1	2	3	4	5
13. Opportunity I have to suggest new ideas	1	2	3	4	5
14. Recognition I receive for my work	1	2	3	4	5
15. Control I have over my work and assignments	1	2	3	4	5
16. Opportunity my job provides for me to remain current in my field	1	2	3	4	5
17. Fairness of promotion	1	2	3	4	5
18. Consistency of my organization's policies and practices	1	2	3	4	5
19. Power I have in my job	1	2	3	4	5
20. Opportunity to do work I consider important	1	2	3	4	5
21. Involvement in my organization's decision making	1	2	3	4	5
22. Fairness of pay raises	1	2	3	4	5

Step 3: Tabulate the responses for each facet indicated by completing the following questions.

Job Properties: Ratings for questions 1,2,3,8,9,16,20 = _____ Divided by 7 = _____
Organizational Policies and Practices: Ratings for questions 5,6,7,17,22 = _____ Divided by 5 = _____
Power and Control: Ratings for questions 4,13,15,19,21 = _____ Divided by 5 = _____
Relationships with Others: Ratings for questions 11,12 = _____ Divided by 2 = _____
Other Facets of the Work Situation: Ratings for questions 10,14,18 = _____ Divided by 3 = _____

Step 4: Compare the scores of the two respondents. How do the differences in their scores reflect differences in their attitudes?

Step 5: Interview each respondent to determine the causes and consequences of at least one of these attitudes toward their jobs.

1. What beliefs have influenced their attitudes toward their jobs?

2. What values have influenced their attitudes toward their jobs?
3. What behaviors (intended or actual) resulted from positive attitudes? negative attitudes?
4. How can dysfunctional behaviors be altered?

These questions were drawn from the alumni questionnaire in J. R. Gordon, *The Congruence Between the Job Orientation and Job Content of Management School Alumni,* doctoral dissertation, Massachusetts Institute of Technology, 1977.

Activity 2–6   Bill Creighton

Step 1: Read the Bill Creighton case.

On the evening of November 12, 1986, Bill Creighton, senior associate, and Mark Finney, administrative associate at Sterling Bank, vented their frustrations in Finney's Wall Street office. Finney had been avoiding Bill for several days until Creighton finally caught up with him at 8:00 P.M. just as Finney was leaving for home. Creighton was frustrated because Finney was not giving him any meaningful assignments. Finney was tired of taking heat for "the unknown Canadian." After a relatively charged but short exchange, Finney told Creighton that he should do something for himself because Finney could not help him.

The temporary transfer Bill had pushed so hard for in Toronto was quickly blowing up into a nightmare. He knew that he would have to straighten things out in a hurry or waste six months in New York and put a black mark on his otherwise unblemished record.

INVESTMENT BANKING
By the 1980s, several hundred banking organizations around the world were providing an increased array of investment banking products and services. Some organizations were exclusively investment banks (such as New York based Salomon Brothers), while others provided both investment banking and commercial banking products and services. The Sterling Bank was a British commercial bank whose main thrust in recent years had been investment banking. Sterling operated a Schedule B bank in Canada and a commercial bank in the U.S. The Canadian operations were headquartered in Toronto, while the U.S. operations were headquartered in New York. In Canada, Sterling competed primarily with the investment bank oriented Schedule B banks as well as the Canadian investment dealers. In the U.S., Sterling competed primarily with the large U.S. commercial banks (such as Citicorp, Bankers Trust, and Morgan Guaranty) and the large U.S. investment banks (such as Salomon Brothers and First Boston Corporation).

Investment banking was an intermediary role that involved selling debt and equity securities to retail clients and institutions, raising debt and equity capital for companies that required financing, advising client organizations on financial transactions such as mergers & acquisitions and providing general financial advice on how firms should manage their balance sheets. Investment banks and the investment banking divisions of the commercial banks were typically divided into the following major areas: (1) Corporate Finance involved developing and marketing financial products that allowed firms to raise debt and equity capital. The corporate finance group acted as underwriters and assumed the risk of issuing new capital. This function typically had the highest profit margins because the compensation reflected the underwriting risk. Corporate Finance also included the highly profitable mergers & acquisitions function which acted on behalf of clients who were interested in making acquisitions or who were the targets of takeover bids. (2) Trading and Sales distributed the new issues generated by Corporate Finance and responded to clients' needs to purchase securities. Trading and Sales included debt and equity transactions that were executed in institutional and retail markets. (3) Research conducted research on a wide range of financial securities. Research findings were made available to clients and were used to support decisions in the Corporate Finance and Sales and Trading functions.

By 1986, the investment banking industry was undergoing several fundamental changes. Firms were becoming larger and more international. The industry was being deregulated, and competition was increasing. As a result, risk and returns were at all time highs, and MBAs were being lured with incredibly lucrative salaries and bonuses. In addition, the industry was under close scrutiny because of some high profile insider trading scandals, in which some very senior Wall Street bankers were found guilty of illegally earning astronomical profits. Because the industry was driven by huge profits, many observers concluded that investment bankers were driven by greed. It was not unheard of for young investment bankers to earn hundreds of thousands of dollars per year. The most successful investment bankers earned millions of dollars per year. Most of that income was earned through annual bonuses. Bonus formulae varied from firm to firm, but most depended on the firm's profitability, the department's profitability, and the individual's contribution. Some firms encouraged teamwork by weighting bonuses for team results. Other firms fostered "star systems" where individuals were rewarded primarily for individual effort. Because every investment banking deal demanded highly specialized skills from several areas, cooperation among colleagues was key to succeeding and earning the really big money. Investment bankers were bright (usually graduating from the top of their class), aggressive, and focused; most bankers logged more than 60 hours per week, and 100 hours per week was not uncommon, particularly for the younger bankers.

BILL CREIGHTON

Bill started his investment banking career in the summer of 1983 when he joined Anderson Clarke Limited, a major Canadian investment dealer. Previously, he had earned a commerce degree from a small U.S. college [and] spent a year in the finance department of a large Canadian packaged goods company. He earned his MBA from the University of Western Ontario in 1982 and was a research assistant for a senior faculty member in finance for one year. Bill was Canadian but had been exposed to many cities in North America because of the extensive traveling his father had done when Bill was growing up. Bill joined Anderson Clarke at age 25 and spent just over two years in the Corporate Finance department working on a variety of investment banking deals. During that time, Bill established himself as bright, keen, and ambitious. He saw himself as a "mad professor: I was fun and unconventional. I was the only one who could walk into a senior executive's office and baffle him because I treated him like one of the guys instead of some demigod." The combination of Bill's likable manner and his outstanding work earned him considerable respect in Anderson Clarke. In particular, Brian Nelson, the firm's most senior investment banker, became Bill's mentor.

The Sterling Bank made a strong push in Canada in the spring of 1984. They brought in a new senior management team and lured Nelson away from Anderson Clarke to become their new Canadian president and spearhead their investment banking thrust. Bill remembered being shocked by Nelson's decision to leave Anderson Clarke: "He didn't say a word to any of us about it and then boom, he's gone. I feel as though he betrayed our team and he betrayed me." Bill did not hear from Nelson until the spring of 1985 when Nelson offered Bill a job with Sterling in Toronto. Bill was happy with Anderson Clarke and rejected Nelson's initial offer. But Nelson persisted for several months and eventually got Bill's interest by adding a sweetener: If he came to Sterling, Bill could spend six months to a year in Sterling's New York or London office. Bill knew that some experience in New York would really round out his development, so he joined Sterling in August 1985.

ADJUSTING TO STERLING

Bill and Nelson agreed that it would be appropriate for Bill to spend two or three months with Sterling in Toronto and then transfer to New York in December or January. That would allow Bill to get to know Sterling and vice versa. Other than Nelson, Bill did not know anyone else in Sterling. Unlike at Anderson Clarke, Nelson did not work closely at all with Bill. In fact, Bill and Nelson did not work on any deals together. Bill's new boss was Howard MacIntosh, an executive vice president. MacIntosh was also a relatively new member of Sterling's senior management team. Although MacIntosh and Nelson got along, they had very different operating styles. Nelson was a consummate investment banker: He understood the technical aspects of all of his deals and was smooth as silk in managing his clients. He was the perfect senior statesman for Sterling. MacIntosh was different. He had been with a large, established Canadian investment dealer for his entire career and had distinguished himself as a strong marketing person. Whereas Nelson was calm and cool, MacIntosh was emotional and sometimes brash. Bill described MacIntosh as "a bull in a china shop. At times, he had very little tact. But if he liked you, he could be just like a teddy bear."

Initially, MacIntosh saw Bill as Nelson's boy and rode Bill very hard for the first couple of months. It was not uncommon for MacIntosh to raise his voice or yell at someone to make a point. Bill recalled doing his first financial analysis for MacIntosh and MacIntosh screaming: "What the hell is this garbage? That's not the way we do it around here. Who taught you this crap anyway?" Even though his analysis was sound, Bill realized that he had to prove himself all over again in Sterling and especially to MacIntosh. Within a few months, Bill had earned MacIntosh's respect. In fact, MacIntosh eventually told Bill that he was "the best associate that I have, and you're the easiest to get along with . . . as long as you think you are being treated fairly."

NEGOTIATING FOR NEW YORK

By the end of November, Bill had the impression that the "powers" at Sterling were not keen on sending him to New York. As Nelson once told Bill: "We're not in the habit of hiring people for New York. We don't want them to think that we'll pick the plums off the tree and send them down." Nelson had not told MacIntosh about the New York deal he had struck with Bill until late in October. Moments after MacIntosh had learned of the deal, he called Bill into his office. He told Bill flat out: "Listen, you work for me now, so your deal with Nelson is off. If you want to go to New York, you and I have to renegotiate." As far as Bill was concerned, the deal he had cut with Nelson should be honored. Over the next several weeks, Bill pressed MacIntosh on the issue, and MacIntosh hinted that he *might* get to New York in a year. If he did get there, it would be for no more than three months. In Bill's mind, that would be reneging on the deal. Bill made it clear, without ever explicitly saying it, that if he was not assured of going to New York for 6–12 months he would leave Sterling.

When Bill returned from a week's vacation in late March, MacIntosh told him about his annual performance bonus. Sterling had made its bonus decisions while Bill was on vacation. Bill was not happy with the bonus; in fact, he was extremely disappointed. Before Bill had joined Sterling, Nelson had led him to believe that his total compensation package at Sterling would be considerably higher than his Anderson Clarke package. However, based on the bonus MacIntosh had just given to Bill, the Sterling package was marginally below what the Anderson Clarke package would likely have been. Bill was angry and let MacIntosh know it. In a move apparently to appease Bill, MacIntosh told him that he had changed his mind and would send Bill to New York for six months starting in September. Bill remembered MacIntosh saying: "I don't give anything easily to anyone. You know that's just the way I am." However, MacIntosh's concession on New York didn't entirely satisfy Bill. He was still really steamed about the compensation issue.

Later that same day, Bill got a call from Nelson. Because they no longer worked together, Bill hadn't talked with Nelson for some time. However, Nelson had heard from the grapevine that Bill was really upset and he wanted to find out why. Bill told him that it had been over six months since he joined Sterling, that he hadn't been transferred to New York yet and finally, that his bonus was ridiculous. Bill told Nelson he was really tired of being "jerked around" and he thought that Sterling was not honoring the deal that had brought Bill from Anderson Clarke. Nelson, in his customary unemotional manner, assured Bill that things would work out. After his meeting with Nelson, Bill reasoned that Nelson had called MacIntosh later that day because Nelson was worried about Bill quitting Sterling. In an effort to cool Bill down, Nelson overruled MacIntosh's agreement with Bill and moved the transfer date to May. When Nelson told Bill about the change, Bill told him that he didn't want to leave in May because he was busy on several large Toronto deals, he wouldn't be very busy in New York (investment banking is very slow over the summer months), and a very close friend was transferring to New York in September. Finally after a joint meeting in April, the three of them agreed that Bill would go to New York in September for at least six months.

ARRANGING THE TRANSFER

There were several groups in corporate finance that Bill considered transferring to in New York. He eventually decided that he would learn the most in the High Yield Group and he spoke to MacIntosh about his preference. The High Yield Group was a small, highly focused group that worked exclusively on "junk bonds," which were specialized debt securities that were frequently used to finance leveraged

buyouts.[1] MacIntosh had indicated to Bill that he knew someone in the High Yield Group in New York. In fact, MacIntosh had briefly met Nick Mantia, executive vice president in charge of the U.S. High Yield Group, at a recent meeting of Sterling's executive vice presidents. MacIntosh agreed to arrange things with Mantia. Bill found out later that MacIntosh made a short call to Mantia. Bill guessed that the call went something like the following: "Nick, it's Howard MacIntosh from Toronto. How are you doing? Yeah, we met at the EVP's meeting in Florida last month. Listen, I've got a good young senior associate named Creighton who wants to spend six months with your group. Have you got room for him in September? Great. Why don't you have your administrative associate call him and take care of the details? Thanks a million."

Bill called Mantia several times in August to ask a few questions about the High Yield Group. Mantia was never available, and he didn't return any of Bill's calls. Bill did get two phone calls from Mike Finney, the administrative associate, and they briefly discussed the kind of deals Bill might work on. They also agreed that Bill would attend the High Yield Group weekly meeting on September 16. He could meet the 20-person team, be briefed on the current deals, and then move to New York. Bill attended the 8:00 A.M. meeting on September 16—but arrived 10 minutes late. Nick Mantia was chairing the session and did not stop when Bill arrived. After about an hour Mantia said: "By the way, there's a new guy here. Who is he?" (Bill was the *only* "new guy" in the room; he waved his hand.) "Oh yeah, you're the guy down from Canada aren't you? Tell us something about yourself." Before Bill had finished introducing himself, Mantia rushed out of the boardroom to another meeting. Bill never had the chance to shake his hand. After the two-hour meeting ended, Bill met two people he was going to work with on a deal: Tom Soward, vice president, and Ken Conrad, senior associate. Bill also met Mark Finney. Finney showed Bill his office and asked him to get started right away on the deal with Soward and Conrad. Bill was confused; he was only in New York for the day. He wasn't moving to New York for two more weeks. There had been a misunderstanding. Finney was annoyed; he had rushed around the day before to arrange things for Bill.

ARRIVING IN NEW YORK

Bill finally arrived in New York in the last week of September. It was an intimidating experience. Bill had worked on some New York deals from Canada but he had always been on a team with people he knew. He went into the U.S. High Yield Group as an unknown. He had worked on some leveraged buyout deals in Canada but none that had relied on junk bonds very much. He wondered if he would be up to speed technically in the High Yield Group. He also wondered what barriers might exist because he wasn't part of a "class." During the strong bull markets of the mid-1980s, the large investment banks on Wall Street had hired as many as 100 new associates each year. The incoming "classes" spent their initial training together, helped each other on deals and developed very strong social ties. By working and socializing together, investment banking "classmates" developed a strong sense of professional trust in each other. As an outsider, Bill did not have any such ties and had not yet earned the trust of his High Yield colleagues. Bill spent the first week getting adjusted and trying to meet the rest of his new colleagues. He never did manage to meet Mantia. The High Yield Group was relatively small by Wall Street standards with only 20 professionals, including two executive vice presidents.

Mantia had recently brought in a huge leveraged buy-out deal from Hoyle, Inc., a major international containerized shipping company. It was the biggest and potentially the most profitable deal that the High Yield Group had seen all year. The Hoyle deal was initially staffed by Soward, Conrad, and some analysts (generally, analysts were undergraduate students who worked on Wall Street for two years before returning to graduate school). The Hoyle deal was referred to as a "black hole" deal. It was so big and so complex that it could totally consume as many associates as were thrown into it. In contrast, a normal deal was staffed by a senior or executive vice president, a vice president, and one or two associates. Soward needed some extra bodies for Hoyle and was willing to let Bill assume some relatively small, safe tasks. Even though he was a fourth-year associate and he was more than capable to assume more responsibility on the Hoyle deal, Bill was still an unknown quantity in New York. Bill participated in several team meetings on the Hoyle deal through October and early November. Bill, Soward, and Conrad updated each other during those meetings in Soward's office.

On two occasions, Nick Mantia popped into the meetings and inquired about the progress of the deal. Mantia specifically addressed his questions to either Soward or Conrad even though some of the questions could only be answered by Bill. For those questions, Soward acted like an interpreter, repeating Bill's answer to Mantia. Bill was livid. Mantia was treating him like a total rookie. To make matters worse, Mark Finney, who was responsible for farming out work from the senior and executive vice presidents, was not giving any work to Bill because none of them had asked for him to be on their deals. Bill dropped into Finney's office almost every day to ask about any new work that could be assigned to him. Finney never had anything for him. Bill was frustrated because he was stuck with only a small number of simple tasks and he was being treated like a ghost by the senior people in High Yield, especially Mantia. He had called Howie MacIntosh twice in October and asked him to speak to Mantia. Since Mantia was not speaking to Bill, he never knew if MacIntosh had spoken to Mantia. Bill figured that MacIntosh wasn't anxious to make things easy for Bill in New York. MacIntosh was concerned about losing Bill. In one of their phone calls, MacIntosh

had said: "If you try to end-run me and stay in New York, I'll yank you out of there faster than you can say Sterling Bank."

In their late night meeting on November 12, Bill's frustration came to the surface. Bill was not known for his diplomacy or for flowery language, and he always called a spade a spade:

Bill: Look Mark, I'm tired of sitting around here doing nothing. What the hell is going on? I've been twiddling my thumbs for over a month, I still don't have a secretary and Nick hasn't said boo to me since I've been here.

Mark: So what do you want me to do? You came down here without any credibility—you're not even a vice president. No one from Toronto called to even see if you'd arrived, and Mantia's riding my butt because you're not doing anything. You're a bloody thorn in Nick's side, and he's taking it out on me. And no one else is asking for you on their deals. Let's face it Bill—you're a big question mark down here. Why don't you get some backup from your senior guy in Toronto?

Bill: Wait a minute, I just missed making VP for three reasons: I am relatively new to Sterling, they considered it a real perk that I was sent to New York, and, because I am only 28, they didn't want to put any noses out of joint. They told me I am VP quality, but politics got in the way. So I don't think that my capabilities should be an issue.

Mark: Yeah, I agree—your capabilities shouldn't be an issue. In fact Tom (Soward) and Ken (Conrad) are real impressed with your work. But nobody else down here *who counts* knows that.

Bill: I've already spoken to MacIntosh and nothing has changed. I can't get an appointment with Mantia to talk to him. Sonya (Mantia's secretary) treats me like her son, but the bastard doesn't even say hello to me. I've thought about going into his office and talking to him about it.

Mark: Listen, cowboy, this is New York. You don't walk into an EVP's office without his invitation or without an appointment. Those guys are working on billion-dollar deals. They've been known to fire wise-ass associates who have interrupted them.

Bill: I've also talked to Paul Harper (the other executive vice president of the U.S. High Yield Group) about my situation. He said he would speak to you about getting me some more work.

Mark: Harper hasn't said squat to me about you.

Bill: C'mon Mark, I busted my tail to get this transfer to New York. I don't care if I have to call Toronto and have work sent to me; there's no way I'm going to sit on my hands for the next four months. I'm tired of being treated like a first-year associate. And there's no way I'm going back to Toronto before my time is up.

Mark: Suit yourself, Bill. I feel for you but there is nothing I can do. I think you had better do something for yourself. If I were you, I'd work through your senior guy in Toronto. Frankly, it sounds like you've been hung out to dry and he's not doing anything to help you. But you better do something. Listen, I've got to leave now or my wife will kill me. Let me know how things go.

Bill spent the balance of that evening reflecting on his situation. He wondered if he was responsible for the mess he was in—had he mismanaged his bosses? Or had he been mismanaged by them—first Nelson, then MacIntosh, and finally Mantia? Although he was unsure about why certain things had happened, he focused on what he should do the next day. He had already called his parents and some friends in Toronto to talk about the options that were available to him. But he had no idea which option to choose or how *exactly* to exercise the option he chose.

NOTE
1. Leveraged buyouts were acquisitions that were paid for with the unused debt capacity of the *acquired* company. The acquiring company issued bonds with higher than normal yields ("junk bonds") to attract investors and to secure financing for the acquisition. Originally, junk bonds were used by smaller, riskier companies. By 1986, the junk bond market in the U.S. had taken off and major corporations such as B. F. Goodrich and Texaco had issued junk bonds. Junk bonds were not very prevalent in Canada in 1986.

Step 2: Prepare the case for class discussion.

Step 3: Answer each of the following questions, individually or in small groups, as directed by your instructor.

Description
1. What was Bill's perception of MacIntosh? What was his perception of Mantia?
2. How did Bill's perceptions change during the case?
3. What were MacIntosh's and Mantia's perceptions of Bill?
4. How did their perceptions change during the case?
5. How did Creighton's, MacIntosh's, and Mantia's perceptions differ?

Diagnosis
6. What factors affected Creighton's, MacIntosh's, and Mantia's perceptions?
7. What were Bill's attributions of the reasons for Mantia's behavior toward him?
8. What learning occurred during the case?
9. What factors affected the learning?
10. What were Creighton's, MacIntosh's, and Mantia's attitudes toward the situation?
11. How did cultural differences affect the situation?

Prescription
12. How could the situation have been improved?

Step 4: Discussion. In small groups, with the class as a whole, or in written form, share your answers to the questions above. Then answer the following questions:

1. What symptoms suggest that a problem exists?
2. What problems exist in the case?
3. What theories and concepts help explain those problems?
4. How can the problems be corrected?
5. Are the actions likely to be effective?

This case was prepared by Randy Lyons under the direction of Professor Jim Erskine of the Western Business School. Copyright © 1987, the University of Western Ontario.

CONCLUDING COMMENTS In Chapter 1 we suggested that different theoretical perspectives were emphasized in the field of organizational behavior during different decades. In this chapter we have looked at the issue of different perspectives in another way. We have focused on the ways in which different people in organizations often have different perceptions and attributions of any particular event.

In the activities of this chapter, "Facts and Inferences" provided the opportunity to examine factors that influence perception. "A-Plus Aeronautics" offered a chance to test attributional biases. Both the Carol Bevin and Bill Creighton cases illustrated the role of perceptual and attributional distortions in organizational situations. The "Learning Model Instrument" allowed you to assess your own learning style. "Assessing Attitudes toward Work" allowed you to compare and contrast workers' job attitudes and their causes and consequences. Accurate diagnosis requires understanding the way individuals perceive, attribute, learn, and form attitudes. It also requires an understanding of individual differences and development and their significance for managing a diverse work force, as described in the next chapter.

ENDNOTES

[1] E. J. Gibson, Development of perceiving, acting, and acquiring of knowledge. In E. J. Gibson, ed., *An Odyssey in Learning and Perception* (Cambridge, Mass.: MIT Press, 1991).

[2] M. B. Howes, *The Psychology of Human Cognition* (New York: Pergamon, 1990).

[3] D. J. Schneider, Social cognition. In M. R. Rosenzweig and L. W. Porter, eds., *Annual Review of Psychology* 4(2) (1991): 527–561.

[4] Howes, *Psychology of Human Cognition.*

[5] D. L. Medin, Social categorization: Structures, processes, and purposes, *Advanced Social Cognition* 1 (1988): 119–126.

[6] Schneider, Social cognition.

[7] J. R. Pomerantz and M. Kubovy, Theoretical approaches to perceptual organization. In K. R. Boff, L. Kaufman, and J. P. Thomas, eds., *Handbook of Perception and Human Performance*, vol. 2 (New York: Wiley, 1986); I. Rock, The description and analysis of object and event perception. In Boff et al., *Handbook of Perception.*

[8] W. L. Gardner and M. L. Martinko, Impression management in organizations, *Journal of Management* 14(2) (1988): 321–338.

[9] E. Gibson, *Principles of Perceptual Learning and Development* (New York: Appleton-Century-Crofts, 1969).

[10] R. L. Solso, Prototypes, schemata and the form of human knowledge: The cognition of abstraction. In C. Izawa, ed., *Current Issues in Cognitive Processes* (Hillsdale, N.J.: Erlbaum, 1989): 345–368.

[11] Schneider, Social cognition.

[12] S. L. Brodsky, *The Psychology of Adjustment and Well-being* (New York: Holt, Rinehart and Winston, 1988).

[13] G. Haight, Managing diversity, *Across the Board* (March 1990): 22–29; L. Copeland, Learning to manage a multicultural work force, *Training* (May 1988): 49–56.

[14] M. E. Heilman and M. H. Stopeck, Being attractive, advantage or disadvantage? Performance evaluations and recommended personnel actions as a function of appearance, sex, and job type, *Organizational Behavior and Human Decision Processes* 35 (1985): 202–215.

[15] S. G. Redding, Cognition as an aspect of culture and in relation to management processes: An exploratory view of the Chinese case, *Journal of Management Studies* 17(2): 127–148; J. B. Shaw, A cognitive categorization model for the study of intercultural management, *Academy of Management Review* 15(4) (1990): 626–645.

[16] N. J. Adler, *International Dimensions of Organizational Behavior,* 2nd ed. (Boston: Kent, 1991).

[17] E. E. Jones, *Interpersonal Perception* (New York: W. H. Freeman, 1990) is the most recent in a series of articles and books about attribution theory.

[18] E. K. Shaver, *An Introduction to Attribution Processes* (Cambridge, Mass.: Winthrop, 1975).

[19] H. H. Kelley, Attribution theory in social psychology, *Nebraska Symposium on Motivation* 14 (1967): 192–241.

[20] Jones, *Interpersonal Perception.*

[21] Adler, *International Dimensions.*

[22] E. E. Jones and R. E. Nisbett, *The Actor and the Observer, Divergent Perceptions of the Causes of Behavior* (Morristown, N.J.: General Learning Press, 1971).

[23] S. L. Payne and R. A. Giacalone, Social psychological approaches to the perception of ethical dilemmas, *Human Relations* 43 (1991): 649–665.

[24] D. A. Gioia and H. P. Sims, Self-serving bias and actor observer differences: An empirical analysis, *Journal of Applied Social Psychology* 15 (1985): 547–563.

[25] J. Barry, *Moral Issues in Business* (Belmont, Calif.: Wadsworth, 1983).

[26] J. Bartunek, Why did you do that? Attribution theory in organizations, *Business Horizons* 24 (1981): 66–71.

[27] H. H. Kelley and J. L. Michela, Attribution theory and research, *Annual Review of Psychology* 31 (1980): 457–501.

[28] W. B. Swann, Jr., Identity negotiation where two roads meet, *Journal of Personality and Social Psychology* 53 (1987): 1038–1051; Jones, *Interpersonal Perception.*

[29] R. G. Lord and J. E. Smith, Theoretical, information processing, and situational factors affecting attribution theory models of organizational behavior, *Academy of Management Review* 8 (1983): 50–60.

[30] I. Pavlov, *Conditioned Reflexes: An Investigation of the Physiological Activity of the Cerebral Cortex,* trans. and ed. G. V. Anrep (London: Oxford University Press, 1927). Comparable work done in the United States by J. B. Watson is described in *Behaviorism* (New York: Norton, 1924).

[31] B. F. Skinner, *About Behaviorism* (New York: Knopf, 1974); B. F. Skinner, *The Behavior of Organisms* (New York: Appleton-Century-Crofts, 1938).

[32] E. C. Tolman, *Purposive Behavior in Animals and Men* (New York: Appleton-Century-Crofts, 1932).

[33] F. Luthans, *Organizational Behavior,* 4th ed. (New York: McGraw-Hill, 1985); C. C. Manz and H. P. Sims, Vicarious learning: The influence of modeling on organizational behavior, *Academy of Management Review* 6 (1981): 105–113.

[34] A. Bandura, *Social Learning Theory* (Englewood Cliffs, N.J.: Prentice-Hall, 1978).

[35] S. Kumon, Some principles governing the thought and behavior of Japanists (contextuals), *Journal of Japanese Studies* 8 (1984): 5–28.

[36] G. Greenwald, Why are attitudes important? In A. R. Pratkanis, S. J. Breckler, and A. G. Greenwald, eds., *Attitude Structure and Function* (Hillsdale, N.J.: Erlbaum, 1989): 1–10.

[37] S. Oskamp, *Attitudes and Opinions,* 2nd ed. (Englewood Cliffs, N.J.: Prentice Hall, 1991) offers a good overview of the measurement of attitudes.

[38] See M. Fishbein and I. Ajzen, *Beliefs, Attitude, Intention, and Behavior: An Introduction to Theory and Research* (Reading, Mass.: Addison-Wesley, 1975); I. Ajzen, *Attitudes, Personality, and Behavior* (Chicago: Dorsey, 1988).

[39] R. H. Fazio, How do attitudes guide behavior? In R. M. Sorrentino and E. T. Higgins, eds., *Handbook of Motivation and Cognition* (New York: Guilford, 1986): 204–243.

[40] A. R. Pratkanis, The cognitive representation of attitudes. In Pratkanis et al., *Attitude,* pp. 71–98.

[41] Fazio, How do attitudes guide behavior?

[42] D. L. Ronis, J. F. Yates, and J. P. Kirscht, Attitudes, decisions, and habits as determinants of repeated behavior. In Pratkanis et al., *Attitudes,* pp. 213–239.

[43] Originally conceived by L. Festinger, *A Theory of Cognitive Dissonance* (Stanford, Calif.: Stanford University, 1957); and more recently discussed by H. Marcus and R. B. Zajonc, The cognitive perspective in social psychology. In G. Lindzey and E. Aronson, eds., *The Handbook of Social Psychology,* 3rd ed., vol. 1 (New York: Random House, 1985), among others.

[44] Summarized in Oskamp, *Attitudes and Opinions.*

[45] G. Hofstede, Motivation, leadership, and organization: Do American theories apply abroad? *Organizational Dynamics* 9 (Summer 1980): 45–46.

[46] R. T. Jones, B. Jerich, L. Copeland, and M. Boyles, How do you manage a diverse workforce? *Training and Development Journal* (February 1989).

[47] E. A. Locke and G. P. Latham, *A Theory of Goal Setting and Task Performance* (Englewood Cliffs, N.J.: Prentice Hall, 1990).

[48] L. M. Shore and H. J. Martin, Job satisfaction and organizational commitment in relation to work performance and turnover intentions, *Human Relations* 42(7) (1989): 625–638; M. T. Iaffaldano and P. M. Muchinsky, Job satisfaction and job performance: A meta-analysis, *Psychological Bulletin* 97 (1985): 251–273.

RECOMMENDED READINGS

Advances in Social Cognition, vol. 1. Hillsdale, N.J.: Erlbaum, 1988.

Boff, K. R., Kaufman, L., and Thomas, J. P., eds. *Handbook of Perception and Human Performance.* New York: Wiley, 1986.

Davey, G., and Cullen, C., eds. *Human Operant Conditioning and Behavior Modification.* New York: Wiley, 1987.

Gibson, E. J. *An Odyssey in Learning and Perception.* Cambridge, Mass.: MIT Press, 1991.

Klein, S. B., and Mowrer, R. R., eds. *Contemporary Learning Theories, Pavlovian Conditioning and the Status of Traditional Learning Theory.* Hillsdale, N.J.: Erlbaum, 1989.

Pratkanis, A. R., Breckler, S. J., and Greenwald, A. G., eds. *Attitude Structure and Function.* Hillsdale, N.J.: Erlbaum, 1989.

Chapter Outline

Dealing with Work Force Diversity

Learning Objectives

After completing the reading and activities of Chapter 3, students will be able to

1. Comment about the implications of diversity in the work force.

2. Illustrate the nature of ethnic differences.

3. Describe the characteristics of workers that contribute to work force diversity.

4. Define personality and show its significance for personal development and individual behavior in organizations.

5. Trace the stages of personal development and their significance for organizational behavior.

6. Comment about the issues in the career development of members of a diverse work force.

7. Identify the issues involved in managing the interaction of work and family.

8. Diagnose possible sources of role conflict and role ambiguity in organizations and strategies for reducing them.

9. Identify the causes of stress in organizations and ways of using stress constructively.

10. Suggest a protocol for managing diversity in organizations.

The Staffing Problem at Malvern General Hospital

Malvern General Hospital is a teaching hospital in a moderate-sized city in the United States. Recently, Malvern and its competitors have experienced significant shortages of nurses and paraprofessional staff. They also have been seriously under-staffed in many of the support areas, such as housekeeping, food services, and transport, and have even had to hire expensive independent companies to act as subcontractors for these services.

Richard Bridges recently became the vice president in charge of Human Resources, a newly created senior-level position in the hospital. Human Resources had previously been considered a lower-level staff department; now its top job-holder would sit on the executive board of the hospital. Although Richard's career had included many positions in hospital administration, he had spent only a short time earlier in his career as the director of a human resources department in a small, community hospital, where the major function of the department was re-cruiting staff and making sure they were paid appropriately.

Richard knew that his first challenge was to solve the staff shortage problem at Malvern General. Besides having difficulty attracting the right type of staff, the hospital had a high turnover rate. After talking with many of the managers in the hospital, Richard felt that they were not willing to be very flexible in adjusting their hiring criteria to the nature of a changing work force. He also learned that the hospital itself offered no benefits that would attract married professionals with children, such as child care, flexible working schedules, or part-time employment. Potential employees often accepted job offers at other hospitals that offered such benefits, even if Malvern General had a slightly higher pay scale.

Richard knows that one solution to the staffing problem is to tap into new sources of workers, which will result in a more diverse work force. But Bridges knows that the hospital's managers and professional staff have little experience in supervising and working with such employees. He also knows that the hospital must find better ways to meet the unique needs of this more diverse work force. The question remains how to do this.

Richard Bridges faces a problem that many managers will face in the twenty-first century: how to attract, retain, and encourage the productivity of a diverse work force. This task requires managers who can understand the unique characteristics of workers and design programs to meet and enhance them.

We can look at diversity in two different ways. The first way focuses on ethnic and cultural differences associated with different countries or regions in the world. We know, for example, that the Japanese culture spawns very different behaviors from the German culture or the culture of the United States. Throughout this book we highlight such differences in each area discussed; we examine, for example, cross-cultural issues of motivation, leadership, and negotiation, among others. The second way to look at diversity focuses on differences within homogeneous cultural groups. Organization members who have ethnic, gender, and race similarity may differ in personality, development, work-family interactions, and role expectations.

We begin this chapter by illustrating cultural diversity through a description of three ethnic groups. We then comment about gender differences, race in the work-place, and issues associated with older workers. The majority of this chapter then focuses on individual differences, development, role pressures, and stress. We conclude the chapter with brief comments about managing diversity.

ETHNIC DIFFERENCES IN THE DIVERSE WORK FORCE

As organizations become more multinational, the demands for integrating "home-country" and foreign workers will increase. Executives and supervisors must be sensitive to and understand cultural differences as a first step in effectively managing such workers. In addition, in many countries, the immigrant pool of workers is changing and will continue to change dramatically. The permeability of borders created by the European Economic Community, the dissolution of the U.S.S.R., and the creation of a united Germany are among the political factors that influence the changing work force throughout the world. In the United States, for example, organizations will employ increasing numbers of Oriental and Hispanic workers, and to a lesser degree Middle Easterners, Indians, and Russians.

We cannot in a single chapter discuss each ethnic group separately. Instead, the next sections briefly describe three different ethnic groups, their unique characteristics, and their relationship to North Americans.

Japanese

The Japanese culture provides a major counterpoint to the culture of the United States. Oriental in character, Japanese values include an acceptance of the unequal distribution of power, a feeling of being threatened by uncertain or ambiguous situations, the valuing of a tight social framework where loyalty is owed to an in-group such as relatives or coworkers, and a focus on caring for others and the quality of work life.[1] These values greatly contrast with the values of the U.S. culture, which are opposite on all four dimensions. The Japanese use softer, vaguer, less direct language.[2] Saving face is particularly important, and approaching individuals at the highest level in the organization through a third party is considered correct. The Japanese have a different sense of time: They resist deadline pressures and expect group decisions to take time; implementation, however, should follow immediately. Rewards focus more on groups and organizations than on individuals, an approach which complements the Japanese valuing of familial relationships. Japanese organizations emphasize the value of seniority, lifetime employment, and continuous learning.

Eastern Europeans

Recent political events in Eastern Europe make it difficult to predict how the culture of the countries in this part of the world will change in the next decade. The destruction of the Berlin Wall and the demise of the U.S.S.R. have prompted a strong interaction with the West that may eventually overcome any lingering impact of Communist rule on such countries as Hungary, Poland, and the Baltic states. Eastern European workers are experiencing a change from a collectivist to a more individualistic orientation. The cultural and intellectual heritage in many of these countries resembles the backgrounds of many second- and third-generation North Americans, and this similarity may ultimately influence their interactions. The possibility of owning their own businesses, for example, may spur an entrepreneurial spirit and individualism that has not existed for many generations but is common to the rest of Europe and North America.

Latin Americans

Although significant differences exist among citizens of the Central and South American countries, some common themes form the basis of their behavior.[3] First, male Latin Americans personalize all aspects of their lives; they look at family and friends, for example, in terms of personal pride. Second, they subscribe to the *mañana* concept in which everything has an indefinite future. Third, the culture emphasizes *machismo,* or male aggressiveness, which allows men to be forceful, self-confident, and chauvinistic. Fourth, because of political instability in this region, Latin Americans develop a fatalistic attitude that fosters risk taking and the belief in the influence of luck or chance. Fifth, they value good manners, dignity, and warm hospitality. Finally, they accept power distance and submit to authority. Obviously, these values directly contradict the present-oriented, egalitarian, controlling behavior of many North Americans and contribute to the challenge of managing a diverse work force in a United States organization that includes a significant number of Hispanics.

THE GENDER, RACE, AND AGE COMPONENTS OF DIVERSITY

In addition to ethnic differences, three major demographic trends significantly influence the diversity of the work force in the United States. By the year 2000 women and minorities will comprise 85 percent of the net increase in the U.S. work force. These groups, previously underrepresented, will be the majority of the labor pool.[4] Demographics, competition for talent, marketplace demands, and the changing environment are among the factors calling for a diverse work force.[5] In addition, more older workers are remaining employed as a result of the lifting of the mandatory retirement age, among other factors. In this section we briefly comment about the issues related to gender, race, and age in the workplace.

Women in the Workplace

Equal employment and affirmative action legislation of the 1960s and 1970s, the feminist movement of the 1970s and 1980s, and the economic realities faced by women who are single, heads of their families, or members of dual-career families have motivated a dramatic increase in the numbers and percentage of women in the workplace. Even as their representation is increasing, women continue to experience unique concerns and problems.

Women's lives are qualitatively and structurally different from men's lives.[6] Socialized to value affiliation and attachment, they can experience difficulty in organizations that promote competition.[7] Organizational barriers also hinder their performance. Limited access to the executive ranks, difficulty in infiltrating the old-boy network, and lack of suitable child care are among the issues that programs for managing diversity must address.

Race in the Workplace

The percentage of African-Americans in the workplace has increased significantly in the past twenty-five years, prompted largely by affirmative action.[8] Now, many African-American and Caucasian leaders are questioning hiring preferences because they feel that they disadvantage African-Americans in the workplace. Racial stereotypes persist in organizations; even managers who are satisfied with minority workers do not actively recruit them. African-American managers in the executive ranks often feel isolated because of their small numbers. Too often they are treated as tokens rather than as individual performers. Reducing stereotypes and promoting workers on the basis of ability and demonstrated competence is a major challenge of diversity training.

Older Workers

By the year 2001 the baby boomers will begin to reach the age of 55, when the Department of Labor counts them as older workers.[9] Managing older workers also requires overcoming stereotypes. Doubts about their ability to learn, speed of response, creativity, adaptability, and manageability have been disproved by research on older workers. The Japanese, for example, value older workers and show the advantage of using their skills and wisdom. Tailoring jobs to the requirements of older workers who may wish to reduce their time commitment while still remaining actively engaged in organizational life and recognizing their individual competencies are major challenges of managing the diverse work force.

DIVERSITY AND INDIVIDUAL DIFFERENCES

Organizations such as Malvern Hospital must prepare their managers to deal effectively with the new composition of the work force. Understanding individual differences is one step in developing this ability.

Personality

A diverse work force typically includes individuals with a variety of personality types. *Personality* here refers to a set of distinctive personal characteristics, including motives, emotions, values, interests, attitudes, and competencies. These characteristics frequently are organized into patterns that are influenced by an individual's heredity and social, cultural, and family environments.

Personality Dimensions Psychological research has identified a wide range of psychological characteristics that compose an individual's personality. In this section we look at a subset of these characteristics that have been considered significant for organizational behavior.

As one early example, Rotter described the extent to which individuals believe that their behaviors influence what happens to them.[10] *Internalizers* feel that they control their own life and actions; *externalizers* believe others control their lives. Internalizers would agree, for example, that "when I get what I want it's usually because I worked hard for it" and "when I make plans I am almost certain to make them work."[11] Externalizers would agree that "making a lot of money is largely a matter of getting the right breaks" and "it is silly to think that one can really change another person's basic attitudes."[12]

In a second example, early work on Type A or Type B characteristics, which reflect an individual's desire for achievement, perfectionism, competitiveness, and ability to relax, has been related to cardiovascular fitness and stress-proneness. Type A people tend to feel very competitive, be prompt for appointments, do things quickly, and always feel rushed, whereas Type B individuals tend to be more relaxed, take one thing at a time, and express their feelings.[13]

Jungian psychology, which identified two basic personalities, has also had a long-lasting impact on personality diagnosis. The *introverted* person is shy and withdrawn, whereas the *extroverted* person is outgoing and, in extreme cases, often aggressive and dominant.[14] These personality patterns are matched by four problem-solving orientations, shown in Figure 3–1 and described in Table 3–1. Characterizing the personality of workers should help managers to respond to the unique dimensions of each worker's style and better manage a diverse work force.

Measuring Personality Personality is primarily assessed in three ways, generally by trained and certified professionals. Individuals can complete inventories, which are lists of questions that describe the respondent's personality. Second, individuals can complete projective tests in which the respondent describes to the test administrator what he or she sees in a picture or relatively ambiguous stimulus, such as an inkblot. After using a detailed protocol to score the descriptions, individuals are placed along a variety of personality dimensions. In the third assessment approach, a participant's behavior in simulations, role-playing exercises, or stress interviews is observed and scored along a variety of dimensions, such as adaptability, assertiveness, and dominance. These instruments describe personality by looking for repetitive behaviors and attitudes associated with a given personality type.

Figure 3–1 **Problem-Solving Orientations**

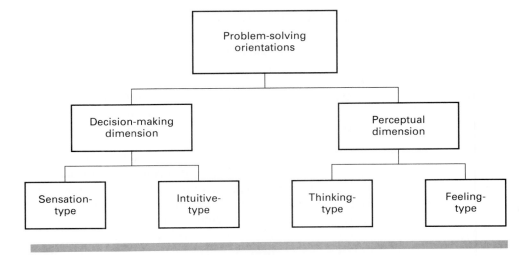

Table 3–1 **Behavioral Clues of Four Personal Styles**

Perceptual Dimensions

Style Characteristic	Sensor	Intuitor
Emphasis	Action, getting things done, wants to see results of efforts quickly	Ideas, concepts, theory, innovation, long-range thinking
Time orientation	Present	Future
Sources of satisfaction	Likes quick results, enjoys making things happen, likes feedback on efforts, likes to be in charge	Derived from world of possibilities, oriented toward problem solving but not terribly interested in implementing solutions
Strengths	Pragmatic, assertive, directional, results-oriented, objective, competitive, confident	Original, imaginative, creative, idealistic, intellectually tenacious, ideological
Weaknesses (if style is overextended)	Doesn't see long range, acts first then thinks, lacks trust in others, domineering, arrogant	Unrealistic, "far out," fantasy-bound, scattered, devious, out of touch, dogmatic, impractical
In clothing	Informal, simple, functional, neat but not fancy	Erratic and hard to predict
In surroundings	Hard-charging, clutter	Futuristic, modern, creative
Typical occupations	Accountants, pilots, bankers, investors, professional athletes, salespeople, models, physicians, land developers	Scientists, researchers, artists, market researchers, writers, corporate planners, "idea" people

The Effect of Personality The description and analysis of an individual's personality or personal style can help us understand the way that individual behaves in organizations and particularly the way that person interacts with others. Assume that a manager has two subordinates: Ralph Jackson is an internalizer, and Zachary Feller is an externalizer. How might these two men differ in their views of the best way to advance in an organization? The first might view advancement as being within his control; the second would view it as being out of his control.

Now consider a manager with a thinking-type personal style. How would the manager begin to deal with a poorly performing employee? He or she likely would perform a logical, systematic inquiry into the situation that focuses on behaviors. Compare this behavior to that of a feeling-type manager in the same situation. He or she might begin by conducting an assessment that focuses first on the employee's feelings. By diagnosing the impact of an individual's personality on an organizational situation we can anticipate the possible consequences and make provisional plans for responding. Such plans are particularly important when dealing with a diverse work force, so that racial, ethnic, general, or personality stereotyping is minimized.

Decision-Making Dimensions

Style Characteristic	Thinker	Feeler
Emphasis	Logic, organization, analysis, systematic inquiry	Human interaction, feelings, emotions
Time orientation	Past, present, future	Past
Sources of satisfaction	Enjoys seeing a problem through to implementing solution; enjoys anything well-organized or methodically thought out	Enjoys "reading between the lines"; social interpersonal contact is sought out
Strengths	Effective communicator, deliberative, prudent, weighs alternatives, stabilizing, objective, rational, analytical	Spontaneous, persuasive, emphatic, grasps traditional values, probing, introspective, draws out feelings of others, loyal
Weaknesses (if style is overextended)	Verbose, indecisive, overly cautious, overanalytical, controlled and controlling, overly serious, rigid	Impulsive, manipulative, over-personalizes, sentimental, postponing, stirs up conflict, subjective
In clothing	Conservative, unassuming, understated, color-coordinated	Colorful, informal, mood-oriented
In surroundings	Correct, nondistracting, tasteful but conventional, organized	Informal, warm, personalized
Typical occupations	Lawyers, engineers, computer programmers, accountants	Entertainers, salespeople, writers, teachers, public relations specialists, nurses, social workers, psychiatrists, psychologists, secretaries, retail business people

Recent research has suggested that the personalities of top executives can help explain dysfunctional organizations.[15] A manager with a neurotic personality is more likely to lead an organization that experiences significant dysfunctions and pathologies. For example, an executive who believes that no one can be trusted often creates an organization in which secrecy and guardedness characterize the culture. Or a manager whose compulsive personality reflects a need for control more often will create an organization that relies too much on formal controls and direct supervision to accomplish the organizational goals. As the number of children in dysfunctional homes increases, the number of dysfunctional adults and potentially dysfunctional managers also increases.[16] While personality and personal style are relatively stable dimensions of individuals, their manifestation may differ during an individual's life, as described in the next section.

Personal Development   Research has suggested that adults, like children, have clearly defined stages of biological, social, family, and career growth and development that may include transition-in, stability, and transition-out periods.[17] Individuals at a particular stage often have common needs or similar ways of coping with and responding to situations they encounter. These ways may be modified by an individual's personality, causing variations within stages. We describe a typical progression here that is common in the United States. But this progression may differ in other countries. Little cross-cultural research has been done regarding personal development, but we might hypothesize that patterns vary in different cultures, according to the expectations of women and older persons; as a function of the financial supports provided for medical care, child care, and other personal needs; and according to opportunities for individuals of various social and economic classes.

Consider, for example, the Orthopedics Department at Malvern General Hospital, a typical U.S. organization. Do you think its physicians, nurses, and other staff respond to their work in the same way? Although different job responsibilities, as well as ethnic, racial, or gender differences, might explain their different reactions, so too might differences in their stage of personal development, as shown in Figure 3–2.

Most staff members who have just completed their professional training or who are holding their first job after high school or college are primarily concerned with getting into the adult world, developing their sense of identity, and building a life that reflects their personality and personal style. They can experiment with various combinations of work and nonwork in their lives: At times they may spend 70 or 80 hours at work, and at other times they may work only the minimum time required.

A nurse such as Jane Shelton, who is in her late twenties, has probably spent much of her twenties establishing her own identity and life-style. Now, approaching the age of thirty, Jane and others like her must review all past commitments and reappraise their personal and career progress to date. Some workers try to make themselves indispensable to their organizations as one way of encouraging employers to provide greater flexibility. Individuals in their thirties typically must come to terms with both career and family concerns. Some staff members may feel pressure to have children. If they already have children, they might experience a dilemma about how much time and energy to devote to family versus career. Other staff members may choose alternative life-styles and seek to gain their acceptance in the workplace. Managers of a diverse work force must develop and implement strategies for easing these dilemmas as a way of retaining productive employees.

The Orthopedics Department may also have some technicians like Joan Andrews on staff. Joan reentered the work force when her children reached school age. Now

Figure 3–2 **Stages of Personal Development**

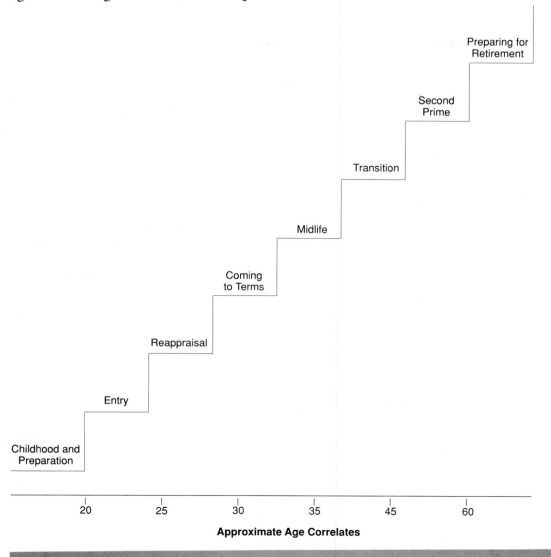

Approximate Age Correlates

she encounters the difficulties of midlife, of being part of the "sandwich generation" where she has responsibility for both her children and aging parents. Or, the department may have technicians like Ted Fabrizzi on the staff. Like some other men in their early forties, Ted has experienced a *midcareer crisis* where he questions the fundamental value, appropriateness, and real accomplishment in his life so far.[18] Individuals at this stage must manage the transition between the two chronological parts of their lives to ensure their personal satisfaction and well-being.

Productivity remains a key issue for men and women in their late fifties, sixties, and even seventies or eighties. They can continue devoting significant energy to work and careers, or they can refocus their energies on retirement. Planning for adjusting to a reduced status and work role requires significant thought and time investment. As we noted earlier, older workers will continue to be a significant source of staff in the next century, and managers must understand their abilities and respond to their needs.[19]

Clearly, then, managers of a diverse work force must understand that individuals tend to confront different issues at each decade of their lives. Further, their abilities to deal with these issues, as well as the organization's success in responding to different needs, will influence both individual and organizational performance. Managers can assist employees by helping them recognize their developmental needs and where possible restructuring the work situation to meet these needs. Obviously, some major changes need to be made at Malvern General Hospital before this restructuring can occur.

CAREER DEVELOPMENT FOR A DIVERSE WORK FORCE

Progress through a series of jobs over a forty- to fifty-year period, accompanied by a set of related attitudes and experiences, characterizes the *careers* of individual employees, which complement their personal development.[20] Recognizing the issues associated with specific career stages, acknowledging the unique issues faced by professional workers, and implementing career development activities in expanding and contracting economies challenge the manager of a diverse work force. Note that the career development described here reflects typical patterns in the United States and is only one prototype for career development. In Israel and other countries with mandatory military service for all men (and women in some cases) the sequence of career stages presented here may be delayed or altered. Countries such as Sweden with liberal maternity and paternity leave policies may also have workers with different career patterns from the one described here.

Career Stages

Figure 3–3 presents one prototypical time line of career development, and Table 3–2 some issues associated with each stage. Note that the ages associated with each stage may vary significantly for different careers and different individuals. Cross-cultural variations may also exist, as noted previously.

Think of the staff in the Psychiatric Unit at Malvern General. Are they likely to be at the same career stage? What do they expect from their jobs in relation to their careers? Will they react in the same way to the requirements of their job and their

Figure 3–3 **Stages of Career Development**

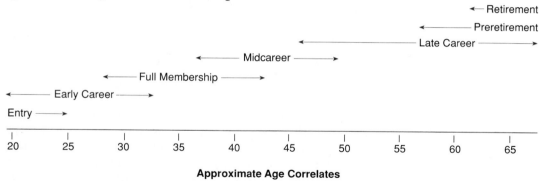

Table 3–2 **Career Stages and Issues**

Stages	Issues	Specific Tasks
Growth, fantasy, exploration	Developing a basis for making realistic vocational choices	Developing and discovering one's own needs and interests
	Obtaining education or training	Getting maximum career information
Entry into world of work	Becoming a member of an organization or occupation	Learning how to look for and secure a job
Basic training	Becoming an effective member quickly	Overcoming the insecurity of inexperience
		Learning to get along with boss and coworkers
Full membership in early career	Accepting the responsibility and discharging duties	Performing effectively
		Accepting subordinate status
	Developing and displaying special skills	Developing initiative and realistic expectations
Full membership, midcareer	Choosing a specialty	Gaining a measure of independence
	Remaining technically competent	Assessing own motives, talents
	Establishing a clear identity	Assessing organizational and occupational opportunities
Midcareer crisis	Reassessing own progress relative to ambitions	Becoming aware of career anchor
	Deciding relative importance of work and family	Making specific choices about the present and future
Late career in nonleadership role	Becoming a mentor	Remaining technically competent
	Broadening interests	Developing interpersonal skills
	Deepening skills	Dealing with younger persons
Late career in leadership role	Using skills and talents for organization's welfare	Becoming more responsible for organization
	Selecting and developing subordinates	Handling power
		Balancing career and family
Decline and disengagement	Learning to accept reduced power and responsibility	Finding new sources of satisfaction
Retirement	Adjusting to more drastic life-style changes	Maintaining a sense of identity and self-worth without job

SOURCE: E. H. Schein, *Career Dynamics: Matching Individual and Organizational Needs*, © 1978, Addison-Wesley Publishing Company, Inc. Adapted from Table 4.1. Reprinted with permission of the publisher.

organization? Individuals in their *first job* try to become effective and accepted members of their organizations as quickly as possible while they learn the job's ropes and routines. They must spend time learning to get along with their boss and coworkers, as well as trying to become an effective member quickly. The nature of the workers' experiences on entering the organization significantly affects their longer term commitment to it.[21]

At the next stage, often known as *early career,* individuals become more concerned with advancement and establishing a career path. They should find a *mentor,* a person who helps influence their movement through the organization and affects their career success by performing functions such as those shown in Table 3–3, or other organizational members who can become part of a *relationship constellation* that provides developmental support to an individual.[22] Mentoring becomes particularly important in a multicultural environment where nonperformance-related factors can block career progress.

Individuals who have experienced extensive mentoring reported receiving more promotions, having higher incomes, and being more satisfied with pay and benefits.[23] Mentoring for women has not occurred to a sufficient degree in the workplace, in part because women do not seek mentors or mentors may not select females.[24] The barriers can be characterized as follows: Women lack access to networks within organizations; women may be viewed as tokens who cannot reach top management; stereotypes and misattributions about women's abilities to manage may reduce the view of their performance; women may be seen as having been socialized to develop personalities alien to management success; cross-gender relationships may be viewed as taboo; and women may rely on ineffective sources of power, reducing their success.[25]

The establishment of formal mentoring programs, the conduct of educational programs about mentoring and career development, and the implementation of more significant changes in organizational structure, norms, and processes are three strat-

Table 3–3   **Mentoring Functions**

Career Functions	Psychosocial Functions
Sponsorship Opening doors. Having connections that will support the junior's career advancement.	*Role modeling* Demonstrating valued behavior, attitudes and/or skills that aid the junior in achieving competence, confidence, and a clear professional identity.
Coaching Teaching "the ropes." Giving relevant positive and negative feedback to improve the junior's performance and potential.	*Counseling* Providing a helpful and confidential forum for exploring personal and professional dilemmas. Excellent listening, trust, and rapport that enable both individuals to address central developmental concerns.
Protection Providing support in different situations. Taking responsibility for mistakes that were outside the junior's control. Acting as a buffer when necessary.	*Acceptance and confirmation* Providing ongoing support, respect, and admiration, which strengthens self-confidence and self-image. Regularly reinforcing both as highly valued people and contributors to the organization.
Exposure Creating opportunities for the junior to demonstrate competence where it counts. Taking the junior to important meetings that will enhance his or her visibility.	*Friendship* Mutual caring and intimacy that extends beyond the requirements of daily work tasks. Sharing of experience outside the immediate work setting.
Challenging work Delegating assignments that stretch the junior's knowledge and skills in order to stimulate growth and preparation to move ahead.	

SOURCE: Reprinted with permission from K. E. Kram, "Mentoring in the Workplace." In D. T. Hall and Associates, eds., *Career Development in Organizations* (San Francisco: Jossey-Bass, 1986), p. 162. © 1986 by Jossey-Bass Inc., Publishers.

egies that have been used to support the mentoring process.[26] Benefits of mentoring to organizations are the transmission of corporate culture and the ability to "deep sense" employees' moods and attitudes.[27] In addition, the organization must encourage all managers to act as mentors by providing training in evaluation, and then reward their mentoring activities.[28]

Workers who are typically in their late twenties or early thirties strive for *full membership in an early career*. The primary emphasis of such individuals must be on performing effectively, accepting responsibility, managing subordinates, discharging duties, and developing special skills. Early research about this stage suggested that young professionals may experience conflicting expectations from their coworkers and bosses, incompetent supervisors, insensitivity to the internal political environment, personal passivity and ignorance of real performance criteria, and dilemmas about loyalty, integrity, commitment, and dependence.[29]

Workers with a somewhat longer employment history at the same stage also have *full membership,* assume additional responsibilities, and become increasingly autonomous. These employees must also assess the extent to which they wish to remain technical or advance into a managerial position. If they choose to remain technical, they must ensure that they maintain up-to-date knowledge in their career field. They also must ensure that they do not become *plateaued performers,* workers who are "stuck" in their present job or level in the organization because the hierarchy narrows and severely limits advancement opportunities or because their job responsibilities never change.[30] For women, the *glass ceiling* may be another manifestation of plateauing. This invisible barrier to movement into top management occurs because of discrimination in the workplace, the inability of women to penetrate the "old boys' network," and the tendency of executives to promote others like themselves.[31]

Midcareer is defined as "the period during one's work in an occupational (career) role after one feels established and has achieved perceived mastery and prior to the commencement of the disengagement process."[32] Those individuals who are between the ages of thirty-five and forty-five may experience a difficult midlife transition in their careers as well as their personal life. The midlife transition may cause individuals to reappraise their life's accomplishments to date. Some men at midcareer experience a need to disrupt their habitual behavior and initiate career exploration, whereas women become concerned with balancing the various aspects of their lives and ensuring that they have not sacrificed too much time with their family in favor of career activities and advancement.[33] Resolving these dilemmas may result in new choices about career and family or an acceptance of old choices as appropriate.

Once past midcareer, individuals in organizations must find a way to continue to contribute. Depending on the person's skills, interests, and motivation, and the organization's culture and goals, such employees might help shape the direction of the organization by acting as a *sponsor* for younger workers. One study of such professionals considered this role a prerequisite for continued career performance.[34]

Table 3–4 and Figure 3–4 summarize our discussion about career stages by plotting a career-stage model for industrial CEOs. But would the same model hold for men and women? Recent research suggests that the same model of career development may not apply to men and women because they differ in career preparation, job opportunities, their role in marriage and childbearing, and the likely interruption of their careers.[35]

Professional Careers   Professional employees, such as scientists, engineers, teachers, and accountants, bring specialized expertise to organizations, frequently as a result of advanced education or special training. They may face different career and organizational issues from

Table 3–4 CEO Career Stages

Exploration (1–5 years)
- 40% change firms searching for the right fit
- 25% move into industrial firms from accounting, law, or government
- Phase ends with promotion to first management position

Development (6–10 years)
- Less interfirm movement; more intrafirm movement
- Movement to other functions and/or cross-functional assignments
- Some assignments as "assistant to" a senior manager
- Promotion to lower middle management

Commitment (11–15 years)
- High level of loyalty to one firm
- International experience attained
- Advancement into middle management continues

Verification (16–20 years)
- Promotion to either division-level management or functional VP level
- Responsibilities change rapidly
- Executive skills are proven

Payback (21–25 years)
- Frequent, broad job changes
- Final grooming or competition for the top
- Experience as senior group or division head, executive VP, chief operating officer, or president

Payoff (beyond 25 years)
- Attainment of the position of chief executive officer

SOURCE: Reprinted with permission from J. E. Piercy and J. B. Forbes, The phases of the chief executive's career, *Business Horizons* (May–June, 1991), p. 22.

those experienced by managerial or other employees. Managers who do not share the same professional background may have difficulty in motivating or supervising these employees and in understanding the autonomy they expect.[36] Managers may also have difficulty acknowledging the technical quality of their work because of their own lack of technical knowledge. Because of their often high commitment to their profession, these employees may appear less committed to their organizations. Top executives at Malvern General Hospital, for example, may perceive the physicians as having competing loyalties. They may also not be able to advance in their organizations without assuming managerial responsibility.[37]

Dual ladders, as shown in Figure 3–5, where individuals can assume increasingly higher positions in the organization (with greater pay, status, and responsibility) with or without assuming managerial or supervisory responsibility, are uncommon in organizations. More recent research suggests that a third option may exist and may become more popular as workers get older. In the *treble ladder* individuals can progress through a series of interesting projects over time rather than through either traditional career path.[38] To ensure the productivity of professionals, top executives must use these and other accommodative mechanisms, including job redesign, professional reward systems, and mentorship for managers.

Implications for Managing   Career effectiveness and the individual job effectiveness that accompanies it often arise from the organization's ability to integrate the employee into the organization

Figure 3–4 **Steps to the Top for CEO**

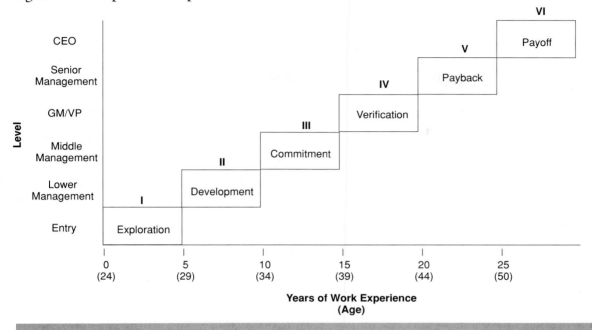

SOURCE: Reprinted with permission from J. E. Piercy and J. B. Forbes, The phases of the chief executive's career, *Business Horizons* (May-June, 1991), p. 21.

and to help that employee make career transitions effectively. Both employees and their managers should assume some career development responsibilities. Employees should know and understand the implications of their own stage of career development for satisfaction and job performance. Managers should provide opportunities to discuss career development issues, give feedback about reasonable expectations for employees, identify employee potential, provide relevant growth opportunities, and link employees to appropriate resources.[39] A lack of such information in addition to the dilemmas experienced at various stages of biosocial, family, and career development may contribute to confusion and conflict in the performance of work and non-work roles.

Managing career development in an environment in which the work force and hence career opportunities are shrinking poses significant challenges to managers. Organizations that once valued low turnover may now foster higher turnover through voluntary severance programs, early retirement options, mandatory employee relocations, or layoffs. Less costly solutions include assuring that plateauing does not occur by transferring employees laterally and redesigning jobs to increase the job holders' responsibilities.

MANAGING WORK AND FAMILY INTERACTIONS

Particularly as women continue to enter the work force in increasing numbers, the interaction between work and family becomes critical for most men and women. Responding to issues created by this interaction is particularly critical in managing a diverse work force in the United States. The traditional family with a working father, stay-at-home mother, and average of 2.2 children is rare in the United States and other countries as well. Nontraditional family styles—including single parents

Figure 3–5 **Example of a Dual Ladder**

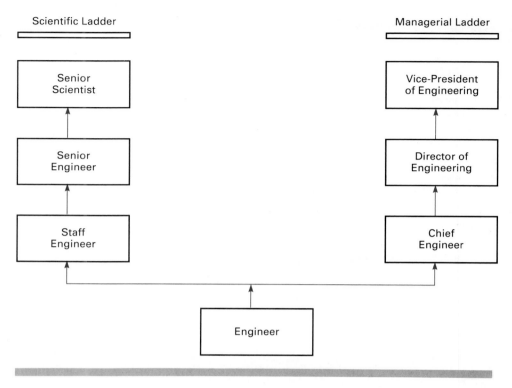

with children, stepfamilies, divorced parents alternating child-rearing responsibilities, and increasing numbers of adult couples with no children—call for greater attention to the work-family interaction. Workplace issues seem to be most critical for adults with child care responsibilities. The United States lags significantly behind other industrialized countries in dealing with these issues.

Family Issues   In this section we describe one set of family concerns. Clearly the basic issues individuals face depend greatly on their age, marital status, and whether they have children. Figure 3–6 illustrates one example of family concerns over time.

A single adult new to the work force enters the adult world, focuses on developing his or her sense of self, and increases his or her independence from parents and extended family. For example, single adults must decide where to live, how much time to spend with parents and friends, and how much time and energy to devote to work and nonwork activities. Other individuals in the early career stage may be learning to live with a spouse, friend, or relative. Balancing personal needs with the needs of another may create performance dilemmas. For example, the demands of one spouse's work may require a geographical relocation that could affect the other spouse's career. Or conflicting work schedules may limit the amount of time husband and wife spend together. Clearly, the choice of a family style, such as whether to be part of a dual-career family, will influence the nature of work involvement and commitment.

Parents of young children often face very real conflicts between their work and home responsibilities. The issue of balance between work and family becomes paramount.[40] In addition to dealing with parenthood emotionally, they must determine a workable division of responsibility because work demands may limit the amount

Figure 3–6 **Family Concerns**

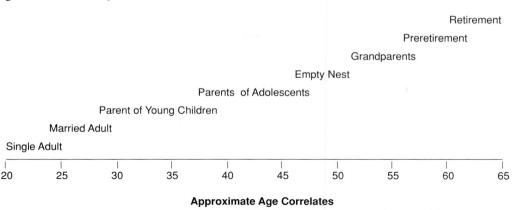

of time either spouse can devote to home responsibilities. Many women at this stage experience so much tension between work and family demands that they seek more flexible working arrangements. Some even leave the work force entirely, often re-sulting in a significant personnel loss for their organization.[41] Finding quality child care becomes a major issue that remains in the forefront for ten to fifteen years of their work life.

Midlife may see either the resolution or exacerbation of these stresses. A mid-career crisis may be compounded by the complex family arrangements; for example, dealing with the independence and possible rebellion of children may reinforce feel-ings of inadequacy or dissatisfaction. Facing the financial strains of college tuition may contribute to stress and cause performance problems. Or, the greater career security sometimes experienced at midlife may free more energy for dealing with family issues. Of course, divorce and its attendant financial requirements may further intensify the stress. After midlife, building enduring relationships may create new challenges.

Individuals in dual-career families often use one or more of the following five strategies for dealing with role pressures.[42] First, family members can develop a commitment to both careers. Second, they build in flexibility at home and on the job, such as by choosing jobs that give them autonomy. Third, they may adjust their priorities about home responsibilities or hire other people to do some of them, such as cooking or cleaning. Fourth, they develop and use good time-management skills, often paring their lives to priority activities. Fifth and finally, they develop career competencies, such as self-assessment, collection of vocational information, goal set-ting, planning, and problem solving to facilitate their mutual career advancement.

Organizational **Responses** Organizations such as Malvern General must find ways to respond to the needs of workers with various family demands. Employers must help workers to balance the various aspects of their lives by easing the interface between work and family. Recent discussion of the feasibility and appropriateness of a *mommy track,* where women have the option of slowing their career advancement during their parenting years, has suggested the complexity of work-family issues.[43] Yet most feel this alternative does not really address the issues.[44] Rather, organizations must become more family-friendly, as shown in Table 3–5 and Figure 3–7. Helping workers set and meet

Table 3–5 **Family-Friendly Companies**

A sampling of companies and the programs they sponsor to meet the family needs of their employees

Company	Rationale for Family Policies	Sampling of Programs
Johnson & Johnson	Recruitment, retention of workers, and stress reduction	Family-care leave and sick days, child care, community child-care centers and subsidies, grants
IBM	Stress reduction	Flexible scheduling, leaves of absence, work-at-home programs, fund to improve quality and supply of child care
Aetna Life & Casualty	Recruitment and retention	Job-sharing, part-time work, flexible hours, school-holiday program, work at home
Corning	Recruitment and retention	Child care, part-time work, summer camps, and after-school programs

SOURCE: Data supplied by Families and Work Institute. From S. Shellenbarger, More job seekers put family needs first, *Wall Street Journal*, November 15, 1991, pp. B1, B12. Reprinted by permission of the *Wall Street Journal*, © 1991 Dow Jones & Company, Inc. All Rights Reserved Worldwide.

priorities, providing flexibility in working arrangements, offering quality child care options, and judging workers in terms of outputs rather than time or effort should facilitate the interaction. Redesigning jobs (Chapter 13) and changing the organizational culture (Chapter 5) to one that supports the diverse work force are also significant organizational responses. At midcareer and late career, offering opportunities for respite and reflection, such as through learning sabbaticals or paid leaves, would also rejuvenate a worker stressed from coping with multiple demands. Reading 3–1, "Promoting Work/Family Balance: An Organization-Change Approach" by Douglas T. Hall, addresses these issues in greater detail.

INDIVIDUAL ROLE PRESSURES

Within the constellation of individual development, job and career activities, and family responsibilities, each person has a prescribed set of activities, or potential behavior, that constitute the *role* that individual performs.[45] The different and multiple roles held by individuals in organizations contribute to the challenge of managing a diverse work force. Building appropriate and consistent expectations of role holders is difficult. Managers must carefully assess individuals on objective performance characteristics and clearly communicate expectations to them. In a global environment, definitions of roles and expectations associated with them may vary among different cultures, countries, or work groups.

Typically, an individual who holds a particular role relates to or interacts with others in comparable or related roles, known as the *role set*. A female may hold the roles of manager, wife, mother, and participant in community activities, and as a manager she may hold the roles of supervisor and subordinate simultaneously. At Malvern General Hospital a nurse interacts with an extensive group of professionals, including other nurses in the department, physicians, members of other departments, and patients and their families who have *expectations* of how the nurse (as a role holder) will think and behave. For example, physicians may expect nurses to provide certain support services and look to orderlies or other department and hospital per-

Figure 3–7 **Is Your Company Family-Friendly?**

The Families and Work Institute created this index to compare work/family policies at large companies. It rates them according to whether they have these options—and gives higher scores for companywide, formal programs.

Policy	Maximum Score
Flexible work arrangements Variable starting and quitting times, part-time work	105
Leaves Length of parental leaves, who's eligible, job guarantees	40
Financial assistance Flexible benefits, long-term-care insurance, child-care discounts	80
Corporate giving/community service Funding for community or national work/family initiatives	60
Dependent-care services Child- and elder-care referral, on-site centers, sick-child programs	155
Management change Work/family training for managers, work/family coordinators	90
Work-family stress management Wellness programs, relocation services, work/family seminars	80
Total possible score:	610

The Top Scorers

Here are the most family-friendly of 188 companies surveyed.* Because all policies may not fit every company, the ideal score is probably below the maximum of 610 points.

Johnson & Johnson	245	John Hancock	175
IBM	223	Warner-Lambert	175
Aetna	195	U.S. West	165
Corning	190	Du Pont	163
AT&T	178	Travelers	158

*Based on policies in place as of spring 1990

SOURCE: Data supplied by Families and Work Institute. Reprinted with special permission from Corporate America is still no place for kids, *Business Week,* November 25, 1991, pp. 234, 236. Copyright © 1991 by McGraw-Hill, Inc.

sonnel for others. Of course, the role holder may or may not conform to these expectations.

Generally, an individual will operate *in role*—that is, according to expectations associated with the role. Occasionally role holders operate out of role and perform activities typically not associated with their roles. In role, a factory worker assembles engines; out of role, he or she delivers heated political orations during work hours. You might say, however, that such behaviors are not really out of role. People often have differing expectations about the activities that are appropriate for a role holder, particularly in a complex, global environment.

Role Conflict   Differing expectations pressure a role holder to perform in one way rather than another and result in *role conflict,* where compliance with one set of pressures hinders or prevents compliance with a different set of pressures. For example, top management may expect an accountant to perform as a detail person and process as many accounts as possible, while at the same time ensuring the highest quality and creativity. Role conflict (and role ambiguity as described in a later subsection) may lead to such dysfunctional work-related behaviors as tension, stress, job dissatisfaction, propensity to leave the organization, and lowered organizational commitment.[46]

Not only is conflict inherent within a single role, but the multiple roles a person plays often create diverse, potentially conflicting expectations. Remember that these roles can be both formal and informal, both work and nonwork. For example, a woman manager who is a wife and mother and a male manager who is a husband and father might experience role conflict when they must deal with a sick child on the same day a mandatory meeting for all managers is scheduled. Each type of role conflict involves implicitly or explicitly pressuring the role holder to change to conform to the senders' expectations. Generally, the more extreme the pressure, the more extensive the conflict. Stress, as described later in this chapter, often results from such conflicts.

Intrasender Conflict   When one person sends a role holder conflicting or inconsistent expectations, *intrasender* role conflict occurs. Computer programmers whose boss tells them on the one hand to write as many lines of code as possible and on the other hand to write programs that are error-free may experience intrasender conflict. At Malvern General Hospital the chief of nursing might direct a nursing supervisor to provide the most state-of-the-art medical care to patients while at the same time minimizing costs.

Intersender Conflict   When different people with whom the role holder interacts have different expectations of him or her, *intersender* conflict occurs. Tax consultants may "hear" different expectations about their role from their clients and the Internal Revenue Service. Lab technicians may receive different instructions about the nature and extent of tests they should provide from their supervisors and from physicians requesting services.

Interrole Conflict   When the expectations associated with different roles a person holds come into conflict, *interrole* conflict occurs. The working mother who has a sick child feels she is expected to be at work and perform her job as well as to be at home and to care for her sick child. Work-family conflict, as we have discussed earlier, arises from insufficient time to perform one or the other role sufficiently, a preoccupation with the role not currently performed, strain caused by one or both roles, and behavior required by one role (for example, aggressiveness or nurturance) that interferes with the performance of the other role.[47] A larger proportion of managerial women than managerial men deal with this conflict by remaining unmarried or childless.[48]

Person-Role Conflict   When the activities expected of a role holder violate the individual's values and morals, *person-role* conflict occurs. The employee who is asked to work on a religious holiday or to participate in activities that contradict his or her moral values may experience this type of conflict. Ethical conflicts, such as experienced by the employee who is asked to distort data to represent the company favorably in an affirmative action report, fall into this category. Management and workers have a joint responsibility for identifying and eliminating such conflicts.

Role Overload   When the expectations sent to a role holder are compatible but their performance exceeds the amount of time or knowledge available to the person for performing the expected activities, *role overload* occurs. A person who holds a full-time job and has too many tasks to complete in the available time likely experiences role overload. So too does a person who is asked to perform tasks that exceed his or her knowledge, skills, or abilities. Overload typifies top management jobs, where the role holder often has more responsibilities than a single individual can handle.

Role Ambiguity   A role holder for whom expectations in that role have not been adequately clarified experiences *role ambiguity*. The new employee who receives no orientation to the job often experiences role ambiguity because he or she lacks complete information about job activities and responsibilities, as well as about the employing organization (organizational socialization activities as described in the next paragraphs address this deficiency). The employee who does not know what activities the organization rewards also may experience role ambiguity. Does the company promote individuals who conform to company policies completely or who take some risks and demonstrate creativity? Does the company value a perfect attendance record over productivity? Does the company reward loyalty and encourage long-term employment?

Organizational Socialization   "Learning the ropes," being taught what the organization values, or being oriented or trained in organizational operations helps reduce role ambiguity for individuals entering new jobs or organizations.[49] Through *organizational socialization* a new member learns the organization's (1) basic goals, (2) preferred *means* to attain those goals, (3) basic *role responsibilities* of the member, (4) *behavior patterns* required for effective role performance, (5) rules or principles that pertain to maintaining the organization's *identity and integrity,* (6) *symbols* and *rituals,* and (7) *meaning of events*.[50] It can occur either formally, through orientation or structured training programs, or informally, through daily interpersonal interactions. Together with individual differences and attributions, early learning experiences and socialization tactics influence newcomers' adjustment to the organization.

Orientation programs frequently provide the initial socialization of organization members. Top managers may meet with new recruits to discuss their philosophy and vision of the organization; the human resources management department may present the organization's rules and standard operating procedures to them; or managers may discuss specific job activities. Subsequent on-the-job training and informal interactions with peers and subordinates reinforce the values, norms, and behavior patterns introduced earlier. For example, continued individualized on-the-job training suggests to a new recruit that the organization values individuality. In contrast, the repetition of rules and procedures reflects a more bureaucratic operating style. Socialization occurs continually, but the process begins again each time an individual makes a transition in an organization by entering a new, often higher, position or a different department.[51]

Dealing with Role Pressures   Action first requires determining whether role conflict, role overload, or role ambiguity exists in given situations, such as those that are likely to exist at Malvern General Hospital. To diagnose the nature of the role pressures we can ask the following questions:

1. Do any symptoms of role conflict, role overload, or role ambiguity, such as dissatisfaction, confusion, or low productivity, exist?
2. How is each person's role defined by the role holder and by relevant others?
3. Are the expectations of the role holder clear?

4. Do any of the role expectations create conflict?
5. How does the organization socialize new members?
6. What are the outcomes of the socialization processes, and are they appropriate to the individuals involved and the situation?

How then does coping occur? Some set new priorities or ignore certain expectations or leave the situation. Strategies for coping with role ambiguity include asking about others' expectations, identifying desired behavior, and learning about the reward system. Others become less satisfied with their work, family, or lives in general, or experience stress and anxiety, as discussed in the next section.

STRESS IN ORGANIZATIONS

Stress refers to a psychological and physiological state that results when certain features of an individual's environment, including noise, pressures, job promotions, monotony, or the general climate, attack or impinge on that person; these features create an actual or perceived imbalance between demand and capability to adjust and result in a nonspecific response.[52] In stress situations individuals experience (1) alarm, (2) resistance, and (3) exhaustion.[53] In the *alarm* stage individuals face a *stressor*—an aspect of the situation that causes a rise in adrenaline or increased anxiety. Stressors include role conflict, role overload, task ambiguity, uncertainty, competition, and other aspects of a work or nonwork situation. If the stressor persists, individuals respond to it during the *resistance* stage. They may deal with the stressor directly or use it to stimulate creative behaviors. When the stressors persist and either result in positive outcomes or create physiological or psychological damage, *exhaustion* has occurred.

Think about a situation in which you experienced stress. How did you feel? What contributed to the stress? What alleviated it? How did you perform when you experienced stress? You may have felt stress, for example, when you had too many tasks to complete in too short a time. Or you may have felt stress when you failed to advance in an organization because of poor supervision, lack of a mentor or sponsor, or the inability to become autonomous in your work. Or you may have experienced stress when you received a promotion and questioned your ability to fulfill your new responsibilities.

The response to stress is quite varied.[54] Some respond by becoming more productive and creative. Have you ever heard a friend or coworker say, "I work best when I have a deadline in sight; I can't do anything productive unless I feel some pressure." This person likely uses the stress resulting from time pressure constructively—to increase his or her productivity. Others experience gastrointestinal, glandular, and cardiovascular disorders or respond to stress by overeating, drinking excessively, or taking drugs. Others become impatient, detached, or filled with despair. Still others experience *burnout,* a particular and intense reaction that is represented by emotional exhaustion, the development of negative or impersonal responses to workers, and loss of self-esteem or low feelings of accomplishment.[55] Such physiological and psychological reactions can decrease a person's satisfaction, creativity, and productivity, and these effects in turn often increase a person's level of stress, thus causing a further decrease in effectiveness.

Causes of Stress

Stress has become increasingly common in organizations, largely because of increased job complexity and increased economic pressures on individuals.[56] Individual career characteristics, such as occupational level, career stage, and stage of adult development, may cause stress. Individuals at the beginning of their career who are trying to establish themselves often experience stress; "midcareer crisis" is virtually synonymous with stress; and even facing the changes of retirement creates significant stress for individuals. Table 3–6 lists the major life-stress events for individuals in the United States, and it also provides a way of calculating the probability that an individual will experience stress-related illness. Table 3–7 lists a set of potential stressors in public accounting. Professional women also experience unique stressors: discrimination, stereotyping, conflicting demands of work and family, and feelings of isolation.[57]

Predicting the level of stress in situations can be difficult, largely because stress is often person-specific and can also be culture-specific. Simple requests for overtime or revisions of completed work may cause stress, whereas managing an organization in a competitive environment may not. Such events may also have varying impact in different cultures.

Let us consider again the situation at Malvern General Hospital described in the introduction to this chapter. We can evaluate the extent of dysfunctional stress there by performing a *stress audit,* which helps identify the symptoms and causes of stress,[58] as shown in Table 3–8.

Dealing with Stress   Diagnosis of stress is obviously the first step in using or reducing it. Effective organizational members must know how to manage stress—when to increase and decrease it by recognizing both its energizing and destructive effects.[59] Managers can encourage productive stress by helping employees build challenge into their work and assume incremental responsibility and autonomy over time. They can also help individuals cope with dysfunctional stress.[60] They can encourage individuals to secure treatment for symptoms of stress. Many organizations offer health protection, health promotion, and wellness programs.[61] They also can redesign jobs or restructure organizations to reduce dysfunctional stress. Or they can change organizational policies and practices, such as by rewarding delegation of responsibilities, positive interpersonal interactions, and constructive conflict resolution.

MANAGING DIVERSITY IN ORGANIZATIONS   Managing diversity begins with valuing individual differences. Richard Bridges at Malvern General Hospital must help the hospital's managers and nonmanagerial employees to develop a sensitivity to, understanding of, and acceptance of individuals with different ethnic and cultural backgrounds and of different races, genders, and ages.

In one set of solutions, educational efforts are the common thread.[62] The first solution is diversity training, which helps individuals understand their own and others' prejudices. At Honeywell, for example, diversity training focuses on four strategies:

- Management development—increase the visibility of, understanding of, and commitment to diversity throughout global Honeywell.
- Organizational development—promote an equitable work environment that values diversity.
- Talent development—obtain horizontal and vertical integration of diversity throughout all functions.
- Individual development—empower individuals to help reduce barriers to reaching their full potential.[63]

A second alternative focuses on career training for minorities to assist them in advancement. A third solution rewards managers who create environments that foster

Table 3–6 **Stress Events**

Complete the scale by circling the mean value figure to the right of each item if it has occurred to you during the past year. To figure your total score, add all the mean values circled (if an event occurred more than once, increase the value by the number of times). Life event stress totals of 150 or less indicate generally good health, scores of 150 to 300 indicate a 35–50 percent probability of stress-related illness, and scores of 300+ indicate an 80 percent probability.

Life Event	Mean Value
1. Death of spouse	100
2. Divorce	73
3. Marital separation from mate	65
4. Detention in jail or other institution	63
5. Death of a close family member	63
6. Major personal injury or illness	53
7. Marriage	50
8. Being fired at work	47
9. Marital reconciliation with mate	45
10. Retirement from work	45
11. Major change in the health or behavior of a family member	44
12. Pregnancy	40
13. Sexual difficulties	39
14. Gaining a new family member	39
15. Major business readjustment	39
16. Major change in financial state	38
17. Death of a close friend	37
18. Changing to a different line of work	36
19. Major change in the number of arguments with spouse	35
20. Taking out a mortgage or loan for a major purchase	31
21. Foreclosure on a mortgage or loan	30
22. Major change in responsibilities at work	29
23. Son or daughter leaving home	29
24. In-law troubles	29
25. Outstanding personal achievement	28
26. Wife beginning or ceasing work outside the home	26
27. Beginning or ceasing formal schooling	26
28. Major change in living conditions	25
29. Revision of personal habits	24
30. Troubles with the boss	23
31. Major change in working hours or conditions	20
32. Change in residence	20
33. Changing to a new school	20
34. Major change in usual type and/or amount of recreation	19
35. Major change in church activities	19
36. Major change in social activities	18
37. Taking out a mortgage or loan for a lesser purchase	17
38. Major change in sleeping habits	16
39. Major change in number of family get-togethers	15
40. Major change in eating habits	15
41. Vacation	13
42. Christmas	12
43. Minor violations of the law	11

SOURCE: Reprinted with permission from *Journal of Psychosomatic Research,* 11, Thomas H. Holmes, Social Readjustment Rating Scale, Copyright 1967, Pergamon Press, Inc.

Table 3–7 Some
Stressors in Public
Accounting

Stressors Related to the Demand/Capability Imbalance
Insufficient background or knowledge (i.e., work is too difficult)
Inability of assigned tasks to maintain interest (i.e., work is not challenging)
Striving for unattainable goals

Stressors Related to the Public Accounting Environment
Working for a national CPA firm
Working in the auditing department
Being a junior accountant or manager
Variations in work load (i.e., too much work, deadlines, idle time)
Up-or-out proposition of CPA firms (i.e., promotion or termination)
Requirement of passing the CPA examination
Requirement of continuing professional education

Stressors Related to Change
New accounting and auditing standards
Tax law changes
Use of microcomputers and new software
Concern over employer merging with another firm

Stressors Related to Time
Variations in work load
Pressures relating to audit or tax deadlines
Overnight travel
Conflicting time demands

Stressors Related to Gender
Concern over job discrimination
Cross-gender relations
Conflicts between home and work
Time conflicts resulting in unique time demands on the woman
Combination of high-stress marriage and high-stress job

Stressors Related to Other Psychological or Social Situations
Self-inflicted stress (personal fears and anxiety)
Being a Type A personality or working with someone with a different personality type
Expectations of peers, supervisors, family, and friends
Lack of control over the job or lack of participation in managerial decisions
Being responsible for the actions of other staff members
Job insecurity and job ambiguity
Career dissatisfaction

SOURCE: Reprinted with permission from L. Piccoli, J. M. Emig, and K. M. Hiltebeitel, Why is public accounting stressful? Is it especially stressful for women? *The Woman CPA* (July 1988), p. 12.

Table 3–8 Stress
Audit Questions

1. Do any individuals demonstrate physiological symptoms?
2. Is job satisfaction low, or are job tension, turnover, absenteeism, strikes, and accident-proneness high?
3. Does the organization's design contribute to the symptoms?
4. Do interpersonal relations contribute to the symptoms?
5. Do career-development variables contribute to the symptoms?
6. What effects do personality, sociocultural influences, and the nonwork environment have on the relationship between the stressors and stress?

individual growth, help develop minority employees, and mentor their advancement in the organization.

A second approach emphasizes structural supports. In particular, two-career couples benefit from flexible work arrangements and flexible benefits.[64] Older workers may also want part-time employment or greater flexibility in their work schedules.

Finally, the organizational culture must support diversity. An organization that does so "reflects the contributions and interests of the diverse cultural and social groups in the organization's mission, operations, products, or services; commits to eradicate all forms of social discrimination in the organization; shares power and influence so that no one group is put at an exploitative advantage; follows through on its broader social responsibility to fight social discrimination and advocate social diversity."[65]

SUMMARY   We began this chapter by sampling some of the ethnic diversity experienced by national and multinational organizations. In particular, we chose three cultural examples: the Japanese, Eastern Europeans, and Latin Americans. Next we looked at demographic differences in the U.S. work force. We looked at women, African-Americans, and older workers.

In the major part of the chapter, we looked at individual differences. We defined personality and considered how individuals with different personalities might function in an organization. We looked at the phases of personal development and how they complement personality in individual functioning. We discussed career development in a diverse work force. We described the nature of work and family interactions. We then examined role pressures experienced by organizational members and the stress that often results. We concluded the chapter with some comments about managing diversity. Table 3–9 summarizes the issues presented in this chapter in a series of diagnostic questions related to individual differences, development, role pressures, and stress.

Table 3–9 **Diagnostic Questions for Personality, Individual Development, Career Development, Work-Family Interaction, Role Pressures, and Stress**

- Do the personality styles of participants fit with the situation?
- Do the personality styles of participants fit with those of other organizational members?
- Do the organizational members experience problems in adult or career development?
- How compatible are the adult and career development stages of various organizational members?
- How effective are the interactions between work and family?
- How does the organization help its members balance work and family responsibilities?
- Do individuals experience role conflict?
- Do individuals experience role overload?
- Are roles clear or ambiguous?
- Do the socialization processes used fit with the situational requirements and help reduce role ambiguity?
- How do managers and other organizational members deal with role pressures?
- Is there stress in the situation?
- Are there mechanisms for effectively managing stress?

Promoting Work/Family Balance: An Organization-Change Approach
Douglas T. Hall

Work/family balance is fast becoming *the* hot career issue of the new decade. With baby boomers well into their 30s and 40s and confronted with a now-or-never situation regarding children, the management ranks are swelling in a new way. Recently I visited a *Fortune* 100 firm's headquarters, where a female executive exclaimed to me, "It seems as if half of my department is either pregnant or out on maternity leave!" In another large company I was told, "Executive row has become maternity row!" Since many of these new two-career parents (both mothers and fathers) are now in quite senior positions, old familiar questions about whether and how one can balance family and career are being reexamined, but with a greater urgency and higher stakes than ever before—for both the individual and the organization.

The depth of corporate and personal concern about this issue was crystallized in an article by Felice Schwartz that appeared in the *Harvard Business Review* (January-February, 1989, pp. 65–76), with the provocative title "Management Women and the New Facts of Life." Two major points in her article drew powerful reactions from a variety of sources: (1) The cost of employing women is greater than that of employing men (because of turnover related to maternity), and (2) to reduce this cost, corporations should provide more flexible employment arrangements for women who want to combine career and family.

On the second point, Schwartz identified two groups of corporate women: "career-primary women" (who put career first and are willing to make sacrifices in their personal lives, such as forgoing children, to reach for the top) and "career-and-family women" (who are "willing to trade some career growth and compensation for freedom from the constant pressure to work long hours and weekends" [p.70]).

This article generated a tremendous amount of interest—and no small degree of controversy. Schwartz, a long-time feminist and supporter of business advancement for women (through her work with the Catalyst organization), was roundly criticized by other feminist leaders on several grounds: for giving (male) executives a ready excuse for denying women promotional opportunities, for "sacrificing" the promotion opportunities of the majority of women (those who want balance) for those of the few who are willing to give up everything else for the career, for presenting only two tracks (a rigid form of flexibility, as author Ellen Goodman called it), for not acknowledging a woman's option to shift gears and increase or decrease her work

involvement at different points in the career, and for appearing to place all of the responsibility for family care on the mother's shoulders. The article and the ensuing reaction were both remarkable: There was something there for everyone to be angry about!

I would like to add my thoughts to the debate and provide a bit of the male perspective. I will examine a few of the issues: First, why has the reaction to Schwartz's article been so explosive? The issue of flexible work arrangements for parents is not new; why has everything suddenly become so polarized? Second, is there a "daddy track"? And, most important, what can organizations do to promote work/family balance?

WHY THE EXPLOSIVE REACTION?

The Schwartz article hit a nerve. What happened? The author is a highly respected, highly effective champion of women's career opportunity in business. The organization she founded, Catalyst, is a nonprofit research and education organization that has conducted landmark studies on women, two-career couples, and corporations for almost 30 years. Women, especially those in the "baby boom" generation, have been moving up through the ranks, and they have been having babies. The business world seems to be adjusting. Why the fuss?

While there are probably a lot of separate reasons for individual responses, I think a lot of the reaction occurred because Schwartz committed the "cardinal sin" of daring to discuss two "nondiscussable" issues: the possibility that (1) career mothers can't "have it all" (when "it" includes fast-track career success and children, and (2) businesses have to make accommodations for career mothers. There's enough in these two ideas to create "equal infuriation opportunity" for business leaders and feminist leaders alike, but the business world is less likely to open up to the press. Both ideas suggest that some sort of compromises will have to be made by individuals (Point 1) and by corporations (Point 2).

The problem is that we have been operating under the assumption (actually, it's a *value position*) that as organizations and society change, we *will* find ways for career women to have it all—executive success, loving spouses, wonderful children, lovely homes, good friends, cared-for parents, and all the rest. Most of the literature on work/family balance recognizes that this is not currently the case and focuses on the search for ways to have it all.

And now in the midst of all of this normative work on *what should be,* along comes Schwartz, who confronts us with *what is,* as she sees it. Her point is that these are the current realities of business (commitment and continuity are required) and parenting (the mother bears most of the responsibility). And people don't like hearing that. Or, at best, we are deeply ambivalent about trying to adapt to these realities. We would rather work to change them.

Not only is the Schwartz article based on the world as it is (as she sees it), in the eyes of her critics, the appearance of her article in an influential journal like the *Harvard Business Review* strongly reinforces the status quo. She is seen as playing into the hands of the current generation of senior executives who are only too happy to have their perceptions of career women confirmed. The article is seen as supporting top management's rationalizations about and resistance to bringing more women into senior executive circles ("Aha! See, they *do* cost us more!"). By providing a second track for women who want work/home balance, they are also off the hook when it comes to accommodating the family needs of fast-track women.

WHY JUST A "MOMMY TRACK"?

Another issue that intrigues me is why all the focus has been on women in relation to parenting. As Representative Pat Schroeder (D., Col.) commented recently, "The last time I checked, most of us here got into the world through the efforts of a mommy *and* a daddy."

What do we know about men's views of work/family balance? (As I sit here with a one-year-old's little fingers competing with mine for the use of this keyboard, I'd be happy to share some personal views, but this analysis calls for a little more detachment!) Much research on two-career couples shows that men, in fact, are concerned about the issue of juggling family and career. We do know that some men make career accommodations for the sake of a career wife or the family. The question is, how many men make career accommodations, and how much accommodating do they do?

The Impact on Men's Careers

The research evidence is mounting that men's careers are, in fact, being affected by family needs. Joseph Pleck in 1985 was one of the first researchers to point out the growing equity in the work loads of men and women at home and on the job. A later study (cited in the *Wall Street Journal,* November 1, 1988) of 1,200 employees at a large Minneapolis firm found that more than 70% of fathers under age 35 reported serious concerns about work/family conflicts with their wives. Sixty percent of the men said these family concerns were affecting their work goals and plans. For example, some men reported their careers were being impacted because they were not seeking promotions and transfers so they could spend more time with their families.

Further data come from studies of work/family issues conducted in recent years at Du Pont. A study in 1985 revealed that work/family conflict was a major impediment to career development at Du Pont, but this impact was felt primarily by female employees; however, a survey in 1988 found that comparable numbers of men and women were concerned with work/family issues. Faith Wohl, co-chair of the task force that conducted the later study, concludes that work/family balance is now an *employee concern,* not just a woman's concern.

Comparable conclusions can be drawn when we look at the levels of fatigue and overload experienced by men and women. Research by Patricia Voyandoff and by Elizabeth Goldsmith has found more similarities than differences between mothers and fathers with respect to work/family conflict. A 1987 study of 1,600 employees in two corporations, conducted by Boston University's Dianne Burden and Brad Googins, also found that men were strongly affected by family responsibilities: 36% of the fathers and 37% of the mothers reported "a lot of stress" in balancing work and family responsibilities. (An additional 11% of the women, however, reported "extreme stress," while none of the men did.) How were their careers affected? Seventy-one percent of the men strongly agreed or agreed that family responsibilities negatively affected employees' careers and ability to advance in the company.

How much time do fathers spend caring for their children? Burden and Googins found that married fathers averaged almost 15 hours a week on childcare, while single fathers averaged almost 18 hours. (The figures for single and married mothers were about 22 and 24 hours, respectively. Single mothers must put in more hours at work, so they spend less time at home with their children.) Among single male parents, 53.8% had sole responsibility for childcare, while close to 30% of the married fathers either had sole responsibility or shared it with spouses. (The comparable figures for single and married mothers were 98% and 94%, respectively.)

Thus, although women spend more time on childcare than men, the fact is that men spend significant amounts of their time caring for their children. Furthermore, men's careers are affected by their parental responsibilities.

The "Invisible Daddy Track"

Why isn't the general public more aware of the effects of childcare on fathers and of fathers' contributions to family responsibilities? My hunch is that it is because fathers keep family care activities to themselves. And in the process many men manage to balance their family responsibilities with a fast-track career. For them, the result is an "invisible daddy track."

Men tend to keep quiet about balance because they want to be seen as dedicated careerists, and thus believe they should not take time out of the workday to spend on childcare. As Googins puts it, "The workplace hasn't changed significantly. The norms are for men that 'If I assume some of this role, not only will my career be impacted but I'm going to be seen as some sort of funny guy' " (*Wall Street*

Journal, Nov. 1, 1988, p. B1). Research has shown that men who take advantage of parental leaves or other flexible work options are seen as eccentrics who are not serious about their careers, in contrast to women who do so. Even in Sweden, the most advanced country with regard to liberal parenting policies, the men, who are paid 90% of their regular salaries for paternity leave, are reluctant to take advantage of parental leaves because of concerns for their future career success. As one young high-achieving father expressed it to me, "You want to project the image of Joe G.E., but you also want to get home in time to play with the kids."

Thus I would submit that a significant proportion of fathers make significant accommodations in their careers for the sake of family, but they do it in nonpublic ways. For example, they may leave work at 5:00 P.M. but take more work home with them. They may turn down an occasional job assignment because it involves too much travel yet give some other reason for their refusal. They may refrain from aggressively going after a particular promotion because it would mean relocating. Men may make a host of small decisions because of family concerns—decisions that affect their career at the margins but do not take them off the fast track. And because their jobs in today's downsized, de-layered organizations have so much more autonomy (along with increased responsibility), they have more freedom to achieve their work results in their own ways, more flexibility to schedule work around family needs. (This is one "silver lining" in all the trauma of today's corporate restructuring.)

This increased autonomy and flexibility may simply mean that the man has freedom to pick *which* 70 hours per week he will work, but this does leave more leeway for family activities. For example, writer Cathy Trost describes the daily routine of Chris Kerns, a lawyer with a Washington, D.C. firm. He picks up his youngest son from a day-care center, heads home for dinner with the family, then goes back to the office to work, often until 2:00 A.M. or later. He reports that his life is busy, but "it feels good."

Furthermore, as baby boomer fathers move up in the hierarchy, they gain even more flexibility. Trost quotes James Levine, director of the Fatherhood Project at Bank Street College: "Men in management and higher-paid jobs have more freedom to act in accordance with changing awareness."

Thus, I would conclude that men are making accommodations to help balance career and family; however, they are managing to do this in quiet, subtle ways, so they are not perceived as being on a daddy track. In contrast to women, they are not using organization programs such as paid parental leave or part-time work (the "building blocks" of the mommy track).

Only 9 of 384 big companies with paid parental leave or part-time work policies report that men take advantage of them. As one human resources executive told Trost, "If a man requested a leave for this purpose, his career would take a dive."

I would argue, then, that whatever time men are putting into family-care responsibilities, many are managing to do so while staying in fast-track careers. This is in striking contrast to their wives, who are seen as having to make a choice between work and family: either the fast track *or* the mommy track. Let's reconsider the need for this all-or-nothing choice.

LESS RIGID FORMS OF FLEXIBILITY

From observing men's accommodations to career and family demands, I think we are learning that a whole continuum of possibilities exists for work/family balance.

• *First, it is possible to make one's work arrangements more flexible through work restructuring.* Much of this can be (and is being) done informally, by agreement between employee and manager.

For example, when work is redesigned to give the employee more autonomy about the methods and pacing of his or her work (while still holding him or her accountable for a high-quality end result), that employee also has more freedom to juggle home and job demands. Or, in a more modest change, even if the company has no formal flextime policy, the manager can agree to a later arrival time and a shorter lunch or can let the employee take work home, even though the company does not officially permit home work. My hunch is that in many well-managed organizations working parents have much greater flexibility than is generally realized because of these "invisible" forms of manager-employee accommodation—and effective managers are retaining successful women in the process. In fact, flexibility has become a powerful reward that a sharp supervisor can use to retain reliable, high-performing employees. The informal organization and the individual supervisor may provide greater sensitivity to work/family issues than the formal organization may even realize.

• *Second, I am sure many women who are clearly on the fast track make the same kinds of private career accommodations that men do.* And senior management is never the wiser. It *is* possible to be a career mom and avoid the mommy track. As one working mother put it, "You can have it all if you're willing to do it all!" The problem is that something has to give, and what usually gives is the mom's own time (for self, for husband, for friends, or for sleep).

A recent study conducted at Mobil, presented at the 1989 Academy of Management meeting, shed light on who these balanced fast trackers are: They are women and men under 35 years of age. In contrast, Mobil found that 80% of the women fast trackers over age 35 did not have children, whereas virtually all of the men in that age group did. Those older female fast trackers ("our bench strength," according to Mobil's employee relations manager, Jean Baderschneider) were the ones who had sacrificed family for the sake of career. The women under age 35 were not prepared to make that family sacrifice. They were struggling to have both family and career. This does not mean that all succeeded in having both with Mobil: The turnover rate for women fast trackers was 2½ times that for the men.

Another source of stress for the woman who is managing to juggle family and fast track is the way she is perceived by her senior male colleagues. Even when a woman makes all of the personal accommodations needed to continue to work at the same pace she did before she became a parent, she is often perceived and treated as a mommy tracker. As one fast-rising female account executive for a major computer company described it:

> Once you have that baby, you're seen differently. I had everything set up to support high-powered work—live-in sitter, a husband who saw my career as the primary one, a job I absolutely loved. Yet I noticed I wasn't being sent to training seminars anymore. I wasn't being given the "plum" assignments anymore. I wasn't put on projects that involved travel. After a while, I realized that I was on an involuntary mommy track!

• *Third, if a woman wants to opt for a formal type of corporate flexibility, she may consider varying forms of "time out" from a career.* A part-time position may entail four days of work a week (as compared with half time, which is what the job sharing advocated by Schwartz entails) or two days; or it may start as three days a week, increase to four after a period of time, and then finally become full time. Time out of work force may extend over a six-month period, a year, three years, or something else. And family-compatible time may take the form of temporary reassignment to work requiring less travel, less evening or weekend work, or work that can be performed solely or partially at home; later, the employee returns to the previous career path.

• *Fourth, greater use should be made of home-based work.* This is especially appropriate for professional work and work for which telecommunications technology can substitute for physical presence. To give a concrete example, IBM has a "Work at Home" program for employees on personal leave of absence (for example, for childcare or eldercare purposes) who want to work part time but cannot report regularly to their work locations. This option does present hazards of potential spillover of work so that it interferes with personal responsibilities, of social deprivation, and of removal from political "loops" at the office, but some of these problems can be overcome. For example, IBM's Work at Home program requires that the employee be at the office at least four consecutive hours each week, which helps alleviate some of these problems. Research indicates that employees who perform home-based work that *supplements* their office work, as opposed to those who perform full-time work at home, are more likely to be satisfied. Working at home is also likely to be most satisfying to people who do not have high needs for affiliation, support, or power (all of which require interaction with other people).

• *Fifth, one's work/family choice should* not *be viewed as a one-time career decision.* Schwartz suggests that employees make the fast track versus work/family balance track decision early in their careers, but this suggestion ignores all the data we have on the ways people's family and career orientations change over time. For example, it is not unusual for a woman to be certain she will return to work after a few weeks' leave—only to decide later to quit the job. As one new mom described her reaction, "I definitely planned to continue my work, but I had no idea how much I would fall in love with this baby!" Conversely, people who fully intend to quit working often decide to go back after a few months or years off. These multiple tracks need to have multiple entrances and exits as well.

Corporate Priorities

Unfortunately, as a result of corporate restructuring and drives for greater productivity, many organizations are working in just the opposite direction: putting pressure, explicit and implicit, on employees to put in more time, stay late at night, come in on weekends, take work home, and so on to help the firm improve its competitive position. The message often given to fast trackers is, "If you want to make it to the top, you've got to sacrifice lots of your personal time." This phenomenon is especially clear in big law firms, where some of the first "two track" systems were observed. For example, in major New York law firms part-time work for lawyers is defined as 9 to 5, Monday through Friday.

My hunch, however, is that this pressure in "lean and mean" corporate organizations will be counterproductive in the long run because it leads to burnout and high turnover. The appropriate focus of corporate pressure should be end results, not employee time or effort. In fact, some of the most productive, best managed firms—such as Du Pont, IBM, Eli Lilly, and Johnson & Johnson—are taking the lead in legitimizing work/family boundaries.

WHAT CAN ORGANIZATIONS DO?

Since space is running short, and it is not possible to resolve the complete conundrum of work/family balance, let me touch on a few of my favorite biases.

Step 1: Set Policy and Values for the Organizational Change Process (Senior Executive Soul-Searching on Values)

At its heart, the work/family problem is an issue of corporate values. It is, in a sense, too easy to set up a corporate task force and implement some recommendations about childcare and flexible leave (although I don't want to minimize the importance of these actions). And the resulting enthusiasm and public recognition make it easy for organizational attention to be diverted from a much more fundamental issue: What is top management's deep-seated attitude about women reaching top-level positions?

One question we need to ask is why organizations have not done much work on work/family issues in the past. My hunch is that part of the real reason is a deep belief on the part of top (male) management that the woman's role really is in the home, not in the boardroom. Despite all of their intellectual—and sincere—commitment to affirmative action, I would argue that many top management groups, made up of white males in their 50s and 60s, simply do not understand how a younger couple could *both* want to have both career and family. And since these executives made it to the top themselves, they simply cannot understand (or respect) people who would be willing to settle for less than that. When top management's basic values and experiences are very much those of the traditional one-earner family with the enabling spouse (wife) at home—and as long as those values remain unexamined—top management will block true progress on the advancement of women and on work/family issues. This leads to the following:

Recommendation #1: Top management should examine its own values and basic assumptions about what a "good" executive is, what a "good" parent is, and what a "good" career is.

Before any organization commissions a task force on work/family issues, the top management group should first go off for a couple of days together, ideally with their wives, and do some self-assessment work on their own values and feelings about these issues.

As preparation for this meeting, each member should be given a set of questions to ask his wife and sons or daughters, to get their views and experiences relating to these matters. These issues are rarely talked about explicitly in the normal course of family conversations, and people usually find them fascinating to discuss at home. They are not necessarily threatening or difficult issues—just not usually addressed. (Often a major source of unfreezing for executives is the experiences of their own families; nothing sensitizes an executive as much as seeing his own daughter face discrimination.)

The goal would be for the executives to clarify and own up to their values—not necessarily to change them, but to consider how they might support younger managers' career styles and lifestyles, which may be quite different from their own. The basic approach here is not one of confrontation, but of *valuing difference,* an approach being used successfully in a variety of organizations. Two days of personal exploration at the top produces much faster progress further down the line, and the honest thoughts revealed give the approach respect and credibility with lower-level managers.

This sort of personal exploration can also lead the top management group to consider other values issues that affect career advancement in the organization. Examples include the value of manager self-direction in pursuing a career, the value of manager input into corporate staffing decisions, the value of providing more and franker career information to young managers, and the value of considering

personal and family circumstances when making personnel decisions. Many good career-development programs get stymied because top management simply does not believe, deep down inside, that these activities are appropriate and/or practical.

As a way of making the issue of women's advancement more central, I propose the following:

Recommendation #2: Top management should focus on how successful its executive succession-planning process is in advancing women; it should not focus primarily on work/family balance.

How does the number of women in top jobs compare with the number five and ten years ago, or with the number of women coming out of M.B.A. programs today (one-half to one-third in most business schools)? Is the turnover of high-potential women 2½ times that of high-potential men, as it was at Mobil? If the primary issue is how successful are we at moving women into the very top executive ranks, then the energy is going to go where it really counts. In the process of working on this "glass ceiling" issue, the work/family issue will be addressed with much more commitment than it would be if it were viewed as an end in itself.

I worry that too much stress on mommy tracks and daddy tracks will drain attention from the real problem and thus take top management "off the hook" by framing the problem as a parent problem, rather than a problem for the corporation. (Indeed, some people have argued that the whole parent track issue plays right into the hands of very traditional senior executives who can look progressive by working on family issues without confronting important issues of discrimination—based not just on gender, but also on race, ethnicity, and other kinds of difference.)

The third recommendation deals with the later stages of the change-implementation process. It is critical to view all of this work as a basic process of organizational change and to apply what we know about effective planned change. Thus, not only should we start at the top (Recommendation #1) and consider work/family in the context of basic system-maintenance needs (Recommendation #2), but the change process should be one that leads to high-commitment and high-performance outcomes, as follows:

Recommendation #3: The change process should be self-reflective and participative, focused on both formal and informal systems.

Just as top managers will kick off the process by examining their own values, any task force or other group that addresses an issue should periodically stop and compare its actions with its own values (or "espoused theories," as researchers Chris Argyris and Donald Schon call them) and, if necessary, take corrective action. This is especially important when personal issues such as family and career are concerned.

And the process should be inclusive, encouraging a

variety of groups throughout the organization to form and address the issue and propose changes in their units. Thus, changes should be encouraged not only at the corporate level, but also at the local plant, office, and unit level.

Change may not always be required: If a sensitive, supportive, "family friendly" plant manager or supervisor has already created new work structures, these should be publicized and recognized. My hunch is that in a lot of locations, work/family conditions are a lot *better* than we think, thanks to good management. By communicating and celebrating this good news, much resistance to change can be overcome.

Step 2: Organizationwide Diagnosis

Once the top management group has reflected on its own values and behavior, the next step is to create corporatewide dialogue about work life, family life, and the meaning of success. I realize this is very inclusive, but we do need more open discussion, flowing from the top group's reflections and policies (Step 1), about how working for the organization affects family life and vice versa. An important way to start is to collect hard data on work/family issues in the organization. For example, consider Du Pont, which has had a major task force (the Work and Family Committee), appointed as a subcommittee of top management's Affirmative Action Committee, working on this issue since July 1987. The committee involved many members of the company in conversations about work and family life as it developed a comprehensive set of recommended policies and practices. Because of this high level of employee involvement, the final recommendations had widespread support. Now major changes are being made—ranging from on-site childcare to flexible work arrangements to manager training in awareness and response to work/family strains. Other firms, such as Merck, Johnson & Johnson, IBM, Stride Rite, and Campbell Soup, have also raised the issue up for dialogue. Thus, we propose:

> *Recommendation #4: Top management should create a task force or committee on work/family issues to promote a corporatewide dialogue.*

> *Recommendation #5: As part of this dialogue, the task force should conduct an organizational survey to assess work/family needs and resources.*

Step 3: Change Implementation

As a result of the dialogue, the organization should implement change to help employees cope with work/home strains. Again, the comprehensive set of recommendations developed by the Du Pont task force could be a model. Some companies need specific services (for example, dependent care, employee-assistance programs, childcare referral information, and flexible benefits). Others may need more flexible work arrangements, as well as more supportive, flexible supervision. Still others may need more flexible human resources management policies (for example, relocation policies, spouse career assistance during relocation, recognition of family needs in relocation decisions, and policies about overtime work and travel). A summary of the Du Pont study is reported in the box on page 105.

I submit that these forms of everyday work flexibility are much more important than the more publicized forms such as mommy tracks or daddy tracks. The most important need for many employees is not to get away from work (through long leaves or part-time work) but to find satisfying ways to combine work and family life. Therefore, it is important that the focus not be just on childcare. If anything, it is too easy for an organization to set up a research and referral service to provide information on childcare services or even for a firm to set up its own center. The much more difficult task is to restructure the everyday work environment so that employees have the autonomy they need to make their own work/family accommodations.

In addition to work, career paths must be restructured. More specifically, we must decouple age and career opportunities. With the coming labor shortage, successful organizations will compete by tapping skills wherever they can be found, and they will be found in a much more diverse work force. In addition to characteristics such as gender, color, and ethnicity, a major form of diversity will be age. As longevity increases and employees desire to extend their working lives, a pool of highly talented older employees will develop. It will be possible—and necessary—to appoint people to management positions at later ages. Firms that arbitrarily rule out promotions past a certain age (for example, 40) will be handicapping themselves. This greater age flexibility will give women and men more years to have families and managerial careers. The addition of these "new work years" may help employees resolve the dilemmas of combining these two parts of life.

As a more specific way of helping employees cope, organizations should legitimize boundaries between work and home. This has been one of the most important outcomes of work/family workshops that I have seen. It is very significant for employees to hear from senior executives, for example, that evenings and weekends are viewed by the company as home and family time, and that people who stay late at the office are *not* seen as super-achievers, but rather as poor time-managers. (Of course this message is even more powerful if it is supported by those senior executives' behavior!)

In a similar vein, many companies no longer expect employees to travel on weekends. Off-site meetings often end by noon on Fridays or start in the afternoon on Mondays. One high-pressure sales organization, whose district managers need to be available to sales reps in the field at all hours, developed a set of guidelines governing when managers should not be called at home (between 5 and 7 P.M. and after 10 P.M.).

Interestingly, employees' need to separate work and family raises questions about the wisdom of corporate on-

Work/Family Issues at Du Pont

Du Pont's corporate Work and Family Committee was formed in July 1987 to "study and make recommendations on work and family issues, with emphasis on childcare." Work/family conflicts were thought to be having a major effect on affirmative action results.

The committee had 19 members, 17 of whom were from a cross section of the corporation, representing different departments, sites, levels, ages, and family situations. Two outside consultants on work/family issues were also involved to conduct research studies.

The committee was divided into three teams: The Internal Issues Team conducted an employee survey and examined existing Du Pont policies that affected work/family balance; the Industry and Government Team surveyed comparison companies, looked at a number of different initiatives in childcare and eldercare, and reviewed present and proposed state and federal legislation for their impact on potential Du Pont initiatives in this area; and the Local Initiatives Team looked at the corporate headquarters area, speaking with other employers, visiting local childcare providers, and analyzing why the marketplace was not supplying the needed services. In April 1988 a similar study was done by a Work and Family Committee at Conoco, Du Pont's energy subsidiary, in Houston.

The employee survey, completed by more than 4,000 employees, found that the needs were great. More than 60% of Du Pont parents with children in childcare said they had difficulty finding care that conformed to their work hours and provided for overtime work. Forty-three percent of all Du Pont children between the ages of 10 and 13 were alone routinely after school. Almost all Du Pont parents reported difficulty finding care for sick children. Parents had difficulty attending teacher meetings and school activities and coping with school closings. More than 70% considered it very important to have a policy to extend sick time

to cover children's illnesses. Almost as many placed high value on flexible hours.

Based on the work of all three teams, the committee made 23 recommendations for action. The major ones were as follows:

1. Communicate better about current work/family practices and policies that already exist.
2. Make managers and supervisors more sensitive to work/family issues. Incorporate work/family topics into training. Make sure that all managers understand company policies relating to work/family issues.
3. Give employees the free time they need for family responsibilities (by using schedule innovations such as part-time work, adjustable work arrangements, and work performed at home).
4. Reexamine the organization's career planning process in light of work/family responsibilities.
5. Increase the impact of benefits through flexible benefits and more options for dependent care (childcare, eldercare, and care for sick children).
6. Exercise leadership in the community to improve the availability of quality childcare (e.g., help create near-site childcare centers; continue to support Child Care Connection, a Delaware referral service; stimulate and provide seed money for after-school and summer programs; work on new programs for sick-child care; support the increased professionalism of childcare providers).
7. Exercise leadership to increase the participation of other business, government, and community organizations to address childcare problems.

The company is currently *implementing* these recommendations. Like any major cultural change, this is a long, difficult, and uneven process, particularly in a decentralized firm such as Du Pont.

Adapted from information in "Diversity: A Source of Strength," Wilmington, DE: Du Pont, Corporate Employee Relations Department, Undated.

site childcare facilities, since these could potentially blur the work/home boundary. Employees may feel pressure to be "on call" and not totally separate from their children during the day or to be at the center at lunchtime, which could present problems for staff members as well as the parents and their colleagues. I realize that this is a complex and controversial issue, but companies do need to take it into account when they consider on-site childcare.

My sense is that the legitimizing of boundaries by top management is much easier done than said. In other words, it's easier than it sounds. In most cases, executives care deeply about their own family life, and they often don't realize that employees interpret their signals regarding the need for commitment and high performance to mean that work should have priority over home. When engaged in dialogue on this point and given feedback, executives often respond strongly and genuinely about the need for good work/home boundaries.

I cannot offer specific recommendations regarding the action stage, since the specifics will vary depending on the outcome of the organizational survey; however, we can say the following:

Recommendation #6: Clear action should be taken based upon the needs identified in the organizational survey. Areas to consider include policies, benefits, work restructuring, management training, career paths, work/home boundaries, and dependent care.

PHASES AND DEPTH OF CHANGE

When working on issues as complex as these, it is important to remember, as researcher Ellen Galinsky and her colleagues, Diane Hughes and Judy David, point out, that organizations tend to work on work/family issues in phases. During the first phase, the organization becomes aware of the issues and develops new formal programs and policies. During the second, it makes changes in corporate culture and the design of work: Work/family commitment is seen as a true business issue, and line managers begin to run the business in a different way to accommodate employees' work/family concerns. At this stage supervisor flexibility and employee autonomy tend to increase. Specific activities like childcare services became just one small part of a holistic approach to management that makes the organization "family friendly," according to Galinsky.

Another consideration is the depth at which the organization intervenes to create change. The work/family issue can be seen as both fairly straightforward and incredibly complex and difficult. Addressing the problem in all of its complexity involves starting at Step 1 (top executive soul-searching), moving through Step 2 (organizationwide diagnosis), and continuing through Step 3 (action). A simpler approach is to start with Step 2, or even Step 3.

While it is probably possible to do some good through simple measures alone (for example, Step 3 measures, such as establishing a parental leave policy), I would encourage top management to start at Step 1—to be bold and examine the basic assumptions underlying the career culture in the organization. In this way the organization has a good opportunity to release tremendous untapped human potential, as younger people begin to see ways of achieving psychological success through a fulfilling career. As a result of top management's greater self-understanding, Steps 2 and 3 will follow much more easily and naturally. With this more integrated organization-change approach, work/family issues will be addressed in ways that have a good chance of becoming part of the basic fabric of the organization.

DISCUSSION QUESTIONS

1. What accommodations have men and women made to career and family demands?
2. Is there or should there be a "daddy track"?
3. What are some possible strategies for improving work/family balance?
4. What can organizations do to assist workers in improving work/family balance?

Activity 3–1

Locus of Control Test

Step 1: Answer the following questions the way you feel. In the column, mark a Y for yes and an N for no next to each question.

_____ 1. Do you believe that most problems will solve themselves if you just don't fool with them?

_____ 2. Do you believe that you can stop yourself from catching a cold?

_____ 3. Are some people just born lucky?

_____ 4. Most of the time do you feel that getting good grades meant a great deal to you?

_____ 5. Are you often blamed for things that just aren't your fault?

_____ 6. Do you believe that if somebody studies hard he or she can pass any subject?

_____ 7. Do you feel that most of the time it doesn't pay to try hard because things never turn out right anyway?

_____ 8. Do you feel that if things start out well in the morning it's going to be a good day no matter what you do?

_____ 9. Do you feel that most of the time parents listen to what their children have to say?

_____ 10. Do you believe that wishing can make good things happen?

_____ 11. When you get punished does it usually seem it's for no good reason at all?

_____ 12. Most of the time do you find it hard to change a friend's opinion?

_____ 13. Do you think that cheering more than luck helps a team to win?

_____ 14. Did you feel that it was nearly impossible to change your parents' minds about anything?

_____ 15. Do you believe that parents should allow children to make most of their own decisions?

_____ 16. Do you feel that when you do something wrong there's very little you can do to make it right?

_____ 17. Do you believe that most people are just born good at sports?

_____ 18. Are most of the other people your age stronger than you are?

_____ 19. Do you feel that one of the best ways to handle most problems is just not to think about them?

_____ 20. Do you feel that you have a lot of choice in deciding who your friends are?

_____ 21. If you find a four-leaf clover, do you believe that it might bring you good luck?

_____ 22. Did you often feel that whether or not you did your homework had much to do with what kind of grades you got?

_____ 23. Do you feel that when a person your age is angry at you, there's little you can do to stop him or her?

_____ 24. Have you ever had a good-luck charm?

_____ 25. Do you believe that whether or not people like you depends on how you act?

_____ 26. Did your parents usually help you if you asked them to?

_____ 27. Have you felt that when people were angry with you it was usually for no reason at all?

_____ 28. Most of the time, do you feel that you can change what might happen tomorrow by what you do today?

_____ 29. Do you believe that when bad things are going to happen they just are going to happen no matter what you try to do to stop them?

_____ 30. Do you think that people can get their own way if they just keep trying?

_____ 31. Most of the time do you find it useless to try to get your own way at home?

_____ 32. Do you feel that when good things happen they happen because of hard work?

_____ 33. Do you feel that when somebody your age wants to be your enemy there's little you can do to change matters?

_____ 34. Do you feel that it's easy to get friends to do what you want them to do?

_____ 35. Do you usually feel that you have little to say about what you get to eat at home?

_____ 36. Do you feel that when someone doesn't like you there's little you can do about it?

_____ 37. Do you usually feel that it was almost useless to try in school because most other children were just plain smarter than you were?

_____ 38. Are you the kind of person who believes that planning ahead makes things turn out better?

_____ 39. Most of the time, do you feel that you have little to say about what your family decides to do?

_____ 40. Do you think its better to be smart than to be lucky?

Step 2: Scoring the Scale.

Using the scoring key below, compare your answers on the previous page to the ones on the key. Give yourself one point each time your answer agrees with the keyed answer. Your score is the total number of agreements between your answers and the ones on the key.

Scoring Key

1. Yes _____		21. Yes _____	
2. No _____		22. No _____	
3. Yes _____		23. Yes _____	
4. No _____		24. Yes _____	
5. Yes _____		25. No _____	
6. No _____		26. No _____	
7. Yes _____		27. Yes _____	
8. Yes _____		28. No _____	
9. No _____		29. Yes _____	
10. Yes _____		30. No _____	
11. Yes _____		31. Yes _____	
12. Yes _____		32. No _____	
13. No _____		33. Yes _____	
14. Yes _____		34. No _____	
15. No _____		35. Yes _____	
16. Yes _____		36. Yes _____	
17. Yes _____		37. Yes _____	
18. Yes _____		38. No _____	
19. Yes _____		39. Yes _____	
20. No _____		40. No _____	

Total
score

Interpreting Your Score

Low Scorers (0–8)—Scores from zero to eight represent the range for about one-third of the people taking the test. As a low scorer, you probably see life as a game of skill rather than chance. You most likely believe that you have a lot of control over what happens to you, both good and bad. With that view, internal-locus-of-control people tend to take the initiative in everything from job-related activities to relationships and sex. You are probably described by others as vigilant in getting things done, aware of what's going on around you, and willing to spend energy in working for specific goals. You would probably find it quite frustrating to sit back and let others take care of you, since you stressed on the test that you like to have your life in your own hands.

Although taking control of your life is seen as the "best way to be," psychologists caution that it has its own set of difficulties. Someone who is responsible for his or her own successes is also responsible for failures. So if you scored high in this direction, be prepared for the downs as well as the ups.

Average Scorers (9–16)—Since you've answered some of the questions in each direction, internal and external control beliefs for you may be situation specific. You may look at one situation—work, for example—and believe that your rewards are externally determined, that no matter what you do you can't get ahead. In another situation, love perhaps, you may see your fate as resting entirely in your own hands. You will find it helpful to review the questions and group them into those you answered in the internal direction and those you answered in the external direction. Any similarities in the kinds of situations within one of those groups?

If so, some time spent thinking about what it is in those situations that makes you feel as though the control is or is not in your hands can help you better understand yourself.

High Scorers (17–40)—Scores in this range represent the external control end of the scale. Only about 15 percent of the people taking the test score 17 or higher. As a high scorer, you're saying that you see life generally more as a game of chance than as one where your skills make a difference.

Step 3: Discussion. In small groups or with the class as a whole, answer the following questions:

Description
1. What was your score?
2. What type of personality does this represent?
3. How does this compare to scores of others in the class?

Diagnosis
4. What behaviors and attitudes is each personality type likely to demonstrate?
5. What are the implications for encouraging organizational effectiveness?

By Stephen Nowicki, Jr., and B. Strickland in *The Mind Test* by Rita Aero and Elliot Weiner (New York: William Morrow, 1981), pp. 20–23. Reprinted with permission.

Activity 3–2

Life Line Exercise

Step 1: Draw a time line that represents the major events in your life (your life line). Represent it in any way you choose, but be sure to identify all key events.

Step 2: Now draw separate life lines for (1) your career, (2) your family, and (3) your biological development.

1. How do they interface?
2. Identify times of stress.
3. Identify key transitions.
4. What effect did these transitions have on your motivation and perceptions at work at the time?

Step 3: Discussion. In small groups or with the entire class, answer the following questions:

Description
1. What elements do the life lines share?
2. How do the life lines differ?

Diagnosis
3. Can you delineate common phases or stages in your careers? in your lives?
4. For each stage identified, specify the key issues members of the group had to confront.
5. Identify the times of greatest stress.
6. What factors contributed to stress at these times?

Prescription
7. For each stage, specify ways stress at that time could be reduced.

Activity 3–3

The Case of the Undecided Accountant

Step 1:   Read the Case of the Undecided Accountant.

INTRODUCTION

Bill Hunter looked at his clock and sighed. It was 11:00 P.M. and there were still four unfinished projects that were sitting on his desk that would have to wait until another day. As he was walking out of the office, he noticed that the light was on in the office of Dave Landis.

Bill: What are you doing up here this time of night, Dave?

Dave: I suppose that I am in the same situation that you are. There are a number of things that just don't seem to get out. I'm trying to clean up some projects so I can see my desk again.

Bill mumbled goodbye and decided to head home. Bill's mind was recalling the events of the past few weeks. He had been promoted by the partnership group of Fitch, Olson & Company to a management position within the firm. He had perceived his promotion to be an important milestone in his accounting career. This was a promotion that had to be approved by the partner group. Secondly, the criteria established to meet the requirements of a manager were quite detailed. However, he was quickly becoming disillusioned with the lack of direction supplied by the partners for the office and the absence of a clearly defined set of objectives for the future. Bill had originally felt that the recent promotion would give him the opportunity to share his concerns and ideas to improve the undesired situations occurring in the office that seemed to be ignored instead of being addressed.

COMPANY BACKGROUND AND ORGANIZATION

Fitch, Olson & Company was a professional partnership of certified public accountants based in Billings, Montana. The company was started by Jim Fitch and Harold Olson in 1962 when they decided to leave the Big-Eight accounting firm of Arthur Andersen to form their own office. Their objective was to remain a smaller accounting firm which could provide personalized, yet high-quality, accounting services for its clientele. The company expanded to start an office in Great Falls, Montana, in 1969 and Casper, Wyoming, in 1976. The expansion to Wyoming had proved to be quite profitable because of the energy-related boom that occurred in Wyoming during the late 1970s. In 1979, Steve Martin replaced Harold Olson as the managing partner of the accounting firm. Martin had been primarily responsible

for exploring the possibilities of expanding into Wyoming and for finalizing the merger with another accounting firm in Casper. Even though Martin was the third-youngest partner at 37, his foresight of the profit potential of an expansion into Wyoming had given him a quick ticket to the top of the company. In 1980, the firm approved an aggressive expansion policy for the next ten years. There were mergers with other accounting firms in 1981, 1982, and 1983 that increased the geographical market of Fitch, Olson & Company to Bismarck, North Dakota, Boise, Idaho, and Denver, Colorado. (See Table 3–10.) Once again the expansion to Bismarck, North Dakota, was influenced by the energy-related boom that was occurring in western North Dakota. The firm decided in 1982 to establish its expansion plans for larger market areas. The long-term objectives became geared toward making Fitch, Olson & Company a large, widely known regional accounting firm in the upper northwest.

The management of Fitch, Olson & Company was based on a one-man, one-vote partnership. This meant that all partners had equal representation within the partnership while discounting such variables as seniority and location. The power structure for the firm was centered around the managing partner and the executive committee. The executive committee consisted of the managing partner, from the Billings office, and the administrative partner from each of the other offices. (See Figure 3–8.)

The power structure has been centered in Billings since the company was founded. The managing partner has always been from the Billings office. In addition, the Billings office has more partners, professional staff, and gross fees than any other office.

GREAT FALLS

The Great Falls office has the image of being the "dark horse" of the firm. The office experienced a strong period

Table 3–10   **Growth of Fitch, Olson & Company**

	Offices	Partners	Employees	Gross Fees
1960	1	2	10	$ 350,000
1970	2	7	40	1,500,000
1980	3	14	85	3,250,000
1983	6	26	150	6,500,000

Figure 3–8 **Organization Chart, Fitch, Olson & Company, October 31, 1983**

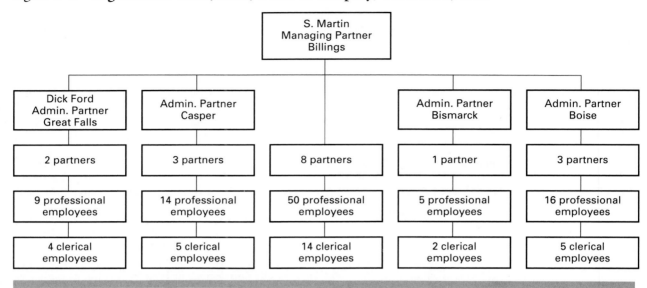

of growth from its inception in 1969 until 1975. Since 1975, the office has experienced little or no growth. (See Figure 3–9.) There has not been an additional partner admitted into the Great Falls office since 1973. The staff size is smaller than in 1975, and growth in gross fees has decreased when considering the inflation factor. This lack of growth was gaining attention and generating more concern from the other offices in the firm. The firm had made it clear that improvement would be expected.

CPA PROFESSION

The CPA profession is based on providing accounting services for individuals and businesses. The profession had its roots in bookkeeping services and tax return preparation. With the beginning of the Securities and Exchange Commission in 1934, there was a new need for independent audits of financial information. There was also an increased awareness by third-party users of financial information, such as financial institutions and governmental agencies, of the need for independent audits. There was a significant increase during the 1970s of people entering the public accounting profession. The following schedule shows the dramatic increase in the number of members of the American Institute of Certified Public Accountants.

Year	Members
1973	95,414
1975	112,494
1977	131,300
1979	149,314
1981	173,900
1983	201,764

Even with the influx of young members into the accounting profession, the main image of the accounting profession is one of conservatism. The conservatism projected was due to the profession's concern about overstating the company's financial position and earnings power in the audit area or, in the tax area, understating the company's tax liability.

There are three main fields within the accounting profession; audit, tax, and management advisory services (MAS). The first two areas are self-explanatory. Management advisory services involves a wide range of services. This can include accounting system reviews, computer system reviews, preparation of accounting manuals, assistance with analysis of computer software, and feasibility studies. Staff titles and responsibilities within the accounting profession are consistent. The titles and experience levels that are consistently used are:

Partner	10+ years
Manager	5–10 years
Supervisor	3–7 years
Senior Staff	1–3 years
Junior Staff	0–2 years

BILL HUNTER

Bill Hunter grew up in a small community in northern Idaho. He selected accounting as his undergraduate area of study mainly because of his interest in working with numbers. He began his career with a small, local accounting firm in Idaho. His work entailed both tax and accounting work mainly for small businesses. He accepted a position with the Great Falls office of Fitch, Olson & Company in 1980.

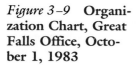

Figure 3–9 **Organization Chart, Great Falls Office, October 1, 1983**

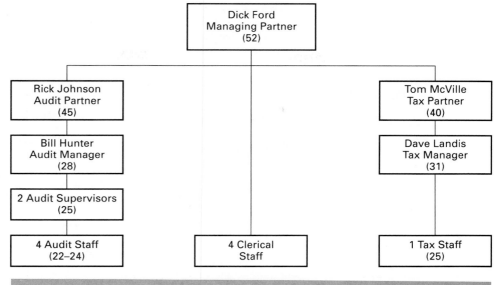

He had become dissatisfied with his present situation and felt that the move to Fitch, Olson & Company would be an excellent move for his career. He would start at the supervisory level in the Great Falls office. He would be the highest audit staff member under the partner because three individuals had left the Great Falls office in 1978 and 1979. This move would promote his career by two to three years and would also provide him the opportunity to provide a large amount of input into the operation of the office.

He was satisfied with his work performance during the three years he had been working at Fitch, Olson & Company. He was comfortable with the trust he had received from the Great Falls partners. He was also satisfied with the working relationships he had developed with other staff members. He felt that his performance had been rewarded when he was promoted to the manager position after only two and one-half years with Fitch, Olson & Company:

I was pleased when I received the announcement that I had been promoted to manager. It was a feeling of satisfaction to know that the partners felt that I should be rewarded with the promotion. However, the feeling becomes confused when I look at what is going on around me. I become frustrated whenever I look around; I'm better off when I just close my eyes.

I know that there are a number of problems in the Great Falls office. That's clear when you see the amount of turnover that has occurred in the office. I've also heard there is increasing pressure to turn around the no-growth situation that has occurred with the management group. I am concerned about the direction, or I should say the lack of direction, that this office is taking. This office is a perfect example of management

by crisis. It becomes frustrating to feel like we are floundering around.

I find myself in an interesting yet sensitive situation. I feel that I have a fair amount of influence in the management group. Because of that, I hear a lot of information from the partners that no other staff person does. Yet, because I'm in a supervisory position, I hear a lot of concerns and complaints from the staff. There have been a number of instances where I've been in the position of knowing what is happening on both sides of a conflict. The confidence both sides show when speaking with me is very satisfying.

Staff motivation seems to be almost nonexistent in the office. Maybe my view that motivated staff would help improve the current situation is too simplistic. The partnership group have goals for the entire firm and there seems to be motivation at the partner level. However, the motivation is not trickling down through the staff. The staff members that do well in the firm do so only because they are high achievers. There is so little interaction between the partners and the staff that even the best people become frustrated with the lack of direction that exists.

The reward system here is interesting in that there seems to be no reward system. The promotions through the firm seem to be delegated on a timetable rather than being given because they are earned. The compensation package meets industry averages when coming out of college. However, the raises for the first four or five years within the firm seem to be structured within very tight guidelines. The differentiation between raises given to the highest producers compared to average employees is very small during this period.

Also, because the firm does not pay overtime, the hardest-working staff members become frustrated at annual reviews when they see the little difference that their efforts have made. In one instance, five people at the same level in one office received exactly the same annual pay increase. I find that incredible and it seems clear to me that this type of system can only be a dissatisfaction to the best staff members. The long-term effect of this policy seems to be that the best people are leaving the firm.

In an optimistic light, I see these problems as a challenge and an opportunity. The promotion to manager is considered a move into the lower rung of the management career ladder of the firm. Managers become more involved with the partners in firm objectives such as marketing efforts. Also, the various offices have monthly partner–manager meetings to discuss what is happening within the office and what should be done to improve the office. This could be an excellent opportunity for me to present various concerns and ideas that I have. I wouldn't feel that this could be an opportunity unless I felt confident about my position in the Great Falls partnership group.

My future with this firm will involve increasing time spent on management responsibilities and assignments. Because of this, I have enrolled in a MBA program. We are currently studying organization theory and behavior. It would be nice if I could find the time to apply what I have learned into what could be done to understand and improve the current situation in this office. . . .

Step 2: Prepare the case for class discussion.

Step 3: Answer the following questions, individually or in small groups:

Description
1. Trace Bill Hunter's career so far.
2. What are Bill's concerns about his recent promotion?
3. What are Bill's concerns about Fitch, Olson & Company?

Diagnosis
4. What problems exist in the Great Falls office?
5. Using your knowledge of career development, evaluate the situation.
6. Using your knowledge of adult development, evaluate the situation.
7. Using your knowledge of personality or personal style, evaluate the situation.
8. Using your knowledge of attribution, evaluate the situation.
9. Using your knowledge of perception, evaluate the situation.
10. What possible stressors are inherent in the situation?

Prescription
11. What should Bill do next?

Step 4: Discussion. In small groups, with the entire class, or in written form, as directed by your instructor, share your answers to the questions in Step 3. Then answer the following questions:

1. What symptoms suggest that a problem exists?
2. What problems exist in the case?
3. What theories and concepts help explain the problems?
4. How can the problems be corrected?
5. Are the actions likely to be effective?
6. What should be done now?

Reprinted by permission of the author, M. Tom Basuray, Professor of Management, Towson State University.

Activity 3–4   CNN Video: Inside Business—Child Care

Step 1: View the CNN segment about child care.

Step 2: Answer each of the following questions, individually or in small groups, as directed by your instructor.

Description
1. Describe the type of child care programs presented in the video.

Diagnosis
2. What challenges do working parents face with regard to child care?

3. How effective are existing child care programs?
4. What responsibilities do companies have to provide child care for their employees?
5. What responses currently exist in the United States and in other countries?

Prescription
5. What changes in child care provisions should be made in corporate America to respond to the needs of working parents?

Activity 3–5

The Dual-Career Couple Dilemma

Step 1:   Read the Dual-Career Couple Dilemma case.

"Well, Fred, I think that about covers the major points of our proposal," said Jim Franklin, "If you accept, we will be pleased to have you in the department." Jim was head of the Management Department at Lawrence State University (LSU).[1] He was speaking by telephone with Fred Johnston, an applicant for a faculty position in business policy at LSU. Fred had published several articles, had presented good student evaluations of teaching, and had received high marks for service activities at his present school. He had also made a positive impression on the LSU management faculty during his recent campus visit. His wife, Alice, was just completing a Ph.D. in English at Warner University where Fred was employed. She had applied for a teaching position in LSU's English Department. Fred responded, "I'm really excited to get your offer, Jim. Lawrence State is on the way up, and I'd like to be a part of its success."

Jim was anxious to get a firm answer from Fred. "How do you think your wife will feel about this?" asked Jim. Fred replied, "Alice told me this morning that she thought she'd prefer Lawrence State over any of the other schools we're looking at. She's not heard anything about a campus interview from Dr. Allen yet, but expects to soon." Dr. Jordan Allen was head of LSU's English department.

Fred continued, "You know, of course, that timing is becoming critical for us. Alice and I are both going to interview at Evergreen College in Wisconsin next week, as I told you." He added that Evergreen seemed to be "really interested" in hiring both of them. Jim knew Evergreen did not have an accredited program in business and felt going there would not be a good career move for a person with Fred's credentials. Fred confirmed this, saying, "The business faculty at Evergreen is very small, and I'd have to teach in both management and marketing. The little town is okay, but there'd be few opportunities for my research and consulting in that setting. Also, they have only an undergraduate program. They're talking about trying to add an MBA. But that seems a long way off."

Still, Fred had made it clear he considered Alice's career fully as important as his own. He explained, "As you know, Alice will have fewer job opportunities than I, given the abundance of English Ph.D.'s relative to the available jobs. So we have to be interested in Evergreen at this point, even though we would rather come to LSU." Fred continued, "Jim, I can't say for sure, of course, but if we both get offers from Evergreen, we'll probably go there."

Jim replied, "I know that you and Alice have a lot to consider in this move. I have stayed in touch with Jordan Allen. He knows we are making you an offer. Hopefully, he'll get on the stick."

"OK, Jim," said Fred, "I'll get back to you after we return from Evergreen next week. Then we'll know if Alice and I have that option—at least I think we will know. But I hope Dr. Allen can at least schedule an interview for Alice soon."

"Fred, I'll call you next Friday. In the meantime, be thinking about our offer. You could have a fine future here at Lawrence," said Jim.

"You know we're seriously considering it, Jim," Fred replied.

"Okay. Good-by Fred," said Jim.

Early the next week, Jordan Allen called Jim to discuss the Johnstons and the status of Alice's application. Another candidate for the position had recently visited the campus and the interview was "almost a disaster." Also, one of the other finalists had withdrawn his application. Indeed, Jordan said he was planning to call Alice that afternoon since "her position on the list had advanced," and she had now become a probable candidate. Jim was pleased to hear this. Filling the business policy slot would really reduce his recruiting woes, and placing Alice seemed to be the only roadblock.

But Jim knew the Johnstons would be leaving the next morning for Wisconsin. It was March 14, late in the recruiting season, and Jim feared Evergreen College might be as anxious as he to close a deal with Fred and Alice. Jim felt he had already violated academic protocol in trying so hard to get Alice placed in the English Department. Yet, he thought all his work with Fred would be for naught unless Jordan gave Alice some affirmation immediately.

BACKGROUND

The Management Department at LSU, like the College of Business generally, had experienced rapid enrollment growth over the preceding five years. A new faculty position in business policy had been approved for the coming year. There were two other management vacancies (due to a retirement and a transfer) which also had to be filled.

Although recruiting consumed a tremendous amount of his time, Jim realized that probably nothing was more important to the department. He knew that a strong faculty was a key element in maintaining accreditation and competing with other schools for good students. Performance and potential in teaching, research, and service were the main selection criteria, but it was also important that new hires be congenial and fit in well with existing faculty.[2]

At LSU, as at many other schools, the faculty hiring process was lengthy and elaborate. It involved a sequence of steps which included securing approval for the position, listing the position with the professional associations, advertising the vacancy in professional journals and newsletters, reviewing and responding to applications, having applicants evaluated by a faculty committee, selecting candidates for campus interviews, arranging and administering campus visits, negotiating with the chosen candidate, and processing the appointment package through the university administrative hierarchy.

The three openings in Jim's department were in human resource management, organizational behavior, and business policy. There were more qualified candidates for jobs in the first two fields, so Jim thought he would be able to fill those jobs. On the other hand, business policy was a rapidly developing field, and demand for qualified policy teachers far exceeded the supply. A position listing in the Academy of Management Placement Roster had resulted in many inquiries about the policy slot, but very few promising applications.[3] Jim had contacted three persons listed in the applicants section of the roster and found no desirable candidate among them. The several unsolicited inquiries he had received were equally unsatisfying. Calls to colleagues at other universities provided several good leads, but only one seemingly qualified person applied. Like most academic department heads, Jim attended several national and regional academic conferences each year and filled out the usual placement forms at the meetings. He could have advertised the policy position in such publications as the *Chronicle of Higher Education* (a newspaper) and the American Assembly of Collegiate Schools of Business *Newsline* (a newsletter), but had not found those media to be very effective in the past.

EARLY CONVERSATIONS

Fred Johnston first called Jim in early October, after seeing the policy job listed at a September meeting. Fred said he had been on the faculty at Warner University for two years and was planning to make a job change. He explained that although his experience at Warner had been generally favorable and that he felt he could have a good future there, his wife, Alice, had to move because Warner had a firm policy of not hiring its own graduates. He and Alice had agreed to consider only places where there were employment opportunities for both.

After describing his general background, qualifications, and professional interests, Fred asked Jim if he felt there might possibly be a "match" of his qualifications and Lawrence State's needs. Jim responded that, indeed, there seemed to be and suggested that Jim send his resume for review by the faculty recruiting committee. He further suggested the two meet at the Allied Southern Business Association (ASBA) meeting in New Orleans in November.

In the meantime, Alice scheduled an appointment with a recruiting representative of Lawrence State's English Department at an upcoming language arts meeting in San Francisco. The opening in the English Department was in technical writing, Alice's minor field of study; her major area was Shakespearian studies.

From Jim's point of view, Fred Johnston had several appealing qualifications. He had completed his doctoral degree at a respected school, had significant teaching experience, and had worked several years in industrial management. Jim much preferred to hire a candidate who had completed the degree, rather than an "ABD" (all but dissertation), since it could take several years to complete the dissertation project and there was always the risk that it would never be finished.[4] Also, because of the work involved in the dissertation, the ABD seldom assumes a full share of departmental duties such as teaching, advising, committee work, and so forth. In addition, an ABD does not formally start any other research projects which might accrue to the credit of the college while involved with the dissertation. Faculty publications had become an important measure of a school's relative stature, and Fred Johnston had already written several professional papers and articles.

CONTINUING DISCUSSIONS

Jim soon received a glowing evaluation of Fred's resume from the faculty recruiting committee. And calls to Fred's references evoked expressions of admiration and respect. The recruitment process continued over the next few months, with admission of recommendation letters and other documentation. It became increasingly clear that Fred Johnston was an exceptional candidate.

Alice was the problem. Jim was concerned about the English Department in their handling of Alice's application, so he checked about faculty vacancies in English at three other colleges in the Lawrence area. But each either anticipated no openings or already filled those which existed.

At the November ASBA meeting, Jim and Fred talked for more than an hour. Fred seemed to be as good as he appeared on paper. And Fred seemed impressed with Lawrence State, which Jim considered just as important.

After Jim returned to the campus, he called Jordan Allen to check on Alice's application. Jordan said that the person who interviewed her at the meeting was favorably impressed, that Alice "certainly hadn't eliminated herself," and that she did seem to have "good potential." However, he said, the recruiting committee ranked four or five applicants ahead of her overall. Jordan noted that Alice was just completing the doctorate, had little teaching experience, and had not published.

Although Jim did not want to try to pressure Jordan to give Alice special consideration, he did emphasize that the Johnston's were looking first at schools which would hire them both. He pointed out that Fred's interest in Lawrence State would surely facilitate the recruiting of his wife, perhaps on favorable terms for the university. Jordan acknowledged this, but said he was relying on his committee. He said they were not ready to invite Alice Johnston in for a campus interview—at least not at that time.

About two weeks later, early in December, Jim called Jordan. "Hello, Jordan," he began, "I wanted you to know that we're inviting Fred Johnston in for a campus interview. Any chance that you are ready to move on Alice's candidacy? We could surely sell them better on Lawrence if we had them both here."

Jordan replied, "No, sorry Jim. We've got two others we're going to look at first, although our list is getting shorter. You're going to bring Dr. Johnston in anyway, right?"

"Yes, we think he'd fit in well here," Jim answered, "And who knows, maybe the Johnstons will decide they can't get exactly what they want. Fred said if he finds something really attractive and the chances look good for his wife they might go ahead and make the decision. So we're going to take the risk and have him in."

"Well, thanks for keeping me posted, Jim," Jordan said, "Let me know how the interview goes with Fred and what you plan to do."

"Will do, Jordan, and call me if you have any developments," Jim replied.

CAMPUS INTERVIEWS

When Fred came in for a day and a half campus visit, Jim had hopes of selling him on Lawrence State on the spot. The interview schedule included a series of meetings with various faculty, college and university administrators, and graduate students. There was also to be a formal presentation on Fred's current research and informal gatherings at meals hosted by the departmental faculty. Jim was generally pleased with the interviews as the faculty, students, and administrators seemed to respond well to Fred.

As Jim drove Fred to the airport, he told Fred that he expected to be able to call him within a couple days with positive news. He stated that he felt the interviews had gone well and that he hoped Fred had retained his interest in the position. Fred replied that he was very much interested, and that he now hoped things would work out for him and Alice at Lawrence State.

The next day Jim talked with members of the faculty recruiting committee and the dean and reviewed the written evaluations by faculty, administrators, and students who had met with Fred or attended his seminar. These evaluations were uniformly favorable, affirming Jim's tentative decision to make Fred an offer. Jim wrote a hiring proposal, which specified the academic rank, salary, and the other major terms and conditions of the appointment. He went over it with the dean and got the necessary approval to make the offer.

Before calling Fred, he decided to give Jordan Allen a call to check on Alice's status and inform him of the imminent offer. When Jim asked about Alice's chances, Dr.

Allen replied that it would be a few days before he would know any more, since their other candidate was due in to interview the next day and the department had high hopes of hiring her. Jim thanked Jordan for the information, and they agreed to keep in close contact. He then made the call to Fred offering him a faculty position (as described in the introduction to the case).

Early the next week, Jim received the call from Jordan Allen with the news that Alice Johnston was being invited for an interview. He was pleased to hear this and, only half kidding, said, "Now, be nice to her during her visit." Jordan replied that they would have to "see how it goes" and that he, too, hoped Alice Johnston would be well received by the faculty. Jordan agreed to call Jim following her interview.

As Jim had promised, he called Fred Johnston on Friday afternoon, one week after he had extended the job offer and following the Johnstons' interviews at Evergreen College in Wisconsin. "Hello, Fred," he said, "I'm calling to follow up on our last discussion about our offer to join the faculty here."

Fred responded: "Jim, I was expecting your call, and I do have some news. Evergreen offered us both contracts before we left the campus. But there are more problems than I thought with the school, at least from my standpoint. There is little summer teaching,[5] limited travel funds, a fifteen-hour teaching load,[6] and, frankly, not much support for research and publication. The salary offers were interesting. They offered me $3,500 less than you did, but promised Alice about $3,000 more than Dr. Allen indicated English could pay. I'm sure they know what they're doing, low balling me and loading up way above market rate on her. She's seen no schools paying quite that much in her field. She was pretty impressed."

"I suppose she would be," said Jim, "But isn't it the total package which should count, not just what one of you gets?"

Fred continued: "I am happy to say Lawrence State has finally scheduled an interview for Alice, next Wednesday. If English makes her a reasonable offer, we're on our way to Lawrence, even if the money package turns out a little less attractive. Timing is now of utmost importance. Evergreen wants our decision by Monday, but I think we can stall them until Friday, after Alice gets back from Lawrence. Alice has explained our situation to Dr. Allen, and he promised to act quickly after her interview."

Jim grimaced, but kept his voice pleasant, "Fred, thanks for the update. I'll call Jordan Allen so that he'll know of our department's continued strong interest in you. I really appreciate your candor in sharing this with me. Let's see, I'll call you back on Friday, or you call me before if there's anything new."

"I'll do it," replied Fred, "Good-by now."

Jim was anxious to hear about Alice's interview with the English Department. His spirits were not lifted by a letter he got the following Wednesday from his back-up candidate for the business policy position. She had accepted another job, noting that she couldn't wait any longer for Lawrence State to act.

Early Thursday morning, Jordan Allen called. "Jim," he began, "Alice Johnston was in yesterday and, well, our feelings about her are rather mixed. She's a pleasant, congenial person. But several members of the recruiting committee think Alice is really more interested in teaching the works of Shakespeare than technical writing. We're a little concerned about the fit. We're not sure what we're going to do, but we have a meeting tomorrow to talk about it."

"Well, Jordan, this news concerns me," Jim replied. "But I will tell you that we can get them both if you offer her a job. I don't think there's any question about it. Then you and I could move on to working on something else! I guess you have to do what's best for you, but it is getting late in the year for us to hire. We'll be sitting here empty-handed for the fall semester if we can't fill this position soon. And I'd guess you'll have to fill your slot in the near future if you're going to?"

"I do appreciate your situation, and we'll be mindful of it in our discussions. We want to cooperate with you as much as possible," said Jordan, "I'll give you a call."

"Thanks, Jordan, and I'll look forward to learning of your decision. Now, help us out if you can."

Jim leaned back in his chair and reflected on what had become a complex and frustrating recruitment and selection experience. Had he done everything he could to increase the chances that Fred would come to LSU? Had he used the right approach in promoting Alice's candidacy for the job in the English Department? He wondered what more he could do? Maybe he should call Alice to inform her of the concerns of the English Department about her teaching interests? Perhaps then she could better "sell" herself to them? Or could he possibly persuade Jordan to use his influence with the committee? Or should he ask the dean to involve the provost[7] who could better consider the university's interest in this matter? Maybe some leverage could be exercised by his office to help the Management Department fill the position? After all, from the university perspective, Fred would be an excellent hire and Alice would surely be an acceptable one, Jim reasoned. Or had he already gone too far in pressuring Jordan?

As Jim packed up his briefcase to leave for the day, he pondered how this situation he'd been wrestling with for six months would come out. Maybe LSU should develop a policy that would promote better cooperation among departments that were recruiting working couples? Jim had recalled a recent faculty position announcement from Oregon State University which had a tagline stating an institutional policy of "being responsive to the needs of dual-career couples." On the other hand, perhaps it would be better to simply avoid recruiting dual-career couples in the future and consider only individual candidates? He wondered.

NOTES

1. Names of institutions and persons in the case are disguised. The university is a comprehensive state institution with about 24,000 students in a southeastern city with a population of over 500,000.

2. Although the evaluation of qualifications in these areas is difficult and subjective, teaching may be judged by student evaluations, peer or administrative evaluations, quality of course syllabi, etc. Research is measured largely by the quality and quantity of one's scholarship reported in professional journals, books, or at professional conferences. Service may be gauged by one's performance in activities of professional associations, professional contributions to the community, and work on university committees or projects.

3. The Academy of Management is the leading academic association in management. It publishes a placement roster in the spring and another in the fall, listing job applicants as well as openings.

4. The typical Ph.D. program includes two or more years of course work beyond the master's degree, comprehensive written and oral examinations, and the dissertation. The dissertation is an advanced treatise, often exceeding 150 pages, based on independent research and demonstrating mastery of the candidate's own subject as well as of the scholarly method. Ph.D. candidates often accept teaching jobs after completing their examinations while working on the dissertation.

5. The usual contract is for nine months, and summer teaching offers a way for many faculty members to earn added income.

6. Nationally accredited business schools generally limit teaching loads to twelve semester hours, nine if a graduate course is included.

7. At LSU, the provost served the function of the academic vice president or vice president, academic affairs at many other universities. Jim and Jordan reported to their respective deans, who in turn reported to the provost with regard to academic matters.

Step 2: Prepare the case for class discussion.

Step 3: Answer each of the following questions, individually or in small groups, as directed by your instructor.

Description
1. Trace each person's career.

Diagnosis
2. What is the major dilemma faced by Jim Franklin?
3. What are Alice Johnston's and Fred Johnston's priorities?
4. Using your knowledge of personal and career development, evaluate the situation.
5. What problems exist for the dual-career couple in the case?
6. What needs must the university meet?

Prescription

7. What should Franklin do?
8. What provisions should the university make for this type of situation?

Step 4: Discussion. In small groups or with the entire class, or in written form, share your answers to the questions above. Then answer the following questions:

1. What symptoms suggest that a problem exists?
2. What problems exist in the case?
3. What theories and concepts help explain those problems?

4. How can the problems be corrected?
5. Are the actions likely to be effective?

This case was prepared by Thomas R. Miller of Memphis State University and Arthur Sharplin of McNeese State University as the basis for class discussion rather than to illustrate either effective or ineffective handling of a managerial situation. All proper names have been disguised. Distributed by the North American Case Research Association. © 1991. All rights reserved to the authors and the North American Case Research Association. Permission to use the case should be obtained from the authors and the North American Case Research Association.

Activity 3–6

Diagnosis of Stress

Step 1: Complete the following questionnaire by checking the appropriate column:

Do You Frequently	Yes	No
1. Neglect your diet?		
2. Try to do everything yourself?		
3. Blow up easily?		
4. Seek unrealistic goals?		
5. Fail to see the humor in situations others find funny?		
6. Act rude?		
7. Make a "big deal" of everything?		
8. Look to other people to make things happen?		
9. Have difficulty making decisions?		
10. Complain you are disorganized?		
11. Avoid people whose ideas are different from your own?		
12. Keep everything inside?		
13. Neglect exercise?		
14. Have few supportive relationships?		
15. Use psychoactive drugs, such as sleeping pills and tranquilizers, without physician approval?		
16. Get too little rest?		
17. Get angry when you are kept waiting?		
18. Ignore stress symptoms?		
19. Procrastinate?		
20. Think there is only one right way to do something?		
21. Fail to build in relaxation time?		
22. Gossip?		
23. Race through the day?		

Do You Frequently	Yes	No
24. Spend a lot of time lamenting the past?		
25. Fail to get a break from noise and crowds?		

Step 2: Score your responses by scoring 1 for each yes answer and 0 for each no answer. Total your score.

1–6: There are few hassles in your life. Make sure, though, that you aren't trying so hard to avoid problems that you shy away from challenges.

7–13: You've got your life in pretty good control. Work on the choices and habits that could still be causing some unnecessary stress in your life.

14–20: You're approaching the danger zone. You may well be suffering stress-related symptoms, and your relationships could be strained. Think carefully about choices you've made, and take relaxation breaks every day.

Above 20: Emergency! You must stop now, rethink how you are living, change your attitudes, and pay scrupulous attention to your diet, exercise, and relaxation programs.

Step 3: Discussion. In small groups or with the class as a whole, answer the following questions:

Description

1. What was your score?
2. How much stress does this represent?
3. How does this compare to scores of others in the class?

Step 4: Think about a stressful situation you have experienced.

1. Describe the situation.
2. What symptoms of stress did you experience at the time?
3. What caused the stress?
4. How did you reduce the stress?

Step 5: Individually or in small groups, offer a plan for coping with or reducing stress.

—————

Source: Adapted with permission from "Stress Index" by A. E. Slaby, M.D., Ph.D., M.P.H., *60 Ways to Make Stress Work for You* (Summit, N.J.: PIA Press, 1988).

CONCLUDING COMMENTS

In this chapter we examined the nature of diversity in organizations in greater detail. We considered different ethnic groups and the role of gender, race, and age in organizations, as well as issues related to personality, individual development, work-family interactions, role expectations, and stress.

We have seen the impact of developmental transitions on performance. You assessed your own personality and commented on issues related to your personal style. You traced your own life line and identified times of crisis. You assessed your current level of stress. In each case, you used a variety of theoretical perspectives to enhance your understanding of the situation. In the Case of the Undecided Accountant and the Dual-Career Couple Dilemma, you translated this understanding into prescriptions for change.

ENDNOTES

[1] G. Hofstede, *Cultural Consequences: International Differences in Work-Related Values* (Beverly Hills, Calif.: Sage, 1984).

[2] This discussion is drawn from P. R. Harris and R. T. Moran, *Managing Cultural Differences,* 3rd ed. (Houston: Gulf, 1991).

[3] *Ibid.*

[4] *Workforce 2000 Report,* U.S. Labor Department, 1987.

[5] L. Copeland, Valuing workplace diversity, *Personnel Administrator* 33 (November 1988): 38, 40; T. H. Cox and S. Blake, Managing cultural diversity: Implications for organizational competitiveness, *Academy of Management Executive* 5(3) (1991): 45–56.

[6] S. Kintner, Older is better, *Women and Therapy* 2(4) (1983): 61–67.

[7] C. Gilligan, *In a Different Voice* (Cambridge, Mass.: Harvard University, 1982).

[8] This discussion is drawn from Race in the workplace: Is affirmative action working? *Business Week,* July 8, 1991, pp. 50–63.

[9] This discussion is drawn in part from W. Kiechel III, How to manage older workers, *Fortune,* November 5, 1990, pp. 183–186.

[10] J. B. Rotter, Generalized expectancies for internal versus external control of reinforcement, *Psychological Monographs* 1, no. 609 (1966): 80.

[11] D. Paulhus, Sphere-specific measures of perceived control, *Journal of Personality and Social Psychology* 44 (1983): 1253–1265.

[12] J. B. Rotter, External control and internal control, *Psychology Today* (June 1971): 37.

[13] M. Friedman and R. Roseman, *Type A Behavior and Your Heart* (New York: Knopf, 1974); M. T. Matteson and C. Preston, Occupational stress, Type A behavior and physical well-being, *Academy of Management Journal* 25 (1982): 373–391; D. C. Glass, *Behavior Patterns, Stress, and Coronary Disease* (Hillsdale, N.J.: Erlbaum, 1977).

[14] C. G. Jung, *Collected Works,* ed. H. Read, M. Fordham, and G. Adler (Princeton, N.J.: Princeton University Press, 1953).

[15] M. F. R. Kets de Vries and D. Miller, Personality, culture, and organization, *Academy of Management Review* 11 (1986): 262–279.

[16] F. S. Hall, The dysfunctional managers: The next human resource challenge, *Organizational Dynamics* 20 (Autumn 1991): 48–57.

[17] H. Levinson, A conception of adult development, *American Psychologist* 41 (1986): 3–13; D. C. Feldman, *Managing Careers in Organizations* (Glenview, Ill.: Scott Foresman, 1988); D. J. Levinson, *The Seasons of a Woman's Life* (New York: Knopf, 1989).

[18] See, for example, Feldman, *Managing Careers in Organizations;* D. T. Hall, Breaking career routines: Midcareer choice and identity development. In D. T. Hall and Associates, eds., *Career Development in Organizations* (San Francisco: Jossey-Bass, 1986).

[19] See Kiechel, How to manage older workers, for a list of stereotypes about older workers that must be dispelled.

[20] D. C. Feldman, Careers in organizations: Recent trends and future directions, *Journal of Management* 15 (1989): 135–156.

[21] J. P. Meyer and N. J. Allen, Links between work experiences and organizational commitment during the first year of employment: A longitudinal analysis, *Journal of Occupational Psychology* 61 (1988): 195–209; D. M. Hunt and C. Michael, Mentorship: A career training and development tool, *Academy of Management Review* 8 (1983): 475–485; K. E. Kram, Phases of the mentor relationship, *Academy of Management Journal* 26 (1983): 608–625.

[22] See K. E. Kram, *Mentoring at Work: Developmental Relationships in Organizational Life* (Glenview, Ill.: Scott, Foresman, 1985); R. Rubow and S. Jansen, A corporate survival guide for the baby bust, *Management Review* (July 1990): 50–52; E. A. Fagenson, The mentor advantage: perceived career/job experiences of proteges versus non-proteges, *Journal of Organizational Behavior* 10 (1989): 309–320; K. E. Kram, Mentoring in the workplace. In D. T. Hall et al., *Career Development in Organizations*.

[23] G. F. Dreker and R. A. Ash, A comparative study of mentoring among men and women in managerial, professional, and technical positions, *Journal of Applied Psychology* 75(5) (1990): 539–546; W. Whiteley, T. W. Dougherty, and G. F. Dreker, Relationship of career mentoring and socioeconomic origin to managers' and professionals' early career progress, *Academy of Management Journal* 34(2) (1991): 331–351.

[24] R. Ragins, Barriers to mentoring: The female manager's dilemma, *Academy of Management Review* 42 (1989): 1–22.

[25] R. A. Noe, Women and mentoring: A review and research agenda, *Academy of Management Review* 13 (1988): 65–78, lists the six barriers; C. A. McKeen and R. J. Burke, Mentor relationships in organizations: Issues, strategies, and prospects for women, *Journal of Management Development* 8(6): 33–42, also discusses mentoring issues for women.

[26] Kram, Mentoring in the workplace, *Mentoring at Work*.

[27] J. A. Wilson and N. S. Elman, Organizational benefits of mentoring, *Academy of Management Executive* 4(4) (1990): 88–94.

[28] D. Jacoby, Rewards make the mentor, *Personnel* (December 1989): 10–14; R. J. Burke and C. A. McKeen, Mentoring in organizations: Implications for women, *Journal of Business Ethics* 9 (1990): 317–332.

[29] R. A. Webber, Career problems of young managers, *California Management Review* 18 (1976): 19–33.

[30] See K. Little, The baby boom generation: Confronting reduced opportunities, *Employment Relations Today* (Spring 1989): 57–63; and D. C. Feldman and B. A. Weitz, Career plateaus reconsidered, *Journal of Management* 14 (1988): 69–80 for current thinking about this issue.

[31] Up against the glass ceiling, *Management Review* (April 1987): 6; A. Morrison, R. White, and E. Van Velsor, *Breaking the Glass Ceiling* (Reading, Mass.: Addison-Wesley, 1987).

[32] D. T. Hall et al., Breaking career routines, *Career Development in Organizations,* p. 133.

[33] A. Howard and D. W. Bray, *Managerial Lives in Transition: Advancing Age and Changing Times* (New York: Guilford, 1988); J. R. Gordon, Adding diversity to the Workforce 2000: Meeting the needs of working mothers at midlife. Paper presented at the seventh annual Women and Work Conference. Arlington, TX, May 1992.

[34] F. W. Dalton, P. H. Thompson, and R. L. Price, The four stages of professional careers: A new look at performance by professionals, *Organizational Dynamics* 6 (1977): 19–42.

[35] L. Larwood and B. A. Gutek, Working toward a theory of women's career development. In B. A. Gutek and L. Larwood, eds., *Women's Career Development* (Newbury Park, Calif.: Sage, 1987), pp. 170–183.

[36] J. A. Raelin, An anatomy of autonomy: Managing professionals, *Academy of Management Executive* 3 (August 1989): 216–228; J. A. Raelin, C. K. Sholl, and D. Leonard, Why professionals turn sour and what to do, *Personnel* 62 (October 1985): 29–41.

[37] See J. Raelin, *Professional Careers* (New York: Praeger, 1983); T. J. Allen and R. Katz, The dual ladder: Motivational solution or managerial delusion? *Research and Development Management* 16 (1986): 185–197; R. Katz, M. L. Tushman, and T. J. Allen, Exploring the dynamics of dual ladders: A longitudinal study, Massachusetts Institute of Technology, Sloan School of Management Working Paper 11–90, August 1990.

[38] T. J. Allen and R. Katz, The treble ladder revisited: Why do engineers lose interest in the dual ladder as they get older? Massachusetts Institute of Technology, Sloan School of Management Working Paper 7–90, July 1990.

[39] B. Leibowitz, C. Farren, and B. L. Kaye, *Designing Career Development Systems* (San Francisco, Jossey-Bass, 1986).

[40] J. R. Kafodimos, Regaining balance, *Executive Excellence* (August 1990): 3–5.

[41] H. Cosell, *Women on a Seesaw* (New York: Putnam and Sons, 1985).

[42] D. T. Hall and J. Richter, Balancing work life and home life: What can organizations do to help? *Academy of Management Executive* 2(3) (1988): 213–223; F. S. Hall and D. T. Hall, Dual careers—How do couples and companies cope with the problems? *Organizational Dynamics* 6 (1978): 57–77.

[43] F. N. Schwartz, Management women and the new facts of life, *Harvard Business Review* (January-February 1989): 65–76.

[44] E. Ehrlich, Is the mommy track a blessing—or a betrayal? *Business Week* (May 15, 1989): 98–99.

[45] See R. L. Kahn, D. M. Wolfe, R. P. Quinn, and J. D. Snoek, *Organizational Stress: Studies in Role Conflict and Ambiguity* (New York: John Wiley, 1964), for the classic discussion. For more recent discussion, see M. Van Sell, A. P. Brief, and R. S. Schuler, Role conflict and role ambiguity: Integration of the literature and directions for future research, *Human Relations* 34 (1981): 43–71; S. E. Jackson and R. S. Schuler, A meta-analysis and conceptual critique of research on role ambiguity and role conflict in work settings, *Organizational Behavior and Human Decision Processes* 36 (1985): 16–78; K. Klenke-Hamel and J. E. Mathieu, Role strains, tension, and job satisfaction influences on employees' propensity to leave: A multi-sample replication and extension, *Human Relations* 43 (1990): 791–807; E. Kemery, A. G. Bedeian, K. W. Mossholder, and J. Touliatos, Outcomes of role stress: A multisample constructive replication, *Academy of Management Journal* 28 (1985): 363–375; and J. Schaubroeck, J. L. Cotten, and K. R. Jennings, Antecedents and consequences of role stress: A covariance structure analysis, *Journal of Organizational Behavior* 10 (1989): 35–58.

[46] C. D. Fisher and R. Gitelson, A meta-analysis of the correlates of role conflict and ambiguity, *Journal of Applied Psychology* 68 (1983): 320–333; A. G. Bedeian and A. A. Armenakis, A path-analytic study of the consequences of role conflict and ambiguity, *Academy of Management Journal* 24 (1981): 417–424.

[47] J. H. Greenhaus and N. J. Beutell, Sources of conflict between work and family roles, *Academy of Management Review* 10 (1985): 76–88.

[48] R. L. Valdez and B. A. Gutek, Family roles—a help or hindrance for working women? In Gutek and Larwood, *Women's Career Development.*

[49] E. Schein, Organizational socialization and the profession of management, *Sloan Management Review* 9 (1968): 1–16; D. C. Feldman, The multiple socialization of organization members, *Academy of Management Review* 6 (1981): 309–318.

[50] Schein, Organizational socialization; R. R. Ritti and G. R. Funkhouser, *The Ropes to Skip and the Ropes to Know,* 3rd ed. (New York: Wiley, 1987).

[51] J. Van Maanen, Golden passports: Management socialization and graduate education, *The Review of Higher Education* 6 (1983): 435–455; D. C. Feldman, Socialization, resocialization, and training: Reframing the research agenda. In I. Goldstein, ed., *Frontiers of Industrial and Organizational Psychology* vol. 3 (San Francisco: Jossey-Bass, 1989).

[52] A. Mikhail, Stress: A psychophysiological conception, *Journal of Human Stress* (June 1981): 9–15.

[53] H. Selye, *The Stress of Life,* 2nd ed. (New York: McGraw Hill, 1976).

[54] See K. Karaseh and T. Theorell, *Healthy Work: Stress, Productivity, and the Reconstruction of Working Life* (New York: Basic Books, 1990); and J. Eckenrode and S. Gore, eds., *Stress between Work and Family* (New York: Plenum, 1990), for a wide-ranging discussion of stress and its effects.

[55] D. Friesen and J. C. Sarros, Sources of burnout among educators, *Journal of Organizational Behavior* 10 (1989): 179–188; W. D. Paine, ed., *Job Stress and Burnout: Research, Theory, and Intervention Perspectives* (Beverly Hills, Calif.: Sage, 1982); R. Golembiewski and R. F. Munzenrider, *Phases of Burnout: Developments in Concepts and Applications* (New York: Praeger, 1988).

[56] D. R. Frew and N. W. Burning, Perceived organizational characteristics and personality measures as predictors of stress/strain in the workplace, *Journal of Management* 13 (1987): 633–646.

[57] D. L. Nelson and J. C. Quick, Professional women: Are distress and disease inevitable? *Academy of Management Review* 10 (1985): 206–218; G. L. Cooper and M. J. Davidson, The high cost of stress on women managers, *Organizational Dynamics* (Winter 1982): 44–53.

[58] M. Kets de Vries, Organizational stress: A call for management action, *Sloan Management Review* 21 (1979): 3–14.

[59] B. Schneider, Organizational behavior, *Annual Review of Psychology* (Washington, D.C.: Annual Reviews, 1985).

[60] T. D. Jick and R. Payne, Stress at work, *Exchange: The Organizational Behavior Teaching Journal* 5 (1980): 50–56.

[61] J. R. Terborg, Health promotion at the worksite: A research challenge for personnel and human resources management. In K. H. Rowland and G. R. Ferris, eds., *Researching Personnel and Human Resource Management,* vol. 4 (Greenwich, Conn.: JAI Press, 225–267; B. D. Steffy, J. W. Jones, and A. W. Noe, The impact of health habits and life-style on the stressor-strain relationship: An evaluation of three industries, *Journal of Occupational Psychology* 63 (1990): 217–229.

[62] G. Haight, Managing diversity, *Across the Board* (March 1990): 22–28.

[63] C. M. Solomon, The corporate response to work force diversity, *Personnel Journal* (August 1989): 49.

[64] How do you manage a diverse workforce? *Training and Development Journal* (February 1989): 13–21.

[65] B. G. Foster, G. Jackson, W. E. Cross, B. Jackson, and R. Hardiman, Workforce diversity and business, *Training and Development Journal* (April 1988): 40.

RECOMMENDED READINGS

Arthur, M. B., Hall, D. T., and Lawrence, B. S., eds. *Handbook of Career Theory*. New York: Free Press, 1989.

Crosby, F. J. *Juggling: The Unexpected Advantages of Balancing Career and Home for Women and Their Families*. New York: Free Press, 1991.

Gilbert, L. A. *Sharing It All: The Rewards and Struggles of Two-Career Families*. New York: Plenum, 1988.

Levinson, H., ed. *Designing and Managing Your Career*. Boston: Harvard Business School Press, 1989.

Liebert, R. M. and Spiegler, M. D. *Personality: Strategies and Issues,* 6th ed. Pacific Grove, Calif.: Brooks/Cole, 1990.

Patel, C. *The Complete Guide to Stress Management*. New York: Plenum, 1991.

Chapter Outline

- **OPENING CASE** *Offering Employees Stock Options They Can't Refuse*

  Needs Theories

  Equity Theory

  Reinforcement Theory

  Expectancy Theory

  Goal-Setting Theory

  Motivating a Multicultural and Multinational Work Force

  The Reward System: Applying Motivation Theories to Practice

- **READING 4–1** *A Contingency Theory of Pay*
  Edward J. Harrick

- **ACTIVITIES**

  4–1   Expectancy Questionnaire

  4–2   Goal-Setting Exercise

  4–3   Feeling Stuck at Hyatt? Create a New Business

  4–4   Motivating Diversity in Middle and Top Management

  4–5   Educational Toys, Inc.

  4–6   Traveler Import Cars, Inc.

Motivating and Rewarding Individuals

Learning Objectives

After completing the reading and activities in Chapter 4, students will be able to

1. Identify, compare, and contrast the major needs theories.

2. Discuss the application of equity theory in the workplace.

3. Comment about the use of various types and schedules of reinforcement.

4. Use expectancy theory and goal-setting theory to diagnose motivational situations.

5. Comment about the relevance of various motivation theories to managing a diverse work force.

6. Note the impact of cross-cultural issues on motivating employees.

7. Comment about the use of wages and benefits in a reward system.

8. Describe and design an incentive system.

9. Discuss the role of employee ownership in the reward system.

10. Specify the characteristics of an effective reward system.

Offering Employees Stock Options They Can't Refuse

At $33,000 a year, Bob Huxford's pay as a corporate chauffeur for Merck & Co. doesn't put him in the same league as P. Roy Vagelos, the company's $7-million-a-year chief executive. But Huxford feels that a new company program that grants stock options to nearly all employees—not just top managers—will give him one thing in common with the boss. "Everybody will take a little more pride in their jobs if they know they have a stake in the company's results," says Huxford.

Merck's program, announced on Sept. 11, puts it in the growing ranks of companies that want employees to own more of their stock. The trend first developed in the early 1980s, when thousands of employers set up Employee Stock Ownership Plans (ESOPs). Other companies began to use stock-purchase plans, which allow workers to buy company shares, often at favorable rates. More recently, some employers have extended stock-option plans to most employees. Although only a handful of major companies have taken this route so far, experts expect many more to follow suit. "I don't think it's just a fad," says Corey Rosen, executive director of the National Center for Employee Ownership.

Whatever the method used, most employers share a similar goal: to enhance employees' concern for the company's overall performance. As many companies push decision-making down the corporate ladder, they're using stock to encourage employees to think like owners. "We want every individual to feel a higher level of personal responsibility for the company's success," says John W. Himes, human-resources vice-president at Du Pont Co., which set up an option plan in February. . . .

"Sharepower." Options aren't cheap for employers. Either they must buy the stock for employees on the open market or issue new shares, which reduces the proportion of the company owned by existing shareholders. Investors in highly capitalized companies, such as Merck, probably won't blanch at the tiny dilution involved. However, those at thinly capitalized companies could balk. What's more, the programs can be expensive to set up. Du Pont has spent several million dollars mapping out its plans and gearing up to communicate details to 136,000 staffers in 53 countries.

Such shortcomings seem remote to many Merck employees: Someone who bought $100 worth of Merck shares in 1970 now holds stock worth some $1,750. If Merck's stock does as well in the next five years, Huxford could pocket a $12,875 gain. Little wonder that he, his wife, his son, and two brothers are all among Merck workers who now regularly scan stock tables.[1]

Merck's offering of stock options addresses some typical motivational concerns, including how to encourage employees to perform at a high level, how to support their involvement in decision making, and how to encourage their commitment to the organization. More generally, motivation issues include how to get desired outcomes from employees—such as productivity, efficiency, involvement in decision making, or organizational loyalty, among others. But, is the opportunity to buy stock likely to affect the motivation of employees at Merck and other companies that offer this option?

What motivates individuals to behave, think, or feel in certain ways? What factors make you or others more willing to work, to be creative, to achieve, to produce?

Theory and research in the area of motivation provide a systematic way of diagnosing the degree of motivation and of prescribing ways of increasing it. In the first half of this chapter, we examine five motivation perspectives: needs theories, equity theory, reinforcement theory, expectancy theory, and goal setting theory. In the second half we consider compensation alternatives and reward systems in organizations.

NEEDS THEORIES

Think again about the situation at Merck. Why does its management think that offering stock options will help motivate its workers? Early motivation theorists would explain such a situation by saying that Merck, Du Pont, and similar companies expect the new program to meet employees' needs—their basic requirements for living and working productively. As the work force in organizations becomes more diverse, recognizing the individuality of needs becomes paramount; identifying and responding to them becomes a critical issue in effective management.

Can you identify Bob Huxford's needs? To do a good job of identifying them, we probably would need to spend a great deal of time talking with Bob and observing his behavior both in and out of the work situation. However, based on the information presented in the introduction, we might conjecture that he has basic physiological needs and safety and security needs that additional pay would satisfy.

In this section we present in brief four of the most popular needs theories: Maslow's hierarchy-of-needs theory, Alderfer's ERG theory, McClelland's need-for-achievement theory, and Herzberg's two-factor theory. Each of these theories describes a specific set of needs the researchers believe individuals have, and each differs somewhat in the number and kinds of needs identified. Table 4–1 identifies the different needs. The theories also differ as to how unfulfilled needs influence motivation, as discussed in the following sections.

Maslow's Hierarchy of Needs

Beginning in 1935, Abraham Maslow developed the first needs theory, and it is still one of the most popular and well-known motivation theories.[2] Maslow stated that individuals have five needs, arranged in a hierarchy from the most basic to the highest level, as shown in Figure 4–1: physiological, safety, belongingness and love, esteem, and self-actualization.

Physiological needs are the most basic needs an individual has. These include, at a minimum, a person's requirement for food, water, shelter, sex, the ability to care for his or her children, and medical or dental coverage. *Safety* needs include a person's desire for security or protection. This translates most directly into concerns for short-term and long-term job security, as well as physical safety on the job. *Belongingness and love* needs focus on the social aspects of work and nonwork situations. Virtually

Table 4–1 List of Needs

Maslow	Alderfer	McClelland	Herzberg
Physiological Safety and security	Existence		Hygiene
Belongingness and love	Relatedness	Need for affiliation	
Self-esteem Self-actualization	Growth	Need for achievement Need for power	Motivators

Figure 4–1 **Maslow's Hierarchy of Needs**

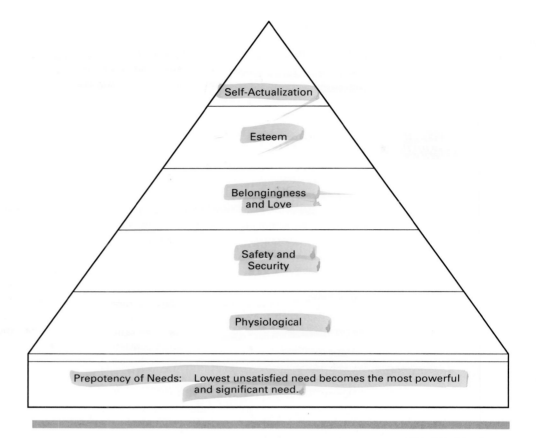

Self-Actualization

Esteem

Belongingness and Love

Safety and Security

Physiological

Prepotency of Needs: Lowest unsatisfied need becomes the most powerful and significant need.

all individuals desire affectionate relationships or regular interaction with others, which can become a key facet of job design. *Esteem* needs relate to a person's desire to master his or her work, demonstrate competence and accomplishments, build a reputation as an outstanding performer, hold a position of prestige, receive public recognition, and feel self-esteem. *Self-actualization* needs reflect an individual's desire to grow and develop to his or her fullest potential. An individual often wants the opportunity to be creative on the job or desires autonomy, responsibility, and challenge.

Responding to Needs   According to needs theory, organizations must meet unsatisfied needs, in ways like those shown in Table 4–2. In Maslow's scheme, the lowest unsatisfied need, starting with the basic physiological needs and continuing through safety, belonging and love, esteem, and self-actualization needs, becomes the *prepotent,* or most powerful and significant, need. Although the order may vary in certain special circumstances, generally the prepotent need motivates an individual to act to fulfill it; satisfied needs do not motivate. If, for example, a person lacks sufficient food and clothing, he or she will act to satisfy those basic physiological needs; hence, this person would most likely work to receive pay or other benefits to satisfy those needs. On the other hand, a person whose physiological, safety, and belongingness needs are satisfied will be motivated to satisfy needs at the next level—the esteem needs. For this person, pay will not motivate performance unless it increases esteem, but a promotion or other changes in a job's title or status, which satisfy esteem needs, are likely to motivate.

Table 4–2 **Mechanisms for Meeting Needs**

Need	Organizational Conditions
Physiological	Pay
	Mandatory breakfast or lunch programs
	Company housing
Safety	Company benefits plans
Security	Pensions
	Seniority
	Pay
	Child care
	Medical and dental benefits
Love	Coffee breaks
Belongingness	Sports teams
Relatedness	Company picnics and social events
Affiliation	Work teams
	Pay
Esteem	Autonomy
	Responsibility
	Pay (as symbol of status)
	Prestige office location and furnishings
Achievement	Job challenge
Competence	Pay
Power	Leadership positions
	Authority
Self-actualization	Challenge
Growth	Autonomy

Managers should understand that the popularity of this theory of motivation stems primarily from its simplicity and logic, not from strong current research support. In general, research indicates that two or three categories of needs, rather than five, exist, and that the relationships, relative importance, and sequences are not consistent from one individual to another.[3] In addition, the ordering of needs may vary in different countries, and thus Maslow's theory may not be universal.

Consider again the case of Bob Huxford. To use Maslow's theory to diagnose the likely effectiveness of the new stock option program on Bob's motivation, we can ask three questions: (1) Which needs have been satisfied? (2) Which unsatisfied need is lowest in the hierarchy? (3) Can those needs be satisfied with the new program? If, for example, his physiological and safety needs have been satisfied, then his social needs become prepotent; if the stock option program can satisfy those needs, then, according to Maslow's theory, it would be motivating.

Alderfer's ERG Theory   The ERG theory addresses one criticism of Maslow's theory by collapsing the hierarchy into three needs, as shown in Figure 4–2: existence, relatedness, and growth.[4] *Existence* includes both physiological and safety needs, and corresponds to Maslow's lower-order needs. *Relatedness* comprises both love and belongingness needs. *Growth* incorporates both esteem and self-actualization needs.

Figure 4–2   **Needs According to ERG Theory**

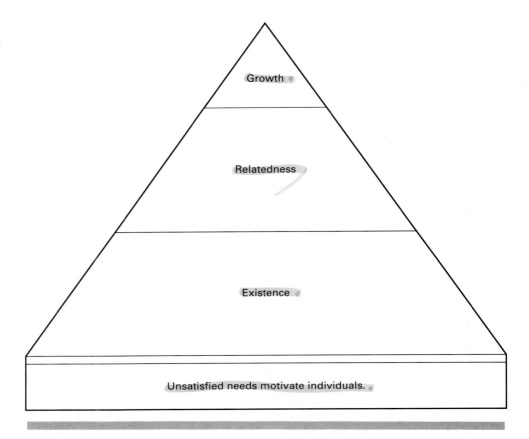

Growth

Relatedness

Existence

Unsatisfied needs motivate individuals.

Individual differences in various needs may be associated with differences in an individual's developmental level, as well as differences in group experiences. For example, after Bob Huxford receives his high school diploma, his existence needs might predominate; as he attains financial security, his needs might shift to primarily relationship ones; later, when he has added financial responsibilities, such as a family or aged parents, satisfying his existence needs may again become important.

The ERG theory also states that unsatisfied needs motivate individuals, and that individuals generally move up the hierarchy in satisfying their needs. For example, individuals with unsatisfied relatedness needs (love and belongingness) would be motivated to produce if their performance resulted in their satisfying these needs. As lower-order needs are satisfied, they become less important, but according to ERG theory, higher-order needs become more important as they are satisfied. For example, increased opportunity for autonomy, which satisfies growth needs, has also increased the requirements for satisfying those needs in the future. If an employee is frustrated in satisfying higher-order needs, such as growth needs, for example, he or she might try instead to satisfy lower-level needs by seeking work situations with social interaction.[5]

Consider, for example, the employee who earns a good salary, has a reasonably high standard of living, and has made many friends at work. According to Maslow and Alderfer this person probably would be motivated to satisfy his or her growth needs. What if in trying to satisfy these needs the individual finds that he or she is continually frustrated in attempts to get more autonomy and responsibility, features of a job that generally encourage individual growth? When asked, the employee now reports that having friends at work and getting together with them outside of work is most important. Frustration in satisfying a higher (growth) need has resulted in a regression to a lower level of (relatedness) needs.

Managerial Responses   In using Alderfer's theory to diagnose motivation situations, such as finding ways to motivate a poorly performing employee to improve his or her productivity or efficiency or to motivate a highly productive employee to continue at or surpass his or her present performance level, we can ask questions similar to those we asked for Maslow, with the addition of three more. First, what needs are the individuals involved in the situation experiencing? Second, what needs have been satisfied, and how have they been met? Third, which unsatisfied need is the lowest in the hierarchy? Fourth, have some higher-order needs been frustrated? Fifth, has the person refocused on a lower-level need? Sixth, how can the unsatisfied needs be satisfied?

McClelland's Trichotomy of Needs   Needs for achievement, affiliation, and power resemble the higher-order needs we have described so far.[6] *Need for achievement* (Nach) is a need to accomplish and demonstrate competence or mastery; a person who continuously asks for and masters increasingly difficult tasks demonstrates a need for achievement. Early and recent research linked this need to effective managerial performance in the United States and abroad.[7] Based on his assumption that he can teach an individual the need for achievement, McClelland and his associates designed and conducted training sessions that teach managers how to act like a person high in need for achievement as a way of increasing performance.

    Need for affiliation (Naff) is a need for love, belonging, and relatedness; a person who seeks jobs high in social interaction shows this need. *Need for power* (Npow) is a need for control over one's own work or the work of others; a person who insists on autonomy in his or her work or who seeks supervisory responsibility likely has a need for power. Other early research showed that male managers with a high need for power tended to run more productive departments than did managers with a high need for affiliation.[8] A person may demonstrate each need overtly or covertly; Bob Huxford may seek a job with more autonomy or may work harder when given it. He may visibly delight in social activities or complain about always working alone. Although each person has all three needs to some extent, only one of them tends to motivate an individual at any given time.

    Figure 4–3 can help identify your own or another's predominant need at any given time. Take a few moments and answer the questions posed here for yourself. Note that occasionally an individual may experience more than one of these needs equally strongly, so you might have equally positive responses to two or more sets of items.

    The projective Thematic Apperception Test (TAT) also measures these needs. The respondent describes what he or she sees as occurring in a series of pictures. What do you see in Figure 4–4? The respondent *projects* his or her needs into the description of the picture. For example, if you viewed the picture as a problem-solving meeting, then you would a receive positive score on need for achievement. If you viewed the picture as being a social gathering, then you would receive a positive score on need for affiliation. If you viewed the picture as being a situation dominated by a single person, then you would receive a positive score on need for power. Professional test administrators have detailed protocols for scoring the pictures included in the TAT and similar tests. Because of the time and skill required

Figure 4–3 **Questions to Identify Need for Achievement, Need for Affiliation, and Need for Power**

1. Do you like situations where you personally must find solutions to problems?
2. Do you tend to set moderate goals and take moderate, thought-out risks?
3. Do you want specific feedback about how well you are doing?
4. Do you spend time considering how to advance your career, how to do your job better, or how to accomplish something important?

If you responded yes to questions 1–4, then you probably have a high need for achievement.

5. Do you look for jobs or seek situations that provide an opportunity for social relationships?
6. Do you often think about the personal relationships you have?
7. Do you consider the feelings of others to be very important?
8. Do you try to restore disrupted relationships when they occur?

If you responded yes to questions 5–8, then you probably have a high need for affiliation.

9. Do you try to influence and control others?
10. Do you seek leadership positions in groups?
11. Do you enjoy persuading others?
12. Are you perceived by others as outspoken, forceful, and demanding?

If you responded yes to questions 9–12, then you probably have a high need for power.

SOURCE: Based on R. M. Steers and L. W. Porter, *Motivation and Work Behavior* (New York: McGraw-Hill, 1979), pp. 57–64. Copyright 1979 by McGraw-Hill, Inc. Reproduced with permission.

in the administration and scoring of the test, its cost is relatively high and only a trained professional can administer and score it.

Can McClelland's theory help us understand why stock options might affect motivation at Merck? To begin, we might assess its employees' needs for achievement, affiliation, and power. Then we can evaluate whether the proposed program might meet some of these needs.

Herzberg's Two-Factor Theory   Frederick Herzberg and his associates described features of a job's content, including responsibility, autonomy, self-esteem, and self-actualization opportunities, known as motivators, which motivate a person to exert more effort and ultimately perform better.[9] Early job redesign efforts focused on increasing these motivators. Because serious criticisms of the theory's rigor and validity have existed, its major contribution is a historical one.[10]

Herzberg and his associates also described hygiene factors, aspects of a job that can meet physiological, security, or social needs, including physical working conditions, salary, company policies and practices, and benefits, that satisfy the lower-order needs, and prevent dissatisfaction. Figure 4–5 illustrates the two components of this theory. Although hygiene factors per se do not encourage individuals to exert more effort, they must be at an acceptable level before motivators can have a positive effect. For example, offering autonomy and responsibility when working conditions and other contextual factors are not resolved results in worker dissatisfaction and limits the occurrence of motivation.

Figure 4-4 **Example of a TAT Picture**

Herzberg's theory has been subjected to significant criticism. This criticism focuses on the research method used to collect data as well as the classification of some factors, especially pay, as both a motivator and a hygiene factor.[11] His theory also ignores individual differences and may overemphasize the importance of pleasure as a desired outcome.

The extent to which current needs theories explain motivation in organizations has been questioned by some researchers who maintain that the concept is difficult to prove or disprove for several reasons.[12] First, needs are difficult to specify and measure. Second, relating needs to various job characteristics, such as a company benefits plans, can be problematic. Third, need-satisfaction models fail to account for variances in individuals' behaviors and attitudes. Fourth, attributing needs to individuals may stem from a lack of awareness of external causes that influence behavior. Finally, applying needs may result in stereotyping individuals and ignore the dynamic quality of individual behavior.

Figure 4–5 **Herz-berg's Theory**

Hygiene Factors *The Environment*		**Motivators** *The Job*	
Job Dissatisfaction	No Job Dissatisfaction	No Job Satisfaction	Job Satisfaction
• Pay • Status • Security • Working conditions • Fringe benefits • Policies and administrative practices • Interpersonal relations		• Meaningful and challenging work • Recognition for accomplishment • Feeling of achievement • Increased responsibility • Opportunities for growth and advancement • The job itself	

EQUITY THEORY   The second major type of motivation theory evolved from social comparison theory. Lacking objective measures of performance or appropriate attitudes, individuals assess and compare their performance and attitudes to others'. *Equity theory* assumes that people assess their job performance and attitudes by comparing both their contribution to work and the benefits they derive from work to the contributions and benefits of a *comparison other,* an individual whom the person selects and who in reality may be like or unlike the person. Bob Huxford, for example, might compare his effort and rewards to other corporate chauffeurs, other professionals in the company, friends or associates in other firms, or even the CEO of the organization.

Determination of Equity   Equity theory further states that a person is motivated in proportion to the perceived fairness of the rewards received for a certain amount of effort.[13] You may have heard your colleague James say, "I'm going to stop working so hard—I work harder than Susan and she gets all the bonuses," or your classmate Sarah say, "Why should I bother studying? Alan never studies and still gets A's—and he's no smarter than I am." James and Sarah have compared their effort and the rewards they received to the effort exerted and rewards received by Susan and Alan. James and Sarah have *perceived* an inequity in the work and school situation; in fact, no actual inequity may exist, but the perception of inequity influences James' and Sarah's subsequent actions.

Specifically, James and Sarah compare their perceptions of two ratios, as shown in Figure 4–6: (1) the ratio of their outcomes to their inputs to (2) the ratio of another's outcomes to inputs. *Outcomes* may include pay, status, and job complexity; *inputs* include effort, productivity, age, sex, or experience. Thus they may compare their pay-to-experience ratio to another's ratio, or their status-to-age ratio to another's. For example, James may feel that he receives $20 for each hour of effort he contributes to the job; in contrast, he may assess that Susan receives $40 for each hour of effort she contributes to the job. James perceives that his ratio of outcomes to inputs (20 to 1) is less than Susan's (40 to 1). In fact, Susan may only receive $10 for each hour of effort she contributes to the job. But, according to equity theory, the facts do not influence motivation; *perceptions* of the situation do. Recent research suggests, however, that equity calculations may be difficult because of cognitive differences in assessment and performance.[14] Instead, individuals look for long-

Figure 4–6 **Equity Theory**

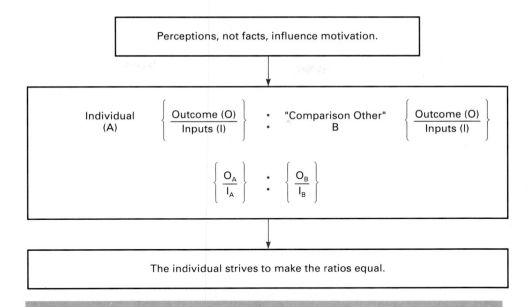

The following content appears within the figure:

Perceptions, not facts, influence motivation.

Individual (A) { Outcome (O) / Inputs (I) } · "Comparison Other" B { Outcome (O) / Inputs (I) }

{ $\frac{O_A}{I_A}$ } · { $\frac{O_B}{I_B}$ }

The individual strives to make the ratios equal.

term rather than short-term parity in work situations; they compare their rank order on merit and rank order on a scale of reward outcomes, and see equity as a goal to work for over time.[15]

Reduction of Inequity

According to equity theory, individuals are motivated to reduce any perceived inequity, as shown in Table 4–3. They strive to make the ratios of outcomes to inputs, O/I, equal.[16] When inequity exists, the person making the comparison strives to make these ratios equal by changing either the outcomes or the inputs, as shown by the calculations in Table 4–4. James, for example, might reduce his inputs (his effort) to make the ratio the same as Susan's. If he cannot change his own inputs or

Table 4–3 **Responses to Inequitable Conditions**

Condition	Responses
$\frac{O_A}{I_A} > \frac{O_B}{I_B}$	A increases inputs A asks for reduced outputs B reduces inputs B asks for increased outputs A or B changes comparison person A or B rationalizes that equity exists A or B leaves the situation
$\frac{O_A}{I_A} < \frac{O_B}{I_B}$	B increases inputs B asks for reduced outputs A reduces inputs A asks for increased outputs A or B changes comparison person A or B rationalizes that equity exists A or B leaves the situation

Table 4–4 **Calculation of Equity**

James' Beliefs	
About James:	About Sarah:
$20 for each hour of effort	$40 for each hour of effort
$\dfrac{\text{Outcomes (J)}}{\text{Inputs (J)}} = \dfrac{20}{1}$ $<$	$\dfrac{\text{Outcomes (S)}}{\text{Inputs (S)}} = \dfrac{40}{1}$

James perceives *inequity* and strives to make the ratios equal.

James changes his inputs and hence his perceptions.

About James:	About Sarah:
$20 for each ½ hour of effort	$40 for each hour of effort
$\dfrac{\text{Outcomes (J)}}{\text{Inputs (J)}} = \dfrac{20}{0.5} = 40$ $=$	$\dfrac{\text{Outcomes (S)}}{\text{Inputs (S)}} = \dfrac{40}{1} = 40$

James perceives *equity*.

outcomes, he might adjust either his *perception* of Susan's outcomes or inputs or his attitude toward the situation by reevaluating her effort or obtaining more accurate information about her pay and adjusting the ratio accordingly.

In theory, the same adjustment process occurs when a person perceives he or she receives too much reward for the input or has too complex a job in comparison to others.[17] If Bob Huxford felt that he were being overpaid relative to his co-workers, would he complain to his bosses? Although early studies suggested that he would, recent research has questioned whether this *overjustification effect* really occurs.[18]

While equity theory basically makes strong intuitive sense, the empirical evidence has been mixed.[19] The concept of *equity sensitivity* in part explains these findings by suggesting that individuals have different preferences for equity (e.g., a preference for higher, lower, or equal ratios) that cause them to react consistently but differently to perceived equity and inequity.[20]

In a sense, equity theory oversimplifies the motivational issues by not explicitly considering individual needs, values, or personalities. This oversimplification becomes particularly important as the work force becomes more diverse. Cross-cultural differences may also occur in preferences for equity, as well as the preferred responses to inequitable situations.

Determining Equity in the Workplace

To determine whether such equity exists in the workplace, we can use a questionnaire such as the Organizational Fairness Questionnaire. Table 4–5 lists some sample items from this instrument. How would Bob Huxford and other employees at Merck respond to these questions? Other concerns about equity can be addressed by answering the questions shown in Table 4–6.

Table 4–5 **Excerpts from Organizational Fairness Questionnaire**

Dimension	Sample Items
Pay rules	• The rules for giving pay raises are not fair to some employees. • The rules for giving pay raises to all employees are fair.
Pay administration	• My supervisor knows who should be promoted and sees that they are promoted if he (or she) can. • My supervisor rates people fairly in giving raises.
Work pace	• People are expected to do a fair day's work in my company. • Some employees can get away with working at a slow speed if they want to in my company.
Pay level	• Persons who have the same education as I have are paid more than I am being paid. • When I compare my pay with the pay of working classmates, my pay is higher than theirs.
Rule administration	• My supervisor will get after workers if they are late to work, play around in the office, or behave badly in other ways. • My supervisor allows workers to tease other employees, be late to their workstations, and act improperly in other ways.
Distribution of jobs	• My supervisor tends to assign unpleasant jobs to those he (or she) doesn't like. • My supervisor sees that everybody in my department does his or her share of the more unpleasant jobs.
Latitude	• In my department, as people learn their jobs, the supervisor lets them make more and more decisions on their own. • In working with me, my supervisor is fair in letting me decide how to do my work.

SOURCE: Reprinted with permission from the Organizational Fairness Questionnaire, by John E. Dittrick.

Table 4–6 **Questions to Assess Equity**

1. What contributions or inputs does the person make to the situation?
2. What is his or her level of education, effort, or experience?
3. What benefits or outcomes does the person receive?
4. What is the level of job complexity, pay, or status of that person?
5. What is the ratio of inputs to outcomes?

REINFORCEMENT THEORY

Reinforcement theory applies behaviorist learning theories, as described in Chapter 2, to motivation. It emphasizes the importance of feedback and rewards in motivating behavior through diverse reinforcement techniques, including positive reinforcement, punishment, negative reinforcement, or extinction.[21]

Types of Reinforcement

First, reinforcement techniques can either encourage or eliminate the desired behavior; second, they can be actively applied or passively used. Table 4–7 shows the four resulting types.

Table 4–7 **Rein-
forcement Options**

Use of Reinforcement	Target Behavior	
	To Encourage Desired Behavior	To Eliminate Desired Behavior
Active	Positive reinforcement	Punishment
Passive	Negative reinforcement (withhold punishment)	Extinction (withhold positive reinforcement)

Positive Reinforcement   Positive reinforcement involves *actively encouraging* a desired behavior by repeatedly pairing desired behaviors or outcomes with rewards or feedback. For example, a person who packs tea sets receives 10 cents for each one packed; the desired behavior—packing the tea sets—is paired with the financial rewards. This feedback *shapes* behavior by encouraging the reinforced or rewarded behavior to recur. If the behavior is not precisely what is desired by a superior or client, repeated reinforcements, resulting in successive approximations to the desired behavior, can move the actual behavior closer to the desired behavior. For example, if a travel agent increases the accuracy of his or her ticketing, the agent's boss might positively comment about the improvement; additional praise might follow if that person makes fewer ticketing errors; praise would continue until the best performance occurred. This behavior would then be reinforced with praise or even financial incentives until it became more or less permanent, but praise would be discontinued if any reversion to previous behaviors occurred.

Punishment   Punishment *actively eliminates* undesirable behaviors by applying an undesirable reinforcer to an undesirable behavior. In this way it differs from negative reinforcement (described in the next section), which rewards the cessation or withdrawal of an undesirable behavior. Using punishment, a female superior officer gives extra, undesirable work to a newly recruited army private who questions a directive about the usage of computers in her job.

How will the private react to punishment? Most likely the recruit will feel bitterness or anger toward the superior or toward the use of computers; this attitude, which results from the use of punishment, may have long-term negative consequences for the private's performance. Punishment often creates secondary consequences of tension and stress and may result in unpredictable and unobservable outcomes, and so it should be used only as a last-resort motivator. Punishment may not permanently eliminate undesired behavior because it does not offer an alternative to the desired behavior. If a worker repeatedly misuses a piece of equipment and receives punishment each time he or she uses the equipment, the behavior may not change because no correct way of using the equipment (an alternative to the desired behavior) is presented.

The undesired behavior also may be offset by positive reinforcement for the same behavior from another source, such as peers.[22] The newly recruited army private's "speaking back" to a superior may be applauded by the other recruits. Or the worker's coworkers may encourage the misuse of equipment, particularly if the worker is otherwise perceived to violate the group's standards for expected and acceptable production (see Chapter 5 for further discussion of group behavior).

Negative Reinforcement   In negative reinforcement, an individual *passively encourages* a desired behavior by withholding punishment. The term *negative* stems from the removal of the individual from a punitive (negative) situation when the desired behavior occurs. The reporter who refuses to name the source of information in a story, is sent to jail (punished), and is then released (removing the punishment) upon naming the source. Releasing (removing) the reporter from his or her punishment (jail) encourages or reinforces the desired behavior (naming the source).

Extinction   Extinction *passively eliminates* an undesired behavior by withholding positive reinforcement. Typically, the failure to apply positive reinforcements causes the desired behaviors to cease. A person who repeatedly works overtime but receives neither compensation, status, nor praise for this added effort likely will stop the overtime hours, depending on other motivating forces at work. By withholding reinforcement, a supervisor may also cause desired behaviors, such as productivity, creativity, and attendance, to stop.

Reinforcement Schedules   The timing and frequency of reinforcement significantly influence its impact. *Fixed and variable schedules* reflect the extent to which reinforcement is regular and known in advance or not. A paycheck is officially administered according to a fixed schedule; the employee receives a paycheck after completing his or her last desired behavior in that time period. Often this type of reinforcer loses the power to motivate good performance because it is received regardless of the individual's behavior. Merit increases, bonuses, and praise are often given on variable schedules. The person giving these rewards does not determine in advance precisely when he or she will comment about an employee's behavior.

Interval and ratio schedules describe the extent to which reinforcement corresponds with a specific time interval (a week, month, or year) or a given number of responses or outputs, such as fifty units of a particular product. Christmas bonuses illustrate reinforcements given according to an interval schedule: They are given once a year at a predetermined time. Piecework rates illustrate reinforcement according to a ratio schedule: Piecework pay is given after a specific number of articles (or responses) are produced.

Table 4–8 illustrates the four schedules that result when these two dimensions are combined and suggests some applications of them. In general, continuous reinforcement along fixed and interval schedules more effectively encourages desired behaviors in the short term; a weekly paycheck motivates workers immediately to perform as desired. Intermittent reinforcement according to variable and ratio schedules more effectively sustains desired behaviors over the long run; not knowing when (or whether) a merit increase in pay will be given tends to motivate workers to continue performing at a high level in hopes such reinforcement will occur. Ensuring performance in the medium run might require adding a fixed-ratio component, such as an incentive program.

Managing Reinforcement Programs   Most frequently a diversity of rewards should be applied, each according to different but complementary schedules. For example, a manager might use the weekly paycheck to encourage attendance, a merit bonus to motivate exceptional behavior, and periodic praise to stimulate day-to-day and longer-term productivity. Adding to the reinforcements on a fixed-interval or fixed-ratio schedule by using either a variable-interval or variable-ratio schedule or both should sustain the already-established desired behaviors. In trying to motivate an employee to show initiative, for example, a manager should begin praising the worker each time he or she demonstrates ini-

Table 4–8 Rein-
forcement Schedules

	Fixed	Variable
Interval	Reinforcement or reward given after the first proper response following a specified period of time	Reinforcement or reward given after a certain amount of time with that amount changing before the next reinforcement
	Weekly or monthly paycheck	Supervisor who visits shop floor on different unannounced days each week Unexpected merit bonuses
Ratio	Reinforcement or reward given after a specified number of proper responses	Reinforcement or reward given after a number of responses with that number changing before the next reinforcement
	Pay for piecework	Praise

tiative, then gradually decrease the use of praise until only exceptional behavior receives comments. This movement from a fixed-ratio schedule to a variable-ratio schedule will sustain behavior over the long term. Organizational behavior management programs have become more common. They have been implemented in a wide range of settings, from insurance companies to private hospitals to furniture manufacturing plants, and have addressed diverse outcomes, from attendance to preventing hazardous conditions to earplug usage.[23] At the same time that the popularity of positive reinforcement has increased, the assignment of reinforcers has become more complicated. What, for example, does the weekly paycheck or the annual Christmas bonus reinforce? Do supervisors praise their subordinates enough or at the best times? Too often, managers hope for one kind of behavior but reward another. They may hope for creative contributions but reward the quantity or timeliness of contributions instead of rewarding creativity.[24] These misguided reward systems, where undesired behaviors are reinforced or perceived to be reinforced, occur because organizational members may substitute measurable outcomes for true organizational goals; managers may overemphasize the visible parts of a task; organizational leaders might deceive subordinates about the outcomes they desire; and managers may feel societal or other pressures to reinforce behaviors they really do not desire.[25]

To diagnose the behavior of workers at Merck or other companies using reinforcement theory, we can ask the questions in Table 4–9. Reinforcement theory should not be applied in isolation; it should be applied in conjunction with the principles of social learning presented in Chapter 2. In addition, rewards or reinforcements must meet an employee's specific needs and be applied equitably.

EXPECTANCY THEORY

Expectancy theory has dominated research about motivation since the early 1970s, principally because it has strong empirical support, integrates diverse perspectives on motivation, and provides explicit ways to increase employee motivation.[26] Perhaps more than the preceding theories, expectancy theory offers a comprehensive view of motivation that integrates many of the elements of the needs, equity, and reinforcement theories.

Table 4–9 Ques-
tions Using Rein-
forcement Theory

1. What behaviors are desired?
2. Are these behaviors observable and measurable?
3. What reinforces these behaviors?
4. When are the reinforcements applied?
5. What are the consequences of these reinforcements?
6. How can the reinforcement pattern be improved?

The Earliest Formulation

Victor Vroom popularized the expectancy theory in the 1960s with his model that stated that motivation was a function of expectancy, valence, and instrumentality:[27]

$$\textbf{Motivation} = E \times V \times I \ (\text{Expectancy} \times \text{Valence} \times \text{Instrumentality})$$

This simple formulation identifies the three basic components of expectancy theory.

E, or *expectancy,* refers to a person's perception of the probability that effort will lead to performance. For example, a person who perceives that if he or she works harder, then he or she will produce more, has a high expectancy. A person who perceives that, if he or she works harder, then he or she will be ostracized by other workers and will not receive the cooperation necessary for performing, has a lower expectancy. A person who sees no link between effort and performance will have zero expectancy. If expectancy is zero, then motivation will be lower than if expectancy is positive.

I, or *instrumentality,* refers to a person's perception of the probability that certain outcomes, positive or negative, will be attached to that performance. For example, a person who perceives that he or she will receive greater pay or benefits if he or she produces has high instrumentality. A person who sees no link between performance and pay will have zero instrumentality. Motivation is a function of the degree of instrumentality, in addition to expectancy and valence.

V, or *valence,* refers to a person's perception of the value of specific outcomes; that is, how much the person likes or dislikes receiving these outcomes. An individual with high esteem needs generally will attach a high valence to a new job title or a promotion. When valence is high, motivation is likely to be higher than when valence is less positive or negative.

The Multiple-Outcome Formulation

Vroom's simplified introduction of expectancy theory was followed in the 1970s by a more complex formulation:[28]

$$\textbf{Motivation} = [E{\rightarrow}P] \times \sum [(P{\rightarrow}O)(V)]$$

Here, E→P refers to the employee's perception of whether effort leads to performance; this is analogous to expectancy. The relation P→O refers to the employee's perception of whether performance leads to outcomes, including fatigue, pay, benefits, job challenge, among others. The variable V refers to the valence, or value attached to the outcome.

We can examine the case of a worker such as Bob Huxford using this formulation of motivation. If Bob perceives that devoting more hours to work will result in his performing better, then E→P will be positive. If he perceives that he receives pay and praise if he performs his job well, then P→O will be positive. If Bob likes receiving money and praise, then V will be positive. We can operationalize this equation by arbitrarily assigning values to each variable, as shown in Figure 4–7.

Figure 4–7 **Calculation of Motivation Using Expectancy, Instrumentality, and Valence: A Simple Example**

If we arbitrarily assign values to

E→P between 0 and 1
P→O between 0 and 1
V between −1 and +1

When all are extremely positive, then

$$E→P = 1, \quad P→O = 1, \quad \text{and } V = 1$$

Motivation = $1 \times 1 \times 1 = 1$, which is high motivation potential.

Assume the worker wins the $20 million lottery, then

$$E→P = 1, \quad P→O = 1, \quad \text{and } V = −1$$

Motivation = $1 \times 1 \times −1 = −1$, which is low motivation potential.

Assume that the worker does not have the tools and techniques for performing the job, then

$$E→P = 0, \quad P→O = 1, \quad \text{and } V = 1$$

Motivation = $−1 \times 1 \times 1 = −1$, which is low motivation potential.

Assume that the worker does not feel that higher performance results in higher pay, then

$$E→P = 1, \quad P→O = 0, \quad \text{and } V = 1$$

Motivation = $1 \times −1 \times 1 = −1$, which is low motivation potential.

Because performance can lead to multiple outcomes, each with different valences or values, each performance-to-outcome expectancy is multiplied by the corresponding valence. For example, consider a female construction worker who knows that if she produces she will receive pay, resulting in one positive performance-to-outcome expectancy. But this worker may also know that if she produces too much, she will be ostracized by her coworkers for being a "rate-buster"; this performance-to-outcome expectancy is much less positive, and probably approaches zero. These products are then summed before being multiplied by the effort-to-performance expectancy.

The Intrinsic–Extrinsic Motivation Formulation

A revised expectancy theory, which was developed in the late 1970s, incorporates the intrinsic and extrinsic outcomes of performing a task.[29] In this model, motivation is reduced if an individual does not value either intrinsic or extrinsic outcomes, or if the person perceives that either the intrinsic or extrinsic performance-to-outcome expectancies are low. For example, the construction worker's motivation will be reduced either if she does not like doing her tasks (intrinsic) or if she does not receive desired rewards (extrinsic) for performing them.

Managerial Application

Although evidence for the validity of the expectancy model is mixed,[30] managers can still use it to diagnose motivational problems or to evaluate effective motivation. (1) Does the individual perceive that effort will lead to performance? (2) Does the individual perceive that certain behaviors will lead to specified outcomes? (3) What values do individuals attach to these outcomes? Answers to these questions should help managers determine the level of an employee's work motivation, then identify any deficiencies in the job situation and prescribe remedies. The expectancy perspective implies the value of equity in the work situation, as well as the importance of consistent rewards; in fact, both equity theory and reinforcement theory have been viewed as special cases of expectancy theory.[31] It also addresses the issue of individual differences and offers the opportunity for quantification of the various facets of motivation. Hence, expectancy theory, more than any other presented so far, offers a comprehensive diagnostic tool.

GOAL-SETTING THEORY

Just as expectancy theory can serve as an integrative view of motivation, so can goal setting. Although extensive research has been conducted on the goal-setting process and its relationship to performance, in this section we highlight only a sample of the findings. *Goals,* which any member of an organization can set, describe a desired future state, such as reduced costs, lower absenteeism, higher employee satisfaction, or specified performance levels. Once established, they can focus behavior and motivate individuals to achieve the desired end state.

Goal Characteristics

Goals can vary in at least three ways: specificity, difficulty, and acceptance. The *specificity* or clarity of goals refers to the extent to which their accomplishment is observable and measurable. "Reducing absenteeism by 20 percent" is a highly specific goal for a manager; "developing subordinates" is a much less specific goal. Goal *difficulty,* or the level of performance desired, can also vary significantly. A salesperson might set a goal to open ten new accounts per month or a goal to open one hundred new accounts; the first goal might be easy, the second extremely difficult. Although goal-setting research originally called for setting moderately difficult goals, now empirical studies indicate that a linear relationship exists between goal difficulty and performance.[32] Empirical studies that combined the two characteristics of goal specificity and difficulty showed that better performance accompanied specific difficult goals than vague, nonquantitative ones.[33] Individuals' *acceptance* of stated goals, or their commitment to accomplishing the goals, may vary. In general, a subordinate is less likely to accept a goal as his or her own and try to accomplish it if a manager assigns the goal rather than *jointly* sets it with the subordinate.[34] Commitment is influenced not only by participation in goal setting, but also by the authority who sets the goals unilaterally or collaboratively, the existence of peer pressure to accomplish the goals, the values, incentives, and rewards associated with goal performance, the person's expectancy of success, and the existence of any self-administered rewards for goal accomplishment.[35] High expectancy (that effort will lead to performance) plus high self-efficacy, or an individual's judgment of his or her ability to accomplish a specified course of action, here a specific goal, also influence commitment, and ultimately performance.[36] Workers tend to increase their goals after success and reduce them after failure.[37] In addition, the analytical strategies used in performing tasks are a key link between goals and performance on complex tasks.[38]

Goal Setting and Performance

Early research indicated that goal-setting programs improve performance at both managerial and nonmanagerial levels over an extended period of time in a variety of organizations.[39] It also recognized the role of feedback as a necessary condition for goal setting; individuals required information about their effectiveness in meeting their goals as part of continuing to work toward them.[40]

More recent research has suggested that performance was a function of employees' ability, acceptance of goals, level of the goals, and the interaction of the goal with their ability.[41] Characteristics of the participants in goal setting, such as their authority or education, may have an impact on its effectiveness; for example, workers are more likely to accept goals from individuals with legitimate authority.[42] Acceptance of the goals also has consequences for how difficult the goals can be; workers are likely to perform a task if the goals are difficult *and* accepted, but not difficult and rejected.[43] When joined with attempts to raise expectancies that effort leads to performance, setting difficult goals can boost productivity.[44] But most research has looked at single goals.[45] Studies of setting multiple goals suggest that accomplishment of one results in some sacrifices of a second, reflecting the limited cognitive capacity of individuals.[46] In very complex jobs, however, goal setting may not be feasible because multiple goals may be necessary. Or goal setting may lead to bureaucratic behavior, where setting the goals becomes an end in itself. The effects of goal setting may also differ across cultures.[47]

Figure 4–8 offers a summary model of the factors that affect performance. Individuals set goals in response to work-related demands placed on them, and the goals in turn lead to performance. The strength of the relationship between goals and performance is affected by the worker's ability, commitment to the task, and receipt of feedback about performance, as well as the complexity of the task and other situational constraints. Further, performance increases when workers pay attention to a task, exert effort on it, and persist over time in doing it. In diagnosing a situation where employees lack motivation to perform the job correctly and effectively, we can analyze the goal-setting behavior in terms of the research just described. We can evaluate each of the factors shown in Figure 4–8 and offer ways of improving them. In particular, we can focus on goals and make three assessments. First, we ask whether the individual has goals. Second, we determine whether the individual accepts his or her goals; such acceptance depends on whether the individuals perceive the goals as reasonable, are themselves self-assured, and have previous successes in accomplishing goals. Third and finally, we must assess whether feedback has been provided en route to goal accomplishment.

Figure 4–8 Summary Model of Goal Setting

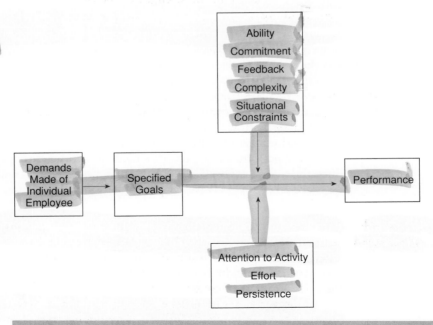

SOURCE: Based on E. A. Locke and G. P. Latham, *A Theory of Goal Setting and Task Performance* (Englewood Cliffs, N.J.: Prentice Hall, 1990).

MOTIVATING A MULTI-CULTURAL AND MULTI-NATIONAL WORK FORCE

Global managers must effectively motivate a diverse work force that has a wide range of needs, values, expectancies, and aspirations. Such managers must be sensitive to these variations and design reward systems that respond to cultural variations.

Cross-Cultural Needs Assessment

Significant cross-cultural differences can exist in predominant needs.[48] The ordering of needs may vary in different countries. For example, workers in countries characterized as high on uncertainty avoidance (for example, Japan) value security over self-actualization.[49] A study of Liberian managers showed that they valued self-esteem and security.[50] Different cultures may also place relatively more value on lower rather than higher needs, or vice versa. In France, belongingness heavily influences motivation, whereas in Holland fairness and in the United States recognition are most influential; U.S. managers were more individually (versus socially) motivated than their Dutch counterparts.[51] Not only must assessment of individual needs be an ongoing process, but strategies for meeting needs must also be tailored to individual countries.

Perceptions of Equity

Differences in individuals' views of equity in a situation may be a function of their cultural background. Although no body of research exists in this area, we know that the U.S. and Canadian cultures deemphasize power distance and emphasize individualism, whereas Oriental and South American countries accept that power is distributed unequally and take a more collectivist orientation.[52] We could predict that equity sensitivity would be greater among individuals from the United States and Canada where power and status differences are less tolerated than among individuals from China, Japan, or South America where power and status differences are more accepted. In addition, the strength of the overcompensation effect may vary in different cultures.

Effective Reinforcers and Rewards in a Global Environment

Different reinforcers may be useful in different cultures. Praise may be valued over pay increases; job flexibility and autonomy over job titles. What principles should guide the effective use of reinforcement theory? Managers can begin by determining the behaviors that are currently rewarded; they can administer a questionnaire to organizational members or interview them to obtain this information; they can review actual rewards given and their circumstances for the previous year or two. If the reward system is incongruent with the organization's goals, then management can change it. This approach eliminates the almost impossible task of selecting only employees whose goals and motives match top management's or training employees so they match.

Cross-Cultural Compensation

The growth of U.S. corporations abroad and of foreign-owned corporations in the United States has created challenges in designing effective and equitable multinational reward systems. Variations in the standard of living in different countries, the need to offer incentives to attract workers to certain locations throughout the world, and the desire to maintain a degree of consistency across work sites influence compensation and other, nonmonetary rewards offered. Selecting rewards that motivate employees in these situations and determining appropriate wages and benefits, as described in the next section, becomes a major challenge for executives of such organizations.

THE REWARD SYSTEM: APPLYING MOTIVATION THEORIES TO PRACTICE

An organization's reward system incorporates the motivational principles described so far into a formal mechanism for improving or reinforcing quality performance. It can also be used to support the organization's strategy.[53] A comprehensive reward system demands a complete analysis of the organizational members and their work situation before choosing and allocating rewards.[54] It should respond to the organization's environment, help accomplish the organization's goals, and relate to the organization's culture. An effective reward system must create a high quality of work life, encourage organizational effectiveness by rewarding better performance, and pay attention to the needs of individuals. It must also avoid creating ethical dilemmas for those individuals it affects.[55] Twelve typical errors in the design of reward systems are shown in Table 4–10. In this book we consider the reward system to include compensation, as well as nonpay components, such as promotions or praise.[56]

The Wage Issue

According to the motivation theories, pay acts as a powerful reward and can motivate workers to perform better.[57] It can meet diverse needs and reinforce desired behaviors. However, because of the complexity and difficulty of applying pay correctly, organizations frequently misuse it as a reward. They may, for example, give all employees the same pay increase, regardless of their performance. Organizations may not satisfy the needs they intend to meet with pay.

Many organizations use systematic wage and salary structures to ensure the equitable and effective distribution of pay. They assign each job to a wage category with an associated pay range; jobholders receive wages within that range. Pay increases also occur in a prescribed fashion as the employee's longevity of employment increases and performance improves.

Top management must decide whether it will assign pay on the basis of jobs held by the workers or the skills or competencies workers have.[58] Job-based pay rewards people for performing specific jobs and moving up the hierarchy, whereas skill-based programs reward people for building more competencies and increasing their skills. Job-based pay reinforces the link between an individual's job and organizational outcomes. It supports a culture that emphasizes bottom-line performance. Skill-based programs support a culture that reflects a concern for individual development and learning and an environment that requires greater flexibility from a relatively permanent work force.[59]

Table 4–10 Errors in Designing Reward Systems

1. Failing to consider the state of the industry.
2. Confusing productivity and quality measures with financial performance.
3. Locking the firm into a rigid sharing formula.
4. Making rewards contingent on a single performance measure.
5. Failing to include all employees in the reward opportunity.
6. Failing to obtain middle management commitment to the reward program.
7. Failing to build necessary management supervisory skills in allocating rewards.
8. Lacking organization input into the design of the reward system.
9. Failing to convince employees that the opportunity to earn rewards is real.
10. Lacking performance feedback.
11. Offering cash awards as the only option.
12. Failing to grant rewards on a timely basis.

SOURCE: Based on M. J. Cissell, Designing effective reward systems, *Compensation and Benefits Review,* November-December 1987.

Wage systems must also consider the market position of the pay offered. If, for example, Merck, Inc., pays on average higher wages than its competitors and learns that a major competitor pays on average lower wages, would Merck's management continue to offer high pay levels? Some companies prefer to take a leadership position in compensation; management of these organizations assumes that paying well will result in their attracting the best people. Others are willing to risk attracting somewhat less qualified workers by offering lower financial rewards. The market position chosen certainly influences the organization's ability to cope with its environment; when a tight labor market exists, organizations with an aggressive, "leader" strategy typically fare best in securing the workers they need. When, on the other hand, labor is very available, these compensation leaders may unnecessarily spend a premium.

Top management must also determine which organizational members will make pay decisions. Responsibility can be decentralized throughout the organization to supervisors or can be centralized and systematized in a corporate compensation system. Communication of compensation decisions varies from very secretive to very open. The processes chosen frequently complement the organization's structure and reinforce its culture.

Distributing Benefits

Although most organizations use benefits to supplement wages, their value in motivating workers is somewhat controversial.[60] They are intended to motivate employees, improve employee morale, reward loyalty, increase job satisfaction, attract good employees, reduce turnover, prevent unionization, enhance employee security, maintain a favorable competitive position, and enhance the organization's image among employees. While profit sharing and bonuses can be directly tied to performance, sick days and some health protectors are increasingly being viewed as essential and separate from the reward system.

In selecting benefits from the wide array, as shown in Table 4–11, managers

Table 4–11 **Examples of Benefits**

Health Protectors	Income Supplements
Medical insurance	Bonuses
Dental insurance	Profit-sharing plans
	Stock bonus plans
Income Protectors	Stock options
Accidental death insurance	
Disability insurance	Other Benefits
Life insurance	Business and professional memberships
Pension	Club memberships
Retirement benefits	Company automobile
Supplementary unemployment benefits	Credit union
Workers' compensation	Day care
	Education costs
Time off with Pay	Flexible work arrangements
Holidays	Recreational facilities
Personal days	Subsidized housing
Maternity or paternity leave	Subsidized meals
Sabbaticals	
Sick leave	
Vacations	

must assess how well each benefit responds to workers' needs and its cost-effectiveness. Some organizations offer *flexible benefits plans,* where workers are given a fixed amount of dollars or points to allocate to various health, pension, vacation, child care, or other benefits. Such a choice prevents the duplication of benefits and ensures that benefits better respond to worker needs. Or some employers create *flexible spending accounts,* which allow workers to pay for benefits with before-tax dollars, thereby creating tax benefits and reducing the "real" cost of the benefits.

Using Incentives

Incentive programs are formalized reward programs that pay an individual or group of individuals for what they produce. They incorporate the motivational principles described earlier in the section on reinforcement theory. If a worker packs shipping containers, then he or she receives a certain amount of money for each container filled; often, the more containers filled, the more pay the worker receives. Or a salesperson receives a fee for each container sold. Piecework systems, commission plans, and merit bonuses are the most common incentive systems; they directly link pay to performance.

Piecework systems tie compensation to individual performance by paying workers for each item produced. *Commissions* link pay to sales levels rather than production rates; individuals may receive a certain percentage of total sales or new sales, or they may receive compensation for reaching a sales quota. *Bonuses* are one-time, lump-sum payments that are tied to exceptional performance. Increasingly, organizations use these instead of merit increases because their cost in the long run is less. Merit increases reward past performance but become a cost of future performance regardless of its quality; a 6 percent merit increase changes the base pay rate and so applies for the rest of a worker's employment in an organization, even if subsequent performance does not merit such a pay level. *Gainsharing* programs, such as the Scanlon Plan, Improshare, or the Rucker Plan, allow workers to share in productivity improvements by earning bonuses based on group performance.[61] Workers typically get a portion of the financial gains on a formula basis. Such programs have been shown to result in increased coordination, teamwork, and knowledge sharing; better meeting of social needs; increased attention to cost savings; increased acceptance of change due to technology and new methodologies; more calls for more efficient management and planning; successful reduction of overtime; increased creativity and sharing of new ideas; and more flexible labor management relations.[62]

Incentives can reinforce organizational goals, and their use supports an emphasis on "bottom-line" performance. Although they can increase productivity and lower production costs, they can also adversely affect the quality of the product, cause workers to trade off long-term for short-term gains, and ignore the means by which individuals attain results.[63] Reading 4–1, "A Contingency Theory of Pay" by Edward J. Harrick, describes these programs in greater detail.

Employee Ownership

Perhaps the ultimate reward to workers is for them to own part of the organization, as described in the introductory scenario. Employee stock ownership and more direct ownership are two such options.[64] Worker-owned cooperatives, such as the Mondragon Cooperatives in Spain, have served as a model for employee ownership of companies in the United States and abroad.[65] In these organizations workers sit on the corporate board and top management teams and thus can exert control over the organization's direction and operation. While these efforts were initially not well received in the United States, recent opportunities for employee ownership have increased.

Worker representation on boards of directors has been viewed as a lesser form of worker ownership. Known as *codetermination,* this structure also gives workers a direct voice in the operation of their companies. Other worker participation ideas, such as work councils, have been incorporated into quality of working life programs, as described in Chapter 13.

Criteria of an Effective Reward System

An effective reward system ties rewards to performance. Individuals who work harder, produce more, or produce better quality outputs should receive more rewards than poorer performers. Reward systems should also offer a sufficient number and diversity of rewards. Some organizations lack the resources to offer sufficient extrinsic rewards to employees to motivate them to perform or to encourage their satisfaction; in these cases, organizations must consider job enrichment or quality of working life programs (see Chapter 13) as ways of increasing intrinsic rewards instead. Note, however, that international cultures differ significantly in terms of wages and other forms of compensation, and in terms of the ratios between the two, complicating the issue of rewards for multinational organizations.[66]

The criteria for the allocation of rewards must be clear and complete. Individual organizational members should know whether they receive rewards for level or quality of performance, attendance, innovativeness, or effort, for example. The criteria for receipt of specific wages, benefits, or incentives must be clearly defined. In addition, different individuals should be treated differently when appropriate. Workers who perform at different levels or who have different needs often should not receive the same rewards. At the same time, management must ensure that workers perceive that an equitable distribution of rewards occurs. Finally, organizational rewards should compare favorably with rewards in similar organizations. For organizations to attract and retain qualified and competent employees they must offer rewards comparable to their competitors.

SUMMARY

Merck, Inc., has given its employees the opportunity to own stock in the company. Such ownership should increase the motivation of workers to perform effectively and efficiently. We have examined this situation by applying diverse motivation theories to help us understand the events.

Using needs theories, such as Maslow's, Alderfer's, McClelland's, and Herzberg's, we hypothesized how this program might meet the needs of various employees. Next, we considered the ways in which equity theory provided insights into the situation. Reinforcement theory focused our attention on the feedback Bob Huxford and other employees receive about their performance. To encourage the type of performance that will help accomplish organizational goals, they must receive valued reinforcers when they behave in appropriate ways. We also used expectancy theory to diagnose the situation at Merck and suggested that employees must perceive expectancies, instrumentalities, valences of ownership, and other rewards to be high. Finally, we examined the role of goal setting as a technique that assists workers in meeting their needs, encouraging equity in the workplace, reinforcing desired behaviors, and ensuring that expectancy, instrumentality, and valence are positive.

In the rest of the chapter we considered the nature of reward systems in organizations. We considered the use of wages, benefits, and incentives in an organization. We concluded by identifying the principles that describe an effective and motivating reward system. The questions in Table 4–12 help diagnose the effectiveness of the reward system, as well as the degree of motivation in an organizational situation.

Table 4–12 Diagnostic Questions to Assess Motivation and Quality of the Reward System

- Do rewards satisfy individuals' needs?
- Are rewards applied equitably and consistently after desired behaviors?
- Do individuals value the rewards they receive?
- Are rewards consistently applied in proportion to performance?
- Do individuals perceive that their efforts correlate with performance?
- Do individuals set goals that are specific and moderately difficult, yet accepted?
- Do individuals receive feedback about their goal accomplishment as part of the organization's reward system?
- What type of reward system exists?
- Does it encourage desired outcomes such as innovation, productivity, or attendance?
- Are benefits and incentive systems effective in motivating desired outcomes?

Reading 4–1

A Contingency Theory of Pay
Edward J. Harrick

Historically, organizations have made efforts to design fair and equitable compensation systems relative to the importance of work performed by their employees. The inherent logic of such designs is difficult to dispute. Yet, many designers of pay systems are moving away from these traditional systems and introducing alternative pay systems that make an effort to link pay with performance.

The design of traditional systems has often started with a philosophical orientation toward pay. This orientation may reflect a desire to lead the market, pay at the market, or lag the market. Several variables affect the philosophical orientation, including the following:

- Ability to pay;
- Competition;
- Supply and demand;
- Technology;
- Willingness to assume risk;
- Attitudes and beliefs about human resources;
- Willingness to invest in the development of employees; and
- Attitude toward profit and risk by board of directors.

The design of sound pay structures should reflect the organization's mission, purpose, long-range goals, and short-run objectives. Further, traditional compensation programs have built pay and benefits systems to support the desires and values of owners and stockholders. Because alternative pay systems provide incremental pay to workers who achieve organizational goals, these systems are valued by owners, stockholders, and employees.

Traditional pay systems include the use of job evaluation techniques to ascertain the relative importance of tasks. Job evaluation leads to the establishment of internal pay equity in an organization. Many organizations also take ex-

ternal equity into consideration, often using salary surveys. In fact, some organizations have chosen to disregard internal equity and build their pay structures around external market conditions. Such an orientation may create a competitive pay structure relative to the labor market, but often disregards inequities in the compensation of individual job incumbents.

Traditional salary structures, for purposes of this article, also provide for salary increases based on cost-of-living indexes or across-the-board salary adjustments based on an organization's ability to pay.

ALTERNATIVE PAY SYSTEMS

Because there is a recognition of the need for improved cost effectiveness and productivity enhancement in the United States, alternative pay systems are becoming more common. Although alternative pay systems have been available for many years, systematic attention has not been directed to the identification of a theory or an integrated model for the application of these systems in practice. As a result, compensation systems are adopted that are unsuitable for the particular circumstances under which an organization is operating, and thus desired goals of motivating employees and improving productivity are not achieved.

Pay strategies should match the situation in which the firm is functioning. This contingency theory of pay, first suggested in an article titled "Strategic Pay Planning" by Bruce Ellig,[1] will provide the conceptual framework for the following discussion.

Pay strategies may be contingent on a number of variables, such as organization life cycle stages, degrees of risk the organization faces at a point in time, and the degrees of cooperation desired among people or units. However, before examining how these factors affect the choice of pay system, we should examine the forms of compensation available to meet these contingencies.

Profit Sharing

Profit-sharing programs, designed to reward performance based on the profitability of the organization, are intended to permit employees to identify more closely with the goals of the organization. As stakeholders, workers are more apt to behave in ways that are in concert with company goals.

Although profit sharing may involve extremely short-term (quarterly) or long-range (tied to a pension program) payouts, these aspects may be combined in programs that provide an initial payout of profits and defer a portion. The value of profit-sharing plans as an incentive is directly related to the extent to which employees view their work behaviors as producing profits. Employee attitudes toward profit sharing will most likely be affected by variables such as the timing of the payout, the age of the employees, the magnitude of the payout, the need for disposable income among employees, and the perceived value of a retirement program by those participating in a deferred-compensation scheme.

Profit-sharing plans may encourage cost-containment efforts and attention to productivity among employees. From the organization's perspective, profit-sharing plans permit compensation to be distributed when the firm is best able to afford payment, when profits exist.

Generally, deferred profit-sharing plans are designed as retirement programs and cover all employees. When this is the case, these programs must comply with the Employee Retirement Income Security Act (ERISA) and are subject to changing tax regulations. Many small firms have found that profit-sharing plans meet their pension needs. Deferred profit-sharing programs also encourage long-term cooperation and commitment.

Profit-sharing plans designed to pay quarterly or annually are most effective when employees can see that their behaviors have an impact on profits. Such programs contain many of the same features as gainsharing. Although in some ways similar to gainsharing (described below), profit sharing, as discussed, may offer deferred-compensation features and distribute a percentage of profits, while gainsharing is based on meeting a goal.

Gainsharing

Gainsharing plans provide for rewards based on whether performance reaches predetermined standards. They are among the oldest known forms of compensation. These programs tie incentives to factors that individuals or groups can control. Most gainsharing plans provide for payment to a work group rather than individual employees.

Trust within the organization is a key variable in the success of gainsharing. Because standards are used to measure performance, cost-accounting methods and techniques must be in place if the program is to function properly.

Further, the organization should have sufficient historical data to permit the establishment of standards. Gainsharing programs seem to work best when the external environment is not subject to unpredictable fluctuations due to seasonal changes, competitive environments, or regulatory climates. Gainsharing plans also seem to be most effective when the workforce is technically competent and interested in employee involvement schemes.[2]

Although Scanlon plans are perhaps the best known gainsharing programs, Rucker and Improshare plans are also available.

Scanlon Plan. A Scanlon plan establishes a ratio of total labor costs divided by sales value of production. A bonus is provided to participants based on reductions in costs below the ratio. Bonus pay is normally distributed monthly. Governance committees, made up of worker representatives and management, oversee the operations of the program. The ultimate success of Scanlon plans frequently rests with these committees.

Rucker Plan. These plans provide a norm or base to measure productivity. This measurement is the output of value added for each dollar of payroll costs. Employee contributions to savings are allocated to a bonus pool with a substantial portion of that pool paid to employees on a monthly basis. A reserve pool, established to account for unforeseen events, is distributed to employees at the end of the accounting period. This incentive program is similar to the Scanlon plan. It has been most successful in organizations with 50 to 800 employees and in which labor and management trust each other.

Improshare Plan. IMproved PROductivity through SHARing (Improshare) plans use industrial-engineering-based productivity measures derived from historical production records. Hourly and salaried employees share productivity gains. Most frequently, the organization retains half the productivity gains and the employees share the remainder. Standards are adjusted for new equipment or technology.[3]

Each of these plans involves the distribution of funds generated by productivity improvements. The method used to calculate the standard, how the standard may be changed, how much of the improvement is shared, and trust in the program administration are important features of all gainsharing plans.

Bonus

Bonus programs provide for cash awards to individuals based on performance over a specific time period. Increasingly, bonuses are being substituted for regular increases in base pay. When this is the case, the future pay of workers is at risk and is variable rather than fixed. Usually individuals, not groups, are eligible for bonuses. Variable compensation programs are advantageous to organizations operating in an environment of high uncertainty because they place individual pay at risk and allow organizations greater financial flexibility. For example, when AT&T was deregulated, it implemented an elaborate bonus program tied to the performance of individual managers. Depending on the manager's level in the organization, from 5% to 20% of his or her pay was placed at risk. The AT&T program provided for both a lump-sum bonus to outstanding performers and a team incentive award.

Bonus programs are attractive when participating employees can control the important variables affecting their performance. In addition, the connection between individual effort, performance, and reward must be clear. These programs seem to have great appeal to managers when clear, unambiguous standards can be established; when individual performance can be measured; and when the individual has control over the critical elements of performance attainment.

Merit Pay

Merit pay programs, which have long been the major form of pay-for-performance used by most organizations, tie future base wage increases to periodic performance evaluations. The major difference between merit pay and the bonus system is that merit pay plans provide for an increase in regular base salary, while bonus systems provide a lump-sum payment at one point in time. Merit pay programs have been in existence for some time and are attractive to employees because they place less of base pay at risk. They are popular in large organizations when environments are stable and certain. The pros and cons of merit pay plans have been widely discussed. Merit pay systems are effective in cases where it is possible to establish performance standards and accurate appraisal systems. In addition, such systems work well when it is possible to closely link rewards with performance and supervisors can be taught to do appraisals and give feedback. Merit pay is useful in situations where increases vary widely.

Merit pay programs do not work well in unionized environments where increases are set by contract or when supervisors are poorly equipped or reluctant to give appraisals. They are also ineffective if the rewards are tenuous from the employee's point of view; a merit increase may seem too small to justify additional effort. They may be unattractive to employers because the increase becomes a permanent part of base pay.

CONTINGENCY THEORY AND PAY

Pay strategies should be designed to accommodate situational variables within the organization's environment. The choice of these strategies is therefore affected by three important internal considerations: (1) the life cycle stage of the organization, (2) the degree of risk assumed by the organization, and (3) the degree of cooperation desired among individuals or units within the organization. Additionally, the specific pay strategies employed are affected by such external factors as competition, labor supply and demand, ability to pay, and assumptions made about human resources.

Organizational Life Cycle

Traditionally, organizations are assumed to go through a four-stage life cycle:

1. Development or formation;
2. Growth;
3. Stability or maturity; and
4. Decline.

Although most organizations follow this cycle, the duration of each phase varies. (Recently attention has also been given to a so-called renewal phase that can provide the impetus to shift the organization to earlier stages of the life cycle model.)

Phase 1: Development or Formation. During the development phase, as the organization is beginning to establish a market and invest capital in plant, equipment, and people, the need to preserve capital is critical. This phase of the life cycle is best served by pay strategies that motivate individual behavior and encourage creativity but preserve necessary funds for capital reinvestment. Consequently, deferred-compensation programs and bonuses would seem to be most effective at this stage.

An organization faces the critical issue of survival during this stage of its life. Strategies that "buy" commitment from employees through attractive growth opportunities such as profit sharing have great appeal. Likewise, bonuses that are largely based on individual contributions but do not increase fixed costs to the organization are attractive. Gainsharing programs are less likely to be successfully introduced because they rely on historical data in the development of fair and equitable standards. Thus, gainsharing may not be as effective as profit-sharing or bonus systems.

Merit pay systems can be, and frequently are, used during this period, although they are not a good choice for organizations in the development phase. Of concern to organizational policy makers is the impact of higher fixed costs that result from merit pay strategies. Instead, bonuses or one-time financial incentives are the best choices for non-deferred compensation because they will not increase base pay and will provide greater financial flexibility during this crucial stage of the organization's life cycle.

Phase 2: Growth. The second phase of the life cycle is characterized by additional capital formation, the infusion of new employees, the utilization of new technologies, and the establishment of a market. The pay strategies that are most appropriate for the growth phase are gainsharing and merit pay because they reinforce behavior that sustains growth and provide that reinforcement more immediately than other systems.

Gainsharing establishes standards of performance (these may be cost reduction, revenue enhancement, or productivity improvement) and rewards the individual or group behavior needed during this period of rapid expansion. Similarly, performance appraisal systems, utilizing sound standards and equitably administered, may achieve similar results. It is generally thought that gainsharing is more appropriate in situations that necessitate a high degree of cooperation and teamwork among individuals and units. However, when work is more a matter of individual responsibility, the preferable strategy is merit pay. It is best to make employees aware that performance is being rewarded.

Bonus and profit-sharing systems are of less value during the growth phase. Profit-sharing programs that provide for quarterly or annual payout are preferable to deferred compensation because the former provide more immediate reinforcement.

During a period of rapid growth, an organization may begin to pay more attention to internal pay equity. However, the least desirable pay strategy during this phase is across-the-board increases to all organizational members. Performance-based differentials in pay increases will reinforce high growth.

Phase 3: Stability or Maturity. The third phase in an organization's life cycle is stability or maturity. Pay strategies should encourage behavior that benefits the organization in the short run during this phase. Efforts should be directed to the retention of competitiveness, market share, and productivity.

At this phase, the intent of any pay strategy is to maintain the organization's status quo relative to the competition. Gainsharing and merit pay systems, designed to encourage specific, short-term results, are the preferred strategies. Because growth is limited during this period, profit-sharing and across-the-board pay structures are of intermediate importance. Particularly if organization members are aware of the limited opportunity for growth, profit-sharing programs should be designed for short-term payouts rather than deferred compensation. If the environment of the organization is somewhat stable and competitive pressures are not acute, this is one of the few times that across-the-board increases for all organization members are attractive. This phase is relatively predictable. Consequently, cost-of-living adjustments can be made with a high degree of certainty that they will not endanger the financial future of the organization. Bonus programs are least desirable during the period of stability because there is a lower probability of bonus funds being generated.

Phase 4: Decline. The fourth stage of the life cycle is the period of decline. Bonus and gainsharing programs are most appropriate during this phase because pay strategies should be oriented toward the short term. Frequently, during this phase an organization's objectives are cost-reduction strategies. Consequently, bonus and gainsharing strategies are useful because they distribute payouts based on results achieved by organization members in terms of profitability, productivity, or revenue.

Merit pay systems are of moderate importance during the decline phase. However, because merit pay provides the opportunity for differential rewards based on performance, it does have some appeal. Profit sharing and across-the-board increases would be the least desirable pay strategies. Profits may be limited in a decline and therefore profit sharing would have little appeal as a motivational technique to increase individual performance. Across-the-board increases would be unattractive because they increase fixed costs at a time when the organization should not sustain cost increases.

Risk and Cooperation

Two other internal variables affect the design of compensation strategies: risk and cooperation. When organizations assume a high degree of risk, the appropriate compensation strategies are those that tie pay swiftly and significantly to the behavior desired. Bonus and merit pay systems seem most appropriate under these conditions. Profit-sharing programs with short-term payout features are also highly effective. Long-term strategies, such as profit sharing, are equally effective. When the organization is risk averse and its environment is predictable and stable, merit pay and gainsharing systems are attractive options because these programs can motivate individuals or groups toward behavior suitable to predictable and desired organizational outcomes.

The last internal variable in the contingency model is the degree of cooperation desired among organization members. Profit-sharing and gainsharing programs encourage teamwork and cooperation because incentives are determined by group performance. At the opposite end, individual bonus programs are the least desirable when cooperation is a goal.

External Considerations

There are many other factors that affect how organizations pay employees. Although it is less likely that these variables will determine the selection of the specific pay strategies discussed above, the issues are important for setting pay levels and in compensation administration. Demand and supply of labor, competitive pay practices, trends in the industry, tax legislation, and the corporation's philosophy about human resources are but a few of these important variables.

NOTES

1. Bruce R. Ellig, "Strategic Pay Planning," *Compensation/ Benefit Review,* July/August 1987, pp. 28–43.
2. Edward E. Lawler, *Pay and Organization Development* (Reading, Mass.: Addison-Wesley Publishing, 1981), p. 144.
3. Richard Henderson, *Compensation Management* (Englewood Cliffs, New Jersey: Prentice-Hall, Inc. 1989).

DISCUSSION QUESTIONS

1. What alternative pay systems are available to organizations?
2. What are the implications for motivation of these alternative pay systems?
3. How should pay relate to an organization's life cycle?

Activity 4–1

Expectancy Questionnaire

Step 1: Answer Questions 1, 2, and 3 by circling the answer that best describes your feelings.

Question 1: Here are some things that could happen to people if they do their jobs *especially well*. How likely is it that each of these things would happen if you performed your job *especially well*? (You may use your job as student.)

	Not at All Likely		Somewhat Likely		Quite Likely		Extremely Likely
a. You will get a bonus or pay increase	(1)	(2)	(3)	(4)	(5)	(6)	(7)
b. You will feel better about yourself as a person	(1)	(2)	(3)	(4)	(5)	(6)	(7)
c. You will have an opportunity to develop your skills and abilities	(1)	(2)	(3)	(4)	(5)	(6)	(7)
d. You will have better job security	(1)	(2)	(3)	(4)	(5)	(6)	(7)
e. You will be given chances to learn new things	(1)	(2)	(3)	(4)	(5)	(6)	(7)
f. You will be promoted or get a better job	(1)	(2)	(3)	(4)	(5)	(6)	(7)
g. You will get a feeling that you've accomplished something worthwhile	(1)	(2)	(3)	(4)	(5)	(6)	(7)
h. You will have more freedom on your job	(1)	(2)	(3)	(4)	(5)	(6)	(7)
i. You will be respected by the people you work with	(1)	(2)	(3)	(4)	(5)	(6)	(7)
j. Your supervisor will praise you	(1)	(2)	(3)	(4)	(5)	(6)	(7)
k. The people you work with will be friendly with you	(1)	(2)	(3)	(4)	(5)	(6)	(7)

Question 2: Different people want different things from their work. Here is a list of things a person could have on his or her job. How *important* is each of the following to you? (You may use your job as student.)

	Moderately Important or Less		Quite Important		Extremely Important		

How important is . . . ?

a.	The amount of pay you get	(1)	(2)	(3)	(4)	(5)	(6)	(7)
b.	The chances you have to do something that makes you feel good about yourself as a person	(1)	(2)	(3)	(4)	(5)	(6)	(7)
c.	The opportunity to develop your skills and abilities	(1)	(2)	(3)	(4)	(5)	(6)	(7)
d.	The amount of job security you have	(1)	(2)	(3)	(4)	(5)	(6)	(7)

How important is . . . ?

e.	The chances you have to learn new things	(1)	(2)	(3)	(4)	(5)	(6)	(7)
f.	Your chances for getting a promotion or getting a better job	(1)	(2)	(3)	(4)	(5)	(6)	(7)
g.	The chances you have to accomplish something worthwhile	(1)	(2)	(3)	(4)	(5)	(6)	(7)
h.	The amount of freedom you have on your job	(1)	(2)	(3)	(4)	(5)	(6)	(7)

How important is . . . ?

i.	The respect you receive from the people you work with	(1)	(2)	(3)	(4)	(5)	(6)	(7)
j.	The praise you get from your supervisor	(1)	(2)	(3)	(4)	(5)	(6)	(7)
k.	The friendliness of the people you work with	(1)	(2)	(3)	(4)	(5)	(6)	(7)

Question 3: Below you will see a number of pairs of factors that look like this:

Warm weather → sweating (1) (2) (3) (4) (5) (6) (7)

You are to indicate by circling the appropriate number to the right of each pair how often it is true for you personally that the first factor leads to the second on your job (or your job as student). Remember, for each pair, indicate how often it is true by circling the number under the response that seems most accurate.

	Never		Sometimes		Often		Almost Always

a.	Working hard → high productivity	(1)	(2)	(3)	(4)	(5)	(6)	(7)
b.	Working hard → doing my job well	(1)	(2)	(3)	(4)	(5)	(6)	(7)
c.	Working hard → good job performance	(1)	(2)	(3)	(4)	(5)	(6)	(7)

Step 2: Using the questionnaire results.

The results from this questionnaire can be used to calculate a work-motivation score. A score can be calculated for each individual, and scores can be combined for groups of individuals. The procedure for obtaining a work-motivation score is as follows:

a. For each of the possible positive outcomes listed in questions 1 and 2, multiply the score for the outcome on question 1 (P → O expectancies) by the corresponding score on question 2 (valences of outcomes). Thus, score 1a would be multiplied by score 2a, score 1b by score 2b, and so forth.

b. All of the 1-times-2 products would be added together to get a total of all expectancies-times-valences.

c. The total should be divided by the number of pairs (in this case, eleven) to get an average expectancy-times-valence score.

d. The scores from question 3 (E → P expectancies) should be added together and then divided by three to get an average effort-to-performance expectancy score.

e. Multiply the score obtained in step c (the average expectancy-times-valence) by the score obtained in step d (the average E → P expectancy score) to obtain a total work-motivation score.

Step 3: Discussion. Answer the following questions in small groups or with the entire class:

Description

1. What score did you receive? Compare it with the scores of other class members.

Diagnosis

2. How motivating is your job?
3. What factors influence your score?
4. How does the content of your job relate to your score?
5. Can you explain the score using expectancy theory?
6. Can you explain the motivation potential of your job using
   a. reinforcement theory?
   b. equity theory?
   c. needs theories?

Prescription

7. How would you improve the motivating potential of your job?

Reprinted by permission from D. A. Nadler and E. E. Lawler III, Motivation: A diagnostic approach. In *Perspectives on Behavior in Organizations*, ed. J. R. Hackman, E. E. Lawler, III, and L. W. Porter. New York: McGraw-Hill, 1977.

Activity 4–2

Goal-Setting Exercise

Step 1: Think about a job you now hold or a job you have held in the past. If you have never been employed think about an "ideal" middle-management job.

Step 2: Answer the following questions about that job:

1. How effective were (are) the methods used by your manager in generating maximum employee work performance? (Circle one)
   A. Highly effective
   B. Moderately effective
   C. Ineffective
2. How satisfied were (are) you with this job?
   A. Highly satisfied

   B. Moderately satisfied
   C. Unsatisfied

Step 3: Complete the job objectives questionnaire.

As employees, each of us has certain objectives that are part of our work. Sometimes, these objectives are spelled out in detail; other times, the objectives are simply intuitively "understood." The following statements refer to your job, and to the objectives that are associated with your job. Read each statement, then circle the number indicating *how untrue* or *how true* you believe each statement to be. (If you prefer, you can think about a job you've had with some organization in the past.)

	Definitely Not True	Not True	Slightly Not True	Uncertain	Slightly True	True	Definitely True
1. Management encourages employees to define job objectives.	−3	−2	−1	0	1	2	3
2. If I achieve my objectives, I receive adequate recognition from my supervisor.	−3	−2	−1	0	1	2	3
3. My objectives are clearly stated with respect to the results expected.	−3	−2	−1	0	1	2	3
4. I have the support I need to accomplish my objectives.	−3	−2	−1	0	1	2	3
5. Achieving my objectives increases my chances for promotion.	−3	−2	−1	0	1	2	3
6. My supervisor dictates my job objectives to me.	−3	−2	−1	0	1	2	3
7. I need more feedback on whether I'm achieving my objectives or not.	−3	−2	−1	0	1	2	3
8. My supervisor will "get on my back" if I fail to achieve my objectives.	−3	−2	−1	0	1	2	3
9. My job objectives are very challenging.	−3	−2	−1	0	1	2	3
10. Management wants to know whether I set objectives for my job or not.	−3	−2	−1	0	1	2	3
11. My supervisor will compliment me if I achieve my job objectives.	−3	−2	−1	0	1	2	3
12. My objectives are very ambiguous and unclear.	−3	−2	−1	0	1	2	3
13. I lack the authority to accomplish my objectives.	−3	−2	−1	0	1	2	3
14. Achievement of objectives is rewarded with higher pay here.	−3	−2	−1	0	1	2	3
15. My supervisor encourages me to establish my own objectives.	−3	−2	−1	0	1	2	3
16. I always have knowledge of my progress toward my objectives.	−3	−2	−1	0	1	2	3
17. My supervisor will reprimand me if I'm not making progress toward my objectives.	−3	−2	−1	0	1	2	3
18. My objectives seldom require my full interest and effort.	−3	−2	−1	0	1	2	3
19. Management makes it clear that defining job objectives is favorably regarded.	−3	−2	−1	0	1	2	3
20. My supervisor gives me more recognition when I achieve my objectives.	−3	−2	−1	0	1	2	3
21. My objectives are very concrete.	−3	−2	−1	0	1	2	3
22. I have sufficient resources to achieve my objectives.	−3	−2	−1	0	1	2	3
23. My pay is more likely to be increased if I achieve my objectives.	−3	−2	−1	0	1	2	3
24. My supervisor has more influence than I do in setting my objectives.	−3	−2	−1	0	1	2	3
25. I wish I had better knowledge of whether I'm achieving my objectives.	−3	−2	−1	0	1	2	3
26. If I fail to meet my objectives, my supervisor will reprimand me.	−3	−2	−1	0	1	2	3
27. Attaining my objectives requires all my skill and know-how.	−3	−2	−1	0	1	2	3

Step 4: For each of the nine "scales" (A through I), compute a total score by summing the answers to the appropriate questions. Be sure to subtract "minus" scores.

Question Number	Question Number	Question Number	Question Number
1. + ( )	3. + ( )	6. + ( )	4. + ( )
10. + ( )	12. + ( )	15. + ( )	13. + ( )
19. + ( )	21. + ( )	24. + ( )	22. + ( )
Total Score	Total Score	Total Score	Total Score
A	B	C	D

Question Number	Question Number	Question Number	Question Number	Question Number
7. + ( )	9. + ( )	5. + ( )	2. + ( )	8. + ( )
16. + ( )	18. + ( )	14. + ( )	11. + ( )	17. + ( )
25. + ( )	27. + ( )	23. + ( )	20. + ( )	26. + ( )
Total Score	Total Score	Total Score	Total Score	Total Score
E	F	G	H	I

Step 5: Next, on the following graphs, write in a large "X" to indicate the total score for each scale.

	-9	-7	-5	-3	-1	1	3	5	7	9
A	-9	-7	-5	-3	-1	1	3	5	7	9
B	-9	-7	-5	-3	-1	1	3	5	7	9
C	-9	-7	-5	-3	-1	1	3	5	7	9
D	-9	-7	-5	-3	-1	1	3	5	7	9
E	-9	-7	-5	-3	-1	1	3	5	7	9
F	-9	-7	-5	-3	-1	1	3	5	7	9
G	-9	-7	-5	-3	-1	1	3	5	7	9
H	-9	-7	-5	-3	-1	1	3	5	7	9
I	-9	-7	-5	-3	-1	1	3	5	7	9

Step 6: In small groups answer the following:

1. What common patterns exist in your questionnaire responses and graph?
2. Do the patterns that are highly effective, moderately effective, and ineffective differ? In what ways?
3. Do the patterns differ for jobs that are highly satisfying, moderately satisfying, and unsatisfying?

Step 7: Discussion. In small groups, with the entire class, or in written form, as directed by your instructor, answer the following:

1. What characteristics of goals and goal setting contribute to effective organizational behavior and satisfying organizational experiences?
2. What characteristics contribute to ineffective behavior and unsatisfying experiences?

Based on Peter Lorenzi, Henry P. Sims, Jr., and E. Allen Slusher, Goal setting, performance and satisfaction: A behavioral demonstration. *Exchange: The Organizational Behavior Teaching Journal* 7 (1982): 38–42.

Activity 4–3   Feeling Stuck at Hyatt? Create a New Business

Step 1:   Read the Feeling Stuck at Hyatt case.

John Allegretti remembers the day last year when he decided to quit. After two years as a switchboard operator and an assistant housekeeping manager at the Hyatt Regency Chicago, Allegretti was chafing at the long grind required to become a hotel manager. "I hated the repetition of my day," he recalls, "and realized that the hotel business just wasn't for me." Instead, the 23-year-old yearned for a more challenging job that also would help the environment. So after months of resumé-writing and interviewing at waste-recycling companies, Allegretti finally landed the job of his dreams—right back at Hyatt.

Anxious to retain Allegretti, Vice-President Don DePorter asked him to head a project to reduce waste at his 2,000-room hotel. Allegretti did so well that Hyatt let him develop and run a new waste-consulting company called International ReCycleCo Inc. Besides several large Hyatts, ReCycleCo now has 24 clients in 8 states. "I've seen John working at 10 A.M. and later that same night at 2 A.M. because he's hyped about it," says DePorter.

LONG HITCH

Figuring out ways to keep employees hyped has become a way of life at Chicago-based Hyatt Hotels Corp., the flagship of the Pritzker family empire. Motivation was less of a problem in the 1960s, when it took as little as three years to become a hotel manager at the fast-growing company. Now, aspiring hoteliers must wait eight years or longer to run even a small hotel.

To keep staffers energized and ideas flowing, the $2.2 billion lodging giant uses everything from monthly worker rap sessions at its hotels to anonymous employee critiques of bosses. As a result, Hyatt is bombarded with staff suggestions to improve hotel service. And a full 60% of its 5,000 managers have been with Hyatt since starting as trainees. That's no mean feat in the nomadic hotel business.

Now, Hyatt is taking its motivation efforts one step further: It's helping employees with novel ideas outside the company's core business to set up freestanding companies. In the past three years, employee suggestions have prompted Hyatt to spin off a half-dozen ventures in such things as party catering, retirement apartment complexes, and sporting-equipment rental shops. And, like Allegretti, the people who help develop the ideas are usually allowed to run the new ventures. They receive startup capital—but they don't get an equity stake. Hyatt sets up the ventures as separate companies largely to let its lean corporate staff concentrate on hotels.

The startups allow Hyatt and its managers to build on some expertise or insight they've acquired in the course of running the hotel business. James E. Jones was director of sales development for Hyatt Hotels when he noticed that professional party planners were getting hefty fees for some of the same services Hyatt could provide, such as catering and entertainment. And thanks to his work at the hotels, Jones had wide contacts in professional sports, a big source of business for event planners. "I was ready to go out on my own with the idea if it wasn't accepted, because I knew it would work," he recalls.

After ordering up a business plan and holding a quick consultation with the Pritzkers, Hyatt Hotels Corp. President Darryl Hartley-Leonard last spring gave Jones $780,000 to see if his dream could be turned into a real business. Eight months later, Jones runs events planner Regency Productions by Hyatt. Regency has already won a contract from the National Football League to manage the corporate hospitality tents at next month's Super Bowl, as well as a contract to handle catering for the 1991 U.S. Open golf tournament. "It's the most challenging time of my life," says Jones, "but it's also the most rewarding, exciting, and phenomenal growth period of my life."

Still, the process can be difficult to manage—particularly for Hyatt's senior executives, who are frequently bombarded with ideas from employees who lack financial or technical skills. Jones, for example, had never drawn up a business plan. Hartley-Leonard found his proposal particularly thin on contingency planning if the venture didn't meet its initial revenue projections. "But you could see his thinker was thinking," the Hyatt president recalls. So rather than pan the idea as naive, he simply sent an excited Jones back to the drawing board to prepare some operating alternatives.

REINED IN

Giving managers plenty of freedom to try out their own ideas can sometimes backfire. Take the general manager of one suburban Chicago Hyatt several years ago who added a club and disco—and named it after himself. Unfortunately, the manager never mentioned his plan to headquarters, which was embarrassed to learn months later about a new disco in its own backyard. Hyatt left the disco and manager in place, though. "If you fire somebody who does that, then nobody else would ever try anything they believed in again," says Hartley-Leonard.

Thomas J. Pritzker agrees. Says the 40-year-old scion who serves as president of Hyatt Corp.: "It's always better have a racehorse you have to rein in than a donkey that you have to whip." As any good jockey knows, the best horses set their own pace.

Step 2: Prepare the case for class discussion.

Step 3: Individually, in small groups, or with the entire class, as directed by your instructor, answer the following questions:

Description
1. Describe the situation at Hyatt.
2. Why did John Allegretti quit?
3. How did Hyatt respond to Allegretti's resignation?

Diagnosis
4. What problems existed at Hyatt?

5. How do (a) needs, (b) equity, (c) reinforcement, (d) expectancy, and (e) goal-setting theories explain the situation?

Prescription
6. What solution did Hyatt offer Allegretti?
7. Why was it effective?

Step 4: Discussion. In small groups, with the entire class, or in written form, share your answers to the questions above. Then answer the following questions:

1. What symptoms suggested that a problem existed?
2. What problems existed in the case?
3. What theories and concepts help explain the problems?
4. How were the problems corrected?
5. Were the actions effective?

J. E. Ellis, Feeling stuck at Hyatt? Create a new business. *Business Week,* December 10, 1990. Reprinted by special permission, copyright © 1990 by McGraw-Hill, Inc.

Activity 4–4

Motivating Diversity in Middle and Top Management

Step 1: Consider the following situation:

You have recently become the chief operating officer of a large high-technology company that specializes in telecommunications. You are very committed to increasing the diversity of your work force, but know that you must develop a master plan to help motivate other managers in the company to support this goal. To date, your organization has included primarily white males born in the United States. The previous COO was reluctant to promote women and minorities into top management because he felt that they would have difficulty fitting into the executive ranks. As a result, there are currently very few women and minorities who hold top-management positions, and about 20 percent who hold middle-management positions. The lower ranks of the organization have a significant number of women

and minorities who have entered the organization in recent years.

Step 2: Individually or in small groups, incorporating your knowledge of motivation theories, design a motivational plan for reaching this goal.

Step 3: Discussion. In small groups or with the entire class, share the plans you developed. Then answer the following questions:

1. What motivation theories have you incorporated into your plans?
2. How do your plans reflect elements of an effective reward system:
3. How effective do you expect these plans to be? Why?

Activity 4–5   Educational Toys, Inc.

Step 1: Read the following description of Educational Toys, Inc.:

Educational Toys is a large toy distributor that relies on "Educational Toy Account Representatives" who sell the products door-to-door or during neighborhood parties rather than through retail outlets. Each account representative has a supervisor who oversees his or her performance. Regional managers supervise from ten to fifteen supervisors each.

To date, the only information used in assessing a regional manager's performance has been the percentage of goods sold by the salespeople in the region. Regional managers receive 5 percent of the worth of the goods the account representatives in their region sell. Recently many managers have complained that they are not rewarded on many of the important parts of their job, such as training and development of account representatives, supervision of the supervisors, and identification of the most appropriate products for their region, among other activities. The supervisors also receive rewards in the form of a 5 percent share of the worth of the goods sold by the account representatives.

Top management of Educational Toys, Inc., has agreed to revise the company's reward system for supervisors and regional managers. They want a system that is relatively easy to administer and consistent across the thirty sales regions of the country.

Step 2: In groups of four to six, design a reward system for the regional managers and supervisors.

Step 3: Discussion. In small groups or with the entire class, share your systems. Then answer the following questions:

1. What do these systems have in common?
2. How do they differ?
3. What are the strengths and weaknesses of each system?
4. What changes would you recommend?
5. What role do the regional managers and supervisors play in the determination of rewards?

Activity 4–6   Traveler Import Cars, Inc.

Step 1: Read the Traveler Import Cars, Inc., case.

BACKGROUND

Randy Traveler had been a partner in Capitol Imports, one of the most prosperous foreign car dealerships in greater Columbus, Ohio, selling expensive European automobiles. His wife, Beryl, a holder of an MBA degree from a respected private university, was a consultant specializing in automobile dealerships.

In 1979, Randy and Beryl decided to go into business for themselves. Since between the two of them they had four decades of automobile dealership experience, they elected to acquire their own dealership. With some luck, they obtained a dealership selling a brand of Japanese cars

that had become known in the United States for its very high quality. Randy became president and Beryl executive vice-president.

EVOLUTION OF THE FIRM

Stage 1

After obtaining the Japanese dealership, Randy and Beryl decided to locate it approximately two miles from Capitol Imports. The decision was made on the basis of immediate availability of a suitable facility. This location, however, was several miles from a major shopping area of any kind, and the closest automobile dealership was Capital Imports. Furthermore, the location was approximately three miles from the nearest interchange of a major interstate highway. Nonetheless, the dealership was located on a busy street within easy access to half a dozen upper-middle-class-to-affluent neighborhoods with residents predisposed to purchasing foreign automobiles with a high quality image.

A number of key employees were enticed by Randy and Beryl to leave Capitol Imports and join Traveler Import Cars. Stuart Graham, who was in charge of Finance and Insurance at Capitol Imports, became general manager at Traveler Import Cars. Before specializing in finance and insurance, Graham was a car salesman. Several mechanics and car salesmen also left Capitol Imports to join Traveler Import Cars. As a rule, the policies and procedures that pertained at Capitol Imports were relied on at Traveler Import Cars, Inc., for the first five years of operations.

No one at Traveler Import Cars was unionized, but the mechanics were given everything that unionized mechanics received at other dealerships in order to remove the incentive to unionize. By everything, it is meant direct compensation, indirect compensation (fringe benefits), and work rules.

Randy and Beryl viewed their dealership as a family. This was in some measure due to the fact that the dealership was part of a Japanese corporation (which viewed its employees as family), and partly due to the beliefs that Randy and Beryl shared about organizations. Randy and Beryl made every effort to involve subordinates in day-to-day decision-making. As tangible evidence of her commitment to democratic leadership, Beryl decided to introduce a quality circle into Traveler Import Cars, Incorporated. This was done by selecting five non-supervisory employees (one from each part of the organization) to meet once a month with Beryl and Stuart Graham in order to discuss problems, possible solutions, and implementation strategies. No training whatsoever regarding quality circles was provided anyone involved with the so-called "quality circle," and this includes Beryl and Stuart.

Stuart Graham, on the other hand, was a benevolent autocrat, although he tried to create the facade of a democratic leader because he understood well Randy and Beryl's leadership preferences. Most employees agreed with Randy and Beryl that Traveler Import Cars was a family. Furthermore, most employees felt free to voice an opinion on anything to Randy, Beryl, and Graham, or to any other supervisor or manager, for that matter.

Stage 2

As long as the dealership was small everything went well, largely because Randy and Beryl made all key decisions, provided daily direction to supervisors and managers (including the general manager—Stuart Graham, who should have been running the dealership on a day-to-day basis), and resolved problems through face-to-face communica-

tions with the involved individuals. As the dealership grew and prospered, it generated enough money for growth. Expanding the dealership rapidly was impractical because of the limited allotment of cars due in large measure to the so-called "voluntary" import quotas by the Japanese car manufacturers. The demand for these cars was so great that cars were even sold from the showroom floor, leaving at times few models for new customers to view.

The first acquisition that Randy and Beryl made was a car leasing company, which they located next to the dealership. Randy elected to spend most of his time building up the car leasing company, leaving the operations of the dealership to Beryl. The second acquisition consisted of another car dealership located approximately ten miles from the original one. The new dealership sold another make of Japanese cars and an expensive European make. The newly acquired dealership was located in the midst of automobile dealerships on a main road, but was housed in inadequate facilities and beset by many problems. Beryl became the chief operating officer of the second dealership as well. Soon after acquiring the second dealership, Randy and Beryl decided to construct new facilities adjacent to the existing ones.

Stage 3

The newly acquired dealership created a great deal of additional work for Beryl, but she understood and accepted that reality because she and Randy knowingly acquired a business that had been plagued by problems prior to acquisition. What bewildered and frustrated Beryl was the fact that the operation of Traveler Import Cars, Inc., took so much of her time as well as physical and psychic energies. After all, it has been five years since she and Randy purchased that dealership. Many key supervisory and managerial personnel now have five years of experience with the dealership, yet the task of running Traveler Import Cars was just as consuming at this time as it was when the dealership was new. Frequently, Beryl would tell one of the managers to do something, but it wouldn't get done. Decisions were reached at management meetings, but they did not get implemented. Programs were initiated, but were frequently permitted to drift and disappear. Important deadlines were being missed with increasing frequency. Mechanics and salesmen were coming to work late and taking excessive lunch breaks with greater frequency. Beryl knew that these problems were not due to insubordination or lack of motivation. Yet, if she did not directly oversee implementation of an important decision, it did not get implemented.

In order to relieve herself of some of the work load, Beryl hired two experienced managers. In order to justify their salaries, however, they spent half of their time at Traveler Import Cars and the other half at the newly acquired dealership. The newly hired managers had good ideas, yet

Beryl was working just as hard as ever, and the problems that motivated Beryl to hire two experienced managers remained practically unchanged. In spite of the problems, the dealership grew as rapidly as the increase in the quota of cars that was allotted to the dealership by the manufacturer permitted. In addition, Traveler Import Cars began wholesaling parts to service stations and car repair shops, and started to lease cars in direct competition with the leasing operation managed by Randy. Although an organizational chart did not exist, it would look like Figure 4–9, if Randy and Beryl bothered to construct one.

About this time, Randy and Beryl's marriage had come undone, and Randy remarried a lady considerably his junior. Even so, Beryl and Randy maintained their business relationship, and were able to work together professionally without visible acrimony. Beryl now had more money than she knew what to do with, and was about to make much more because the newly acquired dealership was being turned

around rapidly, largely due to Beryl's considerable talents, the new facility, and the rapidly recovering economy. Yet Beryl no longer wanted to work as hard as she had in the past.

Beryl understood that Stuart Graham lacked the right stuff to be general manager of a car dealership in a metropolitan area, and she approached Randy on the matter. His response was: "Stuart Graham is too valuable of an asset because Traveler Import Cars, Inc., had generated a $500,000 after-tax profit last year. He must be doing something right."

Even though Beryl had been a consultant to automobile dealerships for twenty years, she decided nonetheless to retain a consultant. Beryl was fortunate to contact a particularly astute consultant by the name of J. P. Muzak. Her request was that Muzak straighten out the quality circle, which she felt wasn't living up to her expectations. Muzak, however, was reluctant to get involved unless he was per-

Figure 4–9 **Organizational Chart of Traveler Import Cars, Inc.**

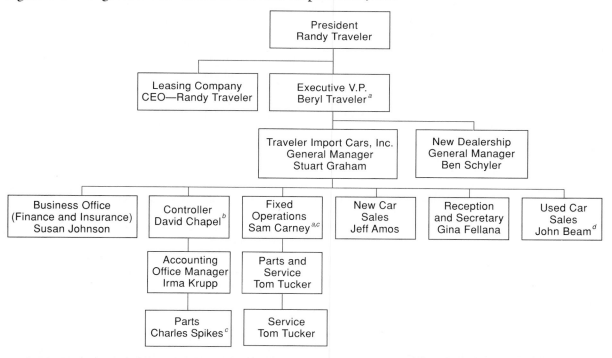

[a]These individuals spent approximately one-half of their time at Traveler Import Cars and one-half at the new dealership.
[b]David Chapel is the controller for Traveler Import Cars, the new dealership, and the leasing company. He spent about one-half of his time at Traveler Import Cars and one-half at the new dealership.
[c]Sam Carney owned and operated his own small business prior to joining Traveler Import Cars, Inc. Charles Spikes was a supervisor at a local office of a national automobile parts distributor before coming to work for Traveler Import Cars, Inc.
[d]John Beam frequently is asked by Randy Traveler to assist with matters pertaining to the leasing company.

mitted to conduct a thorough needs analysis before selecting any kind of intervention strategy. Beryl, after thinking the matter through, assented to Muzak's proposal. The organizational needs analysis relied on confidential structured interviews with all the managers, supervisors, and select nonsupervisory personnel. The summary of Muzak's organization needs analysis follows.

POSSIBLE PROBLEM AREAS
Goals
Although general goals (such as providing the best customer service possible) exist at the organizational level, many individuals report that what is expected of them, in terms of specific and measurable objectives, isn't clearly defined. It is difficult to make a superior happy if the subordinate isn't sure just what it is that the boss wants.

Also, there does not appear to be a philosophy for setting goals. For example, should goals and objectives be imposed unilaterally by the superior on the subordinate, or should the goals and objectives be set jointly between the superior and subordinate?

Organizational Structure
The organizational structure in a number of instances appears to be confusing. Specifically, a number of individuals appear to be reporting to two or more superiors. Irma Krupp reports to David Chapel and Stuart Graham. Tom Tucker reports to Sam Carney and Stuart Graham. Charles Spikes reports to Tom Tucker, Sam Carney, and Stuart Graham. John Beam had Susan Johnson's jobs before he became manager of used cars. David Chapel believes that he reports to the two general managers, to Beryl, and to Randy. Gina Fellana appears to report to everyone.

There is the perception that few managers know what they can do on their own authority and what they must get approved and by whom.

Communications
There appear to be too many meetings and they do not seem to be as productive as they could be. On this point there is a consensus.

A paper flow problem exists in several areas. The Accounting Office at times does not receive properly filled out forms from the Business Office. It appears that Susan Johnson does not have the time to fill out carefully and on a timely basis all the forms and attend to her other finance and insurance duties. The Accounting Office at times does not receive the necessary paper work from New Car Sales. The Parts Department at times doesn't receive on a timely basis the necessary information from New Car Sales.

Some individuals complain that their superiors do not keep them informed. Everything is a secret.

Training and Development
A number of individuals have risen through the ranks into supervisory and managerial positions. Since these individuals have never received formal managerial training, the void must be filled by coaching. In a number of cases, the void has not been filled by coaching, and these persons are learning through trial and error—an expensive and time-consuming way of learning, indeed.

The consensus is that the computer equipment is adequate to the task, but the operators need additional training to realize the potential of the equipment. The mechanics receive the latest training from the manufacturer.

Performance Appraisal
Many people reported that they do not receive a periodic formal appraisal. Thus, their need for performance feedback is frustrated.

Wage and Salary Administration
Numerous individuals have reported that it is the subordinate who has to initiate a wage or salary increase. Most individuals report that they would like to see the superior initiate wage and salary action at least annually. Moreover, a number of individuals are not sure on what basis they are remunerated. The absence of a systematic periodic performance appraisal is responsible, in part, for this perception.

Discipline
In a number of instances, individuals arrive late, take extended lunch breaks, and violate rules with impunity. This creates a demoralizing effect on others.

Control System
The financial control system at the top of the organization appears to be satisfactory. The operational control systems in the rest of the organization are problematic.

Morale
While there is still the feeling that the organization is a family and the best place the employees have ever worked, the feeling is starting to diminish.

Sundry Problems
1. Quality circle may need restructuring along traditional lines.

2. The time it takes to make decisions should be shortened.
3. The organization has difficulty implementing decisions that have been made.
4. Lack of follow-up presents serious problems.
5. Policies and programs are permitted to drift and disappear (motivator board is an example).
6. Managers may not be delegating enough.
7. New car salesmen do not always turn customers over to the Business Office, resulting in loss of revenue to the dealership.
8. Service desk is crucial and it has been a revolving door.

At a meeting, Muzak presented the findings of his needs analysis to the management team of Traveler Import Cars, Inc., and a discussion ensued regarding each of the possible problem areas. Randy Traveler did not attend since he relegated the operation of the dealership to Beryl. At the end of the discussion, the management team agreed that all the problems uncovered by Muzak were real and, if anything, understated.

Muzak did not present at the meeting his assessment of the potential of the key managers. This he did in a private discussion with Beryl. In summary, Muzak concluded that Stuart Graham was too set in his ways to change. Moreover, he displayed too much emotion publicly, and lacked the respect of his subordinates. Jeff Amos was considered by his subordinates to be a nice guy, but was indecisive, lacked firmness, was manipulated by subordinates, and did not enjoy the respect of his subordinates. Tom Tucker was probably in over his head in his present position. He was only a high school graduate, he was not a mechanic, was unsure of himself, and lacked the confidence of his subordinates. Lastly, he was quite impulsive. His previous experience was as a service desk writer (the person to whom the customer explains the car problems and who writes the work order). All the other managers and supervisors were thought to possess the necessary potential which could be realized through training and experience.

Step 2: Prepare the case for class discussion.

Step 3: Individually, in small groups, or with the entire class, as directed by your instructor, answer the following questions:

Description
1. Describe the situation at Traveler Import Cars.
2. Describe Stuart Graham's performance during the case.

Diagnosis
3. What problems existed at Traveler Import Cars?
4. How do (a) needs, (b) equity, (c) reinforcement, (d) expectancy, and (e) goal-setting theories explain the situation?
5. Using your knowledge of perception and attribution, evaluate the situation.
6. Using your knowledge of personality, personal development, and career development, evaluate the situation.
7. Using your knowledge of role pressures and stress, evaluate the situation.

Prescription
8. What changes should be made in this situation?

Step 4: Discussion. In small groups, with the entire class, or in written form, share your answers to the questions above. Then answer the following questions:

1. What symptoms suggested that a problem existed?
2. What problems existed in the case?
3. What theories and concepts help explain the problems?
4. How can the problems be corrected?
5. Are the actions likely to be effective?

CONCLUDING COMMENTS   In this chapter we developed a multifaceted view of motivation. This comprehensive perspective considers the major motivation theories of this century. In assessing the situations in the cases and exercises we considered individuals' needs and organizational responses to those needs; the equitable assignment, appropriate timing, and correct selection of rewards; the expectancy, instrumentality, and valence of various situations; and the type of goals set.

The Expectancy Questionnaire and Goal-Setting Exercise offered tools and techniques for diagnosing motivational level. The cases "Feeling Stuck at Hyatt?" and

"Traveler Import Cars, Inc.," offered the opportunity for diagnosing motivational issues using a comprehensive perspective. Preparing a plan for increasing the diversity of the workplace and designing a more comprehensive reward system for Educational Toys, Inc. helped you integrate the diverse motivation theories and prepare effective reward systems in organizational situations.

ENDNOTES

[1] Excerpted from Offering employees stock options they can't refuse, *Business Week,* October 7, 1991, p. 34. Reprinted by special permission, copyright © 1991 by McGraw-Hill, Inc.

[2] A. H. Maslow, *Motivation and Personality,* 3rd ed. (New York: Harper & Row, 1987).

[3] See M. A. Wahba and L. G. Bridwell, Maslow reconsidered: A review of research on the need hierarchy theory, *Organizational Behavior and Human Performance* 15 (1976): 212–240; V. F. Mitchell and P. Moudgill, Measurement of Maslow's need hierarchy, *Organizational Behavior and Human Performance* 16 (1976): 334–349; E. E. Lawler III, *Motivation in Work Organizations* (Monterey, Calif.: Brooks/Cole, 1973).

[4] C. P. Alderfer, *Existence, Relatedness, and Growth: Human Needs in Organizational Settings* (New York: Free Press, 1972).

[5] F. J. Landy, *The Psychology of Work Behavior,* 3rd ed. (Homewood, Ill.: Dorsey, 1985) compares Maslow's and McClelland's mechanisms of needs satisfaction.

[6] D. McClelland, *The Achieving Society* (Princeton, N.J.: D. Van Nostrand, 1961); D. C. McClelland, *Motives, Personality, and Society: Selected Papers* (New York: Praeger, 1984).

[7] *Ibid.;* S. R. Jenkins, Need for achievement and women's careers over 14 years: Evidence for occupational structure effects, *Journal of Personality and Social Psychology* 53 (1987): 922–932.

[8] D. McClelland and D. H. Burnham, Power driven managers: Good guys make bum bosses, *Psychology Today* (7) (1975): 69–71.

[9] F. Herzberg, B. Mausner, and B. B. Snyderman, *The Motivation to Work* (New York: Wiley, 1959); F. Herzberg, *The Managerial Choice: To Be Efficient and to Be Human* (Salt Lake City: Olympus, 1982).

[10] See B. L. Hinton, An empirical investigation of the Herzberg methodology and two-factor theory, *Organizational Behavior and Human Performance* 3 (1968): 286–309; J. Schneider and E. Locke, A critique of Herzberg's classification system and a suggested revision, *Organizational Behavior and Human Performance* (1971): 441–458.

[11] R. House and L. Wigdor, Herzberg's dual-factor theory of job satisfaction and motivation: A review of the evidence and criticism, *Personnel Psychology* 20 (1968): 369–389, is one example of this criticism.

[12] G. R. Salancik and J. Pfeffer, An examination of need-satisfaction models of job attitudes, *Administrative Science Quarterly* 22 (1977): 427–456.

[13] J. S. Adams, Inequity in social exchange. In *Advances in Experimental and Social Psychology,* Vol. 2, ed. L. Berkowitz (New York: Academic Press, 1965), pp. 267–300. See also E. Walster, W. Walster, and E. Berscheid, *Equity: Theory and Research* (Boston: Allyn and Bacon, 1978).

[14] F. J. Landy and W. S. Becker, Motivation theory reconsidered, *Research in Organizational Behavior* 9 (1987): 1–38.

[15] B. A. Mellers, Equity judgment, A revision of Aristotelian views, *Journal of Experimental Psychology: General* 111 (1982): 242–270; M. H. Birnbaum, Perceived equity in salary policies, *Journal of Applied Psychology* 68 (1983): 49–59.

[16] R. P. Vecchio, Predicting worker performance in inequitable settings, *Academy of Management Review* 7 (1982): 103–110, presents four mathematical models of equity theory.

[17] G. R. Oldham and H. E. Miller, The effect of significant other's job complexity on employee reactions to work, *Human Relations* 32 (1979): 247–260; J. Greenbert and G. S. Leventhal, Equity and the use of overreward to motivate performance, *Journal of Personality and Social Psychology* 34 (1976): 179–190.

[18] D. Schwab, Construct validity in organizational behavior. In *Research in Organizational Behavior,* vol. 2, ed. B. Staw (Greenwich, Conn.: JAI Press, 1980); M. R. Carrell and J. E. Dittrick, Equity theory: The recent literature, methodological considerations, and new directions, *Academy of Management Review* 3 (1978): 202–210; Walster et al., *Equity,* p. 128.

[19] R. E. Kopelman, Psychological stages of careers in engineering: An expectancy theory taxonomy, *Journal of Vocational Behavior* 10 (1977): 270–286; M. R. Carrell and J. E. Dittrich, Employee perceptions

of fair treatment, *Personnel Journal* 55 (1976): 523–524; R. A. Cosier and D. R. Dalton, Equity theory and time: A reformulation, *Academy of Management Review* 8 (1983): 311–319.

[20] R. C. Huseman, J. D. Hatfield, and E. W. Miles, A new perspective on equity theory: The equity sensitivity construct, *Academy of Management Review* 12 (1987): 232–234.

[21] E. L. Thorndike, *Behaviorism* (New York: Norton, 1924); B. F. Skinner, *The Behavior of Organisms: An Experimental Approach* (New York: Appleton-Century, 1938).

[22] S. F. Jablonsky and D. L. DeVries, Operant conditioning principles extrapolated to the theory of management, *Organizational Behavior and Human Performance* 7 (1972): 340–358.

[23] K. O'Hara, C. M. Johnson, and T. A. Beehr, Organizational behavior management in the private sector: A review of empirical research and recommendations for further investigations, *Academy of Management Review* 10 (1985): 848–864.

[24] S. Kerr, On the folly of rewarding A, while hoping for B, *Academy of Management Journal* 18 (1975): 769–783.

[25] *Ibid.*

[26] M. G. Evans, Organizational behavior: The central role of motivation. In J. G. Hunt and J. D. Blair, eds., *1986 Yearly Review of Management of the Journal of Management* (1986): 203–222, counters the overwhelming evidence in support of this theory by suggesting that the identification and assessment of an individual's valences over time remains a problem.

[27] V. H. Vroom, *Work and Motivation* (New York: Wiley, 1964).

[28] D. A. Nadler and E. E. Lawler III, Motivation: A diagnostic approach. In J. R. Hackman, E. E. Lawler III, and L. W. Porter, eds., *Perspectives on Behavior in Organizations* (New York: McGraw-Hill, 1977), pp. 26–38.

[29] B. M. Staw, *Intrinsic and Extrinsic Motivation* (Morristown, N.J.: General Learning Press, 1976), presents an early view; W. E. Scott Jr., J. Farh, and P. M. Podsakoff, The effects of "intrinsic" and "extrinsic" reinforcement contingencies on task behavior, *Organizational Behavior and Human Decision Processes* 41 (1988): 405–425; and P. C. Jordan, Effects of an extrinsic reward on intrinsic motivation: A field experiment, *Academy of Management Journal* 29 (1986): 405–412, present more recent examples.

[30] See L. E. Miller and J. E. Grush, Improving predictions in expectancy theory research: Effects of personality, expectancies, and norms, *Academy of Management Journal* 31 (1988): 107–122; T. R. Mitchell, Expectancy-value models in organizational psychology. In *Expectation and Actions: Expectancy-Value Models in Psychology*, ed. N. T. Feather (Hillsdale, N.J.: Erlbaum, 1982), pp. 293–312.

[31] See J. P. Campbell and R. D. Pritchard, Motivation theory in industrial and organizational psychology. In *Handbook of Industrial and Organizational Psychology*, ed. M. D. Dunnette (Chicago: Rand McNally, 1976).

[32] See, for example, E. A. Locke, E. Frederick, E. Buckner, and P. Bobko, Effect of previously assigned goals on self-set goals and performance, *Journal of Applied Psychology* 69 (1984): 694–699; and E. A. Locke, D. O. Chah, S. Harrison, and N. Lustgarten, Separating the effects of goal specificity from goal level, *Organizational Behavior and Human Decision Processes* 43 (1989): 270–287.

[33] R. Vance and A. Colella, Effects of two types of feedback on goal acceptance and personal goals, *Journal of Applied Psychology* 75 (1990): 68–76.

[34] E. A. Locke, G. P. Latham, and M. Erez, The determinants of goal commitment, *Academy of Management Review* 13 (1988): 23–39.

[35] *Ibid.*

[36] E. A. Locke and G. P. Latham, *A Theory of Goal Setting and Task Performance* (Englewood Cliffs, N.J.: Prentice Hall, 1990).

[37] E. A. Locke, E. Frederick, C. Lee, and P. Bobko, Effect of self-efficacy, goals, and task strategies on task performance, *Journal of Applied Psychology* 69 (1984): 241–251.

[38] *Ibid.*

[39] G. P. Latham and G. A. Yukl, A review of research on the application of goal setting in organizations, *Academy of Management Journal* 18 (1975): 824–845.

[40] See B. D. Bannister and D. B. Balkin, Performance evaluation and compensation feedback messages: An integrated model, *Journal of Occupational Psychology* 63 (1990): 97–111, for a model of intervening variables between feedback and motivation; see also J. R. Larson, The performance feedback process: A preliminary model, *Organizational Behavior and Human Performance* 33 (1984): 42–76; R. C. Liden and T. R. Mitchell, Reactions to feedback: The role of attributions, *Academy of Management Journal* 28 (1985): 291–308.

[41] Locke, Frederick, Buckner, and Bobko, Effect of previously assigned goals.

[42] M. Erez, P. C. Earley, and C. L. Hulin, The impact of participation on goal acceptance and performance: A two-step model, *Academy of Management Journal* 28 (1985): 50–66; Evans, Organizational behavior.

[43] M. Erez and I. Zidon, Effect of goal acceptance on the relationship of goal difficulty to performance, *Journal of Applied Psychology* 69 (1984): 69–78.

[44] D. Eden, Pygmalion, goal setting, and expectancy: Compatible ways to boost productivity, *Academy of Management Review* 13 (1988): 639–652.

[45] Locke and Latham, *Theory of Goal Setting.*

[46] For example, see K. H. Schmidt, U. Kleinbeck, and W. Brockmann, Motivational control of motor performance by goal-setting in a dual-task situation, *Psychological Research* 4 (1984): 129–141.

[47] See, for example, M. Erez and P. C. Earley, Comparative analysis of goal-setting strategies across cultures, *Journal of Applied Psychology* 72 (1987): 658–665.

[48] Such differences do not always exist, as suggested by a comparable level of growth needs among computer programmers in the United States and Singapore, as described by J. D. Conger, Effect of cultural differences on motivation of analysts and programmers: Singapore vs. the United States, *MIS Quarterly* (June 1986): 189–196.

[49] G. Hofstede, Motivation, leadership, and organization: Do American theories apply abroad? *Organizational Dynamics* (Summer 1980): 42–63.

[50] P. Howell, J. Strauss, and P. F. Sorensen, Research note: Cultural and situational determinants of job satisfaction among management in Liberia, *Journal of Management Studies* (May 1975): 225–227.

[51] G. G. Alpander, A comparative study of the motivational environment surrounding first-line supervisors in three countries, *Columbia Journal of World Business* 19(3) (1984): 95–104.

[52] G. Hofstede, *Cultural Consequences of International Differences in Work-Related Values* (Beverly Hills, Calif.: Sage, 1984).

[53] See, for example, D. Lei, J. W. Slocum, Jr., and R. W. Slater, Global strategy and reward systems: The key roles of management development and corporate culture, *Organizational Dynamics* 19 (Autumn 1990): 27–41.

[54] D. B. Balkin and L. R. Gomez-Mejia, Toward a contingency theory of compensation strategy, *Strategic Management* 58 (1987): 169–182, calls for a contingency approach to determining compensation.

[55] See E. Jansen and M. Von Glinow, Ethical ambivalence and organizational reward systems, *Academy of Management Review* 19 (1985): 814–822, for a discussion of possible misfits between individual ethical positions and those maintained by the organizational reward system.

[56] R. M. Kanter, Holiday gifts: Celebrating employee achievements, *Management Review* (December 1986): 19–20, distinguishes between compensation and rewards and offers a list of ways of recognizing employees' accomplishments apart from pay.

[57] See E. E. Lawler III, *Strategic Pay: Aligning Organizational Strategies and Pay Systems* (San Francisco: Jossey-Bass, 1990), for extensive discussion of the role of pay.

[58] G. E. Ledford, Jr., Three cases on skill-based pay: An overview, *Compensation and Benefits Review* 23(2) (1991): 11–23; G. E. Ledford, Jr., and G. Bergel, Skill-based pay case number 1: General Mills, *Compensation and Benefits Review* 23(2) (1991): 24–38; P. V. LeBlanc, Skill-based pay case number 2: Northern Telecom, *Compensation and Benefits Review* 23(2) (1991): 39–56; G. E. Ledford, Jr., W. R. Tyler, and W. B. Dixey, Skill-based pay case number 3: Honeywell Ammunition Assembly Plant, *Compensation and Benefits Review* 23(2) (1991): 57–77.

[59] See E. E. Lawler III, reward systems in organizations. In J. Lorsch, ed., *Handbook of Organizational Behavior* (Englewood Cliffs, N.J.: Prentice-Hall, 1983).

[60] D. E. Bowen and C. A. Wadley, Designing a strategic benefits program, *Compensation and Benefits Review* 21(5) (1989): 44–56.

[61] E. E. Lawler III, Gainsharing theory and research: Findings and future directions. In W. A. Pasmore and R. Woodman, eds., *Research in Organizational Change and Development,* vol. 2 (Greenwich, Conn.: JAI Press, 1988).

[62] *Ibid.*

[63] T. Rollins, Productivity-based group incentive plans: Powerful, but use with caution, *Compensation and Benefits Review* 21(3) (1989): 39–50.

[64] J. L. Pierce and C. A. Furo, Employee ownership: Implications for management, *Organizational Dynamics* (Winter 1990): 32–45.

[65] C. Rosen, Employee stock ownership plans: A new way to look at work, *Business Horizons* 26 (September-October 1983): 48–56, describes a variety of these plans.

[66] A. M. Townsend, K. D. Scott, and S. E. Markham, An examination of country and culture-based differences in compensation practices, *International Business Studies* 2(4) (1990): 667–678.

RECOMMENDED READINGS

Boyett, J. H., and Conn, H. P. *How to Manage and Compensate People to Meet World Competition*. Macomb, Ill.: Glenbridge, 1988.

Lawler, E. E. III. *Strategic Pay: Aligning Organizational Strategies and Pay Systems*. San Francisco: Jossey-Bass, 1990.

Locke, E. A., and Latham, G. P. *A Theory of Goal Setting and Task Performance*. Englewood Cliffs, N.J.: Prentice Hall, 1990.

Manage People, Not Personnel. Boston: Harvard Business School, 1990.

Milkovich, G. T., and Wigdor, A. K., eds. *Pay for Performance: Evaluating Performance Appraisal and Merit Pay*. Washington, D.C.: National Academy Press, 1991.

Chapter Outline

Building Effective Work Teams and Culture

Learning Objectives

After completing the reading and activities in Chapter 5, students will be able to

1. Describe organizational culture and its relationship to team performance.

2. Identify the characteristics of effective teams.

3. Understand the formation of an effective team.

4. Trace the development of an effective team using several models.

5. Describe the contribution of group goals to team effectiveness.

6. Outline the different roles individuals can play in functioning teams.

7. Discuss the ways norms influence group behavior and attitudes.

8. Compare and contrast five communication networks and describe their impact on team performance.

9. Identify issues in the management of teams outside the United States.

10. Comment about the impact of cultural diversity on team effectiveness.

11. Prescribe strategies for building effective teams and improving their performance.

Teamwork at Office Manufacturing, Inc.

Jeffrey Markham recently and unexpectedly became the project leader of the Design Team at Office Manufacturing. This group had been working on a new design for office furniture that included innovations in the product and in the process for manufacturing it. The team had been organized about two years prior to his promotion, and it had worked intensively together during that two-year period. His preliminary review of their progress to date indicated that they might soon make a major design breakthrough that would revolutionize the business of manufacturing office furniture. Three of the ten team members had recently been reassigned to other projects, and two new members would join the seven remaining ones.

Markham replaced Tom Anthony, who had been a fixture at Office Manufacturing for a long time. Tom had handpicked the original ten-person team and had worked intensively with them for the past two years. He called them "my people," and they felt a strong allegiance to him. Markham had spoken with several managers in the company about the team; one person's comments reflected the other managers' feelings about the team: "Tom's group is so 'tight' that we wonder what goes on during their meetings. They tell us they are accomplishing a great deal, but we have yet to see a product."

Jeff Markham prepared for the first meeting with the team by setting some goals for the group and outlining an agenda and time line for them to follow. He wanted to take the progress that they had made so far and quickly turn it into a public demonstration of the design advances. He knew that his management style differed significantly from Tom's, but Jeff felt that he was much better at "getting the product out the door."

He thought he would begin the first meeting by outlining what he thought needed to be done and announcing the names of the two new people he had picked to join the team. As he finished his preparations, he wondered what else he should do to manage the team effectively.

What does Jeff need to do to ensure that the team functions effectively? What difficulties is he likely to encounter in managing the Design Team? In this chapter we examine the features of effectively functioning teams. A *team* is defined here as a group of people in a work setting who must rely on collaboration to accomplish their group's and organization's goals and attain their desired outcomes. It can focus on resolving problems in an ongoing fashion, creatively exploring possibilities or alternatives, or executing well-developed plans, among other things.[1] We begin by looking at the changing culture in organizations that has spawned an interest in using teams to accomplish organizational goals and get the work done. Then we discuss the ways teams form and develop. We next look at group process, which acts as the underpinning of team functioning. We also explore the international dimensions of team management. The chapter concludes with a set of strategies for improving team building, approaches for dealing with culturally diverse work teams, and methods for increasing collaboration among members.

THE CULTURAL CONTEXT

Significant changes in organization culture in the last decade have motivated widespread support for the use of teams to accomplish work-related tasks. At Office Manufacturing, for example, top management relies on a team of professionals to develop a state-of-the-art design process, rather than on individuals working alone or even in parallel. What comprises this *cultural context* in which work teams multiply and flourish?

Definition of Culture

Culture is "(a) a pattern of basic assumptions, (b) invented, discovered, or developed by a given group, (c) as it learns to cope with its problems of external adaptation and internal integration, (d) that has worked well enough to be considered valid and, therefore, (e) is to be taught to new members as (f) the correct way to perceive, think, and feel in relation to these problems."[2] As a concept borrowed by organizational theorists from anthropology, culture can also be viewed as shared meanings or understandings that are largely tacit and unique to group members.[3] It draws attention to facets of organizational life previously unattended to, and through shared interpretations it focuses action.[4]

The discussion in this book emphasizes culture based on organization-wide consensus. Yet recent research suggests two alternative perspectives to this integrative view.[5] A differentiation perspective views organizational culture as a "mosaic of inconsistencies," with meaning shared within subcultural boundaries, such as departments, divisions, or even work teams. A fragmentation perspective tunes into the ambiguities of organizational life. It does not focus on shared meanings or understandings, but rather on what individual organizational members experience.

Managers use culture in a variety of ways.[6] It can, for example, set the stage for the implementation of an organization's business strategy. Culture can also prescribe acceptable ways for managers to interact with external constituencies such as shareholders, the government, or customers. Staffing decisions and performance criteria can flow from the organization's culture. It can also guide the nature of acceptable interpersonal relationships within the company and the selection of an appropriate management style. It also has significance for organizational effectiveness: The culture's strength and consistency, emphasis on employee involvement in decision making, facilitation of corporate adaptability to organizational change, and clarity of mission are key predictors of organizational effectiveness.[7] Currently, managers in many companies view the organizational culture as supporting team-based efforts.

Components of Culture

In determining the nature of organizational culture we can examine it at three levels, as shown in Figure 5–1, and assess its support for team-based activities.[8] We can then look at the ways culture is embedded and transmitted in an organization, as shown in Figure 5–2, to assess its compatibility with work team functioning. We can also analyze its components, as shown in Figure 5–3.

Beliefs, Expectations, and Shared Values Basic organizational philosophy reflects the beliefs, expectations, and shared values of its leaders, as illustrated by the examples in Figure 5–4. Together these drive the organization toward its goals—profit or service, for example. Basic beliefs—which influence employee behavior and attitudes, define success for employees, and establish standards of achievement—may be a function of the requirements of the industry in which the organization functions as well as its national culture.[9]

Figure 5–1   Levels of Culture

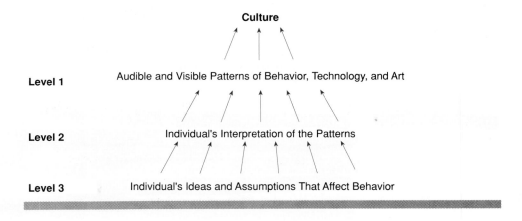

Culture

Level 1   Audible and Visible Patterns of Behavior, Technology, and Art

Level 2   Individual's Interpretation of the Patterns

Level 3   Individual's Ideas and Assumptions That Affect Behavior

Heroes and Heroines   Heroes and heroines transmit culture by personifying its corporate values. Leaders viewed in this way reinforce the basic values of an organization's culture by providing role models, symbolizing their organization to the outside world, preserving the organization's special qualities, setting a standard of performance, motivating employees, and making success attainable and human.[10] Managers who create heroes or heroines foster a set of corporate values that may stabilize the current organization or expedite change.

Myths and Stories   Myths, in this context, are stories about corporate heroes and heroines that facilitate the transmission and embedding of culture. What does the repeated telling of a story about the spectacular rise of a copy editor to the presidency of a major publishing firm suggest about a company's values? Does a story about the heir to the family fortune being the designated company president give the same impression? The themes of such stories provide clues to an organization's culture. For example, an organization whose stories emphasize individuality and competitive

Figure 5–2   How Culture is Embedded and Transmitted

1. Formal statements of organizational philosophy, charters, creeds, materials used for recruitment and selection, and socialization.
2. Design of physical spaces, facades, buildings.
3. Deliberate role modeling, teaching, and coaching by leaders.
4. Explicit reward and status system.
5. Stories, legends, myths, and parables about key people and events.
6. What leaders pay attention to, measure, and control.
7. Leader reactions to critical incidents and organizational crises.
8. Organizational design and structures.
9. Organizational systems and procedures.
10. Criteria used for recruitment, selection, promotion, leveling off, retirement, and "excommunication" of people.

SOURCE: Based on E. H. Schein, The role of the founder in creating organizational culture, *Organizational Dynamics* (Summer 1983).

Figure 5–3 **Components of Culture**

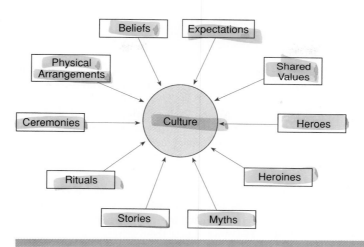

Figure 5–4 **Corporate Mission Statements**

Baxter International

Mission: Our Primary Objective

We will be the leading health-care company by providing the best products and services for our customers around the world, consistently emphasizing innovation, operational excellence and the highest quality in everything we do.

Principles: What We Stand For

We are committed to serving:
- *Customers:* Aggressively meeting customer needs.
- *Employees:* Respecting employees as individuals and providing opportunities for their personal development.
- *Stockholders:* Achieving long-term growth and the best return for our investors.

Through:
- *Teamwork:* Working strongly as a Baxter team.
- *Quality:* Reaching an objective understanding of customer requirements and using all our resources to satisfy those requirements.
- *Business Excellence:* Acting ethically and continually striving for excellence in our performance.

Strategy: The Course We're Taking

We are unique in our product and service breadth and our technological depth. We will use these strengths to:
- Grow our business by providing the best quality in products and services to customers and to suppliers.
- Provide the products and services to deliver effective therapy to patients in lower-cost settings, inside and outside the hospital.
- Creatively apply technology to develop and maintain high-return leadership positions in selected markets worldwide.
- Manage a balanced portfolio of businesses that increases the long-term value of our shareholders' investment.
- Be the best-cost producer by emphasizing innovative technology, cost and quality.

(continued)

Figure 5–4
(Continued)

Johnson & Johnson

Our Credo

We believe our first responsibility is to the doctors, nurses and patients,
to mothers and fathers and all others who use our products and services.
In meeting their needs everything we do must be of high quality.
We must constantly strive to reduce our costs
in order to maintain reasonable prices.
Customers' orders must be serviced promptly and accurately.
Our suppliers and distributors must have an opportunity
to make a fair profit.

We are responsible to our employees,
the men and women who work with us throughout the world.
Everyone must be considered as an individual.
We must respect their dignity and recognize their merit.
They must have a sense of security in their jobs.
Compensation must be fair and adequate,
and working conditions clean, orderly and safe.
We must be mindful of ways to help our employees fulfill
their family responsibilities.
Employees must feel free to make suggestions and complaints.
There must be equal opportunity for employment, development
and advancement for those qualified.
We must provide competent management,
and their actions must be just and ethical.

We are responsible to the communities in which we live and work
and to the world community as well.
We must be good citizens—support good works and charities
and bear our fair share of taxes.
We must encourage civic improvements and better health and education.
We must maintain in good order
the property we are privileged to use,
protecting the environment and natural resources.

Our final responsibility is to our stockholders.
Business must make a sound profit.
We must experiment with new ideas.
Research must be carried on, innovative programs developed
and mistakes paid for.
New equipment must be purchased, new facilities provided
and new products launched.
Reserves must be created to provide for adverse times.
When we operate according to these principles,
the stockholders should realize a fair return.

Johnson & Johnson

Courtesy of Baxter International and Johnson & Johnson.

achievement has a different culture than one whose themes focus on teamwork and collaboration. Consider the implications of a story about Bill Hewlett's visit to a plant one Saturday. Finding "the lab stock area locked, he immediately cut the padlock, leaving a note saying, 'Don't ever lock this door again. Thanks, Bill.' Along with more formal statements of company philosophy, the message soon hits home: at H-P we trust and value you. You're free to be enthusiastic about your job even if it's Saturday, and to innovate and contribute in whatever way you can."[11]

Rituals and Ceremonies   Ceremonies such as retirement dinners or employee-of-the-month awards contribute to corporate culture by dramatizing the organization's basic values; for example, the award of a pin for twenty-five years of service reflects a company that values loyalty. Often linked with a corresponding organizational story, such an event can provide an explanation of new behavior patterns.[12] Such ceremonies can also act as rites of passage, delineating entry into an organization's inner circle. They can also expedite transitions in leadership, such as that experienced by the Design Team; for example, a "new team" breakfast or dinner demarcates the change from the former to current team composition.

Physical Arrangement   The selection and arrangement of offices and furnishings often reveal significant insights into corporate culture. Compare an investment firm that provides only a desk and telephone for its brokers to one that offers private office space to the same jobholders. How might the cultures of these two firms differ? How could the physical arrangements in an organization support teamwork? Desks arranged in a bullpen area or the availability of many conference rooms might reflect such a culture.

The Team Culture   As the problems organizations face have become more complex, individual problem solving has been inadequate. Based in part on the success of the Japanese in manufacturing in the 1970s and 1980s, corporations in the United States and abroad have altered their cultures to encourage teamwork and collaboration. Executives in organizations such as Office Manufacturing create, authorize, and legitimize teams, such as the Design Team, to encourage creativity, facilitate the use of diverse intellectual resources, and inspire multifaceted problem solving.

Table 5–1 contrasts the old and new cultures. Note that the "new" team culture balances empowerment of workers with collaboration.[13] Such a culture can be the source of competitive advantage for an organization. Qualities of successful and well-managed companies have included employee participation in decision making, open communication, emphasis on quality, and use of lean administrative structure,[14] all characteristics that support team performance.

FORMATION OF EFFECTIVE TEAMS   Organizing a work group in an organizational setting does not guarantee quality team performance. Rather, managers must consciously work on building an effective team, which has characteristics such as those shown in Figure 5–5. Why do people join groups and how do their reasons for joining affect team performance? How can managers constitute groups for maximum effectiveness? Individuals may join *formal* groups—those officially sanctioned and organized by managerial or other authority—to accomplish organizational goals, such as departments in organizations or task forces, or to perform specific work tasks. Or individuals may form *informal* groups—those that arise spontaneously in the organization or within formal groups, such as cliques or a network of professionals.

Table 5–1 **Old Versus New Cultures**

Old Environment	New Environment
Person followed orders.	Person comes up with initiatives.
Group depended on manager.	Group has considerable authority to chart its own steps.
Group was a team because people conformed to direction set by manager. No one rocked the boat.	Group is a team because people learn to collaborate in the face of their emerging right to think for themselves. People rock the boat *and* work together.
People cooperated by suppressing their thoughts and feelings. They wanted to get along.	People cooperate by using their thoughts and feelings. They link up through direct talk.

SOURCE: Reprinted with permission from L. Hirschhorn, *Managing the New Team Environment* (Reading, Mass.: Addison-Wesley, 1991).

Figure 5–5 **Some Characteristics of an Effective Work Team**

1. The team shares a sense of purpose or common goals, and each team member is willing to work toward achieving these goals.
2. The team is aware of and interested in its own processes and examining norms operating within the group.
3. The team identifies its own resources and uses them, depending on the team's needs at any given time. At these times the group willingly accepts the influence and leadership of the members whose resources are relevant to the immediate task.
4. Group members continually try to listen to and clarify what is being said and show interest in what others say and feel.
5. Differences of opinion are encouraged and freely expressed. The team does not demand narrow conformity or adherence to formats that inhibit freedom of movement and expression.
6. The team is willing to surface conflict and focus on it until it either is resolved or managed in a way that does not reduce the effectiveness of the individuals involved.
7. The team exerts energy toward problem solving rather than allowing it to be drained by interpersonal issues or competitive struggles.
8. Roles are balanced and shared to facilitate both the accomplishment of tasks and feelings of group cohesion and morale.
9. To encourage risk taking and creativity, mistakes are treated as sources of learning rather than reasons for punishment.
10. The team is responsive to the changing needs of its members and to the external environment to which it is related.
11. Team members are committed to periodically evaluating the team's performance.
12. The team is attractive to its members, who identify with it and consider it a source of both professional and personal growth.
13. Developing a climate of trust is recognized as the crucial element for facilitating all of the above elements.

SOURCE: Reprinted with permission from P. G. Hanson and B. Lubin, Characteristics of an effective work team, *Organization Development Journal* (Spring 1986), published by the O. D. Institute, 11234 Walnut Ridge Road, Chesterfield, Ohio 44026 USA. Reprinted in W. B. Reddy and K. Jamison, eds., *Team Building: Blueprints for Productivity and Satisfaction* (San Diego: NTL Institute and University Associates, 1988), pp 76–87.

Reasons for Group Formation

Consider the reasons you have joined groups in the past. Perhaps you liked the group members, you lived or worked near them, or you valued the goals they accomplished. Groups form when individuals exhibit one or more of the following, as shown in Figure 5–6.[15] First, they may have *common needs* for food, security, esteem, autonomy, creativity, or challenge, among others. Food cooperatives form because individuals want to satisfy their basic needs for food at a low cost. Honorary societies form to meet the esteem needs of students or professionals. Work teams may form because employees have social or creativity needs.

Second, individuals may form groups because of their *common interests*. Engineers employed by different companies often join the same professional group. Faculty members may form a research group because of interest in the same or related area of study. A manager may organize coworkers responsible for the same job into a group.

Third, groups may form because individuals have *common goals* or objectives. A board of directors of a company forms to help the company reach its profitability objectives. A marketing department forms to increase sales of a company's product. An executive forms a task force of individuals with a common goal, such as improving customer service or reducing labor costs. Jeff Markham and Tom Anthony before him constituted the Design Team to develop innovative approaches to furniture design.

Fourth, the *physical proximity* of individuals may cause them to form a group. Employees in the same work area often join together as a social group. Engineers with offices on the same floor become part of project teams more often than do engineers located in different buildings or cities.

Finally, groups may form because of *cultural similarity*. Expatriates frequently develop professional and social groups in their country of residence. New immigrants seek employment in organizations or departments where large numbers of culturally similar workers are employed.

The reason a group forms will influence the nature and quality of its functioning. In the introductory case, for example, the professionals at Office Manufacturing, Inc., formed the Design Team at the direction of the company's top management. We would expect them to have common goals but different needs and interests because of differences in their training, experience, and career stage. We would hypothesize that because of their common goal the members would have similar enthusiasm for the group's work. Their diverse needs and interests, however, may exert a different and even greater influence on the group's performance. The addition of two new members and a project leader, who likely have different needs and interests

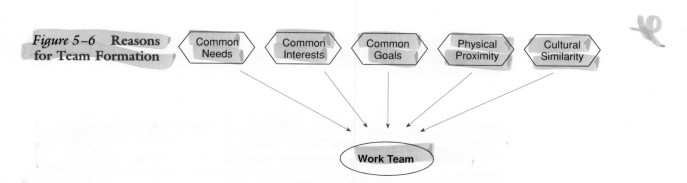

Figure 5–6 **Reasons for Team Formation**

Common Needs · Common Interests · Common Goals · Physical Proximity · Cultural Similarity

Work Team

from the existing group members, will have a significant influence on group functioning. Diagnosing the factors in group formation, then, would help Jeff Markham to predict the ways a group will be likely to act and help him to plan other ways to support functional attitudes and behavior and counteract dysfunctional actions and attitudes. In forming work teams, then, managers such as Jeff Markham should be aware of similarities and dissimilarities of needs, interests, goals, location, and culture of potential group members and their likely consequences.

Group Attractiveness and Cohesion

The attractiveness of group membership increases as the group is viewed as more cooperative, as the prestige experienced by the group is greater, as there is more interaction among its members, as the group's size is smaller, and as others perceive the group as more successful.[16] Though the Design Team is of moderate size and viewed as cooperative, collaborative, and productive, Jeff must ensure that the group continues to be viewed in the same way. He must maintain its attractiveness to its present members, as well as its new and potential members.

Group membership can lose its attractiveness for a variety of reasons. The new members of the Design Team may feel that the group makes unreasonable demands on individuals or that some members dominate the group too often. Other members may feel that too much self-oriented behavior occurs, thereby reducing the attractiveness of group membership. Disagreement can occur during problem solving. Competition might even exist between members, creating a less desirable atmosphere in the group and reducing its attractiveness to all members. When a group no longer meets an individual's needs, dissatisfaction with membership may result. In addition, individuals who are blamed for negative events in the group may perceive themselves to be outsiders and reduce their identification with the group. Obviously, Jeff wants to avoid these dysfunctions and maintain the attractiveness of the team. The lack of attractiveness of membership on a team typically inhibits member efforts to perform well and reach the group's goals.

Cohesiveness develops more easily in small and homogeneous groups; too many changes in membership in a short time hurt cohesion and attractiveness.[17] Workers are often attracted to highly cohesive groups, or ones in which members form a tight bond in interpersonal relations, because such groups are highly committed to the task[18] and provide a strong identity for organizational members. Such groups may experience increased performance, satisfaction, quality of interaction, and goal attainment.[19] As cohesive groups work together they become even more cohesive, resulting in greater likelihood of successful performance.[20] In some situations, however, because increased cohesiveness means increased influence, lowered productivity may result if workers decide to use their influence for dysfunctional rather than functional outcomes.[21] Figure 5–7 incorporates issues of cohesiveness into the steps to becoming a team.

In forming a new team, members should ideally follow four steps.[22] First, each member must determine the priority he or she attaches to participating in the team's activities and assess the personal importance of these activities. In selecting and retaining members of the Design Team, Jeff Markham must ensure their commitment to the group's task and performance, particularly now that the leadership and composition of the team are changing. Second, the members must share and ensure the commonality of their expectations about working on the team. Third, team members must clarify the team's goals and objectives and must agree to a core mission for the team. Finally, the team must quickly agree to basic operating guidelines as a way of finalizing team formation. In constituting a nonpermanent team, such as a task force,

Figure 5–7 **Steps to Becoming a Team**

Values and attitudes

- Explain that the company values employees as people and wants them to develop caring, supportive relationships to make their work more rewarding and productive.
- Work and live by these values.
- Have employees determine what these values mean for how they can work together effectively.

Tasks and rewards

- Assign tasks to groups and indicate that rewards will be given if the group is successful.
- Indicate that employees are expected to share information and ideas and aid each other.
- Provide procedures to coordinate effort.

Deciding that goals are cooperative

- After explaining the rationale and purpose of the task, have employees discuss how it can help them and the company.
- Have employees discuss the task to help them understand that their goals are cooperative.
- Encourage employees to understand each other's aspirations and objectives so that they know how they can help each other.

Working together

- Plan how to share the work efficiently and fairly.
- Develop a policy urging employees to show respect and acceptance of each other.
- Encourage employees to improve their abilities to solve problems, manage conflicts, and work together.

SOURCE: Reprinted with permission from Dean Tjosvold, *Working Together to Get Things Done: Managing for Organizational Productivity* (Lexington, Mass.: Lexington Books, 1986), p. 59.

its originator must similarly constitute the task force, define and allocate resources, and manage day-to-day activities.[23] He or she must select members who have a vested interest in its mission, will be challenged by its task, and have complementary skills.

DEVELOPMENT OF EFFECTIVE TEAMS

Once a group forms, it must resolve a variety of issues before it functions effectively. Tracing the development of groups provides one perspective for assessing a group's progressive performance. We can apply different evaluative standards earlier in a group's existence than later in its development. Managers can then use their understanding of group development to identify and remove obstacles to effective group performance.

The Task-Process Framework

The traditional view of group development traces it along two dimensions.[24] *Task activity* refers to the steps used to perform a task, such as outlining of specifications for new equipment or software. *Group process* refers to the interpersonal interactions needed to accompany and accomplish task activities; it includes the group's goals, expectations of behavior, roles that guide and limit behavior, and patterned ways of interacting, as described later in this chapter. Figure 5–8 diagrams the stages of development along these dimensions. The solid arrows represent typical developmental progression from one stage to the next and within stages. Creating an effective group requires a successful resolution of each stage.

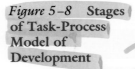

Figure 5–8   Stages of Task-Process Model of Development

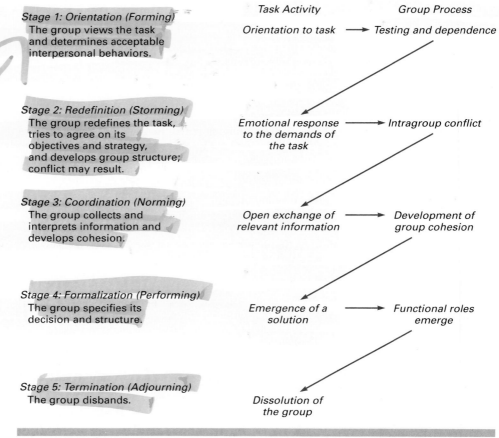

Stage 1: Orientation (Forming)
The group views the task and determines acceptable interpersonal behaviors.

Stage 2: Redefinition (Storming)
The group redefines the task, tries to agree on its objectives and strategy, and develops group structure; conflict may result.

Stage 3: Coordination (Norming)
The group collects and interprets information and develops cohesion.

Stage 4: Formalization (Performing)
The group specifies its decision and structure.

Stage 5: Termination (Adjourning)
The group disbands.

Task Activity	Group Process
Orientation to task	→ Testing and dependence
Emotional response to the demands of the task	→ Intragroup conflict
Open exchange of relevant information	→ Development of group cohesion
Emergence of a solution	→ Functional roles emerge
Dissolution of the group	

SOURCES: Based on A. C. Kowitz and T. J. Knutson, *Decision-Making in Small Groups: The Search for Alternatives* (Boston: Allyn and Bacon, 1980); B. W. Tuchman, Developmental sequences in small groups, *Psychological Bulletin* 63(1965): 384–399; B. W. Tuchman and M. C. Jensen, Stages of small group development revisited, *Group and Organization Studies* 2(1977): 419–427.

Orientation   During the first or *forming* stage, which is typically the shortest stage in normally functioning groups, the group views the task and determines acceptable interpersonal behaviors. As part of the *orientation to task* the group members gather information about the nature of the group's task. At the first meeting of the new Design Team, Jeff and the group should share their perceptions of the group's goal and the activities required to accomplish it.

In the corresponding process step, called *testing and dependence,* group members discover acceptable interpersonal behaviors that facilitate task accomplishment. Members of the Design Team, for example, might try out the roles of agenda setter, encourager, or summarizer, and in general learn the extent to which their efforts now can focus on interpersonal interactions as opposed to task issues. The continuing members must also test whether the interaction pattern established under Tom's leadership will work.

Redefinition   During the second, or *storming,* stage the group redefines the task, tries to agree on its objectives and strategy, and develops group structure, sometimes resulting in conflict. The task activities of this stage focus on team members offering *emotional responses to the demands of the task.* They determine whether they like the task, as well as how committed they are to it. For example, at Office Manufacturing, the continuing members of the Design Team must specify their ongoing commitment to the goals of the newly constituted group.

Disagreements by members of the group in their reactions to the task demands often lead to *intragroup conflict,* the group process dimension of the redefinition stage. Members may differ in the amount of time they will devote to a particular task, the priority they assign to the task, or the means they feel will best accomplish it. The sharper these differences, the greater the intragroup conflict that results. A manager who anticipates differences such as these may be able to reduce the conflict or make it functional for the group.

Coordination   During the *norming* stage the task activities focus on the *open exchange of relevant interpretation and opinions;* group members acknowledge that different emotional responses to the task are legitimate. The stage is often the longest because of the time required for the group to collect and interpret information, and arguments about the meaning of the data occur frequently. Discussions about the nature of the task, alternatives, and possible action may accompany the data analysis. The Design Team's discussion about the types and quality of furniture products and processes, as well as the development of an innovative approach, illustrate the activities of this stage.

Development of group cohesion frequently results from these discussions. The members resolve their differences after an open exchange of relevant interpretations and opinion, and begin to act as a cohesive group. Often groups do not reach this stage, and the group disintegrates.

Formalization   The group specifies the final version of the decision. During the *performing* stage *emergence of a solution* or resolution of the task occurs. At this stage the team must effectively resolve issues that arose at previous stages of group development, including divergent emotional responses to the task and differences in the interpretation of relevant information and opinions, and in proposals for action.

In the process component of this stage, *functional roles emerge* as a way of problem solving. At this time, the assignment of roles that match the group's needs for leadership and expertise, as well as the members' abilities and attitudes, occurs. Jeff Markham must be careful to consider this stage because the roles of members of the team may change with the addition of new members and a new manager.

Termination   *Adjourning* of the group occurs during this fifth stage. Termination may mean the dissolution of the group or its reorientation to other tasks and responsibilities. Table 5–2 shows a contemporary model that parallels and summarizes the task-process model described here. It differs by integrating the two dimensions at each of four stages.[25]

Moving through the Stages   A group may recycle through the stages of development, particularly as changes occur in the group's membership, its task, or the environment. For example, if additional new members are added to the Design Team, the group begins its development anew. Of course, movement through stages that the group has already resolved may occur more rapidly the second time. For example, orientation of a new member may require ten minutes rather than the two hours it

Table 5–2 **Stages of Team Development Model**

	Member Behaviors	Member Concerns	Leader Behaviors
Stage I: *Orientation to* *group and task*	Almost all comments directed to the leader Direction and clarification sought Status accorded to group members based on their roles outside the group Members fail to listen, resulting in nonsequitur statements Issues are discussed superficially, with much ambiguity	Who am I in this group? Who are the others? Will I be accepted? What is my role? What tasks will I have? Will I be capable? Who is the leader? Will he or she value me? Is the leader competent?	Provide structure by holding regular meetings and assisting in task and role clarification Encourage participation by all, domination by none Facilitate learning about one another's areas of expertise and preferred working modes Share all relevant information Encourage members to ask questions of you and one another
Stage II: *Conflict over* *control among* *the group's* *members and* *with the leader*	Attempts made to gain influence, suggestions, proposals Subgroups and coalitions form, with possible conflict among them The leader is tested and challenged (possibly covertly) Members judge and evaluate one another and the leader, resulting in ideas being shot down Task avoidance	How much autonomy will I have? Will I have influence over others? What is my place in the pecking order? Personal level: Who do I like? Who likes me? Issues level: Do I have some support in here?	Engage in joint problem solving; have members give reasons why idea is useful and how to improve it Establish a norm supporting the expression of different viewpoints Discuss the group's decision-making process and share decision-making responsibility appropriately Encourage members to state how they feel as well as what they think when they obviously have feelings about an issue Provide group members with the resources needed to do their jobs, to the extent possible (when this is not possible, explain why)
Stage III: *Group* *formation and* *solidarity*	Members, with one another's support, can disagree with the leader The group laughs together; members have fun; some jokes made at the leader's expense A sense of "we-ness" and attention to group norms is present The group feels superior to other groups in the organization Members do not challenge one another as much as the leader would like	How close should I be to the group members? Can we accomplish our tasks successfully? How do we compare to other groups? What is my relationship to the leader?	Talk openly about your own issues and concerns Have group members manage agenda items, particularly those in which you have a high stake Give and request both positive and constructive negative feedback in the group Assign challenging problems for consensus decisions (e.g., budget allocations) Delegate as much as the members are capable of handling; help them as necessary

Table 5–2 (Continued)

	Member Behaviors	Member Concerns	Leader Behaviors
Stage IV: Differentiation and productivity	Roles are clear and each person's contribution is distinctive	(Concerns of earlier stages have been resolved)	Jointly set goals that are challenging
	Members take the initiative and accept one another's initiatives		Look for new opportunities to increase the group's scope
	Open discussion and acceptance of differences among members in their backgrounds and modes of operation		Question assumptions and traditional ways of behaving
	Challenging one another leads to creative problem solving		Develop mechanisms for ongoing self-assessment by the group
	Members seek feedback from one another and from the leader to improve their performances		Appreciate each member's contribution
			Develop members to their fullest potential through task assignments and feedback

SOURCE: J. Moosbruker, Developing a productive team: Making groups at work work. In W. Brendan Reddy and Kaleel Jamison, eds., *Team Building: Blueprints for Productivity and Satisfaction* (Alexandria, Va.: NTL Institute for Applied Behavioral Science, 1988), pp. 91–92. Reprinted with permission from NTL Institute, copyright 1988.

required to orient the entire group. Or the group may use techniques they previously perfected to exchange relevant information and opinions more effectively and efficiently. A change in the group's goals or in the organization's environment may also cause the group to return to a previous stage. The extent and uniqueness of such changes will influence the speed with which the group moves through stages it has already resolved.

Some groups stick at one stage because they fail to resolve the issues associated with that stage. Arresting at orientation suggests that the group lacks the skill to screen out irrelevant information and behavior. Inability to move beyond coordination often reflects a group with poor information, which hinders effective interpretation. Dilemmas at various stages of development can remain unresolved when a group lacks clear goals, when individual members have incompatible goals, or when group management is dysfunctional.

The Organizational Socialization Approach Group development and organizational socialization occur simultaneously for groups and help us diagnose their developmental progress, as shown in Table 5–3. Newcomers first become oriented to the task and roles by confronting and accepting organizational reality as a result of checking their own expectations and learning behaviors that are rewarded or punished. Second, they attempt to clarify their roles and learn ways to deal with change and ambiguity. Third, they achieve role clarity in the socialization process by exchanging relevant information. Finally, they experience satisfaction and commitment to the organization; the group reaches a solution and develops functional role-related behavior. Again, a manager can use this model to diagnose team development and anticipate and plan for possible impediments to effective functioning.

Table 5–3 **Comparison of Stages of Group Development to Stages of Socialization**

	Group Development[a]	Organizational Socialization[b]
Stage 1: *Orientation*	1. Forming Establish interpersonal relationships Conform to organizational traditions and standards Boundary testing in relationships and task behaviors	1. Getting In (Anticipatory socialization) Setting of realistic expectations Determining match with the newcomer
Stage 2: *Redefinition*	2. Storming Conflict arising because of interpersonal behaviors Resistance to group influence and task requirements	2. Breaking In (Accommodation) Initiation on the job Establishing interpersonal relationships Congruence between self and organizational performance appraisal
Stage 3: *Coordination*	3. Norming Single leader emerges Group cohesion established New group standards and roles formed for members	3. Settling In (Role management) The degree of fit between one's life interests outside of work and the demands of the organization Resolution of conflicts at the workplace itself
Stage 4: *Formalization*	4. Performing Members perform tasks together Establishing role clarity Teamwork is the norm	

[a]Based on B. Tuchman, Developmental sequence in small groups, *Psychological Bulletin* 63 (1965): 384–399.

[b]Based on D. C. Feldman, A contingency theory of socialization, *Administrative Science Quarterly* 21 (1976): 433–454; D. C. Feldman, A practical program for employee socialization, *Organizational Dynamics* 7 (1976): 64–80.

SOURCE: Adapted from J. P. Wanous, A. E. Reichers, and S. D. Malik, Organizational socialization and group development: Toward an integrative perspective, *Academy of Management Review* 9 (1984): 670–683.

Current Thinking about Group Development

The most recent models of group development, including the punctuated equilibrium approach, the team performance model, and the external orientation model, place less emphasis on a continuous developmental progress. Rather, they address more radical adjustments and orientations by the group.

The Punctuated Equilibrium Approach   Based on a field study of task forces, the punctuated equilibrium model questions the stage progression of group development.[26] As shown in Figure 5–9, each group begins with a unique approach to its task that is set in its first meeting and that includes the behaviors and contents that

Figure 5–9 **Punctuated Equilibrium Model**

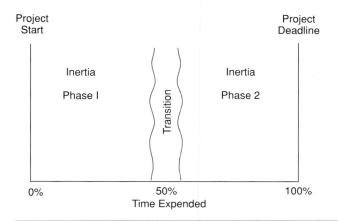

dominate Phase 1. Phase 1 continues until one-half of the allotted time for project completion has expired (regardless of the actual amount of time). At this halfway point, a major transition occurs that includes the dropping of the group's old behavior patterns, the adoption of new ones, and the making of significant progress toward completing the project. A second period of inertia follows in which the groups implement the plans from the transition period. Table 5–4 illustrates the life cycles of the eight task forces studied.

The Team Performance Model As shown in Figure 5–10, the team performance model organizes team development in two distinct phases: the creating stages and the sustaining stages.[27] Individual team members begin by answering the questions "Why am I here?" "Who are you?" and "What are we doing?" Quality answers to these questions should allow decision making, the transition stage. Development then turns to implementation of the decisions or action, followed by high performance, and concludes with a decision about whether and why the team should continue. Note that resolution of the key developmental issue at each stage moves the group into the next stage of development. Unresolved issues result in stagnation or a return to a previous stage. The companion Team Performance Inventory can be used to evaluate teams at these stages.

The work cycle of professional support teams, such as a computer systems group or airline maintenance group, has a different work cycle from other teams, as shown in Figure 5–11.[28]

External Orientation Recent thinking states that models of group development and activities must include external, as well as internal, relationships.[29] For example, development in a new product team is closely linked to project performance. It begins at the creation phase, during which team members talk extensively with people inside and outside the team. Next, a transition from recognizing the potential feasibility of a product to committing to a single product idea occurs. Development, the next stage, includes extensive coordination, focusing first on dealing with technical groups internally and then shifting to efforts directed at building and maintaining relationships with other groups. Technology transfer, the second transition, describes the movement from team to organizational ownership of a product. Diffusion and ending, the final stage, sees a significant increase in external activities as

Table 5–4 **An Overview of the Groups' Life Cycles**

Teams	First Meeting	Phase 1	Transition	Phase 2	Completion
A. Student team A	Agreement on a plan.	Details of plan worked out: client's "growth options."	First draft revised; second draft planned.	Details of second plan worked out: organization design.	Homework compiled into paper, finished, and edited.
B. Student team B	Disagreement on task definition.	Argument over how to define task: challenge vs. follow client's problem statement.	Task defined; case analysis rough-outlined.	Details of outline worked out: affirmative action plan, following client's request.	Paper (drafted by one member) finished; edited.
C. Student team C	One member proposes concrete plan; others oppose it.	Argument over details of competing plans ("structured" vs. "minimal") but no discussion of goals.	Goals chosen; case analysis outlined.	Details of outline worked out: "minimalist" U.S. trade policy.	Homework compiled into paper, finished, and edited.
D. Community fundraising agency committee	Agreement on a plan.	Details of plan worked out: "nonthreatening" self-evaluation for member agencies.	First draft revised; second draft planned.	Details of second plan worked out: explicitly allocations-related evaluation plan.	Report (drafted by two members) edited.
E. Bank task force	Uncertainty about new product; federal regulations unclear.	Team "answers questions"; maps possible account features.	Account completely outlined.	Members work throughout bank on systems, supplies for account.	Account finalized for advertising; bank-wide training planned.
F. Hospital administrators	Team fixes on "trust" theme; uncertain what to do with it for program.	Unstructured trial and rejection of program possibilities; disagreement about goals.	Complete program outlined.	Consultant hired to plan program; team arranges housekeeping details.	Responsibility for final preparations delegated.
G. Psychiatrists and social workers	Leader presents "the givens"; team opposes project.	Subgroup reports presented; members object to all plans; leader rebuts objections.	Disagreement persists; leader picks one plan; redelegates task; dissolves team.		
H. University faculty members and administrators	Team divided on whether to accept project; leader proposes diagnosis as first step.	Structured exploration; diagnosis of situation.	Team redefines task; commits to project.	Computer institute designed (original task) plus system for university computer facilities planning.	Report (written by leader from members' drafts) edited and approved.

SOURCE: Reprinted with permission from C. J. G. Gersick, Time and transition in work teams: Toward a new model of group development, *Academy of Management Journal* 31 (1988): p. 22.

Figure 5–10   **Drexler/Sibbet Team Performance Model**

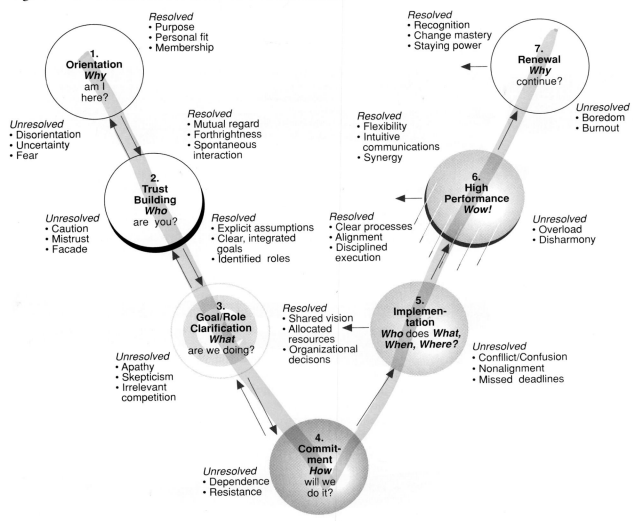

Reprinted with permission, © 1992 Allan Drexler and David Sibbet, Drexler and Associates, Annapolis, MD.

Figure 5–11 **Stages of Professional Support Team Development**	*Scanning*	Team actively scans environment or passively waits for a problem to emerge.
	Diagnosing	Team reformulates the problem in members' terms and language.
	Proposing	Team produces a concrete action proposal a client can implement.
	Handing off	Team delivers proposal or product to client for action or implementation.

the transfer of information and product ownership continues and concludes. Reading 5–1, "Improving the Performance of New Product Teams," discusses external activities in greater detail.

THE UNDERPINNINGS OF GROUP PROCESS

An effective work team has clear, shared goals, strong member participation, good diagnostic skills, the ability to meet leadership needs from within the group, mechanisms for seeking and reaching consensus, the trust of its members, and opportunities for member growth and creativity. Group process, including goals, norms, roles, and structure, contributes to a team's effective functioning.

Goals

What are the goals of the new Design Team? Getting the new products and processes in place within six months might be the group's goal. Specifying a feasible set of activities for instituting the innovations might be its goal instead. Agreement about group goals increases the cohesiveness experienced by the group. Or the group might lack an agreed-upon goal. Instead, the goals of the individuals together might constitute the group's goal. Each member's desire to demonstrate his or her own expertise might constitute the team's goal. What if one group member wants to use performance on the project as a springboard to a job in another company? What would happen if one of the team members wants to sabotage the project? Lack of a clear, performance-related goal as the primary focus of the group is a major cause of team failures.[30]

Goals can be *formal* (specifically stated orally or in writing) or *informal* (implied in the actions of group members). A formal goal of the Design Team is to develop an innovative product line for Office Manufacturing, Inc. An informal goal might be to ensure the input of all group members. As noted in Chapter 4, the most effective goals are difficult, specific, yet accepted by group members. For example, "identifying the specifications for two new product prototypes by January 13" is a more specific objective than "improving the product." The specific objective must be sufficiently difficult and accepted by group members to be useful as a focus of group activity. Numerous specific objectives should comprise the group's goal.

Sometimes the goals of individual members may conflict with the group goals. In such situations, individuals may develop *hidden agendas,* or goals hidden from the group. For example, one member of the Design Team might want to experiment with new CAD-CAM software, even if the time required to learn and use the software is too great for its potential usefulness. Because such hidden agendas can hinder the group's performance, diagnosis of group structure must include a search for and recognition of hidden agendas. Individuals generally should be encouraged to bring them to the surface, and a well-developed group will have mechanisms for resolving them.

Norms

Underlying group development and implicit in group functioning are expectations that guide behavior. A student, for example, is expected to attend classes, prepare homework, and take examinations. A worker is expected to be at work on time, miss work only in case of illness, and put in a "good day's work for a good day's pay." When these expectations are unwritten and informal they are called *norms.*

An *unattainable-ideal norm* describes behavior where "more is better";[31] for example, among policemen the more criminals arrested the better. A *preferred-value norm* describes behavior where either too much or too little of the behavior receives disapproval from group members; assembly line workers who work too fast or too slow may violate a group norm. An *attainable-ideal norm* describes behavior where approval occurs for increasing amounts of behavior until an attainable goal is reached but further goal-oriented behavior lacks value: An advertising executive will receive approval for each new campaign idea he or she generates until the client chooses one of the ideas.

Norms also differ in their centrality to the organizational functioning of the behavior they govern.[32] *Pivotal norms* guide behavior essential to the core mission of the organization. Expectations about the level of production or innovation required of workers fall into this category. *Peripheral norms* guide behaviors that are important, but not essential, to the performance of the organization's goals or mission, such as gathering for lunch in the employee cafeteria. The worker who violates pivotal norms often impedes the accomplishment of organizational goals; therefore, he or she may receive chastisement from superiors, ostracism by coworkers, or lack of loyalty from subordinates. Violation of peripheral norms by employees typically has fewer negative consequences for the worker and the organization.

Norms develop through interaction of group members and reinforcement of behaviors by the group. Generally the expectations of group members are in line with group goals and so are helpful in accomplishing organizational goals. In some cases, however, these expectations do not fit with the organization's goals. Some work groups, for example, insist that their members maintain a certain, often suboptimal, production level to avoid rate busting.

Norms generally develop in one of four ways for behaviors that team members view as important, such as performance, effort, attendance, and even work breaks.[33] Supervisors or coworkers may at one time but not repeatedly *explicitly state* certain expectations. Jeff Markham, for example, might state at the first meeting of the new team that attendance is required at all formally scheduled team meetings; expected attendance at all subsequent meetings may become a norm. *Critical events* in the group's history may also establish norms. If a new leader is appointed to the team, and the members question the leader's authority at the first meeting, questioning the leader's requests and directives may become a norm. Third, the *initial pattern of behavior* may become a norm. If an old member of the group dominates the first team meeting and the rest of the group says little, this pattern may persist at subsequent meetings. Finally, group members may *transfer behavior* from other situations to the group. The relative aggressiveness of some team members and the silence of others may reflect expected behaviors in previous work assignments that they now bring to other group tasks.

Compliance with Norms A group enforces norms that facilitate its survival, help predict the behavior of group members, prevent embarrassing interpersonal problems from arising, express the group's central values, and clarify the group's identity.[34] Teams may encourage or discourage certain behaviors. They can praise a specific level of production or criticize it. Suppose, for example, that one of the Design Team members came to the second meeting with a completed timetable of activities, whereas the remainder of the group came unprepared. If the other group members ignore all suggestions made by the well-prepared member, they may be signaling that such preparation is unexpected and unacceptable. Teams can also apply *sanctions* to encourage norm compliance. Those who follow the norms may receive accolades, emotional support, or acceptance of their ideas. Individuals who do not follow group norms may receive verbal reprimands or ridicule, formal punishments such as fines or firings, or informal actions such as isolation from the group. The Design Team should enforce norms that facilitate meeting the goals set by the group and that help group members to work cooperatively toward the innovative design of furniture.

Compliance with norms tends to increase as the group's size decreases, or as its homogeneity, visibility, or stability increases; members of small, homogeneous groups that are visible and stable experience greater norm compliance than large, heterogeneous groups that lack visibility and stability.[35] Diagnosing a team's norms and its compliance with them helps explain group performance.

Habitual Routines   Recent research suggests that groups develop functionally similar patterns of behavior that affect group performance.[36] In project groups these routines began at the start of the program and persisted halfway through the project.[37] Such routines help groups save time and energy, develop a shared agreement about the situation, develop a shared plan about proceeding, foster coordination, free members to focus on nonroutine challenges, contribute to members' confidence in performing their roles, and reduce the likelihood of their being perceived as deviant. At the same time, habitual routines can reduce performance or decrease the likelihood of innovation if team members fail to alter inappropriate routines.

Team leaders and members must recognize that habitual routines develop when groups import them, create them early in team development, or evolve them over time. Changing such routines often requires significant attention and effort. Impetus for change may occur when groups encounter a novel situation, experience failure, reach a milestone in group life, receive an intervention, or must cope with a change in the group's structure, task, or authority. Both the timing of the change and the tenacity of the routine will affect the ease with which it can be altered.

Roles   Effective team functioning calls for the performance of a wide range of work-related roles and understanding of the role system. Such understanding occurs when team members know their own and others' jobs and assignments and feel they have sufficient room to perform their responsibilities and get the job done independently or by coordinating with others.[38] Although we have discussed role performance, including role conflict and role ambiguity, in Chapter 3, we pursue the idea of work roles further here by examining the functional classification of roles that has been used historically and is still relevant today for analyzing group behavior.

Table 5–5 shows three categories of roles: task, maintenance, and individual.[39] *Task roles,* such as coordinator or initiator, focus on task or goal accomplishment. *Maintenance or group-building roles,* such as harmonizer or encourager, direct the group toward positive member interaction and interpersonal behavior. *Individual or self-oriented roles,* such as blocker or dominator, focus on satisfying an individual's needs and typically distract the group from effective functioning. Some members of the old Design Team, for example, may perform the task role of information giver by sharing their knowledge of various procedures developed so far with new team members. The team leader may be charged with monitoring and taking action by setting directions, designing the group, tuning its context, and providing resources.[40] Another member may perform the maintenance role of encourager by praising the ideas of other team members or the role of gatekeeper by encouraging others' participation. If two group members repeatedly argue with each other, they assume self-oriented roles and may also act as blockers who stubbornly resist others' ideas or as recognition-seekers who call attention to themselves by acting superior.

A group member may perform more than one role, and several members may perform the same role. Frequently a pattern of roles emerges for each group member. By tallying the nature and frequency of role behaviors and individuals' interactions

Table 5–5 **Classification of Group Roles**	*Task-oriented roles*	Initiator	Offers new ideas or suggests solutions to problems
		Information seeker	Seeks pertinent facts or clarification of information
		Information giver	Describes own experience or offers facts and information
		Coordinator	Coordinates activities, combines ideas or suggestions
		Evaluator	Assesses the quality of suggestions, solutions, or norms
	Maintenance roles	Encourager	Encourages cohesiveness and warmth, praises and accepts others' ideas
		Harmonizer	Alleviates tension; resolves intragroup disagreements
		Gatekeeper	Encourages participation by others and sharing of ideas
		Standard setter	Raises questions about group goals; helps set goals and standards
		Follower	Agrees and pursues others' activities
		Group observer	Monitors group operations; provides feedback to group
	Individual roles	Blocker	Resists stubbornly; negative; returns to rejected issues
		Recognition seeker	Calls attention to self by boasting, bragging, acting superior
		Dominator	Manipulates group; interrupts others; gains attention
		Avoider	Remains apart from others; resists passively

SOURCE: K. Benne and P. Sheats, Functional roles of group members, *Journal of Social Issues* 2 (1948): 42–47.

in a group, an observer can identify roles played by group members. This diagnosis is prerequisite to the evaluation of group functioning and effectiveness. It can also identify task and maintenance roles not played by any group members but important for group functioning. We can use the first two sets of roles listed in Table 5–5 as a basic checklist of roles that should be performed in groups such as the Design Team. Which roles are not performed by any group members? Which roles are performed ineffectively by group members?

Now think for a moment of a group to which you belong. Which roles did individuals perform at the group's most recent meeting or gathering? What types of behaviors occurred most frequently? Did the extent of task or maintenance role performance fit with the group's purpose and needs? Did a large number of self-oriented behaviors occur? An effective group typically displays both task and maintenance roles in varying amounts, depending on the group's needs. It shows few, if any, individual roles because these tend to detract from effective group functioning. Sometimes, however, even if individuals wish to play more functional roles, other group members may lock them into deviant or isolate roles. Scapegoating and projection by other group members can prevent an individual from adapting to the group's requirements. In addition, some members become dependent on other group members for approval or direction, causing dysfunctional behavior.

Effective managers can diagnose roles needed and played within a group. They can then act to reduce dysfunctional and increase functional role performance. Changing the roles of group members might require a structured intervention, such as training of group members or formal analysis of their role performance.

Structural Configuration

The group's structural configuration describes the relatively permanent role interactions in groups. These arrangements reflect the nature of communication among role holders and can contribute to a group's cohesiveness. Figure 5–12 illustrates five such communication patterns or networks. The wheel network has a single person who alone communicates with all others in the work group. The Y network (particularly if we invert it) and the chain network resemble the chain of command in a group. Communication flows up and down a hierarchy, with little skipping of levels or communication outside the hierarchy. The circle resembles the chain except the communication loop is closed; for example, the lowest-level member of a group may have a top manager as a mentor and communicate with him or her. In the completely connected network, all group members regularly communicate with all other members. Additional configurations, such as a star or a barred circle (where two additional points are connected across the circle) represent variations of these.[41]

The structural networks differ in the way information is exchanged and in the characteristics of the network members. Figure 5–12 summarizes the performance of various networks along these dimensions. The *speed* of information exchange and ultimately of problem solving tends to be slowest in the Y, chain, and circle networks, somewhat faster in the completely connected, and fastest in the wheel. In the wheel configuration, for example, information exchange occurs relatively quickly between the center position and peripheral ones; it flows somewhat slower among the spoke positions because the center acts as an intermediary.

Figure 5–12 Communication Networks and Their Characteristics

Network:

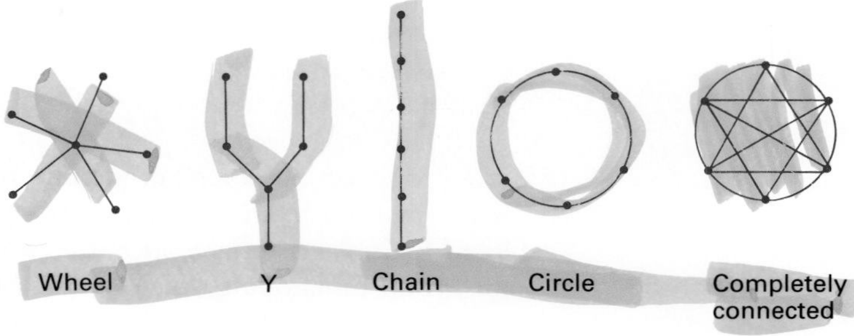

	Wheel	Y	Chain	Circle	Completely connected

Characteristics of Information Exchange:

	Wheel	Y	Chain	Circle	Completely connected
Speed	Fast	Slow	Slow	Slow	Fast-Slow
Accuracy*	Good	Fair	Fair	Poor	Good
Saturation	Low	Low	Moderate	High	High

Characteristics of Members

	Wheel	Y	Chain	Circle	Completely connected
Overall satisfaction	Low	Low	Low	High	High
Leadership emergence	Yes	Yes	Yes	No	No
Centralization	Yes	Yes	Moderate	No	No

*These accuracy estimates may change according to the nature and complexity of the task.

SOURCE: Based on A. Bavelas, Communication patterns in task-oriented groups, *Journal of Accoustical Society of America* 22 (1950): 725–730.

The *accuracy* of problem solving by the group—that is, the extent, frequency, and type of mistakes made—depends in part on the nature of the task. While accuracy of a very complicated task may be greater in a completely connected than in a wheel network, the reverse may be true for a very simple task where too great an exchange of information in the completely connected network may distort the information disseminated.

The *saturation* of the network, or the amount of information passed along the network's segments, ranges from lowest in the wheel or Y to highest in the circle and completely connected networks. Networks with low saturation tend to have a single, relatively central node that acts as a focus of information and limits the amount of information passed along the rest of the segments. In the highly saturated networks, in contrast, information passes relatively equally through all segments.

Member satisfaction overall seems to be higher in the circle and completely connected networks than in the other three. This satisfaction may also be associated with the sharing of leadership responsibility and the decentralized decision making in groups with those structural configurations, as well as the difficulty in isolating group members.

Leadership emerges most naturally in central positions of the wheel, Y, and chain networks. Here individuals who hold positions that link to at least two other positions tend to collect more information and hence can exert greater influence over other group members. The existence of *centralization* of decision making in the group—that is, whether a single person has primary responsibility for decision making as opposed to being decentralized to many members of the group—resembles the emergence of leadership in the networks.

Of course, a single network does not precisely describe communication in a group; more often a team uses variants of several networks. Identifying the predominant structural configuration, however, helps us explain or predict the performance and satisfaction of the group and its members and provides a useful diagnostic tool for identifying potential behavior problems. In the Design Team, for example, a wheel configuration may be best when the new group is first convened so that the leader can convey a large quantity of information to the team members as rapidly as possible. But when the group must identify and evaluate alternatives for the new products and processes, more discussion is essential, and a completely connected network would be more appropriate. Effectiveness occurs when a *fit* exists between the network, group member, and task characteristics. Chapters 7 and 11 examine the network approach to interpersonal interactions in greater detail by discussing its application to communication and organizational design.

CULTURAL DIVERSITY AND TEAM EFFECTIVENESS

Diversity of group members with regard to age, sex, race, or ethnic origin can have consequences for group performance. Specifically they may have different needs, interests, and goals, as well as bring different experiences and perspectives to the situation. Although groups composed of individuals with diverse cultural backgrounds can have special difficulties in functioning, the diversity can also enrich their performance.

Table 5–6 summarizes the advantages and disadvantages of cultural diversity in groups.[42] Multiculturalism brings diverse perspectives to the organization, resulting in multiple interpretations, greater openness to new ideas, increased flexibility, increased creativity, and improved problem-solving skills. Cultural diversity fosters increased creativity but requires careful conversations to ensure all members are understood; this process can result in better decisions and ultimately improved group

Table 5–6 **Advantages and Disadvantages of Cultural Diversity in Teams**

Advantages	Disadvantages
Culturally synergistic advantages: organizational benefits from multiculturalism	Disadvantages due to cultural diversity: organizational costs due to multiculturalism
Expanding meanings 　Multiple perspectives 　Greater openness to new ideas 　Multiple interpretations Expanding alternatives 　Increasing creativity 　Increasing flexibility 　Increasing problem-solving skills	Diversity increases 　Ambiguity 　Complexity 　Confusion Difficulty converging meanings 　Miscommunication 　Hard to reach a single agreement Difficulty converging actions 　Hard to agree on specific actions
Culture-specific advantages: benefits in working with a particular country or culture	Culture-specific disadvantages: costs in working with a particular country or culture
Better understanding of foreign employees Ability to work more effectively with 　particular foreign clients Ability to market more effectively to specific 　foreign customers Increased understanding of political, social, 　legal, economic, and cultural environment 　of foreign countries	Overgeneralizing 　Organization policies 　Organization practices 　Organization procedures Ethnocentrism

SOURCE: From Nancy J. Adler, *International Dimensions of Organizational Behavior,* 2nd ed. (Boston: PWS-Kent, 1991), p. 99. © by Wadsworth, Inc. Reprinted by permission of PWS-Kent Publishing Company, a division of Wadsworth, Inc.

effectiveness. It facilitates dealing with a particular country or culture because the team likely has someone who understands the "foreign" environment and workers. At the same time, the diverse perspectives in a multicultural group may increase the ambiguity, complexity, or confusion in situations; the group may not be able to reconcile different perspectives and use them constructively. Miscommunication and difficulty in reaching an agreement may result. Diversity can also cause decreased group cohesion resulting from such miscommunication and mistrust, which results in decreased ability to reach decisions and consequently decreased effectiveness.

INTERNATIONAL AND MULTI-CULTURAL DIMENSIONS OF TEAM MANAGEMENT

The society in which an organization operates provides a clue to organizational cultures there, which in turn provides the context for team functioning.[43] Consider, for example, the difference between U.S. and Japanese cultures and their implications for corporate culture. Many U.S. companies reflect a cultural orientation of individualism, whereas Japanese companies typically reflect their culture's collective orientation. These cultures would provide a significantly different context for the teamwork Jeff Markham must encourage. Now compare the U.S. and Scandinavian cultures, with their respective emphases on capitalism and socialism. Again, teamwork is more compatible with Scandinavian than U.S. culture. Some cultural systems accept change more rapidly than others; thus the state of the technological, economic, and social development of a nation affects its organizational culture. In Arab cultures, personal relationships and trust are primary and might provide a different context for team functioning than other countries.[44]

Culturally diverse teams have the potential for ineffective and effective perform-ance, depending on the nature of their task, stage of development, and the manage-ment of diversity. Diverse groups are advantageous in performing innovative tasks and less useful in completing routine tasks. Table 5–7 lists six questions for evalu-ating the effectiveness of a multicultural team. Diversity makes the processes of trust building and consensus building that are key to early and late stages of team devel-opment more difficult, but it facilitates the creation of ideas often associated with the middle stages of group development.[45] Group dynamics poses special challenges because managers cannot assume that organizational practices in one country apply equally well to those in another.

INCREASING WORK TEAM EFFECTIVENESS

How can Jeff Markham ensure that the Design Team will function effectively? Man-aging the organization's culture, improving group performance, implementing team building strategies, and encouraging collaboration among team members should ex-pedite team functioning.

Managing the Organization's Culture

We can diagnose an organization's culture to determine its fit with organizational goals and ability to relate effectively to the organization's environment. We can also assess its support for team-building activities. If the fit is a poor one, can culture be changed?

We can follow five guidelines for instituting such changes.[46] Changing an or-ganization's culture first requires a clear vision of the organization's future direction and the values and behaviors required to meet it. Second, top management must

---

Table 5–7 **Ques-tions for Evaluating Multicultural Team Effectiveness**

- Do members work together with a common purpose (something that is spelled out and felt by all to be worth fighting for)?
- Has the team developed a common language or procedure (a common way of doing things, a process for holding meetings)?
- Does the team build on what works (learning to identify the positive actions before being overwhelmed by negatives)?
- Does the team attempt to spell out things within the limits of the cultural differences involved (delimit the mystery level by directness and openness regardless of cultural origins of participants)?
- Do the members recognize the impact of their own cultural programming on individual and group behavior (deal with, not avoid the differences in order to create synergy)?
- Does the team have fun (within successful multicultural groups, the cultural differences become a source of continuing surprise, discovery, and amusement rather than irritation or frustration)?

SOURCE: Reprinted with permission from *International Consulting News,* April 1987. Cited in Philip R. Harris and Robert T. Moran, *Managing Cultural Differences,* 3rd ed. (Houston: Gulf, 1991), p. 197. Copyright © 1991 by Gulf Publishing Company, Houston, TX. Used with permission. All rights re-served.

support the culture change. Top management must be open to team ideas, be prepared to divest responsibility and authority to teams, involve the teams early in planning, be prepared for feelings of anxiety, be genuine in supporting the team, show commitment to teamwork by removing obstacles, and be prepared to invest time and money in team activities.[47] Third, top managers must model the new culture for subordinates in and through their own behavior. They must represent the desired values, expectations, and behaviors. Fourth, changes in an organization's structure, human resource systems, and management styles and practices must support the shift in culture. If an organization assumes an egalitarian, people-oriented culture, managers must encourage, measure, and reward worker participation in decision making. If an organization assumes a more authoritarian, production-oriented culture, managers must encourage, measure, and reward worker obedience to authority and "bottom-line" performance. Fifth and finally, members of the organization must be able to fit with the new culture. Doing so may require selection and socialization of newcomers—and termination of misfits; the merger of two organizations or a radical cultural change in a single organization is likely to result in some employee casualties.

Some researchers have suggested that different processes may be required to change different cultures, depending on a given organization's stage of development, orientation, ability to change, experience with alternate cultural frameworks, and history.[48] Figure 5–13 shows one model of culture change.[49] Managers here intervene at the points of behavior, justifications of behavior, cultural communications, hiring, and termination. Figure 5–14 shows a second alternative.[50] Phase I begins the process by analyzing the current culture and setting objectives; Phase II involves

Figure 5–13 **How Culture Tends to Perpetuate Itself**

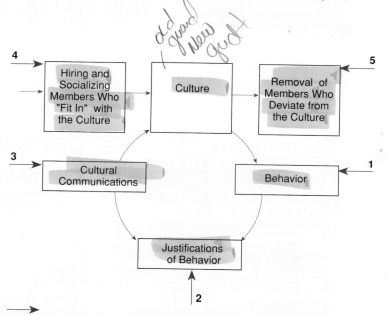

Managers seeking to create cultural *change* must intervene at these points. Conversely, managers seeking to *maintain* the prevailing culture must counteract any such intervention by others and prevent any weakening of these processes.

SOURCE: Reprinted with permission from V. Sathe, How to decipher and change culture. In R. H. Kilmann, M. J. Saxton, R. Serpa, and associates, eds., *Gaining Control of Corporate Culture* (San Francisco: Jossey-Bass, 1985), p. 245.

Figure 5–14 **The Normative Systems Change Process**

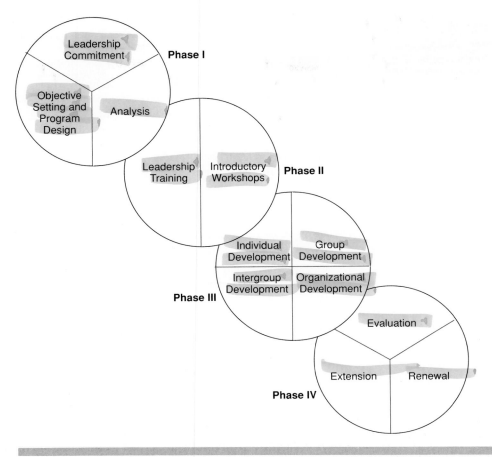

SOURCE: Reprinted with permission from R. F. Allen, Four phases for bringing about cultural change. In R. H. Kilmann, M. J. Saxton, R. Serpa, and associates, eds., *Gaining Control of Corporate Culture* (San Francisco: Jossey-Bass, 1985), p. 337.

putting those affected by the change into training and educational programs; Phase III focuses on systematically modifying the culture; Phase IV concludes with evaluation and revision of the change process. Every view of change calls for careful diagnosis of current culture by managers and other organizational members before designing and implementing change efforts.

Improving Group Performance

How can the team members improve their group's performance? Group members can contribute to better group performance by exerting more effort, bringing sufficient knowledge to the task, and using appropriate strategies for performing the task.[51] Table 5–8 identifies areas that can be altered to improve these conditions. For example, adjusting the group composition will help ensure that the group has sufficient knowledge and skills. Adjusting the organizational reward system should motivate ample effort.

Recent research addressed at a group's external interactions suggests that team building must consciously consider the group's tasks. For a group that needs outside resources, support, or information, such as consulting teams or product development teams, focusing only on internal processes may be insufficient or even counterpro-

Table 5–8 **Points of Leverage for Creating Conditions That Enhance Group Task Performance**

Process Criteria of Effectiveness	Points of Leverage		
	Group Structure	Organizational Context	Coaching and Consultation
Ample effort	Motivational structure of group task	Organizational reward system	Remedying coordination problems and building group commitment
Sufficient knowledge and skill	Group composition	Organizational education system	Remedying inappropriate "weighting" of member inputs and fostering cross-training
Task-appropriate performance strategies	Group norms that regulate member behavior and foster scanning and planning	Organizational information system	Remedying implementation problems and fostering creativity in strategy development

SOURCE: Reprinted with permission from J. R. Hackman, ed., *Groups That Work (And Those That Don't)* (San Francisco: Jossey-Bass, 1989), p. 13.

ductive.[52] External strategies, including *informing* by concentrating on internal processes and then communicating about the group's activities, *parading* by emphasizing internal team building and external visibility, and *probing* by interacting externally to learn about the environment, may be essential.

Strategies for Team Building

Improving the performance of work teams may also require implementing a variety of team-building activities. Managers or other organizational members can begin by collecting data about team functioning. They can use process observation, in which the process observer collects data about communication, decision making, and leadership in a team.[53] He or she records information about group norms and roles by tabulating who talks to whom, how frequently, and about what topics. Other data collection activities include brainstorming and various forms of interviewing and questionnaire administration. Team members must identify the problems they experience with group behavior and task performance. They might describe, for example, uneven participation by various group members or lack of appropriate skills for task performance as group problems. The administration of interviews and questionnaires to group members also provides information about the effectiveness of team performance.

After the data are collected, team members receive a compilation of the findings. A process consultant may help set an agenda for team action, coach the group or its members in effective interpersonal processes, or offer recommendations for more effective performance. This feedback and discussion of results is intended to help the team face their problems, evaluate their behaviors, and identify their challenges for future performance by answering questions such as the following:

- What is it like to work here?
- What helps or hinders working together?
- What is our job and our responsibilities?
- What are our expectations of our team and each other?
- What changes could be made to improve performance?
- What does each group member need to do differently?
- What can this unit do to work more cooperatively?
- How do other teams or work units perceive us, and vice versa?
- What commitment is each member willing to make to increase our effectiveness?[54]

Following data collection and feedback, team-building interventions provide opportunities for individuals to practice acting collaboratively and creatively. The team may use techniques such as brainstorming, NGT, or the delphi technique for improving group decision making and creative problem solving. Or they may use techniques designed to increase trust, improve communication, and encourage confrontation of conflict.[55] These include checking perceptual differences, practicing active listening, giving better feedback, third-party interventions, and redesigning jobs.

Self-directed work teams, or those groups of highly trained employees fully responsible for producing a major piece of finished work, pose different issues.[56] Team building must include planning for a transfer of operational decision-making authority from managers to the work teams themselves. Training must address the unique needs of managers and team members. Clear standards form the basis for measuring team performance, and the culture must support this way of doing work and accomplishing the organization's goals.

Building an Effective Multicultural Team

The protocol for building an effective multicultural team does not differ significantly from the general guidelines for team development. Managers should use diversity to enhance productivity while simultaneously addressing possible dysfunctions that accompany diversity.[57] They should select team members on the basis of their task-related skills, not their ethnic characteristics. Mutual respect should be developed by minimizing cultural stereotypes. Groups must then acknowledge cultural differences and strive to overcome any barriers these create early in the team's existence. The group's leadership must identify a superordinate goal as soon as possible, as well as neutralize power differences based on cultural background. Finally, managers should use quality feedback to reinforce desired group behaviors and extinguish undesirable behaviors and attitudes.

Increasing Collaboration among Team Members

The ability to work together is a prerequisite for team functioning. Facilitating collaboration may be a major challenge for organizations. Table 5–9 lists the steps that empower team members and support collaboration. Creating a culture that supports collaboration is a key step. Such a culture rewards honesty, integrity, willingness to share, receptivity to information and ideas, consistency, and respect for others.[58] Trust is a particularly important ingredient; it allows members to remain focused on the problem, encourages better communication and coordination, improves the quality of the results of collaboration, and encourages team members to pick up the slack for one another and consequently to improve overall team performance.[59] "Trust and collaboration come from (team members) being involved in planning the attack, working out the strategy for accomplishing the goal, and knowing what the team's approach is going to be and how it all fits together—recognizing that achieving the

Table 5–9 **Steps to Positive Power in Teams**

Team members must recognize each other's abilities and exchange them to accomplish tasks and solve problems.

1. Team members together recognize, emphasize, and clearly understand that their goals are cooperative. They know that as others reach their goals, they too are successful. Important cooperative goals lay the foundation for the following activities.
2. Members indicate the abilities and resources needed to accomplish team goals and aspirations.
3. Team members identify and demonstrate their knowledge, ideas, and other strengths. They know each other's abilities.
4. Employees indicate how they can use each other's abilities to reach the team's goals, accomplish its tasks, and meet their own aspirations.
5. Aware of their cooperative goals and valued abilities, team members agree to exchange resources. These exchanges should be timely, fair, and enhancing.
   - Abilities are valued at a particular time; information useful at one time is noise at another. Employees let each other know when they need the others' abilities.
   - Fairness demands that everyone give as well as receive.
   - Resources should be given so that the receiver does not feel belittled. Exchanges help members to feel confident that they have important assets and that they can rely on others for assistance.
6. As they collaborate, team members help each other to learn and develop skills.
7. The team celebrates its accomplishments and recognizes that everyone contributed to the group's success.

SOURCE: Reprinted with permission from D. Tjosvold, *Working Together to Get Things Done: Managing for Organizational Productivity* (Lexington, Mass.: Heath, 1986), pp. 88–89. Copyright 1986 by Macmillan Publishing Co., a Division of Macmillan, Inc.

goal is going to depend on how well the team works together in developing and implementing its strategy."[60] Finally, implementing a reward system that supports collaboration is critical. Through compensation, praise, or other reinforcers, organizational members must receive a clear message that collaboration is a priority.

SUMMARY

The workplace of the year 2000 will emphasize job performance by multicultural teams of workers. In this chapter we examined the factors that affect the functioning of such teams. We began by discussing the changing culture of organizations that fosters work by teams. We described its characteristics and links to team performance. We examined the reasons for team formation and identified the influences on group attraction and cohesion. We looked at team development over time from several perspectives that help diagnose dysfunctions in team performance.

Next we considered four aspects of group process that underlie team performance: goals, norms, roles, and structure. We compared and contrasted individual goals with group goals and showed how group goals influence team performance and effectiveness. We examined the nature and impact of norms, as well as influences on compliance in groups. We described the types of functional roles group members can hold. We studied a series of structural configurations in which interaction occurs in groups and their implications for information processing, team performance, and member satisfaction.

We then considered issues faced by groups that operate in the international arena and looked at the impact of cultural diversity on team effectiveness. The chapter concluded with a series of approaches for improving work team effectiveness, in-

Table 5–10 **Questions for Diagnosing Culture and Team Effectiveness**

- What type of culture exists in the organization?
- What components reinforce the culture?
- Does the culture reinforce team performance?
- Did the team form effectively?
- How effectively did the team deal with all stages of development?
- What are the team's norms, and are they functional?
- What roles did the team perform, and are they functional?
- Are individual and team goals appropriate and congruent?
- Is the team's structural configuration appropriate to the task, people, and information processing needs of the team?
- Does the team function well in a multinational and multicultural environment?
- What strategies does or should the team use to improve its effectiveness?

cluding strategies for increasing group performance, building effective teams, and facilitating collaboration among team members. Table 5–10 lists a set of diagnostic questions that help build effective teams.

Reading 5–1

Improving the Performance of New Product Teams
Deborah Gladstein Ancona and David Caldwell

An increasingly competitive global economy, coupled with rapid technological change, has made improvements in new product development a necessity. Strategies of being "first-to-market" or a "quick second" are increasingly seen as the most effective approaches for competing with both foreign and domestic rivals.[1]

Proposed techniques for speeding up the development process are diverse, ranging from increased use of new technologies such as CAD/CAM, to changing the structure of the organization, to reorganizing the teams responsible for actual development and testing of the new product.[2,3,4] What many of these techniques have in common is their attempt to improve the coordination among the different functions in the organization. A good deal of research[5] suggests that much of the delay in product development comes from the difficulty in coordinating the efforts of the various groups that must contribute to the development of a new product. Examples abound of the difficulties of ensuring that product designs can be easily manufactured, or of failing to include important information from marketing or sales and service early in the design process.

Perhaps the most common approach for speeding up the product development process is the use of a *team* to design the new product rather than assigning the design and development work to a single individual. As products become more complex, it is no longer possible for a single engineer or scientist to complete a project alone. In addition, the use of a cross-functional team has the potential to improve inter-unit coordination, to allow for project work to be done in parallel, not just sequentially, and to reduce delays due to the failure to include the necessary information from throughout the organization.[6]

If new product teams are able to fulfill their promise of shortening the product development cycle, they must develop the ability to obtain information and resources from diverse sources both inside and outside the organization. Without detailed technical, market, political, and financial information it is unlikely that the new product will meet both customer needs and the expectations of others in the organization. In addition to simply collecting information from diverse sources, teams must also interact with others in the organization to negotiate delivery deadlines, coordinate or synchronize work flow, obtain support from upper levels of management, and smoothly transfer the "ownership" of the new product to manufacturing, marketing and other groups. What this suggests is that developing an understanding of *how* teams deal with other groups can have important implications for helping improve the performance of these teams.

Boundary management is the process by which teams manage their interactions with other parts of the organization. It refers to lateral communications with other functional groups as well as with people further up the division or corporate hierarchy. Boundary management not only refers to communications or interactions that the team initiates but also to how the team responds to input from others.

In short, it describes the entire set of interactions a team must undertake in dealing with others upon whom it is dependent for information or resources or with whom it must coordinate to complete its assignment. How a team manages its boundaries can affect the team's performance.

This article reports some general findings from a study of the boundary management activities of 45 new product teams in five high-technology companies (see Table 5–11). We will lay out the patterns of activities teams use to coordinate with other parts of the organization and indicate how these patterns can influence both the internal functioning of the team and its overall performance. Then we will conclude with recommendations for managers who wish to improve the product development process.

MANAGING ACROSS THE TEAM'S BOUNDARY

Before describing how team members interact with others, it is useful to know that the members of the 45 teams spend, on average, about 48 percent of their time working alone, 38 percent of their time working with other team members, and only 14 percent of their time working with outsiders. Although the average time individuals spend working with outsiders is low, this is somewhat misleading. Viewing the distributions we find that certain team members spend a great deal of their time (in some cases, as much as 90 percent) working on problems that cross the team boundary, while others are totally isolated from outsiders.

The first major finding of our study is that new product team members engage in four distinct sets of activities

Table 5–11   **How the Study Was Conducted**

The study from which our descriptions of boundary management in new product teams are drawn was conducted in two phases. The first phase consisted of 38 interviews with new product team managers at seven companies in the computer, integrated circuit and analytical instrumentation industries. In addition to the interviews, all members of two teams kept logs of all of their external activities over a two-week period. In this initial phase, our goals were to understand the complete task the team faces and catalogue the complete set of activities that group members carry out with other parts of the organization.

In the second phase of the study, questionnaires were distributed to members of 45 new product development teams in five companies. Four hundred and nine people responded. We also asked senior division managers to evaluate the performance of each team. The goal of this phase was two-fold. First, we wanted to identify clusters of boundary activity, and second, we wanted to see how activity differed over the development cycle, and for high and low performing teams.—**D.G.A. and D.C.**

with other groups. The four patterns of activity are: ambassador, task coordinator, scout, and guard activity. Examples of each of these patterns are shown in Table 5–12.

1. *Ambassador* activities are those aimed at representing the team to others and protecting the team from interference. The team leader typically takes on these responsibilities, although they are often shared by several experienced team members. Ambassador activities are most often directed toward influencing individuals at upper levels in the organization and are directed toward one of four aims.

The first aim is buffering or protecting the team. In our sample, people reported that they spend time absorbing pressure from high levels and protecting the team from "political" pressures. As one interviewee pointed out, he tried to follow the lead of Tom West as described in the book *Soul of a New Machine* and "not pass on the garbage and the politics" to his team.

The second aim of the ambassador is building support for the team. This frequently means "talking up the team" in order to build the enthusiasm of outsiders and attempting to obtain resources the team feels it needs. Related to this is the third aim of ambassador activity which is reporting the team's progress to those higher in the organization.

Table 5–12   **Examples of Ambassador, Task Coordinator, Scout, and Guard Activities**

Ambassador:

"Near the end I talked to the top management group a lot. I tried to protect the group from that kind of pressure though. It's like Tom West said, 'we won't pass on the garbage and the politics.' "

"The first thing I did was to talk to lots of people to find out what they thought the product was and how to get there. . . . I started out with the guy who brought me here, he sent me to someone else, and so it went that I came to talk to a lot of high and middle level people. . . . So I gained knowledge about details of what the product ought to be, who the players were, what they did and what they wanted."

Task Coordinator:

"After a few weeks we had a design review with all of R&D. We just wanted to make sure that we weren't going off in crazy directions."

"At this point we have to use the test line, which is a shared resource so there's a lot of competition to use it. I have one guy who checks the schedule every morning so we know of any holes that we can fill."

Table 5–12 *(Continued)*

"We had to explain (to manufacturing) how certain things worked. I had lots and lots of meetings about the status of the project. We wanted some last minute changes on the machine, but manufacturing was not able or not willing to put it in all the machines. There were great arguments. . . . By April we had worked out a compromise agreement."

Scout:

"We have a kind of detector. . . . She spends time with outside groups to detect problems so they can be dealt with quickly."

"I have been to several meetings with the marketing representative—although it's not clear that he knows exactly what the marketplace is ready for. We're thinking about making some customer visits."

Guard:

"So we set up living quarters and moved the team away. That kind of intensity needed to be isolated. People kept coming over and saying, 'How's it going? What are you up to now?' That was at best distracting and at worst like being in a pressure cooker."

The final aim is developing an understanding of the company strategy and of the potential threats or opposition the team might face. The ambassador attempts to find answers to questions such as: What is the current product strategy? How can the product we are developing fit that strategy? How can we win over those who oppose this project?

2. *Task coordinator* is the name given to the second set of activities we identified. In contrast to those taking on the ambassador activities, people taking on these activities communicate laterally rather than up the organization. In our sample, the primary communication links were with manufacturing and other parts of R&D, and to a lesser extent, marketing. The activities of the task coordinator are aimed at coordinating the team's efforts with others. Examples include discussing design problems with others, obtaining feedback about the team's progress, and getting information about the progress other functional groups are making in accomplishing goals. Coordination planning is often accompanied by negotiating. This might involve attempting to get another group to speed up the development of a component or to share data with the team.

These activities may change over the life of a project.

In some teams, members describe a process of building relationships with other groups early in the product development process, well before coordination or negotiation are necessary. By doing this, team members are able to establish personal links with other groups before conflicting demands and deadlines put pressure on relationships. People who have high levels of ambassador or task coordinator activities spend more time working with outsiders and less time working alone than do other individuals. These individuals take on a higher percentage of the team's interactions with outsiders than others.

3. *Scouts* act like a scout on an expedition; that is, they go out from the team to bring back information about what is going on elsewhere in the organization. Scout activities are much less focused than task coordinator activities. Rather than having a specific schedule to work out, or seeking specific feedback on a particular piece of work, these activities involve more general scanning. Scouting provides general information about markets, technology and competition.

Individuals taking on these activities communicate more frequently with the marketing and sales functions than do individuals carrying out other activities. Scout duties are taken on more frequently by those who have experience in marketing and sales functions, and are seldom taken on by people who have spent their careers in manufacturing. Scout activities appear to be most important in the early phases of product development when the specifications of the new product are still being defined.

4. *Guard* activities differ from the others in that they are designed to keep information and resources inside the group and prevent others from drawing things out of the group. Not surprisingly, people taking on the guard role do not have significant amounts of communication with other functions or levels, and many of the communications they do have are designed to block or head off the requests of others. A key guard activity is keeping information secret. High levels of guard activity are most often found in teams working on high-priority projects or in organizations where product teams are highly competitive. An extreme form of guard activity is for a team to isolate itself and attempt to form its own "skunkworks."

In each team we studied, we observed different amounts of these boundary activities and different patterns of how these activities were distributed among team members. Some teams have broad communication networks with other parts of the organization while others are virtually isolated. Within teams, there are differences in how activities are split among team members. In some teams, the activities are widely distributed across individuals. In other teams, the activities are confined to a few individuals. Of particular interest is that people were seldom formally assigned to take on these activities.

CHANGING BOUNDARY ACTIVITIES

Our second major finding is that boundary management activities must differ across the product development cycle if the new product team is to be successful. Based on our early interviews with team leaders, we divided the development process into three phases: creation, development and diffusion. Each of the phases poses a different set of demands which the team must meet; as the demands of the task change, so must the pattern of the team's interactions with other groups.

The first phase, *creation,* is the early period of the product development cycle when the product idea is being formulated and the team organized. It is a time when the dominant activity is that of *exploration.* The team must consider many technical possibilities, integrate marketing data into technical considerations, and develop support for the product within the organization. During this time, we observed higher levels of ambassador, task coordinator, and scout activities in successful teams. During this phase, teams must collect large amounts of information: technical information about what is feasible; market information about what products are selling well; and political information about who in the organization supports the project and what resources will be available. In addition, many successful teams had members begin building relations with individuals in other functional areas to facilitate interactions later in the process.

For a team to enter the second phase, *development,* the project must have received some organization support and commitment. Product specifications have been agreed upon, and the major task of the team is to develop a prototype. The dominant activity during this time is *exploitation* of the information and resources the team has previously acquired. During this period, the team struggles to find the most efficient way to coordinate members and get the prototype finished. During this phase, the high levels of ambassador and scout activities seen during the creation phase are reduced. Successful teams reduce the incorporation of new ideas from outsiders so that the team can set schedules and get technical problem solving under way. Task coordination remains a dominant activity for these teams.

The few teams in our sample that failed and were disbanded before completing the project upon which they were working, failed because they were unable to change the work patterns that developed in Phase 1. These teams were unable to commit to a single plan of action but rather kept changing the product idea, schedules and team composition in response to continuing input from outsiders.

A change of boundary activities takes place again during the third phase, *diffusion.* This phase can be referred to as a technology transfer point in that the prototype, technical expertise, and enthusiasm and excitement for the product must be transferred from the team to other groups in the organization, particularly sales, marketing and manufacturing. During this phase, the important task of the team becomes that of *exportation* of the work that has already been completed. In our sample of teams, the diffusion phase was characterized by the highest levels of external interaction. Here teams need to convince manufacturing that their product should take priority, and they must get marketing to have the documentation ready on time. Unfortunately, many team members are "burnt out" or have moved on to other projects and are not prepared for the surge of activity needed at this time.

BOUNDARY ACTIVITIES AND TEAM PERFORMANCE

The third major finding of our study is that high-performing product development teams generally carry out more external activity than low-performing teams, even when controlling for the phase of the project. More specifically, high levels of scout activity are only important early in the process, while ambassador and task coordinator activity remain linked to performance throughout the product development cycle. High performers interacted more frequently than low performers with manufacturing, marketing, R&D, and top division management during all phases of activity. Members of high-performing teams did not simply react to communications from others; they were more likely to be the initiators of communication with outsiders than those individuals on low-performing teams.

In contrast, internal team dynamics were not related to performance in our study. High-performing teams were *not* distinguished by clearer goals, smoother work-flow among members, or a greater ability to satisfy the individual goals of the team members. In short, there was very little difference in the internal operations of high- and low-performing teams. In fact, in teams with high levels of interaction with outsiders, conflict between team members was higher than in teams with less boundary activity.

This is not to suggest that teams do not have to consider their internal operations. In fact, to successfully integrate information from outside sources and deal with the complexities in organizing and managing interactions with other groups, attention to the group's internal processes becomes critical. However, it is the external activities that are linked to high performance.

Perhaps as interesting as the findings themselves were the reactions of team members and leaders to those findings. When we interviewed members of these top-performing teams, they frequently reported that communication with top management was necessary in order to obtain resources, to present their proposals in line with current corporate thinking, and to build a reputation for excellent work that could be spread throughout the firm. Yet, when the pivotal role of ambassadorial activity was reported, members were often surprised and disappointed in the role that "politics" played in successful products. Leaders were not at all surprised by this finding and saw their ambassadorial activity as a critical mechanism to move the product across functional lines and through the organization.

Team members also viewed it as somewhat paradoxical that large amounts of time spent working outside the group can facilitate the group's effort. A number of engineers complained about the management responsibilities they had to assume, bemoaned the fact that they were being called upon to move beyond their technical assignments, and worried that spending time away from the team would negatively affect the product. Our results did not indicate this to be true.

WHAT TO DO

Although teams are currently touted as a mechanism for speeding up the product development process, this study suggests that putting a team structure in place is only the first step in a longer process. Team members also need to be educated to consider boundary management as an important part of their task. As authority and responsibility get delegated down through the organization to facilitate flexibility and speed, team members have to convince the rest of the organization that they have the right product, and they must move that product through creation, development and diffusion. Finding the best design is no longer enough. Team members first need to be convinced that ambassador, task coordinator, and scout activities are needed to both improve their product and get it to market in time to make a difference.

Yet even if convinced of their value, team members may not have the skills necessary to carry out such activities. For these people, training is suggested. This might take the form of classroom training where team members would struggle with cases of critical cross-functional problems and role play solutions, as well as apprenticeship programs whereby those with appropriate skills could model their boundary activity to an observant trainee. As an interim measure, liaison managers could be assigned to act as links between multiple product teams and various functional areas until the necessary skills are diffused throughout the organization. Furthermore, future recruitment decisions would have to reflect the need for individuals who could carry out ambassador, task coordinator, and scout activities.

These recommendations involve the individual members of the new product team. Yet cross-functional teams often face an organization that has rewards, norms, structures, and management that work to push members into old patterns of activity. The iron curtain that may exist among functions works to encourage the marketer not to trust the engineer. The fact that a team member is evaluated by a functional manager decreases commitment to the team.

This suggests that change at the individual and group level is not enough. New product teams may need to be moved out of the traditional environment into a new one where rewards are based on output and coordination, and the old modes of working are discouraged. In order to diffuse these innovations into the rest of the organization, broad changes in structure and culture are required. To catalyze such changes, we would look to new information technologies which network individuals across traditional boundaries, and to new management tools such as quality function deployment, which orchestrates interaction and understanding across functions. The new organization would have the language, vision and rewards to support a set of interconnected teams whose task is both quality design and efficient pooling of technical, market, manufacturing and sales expertise.

CONCLUSIONS

The change process we have described is going to be a long and difficult one. Frustrations are already apparent in many companies. However, if teams are to be the kernel of the structures of the future, such actions may be necessary. As our study suggests, the importance of boundary management in these teams should not be underestimated. Improving the ability of new product team members to carry out ambassador, scout, and task coordinator activity and to manage their relationships with others has the potential to shorten the product development cycle and help companies improve their competitive positions.

REFERENCES

1. Porter, M. E. (1987). "From competitive advantage to corporate strategy." *Harvard Business Review,* 65(3), pp. 43–59.
2. Clark, K. B. (1988). "Managing technology in technology competition: the case of product development in response to foreign entry." In A. M. Spence and H. A. Hazard (eds.) *International Competitiveness:* 27–74, Cambridge, MA: Ballinger.
3. Kanter, R. M. (1983). *The change masters: innovation for productivity in the American corporation.* New York: Simon and Schuster.
4. Sasser, W. E. and N. H. Wasserman (1984). *From design to market: the new competitive pressure.* Harvard Business School working paper.
5. Dougherty, D. (1987). *New products in old organizations: the myth of the better mousetrap in search of the beaten path.* Ph.D. Dissertation, Sloan School of Management, MIT.
6. Kasanjian, R. K. & R. Drazin (1986). "Implementing Manufacturing Innovations: Critical Choices of Structure and Staffing Roles." *Human Resource Management* 25(3), pp. 385–403.

DISCUSSION QUESTIONS

1. What can product teams do to shorten the product development cycle?
2. Describe and illustrate the four patterns of activities by which members of new product teams engage with other groups.
3. What are the stages of boundary-spanning activities and their implications for team performance?

Reprinted with permission from *Research Technology Management* 33(2) (March-April 1990): 25–29. Copyright © 1990 by Industrial Research Institute, Inc.)

Management Practices Also Need Passports

Activity 5–1

ADVANCE PREPARATION
Gather role sheets for each person.

INTRODUCTION
Culture clashes abound in today's global economy. Managers at all levels are being challenged, many for the first time, to do a better job of dealing with peers, subordinates, and bosses from other countries. Many scholars predict that what we see today with regard to "culture clashes" is but the tip of the interpersonal iceberg as we move toward the twenty-first century.

Step 1: Assign role plays to individuals, allowing them some time to read and prepare for the role playing. The preparation can be done outside of class. For each pair of roles, the U.S. manager's role can be assigned to an American student, and if foreign students are available, the foreign role players may be matched closely or approximately to their ethnic background.

Step 2: Form groups of three: two role players and one observer. The role player in whose office the role play is to occur must set up the meeting place—that is, arrange desk, chairs, and so on. The observer's task is to observe the behavior of the role players and after the role playing is concluded to ask the role players such questions as (a) Why did you behave the way you did? (b) What perceptions do you hold about the other's culture? Why? (c) What assumptions did you make about the other's culture? Why?

Step 3: Conduct the role plays. Optionally, a second and third round may be done with different roles, allowing role players and observer to rotate.

Step 4: The observers debrief the role players.

Step 5: Discussion. In small groups or with the class as a whole answer the following questions:

Description
1. Describe the behavior observed. What did each role player say and do?

Diagnosis
2. Evaluate the effectiveness of the role players' actions.
3. What role did cultural differences play in their behavior and attitudes?

Prescription
4. How could their interactions be improved?

Reprinted by permission of the authors: John F. Veiga, John N. Yanouzas, and Stan Bazan of the University of Connecticut, Storrs, CT 06269-2041.

The Reporter

Activity 5–2

Step 1: Read the *The Reporter* case.

The Reporter recently celebrated its thirteenth year as the student newspaper at State College. While it has experienced its share of ups and downs, it has always been published on time. In 1983 its staff was awarded the Red Key Student Organization of the Year Award for its outstanding performance and contribution to the college community. On October 20, 1985, *The Reporter* staff failed to print a weekly edition. This was the first time in its history that the paper had not met its deadline.

BACKGROUND
Until 1964, the campus newspaper's banner read *Exec*. This title epitomized the college founder James D. Atherton's commitment to develop and educate affluent young men into wealthy business executives and leaders in the field.

With the advent of the 1970s, State College underwent drastic changes; it began admitting women into the school. At the same time, the newspaper underwent a major change. Now there are approximately 1,650 full-time undergraduate students pursuing the Bachelor of Science degree in management and about 2,000 graduate students pursuing the Master of Business Administration degree. Of the total enrollment, approximately 1,060 are women.

Traditionally, all student organizations receive operating funds by submitting annual budgets to the Student Government Executive Board. All budgets list the amount required to conduct operations as well as that necessary to sponsor student-related events. The Government Board must then allocate student activities fees (independent of college administration) as equitably as possible.

In 1973 the *Exec* assumed its current identity, *The Reporter*. Previously, the *Exec* had received insufficient operating funds whenever it had printed unfavorable information about student government. In order to operate efficiently and effectively, *The Reporter* had committed itself to accepting funds from the college treasurer directly. Today its management is completely responsible for its operations, future development, and all debts incurred.

OPERATIONS

The Reporter, a student newspaper for and by students, links 3,000 individuals on and off campus at all levels of State's hierarchy including students, college staff, administrators, corporation officers, and trustees. The newspaper is published every Thursday during the fall and spring semesters with the exception of vacations and final exam periods. Members of the staff, comprised solely of students and a faculty adviser, are responsible for financial operations and planning, editorial content and policy, production, layout design, and circulation. The staff controls and performs all operations except for printing; printing services are contracted with an offset printer.

Organized along functional lines (Figure 5–15), general operations are overseen by the editor-in-chief. Each associate editor and all managers serve as the "movers" of the organization.

The editor-in-chief is elected by staff members to the post for a one-year period beginning in April; the transition month of May allows the newly elected editor-in-chief and staff members the opportunity to run the paper with the previous staff available to offer advice and support.

A successful candidate for the editor-in-chief position has made significant contributions to the organization by performing exceptionally in any functional area, has impeccable writing skills and command of grammar rules, and has a sincere commitment to task achievement.

Much like the student government president, *The Reporter* editor represents the entire student body. The editor acts as a liaison between the student body and college administration, faculty, and trustees. As part of the position, the editor serves as a member of the Trustee's Committee on Student Affairs which is comprised of both graduate and undergraduate student body presidents, one government-appointed student representative from each school, student judicial court chairperson, Greek Council President, the vice-president for student affairs, a faculty member, and the deans of students and student activities.

The editor's role on this committee is to summarize the issues that affect campus life. While the trustees may be aware of some issues, the editor relates the implication of any given policy or event, and the impact upon students' routines, morale, and attitudes. The editor also provides trustees with input through discussing letters to the editor. Letters, submitted by State community members, express attitudes, values, beliefs, and ways that a situation may be dealt with effectively.

Serving as a common bond between all persons affiliated with State College, from students to trustees, the newspaper is the student's formal mouthpiece. The newspaper enables students to get readers to know facts and feelings related to student concerns. The newspaper may be likened to a barometer that measures the general atmosphere of the student body.

ORGANIZATIONAL STRUCTURE
Business Manager
Working closely with the editor is the business manager. Together they monitor the newspaper's financial affairs, al-

Figure 5–15 **Organizational Structure**

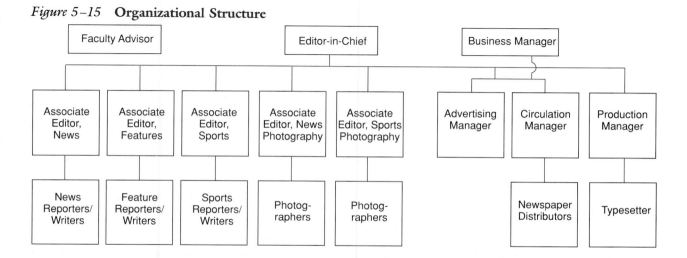

locating funds to support various functions. Only two variable sources of income beyond the student activities fees generate subscription revenue. They are alumni and parent readership and advertising revenue from local merchants (historically accounting for only 10 percent of operating funds). With approximately 90 percent of the newspaper's circulation confined to the campus, subscription and advertising revenue potential remains relatively low. Insightful planning is essential, otherwise spending more than available would result in the newspaper's shutdown. All debt incurred would be paid with funds from the following year's activities fees.

On the operations side, the business manager establishes the schedule for the collection of accounts receivable and the payment of accounts payable. At the editor's request, the business manager monitors the use of inventory and receives price quotes from various graphic supply houses. By comparing quotes and assessing the organization's needs, the business manager selects the most economical ones.

Finally, this position requires its incumbent to work closely with the college comptroller and treasurer in obtaining funds from the school when needed. Together they determine the optimum means of managing the funds for both short- and long-term requirements.

Associate Editors

Selected by the current editor, the associate editors are responsible for working with the editor frequently. Commitment to task completion, an affinity for writing, and adeptness in organizing people are the minimum requirements for a successful candidate. The news, features, and sports editors all determine their respective strategy, ensuring that each area complements the other stylewise. The associate editors coordinate the number of pages to be used by each.

Individually, each associate editor works with the editor to make certain that the information is objective, well-balanced, and of significance to the readers by answering how, what, why, when, who, and where. Key to any mission is that every story be followed up in subsequent issues, highlighting the impact upon the community, and the implications of both the short-run and the long-run.

Responsible for organizing, developing, and maintaining a staff of peers, each associate editor must establish source contacts from among students, college staff, faculty, and administration. The associate editor then works with each writer, providing support, information, and editorial assistance.

Advertising Manager

The advertising manager generates additional revenue by communicating with local merchants via telephone, letter, or in person. Accounts are won by eliciting a need in the advertiser's minds, communicating to them that a desire exists for the service or product, and convincing them that a handsome return on investments will follow.

Selling is one aspect of the advertising manager's position. Graphic layout is another. While some sponsors submit camera-ready mechanicals, others request that the advertising manager design the ad. Finally, both advertising manager and business manager work together to ensure that payment is received and that additional work is not provided for delinquent accounts.

Circulation Manager

Primary responsibilities of the circulation manager include delivering the mechanical (a mockup of a newspaper issue from which the printer takes photographs for offset printing) to the printer and delivering the printed copies to campus for distribution. With a staff of three or four students, newspapers are placed in students' campus mailboxes, handed to the campus mail center for distribution, to college faculty and administration, and dropped off at various high traffic locations on campus for public reading. For off-campus subscribers, the circulation manager prepares labels extracted from a computer program.

Soliciting for new subscriptions is limited. Feedback indicates that parents and alumni are not interested in day-to-day events on campus. Off-campus subscriptions equal a very small proportion of total circulation. The marginal revenue generated usually covers both fixed and variable expenses, contributing nothing to the newspaper's development.

STATE'S ENVIRONMENT AND ITS STUDENTS

With approximately 30 percent of State's undergraduate students as commuters, the college is classified as a residence campus. Despite its heavy concentration of resident students, the college community, according to former editor (1984–1985) Jack Dolan, is far from cohesive:

> The students at State generally do not get very involved in community activities like the newspaper or government. For the most part, students have off-campus jobs and commitments that they feel are more instrumental to securing a lucrative job after graduation. I've asked many students why they have not gotten involved in community activities. Their feeling is that it is something a person does in high school as a means to present impressive credentials to admission committees of prestigious colleges and universities.

The typical *Reporter* staff member does not fit into the mold which Dolan perceives. Rather, the student displays a greater degree of curiosity and expresses a greater concern about issues affecting the college community as a whole. A staff member tends to possess a higher degree of motivation than others. Additionally, a staff member realizes the benefit of involvement with the newspaper; potential employers generally view extracurricular participation as a predictor of high motivation and a desire to learn varied tasks. The newspaper also provides students with the opportunity to express themselves in such ways as writing, photography, and designing the layout format. *The Reporter* is a learning ground for budding leaders, and allows students to integrate the academic side of management with the realities of running an organization.

TWO CASES IN POINT
1984–1985

Led by Jack Dolan who served as editor during his junior year, *The Reporter* staff was comprised of forty active participants. Upon assuming the role of editor in April 1984, Dolan set out to build the remaining staff of twenty students to a greater size. During the previous year, much of the staff was doubling up in duties performed. For example, during the 1983–1984 administration, Dolan, who served as news editor, also assumed the responsibility for typesetting. Since most viewed this task as dull, volunteers were hard to come by.

Commenting on his decision to enlarge the staff, Dolan stated,

> With the pressure of academics, social concerns, and changing priorities, doubled responsibility just did not allow many of the staff enough room to breathe. In fact, morale suffered because of it. Not only was there a general lack of camaraderie, but the quality of the paper in comparison to previous editions also suffered. Bottom line, the lack of sufficient staffing made working on the paper unappealing. Staying up until 5 A.M. (from noon of the previous day) to produce the mechanical took out all the fun and clouded any benefits to be gained.

Dolan involved himself in every aspect of the newspaper. By working closely with individuals, he sought not only to assist staff members in producing an informative vehicle of communication, but he also discussed the ways in which involvement benefited the individual.

Mindful of the entire staff, Dolan believed that exceptional work by individuals contributed nothing to the entire organization. Teamwork, Dolan felt was imperative. Standards and formats were not determined by any single person. By encouraging communication among each other, generally agreed upon standards and formats were devised. Given the staff members' raw ability and the available equipment with which to work, Dolan often worked in a particular functional area in order to realize realistic goals.

1985–1986

In the spring of 1985, Jean Beene, then a junior, assumed the responsibilities of *The Reporter* editorship. Having served as news editor in 1984–1985, Beene was a writer on the news staff in 1983–1984. A marketing major, Beene felt the role of editor would enable her to test lessons learned in class while accepting a management role in her area of interests.

Except for the news and sports photography editors and business manager, all other management positions were filled by students who had either never worked on the staff or who had worked as reporters/photographers under an associate editor. With the exception of the news and sports photography editor, business manager, advertising manager, and circulation manager, the other associate editors were entering their second year at the college. The 1985–1986 staff totalled twenty volunteers.

With the new staff's first issue just one week away, no attempt had been made to formulate strategies or policies. It was just expected that the functional areas would guess correctly the number of pages to be filled. No meeting had been called to set direction for the associate editors.

As the first issue was in production, the previous editors visited in order to answer any questions the new staff might have had. With production a few hours behind the pace kept during the previous year, Dolan asked Beene, "Jean, I know it is your first issue as editor. Perhaps I can help you out a little so that you (the staff) will not have to stay up all night. Do you mind?"

Beene responded, "Thanks for the offer, Jack. But, it'll be fine. We're new and we're learning." For the remaining few issues before the end of the semester, the staff had produced issues of quality above that of other new staffs in their respective initial periods.

During the summer there had been no contact between the new staff members, except for a note sent by Beene indicating that all associate editors and managers would return to campus three days before new student orientation. Normally, the early return was used by *The Reporter* management to compile an issue for new students that previewed fall sports, student organizations, the orientation program, and key college staff and administrators with whom new students might need to consult. Also included in the note was a time and place for a staffing meeting.

At the staff meeting, Beene welcomed everyone back. She stated that the format for the new issue would be the same as produced during previous years. She asked the editors to make plans for storywriting; the previous year's deadlines would apply. Without further specification, the meeting was adjourned.

As the semester progressed, there was no mention of the traditional *Reporter* open house, designed to have students meet with the management staff, and to afford students the opportunity to learn how they could contribute to the organization. While most reporters from the previous year had graduated, few of the underclass students continued with the paper in the fall of 1985. Contributors to the newspaper plummeted from forty students to twenty students.

Normally a twelve-page paper, eight pages seemed to become the norm (the mechanics of newspaper construction necessitate that an issue be done in increments of four pages). No longer was the production of an issue finished the day before publication at 11 P.M. The average time lapsed to about 3:30 A.M. the day of publication, just a few hours before the printer's 6 A.M. deadline. Students on campus stated that the paper was not as informative as it had been in the past. Clubs no longer sent messages about events and meetings. Traditionally, the newspaper had been the primary vehicle for such communication. The staff members' morale was on the decline.

A CRITICAL INCIDENT

On October 20, *The Reporter* was not published for the first time in its history. At 11 P.M. on its production night, Dolan had gone down to the newspaper's production office at the request of an associate editor. According to Dolan, "The associate editors were quite upset, stating that they were sick of the conditions." Due to understaffing, none of the typesetting had been done (typesetting for an eight-page paper requires about ten hours of labor). After that, layout normally takes four hours. The printer's deadline was only eight hours away.

Beene was determined to put out a paper that week. Even though production was at a standstill, she insisted that they would make it. Everyone knew it was physically impossible. And since the printer runs copy only on Thursday, the outcome was certain. An emergency meeting was held among *The Reporter* staff members.

Step 2: Prepare the case for class discussion.

Step 3: Answer the following questions individually, in small groups, or with the class as a whole, as directed by your instructor:

Description
1. Why did *The Reporter* fail to publish?
2. How did each of the staff members contribute to the situation?

Diagnosis
3. What was the culture of this newspaper?

4. Did the culture facilitate team performance?
5. Did the staff develop into a team?
6. Evaluate the team performance. Apply the following conceptual frameworks in your analysis: (a) team formation, (b) team development, and (c) group process, including norms, roles, goals, and structure.
7. Did the group experience perceptual or attributional problems?
8. How did personal differences in group members affect the team's performance?
9. Did the staff experience motivation problems?

Prescription
10. What changes should have been made?
11. How can the staff become a team in the short run and long run?

Action
12. What issues should be considered in implementing this prescription?

Step 4: Discussion. In small groups, with the entire class, or in written form, share your answers to the questions above. Then answer the following questions:

1. What symptoms suggest that a problem exists?
2. What problems exist in the case?
3. What theories and concepts help explain the problems?
4. How can the problems be corrected?
5. Are the actions likely to be effective?

Reprinted with permission from The reporter, by Joseph J. Martocchio, in R. S. Schuler, ed., *Case Problems in Management and Organizational Behavior* (St. Paul: West, 1991). This case is based upon a real-life situation. It should serve as the basis for classroom discussion. Its purpose is not to convey what is effective or ineffective management. In this spirit, all proper names, dates, and vital information have been changed.

Activity 5–3   Paper Tower Exercise

Step 1: Your instructor will organize the class into groups of five to eight people.

Step 2: Each group will receive one twelve-inch stack of newspapers and one roll of masking tape. The groups have twenty minutes to plan a paper tower that will be judged on the basis of three criteria: height, stability, and beauty. No physical work is allowed during the planning period.

Step 3: Each group has thirty minutes for the actual construction of the paper tower.

Step 4: Each group should sit near its tower. Your instructor will then direct you to individually examine all the paper towers. Your group must then come to a consensus as to which tower is the winner. A spokesperson from your group should report its decision and the criteria the group used in reaching it.

Step 5:   Discussion. In your small groups, answer the following questions:

1. What percent of the plan did each member of your group contribute?
2. Did your group have a leader? Who? How was he or she chosen?
3. Which of the following best describes your role in the planning session: dominator, facilitator, inventor, design engineer, questioner, clarifier, negativist, humorist, artist? Which describes your role in the building session?
4. How did the group generally respond to the ideas that were expressed?
5. List specific behaviors exhibited during the planning and building session that you felt were helpful to the group.
6. List specific behaviors exhibited during the planning and building session that you felt were dysfunctional to the group.

Step 6:   Discussion. With the entire class, answer the following questions:

1. How did the groups' behavior differ?
2. What characterized effective groups?
3. How does your knowledge of group dynamics, specifically norms, roles, goals, and structure, explain your own and other groups' behavior?
4. How could the behavior of the groups be improved?

This exercise is based on "The Paper Tower Exercise: Experiencing Leadership and Group Dynamics" by Phillip L. Hunsaker and Johanna S. Hunsaker, unpublished manuscript. A brief description is included in *Exchange: The Organizational Behavior Teaching Journal* 4(2) (1979): 49. Reprinted by permission of the authors.

Activity 5–4

Group Meeting at the Community Agency

ADVANCE PREPARATION
Gather role sheets for each character and instructions for observers. Set up a table in front of the room with five chairs around it, arranged in such a way that participants can talk comfortably and have their faces visible to observers. Read the following introduction and cast of characters:

INTRODUCTION
The Community Agency is a role-play exercise of a meeting between the chairman of the board of a social service agency and four of his subordinates. Each character's role is designed to recreate the reality of a business meeting. Each character comes to the meeting with a unique perspective on a major problem facing the agency as well as some personal impressions of the other characters developed over several years of business and social associations.

THE CAST OF CHARACTERS

John Cabot, the chairman, was the principal force behind the formation of the Community Agency, a multi-service agency. The agency employs 50 people, and during its nineteen years of operations has enjoyed better client relations, a better service record, and a better reputation than other local agencies because of a reputation for high-quality service at a moderate cost to funding agencies. Recently, however, competitors have begun to overtake the Community Agency, resulting in declining contracts. John Cabot is expanding every possible effort to keep his agency comfortably at the top.

Ron Smith, director of the agency, reports directly to Cabot. He has held this position since he helped Cabot establish the agency nineteen years ago.

Joan Sweet, head of client services, reports to Smith. She has been with the Agency twelve years, having worked before that for HEW as a contracting officer.

Tom Lynch, head community liaison, reports to Joan Sweet. He came to the Community Agency at Sweet's request, having worked with Sweet previously at HEW.

Jane Cox, head case worker, also works for Joan Sweet. Cox was promoted to this position two years ago. Prior to that time, Jane had gone through a year's training program after receiving an MSW from a large urban university.

TODAY'S MEETING
John Cabot has called the meeting with these four managers in order to solve some problems that have developed in meeting service schedules and contract requirements. Cabot must catch a plane to Washington in half an hour; he has an appointment to negotiate a key contract that means a great deal to the future of the Community Agency. He has only 20 minutes to meet with his managers and still catch the plane. Cabot feels that getting the Washington contract is absolutely crucial to the future of the agency.

Step 1:
1. Five members from the class are selected to roleplay one of the five characters.
2. All other members act as observers.
3. All participants read the introduction and cast of characters.

4. The participants study the roles. All should play their roles without referring to the role sheets.
5. The observers read the instructions for observers.

Step 2:
1. When everyone is ready, John Cabot enters his office and joins the others at the table, and the scene begins.
2. Allow twenty minutes to complete the meeting. The meeting is carried to the point of completion unless an argument develops and no progress is evident after ten or fifteen minutes of conflict.

Step 3:   Discussion. In small groups or with the class as a whole answer the following questions:

Description
1. Describe the group's behavior. What did each member say? do?

Diagnosis
2. Evaluate the effectiveness of the group's performance.
3. What effects did such characteristics as group development, goals, roles, norms, and structural configuration have on its effectiveness?
4. Did any problems exist in leadership, power, motivation, communication, or perception?

Prescription
5. How could the group's effectiveness be increased?

Acton-Burnett, Inc.

Step 1:   Read the Acton-Burnett, Inc., case.

Bringing Acton-Burnett's June 12 executive committee meeting to a close, Hale Acton, III, chief executive officer and chairman of the board, asked Casey Ryan, vice president of marketing, and John Keene, vice president of corporate planning, to seriously reexamine the company's procedures for forecasting sales. Acton hoped that improved product demand projections would lead to better inventory control, financial planning and factory scheduling. Acton-Burnett had suffered significant losses in the first quarter of 1975 and expected even greater losses in the second quarter (the first losses the company had experienced since 1936). Acton felt that poor forecasting was one of several underlying factors contributing to the firm's current, poor performance.

   Ryan and Keene met subsequently with Robert Herd, president and chief operating officer, to briefly discuss his ideas on the subject. The two men then decided to form a task force to investigate the forecasting problem. Ryan and Keene agreed to put David Baker, a recent graduate of Stanford's Graduate School of Business, in charge of the task force. Baker had been with Acton-Burnett for two years and was currently a special assistant to John Keene. Prior to his present assignment, Baker had worked as a financial analyst in Keene's financial planning group, and was now assigned to Keene's market planning group. The assistant to market planning was an intentional move on Keene's part to broaden Baker's exposure to different aspects of Acton-Burnett's business. Baker was regarded by both Keene and Ryan as an especially promising and capable individual.

COMPANY BACKGROUND
Acton-Burnett was the third largest U.S. producer of precious metal alloys and other specialized alloys for commercial and industrial use; its 1974 sales exceeded $400 million. The company was headquartered in Chicago and had four major sales offices and five plants dispersed throughout the United States. Its products included alloys of silver, gold, platinum, and other precious or rare metals. The company sold its alloys in the form of ingots, bars, coil, strip and wire. Most of its raw material was purchased from abroad. Acton-Burnett sold its products to a wide range of customers, including dealers in precious metals, jewelry manufacturers, scientific firms, and industrial companies which used precious metals or special alloys in the manufacture of instruments and other devices.

   The company's present difficulties were precipitated by two sets of related events. The first was the 1974–1975 recession which had affected the company's sales to both industrial customers and jewelry manufacturers. The second factor was the rapid escalation which had occurred in the price of gold during the last six months of 1974. During 1974, the U.S. Congress had enacted legislation making it legal for private individuals and institutions to own and sell gold after January 1, 1975. Many industry sources felt that international gold speculators had intentionally driven up the price of gold during late 1974 in anticipation of a rush on gold by private U.S. investors. However, when the "public market" for gold opened in January, the expected demand did not materialize and the price of gold fell rapidly. The combination of the declining price of gold in early 1975 and Acton-Burnett's overly optimistic sales forecasts for the first two quarters of 1975 had resulted in excessive inventories of overvalued gold and sizable losses.

Acton-Burnett's current problems stood in dramatic contrast with the company's recent record of outstanding growth and profitability. The company had been founded by Acton's great-grandfather in 1881 and had always enjoyed a reputation for being a quality supplier of precious metals. However, during Hale Acton, III's ten-year stewardship as chief executive officer, the firm had quadrupled in size and had become the most profitable firm in the industry. Acton attributed this recent success to the company's aggressive marketing efforts and to an infusion of "professionally" trained managers into the company's organization. Under Acton and Herd's direction, the company was the first firm in the precious metals industry to develop a marketing organization in which market managers and product managers were responsible for focusing on specific market segments and applications. (Herd had been vice president of marketing prior to his promotion to president in 1973.)

Despite his family's obvious influence in the company, Acton had "come up through the ranks" and had a solid grounding in the business. Prior to becoming president of the company in 1965, Acton had attended the Advanced Management Program of the Harvard Business School. This experience had convinced him that several ideas he had developed over the years about marketing alloys were feasible, and he returned to Acton-Burnett determined to create a marketing organization and to hire business school-trained managers. In the ten years that followed, Hale Acton had hired a number of MBAs from Harvard, Stanford, Wharton, Columbia, and Dartmouth. It was generally acknowledged that many of these MBAs were received with some resistance from the "old-timers," although several of them had gained considerable influence and success within the company, including Ryan (a Harvard MBA) and Keene (a Dartmouth MBA), both of whom were now vice presidents.

FORMATION OF THE TASK FORCE

After some discussion, Keene and Ryan concluded that the major area for the task force to study should be the marketing division, because it was the four market managers who made the final forecasts for product demand. The market managers based their forecasts on information they received from their product managers, the vice president of Sales, the vice president of manufacturing, and the macroeconomic forecasts made by the vice president of economic analysis and forecasting. (See Figure 5–16 for an organization chart of Acton-Burnett.)

Having decided on the task force's mandate, Ryan and Keene met with Baker and described the problem as they saw it. Ryan said that he would appoint three product managers to the task force to represent the marketing division. He suggested that it would not be necessary to involve the market managers (to whom the product managers reported) because they were currently very busy and had been resistant to similar changes in the procedures in the past. Keene, in turn, said that he would ask Vincent Ernst, vice president of sales, to appoint a representative from sales to the task force. He also suggested that two others, in addition to Baker, be assigned from corporate planning. The first was Cynthia Schrafft, a young Harvard MBA, who Keene felt would add analytic strength to the group; and the second was Jason Cassis, a man in his mid-fifties, who Keene thought would add "balance" because he was an "old-timer" and would be able to relate well to the product managers. Keene also added that he would ask Dr. Walter Hunneuus, vice president of Economic Analysis, to also appoint a representative from his group.

The three men then agreed that the task force would report back to Keene, Ryan and the market managers on August 4. After the August 4 presentation, Keene would arrange for a subsequent presentation to the president and chairman of the board later in the month.

INITIAL MEETING OF THE TASK FORCE

A week after his discussion with Keene and Ryan, Baker had his first meeting with the newly appointed task force. Its members included (in addition to himself, Cynthia Schrafft and Jason Cassis) the three product managers from the marketing division, Steve Eldredge, an economic analyst from Dr. Hunneuus's group, and Ezra Bowe, a special assistant to the vice president of sales. (Please see Figure 5–17 for the names and positions of the task force members.)

The three product managers were all men in their middle to late forties and were obviously uneasy at the beginning of the meeting. Baker had had few prior contacts with them and did not know them well. By contrast, he knew Cynthia Schrafft and Jason Cassis fairly well because they also worked for Keene in corporate planning. Baker had previously worked with Schrafft and had come to admire her analytic ability, quickness, and perceptiveness. Although he had never worked directly with Cassis, he knew that Cassis was widely respected within the company for his competence, knowledge, and thoughtfulness.

Steve Eldredge, the representative from the economic analysis and forecasting group, was a Wharton MBA and a contemporary of Baker and Schrafft. Baker had once worked with Eldredge on a project before Eldredge had been transferred from Corporate Planning to Dr. Hunneuus's group. Baker had found this experience to be less than satisfying, with he and Eldredge disagreeing over several issues while working together.

Ezra Bowe, the representative from the sales division, was in his late fifties and had spent all of his career in sales. His last five years had been as a "trouble shooter," and special assistant to the vice president of Sales. Bowe, like Cassis, was well-liked and widely respected within the company.

The meeting had a slow and awkward beginning, with

Figure 5–16 Acton-Burnett, Inc., Simplified Organization Chart

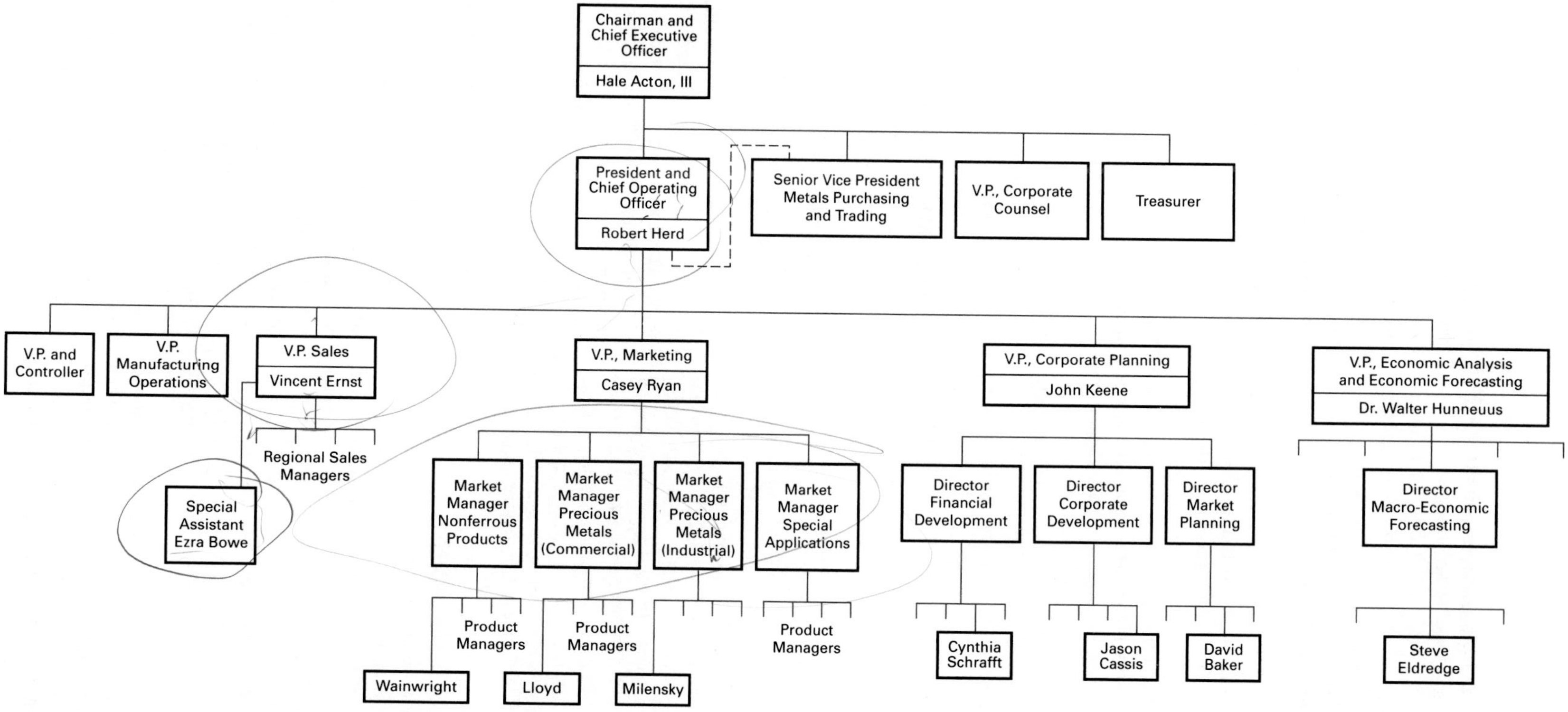

Figure 5–17   **Acton-Burnett, Inc., Forecasting Task Force**

David Baker, 28, Chairman: Marketing Planning analyst and Assistant to the Vice President of Corporate Planning. (Stanford MBA)

Cynthia Schrafft, 27: Financial Planning analyst. Representative of Corporate Planning. (Harvard MBA)

Jason Cassis, 54: Corporate Development specialist. Representative of Corporate Planning. (B.S., Missouri School of Mines, Rolla)

Peter Wainwright, 47: Product manager (Nonferrous Products Market Group). Representative of Marketing Division. (B.S., Wayne State)

Charles Lloyd, 43: Product manager (Precious Metals, Commercial Applications Market Group). Representative of Marketing Division. (B.S., Illinois Institute of Technology)

Charles Milensky, 48: Product manager (Precious Metals, Industrial Applications Market Group). Representative of Marketing Division. (Bronx High School of Science)

Ezra Bowe, 58: Special Assistant to the Vice President of Sales. Representative of the Sales Division. (B.M.S., Massachusetts Maritime Academy)

Stephen Eldredge, 29: Economic analyst. Representative of the Economic Analysis and Economic Forecasting Group. (MBA, Wharton)

Ezra Bowe, Cynthia Schrafft, and the three product managers saying almost nothing. In contrast, Steve Eldredge was quite vocal and emphatic about the need to develop a model for the internal forecasting process. Eldredge argued that it was essential for the task force to identify the basic underlying assumptions upon which the present product demand forecasts were based, and then to make a model of the entire process. Schrafft finally interrupted Eldredge to say that although she agreed a forecasting model might be useful in the future, she thought the creation of such a model should not be the task force's purpose. Rather, it should be one of the recommendations that the task force might make based on what they found. She also added that it was much more difficult to develop a single-firm forecasting model than it was to develop the macroeconomic models which Dr. Hunneuus and his group worked with.

After a long pause, Jason Cassis suggested that the task force divide up its work so that he and the three product managers could concentrate on the Marketing Division and Eldredge could concentrate on gathering whatever "hard data" he felt were necessary for a model. Baker thought that this was a good idea. He then asked Cynthia Schrafft and Ezra Bowe if they would be willing to concentrate on the Sales Division's inputs into the forecast. Schrafft and Bowe exchanged ideas briefly and then agreed to take responsibility for this part of the project. Shortly thereafter, the meeting adjourned, the consensus being that individual subgroups would stay in contact with Baker.

PREPARATION OF THE TASK FORCE REPORT

In the following five weeks, Baker spent much of his time working with Cassis and the three product managers on the Marketing Division's part of the study and with Schrafft and Ezra Bowe on the Sales Division's part. Cassis and the product managers worked well together and Baker found his meetings with them to be enjoyable and, at times, exciting. He also found that he, Schrafft and Bowe enjoyed working together and that the three of them were making considerable progress in identifying how the regional sales managers prepared the sales estimates which they gave to the vice president of Sales (which, in turn, constituted the Sales Division's inputs to the market managers). Eldredge, on the other hand, spent most of his time traveling to the various sales offices gathering data on historic sales trends as well as interviewing all of the product managers in the company headquarters. Baker's exchanges with Eldredge were brief and infrequent and occasionally, strained. Baker suspected that Eldredge resented Baker's more rapid progress within the company. He had also heard through the grapevine that Eldredge's boss, Dr. Hunneuus, was disturbed that he had not been asked by Acton to look at the forecasting problem, or by Keene and Ryan to head the task force. Several of Eldredge's comments reinforced Baker's suspicions, since Eldredge made it clear that the internal product demand forecasting should be done by Hunneuus's group instead of the market managers.

By July 23, Baker felt that the group had made enough progress to report back to Keene, Ryan and the market managers. The next day, he called the task force together to exchange their findings and to discuss a strategy for presenting their recommendations to Ryan and Keene on August 4. All of the task force members attended except Eldredge who was in New York City gathering sales data and could not make the meeting. Cassis and the three product managers were quite enthusiastic about several recommendations that they were sure would improve the quality of the product demand forecasts. Bowe and Schrafft also reported that they had found what they described as "some systematic biases" in the Sales Division's inputs into the forecast. However, they felt that they needed more time before they could make any specific recommendations. They did not think that they could make some "recommendations of a general nature" at the August 4 presentation.

After the meeting ended, Ezra Bowe took Baker aside and explained that the information he had on how the regional managers made their sales estimates was quite sensitive, and that he needed to discuss it with Vincent Ernst, the vice president of sales, before proceeding further. Bowe said that he would first prepare a report of his findings for only Baker and Schrafft to look at; then, after the three had discussed it, he would take the report to Ernst. He said that he did not yet have all the information necessary and that the report would probably not be ready before the August 4 presentation. He also added that it would take several discussions with Ernst before his findings could be presented to the rest of the task force because he thought his report would place the Sales Division in an embarrassing situation. He expected, however, that once Ernst understood the report and its implications, some significant changes could be made to improve the Sales Division's inputs into the market manager's forecasts. He also felt that Ernst would support these recommendations. Schrafft joined Bowe and Baker partway through their conversation, and she concurred that all of this work could not possibly be completed by August 4. She suggested that their general recommendations be followed up at a later date with more specific recommendations after Bowe had discussed his report with Ernst.

During the following week, Jason Cassis and the product managers spent most of their time preparing for the presentation, while Ezra Bowe worked as rapidly as he could on his report. Cynthia Schrafft, in addition to consulting with Bowe on the report, concentrated on preparing some general recommendations about the Sales Division's input into the forecast.

Baker had spoken with Eldredge as soon as he returned from New York and briefed him on the results of the earlier meeting. Eldredge agreed to outline a proposal for the development of an internal planning model as his part of the August 4 presentation. Eldredge added that gathering his data had been a frustrating experience and that he suspected that the regional sales managers were hiding information from him.

THE AUGUST 4 REPORT OF THE TASK FORCE

Prior to the task force's oral presentation on August 4, Baker, Cassis and the three product managers agreed that Cassis should be the one to report his subgroup's findings and recommendations. The three product managers felt that if they made the presentation it would put them in an awkward position with their bosses, the market managers, because several of their conclusions were critical in nature. Baker agreed with this strategy. He also decided (with the approval of the other members of the task force) on a tentative agenda. The plan was for Baker to begin the oral report with a fifteen-minute summary of the group's purpose, what they saw as the general problems, and their major recommendations. He was to be followed by Eldredge, who would recommend that an internal forecasting model be developed to assist the market managers in making their individual product demand forecasts. Eldredge would also report on the historic sales data and on what he thought

were the critical underlying assumptions which would have to be clarified in developing an internal forecasting model. Then, Cassis would report his subgroup's findings on how the Marketing Division should restructure its procedures for making future product demand forecasts. After Cassis's report was completed, Schrafft would present her general recommendations concerning the Sales Division's inputs into the product demand forecasts.

The presentation was scheduled to last from 10:00 A.M. to 1:00 P.M. in Casey Ryan's office. Baker had arrived at his own office at 8:00 A.M. to go over his notes and flip charts. Shortly after 9:00, Ezra Bowe came into Baker's office with a copy of the report he had been working on all week. Bowe had stayed up most of the night typing it himself so that Baker could see it before going into the meeting. Baker skimmed the six summary statements on the first page and was indeed surprised by what they said. It was clear that the regional sales managers were consistently overstating their sales estimates in order to ensure adequate inventory and rapid delivery. He called Schrafft on the telephone and the three decided to discuss Bowe's report the next day, but not to report any of its findings at the presentation.

The presentation began promptly at 10:00 A.M. Everyone seemed very much at ease except for the three product managers. The meeting went smoothly until Eldredge finished his portion of the presentation. Eldredge asked if there were any questions and one of the market managers said he hoped that what the others had to say would be more relevant than Eldredge's recommendations. He added, "You guys in Hunneuus's group can't even forecast what the economy is going to do; how the hell are you going to tell me what our customers are going to do with your models?" The other market managers laughed at this remark, and to save Eldredge further embarrassment, Baker said that Eldredge's recommendations would make more sense after the market managers heard the other reports.

Cassis then presented the report on the Marketing Division's procedures for forecasting product demand and the task force's recommendations on how they should be changed. During Cassis's presentation, the product managers asked him several questions of a clarifying nature which Baker felt were useful in getting certain points across to the market managers. At the conclusion of Cassis's presentation, Lloyd, one of the product managers, said that all three of them felt that the conclusions and recommendations were sound and that they were prepared as individuals to "stand solidly behind them" and take "personal responsibility" for their consequences.

Following this remark, Ryan, the vice president of Marketing, asked his market managers what they thought of Cassis's report. One of them said he thought the recommendations might improve the forecasts, while the other three said that the recommendations could not possibly work. Their comments included such arguments as the recommendations would not allow enough room for necessary subjective factors, and that the new procedures would involve too much red tape. The discussion became quite heated, with most of the questions being addressed to Cassis. Several times, the product managers were cut off by their bosses in their attempts to answer questions or clarify certain points. Finally, one of the market managers said to Cassis, "Jason, frankly, I'm amazed that this kind of nonsense could come from you. I would expect it from a tenderfoot like Baker or Schrafft or Eldredge, but from you? You've been around here long enough to know our business better than to come up with this nonsense." A second market manager added, "Look, I'm just getting things under control again so we won't lose money next quarter. The last thing I need is this garbage." He then turned to Ryan and said, "In no way am I going to swallow this stuff." Ryan began to respond, when Keene interrupted to say that he thought tempers were hot and that the recommendations were not as controversial as they might first appear to be. He suggested that the meeting be adjourned until 3:00 to give everyone a chance to cool off and think things over. Ryan agreed that the suggestion was a good one and the meeting ended at 11:30.

Keene asked Baker to remain after everyone else had left. Keene then closed the door and said to Baker, "We've got one hell of a mess here, and you better figure out what you're going to do at 3:00. In the meantime, Ryan and I will put our heads together and see what we can come up with." Baker picked up his notes and left.

When Baker returned to his own office, he found Eldredge sitting at his desk thumbing through the report that Ezra Bowe had left for him earlier in the morning. Baker explained that the report had been loaned confidentially to Baker for study purposes only, and that Bowe had told him that he had to discuss the report with his boss before presenting it to the full task force. Baker added that none of the report's data would be presented in the afternoon meeting, except in the most general terms. Baker continued by saying that it was important to respect Bowe's wishes and that the report would be shared with the task force when the time was right. Eldredge responded by saying that Bowe's data would certainly have made his own task much easier. He said he had suspected all along that the regional sales managers had been withholding information from him. Eldredge added that he had come by to say that he was angry that he had not received more support from Baker and Schrafft when the market managers had attacked him during the morning meeting. Baker explained his rationale for wanting to move the discussion on to another topic, and that one of his reasons for doing this was to get Eldredge out of the tough spot that he was in. He said he was sorry that Eldredge had interpreted it as a lack of support. Eldredge accepted his apology and left.

A few moments later, Schrafft came in to ask Baker to join her for lunch. The two spent most of their lunch discussing what Baker should do when the meeting reconvened at 3:00. After lunch, Schrafft accompanied Baker back to his office where they found Dr. Hunneuus waiting at Baker's door. Hunneuus said that he wanted some information on two of the points that Bowe had made on the first page of his report. Baker noticed that Hunneuus was holding a piece of yellow-lined paper with Bowe's six major points written on it. Hunneuus stated that he needed this information for a meeting that he had scheduled for 4:00 with Vincent Ernst, the sales vice president (and Bowe's boss), to get "some real progress going on the forecasting problem." Baker replied that it was impossible to give him that data, and that the report was considered confidential. Hunneuus smiled and asked how company information could be thought of as confidential when it was a corporate vice president who was asking for it. Hunneuus left by saying that he would get the information he needed from Ernst himself when they met at 4:00.

Schrafft, who had overheard Baker's exchange with Hunneuus, seemed incredulous at what had transpired. Baker explained that Eldredge had seen the report before lunch and that he had explained its confidentiality to him. Eldredge had presumably understood the situation, although he had not actually said that he would keep it confidential. Schrafft was by now quite angry, and said that if Ezra Bowe was in any way hurt or compromised by this turn of events, that it would be Baker's responsibility. She said that Bowe had taken a personal risk in sharing the information with them and that if Bowe ended up in trouble because of it, Baker's word would not "be worth a plugged nickel" in the future. Baker attempted to again explain what had happened, but Schrafft cut him off by saying, "You've got a problem, man, which you'd better fix in a hurry."

Step 2: Prepare the case for class discussion.

Step 3: Answer the following questions individually, in small groups, or with the class as a whole, as directed by your instructor:

Description

1. Describe the interactions among members of the task force.
2. What occurred at the initial meeting of the task force?
3. How were responsibilities for preparing the task force's report allocated?
4. Why did Schrafft give Baker an ultimatum?

Diagnosis

5. In what culture did the task force function?
6. Do members of the task force function as a team?
7. Is the task force an effective team?
8. Evaluate the group dynamics in the task force. Apply the following conceptual frameworks in your analysis: (a) goals, (b) norms, (c) roles, and (d) structure.
9. Did the task force experience perceptual or attributional problems?
10. How did personal differences in task force members affect their performance?

11. Did the task force members experience motivation problems?

Prescription

12. What changes should have been made?

13. How can the staff become a team in the short run and long run?

Action

14. What issues should be considered in implementing this prescription?

Activity 5–6   **Team Behavior Analysis**

Step 1: Select a team to observe. Justify that it qualifies as a team.

Step 2: Spend at least five hours observing the team.

Step 3: Describe the team's behavior. Keep a log of your observations.

Step 4: Diagnose the team's behavior.

1. Describe its culture.
2. Trace its formation and development.
3. Identify its goals, norms, roles, and structure, and evaluate them.
4. Diagnose the team's overall effectiveness.

Step 5: Prescribe a plan for improving the team's effectiveness.

Step 6: Discussion. In small groups or with the class as a whole, or in writing, share your observations and analyses. Then consider the following questions:

1. What similarities are there among the teams? What differences? Can you develop profiles of types of teams?
2. What do effective teams look like? What do ineffective teams look like?
3. Trace the formation, development, and group dynamics of effective and ineffective teams. Compare and contrast the features of such teams.
4. Identify key elements in plans for increasing team effectiveness.

CONCLUDING COMMENTS

Organizations are increasingly relying on work teams to perform many kinds of jobs. Senior-level management teams are also becoming increasingly common.[61] Effective teams must succeed in dealing with informational, decisional, operational, and interpersonal aspects of group process. Managers who lead work teams must avoid the following five mistakes:

1. Calling the performing unit a team but really managing members as individuals.
2. Failing to maintain the balance of authority between management and the team.
3. Failing to provide the team with appropriate amounts (neither too much nor too little) of structure for accomplishing the task.
4. Failing to provide organizational supports for accomplishing challenging team objectives.
5. Assuming members have the required competence to work well as a team.[62]

Groups help humanize the workplace, delineate the social reality for organizational members, generate and enforce norms, voice members' concerns, exert influence within and outside the organization, and coordinate resources for task performance.[63] These features and functions permeate any discussion of team forma-

Table 5–13 **Special Risks and Opportunities for Work Teams**

	Risks	Opportunities
Top Management Teams	Underbounded; absence of organizational context	Self-designing; influence over key organizational conditions
Task Forces	Team and work both new	Clear purpose and deadline
Professional Support Groups	Dependency on others for work	Using and honing professional expertise
Performing Groups	Skimpy organizational supports	Play that is fueled by competition and/or audiences
Human Service Teams	Emotional drain; struggle for control	Inherent significance of helping people
Customer Service Teams	Loss of involvement with parent organization	Bridging between parent organization and its customers
Production Teams	Retreat into technology; insulation from end users	Continuity of work; ability to hone both the team design and the product

SOURCE: Reprinted with permission from J. R. Hackman, ed., *Groups That Work (And Those That Don't)* (San Francisco: Jossey-Bass, 1989), p. 489.

tion and development, norms, roles, goals, and structural configuration. Table 5–13 shows the special risks and opportunities for a variety of work teams. They function within the context of the organization's culture, which may be a function of the national culture. You experienced some of the potential clash of cultures in the role plays of "Management Practices Also Need Passports." You continued your analysis of teams and cultures in observing the groups in the Community Agency and Paper Tower exercises and analyzing team performance in *The Reporter* and Acton-Burnett, Inc., cases.

In these activities, as well as in Team Behavior or Analysis, you also proposed strategies for building an effective team. You may have offered approaches that influence the interpersonal processes and encourage new group social norms. Or you may have proposed technical and procedural interventions, which primarily seek to alter technical skill levels and task-related norms. Finally, you may have offered cultural changes, which focus on changing the environment in which teams function.

ENDNOTES

[1] C. E. Larson and F. M. J. LaFasto, *Team Work: What Must Go Right/What Can Go Wrong* (Newbury Park, Calif.: Sage, 1989).

[2] See E. H. Schein, Organizational culture, *American Psychologist* 45(2) (1990): 109–119.

[3] N. C. Morey and F. Luthans, Refining the displacement of culture and the uses of scenes and themes in organizational studies, *Academy of Management Review* 10 (1985): 219–229; M. R. Louis, Organizations as culture-bearing milieux. In L. R. Pondy R. J. Boland, Jr., and H. Thomas, eds., *Organizational Symbolism* (Greenwich, Conn.: JAI, 1980).

[4] G. Morgan, *Images of Organizations* (Beverly Hills, Calif.: Sage, 1986).

[5] J. Martin and D. Myerson, Organizational culture and the denial, channeling, and acknowledgement of ambiguity. In L. R. Pondy, R. J. Boland, Jr., and H. Thomas, eds., *Managing Ambiguity and Change* (New York: Wiley, 1988); and D. Meyerson and J. Martin, Cultural change: An integration of three different views, *Journal of Management Studies* 24 (1987): 623–647, provide the original categorization of perspectives. P. J. Frost, L. F. Moore, M. R. Louis, C. C. Lundberg, and J. Martin, eds., *Reframing Organizational Culture* (Newbury Park, Calif.: Sage, 1991), offers additional discussion and examples.

[6] L. Schein, *A Manager's Guide to Corporate Culture* (New York: Conference Board, 1989).

[7] See D. L. Denison, *Corporate Culture and Organizational Effectiveness* (New York: Wiley, 1990), for a detailed examination of this relationship.

[8] V. Sathe, *Culture and Related Corporate Realities* (Homewood, Ill.: Irwin, 1985).

[9] G. G. Gordon, Industry determinants of organizational culture, *Academy of Management Review* 16(2) (1991): 396–415.

[10] T. E. Deal and A. A. Kennedy, *Corporate Cultures* (Reading, Mass.: Addison-Wesley, 1982).

[11] Morgan, *Images of Organizations,* p. 124.

[12] S. L. Solberg, Changing culture through ceremony: An example from GM, *Human Resource Management* 24 (Fall 1985): 329–340.

[13] L. Hirschhorn, *Managing the New Team Environment: Skills, Tools, and Methods* (Reading, Mass.: Addison-Wesley, 1991).

[14] J. Moskowitz, Lessons from the best companies to work for, *California Management Review* 27 (Winter 1985): 42–47; J. O'Toole, Employee practices at the best managed companies, *California Management Review* 28 (Spring 1985): 35–66.

[15] R. W. Napier and M. K. Gershenfeld, *Groups: Theory and Experience,* 4th ed. (Boston: Houghton Mifflin, 1989).

[16] *Ibid.*

[17] N. Rosen, *Teamwork and the Bottom Line* (Hillsdale, N.J.: Erlbaum, 1989).

[18] P. S. Goodman, E. Ravlin, and M. Schmenlie, Understanding groups in organizations. In L. L. Cummings and B. M. Staw, eds., *Research in Organizational Behavior,* vol. 9 (Greenwich, Conn.: JAI, 1987).

[19] D. Norris and R. Niebuhr, Group variables and gaming success, *Simulation and Games* 11 (1980): 301–312; L. Wheeless, V. Wheeless, and F. Dickson-Markham, A research note: The relations among social and task perceptions in small groups, *Small Group Behavior* 13 (1982): 373–384.

[20] Napier and Gershenfeld, *Groups.*

[21] *Ibid.*

[22] W. G. Dyer, *Team Building: Issues and Alternatives,* 2nd ed. (Reading, Mass.: Addison-Wesley, 1987).

[23] S. D. Van Raalte, Preparing the task force to get good results, *Advanced Management Journal* 47 (Winter 1982): 11–19.

[24] B. W. Tuchman, Developmental sequences in small groups, *Psychological Bulletin* 63 (1965): 384–399; N. R. F. Maier, *Problem Solving and Creativity in Individuals and Groups* (Belmont, Calif.: Brooks/Cole, 1970); R. F. Bales and F. L. Strodtbeck, Phases in group problem solving, *Journal of Abnormal and Social Psychology* 46 (1951): 485–495; B. W. Tuchman and M. C. Jensen, Stages of small group development revisited, *Group and Organization Studies* 2 (1977): 419–427.

[25] J. Moosbruker, Developing a productive team: Making groups at work work. In W. B. Reddy and K. Jamison, eds., *Team Building: Blueprints for Productivity and Satisfaction* (Alexandria, Va.: NTL Institute for Applied Behavioral Science, 1988).

[26] Discussion of this model is based on C. J. G. Gersick, Time and transition in work teams: Toward a new model of group development, *Academy of Management Journal* 31 (1988): 9–41.

[27] A. B. Drexler, D. Sibbet, and R. H. Forrester, The team performance model. In Reddy and Jamison, *Team Building.*

[28] J. R. Hackman, ed., *Groups That Work (And Those That Don't)* (San Francisco: Jossey-Bass, 1989).

[29] D. G. Ancona and D. F. Caldwell, Information technology and work groups: The case of new product teams. In J. Galegher, R. E. Kraut, and C. Egido, eds., *Intellectual Teamwork: Social and Technological Foundations of Cooperative Work* (Hillsdale, N.J.: Erlbaum, 1990).

[30] Larson and LaFasto, *Team Work.*

[31] J. Jackson, A conceptual and measurement model for norms and values, *Pacific Sociological Review* 9 (1966): 35–47, describes the three types discussed here.

[32] E. F. Huse and J. L. Bowditch, *Behavior in Organizations: A Systems Approach,* 2nd ed. (Reading, Mass.: Addison-Wesley, 1977).

[33] D. C. Feldman, The development and enforcement of group norms, *Academy of Management Review* 9 (1984): 47–53.

[34] *Ibid.*

[35] Napier and Gershenfeld, *Groups.*

[36] This discussion of habitual routines is based on C. J. G. Gersick and J. R. Hackman, Habitual routines in task-performing groups, *Organizational Behavior and Human Decision Processes* 47 (1990): 65–97.

[37] Gersick, Time and transition in work teams.

[38] Hirschhorn, *Managing the New Team Environment.*

[39] K. D. Benne and P. Sheats, Functional roles of group members, *Journal of Social Issues* 4 (1948): 473–506.

[40] J. R. Hackman and R. E. Walton, Leading groups in organizations. In P. S. Goodman and Associates, eds., *Designing Effective Work Groups* (San Francisco: Jossey-Bass, 1986).

[41] See R. S. Ross, *Small Groups in Organizations* (Englewood Cliffs, N.J.: Prentice-Hall, 1989); R. R. Ross and M. G. Ross, *Relating and Interacting* (Englewood Cliffs, N.J.: Prentice-Hall, 1982); M. E. Shaw, Communication networks fourteen years later. In *Group Processes,* L. Berkowitz, ed. (New York: Academic Press, 1978).

[42] N. J. Adler, *International Dimensions of Organizational Behavior,* 2nd ed. (Boston: PWS-Kent, 1991).

[43] C. J. Fombrun, Corporate culture and competitive strategy. In C. J. Fombrun, N. M. Tichy, and M. Devanna, eds., *Strategic Human Resource Management* (New York: Wiley, 1984).

[44] P. R. Harris and R. T. Moran, *Managing Cultural Differences,* 3rd ed. (Houston: Gulf, 1991).

[45] Adler, *International Dimensions.*

[46] H. Schwartz and S. Davis, Matching corporate culture and business strategy, *Organizational Dynamics* (Summer 1981): 30–48.

[47] C. Hastings, P. Bixby, and R. Chandhry-Lawton, *The Superteam Solution: Successful Teamworking in Organizations* (Aldershot, England: Gower, 1986).

[48] A. L. Wilkins and W. G. Dyer, Jr., Toward culturally sensitive theories of cultural change, *Academy of Management Review* 13 (1988): 522–533; E. H. Schein, *Organizational Culture and Leadership* (San Francisco: Jossey-Bass, 1985).

[49] V. Sathe, How to decipher and change corporate culture. In R. H. Kilmann, M. J. Saxton, R. Serpa, and associates, eds., *Gaining Control of the Corporate Culture* (San Francisco: Jossey-Bass, 1985).

[50] R. F. Allen, Four phases of bringing about cultural change. In Kilmann et al., *Gaining Control.*

[51] Hackman, *Groups That Work.*

[52] D. G. Ancona, Outward bound: Strategies for team survival in an organization, *Academy of Management Journal* 33 (1990): 334–365.

[53] E. H. Schein, *Process Consultation,* 2nd ed. (Reading, Mass.: Addison-Wesley, 1988).

[54] P. R. Harris and R. T. Moran, *Managing Cultural Differences,* 2nd ed. (Houston: Gulf, 1987), pp. 174–175.

[55] U. Merry and M. E. Allerhand, *Developing Teams and Organizations: A Practical Handbook for Managers and Consultants* (Reading, Mass.: Addison-Wesley, 1977).

[56] J. D. Orsburn, L. Moran, E. Musselwhite, and J. H. Zenger, *Self-Directed Work Teams: The New American Challenge* (Homewood, Ill.: Irwin, 1990).

[57] Adler, *International Dimensions.*

[58] Larson and LaFasto, *Team Work.*

[59] *Ibid.*

[60] *Ibid,* p. 93.

[61] J. S. Lublin, Companies form teams to expedite decisions, *Wall Street Journal,* December, 20, 1991, p. B1.

[62] Hackman, *Groups That Work.*

[63] R. E. Walton and J. R. Hackman, Groups under contrasting management strategies. In Goodman and Associates, *Designing Effective Work Groups.*

RECOMMENDED READINGS

Denison, D. *Corporate Culture and Organizational Effectiveness.* New York: Wiley, 1990.

Frost, P. J., Moore, L. F., Louis, M. R., Lundberg, C. C., and Martin, J., eds. *Reframing Organizational Culture.* Newbury Park, Calif.: Sage, 1991.

Galegher, J., Kraut, R. E., and Egido, C. *Intellectual Teamwork: Social and Technological Foundations of Cooperative Work.* Hillsdale, N.J.: Erlbaum, 1990.

Hackman, J. R., ed. *Groups That Work (And Those That Don't).* San Francisco: Jossey-Bass, 1989.

Hirschhorn, L. *Managing in the New Team Environment: Skills, Tools, and Methods.* Reading, Mass.: Addison-Wesley, 1991.

Napier, R. W., and Gershenfeld, M. K. *Groups: Theory and Experience,* 4th ed. Boston: Houghton Mifflin, 1989.

Reddy, W. B., and Jamison, K., eds. *Team Building: Blueprints for Productivity and Satisfaction.* Alexandria, Va.: NTL Institute for Applied Behavioral Science, 1988.

Chapter Outline

- **OPENING CASE** *The Downsizing Decision at Acme Products, Inc.*

  The Context of Decision Making

  The Decision Makers

  Types of Decisions

  Information and Decision Making

  The Characteristics of Effective Decisions

  The Rational Decision-Making Process

  Alternatives to the Rational Decision-Making Process

  Individual versus Group Decision Making

  Barriers to Decision-Making Effectiveness

  Cognitive Biases in Decision Making

  Ways to Improve Decision Making

- **READING 6–1** *Agreement and Thinking Alike: Ingredients for Poor Decisions*

  Richard A. Cosier and Charles R. Schwenk

- **ACTIVITIES**

  6–1 Anatomy of a Tragedy

  6–2 Wilderness Survival Worksheet

  6–3 Decision Making in Groups

  6–4 How Biased Is Your Decision Making?

  6–5 Dave Stewart

  6–6 Ethical Decision Making

Analyzing and Improving Decision Making

Learning Objectives

After completing the reading and activities in Chapter 6, students will be able to

1. Delineate the context of decision making.

2. Identify the types of decision makers in organizations.

3. Discuss the impact of a multinational and multicultural context on decision making.

4. Compare and contrast two types of decisions and offer approaches for making each of them.

5. Cite the criteria of effective decisions and apply them to a decision.

6. Comment about the characteristics of an ethical decision.

7. Trace the steps in the rational decision-making process.

8. Offer a complementary four-step process to the rational decision-making process.

9. Contrast the rational process to alternative decision-making processes.

10. Compare and contrast the value and use of individual and group decision making.

11. Describe the barriers to effective decision making and suggest ways of overcoming them.

12. Offer three strategies for improving individual decision making.

• •

The Downsizing Decision at Acme Products, Inc.

Carl Shigatsu recently became the managing director of Acme Products, a major manufacturer and distributor of electronics products in the United States. The U.S. division had 4,000 employees in seven plants located across the United States and a central headquarters operation. Business had boomed during the 1980s, but like many of its competitors Acme was experiencing significant profitability problems in the new decade.

Shigatsu had been selected because of his previous successes in turning around similar problems in Japan. He had been schooled in Japan and the United States, and had spent part of his career working for a subsidiary of Acme in Japan, but he had also spent a number of years working for Acme's competitors in the United States. Shigatsu took over his new position knowing that he would have to make some significant changes.

During his first month on the job, it became clear to him that the 1980s had meant more than just a boom in profits. Hiring had been expansive, and at least two of the plants had been built without a careful analysis of their utilization in times of decline. When he compared the revenues to the costs of personnel and equipment, he knew that he would be faced with some hard decisions.

Carl's mandate from the board of directors was to cut costs and increase profits. He quickly identified three ways of accomplishing these goals. First, he could close one or more plants. Second, he could reduce the number of employees at each plant. Third, he could cut the staff at corporate headquarters, including the sales and service people. Shigatsu knew that further study of the situation might suggest other problems and possibilities, but he also knew he needed to act quickly and decisively to stem the flow of red ink.

• • • • • • • • • • • • • • • • • • • •

*H*ow should Shigatsu proceed? How should he manage the decision-making process? In this chapter we begin by examining the context of decision making and the nature of decision makers, focusing particularly on issues associated with managing a global and multicultural work force. Next we look at the types of decisions managers and other organizational members make and the information they use to make the decisions. Then we specify the characteristics of effective decisions, including issues of quality, acceptance, and ethical decision making. We next consider several prototypes for an effective decision-making process. We also compare and contrast individual and group decision making. Finally, we discuss the barriers to decision making and cognitive biases in decision making, and we propose ways of overcoming them and making more effective decisions.

THE CONTEXT OF DECISION MAKING   Decision making occurs at individual, group, and organizational levels. Since many organizations operate in a global environment, decision makers must be prepared to function in complicated and ambiguous situations. Dealing with the intense competition in the marketplace and the rapidly changing economic, social, political, and technological environment requires decision makers to have a readily accessible and effective process for making decisions. Environmental conditions may increase the complexity of the decision-making process and limit an organization's ability to control the outcomes of its decisions.[1]

THE DECISION MAKERS

Individuals or groups of individuals with a set of skills, knowledge, experiences, and values make decisions in organizations. Obviously the skills, knowledge, and experiences correlate with the type and amount of expertise an individual or group brings to decision making. The personal value systems of individuals influence the decision-making process and outcomes by affecting perceptions of situations, problems, individual and organizational success, the choice process, interpersonal relations involved in decision making, limits of ethical behavior, and acceptance of organizational goals.[2]

Personal style also plays a major role in decision making. Figure 6–1 shows one model of style. It considers the dimensions of cognitive complexity, or an individual's ability to tolerate ambiguity, and values orientation, or the propensity for logical as

Figure 6–1 **Cognitive Decision Style Model, Showing the Two Dimensions and their Interpretations**

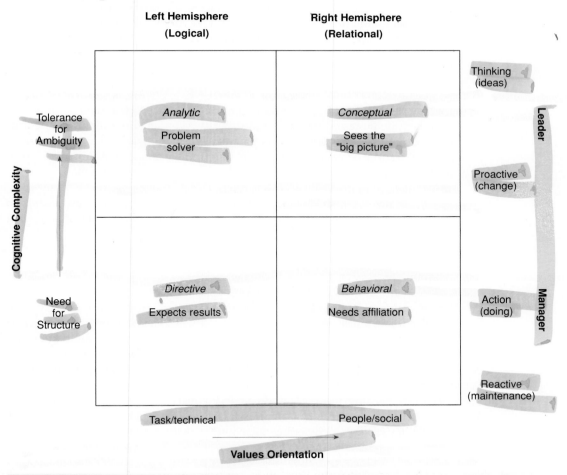

Source: Reprinted with permission from D. Shackleton, L. Pitt, and A. S. Marks, Managerial decision styles and Machiavellianism: A comparative study. *Journal of Managerial Psychology* 5(1) (1990): p. 10.

opposed to relational thought.[3] High cognitive complexity also describes a leader who is proactive and has a high tolerance for ambiguity; low cognitive complexity depicts a manager who is action oriented and reactive, and has a high need for structure. The resulting four styles suggest the way a decision maker would approach the decision-making process. Groups of decision makers may use a common or hybrid style; analyzing its appropriateness is one element in diagnosing decision-making effectiveness. An individual's personality may further affect the attitude toward uncertainty and risk, as well as his or her perception of the decision and the decision-making process.[4]

TYPES OF DECISIONS

Consider the types of decisions made consciously (or unconsciously) by managers such as Carl Shigatsu. Obviously he makes staffing, budgeting, product, and other policy decisions; he might also be involved in advertising decisions, decisions about plant openings or closings, or even issues related to the management of particular employees. Now think for a moment about the types of decisions other managers—and employees—at Acme make. Although such decisions can be classified in a variety of ways, including managerial–nonmanagerial, work–nonwork, organization–group/individual, policy–one-time, formal–informal, and routine–nonroutine, one useful way of thinking about such decisions is whether they are programmed or nonprogrammed.

Programmed Decisions

In making *programmed* decisions, individuals devise specific solutions to problems that are relatively structured. Sometimes decisions become programmed because they have been repeatedly tested through past experience; other times they become programmed because the problem and its parameters are so clearly defined. Decisions about the allocation of overtime hours in unionized plants, for example, are programmed because standard operating procedures exist for solving them.

In making programmed decisions, individuals typically have rules of thumb or heuristics for solving the problem. They may have had significant experience in making the same decision and can relatively automatically follow a set of steps that result in an appropriate outcome.

Nonprogrammed Decisions

Nonprogrammed decisions are unstructured, sometimes new and unique, and require special treatment. Shigatsu's decision about whether and how to downsize Acme Products is a nonroutine and nonprogrammed decision. Although Carl may have been involved previously in making a similar downsizing decision, the particular circumstances he encounters at Acme sufficiently differ from other profitability problems that established policies or precedents are not really helpful. Nonprogrammed decisions can be problematic and challenging for managers and other organizational members because they often must find innovative solutions to difficult problems. Such decisions become more common as individuals move up the organization's hierarchy. Because no precedent may exist for making such decisions, a quality decision-making process, as described later in this chapter, is very important.

Decision makers must seek creative ways of making nonprogrammed decisions because they cannot rely on either their own or others' experience or standard solutions. Note that making a nonprogrammed decision often requires time, expertise, and creativity, since the decision maker is breaking new ground.

INFORMATION AND DECISION MAKING

Effective decision making requires an individual to secure and use high-quality and complete information. One way of describing information is to categorize it as basic, elaborating, or performance data,[5] as described in Table 6–1. *Basic* data include the list of alternatives from which choices are made and the criteria used to evaluate each alternative. Shigatsu, for example, must gather information about the company's options for reducing costs, describe several possible future scenarios, and decide how to assess the quality of each scenario. *Elaborating* data provide more insight into the future conditions and criteria for evaluating them. *Performance* data include the likely consequences of various alternatives as well as the constraints that affect them. Shigatsu, for example, must assess the economic ramifications of continuing versus not continuing to distribute particular products, or maintaining certain plants in operation.

If managers and organizational members behaved rationally, they would collect sufficient information to allow them to discriminate among alternative choices. But do individuals behave in this way? Too often individuals tend to use accessible information rather than to continue seeking quality information.[6] Although using only readily accessible information can save time, it can also contribute to faulty decision making. Carl Shigatsu must be sure to collect comprehensive information about various costs, expenditures, and revenues before making the downsizing decision. He likely will rely on other managers and employees at Acme to provide many of these data. These organizational members must recognize that the quality of information they can readily acquire, such as reports from coworkers, offhand comments by other employees, or one-time observations of behavior, may be inferior to the information potentially available and actually may not be adequate for the situation.

Individuals also vary in their access to information; for example, they can draw more easily on information that caused an emotional reaction, is specific to the given situation, was received most recently, and is most accessible to them.[7] Even when decision makers gather information, they may not use it in decision making. Managers must ensure that they collect reliable and relevant information and allow sufficient time to use the information once they collect it. Recognizing constraints imposed by the nature of the decision and collecting and using quality information contribute to effective decision making.

Table 6–1 **Types of Information**

Basic Data
1. What are the alternatives?
2. What are the future conditions that might be encountered?
3. What are the criteria to be used in evaluating alternatives?

Elaborating Data
1. What are the probabilities of the future conditions?
2. What is the relative importance of the various criteria?

Performance Data
1. What are the payoffs (or costs) associated with various outcomes?
2. What are the constraints on the payoffs or costs?

SOURCE: G. Huber, *Managerial Decision Making* (Glenview, Ill.: Scott, Foresman, 1980), pp. 257–258.

THE CHARAC-
TERISTICS OF
EFFECTIVE
DECISIONS

Effective decisions combine at a minimum high quality, acceptance by the decision makers and other stakeholders, and ethical appropriateness, as shown in the effectiveness triangle of Figure 6–2.

Quality of the Decision

A good-quality decision brings about the desired result while meeting relevant criteria and constraints. What would constitute a good-quality decision about the situation at Acme? Certainly a decision that reduces costs while maintaining profits would be considered a good-quality one. Also, a decision that met the needs of those affected by the decision, including stockholders, top management, and workers, would qualify. So too would a decision that meets the financial, human, time, and other constraints existing in the situation.

The quality of the decision depends in part on the level of the decision maker's technical or task skills, interpersonal or leadership skills, and decision-making skills, as shown in Figure 6–3. *Technical or task skills* refer to the individual's knowledge of the particular area in which the decision is being made—the technical aspects of the work operations. In the decision Carl must make about downsizing, task skills refer to a knowledge of labor costs, projected revenues, product information, and plant overhead costs. *Interpersonal or leadership skills* relate to the way individuals lead, communicate with, motivate, and influence others. Carl Shigatsu for example, must be able to get the other managers at Acme, as well as many of the employees, to accept the decision for which he is responsible. Effective communication, as described in Chapter 7, should facilitate understanding and acceptance of the decision in the implementation. *Decision-making skills* are the basic abilities to perform the components of the decision-making process, including situational analysis, objective setting, and generation, evaluation, and selection of alternatives, as described later in this chapter.

Acceptance of the Decision

Carl Shigatsu and any advisers he involves in the decision making must produce a decision that they and the rest of the company can accept—one they are willing to

Figure 6–2 **Effectiveness Triangle**

Figure 6–3 **Quality of Decision Making**

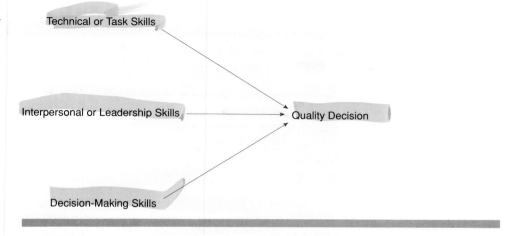

Technical or Task Skills

Interpersonal or Leadership Skills ⟶ Quality Decision

Decision-Making Skills

"live with" and use as the basis of further action. For example, closing two plants may be a high-quality decision, but the union may oppose it so much that the union members would cripple the work at other Acme plants. Alternatively, redesigning the sales job and laying off part of the sales support staff may be a high-quality decision, but the customers may resist the change because they feel Acme will not respond to problems in a timely fashion.

Ethical Decision Making

In addition to evaluating a decision in terms of its quality and acceptance, we can also assess how well it meets the criterion of ethical justness. "Ethical issues are ever present in uncertain conditions where multiple stakeholders, interests, and values are in conflict and laws are unclear."[8]

Consider, for example, the situation experienced by Johnson & Johnson during the Tylenol tampering in the 1980s. Top management faced the decision of whether to pull millions of dollars of inventory from store shelves at a major financial loss to the company or to ignore the situation. What decision did the executives make? They pulled Tylenol in a variety of forms from the shelves, stating that it was the only choice. Such ethical decision making should be *de rigeur* in organizations, but often is not. Now consider the decision made by Exxon's top management regarding the cleanup in Alaska of the *Valdez* oil spill. The ethical appropriateness of their decision has been widely criticized.

Managers and employees can assess whether the decisions they make are ethical by applying personal moral codes or society's codes of values; they can apply philosophical views of ethical behavior; or they can assess the potential harmful consequences of behaviors to certain constituencies. In the Tylenol situation, top management appeared to apply at least one and probably all of these criteria in selecting the action they chose. One way of thinking about ethical decision making suggests that a person who makes a moral decision must first recognize the moral issue where a person's actions can hurt or help others, second make a moral judgment, third decide to attach greater priority to more concerns than financial or other concerns, or establish their moral intent, and finally act on the moral concerns of the situation by engaging in moral behavior.[9] In making a decision managers can use the checklist shown in Figure 6–4. Managers certainly should assess whether their own and others' decisions meet ethical standards before implementing them.

The cultural context may affect the classification of a decision as ethical or not. What is viewed as unethical behavior, such as taking bribes, in one country may be

Figure 6–4 **General Ethical Checklist**

	Yes	No
1. "Does my decision treat me, or my company, as an exception to a convention that I must trust others to follow?"	—	—
2. "Would I repel customers by telling them?"	—	—
3. "Would I repel qualified job applicants by telling them?"	—	—
4. "Have I been cliquish?" (If "Yes," answer questions 4a through 4c. If "No," skip to question 5.)	—	—
4a. "Is my decision partial?"	—	—
4b. "Does it divide the constituencies of the company?"	—	—
4c. "Will I have to pull rank (use coercion) to enact it?"	—	—
5. "Would I prefer to avoid the consequences of this decision?"	—	—
6. "Did I avoid any of the questions by telling myself that I could get away with it?"	—	—

SOURCE: Reprinted with permission from M. R. Hyman, R. Skipper, and R. Tansey, Ethical codes are not enough, *Business Horizons* (March-April 1990), p. 17.

viewed as ethical in another. How would you act if you believed taking a bribe was unethical but it was common practice in the country where you worked? The decision maker has basically two options for resolving this dilemma: either invoking his or her personal beliefs or following the norms of the culture in which the company is located.

THE RATIONAL DECISION-MAKING PROCESS

In many situations, using a rational, step-by-step decision-making process increases the likelihood that a high-quality, accepted, and ethical decision will result.[10] In this section, we first consider a six-step approach in detail and then briefly examine a four-step sequence.

The Six-Step Approach

Consider the decision that Carl Shigatsu must make at Acme Products. He can proceed to a solution by performing the six steps shown in Figure 6–5 and described in Table 6–2: situational analysis, objective setting, generation of alternatives, evaluation of alternatives, making the decision, and evaluation of the decision.

Analyzing the Situation Decision making first requires the recognition that there is a problem to be solved or a decision to be made, followed by the exploration and classification of the decision situation.[11] Decision making then requires asking such questions as (a) What are the key elements of the situation? (b) What constraints affect the decision? and (c) What resources are available? How would Carl Shigatsu answer these questions? The key elements include the past performance of various plants and workers, the sales history of the company, the projected sales forecasts, the overhead costs of plant operation, and the likely cost of living, among others. Carl must consider previous efforts to reduce costs at Acme and the employees' and customers' reactions to them. He must investigate the current situation of competitors and the likely impact their actions will have on Acme.

Constraints on the decision will include the laws that affect employment and plant closings and the availability of alternative sources of capacity if he misestimates

Figure 6–5 **The Six-Step Decision-Making Process**

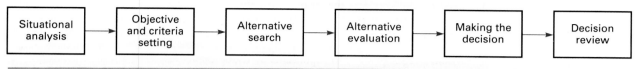

demand. While limitations on resources can act as a constraint on the decisions made in this situation, the nature of financial, personnel, and time resources should also act as criteria for selecting among alternatives. Offering early retirement may have different time and financial implications than offering voluntary severance programs or just closing plants and laying off workers. From this situational analysis, the decision maker begins to formulate the issues to be addressed. Clearly, in the situation at Acme Products, the problems focus on dealing with the oversupply of workers and the lack of product demand.

Table 6–2 **Sample Diagnostic Questions for the Six-Step Decision-Making Process**

Phase I	Situational analysis	What are the key elements of the situation?
		What constraints affect the decision?
		What resources are available?
Phase II	Objective setting	Is the problem stated clearly?
		Do group members understand what they will work on?
		By what criteria will decision making be judged?
Phase III	Search for alternatives	Are those individuals most involved in the problem also involved in the decision making?
		Has complete information been sought? Are information holders involved in the decision making?
		Is a diversity of means used to generate ideas?
		Are all ideas encouraged, regardless of their content?
Phase IV	Evaluation of alternatives	Do participants recognize that the process has switched to evaluation?
		Are criteria for assessment clearly specified and understood by group members?
		Are differences of opinion included in the evaluation?
		Are some alternatives pilot-tested?
Phase V	Making the decision	Are group members clear that selection is occurring?
		Are they aware if they are satisficing or optimizing?
		Are action plans made to fit with the decision?
		Are group members committed to the decision?
Phase VI	Evaluation of the decision	Are responsibilities for data collection, analysis, and reporting clearly assigned?
		Does a comprehensive evaluation plan exist?
		Does an evaluation schedule exist?

Setting Objectives   The way the decision makers frame the problem has a significant impact on its ultimate resolution. Subsequent steps may differ, for example, if Shigatsu frames the problem as cost reduction, revenue maximization, or merely a downsizing problem. Errors in problem definition may be hard to identify and even harder to correct.[12] The decision maker should carefully identify the goals and objectives that the decision must accomplish and specify the criteria that will be used to assess its quality, acceptance, and ethical appropriateness. Table 6–3 lists a set of such criteria. For example, Shigatsu might focus on the objective of reducing costs by 30 percent or increasing revenues by the same amount. He might focus on subobjectives of reducing the work force by 20 percent or offering two new product lines. A university president might set a goal of increasing student enrollment by 10 percent. A marketing specialist might set a goal of reducing advertising costs by $10,000 without decreasing the advertising's effectiveness. The accomplishment of these and similarly set goals serves as one measure of the effectiveness of the decision and the decision process.

Often, decision makers err at this step by confusing action plans with objectives. Decision makers must first set their goals and then determine ways of accomplishing them. For example, offering all workers voluntary severance pay is one way of accomplishing the goal of reducing the work force by 20 percent. In this case, the program is not the goal, but a means to a goal.

When possible, decision makers should establish objectives that specify observable and measurable results. Certainly, reducing turnover, absenteeism, and costs, or

Table 6–3   **Set of Criteria for Evaluating Objectives**

1. *Relevance.* Are the objectives related to and supportive of the basic purposes of the organization?
2. *Practicality.* Do the objectives recognize obvious constraints?
3. *Challenge.* Do the objectives provide a challenge for managers at all levels in the organization?
4. *Measurability.* Can the objectives be quantified, if only in an order-of-importance ranking?
5. *Schedulability.* Can the objectives be scheduled and monitored at interim points to ensure progress toward their attainment?
6. *Balance.* Do the objectives provide for a proportional emphasis on all activities and keep the strengths and weaknesses of the organization in proper balance?
7. *Flexibility.* Are the objectives sufficiently flexible or is the organization likely to find itself locked into a particular course of action?
8. *Timeliness.* Given the environment within which the organization operates, is this the proper time to adopt these objectives?
9. *State of the art.* Do the objectives fall within the boundaries of current technological development?
10. *Growth.* Do the objectives point toward the growth of the organization, rather than toward mere survival?
11. *Cost effectiveness.* Are the objectives cost effective in that the anticipated benefits clearly exceed the expected costs?
12. *Accountability.* Are the assignments for the attainment of the objectives made in a way that permits the assessment of performance on the part of individual managers throughout the organization?

SOURCE: Reprinted from E. Frank Harrison, *The Managerial Decision Making Process,* 3rd ed. (Boston: Houghton Mifflin, 1987), p. 41. Copyright © 1987 by Houghton Mifflin Company. Used with permission.

increasing profits and productivity, by specified percentages or amounts are objectives that are observable and measurable. Introducing new products or eliminating other product lines are also observable and measurable. Objectives related to employee attitudes, such as satisfaction, commitment, or involvement, may be more difficult to measure and observe. Similarly, expressing objectives related to the effectiveness of work processes, employee performance, or personnel practices in observable and measurable ways may require skillful crafting by the decision maker, consistent with scientific standards of validity. Criteria for assessing the decision might be its cost, ease of implementation, degree of acceptance by workers, and so on, and should also be measurable.

Searching for Alternatives The decision maker specifies a set of realistic and potentially acceptable solutions to the problem or numerous ways of meeting the objectives specified earlier. What alternatives are available to Carl Shigatsu and his managers? He can close no plants but offer early retirement incentives or a voluntary severance program; he can close one or two plants and lay off or transfer some or all of the affected workers; he can increase research and development and product advertising and hope that sales will increase; he can reduce the sales force or other nonmanufacturing personnel. Techniques for improving the generation of alternatives are described later in this chapter. Decision makers may err at this stage by not using information they have gathered, ignoring additional information they have requested, looking for information to support decisions after a decision has been made, and gathering irrelevant information.[13]

Evaluating Alternatives The decision maker appraises each alternative. Criteria for evaluation include the alternative's feasibility, cost, and reliability. In addition, the decision maker must assess the risks involved and the likelihood of certain outcomes for each alternative. What other criteria might be used in evaluating the alternatives Shigatsu and his colleagues face? Are there other criteria that might be relevant in this situation? Looking at Table 6–4, we see an evaluation of a set of alternatives Shigatsu and his colleagues might select to deal with the situation at Acme. We can see that they likely differ in cost, feasibility, possible adverse consequences, and probability of success in solving the problem.

Table 6–4 **Evaluation of Alternatives Open to Carl Shigatsu**

Alternative	Cost	Feasibility	Likelihood of Adverse Consequences	Relative Probability of Success in Solving Problem
Close two plants	Low	High	High	High
Lay off workers at several plants	Low	Moderate	Moderate	Moderate
Offer early retirement or voluntary severance programs	Moderate	Moderate	Moderate	Low
Phase in new products over two to five years	High	Moderate	Low	Low

Quantifying the alternatives can systematize their evaluation, dramatize differences among them, and even improve the quality of decision making. For example, we might score each of these four alternatives on its feasibility, cost, potentially adverse consequences, and probability of success. Summing the scores for each alternative then would allow us to rank-order them and ultimately select the highest ranked one. The process assumes that the criteria are equally weighted, that the numerical values are exact, and that ranks alone are sufficient to provide the best choice. More sophisticated statistical techniques can also be used for such an evaluation. Obviously this approach to quantifying the evaluation of alternatives is highly subjective because the decision maker's rating of each criterion is incorporated into the overall evaluation. Recent research suggests that decision makers evaluate alternatives using a *compatibility test*.[14] In decision making, which can be either intuitive or deliberative, the decision maker compares each alternative with a set of standards, such as values, morals, beliefs, goals, and plans, called *images*. The decision maker rejects incompatible alternatives and adds compatible ones to the set of feasible alternatives.

Making the Decision   Ideally, a decision maker should select the optimal, or best, alternative. Note, however, that the decision maker's knowledge, abilities, and motivation will affect the choice.[15] In addition, as for those listed in Table 6–4, each alternative has disadvantages as well as advantages. If the cost criterion outweighs all others, then closing plants and laying off workers would be the best decision. If a moderate cost is acceptable and low likelihood of adverse consequences is desired, then offering early retirement or voluntary severance programs or phasing in new products over two to five years would be a better decision.

Evaluating the Decision   Review of the decision is an essential step in effective decision making. Too often, selecting an alternative and reaching a decision comprise the final step. Individuals must pause and recheck their decisions and the process that led to them as one way of increasing their effectiveness. Once Shigatsu determines how to handle the situation he faces, he must review the steps that led to that decision. Where possible, he might check his thinking with another person. Together they can evaluate the planned implementation of the decision by assessing its likely or actual outcomes and comparing them to the objectives set earlier. Evaluation done prior to implementation is part of decision making. Evaluation performed after implementation is part of management control and may call for corrective action and follow-up.

The Four-Step Model   Figure 6–6 and Table 6–5 show a complementary four-step process.[16] Decision makers begin by *exploring* the situation for possible problems. This stage includes specifying the core problems, setting objectives, and generating alternatives. Stage 2 focuses on *assessing options* and corresponds to the evaluation of alternatives in the six-step model. Here decision makers generate criteria for assessing the alternatives and consider factors that might influence effectiveness of the decision outcomes; they then examine each alternative in this context. *Testing assumptions,* Stage 3, means reviewing individuals' values, their attitudes toward risk, and the trade-offs they made in assessing alternatives. This stage would involve investigating Shigatsu's values and the trade-offs he made in evaluating the options of plant closings, layoffs with no closings, and others. Decision makers subject their assumptions to analysis to identify more clearly the range of possible outcomes. Finally, in Stage 4 decision makers assess the outcomes that result from the decision and try to identify missed

Figure 6–6 **Four-Step Decision-Making Process**

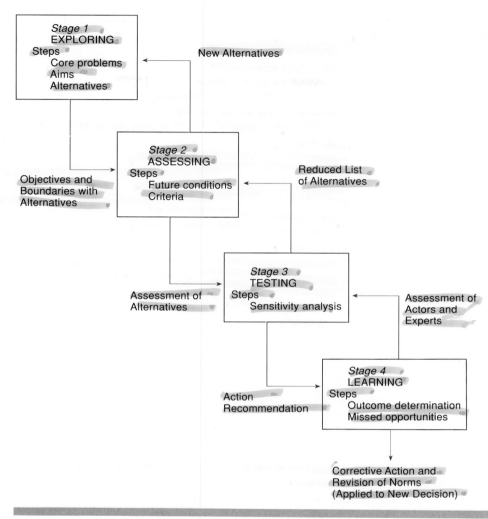

SOURCE: Reprinted with permission from P. C. Nutt, *Making Tough Decisions* (San Francisco: Jossey-Bass, 1989), p. 335.

opportunities. Shigatsu and his colleagues might have overlooked a new product opportunity, for example, that would have allowed the plant to remain open. *Learning* should result from this assessment and search.

Cross-Cultural Issues in Rational Decision Making

A culture's underlying values may affect problem recognition. U.S. managers, for example, see situations as problems to be solved, but Thai and Indonesian managers perceive that a situation should be accepted as is, not changed.[17] The values may also affect the type of alternatives they selected. We might hypothesize, for example, that European countries may rely more on historical patterns as the source of alternatives; more future-oriented cultures, such as Israel, may generate more new, untested alternatives.[18]

The speed of and responsibility for decision making is also culturally based.[19] The United States tends to be characterized by more rapid decision making, whereas many Middle Eastern cultures, such as Egypt, downplay time urgency. Responsibil-

Table 6–5 **Analytical Decision Process**

Exploring Stage
Step 1   Identify problem
Step 2   Explore problem
Step 3   Establish objectives
Step 4   Develop a list of alternatives
Step 5   Consider ethical concerns
Outcome: A bounded decision, with objectives and alternatives

Assessing Stage
Step 6   Use objectives to specify criteria
Step 7   Uncover future conditions, establish likelihoods, and select decision rule
Step 8   Organize with a decision tree
Step 9   Value alternatives, using criteria tied to future conditions
Step 10   Value additional information
Outcome: Assessment of the alternatives

Testing Stage
Step 11   Apply sensitivity analysis to future conditions
Step 12   Apply sensitivity analysis to criteria
Step 13   Select best alternative
Outcome: Action

Learning Stage
Step 14   Determine outcome
Step 15   Appraise performance and process
Step 16   Use decision analysis for recurring significant decisions
Outcome: Reflection on results and process used

SOURCE: Reprinted with permission from P. C. Nutt, *Making Tough Decisions* (San Francisco: Jossey-Bass, 1989), p. 175.

ity for decisions may rest on the individual, as in the United States, or with a group, as in Japan. Factors considered irrelevant in the United States, such as face-saving, can be crucial in the decision processes of Oriental groups. Decisions can also be made at various levels in the hierarchy. For example, Swedish workers are more comfortable with decentralized decision making than are Indian or French employees; and in Africa, middle managers rarely delegate authority.[20]

ALTERNATIVES TO THE RATIONAL DECISION-MAKING PROCESS

Some researchers have argued that the decision-making process just described does not adequately consider the complexity and ambiguity of organizational life. In this section we present three alternative models from the array available that highlight specific difficulties with the rational process presented and may cause individuals to adjust the rational process in certain situations.

Simon's Bounded Rationality

Herbert Simon, a Nobel Prize winner, was an early critic of the rational model.[21] In his three-step decision process, the decision maker first scans the environment for conditions that call for a decision. Shigatsu operates at this *intelligence* stage when he listens to reports from various managers, analyzes the subsidiary's budgets and product lines, and generally monitors the workplace. In the second step, the decision maker *designs* possible solutions to the problem; he or she develops and analyzes possible courses of action. Finally, the decision maker must make a *choice* among the available alternatives. Here in the interests of efficiency and because of an individual's limited information-processing capability, the decision maker will *satisfice,* or sacrifice the optimal for a solution that is satisfactory or "good enough."

Simon's bounded rationality approach places greater emphasis on the creative generation of reasonable alternatives to identify possible solutions and less on evaluation of alternatives to identify an optimal one than the basic decision-making model. Finding the best alternative, as required by the rational model, may be unrealistic because of conflicting aspects of the situation, such as constituencies with opposing objectives, lack of information, time and cost constraints, communication failures, precedent, or perceptual limitations,[22] making satisficing an appropriate and effective strategy.

Decision Making by Objection

In the model known as decision making by objection, the decision makers do not seek an optimal solution to a problem, but a course of action that does not have a high probability of making matters worse.[23] The decision makers first produce a rough description of an acceptable resolution of the situation. Then they propose a course of action, accompanied by a description of the positive outcomes of the action. Objections to the action are raised, further delimiting the problem and defining an acceptable resolution. The decision makers repeat this process, creating a series of courses of action, each one having fewer objections than the previous one. Carl Shigatsu might choose to focus first on a single course of action, such as closing two plants, and decide whether it is acceptable, then offer an improved alternative.

The "Garbage Can" Model

In contrast to the decision-making process proposed earlier, the "garbage can" model emphasizes the unsystematic quality of much decision making in organizations.[24] In an organization with unclear goals, uncertain means of achieving the goals, and changing participants in decision making, a diverse set of problems and solutions are presented simultaneously. The decision maker should recognize that serendipitous decisions may occur. Sometimes decisions fit solutions to problems in a way that resolves the problem, removing both the problem and solution from further consideration. The researchers note that this matching often occurs somewhat at random, and use the image of participants dumping problems and solutions into a "garbage can" to reflect how problems and solutions may be mixed together, as shown in Figure 6–7. If solutions and problems meet at the right time to make a choice, a rational outcome or choice is made; otherwise no decision results.[25] "Since solutions go in search of problems, the stream of problems must coincide with the stream of solutions for the optimal decisions to be made."[26] More recent expansions of this model try to make the decision maker a more explicit part of the action by citing him or her as able to take advantage of opportunities when problems and solutions match.[27] For example, Acme Products may unexpectedly market a "hot product" that meets both revenue and cost objectives and thus resolve Shigatsu's problem. The mapping of problems to solutions may be one-on-one, every combination allowed, or selective access of some problems to solutions or vice versa.[28]

More commonly, individuals make decisions by oversight or flight. When participants focus their attention on significant problems, they often find that they can make a decision about a new, less significant problem quickly, without considering it in depth. Or, solving the new problem may unintentionally result in a solution of the original problem. In trying to decide how to handle the downsizing problem, for example, Shigatsu may need to meet environmental protection guidelines that determine the type of employees Acme must have.

Figure 6–7 **Garbage Can Model of Decision Making**

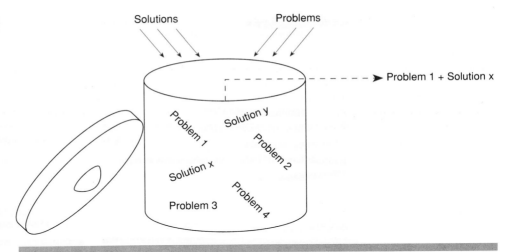

INDIVIDUAL VERSUS GROUP DECISION MAKING

The decision-making process described so far can apply to decisions made by individuals or groups. Yet, group decision making brings different resources to the task situation than does individual decision making. Table 6–6 presents a summary of these advantages and disadvantages of group decision making, and Table 6–7 summarizes the differences between individual and group decision making.

The Advantages and Disadvantages of Group Decision Making

When a group makes a decision, a synergy occurs that causes the group decision to be better than the sum of the individual decisions. The involvement of more than one individual brings additional knowledge and skills to the decision, and it tends to result in higher quality decisions.[29]

Cultural Diversity As the group becomes more diverse (attitudinally, behaviorally, and culturally), the advantage of cultural diversity increases. "Cultural diversity provides the biggest asset for teams with difficult, discretionary tasks requiring innovation. Diversity becomes least helpful when working on simple tasks involving repetitive and routine procedures."[30]

Time Required Group decision making generally takes more time than decision making by individuals. The exchange of information among many individuals, as well as effort spent on obtaining consensus, is time consuming. Sometimes, to reach a decision more quickly or to reach a decision all group members will accept, groups satisfice rather than optimize.

Riskiness of Decisions Early research suggested that groups tend to make riskier decisions.[31] More recent research suggests that this *risky-shift* phenomenon is actually a *polarization* phenomenon. Groups become more extreme in the direction of the initial predominant view.[32] Because no single person shoulders the consequences of a decision made by a group, individuals may feel less accountable and will accept more risky or extreme solutions.

Recognizing Expertise Groups may ignore individual expertise, opting instead for group consensus. Particularly as a member of a group of peers, an individual may be reluctant to discriminate among individuals on the basis of their expertise. Groups

Table 6–6　**Advantages and Disadvantages of Group Decision Making**

Advantages	Disadvantages
Brings multiple knowledge and skills to the decision	Requires more time
Expedites acceptance by the group	Ignores individual expertise, at times
Generally results in higher quality decisions	Satisfices even when better decision is possible
Increases commitment to decisions	Encourages riskier decisions
	Creates possibility of groupthink

then may develop *groupthink*—a mode of thinking with a norm of concurrence-seeking behavior—as described in the next section.[33] When group members choose a colleague's solution that they consider to be good, the resulting decision equals the quality of a decision obtained by group decision making and is no riskier than a group decision.[34] But the effectiveness of such a "best-member strategy" depends on the probability of the group's selecting the real best member and on the potential for subjectivity in the solution.[35] Even then, recent research suggests that many groups can perform better than the most knowledgeable member.[36]

Groupthink　Irving Janis first identified *groupthink* as a factor that influenced the misguided 1961 Bay of Pigs invasion.[37] The symptoms of groupthink, as listed in Table 6–8, arise when members of decision-making groups try to avoid being too critical in their judgment of other group members' ideas and focus too heavily on developing concurrence. It occurs most frequently in highly cohesive groups, particularly in stressful situations. Multicultural groups experience it less frequently because of their inherently different perspectives. For example, group members experiencing groupthink may feel invulnerable to criticism and hence believe that any action they take or decision they make will be positively received. They may also ignore external criticism, choosing instead to rationalize their actions or decisions as

Table 6–7　**Comparison of Group and Individual Decision Making**

Factor	Group	Individual
Type of problem or task	When diverse knowledge and skills are required	When creativity or efficiency is desired
Acceptance of decision	When acceptance by group members is valued	When acceptance is not important
Quality of the solution	When several group members can improve the solution	When "best member" can be identified
Characteristics of individuals	When group members have experience working together	When individuals cannot collaborate
Climate of the decision making	When the climate is supportive of group problem solving	When the climate is competitive
Amount of time available	When relatively more time is available	When relatively little time is available

Table 6–8 Symptoms of Groupthink

Invulnerability	Members feel they are safe and protected from dangers, ostracism, or ineffective action.
Rationale	Members ignore warnings by rationalizing their own or others' behavior.
Morality	Members believe their actions are inherently moral and ethical.
Stereotypes	Members view opponents as truly evil or stupid and thus unworthy of or incompetent at negotiations around differences in beliefs or positions.
Pressure	Members pressure all individuals in the group to conform to the group's decision; they allow no questioning or arguing of alternatives.
Self-censorship	Members do not express any questions about the group's decision.
Unanimity	Members perceive that everyone in the group has the same view.
Mindguards	Members may keep adverse information from other members that might ruin their perceptions of consensus and the effective decision.

SOURCE: Based on I. Janis, Groupthink, *Psychology Today*, June 1971.

optimum. Some group members may also pressure other group members to agree with the group's decision; deviant opinions are either ignored or not tolerated; members can neither question views offered nor offer disconfirming information. Recent research posits, however, that groupthink alone does not explain decision fiascoes. It ignores a group's tendency to exaggerate the value, relevance, and perceived quality of the members' initial decision.[38] Still, when faced with threats, groups of executives likely procrastinate, "pass the buck," or support other members' rationalizations about the appropriate decision.[39]

Choosing Group Decision Making   In deciding whether to use a group or individual decision-making process, decision makers should evaluate the type of problem, the importance of its acceptance, the desired solution quality, the individuals involved, the organizational culture, and the time available, as shown in Figure 6–8.

Type of Problem   Group decision making is superior when a task or problem requires a variety of expertise, when problems have multiple parts that can be addressed by a division of labor, and when problems require estimates. Individual decision making results in greater creativity as well as more efficiency if policy dictates the correct solution. Individual decision making also tends to lead to more effective decisions for problems that require completion of a series of complex stages, so long as the individual receives input from many sources, because it allows better coordination of the phases in solving the problem.[40] At Acme Products, for example, the main decision Shigatsu and his colleagues must make is how to reduce costs. This type of problem requires diverse knowledge and skills, creativity, and completion of a series of complex stages, calling most likely for a combination of individual and group decision making.

Importance of Decision Acceptance   Group decision making more often leads to acceptance than does decision making by individuals. In addition, since individuals involved in making a decision generally become committed to the decision, use of group consensus expedites acceptance of the decision by the group, thereby increas-

Figure 6–8 **Individual versus Group Problem Solving**

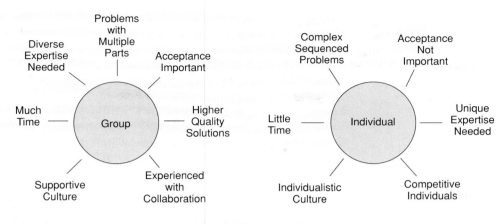

ing individual and group commitment to the decision. Acceptance of the decision about cost reductions at Acme by various managers and employees likely will affect its implementation in the short run. In the long run, Shigatsu can probably replace any employees who impede the decision. Some attempt to confer with a variety of individuals also helps to reduce any stress related to the decision.[41]

Solution Quality   Group decision making generally leads to higher quality solutions unless an individual's expertise in the decision area is identified in the beginning. At Acme the diverse expertise of team members should improve the solution. Finding a way to solicit a range of ideas would be appropriate.

Individuals Involved   The personalities and capabilities of the people involved in the decision will help or hinder group decision making. Some individuals have difficulty collaborating in a group setting, whereas others are used to dealing with diverse viewpoints and attitudes. Also, groups can ignore individual expertise, creating tension, distrust, and resentment, which can hinder the identification of effective solutions. We have little information about the personalities and capabilities of Acme's managers and employees. So, we have no reason to assume that anyone could not collaborate or would ignore individual expertise, allowing Shigatsu to use either decision method.

Organizational Culture   The organizational culture provides a context in which the rational or alternative decision making processes occur. Supportive climates (see Chapter 7) encourage group problem solving; competitive climates stimulate individual responses. In countries outside the United States, where group-oriented behavior is more valued and rewarded, group decision making occurs more frequently than decision making by individuals.[42]

Time   The amount of time available will determine whether group problem solving is feasible because group decision making takes much more time than individual decision making. Acme must solve the cost problem quickly if they are to remain competitive. This time frame may limit the amount of group consultation possible.

BARRIERS TO DECISION-MAKING EFFECTIVENESS

Blocks to decision-making effectiveness include addressing the wrong problem, failing to use participation, being distracted by conspicuous alternatives, overreacting to stress and home pressures, overusing judgment and intuition, ignoring values, erring in subjective estimates, failing to use analysis, lacking skills for communicating results, ignoring ethics, and not learning about failures.[43] Groups may also make faulty decisions because they do not assess the situation correctly and fail to recognize a potentially problematic situation, set inappropriate goals and objectives, do not evaluate alternatives accurately, use flawed information, and reason incorrectly from available data.[44] In addition, groups may make false assumptions, misperceive key issues, violate procedural norms, and allow high-status individuals to dominate the decision making.[45] Which of these exists at Acme Products? Shigatsu, for example, may not be able to determine whether plant utilization or worker salaries contribute more to the cost. His information may be insufficient, causing him to inappropriately restrict the alternatives considered. Shigatsu must be sure to analyze the environment to determine the pressures and constraints it places on decision making. He should also evaluate his own personal motivation to reach a quality decision, his risk-proneness, and his problem-solving skills.

COGNITIVE BIASES IN DECISION MAKING

The variety of backgrounds and experiences individuals and groups have are both resources in decision making and sources of bias. Individuals frequently make errors in estimating probabilities, reasoning about the cause of behaviors, and thinking about risk in situations.[46] These errors occur because decision makers use simplifying strategies, called *heuristics,* to guide their judgments in decision making.[47] Individuals overestimate the likelihood of an event if they can easily recall instances of it; such "availability" results in systematic bias in estimating frequencies. A manager may overestimate the likelihood of a staff cutback rather than an expansion if he or she has only experienced the former. Individuals also tend to overestimate the likelihood of disasters and underestimate the probability of more common events.[48] They also incorrectly value the size of a sample of observations; they give as much or more credence to small samples than to larger, more representative, ones. They might consider the rate of performance problems in a group of ten bookkeepers more representative of the organization than the rate in a group of fifty-five data entry clerks, when in fact the reverse is true.

Still others ignore the base rate, or the historical rate at which certain events occur. They assume, for example, that if no manager has been promoted in the last year, but five have been promoted for each of the previous ten years, that management promotions are very rare. Different framing of the same problem may result in a different decision: Individuals are more risk averse when seeking gains, but risk prone when avoiding losses, even if the probability of each is identical. Table 6–9 lists eight questions about framing the problems and their effects. We also assume that we know more about uncertain events than we do, further biasing our evaluation of alternatives. Table 6–10 lists these and other cognitive biases.

WAYS TO IMPROVE DECISION MAKING

How can decision makers overcome barriers, reduce biases, and make more effective decisions. In this section we examine five techniques that can improve decision making: brainstorming, the nominal group technique, the Delphi technique, consensus mapping, and creative thinking.

Table 6–9 Summary Descriptions of Eight Effects of Framing

Organizing Question	Description of How Most People Are Affected
1. How are your decisions affected by the framing of choices?	Individuals tend to be risk averse to positively framed choices and risk seeking to negatively framed choices.
2. How are your decisions affected by the framing of outcomes?	After individuals gain or lose some commodity, future decisions (in the short term) are evaluated . . . in reference to the current sure loss or gain position.
3. How are your decisions affected by the framed pseudocertainty and certainty of choices?	Individuals value the reduction of uncertainty more when the outcome was initially certain than when it was merely probable.
4. How do you differentially respond to "paying premiums" versus accepting sure losses?	Certain losses are more attractive when *framed* as insurance premiums than when *framed* as monetary losses.
5. How is your evaluation of the quality of a transaction affected by the frame in which it is presented?	Individual purchasing behavior is affected by acquisition utility and transactional utility. *Acquisition utility* is associated with the value that the individual places on the commodity. *Transactional utility* refers to the quality of the deal, in reference to what the item "should" cost.
6. How are your decisions affected by summing gains and losses?	Individuals value a series of small gains more than a single gain of the same summed amount. In addition, individuals lose less value by one large loss than by an identical loss suffered in multiple smaller parts.
7. How does the frame of the problem affect how much your time is worth?	Individuals value their time at extremely different rates, depending on social norms, transactional utility, anchor points based on market values, and expectations of how much "work" they should do in a given time period.
8. How rational are your intertemporal choices?	Individuals show a number of inconsistencies in making decisions about whether to take a good thing now or delay, as well as about whether to accept a bad outcome now or delay this negative event.

SOURCE: M. Bazerman, *Judgment in Managerial Decision Making,* 2nd ed. (New York: Wiley, 1990), p. 69. Copyright © 1990 by John Wiley & Sons, Inc. Reprinted by permission.

Table 6–10 Summary of Cognitive Biases

Bias	Description
Biases Emanating from the Availability Heuristic	
1. Ease of recall	Individuals judge events that are more easily recalled from memory, based upon vividness or recency, to be more numerous than events of equal frequency whose instances are less easily recalled.
2. Retrievability	Individuals are biased in their assessments of the frequency of events based upon how their memory structures affect the search process.
3. Presumed associations	Individuals tend to overestimate the probability of two events co-occurring based upon the number of similar associations that are easily recalled, whether from experience or social influence.
Biases Emanating from the Representativeness Heuristic	
4. Insensitivity to base rates	Individuals tend to ignore base rates in assessing the likelihood of events when any other descriptive information is provided—even if it is irrelevant.
5. Insensitivity to sample size	Individuals frequently fail to appreciate the role of sample size in assessing the reliability of sample information.
6. Misconceptions of chance	Individuals expect that a sequence of data generated by a random process will look "random," even when the sequence is too short for those expectations to be statistically valid.
7. Regression to the mean	Individuals tend to ignore the fact that extreme events tend to regress to the mean on subsequent trials.
8. The conjunction fallacy	Individuals falsely judge that conjunctions (two events co-occurring) are more probable than a more global set of occurrences of which the conjunction is a subset.
Biases Emanating from Anchoring and Adjustment	
9. Insufficient anchor adjustment	Individuals make estimates for values based upon an initial value (derived from past events, random assignment, or whatever information is available) and typically make insufficient adjustments from that anchor when establishing a final value.
10. Conjunctive and disjunctive events bias	Individuals exhibit a bias toward overestimating the probability of conjunctive events and underestimating the probability of disjunctive events.
11. Overconfidence	Individuals tend to be overconfident of the infallibility of their judgments when answering moderately to extremely difficult questions.
Two More General Biases	
12. The confirmation trap	Individuals tend to seek confirmatory information for what they think is true and neglect the search for disconfirmatory evidence.
13. Hindsight	After finding out whether or not an event occurred, individuals tend to overestimate the degree to which they would have predicted the correct outcome.

SOURCE: M. Bazerman, *Judgment in Managerial Decision Making,* 2nd ed. (New York: Wiley, 1990), pp. 40–41. Copyright © 1990 by John Wiley & Sons, Inc. Reprinted by permission.

Brainstorming Groups or individuals use brainstorming when creativity is needed to generate many alternatives for consideration in decision making. In brainstorming, they list as many alternatives as possible without simultaneously evaluating the feasibility of any alternative. For example, Shigatsu might charge a task force with listing all ways of reducing costs at Acme. The absence of evaluation encourages group members to generate rather than defend ideas. Then, after ideas have been generated, they are evaluated, and decisions are made. Although brainstorming can result in many shallow and useless ideas, it can also push members to offer new ideas. It works best when individuals have a common view of what constitutes a good idea, but it is harder to use when specialized knowledge or complex implementation is required.[49]

Nominal Group
Technique The nominal group technique (often referred to as NGT) is a structured group meeting that helps resolve differences in group opinion by having individuals generate and then rank-order a series of ideas in the problem-exploration, alternative-generation, or choice-making stage of group decision making.[50] A group of individuals is presented with a stated problem. Each person individually offers alternative solutions in writing. The group then shares the solutions and lists them on a blackboard or large piece of paper, as in brainstorming. The group discusses and clarifies the ideas. They then rank and vote their preference for the various ideas. If the group has not reached an agreement, they repeat the ranking and voting procedure until the group reaches some agreement. Figure 6–9 illustrates the steps. Table 6–11 presents a leader guide for NGT meetings.

Figure 6–9 **Steps in Nominal Grouping**

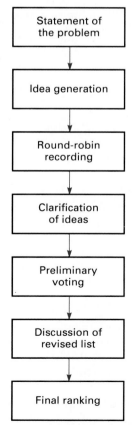

Table 6–11 **Leader Guide for NGT Meetings**

Step 1. Silent Recording
1. Present a written problem statement and a written outline of all process steps.
2. Resist all but process clarifications.
3. Maintain atmosphere by also writing in silence.
4. Discourage members who attempt to talk to others.

Step 2. Round-Robin Recording
1. Indicate the purpose of Step 2 (to create a record of the meeting).
2. Ask members to present their problems briefly and clearly.
3. Accept variations on a theme, but discourage duplicate items.
4. Ask if an idea has been correctly recorded to gain approval before proceeding.
5. Keep the list visible to all members by taping it on the wall.

Step 3. Interactive Discussion
1. Indicate this step's purpose (to explain and consolidate).
2. Skirt arguments, but accept both opinions when a difference arises.
3. Give all items some consideration.
4. Encourage elaborations from everyone without reference to who proposed them.
5. Gain the group's agreement to merge similar ideas, keeping the ideas separate when the group objects.

Step 4. Prioritization
1. Indicate the purpose of Step 4 (to set priorities).
2. Explain the procedure.

SOURCE: Adapted from A. L. Delbecq, A. Van de Ven, and D. H. Gustafson, *Group Techniques for Program Planning* (Middleton, Wis.: Greenbrier, 1986). Reprinted with permission from P. C. Nutt, *Making Tough Decisions* (San Francisco: Jossey-Bass, 1989), p. 364.

A more recent version of the NGT, the improved nominal group technique, emphasizes anonymity of input, pursuing a single purpose in any one group meeting, collecting and distributing inputs before a meeting, and delaying evaluation until all inputs are displayed.[51] It also assures opportunities for discussing displayed items before voting and limiting discussion to their pros and cons, allowing any individual to reword items, always using anonymous voting, and providing a second vote option.

The size of the group and the diverse expertise of its members increases the usefulness of the NGT. It encourages each group member to individually think about and offer ideas about the content of a proposal and then directs group discussion. It moves the group toward problem resolution by focusing on top-ranked ideas and eliminating less valued ones systematically. The NGT also encourages continued exploration of the issues, provides a forum for the expression of minority viewpoints, gives individuals some time to think about the issues before offering solutions, and provides a mechanism for reaching a decision expediently through the ranking-voting procedure.[52] It fosters creativity by allowing extensive individual input into the process. Strong personality types will dominate the group less often because of the opportunity for systematic input by all group members. It encourages innovation, limits conflict, emphasizes equal participation by all members, helps generate consensus, and incorporates the preferences of individuals in decision-making choices.[53]

Delphi Technique   Basically, the Delphi technique structures group communication in dealing with a complex problem into four phases: first, exploration of the subject by individuals;

second, reaching understanding of the group's view of the issues; third, sharing and evaluation of any reasons for differences; and fourth, final evaluation of all information.[54] In the conventional Delphi, as shown in Figure 6–10, a small group designs a questionnaire, which is completed by a larger respondent group; the results are then tabulated and used in developing a revised questionnaire, which is again completed by the larger group. Thus the results of the original polling are fed back to the respondent group to use in subsequent responses. This procedure is repeated until the issues are narrowed, responses are focused, or consensus is reached. In another format, a computer summarizes the results and thus replaces the small group. Such group decision support systems have increased the focus on the task or problem, the depth of analysis, communication about the task and clarifying information and conclusions, effort expended by the group, widespread participation of group members, and consensus reaching.[55]

Delphi is very useful in a variety of circumstances.[56] First, if the decision makers cannot apply precise analytical techniques to solving the problem but prefer to use subjective judgments on a collective basis, Delphi can provide input from a large number of respondents. Second, if the individuals involved have historically failed to communicate effectively in the past, the Delphi procedures offer a systematic method for ensuring that their opinions are presented. Third, the Delphi does not require face-to-face interaction and thus succeeds when the group is too large for such a direct exchange. Fourth, when time and cost prevent frequent group meetings or when additional premeeting communication between group members increases the efficiency of the meetings held, the Delphi technique offers significant value for decision making. Fifth, the Delphi can overcome situations where individuals greatly disagree or where the anonymity of views must be maintained to protect group members. Finally, the Delphi technique reduces the likelihood of groupthink; it

Figure 6–10 **Steps in the Delphi Technique**

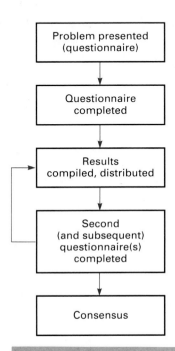

prevents one or more members from dominating by their numbers or the strength of their personality.

Consensus Mapping

Consensus mapping, which works best with multidimensional, complex problems that have interconnected elements and many sequential steps, begins after a task group has developed, clarified, and evaluated a list of ideas.[57] First, a person acting as a facilitator encourages participants to search for clusters and categories of listed ideas. This search for structure includes the listing and discussion of alternative clusters and categories by the entire group or subgroups and then production of a single classification scheme by group members working as a group or in pairs or trios. Then the facilitator consolidates the different schemes developed by subgroups into a representative scheme that acts as a "straw-man map" for the entire group. Group members next work to revise the straw man into a mutually acceptable solution. When there is more than one task group, a representative from each task group presents its revised map to members of other task groups. Finally, representatives from each task group produce a single, consolidated map or solution.

Since this technique works best for consolidating results from several task forces or project groups, Carl Shigatsu would need to consider whether he wanted to proceed in this fashion. He could use the technique if he assigned several groups the task of developing a way of meeting the cost-reduction objectives.

Creative Thinking

Creativity in decision making is concerned with changing traditional patterns of thinking. Individuals try to restructure a pattern to reassemble it and view the problem differently. Like brainstorming, which is a type of creative or lateral thinking, such thinking should focus on the generation of ideas, not on the evaluation of alternatives. Suspending judgment about the correctness of an alternative facilitates creative thinking.[58] Individuals can delay judgment about the relevance of information to the decision being considered, the validity of an idea for themselves or others, or the validity of an idea offered by another person. Delaying judgment encourages ideas to survive longer and spawns other ideas. It also motivates other people to offer ideas they normally would reject and stimulates new ideas, and it may result in the development of a new, more useful frame of reference for assessing them. Figure 6–11 shows these and other actions that help and hinder creative problem solving.

Individuals can use a variety of techniques to encourage their creative thinking. First, they can use alternative thinking languages, such as expressing a problem in mathematical rather than verbal language or using visual models rather than verbal expressions of a problem. For example, we might suggest that Shigatsu express his alternatives graphically—in the form of a decision tree, for example. Decision makers can also develop a questioning attitude as a way of gaining additional information. They might also make lists as a way of increasing their ability to process the information gained. Creative decision makers repeatedly challenge their assumptions; for example, Shigatsu or any of his colleagues might repeatedly ask the questions "why" about information gathered. Or other individuals or group members might take a *devil's advocate approach* to evaluating alternatives and choosing final solutions to a problem. Reading 6–1, "Agreement and Thinking Alike: Ingredients for Poor Decisions," shows the value of taking the devil's advocate and dialectic methods for improving decision making. Creating analogies, reversing situations, and breaking alternatives into their component parts also foster more creative decision making. These techniques and those described earlier reduce the perceptual, emotional, cultural, environmental, intellectual, and expressive blocks that hinder effective decision making.[59]

Figure 6–11   **Actions That Enhance and Hinder Creative Problem Solving**

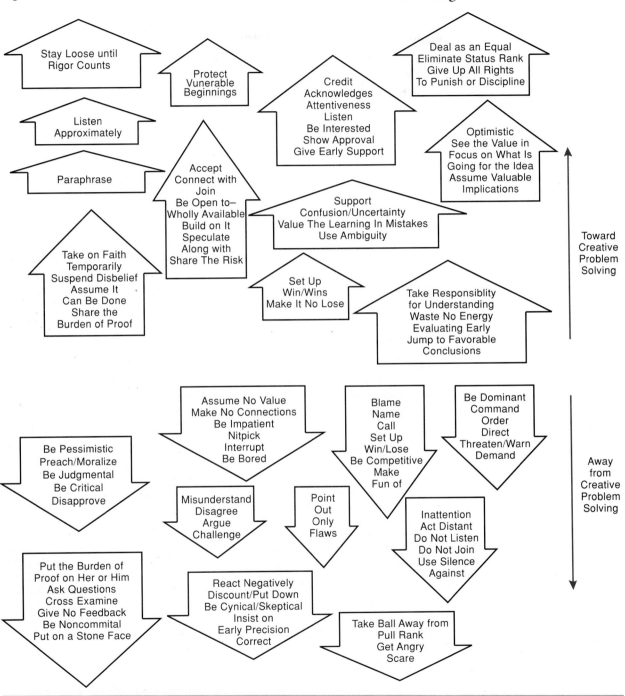

SOURCE: Reprinted with permission from James L. Adams, *The Care and Feeding of Ideas: A Guide to Encouraging Creativity* (Reading, Mass.: Addison-Wesley, 1986), pp. 185–186. Copyright © 1986 by James L. Adams. Reprinted by permission of Addison-Wesley Publishing Company.

Table 6–12 **Diagnostic Decision-Making Questions**

- What type of decision is being made?
- What types of information have been collected for making the decision?
- Do organizational members make high-quality, accepted, ethical decisions?
- Do the decision makers follow the basic process of decision making?
- Do ways of dealing with the limitations of the process exist?
- Is the group appropriately involved in decision making?
- What barriers are there to effective decision making?
- What techniques can be used to overcome these barriers?

SUMMARY   Decision making is a basic process in organizational behavior. In this chapter we described the nature of the decision being made and the information used in decision making at Acme Products. We noted that to make such decisions effectively individuals must have technical, interpersonal, and decision-making skills. We outlined a basic decision-making process that helps improve the quality of a decision and encourage its acceptance by others. Decision makers must systematically analyze the situation; set objectives; generate, evaluate, and select alternatives; make the decision; and evaluate the decision made. We also identified some limitations to the rational process and examined Simon's concept of bounded rationality, decision making by objection, and the "garbage can" model of decision making.

   The chapter next compared decision making by individuals and groups. The advantages and disadvantages of group decision making were presented, and the factors that affect the extent of involvement were cited. We then identified some barriers to effective decision making. The chapter concluded by offering ways to overcome these barriers. Answering the questions in Table 6–12 should help increase the effectiveness of decision making by managers and other organizational members.

Reading 6–1

Agreement and Thinking Alike: Ingredients for Poor Decisions
Richard A. Cosier and Charles R. Schwenk

Most of us believe that a major objective in organizations is to foster agreement over decisions. After all, agreement indicates cohesion and homogeneity among employees. People who are in agreement with each other are satisfied and secure.

   There is growing evidence that suggests conflict and dissent are what organizations *really* need to succeed.[1] Corporate decisions should be made after thoughtful consideration of counterpoints and criticism. People with different viewpoints must be encouraged to provide thoughts on important decisions. Widespread agreement on a key issue is a red flag, not a condition of good health.

   There is an old story at General Motors about Alfred Sloan. At a meeting with his key executives, Sloan proposed a controversial strategic decision. When asked for comments, each executive responded with supportive comments and praise. After announcing that they were all in apparent

agreement, Sloan stated that they were not going to proceed with the decision. Either his executives didn't know enough to point out potential downsides of the decision, or they were agreeing to avoid upsetting the boss and disrupting the cohesion of the group. The decision was delayed until a debate could occur over the pros and cons.

   Some contemporary managers, however, recognize the benefits of conflict. Gavin Rawl, chief executive officer at Exxon, follows a policy of "healthy disrespect," according to *Business Week*.

   Even as he rose through the Exxon hierarchy, however, Rawl always had a healthy disrespect for bureaucracy. The company was obsessed with consensus. Proposals would wend their way through a maze of committees and task forces, through layers of staff. As Senior Vice-President Charles R. Sitter says: "In a large organization, good ideas have lots of foster parents, and the bad decisions produce lots of orphans." Consensus, after all, is safer: The footprints are covered.[2]

Another example is the flamboyant Scott McNealy, Sun Microsystems' chief executive officer. McNealy encourages noisy, table-pounding meetings and debate among senior executives. Dissent and opinion is a natural part of the "controlled chaos."[3]

These managers, like others, have recognized the need to allow different viewpoints and critical thinking into organizational decisions. The type of conflict that is encouraged involves different interpretations of common issues or problems.[4] This "cognitive conflict" was noted as functional many years ago by psychologist Irving Janis. Janis, in his famous writings on groupthink, pointed out that striving for agreement and preventing critical thought frequently leads to poor decisions such as those made during the Bay of Pigs invasion and the defense of Pearl Harbor.

Cognitive conflict can arise in two ways: 1) It can reflect true disagreement among managers and surface through an open environment which encourages participation, or 2) It can be programmed into the decision-making processes and forced to surface, regardless of managers' true feelings. Although both methods may be effective, the second is decidedly less common. Given the potential benefits of programmed conflict in organizational decision-making, companies would do well to implement it. While elements of both methods of conflict generation are reviewed, means for encouraging programmed conflict is a major focus in this article.

ALLOWING TRUE DISAGREEMENT

Allowing disagreement to surface in organizations is exemplified by Jack Welch at General Electric. *Business Week* observed:

> Welch, though, is convinced he can reach his aims. Like a man obsessed, he is driving G.E. through drastic fundamental change. Once formal, stable, gentlemanly, the new G.E. is tough, aggressive, iconoclastic. "It's a brawl," says Frank P. Doyle, senior vice-president for corporate relations. "It's argumentative, confrontational." Working there can be a shock to newcomers. "There's a much higher decibel level here. I told Jack what passes for conversation here would be seen as a mugging by RCA people," Doyle says.[5]

The planning process involves scrutiny and criticism at G.E. Suggestions are expected and frequently offered and people are encouraged by Welch to speak their minds. This is consistent with organizational case studies that note the value of "forthright discussion" versus behind the scenes politicking in determining organizational strategy. In one case, the vice president for manufacturing and finance at a company showing strong performance stated:

> You don't need to get the others behind you before the meeting. If you can explain your view (at the meeting), people will change their opinions. Forefront (the fictitious name of the company) is not political at this point. But, you must give your reasons or your ideas don't count. (VP of manufacturing).
>
> There is some open disagreement—it's not covered up. We don't gloss over the issues, we hit them straight on. (VP of finance).[6]

Several studies on strategic decision-making show that in general, successful companies advocate open discussions, surfacing of conflict, and flexibility in adopting solutions. Other studies, however, suggest that strategy is facilitated by consensus. This contradiction raises an important issue. Consensus may be preferred for smaller, non-diversified, privately held firms competing in the same industry while larger firms dealing with complex issues of diversification may benefit from the dissent raised in open discussions. Larger firms in uncertain environments need dissent while smaller firms in more simple and stable markets can rely on consensus. In addition, Dess concludes, "organizations competing within an industry experiencing high growth may benefit from a relatively high level of disagreement in assessing the relative importance of company objectives and competitive methods."[7]

Examples of the benefits of conflict in tactical problem-solving (short-term) situations are also common. Bausch and Lomb have established "tiger teams" composed of scientists from different disciplines. Team members are encouraged to bring up divergent ideas and offer different points of view. Xerox uses round table discussions composed of various functional experts to encourage innovation. Compaq expects disagreement during all stages of new product development. Stuart Gannes, writing in *Fortune*, explains, "But at Compaq, instead of just arguing over who is right, we tear down positions to reasons. And when you get to reasons you find facts and assumptions."[8] Apple Computer, Ford Motor Co., Johnson and Johnson, and United Parcel Service are other examples of companies that tolerate conflict and debate during decisions.

In general, successful leaders seem to encourage managers to speak their minds. While this allows conflict into decision-making, it carries a potential high cost. Positions are frequently tied to people and competitive "zero-sum" situations in which perceived winners and losers are likely to develop. Clearly, "losers" are less likely in future discussions to give their opinions.

Also, unprogrammed conflict is likely to be emotional and involve personal feelings. Lingering dislikes and rivalries are possible after higher emotional interchanges. Coalitions form and long-term divisiveness ensues.

Corporate time and money may have to be diverted from problem-solving to resolving emotional conflicts between managers.

What may, in fact, be needed is programmed conflict that raises different opinions *regardless of the personal feelings of the managers.* Although research exists supporting some options for programmed conflict, few, if any, examples exist in the corporate world.

PROGRAMMED CONFLICT

The Devil's Advocate

What can leaders do to experience the benefits associated with conflict in decision-making, while minimizing the cost? Two options with potential are the devil's advocate and dialectic methods for introducing programmed conflict into organizational decisions.

The usefulness of the devil's advocate technique was illustrated several years ago by psychologist Irving Janis when discussing famous fiascos. Janis attributes groupthink—the striving for agreement instead of the best decision in a group—to decisions such as were made during the Bay of Pigs and Pearl Harbor.[9] Watergate and Vietnam are also often cited as examples. Janis recommends that everyone in the group assume the role of a devil's advocate and question the assumptions underlying the popular choice. Alternatively, an individual or subgroup, could be formally designated as the devil's advocate and present a critique of the proposed course of action. This avoids the tendency of agreement interfering with problem solving. Potential pitfalls are identified and considered before the decision is final.

While Janis' observations are generally well known and accepted, corporate implementation of devil's advocacy as a formal element in decision-making is rare. This is despite recent research that supports the benefits of devil's advocacy.[10] The conflict generated by the devil's advocate may cause the decision maker to avoid false assumptions and closely analyze the information. The devil's advocate raises questions that force an in-depth review of the problem-solving situation.

A devil's advocate decision program (DADP) can take several forms. However, all options require that an individual or group be assigned the role of critic. It needs to be clear that the criticism must not be taken personally, but is part of the organizational decision process.

The devil's advocate is assigned to identify potential pitfalls and problems with a proposed course of action. The issue could relate to strategic planning, new product development, innovation, project development, or of other problems not amenable to programmed solutions. A formal presentation to the key decision makers by the devil's advocate raises potential concerns. Evidence needed to address the critique is gathered and the final decision is made and monitored. This DADP is summarized in Figure 6–12.

It is a good idea to rotate people assigned to devil's advocate roles. This avoids any one person or group being identified as the critic on all issues. The devil's advocate role may be advantageous for a person and the organization. Steve Huse, chairperson and CEO of Huse Food Group,

Figure 6–12 A Devil's Advocate Decision Program

1. A proposed course of action is generated.
   ↓
2. A devil's advocate (individual or group) is assigned to criticize the proposal.
   ↓
3. The critique is presented to key decision makers.
   ↓
4. Any additional information relevant to the issues is gathered.
   ↓
5. The decision to adopt, modify, or discontinue the proposed course of action is taken.
   ↓
6. The decision is monitored.

states that the devil's advocate role is an opportunity for employees to demonstrate their presentation and debating skills. How well someone understands and researches issues is apparent when presenting a critique.[11] The organization avoids costly mistakes by hearing viewpoints that identify pitfalls instead of foster agreement.

Often, a devil's advocate is helpful in adopting expert advice from computer-based decision support systems. Behavioral scientists Cosier and Dalton suggest that computer-based decisions may be more useful if exposed to a critique than simply accepted by managers.[12]

The Dialectic

While the DADP lacks an "argument" between advocates of two conflicting positions, the dialectic method (DM) programs conflict into decisions, regardless of managers' personal feelings, by structuring a debate between conflicting views.

The dialectic philosophy, which can be traced back to Plato and Aristotle, involves synthesizing the conflicting views of a thesis and an antithesis. More recently, it played a principal role in the writings of Hegel who described the emergence of new social orders after a struggle between opposing forces. While most of the world's modern legal systems reflect dialectic processes, Richard O. Mason was one of the first organization theorists to apply the dialectic to organizational decisions.[13] He suggested that the decision maker consider a structured debate reflecting a plan and a counterplan before making a strategic decision. Advocates of each point of view should present their assumptions in support of the argument.

The benefits of DM are in the presentation and debate of the assumptions underlying proposed courses of action. False or misleading assumptions become apparent and decisions based on these poor assumptions are avoided. The value of DM, shown in Figure 6–13, for promoting better understanding of problems and higher levels of confidence in decisions is supported by research.[14]

Critics of DM point to the potential for it to accentuate who won the debate rather than the best decision. Compromise, instead of optimal decisions, is likely. Managers will require extensive training in dialectic thinking and philosophy. Supporters of DADP argue that a critique focuses the decision-maker on issues while the dialectic focuses more on the process of structural debate. Nevertheless, Cosier and Dalton suggest that DM may be the best method to use under the worst decision-making condition—high uncertainty and low information availability. The dialectic may be a good way to define problems and generate needed information for making decisions under uncertainty. When information is available and causal relationships are known, computer-assisted or devil's advocate methods are preferred.

PROGRAMMED AND UNPROGRAMMED CONFLICT

It is not a major breakthrough in management advice to suggest that conflict can improve decisions, although it is useful to remind managers of the need to allow dissent. It is, however, uncommon for managers to formally program conflict into the decision-making process. Thus, regardless of personal feelings, programmed conflict requires managers to challenge, criticize, and generate alternative ideas. Compared to conflict that is allowed to naturally surface, programmed conflict may reduce negative emotional by-products of conflict generation since dissent is no longer "personal." It also insures that a comprehensive decision framework is applied to important problems and issues.

Two options for implementing programmed conflict

Figure 6–13 **The Dialectic Decision Method**

1. A proposed course of action is generated.
   ↓
2. Assumptions underlying the proposal are identified.
   ↓
3. A conflicting counterproposal is generated based on different assumptions.
   ↓
4. Advocates of each position present and debate the merits of their proposals before key decision makers.
   ↓
5. The decision to adopt either position, or some other position, e.g., a compromise, is taken.
   ↓
6. The decision is monitored.

are based on the devil's advocate (DADP) and dialectic (DM) methods. We challenge managers to formally encourage controversy and dissent when making important choices under uncertain conditions. Encouraging "yes sayers" and complacency promotes poor decisions and lack of innovative thinking in organizations.

ENDNOTES

1. Conflict has been frequently presented as a positive force in textbooks. See, for example, Peter P. Schoderbek, Richard A. Cosier, and John C. Aplin, *Management,* San Diego: Harcourt, Brace, and Jovanovich, 1988, 511–512.
2. "The Rebel Shaking Up Exxon," *Business Week,* July 18, 1988, 107.
3. "Sun Microsystems Turns on the Afterburners," *Business Week,* July 18, 1988, 115.
4. Tjosvold uses the term "controversy" to describe this type of conflict. He differentiates controversy from conflicts of interest which involves the actions of one person blocking the goal attainment of another person. See Dean Tjosvold, "Implications of Controversy Research for Management," *Journal of Management,* Vol. 11, 1985, 22–23.
5. "Jack Welch: How good a manager?" *Business Week,* Dec. 14, 1987, 94.
6. Kathleen M. Eisenhardt and L. J. Bourgeois III, "Politics of Strategic Decision Making in High-Velocity Environments," *Academy of Management Journal,* Vol. 31, 1988, 751–752.
7. Gregory G. Dess, "Consensus on Strategy Formulation and Organizational Performance: Competitors in a Fragmented Industry," *Strategic Management Journal,* Vol. 8, 1987, 274.
8. Stuart Gannes, "America's Fastest-growing Companies," *Fortune,* May 23, 1988, 29.
9. See Irving L. Janis, *Victims of Groupthink,* Boston: Houghton-Mifflin, 1972.
10. See, for example, Richard A. Cosier, "Methods for Improving the Strategic Decision: Dialectic Versus the Devil's Advocate," *Strategic Management Journal,* Vol. 16, 1982, 176–184.
11. Steve Huse, chairperson and CEO of Huse Food Group Inc., shared these observations in an interview with the senior author.
12. A model is developed which recommends methods of presenting information based upon conditions of uncertainty and information availability in Richard A. Cosier and Dan R. Dalton, "Presenting Information Under Conditions of Uncertainty and Availability: Some Recommendations," *Behavioral Science,* Vol. 33, 1988, 272–281.
13. Richard O. Mason, "A Dialectical Approach to Strategic Planning," *Management Science,* Vol. 15, 1969, B403–B414.

14. Ian I. Mitroff and J. R. Emshoff, "On Strategic Assumption-making: A Dialectical Approach to Policy and Planning," *Academy of Management Review,* Vol. 4, 1979, 1–12.

DISCUSSION QUESTIONS

1. Why should managers allow disagreements to surface in organizations?

2. How can programmed conflict improve decisions in organizations?

3. What options are available for creating programmed conflict in organizations?

Reprinted with permission from *Academy of Management Executive* 4(1) (1990): 69–74.

Activity 6–1

Anatomy of a Tragedy

Step 1: Read the Anatomy of a Tragedy case.

Six days after the Challenger disaster, on Feb. 3, 1986, President Reagan appointed a commission and charged it with reviewing the accident's circumstances, determining its probable cause, and recommending measures toward preventing another such disaster. Known as the Rogers commission after its chairman, former Secretary of State William P. Rogers, it had 120 days to work.

On June 6, the commission announced its conclusion: The immediate physical cause of Challenger's destruction was "a failure in the joint between the two lower segments of the right Solid Rocket Motor," the report said. "The specific failure was the destruction of the seals that are intended to prevent hot gases from leaking through the joint during the propellant burn. . . ."

But contributing to the accident was, in the commission's now-famous words, the fact that "the decision to launch the Challenger was flawed." The report continued: "Those who made that decision were unaware of the recent history of problems concerning the O-rings and the joint and were unaware of the initial written recommendation of the contractor advising against the launch at temperatures below 53 degrees Fahrenheit and the continued opposition of the engineers at Thiokol after the management reversed its position." It faulted the management structure of both Thiokol and NASA for not allowing such information to flow to the people who needed to know it.

After the Rogers commission report was released, the U.S. House of Representatives' Committee on Science and Technology spent two months conducting its own hearings and reached its own conclusions in November 1986. Although the House committee agreed with several of the Rogers commission's conclusions, it also stated that "the fundamental problem was poor technical decision-making over a period of several years by top NASA and contractor personnel."

The House committee pointed out that ". . . information on the flaws in the joint design and on the problem encountered in missions prior to 51-L was widely available

and had been presented to all levels of Shuttle management." But the committee's report continued: "The NASA and Thiokol technical managers failed to understand or to fully accept the seriousness of the problem. There was no sense of urgency on their part to correct the design flaws in the SRB. No one suggested grounding the fleet. . . . Rather NASA chose to continue to fly with a flawed design and to follow a measured, 27-month corrective program," leading to a new type of joint proposed for later missions—the capture joint. The committee came to the conclusion that the problem surrounding the field-joint O-rings had been recognized soon enough for it to have been corrected, but that no correction was made, because "meeting flight schedules and cutting cost were given a higher priority than flight safety."

The findings both of the Rogers commission and of the House committee suggest a fundamental question that neither investigation addressed: just how could NASA—an organization with a reputation for ingenuity, good design, meticulous engineering, reliability, and safety—have found itself in a position where it repeatedly overlooked the obvious until disaster struck?

WHY WASN'T THE DESIGN FIXED?

Design of the joint was not changed, say Thiokol and NASA engineers and managers, because it was assumed the joint would behave like the similar joints on the Titan boosters. "In an overall sense," said Thiokol's Joe Kilminster last December, "the comfort zone, if you will, was expanded because of the fact that the shuttle joint was so similar to the Titan joint, and its many uses had shown successful operation. That's why a lot of—I guess 'faith' is the right word—was based on the fact that the Titan had had all these tests and successful experience."

Furthermore, Boisjoly pointed out: "The working troops—and I consider myself one of the working troops—had no knowledge of the thing being changed to a Criticality 1. So far as we were concerned, we had two seals that were redundant. . . . So either you believe that you fly, or you don't believe it and shut the program down."

WHY WASN'T EROSION SEEN AS A DANGER SIGN?

By 1985, erosion and blow-by had come to be accepted as normal—to the point where, in the Level I flight-readiness review for STS 51-L that analyzed the results of the preceding flight STS 61-C, NASA's Mulloy noted there were "no 61-C flight anomalies" and "no major problems or issues," in spite of the fact that there had been erosion or blow-by in three joints. Although some engineers were beginning to be alarmed about the frequency of the erosion—especially after an analysis of the results of STS 51-B in April 1985 disclosed that the secondary O-ring of a nozzle joint had been eroded as well as its primary—they received little support from NASA or Thiokol.

In July 1985, for example, Thiokol's unofficial task force was told to solve the O-ring erosion problems for both the short and long term. But in a memorandum of July 31, Boisjoly noted the group's "essential nonexistence" and asked that it be officially endorsed. He wrote that the consequences of not dealing with the seal problems "would be a catastrophe of the highest order—loss of human life."

By October, however, one task-force member was dismayed enough to write a note to Allan McDonald: "HELP! The seal task force is constantly being delayed by every possible means. . . . This is a red flag." And around the same time Boisjoly went to Kilminster and, as he now recalls, "pleaded for help." But remembering that meeting, Boisjoly said: "And quite frankly, when we were leaving the room he [Kilminster] said, 'Well, it was a good bullshit session anyway.' And that was the end of it." Boisjoly now says he didn't use exactly those words when describing, in his weekly activity report of Oct. 4, 1985, his problem in obtaining support from Kilminster. "But I had it in my notebook. I was really ticked because we were pleading for help and we couldn't get it. We were fighting all the major inertia in the plant, just like everybody else, and yet we were supposed to be this tiger team to get a very severe problem solved." Kilminster, Boisjoly now says, "just didn't basically understand the problem. We were trying to explain it to him, and he just wouldn't hear it. He felt, I guess, that we were crying wolf."

OPERATIONAL: AND THEN WHAT?

"There's just no way that I can understand in God's green earth that an airline could undertake with its normal procedures the operation of the space shuttle," said former Apollo astronaut Frank Borman, now vice-chairman of Texas Air Corp. in Las Cruces, N.M. "When NASA came out with the request for a proposal from airlines to run the shuttle like it was a [Boeing] 727, I called them and I told them they were crazy. The shuttle is an experimental vehicle, and will remain an experimental, highly sophisticated vehicle on the edge of technology."

In the early 1980s there was much discussion about whether it made sense for NASA, a research and development agency, to run what was already being viewed as a common carrier, and proposals were solicited from airlines for operating agreements. "NASA's highest priority is to make the Nation's Space Transportation System (STS) fully operational and cost-effective in providing routine access to space." So stated National Security Decision Directive 42, in 1982, and Directive 144, in 1984. The directives set as a goal "a flight schedule of up to 24 flights per year with margins for routine contingencies attendant with a flight-surge capability."

The goal of being operational also changed NASA's philosophy on crew safety, as is seen from a 1985 report produced by Rockwell International for NASA's Langley Research Center, in Hampton, Va., titled "Space Station Crew Safety Alternatives Study." Wrote the Rockwell authors: "It is interesting to trace the evolution of crew safety philosophy [from Apollo through shuttle] and to understand the reasons for this evolution. The emphasis has gone historically in two directions: (1) a tendency to go from escape and rescue measure (e.g., abort systems) toward obtaining inherent safety (i.e., reduce/eliminate threats); and (2) an increasing interest in saving not only the crew, but also the very valuable space systems. We expect these trends to continue as space operations mature and become more routine."

This emphasis on eliminating or controlling threats rather than escaping from them is consistent with airline mentality. "You don't put parachutes on airlines because the margin of safety is built into the machine," said Borman, for 17 years president of Eastern Airlines. But, he pointed out, "The 727 airplanes that we fly are proven vehicles with levels of safety and redundancy built in"—levels, he said, that the space shuttle comes nowhere near to. The way Borman sees it, the shuttle is "a hand-made piece of experimental gear."

Nevertheless, people both within and outside NASA began to treat the shuttle like an airplane, with an attendant psychological casualness about its mechanical safety. Harold Finger, formerly NASA's associate administrator for organization and management and now president of the U.S. Committee for Energy Awareness in Washington, D.C., said the NASA successes may have led to a lack of vigilance and high-level knowledge of potential danger.

WHY NO SECOND SOURCES?

Ever since the start of the shuttle program, other manufacturers had been after NASA to let them be second sources for the boosters, the largest market anywhere for solid-fuel rocket motors. Congress had also wanted a second source, for national security reasons, so that the shuttles would be available for military payloads in the event of a work stoppage or accident at Thiokol.

Obedient to the U.S. Competition in Contracting Act, NASA announced on Dec. 26, 1985—less than a month before Challenger's original launch date—a set of rules under which other manufacturers could bid to become a second source for the boosters. Although the bidding rules favored Thiokol in many ways, the announcement, Levin said, still threatened "a very fat contract. . . . Why did Thiokol management surrender on the night of Jan. 27? They didn't have to," he said—except for the fact that they were in the midst of negotiating the next production buy, and they were being threatened with a second source in connection with that buy, "Thus, keeping this customer happy was very important," Levin said.

THE NASA/CHALLENGER INCIDENT

NASA and Thiokol were aware of the likely impact of redesigning the booster joint from the ground up at least six months before Challenger's last flight. On July 23, 1985, NASA budget analyst Richard C. Cook sent a memorandum to his superior, Michael Mann. It was clear that the booster seal threatened flight safety, Cook wrote. If the cause of the problems required a major redesign, it "would lead to the suspension of Shuttle flights, redesign of the SRB [solid-fuel rocket booster], and scrapping of existing stockpiled hardware. The impact on the FY 1987–8 budget could be immense."

Within Thiokol, Boisjoly wrote in his weekly report of July 22, 1985, that the company needed to focus attention on the problem. Otherwise, "We stand in danger of having one of our competitors solve our problem via an unsolicited proposal. This thought is almost as horrifying as having a flight failure before a solution is implemented to prevent O-ring erosion."

HOW DID NASA AND THIOKOL VIEW THE ODDS?

"No data conclusively showed that low temperatures would increase the risk," said NASA's Mulloy. "I agree with the House committee that continually taking that risk was bad engineering judgment, but that bad judgment started long before the teleconference that night of Jan. 27, and had the highest levels of NASA management participating in it."

Marshall propulsion engineer Ben Powers said that, at the time, "my understanding was that the [booster] motor was qualified [down] to 31° [F]." However, he recalled little surprise in finding that the Thiokol engineers were now stating that it should not be flown in conditions that cold. The Jan. 27 teleconference, he said, was the first time his attention had been directed to it. "The emphasis was not enough earlier on."

According to Thiokol's Kilminster, "All the tests that showed that the resiliency of the [primary] O-ring was lower at low temperature did not include the effects of pressure acting on it during the motor-ignition pressure rise. This pressure acting on the O-ring tended to move it into a sealing position," he said. "We felt—based on all the test experience we had to that point, plus flight experience—that pressure caused the O-ring to operate as it was designed to operate, even in some of the static tests that were relatively cold—40° F."

Mulloy, in recalling his own reasoning about the launch conditions, said he argued: "We've been addressing this problem of O-ring erosion *every* launch. What is *different* this time? What was different was temperature. What is the effect of temperature? Our conclusion was that there is no correlation between low temperature and O-ring erosion—in fact, our worst erosion was at one of the highest temperatures.

"I concluded that we're taking a risk every time," Mulloy said. "We all signed up for that risk. And the conclusion was, there was *no* significant difference in risk from previous launches. We'd be taking essentially the same risk on Jan. 28 that we have been ever since we first saw O-ring erosion," he said.

The fact that data linking low temperature to increased O-ring problems were uncertain may have had an underappreciated role. "In the face of uncertainty, people's preferences take over," said Dennis Mileti, professor of sociology and director of Colorado State University's Hazards Assessments Laboratory at Fort Collins, Colo. The risk is denied, discounted, and the chance is taken. . . . "This is not unique. It's just like any of us getting on an airplane—we all know that airplanes crash, but in our hearts we don't believe that the one we get on will crash."

Uncertainty over the effect of cold on the seal came about in several ways. There was no launch-commit criterion for the booster joint with regard to temperature. Also, Boisjoly later noted, there was "no graph plotting flights, with or without erosion as a function of temperature," that might have enabled the engineers to assess whether or not there was a correlation.

Moreover, there was, and continues to be, uncertainty over what temperatures had been specified in the design criteria for the entire shuttle. McDonald and Lund of Thiokol both now say that the only specification they knew of called for the booster to operate between 40 and 90° F—although even what those limits referred to was unclear: Did it apply to the ambient temperature or to the propellant's mean bulk temperature inside each booster? Thiokol engineers say they never knew of a "higher-level spec," set at Johnson Space Center that called for the entire shuttle system to function at ambient temperatures from 31 to 99° F.

Mulloy calls that uncertainty "nonsense." Thiokol wrote the end-item specifications, he said, with 40 to 90° set for the propellant's mean bulk temperature, 31 to 99° for the ambient temperature, 21° for the external tank-booster strut interface, and 25° for the joint between the booster's aft and aft-center sections—the joint that failed on Challenger. Nonetheless, everyone at NASA up to Jesse Moore seems to have assumed that because specifications did exist, the entire shuttle met them. There also seems to have been confusion over the establishment of launch-commit criteria, as well as over when the criteria could be waived.

No one either at Thiokol or at NASA knew for sure how the O-rings would respond to cold, said Mulloy. He pointed out that the Viton rubber O-rings had never been tested below 50° F, mainly because the material had been designed to withstand the heat of combustion gases rather than the chill of winter launches. The Viton was formulated to military specifications for use between − 30 and + 500° F, but NASA did no tests of its own to see whether the O-rings met those specifications.

Even opposition by several Thiokol engineers to sending up the shuttle in freezing weather was not, in itself, seen as sufficient reason to scrub the launch, because experience itself is an uncertain guide. "When I was working as [NASA's] deputy administrator, I don't think there was a single launch where there was some group of subsystem engineers that didn't get up and say 'Don't fly,'" said Hans Mark, now chancellor of the University of Texas system in Austin. "You always have arguments."

WHAT ROLE DID NASA'S SAFETY OFFICE PLAY?

The Rogers commission noted the absence of safety personnel in making the decision to launch Challenger. Arnold Aldrich told the commission of five distinct failures that contributed to the decision, four of them relating to safety, reliability, and quality assurance. There was, he said, a lack of problem-reporting requirements, and a failure to involve NASA's safety office in critical discussions.

Indeed, NASA's own corporate architecture contributed to those problems. Safety, reliability, and quality assurance was the responsibility of NASA's chief engineer, Milton Silveira, at headquarters in Washington. As NASA's hub, the headquarters directs the 16 field centers and facilities all over the country. According to the Rogers commission, one of Silveira's headquarters staff of 20 devoted one-quarter of his time to space-shuttle concerns; another spent only one-tenth of his time on flight-safety issues.

"In the early days of the space program we were so damned uncertain of what we were doing that we always got everybody's opinion," said Silveira. "We would ask for continual reviews, continual scrutiny by anybody we had respect for, to look at this thing and make sure we were doing it right. As we started to fly the shuttle again and again, I think the system developed false confidence in itself and didn't do the same thing."

WAS NASA OR THIOKOL PRESSURED TO LAUNCH?

The push was on for 15 launches in 1986 and 24 launches a year by 1990. "That can't help but influence the degree of risk that one would take," said Mulloy. "But to me that is a self-imposed thing. You make a commitment and you try your damnedest to meet it. It's probably self-imposed professional pride—doing what you, by God, said you were going to do."

But the House committee report stressed the likely result of such a punishing schedule: "The pressure on NASA to achieve planned flight rates was so pervasive that it undoubtedly adversely affected attitudes regarding safety. . . . Operating pressures were causing an increase in unsafe practices," such as shortcuts in established launch-preparation procedures to save time.

The very day of the disaster brought speculation about pressure from the White House to have Challenger launched in time for President Reagan's State of the Union message, scheduled for that evening. NASA officials told the Rogers commission, however, that there was no such outside pressure and after a short discussion, the commission concluded that "the decision to launch the Challenger was made solely by the appropriate NASA officials without any outside intervention or pressure."

"I don't have any personal first-hand knowledge about presidential pressure, but circumstances and events were suggestive of pressure from the White House," said Traficant in August. "Whether or not there was any direct intent to apply pressure to have [the shuttle] launched in a timely way to orchestrate it with the State of the Union message, I believe NASA *perceived* that these types of timetable are important."

Richard C. Cook, the former NASA budget analyst who wrote the memorandum of July 23, 1985, warning of the possible effects of the joint's design, believes there was political pressure. In a 137-page report Cook stated: "The reason NASA overruled contractor engineers and lost Challenger was because they wanted to get the shuttle into the air by the time of the President's State of the Union Message, which mentioned the teacher in space. I believe that without political motivation, the accident would not have happened," he stated, adding: "I believe that the reason the White House formed its Presidential commission was to cover that up . . . and that there is perjury by NASA officials in the commission hearings."

In support of Dennis Mileti's theory that in the face of uncertainty people opt for their preferences, Levin said: "None of these folks that decided to fly Challenger wanted those people to die. None of them in their hearts would acknowledge that they were doing something stupid, evil, or rotten. We're not talking about murderers. We're talking about people who took a desperately high risk with other people's money, other people's lives—hoping like hell that the good luck that had always attended NASA activities would hold."

WHY DIDN'T THEY TALK TO EACH OTHER?

The Rogers commission perceived a lack of communication between engineers doing technical work at Thiokol and the top NASA managers who made the launch decisions. This breakdown meant that no information flowed on known problems with the booster joint—not only during the decision to launch Challenger, but also during the entire design and development process.

Hans Mark, widely regarded for his insight and skill in technology management, has observed: "The only criticism that I have of the [Rogers commission] report is that they laid more blame on the lower-level engineers and less blame on the upper-level management than they should have. As with most of those commissions, the guys on the bottom took the rap. They quote [associate administrator for space flight Jesse] Moore and [administrator James] Beggs and a few others saying they didn't know about the O-ring problems, which I find awfully hard to believe. I mean, hell, I knew about it two years before the accident and even wrote a memo about it. I just find it very hard to believe."

Robert Boisjoly at Thiokol, Ben Powers at NASA, and other technical people assert they did as much as they felt they could to air their concerns about the joint, short of risking being fired. They saw themselves as loyal employees, believing in the chain of command. Boisjoly told the Rogers commission: "I must emphasize, I had my say, and I never take [away] any management right to take the input out of an engineer and then make a decision based upon that input, and I truly believe that. . . . So there was no point in me doing anything any further."

And Powers said in an interview: "You don't override your chain of command. My boss was there; I made my position known to him; he did not choose to pursue it. At that point it's up to him; he doesn't have to give me any reasons; he doesn't work for me; it's his prerogative." And at least two others, asked by the Rogers commission why they did not voice their concerns to someone other than their immediate superior, replied in virtually identical language: "That would not be my reporting channel."

Following the chain of command is regarded favorably by managers and organizational theorists. But Harold Finger of the Committee for Energy Awareness warned: "You must organize for multiple lines of communication. You cannot be in a situation of any nature where you are limited by the requirement for a single reportage. In my mind, that's exactly what happened in the shuttle accident. There was no deliberate built-in system of multiple communications. Therefore, when objections were registered to somebody at Marshall or Houston or Kennedy, and he determined it didn't have to go up, it didn't go up."

Furthermore, even if the lower-level managers do pass the technical staff's concerns up the chain, they may make crucial modifications. "The fact that people are in a hierarchy tends to amplify misperceptions," said William H. Starbuck, ITT professor of creative management at New York University's Graduate School of Business Administration. "A low-level person has a fear that something might happen and reports it to a higher level. As it goes up the hierarchy, information gets distorted, usually to reflect the interests of the bosses."

WHAT ABOUT NASA'S SUCCESS STORY?

It is human nature to believe that success breeds success, when in some situations success may lead directly to failure. One of those situations is when people in an organization feel they have a problem licked. Said NYU's Starbuck: "As a company goes along and is successful, it assumes that success is inevitable. NASA had a history of 25 years of doing the impossible.

"My speculation is that this history made NASA come to have two points of view," Starbuck said. "First, risks as presented by engineers are always overstated—the actual risk is much smaller than it appears. Second, there is something magical about this group of people at NASA that can somehow surmount these risks. I think they developed a feeling of invulnerability."

Otto Lerbinger, professor of communications at Boston University, characterized this feeling that nothing can go wrong as "the Titanic syndrome." On the Titanic, he said, everyone felt that safety had been taken care of. "They even felt they didn't need lifeboats for everyone because the ship was unsinkable." It was the kind of situation where Lerbinger would see complacency setting in. "People make convenient assumptions because they want to move on. They note risks involved, but forget their assumptions and forget the risks they originally recognized," he said.

Starbuck, Lerbinger and Colorado State University's Dennis Mileti all sense that such feelings of invulnerability can gradually lead an organization to take greater chances. Starbuck mentioned a cut in the number of NASA inspectors assigned to oversee contractor's work, and the decrease in the safety, reliability, and quality assurance staff, disproportionate to other NASA staff cuts over the 15-year shuttle program.

All three experts mentioned NASA's shaving safety margins to increase shuttle payloads. "You build a bridge and it works, and so you figure on the next one you can trim it," said Starbuck. "That exceeds expectations, so you trim a bit more on the next one, until you build one that collapses." With the shuttle, he said, increasing amounts of O-ring erosion came to be accepted as normal.

John Hodge, who recently retired as NASA's acting associate administrator for space stations, said: "The problem is everybody thinks of engineering as an exact science. I think one of the real problems that we've had at NASA is that the more successful we are, the more people believe it's an exact science—and it isn't. There's a great deal of trade-off on design, and a great deal of judgment involved in engineering, and there always will be."

WHAT LESSONS HAVE BEEN LEARNED?

For Lawrence Mulloy, there are two major lessons to be learned from Challenger. "The paramount lesson is to assure that a product one sets the specs for and procures is designed, qualified, and certified to actually meet the design requirements," he said. "The fact that the booster was to function in 31° F ambient temperatures was flat missed. Whether that caused the accident is academic, but the fact was that is was missed."

Second, said Mulloy, "Be very, very careful in using subscale tests and analytical techniques to justify continuing operations on a flight vehicle where the component is not operating as you designed it to operate. Be careful in rationalizing the acceptance of anomalies you didn't expect."

According to Boston University's Lerbinger, corporate cultures try to ignore the unpleasant, and this has to be counteracted by deliberately creating a culture that encourages people to bring up unpleasant information. "In a group trying to move ahead with a decision, you find that those people that have anything negative to say are unpopular," said Lerbinger. "So a manager deliberately has to *encourage* people taking the devil's advocate position. In a crisis situation, somebody has got to think about the possibility of something going wrong, and to use a worst-case scenario approach."

Erasmus Kloman, retired consultant for the National Academy of Public Administration in Washington, has written six management studies of NASA. "The way to minimize uncertainty is to have an environment where bad news can travel up," he said. "Where there's that, there's trust and confidence."

Time and again there is the tendency to kill the messenger bringing bad news, rather than punish the wrongdoers. This was pointed out by NYU's Starbuck as well as by Myron Peretz Glazer, professor of sociology at Smith College in Northampton, Mass.

After the Challenger disaster Roger Boisjoly found he was ostracized within Thiokol and no longer allowed to work with NASA. In July he was put on permanent leave. Allan McDonald was initially stripped of his staff; later Thiokol sent out a press release that he was in charge of redesigning the booster joint. "They made it sound as if Al was heading up the whole thing, but that's a bunch of baloney," said Boisjoly. "He got his old job back, period."

"That's a very normal story," said Starbuck. "It's very typical for a whistleblower to be punished by an organization." Lerbinger agreed, pointing out that objections to Thiokol's determination to launch would be seen as "organizational treason."

On the other hand, as far as Thiokol and NASA were concerned, "The price was not nearly as heavy as one would have expected," said Glazer. "If one looks at the costs involved and the risks people took, it was the most disastrous thing that could have happened, yet they walked away okay." Glazer pointed out that William Lucas retired, by no means in disgrace, as director of Marshall Space Flight Center, shortly after the Challenger disaster. Research by Glazer and Penina Migdal Glazer for a book on whistleblowers shows, Glazer said, that "People who hung tough with their organization managed to do very well. Hanging in there and not protesting is valued highly. They manage to survive because of their fundamental and correct belief that the organization will protect them."

In fact, Starbuck said, "Thiokol's management worries me even more than NASA's. It's Thiokol where one manager said to another, 'Take off your engineering hat and put on your management hat.' They are the ones who should have looked into the questions surrounding the O-ring."

When no penalty is foreseen for being careless or doing wrong, the very behavior that should be prevented is actually enforced. Thus penalties have to be clarified and exacted, said attorney Robert Levin. "One of the things that's clear to me is that engineers do not speak the same language as managers," he said. "And engineers as a group are not politically savvy. What I would very much like to come out of all this—legislatively or otherwise—is that the next time this kind of dispute comes up, one of these engineers can say 'Damn it! Look what it *cost* Thiokol.' Now you're talking the language those folks understand."

Levin pointed out that not only is Thiokol reluctant to pay the $10 million penalty to NASA stipulated in its contract in the event of such a disaster, but "Thiokol has received millions of dollars as a result of this disaster; they're getting paid for the redesign."

The fact that there are few real penalties to organizations that commit avoidable errors also concerns Boston University's Lerbinger. "It's almost political law," he said. "Public memory is short. That puts managers in a position where they can *ignore* safety unless there is some reinforcement that gets public opinion aroused again."

Step 2: Prepare the case for class discussion.

Step 3: Answer each of the following questions, individually or in small groups, as directed by your instructor:

Description
1. Briefly describe the decisions made in the NASA *Challenger* incident.
2. Describe the major individuals involved in the decision making.

Diagnosis
3. What situation did those involved in the design of the *Challenger* face?
4. What were their objectives?
5. What alternatives were considered?
6. How completely were the alternatives evaluated?
7. Was a quality decision reached?
8. Did groupthink exist?
9. Was an ethical decision reached?

Prescription
10. How could more effective decisions have been made?
11. What techniques could those involved in the *Challenger* project have used to improve decision making?

Action

12. What were the long-run implications of the decisions made?

Step 4: Discussion. In small groups, with the entire class, or in written form, share your answers to the questions above. Then answer the following questions:

1. What symptoms suggested that a problem existed?

2. What problems exist in the case?

3. What theories and concepts help explain those problems?

4. How could the problems have been corrected?

5. Would the actions have been effective?

© 1987 IEEE. Reprinted, with permission, from *IEEE Spectrum*, vol. 24 (2), February 1987, pp. 44–51.

Activity 6–2

Wilderness Survival Worksheet

Step 1: Read the following instructions:

Directions: Here are twelve questions concerning personal survival in a wilderness situation. Your first task is to *individually* select the best of the three alternatives given under each item. Try to imagine yourself in the situation depicted. Assume that you are alone and have a minimum of equipment, except where specified. The season is fall. The days are warm and dry, but the nights are cold.

After you have completed the task individually, you will again consider each question as a member of a small group. Both the individual and group solutions will later be compared with the "correct" answers provided by a group of naturalists who conduct classes in woodland survival.

	Your Answer	*Your Group's Answer*	*Expert Answer*
1. You have strayed from your party in trackless timber. You have no special signaling equipment. The best way to attempt to contact your friends is to: a. Call for "help" loudly but in a low register. b. Yell or scream as loud as you can. c. Whistle loudly and shrilly.	C	A	A
2. You are in "snake country." Your best action to avoid snakes is to: a. Make a lot of noise with your feet. b. Walk softly and quietly. c. Travel at night.	A	A	
3. You are hungry and lost in wild country. The best rule for determining which plants are safe to eat (those you do not recognize) is to: a. Try anything you see the birds eat. b. Eat anything except plants with bright red berries. c. Put a bit of the plant on your lower lip for five minutes; if it seems all right, try a little more.	C	A	
4. The day becomes dry and hot. You have a full canteen of water (about one liter) with you. You should: a. Ration it—about a capful a day. b. Not drink until you stop for the night, then drink what you think you need. c. Drink as much as you think you need when you need it.	A	A	C

	Your Answer	*Your Group's Answer*	*Expert Answer*

5. Your water is gone; you become very thirsty. You finally come to a dried-up watercourse. Your best chance of finding water is to:
   a. Dig anywhere in the stream bed.
   b. Dig up plant and tree roots near the bank.
   c. Dig in the stream bed at the outside of a bend.

Your Answer: C   Your Group's Answer: B

6. You decide to walk out of the wild country by following a series of ravines where a water supply is available. Night is coming on. The best place to make camp is:
   a. Next to the water supply in the ravine.
   b. High on a ridge.
   c. Midway up the slope.

Your Answer: C   Your Group's Answer: B

7. Your flashlight glows dimly as you are about to make your way back to your campsite after a brief foraging trip. Darkness comes quickly in the woods and the surroundings seem unfamiliar. You should:
   a. Head back at once, keeping the light on, hoping the light will glow enough for you to make out landmarks.
   b. Put the batteries under your armpits to warm them, and then replace them in the flashlight.
   c. Shine your light for a few seconds, try to get the scene in your mind, move out in the darkness, and repeat the process.

Your Answer: C   Your Group's Answer: C

8. An early snow confines you to your small tent. You doze with your small stove going. There is danger if the flame is:
   a. Yellow.
   b. Blue.
   c. Red.

Your Answer: A   Your Group's Answer: B

9. You must ford a river that has a strong current, large rocks, and some white water. After carefully selecting your crossing spot, you should:
   a. Leave your boots and pack on.
   b. Take your boots and pack off.
   c. Take off your pack, but leave your boots on.

Your Answer: A   Your Group's Answer: A

10. In waist-deep water with a strong current, when crossing the stream, you should face:
   a. Upstream.
   b. Across the stream.
   c. Downstream.

Your Answer: A   Your Group's Answer: B

11. You find yourself rimrocked; your only route is up. The way is mossy, slippery rock. You should try it:
   a. Barefoot.
   b. With boots on.
   c. In stocking feet.

Your Answer: C   Your Group's Answer: A

12. Unarmed and unsuspecting, you surprise a large bear

	Your Answer	Your Group's Answer	Expert Answer
	C	C	

prowling around your campsite. As the bear rears up about ten meters from you, you should:

a. Run.

b. Climb the nearest tree.

c. Freeze, but be ready to back away slowly.

Individual Score _____ C _____

Step 2: Wilderness Survival Group Consensus Task:

Directions: You have just completed an individual solution to Wilderness Survival. Now your small group will decide on a group solution to the same dilemmas. A decision by consensus is difficult to attain, and not every decision may meet with everyone's unqualified approval. There should be, however, a general feeling of support from all members before a group decision is made. Do not change your individual answers, even if you change your mind in the group discussion.

Step 3: Scoring Sheet:

Directions:

1. As your instructor reads the experts' answers, record these in the Expert Answer column of the Wilderness Survival Worksheet.
2. Compare these "correct" answers with your individual answers, and record the number of questions you answered correctly in the Individual Score space provided at the end of the Wilderness Survival Worksheet.
3. Compare the experts' answers with your group's answers, and record the number of questions the group answered correctly in the Group Score space provided on the chart below.
4. Compute your group's Average Individual Score by adding the Individual Scores of all group members and dividing by the number of members in your group. Record the result on the chart below.
5. Compute your Asset/Liability Score by subtracting the Average Individual Score from the Group Score, and record the result on the chart. If the result is positive,

your group was more effective than the individual group members would have been working independently. In other words, the group capitalized on the "assets" of group problem solving. If the result is negative, your group did not capitalize on its assets, but fell prey to the "liabilities" of group problem solving.

6. Poll your group to find the highest and lowest individual scores. Record this range on the chart below. If any of the group members scored higher than the group, that individual would have performed better working alone than with the group. That individual was also unable to adequately influence the group.
7. Select a spokesperson to report your (a) Range of Individual Scores, (b) Average Individual Score, (c) Group Score, and (d) Asset/Liability Score.

Scoring Chart

Range of Individual Scores	
Average Individual Score	
Group Score	
Asset/Liability Score	

Step 4: Discussion. What do these scores suggest? How could your groups have made more effective decisions?

Reprinted from J. William Pfeiffer and John E. Jones (Eds.), *The 1976 Annual Handbook for Group Facilitations* (San Diego, Calif.: Pfeiffer & Company, 1976). Used with permission.

Activity 6–3

Decision Making in Groups

Step 1: Your instructor will organize the class into nominal groups of five to eight people and present the task to you.

Step 2: Write your own ideas about the problem on a piece of paper.

Step 3: In the small groups, each person should contribute one idea and list it on a flip chart. This type of sharing should continue until all ideas are publicly recorded.

Step 4: Where necessary, briefly clarify each idea by means of examples and explanations, but do not debate for relative merits. Eliminate duplicate ideas and refine global ideas into two or more specific items.

Step 5: As individuals, rank or classify all ideas in writing according to criteria specified by the instructor.

Step 6: Tabulate and summarize all individual evaluations to produce a group decision.

Step 7: With the entire class, share the decisions you reached.

Step 8: The instructor will select a panel of experts (usually the entire class) who are informed about the task.

Step 9: You will receive a question or questionnaire to complete in writing.

Step 10: Your instructor or appointed members of the class will tabulate and summarize the data.

Step 11: The instructor will feed back and discuss the summarized data with the class.

Step 12: The instructor may repeat Steps 9, 10, and 11 until some consensus is reached about the task or problem.

Step 13: With the entire class, share the decisions you reached.

Step 14: Your instructor will organize you into small groups of five to eight individuals.

Step 15: Each group will receive a problem or task.

Step 16: As a group, you are to brainstorm possible solutions to the problem; list all ideas without discussion on a large piece of newsprint.

Step 17: Using these ideas, reach consensus about a decision.

Step 18: With the entire class, share the ideas you generated.

Step 19: Discussion. In small groups, with the entire class, or in written form, as directed by your instructor compare and contrast the three approaches to decision making.

1. How did the approaches differ? How were they similar?
2. Which approach resulted in the most effective decisions?
3. Under what circumstances would each approach be effective? ineffective?
4. Offer ways of improving the effectiveness of the decision-making processes you used.

Based on Curtis W. Cook, Nominal group methods enrich classroom learning. *Exchange: The Organizational Behavior Teaching Journal* 5 (1980): 33–36.

Activity 6–4   How Biased Is Your Decision Making?

Step 1: Answer each of the following problems:

1. A certain town is served by two hospitals. In the larger hospital about 45 babies are born each day, and in the smaller hospital about 15 babies are born each day. Although the overall proportion of boys is about 50 percent, the actual proportion at either hospital may be greater or less than 50 percent on any day. At the end of a year, which hospital will have the greater number of days on which more than 60 percent of the babies born were boys?
   a. The large hospital
   b. The small hospital
   c. Neither—the number of days will be about the same (within 5 percent of each other)
2. Linda is 31, single, outspoken, and very bright. She majored in philosophy in college. As a student, she was deeply concerned with discrimination and other social issues, and participated in antinuclear demonstrations. Which statement is more likely:
   a. Linda is a bank teller
   b. Linda is a bank teller and active in the feminist movement
3. A cab was involved in a hit-and-run accident. Two cab companies serve the city: the Green, which operates 85 percent of the cabs, and the Blue, which operates the remaining 15 percent. A witness identifies the hit-and-run cab as Blue. When the court tests the reliability of the witness under circumstances similar to those on the night of the accident, he correctly identifies the color of a cab 80 percent of the time and misidentifies it the other 20 percent. What's the probability that the cab involved in the accident was Blue, as the witness stated?
4. Imagine that you face this pair of concurrent decisions.

Examine these decisions, then indicate which choices you prefer:

Decision I.

Choose between:
a. a sure gain of $240
b. a 25 percent chance of winning $1,000 and a 75 percent chance of winning nothing

Decision II.

Choose between:
c. a sure loss of $750
d. A 75 percent chance of losing $1,000 and a 25 percent chance of losing nothing

Decision III.

Choose between:
e. a sure loss of $3,000
f. an 80 percent chance of losing $4,000 and a 20 percent chance of losing nothing

5. You've decided to see a Broadway play and have bought a $40 ticket. As you enter the theater, you realize you've lost your ticket. You can't remember the seat number, so you can't prove to the management that you bought a ticket. Would you spend $40 for a new ticket?

You've reserved a seat for a Broadway play for which the ticket price is $40. As you enter the theater to buy your ticket, you discover you've lost $40 from your pocket. Would you still buy the ticket? (Assume you have enough cash left to do so.)

6. Imagine you have operable lung cancer and must choose between two treatments—surgery and radiation therapy. Of 100 people having surgery, 10 die during the operation, 32 (including those original 10) are dead after one year, and 66 after five years. Of 100 people having radiation therapy, none dies during treatment, 23 are dead after one year and 78 after five years. Which treatment would you prefer?

Step 2: Your instructor will give you the correct answer to each problem.

Step 3: Discussion. In small groups, with the entire class, or in written form, as directed by your instructor, answer the following questions:

Description
1. How accurate were the decisions you reached?

Diagnosis
2. What biases were evident in the decisions you reached?

Prescription
3. How could you improve your decision making to make it more accurate?

From D. Kahnemann and A. Tversky, Rational choice and the forming of decisions, *Journal of Business* 59 (4) (1986): 5251–5278; A. Tversky and D. Kahnemann, The framing of decisions and the psychology of choice, *Science* 211 (1981): 453–458; D. Kahnemann and A. Tversky, Extension needs intuitive reasoning, *Psychological Review* 90 (1983): 293–315; K. McKean, Decisions, decisions, *Discover Magazine,* June 1985.

Activity 6–5 **Dave Stewart (S)**

Step 1: Read the Dave Stewart (S) case.

Dave Stewart was a leasing agent for a major real estate development firm. A leasing agent sold office and warehouse space or locations for new construction to businesses, and also negotiated with such clients over terms and conditions of contracts. Dave was his firm's primary contact in a business deal involving D. B. Snow, a company that had decided to lease or buy new facilities from Dave's firm. He ran into three troublesome situations over this one deal:

1. D. B. Snow wanted a ten-year lease term on the property and buildings, with an option to buy it all after five years, instead of leasing for a second five-year period. Snow and Dave agreed that the purchase price—should Snow decide to buy the leased facilities—would be equal to the expenses for certain property improvements that Dave's firm had incurred prior to its leasing arrangement with Snow. Dave knew that the actual amount his company had paid for improvements totaled $600,000, but his boss, Tom, instructed him to tell Snow that the improvements had cost $900,000. Tom also told Dave that he should back down from the $900,000 bluff only if Snow questioned the figure.

2. Snow had signed a separate contract with Dave's firm that required the firm to reserve some land adjacent to Snow's leasing location for a future administrative building. Both Dave and Snow had thought there was enough land available for future construction, but Dave discovered later that a sewer easement and flood plain limited the available land and prohibited future construction of the administrative building. Snow had chosen Dave's building location over competing locations partly be-

cause it had been told that this land would be available. Tom told Dave to keep quiet about his discovery and to have architectural drawings prepared showing this adjacent building, which couldn't be built.

3. A local broker had represented Snow in its move to the new leasing location. This broker's standard commission was 4 percent of the gross lease amount over the whole lease term. Both Dave and his boss Tom knew that the broker expected to be paid according to the standard commission on the basis of the full ten-year lease term ($240,000), even though Snow had the option to buy out after five years. Several weeks after Snow's lease was signed, Tom told Dave to tell the broker that, because Snow had the option to buy out after the fifth year, the arrangement represented the equivalent of a five-year lease. Consequently, Dave's firm would pay the broker only half the commission he expected—$120,000 instead of $240,000.

Dave had much to think about as he faced the decisions he had to make about how to handle the D. B. Snow deal. His boss expected him to carry out his orders without question; Dave knew that a fellow leasing agent in the same office wouldn't even think twice before doing so. Dave was paid $50,000 annually by his firm, and he needed the money badly: he still had school debts to pay off; he had almost no savings; he and his wife had just had their first baby. If he followed his conscience, he would jeopardize his position with his employer and maybe face a personal financial crisis.

Step 2: Prepare the case for class discussion.

Step 3: Answer each of the following questions, individually or in small groups, as directed by your instructor:

Description
1. Describe the situation faced by Dave Stewart.

Diagnosis
2. What decisions must Dave Stewart make?
3. What information is available for use in the decision making?
4. What ethical issues does he face?

Prescription
5. What process should Dave use in making the decisions?
6. What advantages do individual and group decision making offer?
7. How can he ensure that he makes a high-quality, accepted, ethical decision?

Action
8. What outcomes are likely from each possible decision?

Step 4: Discussion. In small groups, with the entire class, or in written form, share your answers to the questions above. Then answer the following questions:

1. What symptoms suggest that a problem exists?
2. What problems exist in the case?
3. What theories and concepts help explain those problems?
4. How should the situation be handled?

This material was prepared by Stephen B. Cook, Research Assistant, under the supervision of Lynda Sharp Paine, Visiting Assistant Professor, and Henry W. Tulloch, Executive Director, Olsson Center for Applied Ethics. The case is a simplified version of "Dave Stewart (A)," UVA–E–024. Copyright © 1984 by the Darden Graduate Business School Foundation, Charlottesville, Va. IBM:E–023.

Activity 6–6   Ethical Decision Making

Step 1: Read Cases 1–4. For each case, first decide what you would do and why. In doing this, consider what information you would use to investigate the question, what alternatives you would consider, and what criteria you would use in making your decision.

CASE 1: SALES REPRESENTATIVE IN THE MIDDLE EAST
You are the sales representative for your construction company in the Middle East. Your company has bid on a substantial project which it wants *very much* to get. Yesterday, the cousin of the minister who will award the contract sug-

gested that he might be of help. You are reasonably sure that with his help the chances of getting the contract would increase. For his assistance, the minister expects $20,000. You would have to pay this in addition to the standard fees to your agent. If you do not make this payment to the minister, you are certain that he will go to your competition (who have won the last three contracts), and they *will* make the payment (and probably get this contract, too).

Your company has no code of conduct yet, although a committee was formed some time ago to consider one. The government of your country recently passed a Business Practices Act. The pertinent paragraph is somewhat vague, but implies that this kind of payment would probably be a violation of the act. The person to whom you report, and those above him, do not want to become involved. The decision is yours to make.

CASE 2: HAZARDOUS MATERIALS IN WEST AFRICA

For one year now, you have been international vice president of a multinational firm that produces and markets chemicals. The minister of agriculture in a small developing country in West Africa has requested a series of large shipments over the next five years of a special insecticide that only your firm prepares. The minister believes that this chemical is the only one that will rid one of his crops of a new infestation that threatens to destroy it. You know, however, that one other insecticide would probably be equally effective; it is produced in another country and has never been allowed in your own country.

Your insecticide, MIM, is highly toxic. After years of debate, your government has just passed a law forbidding its use in your country. There is evidence that dangerous amounts are easily ingested by humans through residue on vegetables, through animals that eat the crops, and through the water supply. After careful thought, you tell the minister about this evidence. He still insists on using it, arguing that it is necessary and it will be used "intelligently." You are quite sure that, ten years from now, it will begin to damage the health of some of his people.

Both the president and the executive vice president of your firm feel strongly that the order should be filled. They question the government's position, and they are very concerned about the large inventory of MIM on hand and the serious financial setback its prohibition will cause the company. They have made it clear, however, that the decision is up to you.

Note: While the company has a code of conduct and your government has a Business Practices Act, neither covers hazardous materials.

CASE 3: THE SOUTHEAST ASIAN ADVERTISING CAMPAIGN

You are the new marketing manager for a very large, profitable international firm that manufactures automobile tires. Your advertising agency has just presented for your approval elaborate plans for introducing a new tire into the Southeast Asian market. The promotional material clearly implies that your product is better than all local products. In fact it is better than some, but not as good as others. This material tries to attract potential buyers by explaining that for six months your product will be sold at a "reduced price." Actually, the price is reduced from a hypothetical amount that was established only so it could be "reduced." The ad claims that the tire has been tested under the "most adverse" conditions. In fact it has not been tested in the prolonged heat and humidity of the tropics. Finally, your company assures potential buyers that, riding on your tires, they will be safer in their car than ever before. The truth is, however, that they could have been equally safe on a competitor's tire that has been available for two years.

You know your product is good. You also know the proposed advertising is deceptive. Your superiors have never been concerned about such practices, believing they must present your products as distinctive in order to achieve and maintain a competitive edge. They are counting on a very favorable reception for this tire in Southeast Asia. They are counting on you to see that it gets this reception.

Whether you go with the proposed advertising or not is up to you. Your company has a code of conduct and your government has a Business Practices Act, but neither covers advertising practices.

CASE 4: CULTURAL CONFLICT IN THE MIDDLE EAST

You were quite upset last week when you read a strong editorial in the *New York Times,* written by a prominent journalist, that was highly critical of your company, especially its major project in a conservative Moslem country.

As the international vice president, you are responsible for this project, which is the building and running of a large steel plant. Based on the figures, this plant makes a lot of sense, both for your company and for the government of the country that approved the project. But as the journalist pointed out, it is to be built in a rural area and will have a very disruptive effect upon the values and customs of the people in the whole region. There will be many consequences. The young people from the other towns will move to work at the plant, thereby breaking up families and eliminating their primary source of financial and personal security. Working the second or third shift will further interfere with family responsibilities, as well as religious observances. Working year round will certainly mean that many people will be unable to return home to help with the harvest. As the young people will be paid more and more, they will gain more influence, thereby overturning century old patterns of authority. And, of course, the Westerners who will be brought in will probably not live up to the local moral standards and will not show due respect for local women.

The journalist ended by charging your company with "cultural imperialism" and claiming that your plant, if actually built and put into operation, would contribute to the disruption of the traditional values and relationships that have provided stability for the country through many generations.

You had known there would be some social changes, but you did not realize how profound they could be. You have now examined other evidence and discovered that a factory built several years ago by another foreign firm in a similar location is causing exactly these problems—and more. Widespread concern in the country over these problems is one reason for the increasing influence of traditionalists and nationalists in the country, who argue for getting rid of all foreign firms and their disruptive priorities and practices.

Your company has a code of conduct and your government has a Business Practices Act, but neither deals with the destruction of traditional values and relationships. You are on your own here. A lot is at stake for the company, and for the people of the region into which you had planned to move. The decision is yours.

Step 2: In groups of four to six students, reach consensus about how to handle each situation.

Step 3: Discussion. In small groups, with the entire class, or in written form, as directed by your instructor, answer the following questions:

Description
1. What decisions did each group reach?

Diagnosis
2. How ethical were the decisions reached?
3. What criteria did you use to evaluate the decisions?

Prescription
4. How could you improve your decision making to make it more ethical?

_____

From Nancy J. Adler, *International Dimensions of Organizational Behavior,* 2d ed. (Boston: PWS-Kent Publishing Company, 1991). © by Wadsworth, Inc. Reprinted by permission of PWS-Kent, a division of Wadsworth, Inc.

CONCLUDING COMMENTS

Decision making occurs in increasingly complex and ambiguous situations, calling for excellent technical, interpersonal, and decision-making skills by individuals and groups responsible for decisions. The quality of information is a key ingredient in effective decision making. Information is used in analyzing the situation, setting objectives, and choosing appropriate alternatives to comprise the decision. The quality of information can be influenced through improved data collection, objectifying perceptions, and reducing misattributions. In the NASA *Challenger* case you saw the impact of an ineffective decision-making process and offered ways the design groups could have improved their outcome. You tried various group decision-making techniques in Decision Making in Groups. You also compared group to individual decision making in the Wilderness Survival Exercise.

People's perceptions of and attributions for particular events and people affect the way they make decisions. In How Biased Is Your Decision Making you considered the types of biases that affect decision making. In Ethical Decision Making and the Dave Stewart case you examined the ethical issues associated with decision making.

ENDNOTES

[1] E. F. Harrison, *The Managerial Decision Making Process,* 3rd ed. (Boston: Houghton Mifflin, 1987).

[2] G. W. England, Personal value systems of American managers, *Academy of Management Journal* (March 1967), was an early writer about this relationship.

[3] A. J. Rose, R. O. Mason, and K. E. Dicken, *Strategic Management: A Methodological Approach* (Reading, Mass.: Addison-Wesley, 1987).

[4] Harrison, *Managerial Decision Making Process.*

[5] G. P. Huber, *Managerial Decision Making* (Glenview, Ill.: Scott, Foresman, 1980): G. P. Huber, Decision support systems: Their present and future applications. In G. R. Ungson and D. N. Braunstein, eds., *Decision-Making: An Interdisciplinary Inquiry* (Boston: Kent, 1982).

[6] C. A. O'Reilly III, Variations in decision makers' use of information sources: The impact of quality and accessibility of information, *Academy of Management Journal* 25 (1982): 756–771.

[7] See M. Bazerman, *Judgment in Managerial Decision-Making,* 2nd ed. (New York: Wiley, 1990), for a summary of the research in this area.

[8] L. K. Trevino, Ethical decision making in organizations: A person-situation interactionist model, *Academy of Management Review* 11 (1986): 601–617.

[9] J. R. Rest, *Moral Development: Advances in Research and Theory* (New York: Praeger, 1986); T. M. Jones, Ethical decision making by individuals in organizations: An issue-contingent model, *Academy of Management Review* 16(2) (1991): 366–395.

[10] See J. Bulhart, *Effective Group Discussion* (Dubuque, Iowa: William C. Brown, 1986); J. T. Wood, G. M. Phillips, and D. J. Pedersen, *Group Discussion: A Practical Guide to Participation and Leadership* (New York: Harper & Row, 1986), for examples.

[11] J. S. Carroll and E. J. Johnson, *Decision Research: A Field Guide* (Newbury Park, Calif.: Sage, 1990).

[12] P. C. Nutt, Types of organizational decision process, *Administrative Science Quarterly* 29 (1984): 414–450.

[13] Ungson and Braunstein, *Decision-Making*.

[14] T. R. Mitchell and L. R. Beach, ". . . Do I love thee? Let me count . . ." Toward an understanding of intuitive and automatic decision making, *Organizational Behavior and Human Decision Processes* 47 (1990): 1–20.

[15] Harrison, *Managerial Decision-Making Process*.

[16] This description is based on P. C. Nutt, *Making Tough Decisions* (San Francisco: Jossey-Bass, 1989).

[17] N. J. Adler, *International Dimensions of Organizational Behavior,* 2nd ed. (Boston: PWS-Kent, 1991).

[18] *Ibid.*

[19] *Ibid.*

[20] P. R. Harris and G. T. Moran, *Managing Cultural Differences,* 3rd ed. (Houston: Gulf, 1991).

[21] H. A. Simon, *The New Science of Management Decision* (New York: Harper, 1960).

[22] The last five reasons are drawn from R. C. Snyder, A decision-making approach to the study of political phenomena. In R. Young, ed., *Approaches to the Study of Politics* (Evanston, Ill.: Northwestern University, 1985).

[23] P. A. Anderson, Decision making by objection and the Cuban Missile Crisis, *Administrative Science Quarterly* 28 (1983): 201–222.

[24] For a discussion of this model see most recently J. G. March and J. P. Olsen, Garbage can models of decision making in organizations. In J. G. March and R. Weissinger-Baylon, eds., *Ambiguity and Command* (Marshfield, Mass.: Pitman, 1986), pp. 11–53; and earlier works including M. D. Cohen, J. G. March, and J. P. Olsen, A garbage can model of organizational choice, *Administrative Science Quarterly* 17 (1972): 1–25; J. G. March and J. Olsen, *Ambiguity and Choice in Organizations* (Bergen, Norway: Universitetsforlaget, 1976).

[25] M. Masuch and P. LaPotin, Beyond garbage cans: An AI model of organizational choice, *Administrative Science Quarterly* 34 (1989): 38–67.

[26] L. M. Lovata, Behavioral theories relating to the design of information systems, *MIS Quarterly* (June 1987): 147–149.

[27] Masuch and LaPotin, Beyond garbage cans.

[28] *Ibid.*

[29] Recent research continues to confirm this observation. See, for example, J. P. Wanous and M. A. Youtz, Solution diversity and the quality of group decisions, *Academy of Management Journal* 29 (1986): 149–159; and P. C. Bottinger and P. W. Yetton, An integration of process and decision scheme explanations of group problem solving performance, *Organizational Behavior and Human Decision Processes* 42 (1988): 234–249.

[30] N. J. Adler, *International Dimensions of Organizational Behavior,* 1st ed. (Boston: Kent, 1986), p. 113.

[31] K. Dion, R. Baron, and N. Miller, Why do groups make riskier decisions than individuals? In L. Berkowitz, ed., *Advances in Experimental Social Psychology,* vol. 5 (New York: Academic Press, 1970), presents some of the earliest work in this area; see Bazerman, *Judgment in Managerial Decision-Making,* for recent discussion of this phenomenon.

[32] H. Lamm and D. G. Myers, Group-induced polarization of attitudes and behaviors. In L. Berkowitz, ed., *Advances in Experimental Social Psychology,* vol. 11 (New York: Academic Press, 1978).

[33] I. Janis, Groupthink, *Psychology Today,* June 1971.

[34] P. W. Yetton and P. C. Bottinger, Individual versus group problem solving: An empirical test of a best-member strategy, *Organizational Behavior and Human Performance* 29 (1982): 307–321.

[35] H. J. Einhorn, R. M. Hogarth, and E. Klempner, Quality of group judgment, *Psychological Bulletin* 84 (1977): 158–172.

[36] L. K. Michaelsen, W. E. Watson, and R. H. Black, A realistic test of individual vs. group consensus decision making, *Journal of Applied Psychology* 74(5) (1989): 834–839.

[37] Janis, Groupthink.

[38] G. Whyte, Groupthink reconsidered, *Academy of Management Review* 14 (1989): 40–56; Lamm and Myers, Group-induced polarization.

[39] I. L. Janis and L. Mann, *Decision Making* (New York: Free Press, 1977).

[40] L. N. Jewell and H. J. Reitz, *Group Effectiveness in Organizations* (Glenview, Ill.: Scott, Foresman, 1981).

[41] S. E. Jackson, Participation in decision making as a strategy for reducing job-related stress, *Journal of Applied Psychology* 68 (1983): 3–19.

[42] See, for example, R. T. Pascale, Communication and decision making across cultures: Japanese and American comparisons, *Administrative Science Quarterly* 23 (1978): 91–110.

[43] Nutt, Types of organizational decision process.

[44] R. Y. Hirokawa and D. R. Scheerhorn, Communication in faulty group decision-making. In R. Y. Hirokawa and M. S. Poole, eds., *Communication and Group Decision-Making* (Beverly Hills, Calif.: Sage, 1986).

[45] D. S. Gouran and R. Y. Hirokawa, Counteractive functions of communication in effective group decision-making. In Hirokawa and Poole, *Communication and Group Decision-Making.*

[46] J. D. Mullen and B. M. Roth, *Decision-Making: Its Logic and Practice* (Savage, Md.: Rowman and Littlefield, 1991).

[47] Bazerman, *Judgment in Managerial Decision-Making.*

[48] P. Slovic, B. Fischhoff, and S. Lichtenstein, Behavioral decision theory, *Annual Review of Psychology* 28 (1977): 1–39.

[49] J. L. Adams, *The Care and Feeding of Ideas: A Guide to Encouraging Creativity* (Reading, Mass.: Addison-Wesley, 1986).

[50] G. P. Huber, *Managerial Decision Making* (Glenview, Ill.: Scott, Foresman, 1980); and A. Delbecq, A. Van de Ven, and D. Gustafson, *Group Techniques for Program Planning* (Glenview, Ill.: Scott, Foresman, 1975), provide an early discussion. See J. B. Thomas, R. R. McDaniel, Jr., and M. J. Dooris, Strategic issue analysis: NGT + decision analysis for resolving strategic issues, *Journal of Applied Behavioral Sciences* 25(2) (1989): 189–200, for more recent examples.

[51] W. M. Fox, Anonymity and other keys to successful problem-solving meetings, *National Productivity Review* 8(2) (1989); W. M. Fox, The improved nominal group technique (INGT), *Journal of Management Development* 8(1) (1989): 20–27.

[52] A. Van de Ven and A. L. Delbecq, Nominal versus interacting group processes for committee decision-making effectiveness, *Academy of Management Journal* 14 (1971): 203–212.

[53] J. G. Mahler, Structured decision making in public organizations, *Public Administration Review* (July/August 1987): 336–342.

[54] A. L. Delbecq, A. Van de Ven, and D. H. Gustafson, *Group Techniques for Program Planning* (Middleton, Wis.: Greenbrier, 1986); D. R. Anderson, Increased productivity via group decisionmaking, *Supervision* (September 1990): 6–10.

[55] K. L. Kraemer and A. Pinsonneault, Technology and groups: Assessment of the empirical research. In J. Galegher, R. E. Kraut, and C. Egido, eds., *Intellectual Teamwork* (Hillsdale, N.J.: Erlbaum, 1990): 375–405.

[56] H. A. Linstone and M. Turoff, eds., *The Delphi Method: Techniques and Applications* (Reading, Mass.: Addison-Wesley, 1975).

[57] S. Hart, M. Boroush, G. Enk, and W. Hornick, Managing complexity through consensus mapping: Technology for the structuring of group decisions, *Academy of Management Review* 10 (1985): 587–600.

[58] E. DeBono, *Lateral Thinking: Creativity Step by Step* (New York: Perennial Library, 1990); E. DeBono, *Lateral Thinking for Management: A Handbook of Creativity* (New York: American Management Association, 1971).

[59] J. L. Adams, *Conceptual Blockbusting: A Guide to Better Ideas,* 2nd ed. (New York: W. W. Norton, 1979).

RECOMMENDED READINGS

Adams, J. L. *The Care and Feeding of Ideas: A Guide to Encouraging Creativity.* Reading, Mass.: Addison-Wesley, 1986.

Bazerman, M. *Judgment in Managerial Decision-Making,* 2nd ed. New York: Wiley, 1990.

Harrison, E. F. *The Managerial Decision Making Process,* 3rd ed. Boston: Houghton Mifflin, 1987.

March, J. G., ed. *Decisions and Organizations.* New York: Basil Blackwell, 1988.

Mullen, J. D., and Roth, B. M. *Decision-Making: Its Logic and Practice.* Savage, Md.: Rowman and Littlefield, 1991.

Nutt, P. C. *Making Tough Decisions.* San Francisco: Jossey-Bass, 1989.

Chapter Outline

Developing Better Communication

Learning Objectives

After completing the reading and activities in Chapter 7, students will be able to

1. Describe, illustrate, and identify the communication process and diagnose dysfunctions in it.

2. Discuss the role of language, listening, noise, and feedback in communication.

3. Compare and contrast communication that occurs upward, downward, and laterally, and offer strategies for communicating effectively in each direction.

4. Discuss how interpersonal relationships affect the accuracy of communication.

5. Comment about the nature and impact of informal communication.

6. Identify the key issues for effective multicultural and multinational communication.

7. Specify the barriers to effective communication and propose strategies for reducing them.

8. Specify and illustrate the dimensions of a supportive communication climate.

9. Compare an assertive style to aggressive and passive styles and illustrate its use.

10. Show how active listening contributes to effective communication.

11. Offer guidelines for increasing the effectiveness of interviews in organizations.

Communication at Mattel and Brook Furniture Rental

Radical changes have . . . transformed Mattel since John Amerman became CEO of the California-based toy company in 1987. The second day on the job, he told employees he was letting in some "fresh air" and that the new watchword at Mattel was to be "fun." At the time Mattel was an out-of-control money loser that had spent big to introduce a series of toys that bombed. Morale was low. Amerman asked his work force to help him turn the company around and assured them it could be done with a minimum of chaos if they worked in teams and tried to enjoy themselves.

The cheerful, white-haired CEO began wandering around the place, eating in the cafeteria, and meeting regularly with employees. The results were gratifying. For example, when he asked for suggestions on how to eliminate some layers in the organization, to his surprise many employees recommended that their departments be pruned or totally scrapped. Taking their advice, he cut out six layers from the hierarchy. Some people took early retirement, others were transferred to new departments, and a few were laid off.

Amerman often speaks without a written script. But he develops "a structured format" in his mind and rehearses what he's going to say while driving to work. Says he: "Everyone is so sleepy on the freeway, they don't pay attention to me talking to myself."

Mattel rebounded from a loss of $113 million in 1987 to record earnings of $91 million in 1990. To announce earnings results to the work force in 1989, Amerman put together a rap routine: "Supersonic motivating toys we're creating / Everybody knows that Mattel's devastating," grooved the CEO, his backup chiming in. It brought the house down. Recalls Amerman: "All of the employees came up and hugged me. It was like I hit the home run in the ninth inning of the seventh game of the World Series."

The next year the CEO spruced up his stage act. He recruited his top two lieutenants to put on a Las Vegas-style revue. All three executives donned tuxedos and glittery top hats. Dubbing themselves the "Toy Boys," they pranced and sang new lyrics to old tunes, like "There's No Business Like Toy Business." They concluded the show by announcing that all 1,100 rank-and-file headquarters employees would receive a bonus of two weeks pay that was to come out of senior management's bonus pool. A good idea, says communication experts: Acts like sharing bonuses validate management's claim that it is working together with employees toward a common objective.

Bob Crawford, founder and CEO of fast-growing Brook Furniture Rental (1991 estimated sales: $50 million), puts great emphasis on two-way communications. In particular, he has strived to create an atmosphere where employees speak openly, without fear of reprisal. "People will put every effort into advancing the business if they can communicate their ideas freely," argues Crawford, 52, who began his career at Procter & Gamble 25 years ago. Communications consultant Richard Bevan of Towers Perrin agrees: "It's nuts if you don't involve employees; they are the only people who can fix the business."

When Crawford walks through his company's huge warehouses, he greets every worker by name and chats about work or personal matters. Newly hired salesmen are shocked to find Crawford leading many of their training sessions and soliciting their ideas to improve the company.

Crawford even finds time to accompany members of his 150-odd sales force when they call on accounts. He still gets a charge from the reaction of customers who tell him that he is the first company president to call on them. "In this impersonal society, people want a personal touch," he reasons.

Listening is Crawford's most powerful communications tool, he notes, and he urges his staff to attend carefully to what both customers and employees have to say: "The secret of good human dynamics is a balance between talking and listening. You need to absorb data before imparting information." Listening does not come easily, he warns. Even now Crawford concedes that he must constantly remind himself to concentrate. Remembering names is especially difficult, he admits.[1]

• • • • • • • • • • • • • • • • • •

W hy are Amerman and Crawford unique managers? What has been happening at Mattel and Brook Furniture Rental? What factors contribute to the effective communication in these organizations?

In this chapter we examine the nature of effective communication, a central organizational process that can occur at the intrapersonal, interpersonal, intragroup, intergroup, organizational, and public levels. As a linking mechanism among the different organizational subsystems, communication is a central feature of the *structure* of groups and organizations. It builds and reinforces interdependence between various parts of the organization.

The chapter first describes the communication process and then its five components: encoding, transmission, decoding, noise, and feedback. Next it looks at downward, upward, and lateral communication. Then it discusses how interpersonal relations and attitudes affect the quality of communication, as well as issues of informal communication. The chapter then turns to multicultural and multinational communication. It continues by presenting a set of strategies for improving communication accuracy. The chapter concludes with a discussion of a special type of communication in organizations—interviewing.

THE COMMUNICA-TION PROCESS

Perception, attribution, motivation, individual personality and personal development, group characteristics, and organizational factors all affect the way individuals transmit information and receive information transmitted by another. We begin with a simple example of the communication process. A subordinate recently asked her boss how long an upcoming project would be. The boss answered by stating, "Ten weeks." When the subordinate asked that simple question, and the boss responded, they both participated in a complex communication process.

In communication, an *input* is *transformed* by *encoding* and *decoding,* resulting in another meaning, or *output,* which is *fed* back to the sender.[2] Figure 7–1 pictures the steps of the process. Each of these steps should follow three principles of ethical communication:

1. Organization members should not intentionally deceive one another.
2. Organization members' communication should not purposely harm any other organization member or members of the organization's relevant environment.
3. Organization members should be treated justly.[3]

Figure 7–1 **The Communication Process**

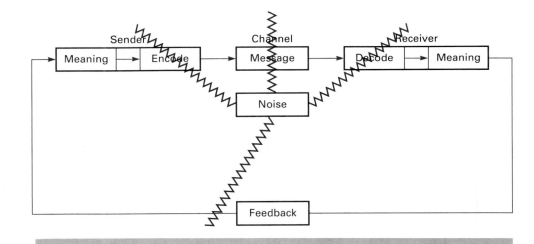

ENCODING: VERBAL AND NONVERBAL COMMUNICATION

Once a person has a meaning to convey, he or she needs to determine the means to convey that meaning—the way to *encode* it. The sender uses his or her own *frame of reference* as the background for encoding information. It includes the individual's view of the organization or situation as a function of personal education, interpersonal relationships, attitudes, knowledge, and experience.

Going back to the boss-subordinate example, first the subordinate had a meaning she wished to convey: The boss later learned that she wanted to determine the content and comprehensiveness of the project—she did not want to know its length but rather its scope. Notice that this meaning differs from the question she asked. Next, she had to decide how to encode this meaning. She had to decide, for example, an efficient way of getting the needed information. She considered, probably unconsciously, whom she should ask: her boss, a coworker, another manager. Should she ask the question by phone, in a letter, or directly? What specific question should she ask so that she would be understood? What nonverbal messages (e.g., an attitude of pleading? of arrogance? of total ignorance?) should accompany her question? How else might the subordinate have encoded this message? She might have asked what tasks would be included in the project, or what were its desired outcomes. In encoding the message, the subordinate should have considered what was the most effective way to convey her desire for certain information.

Now consider the situation at Mattel or Brook Furniture. What messages do you think the CEOs wanted to send to their employees? How successfully did they communicate these messages to them? How, for example, did Amerman encode his message of "having fun" to his employees?

The Use of Language

The choice of words or language in which a sender encodes a message will influence the quality of communication. Because language is a symbolic representation of a phenomenon, room for interpretation and distortion of the meaning exists. Consider an instructor who decides to present an entire class in a foreign language that few or none of the students understand. Consider a salesperson who describes a product using so many technical specifications that his or her client cannot easily determine the product's characteristics. Think about a manager whose directions are so ambiguous that his or her subordinate cannot determine the most appropriate way of acting. In each of these cases, the inappropriate use of language can limit the quality of effective communication. People can use the same words but attribute different meanings to them; such *bypassing* can occur in cross-cultural situations or in stressful situations.[4] Reading 7–1, "Bypassing in Managerial Communication," discusses this concept in greater detail.

A sender can create misunderstandings by using language in a number of ways.[5] The sender may use words that are too abstract and have many mental images associated with them. Or the sender may overgeneralize messages and fail to recognize subtleties. As noted earlier, the use of jargon frequently creates misunderstandings, as does the use of slang or colloquialisms in speech. Some senders consciously use messages to confuse the issue. Others leave information out of messages. Both Amerman and Crawford seem to take great care to avoid such misunderstandings. They spend a great deal of time talking with their employees face-to-face in formal and informal situations.

Misuses of language are especially common between superiors and their subordinates. For example, a subordinate can create misunderstandings by distorting information upward: telling the boss only good news, paying the boss compliments whenever possible, always agreeing with the boss, avoiding offering personal opinions different from the boss's, insulating the boss from information detrimental to him or her, covering up information potentially damaging to oneself, and selecting words that project only favorable impressions.[6] The boss can create misunderstandings by withholding information or omitting the emotional content of a message.

Nonverbal Communication

The use of gestures, movements, material things, time, and space can clarify or confuse the meaning of verbal communication. For example, the kind of facial expressions that accompany a request for time off may indicate its importance or frivolity. If an interviewer arrives at an interview late, the interviewee may interpret any comments as less sincere than if the interviewer is prompt. Or a salesperson may use props to illustrate aspects of a sales pitch.

Nonverbal cues serve five functions.[7] They *repeat* the message the individual is making verbally; an individual who nods after he or she answers affirmatively confirms the verbal message with the nonverbal gesture. They can *contradict* a message the individual is trying to convey; an individual who pounds the table while stating that he or she does not care about the situation being discussed uses verbal and nonverbal communication that disagree; the nonverbal communication may, in some cases, be more powerful or accurate than the verbal communication. Nonverbal cues may also *substitute* for a verbal message; an individual with "fire in his eyes" conveys information without using verbal messages. They may add to or *complement* a verbal message; a supervisor who beams while giving praise increases the impact of the compliment to the subordinate. Or, nonverbal communication may *accent* or underline a verbal message; for example, speaking very softly or stamping your feet shows the importance an individual attaches to a message.

Senders must recognize the significance of nonverbal communication and use it to increase the impact of their verbal communication. They must also recognize that nonverbal signals may give a message that is different from the one they intend. For example, English-speaking managers who supervise non-English-speaking workers often experience this problem.[8] A gesture, for example, may have different meanings in different cultures. Consider the A-OK gesture, or the thumb and forefinger circled: In the United States it means that things are fine; in Brazil it is an obscene gesture; in Japan it means money.[9]

TRANSMISSION AND ELECTRONIC MEDIA

The actual transmission of the message follows the encoding; the sender must convey the message to the receiver. Here, the subordinate went to her boss's office. She walked in and asked how long the project would be. Thus the transmission of her message took place primarily by verbal channels. In determining the appropriateness of this medium, the subordinate should consider among other factors the medium's richness, as determined by its speed of feedback, variety of communication channels, extent of personal interactions, and richness of language.[10] As tasks become more ambiguous, managers should increase the richness of the media they use; for example, they should send nonroutine and difficult communications through a rich medium, such as face-to-face communication, and routine simple communications through a lean medium, such as a memo.[11] They should also use rich media to increase personal visibility and implement company strategies.[12] Table 7–1 shows the advantages and disadvantages of an array of media. At Mattell, Amerman's use of a rap song and sponsorship of a Las Vegas–style review involved a creative use of channels of communication. He could also have talked to his employees individually or sent them a written memorandum. Would these channels have been as effective? Probably not.

Using Electronic Media

The widespread availability of electronic media for communication, including messaging and conferencing systems, has had a significant impact on the accessibility of information and the speed of transmission. Table 7–2 lists the features of various electronic media.

Management information systems, now using computer-based software programs, also facilitate communication by making large quantities of information available and assisting in its analysis. Executive Information Systems and Group Decision Support Systems expand communication beyond a single sender for gathering, filtering, and sharing information and for supporting decision making.[13] Some organizations have information specialists who make relevant information available to

Table 7–1 **Effectiveness of Communication Media**

	Generally Available	Relatively Low Cost	High Speed	Immediate Interaction	High Impact and Attention
Written					
Letters	×	×			
Memos and reports			×		×
Telegrams			×		×
Fax			×	×	×
Newspapers and magazines	×				
Handbooks and manuals	×	×			
Bulletins and posters	×	×			
Inserts and enclosures	×	×			×
Oral					
Telephone	×	×	×	×	×
Intercom and paging	×		×		×
Closed-circuit TV				×	×
Conferences and meetings	×			×	
Speeches	×			×	

SOURCE: Adapted from Dale A. Level, Jr., and William P. Galle, Jr., *Business Communications: Theory and Practice* (Homewood, Ill.: Business Publications, Inc./Richard D. Irwin, Inc., 1988), pp. 91, 93. Reprinted with permission.

Table 7–2 **Features of Various Electronic Media**

Type of Media	Brief Description	Type of Communication Supported	Timing and Geography	Typical Features
Messaging Systems				
(1) Voice messaging	Augmentation for telephone communication Ability to leave and retrieve voice or synthesized voice messages	One-to-one One-to-many	Asynchronous Time independent Geographic distribution	Message forwarding Distribution lists Message storage and retrieval Message editing
(2) Electronic messaging (EMS)	Substitution for telephone or face-to-face User creates a written document using a computer terminal or the equivalent	One-to-one One-to-many	Asynchronous Time independent Geographic distribution	Message creation and editing User receives messages in an electronic in-basket; messages may be answered, filed and/or discarded Message storage and retrieval Distribution lists Message forwarding
Conferencing Systems				
(1) Audio and audiographic	Similar to telephone conference call Participants cannot see each other May have visual aids Substitution for face-to-face meeting, travel	Group	Synchronous Geographic distribution	Ability to transmit graphic materials accompanying a meeting
(2) Video	Substitution for face-to-face meeting, travel Transmits voice and images of participants Can be one-way or two-way	Group	Synchronous Geographic distribution One-way in multiple locations Two-way in two locations only	Images of speaker and images of other participants displayed simultaneously Graphical materials also displayed
(3) Computer	Substitution for face-to-face meeting, travel Meetings conducted using text (no audio, no video)	Group One-to-one	Synchronous or asynchronous Time independent Geographic distribution	Text editing, storage and retrieval Transcript of proceedings maintained Ability for private communication among participants Ability to poll conference participants and collect results of a vote Bulletin boards Preparation and editing of shared documents

(continued)

Table 7–2 *(Continued)*

Type of Media	Brief Description	Type of Communication Supported	Timing and Geography	Typical Features
Integrated Systems	Substitution for telephone or face-to-face Augmentation of traditional written communication Provides support for messaging, word processing, data processing, and administrative activities using a single interface	One-to-one One-to-many	Asynchronous Time independent Geographic distribution	Same features as electronic messaging Ability to create, edit, store and retrieve, and transmit formal documents Electronic calendars and scheduling Ability to retrieve shared documents Support for traditional data processing

SOURCE: M. J. Culnan and M. L. Markus, Information technologies. In F. Jablin, L. Putnam, K. Roberts, and L. Porter, eds., *Handbook of Organizational Communication: An Interdisciplinary Perspective* (Newbury Park, Calif.: Sage, 1987), pp. 424–425. Copyright © 1987 by Sage Publications, Inc. Reprinted by permission.

organization members.[14] Other organizations integrate the use of management information systems technologies into the regular performance of jobs at all levels in the organization.

Amount of Information

Organizational and personal factors influence the amount of information transmitted. Ideally individuals involved in the communication process receive an appropriate amount of information. Sometimes, they may receive too little information, called *underload,* or too much information, called *overload.* Figure 7–2 illustrates the personal and organizational factors that influence the information transmitted. Jobholders who require limited coordination with others, experience great physical distance from others, have highly routine jobs with few time constraints and few decisions to be made, and have a low ability and desire to communicate typically experience underload.[15] Jobholders who require extensive coordination to do the job, experience close physical proximity to others, have unique job requirements with few time constraints and many decisions to be made, and have a high ability and desire to communicate are more likely to experience overload. Underload can result in alienation, lack of motivation, and apathy; overload can cause high stress, confusion, and mistakes. Figure 7–3 shows a model of the causes and consequences of communication load. Table 7–3 lists ways of improving the use of information in communication.

DECODING AND LISTENING

Not only does the sender influence the effectiveness of communication, but the quality of listening by the receiver also helps determine communication quality. The boss in our example performed the next step of the communication process. She needed to decode the message she had received—to attach some meaning to it. An individual's decoding of a message, like encoding, depends on his or her frame of reference. She might have interpreted her subordinate's question in several different ways, again based on her frame of reference. She might, for example, have viewed

Figure 7–2 **Organizational and Personal Variables Influencing Both Underload and Overload**

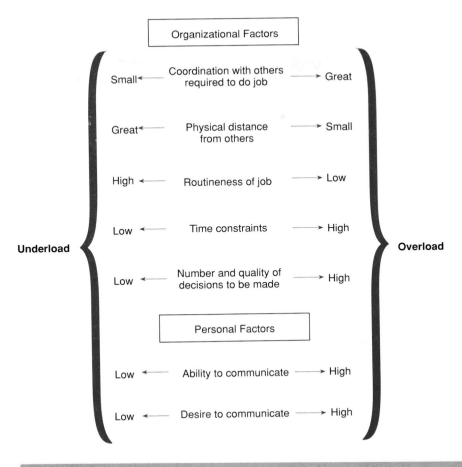

Source: J. W. Gibson and R. M. Hodgetts, *Organizational Communication: A Managerial Perspective,* 2nd ed. (New York: HarperCollins, 1991), p. 281. Copyright © 1991 by Harper & Row, Publishers, Inc. Reprinted by permission of HarperCollins Publishers.

the subordinate's question as a plea for an easy work load; or the boss might have felt that the subordinate literally wanted the information she requested—the number of weeks the project would require. If there had been conflict between the subordinate and her boss, the boss might have interpreted the question as something meant to annoy her or distract her from her work, or as something that would support the boss's view of her subordinate as incompetent. If her usual perception was that her subordinate was a hard worker, then she might have interpreted the question as another indication of her industriousness.

Listening Skills   Crawford at Brooks Furniture emphasized the importance of listening: Collecting data is the first step in quality communication. Receivers can listen in directing, judgmental, probing, smoothing, or active ways, as described in Table 7–4.[16] In effective listening the receiver practices active listening by trying to understand both the facts and the feelings being conveyed. It requires determining what the speaker is trying to say from his or her own viewpoint.[17] Consider a subordinate who asks to leave an hour early from work. Noting both verbal and nonverbal cues the manager should determine the feelings—of worry, fatigue, or frustration, for example—

Figure 7–3   **Communication Load: A Working Model**

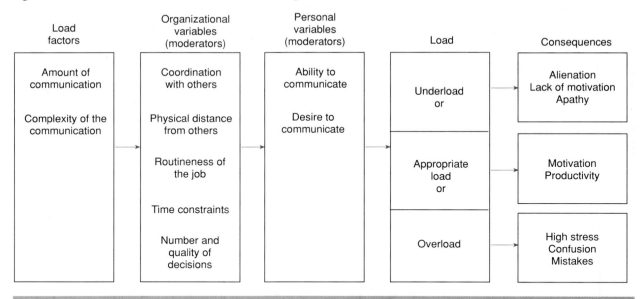

SOURCE: J. W. Gibson and R. M. Hodgetts, *Organizational Communication: A Managerial Perspective,* 2nd ed. (New York: Harper-Collins, 1991), p. 283. Copyright © 1991 by Harper & Row, Publishers, Inc. Reprinted by permission of HarperCollins Publishers.

Table 7–3   **Increasing the Efficiency of Information Use**

Category	Question
Physical Setting	Can the physical setting be changed to improve information processing capabilities? For example, ergonomically designed chairs have been shown to increase employee productivity.
	Can office noise and distractions be decreased?
	Can the physical layout of the office be changed to increase or decrease certain types of information flow?
Filtering Devices	Can bulletin boards be more clearly organized? Are specific individuals solely responsible for certain boards?
	Can different types of written messages be color coded by priority or urgency level?
	Can simple screening devices be used to eliminate "junk mail"?
Technical Devices	Can software be purchased that speeds up the information flow? Building a data base of typical questions and answers may be a way to free up the time of experts so they do not spend all their time answering routine questions.
	Can videotapes be used as a training devise instead of personal trainers?
	Can audio cassette tapes be used to brief employees while they drive?
	Can the phone system be made more efficient with new features?
User Behavior	Can those who desire information serve their own needs [as] in a library or supermarket?
	Can simple verbal reminders of meetings be used instead of memos?
	Can regularly requested information be put into a form that is more easily and efficiently disseminated, [as] in a pamphlet or Question/Answer sheet?

SOURCE: P. G. Clampitt, *Communicating for Managerial Effectiveness* (Newbury Park, Calif.: Sage, 1991), p. 105. Copyright © 1991 by Sage Publications, Inc. Reprinted by permission.

Table 7–4 **Types of Listening**

Type	Function	Example
Directing	Leads the speaker by guiding the limits and direction of conversation.	If I were you, I'd just ignore it.
Judgmental	Introduces personal value judgments into the conversation; injects personal values or opinions.	You're absolutely right; Tom is impossible to get along with.
Probing	Asks a lot of questions in an attempt to get to the heart of the matter.	When did all this start? What do you want me to do about it?
Smoothing	Pats the speaker on the head and makes light of his or her problems; urges conflict resolution.	You and Tom just had a bad day; don't worry—tomorrow it will all be forgotten.
Empathic/Active	Tries to create an encouraging atmosphere for the speaker to use in expressing and solving the problem; tends to feed back neutral summaries of what they have heard.	It seems that you are troubled by the fact that you and Tom don't get along.

SOURCE: J. W. Gibson and R. M. Hodgetts, *Organizational Communication: A Managerial Perspective,* 2nd ed. (New York: HarperCollins, 1991), pp. 68–69. Copyright © 1991 by Harper & Row, Publishers, Inc. Adapted with permission of HarperCollins Publishers.

underlying the question. The listener must next acknowledge these feelings; the manager must respond to both the question and the feelings expressed. Listeners must recognize the importance of nonverbal communication and look for nonverbal cues that support or contradict verbal information. Table 7–5 offers additional guidelines for listening.

NOISE

Many decodings reflect some *noise* or interference in the communication process, some distortions of the message sent and received. They suggest that some factors, such as conflict between the boss and the subordinate or the boss's attribution of the subordinate's industriousness, could affect the boss's understanding of the messages in such a way that she did not "hear" what the subordinate intended. Noise can include physical noise that interferes with transmission, such as static on a telephone line or the noise created by office or plant machinery. But noise may be inaudible. The presence of a silent third party during a conversation may act as noise that distracts the receiver from hearing what the speaker said. Or the frame of reference of the receiver may cause that person to hear the message in a way other than the one in which it was intended. Noise can also include characteristics of senders or receivers, such as their socioeconomic background, experience, education, or value system.

What types of noise likely exist in communications described in the opening case? Differences in roles in the organization may create noise. Biases in their attributions for poor performance may create noise. So too may various perceptual predispositions, such as different personal and organizational goals, attitudes, and

Table 7–5 **Guidelines for Listening**

1. Listen patiently to what the other person has to say, even though you may believe it is wrong or irrelevant. Indicate simple acceptance (not necessarily agreement) by nodding or injecting an occasional "um-hm" or "I see."
2. Try to understand the feeling the person is expressing, as well as the intellectual content. Most of us have difficulty talking clearly about our feelings, so careful attention is required.
3. Restate the person's feeling, briefly but accurately. At this stage, simply serve as a mirror and encourage the other person to continue talking. Occasionally make summary responses such as "You think you're in a dead-end job," or "You feel the manager is playing favorites"; but in doing so, keep your tone neutral and try not to lead the person to your pet conclusions.
4. Allow time for the discussion to continue without interruption and try to separate the conversation from more official communication of company plans. That is, do not make the conversation any more "authoritative" than it already is by virtue of your position in the organization.
5. Avoid direct questions and arguments about facts; refrain from saying, "That's just not so," "Hold on a minute, let's look at the facts," or "Prove it." You may want to review evidence later, but a review is irrelevant to how a person feels now.
6. When the other person does touch on a point you do want to know more about, simply repeat his or her statement as a question. For instance, if the person remarks, "Nobody can break even on his expense account," you can probe by replying, "You say no one breaks even on expenses?" With this encouragement he or she will probably expand on the previous statement.
7. Listen for what isn't said—evasions of pertinent points or perhaps too-ready agreement with common clichés. Such omissions may be clues to a bothersome fact the person wishes were not true.
8. If the other person appears genuinely to want your viewpoint, be honest in your reply. But in the listening stage, try to limit the expression of your views because these may condition or suppress what the other person says.
9. Focus on the content of the message; try not to think about your next statement until the person is finished talking.
10. Don't make judgments until all information has been conveyed.

orientations. Amerman's and Crawford's previous management experience in similar situations may create noise.

Gender Differences in Communication

Recent research suggests that men and women communicate differently.[18] A classic story illustrates a basic difference between male and female communication. A man and a woman were driving to a meeting at a location that they had never visited before. After fifty minutes of driving around in circles, the woman was visibly upset. When asked why, she responded that she was not upset about being lost, but was furious that her male companion had repeatedly refused to stop and ask directions. Women ask for information, and men resist asking for it.[19]

In one study women sounded more polite but also were more uncertain, whereas men used more informal pronunciations, sounded more challenging, direct, and authoritative; the feminine style was more accommodating, intimate, collaborative, and facilitative, whereas the male style was more action-oriented, informational, and controlling.[20] Recognizing such differences should facilitate more accurate diagnosis of communication problems.

FEEDBACK Compare the diagram of the communication process shown in Figure 7–4 to that shown in Figure 7–1. How do they differ? Two-way communication, as shown in Figure 7–1, emphasizes the role of feedback in the process. *Feedback* refers to an acknowledgement by the receiver that the message has been received; it provides the sender with information about the receiver's understanding of the message being sent. The boss's feedback to the subordinate—in which she provided only the length of the project—indicated an inaccurate understanding. If the boss had told the subordinate that the project will involve a detailed feasibility study and cost analysis, the boss would have conveyed a different understanding.

Often one-way communication occurs between managers and their subordinates. Because of inherent power differences in their positions (see Chapter 9) managers may give large quantities of information and directions to their subordinates without providing the opportunity for the subordinates to show their understanding or receipt of the information. These managers often experience conflict between their role as authorities and a desire to be liked by subordinates. Other managers have relied on the use of written memoranda as a way of communicating with subordinates. In addition to the inherent lack of feedback involved in this format, the use of a single channel of communication also limits the effectiveness of communication.

Why do some managers not involve their subordinates in two-way communication? In some situations, managers do not trust their subordinates to contribute effectively. In other situations, lack of self-confidence by the manager makes him or her appear uninterested in or unconcerned about subordinates' opinions. Or superiors assume that subordinates have the same goals as their bosses, and thus feel that input from the subordinates is not required.

What is your attitude toward feedback? You can assess it by completing the questionnaire shown in Figure 7–5. The higher your score, the more discomfort you feel in giving feedback. Recognizing a discomfort about giving or receiving feedback is a key step in eliminating this barrier and improving the quality of managerial communication. Encouraging feedback from subordinates helps show subordinates that you are concerned about them as individuals, in ways that go beyond merely ensuring that they produce.

Subordinates also have responsibility for encouraging two-way communication. While superiors may attempt to protect their power positions, subordinates attempt to protect the image their boss holds of them. Frequently, for example, subordinates withhold negative information about themselves or their activities. Or they may fail to inform their superior about their needs and values. Other subordinates mistrust their superiors and so withhold any information from them. Why do these situations arise? Some subordinates may assume that they and their bosses have different goals. Others mistrust their bosses. Still others lack persistence in seeking responses from their supervisors. Impression management may play a role in whether individuals seek feedback. They may assess in what way asking for feedback will be interpreted and how the resulting information will affect each person's public image.[21] Subor-

Figure 7–4 **One-Way Communication**

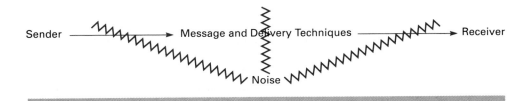

Sender ———→ Message and Delivery Techniques ———→ Receiver

Noise

Figure 7–5 **Attitude toward Feedback: Feedback Questionnaire**

Indicate the degree of discomfort you would feel in each situation given below, by circling the appropriate number:
1—high discomfort; 2—some discomfort; 3—undecided; 4—very little discomfort; 5—no discomfort.

1 2 3 4 5   1. Telling an employee who is also a friend that he or she must stop coming to work late.

1 2 3 4 5   2. Talking to an employee about his or her performance on the job.

1 2 3 4 5   3. Asking an employee if he or she has any comments about your rating of his or her performance.

1 2 3 4 5   4. Telling an employee who has problems in dealing with other employees that he or she should do something about it.

1 2 3 4 5   5. Responding to an employee who is upset over your rating of his or her performance.

1 2 3 4 5   6. An employee's becoming emotional and defensive when you tell him or her about mistakes in the job.

1 2 3 4 5   7. Giving a rating that indicates improvement is needed to an employee who has failed to meet minimum requirements of the job.

1 2 3 4 5   8. Letting a subordinate talk during an appraisal interview.

1 2 3 4 5   9. An employee's challenging you to justify your evaluation in the middle of an appraisal interview.

1 2 3 4 5   10. Recommending that an employee be discharged.

1 2 3 4 5   11. Telling an employee that you are uncomfortable in the role of having to judge his or her performance.

1 2 3 4 5   12. Telling an employee that his or her performance can be improved.

1 2 3 4 5   13. Telling an employee that you will not tolerate his or her taking extended coffee breaks.

1 2 3 4 5   14. Telling an employee that you will not tolerate his or her making personal telephone calls on company time.

dinates must show that they, too, are willing to build relationships with their superiors. Figure 7–6 provides a feedback checklist.

Consider the situation at Mattel and Brook Furniture. Does quality feedback facilitate communication? The case implies that the CEOs listen to what the subordinates say and acknowledge the ideas that they use and do not use, as well as explain their reasoning. Crawford explicitly notes the importance of two-way communication at Brook.

THE DIRECTION OF COMMUNICATION

Both Amerman's and Crawford's successful communication is a function of their ability to encourage subordinates to participate actively in the communication process. Clearly both executives understand the significance of the direction of communication. Although structural factors facilitate and direct communication to a high degree in organizations, these hierarchical arrangements contribute to communication difficulties in organizations as well. Centralization of authority at the higher levels of the organization restricts the dissemination of information. Some organizational members may have access to more information than others; some subunits may have different information from other subunits. Since some people either know much more or possess different information, centralization, which discourages shared information, increases the potential for misunderstandings among the various subunits. The extent to which organizations have specialized work groups also influences the quality of communication. Where differences exist between departments in their goals and expertise, communication among peers may be limited.

Figure 7–6 **Feedback Checklist**

Feedback should . . .

_____ 1. Occur as soon as possible and allow ample time for discussion.
_____ 2. Be done in a private setting.
_____ 3. Not be given when the staff member or supervisor is upset, frustrated, or tired.
_____ 4. Initially be descriptive as opposed to evaluative.
_____ 5. Be specific.
_____ 6. Focus on behaviors and not personality.
_____ 7. Demonstrate interest in the staff member.
_____ 8. Use factual information and open-ended, probing questions.
_____ 9. Be given in relation to an expectation or a related task.
_____ 10. Demonstrate effective preparation by the supervisor.
_____ 11. Ensure that the supervisor and staff member understand what has been discussed.
_____ 12. Reflect adequate collection of information and preparation by the supervisor.
_____ 13. Encourage input from the staff member.
_____ 14. Address both effective performance and areas for needed improvement.
_____ 15. Note the consequences of not effectively addressing a performance problem.
_____ 16. Use effective verbal and nonverbal communication skills.
_____ 17. Encourage self-evaluation by the staff member.
_____ 18. Respect the dignity and opinions of the staff member.
_____ 19. Exhibit a trusting climate.

SOURCE: L. W. Hillman, D. R. Schwandt, and D. E. Bartz, Enhancing staff members' performance through feedback and coaching, *Journal of Management Development* 9(3) (1990): 24. Reprinted by permission of MCB University Press Ltd.

Downward Communication

Managers use this type of communication to disseminate information and directives to subordinates. Using downward communication to share both good news and bad news with employees, they should provide for feedback from lower-level workers about the message they "heard." Encouraging face-to-face communication between all levels of managers and employees through plant visits or management-employee discussion groups, publishing company newsletters, and even introducing a communication hot line in the organization can facilitate accurate downward communication. Table 7–6 shows the subjects of most and least interest to a group of subordinates.

Too often, however, downward communication becomes one-way, with no provision for feedback. Although most managers may intend to communicate accurately to their subordinates, some may consciously or unconsciously distort downward communication. Power differences, as discussed in Chapter 9, can result in distortions: Managers can withhold, screen, or manipulate information.[22] What results from this type of communication? Subordinates can become very distrustful of their managers and circumvent them to obtain accurate information. They may rely instead on rumors, obtaining equally distorted and potentially harmful information. In some organizations, downward communication between bosses and their immediate subordinates is relatively accurate, but information from top management fails to pass accurately through the hierarchy and reach the lower-level employees; managers may adjust or delay it along the way so it better fits their objectives. In addition, managers and subordinates may differ in their perceptions of the quality of

Table 7–6 **Subjects That Are of Most and Least Interest to Survey Respondents**

Rank	Subject	Combined Very Interested/ Interested Responses (percent)
1	Organizational plans for the future	95.3
2	Productivity improvement	90.3
3	Personnel policies and practices	89.8
4	Job-related information	89.2
5	Job advancement opportunities	87.9
6	Effect of external events on my job	87.8
7	How my job fits into the organization	85.4
8	Operations outside of my department or division	85.1
9	How we're doing vs. the competition	83.0
10	Personnel changes and promotions	81.4
11	Organizational community involvement	81.3
12	Organizational stand on current issues	79.5
13	How the organization uses its profits	78.4
14	Advertising/promotional plans	77.2
15	Financial results	76.4
16	Human interest stories about other employees	70.4
17	Personal news (birthdays, anniversaries, etc.)	57.0

SOURCE: Julie Foehrenback and Karen Rosenberg, "How Are We Doing?" *Journal of Communication Management* 12(1) (1982): 7.

downward communication. In one study of 923 managers and 4,708 subordinates in a large company in the communications industry, significant differences existed in their answers to questions such as "In work group meetings, to what extent do you make sure that there is frank and open exchange of ideas?" and "When tasks or projects are assigned, how clearly and thoroughly do you explain them?"[23]

Although open communication has been considered a panacea for many organizational problems, some researchers have argued that characteristics of the individuals involved, their relationships, and the organization and environment in which they function should influence how open communication should be.[24] Disclosure and directness can backfire if, for example, subordinates are not prepared to receive the information being sent, or managers are unwilling to deal with subordinates' reactions. Can you think of a situation where such problems might occur?

Upward Communication

Encouraging ongoing upward communication as part of the organization's culture can minimize such dysfunctional consequences. Primarily a feedback vehicle, upward communication refers to messages sent from subordinates to their bosses. Top and middle management must create a culture that promotes honest upward communication as a way of counteracting employees' tendencies to hide potentially damaging information. Such a culture encourages employee participation in decision making, rewards openness, and limits inflexible policies and arbitrary procedures. Acting constructively on information communicated upward reinforces its future occurrence and limits executive isolation.

How would you describe and evaluate upward communication at Mattel and Brook Furniture Rental? Are subordinates able to communicate their ideas to the

CEO? Does the CEO then provide feedback to the workers about the implementation of these ideas? Both CEOs create the opportunities for upward communication through their informal interactions with workers in the cafeteria, at training sessions, and in the warehouses. Crawford's emphasis on listening reflects his concern for facilitating upward communication.

Managers need to be encouraged to share information about their attitudes, work developments, and even mistakes with their bosses because this type of communication can increase personal and organizational effectiveness. Overemphasizing downward communication, remaining office-bound, and improperly delegating responsibilities can increase executive isolation.[25] Both Amerman and Crawford understand the importance of upward communication.

Lateral Communication

Sharing of information, engaging in problem solving, and coordinating the work flow with employees at their same level in the organization complements both downward and upward communication. While some messages need to go through formal channels, many can be handled through informal channels, or laterally. Workers assembling different parts of a product may coordinate the use of inventories by lateral (or horizontal) communication; sales representatives may discuss field problems with technical services personnel; the divisional marketing vice president may resolve sales problems by gathering information from other divisional marketing executives. Communication directly between the subordinates typically has greater speed and accuracy, although distortions can still occur in encoding, transmission, or decoding. Although subordinates in different or distant departments may have historical problems communicating directly, the proliferation of electronic communication devices should remove some obstacles. Still, in some cases, managers may insist that workers rely on the hierarchy for an exchange of information—for example, passing it from subordinate to manager to top manager to second manager to second subordinate.

Gatekeepers and Boundary Spanners Special roles in the organization can facilitate accurate lateral communication. *Gatekeepers* screen information and access to a group or individual.[26] Situated at the crossroads of communication channels, these positions act as nerve centers where they switch information among people and groups. Staff specialists, such as human resources professionals, project managers, or marketing support staff, may fill such roles. Managers also act as gatekeepers, sharing information with subordinates, superiors, and peers.

Boundary spanners link an organization or an organizational unit to its external environment.[27] A purchasing agent, sales representative, or public relations director, for example, can act as a communication link between a department's or organization's internal and external environments. They serve the roles of information processor and representative for an organization or its subunits to others outside the unit's boundary, and may communicate extensively with professionals outside the parent organization. They differ from gatekeepers in their emphasis on facilitating the exchange of information rather than acting primarily as a screening device for incoming and outgoing information.

INTERPERSONAL RELATIONS AND INFORMAL COMMUNICATION

The relationship between the two people (or two groups) communicating, as well as the type of climate they create during their communication, affects the accuracy with which messages are given and received. The sender's and receiver's *trust* of and *influence* over each other, the sender's *aspirations* regarding upward *mobility* in the organization, and the *norms and sanctions* of the group(s) to which the sender and receiver belong influence the quality of communication.[28] When people trust each other, their communication tends to be more accurate and open; when they distrust each other, they are more likely to be secretive or hesitant to talk openly. If Amerman and Crawford trust their subordinates, for example, they are more likely to present significant organizational issues to them for discussion than to just deliver information about the future of the company as a *fait accompli*. When the receiver has considerable influence over the sender, the sender's communications are likely to be somewhat guarded, often because the sender distrusts the receiver. At both Mattel and Brook Furniture, the CEOs have communicated extensively to ensure that the receivers (their subordinates) do not distrust them and are willing to communicate honestly. This policy may explain the subordinates' willingness to share their views with their bosses and may reduce the tendency for upwardly mobile senders to alter communication in a way that helps their personal advancement. Even so, group norms and sanctions may limit the amount or type of information people feel they can legitimately discuss. Amerman and Crawford have tried to establish a corporate culture in which it is acceptable for work groups to talk about personal, group, and organizational failures.

The informal organization also creates a communication pattern, known as the *grapevine*. Carrying information outside the official channels, the grapevine can either supplement or replace the organizational hierarchy as a communication conduit. The grapevine can provide information about employee attitudes, serve as an emotional outlet for workers, and even spread true information, but it can also disseminate rumors and false information.[29] Table 7–7 lists a series of observations about the grapevine. Managers and other organizational members must recognize that the grapevine is alive and functioning in all organizations.

Attitudes of each person or group toward collaboration and competition can also affect the quality of communication. Parties with competitive attitudes define conflict as win-lose, pursue only their own goals, understand and overemphasize their own needs, and emphasize only differences in positions and superiority of their own position.[30] Particularly when one or both individuals or groups takes a competitive attitude, communication between them can project this "we-they" or "win-lose" perspective. A we-they attitude can polarize the interacting groups and thus establishes a communication barrier between them.

Communication Networks

Networks represent the patterns of communication relationships throughout an organization. They can constitute the structural underpinnings of a group, as discussed in Chapter 5, or represent more interacting individuals or groups. *Total systems networks* describe the communication patterns throughout the entire organization; *clique networks* describe groups of individuals who communicate exclusively with each other; *personal networks* represent individuals who communicate with a specific other person or persons.[31] Networks vary in size, completeness—the extent to which all individuals in a network are interconnected, dispersion—the extent of dominance by an individual or clique, and openness—the amount of contact a network has with its environment.[32] Network analysis maps the pattern of interactions, often with the help of a computer, as shown in Figure 7–7. It identifies groups or clusters that comprise the network, individuals who link the clusters, and other network members.[33] Network analysis allows diagnosis of communication patterns and consequently communication effectiveness, but it also provides a template for electronic messaging that in turn facilitates horizontal, vertical, and lateral linkages.

Table 7–7 **Observations about the Grapevine**

1. The grapevine is a significant part of an organizational communication system with regard to (a) quantity of information communicated and (b) quality of information, such as its importance and its effects on people and performance.
2. The quality of management decisions depends on quality of information inputs that management has, and one useful input is information from the grapevine.
3. Successful communication with employees depends on (a) understanding their problems, (b) understanding their attitudes, and (c) determining gaps in employee information (the grapevine is a valuable source of these kinds of inputs).
4. The quality of management decisions is significantly affected by management's success in listening to and interpreting the grapevine.
5. The quality of management communication programs is significantly affected by management's capacity to understand and to relate to the grapevine.
6. The grapevine cannot be suppressed or directly controlled, although it may be influenced by the way management relates to it.
7. The grapevine has both negative and positive influences in an organization.
8. The grapevine can provide useful inputs even when information it carries is known to be incorrect.
9. In normal organizational situations, excluding situations such as strikes and disasters, the grapevine on the average carries more correct information than inaccurate information.
10. The grapevine carries an incomplete story.
11. Compared with most formal communications, the grapevine tends to speed faster through an organization, so it can affect people very quickly.
12. Grapevine communications are *caused*.
13. Men and women are approximately equally active on the grapevine.
14. Nonverbal communication is significant in interpreting verbal grapevine communication.
15. Informal leaders often serve as message centers for receiving, interpreting, and distributing grapevine information to others.
16. Typical grapevine activity usually is not a sign of organizational sickness or health; that is, grapevine activity is a normal response to group work.

SOURCE: From P. V. Lewis, *Organizational Communication: The Essence of Effective Management*, 3rd ed. (New York: Wiley, 1987), pp. 47–48. Reprinted by permission of the publisher.

MULTICULTURAL AND MULTINATIONAL COMMUNICATION ISSUES

Cross-cultural issues may affect the quality of communication. For example, differences in norms for the appropriate amount of interpersonal space exist in different cultures. Effective communication requires deciphering basic values, motives, aspirations, and assumptions across geographical, occupational, functional, or social class lines. It also means seeing one's own culture as different, but not necessarily better.[34] Cross-cultural miscommunication occurs when a receiver misunderstands the message transmitted by a sender of another culture. Consider the following example:

> An American company eager to do business in Saudi Arabia sent over a sales manager to "get something going." . . . The salesman learned that he had repeatedly insulted his contacts by his impatience, refusal of coffee, the "all business talk" attitude and aggressive selling. Even incidental acts such as handing people paper with his left hand, and exposing the side of his shoe while sitting on the floor were improper Saudi customs.[35]

Or consider the following example:

Figure 7–7 **Communication Network of an Organization**

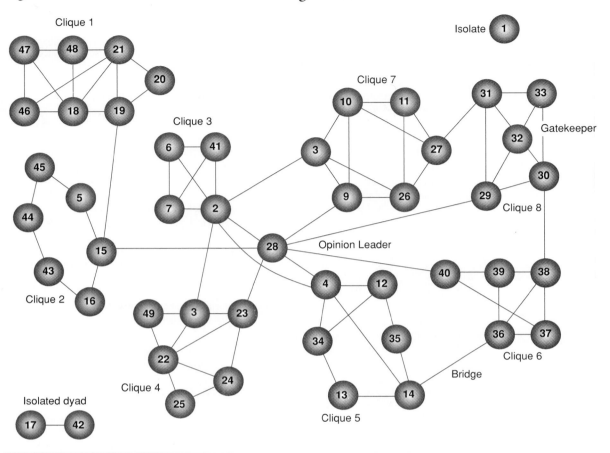

SOURCE: Reprinted with permission from Gary L. Kreps, *Organizational Communication,* 2nd ed. (New York: Longman, 1990), p. 223. Copyright © 1990 by Longman Publishing Group.

You are negotiating a contract with a Japanese company and during the meetings there are times of silence on the part of the Japanese negotiating team. The negotiations, from your perspective as an American, appear to be proceeding at an unusually slow pace and even the simplest decisions or commitments appear to take an inordinate amount of time. You begin to push a little harder and your frustrations mount as you begin to hear statements from the Japanese such as, "it will take a little more time," and "this is quite difficult."[36]

What types of miscommunication occurred here because of cultural differences? Now consider a study of 436 People's Republic of China managers, which found that formality dominated their daily exchanges.[37] What communication dysfunctions might result in their interactions with managers from the United States who are often comfortable using first names and more informal interactions? Even American managers at Japanese-owned companies in the United States have experienced communication problems due to the language barrier.[38]

The compatibility or incompatibility of the verbal and nonverbal styles used to communicate can also influence the effectiveness of intercultural communication.

Verbal styles differ along a variety of dimensions.[39] Japanese camouflage the speaker's true intent in an indirect style, use role-centered or contextual language, and are receiver oriented. The Arabs use an elaborate style or very expressive language in everyday communication. In contrast, North American communication can be described as direct, personal, instrumental, and succinct. Nonverbal communication also varies in cultures because individuals attach different meanings to interpersonal space, touch, and time. For example, interpersonal distance is low among South Americans, Southern and Eastern Europeans, and Arabs, and high among Asians, Northern Europeans, and North Americans.[40]

To ensure quality communication, communicators should first assume that cultural differences exist, and they should try to view the situation from the perspective of their foreign colleagues.[41] They can then adjust their encoding or decoding, their use of language or listening skills, to respond to likely differences. Knowledge of the characteristics of diverse cultures facilitates such an adjustment. A cultural integrator—a person who understands differences in a society from the home country and the ways the organization can adapt to them—can also reduce the barrier of inadequate cross-cultural sensitivity.[42] Companies can select a cultural integrator from among home-country nationals familiar with the host country or host-country nationals familiar with the home-country culture and firm's operations. Consider, for example, how a cultural integrator might help the salesman trying to do business in Saudi Arabia described earlier. Until all individuals have cross-cultural sensitivity, such special arrangements may be necessary for quality multicultural communication.

IMPROVING COMMUNICATION ACCURACY

What can individuals do to improve their communication in both formal and informal settings? In this section we examine three ways of increasing communication effectiveness: creating a supportive communication climate; using an assertive communication style; and using active listening techniques.

Creating a Supportive Communication Climate

In communicating with their employees, both John Amerman and Bob Crawford know they must create a trusting and supportive environment. Creating such a climate has the objective of shifting from *evaluation* to *problem solving* in communication. They must avoid making employees feel defensive, that is, threatened by the communication. Superiors, subordinates, and other communicators can create such an atmosphere in six ways,[43] as summarized in Table 7–8.

1. They use descriptive rather than evaluative speech and do not imply that the receiver needs to change. Amerman might describe which programs proposed by subordinates he supports and opposes, rather than merely evaluating them as good or bad.
2. They take a problem orientation, which implies a desire to collaborate in exploring a mutual problem, rather than trying to control or change the listener. At training sessions, Crawford attempts to solicit the salespeople's ideas to improve the company.
3. They are spontaneous and honest, and reveal their goals, rather than appearing to use "strategy" that involves ambiguous and multiple motivations. Amerman would openly discuss his restructuring efforts rather than implement them surreptitiously.
4. They convey empathy for the feelings of their listener, rather than appearing unconcerned or neutral about the listener's welfare. They give reassurance that they are identifying with the listener's problems, rather than denying the

Table 7–8 **Climate Dimensions**

Dimensions of Supportive Climate	Dimensions of Defensive Climate
Description—giving and asking for information	Evaluation—praising, blaming, passing judgment, calling for different behavior
Problem Orientation—jointly collaborating in defining problems and seeking solutions	Control—attempting to persuade others by imposing your personal attitudes on them
Spontaneity—dealing with others honestly and without deception	Strategy—manipulating others
Empathy—identifying with others' positions or problems	Neutrality—showing lack of concern for others
Equality—deemphasizing status and power differences, respecting others	Superiority—reflecting dominance over others
Provisionalism—postponing taking sides and being open to new information and interpretations	Certainty—being dogmatic, wanting to win rather than solve a problem

SOURCE: Based on J. R. Gibb, Defensive communication, *ETC: A Review of General Semantics* 22 (1965).

legitimacy of the problems. Both Amerman and Crawford try to demonstrate a clear understanding of their workers' perspectives.

5. They indicate that they feel equal rather than superior to the listener. Thus they suggest that they will enter a shared relationship, not simply dominate the interaction.

6. Finally, they communicate that they will experiment with their own behavior and ideas, rather than be dogmatic about them. They do not give the impression that they know all the answers and do not need help from anyone. Neither Amerman nor Crawford operates in isolation; they try to collaborate to reach the best solution for their company's future.

In addition, supportive communication emphasizes a congruence between thoughts and feelings, and communication.[44] An individual who feels unappreciated by a supervisor, for example, must communicate that feeling to the supervisor, rather than deny it or communicate it inaccurately. Communication must also validate an individual's importance, uniqueness, and worth. Nondefensive communication "recognizes the other person's existence; recognizes the person's uniqueness as an individual, rather than treating him or her as a role or a job; acknowledges the worth of the other person; acknowledges the validity of the other person's perception of the world; expresses willingness to be involved with the other person, at least during the communication."[45]

The Johari Window Model Interpersonal communication can be improved by encouraging individuals to communicate using as complete knowledge of themselves and others as possible. The *Johari window* provides an analytical tool that individuals can use to identify information that is available for use in communication.[46] Figure 7–8 illustrates this model of interpersonal knowledge. Note that information about an individual is represented along two dimensions: (1) information known and unknown by the self and (2) information known and unknown by others.

Figure 7–8 **Johari Window**

	Known by Self	Unknown by Self
Known by Others	Open self	Blind self
Unknown by Others	Concealed self	Unknown self

SOURCE: Based on a model developed by Drs. Joseph Luft and Harry Ingham and described in *The Personnel Relations Survey* by Jay Hall and Martha S. Williams, Telometrics International, The Woodlands, Texas.

Together these dimensions form a four-category representation of the individual. The *open* self is information known by the self and known by others. Both Amerman and Crawford share their view of their company's future with their subordinates. The *blind* self is information unknown by the self and known by others, such as others' perceptions of your behavior or attitudes. We do not have a clear sense of either executive's blind self, but more careful interaction with them may reveal it. The *concealed* self is information known by you and unknown by others; secrets we keep from others about ourselves fall into this category. Either CEO's opinions about the best way to accomplish goals of restructuring or improving performance may remain part of his concealed self to ensure that he hears worker perspectives. Finally, the *unconscious* self is information that is unknown to the self and unknown to others. To ensure quality communication, in most cases an individual should communicate from his or her open self to another person's open self and limit the amount of information concealed or in the blind spot. Guarded communication may be appropriate, however, if one party has violated trust in the past, if the parties have an adversarial relationship, if power and status differentials characterize the culture, if the relationship is transitory, or if the corporate culture does not support openness.[47]

Using an Assertive Communication Style

An *assertive* style, which is honest, direct, and firm, also improves communication. With this style a person expresses personal needs, opinions, and feelings in honest and direct ways and stands up for his or her rights without violating the other person's.[48] Assertive behavior is reflected in the content and the nonverbal style of the message. The assertive delegator, for example, "is clear and direct when explaining work to subordinates, doesn't hover, [and] . . . criticizes fairly, objectively, and constructively."[49]

Consider the situation of a boss whose subordinate has missed two important deadlines in the last month. How would the boss respond assertively? The boss might say to the worker: "I know you missed the last two deadlines. Is there an explanation I should know? You must meet the next deadlines. You should have let me know the problems you were facing and explained the situation to me, rather than saying nothing." Note that an assertive response can include the expression of anger, frustration, or disappointment.

We can contrast the assertive approach to nonassertive and aggressive styles, as summarized in Table 7–9. *Nonassertive* communication describes behavior where the sender does not stand up for personal rights and indicates that his or her feelings are unimportant; the person may be hesitant, apologetic, or fearful. In the situation of a missed deadline, nonassertive behavior might involve saying nothing to your worker, hoping the situation would not recur. Individuals act nonassertively because they may mistake assertion for aggression, mistake nonassertion for politeness or

Table 7–9 **A Comparison of Nonassertive, Assertive, and Aggressive Communication**

	Nonassertive (No Influence)	Assertive (Positive Influence)	Aggressive (Negative Influence)
Verbal	Apologetic words. Veiled meanings. Hedging; failure to come to the point. Rambling; disconnected. At a loss for words. Failure to say what you really mean. Qualifying statements with "I mean," "you know."	Statement of wants. Honest statement of feelings. Objective words. Direct statements, which say what you mean. "I" messages.	"Loaded" words. Accusations. Descriptive, subjective terms. Imperious, superior words. "You" messages that blame or label.
Nonverbal General demeanor	Actions instead of words, hoping someone will guess what you want. Looking as if you don't mean what you say.	Attentive listening behavior. Generally assured manner, communicating caring and strength.	Exaggerated show of strength. Flippant, sarcastic style. Air of superiority.
Voice	Weak, hesitant, soft, sometimes wavering.	Firm, warm, well modulated, relaxed.	Tense, shrill, loud, shaky; cold, "deadly quiet," demanding; superior, authoritarian.
Eyes	Averted, downcast, teary, pleading.	Open, frank, direct. Eye contact, but not staring.	Expressionless, narrowed, cold, staring; not really "seeing" others.
Stance and posture	Leaning for support, stooped, excessive head nodding.	Well balanced, straight on, erect, relaxed.	Hands on hips, feet apart. Stiff and rigid. Rude, imperious.
Hands	Fidgety, fluttery, clammy.	Relaxed motions.	Clenched. Abrupt gestures, fingerpointing, fist pounding.

SOURCE: Reprinted with permission of the publisher, from *Mastering Assertiveness Skills,* page 15. © 1984 Elaine Zuker. Published by AMACOM, a division of American Management Association, NY. All rights reserved.

being helpful, refuse to accept their personal rights, experience anxiety about negative consequences of assertiveness, or lack assertiveness skills.[50]

Aggressive communication stands up for an individual's rights without respecting the rights of the other person. Aggressive behavior attempts to dominate and control others by sounding accusing or superior. In the situation of the missed deadlines, an aggressive response might be "You always miss deadlines. You're taking advantage of me and the situation. If you miss another deadline, you're fired." While such a response may result in the desired behavior in the short run, its long-term consequences likely will be dysfunctional, resulting in distrust between boss and subordinate, uncontrollable anger, and even sabotage by the worker. Men often mislabel assertive communication by women as aggressive because the honesty and directness does not fit with their preconceptions about female behavior.

Using Active Listening Techniques   Active listening, which requires understanding both the content and the intent of a message, can be facilitated by paraphrasing, perception checking, and behavior description.

Paraphrasing   The receiver can *paraphrase* the message conveyed by the sender by stating in his or her own way what the other person's remarks convey. For example, if the sender (Amerman) states, "I don't like the work you have been doing," the receiver (e.g., his subordinate) might paraphrase it as "You are saying that you are dissatisfied with my performance," or the receiver might paraphrase it as "You are saying that you want to assign me different types of work to do." Note that these ways of paraphrasing the original message suggest very different understandings of the original statement. The sender, upon receiving this feedback from the receiver, can then clarify his or her meaning.

Perception Checking   Alternatively, the receiver may perception-check—that is, describe what he or she perceives as the sender's inner state at the time of communication to check his or her understanding of the message. For example, if the sender states, "I don't like the work you have been doing," the receiver might check his or her perception of the statement by asking, "Are you dissatisfied with me as an employee?" or, "Are you dissatisfied with the quantity of my output?" Note that answers to these two questions will identify different feelings.

Behavior Description   A third way of checking and clarifying is through behavior description. Here the individual reports specific, observable actions of others without making accusations or generalizations about their motives, personality, or characteristics. Similarly, description of feelings, where the individual specifies or identifies feelings by name, analogy, or some other verbal representation, can increase active listening. For example, to help others understand you as a person, you should describe what others did that affects you personally or as a group member. Then you can let others know as clearly and unambiguously as possible what you are feeling.

INTERVIEWS

Communication problems are most acute when organizational members conduct some type of employee evaluation, such as an employment interview or a performance appraisal. In employment interviews the communicators transmit information that allows them to make decisions about the fit between a job applicant and an available position. In performance appraisal, the supervisor and subordinate share information about the subordinate's performance to date and future development.

Types of Questions

The interviewer can ask open-ended questions or closed-ended questions. *Open-ended* questions—such as "Tell me about your experience in financial analysis" and "What do you consider your weaknesses as an employee?"—allow the interviewee to structure the response to the question and present information that he or she feels is important. *Closed-ended* questions—such as "Tell me the first thing you would say to a potential customer" and "How many employees have you supervised during the past year?"—allow the interviewer to focus a response more precisely. An interview can move from open-ended questions to closed-ended questions, alternate the two types of questions, or begin with closed-ended questions and end with open-ended ones. Figure 7–9 offers one example of the structure of an interview.

The types of questions asked must also be geared to the nature of the position to be filled. Table 7–10 offers questions for interviewing supervisory and executive candidates. In most interviews the interviewer tries to make the interviewee feel at ease by beginning with questions that are relatively easy to answer and then moving on to questions that the interviewee may find more difficult.

Figure 7–9 **Sample Interview Guidelines for a Selection Interview**

Opening

- Give a warm, friendly greeting—smile.
- Names are important—yours and the applicant's. Pronounce it correctly and use first and last names consistently. Tell the applicant what to call you and then ask the applicant for his or her preferred form of address.
- Talk briefly about yourself (your position in the company and then your personal background, hobbies, interests, etc.) to put the applicant at ease so that she or he might reciprocate with personal information.
- Ask the applicant about hobbies, activities, or some other topic that you believe will be of interest to "break the ice."

Structure the Interview

- State the purpose of interview: "The purpose of this interview is to discuss your qualifications and to see whether they match the skills needed to work as a selection interviewer. First, let's talk about your work experience and next your education and training. Then I will give you a preview of what the interviewer's job is really like. Finally, there will be a chance to ask about anything you want. How's that?"
- Since you plan to take notes, mention this to the applicant: "By the way, I will be taking some notes during the interview so that I don't miss any pertinent information that may come from our discussion. Okay?"

Work Experience: Most Relevant Job

- Use this comprehensive opening question: "Let's talk about your work experience. How about starting with the job that you feel gave you the best preparation for working as a selection interviewer. Tell me all about the job: how you got it, why you chose it, your actual job duties, what you learned on the job, the hours and your attendance record, the pay, why you left (or are leaving), and things like that."
- Probe and follow up to cover each of these items thoroughly: how the applicant got the job, reasons for choosing it, job duties, etc.
- Summarize the major facts and findings from the applicant's most relevant job. For example: "Let me summarize what we have covered to make sure that I've got it right. You worked as a _____ where most of your time was spent doing _____ and _____, and you used these skills, _____ and _____. You chose the job because of _____ and your reasons for leaving it are _____ and _____. Anything else to add?"

Other Work Experience

- If time is available, discuss other jobs the applicant has held that might be pertinent. Get a brief overview of each job the applicant has held. Emphasize jobs held in the last five years or less, since older experience is less likely to be relevant for your decision.
- Ask the work experience questions you specifically prepared for this applicant when you planned the interview.
- Summarize your major findings about all jobs. When the summary is satisfactory to the applicant, go on to discuss education and training.

After the Interview

- Take time to write summary notes immediately. Describe the applicant's behavior and the impressions he or she created. Cite facts and specific incidents from the interview or from the person's work or educational history.
- Wait a day and then complete the Evaluation Form.

SOURCE: From Milton D. Haskel, "Employment interviewing." In Kendrith M. Rowland and Gerald R. Ferris, *Personnel Management.* Copyright © 1982 by Allyn and Bacon. Reprinted with permission.

Collecting Performance Data Increasing the effectiveness of communication and the reliability of appraisals requires supervisors to obtain more complete descriptions of subordinate behavior. When organizational members rely on a single source of information, persistent biases occur. One study indicated that raters who had a positive affect toward ratees were most lenient and those with a negative affect were least lenient.[51] Another suggested that the raters who thought workers did well in one area, such as dependability, tended to think the employee did well in several areas.[52] Maintaining a daily or weekly record of employee performance helps reduce such biases.

Table 7–10 **Interview Questions for Supervisors and Executives**

Questions for a Supervisory Candidate:
1. Why do you want to be a supervisor?
2. What are the functions and duties of a supervisor as you see them?
3. What personal characteristics and other qualifications do you have that would help you to become a good supervisor?
4. How do you feel about taking on the added responsibilities and demands that come with a supervisory job?
5. Do you think you could be a supervisor in any department other than your own? Where?
6. If you were a supervisor, could you motivate subordinates and take disciplinary action against employees, including former coworkers, if necessary? How would you handle, say, a worker with a high rate of absence?

Questions for an Executive Candidate:
1. What criteria would you (a) use in measuring your own performance over the next year and the following years, (b) like your performance measured by, and (c) use in measuring your superior's performance and your relation to him or her?
2. Assume we faced a significant cut in expenditures—for example, 10 to 20 percent within a year or two. How would you go about planning and implementing such a cut in the areas of your responsibility?

SOURCE: Based on W. T. Woltz, How to interview supervisory candidates from the ranks, *Personnel* 57 (September-October 1980): 31–48; and S. G. Ginsburg, Preparing for executive position interviews— Questions the interviewer might ask or be asked, *Personnel* 57 (July-August 1980): 31–44.

Guidelines for Effective Interviewing

Conducting interviews effectively requires the manager to share facts about actual job-related behaviors as they occur rather than from memory. In a selection interview, for example, both parties might focus on information presented in the résumé or in work samples provided by the applicant. In a performance appraisal meeting, the discussion should rely on direct observational data rather than hearsay reports; it should describe specific behavior rather than make evaluative statements or describe an individual's personality. Supervisors should express both positive and negative behaviors and use the same basic form and level of detail for each subordinate.

SUMMARY

In this chapter we examined the basic communication process. The sender encodes a message and transmits it through channels to the receiver who decodes the message. We illustrated each step in an exchange between a boss and her subordinate. We also discussed successful communication by John Amerman of Mattell and Bob Crawford of Brook Furniture Rental. Feedback from the receiver to the sender indicates whether any message was received and what it was. Noise often distorts communication. We looked at the impact of organizational structure on communication, and also compared and contrasted downward, upward, and lateral communication. The chapter then discussed interpersonal relationships and the quality of communication. We also considered multicultural and multinational issues in communication.

Communication can be improved by creating a supportive climate, using an assertive style, and practicing active listening techniques. Interviews pose special challenges for effective communication in organizations. Table 7–11 highlights the major points in this chapter by offering a series of diagnostic questions to use in assessing communication effectiveness.

Table 7–11 **Diagnostic Questions about Communication**

- What encoding and decoding errors occur in communication?
- Do senders use effective language?
- Does nonverbal communication reinforce or contradict the message being sent?
- What type of listening is occurring?
- How effective is listening?
- What media are the most appropriate for transmission?
- What types of noise exist in the organization?
- Does two-way communication exist?
- How effective are downward, upward, and lateral communication?
- What special roles exist to facilitate communication?
- Does the organization's structure help or hinder communication?
- Do interpersonal relations help or hinder communication?
- Are information communication mechanisms functional?
- Are the attitudes of communicating parties compatible?
- What types of communication networks exist, and are they functional?
- Does communication consider the diversity of the parties?
- Does communication lack cross-cultural sensitivity?
- Is the climate supportive or defensive?
- Do individuals use assertive, nonassertive, or aggressive communication?
- Do individuals practice active listening?

Reading 7–1

Bypassing in Managerial Communication
Jerry Sullivan, Naoki Kameda, and Tatsuo Nobu

When Jane Brady arrived at the plant one morning, her new boss, Mr. Sato, looked worried. He had only recently arrived in the United States on his first tour of duty outside of Japan. However, his English was good and his superiors were confident that he could handle the job.

"Why so glum, Mr. Sato?" asked Jane, as she seated herself across from him in his office for their morning conference.

"Last night I received a telex from Tokyo," he replied. "Here, take a look."

She reached across the desk and took the paper. The message was short and assertive, just like all the others she had seen in her two years working for Kumitomo America, a firm organized to supply the Japanese parent with printing machinery for its giant publishing business in Japan.

YOU MUST NOT LET INVENTORY BUILD UP. YOU MUST MONITOR CARRYING COSTS AND KEEP THEM UNDER CONTROL. SHIP ANY JOB LOTS OF MORE THAN 25 UNITS TO US AT ONCE.

As she read the letter she nodded. "This is no problem, Sato-san. I can get right on it."

"How many lots do we have to ship? I want to get them out of here right away."

Jane consulted a printout in the manila file folder she had with her. "No problem. We've only got three lots. I'll start the paperwork and get everything moving today. They'll be on the ship in Portland within two weeks."

Mr. Sato smiled weakly. He liked Americans, but he had been told that they were generally not as trustworthy as Japanese. It wasn't that they were bad people. It was just that they saw everything as a deal or an arrangement—you do this for me and I'll do this for you. They didn't do things simply because they were sincere. Miss Brady, however, seemed different. She always did the job, and he didn't have to spell everything out for her. All he needed to do was give her a general goal and she took care of the rest. He relaxed, turning his attention to the important trip to New York he would soon undertake.

Six weeks later Jane was at the other end of the plant when the summons came. She hurried to Sato's office. He sat behind his desk, his face a mask. She knew something was wrong.

"I thought you were a good person, Miss Brady," he said sadly. "This is very bad." He handed her a telex.

WHY DIDN'T YOU DO WHAT WE TOLD YOU?
YOUR QUARTERLY INVENTORY REPORT IN-
DICATES YOU ARE CARRYING 40 LOTS
WHICH YOU WERE SUPPOSED TO SHIP TO
JAPAN. YOU MUST NOT VIOLATE OUR
INSTRUCTIONS.

Jane could not believe what she was reading. "Sir, I
shipped every lot more than 25. Those were my orders and
I carried them out."

Mr. Sato grabbed the telex out of her hand. "What
about this? This doesn't lie," he shouted. "I checked this
morning. We have 40 lots of more than 25 units each."

"That's not so. We don't."

"We do!"

"No, we don't!"

They stared at each other. Finally Jane said softly,
"Please, let's go and look."

Sato got up silently, and Jane followed him out of the
office. In the warehouse they began with the first lot. Both
of them counted. There were 25 units in the lot.

"Miss Brady, why didn't you ship this lot as you were
told to do?"

Her eyes widened. She felt herself losing control. Before answering she breathed deeply. "Tokyo's instructions
referred to lots of more than 25. Is that correct?"

"Yes, exactly."

"Well, this lot only has 25. In fact, many of the lots
are like this one. They have 25 units."

"But you should have shipped them," he said, his voice
tightening. "You should ship anything that's 25, 26, 27 and
so forth."

"What? Since when does 'more than 25' include 25?"

His face became twisted in a look of withering scorn.
"More than 25 always includes 25. It's simple enough. Once
again, your American education system has let you down."

"How dare you! Why don't you take the trouble to
learn English if you are going to work in this country?"

They glared at each other. Sato sighed, "I think we
need to have a long talk, Miss Brady." She nodded.

Mr. Sato and Miss Brady are not bad managers. They
do not really have serious problems with communicating in
English. And they don't have debilitating personality differences. Yet in their "long talk" that's what will be discussed. What's really gone wrong for them is that they have
"bypassed" each other. Bypassing occurs when people miss
each other with their meanings. They use the same words
but attribute different meanings to them.

When one of the Japanese authors of this article was
an MBA candidate at an American university, he was pen-
alized by an American professor over the "more than 25"
bypassing problem. The professor could not accept the fact
that in Japan "more than X" very often includes X. He was
a bit like the British philosopher in the middle ages who
could not understand why the French persisted in saying
chien when everyone knew the word was "dog."

Bypassing is a serious problem in managerial communications, and in the emerging era of globalism the problem
is bound to get worse. We have been collecting bypassing
examples in business communications in Japan, the United
States, and other countries. Our findings suggest that the
causes of bypassing are the same in all languages, as is the
potential seriousness of the consequences. Bypassing can be
avoided if managers become aware of it as a problem and
follow a few simple rules of thumb in their communications.

CONSEQUENCES OF BYPASSING BETWEEN SUPERIOR AND SUBORDINATE

You are walking down the corridor, a place where you've
noticed much of the communicating in your firm occurs.
Suddenly, the vice president of operations rushes out of his
office. He is obviously late for an important meeting. As
he hotfoots it down the corridor, he sees you. "Say, Phil,"
he says as he breezes by, "how about that report for production planning? Don't they want it soon?" Before you
can respond he has popped into another office and shut the
door. You heard the words he uttered. He was "informing"
you that production planning needed the report soon. You
decide to get in touch with them to find out when they
want it.

However, was the vice president simply informing you?
In fact, he could have been doing any of a number of things.
He could have been implying one of several possible
messages.

Directing: "You should get the report to them now.
That's an order."

Suggesting: "I suggest that we consider getting the
report out now."

Requesting: "Can you do the report now? Let me know
if you can't."

Informing: "A report is needed soon by production
planning."

Questioning: "Does production planning want the report soon?"

In the army, when the sergeant says, "Hey, you guys
wanna charge that hill?" it will be clear to most of the troops
that he is not asking. He's telling, dog face. In business,
communications are not quite that simple, and messages
can easily be misunderstood. Assume now that the vice
president was directing when you thought he was informing. Instead of putting the pedal to the metal and getting
the report out, you will casually approach production planning, enjoy a leisurely conversation over coffee, and then
do the report by the agreed-on date. Sometime during the
next day or two you will receive a phone call that will sound
something like this:

Vice president: "Phil, where the hell is my copy of that
report for production planning? I needed it yesterday."

Phil: "But I spoke with production planning, and they
said it would be okay to have it to them tomorrow. I'm
just writing it now."

Vice president: "That's not good enough, Phil. I told you to get it done yesterday."

Phil (biting his tongue): "Yes, sir. I'll have it to you in an hour."

Step back now from the role of Phil and analyze the situation with us. When the short conversation between Phil and the vice president had ended, both parties moved on with the belief that they were in harmony with each other. *Wa* prevailed, as the Japanese say. But in fact the two managers only had achieved apparent agreement. The apparent agreement is bypassing, and it leads to erroneous expectations by each person about the near-term behavior of the other person. Because of bypassing and the resulting failed expectations, serious conflicts can occur which may threaten *wa* and even damage careers.

Negative Performance Attributions

In the case above, the vice president will be angry and vent his spleen on Phil. But that may not be the end of it. He may attribute the lack of task accomplishment to lack of effort on Phil's part and form a strong image of him as an unmotivated subordinate. Research has shown that the impact of one vivid piece of evidence may be relied on more than a whole distribution of outcomes. This is called "the law of small numbers," in contrast to the law of large numbers, which requires the use of means to make inferences. Bypassing tends to create sharply delineated, memorable conflicts that are then overweighted in the formation of performance judgments.

Here's another example from our collection:

An employer asked me to put 500 checks "in order, with the smallest one on top and the largest one on the bottom." I diligently proceeded to collate the checks by the amount they were written for. Upon completion and presentation to my boss, I found out that he wanted them sorted by check number, not amount. We bypassed on our meanings of smallest and largest, and therefore I wasted my initial effort.

This woman is annoyed that she misdirected her effort. She ought to be worried about her boss forming a judgment that she is a careless, unmotivated employee.

In our experience, junior managers who have experienced bypassing with seniors often do not understand the danger they face. They usually assume that a simple communications problem has occurred, something that can be easily corrected by a follow-up communication. Their assumption is correct as far as it goes. But they fail to take into account a common reaction of senior managers to bypassing. They do not tend to identify a miscommunication as such. Rarely is conflict attributed to misunderstanding born of bypassing. Negative attributions of poor subordinate motivation are more common.

Personality Differences

Another frequent response to bypassing-induced conflict is the conclusion that "personality differences" are the source of the problem rather than a blundering misuse of language by both parties.

Recently the staff I have been working with went through mid-quarter evaluations. Most of them were given ratings which management considered "very good," but since this staff group is primarily over-achievers, some of them felt that their evaluations were poor because they were not in the top category. They began to get defensive about their work. It was quite annoying. I had to point out to them that nothing short of perfection would reach the top category.

The superior and his subordinates here have bypassed (and from the look of it are still bypassing) on the meaning of scale. The boss is using a 5-point scale anchored by "poor" and "excellent." "Very good" is a 4. The staff, however, sees only a 2-point scale, with the low end ("very good") meaning poor performance. A rating of "very good" for them was a slap in the face, and it provoked several to complain. The fact that they "annoyed" the manager may lead him to conclude that "personality differences" are beginning to threaten his work unit (a decline in *wa* again) and that he will have to take action. Sometimes managers would rather blow themselves and their team up rather than admit to routine sloppiness in communication.

Lack of Expertise

Bypassing occurs in all languages. Here is an example from Taiwan.

We had a new job site in a town 25 miles from Taipei. One day the general manager called me and said, "Give me a list of equipment over $100 in the new office by tomorrow." I worked overtime to list every piece of equipment over $100 we used in the new job site. It was more than 1000 items. But I later found out that what the general manager wanted was a list of office equipment and furniture over $100 in the new office.

This manager may be judged not up to the job by his boss. Perhaps he is, perhaps he isn't. Whatever the case, the boss is unlikely to take his own poor communicating into account when he makes his judgment.

WHY DOES BYPASSING OCCUR?

Bypassing occurs (1) because managers assume that meanings are in words rather than people, (2) because they think they can communicate in stress conditions with the same degree of success as in non-stress situations, and (3) because they treat communicating as easier than it is.

Meanings Are Not in Words

An old academic gag in philosophy departments is to lock the junior graduate students in a classroom and not let them out until they have written every definition of the word "paint" on the blackboard. Every time the professor checks on them, he tells them one definition they've missed and says that their list is still incomplete. The game goes on until the students give up. It never ends with a complete list. The point is that people construct the meanings of words, and there can be almost as many meanings of a common word as there are groups of people who will agree on a word's meaning.

Managers often hold implicit beliefs, first, that words have inherent meanings and, second, that there is only one meaning per word. Take the word, "bachelor." What does it mean? An unmarried adult male, right? Okay, is Tarzan a bachelor? Or the pope? How about two gays living together in a relationship? Some people will say they are all bachelors, whereas others will defend to the death their belief that they are not. The meaning of the word bachelor depends on who is talking to whom and on what they decide the meaning will be.

Let's look at the word "revenue" as it is used in the United States and Japan. Technically speaking, revenue is an increase in owner's equity based on an irrevocable exchange between the business and a customer. In Japan, however, a sale may occur and be recorded as revenue. But at some later date the goods may be sent back and the money returned. A sale is often contingent upon the maintenance of mutual trust between buyer and seller. If trust is threatened, the sale may be deemed inappropriate. Transactions, then, sometimes are trials rather than verifiable exchanges, yet the money passed from one person to the other is called revenue in Japan even though it would not be called so in the U.S.

In this case the meaning of revenue resides not in the word but in the culture of the people. American financial and accounting managers who believe they invented the language of business would do well to pay attention to the bypassing problems they may encounter in other countries where business terms have different meanings.

When one of the Japanese authors was doing some business with an American firm a few years ago, he tried to head off bypassing problems by asking for their definitions of key terms that would be used in their trade correspondence. For "delivery" the CEO replied, "I take this to mean delivery to the store. So if I promise a September delivery, it means I will deliver products to the customer's store in September." For a Japanese trader this is not what delivery means. To him it refers to the shipment of the goods on board a vessel. Several serious problems were resolved because of this clarification.

Whole deals can be lost because of bypassing. The president of a wood cabinet factory in New Zealand recently flew to New York for an appointment with a vice president of a large audio/electronics company. The New Zealander wanted the company to give him a chance to produce speaker systems at his factory in Auckland. He asked the vice president to visit the factory to see how well prepared it was for the business, proposing that all expenses be paid during his stay in Auckland and a return ticket be sent to him. The New Zealander returned to his hotel to await a decision. After several days without a response he thought he had lost the business. In a last ditch effort he called the vice president. "Well, my boss hasn't given me an okay yet," he said. "He feels he can't justify buying a one-way ticket from New York to Auckland for me." The astonished New Zealander pointed out that he would pay both ways. After some discussion they realized that New Zealanders say "return trip ticket" while Americans say "round trip ticket."

This case is a good example of the meanings problem. The American heard the phrase "return trip ticket." The logic of the situation and common business custom should have led him to conclude that a round trip was offered. Instead, he was guided by implicit rules that state that meanings are in words and only one meaning is attached to a word. The American vice president probably felt a bit foolish over this incident. He need not; virtually all human beings are guided by the same rules until experience or education teaches them that meanings are in people and contexts, not words.

The Worlds of Stress and Non-stress

When we need to communicate with another manager when time is short or we don't have all the data needed, we are likely to experience stress, an unpleasant anxiety about our ability to cope. Mostly we learn to endure the stress and get on with the job. Sometimes a bit of stress even sharpens our wits and helps us perform better. But a lot of stress at one time or continued stress over a period of time may lead to bypassing, subsequent failed expectations, and devastating repercussions. Why is bypassing more likely under high stress conditions? To answer the question we need to recognize that our minds live in different worlds in stressful and non-stressful situations. In the non-stressful world we conceptualize in fuzzy prototypes. We have a basic image of a bird, for example, and can identify most creatures as birds or not birds. When we come to a problem creature like an ostrich, which doesn't fly, we pause and think for a bit, and either categorize it or express uncertainty. The ostrich is out in the margins of our prototype and can be included or excluded, depending on the nature of the task, the context, our needs, and the importance of categorizing in a way acceptable to people we consider important. Under stress, however, our conceptualizing changes and becomes very Aristotelian. In Aristotle's logic an entity either is or isn't a member of a category. An ostrich is either a bird or a non-bird. There is no middle ground.

Assume that a young manager is attending a meeting of senior executives. She is very nervous. Suddenly, the CEO turns to her and says, "What's the value of that new die press over in your shop?" Under better conditions she would vaguely recall that asset value can be defined in terms of historical cost, historical cost modified by changes in the price level, replacement cost, or market value. These various ways of establishing value would influence her thinking; she probably would develop a hazy notion of value in terms of dollars or perhaps a reference point (it's more or less than some other, easily valued machine). Under stress, however, she identifies two categories: value (with one number in the category) and not-value (with all other numbers in it). She then quickly fixes on the first number that makes some sense (perhaps the historical cost) and slots it. That becomes the value she communicates. Instead of a range she reports a unitary statistic to the CEO, who treats that value as if it is the value with a probability of .99 because under stress the junior manager has spoken with much more assertive confidence than is warranted. They have bypassed, because both are in apparent agreement when in fact they do not really agree on what was said. After the meeting the CEO will recall that the junior manager said that the value of the die press was exactly $150,000. The junior manager, who has reverted to thinking under non-stress conditions, will recall reporting the value as "somewhere in the neighborhood of $150,000." She will be surprised and hurt when the CEO holds her to that number, and her backtracking and hedging will not be taken kindly.

Under stress we become either-or thinkers and communicate accordingly, often quite assertively. When the stress is reduced, we revert to fuzzy prototyping, but we don't realize what we've done. And those with whom we've been communicating don't realize it either. Bypassing in these conditions could be reduced if we recognized when stress conditions prevail and took with a grain of salt the clear, concrete meanings seemingly attached to words by our colleagues. Behind every strong assertion uttered in a stressful meeting lies a fuzzy prototype outside of the meeting.

Communicating Is Hard

Many managers treat communication as easy. That is not quite correct. It is usually easy to undo a miscommunication, and if it isn't, the consequences are usually trivial. We are constantly failing to get our message across, constantly adding on new messages to correct the failures, and constantly failing again without suffering severely. This process lulls us into a belief that communicating is simple. To see how wrong this belief can be, let's look at the usage of two simple words, "soon" and "immediately." We recently worked with the managers in a public accounting firm. We asked each of them to tell us the maximum amount of time attached to each of the words. Responses are listed in Table 7–12.

Notice that immediately means anywhere from "right now" to "one week" in this firm, with "end of the day" as the most frequent response. When the "right now" boss tells the "one week" subordinate to get project X finished "immediately," the subordinate will salute and finish it up by the end of that week. We described above the conflict and harsh repercussions that will occur. The problem could have been avoided if both parties had been less casual about their interaction and recognized that most adjectives and adverbs are quite vague. Just because words are short and frequently used does not mean that a communication using

Table 7–12 **Responses**

	Immediately	Soon
Right now	3	
One hour	7	
Two–six hours	4	
End of day	16	
Twenty-four hours	3	2
1.5–3 days	2	3
End of week	2	
One week	4	10
Two–three weeks		4
One month		4
Two–six months		5
One year		7

the words is going to be easy. By the way, imagine the interactions that occur when the seven managers who define soon as anytime up to a year sit down with the managers who see it as within 24 hours.

Some of the shortest, most frequently used words deal with uncertainty—words like "probable," "possible," and "likely." MBAs are taught the concept of expected value, in which each possible outcome is multiplied by its probability. In the real world, however, beliefs about uncertainty are almost never expressed as numbers on a scale from 0 to 1. Rather, a whole set of nouns, adjectives, and phrases are called into play. Recently we asked a group of 30 managers to attach probability ratings to a list of adjectives describing different levels of uncertainty. Figure 7–10 describes their responses. For example, "excellent chance" ranged from .50 probability to .95. "Reasonably possible" went from .30 to .80. The danger of bypassing occurring when these phrases are used is obvious. This is also the case for "likely." Words and phrases like "highly possible," "unlikely," and "very unlikely," however, had narrow ranges and thus specific meanings for the managers. All but one of the phrases lined up on one side of the .50 line, suggesting that most of the words used to describe uncertainty are best thought of as referring to either below .50 or above .50. Managers would have little risk of bypassing when using these terms if they mutually agreed to employ the words only in reference to above or below .50. Before such agreement could occur, however, all parties would have to admit that communicating uncertainty is extremely hard.

AVOIDING BYPASSING

Coping with bypassing once it occurs is all but impossible, since neither party will know that it has occurred until the damage has been done. Consider the plight of a Japanese manager in the United States. In a Portland, Oregon electronics firm the American employees recently criticized the Japanese managers for not offering praise when they did a

Figure 7–10   **Managers' Ratings of Probability of Uncertainty Adjectives**

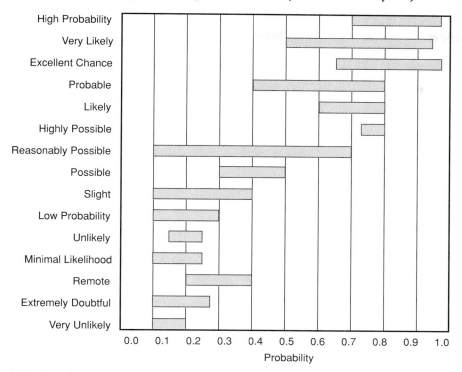

good job. The employees saw the lack of praise as an indication that their foreign employer did not value their excellent productivity. The criticism came as something of a shock to the Japanese president of the firm. He was well satisfied with his employees and thought he had communicated that to them. In Japan, however, satisfaction is often not communicated through praise, since praise carries with it the implied message that one did not really expect such good work in the first place. To praise an employee may be considered an impolite communication! For the Japanese, not offering praise after good work is a way of being civil; for the Americans it is a slap in the face. A better way to deal with bypassing is not to let it occur.

Be alert for vague words or words with multiple meanings. Words like good, bad, soon, immediately, and possibly are dangerous. When a manager hears them, she should always expect a concrete example. Good should never be accepted without evidence of what good means. Managers also need to be alert to words and phrases with multiple meanings that can trigger bypassing. Here's a list we have collected:

- Could or should. Many managers try to avoid sounding too assertive. They tend to substitute could for should ("Perhaps you could look into that rising unit cost data if you have the time this week.") What is in fact a directive may be seen as a suggestion.

- Fact. Our use of fact in the last sentence is harmless enough. But consider this sentence: "The fact of the matter is that the liabilities are excessive." The statement could be a verified observation or simply an offhand opinion.

- Logic. Your accountant tells you, "The logic of this depreciation method is beyond dispute." When he wants to change it six months later, you explode. "If it was logical then, why isn't it now?" you ask. However, you are thinking of logic as referring to a reasoned deduction that holds true as long as the premises are true. Your accountant sees logic as meaning useful. The system was useful then; it isn't now.

- Margin. What one manager thinks of as margin may be gross margin. To another manager, it is net margin.

- Normal. When a manager says, "We have experienced normal operating costs," does he mean desirable or expected costs?

- Help. A young manager was asked by another manager if she could help the next day with a mailing of 1,700 letters for a seminar. She agreed, thinking that help meant being part of a group effort to get the letters out. She discovered the next day that help meant she alone would be responsible for the entire operation.

Paraphrase

Managers should encourage each other to check definitions: "Are you saying that . . . ?" "By return on sales do you mean . . . ?" Although this practice can be tedious, it will uncover most bypassings. As communication expert William V. Haney has noted, paraphrasing doesn't work very well unless a manager is approachable. He must signal to others that the communication channel to him is open, wide, and deep so the timid and reticent as well as the assertive can get through to do their checking.

Use Multiple Channels

Bypassing that occurs during a meeting may be quickly discovered in a follow-up telephone call. It is quite fitting that the telephone, which is the medium in which much dangerous bypassing occurs, should be used to undo it. Exchanges of memos and electronic mail after meetings are always a good idea. E-mail by itself, however, is a menace. Researchers have noted that managers often throw caution and decorum to the winds on E-mail, saying things they ordinarily wouldn't say without a great deal of qualification and expressing themselves in vulgar, often brutish tones.

Don't Fall for Personality Differences as Explanations

It is very easy to explain a conflict born of bypassing as rooted in "personality differences" among American managers. Better to adopt the Japanese practice, in which a manager's personality is not allowed to stand in the way of successful communication. Japanese may be too reticent about facing up to interpersonal conflict, but when they do, they talk it out rather than immediately conclude that no resolution can occur because of personality problems.

Recognize the Complexity of Communication

In conversations we have had with managers, occasionally we hear this remark: "I had to break off my work to talk with one of my subordinates (or customers, suppliers)." Implicit in this statement is the belief that communication is not work. Rather it is some kind of trivial downtime that must be dealt with if work is to be done successfully. American managers are more prone to this idea than Japanese, probably because of their formal training in economic theory. Economic theory emphasizes exchange acts and their outcomes. Except for a few brilliant theorists like A. O. Hirshman, economists have little to say to their students about the actual process of exchange—how it is carried out and maintained through communication. American MBA-trained managers get the idea that communication is not a salient issue in economic reality. Japanese managers, who usually do not enjoy the blessings of a business school education, tend to hold the sensible view that communication is part and parcel of work. Americans, seeing this Japanese behavior, find it odd and call it cultural. It is not.

If communication is trivial downtime, no one is going to put much effort into doing it right. Bypassing will result.

Many American organizations have recognized this problem and taken steps to correct it. Managers are being encouraged to see communication as the major task of the job, and organizational researchers and consultants are beginning to examine theories of rhetoric rather than economic theories as the basics for describing workplace relationships and a source of ideas for improvement. Much more research, for example, is needed on bypassing in cross-cultural settings.

Manage Bypassing in Cross-Cultural Communication

While much needs to be learned, we can offer a number of practices that should reduce bypassing problems in cross-cultural negotiations.

1. When problems come up, don't immediately blame language difficulties. Speaking in English is difficult for Japanese, for instance, and it may cause trouble. But while everyone is alert to syntax, grammar, and using the right technical terms, bypassing over simple words like "soon" may creep in. Watch out for the little words.

2. Discuss basic concepts. Ask each party to exchange a written list of their understandings of key concepts, starting with profit. Then use the first negotiating session to do nothing but build rapport through discussion of the key meanings.

3. Always have at least two people on a team. If one American shows up to negotiate, he or she may face six or seven Japanese. The Japanese are a group-oriented people, but the extra hands perform a valuable function. They listen to the chief negotiators, ready to pick out flaws in the other guy's arguments, but also prepared to spot possible bypassing and correct it.

4. Assume the worst. Bypassing is all but inevitable, even under the best conditions, when people from different cultures communicate. It may be wise to respect the American practice of getting it all in writing, a procedure that will force common meanings to be established.

Treat Stress-Influenced Assertions Warily

In stress-laden meetings, managers who hear a statement are likely to assign a much greater truth value to it than the speaker of the statement will after the meeting. It is better to accept all statements made in meetings or under pressure with a grain of salt. In this way speakers and listeners will find themselves in agreement over claims and assertions. Without such wariness, apparent agreement over truth values will occur when in fact real differences exist. Furthermore, a specific rule to follow in stressful situations is to treat all uncertainty identifier statements as referring either to likely or unlikely. The belief that more subtle gradations can be established will lead to a "highly probable," "quite strong" likelihood of bypassing.

Workplace harmony is not just a function of good incentives, adequate planning, suitable controls, strong leaders, and motivated employees. It requires successful, not

"Profit" in Japan and the United States

During the past decade Japanese direct investment in the United States has soared. Many investments require lengthy negotiations in which problems arise because of differing cultural values, organizational focus, and economic goals. Conflicts over profit (how to divide it up, appropriate targets, growth objectives) can become quite heated. Most profit problems are economic issues, but could it be that some are really rooted in bypassing? If Japanese and American businesspeople have differing concepts of profit and don't realize it, they may bypass in negotiations and get into conflict.

To explore the concept of profit, we developed a survey questionnaire and administered it to Japanese and American business students. In the questionnaire an attempt was made to implicitly offer all conventional definitions of profit and record the responses of subjects to those definitions. The definitions are as follows:

1. *Businessmen's Profits*. Profit was defined as "the difference between revenues and expenses (including taxes) of a business at the end of each year." Economists refer to this as the businessman's definition of profit—an everyday conventional use of the term for noneconomists.
2. *Owner's Surplus*. Here profit was "the money the owner of the business keeps at the end of each year." Once again, this definition was offered as a conventional noneconomic characterization.
3. *Retained Earnings*. Profit is "the money left over at the end of each year which the company uses to invest in new equipment, new products, or new markets."
4. *Economic Profit*. Profit is "the money the businessman gets as a reward from society for taking the financial risks which are needed to produce the society's goods and services." This definition is usually referred to as the pure economic concept of profits.
5. *Society's Investment in the Future*. Here profit is "the money society uses to develop the future." This definition was developed from the work of Peter Drucker, who has written extensively on profits as investment in the future.
6. *Monopolistic Profits*. Profit is "the money which businesses get when they act to deliberately hold back goods and services as a way of driving up prices."
7. *Rewards for Innovation*. Profits are "the money which businessmen receive as a reward from society for being creative and for developing new and improved products." This definition parallels that of those economists who have characterized profit as gains generated by creative managerial innovation.

Our questionnaire was filled out by 172 business students in Tokyo and 106 in Seattle. For each statement about profit they responded on 7-point scales anchored by strongly disagree (1) and strongly agree (7). We approached business students instead of managers because they were less likely to be influenced by corporate culture or the writings of business gurus. Their idea of profit would reflect a basic societal conceptualization.

Table 7–13 shows the American and Japanese students rejected (means less than 4) owner's surplus and monopolistic profits as elements of the concept. They agreed on what profit is not. To find out what profit is, we analyzed the responses. For the Americans, four factors emerged. First, profit is the reward for innovation and risk taking. Second, profit is society's investment in the future. Third, it is the money the owner uses to invest in new equipment, new products, and other items. Fourth, it is simply the difference between revenues and expenses. For the Japanese, only one factor emerged. Profit is the reward to businessmen for taking risks to produce innovations society needs to develop the future. The American students had multiple concepts of profit, some emphasizing personal gain, some social value. To the Japanese, however, only one concept of profit exists, and in it social and self interest are the same.

If Japanese have a unidimensional concept of profit and Americans a multidimensional concept, then the possibility of bypassing as the source of communications problems regarding profit negotiations must be considered. Not only can there be negotiating problems based on different organizational goals, but also problems based on different individual conceptual structuring. If failure to finally agree on a mutually beneficial investment occurs because of difficulties in discussions over profit, the

Table 7–13 **Agreement on Definitions of Profit**

	American (N = 106)	Japanese (N = 172)
Businessmen's Profit	5.61	4.89
Owner's Surplus	3.29	3.74
Retained Earnings	4.09	4.65
Economic Profits	4.77	4.54
Society's Investment in the Future	4.20	4.97
Monopolistic Profits	2.61	3.63
Rewards for Innovation	4.83	5.08

cause of the difficulties may not be two different organizations having two different goals for profit generation. In fact, failure can occur even when the organizations have similar interests if the negotiators are burdened with different culture-bound concepts of the term "profit."

For example, an American who has adopted the concept of profit as personal gain for the corporate owners may think he is in agreement with his Japanese counterpart during initial negotiations over dividend policies for a new joint venture. Later, however, when he finds that the Japanese is projecting much lower cash dividends than he expected, he may feel betrayed. The Japanese will be confused, because he is plowing profits back into technology development that has long-term social gain. To him the social gain is the same thing as corporate gain. A sense of betrayal pitted against confusion can lead to failure in the negotiations, and bypassing born of differing concepts of profit is the cause.

The American doing business with the Japanese ought to realize that he needs to define what he means by profit before he negotiates—so he meets the Japanese conception with one of his own. Clear definition of terms, even if the definitions conflict, is absolutely necessary for successful communications. It is important for the American to understand that his definition of profit as solely corporate gain—involving as it will the maximization of short-term gains—conflicts with the Japanese definition, which necessarily involves a long-term view of things. This realization can stimulate fruitful negotiations and possibly consensus. Without it both parties may bypass—talk past each other and initially delude themselves that understanding has occurred.

---

just frequent or lengthy, communication. Indeed, in a firm where managers are insensitive to the bypassing problem, the less communication the better. Chances of serious conflicts will be reduced. Firms dominated by highly trained technical people ("propeller heads," as one of our colleagues calls them) who think of communication issues as soft-core probably ought not to encourage too much communication under the guise of encouraging participation or building corporate culture. Such efforts simply will lead to more frequent bypassing occurrences and more conflict when expectations of others are formed and not borne out. Technical managers in these firms often have vast technical vocabularies in which they place much more faith than is warranted. No one has ever developed a perfectly performing language (and no one is likely to), yet specialists often treat their technical language apparatus as functioning at an optimal level. In these situations the possibility of bypassing is not accepted and the problem is ignored. The first step required to develop better communication in these and similar organizations is to convince managers that words do not have inherent meanings and that context is crucial in understanding what another person means. Once that barrier is hurdled, managers are ready to recognize the dangers of bypassing. When bypassing sensitivity has been developed, then participatory management, team building, and culture making all will become functional.

DISCUSSION QUESTIONS

1. Give three examples of bypassing.
2. What are the consequences of bypassing between a supervisor and a subordinate?
3. What are the consequences between individuals with different cultural backgrounds?
4. Why does bypassing occur?
5. Offer five strategies for avoiding bypassing.

Reprinted with permission from *Business Horizons* 34(1) (January-February 1991): 71–80.

Activity 7–1

Isabel Stewart

Step 1:   Read the Isabel Stewart case.

Isabel Stewart, 39, was a member of the partnership at Austin & March, one of Philadelphia's largest and most prestigious law firms. A graduate of Harvard Law School, Stewart worked in the tax department, a highly specialized legal area that had doubled in size during the 1980s. Stewart had been made a partner in 1987, despite a recent maternity leave and the fact that she was by a margin of several years the youngest associate to be promoted.

In 1990 Austin & March employed 300 attorneys and an equal number of support staff. Sixty-four lawyers at the firm—fifty-eight men and six women—had partner status. Clients included large corporations, financial institutions, and public agencies, as well as smaller privately owned businesses. During the late 1980s, the real estate and corporate departments had generated substantial business for the firm, but more recently volume in these areas had begun to decline, while the legal work connected with bankruptcy and litigation increased.

Isabel Stewart occupied a spacious office overlooking the river. Her annual compensation was larger than many of her peers due to the highly specialized nature of her work. Nonetheless Stewart was dissatisfied; in the last several months a more junior male lawyer had been able to secure what she regarded as better work. She was convinced that she was being excluded from the "big deal" cases and that her career would suffer as a consequence:

> I'm worried because I have the sense that I am losing ground to someone who has only been here a few years. We do some big transactions, with mega-bills, and I find myself competing for a chunk of those with the guy in the next office. There is a limited universe of high-profile deals, and he markets against me the way he would market against a competing firm. It's in his interests to get more of those deals and for me to get fewer—the more you get, the more money you make.
>
> The head of the department said I should just accept it: "He may always make more money than you, and to set yourself up in competition with him is a bad move, because you may lose." That really gets me riled! I work as hard. I'm smarter. I have been here for ten years and I have cultivated those relationships for a long time, and I guess that I just think that people should be more loyal.

PERSONAL AND CAREER BACKGROUND

Isabel Stewart graduated from college in 1977 with a degree in mathematics and from Harvard Law School in 1980. Stewart was married and had two young sons; her husband was a faculty member in the history department at Princeton.

At Harvard, Stewart had distinguished herself in tax courses, receiving an A+ [in] Corporate Tax Law. Stewart joined the tax department at Austin & March after graduation.

As an associate, Isabel was able to work with a number of the firm's senior lawyers: "As a tax lawyer you work with people in other departments, and I had close working relationships with a lot of people in the firm," she explained. "I had a lot more contacts with other partners than most associates."

She did, however, find one of the two partners who ran the tax department difficult to work with. Ralph Egan was six years older than she, a specialist in corporate tax, and according to Isabel, a person who liked to be in control:

> On the surface Ralph is very gregarious. He doesn't scream or yell. But he likes to be right all the time. He has a reputation for being difficult.
>
> I worked with him a little at the very beginning. He asked me to research a question, so I went to the library, did the research, and wrote him a seven-page memo. He raked me over the coals when he saw it. "I don't want this, I want the equivalent of a Law Review article, with footnotes!" Then he took ideas out of my memo and used them as his own.

Later Isabel was approached by a young lawyer in another department about a corporate tax issue. It developed that they were going to have to get an opinion, for which a partner was needed. Isabel approached one partner, who said, "I don't know, ask Ralph." Knowing that problems might result from Egan's involvement, but wanting to remain in charge of the project, Isabel organized a meeting early in the process in order to circumvent any complications. She prepared both an analysis of the issue and recommendations regarding the opinion and solicited the approval of the partner from the other department. On the day of the meeting this partner was ill, but the meeting went well and Ralph Egan gave his approval. However,

> Six weeks later, when we were really down to the wire, Ralph called me and said, "I have some problems with this. I don't think we can get an opinion." The client was getting upset. I was looking like an idiot. And it turned out that all Ralph's issues were straw men.
>
> His approach is to get you out on a limb and then saw it off. He puts things off and it makes you look bad in front of other people. On the surface he was very pleasant about it. "Isabel, you've got to pay more attention to these things." This is after I had gotten everything lined up ahead of time, got him signed off early, had the partner from corporate in agreement, and still it didn't work. Then, later, I botched a couple of things he asked me to do because he made me so upset, feel so insecure. So that cut me off from a lot I wanted to do.
>
> A number of people have had problems with him. He's only six years senior to me, so I guess at the time I started he wasn't so secure himself. When I was made partner he called me in and told me, "I didn't support you as a candidate, but that's all behind us. Welcome to the partnership." It seems like we get along but it's all below the surface. He seems so reasonable, so rational, that when you start screaming, you are the one out of control.

Isabel was made a partner on schedule, despite her maternity leave and the dissenting vote of Ralph Egan. At the time she was the youngest partner and one of only three women in the partnership. Isabel felt that she had done enough good work for a number of lawyers in the firm that there was sufficient support for the decision to promote her.

Although she had specialized in corporate tax, work in that area never materialized. "There were a lot of men who would get involved in the corporate department, but when I asked about it people would say there isn't much of that work," Isabel recalled. "It was all very vague." Further, the one partner with whom Isabel did not get along did most of that work, and from the start she became much more heavily involved in other areas, such as partnership tax law. But in recent years corporate tax had become a major legal area, and Stewart was eager to get involved. She found herself hindered, however, by both a lack of hands-on experience and an unwillingness on the part of key people to include her in corporate tax transactions.

> I am missing big pieces of substantive knowledge that didn't get developed over the years. But I can work with associates who have the knowledge—I have the managerial and decision-making skills needed to understand it. But there is little reason to come to someone who is playing catch-up.
>
> So I am looking for opportunities to jump in. This week, for example, for a company that was going public, there was a question on net operating losses that came up at the last minute. It's a classic corporate tax kind of question, so I did some work on it. That may happen again, but it is not going to be easy.

When asked why she was so intent on doing this kind of work, Stewart responded that, in addition to the intellectual appeal, it was important work in career terms:

> Part of the appeal is that I have been shut out of it, and I don't like that. Damn it, I'm not going to let them do that to me! I'm going to prove that I can do it. It can be lucrative work for clients who can pay for the kind of planning and in-depth research we like to do. It's a big source of that kind of business. So being excluded from it is potentially harmful.

Stewart explained that, although attracting new clients was desirable, corporate clients typically did not come in through the tax department.

> Corporate clients come in through the corporate department. I don't work on attracting new business, but it is going to become more and more of a prerequisite for becoming a partner. Certainly there is a reward system built around people bringing in business. No one tells you you have to bring in business—you are not under direct pressure from your boss. The pressure comes from the fact that if you don't bring in business, if you don't work on very high-profile, profitable cases, your compensation is going to suffer. That's the form the pressure takes: it's a piece of being a very well-respected, well-compensated partner.

Stewart was increasingly aware of the competition within the office for high-profile work, and she explained that she was trying to figure out how the process worked:

> There is not a God up there who says, OK, there are two people of equal ability and they each ought to get their fair share. It goes to the people who manage to pull it in. There is competition for clients both inside and outside the firm.
>
> I have been talking to people. Some people say I am imagining things. Others say I should just accept it.
>
> I may not play squash, or do the old boy stuff,

but I think I am pretty easy to get along with. It's not that I have negative qualities—it's that I don't have positive ones—that high energy level and enthusiasm.

Isabel told the following anecdote to illustrate the kind of "positive" qualities she believed were required at Austin & March:

> John, a fellow I know in another department, told me a story about a piece of work he had that he thought he would give to a friend of his, Steve. He knew Steve was in competition with another associate and had some catching up to do. So he went to his friend with the work, and his friend said, "Gee, I don't know if I can do it, I guess I can." John said, "Steve is my friend." I had the feeling that if he did it he was going to be doing me a favor, and I don't want him doing me favors just because he's my friend. So he went to Pete, the other guy. Pete goes, "Oh, yeah! That sounds great! I'd really liked to do that." Pete perceived the work as an opportunity. Steve would do it, but as a favor. He perceived it only as something else that had to be done. So John gave the work to Pete. Then Steve got mad because he thinks he is competing with Pete.
>
> So I thought about that and realize that I do favors, instead of, "Wow, that's a really interesting project, tell me about it." I had never thought of every project as an opportunity. I thought every project is something I have to do. I don't mind doing it, it's my work. But I didn't see it in terms of making the person feel that their work is fascinating, the most important thing I had to do.
>
> I tend to do too many things, which means that things sit for awhile and I do it only at the last minute. I'm not right on top of things. I've also noticed that the guy next door has a clean desk. Something hits his desk, it's off his desk. He doesn't work on as many things, but he can be much more responsive. I was cultivating lots and lots and lots of contacts, thinking that the more goodwill I built up with more people, the better off I would be.
>
> It doesn't matter how smart you are if you don't get the work out the right way. I thought if I did good work everyone would know it. Now I am trying to figure out the external things. This is not a place where people tell you much of anything.

Isabel Stewart talked at length about how she had been trained to behave, and she had gradually begun to realize that a different set of characteristics from those she had learned were required in her current milieu:

> If you look at the people who are successful here, one of the key characteristics is energy level. Just pure, raw energy, almost to the point of craziness. I have two little boys and they have that kind of run-around, crazy energy. There is a male model by which you attack

your work, you go after it, you kill it. It's very different from the way I approach work. There is a frenetic style—just moving from one thing to another quickly, moving fast, jumping around the room, and working long hours.

I think that that kind of style is what sells. That is what makes people comfortable. But women don't approach work that way. If they did, they probably wouldn't make it, because they would be viewed as too hard to get along with. Women who behaved like that were filtered out years ago.

I had a conversation just yesterday with two lawyers about another lawyer. What the men said was, "She's too aggressive. There's no softness to her. She backs people into corners and leaves them with no way out." What they really were saying was that she has bad judgment in managing situations. But would they be so bothered if she were a man? No. But with a woman they assume any negative traits are female, so she won't change.

So we are left with a bunch of relatively passive women in the upper ranks. But now we are being measured against a standard that is much more male.

Isabel talked about how her own working style differed from that of her male colleagues. For her it was critical to study legal problems from both her and her client's point of view, and to provide the client with several options and an assessment of the relative value of each. The men at Austin & March, however, tended to propose one specific legal approach, and most often an approach in which they were personally invested.

The guy in the next office—Mike Horn—is extraordinarily masculine in his approach. There is a right answer to a problem for everybody. I'll say, wait a minute, that might make sense for this client, but mine has another set of problems. Mike doesn't tolerate that kind of ambiguity. There has to be a right answer.

Well, the problem is, that when one of the partners from the corporate department is working with both of us on the same issue but for different clients, it makes him nervous: "Gee, Mike thinks that there is an absolute right answer. Why is Isabel being so wishy-washy about it?"

I may come up with a better answer more often, because I am willing to hand-craft a solution for a particular client, whereas he says, this is the right answer, and we'll do it this way for everybody!

The other thing that goes on is that, if someone brings a problem to me, and they basically don't have a problem—I look it over, and say, well, there's this issue, and there's that issue, but I think basically that the way you've done it is one of several different ways to do it. There are three choices, all relatively equal; the client has chosen one, which may suit his business

objectives a bit better, so I say, fine, if that suits his business objectives, the others are not so much better from a tax point of view that it is worth switching him into one of the other two modes. But what Mike will do is, every single time, he'll switch it. Every time. It's, "You've got to do it my way!" They have to put their mark on the transaction. It's like dogs—it's the peeing on the tree. You're marking out your territory: This is my tree!

But this too makes people uncomfortable when they deal with me. I'm not changing things enough. They think what a tax lawyer does is change things around—how come she doesn't make any changes? She must not be seeing things. Mike must be seeing more things, or understanding this better.

Most clients are more comfortable with the style they understand, and it is a very dominating kind of style. But I'm capable of being very definitive. If a client is uncomfortable with choices I can move into that mode. "This is what we'll do." But one risk is, if you do things that way, you may end up in a power play with someone just like you on the other side. If you both come out with, "This is the way it's got to be!" you're going to end up with a clash. So I am more likely to get the lay of the land, get a sense of what the client wants me to do. Do they want me to present them with all the options and accompanying analysis?

When I deal with lawyers in this office, I always assume, which is probably a mistake, that they can tolerate the kind of analytic process that I'm going through, and that I should show them—we are on the same team, and there is no reason for me to hide that from view. We're all working together to get a particular solution for a particular client, and I ought to lay all my cards on the table. But I get the sense that many people here feel more comfortable with someone who imposes a structure on them. I don't know what to do about that.

When asked what she thought clients who were paying large sums for legal advice expected from their attorneys, both in terms of behavior and content, Isabel said that she was no longer certain:

What do clients expect? I don't really know. I thought they wanted someone with technical knowledge who could help them make a decision, not make it for them. These are sophisticated people who understand their business better than I do. I only understand a piece of it. I'm a specialist.

I had a conversation with a friend who is a professor. He was adamant that people want to be told what to do. They don't want their doctor giving them five choices. He hires people to make decisions.

I know what clients should want. I think you should go for the best outcome, and if it doesn't work have a fall-back position. But do you really want to make everyone stand on their heads? It is easier for me to adjust my approach with clients after I get certain signals from them. Where I fall down is inside the office. I feel like I should be able to be honest, to let my guard down, to explain the process. But I get in trouble doing this.

There is one guy in the corporate department I don't get along with, and I'm beginning to realize that I make him nervous. He's losing confidence in me. For example, last Thursday we had a conference with a client and it went very well. The client asked hard questions and I thought I answered them. But I also was supposed to have answers to lots of procedural questions. One of them was whether it takes 30 or 60 days to line up an appeal, but as the event is two years off I didn't bother with that one. I knew the client didn't care. But the other guy lashed out at me: "You don't know?" He seems motivated by fear. He comes from another firm and it seems to be cultural. With him you have to know all the answers. He was afraid I'd screw up.

We all have our own internal sense of risk assessment. We're dealing with situations where we are trying to figure out how the IRS will apply a particular rule to a particular situation. There aren't any answers. The relative risk assessment is a very subjective thing. Plus, it's one element in a business deal. Is it worth changing the business deal some way in order to get slightly better tax position? I would tend to tolerate more risk, or to see that the shades are very fine—"It's a bit better, but not much." I may be creating more tax risk because I am not willing to impose my will. I say, "It might be 5% better if you did this, but you make the choice, because you can better assess what it is going to do to the business deal."

I tend to look at the whole things as pieces of one puzzle, whereas a man would tend to look at his one little piece, and say, "I can make this better."

I can understand changing certain kinds of behavior, being more aggressive, being on top of things, making everyone feel more important. Acting that way won't fundamentally change who I am or how I look at things. But with problem-solving, I don't see any utility or benefit to doing things the male way. I tend to like my way!

Isabel acknowledged that another key area in which she differed from her male colleagues was in her ability to sell herself, and to take personal risks in the process:

I have avoided a lot of things that would have done me good. I have always been very shy—in college I couldn't even talk to a professor—and it is uncomfortable for me to have lunch with clients, or to insert myself into their life. It doesn't feel natural to me. If a client called me and said, "There is this group called Philadelphia Women in Real Estate, do you want to come?" I would say I was too busy. But I'm trying now to view things like that more as opportunities. I've been doing a lot of speaking. I gave a speech at a real estate institute, and unlike the old days I stayed after and tried to meet the people and make contacts.

One thing I have noticed is that the people who are very successful at marketing don't have very much self-awareness. People that do the best never question themselves. They just do it. The world is divided into people who like them, and people who are jerks. It's very simple—you either like me, or you are a jerk! They don't worry about the jerks. But if I stick my neck out and nothing comes from it, I want to crawl into a hole and not get back out!

I know that I have set up blocks to certain kinds of work. Mike is able to get work off his desk, but when I get something new, I say, I'm not up to that right now. It is a resistance due to lack of confidence. Mike doesn't have that hurdle to get over.

We women coming into the professions and business wanted to be invisible, so we learned one kind of behavior in order to succeed at one stage. But this same behavior makes you fail at the next stage.

Isabel summarized what she perceived as her own career problems at Austin & March:

I was only 24 when I came to work here, and I probably wasn't a very mature 24. I'm still carrying the "immature me" image here with a lot of people. I could go to the firm across the street and not have that baggage, but here I can't get rid of it. Mike came in at 34 and was fully developed. He didn't have the ghosts. I was the youngest in my class and for two years the youngest partner. So that has affected people's sense of who I am.

For me the glass ceiling is an inability to project growth and development. With men, they can see the possibilities for growth and so they influence them to develop the positive qualities, to grow in certain ways. But they can't project the same way with women. They think our qualities are fixed because they are female ones.

I've changed, but people don't understand how much I have changed. Most partners remember me then. Success or failure now depends upon how those senior partners think of me, what is locked in their collective memory.

I could have left and joined another firm if I wanted to do more corporate tax work. But I feel loyalty and ties to my clients. I can't jump around just because I am building a career. Relationships are important.

I know I am not going to be happy saying, "I make a lot of money, I'll just do my stuff." No, it will really get to me. I have to find a way to use what I do to be successful.

Step 2: Prepare the case for class discussion.

Step 3: Answer each of the following questions, individually or in small groups, as directed by your instructor:

Description
1. Briefly describe the situation at Austin & March.
2. How would you describe the relationship between Isabel and Ralph, and between Isabel and the other attorneys?

Diagnosis
3. What type of communication dysfunctions exist at Austin & March?
4. Did two-way communication occur?
5. What barriers to communication exist?
6. How did Isabel's power influence her ability to communicate?
7. What was the interaction between Isabel's communication style and her career development?

Prescription
8. What techniques could be used to improve communication?

Step 4: Discussion. In small groups, with the entire class, or in written form, share your answers to the questions above. Then answer the following questions:

1. What symptoms suggest that a problem exists?
2. What problems exist in the case?
3. What theories and concepts help explain those problems?
4. How can the problems be corrected?
5. Are the actions likely to be effective?

This case was prepared by Jeanne D. Stanton for the Institute for Case Development and Research, Simmons Graduate School of Management, Boston, MA 02215. Copyright © 1991 by the President and Trustees of Simmons College. Reprinted by permission.

Activity 7–2 | **Diagnosing Communication**

Step 1: Think about a work situation in which you have been or are currently involved.

Step 2: Complete the following questions about that situation:

1. I Think My Communication with My Subordinates:

	7 6 5 4 3 2 1	
Increases my credibility		Decreases my credibility
Is precise		Is imprecise
Is clear		Is unclear
Answers more questions than it raises		Raises more questions than it answers
Is effective		Is ineffective
Is competent		Is incompetent
Is productive		Is unproductive
Gets the results I want		Does not get the results I want
Is impressive		Is unimpressive
Creates a positive image of me		Creates a negative image of me
Is good		Is bad
Is skillful		Is unskillful
Is relaxed		Is strained
Is self-rewarding		Is not self-rewarding
Does not embarrass me		Does embarrass me

Total Score _____

2. I Think My Communication with My Supervisor:

	7 6 5 4 3 2 1	
Increases my credibility		Decreases my credibility
Is precise		Is imprecise
Is clear		Is unclear
Answers more questions than it raises		Raises more questions than it answers
Is effective		Is ineffective
Is competent		Is incompetent
Is productive		Is unproductive
Gets the results I want		Does not get the results I want
Is impressive		Is unimpressive
Creates a positive image of me		Creates a negative image of me
Is good		Is bad
Is skillful		Is unskillful
Is relaxed		Is strained
Is self-rewarding		Is not self-rewarding
Does not embarrass me		Does embarrass me

Total Score _____

3. I Think My Communication with My Peers:

	7 6 5 4 3 2 1	
Increases my credibility		Decreases my credibility
Is precise		Is imprecise
Is clear		Is unclear
Answers more questions than it raises		Raises more questions than it answers
Is effective		Is ineffective
Is competent		Is incompetent
Is productive		Is unproductive
Gets the results I want		Does not get the results I want
Is impressive		Is unimpressive
Creates a positive image of me		Creates a negative image of me
Is good		Is bad
Is skillful		Is unskillful
Is relaxed		Is strained
Is self-rewarding		Is not self-rewarding
Does not embarrass me		Does embarrass me

Total Score _____

Step 3: Score each question by adding the numbers for the responses you gave. If your total score for a question is 15–36, you have analyzed yourself as a very ineffective communicator; if your score is 37–58, you have analyzed yourself as an ineffective communicator; if your score is 59–80, you have analyzed yourself as an effective communicator; if your score is 81 or above, you have analyzed yourself as a very effective communicator.

Step 4: Discussion. In small groups, with the entire class, or in written form, as directed by your instructor, answer the following questions:

Description
1. In which type of communication are you most effective? least effective?

Diagnosis
2. What are your deficiencies as a communicator?

Prescription
3. How could you improve your communication?

Reprinted with permission from L. Sussman and P. D. Krivonos, *Communication for Supervisors and Managers*. Sherman Oaks, Calif.: Alfred Publishing, 1979.

Activity 7–3

Are You Really Listening?

Step 1: Below are some statements that were made by employees to their manager. Read each statement and select the response that best represents active listening by placing an X next to it.

1. Each day brings new problems. You solve one and here comes another. . . . What's the use?
   _____ a. I'm surprised to hear you say that.
   _____ b. That's the way it is. There's no use getting upset over it.
   _____ c. I know it's frustrating and sometimes discouraging to run into problem after problem.
   _____ d. Give me an example so I know what you're referring to.

2. At our meeting yesterday, I was counting on you for some support. All you did was sit there and you never said anything!
   _____ a. I was expecting you to ask for my opinion.
   _____ b. You're evidently upset with the way I handled things at the meeting.
   _____ c. Hey, I said some things on your behalf. You must not have heard me.
   _____ d. I had my reasons for being quiet.

3. I don't know when I'm going to get that report done. I'm already swamped with work.
   _____ a. See if you can get someone to help you.
   _____ b. All of us have been in that situation, believe me.
   _____ c. What do you mean swamped?
   _____ d. You sound concerned about your workload.

4. I've been scheduled to be out of town again on Friday. This is the third weekend in a row that's been messed up!
   _____ a. Why don't you talk with someone higher up and get it changed?
   _____ b. Going on the road must be a burden to you.
   _____ c. Everyone has to be on the road—it's part of the job.
   _____ d. I'm sure this is the last trip you'll have to make for a while.

5. It seems like other people are always getting the easy jobs. How come I always get the hard ones?
   _____ a. You feel I'm picking on you and that I'm being unfair in assigning work.
   _____ b. What evidence do you have for saying that?
   _____ c. If you'd look at the work schedule, you'd see that everyone has hard and easy jobs.
   _____ d. What about that job I gave you yesterday?

6. When I first joined this company, I thought there would be plenty of chances to move up. Here I am, four years later, still doing the same thing.
   _____ a. Let's talk about some of the things you could do to be promoted.
   _____ b. Maybe you just haven't worked hard enough.
   _____ c. Don't worry, I'm sure your chance will come soon.
   _____ d. Getting ahead must be important to you. You sound disappointed.

7. Performance evaluations are here again. I wish I could just give all my people good ratings—it sure would be easier.
   _____ a. I know, but that's not possible.
   _____ b. We all feel that way; don't get upset over it.
   _____ c. Performance evaluations seem to bother you.
   _____ d. Just do the best you can.

8. It's the same old thing day in and day out. Any child could do this job!
   _____ a. Your work is evidently getting you down and making you feel useless.
   _____ b. I always thought you liked your job.
   _____ c. What good is complaining going to do?
   _____ d. If you've got some ideas on improving your job, I'll be happy to listen.

9. I really appreciate getting the promotion. I just hope I can do the job.
   _____ a. Don't worry. I'm sure you'll get better as you get more experience.
   _____ b. What makes you think you can't do the job?
   _____ c. Don't worry. Most people have those same feelings.
   _____ d. I'm sure you can do it, or you wouldn't have been promoted.

10. I'm tired. That last sale really wore me out. I don't think I can handle another customer.
   _____ a. Sure you can. Just rest a few minutes and you'll be fine.
   _____ b. What have you been doing that's gotten you so tired?
   _____ c. You sound like you're exhausted.
   _____ d. We all get feeling that way; don't worry about it.

Step 2: Your instructor has information about the appropriate responses. You can verify your answers with these data.

Step 3: Two volunteers are to be selected. These volunteers will be asked to role-play a common communications encounter. Everyone else is to act as observers.

Step 4: As observers, be prepared to discuss the following issues:

1. Did the situation seem to be satisfactorily resolved?
2. How did active listening help resolve it? Why?
3. What barriers, if any, emerged during this activity?

4. How might you make use of this technique in interpersonal communication?

_____

Excerpt from *Organizational Behavior: Learning Guide/Experimental Exercises* by Bruce Kemelgor, copyright © 1988 by the Dryden Press, a division of Holt, Rinehart, and Winston, Inc., reprinted by permission of the publisher.

Activity 7–4

Communicating Assertively

Step 1: The following questions will be helpful in assessing your assertiveness.* Be honest in your responses. All you have to do is draw a circle around the number that describes you best. For some questions the assertive end of the scale is at 0, for others at 4. Key: 0 means no or never; 1 means somewhat or sometimes; 2 means average; 3 means usually or a good deal; and 4 means practically always or entirely.

1. When a person is highly unfair, do you call it to attention?   0 1 2 3 4
2. Do you find it difficult to make decisions?   0 1 2 3 4
3. Are you openly critical of others' ideas, opinions, behavior?   0 1 2 3 4
4. Do you speak out in protest when someone takes your place in line?   0 1 2 3 4
5. Do you often avoid people or situations for fear of embarrassment?   0 1 2 3 4
6. Do you usually have confidence in your own judgment?   0 1 2 3 4
7. Do you insist that your spouse or roommate take on a fair share of household chores?   0 1 2 3 4
8. Are you prone to "fly off the handle"?   0 1 2 3 4
9. When a salesman makes an effort, do you find it hard to say "No" even though the merchandise is not really what you want?   0 1 2 3 4
10. When a latecomer is waited on before you are, do you call attention to the situation?   0 1 2 3 4
11. Are you reluctant to speak up in a discussion or debate?   0 1 2 3 4
12. If a person has borrowed money (or a book, garment, thing of value) and is overdue in returning it, do you mention it?   0 1 2 3 4
13. Do you continue to pursue an argument after the other person has had enough?   0 1 2 3 4
14. Do you generally express what you feel?   0 1 2 3 4
15. Are you disturbed if someone watches you at work?   0 1 2 3 4
16. If someone keeps kicking or bumping your chair in a movie or a lecture, do you ask the person to stop?   0 1 2 3 4
17. Do you find it difficult to keep eye contact when talking to another person?   0 1 2 3 4
18. In a good restaurant, when your meal is improperly prepared or served, do you ask the waiter/waitress to correct the situation?   0 1 2 3 4
19. When you discover merchandise is faulty, do you return it for an adjustment?   0 1 2 3 4
20. Do you show your anger by name-calling or obscenities?   0 1 2 3 4
21. Do you try to be a wallflower or a piece of the furniture in social situations?   0 1 2 3 4
22. Do you insist that your property manager (mechanic, repairman, etc.) make repairs, adjustments or replacements which are his/her responsibility?   0 1 2 3 4
23. Do you often step in and make decisions for others?   0 1 2 3 4
24. Are you able openly to express love and affection?   0 1 2 3 4
25. Are you able to ask your friends for small favors or help?   0 1 2 3 4
26. Do you think you always have the right answer?   0 1 2 3 4

27. When you differ with a person you respect, are you able to speak up for your own viewpoint? 0 1 2 3 4
28. Are you able to refuse unreasonable requests made by friends? 0 1 2 3 4
29. Do you have difficulty complimenting or praising others? 0 1 2 3 4
30. If you are disturbed by someone smoking near you, can you say so? 0 1 2 3 4
31. Do you shout or use bullying tactics to get others to do as you wish? 0 1 2 3 4
32. Do you finish other people's sentences for them? 0 1 2 3 4
33. Do you get into physical fights with others, especially with strangers? 0 1 2 3 4
34. At family meals, do you control the conversation? 0 1 2 3 4
35. When you meet a stranger, are you the first to introduce yourself and begin a conversation? 0 1 2 3 4

Step 2: Scoring. Look at your responses to questions 1, 2, 4, 5, 6, 7, 9, 10, 11, 12, 14, 15, 16, 17, 18, 19, 21, 22, 24, 25, 27, 28, 30, and 35. These questions are oriented toward *nonassertive* behavior. Do your answers to many of these items tell you that you are rarely speaking up for yourself? Or are there perhaps some specific situations which give you trouble?

Look at your responses to questions 3, 8, 13, 20, 23, 26, 29, 31, 32, 33, and 34. These questions are oriented toward *aggressive* behavior. Do your answers to many of these questions suggest you are pushing others around more than you realized?

You may examine your *assertive* responses by noting how often you answered 3 or 4 to the questions in the first paragraph and 0 or 1 to the questions in the second paragraph. In short, it is assertive to "usually" take the action described in the first group of items, and to rarely do those things described in the second set of items.

Step 3: Check the statement indicating your most likely response to each situation below.†

1. When there's an unpleasant job that has to be done, I . . .
   a. do it myself.
   b. give it as punishment to someone who's been goofing off.
   c. hesitate to ask a subordinate to do it.
   d. ask someone to do it just the same.
2. When the boss criticizes me, I . . .
   a. feel bad.
   b. show her where she's wrong.
   c. try to learn from it.
   d. apologize for being stupid.
3. When an employee isn't working out, I . . .
   a. give him rope to hang himself.
   b. do everything I can to help him work out before I have to fire him.
   c. put off firing him as long as possible.
   d. get rid of him as quickly as possible if the guy is no good.

4. When my salary increase isn't as large as I think it should be, I . . .
   a. tell the boss in no uncertain terms what to do with it.
   b. keep quiet about it.
   c. say nothing, but take it out on the boss in other ways.
   d. feel bad.
5. When a subordinate continues to ignore instructions after I've explained something for the third time, I . . .
   a. try to give her something else to do.
   b. keep telling her until she does it.
   c. tell her that if she doesn't do it right this time, she's out the door.
   d. try to explain it in a different way.
6. When the boss rejects a good idea of mine, I . . .
   a. ask why.
   b. walk away and feel bad.
   c. try it again later.
   d. think about joining the competition.
7. When a co-worker criticizes me, I . . .
   a. give her back twice the dose she gave me.
   b. avoid her in the future.
   c. feel bad.
   d. worry that she doesn't like me.
8. When someone tells a joke I don't get, I . . .
   a. laugh with the rest of the group.
   b. say it was a lousy joke.
   c. say I didn't get it.
   d. feel stupid.
9. When someone points out a mistake I've made, I . . .
   a. sometimes deny it.
   b. feel guilty as hell.
   c. figure it's only human to make mistakes now and then.
   d. dislike the person.
10. When a subordinate fouls up a job, I . . .
    a. blow up.
    b. hate to tell him about it.
    c. hope that he'll do it right the next time.
    d. don't give him that job to do again.

11. When I have to talk to a top executive, I . . .
    a. can't look the person in the eye.
    b. feel uncomfortable.
    c. get a little nervous.
    d. enjoy the interchange.
12. When a subordinate asks me for a favor, I . . .
    a. sometimes grant it, sometimes not.
    b. feel uncomfortable if I don't grant it.
    c. never grant any favors if I can help it. It sets a bad precedent.
    d. always give in.

Step 4: Scoring.

1. Nonassertive managers hate to ask people to do unpleasant work, and they often wind up doing it themselves (answers *a* and *c*). The aggressive manager might give such odious tasks as punishments (answer *b*). The assertive manager might hesitate to ask the subordinate, but would ask just the same (answer *d*).

2. The aggressive manager argues with the boss when criticized (answer *b*). Feeling bad or guilty, though a common reaction, is a nonassertive response (answer *a*). But apologizing for being stupid is the limit (answer *d*). The assertive response, assuming the criticism is valid, is to try to learn from the remark (answer *c*).

3. The hard-nosed, authoritarian manager would get rid of a "bad" employee as quickly as possible (answer *d*). The nice-guy manager would put if off—forever, if possible (answer *c*)—and would give the poor performer rope to hang himself so the manager would feel justified in firing him (answer *a*). The assertive manager would try hard to help the employee work out, but would fire him in the end if necessary (answer *b*).

4. When people don't like a situation, but they say nothing about it, resentment builds up in them. This resentment often leads to forms of passive aggression; they "get back" in other, devious ways. Answers *b, c* and *d* are compliant reactions. Choice *a* is an aggressive reaction. No assertive choice was given here.

5. Choices *b* and *d* are both assertive ones. Choice *a*—giving the employee something else to do—is evading responsibility and a compliant reaction. Threatening is the hard-guy approach (answer *c*).

6. Planning to join the competition is passive aggression: "I'll get even; they'll be sorry!" Choices *a* and *c* are assertive responses.

7. Choice *a*—"giving her back twice the dose she gave me"—is the aggressive response. Choices *b, c,* and *d* are all nonassertive. No assertive choice was given here.

8. Choices *a* and *d* are nonassertive responses. Assertive people are not afraid to say they didn't get the joke (answer *c*). The aggressive person blames the guy for telling a lousy joke (answer *b*).

9. A common reaction when someone points out a mistake we have made is to feel guilty, to dislike the person for telling us about it, and perhaps even to deny we did it. But assertive people know they have the right to make mistakes.

10. Blowing up at an employee is a tough-guy approach, showing no respect for the employee's rights and feelings (answer *a*). Choices *b, c,* and *d* are all nonassertive responses to this problem. No assertive response was given.

11. It's normal to be a little nervous when you have to talk to an executive, but feeling so uncomfortable that you can't even look the person in the eye is extreme nonassertiveness. If you enjoy the interchange, that's assertive (answer *d*). And that's great.

12. Managers who don't feel comfortable negotiating with subordinates sometimes make a policy of not granting any favors. Nice-guy managers just about always grant favors and feel uncomfortable if they don't. The assertive manager feels free to say yes or no, depending on the circumstances (answer *a*).

Step 5: Discussion. Compare your responses to the questions in Steps 1 and 3. How assertive are you? In what situations do you act assertively? nonassertively? aggressively? How can you act more assertively? Individually, in small groups, or with the entire class, offer three to five strategies for acting more assertively.

Step 6: The instructor will divide the class into groups of three and assign each group one of the following communication styles: assertive, nonassertive, or aggressive. Your group should prepare a short role play that illustrates how you would respond to the following situation in your assigned style. (The instructor or another member of the class will assume the role of your boss during the role play.)

Your boss has recently given you an assignment that you neither like nor feel you have the qualifications to perform. You will be meeting with the boss on another matter in ten minutes and must decide whether and how to express your reaction to the assignment.

Step 7: Discussion. Compare the role plays. How was the communication the same? different? Which role plays illustrated effective communication? ineffective communication? Why?

---

*From *Your Perfect Right: A Guide to Assertive Living* (Sixth Edition) © 1990 by Robert E. Alberti and Michael L. Emmons. Reproduced by permission of Impact Publishers, Inc., P.O. Box 1094, San Luis Obispo, CA 93406. Further reproduction prohibited.

†Excerpted by permission of the publisher from *Mastering Assertiveness Skills* pp. 74–77 © 1983 Elaine Zuker. Published by AMACOM, a division of American Management Association, New York. All rights reserved.

Activity 7–5 Karl Müller (A)

Step 1: Read the Karl Müller (A) case.

LEADERSHIP AND PERFORMANCE MANAGEMENT

First Performance Review

Despite being a bit nervous, Karl Müller felt well prepared for his year-end performance review which was to take place the next day. Karl had joined Roche, a large pharmaceutical corporation, about ten months earlier, in July 1988, as a group chief. (See the partial organization chart in Figure 7–11.) His group was responsible for developing state-of-the-art testing procedures in cardiovascular research. Müller's duties also included routine testing of new compounds (in vivo and in vitro), data collection, and preparation of written and oral reports.

Robert Jackson, his boss (Section Head), had asked Karl to plan for the review by assessing his own performance, comparing it with the established expectations. He knew that his boss would use the Model Format to plan and conduct the Performance Review. (See the basic Performance Management Model in Figure 7–12.)

Karl viewed his performance over the past ten months positively, believing that he had excelled in most areas. There

were, of course, a few performance expectations which had not been met fully, but Karl felt that there had usually been sound reasons or that those areas were clearly less important than the ones where he had excelled. In Karl's opinion, the areas of excellence should compensate for those of less acceptable performance. However, Karl was not at all sure that his boss would see it that way and thus was anxious.

Because of his academic training, his previous experience, his technical skills, his creativity in problem solving and his fine publication record, Karl Müller had a great deal of confidence in himself. He believed that he had a successful career in front of him, but he was concerned that a poor initial performance review might formally and informally label him in a way which could hinder his future.

Karl had a great deal of respect for Robert Jackson, who had been employed by the company for 16 years. Jackson was extremely competent in his field and enjoyed a high reputation both inside and outside the company. In fact, Jackson's recognized leadership in the field of cardiovascular research had been a factor in Müller's application for employment. Karl very much wanted to develop a close working mentor relationship with his boss and thereby learn from his knowledge and skills. However, it seemed to Karl

Figure 7–11 **Organization Chart**

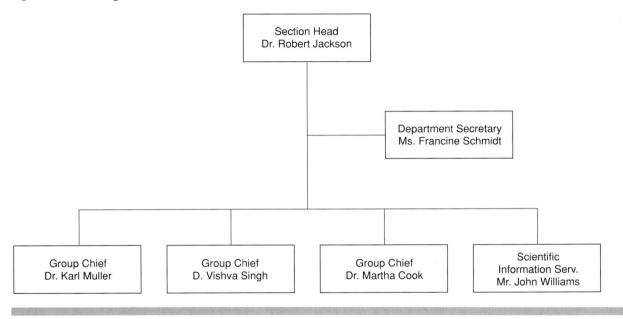

Figure 7–12 **Performance Management Model**

Basic Principles

Performance management at Roche is an *ongoing process* based on having two-way communication between managers and their staff. Managers review other managers, supervisors.

The Process

Performance management consists of three major activities:

- Planning
- Coaching
- Reviewing

Planning

Performance planning starts normally at the beginning of the new work year or planning cycle. It should also occur when a person:

- Joins the company;
- Transfers to a new work group;
- Takes on a new job;
- Has significant changes in current responsibilities.

The main objectives of planning are:

1. To clarify the person's duties and responsibilities;
2. To explain how he/she fits into the overall duties of the unit;
3. To determine the work expectations in terms of performance goals and standards, which should be both realistic and challenging as well as measurable (expected results);
4. To identify individual and personal expectations and what support he/she needs to perform well (development needs);
5. To show how the individual's contributions fit into the work plan of the unit.

Coaching

It is the manager's responsibility to monitor his/her staff's performance on an ongoing basis, not just once a year. It is the manager's responsibility to:

- Adapt the work expectations according to the evolution of the work plan during implementation;
- Create the right environment so that the employee can perform at the highest level;
- Track performance against expectations, spot particular strengths and build on them, recognize weaknesses and opportunities for improvement, provide feedback, support recognition, reinforcement, training and counseling as required.

Reviewing

Minimum of once a year, the manager should sit with the employee and review his/her performance, analyzing the actual results against expectations (agreed goals and standards).

The purpose of the review is to:

1. Confirm and reinforce the performance, coaching and feedback discussions which have taken place throughout the year;
2. Agree on ways to enhance, improve or correct performance;
3. Take stock and *learn* from the past twelve months;
4. Establish a base for setting future performance targets;
5. Discuss career goals and development needs for the future.

An effective review should conclude by summarizing the learning points, identifying the employee's strengths and weaknesses, and agreeing on new performance goals.

Figure 7–12 (Continued)

Note: The annual review is different and should take place separately from discussions about pay or merit increase. While both should be based on performance, other factors (i.e., monies available, policies and guidelines, etc.) exist in pay/merit situations. Trying to combine these discussions generally leads to:

- Overemphasis on how the money was allocated;
- Defensiveness and justification arguments;
- Comparing performance of others in the group, other groups;
- Questions about "fairness";
- Focusing almost totally on the past rather than the present and immediate future.

that this goal might not be realistic. Jackson was somewhat aloof, and his leadership style and interpersonal skills made Karl hesitate to ask for help. He feared that Jackson might judge him to be less competent than he felt he was. Also, Karl found that Jackson communicated poorly. Karl was never completely sure what Jackson wanted, following up for clarification was difficult, and Jackson never provided any direct or specific feedback afterwards. Karl would have liked to break through that apparent barrier and have access to Jackson's enormous wealth of talent. Karl also wanted his tenure in Jackson's section to be productive. Jackson's standards were high, but he did reward performance, and Karl was confident that in the end his expertise would be recognized.

Müller Analyzes His Own Performance
In preparing for the next day's meeting with his boss, Karl sought the right balance between trying to develop a closer working relationship by candidly discussing his performance, especially the areas needing improvement, with a desire to impress Jackson with his talent, skill and accomplishments to date.

Soon after Karl had joined the company, Jackson asked him to develop a new in vitro test for assessing antihypertensive activity, one that would be significantly faster and would present the results in a practical fashion, as the present method was rapidly becoming obsolete. Karl had immediately contacted one of the other group chiefs to obtain information on current testing methods and capabilities. Since then, Karl had been working evenings and sometimes on weekends studying potential new methodology as well as trying to determine the assets and liabilities of present methods. Indeed, at first Karl had not been completely knowledgeable about the current methods and old technology (some of which were unique), and it had required a bit more study than he had anticipated. Nevertheless, Karl had been truly excited about the opportunity to make a significant contribution to the section so early in his tenure.

After a few months, when Jackson began asking questions about the project, it was obvious to Karl that his boss apparently did not understand that most of Karl's time was being spent on planning and investigation in order to have a more effective and precise end result. Moreover, Jackson had never given a clear due date but, based on similar assignments in past job experiences, Karl believed he was on target. He had even tried once to clarify the due date, but Jackson had been unresponsive.

Then Karl realized that time could have been saved by seeking more help about current methods from the other group chief or from Jackson himself. However, given his newness to the section and Jackson's style, Karl had not felt comfortable about asking for help at that time.

Karl Müller's approach for developing the test had eventually been formulated. He admitted that if Jackson had clarified the expected completion date sooner, he might have taken a less complex approach. However, since Karl felt committed to the route he had chosen, it seemed better to continue with it, finishing late, rather than make a fresh start. Actually, it looked promising that Karl's creative solution would enable the final procedure to offer many advantages beyond the original request. Karl estimated he would need about four more months to accomplish this goal. In the long run, he considered the delay was worth it, even without the added efficiency he might have gained by consulting more often with Jackson or his colleagues.

Performance Standards
Since Müller had arrived only 10 months earlier, he had not been present when Jackson and his staff had discussed all the performance expectations at the beginning of the year. Thus, Karl was not sure how his boss viewed his performance compared to the nine established performance standards or what importance Jackson placed on each one. Karl assessed them as follows:

1. *Record Keeping*
For Karl Müller, record keeping was an essential part of the job, and he emphasized it with the people who worked in his area. In fact, he believed that this standard, which depended on accurate, well-organized and easily retrievable

information, should have been weighted higher than some others like report writing. Müller was very proud of his accomplishments in record keeping. He had installed some forms and systems which had made data analysis and data reduction more efficient, thus enabling reports to be compiled more rapidly. Performance in this area had directly contributed to productivity and, Karl believed, should compensate for some of the problems he had had with lesser standards.

2. *Productivity and Planning*
For the most part, Karl felt he was sufficiently productive. Expectations were clear, due to written schedules, especially with the routine testing that his group performed. As Karl did not have to depend on others for regular performance feedback, he had more flexibility and independence. In fact, Karl had been able to beat three target dates through creative problem solving, good planning and hard work. Perhaps Jackson did not know about the third early completion, as he had been out of the country on an extended trip. Karl had, however, received an appreciative phone call from the project manager. Thus, Karl was justifiably proud of his record in this area.

3. *Quality*
All GLPs (Good Laboratory Practices) had been met, and each procedure had been executed using the most exacting levels of qualitative standards. Karl felt that he and his staff had achieved a high productivity level while maintaining excellent quality.

4. *Written Reports*
Müller was not sure how much Jackson valued this standard. At first, Karl had not understood the approved outline, but after some assistance from his peers, he had grasped it. Karl only realized that his reports had been done incorrectly when several were rejected, although specific reasons had never been clearly stated. Overall, Müller felt that the actual reports were acceptable, but he did recognize some weaknesses existed. More graphics and tables could have been used to clarify the subject matter. He also knew that he could improve his basic writing skills; he needed better organization and a more logical flow between sections, leading to a final set of recommendations and conclusions. However, the content of his reports was conceptually strong and based on solid scientific skills. Karl also had a fine record of publications to his credit.

5. *Oral Presentations*
As with his written reports, Karl's oral presentations were based on the results of a strong scientific foundation. Müller did not feel as limited by this medium as he did by the written report. He could clarify points, reference data and interact with members of his audience more easily. Moreover, their immediate feedback and reactions enabled him to be more responsive. Karl found it stimulating to speak in front of groups. He spent a lot of time preparing his oral reports because he believed that he might be influencing important scientific decisions. But, here again, he was not sure how Jackson viewed this standard.

6. *Teamwork*
Karl ran a team-oriented group. Even when they functioned independently, they were aware of each other's projects, ready to help if necessary. When they collaborated on an assignment, Karl always encouraged developing a strong partnership. He kept the group fully informed through work team meetings about more global issues, so they knew where their work fitted into the larger research and business picture. Karl also organized group discussions about technical problems in order to seek creative solutions and maintain high motivation. Müller wanted this style to be the section norm, not only with other groups, but especially with regard to Jackson's leadership style. Karl himself had no doubt about the relationship between his approach to his group and resulting productivity.

7. *Service*
Karl knew service was a problem area. His labs had conducted some routine testing for other departments, and there had been complaints that he had not responded quickly enough to requests which were apparently of high priority. Karl thought that this was another area where Jackson could be more explicit about which people and which projects should have priority. Karl was sure that once the new testing procedure he was developing came on line, normally accepted backlogs would become a thing of the past. He even anticipated getting "extra service credit" in this area.

8. *Housekeeping and Safety*
Müller knew it was important to maintain a high level of performance in this area, and he believed he was exemplary.

9. *Professional Development*
Karl felt that he and his group were maintaining the "state of the art" adequately. He kept up with journal articles and attended selective seminars regularly. He hoped that he could expand the literature coverage of his group by delegating more to his subordinates.

Müller's Conclusions
Müller was confident that he had performed well, a fact which he assumed would become clear to Jackson during their discussion. Karl hoped that the areas needing improvement could be examined and discussed more openly than they had been to date. He felt that a mutual exchange would allow him to explain his problems and also learn how Jackson viewed his performance. He was convinced that such a dialogue would enable him to clarify Jackson's expectations and their relative value and priority.

Figure 7–13 **The Roche Leadership Charter**

(A consolidation of input from group work during management training sessions)

An effective Roche leader is someone who:
1. Is honest and leads by example;
2. Communicates (has a vision, speaks clearly and listens carefully);
3. Gives directions when necessary, sets realistic goals for him/herself and with the team, provides challenges, monitors performance, gives feedback, and provides recognition and reward;
4. Gets things implemented (cuts through bureaucracy);
5. Coaches and supports his/her team members;
6. Creates an environment where people can perform at the highest level and gets their commitment;
7. Delegates (assigns the right tasks to the right people and helps them use and develop their talents);
8. Informs and stimulates information sharing;
9. Creates an atmosphere where new and unconventional ideas can develop and lead to innovative change;
10. Encourages teamwork (within and with other units), the "WE" culture.

Figure 7–14 **Performance Review Skills (For the Employee)**

The performance review has three phases:

- Planning the review
- Implementing the review
- Learning from the review

Planning
Prepare your review meeting focusing on the following:

- What did you do very well? (your strengths)
- Where were you a bit weak? (improvement areas)
- What do you suggest for the future?

Try to be as factual as possible, take some notes, avoid the "justification" syndrome or being on the defensive, be positive and approach the meeting as a learning experience. Review what you have achieved against the expected results.

Implementing
During the review meeting, be ready to:

1. Present your views to the manager *before* getting his/her reactions to your performance.
2. Listen to your supervisor's perceptions regarding your strengths and weaknesses (record them as they are presented to you).
3. Discuss and resolve differences (be analytical, avoid being emotional, control the process so it is as constructive as possible).
4. Summarize the meeting.
5. Agree on new expectations (including personal ones).

Learning
Immediately after the meeting, write down:

- Agreements;
- Commitments (from both sides);
- The action plan you will implement;
- What you learned from the review;
- What your future prospects are.

Karl also had two other goals. Since the company was placing increased importance on good leadership and management skills, Karl wanted to discuss his ideas with Jackson. Karl's previous employer had valued his supervisory and management skills, and therefore Karl felt strong in this area. Jackson had mentioned that he wanted everyone with supervisory responsibilities who reported directly to him to participate in establishing standards for effective leadership and management. He had handed out copies of a leadership charter (see Figure 7–13) that had been prepared during a research management training program and had asked each one to use it as a basis for developing this standard. If time permitted, Karl wanted to discuss the charter with Jackson. His second goal was to reach an agreement or understanding regarding the need for better communication, feedback and, hopefully, the beginning of the mentor relationship he desired.

At the end of his own assessment, Karl was still nervous about this first review. Although he had finished the first phase of a performance review (planning), he still was expected to participate fully in the discussion, and this required different skills (see the Performance Review skills in Figure 7–14). However, since he felt well prepared, Karl was determined to be candid and specific, if given the opportunity. He really wanted Jackson to see him as an asset to his section and the company.

Step 2: Prepare the case for class discussion.

Step 3: Answer each of the following questions, individually or in small groups, as directed by your instructor:

Description
1. Briefly describe Karl's view of his performance.
2. How would you describe the relationship between Karl and his boss?

Diagnosis
3. How effective is communication at Roche? What dysfunctions exist?

4. What barriers to communication exist?
5. Using your knowledge of motivation, perception, and attribution, evaluate Karl's performance.

Prescription
8. How should Karl proceed in the appraisal interview?

Step 4: The instructor should divide the class into groups of two—Müller and Jackson. Your instructor will then distribute a case describing Jackson's view to each person playing him. Both Müller and Jackson should spend five to ten minutes "getting in role."

Step 5: The two participants will conduct the role play.

Step 6: Discussion. In small groups, with the entire class, or in written form, share your answers to the questions above. Then answer the following questions:

1. What symptoms suggest that a problem exists?
2. What problems exist in the case?
3. What theories and concepts help explain those problems?
4. How can the problems be corrected?
5. Are the actions likely to be effective?

This case was developed in cooperation with Hoffmann–La Roche, Inc., Nutley, N.J. It was prepared by Béatrice Balthazart under the supervision of Professor Pierre Casse as a basis for class discussion rather than to illustrate either effective or ineffective handling of an administrative situation. Copyright © 1989 by IMEDE, Lausanne, Switzerland. The International Institute for Management Development (IMD), resulting from the merger between IMEDE, Lausanne, and IMI, Geneva, acquires and retains all rights. Reproduced by permission.

Activity 7–6 **CNN** Video: Hechinger Hardware and Home Improvement

Step 1: View the CNN video segment about Hechinger Hardware.

Step 2: Discussion. In small groups or with the entire class, answer the following questions:

1. What is Hechinger's philosophy about communication?

2. How does he implement this philosophy?
3. What indications suggest that it positively affects workers and customers?
4. What three lessons about how an organizational member should communicate did you learn from this video?

CONCLUDING COMMENTS

Ineffective communication may be the biggest problem facing organizations. People's perceptions of and attributions for particular events and people affect the way they communicate with each other—the way they send messages and receive them. When different people have different perceptions, slipups and misunderstandings can occur in their communication.

In this chapter you had the opportunity to diagnose communication in a work situation in which you have been involved as well as in the Isabel Stewart case and the Hechinger Hardware video segment. You also examined communication in a performance appraisal interview in the Karl Müller case. In "Are You Really Listening?" and "Communicating Assertively," you practiced strategies for increasing your communication effectiveness.

ENDNOTES

[1] Excerpted from F. Rice, Champions of communication, *Fortune* (June 3, 1991): 111–120. Reprinted by permission from *Fortune* magazine; © 1991 The Time Inc. Magazine Company. All rights reserved.

[2] K. J. Krone, F. M. Jablin, and L. L. Putnam, Communication theory and organizational communication: Multiple perspectives. In F. Jablin, L. Putnam, K. Roberts, and L. Porter, eds., *Handbook of Organizational Communication: An Interdisciplinary Perspective* (Newbury Park, Calif.: Sage, 1987); P. G. Clampitt, *Communication for Managerial Effectiveness* (Newbury Park, Calif.: Sage, 1991).

[3] G. L. Kreps, *Organizational Communication,* 2nd ed. (New York: Longman, 1990).

[4] J. Sullivan, N. Kameda, and T. Nobu, Bypassing in managerial communication, *Business Horizons* 34(1) (1991): 71–80.

[5] W. V. Haney, *Communication and Organizational Behavior* (Homewood, Ill.: Irwin, 1979).

[6] D. Fisher, *Communication in Organizations* (St. Paul, Minn.: West, 1981).

[7] See M. L. Knapp, *Nonverbal Communication in Human Interaction* (New York: Holt, Rinehart and Winston, 1972); P. Ekman, Communication through nonverbal behavior. In S. S. Tomkins and C. E. Izard, eds., *Affect, Cognition, and Personality* (New York: Springer, 1965).

[8] C. L. McKenzie and C. J. Qazi, Communication barriers in the workplace, *Business Horizons* 26 (March-April 1983): 70–72.

[9] P. R. Harris and R. T. Moran, *Managing Cultural Differences,* 3rd ed. (Houston: Gulf, 1991).

[10] R. L. Daft and R. H. Lengel, Organizational information requirements, media richness and structural design, *Management Science* 32 (1986): 554–571.

[11] R. H. Lengel and R. L. Daft, The selection of communication media as an executive skill, *Academy of Management Executive* 2 (1988): 225–232.

[12] *Ibid.*

[13] R. C. Huseman and E. W. Miles, Organizational communication in the information age, *Journal of Management* 14(2) (1988); 181–204.

[14] Kreps, *Organizational Communication.*

[15] The discussion of load is primarily based on J. W. Gibson and R. M. Hodgetts, *Organizational Communication: A Managerial Perspective,* 2nd ed. (New York: HarperCollins, 1991).

[16] *Ibid.*

[17] D. B. Rogers and R. E. Farson, Active listening. In D. Kolb, I. Rubin, and J. McIntire, eds., *Organizational Psychology: Readings on Human Behavior in Organizations* (Englewood Cliffs, N.J.: Prentice-Hall, 1984).

[18] See, for example, D. Tannen, *You Just Don't Understand: Women and Men in Conversation* (New York: William Morrow, 1990); S. S. Case, Cultural differences, not deficiencies: An analysis of managerial women's language. In S. Rose and L. Larwood, eds., *Women's Careers: Pathways and Pitfalls* (New York: Praeger, 1988).

[19] Tannen, *You Just Don't Understand.*

[20] Case, Cultural differences.

[21] E. W. Morrison and R. J. Bies, Impression management in the feedback-seeking process: A literature review and research agenda, *Academy of Management Review* 16(3) (1991): 522–541.

[22] P. V. Lewis, *Organizational Communication: The Essence of Effective Management* 3rd ed. (New York: Wiley, 1987).

[23] M. E. Schnake, M. P. Dumler, D. S. Cochran, and T. R. Barnett, Effects of differences in superior and subordinate perceptions of superiors' communication practices, *Journal of Business Communication* 27(1) (1990): 37–50.

[24] E. M. Eisenberg and M. G. Witten, Reconsidering openness in organizational communication, *Academy of Management Review* 12 (1987): 418–426.

[25] Lewis, *Organizational Communication*.

[26] Kreps, *Organizational Communication*.

[27] H. Aldrich and D. Herker, Boundary-spanning roles and organization structure, *Academy of Management Review* 2 (1977): 217–230.

[28] C. A. O'Reilly and L. R. Pondy, Organizational communication. In *Organizational Behavior,* ed. S. Kerr (Columbus, Ohio: Grid, 1979).

[29] Lewis, *Organizational Communication*.

[30] D. W. Johnson and F. P. Johnson, *Joining Together: Group Theory and Group Skills* (Englewood Cliffs, N.J.: Prentice-Hall, 1975).

[31] E. Rogers and R. Agarwala-Rogers, *Communication in Organizations* (New York: Free Press, 1976).

[32] P. R. Monge, J. M. Brismier, A. L. Cook, P. D. Day, J. A. Edwards, and K. K. Kriste, Determinants of communication structure in large organizations. Paper presented at the meeting of the International Communication Association, Portland, May 1976. Cited in Kreps, *Organizational Communication*.

[33] P. R. Monge and E. M. Eisengerg, Emergent communication networks. In Jablin et al., *Handbook of Organizational Communication*.

[34] E. H. Schein, Improving face-to-face relationships, *Sloan Management Review* (Winter 1981): 43–52.

[35] L. Copeland, Making costs count in international travel, *Personnel Administrator* (July 1984): 47.

[36] Harris and Moran, *Managing Cultural Differences*.

[37] W. W. Hildebrandt, A Chinese managerial view of business communication, *Management Communication Quarterly* 2 (November 1988): 217–234.

[38] U.S.-Japanese management enters a new generation, *Management Review* (February 1991): 42–45.

[39] W. B. Gudykunst and S. Ting-Toomey, *Culture and Interpersonal Communication* (Newbury Park, Calif.: Sage, 1988).

[40] N. Sussman and H. Rosenfeld, Influence of culture, language, and sex on conversational distance, *Journal of Personality and Social Psychology* 42 (1982): 66–74.

[41] N. J. Adler, *International Dimensions of Organizational Behavior,* 2nd ed. (Boston: PWS-Kent, 1991).

[42] R. C. Maddox and D. Short, The cultural integrator, *Business Horizons* 31 (November-December 1988): 57–59.

[43] J. R. Gibb, Defensive communication, *ETC: A Review of General Semantics* 22 (1965).

[44] W. G. Dyer, *The Sensitive Manipulator* (Provo, Utah: Brigham Young University Press, 1980).

[45] D. A. Whetton and K. W. Cameron, *Developing Management Skills* (Glenview, Ill.: Scott, Foresman, 1984), p. 209.

[46] J. Hall, Communication revised, *California Management Review* 15 (1973); J. Luft, *Group Processes: An Introduction to Group Dynamics* (Palo Alto, Calif.: Mayfield, 1970).

[47] L. Sussman, Managers: On the defensive, *Business Horizons* 34(1) (1991): 81–87.

[48] R. E. Alberti and M. L. Emmons, *Your Perfect Right* (San Luis Obispo, Calif.: Impact, 1982).

[49] E. Zuker, *Mastering Assertiveness Skills* (New York: AMACOM, 1983), p. 79.

[50] A. J. Lange and P. Jakubowski, *Responsible Assertive Behavior* (Champaign, Ill.: Research Press, 1976).

[51] A. S. Tsui and B. Barry, Interpersonal affect and rating errors, *Academy of Management Journal* 29 (1986): 586–599.

[52] See, for example, R. Jacobs and S. W. J. Kozlowski, A closer look at halo error in performance ratings, *Academy of Management Journal* 28 (1985): 201–212.

RECOMMENDED READINGS

Asante, M. K., and Gudykunst, W. M. *Handbook of Intercultural Communication*. Newbury Park, Calif.: Sage, 1989.

Clampitt, P. G. *Communicating for Managerial Effectiveness*. Newbury Park, Calif.: Sage, 1991.

Corman, S. R., Banks, S. P., Bantz, C. R., and Mayer, M. E., eds. *Foundations of Organizational Communication: A Reader*. New York: Longman, 1990.

Gibson, J. W., and Hodgetts, R. M. *Organizational Communication: A Managerial Perspective*, 2nd ed. New York: HarperCollins, 1991.

Goldhaber, G. *Organizational Communication*, 5th ed. Dubuque, Iowa: Wm. C. Brown, 1990.

Kreps, G. L. *Organizational Communication*, 2nd ed. New York: Longman, 1990.

Stewart, C. J., and Cash, W. B., Jr. *Interviewing: Principles and Practices*, 5th ed. Dubuque, Iowa: Wm. C. Brown, 1988.

Chapter Outline

Evaluating Leadership and Leading Effectively

Learning Objectives

After completing the reading and activities in Chapter 8, students will be able to

1. Comment about the issues for leading in a global environment.

2. Show how trait theories contributed to our understanding of effective leadership.

3. Specify the behavioral dimensions of leadership and diagnose their existence.

4. Describe the nature of managerial work.

5. Describe the early situational theories and their implications for effective leadership.

6. Describe contemporary leadership theories and their implications for effective leadership.

7. Describe the attribution model of leadership and its significance for leadership effectiveness.

8. Discuss possible substitutes for leadership and their impact on organizational behavior.

9. Offer a prescription for becoming a transformational leader.

10. Describe superleadership and its implications for effective leadership.

11. Offer a protocol for leading a diverse work force.

12. Offer a strategy for effective leadership.

Leading Manufacturing Workers to Improved Performance

Last fall, Tellabs, Inc., a maker of sophisticated telephone equipment, received an important order that would have to be completed by the end of the year. Instead of simply posting overtime notices, as would happen in many factories, Grace Pastiak called a meeting of the plant's workers.

"I knew that it was getting into the holiday season and many of the people would have family demands," said Mrs. Pastiak, director of manufacturing for one of three operating divisions.

Standing on a ladder in the middle of the plant, she spoke to the workers. "I gave them some choices," she said. "I said we could tell marketing we could only do half. We could bring in contract labor, or we could shift some production outside. After we talked about it, they said, 'Go for it' and that's what we did." The workers readily put in overtime to get the job done on time.

Mrs. Pastiak, appears to be not just another plant manager. Instead of writing memoirs or limiting her discussions to one or more lieutenants, she prefers a more personal approach. She communicates directly with her people on the plant floor, trying to infect them with a zeal for producing high-quality products. And she fiddles endlessly in search of a better production set-up. . . .

"I have the bias that people do better when they are happy," said Mrs. Pastiak, who attributes her style in part to her education in sociology and early jobs in social work. "The old style of beating on people to get things done does not work." . . .

Mrs. Pastiak is regarded by both her bosses and subordinates as an effective manager, and the numbers seem to back this up. She meets production targets 98 percent of the time, compared with an industry standard that she puts near 90 percent. And it is a record she keeps without seeming to be preoccupied with the output, attendance and cost reports that are the production manager's staples. . . .

Speaking to factory workers gathered in a conference room, she bubbles with enthusiasm as she goes over her personal formula for improving quality by systematic problem solving. An astute instructor making sure her students get the message, she repeatedly focuses their attention: "What is the purpose? What is the process? And what is the payoff?"[1]

Why is Grace Pastiak considered an effective leader? In this chapter we look at both the historical and contemporary theories about leadership, show how they explain Pastiak's effectiveness, and discuss their implications for effective leadership in a global environment. We consider an array of theories, and take an eclectic approach by using several of them for a multifaceted diagnosis of leadership effectiveness.

LEADING IN A GLOBAL ENVIRONMENT

A global manager is a sensitive, innovative, and participative leader who can communicate interculturally, builds on cultural differences through international collaboration, and leads change in the organization to improve intercultural performance.[2] Such a manager must continuously acquire current information about the culture in which he or she is functioning and adapt his or her leadership style to it.

Figure 8–1 shows one clustering of countries based on the importance of work, satisfaction with work, attitudes toward work, personal values, and interpersonal values. Leadership in particular seems to be a function of four dimensions along which these countries can differ: (1) traditionalism versus modernity, (2) particularism (institutional obligations to family and friends) versus universalism (institutional obligations to society), (3) idealism versus pragmatism, and (4) collectivism versus individualism.[3] Consider two studies. One study compared the self-reported behav-

Figure 8–1   **Synthesis of Country Clusters**

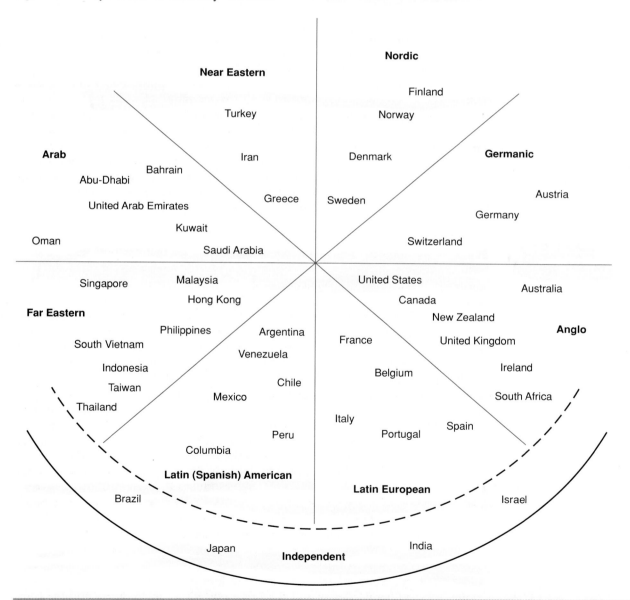

SOURCE: Reprinted with permission from S. Ronen and O. Shenkar, Clustering countries on attitudinal dimensions: A review and synthesis, *Academy of Management Review* 10 (1985): 449.

iors of American expatriate managers in Hong Kong, American managers in the United States, and Hong Kong Chinese managers in Hong Kong.[4] The results showed that American managers in Hong Kong reported behaviors similar to those of American managers in the United States; although these behaviors were positively related to job performance in the United States, they were not linked to performance in Hong Kong. A second study suggested that management in the Republic of China is influenced by different prevailing forces than elsewhere, including socialism, feudalistic values, and the use of side payments. Because of this context, managers try to establish warm relations with each worker, do favors for workers, take a family orientation, and push for reform.[5]

Countries differ in their views of the traits of effective leaders. North Americans value charisma, but West Germans do not.[6] Managers must also recognize that leadership should fit with the specific culture in which it is occurring; for example, participative management either does not work for all cultures or must be adapted to a particular culture.[7]

Today, corporate visions must become transnational, and managers must be able to adjust their style when working with individuals from other countries.[8] The need becomes particularly obvious with the breakdown of national boundaries and the demise of international superpowers. In multinational organizations, executives can place parent-country nationals, home-country nationals, or third-country nationals in leadership positions. These leaders bring cultural biases to the organizational situations that likely influence their effectiveness. In the rest of this chapter we focus primarily on leadership in the United States, but acknowledge areas where cultural differences will influence leadership effectiveness.

THE TRAIT PERSPECTIVE

Trait theory suggests that we can evaluate leadership and propose ways of leading effectively by considering whether an individual possesses certain personality traits, social traits, and physical characteristics.[9] Popular in the 1940s and 1950s, trait theory attempted to predict which individuals successfully became leaders and then whether they were effective. Leaders differ from nonleaders in their drive (achievement, ambition, energy, tenacity, and initiative), desire to lead, honesty and integrity, self-confidence, cognitive ability, and knowledge of business.[10] Even the traits judged necessary for top, middle, and low-level management differed among leaders of different countries; for example, United States and British managers valued resourcefulness, the Japanese intuition, and the Dutch imagination, but for lower and middle managers only.[11] Leaders' traits and skills also included those shown in Figure 8–2. Does Grace Pastiak have such traits? Does she interact often and well with others? Does she show patience, tact, and sympathy? Is she tall, neither too heavy or too thin, and physically attractive? Does she demonstrate social maturity?

Now, can you think of any individuals whom you consider effective leaders but who lack these characteristics? Skills, vision, and the ability to implement the vision are necessary to transform traits into leadership behavior.[12] Individual capability, which is a function of background predispositions, preferences, cognitive complexity, and technical, human relations, and conceptual skills also contribute.[13]

The use of the trait approach has more historical than practical interest to managers, even though recent research has once again tied leadership effectiveness to leader traits. One study of senior management jobs suggests that effective leadership requires a broad knowledge of and solid relations within the industry and the company, an excellent reputation, a strong track record, a keen mind, strong interpersonal skills, high integrity, high energy, and a strong drive to lead.[14] In addition,

Figure 8–2 **Traits and Skills Found Most Frequently to Be Characteristic of Successful Leaders**

Traits	Skills
Adaptable to situations	Clever (intelligent)
Alert to social environment	Conceptually skilled
Ambitious and achievement-oriented	Creative
Assertive	Diplomatic and tactful
Cooperative	Fluent in speaking
Decisive	Knowledgeable about group task
Dependable	Organized (administrative ability)
Dominant (desire to influence others)	Persuasive
Energetic (high activity level)	Socially skilled
Persistent	
Self-confident	
Tolerant of stress	
Willing to assume responsibility	

SOURCE: Reprinted with permission from Gary Yukl, *Leadership in Organizations,* 2nd ed. (Englewood Cliffs, N.J.: Prentice Hall, 1989), p. 176. Copyright © 1989 by Prentice Hall.

some view the transformational perspective described later in this chapter as a natural evolution of the earlier trait perspective.

THE BEHAVIORAL VIEW

Limitations in the ability of traits to predict effective leadership caused researchers during the 1950s to view a person's *behavior* rather than that individual's personal traits as a way of increasing leadership effectiveness. This view also paved the way for later situational theories.

The types of leadership behaviors investigated typically fell into two categories: production oriented and employee oriented. *Production-oriented leadership,* also called concern for production, initiating structure, or task-focused leadership, involves acting primarily to get the task done. A supervisor who tells his or her subordinates that they should do "everything they can to get the job done on time" demonstrates production-oriented leadership. So does a manager who uses an autocratic style or fails to involve workers in any aspect of decision making. *Employee-oriented leadership,* also called concern for people or consideration, focuses on supporting the individual workers in their activities and involving the workers in decision making. A boss who demonstrates great concern for his or her workers' satisfaction with their jobs and commitment to their work has an employee-oriented leadership style. Such a superior often involves workers in departmental decisions.

Studies in leadership at Ohio State University, which classified individuals' style as initiating structure or consideration, examined the link between style and grievance rate, performance, and turnover, as shown in Table 8–1.[15] *Initiating structure* reflects the degree to which the leader structures his or her own role and subordinates' roles toward accomplishing the group's goal through scheduling work, assigning employees to tasks, and maintaining standards of performance. *Consideration* refers to the degree to which the leader emphasizes individuals' needs through two-way communication, respect for subordinates' ideas, mutual trust between leader and subordinates, and consideration of subordinates' feelings. Although leaders can choose the style to fit the outcomes they desire, in fact, to achieve desirable outcomes on all three dimensions of performance, grievance rate, and turnover, the research suggested that managers should strive to demonstrate both initiating structure and con-

Table 8–1 Out-
comes of the Ohio
State Leadership
Studies' Behavioral
Model

		Manager's Initiating Structure	
		High	Low
Manager's Consideration	High	High performance Low grievance rate Low turnover	Low performance Low grievance rate Low turnover
	Low	High performance High grievance rate High turnover	Low performance High grievance rate High turnover

sideration. How well did Grace Pastiak fit this model of effective leadership? She seemed to be high on both dimensions, emphasizing both consideration for her employees and structuring of tasks to ensure that the work was accomplished.

A series of leadership studies at the University of Michigan, which looked at managers with an employee orientation and a production orientation, yielded similar results.[16] In these studies, which related differences in high-productivity and low-productivity work groups to differences in supervisors, highly productive supervisors spent more time in planning departmental work and in supervising their employees; they spent less time in working alongside and performing the same tasks as subordinates, accorded their subordinates more freedom in specific task performance, and tended to be employee oriented.[17] Clearly, Grace Pastiak's behavior also fits with the findings of this research. She spends time in planning and supervising, but also allows her subordinates discretion in task performance.

A thirty-year research study in Japan examined *performance* and *maintenance* leadership behaviors.[18] Performance here refers specifically to forming and reaching group goals through fast work speed; outcomes of high quality, accuracy, and quantity; and observation of rules. Maintenance behaviors preserve the group's social stability by dealing with subordinates' feelings, reducing stress, providing comfort, and showing appreciation. The Japanese, according to this and other studies, prefer leadership high on both dimensions over performance-dominated behavior except when work is done in short-term project groups, subordinates are prone to anxiety, or effective performance calls for very low effort.[19]

MANAGERIAL ROLES

Henry Mintzberg's study of chief executive officers suggested a different way of looking at leadership.[20] He observed that managerial work encompasses ten roles: three that focus on *interpersonal* contact—(1) figurehead, (2) leader, (3) liaison; three that involve mainly *information processing*—(4) monitor, (5) disseminator, (6) spokesman; and four related to *decision making*—(7) entrepreneur, (8) disturbance handler, (9) resource allocator, and (10) negotiator. Table 8–2 offers a brief description of each role; note that almost all roles would include activities that could be construed as leadership—influencing others toward a particular goal. In addition, most of these roles can apply to nonmanagerial positions as well as managerial ones. The role approach resembles the behavioral and trait perspectives because all three call for specific types of behavior independent of the situation; however, the role approach is more compatible with the situation approach and has been shown to be more valid than either the behavioral or trait perspective.

Table 8–2 **Mintz-berg's Roles**

Role	Description
Figurehead	The manager, acting as a symbol or representative of the organization, performs diverse ceremonial duties. By attending Chamber of Commerce meetings, heading the local United Way drive, or representing the president of the firm at an awards banquet, a manager performs the figurehead role.
Leader	The manager, interacting with subordinates, motivates and develops them. The supervisor who conducts quarterly performance interviews or selects training opportunities for his or her subordinates performs the role of leader. This role emphasizes the socioemotional and people-oriented side of leadership and deemphasizes task activities, which are more often incorporated into the decisional roles.
Liaison	The manager establishes a network of contacts to gather information for the organization. Belonging to professional associations or meeting over lunch with peers in other organizations helps the manager perform the liaison role.
Monitor	The manager gathers information from the environment inside and outside the organization. He or she may attend meetings with subordinates, scan company publications, or participate in companywide committees as a way of performing this role.
Disseminator	The manager transmits both factual and value information to subordinates. Managers may conduct staff meetings, send memoranda to their staff, or meet informally with them on a one-to-one basis to discuss current and future projects.
Spokesperson	The manager gives information to people outside the organization about its performance and policies. He or she oversees preparation of the annual report, prepares advertising copy, or speaks at community and professional meetings.
Entrepreneur	The manager designs and initiates change in the organization. The supervisor who redesigns the jobs of subordinates, introduces flexible working hours, or brings new technology to the job performs this role.
Disturbance handler	The manager deals with problems that arise when organizational operations break down. A person who finds a new supplier on short notice for an out-of-stock part, who replaces unexpectedly absent employees, or who deals with machine breakdowns performs this role.
Resource allocator	The manager controls the allocation of people, money, materials, and time by scheduling his or her own time, programming subordinates' work effort, and authorizing all significant decisions. Preparation of the budget is a major aspect of this role.
Negotiator	The manager participates in negotiation activities. A manager who hires a new employee may negotiate work assignments or compensation with that person.

SOURCE: These roles are drawn from H. Mintzberg, *The Nature of Managerial Work* (Englewood Cliffs, N.J.: Prentice-Hall, 1979).

Though not all managers will perform every role, some diversity of role performance must occur. Managers can diagnose their own and others' role performance and then offer strategies for altering it. Table 8–3 shows the most frequent roles played by a variety of managers. The choice of roles will depend to some extent on the

Table 8–3 **Eight Managerial Job Types**

Managerial Job Type	Key Roles	Examples
Contact person	Liaison, figurehead	Sales manager Chief executives in service industries
Political manager	Spokesperson, negotiator	Top government, hospital, university managers
Entrepreneur	Entrepreneur, negotiator	Owner of small, young business CEO of rapidly changing, large organization
Insider	Resource allocator	Middle or senior production or operations manager Manager rebuilding after crisis
Real-time manager	Disturbance handler	Foreman Head of organization in crisis Head of small, one-manager business
Team manager	Leader	Hockey coach Head of R&D group
Expert manager	Monitor, spokesperson	Head of specialist group
New manager	Liaison, monitor	Manager in a new job

SOURCE: Adapted from H. Mintzberg, *The Nature of Managerial Work* (Englewood Cliffs, N.J.: Prentice-Hall, 1973).

manager's specific job description and the situation in question. For example, Figure 8–3 shows that managing individual performance and instructing subordinates are less important for middle managers than for first-line supervisors, and less important for executives than for either lower level of manager.[21]

Two other sets of managerial behaviors are shown in Tables 8–4 and 8–5. The Leader Observation System (LOS) identifies a second set of managerial behaviors derived from observations of those in managerial positions with supervisory responsibilities.[22] The Integrating Taxonomy includes behaviors shown to be related to managerial effectiveness.[23]

Consider some managers you have observed. Now consider your own performance in managerial roles. Finally, consider Grace Pastiak's performance. What roles did a manager perform in each of these situations? Did the managers limit themselves to one or two roles, or perform a range or roles? Should they have performed some roles more frequently? Should they have performed some less frequently? Mintzberg's view of managerial behavior, as well as the LOS categories, offer a diagnostic perspective that allows managers to develop a protocol for action. Introducing the leadership style that fits best with the situation, as described in the next sections, strengthens this protocol.

EARLY SITUATIONAL THEORIES

Contingency or situational models differ from the earlier trait and behavioral models in asserting that no single way of leading works in all situations. Rather, appropriate behavior depends on the circumstances at a given time. Effective managers diagnose

Figure 8–3 **Supervising Individuals**

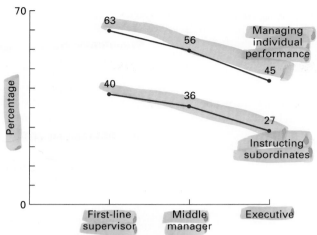

Numbers refer to the percentage of managers who said the task was of "the utmost" or "considerable" importance.

SOURCE: Reprinted with permission from A. I. Kraut, P. R. Pedigo, D. D. McKenna, and M. D. Dunnette, The role of the manager: What's really important in different management jobs, *Academy of Management Executive* 3(4) (1989): 287.

the situation, identify the leadership style that will be most effective, and then determine whether they can implement the required style. Early situational research suggested that subordinate, supervisor, and task considerations affect the appropriate leadership style in a given situation, as shown in Table 8–6. The precise aspects of each dimension that influence the most effective leadership style vary.

McGregor's Theory X and Theory Y

One of the older situational theories—McGregor's Theory X–Theory Y formulation—calls for a leadership style based on individuals' assumptions about other individuals, together with characteristics of the individual, the task, the organization, and the environment.[24] Although managers may have many styles, Theories X and Y have received the greatest attention. *Theory X* managers assume that people are lazy, extrinsically motivated, and incapable of self-discipline or self-control, and that they want security and no responsibility in their jobs. *Theory Y* managers assume people do not inherently dislike work, are intrinsically motivated, exert self-control, and seek responsibility. A Theory X manager, because of his or her limited view of the world, has only one leadership style available: autocratic. A Theory Y manager has a wide range of styles in his or her repertoire. Figure 8–4 summarizes this contingency perspective. It illustrates the way assumptions influence action tendencies, which together with internal and external modifiers should prescribe effective leadership behavior.

How can a manager use McGregor's theory for ensuring leadership effectiveness? What prescription would McGregor offer for improving the situation? If a manager had Theory X assumptions, he would suggest that the manager change them and would facilitate this change by sending the manager to management development programs. If a manager had Theory Y assumptions, McGregor would advise a diagnosis of the situation to ensure that the selected style matched the manager's assumptions and action tendencies, as well as the internal and external influences on the situation.

Table 8–4   **The LOS Categories and Behavioral Descriptors**

1. **Planning/Coordinating**
   a. setting goals & objectives
   b. defining tasks needed to accomplish goals
   c. scheduling employees, timetables
   d. assigning tasks and providing routine instructions
   e. coordinating activities of each subordinate to keep work running smoothly
   f. organizing the work

2. **Staffing**
   a. developing job descriptions for position openings
   b. reviewing applications
   c. interviewing applicants
   d. hiring
   e. contacting applicants to inform them of being hired or not
   f. "filling in" where needed

3. **Training/Developing**
   a. orienting employees, arranging for training seminars, etc.
   b. clarifying roles, duties, job descriptions
   c. coaching, mentoring, walking subordinates through task
   d. helping subordinates with personal development plans

4. **Decision Making/Problem Solving**
   a. defining problems
   b. choosing between 2 or more alternatives or strategies
   c. handling day-to-day operational crises as they arise
   d. weighing the trade-offs; cost benefit analyses
   e. actually deciding what to do
   f. developing new procedures to increase efficiency

5. **Processing Paperwork**
   a. processing mail
   b. reading reports, in-box
   c. writing reports, memos, letters, etc.
   d. routine financial reporting and bookkeeping
   e. general desk work

6. **Exchanging Routine Information**
   a. answering routine procedural questions
   b. receiving and disseminating requested information
   c. conveying results of meetings
   d. giving or receiving routine information over the phone
   e. staff meetings of an informational nature (e.g., status updates, new company policies, etc.)

7. **Monitoring/Controlling Performance**
   a. inspecting work
   b. walking around and checking things out, touring
   c. monitoring performance data (e.g., computer printouts, production, financial reports)
   d. preventive maintenance

8. **Motivating/Reinforcing**
   a. allocating formal organizational rewards
   b. asking for input, participation
   c. conveying appreciation, compliments
   d. giving credit where due
   e. listening to suggestions
   f. giving positive performance feedback
   g. increasing job challenge
   h. delegating responsibility & authority
   i. letting subordinates determine how to do their own work
   j. sticking up for the group to superiors and others, backing a subordinate

9. **Disciplining/Punishing**
   a. enforcing rules and policies
   b. nonverbal glaring, harassment
   c. demotion, firing, layoff
   d. any formal organizational reprimand or notice
   e. "chewing out" a subordinate, criticizing
   f. giving negative performance feedback

10. **Interacting With Outsiders**
    a. public relations
    b. customers
    c. contacts with suppliers, vendors
    d. external meetings
    e. community-service activities

11. **Managing Conflict**
    a. managing interpersonal conflict between subordinate or others
    b. appealing to higher authority to resolve a dispute
    c. appealing to 3rd-party negotiators
    d. trying to get cooperation or consensus between conflicting parties
    e. attempting to resolve conflicts between subordinate and self

12. **Socializing/Politicking**
    a. nonwork related chit chat (e.g., family or personal matters)
    b. informal "joking around," B.S.
    c. discussing rumors, hearsay, grapevine
    d. complaining, griping, putting others down
    e. politicking, gamesmanship

SOURCE: From F. Luthans and D. L. Lockwood, Toward an observation system for measuring leader behavior in natural settings. In J. G. Hunt, ed., *Leader: A New Synthesis* (New York: Sage, 1984). Reprinted by permission of Sage Publications, Inc.

Table 8–5 Definition of Managerial Behavior Categories in the Integrating Taxonomy

Networking: Socializing informally, developing contacts with people who are a source of information and support and maintaining relationships through periodic interaction, including visits, telephone calls, and correspondence, and attendance at meetings and social events.

Supporting: Acting friendly and considerate, showing sympathy and support when someone is upset, listening to complaints and problems, looking out for someone's interests, providing helpful career advice, doing things to aid someone's career advancement.

Managing conflict and team building: Encouraging and facilitating constructive resolution of conflict, fostering teamwork and cooperation, and building identification with the organizational unit or team.

Motivating: Using influence techniques that appeal to emotions, values, or logic to generate enthusiasm for the work and commitment to task objectives, or to induce someone to carry out a request for support, cooperation, assistance, resources, or authorization; also, setting an example of proper behavior by one's own actions.

Recognizing and rewarding: Providing praise, recognition, and tangible rewards for effective performance, significant achievements, and special contributions; expressing respect and appreciation for someone's accomplishments.

Planning and organizing: Determining long-range objectives and strategies for adapting to environmental change, identifying necessary action steps to carry out a project or activity, allocating resources among activities according to priorities, and determining how to improve efficiency, productivity, and coordination with other parts of the organization.

Problem solving: Identifying work-related problems, analyzing problems in a systematic but timely manner to determine causes and find solutions, and acting decisively to implement solutions and deal with crises.

Consulting and delegating: Checking with people before making changes that affect them, encouraging suggestions for improvement, inviting participation in decision making, incorporating the ideas and suggestions of others in decisions, and allowing others to have substantial discretion in carrying out work activities and handling problems.

Monitoring operations and environment: Gathering information about the progress and quality of work activities, the success or failure of activities or projects, and the performance of individual contributors; also, determining the needs of clients or users, and scanning the environment to detect threats and opportunities.

Informing: Disseminating relevant information about decisions, plans, and activities to people who need it to do their work, providing written materials and documents, answering requests for technical information, and telling people about the organizational unit to promote its reputation.

Clarifying roles and objectives: Assigning tasks, providing direction in how to do the work, and communicating a clear understanding of job responsibilities, task objectives, deadlines, and performance expectations.

SOURCE: Reprinted with permission from Gary Yukl, *Leadership in Organizations,* 2nd ed. (Englewood Cliffs: Prentice Hall, 1989), pp. 129–130. Copyright © 1989 by Prentice Hall.

Fiedler's Theory

While McGregor's theory provided a transition from behavioral to situational theories, Fred Fiedler developed and tested the first leadership theory explicitly called a contingency (or situational) model. He argued that changing an individual's leadership style is quite difficult, but that organizations should put individuals in situations that fit with their style.[25] Fiedler's theory suggests that managers can choose between two styles: task oriented and relationship oriented. Then the natur

Table 8–6 **Influ-
ences on Leadership
Style**

Dimension	Description
Subordinate considerations	Expertise, experience, competence, knowledge of job, hierarchical level of occupied position, expectations concerning leader behavior, perceived organizational independence, and psychological aspects.
Supervisor considerations	The similarity of attitudes and behavior to those of higher management, and the degree of upward influence.
Task considerations	The degree of time urgency, amount of physical danger, permissible error rate, presence of external stress, degree of autonomy, degree of job scope, importance and meaningfulness of work, and degree of ambiguity.

Figure 8–4 **How Theory Y Relates to Managerial Style and Behavior**

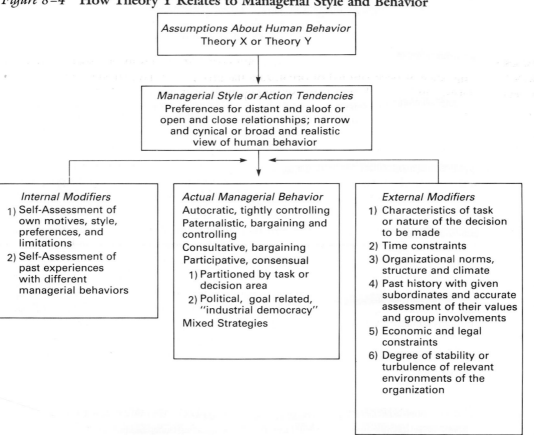

chein, The Hawthorne studies revisited: A defense of Theory Y, Sloan School of Management Working Paper #756–. Massachusetts Institute of Technology, December, 1974, p. 3.

leader-member relations, task structure, and position power of the leader influences whether a task-oriented or a relationship-oriented leadership style is more likely to be effective. *Leader-member* relations refer to the extent to which the group trusts and respects the leader and will follow the leader's directions. *Task structure* describes the degree to which the task is clearly specified and defined or structured, as opposed to ambiguous or unstructured. *Position power* means the extent to which the leader has official power, that is, the potential or actual ability to influence others in a desired direction owing to the position he or she holds in the organization.

Table 8–7 shows the style recommended as most effective for each combination of these three situational factors based on the degree of control or influence the leader can exert in his or her leadership position. In general, high-control situations (I, II, and III) call for task-oriented leadership because they allow the leader to take charge. Low-control situations (VII and VIII) also call for task-oriented leadership because they require rather than allow the leader to take charge. Moderate-control situations (IV, V, VI, and VII), in contrast, call for relationship-oriented leadership because the situations challenge leaders to get the cooperation of their subordinates.[26] But cross-cultural differences exist in this fit: High-performance Philippine managers were task oriented, but high-performance managers in Hong Kong were relations oriented.[27] In spite of extensive research to support the theory, critics have questioned the reliability of the measurement of leadership style and the range and appropriateness of the three situational components.[28]

CONTEMPORARY SITUATIONAL LEADERSHIP

Some researchers have suggested that leadership strategies in one sociocultural setting, such as occupational or organizational group, will have strong underlying similarities and must change as the setting changes over time.[29] For example, in Taiwan, directive leadership had a strong positive correlation with subordinate satisfaction

Table 8–7 **Fiedler's Model of Effective Leadership**

	Description of the Situation				
	Leader–Member Relations	Task Structure	Power Position	Example	Effective Leadership Style
I	Good	Structured	Strong	Bomber crew	Task-oriented
II	Good	Structured	Weak	Basketball team	Task-oriented
III	Good	Unstructured	Strong	ROTC	Task-oriented
IV	Good	Unstructured	Weak	Board of directors of cooperative	Relations-oriented
V	Poor	Structured	Strong	Antiaircraft artillery crew	Relations-oriented
VI	Poor	Structured	Weak	Surveying team	Relations-oriented
VII	Poor	Unstructured	Strong	ROTC	Either
VIII	Poor	Unstructured	Weak	Management teams	Task-oriented

SOURCE: Adapted from F. E. Fiedler, *A Theory of Leadership Effectiveness* (New York: McGraw-Hill, 1967), p. 37. Reprinted with permission.

for those who believed Chinese values, but had almost no correlation for those without strong Chinese cultural beliefs.[30] Other research suggests that the effect of leader behaviors on unit performance is altered by such intervening variables as the effort of subordinates, their ability to perform their jobs, the clarity of their job responsibilities, the organization of the work, the cooperation and cohesiveness of the work group, the sufficiency of resources and support provided to the group, and the coordination of work group activities with those of other subunits.[31] Thus leaders must respond to these and broader cultural differences in choosing an appropriate style. A leader-environment-follower interaction theory of leadership notes that effective leaders first analyze deficiencies in the follower's ability, motivation, role perception, and work environment that inhibit performance and then act to eliminate these deficiencies.[32]

Path-Goal Theory   According to path-goal theory, the leader attempts to influence subordinates' perceptions of goals and the path to achieve them.[33] Leaders can then choose among four styles of leadership: directive, supportive, participative, and achievement-oriented, as shown in Table 8–8. In selecting a style, the leader acts to strengthen the expectancy, instrumentality, and valence of a situation, respectively, by providing better machinery or training for workers; reinforcing desired behaviors with pay, praise, or promotion; and ensuring that the workers value the rewards they receive or that the rewards offered are valued by the workers.

Choosing a Style   Choosing a style requires a quality diagnosis of the situation to decide what leadership behaviors would be most effective in attaining the desired outcomes. The appropriate leadership style is influenced first by *subordinates' characteristics,* particularly the subordinates' abilities and the likelihood that the leader's behavior will cause subordinates satisfaction now or in the future; and second by

Table 8–8 **Styles of Leadership for Path-Goal Theory**

Style	Description
Directive	The leader informs subordinates what is expected of them, gives specific guidance as to what should be done, and shows how to do it. A manager demonstrates directive leadership if he or she provides subordinates with a plan of activities, as well as a complete set of written instructions for implementing them.
Supportive	The leader is friendly and approachable and shows concern for the status, well-being, and needs of subordinates. A supervisor with an "open-door policy" who encourages subordinates to come to him or her with any and all problems has this style.
Participative	The leader consults with subordinates, solicits their suggestions, and takes suggestions into consideration before making a decision. Any boss who makes decisions by group consensus uses this style.
Achievement-Oriented	A leader sets challenging goals, expects subordinates to perform at their highest level, continuously seeks improvement in performance, and shows a high degree of confidence that the subordinates will assume responsibility, put forth effort, and accomplish challenging goals.

the *environment,* including the subordinates' tasks, the formal authority system, the primary work group, and the organizational culture.[34] According to this theory, the appropriate style for Grace Pastiak, for example, depends on her subordinates' skills, knowledge, and abilities, as well as their attitudes toward her. It also depends on the nature of their activities, the lines of authority in the organization, the integrity of their work group, and the task technology involved. The most desirable leadership style helps the individual achieve satisfaction, meet personal needs, and accomplish goals, while complementing the subordinates' abilities and the characteristics of the situation.

Table 8–9 offers a sample of situations in which each type of leadership style likely results in desirable outcomes. The right-hand columns indicate whether each of the four prototype leadership styles fits with the feature of the situation listed in the left-hand column when considered independently of other situational characteristics. For example, only directive leadership is inappropriate when the task is structured because directive leadership is redundant and does not complement either the subordinates' needs or characteristics of the situation. For subordinates with high achievement needs, in contrast, only an achievement style will satisfy their needs. Application of the path-goal theory, then, requires first an assessment of the situation, particularly its participants and environment, and second a determination of the most congruent leadership style. Even though the research about path-goal theory has yielded mixed results,[35] it can provide a leader with help in selecting an effective leadership style by using the diagnostic questions in Table 8–10.

Table 8–9 **Effective Leadership Styles under Different Conditions**

Sample Situational Characteristics	Leadership Styles			
	Directive	Supportive	Achievement	Participative
Task				
Structured	No	Yes	Yes	Yes
Unstructured	Yes	No	Yes	No
Clear goals	No	Yes	No	Yes
Ambiguous goals	Yes	No	Yes	No
Subordinates				
Skilled in task	No	Yes	Yes	Yes
Unskilled in task	Yes	No	Yes	No
High achievement needs	No	No	Yes	No
High social needs	No	Yes	No	Yes
Formal authority				
Extensive	No	Yes	Yes	Yes
Limited	Yes	Yes	Yes	Yes
Work group				
Strong social network	Yes	No	Yes	Yes
Experienced in collaboration	No	No	No	Yes
Organizational culture				
Supports participation	No	No	No	Yes
Achievement-oriented	No	No	Yes	No

Table 8–10 **Path-Goal Questions**

1. What is the nature of the environment, the subordinates' tasks, the formal authority system, and the primary work group?
2. What are the subordinates' abilities and leadership preferences?
3. Which style responds to the environmental contingencies?
4. Which style enhances the subordinates' characteristics?
5. Does the leader use the style called for by various contingencies? If not, how can the leader resolve the difference? If there is a mismatch, then either the situation or the leader must be changed.

The Vroom-Yetton Model

The Vroom-Yetton theory consists of a procedure for determining the extent to which leaders should involve subordinates in the decision-making process.[36] The manager can choose one of five approaches that range from individual problem solving with available information to joint problem solving to delegation of problem-solving responsibility (see Table 8–11 for a summary).

Selection of the appropriate decision process involves assessing six factors: (1) the problem's quality requirement, (2) the location of information about the problem, (3) the structure of the problem, (4) the likely acceptance of the decision by those affected, (5) the commonality of organizational goals, and (6) the likely conflict regarding possible problem solutions. Figure 8–5 illustrates the original normative model, expressed as a decision tree. To make a decision, the leader asks each question, A through H, corresponding to each box encountered, from left to right, unless questions may be skipped because the response to the previous question leads to a later one. For example, a no response to question A allows questions B and C to be skipped; a yes response to question B after a yes response to question A allows question C to be skipped. Reaching the end of one branch of the tree results in identification of a problem type (numbered 1 through 18) with an accompanying set of feasible decision processes. When the set of feasible processes for group problems includes more than one process (e.g., a "no response" to each question results in problem type 1, for which every decision style is feasible), final selection of the single approach can use either minimum number of hours (group processes AI, AII, CI, CII, and GII are preferred in that order), or maximum subordinate involvement (GII, CII, CI, AII, AI are preferred in that order), as secondary criteria. A manager who wishes to make the decision in the shortest time possible, and for whom all processes are appropriate, will choose AI (solving the problem himself or herself using available information) over any other process. A manager who wishes to maximize subordinate involvement in the decision making as a training and development tool, for example, will choose DI or GII (delegating the problem to the subordinate, or together with subordinates reaching a decision) if all processes are feasible and if time is not limited. Similar choices can be made when analyzing individual problems. Research has shown that decisions made using processes from the feasible set result in more effective outcomes than those not included.[37]

The recent reformulation of this model uses the same decision processes—AI, AII, CI, CII, GII, GI, DI—as the original model, as well as the criteria of decision quality, decision commitment, time, and subordinate development.[38] It differs by expanding the range of possible responses to include probabilities, rather than yes or no answers to each diagnostic question, and it uses a computer to process the data. Although both formulations of this model provide a set of diagnostic questions for analyzing a problem, they tend to oversimplify the process. Their narrow focus

Table 8–11 **Decision-Making Processes**

For Individual Problems	For Group Problems
AI You solve the problem or make the decision yourself, using information available to you at that time.	**AI** You solve the problem or make the decision yourself, using information available to you at that time.
AII You obtain any necessary information from the subordinate, then decide on the solution to the problem yourself. You may or may not tell the subordinate what the problem is, in getting the information from him. The role played by your subordinate in making the decision is clearly one of providing specific information which you request, rather than generating or evaluating alternative solutions.	**AII** You obtain any necessary information from subordinates, then decide on the solution to the problem yourself. You may or may not tell subordinates what the problem is, in getting the information from them. The role played by your subordinates in making the decision is clearly one of providing specific information which you request, rather than generating or evaluating solutions.
CI You share the problem with the relevant subordinate, getting his ideas and suggestions. Then *you* make the decision. This decision may or may not reflect your subordinate's influence.	**CI** You share the problem with the relevant subordinates individually, getting their ideas and suggestions without bringing them together as a group. Then *you* make the decision. This decision may or may not reflect your subordinates' influence.
GI You share the problem with one of your subordinates, and together you analyze the problem and arrive at a mutually satisfactory solution in an atmosphere of free and open exchange of information and ideas. You both contribute to the resolution of the problem with the relative contribution of each being dependent on knowledge rather than formal authority.	**CII** You share the problem with your subordinates in a group meeting. In this meeting you obtain their ideas and suggestions. Then, *you* make the decision which may or may not reflect your subordinates' influence.
DI You delegate the problem to one of your subordinates, providing him with any relevant information that you possess, but giving him responsibility for solving the problem by himself. Any solution which the person reaches will receive your support.	**GII** You share the problem with your subordinates as a group. Together you generate and evaluate alternatives and attempt to reach agreement (consensus) on a solution. Your role is much like that of chairman, coordinating the discussion, keeping it focused on the problem, and making sure that the critical issues are discussed. You do not try to influence the group to adopt "your" solution and are willing to accept and implement any solution which has the support of the entire group.

Source: Reprinted by permission from V. H. Vroom, and A. G. Jago, Decision-making as a social process: Normative and descriptive models of leader behavior, *Decision Sciences* 5 (1974): 745.

on the extent of subordinate involvement in decision making also limits their usefulness.

The Life Cycle Model   In an attempt to integrate previous knowledge about leadership into a prescriptive model of leadership style, this theory cites the *readiness of followers*—defined as their ability and willingness to accomplish a specific task—as the major contingency that influences appropriate leadership style.[39] Follower readiness incorporates the follower's level of achievement motivation, ability and willingness to assume responsibility for his or her own behavior in accomplishing specific tasks, and education and experience relevant to the task. The model combines *task* and *relationship* behavior to yield four possible styles, as shown in Figure 8–6. Leaders should use a *telling* style, and provide specific instructions and closely supervise performance, when followers

Figure 8–5   **Decision Process Flow Chart for Both Individual and Group Problems**

A. Is there a quality requirement such that one solution is likely to be more rational than another?
B. Do I have sufficient info to make a high quality decision?
C. Is the problem structured?
D. Is acceptance of decision by subordinates critical to effective implementation?
E. If I were to make the decision by myself, is it reasonably certain that it would be accepted by my subordinates?
F. Do subordinates share the organizational goals to be attained in solving this problem?
G. Is conflict among subordinates likely in preferred solutions? (This question is irrelevant to individual problems.)
H. Do subordinates have sufficient info to make a high quality decision?

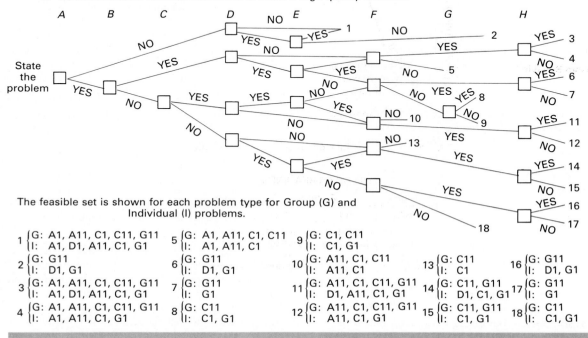

The feasible set is shown for each problem type for Group (G) and Individual (I) problems.

1 { G: A1, A11, C1, C11, G11
    I: A1, D1, A11, C1, G1

2 { G: G11
    I: D1, G1

3 { G: A1, A11, C1, C11, G11
    I: A1, D1, A11, C1, G1

4 { G: A1, A11, C1, C11, G11
    I: A1, A11, C1, G1

5 { G: A1, A11, C1, C11
    I: A1, A11, C1

6 { G: G11
    I: D1, G1

7 { G: G11
    I: G1

8 { G: C11
    I: C1, G1

9 { G: C1, C11
    I: C1, G1

10 { G: A11, C1, C11
     I: A11, C1

11 { G: A11, C1, C11, G11
     I: D1, A11, C1, G1

12 { G: A11, C1, C11, G11
     I: A11, C1, G1

13 { G: C11
     I: C1

14 { G: C11, G11
     I: D1, C1, G1

15 { G: C11, G11
     I: C1, G1

16 { G: G11
     I: D1, G1

17 { G: G11
     I: G1

18 { G: C11
     I: C1, G1

SOURCE: Reprinted from V. H. Vroom and A. G. Jago, Decision making as a social process: Normative and descriptive models of leader behavior, *Decision Sciences* 5 (1974): 748.

are unable and unwilling or insecure. Leaders should use a *selling* style, and explain decisions and provide opportunity for clarification, when followers have moderate-to-low readiness. Using a *participating* style, where the leader shares ideas and helps facilitate decision making, should occur when followers have moderate-to-high readiness. Finally, leaders should use a *delegating* style, and give responsibility for decisions and implementation to followers, when followers are able, willing, and confident.

Although some researchers have questioned the conceptual clarity, validity, robustness, and utility of the model, as well as the instruments used to measure leadership style, others have supported the utility of the theory.[40] For example, the Leadership Effectiveness and Description Scale (LEAD) and related instruments, developed to measure leadership style by the life cycle researchers, are widely used in industrial training programs. Managers can use the situational model analytically to understand leadership deficiencies and combine it with the path-goal model to prescribe the appropriate style for a variety of situations. Grace Pastiak, for example, could assess the readiness of the members of the project team and choose the appropriate style for leading them. Most likely she learned that many of them have moderate

Figure 8–6 **Model of Situational Leadership**

Task Behavior

The extent to which the leader engages in defining roles telling what, how, when, where, and if more than one person, who is to do what in
• Goal-setting
• Organizing
• Establishing time lines
• Directing
• Controlling

Relationship Behavior

The extent to which a leader engages in two-way (multi-way) communication, listening, facilitating behaviors, socioemotional support
• Giving support
• Communicating
• Facilitating interactions
• Active listening
• Providing feedback

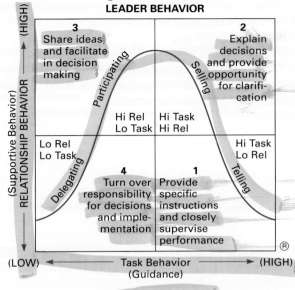

Decision Styles

1
Leader-made decision

2
Leader-made decision with dialogue and/or explanation

3
Leader/follower-made decision or follower-made decision with encouragement from leader

4
Follower-made decision

Ability has the necessary knowledge, experience and skill

Willingness has the necessary confidence, commitment, motivation

When a Leader Behavior is used appropriately with its corresponding level of readiness, it is termed a High Probability Match. The following are descriptors that can be useful when using Situational Leadership for specific applications:

S1	S2	S3	S4
Telling	Selling	Participating	Delegating
Guiding	Explaining	Encouraging	Observing
Directing	Clarifying	Collaborating	Monitoring
Establishing	Persuading	Committing	Fulfilling

to high readiness, calling for a participating or delegating style. Her implementation of such a style helps explains the high level of group performance.

NONSITUA-TIONAL, CONTEMPORARY MODELS

Recently, organizational theorists have explained leadership in terms of nonsituation-based models. We examine three of these approaches—exchange theory, the attributional model, and substitutes for leadership.

Exchange Theory The vertical dyad linkage model of leadership emphasizes the leader's interaction with the group he or she supervises, and with superiors.[41] The leader exchanges resources, such as increased job latitude, influence on decision making, and open communication, for members' commitment to higher involvement in organizational functioning.[42] By behaving to increase the exchange of resources between leaders and members, a leader can increase follower productivity, job satisfaction, and satisfaction with supervision.

According to this research, leaders behave differently toward two types of followers.[43] The *cadre* or in-group includes a small group of trusted subordinates to whom the leader allows a great deal of latitude because of personal compatibility, perceived competence, and dependability. The *hired hands* or out-group includes all subordinates to whom the leader allows little latitude. The cadre experienced higher performance ratings, reduced propensity to quit, greater satisfaction with supervision, and improved actual job performance. Managers who belonged to their boss's in-group were more able to establish in-group relations with subordinates.[44] Supervisors also made internal attributions about their followers consistent with the perceived status of the subordinates as in-group or out-group members, suggesting the relationship of exchange theory to attribution theory.[45] Grace Pastiak, for example, clearly treats her subordinates as part of the cadre of significant advisers in the workplace, thereby explaining their positive attitudes and accompanying performance.

The research on exchange theory has been criticized because it relies on a narrow data base, does not explain how individuals become part of the in-group, does not sufficiently study the organizational outcomes associated with the exchange relationship, and operationalizes the nature of the leader-subordinate or leader-boss exchange in diverse and inconsistent ways.[46] Yet, it encourages managers and other organizational members to diagnose the *status* of followers vis-à-vis leaders in choosing a leadership style. It is important that the leader not develop such differentiated relationships that members of the out-group question whether they really have an opportunity to advance in the organization. The leader must ensure that he or she develops trusting, supportive, respectful relations with both groups of subordinates.[47]

Attributional Model

Attribution theory suggests that a leader's judgment about his or her followers is influenced by the leader's attribution of the causes of the followers' behaviors.[48] Effective leaders must recognize biases in their attributions and consequent actions: They link themselves with successes in the group and remove themselves from failures by manipulating their attributions of subordinates' behavior in the desired direction.[49] They might, for example, suggest to subordinates that the group's success was due to the interpersonal support or skills of the leader, and that the group's failure was due to time constraints, lack of resources, or absence of member skills. Or, leaders may more often attribute poor performance to a subordinate when that person had a poor work history than when the subordinate had a good one.[50] Recent research suggests that after a leader acts in accordance with his or her attributions of followers' behavior, followers may adjust their attributions of leader behavior in terms of their view of the appropriateness of the leader's responses.[51]

In diagnosing the situation, the leader must consider whether the behavior is distinctive or unique to a particular task, the consistency or frequency of the behavior, and the extent to which other followers demonstrate the same behavior. Behavior viewed as distinctive, inconsistent, and of high consensus is more likely attributed to characteristics of the situation than to the person, and the leader would act accordingly. A leader is more likely to attribute subordinate behavior to the situation when (1) the subordinate has no prior history of poor performance on similar tasks, (2) the subordinate performs other tasks effectively, (3) the subordinate is doing as well as other people who are in a similar situation, (4) the effects of failures or mistakes are not serious or harmful, (5) the manager is dependent upon the subordinate for his or her own success, (6) the subordinate is perceived to have other redeeming qualities (popularity, leadership skills), (7) the subordinate has offered excuses or an apology, or (8) there is evidence indicating external causes.[52]

Figure 8–7 summarizes this attributional model of leadership. Although the attributional model of leadership poses some definitional and measurement problems,[53] understanding the correct attributions should result in implementation of more appropriate actions.

Substitutes for Leadership Certain individual, task, and organizational variables prevent the leader from affecting subordinate attitudes and behaviors in an effective manner.[54] Substitutes for leadership, or characteristics that negate leadership influence, are those that structure the task for the followers or give them positive support for their actions. They include characteristics of subordinates, task, and organization, as shown in Figure 8–8. One study of nursing work indicated that the staff nurse's education, the cohesion of the nurses, and the work technology substituted for the head nurse's leadership behaviors in determining the staff nurse's performance; more-educated nurses, for example, could work autonomously, without leadership by the head nurse.[55]

Substitutes for leadership can serve a second function: they can compensate for ineffective leadership. Closely knit teams of highly trained individuals, work with high intrinsic satisfaction, computer technology, and extensive professional education can substitute for traditional formal leadership, as shown in Figure 8–9.[56] For example, developing collegial systems of guidance, redesigning jobs to increase performance feedback, or increasing the professionalism of subordinates can substitute for leader directiveness and supportiveness.[57]

Consider once more the opening scenario. Where the task is clear and the staff members have extensive professional training, the need for the hierarchical superior to play a dominant role may be minimized because the group members and the task can be a source of structuring and supporting behavior.

Figure 8–7 **An Attributional Leadership Model**

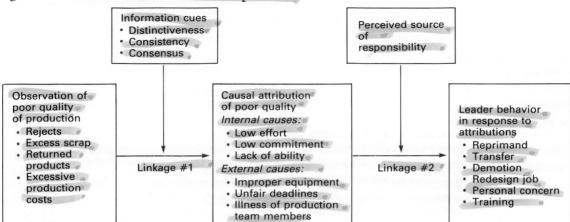

SOURCE: Adapted from Terence R. Mitchell and Robert E. Wood, An empirical test of an attributional model of leader's responses to poor performance. In *Academy of Management Proceedings,* ed. Richard C. Huseman, 1979, p. 94.

Figure 8–8 **Substitutes for Leadership**

	Will Tend to Neutralize	
Characteristic	Relationship-Oriented, Supportive, People-Centered Leadership: Consideration, Support, and Interaction Facilitation	Task-Oriented, Instrumental, Job-Centered Leadership: Initiating Structure, Goal Emphasis, and Work Facilitation
Of the subordinate		
1. ability, experience, training, knowledge		×
2. need for independence	×	×
3. "professional" orientation	×	×
4. indifference toward organizational rewards	×	×
Of the task		
5. unambiguous and routine		×
6. methodologically invariant		×
7. provides its own feedback concerning accomplishment		×
8. intrinsically satisfying	×	
Of the organization		
9. formalization (explicit plans, goals, and areas of responsibility)		×
10. inflexibility (rigid, unbending rules and procedures)		×
11. highly specified and active advisory and staff functions		×
12. closely knit, cohesive work groups	×	×
13. organizational rewards not within the leader's control	×	×
14. spatial distance between superior and subordinates	×	×

SOURCE: From S. Kerr and J. M. Jermier, Substitutes for leadership: Their meaning and measurement, *Organizational Behavior and Human Performance* 26 (December 1978): 375–403. Copyright © 1978 by Academic Press, Inc. Reprinted with permission.

TRANSFOR-MATIONAL LEADERSHIP AND SUPER-LEADERSHIP

Recent thinking about effective leadership has supplemented the situational approach with a revival of trait theory that emphasizes the importance of a leader's charisma and his or her ability to use personal influence to facilitate individual development.

Transformational Leadership

A *charismatic* or *transformational* leader uses charisma to inspire his or her followers. He or she talks to followers about how essential their performance is, how confident he or she is in the followers, how exceptional the followers are, and how he or she expects the group's performance to break records.[58] Mary Kay Ash (Mary Kay Cosmetics), Lee Iacocca (Chrysler), and Steven Jobs (Apple Computer), among others, have been described as this type of leader. Such leaders use dominance, self-confidence, a need for influence, and conviction of moral righteousness to increase their charisma and consequently their leadership effectiveness.[59] While charismatic leadership has been criticized as a concept because of difficulty in defining and operationalizing it,[60] recent research characterizes it as shown in Table 8–12.

Figure 8–9 Coping Strategies for Selected Leadership Problems

Problem	Coping Strategy
Coordination problems among workers	Use self-managed teams
Resistance to leadership attempts	Use peer decision-making systems
Lack of recognition for quality performance by leader	Use job enrichment or offer other types of rewards
Inconsistent leader behavior	Use team goal-setting
Frequently changing leadership	Use staff as back-up resources

SOURCE: Based on J. P. Howell, D. E. Bowen, P. W. Dorfman, S. Kerr, and P. M. Podsakoff, Substitutes for leadership: Effective alternatives to ineffective leadership, *Organizational Dynamics* (Summer 1990), pp. 28–29.

Table 8–12 **Behavioral Components of Charismatic and Noncharismatic Leaders**

	Noncharismatic Leader	Charismatic Leader
Relation to Status Quo	Essentially agrees with status quo and strives to maintain it	Essentially opposed to status quo and strives to change it
Future Goal	Goal not too discrepant from status quo	Idealized vision which is highly discrepant from status quo
Likableness	Shared perspective makes him/her likable	Shared perspective and idealized vision makes him/her a likable and honorable hero worthy of identification and imitation
Trustworthiness	Disinterested advocacy in persuasion attempts	Disinterested advocacy by incurring great personal risk and cost
Expertise	Expert in using available means to achieve goals within the framework of the existing order	Expert in using unconventional means to transcend the existing order
Behavior	Conventional, conforming to existing norms	Unconventional or counternormative
Environmental Sensitivity	Low need for environmental sensitivity to maintain status quo	High need for environmental sensitivity for changing the status quo
Articulation	Weak articulation of goals and motivation to lead	Strong articulation of future vision and motivation to lead
Power Base	Position power and personal power (based on reward, expertise, and liking for a friend who is a similar other)	Personal power (based on expertise, respect, and admiration for a unique hero)
Leader-Follower Relationship	Egalitarian, consensus seeking, or directive	Elitist, entrepreneur, and exemplary
	Nudges or orders people to share his/her views	Transforms people to share the radical changes advocated

SOURCE: Reprinted with permission from A. Conger and R. N. Kanungo, Toward a behavioral theory of charismatic leadership in organizational settings, *Academy of Management Review* 12 (1987): 641.

A transformational leader changes an organization by recognizing an opportunity and developing a vision, communicating that vision to organizational members, building trust in the vision, and achieving the vision by motivating organizational members, as shown in Figure 8–10. The leader helps subordinates recognize the need for revitalizing the organization by developing a felt need for change, overcoming resistance to change, and avoiding quick-fix solutions to problems. Encouraging subordinates to act as devil's advocates with regard to the leader, building networks outside the organization, visiting other organizations, and changing management processes to reward progress against competition also help them recognize a need for revitalization. Individuals must disengage from and disidentify with the past, as well as view change as a way of dealing with their disenchantments with the past or the status quo. The transformational leader creates a new vision and mobilizes commitment to it by planning or educating others. He or she builds trust through demonstrating personal expertise, self-confidence, and personal commitment. The charismatic leader can also change the composition of the team, alter management processes, and help organizational members reframe the way they think about the organizational situation. The charismatic leader must empower others to help achieve the vision. Finally, the transformational leader must institutionalize the change by replacing old technical, political, cultural, and social networks with new ones, as shown in Figure 8–11. For example, the leader can identify key individuals and groups, develop a plan for obtaining their commitment, and institute a monitoring system for following the changes. Or he or she can specify cultural values to change and the main holders of those values, and then design and implement a plan for making the cultural change. One study of 24 CEOs concluded that their agenda involved creating a context for change, building commitment to and ownership of the change, and balancing stability and innovation.[61]

A transformational leader motivates subordinates to achieve beyond their original expectations by increasing their awareness about the importance of designated outcomes and ways of attaining them, by getting workers to go beyond their self-interest to that of the team, organization, or larger society, and by changing or expanding the individual's needs.[62] Subordinates report that they work harder for such leaders.[63] In addition, such leaders are judged higher in leadership potential by their subordinates.[64] We can contrast a transformational leader to the more common

Figure 8–10 **Stages in Charismatic Leadership**

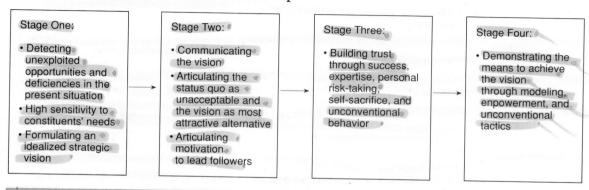

Stage One:	Stage Two:	Stage Three:	Stage Four:
• Detecting unexploited opportunities and deficiencies in the present situation • High sensitivity to constituents' needs • Formulating an idealized strategic vision	• Communicating the vision • Articulating the status quo as unacceptable and the vision as most attractive alternative • Articulating motivation to lead followers	• Building trust through success, expertise, personal risk-taking, self-sacrifice, and unconventional behavior	• Demonstrating the means to achieve the vision through modeling, enpowerment, and unconventional tactics

SOURCE: J. A. Conger and R. N. Kanungo, *The Charismatic Leader: Behind the Mystique of Exceptional Leadership* (San Francisco: Jossey-Bass), p. 27. Copyright © 1989 by Jossey-Bass, Inc., Publishers. Reprinted with permission.

Figure 8–11 Transformational Leadership: A Three-Act Drama

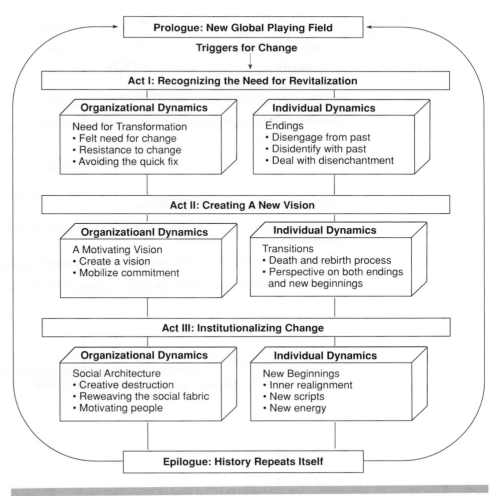

Prologue: New Global Playing Field

Triggers for Change

Act I: Recognizing the Need for Revitalization

Organizational Dynamics

Need for Transformation
• Felt need for change
• Resistance to change
• Avoiding the quick fix

Individual Dynamics

Endings
• Disengage from past
• Disidentify with past
• Deal with disenchantment

Act II: Creating A New Vision

Organizatioanl Dynamics

A Motivating Vision
• Create a vision
• Mobilize commitment

Individual Dynamics

Transitions
• Death and rebirth process
• Perspective on both endings and new beginnings

Act III: Institutionalizing Change

Organizational Dynamics

Social Architecture
• Creative destruction
• Reweaving the social fabric
• Motivating people

Individual Dynamics

New Beginnings
• Inner realignment
• New scripts
• New energy

Epilogue: History Repeats Itself

SOURCE: From N. M. Tichy and M. A. Devanna, *The Transformational Leader,* 2nd ed. (New York: Wiley, 1990), p. 28. Copyright © 1990 by John Wiley and Sons, Inc. Reprinted by permission.

transactional leader, as shown in Figure 8–12. Colleagues and subordinates consider transformational leaders to be effective more often than transactional leaders.[65]

But a "dark side" to charismatic leadership may exist if the leader overemphasizes devotion to himself or herself, makes personal needs paramount, or uses highly effective communication skills to mislead or manipulate others.[66] Such leaders may be so driven to achieve a vision that they ignore the costly implications of their goals; for example, Robert Campeau's blind ambition caused the downfall of two major department store chains plus his own empire.[67] Figure 8–13 shows these and other sources of a failed vision. Early diagnosis of such conditions may help limit their dysfunctional consequences. Further, cultural differences exist in the impact of transformational leadership. One study showed, for example, that charismatic leadership had a greater impact on North American than on Mexican workers.[68]

A boss who is a transformational leader motivates subordinates to do better than they expected in three ways.[69] First, the leader raises their consciousness about the importance of certain outcomes, such as high productivity or efficiency. Second, he or she shows the value of workers' concentrating on their work team's good rather

Figure 8–12 Characteristics of Transformational and Transactional Leaders

Transformational Leader

Charisma: Provides vision and sense of mission, instills pride, gains respect and trust.

Inspiration: Communicates high expectations, uses symbols to focus efforts, expresses important purposes in simple ways.

Intellectual Stimulation: Promotes intelligence, rationality, and careful problem solving.

Individualized Consideration: Gives personal attention, treats each employee individually, coaches, advises.

Transactional Leader

Contingent Reward: Contracts exchange of rewards for effort, promises rewards for good performance, recognizes accomplishments.

Management by Exception (active): Watches and searches for deviations from rules and standards, takes corrective action.

Management by Exception (passive): Intervenes only if standards are not met.

Laissez-Faire: Abdicates responsibilities, avoids making decisions.

SOURCE: Reprinted by permission of publisher, From transactional to transformational leadership: Learning to share the vision, *Organizational Dynamics* (Winter 1990): 22. American Management Association, New York. All rights reserved.

than on their personal interest. Third, the leader raises the workers' need levels so that they value challenges, responsibility, and growth. Managers identified as top performers rated higher on transformational leadership than a group of ordinary managers.[70] CEOs of major business divisions of corporations who succeeded in developing new businesses differed from those who attempted new business development and failed.[71] They inspired pervasive commitment through the division by insisting that the entire division pursue new business development, making new business development part of the job and not the object of special rewards, demonstrating intense, undistracted, and long-term personal commitment to new business development, and assigning the best people to new business development. They built confidence among their subordinates by helping them increase their competence and giving them the freedom to take initiative. They applied appropriate discipline to the process by carefully selecting the new venture, using the appropriate strategy, and managing failures. Because some research suggests that the charisma of a leader also cascades to his or her followers,[72] training higher managers in transformational skills should have a more widespread impact than training only lower level managers.

Figure 8–13 The Sources of Failed Vision

The vision reflects the internal needs of leaders rather than those of the market or constituents.

The resources needed to achieve vision have been seriously miscalculated.

An unrealistic assessment or distorted perception of market and constituent needs holds sway.

A failure to recognize environmental changes prevents redirection of the vision.

SOURCE: Reprinted by permission of publisher. J. A. Conger, The dark side of leadership, *Organizational Dynamics* (Autumn 1990): 45. American Management Association, New York. All rights reserved.

Does Grace Pastiak demonstrate this type of leadership? Certainly she takes a developmental orientation toward her followers by elevating their potential, sets examples, assigns tasks on an individual basis, increases subordinate responsibilities, delegates challenging work, serves as a role model, keeps subordinates informed, provides intellectual stimulation, seeks ways of acting, and is proactive.[73]

Superleadership

The *superleader* goes one step beyond the transformational leader; he or she helps followers to discover, use, and maximize their abilities.[74] Similar to the transformational leader, the superleader empowers followers to contribute fully to organizations.

Superleadership begins with *self-leadership*. "Self-leadership is the influence we exert on ourselves to achieve the self-motivation and self-direction we need to perform."[75] Table 8–13 lists a set of strategies that facilitate self-leadership.

A superleader tries to make subordinates into self-leaders, as shown in Figure 8–14. Accordingly, the superleader shifts from receiving assigned goals, external reinforcement of behavior, external criticism, and external job assignments, to creating self-set goals, internal reinforcement of behavior, self-criticism, and self–job assignments. The superleader models self-leadership for subordinates by establishing himself or herself as a credible model, displaying self-leadership, encouraging others to rehearse and then produce self-leadership behaviors, and motivating such behavior

Table 8–13 Self-Leadership Strategies

Behavior-Focused Strategies

Self-Observation—observing and gathering information about specific behaviors that you have targeted for change

Self-Set Goals—setting goals for your own work efforts

Management of Cues—arranging and altering cues in the work environment to facilitate your desired personal behaviors

Rehearsal—physical or mental practice of work activities before you actually perform them

Self-Reward—providing yourself with personally valued rewards for completing desirable behaviors

Self-Punishment/Criticism—administering punishments to yourself for behaving in undesirable ways

Cognitive-Focused Strategies

Building Natural Rewards into Tasks—self-redesign of where and how you do your work to increase the level of natural rewards in your job. Natural rewards that are part of rather than separate from the work (*i.e.*, the work, like a hobby, becomes the reward) result from activities that cause you to feel:
  a sense of competence
  a sense of self-control
  a sense of purpose

Focusing Thinking on Natural Rewards—purposely focusing your thinking on the naturally rewarding features of your work

Establishment of Effective Thought Patterns—establishing constructive and effective habits or patterns in your thinking (*e.g.*, a tendency to search for opportunities rather than obstacles embedded in challenges) by managing your:
  beliefs and assumptions
  mental imagery
  internal self-talk

SOURCE: Reprinted by permission of publisher from C. C. Manz and H. P. Sims, Jr., *Superleadership: Beyond the myth of heroic leadership, Organizational Dynamics* (Spring 1991): 24. American Management Association, New York. All rights reserved.

Figure 8–14 **The Seven-Step Process of SuperLeadership**

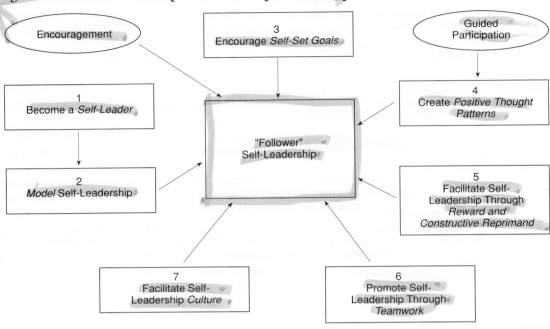

through incentives. Creating productive thought patterns is also an important step. This process includes the following steps:

1. Observing and recording existing beliefs and assumptions, self-verbalization, and mental imagery patterns.
2. Analyzing the functionality and constructiveness of the beliefs, self-talk, and imagery patterns uncovered in step 1.
3. Identifying and developing more functional and constructive beliefs and assumptions, self-verbalizations, and mental images to substitute for dysfunctional ones.
4. Substituting the more functional thinking for the dysfunctional thoughts experienced in actual situations. For example, new, more constructive assumptions, ways of talking to oneself, and mental images of the likely outcome of an encounter can be worked out and written on paper. Then this new mental plan can be worked through when faced with particularly troubling repetitive situations, such as difficulties with an assertive and creative subordinate who arouses personal feelings of threat.
5. Continued monitoring and maintenance of beliefs, self-verbalizations, and mental images over time. This final component of the process feeds back into the functionality and constructiveness analysis in step 2, and the process is continuously repeated.[76]

Rewards for a self-leader ultimately include natural rewards that stem from the task, such as a sense of competence and increased responsibility, as well as self-administered rewards, such as self-recognition, self-praise, and self-congratulations. Figure 8–15 summarizes the components and impact of superleadership.

Figure 8–15 **The SuperLeadership Approach**

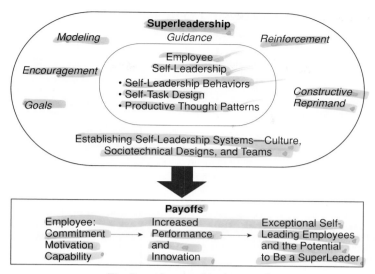

The SuperLeadership Approach

SOURCE: Reprinted with permission from C. C. Manz and H. P. Sims, Jr., *SuperLeadership: Leading Others to Lead Themselves* (New York: Prentice-Hall Press, 1989, and Berkeley Books, 1990).

THE INFLUENCE OF A DIVERSE WORK FORCE ON LEADERSHIP

The theories we have described so far offer numerous ways to answer the questions "How does an individual lead effectively?" and "What is effective leadership?" There is no single correct answer to either of these questions. The increasing multinationalism and multiculturalism of organizations pose significant challenges for any leader or manager.

The new flattened organizations, with empowered workers, may call for a new type of leadership. Some argue that women may be better suited to run the companies of the 1990s and beyond.[77] Others suggest that no consistent differences exist between male and female managers' behavior, although differences in the evaluation of the behaviors may occur.[78] Reading 8–1, "Ways Women Lead," offers some of the controversial findings in this area.

Research about other minorities in leadership and follower roles is more limited.[79] Their underrepresentation in the work force and particularly in management positions may contribute to this dearth of information. Differences in education, family background, values, and needs may influence the leadership styles they use and therefore confound the assessment of their effectiveness.

Leading a diverse work force complements but differs from managing one, as suggested by Figure 8–16. Managers must develop both leadership and management skills as a way of encouraging organizational effectiveness.

SUMMARY

Environmental and organizational changes have contributed significantly to the importance of adequate leadership. Yet, few comprehensive prescriptions for effective leadership exist. Historically, research first linked effective leadership to traits of individuals. Next, leadership was associated with two types of behavior: initiating structure (production orientation) and consideration (employee orientation). Then situational approaches to leadership, which report that the nature of effective leadership depends on particular features of the situation, such as leader-member relations, the structure of the situation, the needs of subordinates, and the readiness of

Figure 8–16 **Kotter's General Comparison of Leadership and Management**

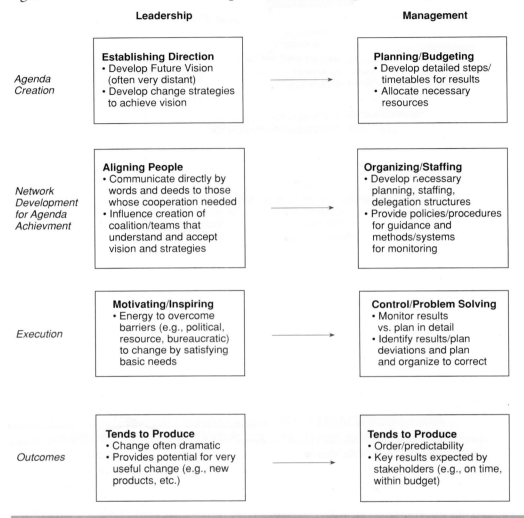

	Leadership	**Management**

Agenda Creation

Establishing Direction
• Develop Future Vision (often very distant)
• Develop change strategies to achieve vision

Planning/Budgeting
• Develop detailed steps/ timetables for results
• Allocate necessary resources

Network Development for Agenda Achievment

Aligning People
• Communicate directly by words and deeds to those whose cooperation needed
• Influence creation of coalition/teams that understand and accept vision and strategies

Organizing/Staffing
• Develop necessary planning, staffing, delegation structures
• Provide policies/procedures for guidance and methods/systems for monitoring

Execution

Motivating/Inspiring
• Energy to overcome barriers (e.g., political, resource, bureaucratic) to change by satisfying basic needs

Control/Problem Solving
• Monitor results vs. plan in detail
• Identify results/plan deviations and plan and organize to correct

Outcomes

Tends to Produce
• Change often dramatic
• Provides potential for very useful change (e.g., new products, etc.)

Tends to Produce
• Order/predictability
• Key results expected by stakeholders (e.g., on time, within budget)

SOURCE: Reprinted with permission from J. P. Kotter, *A Force for Change: How Leadership Differs from Management* (New York: Free Press, 1990), p. 6.

followers, predominated. Today, the situational approach remains viable, although other models, including exchange theory, attributional theory, substitutes for leadership, and superleadership, complement it. In addition, the call for the transformational leader remains loud.

In this chapter we have examined each of these perspectives in turn. We have shown the way trait, behavioral, situational, nonsituational, transformational, and superleadership theories separately and together explain the leadership effectiveness of Grace Pastiak at Tellabs, Inc. We have examined the nature of leadership required to manage a diverse work force in a multinational and multicultural environment. We have described the value and the liabilities of various theories and have shown how they can assist in diagnosing a situation and increasing leadership effectiveness. Table 8–14 highlights key issues presented in this chapter by listing a series of diagnostic questions.

Table 8–14 Diag-
nostic Questions for
Evaluating Leader-
ship Effectiveness

- Do the managers have the traits necessary for effective leadership?
- Do the managers display the behaviors required for effective leadership?
- Do managers exhibit balanced managerial roles?
- Do the leaders encourage the appropriate amount of participation in decision making?
- Does the leadership style fit with the nature of the task, leader–member relations, and the position power of the leader?
- Is leadership superfluous to the situational features and the followers' needs?
- Does it meet their needs?
- Does the leadership style fit with the maturity of the followers?
- Do followers attribute attitudes to the leaders accurately?
- Do transformational leaders exist?
- Do superleaders exist?

*Reading
8–1*

Ways Women Lead
Judy B. Rosener

Women managers who have broken the glass ceiling in medium-sized, nontraditional organizations have proven that
effective leaders don't come from one mold. They have
demonstrated that using the command-and-control style of
managing others, a style generally associated with men in
large, traditional organizations, is not the only way to
succeed.

The first female executives, because they were breaking
new ground, adhered to many of the "rules of conduct"
that spelled success for men. Now a second wave of women
is making its way into top management, not by adopting
the style and habits that have proved successful for men but
by drawing on the skills and attitudes they developed from
their shared experience as women. These second-generation
managerial women are drawing on what is unique to their
socialization as women and creating a different path to the
top. They are seeking and finding opportunities in fast-
changing and growing organizations to show that they can
achieve results—in a different way. They are succeeding because of—not in spite of—certain characteristics generally
considered to be "feminine" and inappropriate in leaders.

The women's success shows that a nontraditional leadership style is well suited to the conditions of some work
environments and can increase an organization's chances of
surviving in an uncertain world. It supports the belief that
there is strength in a diversity of leadership styles.

In a recent survey sponsored by the International
Women's Forum, I found a number of unexpected similarities between men and women leaders along with some important differences. (For more on the study and its findings,
see Figure 8–17, "The IWF Survey of Men and Women
Leaders.") Among these similarities are characteristics related to money and children. I found that the men and
women respondents earned the same amount of money (and
the household income of the women is twice that of the
men). This finding is contrary to most studies, which find
a considerable wage gap between men and women, even at
the executive level. I also found that just as many men as
women experience work-family conflict (although when
there are children at home, the women experience slightly
more conflict than men).

But the similarities end when men and women describe
their leadership performance and how they usually influence those with whom they work. The men are more likely
than the women to describe themselves in ways that characterize what some management experts call "transactional"
leadership.[1] That is, they view job performance as a series
of transactions with subordinates—exchanging rewards for
services rendered or punishment for inadequate performance. The men are also more likely to use power that comes
from their organizational position and formal authority.

The women respondents, on the other hand, described
themselves in ways that characterize "transformational"
leadership—getting subordinates to transform their own self-
interest into the interest of the group through concern for
a broader goal. Moreover, they ascribe their power to per-

Figure 8–17 **The IWF Survey of Men and Women Leaders**

The International Women's Forum was founded in 1982 to give prominent women leaders in diverse professions around the world a way to share their knowledge with each other and with their communities and countries. The organization now has some 37 forums in North America, Europe, Asia, Latin America, and the Middle East. To help other women advance and to educate the public about the contributions women can and are making in government, business, and other fields, the IWF created the Leadership Foundation. The Foundation commissioned me to perform the study of men and women leaders on which this article is based. I conducted the study with the help of Daniel McAllister and Gregory Stephens (Ph.D. students at the Graduate School of Management at the University of California, Irvine) in the spring of 1989.

The survey consisted of an eight-page questionnaire sent to all the IWF members. Each respondent was asked to supply the name of a man in a similar organization with similar responsibilities. The men received the same questionnaire as the IWF members. The respondents were similar in age, occupation, and educational level, which suggests that the matching effort was successful. The response rate was 31%.

The respondents were asked questions about their leadership styles, their organizations, work-family issues, and personal characteristics. The following are among the more intriguing findings, some of which contradict data reported in academic journals and the popular press:

- The women earn the same amount of money as their male counterparts. The average yearly income for men is $136,510; for women it is $140,573. (Most other studies have shown a wage gap between men and women.)
- The men's household income (their own and their spouse's) is much lower than that of the women—$166,454 versus $300,892. (Only 39% of the men have full-time employed spouses, as opposed to 71% of the women.)
- Both men and women leaders pay their female subordinates roughly $12,000 less than their male subordinates with similar positions and titles.
- Women are more likely than men to use transformational leadership—motivating others by transforming their self-interest into the goals of the organization.
- Women are much more likely than men to use power based on charisma, work record, and contacts (personal power) as opposed to power based on organizational position, title, and the ability to reward and punish (structural power).
- Most men and women describe themselves as having

an equal mix of traits that are considered "feminine" (being excitable, gentle, emotional, submissive, sentimental, understanding, compassionate, sensitive, dependent), "masculine" (dominant, aggressive, tough, assertive, autocratic, analytical, competitive, independent), and "gender-neutral" (adaptive, tactful, sincere, conscientious, conventional, reliable, predictable, systematic, efficient).

- Women who do describe themselves as predominately "feminine" or "gender-neutral" report a higher level of followership among their female subordinates than women who describe themselves as "masculine."
- Approximately 67% of the women respondents are married. (Other studies report that only 40% to 50% of women executives are married.)
- Both married men and married women experience moderate levels of conflict between work and family domains. When there are children at home, women experience only slightly higher levels of conflict than men, even though they shoulder a much greater proportion of the child care—61% of the care versus 25% for the men.

sonal characteristics like charisma, interpersonal skills, hard work, or personal contacts rather than to organizational stature.

Intrigued by these differences, I interviewed some of the women respondents who described themselves as transformational. These discussions gave me a better picture of how these women view themselves as leaders and a greater understanding of the important ways in which their leadership style differs from the traditional command-and-control style. I call their leadership style "interactive leadership" because these women actively work to make their interactions with subordinates positive for everyone involved. More specifically, the women encourage participation, share power

and information, enhance other people's self-worth, and get others excited about their work. All these things reflect their belief that allowing employees to contribute and to feel powerful and important is a win-win situation—good for the employees and the organization.

INTERACTIVE LEADERSHIP
From my discussions with the women interviewees, several patterns emerged. The women leaders made frequent reference to their efforts to encourage participation and share power and information—two things that are often associated with participative management. But their self-description went beyond the usual definitions of participation.

Much of what they described were attempts to enhance other people's sense of self-worth and to energize followers. In general, these leaders believe that people perform best when they feel good about themselves and their work, and they try to create situations that contribute to that feeling.

Encourage Participation

Inclusion is at the core of interactive leadership. In describing nearly every aspect of management, the women interviewees made reference to trying to make people feel part of the organization. They try to instill this group identity in a variety of ways, including encouraging others to have a say in almost every aspect of work, from setting performance goals to determining strategy. To facilitate inclusion, they create mechanisms that get people to participate and they use a conversational style that sends signals inviting people to get involved.

One example of the kinds of mechanisms that encourage participation is the "bridge club" that one interviewee, a group executive in charge of mergers and acquisitions at a large East Coast financial firm, created. The club is an informal gathering of people who have information she needs but over whom she has no direct control. The word *bridge* describes the effort to bring together these "members" from different functions. The word *club* captures the relaxed atmosphere.

Despite the fact that attendance at club meetings is voluntary and over and above the usual work demands, the interviewee said that those whose help she needs make the time to come. "They know their contributions are valued, and they appreciate the chance to exchange information across functional boundaries in an informal setting that's fun." She finds participation in the club more effective than memos.

Whether or not the women create special forums for people to interact, they try to make people feel included as a matter of course, often by trying to draw them into the conversation or soliciting their opinions. Frieda Caplan, founder and CEO of Frieda's Finest, a California-based marketer and distributor of unusual fruits and vegetables, described an approach she uses that is typical of the other women interviewed: "When I face a tough decision, I always ask my employees, 'What would you do if you were me?' This approach generates good ideas and introduces my employees to the complexity of management decisions."

Of course, saying that you include others doesn't mean others necessarily feel included. The women acknowledge the possibility that their efforts to draw people in may be seen as symbolic, so they try to avoid that perception by acting on the input they receive. They ask for suggestions before they reach their own conclusions, and they test— and sometimes change—particular decisions before they implement them. These women use participation to clarify their own views by thinking things through out loud and to ensure that they haven't overlooked an important consideration.

The fact that many of the interviewees described their participatory style as coming "naturally" suggests that these leaders do not consciously adopt it for its business value. Yet they realize that encouraging participation has benefits. For one thing, making it easy for people to express their ideas helps ensure that decisions reflect as much information as possible. To some of the women, this point is just common sense. Susan S. Elliott, president and founder of Systems Service Enterprises, a St. Louis computer consulting company, expressed this view: "I can't come up with a plan and then ask those who manage the accounts to give me their reactions. They're the ones who really know the accounts. They have information I don't have. Without their input I'd be operating in an ivory tower."

Participation also increases support for decisions ultimately reached and reduces the risk that ideas will be undermined by unexpected opposition. Claire Rothman, general manager of the Great Western Forum, a large sports and entertainment arena in Los Angeles, spoke about the value of open disagreement: "When I know ahead of time that someone disagrees with a decision, I can work especially closely with that person to try to get his or her support."

Getting people involved also reduces the risk associated with having only one person handle a client, project, or investment. For Patricia M. Cloherty, senior vice president and general partner of Alan Patricof Associates, a New York venture capital firm, including people in decision making and planning gives investments longevity. If something happens to one person, others will be familiar enough with the situation to "adopt" the investment. That way, there are no orphans in the portfolio, and a knowledgeable second opinion is always available.

Like most who are familiar with participatory management, these women are aware that being inclusive also has its disadvantages. Soliciting ideas and information from others takes time, often requires giving up some control, opens the door to criticism, and exposes personal and turf conflicts. In addition, asking for ideas and information can be interpreted as not having answers.

Further, it cannot be assumed that everyone wants to participate. Some people prefer being told what to do. When Mary Jane Rynd was a partner in a Big Eight accounting firm in Arizona (she recently left to start her own company—Rynd, Carneal & Associates), she encountered such a person: "We hired this person from an out-of-state CPA firm because he was experienced and smart—and because it's always fun to hire someone away from another firm. But he was just too cynical to participate. He was suspicious of everybody. I tried everything to get him involved—including him in discussions and giving him pep talks about how we all work together. Nothing worked. He just didn't want to participate."

Like all those who responded to the survey, these women are comfortable using a variety of leadership styles. So when participation doesn't work, they act unilaterally.

"I prefer participation," said Elliott, "but there are situations where time is short and I have to take the bull by the horns."

Share Power and Information

Soliciting input from other people suggests a flow of information from employees to the "boss." But part of making people feel included is knowing that open communication flows in two directions. These women say they willingly share power and information rather than guard it and they make apparent their reasoning behind decisions. While many leaders see information as power and power as a limited commodity to be coveted, the interviewees seem to be comfortable letting power and information change hands. As Adrienne Hall, vice chairman of Eisaman, Johns & Laws, a large West Coast advertising firm, said: "I know territories shift, so I'm not preoccupied with turf."

One example of power and information sharing is the open strategy sessions held by Debi Coleman, vice president of information systems and technology at Apple Computer. Rather than closeting a small group of key executives in her office to develop a strategy based on her own agenda, she holds a series of meetings over several days and allows a larger group to develop and help choose alternatives.

The interviewees believe that sharing power and information accomplishes several things. It creates loyalty by signaling to coworkers and subordinates that they are trusted and their ideas respected. It also sets an example for other people and therefore can enhance the general communication flow. And it increases the odds that leaders will hear about problems before they explode. Sharing power and information also gives employees and coworkers the wherewithal to reach conclusions, solve problems, and see the justification for decisions.

On a more pragmatic level, many employees have come to expect their bosses to be open and frank. They no longer accept being dictated to but want to be treated as individuals with minds of their own. As Elliott said, "I work with lots of people who are bright and intelligent, so I have to deal with them at an intellectual level. They're very logical, and they want to know the reasons for things. They'll buy in only if it makes sense."

In some cases, sharing information means simply being candid about work-related issues. In early 1990, when Elliott hired as employees many of the people she had been using as independent contractors, she knew the transition would be difficult for everyone. The number of employees nearly doubled overnight, and the nature of working relationships changed. "I warned everyone that we were in for some rough times and reminded them that we would be experiencing them together. I admitted that it would also be hard for me, and I made it clear that I wanted them to feel free to talk to me. I was completely candid and encouraged them to be honest with me. I lost some employees who didn't like the new relationships, but I'm convinced that being open helped me understand my employees better, and it gave them a feeling of support."

Like encouraging participation, sharing power and information has its risks. It allows for the possibility that people will reject, criticize, or otherwise challenge what the leader has to say or, more broadly, her authority. Also, employees get frustrated when leaders listen to—but ultimately reject—their ideas. Because information is a source of power, leaders who share it can be seen as naive or needing to be liked. The interviewees have experienced some of these downsides but find the positives overwhelming.

Enhance the Self-worth of Others

One of the by-products of sharing information and encouraging participation is that employees feel important. During the interviews, the women leaders discussed other ways they build a feeling of self-worth in coworkers and subordinates. They talked about giving others credit and praise and sending small signals of recognition. Most important, they expressed how they refrain from asserting their own superiority, which asserts the inferiority of others. All those I interviewed expressed clear aversion to behavior that sets them apart from others in the company—reserved parking places, separate dining facilities, pulling rank.

Examples of sharing and giving credit to others abound. Caplan, who has been the subject of scores of media reports hailing her innovation of labeling vegetables so consumers know what they are and how to cook them, originally got the idea from a farmer. She said that whenever someone raises the subject, she credits the farmer and downplays her role. Rothman is among the many note-writers: when someone does something out of the ordinary, she writes them a personal note to tell them she noticed. Like many of the women I interviewed, she said she also makes a point of acknowledging good work by talking about it in front of others.

Bolstering coworkers and subordinates is especially important in businesses and jobs that tend to be hard on a person's ego. Investment banking is one example because of the long hours, high pressures, intense competition, and inevitability that some deals will fail. One interviewee in investment banking hosts dinners for her division, gives out gag gifts as party favors, passes out M&Ms at meetings, and throws parties "to celebrate ourselves." These things, she said, balance the anxiety that permeates the environment.

Rynd compensates for the negativity inherent in preparing tax returns: "In my business we have something called a query sheet, where the person who reviews the tax return writes down everything that needs to be corrected. Criticism is built into the system. But at the end of every review, I always include a positive comment—your work paper technique looked good, I appreciate the fact that you got this done on time, or something like that. It seems trivial, but it's one way to remind people that I recognize their good work and not just their shortcomings."

Energize Others

The women leaders spoke of their enthusiasm for work and how they spread their enthusiasm around to make work a challenge that is exhilarating and fun. The women leaders talked about it in those terms and claimed to use their enthusiasm to get others excited. As Rothman said, "There is rarely a person I can't motivate."

Enthusiasm was a dominant theme throughout the interviews. In computer consulting: "Because this business is on the forefront of technology, I'm sort of evangelistic about it, and I want other people to be as excited as I am." In venture capital: "You have to have a head of steam." In executive search: "Getting people excited is an important way to influence those you have no control over." Or in managing sports arenas: "My enthusiasm gets others excited. I infuse them with energy and make them see that even boring jobs contribute to the fun of working in a celebrity business."

Enthusiasm can sometimes be misunderstood. In conservative professions like investment banking, such an upbeat leadership style can be interpreted as cheerleading and can undermine credibility. In many cases, the women said they won and preserved their credibility by achieving results that could be measured easily. One of the women acknowledged that her colleagues don't understand or like her leadership style and have called it cheerleading. "But," she added, in this business you get credibility from what you produce, and they love the profits I generate." While energy and enthusiasm can inspire some, it doesn't work for everyone. Even Rothman conceded, "Not everyone has a flame that can be lit."

PATHS OF LEAST RESISTANCE

Many of the women I interviewed said the behaviors and beliefs that underlie their leadership style come naturally to them. I attribute this to two things: their socialization and the career paths they have chosen. Although socialization patterns and career paths are changing, the average age of the men and women who responded to the survey is 51— old enough to have had experiences that differed *because* of gender.

Until the 1960s, men and women received different signals about what was expected of them. To summarize a subject that many experts have explored in depth, women have been expected to be wives, mothers, community volunteers, teachers, and nurses. In all these roles, they are supposed to be cooperative, supportive, understanding, gentle, and to provide service to others. They are to derive satisfaction and a sense of self-esteem from helping others, including their spouses. While men have had to appear to be competitive, strong, tough, decisive, and in control, women have been allowed to be cooperative, emotional, supportive, and vulnerable. This may explain why women today are more likely than men to be interactive leaders.

Men and women have also had different career opportunities. Women were not expected to have careers, or at least not the same kinds of careers as men, so they either pursued different jobs or were simply denied opportunities men had. Women's career tracks have usually not included long series of organizational positions with formal authority and control of resources. Many women had their first work experiences outside the home as volunteers. While some of the challenges they faced as managers in volunteer organizations are the same as those in any business, in many ways, leading volunteers is different because of the absence of concrete rewards like pay and promotion.

As women entered the business world, they tended to find themselves in positions consistent with the roles they played at home: in staff positions rather than in line positions, supporting the work of others, and in functions like communications or human resources where they had relatively small budgets and few people reporting directly to them.

The fact that most women have lacked formal authority over others and control over resources means that by default they have had to find other ways to accomplish their work. As it turns out, the behaviors that were natural and/or socially acceptable for them have been highly successful in at least some managerial settings.

What came easily to women turned out to be a survival tactic. Although leaders often begin their careers doing what comes naturally and what fits within the constraints of the job, they also develop their skills and styles over time. The women's use of interactive leadership has its roots in socialization, and the women interviewees firmly believe that it benefits their organizations. Through the course of their careers, they have gained conviction that their style is effective. In fact, for some, it was their own success that caused them to formulate their philosophies about what motivates people, how to make good decisions, and what it takes to maximize business performance.

They now have formal authority and control over vast resources, but still they see sharing power and information as an asset rather than a liability. They believe that although pay and promotion are necessary tools of management, what people really want is to feel that they are contributing to a higher purpose and that they have the opportunity as individuals to learn and grow. The women believe that employees and peers perform better when they feel they are part of an organization and can share in its success. Allowing them to get involved and to work to their potential is a way of maximizing their contributions and using human resources most efficiently.

ANOTHER KIND OF DIVERSITY

The IWF survey shows that a nontraditional leadership style can be effective in organizations that accept it. This lesson comes especially hard to those who think of the corporate world as a game of survival of the fittest, where the fittest is always the strongest, toughest, most decisive, and powerful. Such a workplace seems to favor leaders who control people by controlling resources, and by controlling people, gain control of more resources. Asking for information and sharing decision-making power can be seen as serious disadvantages, but what is a disadvantage under one set of circumstances is an advantage under another. The "best" leadership style depends on the organizational context.

Only one of the women interviewees is in a traditional, large-scale company. More typically, the women's organizations are medium-sized and tend to have experienced fast growth and fast change. They demand performance and/or have a high proportion of professional workers. These organizations seem to create opportunities for women and are hospitable to those who use a nontraditional management style.

The degree of growth or change in an organization is an important factor in creating opportunities for women. When change is rampant, everything is up for grabs, and crises are frequent. Crises are generally not desirable, but they do create opportunities for people to prove themselves. Many of the women interviewees said they got their first break because their organizations were in turmoil.

Fast-changing environments also play havoc with tradition. Coming up through the ranks and being part of an established network is no longer important. What is important is how you perform. Also, managers in such environments are open to new solutions, new structures, and new ways of leading.

The fact that many of the women respondents are in organizations that have clear performance standards suggests that they have gained credibility and legitimacy by achieving results. In investment banking, venture capital, accounting, and executive placement, for instance, individual performance is easy to measure.

A high proportion of young professional workers—increasingly typical of organizations—is also a factor in some women's success. Young, educated professionals impose special requirements on their organizations. They demand to participate and contribute. In some cases, they have knowledge or talents their bosses don't have. If they are good performers, they have many employment options. It is easy to imagine that these professionals will respond to leaders who are inclusive and open, who enhance the self-worth of others, and who create a fun work environment. Interactive leaders are likely to win the cooperation needed to achieve their goals.

Interactive leadership has proved to be effective, perhaps even advantageous, in organizations in which the women I interviewed have succeeded. As the work force increasingly demands participation and the economic environment increasingly requires rapid change, interactive leadership may emerge as the management style of choice for many organizations. For interactive leadership to take root more broadly, however, organizations must be willing to question the notion that the traditional command-and-control leadership style that has brought success in earlier decades is the only way to get results. This may be hard in some organizations, especially those with long histories of male-oriented, command-and-control leadership. Changing these organizations will not be easy. The fact that women are more likely than men to be interactive leaders raises the risk that these companies will perceive interactive leadership as "feminine" and automatically resist it.

Linking interactive leadership directly to being female is a mistake. We know that women are capable of making their way through corporations by adhering to the traditional corporate model and that they can wield power in ways similar to men. Indeed, some women may prefer that style. We also know from the survey findings that some men use the transformational leadership style.

Large, established organizations should expand their definition of effective leadership. If they were to do that, several things might happen, including the disappearance of the glass ceiling and the creation of a wider path for all sorts of executives—men and women—to attain positions of leadership. Widening the path will free potential leaders to lead in ways that play to their individual strengths. Then the newly recognized interactive leadership style can be valued and rewarded as highly as the command-and-control style has been for decades. By valuing a diversity of leadership styles, organizations will find the strength and flexibility to survive in a highly competitive, increasingly diverse economic environment.

DISCUSSION QUESTIONS

1. How have women executives changed their leadership style over time?
2. How do men and women leaders describe their leadership?
3. What are the roots of women's leadership style?

ENDNOTE

1. Transactional and transformational leadership were first conceptualized by James McGregor Burns in *Leadership* (New York: Harper & Row, 1978) and later developed by Bernard Bass in *Leadership and Performance Beyond Expectations* (New York: Free Press, 1985).

Reprinted with permission from Harvard Business Review 68 (November-December): 119–125.

Activity 8–1

Leadership Style Inventory

Step 1: Complete the following questionnaire:

This inventory is designed to provide you with personal data about the frequency with which you tend to select particular leadership behaviors. As you fill out the inventory, give a high rank to those words which best describe the way you most often behave as a leader and a low rank to the words which describe the way you least often behave as a leader.

You may find it hard to choose the words that best describe your leadership behavior because there are no right or wrong answers. Different behaviors described in the inventory are equally good.

There are nine sets of four words listed below. *Rank-order* the four words in each set across the page, assigning a 4 to the word which best describes your leadership behavior, a 3 to the next best, a 2 to the next best, and a 1 to the word which is least descriptive of your behavior as a leader. *Be sure to assign a different rank number to each of the four words in each set*. Do not make ties.

	A		*B*		*C*		*D*
1.	3 Forceful	4 Negotiating	1 Testing	2 Sharing
2.	4 Decisive	3 Teaching	1 Probing	2 Unifying
3.	4 Expert	2 Convincing	1 Inquiring	3 Cooperative
4.	4 Resolute	3 Inspirational	1 Questioning	2 Giving
5.	4 Authoritative	3 Compelling	2 Participative	1 Approving
6.	2 Commanding	4 Influential	1 Searching	2 Collaborating
7.	3 Direct	4 Persuasive	2 Verifying	1 Impartial
8.	1 Showing	3 Maneuvering	4 Analytical	2 Supportive
9.	3 Prescriptive	4 Strategic	1 Exploring	2 Compromising

Words Numbered:
2 3 4 5 7 8 = _____

Words Numbered:
1 3 6 7 8 9 = _____

Words Numbered:
2 3 4 5 8 9 = _____

Words Numbered:
1 3 6 7 8 9 = _____

Column A (Tell Score)	Column B (Sell Score)	Column C (Consult Score)	Column D (Join Score)

Scoring. Each column corresponds to a different leadership behavior: Column A—Tell; Column B—Sell; Column C—Consult; Column D—Join. To determine how frequently you use each of these behaviors, insert on the lines directly below each column how you ranked the designated words. For example, in Column A (the "Tell" column), words numbered 2, 3, 4, 5, 7, 8 are designated. Now do the same for the other three columns. After you have completed this, add up the numbers on each line to get column scores.

Step 2: Complete the Leadership Scoring and Profile Sheet as directed.

Your Present Leadership Repertoire. The chart on the next page can be developed into a graphic profile of your present repertoire of leadership behavior. Shade in the area which corresponds to each of your scores from the inventory above. For example, if you scored 15 on *TELL* behavior, then shade the area up to the 15 on the chart under *TELL*. The ruled-in percentile provides you a way of comparing yourself to other managers who have taken the inventory. The percentiles are keyed to indicate the number of managers who scored *below* a particular score. For example, a score of 17 on *TELL* means over 80% of the managers tested use a *TELL* behavior less frequently than you do.

Your Leadership Inclinations. Two additional scores may be obtained from the inventory: Manipulativeness and Emphasis on Human Resources. To obtain these, complete the

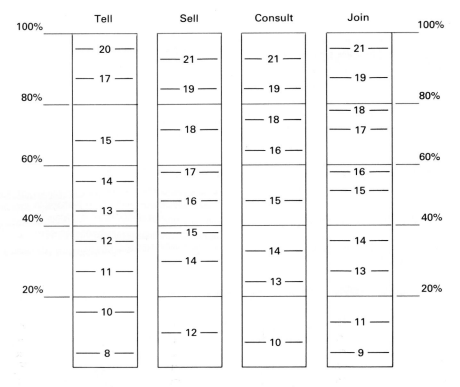

following calculations by first inserting your Tell, Sell, Consult and Join scores on the lines below.

Manipulativeness = *Sell + Consult − Tell − Join*
= _____ (Preserve minus sign if any)

Human Resources = *Join + Consult − Tell − Sell*
= _____ (Preserve minus sign if any)

These scores may now be charted below. (Note that it is possible to chart a negative score.)

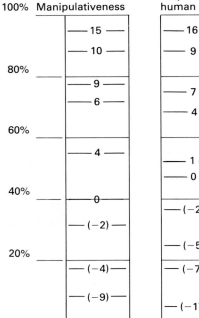

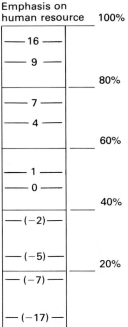

Step 3: Interpret the scores.

Figure 8–18 depicts four primary ways a leader may choose to behave in a given situation. The rectangle represents the amount of authority a leader has in a particular situation so that "Tell" represents a point on the continuum where maximal use of authority is made by the leader and minimal freedom is given to subordinates in the decision-making process. Each of these primary leadership behaviors is more fully explained in Table 8–15.

WHAT THE TELL, SELL, CONSULT AND JOIN SCORES MEAN

Your Tell, Sell, Consult and Join scores indicate the frequency with which you use each of the primary leadership behaviors. In part, your use of these behaviors reflects how you see yourself, your subordinates and your current work situation. For example, if you work in an environment where subordinates are perceived as mature and experienced, then chances are you are going to use more frequently Consult and Join behaviors. On the other hand, if you have little tolerance for ambiguity, then you may tend to frequently use Tell and Sell behaviors. Your scores are also a reflection, in part, of your leadership inclinations. Generally, people tend to emphasize leadership behaviors which fit their personality or which they have learned work for them or with which they feel comfortable. Some managers, by their very nature, find it very hard to be assertive and use a tell approach, while others are very comfortable behaving that way. The point to remember is that your present repertoire of leadership behavior is *not* an unchangeable part of your personality but rather represents how you presently choose

to behave on the job. Hence, it is more important to begin to explore why you emphasize the behaviors you do and whether or not such behaviors are the most effective than to conclude "that's just the way I am." In addition, you will want to explore why you tend to use less frequently some of the leadership behaviors. On pages 366–367, there is a place set aside for you to consider which forces tend to shape your leadership inclinations.

WHAT THE MANIPULATIVENESS AND HUMAN RESOURCES SCORES MEAN

The manipulativeness score measures the degree to which the leader attempts to gain subordinate's acceptance of his or her decisions. Manipulation, as defined by the dictionary, is "artful management of control." It is in this context that manipulativeness is used here and not in the context of unfair or dishonest acts. If we examine the beliefs underlying the Tell and Sell behavior in Table 8–15, we find the primary difference between Tell and Sell is that in Sell the leader also "seeks to reduce any resistance through persuasion"— hence, a manipulative act is added to Sell. Similarly, the difference between Consult and Join is the leader's belief that consulting subordinates is useful in order "to increase subordinate's ownership and commitment"—hence, Consult also involves a manipulative act. If you score high on manipulativeness, it may be because you have experienced a strong need to insure subordinate acceptance of your decisions or because you perceive your subordinates or work setting necessitate such behavior. While some managers tend to employ manipulative behavior, even when such behavior is really unnecessary, whether or not you tend to do so

Figure 8–18 **Continuum of Leader Behavior**

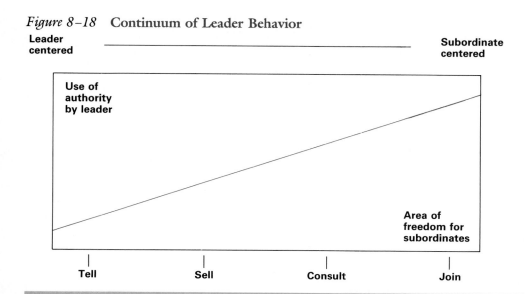

SOURCE: Based largely on R. Tannenbaum and W. H. Schmidt, How to choose a leadership pattern, *Harvard Business Review* (March-April 1958): 95–101. In the original article, Tell was represented by position 1; Sell by position 2; Consult by positions 3, 4, and 5; and Join by positions 6 and 7.

Table 8–15 **A Description of Leader Behaviors**

Leadership Behavior	Action Taken	Underlying Beliefs
Tell	Leader identifies the problem, considers alternative solutions and announces the final decision to subordinates for implementation.	Leader feels subordinate participation in the decision is unnecessary, unwarranted or not feasible. Hence, no opportunity to participate is provided.
Sell	Leader takes responsibility for identifying the problem and determining the final decision. But rather than simply announcing the decision the leader takes the added step of trying to persuade subordinates to accept the decision.	Leader recognizes the potential for subordinate resistance from merely announcing the final decision and therefore *seeks to reduce any resistance through persuasion*.
Consult	Leader identifies the problem, consults subordinates for possible solutions and then announces the final decision.	Leader recognizes the potential value of *effectively culling ideas* from subordinates and believes such action will *increase subordinate's ownership and commitment* to the final solution.
Join	Leader defines the problem and then joins subordinates in making the final decision. The leader fully shares decision-making authority with subordinates.	Leader believes subordinates are capable of making high-quality decisions and that subordinates want to do the right thing. The leader believes human resources are best utilized when decision-making authority is fully shared.

depends upon a careful diagnosis of the forces in your work setting. Do you tend to frequently Sell or Consult even when Telling is all that is necessary? Do you tend to avoid Join situations because you don't want to give up control even though Joining is called for? Do you use manipulative behaviors because you are comfortable doing so or because your situation or subordinates necessitate such action?

The human resources score measures the tendency of the leader to use behaviors which reflect confidence in his or her subordinates' ability to make decisions. As one moves to the right on the leadership continuum, in Figure 8–18, there is an increasing emphasis placed on the use of subordinates as resources. Hence, the leader who relies more on Consult and Join rather than Tell and Sell tends to utilize subordinates more often in joint decision-making situations. Again, to what extent you rely on these behaviors because of your own tendencies or out of real necessity should be carefully evaluated by you.

WHICH BEHAVIORS ARE BEST?

By now it should be clear that one leadership behavior is no better than any other—to be effective the leader must be able to choose correctly the behavior that a particular work situation calls for *and* be effective in the use of that behavior. While this instrument cannot help you decide how to behave, it can help you examine more carefully your

present leadership inclinations and help you begin to explore whether or not it might be useful to begin developing other behaviors. For example, if you frequently use Tell and Sell behaviors, you might want to think about why you tend to favor these over Consult and Join. Are you uncomfortable with less directive behaviors? Do your subordinates have difficulty working independently? Or does the nature of the job require acting this way? In general, the more you understand why you choose the leadership behaviors you do, the more potentially effective you can be as a leader. And, much like the golfer, the more you are comfortable and skilled using the various clubs available to you, the greater your potential versatility in selecting a behavior that is likely to be effective. Below, space is provided for some personal reflection and analysis of your present work situation.

Personal Analysis

A. I tend to frequently use (_____ Tell; _____ Sell; _____ Consult; _____ Join) behaviors because of:

1st, the way I see myself _____

_____

_____

2nd, the way I see my subordinates _____

3rd, the way I see my work situation _____

_____

_____

B. I tend to less frequently use (_____ Tell; _____ Sell; _____ Consult; _____ Join) behaviors because of:

1st, the way I see myself _____

_____

_____

2nd, the way I see my subordinates _____

_____

3rd, the way I see my work situation _____

_____

_____

Step 4: Discussion. In small groups or with the class as a whole, answer the following questions:

Description
1. What does your profile look like?
2. Does your profile surprise you?

Diagnosis
3. How would you act if you were Grace Pastiak, described in the introduction to the chapter?
4. Compare the profiles of people with the same action plans. Do they have the same leadership style?
5. Compare the profiles of people with different action plans. Do they have the same leadership style?
6. How well does your profile predict the nature of your actions?
7. Think of two situations you have faced. What leadership style fits best with those situations?

_____

Reprinted with the permission of the author, John F. Veiga, University of Connecticut; Storrs, CT 06269.

Activity 8–2 Peter Knudtsen

Step 1: Read the Peter Knudtsen case.

Peter Knudtsen paused while packing his suitcase to enjoy the view of Lac Leman from the third-floor window of his room in the Hotel Royal-Savoy in Lausanne.

"What a magnificent sight!" he mumbled softly to himself, as he recalled the shifting moods of the lake and mountains during his many weeks in that room.

Peter couldn't help but remember the incredibly clear evenings when the lights of Evian on the south shore of the lake had sparkled like a thousand diamonds. He also recalled the mornings like this one when the rain and fog had cleared to reveal a bright new cover of snow on the Alps and the beautiful winter sunsets when he could nearly see Geneva almost 50 kilometers to the west.

The unusually mild and sunny December morning in Lausanne triggered some thoughts of the long hours of darkness and cold in Norstrand, the suburb of Oslo where he lived with his wife Grethe. And as he returned his attention to folding a shirt carefully into his suitcase he wondered what he could find as a welcoming present for Grethe when she arrived in Geneva that evening. While Peter had been too busy to miss his wife during the long days of classes and study at the IMEDE Management Development Institute, he was very excited that she had decided to travel to Lausanne for his graduation on Wednesday.

Having finished packing the majority of his clothes, Peter began organizing the large stacks of cases and other course materials he had accumulated during the 19-week Program for Executive Development (PED).

As he sorted through some of the cases from early in the program . . . *Hedblom* . . . *American Motors* . . . *Benihana* . . . *Bobst* . . . *Bulldurhan* . . . he laughed silently about his anxiety during the opening weeks of PED. While he had been overwhelmed by the huge weekly packets of material in August, he now reflected on how easy it was for him to identify the critical issues in a 30- or 40-page business case. Looking at some financial data in the *Sandoz* series, Peter laughed outloud as he thought, "Gosh. I didn't even know what a balance sheet was in August!"

Looking at the huge masses of course materials, it was hard for Peter to deny that his facility with reading and speaking English had greatly improved. And he undeniably knew a lot more about finance and operations than he had before. In fact, he wondered how this would affect his relationship with the production manager and the controller? In his new position as marketing manager for the Consumer Products Division of Norske Elektro A/S, he would be interacting with those men much more frequently than he had in his former position as group product manager in the Industrial Products Division (see Figures 8–19 and 8–20).

In his former position, Peter had come to despise the financial control system at Norske Elektro. Although he had not been able to articulate the problem clearly prior to his experience at IMEDE, Peter now realized that the system rewarded individual competition among the senior functional managers and prevented interdepartmental collaboration that was so vital to new product development.

Indeed, as Peter continued to package his IMEDE case material for shipment to Norway, he thought for the first time of the parallels between the control system . t Norske Elektro and the system in *Rotch Paper,* one of the accounting cases that he had studied.

While the system at Norske Elektro worked very well to encourage the control of manufacturing costs and to promote efficient production schedules, the control system had made it very difficult for him in his role as group product manager to gain the appropriate support from manufacturing in preparing new product introductions or in processing special orders for important industrial customers.

And although Peter had successfully gained the support of the key production supervisors in granting Peter special "favors," he had regrettably irritated and alienated Bjørn Evju and Erling Guttormsen, his counterparts in the Consumer Electronics Division. Ironically, he must now

count on them for their support in his new position as marketing manager of the Division (see Figure 8–20). He would also need to work on his relationship with the Controller, Trond Falkenberg, with whom Peter had had numerous "shouting matches." Indeed, as marketing manager, Peter would be meeting regularly with Trond and Erik Bekeng to review his division's profitability. Peter hoped that his training at IMEDE would increase his empathy for their function.

Thoughts of the control system at Norske Elektro triggered thoughts of his new boss, Horst Berger, who had designed the financial measurement system nearly 20 years before. Peter's concerns about his new superior intensified as he began to reread a report that he had written for the Organizational Behavior course only weeks before. . . .

THE COMPANY

My company, Norske Elektro A/S, is one of the largest manufacturers and distributors of name-brand consumer electronics, electrical appliances, and industrial instrumentation in Norway.

Our company, a wholly owned subsidiary of a German multinational corporation, employs about 900 persons in its modern factory and administrative offices in Fredrikstad, a small industrial town on the east side of the Oslo fjord.

Though Norske Elektro (NE) is one of the leading companies in its industry in Norway, sales volume in its consumer electronics and appliance business has leveled off and is declining in some segments. And although sales volume and market share in industrial

Figure 8–19   **Norske Electro A/S, Partial Organization, July 1981**

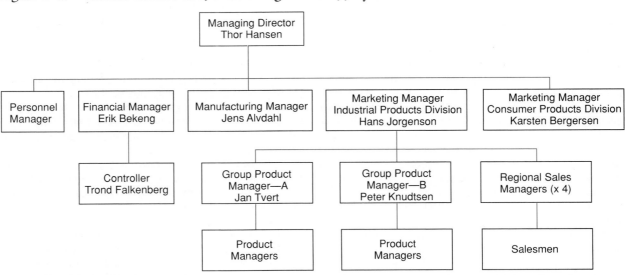

Figure 8–20 **Norske Electro A/S, Partial Organization, January 1982**

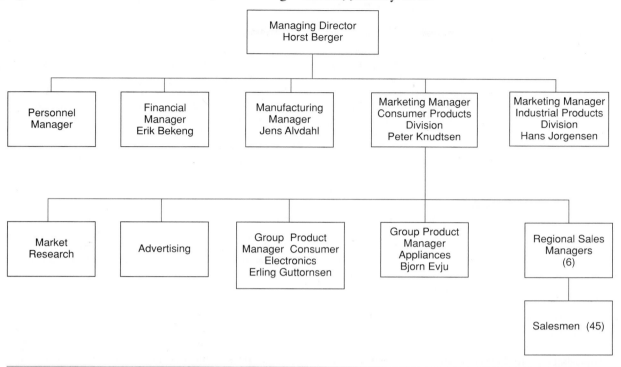

products are strong, the stagnation of the consumer business has created some serious profitability problems in the past few years.

As shown in Figure 8–19, the company is organized along simple functional lines with a managing director serving as "chief executive officer" of the Norwegian operation. In fact, the M/D has always been able to operate with a high degree of autonomy vis-à-vis corporate headquarters in Frankfurt.

THE PEOPLE

Let me start with myself. I was born in 1944 in Norstrand, a small town about one and a half hours south of Oslo. Due to some conflicts with my grandmother (my mother died when I was very young and I was raised by my grandmother) I left home at the age of 15 after completing my education at the local Folke Skole.

I then attended a Fag Skole where I studied to become an electrician and was working in an Oslo manufacturing plant on an apprenticeship when a salesman from Norske Elektro invited me to join the sales force staff as a clerk.

Thus, I entered the company at age 21 at the lowest office clerk level doing record keeping for the in-

dustrial products division. About one year after I was hired, I was asked to supervise a small group of clerks in the sales department, and 3 years later, I joined the sales force.

It was at that time that I remember my first contacts with Horst Berger. The industrial products sales force was expanding rapidly at the time, and I was lucky enough to have the marketing manager recommend me for a promotion to the position of regional sales manager. I remember that Mr. Berger agreed to my promotion; however, reliable sources told me that Mr. Berger had said, "We will replace Knudtsen as soon as we find someone more suitable." I might add that the marketing manager told me about my promotion and not Mr. Berger.

Well, it was not a very exciting start for me in trying to build up an effective sales force, but I tried to understand Mr. Berger's position because I was rather young and inexperienced for a management position.

During the subsequent 7 years I tried to fulfill my assignment as effectively as possible, and I was not replaced. Then about six years ago I was promoted to become group product manager for a group of industrial products with a sales of about SwFr 100 million. It was during this period of time when I started to have more direct contact with Mr. Berger. But before I go on, I should tell you a little more about Mr. Berger and his background.

From what I have heard, Mr. Berger is about 57 years old and is the only son of a wealthy Hamburg industrialist. After attending private schools in Germany, he studied at the Technische Hochschule in Munich where he received an engineering degree. Subsequently he served in the *Deutsche Budeswehr* and later joined the Norske Elektro parent company in one of their manufacturing facilities outside of Frankfurt. As far as I know, he has always been single.

Mr. Berger's career progressed rapidly through various engineering and management positions in the parent company and in 1962, at age 38, he was appointed managing director of Norske Elektro A/S. He served in that capacity until 1976, at which point he was granted a leave of absence from the parent company to serve the government in Bonn in a diplomatic capacity.

When he left the company, Mr. Berger was replaced by Thor Hansen, a dynamic 48-year-old Norwegian who had recently completed the IMEDE PED program and a two-year assignment at corporate headquarters.

Then in August 1981, to everyone's surprise in Frederikstad, Mr. Berger returned to resume his former position as managing director and Thor Hansen was precipitously transferred to an unknown position in Frankfurt.

Finally, as I told you during coffee last month, Karsten Bergersen resigned as marketing manager of the Consumer Products Division, and I was informed that I would be assuming Bergersen's position upon my return in December.

This should be sufficient background to enable you to understand the situation that I will face when I return to Frederikstad.

MR. BERGER'S MANAGEMENT STYLE

As I indicated, I had occasional contact with Mr. Berger several years ago, although most of his contacts were with my boss, the Industrial Products Division marketing manager. However, I would like to describe one of the typical situations I encountered when called into his office by his secretary.

In a typical meeting in Mr. Berger's office, he was sitting behind his huge walnut desk in a large, high-backed leather "executive" chair. In front of his desk were arranged several smaller straight-backed chairs in a straight line to accommodate meeting participants. Usually only the "top five" had direct contact with him. On rare occasions when someone from the next lower level, e.g., the group product manager, was called in, he was greeted by Mr. Berger with a hand shake and a superficial "How are you?" without any real engagement or interest in your answer.

Mr. Berger then initiated the "discussion" by asking one of the individuals present a very specific question. Very often, Mr. Berger would interrupt long before the respondent had finished his answer, and Mr. Berger would elaborate broadly on a certain point which he had heard or meant to hear out of the unfinished answer. He would then elaborate on this idea for 30 minutes to an hour without leaving his guests with an opportunity to interact. As a consequence meetings usually took several hours! To make matters worse, at the end no one had a clear idea what to do when they left or which direction to go because clear decisions were never made.

I do not want to be misunderstood. Mr. Berger is an extremely intelligent person and is highly regarded and respected for his creativity and his public speaking ability. Indeed, he takes numerous opportunities to practice that. I remember one Christmas party in the administrative headquarters when Mr. Berger entered the gathering where about 200 people were celebrating in a cramped room and while they were *standing* with drinks in their hands he proceeded to give a one-and-a-half-hour New Year's address.

In meetings in his office, Mr. Berger creates dozens of ideas within a couple of hours and demands that the senior managers follow up on them. But a few days later when they come back with answers, he might have lost interest in these answers because in the meantime he would have generated a lot of new ideas which he finds more attractive than the ones created a few days earlier.

However, you have to follow them up because in certain cases he will come back to an issue or idea and demand precise answers. Perhaps he does that to clarify his own thinking, but it is really frustrating for his immediate subordinates, and the daily revision of orders causes "shock waves" continually throughout the organization. All in all, I think his management style has, over the years, created "yes-men" out of his key managers.

He also has weekly, monthly, and quarterly profit reviews centered on the analysis of financial data on more than 200 measures such as scrap loss by profit center and shift, sales by product line, and a series of complex ratios which only he understands. Even the controller doesn't seem to understand the system, yet Mr. Berger will call the senior managers into his office and, in "inquisition style," will fire unanswerable questions at them about the "causes" of various ratios which he feels are out of line. I have never attended one of these personally, but will be doing so in my new position.

While this is my impression of Mr. Berger, it may

not be shared by all the managers. Some of the older people in the company who were used to a very paternalistic and authoritarian style seemed to go along with it or at least did not actively resist it. However, most of the managers felt overwhelmingly dominated by him. Perhaps his remarkable appearance—he is over 190 centimeters tall—might have contributed to the feeling.

Personally I was not very concerned about his style of leadership during more than 10 years because Mr. Berger usually did not visit or talk directly to second or third level managers. Thus, the "junior managers," including myself, had few opportunities to build up a close relationship or even talk to him.

It is only fair to point out that Mr. Berger devoted his life totally to the company. I don't think he had any other interests outside of work. On a usual day he would spend 12 hours or more in the office. Starting at the official office time in the morning, he rarely left his office before 8 or 9 o'clock at night. He also expected everyone at the management level to be free to stay at the office as long as he did and to be available at any time including weekends to return to the office without advance notice. I recall situations where he asked managers to stay for the evening who acquiesced even though they had an important evening appointment with their wife or a friend. In such situations I never saw anyone dare to ask if they could leave.

But there was another side of the coin. Instinctively he must have known what people thought of him. I remember one company festivity when he said, after several glasses of wine, "I know nobody likes me here." I could hear an undercurrent of sadness and loneliness, but in the next moment he had himself "under control" again.

Very often I thought about that remark and tried to understand his situation. One important reason seems to me the fact that he became the managing director at a very young age. At the time he had to manage a team of much older and largely Norwegian managers and I suspect he developed his "Theory X" style at a time when he had to establish and assert himself. Another reason could have to do with his experience as an active officer in the German army with its training in authoritarian leadership styles.

When Mr. Berger left for Bonn in 1976, we got a new managing director, Thor Hansen. His management style was highly participative and was clearly what you have called "Model Three" or humanistic-collaborative. For many people, Thor's style was almost a shock because they were now asked for their opinions and their ideas and Thor listened with interest and understanding.

Although it took some time for his subordinates to understand and respond to the new style, they gradually began to actively contribute in meetings and discussions again. While the financial control system remained unchanged, it became an instrument for self-analysis and correction rather than a tool for blame and recrimination.

During the 5 years of Thor's leadership I believe that commitment to the company improved a lot. Problems were discussed freely and with a bit of humor and when no new aspects were forthcoming, Thor would make a decision. When people left Thor's office, a clear decision had been made and everyone knew what to do.

Thor began working at the same time as others and left his office between 5 and 6 P.M. Outside of work he showed a lot of interest in his family and in music and in painting. He also did an excellent job of building up human relations throughout the company and at all levels. For example, he did not hesitate to go directly to the office of a person responsible for a certain task where he would talk to him or her in a friendly "adult-to-adult" manner and in a way which showed respect for the [person's] work. He never left junior managers or employees feeling that they were "subordinates" who were way below the "big boss."

As I mentioned earlier, shortly after my arrival at IMEDE in August, Mr. Berger returned to Frederikstad to reassume his former position as managing director. It was a surprise to everyone, including Thor Hansen, who reluctantly accepted a "transfer" to corporate headquarters.

As expected, the style that Thor had developed was reversed almost immediately. After a couple of months Karsten Bergersen, the marketing manager of the Consumer Products Division, quit in protest. Bergersen had developed a highly effective "counselor" management style with his people and was seen as a kind of participative nurturing parent and adult. Shortly thereafter I received notice from corporate headquarters that I am to take over Bergersen's position upon my return. I don't know if Mr. Berger was consulted on my promotion or if he approves it. However, I had planned to take a two-week vacation with Grethe at Zermatt following PED, and Mr. Berger's secretary called last week to say that Mr. Berger wants me to report to my new position immediately after the end of the program.

As head of marketing for the Consumer Products Division, I will obviously have to interact a lot with Mr. Berger. Assuming that he hasn't changed in the past few years, I will presumably have to adapt myself to his management style. I really don't think it is possible to change a 57-year-old person's management style, but I also don't want to sacrifice my own personality.

Perhaps I should mention that I had an excellent relationship with Thor. He helped develop me for a promotion and sponsored my participation at IMEDE, although the promotion into the consumer products group was rather unexpected. That position will be somewhat challenging for me as I don't know much about the consumer products business as I have spent almost my entire career in the industrial products division, which has a very different product line and marketing strategy.

Also, I developed something of a reputation in my last position for being a "doer-director" and I'm afraid my reputation may precede me. While I felt comfortable with that style in my old job, I'm not sure it is as appropriate to my future position. As you know, group product managers have to "make things happen," and I'm afraid I created some resentments among the financial staff and the product managers in the consumer products division. Finally, I am much younger than most of the people in the consumer products division and will inherit a sales force of "old-timers."

On the one hand, I learned the value of a "counselor" style under Thor Hansen. And yet, on the other hand, I am somewhat naturally inclined to be a "doer-director" and would like to establish my credibility in the new division. Obviously, a "delegator" style won't work, as I don't know anything about the consumer products business, and I wouldn't learn the business by letting others make decisions.

My biggest problem of course will be Mr. Berger. His style will obviously impact what I am able to do with my new people. Also, I have many interests outside of work which developed during Thor Hansen's reign and I really do not want to be available for Mr. Berger at any time of the night or day. I am not his servant. But it may be difficult, because I heard recently via the "grapevine" that the other marketing manager and the manufacturing and finance managers have already "surrendered" to Berger's management style and are playing their roles as they did six years ago. . . .

As Peter neared the end of the report, he was interrupted by a knock at the door. It was Alexander Lischer, one of the other PED participants who had also been living in the hotel.

"How about a beer?" asked Alex. Peter hesitated for a moment, having forgotten where he was, and then smiled and responded, "Sure . . . if you give me some free advice on a personal 'case.' "

"It's a deal," said Alex.

"This is our last Saturday in Lausanne. Why don't we walk down to Ouchy. I need to pick up something for Grethe," said Peter. "You know, she's coming in tonight."

Step 2: Prepare the case for class discussion.

Step 3: Answer the following questions, individually, in small groups, or with the class as a whole, as directed by your instructor:

Description
  1. Describe the leadership style of Horst Berger, Thor Hansen, and Peter Knudtsen.
  2. What is the relationship between these three men's positions?

Diagnosis
  3. Was Berger an effective leader? Was Hansen?
  4. Was Berger an effective manager? Was Hansen?
  5. What situational contingencies should these managers have considered in selecting their leadership style?
  6. What contingencies should Peter Knudtsen consider in selecting a leadership style?
  7. How would you evaluate the quality of communication in this organization?
  8. How well did each manager motivate his employees?

Prescription
  9. What style should Knudtsen use? How should he interact with Berger?

Action
  10. What issues will Knudtsen likely face in his new position?

Step 4: Discussion. In small groups, with the entire class, or in written form, share your answers to the questions above. Then answer the following questions:

  1. What symptoms suggest that a problem exists?
  2. What problems exist in the case?
  3. What theories and concepts help explain the problems?
  4. How can the problems be corrected?
  5. Are the actions likely to be effective?

*Activity
8–3*

Leadership Role Play

Step 1: Divide the class into groups of seven people. Read the general description of the situation below. The instructor will distribute seven roles to each group. Each person in the group should then prepare one role. In preparing for the role play, try to put yourself in the position of the person whose role you are playing.

GENERAL DESCRIPTION OF THE SITUATION

It is August 1, and you are about to have a meeting with the six people you are living with during the summer in an old Victorian house in the city of Medropolis. This city has exciting cultural and educational possibilities, a lovely beach area nearby, a large depressed inner-city area, and a rather conservative political atmosphere.

You are a national group who has come here this summer for various reasons:

Lee West is here for a summer rest after a very demanding work year.
Sandy Brown is a community organizer in the inner city.
Fran Miller is a counselor at an inner city mental health center.
Cam Jones is summer director of curriculum at School District 3 in Medropolis' inner city.
Jan Johnson is teaching summer courses at the medical school.
Brooks Baines is studying philosophy by taking summer courses at the university.
Sam Smith is a secretary in School District 3 for the summer.

You must all return to your homes by August 15. Sandy, Cam, and Fran lived here last year and will continue to live here next year.

You have an important decision to make at this meeting. Mr. Robert Stodge, the superintendent of School District 3, has asked a close friend of yours, Jane Goodenough, for seven people to help him with a census on the weekend of August 12–13. Mr. Stodge is an organization man who cares much about doing what the State Education Director asks of his superintendents. His assistant, David Guitar, loves his work with the people of the district, which he feels is slowly developing a community sense; he is responsible for the organization of the census. It is rumored that several inner-city schools may be consolidated within the next two years, and that School District 3's continued existence may be in question. Your friend has asked you to decide whether or not you will accept this two-day assignment *as a group*. You do not know whether your collection of data will be used responsibly or be a waste of time.

You are to call your friend in a half hour and report your decision. You all agreed when you set the meeting time that you could make your decision in half an hour. (If you don't call Jane within that time, she will call you.)

Step 2: Each group of seven participants should convene the group meeting in part of the room. You have one-half hour to make a decision about whether to conduct the census.

Step 3: Report your group's decision to your instructor.

Step 4: Discussion. Answer the following questions, in small groups or with the entire class:

Description
1. Characterize each participant. How are they similar? different?

Diagnosis
2. What problems did you encounter in reaching agreement? Why?
3. Did a leader emerge?
4. Was the leader effective?
5. Using your knowledge of leadership theories, analyze the leadership you experienced.
6. Did you experience stress?
7. Did you experience issues of adult development?
8. Using motivation, communication, and perceptual theories, explain the outcomes of the meeting.

Reprinted by permission of Sara Ann Rude, St. Louis, Missouri.

Activity 8–4

A Matter of Style

Step 1: Read the case "A Matter of Style."

In his comfortable office on the 22nd floor of a modern office tower in downtown Toronto, Norman Russell, vice president of corporate personnel for the Global Bank, was deep in thought. He was concerned about the problem of increasingly high staff turnover in certain key sectors of the bank's operations, in the face of potentially significant shortages of qualified personnel. Norman remembered that Stuart North, AVP credit at the Mid-City branch, had been strikingly successful in reducing the rate of turnover in his department during the past year (1980–81). The VP personnel wondered if he could learn something from Stuart to help him deal effectively with staff turnover throughout the entire organization.

Norman Russell was especially concerned about possible repercussions from the recent passage of the Canadian Bank Act which would allow foreign banks to obtain Canadian charters. As many as 50 foreign banks were expected to establish operations in Canada during 1981/82, drawing most of their personnel from existing Canadian banks. Because the newcomers planned to concentrate on wholesale banking, their manpower needs were expected to be greatest in two areas—in operations raising funds for lending, and even more so in departments that loan money (e.g., Stuart North's credit department). Norman knew that corporate head-hunters were already attempting to entice experienced middle managers away from their present positions in the Global Bank's money market and foreign exchange trading departments, and from its commercial credit department. Salaries for these specialities were rising rapidly, and a shortage of middle managers was threatening to become acute throughout the entire financial community.

Established in 1902, the Global Bank operated 279 Canadian branches from its Toronto headquarters. Mid-City was the bank's largest branch—495 employees shared space in the cavernous ground floor customer service area ("bigger than a football field!") and in offices on several floors of the bank's head office building. Fifty-five of the Mid-City staff worked in the credit department, considered the senior or prestige area of the branch. The other 440 employees staffed various departments related to the administration of the branch (see Figure 8–21).

Of the credit department's 45 lenders, 60 percent were university graduates, many of them MBAs. The others were "career bankers" who had been trained on the job in many different aspects of banking operations. They were people whose ability and experience had brought them promotion to the senior credit level. Fifteen of the older and more experienced lenders were corporate accounts officers, re-

sponsible for the bank's largest and most complex accounts. The remaining 30 lenders were in charge of commercial credit accounts. All credit personnel were organized in teams (see Figure 8–22) headed by senior credit managers.

The AVP credit, Stuart North, was a "career banker"—a 25-year Global Bank employee who had left high school after completing grade 10 to join a northern Ontario branch as a junior clerk. He had worked successfully for the bank in many different locations, in various positions: ledger keeper, clerk-teller, assistant accounts manager, training school teacher, accountant, office manager, personal loan officer, branch manager, credit supervisor, and district credit manager. Stuart was appointed to the Mid-City position in November 1979, replacing the former AVP credit who had left the Global Bank to work for a private company.

The clients of the Mid-City credit department were law and accounting firms, advertising agencies, management consulting firms, nonprofit organizations, publishers and printers, various types of privately owned businesses, personal holding companies, real estate management firms, insurance-related companies, etc., including many multinational corporations. Each client was "attached" to part of a credit team, and was made the specific responsibility of one lender within that subgroup. Customers tended to phone their own particular lender with *all* of their banking requests, whether credit-related or not. As a result, lenders were very involved in the total administration of each account, which required attention to many banking details in addition to its credit requirements. The relatively new designation for a lender, "account manager," acknowledged this expanded function of the Bank's credit personnel.

On May 6, 1981, Norman contacted Stuart North, who readily agreed to talk with him about his experiences as AVP credit. The following day, Norman walked through the bustling activity of Mid-City's public business area, past closely situated desks of credit department personnel, into Stuart's uncluttered oak-paneled office. Stuart greeted him warmly, and the two men were soon comfortably ensconced in easy chairs on either side of a large, bare, leather-topped desk. What follows is a summary of Stuart's responses to Norman's questions:

Norman: You've established an excellent track record here, Stuart—how did you do it? What have you got that your predecessor lacked?

Stuart: I believe it's all related to how you work with people, Norm, and that's a matter of style, I guess. But please don't misunderstand me—there was nothing basically wrong with the way

Figure 8–21   **Organization of Mid-City Bank, January 1981**

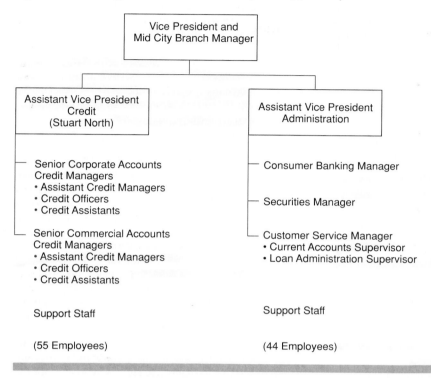

Vice President and
Mid City Branch Manager

Assistant Vice President
Credit
(Stuart North)

Assistant Vice President
Administration

Senior Corporate Accounts
Credit Managers
• Assistant Credit Managers
• Credit Officers
• Credit Assistants

Senior Commercial Accounts
Credit Managers
• Assistant Credit Managers
• Credit Officers
• Credit Assistants

Support Staff

(55 Employees)

Consumer Banking Manager

Securities Manager

Customer Service Manager
• Current Accounts Supervisor
• Loan Administration Supervisor

Support Staff

(44 Employees)

things were going under the former AVP credit. This place always runs and continues to grow, regardless of who's in charge. But things can

Figure 8–22   **Mid-City Credit Department Account Managers: Team Organization Chart, November 1979**

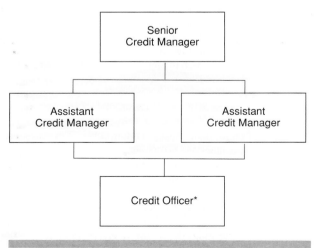

Senior
Credit Manager

Assistant
Credit Manager

Assistant
Credit Manager

Credit Officer*

* A training position, with lending authority.

always be better, and I feel that my predecessor may have directed too much time and effort to unproductive areas. I, myself, am interested in the whole of banking. I think my background reflects this. I don't think of myself as a specialist in credit, and there's still a lot I don't know about it. I consider myself to be a banker, a balanced banker.

As for my job—I'm responsible for the multimillion-dollar credit portfolio of this branch, and for the training and development of my people. My goal is to have my people ready for transfer within two years—only if they're competent, of course. And it's absolutely essential to me that all transferees from Mid-City credit get recognized by Global for their achievements, and are promoted accordingly within the Bank.

Business development is also part of a credit AVP's job, but my people do the business development here. I have to do a balancing act among other priorities. We're on zero manpower growth, which is a problem, though not an insurmountable one. I don't have anyone below me to pass work on to—but when you're moving the paper and not working late, it's difficult to justify hiring another person.

My concept of my job as a manager is to

think basics at first, and move it out from there. And I'm an action-oriented person. You can have all the meetings you want, but if you don't *act*, what's the use? And the Global Bank has done a good job of giving me training, providing me with a broad base of banking knowledge. That base is essential—as I tell my people, if you want to start at the second floor level, sooner or later you'll discover that you don't have a basement!

Norman: What kind of problems did you have when you first arrived at the Mid-City branch?

Stuart: When I came here on November 1, 1979, the problem areas were basically within the commercial credit accounts group. The corporate accounts group is a very senior group with a lot more experienced staff, and they are good at resolving their own problems. But we have many new university grads in commercial credit, and we're training a lot of people who are brand new to the bank. I've noticed that the MBAs coming in want to be "credit animals." They don't want to deal with detail, or take time to learn the basics. My approach to them is, "You've proved you have the ability to learn—now let's put it into practice!"

One of the first things I noticed after I got here was the excessive working hours of credit personnel. During my first week, I made no comment as I signed all their letters of permission for Security, giving them authorization for night and weekend overtime work at their desks. During my second week, I explained to everyone that I was unimpressed with overtime work. And I let them know what *does* impress me— no working late, growth in volume, and doing nine hours' work in seven. Soon there were no more requests for weekend authorizations. But they're an extremely conscientious group, with a very sincere interest in their jobs, and I still sometimes have to go out there and say, "I'm not impressed. Go home!" My feeling is that when they're working too much, giving up their personal life, poor morale results. Their concentration and working relationships at the bank are bound to suffer.

Norman: If I remember correctly, staff turnover was a big issue then.

Stuart: Yes, the high rate of staff turnover was the main problem I focused on during those initial weeks. The year before I came on the scene, seven credit people left to join other financial institutions. As you know, that's really excessive! In this business, you accept one or two losses a year as the norm—not everybody's suited to banking, and right now, with a lot of new banks coming on stream, the head-hunters are avidly soliciting our staff. My people tell me they get upwards of two to three calls a week, offering extra money and perks. My job is to keep everything else in perspective and give them the best possible conditions that they can have, in order to keep them with Global—and that doesn't necessarily have to be monetary.

Norman: What did you do about that problem?

Stuart: Beginning in November 1979, I met as soon as possible with all of the teams, trying to identify what I had to work with. I met with every team singly, then with separate smaller groups of seniors, assistant managers, and credit officers. We met in neutral territory at the round table in the conference room on the 20th floor of the tower, and I asked for their input about problems and solutions. I made no promises, but very carefully considered what they had to say. Incidentally, I was surprised to discover that most of them had never met with senior management before.

I got different input from each group. The seniors had just about accepted the status quo, and the assistants had started to accept; but the credit officers weren't ready to accept anything yet, so they gave me very good input. Even today I get the most useful input from my credit officers. They're new blood, more likely to be free thinkers who won't accept things just because you tell them this is the way it *is*.

I talked with individuals, too, like the assistant who had submitted his resignation before I arrived. I asked him into my office and inquired about his reasons for leaving. Part of what he told me related to lack of challenge. He said that when he looked back at the end of a week, he couldn't identify anything meaningful he had done. He'd made his "quota" of loans, but they were mostly personal loans, nothing to challenge his credit ability. And he estimated that 70 percent of his time was spent in administration duties; he wasn't getting involved in the commercial credit he had anticipated. He said he received "no feeling of accomplishment or recognition" as a Mid-City assistant credit manager.

I noticed how the senior credit managers did their job. Specifically, a senior is responsible for a portion of the portfolio, for training staff, for business development, and for the extension of credit. And the officer is responsible to see that the team operates effectively. It seemed to me that the seniors were abdicating their leadership role—busily dealing with customers and writing up loan applications, but never having time to do the training and development function with their subordinates. The new people weren't getting the training they needed. They were left pretty much on their own, to learn almost by osmosis.

I observed and listened a lot, my first three months on the job. Then, I acted. We eliminated two teams! On February 15, 1980, I released four people from our department for transfer within Global. Accounts were reallocated, workloads were redistributed, the phones were changed, and we began using a new computerized reporting system.

We restructured the remaining teams. The seniors didn't like the structure I originally suggested, so after due consideration, I accepted *their* recommendation. I thought it was a good suggestion, and it was *theirs—they* had to make it work! Instead of two assistant managers sharing a credit officer, we added another credit officer (now termed account officer) and an administration assistant (see Figure 8–23). The credit administration assistant is a nonlending

position, performing clerical assistance for the team—getting statistical information, keeping records, etc. Under the new concept, the team is dealing more with credit and less with administration, and can move paper at a more rapid pace than before. And there's much better utilization of the seniors now, with their expertise applying to five people instead of three. The seniors—"account managers," now—are starting to make management decisions, which gives *me* more freedom as a departmental manager.

And I revised their work priorities. Previously, the seniors had been operating with credit as their top priority. I clearly stated that their new priorities were to be (1) training of their subordinates, (2) business development, and (3) credit, in that order. The new priorities for the assistants became (1) the training of account officers, (2) credit, and (3) business development.

My releasing four from my department was to provide the challenge they were seeking. I know that seems contradictory—with excessive staff turnover and excessive working hours, you'd think staff should be *added*. I took the reverse approach. They wanted challenge, I'd *give* them challenge! And when restructuring lifted some of the administrative load, the credit personnel became far more effective. Without increasing staff, we have increased business. Volumes are up, and their hours have continued to reduce! Now I'm hearing, "My people are tired, drained, every day—but they feel more challenged, more fulfilled."

Norman: I'd like to hear about any other things you've done to provide a "challenge" for your people.

Stuart: We have instituted some new reporting systems to give the credit personnel information about how well they're doing, and to help them establish future goals. For instance, I distribute to all team members a monthly statement of the number of commercial loans that have expired so far this year, and how many expiries are projected for the balance of the year. I break the numbers down according to team responsibility. For example, Team 1 had 12 expired credits as of April 30, 1981, with 33 expiries projected for May, whereas Team 4 had 10 expiries, and 22 projected for May. This information stimulates the teams to look ahead and plan accordingly, as well as to look back and deal with the old expiries. I question each team about the

Figure 8–23 **Mid-City Credit Department Account Managers: Team Organization Chart, February 15, 1980**

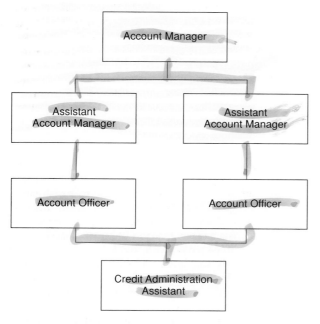

reasons for too-long expires, and why they haven't been renewed.

But the most important thing about circulating such data is so they can see measurable improvement . . . and all the teams want to be low man, introducing a bit of competition. The senior uses this sheet in the team meetings, and I use it as a reporting tool for the vice president's information.

Norman: Do you use any other comparative measurements, Stuart? Classified loans, for example?

Stuart: Yes, we measure the classified loan portfolio—the "bad loans"—because as you know, the extent of a team's classified loan portfolio is an indicator of its credit judgment. So I recently circulated these figures* indicating that the quality of our lending is good . . . and it's getting better all the time.

Time management is a recurring problem. Along with monitoring their progress, credit people have to be taught techniques to best manage their work time. They get more help from their seniors with this aspect, now, but there's always room for improvement. I try to pass on some of my time-saving tricks—I dictate off a point-form synopsis, and if I'm tired and not absorbing what I'm reading late in the day, I put it away and do something else.

I used to hear about the "guidance and direction" the lenders received from the former AVP in the form of comments written in black felt markers across every application. This was perceived as criticism, not guidance, although I've been told that they never spoke to the previous AVP about it. Well, everybody's management style is different—my predecessor liked a black felt pen, but I never use a black felt pen, because it was so detested out there.

Norman: What form of communication do *you* favor?

Stuart: I try to give my staff regular feedback. For instance, whenever a particularly good application crosses my desk, I'll take it down to that credit person and say, "That was a hell of a nice write-up you did on this account!" I'm careful to bring my staff into my office regularly, too, not only for their quarterly reviews. As a result, I get much more input from them. And my door's always open . . . they're usually lined up to get in here. They know I'm receptive, and that's important.

Mid-City credit has always been a large profit maker for Global Bank, and it grows every year. It operated reasonably well before I came, now it operates better. In the past 14 months we've seen an account growth of 12 percent, and our dollar growth is up 26 percent. We've increased productivity to probably the best we're going to get. You can always improve it more, but at what cost? It's a finely tuned "machine" out there. We have a very clean portfolio, so we know our base of loans is good; now we can look forward to *controlled* growth. We're going after the marketplace in a planned way, making major changes throughout the entire department. The changes involve radically restructuring our credit account teams—but that's another story.

For the time being, I'm preparing for these coming changes in my usual manner, via the "planned information leak." When I'm not able to *do* something right away, I keep enthusiasm and excitement high by leaking out bits of information—when you tell one, you've told them all. Then I examine the feedback I get, to see if I'm on the right track or not. When I hear what they're concerned about, I can leak out some more information to compensate for that. It really works!

And I'll soon be talking to each one individually, because I'll need a two-year commitment through the change period. That'll be hard for some of them to give, because they're fast-trackers—they want to be VPs or presidents next year. But I'll also be telling them that our new concept will be the best thing in banking, and we'll have a waiting list of people wanting to come in with us! I don't know if we will or not, but it sounds good . . . *I* believe it's an exciting concept, anyway.

I like the people in my department. We all get together for a weekend at my cottage at least once a year, where we relax and have a lot of fun. And they often ask me to social gatherings among themselves. I go if I'm invited, but it doesn't bother me if I'm not. You know there is more of that sort of activity than I could possibly keep up with, and I do enjoy my home life. My wife and four teenagers appreciate the fact that I manage to keep as many of my evenings and weekends free of work-related commitments as possible.

The "top three" of us—the VP, AVP administration, and myself—work really well

*Mid-City classified loans:

October 1979	72 classified loans
March 1980	66 classified loans
October 1980	51 classified loans
March 1981	45 classified loans

together. I take the same daily commuter train as the other assistant VP, so we're able to do a lot of business in an informal manner. And the vice president is probably the freest thinker I've ever met. The motto now is "Think Wild" . . . and you wouldn't believe how wild we think!

Norman: *(laughing with Stuart):* You really enjoy your work, don't you?

Stuart: That's for sure! The Global Bank has been an excellent place for me to work and advance— personally, professionally, and financially. I grew up in a low-income family, and financial security has always been extremely important to me. Well, I've achieved that! I'm sure that my somewhat relaxed outlook on life is partly due to my currently secure financial situation. Also, I feel very comfortable as a member of this organization. It has been good to me, and I feel very much a part of it.

You know, banking has such variety to it. Once you're into it, it's in your blood. I just love it! Every day is different. I have a great sense of freedom in my job, along with a lot of responsibility—I've got to move the paper, of course. And I learn something every day. I don't think the learning process ever stops.

Norman: Thanks very much, Stuart. I appreciate your sharing your thoughts with me. . . . You know, I can't help wondering how the credit people in your department view the events of the past year or so.

Stuart: Why not ask them? Take whatever time you need—or can get—with any of my people who are available today.

Norman randomly selected two names (Donna Morrison and Tony Walmer) from the list of credit account managers. Later that day he spent a half hour or so talking with each person. Their comments are summarized below:

Donna Morrison

I joined the Global Bank as an MBA grad in 1978. After a short stint in administration, followed by four months of commercial credit training, I was posted to the Mid-City branch as a credit officer. I've been here since shortly after Stuart's arrival.

Before Stuart came, turnover was a serious problem. I was told that credit officers were doing too much "gofer" work, and there were a lot of dissatisfied MBAs. People were leaving for other financial institutions because they just weren't being rewarded on the job. And I received the impression that the former AVP credit didn't care very much. He walked through the branch without taking any specific interest in credit people as individuals or as a employees of the bank.

When he first arrived, Stuart took a good look around. Morale was a top priority in his book, so he started out to determine why morale was low, and what he could do to improve the situation. He called many meetings and listened to our suggestions. Then he restructured our corporate and commercial accounts teams. The idea was to spread the administrative work between two account officers each responsible to one assistant, instead of one responsible to two.

But the biggest change was in the AVP's style. Stuart is definitely concerned about his employees, and their performance within the Mid-City branch, and their career development within the bank as a whole. His different management approach has completely changed the atmosphere within the department. It's a very "open door" policy now—you're welcome to take any complaints, suggestions, criticisms, protests, in to Stuart, knowing full well that you'll be listened to. The bank isn't the sort of institution that changes rapidly—it's still fairly conservative—but at least it's nice to know there's an ear you can bend and you'll probably get some valuable feedback. It makes you feel better that there is somebody at that executive level who will listen.

People now seem quite happy and enthused to be here, and I think that's a direct result of the changes that were made. We can now see what's expected of us, where we are likely to go, and we're being involved more in our own career planning and development.

We all trust and respect Stuart's expert credit judgement. And Stuart's *honest* with us—he doesn't sugarcoat the facts. He gives as honest an answer as he possibly can . . . which often isn't satisfying, though I know he's not at liberty to jeopardize other plans by telling too much too soon. And Stuart continues to make a concerted effort to involve us in determining how the department *should* be functioning.

Tony Walmer

I've been with the Global Bank for 12 years, in commercial credit for three. I was a credit officer when Stuart first came here in 1979, and I've since become an assistant account manager. The organizational changes Stuart introduced are working out well, but the big change is his style of communication.

Stuart really *lives* the "open door" concept. He lets us know that he's always free to speak with any of us, unlike the previous AVP. Stuart listens to everybody, he talks to everybody, and he's willing to make changes based on our recommendations. He tries to be completely fair—he can't be, *all* the time, but he tries to be, and we know and appreciate that.

Another thing about Stuart—he got our confidence at the outset because as soon as he arrived, instead of a senior correcting us on our credit, Stuart would sit down with each person individually and point out ways we could improve. He was never afraid to correct us or give us guidance, and he did it in such a helpful way that nobody resented it. And we have a lot of respect for Stuart's knowledge of credit. Everyone knows that he has exceptional ability in the credit area, without question. Also, he has come up with some unique ideas, including the exciting reorientation concept that's in the mill right now.

For me personally . . . I'm working differently now. I spend much less time writing credit applications—Stuart doesn't want elaborate "stories," only the facts. And in the past, I was afraid to come out and make decisions and take a strong stand. Well, now I don't back down at all, and that's supported by Stuart. If you're doing a good job, he supports and reinforces you. He's got the respect of everybody in the department.

Stuart introduced some changes in systems—follow-up systems, monitoring systems—to save us time, and also inject a little competition among the teams. And hours have changed considerably, with the average person now working only until 4:30, or 5 P.M. at the latest. I took a lot of work home during my first year—no more! But the key to the way we operate now is the openness of Stuart's style. . . . The difference is mainly a matter of style.

As he returned to his office, Norman thought about his conversations with Stuart, Donna, and Tony. "How can I use what I've learned today," he mused, "to help me do my job better—especially in dealing with the issue of staff turnover?"

Step 2: Prepare the case for class discussion.

Step 3: Answer the following questions, individually, in small groups, or with the class as a whole, as directed by your instructor:

Description
1. Describe the actions that Stuart North took after becoming the AVP credit.
2. Describe Stuart's leadership style.

Diagnosis
3. Was Stuart an effective leader?
4. Using the various role classifications, how would you evaluate Stuart as a manager?
5. Did Stuart motivate his employees effectively?
6. Evaluate the quality of communication and decision making in this case?
7. What situational contingencies affected Stuart's leadership style?

Prescription
8. What can Norman learn from Stuart's leadership and management behaviors?

Action
9. What issues will Norman face in translating Stuart's style?

Step 4: Discussion. In small groups, with the entire class, or in written form, share your answers to the questions above. Then answer the following questions:

1. What symptoms suggest that a problem exists?
2. What problems exist in the case?
3. What theories and concepts help explain the problems?
4. How can the problems be corrected?
5. Are the actions likely to be effective?

Case material of the Western School of Business Administration is prepared as a basis for classroom discussion. This case was prepared by Eileen D. Watson, Research Associate, Western Business School, under the direction of Professor Richard C. Hodgson. All names have been disguised. Copyright © 1981, The University of Western Ontario.

Activity
8–5

CNN Video: **Protocol for Leadership**

Step 1: Using your knowledge of leadership theory, formulate a ten-point plan for effective leadership of a national airline that has grown in the last twenty years to become the ninth largest in the United States.

Step 2: View the videotape about Herb Kelleher, president of Southwest Airlines.

Step 3: In groups of four or five, compare Herb Kelleher's leadership behavior to the protocol you developed. Did he act as an effective leader?

Step 4: Based on your conversations, revise your ten-point leadership plan.

Step 5: Compare the revised plans of different groups in the class. Consider similarities and differences. Which theories were most useful in formulating the plan?

Activity 8–6

Managing for the '90s

Step 1: Read the following description of the changes at United Technologies:

WHERE 1990s-STYLE MANAGEMENT IS ALREADY HARD AT WORK

It was with some urgency that Robert F. Daniell, the newly appointed CEO of United Technologies Corp., summoned his top executives in March of 1986. Just weeks after taking the reins from predecessor Harry J. Gray, Daniell called a management powwow at the Jupiter Beach Hilton in Florida. The subject? UTC's shaky future. Customers of its Pratt & Whitney jet engines, outraged by lousy service, were defecting in droves to archrival General Electric Co. Market shares at UTC's once-dominant Otis elevator unit and Carrier air-conditioning company were evaporating. Profits had hit a 13-year low. "Things had to change," says Daniell.

Unlike management meetings under the iron-fisted Gray regime, however, there was no lecturing from Daniell. Instead, a Boston consultant moderated a roiling discussion in which managers put forth their remedies: Dump divisions wholesale, diversify, pump up research-and-development spending. "Just the fact that we went through all of that yelling and screaming was unusual," says one executive who attended. After two days, Daniell and his team decided to remake UTC—to level its autocratic structure and bring more of its 186,800 employees into the decision-making process. The ultimate goal: to get UTC's haughty culture to take marching orders from its customers.

Worker empowerment. Team-building. Getting close to your customer. While a lot of companies are just starting to talk about such methods, Bob Daniell is already proving that they can work wonders on the bottom line. The changes are nowhere more apparent than at jet-engine maker Pratt & Whitney Co., which pulls in more than half of UTC's operating profit. Orders have increased eightfold, to nearly $8 billion, since 1987. Overall, UTC has been a rather sluggish performer. While the company has rebounded from the drubbing it took in a 1986 restructuring, its profits this year—at $675 million on revenues of $20 billion—will be just slightly better than in 1984. But UTC is poised to take off. Spurred by Pratt & Whitney's swelling engine orders, the company's net profits are expected by analysts to jump nearly 16% in 1990, to $785 million. Wall Street's response? UTC's stock, at about 56, has risen 37% in the past year—almost twice the pace of its aerospace and defense industry brethren.

A Listener
Daniell will be hard-pressed to keep up the pace. Pratt & Whitney is duking it out with some formidable competitors, most notably GE and Rolls-Royce PLC. And those companies are hard at work on new engines that could grab business from Pratt. What's more, to sustain a new era of brisk growth for UTC, Daniell must apply the lessons learned at Pratt & Whitney to some of the company's divisions that are still lackluster.

Daniell isn't alone in his vision of how to energize a company. As far as the organizational gurus are concerned, he's doing exactly what Corporate America needs to do to get through the next decade (table below). "In the 1990s,

A CEO's Checklist for Managing in the '90s

In the more competitive business environment of the 1990s, companies will have to be more flexible, move faster, and tap every last bit of talent in the organization. Case in point: Bob Daniell's reinvigoration of United Technologies Corp. Here are the secrets of his success.

Flatten the Hierarchy Daniell leveled a Byzantine corporate structure by cutting many layers of decision-making. At Pratt & Whitney, for instance, he cut eight levels of management to as few as four

Empower Your Workers Managers pushed decision-making down. For instance, field representatives at Pratt & Whitney now make multimillion-dollar decisions about reimbursing customers on warranty claims. Before, they would wait for approvals from numerous layers above

Get Close to Your Customers This is Daniell's battle cry. Worker empowerment helps, but the imperative goes even further than that. For instance, Pratt & Whitney lends some of its top engineers to customers for a year—and pays their salaries

Train, Train, Train Daniell uses training to revamp corporate culture. More than 5,000 senior and middle managers are getting at least 40 hours of classroom work. In some classes, customers are brought in for gripe sessions and a problem-solving team gathered from many different departments must come up with solutions

organization—the team—is the competitive weapon," says Rosabeth Moss Kanter, a consultant and professor at Harvard Business School. There's little choice. Pacific Rim countries will force production costs still lower. And these feisty new competitors will turn up the heat on the U.S.—and Japan—when it comes to innovation.

In many ways, Daniell is the antithesis of conglomerate-era, empire-building managers, making UTC the kind of case study that business schools love to scrutinize. In 10 years, former Chairman Gray built UTC from a $2 billion company into an $18 billion manufacturer of goods ranging from military helicopters to shopping-mall escalators. He ran his empire largely by the numbers—and treated his people with all the finesse of a feudal lord.

By contrast, Daniell is low-key, a listener. When he gets passionate, it's usually about his effort to make employees feel like proprietors. He's a builder—but of a different sort than his predecessor. Daniell is an operations guy who's willing to get his hands dirty. Before taking the top job, he turned around UTC's Sikorsky Aircraft Div., where he started his career as a helicopter engineer 33 years ago.

Daniell holds little regard for the trappings of corporate power. As chief operating officer in 1985, he didn't bother to return a questionnaire of personal data requested by *Who's Who*. When he became CEO in 1986, executives stopped using the heliport atop headquarters, and after he was named chairman in 1987, the guards at headquarters hung up the guns they had worn. Gray and Daniell are "two completely different personalities," says T. Mitchell Ford, a UTC director who is the retired chairman of Emhart Corp. Gray declined to be interviewed for this story.

No-Fault Bosses

When Daniell finally became CEO, he inherited a divided, argumentative management. Executives were too frightened to admit mistakes, and they directed their staffs like armies. All the way down the line, staffers refused to take responsibility for errors.

First, Daniell had some financial problems to wrestle with. He began auctioning off $1.5 billion in assets and cutting staff. "These were fundamental blocking and tackling moves, but that wasn't really the problem," he says. He had to rid the company of the complacency that had allowed GE to start snatching away business from Pratt & Whitney.

The jet-engine division was No. 1 for so long its managers had forgotten that sales don't come automatically. An incident in 1983 made that painfully clear. The Air Force, one of the engine maker's biggest customers, was dissatisfied with Pratt's work on the F-100 engines for its two main fighters, the F-15 Eagle and F-16 Falcon. It had opened bidding on the contract to GE—a real slap at Pratt & Whitney. The contract had been bringing in about $1 billion in revenues annually, nothing to sniff at. Yet Pratt & Whitney's president at the time, Robert J. Carlson, was quoted in the Sunday magazine of *The Hartford Courant,* the division's hometown paper, saying: "It won't mean a tinker's goddamn whether the F-100 stays or goes, not one damn thing." Even when reminded of the incident recently, Carlson defends his attitude. He says he believed then that a resurgence in commercial engine sales would soon eclipse the Air Force business. He was proven right, but that didn't help at the time. The Air Force awarded 75% of its orders to GE.

For Daniell, who was then a senior vice-president, Pratt's arrogance "was brought into crystal-clear focus." By the time he became CEO, the cavalier attitude toward customers was crippling the commercial engine division. Pratt had always been UTC's crown jewel—even during the Gray regime. Over 10 years, UTC had pumped $2 billion into a new generation of engines, which were introduced in 1986. But customers weren't interested—they couldn't get service

United Technologies' Far-flung Lineup

Division	Products	Revenues as Percent of Total	Operating Profit Margin
Pratt & Whitney	Jet engines	34.0%	10.8%
Flight Systems	Helicopters, radar, flight controls	19.0	−0.4%
Carrier	Air conditioners	19.0*	4.5%*
Otis	Elevators	17.0*	7.5%*
Industrial	Auto parts, wire	11.0	10.5%

*Estimates

Data: Company Reports, Oppenheimer & Co.

for the engines they had. Spare parts arrived months late Engineering advice took forever to obtain. And when customers suggested minor changes in service or design, they got such icy retorts as: "You don't know what you're talking about," says Kenneth Johnson, Pratt's vice-president for customer support.

Old Story

Worse, the delays were costing customers plenty as their airliners sat on the ground. At American Airlines Inc., as much as 30% of Pratt's spare parts arrived late, while fewer than 10% of other companies' deliveries ran late. "It was ulcer-producing," says David L. Kruse, American's vice-president for maintenance and engineering. Some customers rebelled. UAL Corp. threatened in 1986 that if Pratt didn't ship parts and answer questions faster, UAL would never buy another Pratt engine, Johnson says.

Pratt, once master of the jet-engine market, saw orders slip to 26% of the total in 1987, compared with GE's 47%. The strongest kick in the pants, however, came in December, 1987, when longtime customer Japan Air Lines Co. ordered more than $1 billion in engines for 747s from GE. It was the same old story: slow service. Daniell didn't wait for excuses. He went to Japan and personally apologized to JAL's top officials.

Daniell warned his managers that he shouldn't have to apologize again. He pushed his manufacturing executives out on a limb by going public with a series of brutally frank ads. One showed a jetliner tethered by red tape to the tarmac and was emblazoned with the tagline: "Excuses just won't fly. Our bureaucracy shouldn't be your hang-up." Daniell and aerospace head Arthur E. Wegner humbled the managers further by making them pay for the *mea culpa* out of their own budget.

At the same time, Daniell was working on a long-term goal: changing Pratt's by-the-book structure. Dictatorial management and a Byzantine approval process made employees feel powerless. Take the case of an airplane builder who wants to mount an engine a fraction of a millimeter closer to the wing than the blueprint specifies. Normally, a good engineer at Pratt could just eyeball the blueprint and give the customer the nod for such a change. But until Pratt changed the system in February, 1988, the request would wind through nine departments, including a committee that met only once a week. "They had to submit mountains of paper," says William J. Garvey, a Pratt manager who helped abbreviate the process.

Now, the design engineer makes the decision and only needs to get three signatures. Says Garvey: "It's all part of quality—taking responsibility." As a result, average response time has gone from 82 days to 10, and the request backlog has shrunk from 1,900 cases to fewer than 100.

Daniell went further with his campaign to improve service. He increased the number of service representatives in the field by nearly 70%—despite 30% staff cuts in the rest of the company. JAL, for one, got a special service center near Tokyo to meet its needs alone. Field reps also were given authority to approve multimillion-dollar warranty replacements on the spot, instead of waiting weeks for the O. K. from headquarters. Before the changes, airframe makers were forced to shut down their assembly lines up to 40 times a month because a Pratt part was missing. Now, Pratt causes only two work stoppages a month on average, and some months pass without any.

Training is also a big part of Daniell's shakeup of the culture. As part of the course work, customers actually come in for gripe sessions, and managers are gathered from all departments to solve problems. In another novel program, Pratt lends out about a dozen of its most talented young engineers to customers for a one-year hitch while paying their salaries. In the first year of the program, for example, a Pratt engine expert worked in the maintenance-engineering department of Northwest Airlines Inc. Back from the stint in July, he has been able to help Pratt revamp the engineering manuals that go with new engines.

Some customers have found the improvement startling. In mid-August, Howard La Grange, vice-president at Aviall of Texas Inc., which overhauls airplanes under contract, needed a scarce engine part to repair a Chinese airliner. A Pratt service representative heard about the problem and called to ask how he could help. He offered to ship three new turbines—which would have cost Pratt roughly $3 million—in order to tide over Aviall until the part could be machined. La Grange eventually found a less costly solution, but he couldn't believe the improvement in service. "I almost laughed a little and asked him what the hell he was doing."

Not Done Yet

That's the good news. The bad news is that Pratt has plenty more work ahead. Many employees are livid about staff cuts. And some middle managers grouse that they haven't seen enough of a change in top management's attitude. They complain, says Michael M. Michigami, former president of UT Control Systems, that Pratt's bureaucracy is still stifling: "We hear the words. We see a little bit. We don't see enough." And customer complaints have yet to vanish. A JAL official says that parts still arrive late at times. Even Daniell admits service isn't where he wants it to be. Says one director: "You can't turn around a 3,000-horsepower locomotive in a microsecond."

Still, now that Pratt has largely repaired its customer relationships, it has been able to turn up the heat on its competition. It is battling GE and Rolls-Royce, among others, for engine orders that could amount to $60 billion over the next five years. While Pratt must keep playing catch-up on service with GE, long the industry model, its marketing edge is becoming more and more apparent. Pratt's entirely new generation of engines stands out from its competition's offerings, which are upgrades of old models.

Pratt now offers the widest range of engines for commercial jet aircraft. There is the PW4000 for widebody planes such as the 767 and 747. The V2500 (developed under a joint venture with Rolls and other European partners) is for narrow bodies such as A-320s. And it has the PW2000 for intermediate-body planes such as 757s. Pratt's new engines have been in the market long enough to show that the kinks are worked out and that they're technologically superior to the competition, says David S. Gardner, an analyst at Nomura Securities International Inc.

Prop Wash

Pratt's top seller, the PW4000, cuts fuel consumption by a wide margin, is more cheaply maintained, and can be changed much more quickly than its predecessor. Also, it can be easily souped up for planes designed for the 1990s. GE is planning a counterattack with an unducted fan engine, which uses a propeller in the jet core to cut fuel consumption by as much as 40%. Daniell is keeping up Pratt's high level of development spending—and is in the race on this front. However, the industry may not be ready for the fancy new design until nearly 2000.

GE disputes that Pratt's new engines are superior, but the numbers tell the story. The PW4000, for instance, has won 70% of the orders on widebodies since its introduction in early 1986, Gardner points out. And nearly 40% of those sales went to airlines that had used GE engines. As a result, Pratt is increasing its market share—grabbing about 40% in 1989, up from 29% in 1988. GE's share has been whittled from 33% to 29%, says Gardner.

Daniell can't stop with improving Pratt. He has instituted the same training and service-improvement programs throughout the company, but an upswing in results for some divisions has been slower in coming. The troubled Norden radar unit has forced some write-downs, and Daniell will sell it eventually. And for years, cash generated by UTC's Carrier air-conditioning and Otis elevator units was siphoned off by headquarters. Their technology fell behind, and market shares and profit margins suffered. Carrier, also hit by rampant price-cutting, has stepped up its R&D spending in the past two years and is revamping its product line. New division head George A. L. David made his agenda clear: "My appetite is for innovation." By next year, 90% of sales will come from newly designed products such as a

home furnace that contains a microprocessor to diagnose any glitches that arise. At Otis, the R&D budget and staff next year is scheduled to be triple what it was three years ago.

Even if the resurgence of Pratt & Whitney keeps up, Daniell can expect Otis and Carrier to keep his management skills sharp. But maybe that's not such a bad thing. For, as he sees it, the greatest danger to a company can be the arrogance bred of success. "It's very hard," says Daniell, "to behave as No. 1 for very long" and stay there. In other words, his goal is to keep UTC acting like the underdog—even when it's on top of the heap.

Step 2:   List the steps that Bob Daniell took to reinvigorate United Technologies.

Step 3:   Indicate which roles of the manager he performed on a regular basis. Rank-order the roles in terms of priority.

Step 4:   Select a manager to observe.

Step 5:   Keep a diary of the manager's activities for as long as one day. Observe him or her as much as possible during that day.

Step 6:   Indicate which roles of the manager he or she performed. Rank-order the roles in terms of frequency.

Step 7:   Discussion. Compare and contrast the activities of the two managers. Compare their patterns of priority activities.

Description
1. Which activities did each manager perform?

Diagnosis
2. Which roles did each manager perform? Which roles did each manager omit?
3. Was each manager effective? Why or why not?

Prescription
4. Which roles should the manager perform to become more effective?

Reprinted from *Business Week* (October 23, 1989): 92–93, 96, 98, 100, by special permission, copyright © 1989 by McGraw-Hill, Inc.

CONCLUDING COMMENTS

This chapter has attempted to dispel five common myths about leadership: (1) that leadership is a single personality trait, (2) that leaders should be smart but not too smart, (3) that leaders are leaders and mostly alike, (4) that once a leader, always a leader, and (5) that a good leader brings to leadership everything required for effective performance.[80] We have reviewed diverse theories that help prescribe effective leadership. Although leadership is a very complex phenomenon, we can use such theories to help us evaluate leadership and offer ways of encouraging its effectiveness.

Activities in this chapter let you evaluate your own leadership style and then practice leadership in a role play. Analysis of the cases of Peter Knudtsen and "A Matter of Style" provided opportunities for you to apply diverse perspectives on leadership and management. You also developed a leadership protocol using the video about Herb Kelleher of Southwest Airlines and offered a strategy for "Managing in the 90s" based on Bob Daniell's changes at United Technologies.

The relationship between leaders and followers is changing. Together they must deal with the challenges posed by a global economy and a diverse work force. Sharing leadership responsibility by empowering workers is a key ingredient.

ENDNOTES

[1] J. Holusha, Grace Pastiak's 'web of inclusion,' *New York Times,* Sunday, May 5, 1991, section 3, pp. 1, 6. Copyright © 1991 by The New York Times Company. Reprinted with permission.

[2] P. R. Harris and R. T. Moran, *Managing Cultural Differences,* 3rd ed. (Houston: Gulf, 1991).

[3] B. M. Bass, *Bass & Stogdill's Handbook of Leadership: Theory, Research, and Managerial Applications,* 3rd ed. (New York: Free Press, 1990).

[4] J. S. Black and L. W. Porter, Managerial behaviors and job performance: A successful manager in Los Angeles may not succeed in Hong Kong, *Journal of International Business Studies* 22(1) (1991): 99–114.

[5] J. A. Wall, Jr., Managers in the People's Republic of China, *Academy of Management Executive* 4(2) (1990): 19–32.

[6] N. J. Adler, *International Dimensions of Organizational Behavior,* 2nd ed. (Boston: PWS-Kent, 1991).

[7] G. Hofstede, Motivation, leadership, and organization: Do American theories apply abroad? *Organizational Dynamics* (Summer 1980): 42–63; N. Foy and H. Gadon, Worker participation contrasts in three countries, *Harvard Business Review* (May-June 1976): 71–84.

[8] Adler, *International Dimensions.*

[9] J. C. Barrow, The variables of leadership: A review and conceptual framework, *Academy of Management Review* 2 (1977): 231–235.

[10] S. A. Kirkpatrick and E. A. Locke, Leadership: Do traits matter? *Academy of Management Executive* 5(2) (1991): 49.

[11] B. M. Bass, P. C. Burger, R. Doktor, and G. V. Barrett, *Assessment of Managers: An International Comparison* (New York: Free Press, 1979).

[12] Kirkpatrick and Locke, Leadership.

[13] J. G. Hunt, *Leadership: A New Synthesis* (Newbury Park, Calif.: Sage, 1991).

[14] J. P. Kotter, *The Leadership Factor* (New York: Free Press, 1988), p. 30.

[15] R. M. Stogdill and A. E. Coons, eds., *Leader Behavior: Its Description and Measurement* (Columbus: Ohio State University Bureau of Business Research, 1957).

[16] E. Fleishman, E. F. Harris, and R. D. Burtt, *Leadership and Supervision in Industry* (Columbus: Ohio State University Press, 1955); E. Fleishman and E. F. Harris, Patterns of leadership behavior related to employee grievances and turnover, *Personnel Psychology* 1 (1959): 45–53.

[17] R. L. Kahn and D. Katz, Leadership practices in relation to productivity and morale. In *Group Dynamics*, ed. D. Gartwright and A. Zander (Evanston, Ill.: Row, Peterson, 1953), pp. 585–611.

[18] J. Misumi and M. F. Peterson, The performance-maintenance (PM) theory of leadership: Review of a Japanese research program, *Administrative Science Quarterly* 30 (1985): 198–223.

[19] Bass, *Bass & Stogdill's Handbook of Leadership.*

[20] H. Mintzberg, *The Nature of Managerial Work,* 2nd ed. (Englewood Cliffs, N.J.: Prentice-Hall, 1979).

[21] A. I. Kraut, P. R. Pedigo, D. D. McKenna, and M. D. Dunnette, The role of the manager: What's really important in different management jobs, *Academy of Management Executive* 3(4) (1989): 286–293.

[22] F. Luthans and D. L. Lockwood, Toward an observation system for measuring leader behavior in natural settings. In J. G. Hunt, D. Hosking, C. A. Schriesheim, and R. Stewart, eds., *Leaders and Managers: International Perspectives on Managerial Behavior and Leadership* (New York: Pergamon, 1984).

[23] G. A. Yukl, *Leadership in Organizations,* 2nd ed. (Englewood Cliffs, N.J.: Prentice-Hall, 1989).

[24] D. McGregor, *The Human Side of Enterprise* (New York: McGraw-Hill, 1961); E. H. Schein, The Hawthorne studies revisited: A defense of Theory Y, Sloan School of Management Working Paper #756–74 (Cambridge: Massachusetts Institute of Technology, 1974), p. 3.

[25] F. E. Fiedler and M. M. Chemers, *Improving Leadership Effectiveness: The Leader Match Concept,* 2nd ed. (New York: Wiley, 1984).

[26] F. E. Fiedler and J. E. Garcia, *New Approaches to Effective Leadership* (New York: Wiley, 1987).

[27] M. Bennett, Testing management theories culturally, *Journal of Applied Psychology* 62 (1977): 578–581.

[28] R. Singh, Leadership style and reward allocation: Does least preferred coworker scale measure task and relationship orientation? *Organizational Behavior and Human Performance* 32 (1983): 178–197.

[29] N. W. Biggart and G. G. Hamilton, An institutional theory of leadership, *Journal of Applied Behavioral Sciences* 234 (1987): 429–441.

[30] P. W. Dorfman and J. P. Howell, Dimensions of national culture and effective leadership patterns, *Advances in International Comparative Management* 3 (1988): 127–150.

[31] Yukl, *Leadership in Organizations.*

[32] J. C. Wofford and T. N. Srinivasan, Experimental tests of the leader-environment-follower interaction theory of leadership, *Organizational Behavior and Human Performance* 32 (1983): 35–54.

[33] R. J. House, A path-goal theory of leader effectiveness, *Administrative Science Quarterly* 16 (1971): 321–338; and R. J. House and T. R. Mitchell, Path-goal theory of leadership, *Journal of Contemporary Business* (Autumn 1974): 81–97.

[34] R. J. House and M. L. Baetz, Leadership: Some empirical generalizations and new research directions. In B. M. Staw, ed., *Research in Organizational Behavior* (Greenwich, Conn.: JAI Press, 1979): 341–423.

[35] J. Indvik, Path-goal theory of leadership: A meta-analysis, *Proceedings of the Academy of Management* (1986): 189–192; J. Fulk and E. R. Wendler, Dimensionality of leader-subordinate interactions: A path-goal investigation, *Organizational Behavior and Human Performance* 30 (1983): 241–263; G. A. Yukl and J. Clemence, A test of path-goal theory of leadership using questionnaire and diary measures of behavior, *Proceedings of the Twenty-First Annual Meeting of the Eastern Academy of Management* (1984): 174–177.

[36] V. H. Vroom and P. W. Yetton, *Leadership and Decision Making* (Pittsburgh: University of Pittsburgh Press, 1973) is the original version; V. H. Vroom and A. G. Jago, *The New Leadership: Managing Participation in Organizations* (Englewood Cliffs, N.J.: Prentice-Hall, 1988) is the most recent version.

[37] R. H. G. Field, A test of the Vroom-Yetton normative model of leadership, *Journal of Applied Psychology* 67 (1982): 523–532.

[38] Vroom and Jago, *The New Leadership.*

[39] P. Hersey and K. H. Blanchard, *Management of Organizational Behavior,* 5th ed. (Englewood Cliffs, N.J.: Prentice-Hall, 1988).

[40] R. P. Vecchio, Situational leadership theory: An examination of a prescriptive theory, *Journal of Applied Psychology* 72 (1987): 444–451; C. L. Graeff, The situational leadership theory: A critical view, *Academy of Management Review* 8 (1983): 285–291; D. C. Lueder, Don't be misled by LEAD, *Journal of Applied Behavioral Science* 21 (1985): 143–151; D. C. Lueder, A rejoinder to Dr. Hersey, *Journal of Applied Behavioral Science* 21 (1985): 154; P. Hersey, A letter to the author of "Don't be misled by LEAD," *Journal of Applied Behavioral Science* 21 (1985): 152–153.

[41] F. Dansereau, G. Graen, and W. J. Haga, A vertical dyad-linkage approach to leadership within formal organizations: A longitudinal investigation of the role-making process, *Organizational Behavior and Human Performance* 23 (1975): 46–78; J. Cashman, F. Dansereau, G. Graen, and W. J. Haga, Organizational understructure and leadership: a longitudinal investigation of the managerial role-making process, *Organizational Behavior and Human Performance* 15 (1976): 278–296.

[42] T. B. Scandura and G. B. Graen, Moderating effects of initial leader-member exchange status on the effects of a leadership intervention, *Journal of Applied Psychology* 69 (1984): 428–436.

[43] D. Duchon, S. G. Graen, and T. D. Table, Vertical dyad linkage: A longitudinal assessment of antecedents, measures, and consequences, *Journal of Applied Psychology* 71 (1986): 56–60.

[44] Cashman et al., Organizational understructure and leadership.

[45] R. L. Heneman, D. B. Greenberger, and C. Anonyuo, Attributions and exchanges: The effects of interpersonal factors in the diagnosis of employee performance, *Academy of Management Journal* 32 (1989): 466–476.

[46] R. M. Dienesch and R. C. Liden, Leader-member exchange model of leadership: A critique and future development, *Academy of Management Review* 11 (1986): 618–634; R. P. Vecchio and B. C. Gobdel, The vertical dyad linkage model of leadership: Problems and prospects, *Organizational Behavior and Human Performance* 34 (1984): 5–20.

[47] Yukl, *Leadership in Organizations.*

[48] J. C. McElroy, A typology of attribution leadership research, *Academy of Management Review* 7 (1982): 413–417.

[49] B. Calder, An attribution theory of leadership. In *New Directions in Organizational Behavior,* ed. B. H. Staw and G. R. Salancik (Chicago: St. Clair Press, 1977).

[50] T. Mitchell and R. Wood, Supervisor responses to subordinates' poor performance: A test of the attributional model, *Organizational Behavior and Human Performance* 25 (1980): 123–138.

[51] M. Martinko and W. L. Gardner, The leader/member attribution process, *Academy of Management Review* 12 (1987): 235–240.

[52] Yukl, *Leadership in Organizations,* p. 168.

[53] J. C. McElroy and C. B. Shrader, Attribution theories of leadership and network analysis, *Journal of Management* 12 (1986): 351–362.

[54] S. Kerr and J. M. Jermier, Substitutes for leadership: Their meaning and measurement, *Organizational Behavior and Human Performance* 22 (1978): 375–403; J. D. Ford, Departmental context and formal structure as constraints on leader behavior, *Academy of Management Journal* 24 (1981): 274–288; J. P. Howell and P. W. Dorfman, Substitutes for leadership: Test of a construct, *Academy of Management Journal* 24 (1981): 714–728; and J. P. Howell and P. W. Dorfman, Leadership and substitutes for leadership among professional and nonprofessional workers, *Journal of Applied Behavioral Sciences* 22 (1986): 2946.

[55] J. E. Sheridan, D. J. Vredenburgh, and M. A. Abelson, Contextual model of leadership influence in hospital units, *Academy of Management Journal* 27 (1984): 57–78.

[56] J. P. Howell, D. E. Bowen, P. W. Dorfman, S. Kerr, and P. M. Podsakoff, Substitutes for leadership: Effective alternatives to ineffective leadership, *Organizational Dynamics* (Summer 1990): 21–38.

[57] *Ibid.*

[58] The discussion here is based on J. Conger, *The Charismatic Leader* (San Francisco: Jossey-Bass, 1989); N. M. Tichy and D. O. Ulrich, The leadership challenge: A call for the transformational leader, *Sloan Management Review* 26 (1984): 59–68; and N. M. Tichy and M. A. Devanna, *The Transformational Leader,* 2nd ed. (New York: Wiley, 1990).

[59] R. J. House, A 1976 theory of charismatic leadership. In J. G. Hunt and Larson, eds., *Leadership: The Cutting Edge* (Carbondale, Ill.: Southern Illinois University Press, 1977).

[60] A. R. Willner, *The Spellbinders: Charismatic Political Leadership* (New Haven, Conn.: Yale University Press, 1984): A. Conger and R. N. Kanungo, Toward a behavioral theory of charismatic leadership in organizational settings, *Academy of Management Review* 12 (1987): 637–647.

[61] H. R. Jonas, R. E. Fry, and S. Srivastva, The office of the CEO: Understanding the executive experience, *Academy of Management Executive* 4(3) (1990): 36–48.

[62] B. M. Bass, *Leadership and Performance Beyond Expectations* (New York: Free Press, 1985).

[63] B. J. Avolio and B. M. Bass, Transformational leadership, charisma, and beyond. In J. G. Hunt, B. R. Baliga, H. P. Dachler, and C. A. Schriesheim, eds., *Emerging Leadership Vistas* (Lexington, Mass.: Lexington Books, 1988).

[64] J. Hater and B. M. Bass, Superiors' evaluations and subordinates' perceptions of transformational and transactional leadership, *Journal of Applied Psychology* 73 (1988): 695–702.

[65] B. M. Bass, From transactional to transformational leadership: Learning to share the vision, *Organizational Dynamics* (Winter 1990): 19–31.

[66] Conger, *Charismatic Leader;* J. A. Conger, The dark side of leadership, *Organizational Dynamics* (Autumn 1990): 44–55.

[67] Conger, Dark side of leadership.

[68] J. P. Howell and P. W. Dorfman, A comparative study of leadership and its substitutes in a mixed cultural work setting, Unpublished manuscript. Cited in Bass, From transactional to transformational leadership.

[69] Bass, Leadership, Good, better, best, *Organizational Dynamics* 12 (Winter 1985): 26–40.

[70] J. J. Hater and B. M. Bass, Superiors' evaluations and subordinates' perceptions of transformational and transactional leadership, *Journal of Applied Psychology* 73 (1988): 695–702.

[71] I. C. MacMillan, New business development: A challenge to transformational leadership, *Human Resource Management* 26 (1987): 439–454.

[72] B. M. Bass, D. A. Waldman, B. J. Avolio, and M. Bebb, Transformational leadership and the falling dominoes effect, *Group and Organization Studies* 12 (March 1987): 73–87.

[73] Bass, Leadership, Good, better, best.

[74] C. C. Manz and H. P. Sims, Jr., Superleadership: Beyond the myth of heroic leadership, *Organizational Dynamics* (Spring 1991): 18–35; C. C. Manz and H. P. Sims, Jr., *Superleadership: Leading Others to Lead Themselves* (New York: Prentice-Hall Press, 1989).

[75] Manz and Sims, Superleadership, p. 23.

[76] C. C. Manz and C. P. Neck, Inner leadership: Creating productive thought patterns, *Academy of Management Executive* 5(3) (1991): 91.

[77] J. Fierman, Do women manage differently? *Fortune* (December 17, 1990): 115–118.

[78] See, for example, J. Adams and J. D. Yoder, *Effective Leadership for Women and Men* (Norwood, N.J.: Ablex, 1985); C. M. Seifert, Reactions to leaders: Effects of sex of leader, sex of subordinate, method of leader selection, and task outcome. *Dissertation Abstracts International* 45 (12B) (1986): 3999.

[79] See Bass, From transactional to transformational leadership.

[80] K. E. Clark and M. B. Clark, eds., *Measures of Leadership* (Greensboro, N.C.: Center for Creative Leadership, 1990).

RECOMMENDED READINGS

Bass, B. M. *Bass & Stogdill's Handbook of Leadership: Theory, Research, and Managerial Applications,* 3rd ed. New York: Free Press, 1990.

Clark, K. E., and Clark, M. B., eds. *Measures of Leadership.* Greensboro, N.C.: Center for Creative Leadership, 1990.

Conger, J. A. *The Charismatic Leader.* San Francisco: Jossey-Bass, 1989.

Hitt, W. D. *Ethics and Leadership: Putting Theory into Practice.* Columbus: Batelle, 1990.

Hunt, J. G. *Leadership: A New Synthesis.* Newbury Park, Calif.: Sage, 1991.

Manz, C. C., and Sims, H. P., Jr. *Superleadership: Leading Others to Lead Themselves.* New York: Prentice-Hall Press, 1989.

Tichy, N. M., and Devanna, M. A. *The Transformational Leader,* 2nd ed. New York: Wiley, 1990.

Yukl, G. A. *Leadership in Organizations,* 2nd ed. Englewood Cliffs, N.J.: Prentice-Hall, 1989.

Using Power and Negotiating

Learning Objectives

After completing the reading and activities in Chapter 9, students will be able to

1. Show the relationship between power and dependence.

2. Diagnose the extent, location, and types of power in an organization.

3. Cite causes of powerlessness and strategies for empowering others.

4. Discuss the role of informal networks, alliances, and trade relations in securing power.

5. Offer ways of securing more power and discuss the ethical issues involved.

6. Describe international issues in the securing and use of power.

7. Compare and contrast the distributive and integrative bargaining paradigms.

8. Outline an effective negotiating process.

9. Specify the major issues for effective cross-cultural negotiation.

Power and Negotiations at the Publishing Company

Shelby McIntyre has recently joined the publishing firm of Webster and Snow as a senior editor in the science division. She had spent a number of years in various editorial positions in companies similar to Webster and Snow, but most recently had worked as a consultant for a company specializing in the use of electronic media in the publishing industry. Shortly after her arrival at W&S, one of her authors requested the computer disk from the previous edition of a book to use in revising it.

Shelby felt very strongly that all book revisions should be prepared and submitted to W&S on a disk. To expedite this process for revisions, the typesetting firm would have to "download" the disk into a usable format and send it to the author. When Shelby asked her boss, Sarah Milton, how to secure the disk for her author, Sarah informed Shelby that this had never been done before and agreed that it was a great idea. Sarah also told Shelby that she would have to work with the production department to secure the disk, since at W&S only the production department worked with the typesetter, who was a subcontractor to the firm. When Shelby asked her counterpart in the production department, John Halverston, to secure the disk, he told her that it would not be possible.

Shelby did not believe that this was the right answer and continued to prod John into finding a way to get the typesetter to download and then release the disk. After a rather heated discussion about "sticking to her own business," Shelby finally convinced John to ask the typesetting firm, and its representative Jeremy Gates, about the cost of downloading. Two months later, after numerous calls to John, who kept stalling, he finally told her that it would cost between $500 and $1,000. Shelby had a hard time believing this statement because she knew that to download the fifteen files she needed would take at most two hours of relatively unskilled (and hence low-paid) labor; even at $50 an hour plus $10 for the cost of the disks, the profit for the typesetting firm seemed out of proportion to the task. John had also told her that he was not sure that the typesetter would be able to provide the text in a form useful to her author. Since W&S gave most of their typesetting to the firm, Shelby could not understand why they were so reluctant to provide the disks she needed.

Shelby's promise to her author to secure the disks had already delayed the publication schedule of the book by at least two months. Now, she had to decide what to do next.

- - - - - - - - - - - - - - - - - -

Power is the potential or actual ability to influence others in a desired direction. An individual, group, or other social unit has power if it controls information, knowledge, or resources desired by another individual, group, or social unit.[1] Who has power in the situation described at W&S publishing? Recognizing, using, and dealing with power differences is implicit in *negotiation,* which is a process for reconciling different, often incompatible interests, of interdependent parties. At W&S, Shelby McIntyre, John Halverston, and Jeremy Gates engage in negotiations about producing the computer disk. How well does each one use power and negotiating skill to reach a satisfactory agreement?

In the rest of this chapter we examine power and negotiations. We begin by considering the reasons individuals or groups exert power. We then examine the sources from which they derive power. We also discuss power in the international arena. Next, we examine the use of negotiation. We describe two bargaining paradigms, the negotiation process, and strategies and tactics of negotiations. We conclude with cross-cultural issues relating to negotiation in organizations.

POWER IN THE ORGANIZATION

Organizational researchers have increasingly cited the value of identifying and using power behavior to improve individual and organizational performance, even calling its development and use "the central executive function."[2] Theorists and practitioners have transformed an early view of power, which considered it evil and as mainly stemming from coercion,[3] into a model of viable political action in organizations. Yet, while functional and advantageous in many situations, power behavior can also create conflict, which frequently is dysfunctional for the organization.

Different individuals and groups within and outside the organization can exert power. Individual employees, including top and middle management, technical analysts and specialists, support staff, and other nonmanagerial workers, can influence the actions an organization takes to reach its goals. Formal groups of employees, such as various departments, work teams, management councils, task forces, or employee unions, as well as informal groups, such as those workers with offices near each other or those who see each other socially, can similarly exercise power. In addition to individuals or groups within the organization, nonemployees may try to influence the behavior of an organization and its members. Owners, suppliers, clients, competitors, employee associations (e.g., unions and professional associations), the general public, and directors of the organization may exert power that affects the organization.[4]

Individuals can exert influence in a variety of ways.[5] They may exert regular, ongoing influence, such as when managers demonstrate authority over subordinates. Or, they can make attempts to exert influence periodically, when unique circumstances occur, such as the expiration of a labor contract or a change in the economic or technological environment. Influence can also focus on specific individuals, groups, or even events, or it can occur more generally, with the entire work situation as a target. Some individuals use their charisma or network of contacts to create personal influence, while others remain more detached—they may try to influence rules, regulations, policies, and procedures rather than individuals. Influence attempts also vary in their formality; calling a meeting to discuss and resolve a major organizational problem differs from trying to handle it informally over coffee, in the hallways, or without systematic planning and implementation. Finally, attempts to exert influence can be constructive or destructive. How would you characterize the situation at W&S publishing? We can begin our diagnosis of power by identifying those exerting influence.

Ethical Issues

How legitimate is the use of power in organizations? Certainly the Machiavellian view of power, with its manipulative and autocratic connotations, raises questions about the ethics of power. The abuse of power has been a favorite topic in political arenas—remember Richard Nixon's Watergate scandal or the earlier Teapot Dome scandal in Warren Harding's administration?

But the use of power so long as it does not abuse the rights of others has been encouraged in organizations. It helps managers attain organizational goals, facilitate their own and others' accomplishments, and expedite effective competition in the workplace. Power, when viewed as potential or actual influence, is an essential part of effective leadership and management.

Managers must establish guidelines for the ethical use of power in their organizations. They and other organizational members must emphasize its contribution to organizational effectiveness and control its abuses. Ensuring that the rights of all organizational members are guaranteed is one criterion for its ethical use.

POWER AND DEPENDENCE

We can initially diagnose power by measuring the extent or force of the dependence that flows in the opposite direction from power in a relationship.[6] In other words, the power that A has over B is determined by the degree of dependence that B has on A. Individuals may initiate an act of power to counteract their job-related dependence.

Nature of Dependence

Dependence arises in part because a person, group, or organization relies on another person, group, or organization to accomplish his, her, or its tasks. It may also arise for other reasons, such as a previous history of assistance by one person or a psychological reliance by one person on another. A subordinate depends on his or her boss for directions and resources. A supervisor in turn depends on his or her subordinates for assistance in accomplishing a task and identifying obstacles to achieving a work group's goal. The person being relied or depended upon automatically has some power—potential or actual ability to influence the other. Individuals who are dependent attempt to secure power to neutralize their dependence on others.

What types of dependence does Shelby McIntyre have? Among others, she relies on the authors to provide manuscripts to sell and on the production staff to transform the manuscripts into books. She also depends on her boss for some direction, as well as other managers who have input into the editorial and publication process. What dependences does John Halverston show? He clearly relies on Shelby providing manuscripts from the authors with whom she works. Each of these individuals, as well as the groups to which they belong, has some degree of power over the others because of the dependence inherent in their relationships. And each person or group attempts to secure more power to neutralize the power that accompanies the dependence.

Now consider a job that you have held. On whom did you depend in performing your work? Did you depend on your boss, your coworkers, customers, or maybe the owner of the company? A jobholder's dependence is related to characteristics of the organization and its environment. Dependence increases as the organization becomes larger, causing greater reliance on specialties that result from division of labor. As the uncertainty of the environment increases or the organization's dependence on it grows, managers also become more dependent on others to facilitate environmental interactions, thus reducing their relative power compared to others. As the organization's goals become more ambitious, managers become more dependent on others involved in coordinating their actions to accomplish these goals, and need to find ways to increase their power. Technology also contributes to dependence by increasing specialization and hence to managers' dependence on specialists. Finally, dependence is a function of the formal structure, measurement systems, and reward systems in organization. For example, diffusing authority throughout the organization to individuals other than the manager creates greater managerial dependencies and calls for power behavior by the manager.

Dealing with Dependence

Individuals engage in power-oriented behavior to reduce their dependence on others; they also try to increase the dependence of others on them, thus increasing their own relative power. A technician who must rely on his or her boss for pay raises may reduce his or her dependence by developing power as a result of becoming indispensable to the boss, such as by acquiring unique expertise or knowledge. Or, the director of purchasing may attempt to reduce his or her dependence on a supplier by finding alternative sources of goods or services. To cope with dependence, managers draw from bases of power and establish trade relations and alliances, as described later in this chapter.

Diagnosing dependence is a key step in understanding and using power. A power/dependence analysis, as shown in Figure 9–1, facilitates diagnosis. Consider once more the introductory scenario. Can you do a power/dependence analysis for this situation? Figure 9–2 offers examples of possible dependence diagrams based on the limited information presented in the opening scenario; they show dependence in only a single direction, although obviously some degree of mutual dependence exists. According to these diagrams, who has the greatest need to exert power on an ongoing basis? Both Shelby McIntyre and John Halverston rely on a relatively large number of constituencies. They probably use many sources of power to reduce their dependence. But Shelby's dependence on John has increased with her desire to obtain the computer disk. Because she has increased her dependence, she also has increased her need for and actual exertion of power.

You might consider other people to whom we typically attribute power: the president of the United States or the head of a large corporation. What would their dependence diagrams look like? What would their power/dependence analysis reveal? This type of dependence analysis essentially derives from the association of power with dependence in social relationships.

POWER AS EXCHANGE

Recent definitions of power have described power as a property of a social relationship. This definition derives from a historical view of power as an exchange process[7]—where a person who commands services needed by others exchanges them for compliance with his or her requests. For example, the supervisor exchanges time off for high-quality performance by the workers. Management accedes to union demands to avoid a strike. Viewing power as a function of ties of dependence or interdependence is describing an exchange relationship in another way.[8] For example, a supervisor often has power because the subordinates depend on him or her for rewards—the supervisor exchanges rewards for good performance. In the exchange relationship, each party exercises a kind of power in providing something of value to the other.

Figure 9–1 **Questions for Power/Dependence Analysis**

1. Whom do you really depend on?
2. How important is each dependency?
3. What is the basis of each dependency?
4. Are any of these dependencies obviously inappropriate or dysfunctional?
5. What has created that pattern of dysfunctional dependence?
6. How much effective power-oriented behavior do you engage in?
7. Is that enough to cope well with the dependencies in the job?
8. Does the manner in which you generate or use power have any negative consequences for the organization?
9. What are the negative consequences?

Source: Based on J. P. Kotter, Power, success, and organizational effectiveness, *Organizational Dynamics* 6 (1978): 27–40.

Figure 9–2 **Dependence Diagrams for W&S Situation**

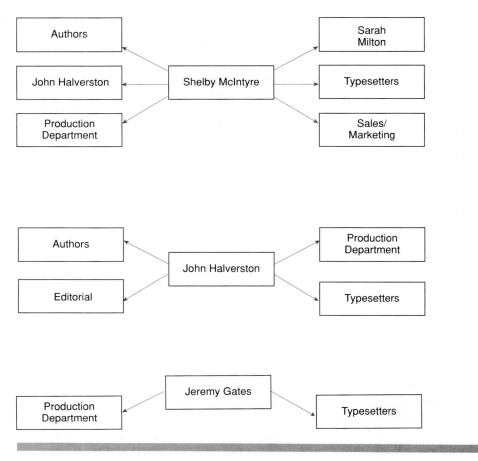

A social exchange network exists when an individual or group negotiates with another over the allocation of valued resources.[9] Managers spend more time making deals, interacting across departments, and even exchanging resources across organizational boundaries.[10] Consider the negotiations between Shelby McIntyre and John Halverston over the computer disk; their discussion revolves in part around the allocation of resources to the downloading of the files. We discuss the control of resources as a source of power in greater detail later in this chapter.

INDIVIDUAL NEEDS, PERSONALITY, AND POWER

A third way of viewing power, in addition to a response to dependence or as part of an exchange relation, looks at individual needs for power, as described in Chapter 4. The *need for power* is an individual motivator that causes a person to seek and build power.[11] You may recall that individuals with a high need for power try to influence and control others, seek leadership positions in groups, enjoy persuading others, and are perceived by others as outspoken, forceful, and demanding. Often politicians, top managers, or informal leaders are perceived as having a high need for power. Do any individuals in the opening case have a high need for power? Because the case does not provide sufficient data for us to answer this question, we would need to gather additional data to verify the individual needs.

An individual's personality can also affect their exertion of power and influence. One recent study showed, for example, that personality explains the type of influence tactics used: People high on Machiavellianism more often used nonrational and indirect tactics (e.g., deceit, thought manipulation), and people low in Machiavellianism more often used rational and direct tactics (e.g., reason, persistence, assertion). Those high on need for approval used rational and indirect tactics (e.g., hinting, compromise, bargaining), and those low on need for approval used nonrational and direct tactics (e.g., threat, evasion, reward).[12]

POWER RELATIONS

Most influence attempts we have described are directed downward in the organization. Managers, for example, can give direct orders to subordinates, establish guidelines for their decision making, approve or reject subordinates' decisions, or allocate resources to them. Individuals can also exert upward influence. To promote or protect their self-interests, they can control the type of information passed to superiors or withhold information they feel is detrimental to themselves. Occasionally workers will punish or reward their superiors—by withholding or providing a quality work effort, for example. Managing the boss effectively requires understanding and responding to his or her needs.[13]

Lateral influence can also occur. Peers can offer advice or provide service; or they can use power to control others. Influence attempts between entities at the same level, such as functional departments, line and staff groups, or labor and management, often result in competition.[14] The parties often resort to power struggles which result from the tendency to try to strengthen one's own power vis-à-vis the other party's. As the parties' interdependence increases, they can less afford conflict. Thus they may rely more on negotiation and cooperation, rather than on a power struggle, to resolve their differences.

Powerlessness

Powerlessness can occur in organizations as a result of various organizational factors, such as characteristics of the reward system, aspects of job design, and the style of the supervisor.[15] Significant organizational changes, excessive competition, an impersonal bureaucratic climate, or poor communications can contribute to the powerlessness of an organization member. Lack of either competence-based or innovation-based rewards or unappealing rewards can also inspire such feelings. Jobs with low task variety, unrealistic goals, too many rules, low opportunities for advancement, or lack of appropriate resources affect powerlessness. Finally, an authoritarian supervisor who emphasizes failure or lacks reasons for his or her actions exacerbates such a situation.

Recent research suggests that women in management have experienced powerlessness because of a combination of formal and informal practices that put them into low-power positions;[16] these same practices extend to men. Symptoms of such powerlessness include a jobholder receiving overly close supervision, being rules-minded and overly concerned with routines, and doing all work himself or herself.

As the work force becomes more diverse, managers are challenged to ensure that they do not contribute to the powerlessness of a jobholder. By being patronizingly overprotective, failing to provide signs of managerial support, assuming that an employee does not know the ropes, ignoring the jobholder in informal socializing, and failing to provide organizational supports, managers contribute to such powerlessness.[17] The likelihood of doing so seems to increase with minorities and women, and must be carefully avoided. Acquiescence is a response strategy frequently used by individuals in powerless jobs; women use it more often than men.[18] They fail to note that they can use the more powerful strategies of negotiation, coalition formation, and persuasion in these situations.

Empowering Others

Recent research suggests that individuals often can increase their own power by sharing power with others.[19] Managers can facilitate the sharing by helping subordinates in particular to tap into the sources of power described in this chapter. They can also give them empowering information, such as providing emotional support, offering words of encouragement, serving as a role model, and facilitating successful mastery of a task.[20] Table 9–1 shows different strategies for the empowering process for leaders and managers. Other strategies for a manager include providing a positive emotional atmosphere, rewarding staff achievements in visible and personal ways, expressing confidence in subordinates' abilities, fostering initiative and responsibility, and building on success.[21]

At General Electric, for example, top executives are relinquishing some of their power.[22] In 1991, one-eighth of the work force participated in a *Work-out,* a program begun in 1989 in which "participants can get a mental workout; they can take unnecessary work out of their jobs; they can work out problems together."[23] At a neutral site, 40–100 people discuss problems, propose solutions, and prepare a formal presentation of their proposals that they deliver to their boss on the final, third day of the forum. The boss is expected to respond to each proposal on the spot. Ideally, and in practice, the process empowers the workers, and the proposals save GE money.

What gives the people at W&S publishing the ability to influence others in the direction they desire? They derive their power from the sources in Figure 9–3: the position they hold, their personal characteristics, the resources or information they can access and control, and informal networks, trade relations, or alliances they form.

Table 9–1 **Differences in the Empowering Process as a Function of Role: Leaders Compared with Managers**

Empowering Process	Leaders	Managers
Providing direction for followers/subordinates	Via ideals, vision, a higher purpose, superordinate goals	Via involvement of subordinates in determining paths toward goal accomplishment
Stimulating followers/subordinates	With ideas	With action; things to accomplish
Rewarding followers/subordinates	Informal; personal recognition	Formal; incentive systems
Developing followers/subordinates	By inspiring them to do more than they thought they could do	By involving them in important decision-making activities and providing feedback for potential learning
Appealing to follower/subordinate needs	Appeal to needs of followership and dependency	Appeal to needs for autonomy and independence

SOURCE: Reprinted with permission from W. W. Burke, Leadership as empowering others. In S. Srivastva and Associates, *Executive Power* (San Francisco: Jossey-Bass, 1986), p. 73.

Figure 9–3 **Sources of Power**

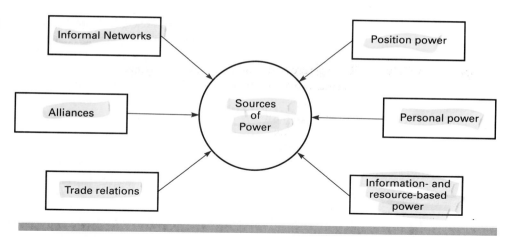

POSITION POWER Individuals frequently derive power from the position or job they hold in an organization, as shown in Figure 9–4.

Authority Possessing *legitimate* power, managers can exert influence over others simply because of the authority associated with their job. It results in subordinates obeying rules or orders given by a manager because they view them as legitimate owing to the position the manager holds. Lower level supervisors can also have authority that gives them power. Such jobholders provide direction for and control over the work done by their subordinates simply because of their relative position in the hierarchy. One study showed that as a supervisor's legitimate power increased, a subordinate's compliance increased, but his or her satisfaction with supervision decreased.[24] Do Shelby and John have legitimate authority? Probably they have such power over their subordinates, but not with regard to each other.

Centrality Power accrues to other positions because of their centrality. The more the activities of a position are linked and important to those of other individuals or subunits, the greater their centrality.[25] A superintendent of schools, for example, has greater centrality than the school committee because the activities of more jobs are linked to him or her than to the elected officials. Sometimes a job that lacks official authority can develop position power because it becomes central to other positions. The administrative assistant to the chief executive officer of a company can develop such centrality. Consider too the position power of the chief of staff to the president of the United States. While he (or she in the future) has some power because of his or her place in the hierarchy, he or she also controls access to the president and acquires power because of this centrality.

Control of Rewards and Punishments Individuals with position power frequently add to their authority because they control the delivery of rewards in the organization. An individual who has control over organizational rewards, including pay raises, status, and desirable work assignments, as well as praise, recognition, or group sanctions, may use them to encourage compliance by others with desired behaviors or goals. A manager might also force individuals to behave in certain ways by punishing them. He or she might demote or dismiss them, increase the supervision they receive, or withhold compensation or

Figure 9–4 **Position Power**

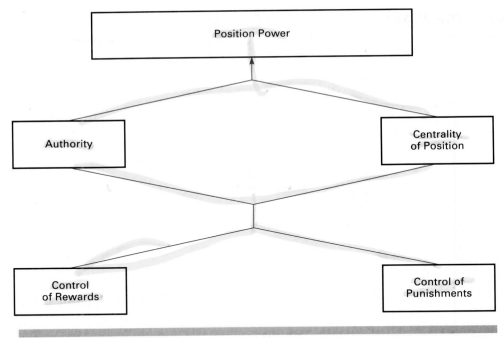

promotions. A manager effectively uses this power if his or her subordinates believe that obeying the manager will result in the receipt of extrinsic or intrinsic rewards.

PERSONAL POWER

Personal power is based on the knowledge or personality of an individual that allow him or her to influence the behavior of others, as shown in Figure 9–5.

Expertise An individual who has unique or special knowledge, skills, and experience may use this expertise as a source of influence and as a way of building personal power. A physician can influence patients to act in certain ways because he or she exerts expert power when giving advice based on medical knowledge. A computer specialist can influence non-technical staff to act in ways he or she desires because of the special knowledge of computers he or she has that may be critical to the rest of the staff. As organizations have become increasingly technology-oriented, technical support staff have acquired increased power in organizations.

Charisma Some individuals influence others because they have charisma or because others identify with them. An individual with charisma often exerts power because he or she attracts others to follow. A movie star, politician, or any organizational member with a charismatic personality may use this base of power. A person who identifies with another person can be influenced by that individual; the person being identified with exerts power.

Does anyone in the introductory scenario have charismatic power? To achieve a precise assessment of their use of this source, we must observe them in person or gather more data about their personalities and behaviors.

Coercion If a manager can exert power over a person because that person fears him or her, the manager is using coercive power. The president of a company where workers

Figure 9–5 Personal Power

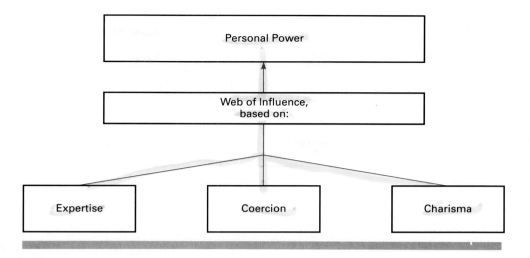

are on strike could threaten to replace any striking workers or take the company into bankruptcy, and thus has coercive power. Can you think of other individuals you know who exert such power? How effectively do they influence behavior in a direction they desire?

The use of coercive power often has secondary, dysfunctional consequences. It can create ongoing stress and anxiety for workers. In extreme cases it can encourage them to increase their absenteeism, increase the rate of turnover, and even commit sabotage in the workplace.

RESOURCE- AND INFORMATION-BASED POWER

Access to resources or information provides a third major source of influence. This differs from expert power in its greater transience—expertise is more permanent than information-based power. For example, the first individuals to learn to use a new computer system may provide rapid assistance to other organizational members and secure both resource- and information-based power, as well as demonstrate expert power. The power of organizational subunits, such as individual managers, union leaders, or the executive committee, is a function of their ability to cope with uncertainty and their unsubstitutability, among other things.

Control of Resources and Information

Power may come from the control of scarce resources, such as money, materials, staff, or information. Individuals who formulate rules to regulate the possession of resources, as well as those who actually possess, allocate, and use the resources, will acquire power.[26] The person who determines or administers the budget controls resources and secures power. Workers who control the scheduling of prized machinery or allocation of computer equipment can also acquire resource-based power. In addition, a unit's centrality may interact with its power and its ability to acquire internal resources in an organization.[27]

Individuals also implement power by making choices in the identification and use of resources along three dimensions: internal-external, vertical-lateral, and legitimate-illegitimate.[28] Along the *internal-external* dimension, people may rely on resources internal to the organization, such as exchanging favors or forming networks with other employees. When these sources fail or become inadequate, individuals may turn outside the organization for resources, such as by joining professional organizations or forming alliances outside the organization. The *vertical-lateral* dimension refers to individuals exerting influence by relating to superiors or subordinates rather than peers. Mentor-protégé activities occur vertically in the organization; coalition formation occurs laterally. The *legitimate-illegitimate* dimension contrasts normal to extreme behavior. For example, most organizational members view forming coalitions as legitimate and sabotaging production as illegitimate. Which strategies should Shelby McIntyre use?

Coping with Uncertainty

Some organizational members help others reduce uncertainty in the workplace caused by unclear task demands, a rapidly changing environment, introduction of new technology, or an ambiguous organizational structure. Managers or nonmanagerial employees who can reduce the ambiguity in these and other situations may acquire power. Employees in a chemical plant who know the relevant regulations of the Environmental Protection Agency may secure information-based power because they help others cope with uncertainty. So may managers who acquire information about pending layoffs, introduction of new technology, or budgetary shortfalls. Consider an agency in state government that experiences a 15 percent budget cutback. The manager who knows which if any workers will lose their jobs because of the deficit and arranges for transfers or retraining for them helps them cope with uncertainty and hence has power. Or consider the role a research and development department can play in bringing a new technology "on-line" in a company. Not only can the department's members educate workers to its use, but they can also modify it to meet product demands and organizational needs. This department would gain power not only from their expertise but also from their ability to use it to help other members clarify the significance of and respond effectively to environmental and organizational changes. In general, the more an individual or group copes with uncertainty, the more power it has.

Boundary-spanner roles (see Chapters 7 and 11 for further discussion) have significant power potential. Individuals in such roles as public relations director or purchasing agent deal with the outside environment for the benefit of the organization's members. Their ability to cope with uncertainty for others is one source of power; the ability to channel or control information going to the organization's members is another. Identification of boundary spanners and diagnosis of their effectiveness in this role, then, are important means of assessing power in organizations.

Does either Shelby or John cope with uncertainty for others? If John could guarantee that Shelby would receive the disks she desires, he would cope with uncertainty for her in dealing with the typesetter and would have more potential power.

Unsubstitutability

In general, the less substitutable the activities of an individual or group in an organization are, the more power it has. Consider an organization in which you have worked. Who or which group performed activities that no one else could readily perform? The president was probably less substitutable than a clerical worker. The chief financial officer may have been more substitutable than the director of product development. Members of the MIS or EDP departments might also have lacked substitutability because of their unique knowledge. A unit that can bring resources into the organization from the outside may also have low substitutability.

Who in the W&S situation has power because of their lack of substitutability? The typesetter has power because he holds the typeset copy of the manuscript and therefore is unsubstitutable. In editorial matters, Shelby McIntyre might be unsubstitutable. Of course, unsubstitutability as a source of power interacts with other sources, affecting the relative power of each person or group in a situation.

The use of power can have positive consequences when the person who controls information or resources gives related jobholders open access to the resources or information. Political alliances with sponsors, peers, and subordinates, as described later in this chapter, can also facilitate the effective sharing of power.

INFORMAL NETWORKS, ALLIANCES, AND TRADE RELATIONS

Individuals and groups can acquire power by increasing their contacts with others. They can build informal networks, foster alliances, and create trade relations.

Informal Networks

Informal networks play a significant role in the exercise of power. The operation of the informal network may result in transfer of legitimate authority from a supervisor to an influential subordinate. To identify the informal network, we can ask the following questions: (1) Who has relevant information? (2) To whom does that person communicate the information? (3) How many others have access to it? (4) What potential sources of power exist in the team? Developing an informal network of contacts requires spending scheduled and unscheduled time meeting with coworkers and other organizational members. Dealing with and penetrating the "old-boys' network" in organizations has been a major challenge faced by upwardly mobile women executives.

Trade Relations

Reciprocity and lateral exchange form trade relationships that contribute to the accruing and exercising of power. Managers participate in trade relationships with lateral network members to get their jobs done.[29] They can enhance their power by (1) using their reputation for making things happen, (2) forming alliances, (3) holding a position with legitimate authority, and (4) developing a favored status vis-à-vis other peers.[30] Consider the relationship between editorial and production at W&S. What peers are indispensable to Shelby's attempts to secure the disk for her author? Certainly she must engage the support of the head of production if the negotiations are to succeed. How can Shelby gain more power using trade relations? For example, she might consider using her reputation or forming alliances as a way of gaining power.

Alliances

Forming alliances addresses the issue faced by organizational members of finding a way to create influence without having or using formal authority.[31] Managers then act as integrators or facilitators; they devote larger amounts of time to boundary-spanning activities.[32] Alliances between two or more individuals form when they have resources or favors to exchange. Such reciprocity can occur among peers, between supervisor and subordinate, or among members of different organizations. They might exchange any of the "currencies" shown in Table 9–2. In making the exchange, a person using influence needs to view the other as a potential ally and understand his or her world; the influencer must also know how to use exchange, focus on effectiveness, and use a repertoire of influence approaches.[33]

Alliances can be organized as a coalition, "an interacting group of individuals, deliberately constructed, independent of formal structure, lacking its own internal formal structure, consisting of mutually perceived membership, issue oriented, focused on a goal or goals external to the coalition, and requiring concerted member action."[34] Allies frequently join into a coalition to support a mutual interest. They bring their larger pool of resources to the situations, including greater expertise and commitment. They often act politically to support or oppose an organizational program, policy, or change. Negotiations play a major role in their actions.

Let us look at the introductory scenario again. What types of power do the

Table 9–2 **Commonly Traded Organizational Currencies**

Inspiration-Related Currencies	
Vision	involved in a task that has larger significance for the unit, organization, customers, or society.
Excellence	Having a chance to do important things really well.
Moral/Ethical Correctness	Doing what is "right" by a higher standard than efficiency.
Task-Related Currencies	
Resources	Lending or giving money, budget increases, personnel, space, and so forth.
Assistance	Helping with existing projects or undertaking unwanted tasks.
Cooperation	Giving task support, providing quicker response time, approving a project, or aiding implementation.
Information	Providing organizational as well as technical knowledge.
Position-Related Currencies	
Advancement	Giving a task or assignment that can aid in promotion.
Recognition	Acknowledging effort, accomplishment, or abilities.
Visibility	Providing chance to be known by higher-ups or significant others in the organization.
Reputation	Enhancing the way a person is seen.
Importance/Insiderness	Offering a sense of importance, of "belonging."
Network/Contacts	Providing opportunities for linking with others.
Relationship-Related Currencies	
Acceptance/Inclusion	Providing closeness and friendship.
Personal Support	Giving personal and emotional backing.
Understanding	Listening to others' concerns and issues.
Personal-Related Currencies	
Self-Concept	Affirming one's values, self-esteem, and identity.
Challenge/Learning	Sharing tasks that increase skills and abilities.
Ownership/Involvement	Letting others have ownership and influence.
Gratitude	Expressing appreciation or indebtedness.

SOURCE: Reprinted, by permission of publisher, from A. R. Cohen and D. L. Bradford, Influence without authority: The use of alliances, reciprocity, and exchange to accomplish work, *Organizational Dynamics* (Winter 1989): 11. © 1989. American Management Association, New York. All rights reserved.

people have? Figure 9–6 summarizes the sources of power each person or group probably uses. Note that the individuals and groups use multiple sources of power. Generally, however, some sources are viewed as having a greater effect than others and as being more appropriate in certain situations. Typically, however, the more bases of power an individual can draw on, the more powerful that person is.

POWER IN THE INTERNATIONAL ARENA

We noted earlier in this book that countries differ significantly along the dimension of *power distance*, or the extent to which inequality in power is accepted.[35] In high-power-distance countries, such as India, Mexico, and France, subordinates accept the unequal distribution of power; they frown on subordinates who bypass their bosses. In low-power countries, such as Austria, Denmark, and Sweden, bypassing superiors is expected.

> An American executive went to London to manage the company's British office. Although the initial few weeks were relatively uneventful, one thing that both-ered the executive was that visitors were never sent directly to his office. A visitor first spoke with the receptionist, then the secretary, then the office manager, and finally was escorted by the office manager to see the American. The American was annoyed with this practice, which he considered a total waste of time. When he finally spoke with his British employees and urged them to be less formal, sending visitors directly to him, the employees were chagrined.
>
> After a number of delicate conversations, the American executive began to understand the greater stress on formality and hierarchy in England. He slowly learned to ignore his feelings of impatience when the British used their proper channels for greeting guests. As a result, visitors continued to see the reception-ist, secretary, and office manager before being sent in to meet the American.[36]

Other cross-cultural differences in power behavior may accompany variations in power distance. We know, for example, that individuals differ in their attitudes toward power and in their abilities to use it.[37] Most likely these differences may be cross-culturally determined. The predominant or most useful bases of power may also be culturally linked. Those in the United States may favor charisma, while the Japanese may favor legitimacy.

Figure 9–6 Sources of Power at W&S

Shelby McIntyre
Authority
Control of rewards and punishments
Expertise

John Halverston
Authority
Control of rewards and punishments
Expertise
Access to resources
Control of information
Coping with uncertainty
Unsubstitutability

Sarah Milton
Authority
Control of rewards and punishments
Expertise
Control of information
Coping with uncertainty

Jeremy Gates
Control of information
Coping with uncertainty
Unsubstitutability

**USE OF
NEGOTIATION**

Negotiation is a process by which two or more parties attempt to reach an agreement that is acceptable to both parties about issues on which they apparently disagree. Negotiations typically have four key elements.[38] First, the two parties involved in negotiating demonstrate some *degree of interdependence*. The editorial and production departments at W&S demonstrate dependence to produce finished books. In addition, Shelby depends on John to secure the computer disk she needs. Power influences such interdependence and affects the relative ability of Shelby and John to exercise their preferences. Second, some *perceived conflict* exists between the parties involved in the negotiations. Shelby and John differed in their view about the necessity of making a computer disk of the manuscript available to the author. Third, the two parties have the potential to participate in *opportunistic interaction*. Each party tries to influence the other through various negotiating actions. Each party cares about and pursues its own interests, by trying to influence decisions to its advantage. Finally, the *possibility of agreement* exists.

In what types of negotiations have you participated? You may have negotiated an increase in salary from your employer. You may have negotiated a different grade from a professor. You may have read about negotiations between union and management. In the political arena, bargaining and negotiations are particularly important. Interest groups or political parties use power to accomplish their goals. Political figures may even concern themselves more with power development than with their management responsibilities.[39]

Managers or other organizational members often choose an interaction strategy that considers the extent of their concern about their own and the other party's outcomes. Research suggests, as shown in Figure 9–7, for example, that a party with a high concern about both parties' outcomes will take a problem-solving approach. A party with a low concern about its own outcomes and high concern about the other party's will yield to the other. A party with a high concern about its own outcomes and a low concern about the other party's will contend for its own preferences. A party with a low concern about its own and the other's outcome will not act.[40] Thus managers and other parties should recognize the range of negotiating styles available to them and the situations in which each style is likely to be used and appropriate.

**BARGAINING
PARADIGMS**

The negotiating process demonstrates a fundamental tension between the *claiming* and *creating* of value.[41] Value claimers view negotiations purely as an adversarial process. Each side tries to *claim* as much of a limited pie as possible by giving the other side as little as possible. Each party claims value through the use of manipu-

Figure 9–7 Nego-
tiating Approaches

		Concern about Own Outcomes	
		High	Low
Concern about Others' Outcomes	High	Problem-solving approach	Yield to other party
	Low	Contend for own preferences	No action

SOURCE: Based on D. G. Pruitt, Strategic choice in negotiation, *American Behavioral Scientist* 27 (November-December 1983): 167–194.

lative tactics, forcible arguments, limited concessions, and hard bargaining. Value creators, in contrast, call for a process that results in joint gains to each party. They try to *create* additional benefits for each side in the negotiations. They emphasize shared interests, developing a collaborative relationship, and negotiating in a pleasant, cooperative manner.

A negotiator incorporates these strategies singly or in combination in one of two basic paradigms. *Distributive bargaining* takes an adversarial or win-lose approach. *Integrative bargaining* takes a problem-solving or win-win approach.

Distributive Bargaining

The classical view considers bargaining as a win-lose situation, where one party's gain is the other party's loss. Known also as a zero-sum type of negotiation, because the gain of one party equals the loss of the other and hence the net adds to zero, this approach characterizes the purchase of used cars, property, and other material goods in organizations. It has also been applied to salary negotiations or labor-management negotiations.

Distributive bargaining emphasizes the claiming of value. The choice of opening offers, the ability to influence the opponent to view the situation in a way favorable to the negotiator, and the careful planning of offers and counteroffers can influence the ability to claim value and "win" the negotiation. Power plays a key role in succeeding in distributive bargaining because it increases a party's leverage and ability to shape perceptions.

Integrative Bargaining

Recent research encourages negotiators to transform the bargaining into a win-win situation.[42] Here both parties gain as a result of the negotiations. Known also as a positive-sum type of negotiation, because the gains of each party yield a positive sum, this approach has recently characterized international negotiations, labor-management negotiations, and specific job-related bargaining. Integrative bargaining will occur at W&S if Shelby and John can reach a solution that is acceptable to both of them.

THE NEGOTIATION PROCESS

We can identify four basic steps in an effective negotiation for either distributive or integrative bargaining, as shown in Figure 9–8. First, the parties *prepare* for the negotiations. Second, they determine their *best alternative* to a negotiated settlement.

Figure 9–8 **Steps in Negotiation**

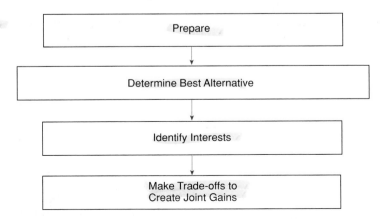

Third, they identify their own and the other party's *interests*. Fourth, they make *trade-offs* and in integrative bargaining attempt to create *joint gains* for the parties involved.

Preparation   Preparation for the negotiation described in the introduction should have begun long before Shelby requested the computer disks. Each party should have gathered information about the other side—its history, likely behavior, previous interactions between editors and production, and other agreements reached by the parties.

Evaluation of   Each party must determine the range of acceptable agreements. The two sides at-
Alternatives   tempt to identify the *bargaining range* and reach an agreement within it. Consider the issue of wages at a unionized company. Assume that the employees represented by a union want a $4.00 per hour wage increase but will settle for $3.00. Figure 9–9(A) illustrates their target price ($4.00) and resistance price ($3.00). Now assume management wants to pay $1.00 more per hour, but is willing to pay $2.00 more. Figure 9–9(B) illustrates management's target price ($1.00) and resistance price ($2.00). The *bargaining range* is the prices where both sides can satisfy their

Figure 9–9 **Hypo-thetical Bargaining Ranges for Wage Demands**

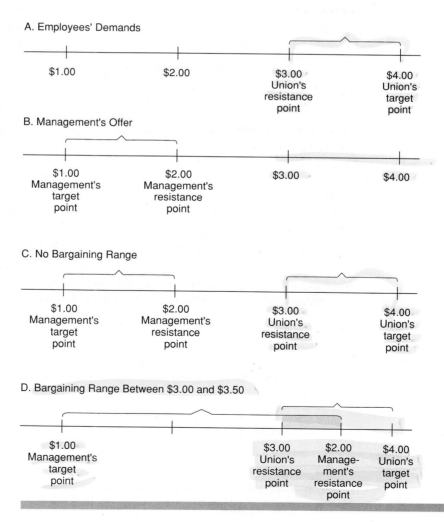

wishes; it is the overlap between the parties' resistance points. Figure 9–9(C) shows that no bargaining range exists for the employees and management given these resistance points. If, however, the employees' union convinces management's representatives that their services are more valuable than they originally thought, management may raise its resistance point to $3.50 as shown in Figure 9–9(D); then a bargaining range exists between $3.00 and $3.50. Figure 9–10 describes the min-max strategy.

The bargainers determine the options acceptable to them and also identify their best alternative if a negotiated settlement is not reached. For some employees, for example, striking might be their best alternative. For others, securing a position outside the company might be the best alternative. The cognitive biases that affect decision making (see Chapter 6) also influence negotiations. The way a negotiator frames a situation (e.g., describing it as a gain or a loss), the nature of the initial anchoring or starting value, the availability of instances of an event (the frequency of unlikely events), and overconfidence in judgment abilities will also affect the assessment of alternatives.[43]

Identifying Interests
Negotiators act to satisfy their own interests. Often in doing so they ignore or simplify the views of their opponents, especially when forced to consider uncertain future events.[44] They must also assess the other party's interests and then decide how they will respond to the others' interests in their offers. Accurately assessing a party's own and another party's interests is essential in effective negotiations.

Even though negotiators try to reach agreements on a specific position on a specific issue, more than one position may actually respond to their interests. The underlying interests are generally broader and may be satisfied with different positions. Employees may argue for a specific wage increase, but their underlying aim may really be the removal of certain managers. Managers' interests can include their reputation, relationship with other parties, long-term organizational goals, various precedents, or even the bottom line. Effective negotiations call for satisfying interests by identifying and exploring a range of positions held on specific issues.

In assessing what interests are at stake, managers can use the following advice.[45] First, they should consider both tangible interests and subtler interests, such as reputation, fairness, and precedent. Second, they should separate interests from issues and positions. Meeting esteem needs differs, for example, from insisting on a 10 percent pay increase. Third, they must recognize that interests may have either intrinsic or instrumental value. Increased autonomy may have value by itself or may be viewed as a means to accomplish other personal goals. Fourth, they must understand that interests depend on perceptions, which are subjective. Finally, they should note that interests and issues can change intentionally or accidentally.

Figure 9–10 **Min-Max Strategy**

What is the minimum I can accept to resolve the conflict?
What is the maximum that I can ask for without appearing outrageous?
What is the maximum I can give away?
What is the least I can offer without appearing outrageous?

What is the minimum the other party can accept to resolve the conflict?
What is the maximum the other party can ask for without appearing outrageous?
What is the maximum the other party can give away?
What is the least the other party can offer without appearing outrageous?

SOURCE: Based on R. Gourlay, Negotiations and bargaining, *Management Decision* 25(3) (1987): 23.

Making Trade-offs and Creating Joint Gains

Bargainers use trade-offs to satisfy their own and others' interests. Recent labor-management negotiations have traded wage increases for job security provisions. Either position (increased wages or better job security) would meet the interests of maintaining a certain standard of living. One way to assess trade-offs is to begin by identifying the best and worst possible outcomes, next to specify possible increments that trade-offs can reflect, and finally to consider how the increments relate to the key issues. Besides making trade-offs as a way of reaching a satisfactory negotiating outcome, integrative bargaining attempts to create gains for both parties. A party may offer something relatively less valuable to it but more valuable to the other party. The parties may build on shared interests. They may also use economies of scale to create joint gains. The following describes ways of creating join gains in a variety of circumstances:

- Differences in *relative valuation* can lead to exchanges, directly or by "unbundling" (considering separately) differently valued interests.
- Differences in *forecasts* can lead to contingent agreements when (1) the items under negotiation are uncertain and themselves subject to different probability estimates, or when (2) each party feels that it will fare well under and perhaps can influence a proposed contingent resolution procedure.
- Differences in *risk aversion* suggest insurancelike risk-sharing arrangements.
- Differences in *time preference* can lead to altered patterns of payments or actions over time.
- Different *capabilities* can be combined.
- Other differences (evaluation criteria, precedence and substance, constituencies, organizational situation, conceptions of fairness, and so on) can be fashioned into joint gains.
- *Mutually preferred positions* on single issues can create common value.
- *Shared interests* on a range of settlements can be made salient or linked to create common value.
- *Economies of scale* can lead to the creation of private and common value.[46]

In addition, negotiators must overcome the idea that a fixed pie of outcomes exists, must counteract nonrational escalation of conflict that can occur, must pay attention to others' cognitions, and must avoid devaluating the others' concessions while overvaluing their own.[47]

NEGOTIATION STRATEGIES AND TACTICS

Three common negotiation strategies exist: competition, collaboration, and subordination, as described in detail in Table 9–3. A party that uses the competitive strategy focuses on its own goals at the expense of the other party's goals. The individual or group may use secrecy, threats, or bluffs as a way of hiding its own goals and uncovering the other party's. This type of strategy frequently accompanies distributive bargaining. The collaborative strategy emphasizes pursuing common goals held by the two parties. Typically used with integrative bargaining, this strategy calls on each party to communicate its needs accurately to the other. Both parties take a problem-solving approach and look for solutions that satisfy both parties. The third strategy describes one party's subordinating its goals, or putting them after the other party's, to avoid conflict. This individual or group becomes overly concerned with the other's goals rather than its own or both parties'. Regardless of the strategy, it is important to attack the problem not the people, treat negotiation as joint problem solving not as a contest, remain open to persuasion and explore interests rather than

Table 9–3 **Characteristics of Negotiation Strategies**

Competitive	Collaborative	Subordinative
1. Behavior is purposeful in pursuing own goals at the expense of the other party.	Behavior is purposeful in pursuing goals held in common with others.	One party consciously subordinates own goals to avoid conflict with other party.
2. Strategy involves secrecy and keeping one's cards close to the vest. It is characterized by high trust in one's self and low trust in the other party.	Strategy calls for trust and openness in expressing one's thoughts and feelings, actively listening to others, and actively exploring alternatives together.	Strategy means that one party is totally open to the extreme of exposing his or her vulnerabilities and weaknesses to the other.
3. Parties have accurate personal understanding of own needs, but publicly disguise or misrepresent them. Neither party lets the other know what it really wants most, so that the other won't know how much it is really willing to give up to attain the goal.	Parties have accurate personal understanding of own needs, and represent them accurately to the other party. Each party has empathy and cares about the needs of the other party.	One party is so concerned with the other's needs that his or her needs are buried or repressed.
4. Parties use unpredictable, mixed strategies and the element of surprise to outfox the other party.	Parties' actions are predictable. While flexible behavior is appropriate, it is not designed to take the other party by surprise.	One party's actions are totally predictable; his or her position is always one that caters to the other party.
5. Parties use threats and bluffs and put each other on the defensive. Each always tries to keep the upper hand.	Parties share information and are honest with each other. They treat each other with mutual understanding and integrity.	One party gives up own position to mollify the other.
6. Search behavior is devoted to finding ways of appearing committed to a position; logical and irrational arguments alike may serve this purpose. Each party engages in destructive manipulation of the other's position.	Search behavior is devoted to finding mutually satisfying solutions to problems; utilizing logical, creative and innovative processes; and developing constructive relationships with each other.	Search behavior is devoted to finding ways to accommodate to position of other party.
7. Success is often enhanced (when teams or organizations are involved on each side) by creating a bad image or stereotype of the other, by ignoring the other's logic, and by increasing the level of hostility. These tend to strengthen in-group loyalty and convince competitors that one means business.	Success demands that bad stereotypes be dropped, that ideas be given consideration on their merit (regardless of sources), and that hostility not be induced deliberately. In fact, healthy, positive feelings about others are both a cause and an effect of other aspects of collaborative negotiations.	Success is determined by minimizing or avoiding all conflict and soothing any hostility. Own feelings are ignored in the interest of harmony.
8. Unhealthy extreme is reached when one party assumes that everything that prevents the other from attaining its goal facilitates movement toward one's own goal; thus each party feels	Unhealthy extreme is reached when one party assumes that whatever is good for others and the group is necessarily good for one's own self, when one cannot distinguish one's identity from that of the group or	Unhealthy extreme is characterized by complete acquiescence to the other's goal at the expense of personal or organizational goals. Concern with harmony results in total avoidance of conflict; the subordi-

(continued)

Table 9–3   (Continued)

Competitive	Collaborative	Subordinative
that an integral part of its goal is to stop the other from attaining its goal.	the other party, or when one party will not take responsibility for itself.	nate party becomes a doormat for the other party.
9. Key attitude/behavior is "I win, you lose."	Key attitude/behavior is "What is the best way to meet the goals of both parties?"	Key attitude/behavior is "You win, I lose."
10. If impasse occurs, a mediator or arbitrator may be required.	If difficulties arise, a facilitator skilled in group dynamics may be used.	If behavior becomes chronic, assertiveness training or a psychotherapist may be used.

SOURCE: Reprinted, by permission from R. W. Johnston, Negotiating strategies: Different strokes for different folks, *Personnel* (March–April 1982).

take a position, create multiple options, and try to improve your alternative if you walk away without a negotiated agreement.[48]

Choice of a strategy may depend on the desired relationship between the negotiating parties and the importance of substantive (content) outcomes to the manager.[49] Figure 9–11 illustrates the way the importance of these two types of outcomes can influence the strategy chosen by one party. In Situation 1, for example, both the relationship outcome and substantive outcome are important to the manager; this situation calls for *trusting collaboration,* where both parties demonstrate openness and seek win-win outcomes. Situation 2 calls for *open subordination* because establishing a relationship overshadows the substantive outcome. Situation 3 demands *firm com-*

Figure 9–11 Considering a Unilateral Negotiation Strategy

	Is the Substantive Outcome Very Important to the Manager?	
	Yes	No
Is the Relationship Outcome Very Important to the Manager? **Yes**	Strategy C1 **Trustingly Collaborate** when both types of outcomes are very important *Situation 1*	Strategy S1 **Openly Subordinate** when the priority is on relationship outcomes *Situation 2*
No	Strategy P1 **Firmly Compete** when the priority is on substantive outcomes *Situation 3*	Strategy A1 **Actively Avoid Negotiating** when neither type of outcome is very important *Situation 4*

SOURCE: Reprinted with permission from G. T. Savage, J. D. Blair, and R. L. Sorenson, Consider both relationships and substance when negotiating strategically, *Academy of Management Executive* 3(1) (1989): 40.

petition to attain the desired substantive results at the expense of the relationship. Situation 4 calls for *active avoidance* of negotiation because the negotiator values neither outcome.

Figure 9–12 offers a decision tree for incorporating the other party's priorities into the strategy selection diagramed in Figure 9–11. The manager asks the following questions in order (from left to right in the figure): (1) Is the substantive outcome very important to the manager? (2) Is the relationship outcome very important to the manager? (3) Is the substantive outcome very important to the other party? (4) Is the relationship outcome very important to the other party? Responses to the questions will indicate the type of negotiation strategy that best fits with the desired outcomes. Additional strategies include (1) *principled collaboration,* where negotiations are based on a set of mutually agreed upon principles; (2) *focused subordination,* where acquiescence occurs only to key needs; (3) *soft competition,* which avoids aggressive tactics and dirty tricks; (4) *passive avoidance,* which involves delegating the negotiations; and (5) *responsive avoidance,* in which standard operating procedures are applied or policies are developed to address the other party's concerns.[50]

Tactics that accompany these strategies can include waiting out the other party; suddenly shifting methods, approach, or argument; taking a unilateral action and thus treating the negotiation outcome as a fait accompli; bland withdrawal; apparent withdrawal; doing the reverse of what is expected; imposing time, dollar, or deadline limits; appearing to move toward one goal when actually moving toward another;

Figure 9–12 **Selecting an Interactive Strategy**

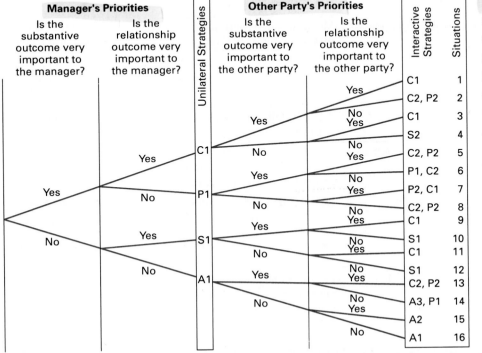

SOURCE: Reprinted with permission from G. T. Savage, J. D. Blair, and R. L. Sorenson, Consider both relationships and substance when negotiating strategically, *Academy of Management Executive* 3(1) (1989): 42.

carefully granting or withholding favors; or showing anger or intimidating the other party.[51]

Table 9–4 describes seven types of negotiators who deliberately choose a style that supports these and other tactics. We can assess the ethical appropriateness of the negotiator's style and tactics by answering two questions: "Are the 'rules' known and accepted?" and "Can the situation be freely entered and left?"[52] More basic questions illuminate the second. Would your self-image remain positive if you used the tactic? How would you feel if someone did it to you? Would you be comfortable advising others to use it? What would happen if everyone who bargained used it? Are there alternative tactics available?

Table 9–4 **Types of Negotiators**

Type	Method
The aggressive-opener negotiator	Discomfort the other side by making cutting remarks about their previous performance, their numbers, their unreasonableness, or anything that can be used to insinuate that the opposition is hardly worth speaking to.
The long-pause negotiator	Listen to the other side but do not answer immediately their propositions but rather appear to give them considerable thought with the result that long silences ensue for the purpose of getting the other to reveal as much of their case as possible without revealing your own.
The mocking negotiator	Mock and sneer your opposition's proposals to get the other side so "uptight" that they say something that they will regret later.
The interrogator	Meet all proposals with searching, prodding questions that are couched in such a way that the opposition feels that they have not thoroughly done their homework; challenge any answers in a confronting manner and ask the opposition to explain further what they mean.
The cloak-of-reasonableness negotiator	Appear to be agreeable and helpful while making impossible demands for the purpose of winning the friendship and confidence of the opposition.
Divide-and-conquer negotiator	Produce dissension among the opposition so that they have to pay more attention to their own internal disagreements rather than the disagreements with the opposition; ally with one member of the team and try to play him or her off against the other members of the team.
Billy Bunter negotiator	Pretend to be particularly dense and by so doing exasperate the opposition in hopes that at least one member of the opposing team will reveal information as he tries to find increasingly simple ways to describe proposals, with each proposal being elaborated and amplified so that Billy Bunter can understand it.

SOURCE: Based on R. Gourlay, Negotiations and bargaining, *Management Decision* 25(3) (1987): 19–20.

CROSS-CULTURAL ISSUES IN NEGOTIATIONS

The assumptions that underlie effective negotiations differ significantly in various parts of the world. Union-management negotiations, for example, would not look the same in Japan or China as they do in the United States. To begin, individual characteristics of negotiators vary in different cultures. Table 9–5 compares American, Japanese, Taiwanese, and Brazilian negotiators.

Table 9–6 describes eleven negotiating tactics and compares their use in three countries. Obviously some cross-cultural differences exist in the verbal tactics of choice. Cultures also differ in nonverbal negotiating tactics of choice. For example, the Japanese rely more on periods of silence than American or Brazilian negotiators, and Brazilian negotiators more often interrupt each other and make direct eye contact with and touch the other party.[53]

The general approach to negotiations in Asia focuses on saving face for the Asians and the other party.[54] Also, being too frank, critical, insincere, impatient, and unadaptable will result in ineffective negotiations. Questions are asked indirectly, not directly: "I've developed a short-cut for manufacturing these garments at a lower cost but ensuring higher quality, and would appreciate any suggestions you have for improving it," not "Can you make this garment cheaper but improve its quality?"

Negotiating with Russians, in contrast, has historically posed different dilemmas.[55] The Russians emphasize building arguments on asserted ideals and deemphasize relationship building. They appeal to ideals and make few concessions. An opponent's concessions are viewed as weaknesses and almost never reciprocated. They have been described as not trying to build a continuing relationship, often offering an extreme initial position, and ignoring any deadlines. Arabs, on the other hand, use primarily an affective rather than an ideological or factual negotiating style.[56] They request and make concessions throughout the negotiating process, and almost always reciprocate an opponent's concessions. Initial positions are extreme, but deadlines are casual; they focus on building a long-term relationship. North

Table 9–5 **Key Individual Characteristics of Negotiators**

American Managers	Japanese Managers	Chinese Managers (Taiwan)	Brazilian Managers
Preparation and planning skill	Dedication to job	Persistence and determination	Preparation and planning skill
Thinking under pressure	Perceive and exploit power	Win respect and confidence	Thinking under pressure
Judgment and intelligence	Win respect and confidence	Preparation and planning skill	Judgment and intelligence
Verbal expressiveness	Integrity	Product knowledge	Verbal expressiveness
Product knowledge	Listening skill	Interesting	Product knowledge
Perceive and exploit power	Broad perspective	Judgment and intelligence	Perceive and exploit power
Integrity	Verbal expressiveness		Competitiveness

SOURCE: Professor John Graham, School of Business Administration, University of Southern California, 1983. Reprinted in N. J. Adler, *International Dimensions of Organizational Behavior,* 2nd ed. (Boston: PWS-Kent, 1991), p. 187.

Table 9-6 **Verbal Negotiating Tactics**

Tactic	Description	Example	Average Number of Times Tactic Was Used in Half-hour Bargaining Sessions in:		
			Japan	United States	Brazil
Promise	I will do something you want me to do, if you do something I want you to do. (conditional, positive)	I will lower the price by $5 if you increase the order by 100 units.	7	8	3
Threat	I will do something you don't want me to do, if you do something I don't want you to do. (conditional, negative)	I'll walk out of the negotiation if you leak this story to the press.	4	4	2
Recommendation	If you do something I want you to do, a third party will do something you want. (third party positive)	If you lower your price, all of the teenagers will be able to buy your product.	7	4	5
Warning	If you do something I don't want you to do, a third party will do something you don't want. (third party negative)	If you don't settle, the press will spill this whole sordid story on the front page of every newspaper in the country.	2	1	1
Reward	I will give you something positive (something you want), now, on the spot. (unconditional, positive)	Let's make it easier on you tomorrow and meet closer to your office. I have really appreciated your willingness to meet at my building.	1	2	2
Punishment	I will give you something negative (something you don't want) now, on the spot. (unconditional, negative)	I refuse to listen to your screaming. I am leaving.	1	3	3
Normative Appeal	I appeal to a societal norm.	Everybody else buys our product for $5 per unit	4	2	1
Commitment	I will do something you want. (unconditional, positive)	I will deliver 100 units by June 15.	15	13	8
Self-Disclosure	I tell you something about myself.	We have had to lay off 100 employees this month. We really need to sign a major contract by the end of the year.	34	36	39
Question	I ask you something about yourself.	Can you tell me more about your Brazilian operation?	20	20	22
Command	I order you to do something.	Lower your price. (or) We are going to talk about delivery now.	8	6	14

SOURCE: Based on John Graham, "The Influence of Culture on Business Negotiations," Tables 1 and 3, *Journal of International Business Studies* 16(1) (Spring 1985): 81–96.

Americans, in contrast, appeal to logic and counter opponents' arguments with objective facts rather than subjective feelings or asserted ideals.[57] They may make small concessions early and then usually reciprocate an opponent's concessions. But they take a moderate initial position, build only a short-term relationship, and value deadlines greatly. Table 9–7 compares these three national styles of persuasion.

In Japan, the negotiating protocol reflects the Japanese tendency to personalize business relations; they prefer to conduct many preliminary get-togethers so they can know the business people with whom they deal.[58] Their negotiations are characterized by politeness, a nonrevealing manner, a nonconfrontational manner, and persistence.[59] Table 9–8 compares the styles of the Japanese to North Americans and Latin Americans. Negotiators must respond to cultural idiosyncrasies about the choice of location, physical arrangements, participants, time limits, and status differences in the bargaining process.[60] They must also recognize the value attached to various tactics. For example, they may differ in their initial offers, the relative use of verbal and nonverbal tactics, and the willingness to employ dirty tricks. In one study, negotiators in Japan and the United States used promises more often and "no's" less often than Brazilian negotiators.[61]

Chinese norms are similar to Japanese norms and are based on the influence of Confucius, which emphasizes harmony, position in the social system, morality, and reliance on kinship.[62] Figure 9–13 presents recommendations for Americans who negotiate with the Chinese. Note that in all intercultural negotiations the parties need to recognize different meanings attached to location, physical arrangements, participants selected, time limits, and status differences.[63]

Table 9–7   **National Styles of Persuasion**

	North Americans	Arabs	Russians
Primary negotiating style and process	Factual: Appeals made to logic	Affective: Appeals made to emotions	Axiomatic: Appeals made to ideals
Conflict: opponent's arguments countered with . . .	Objective facts	Subjective feelings	Asserted ideals
Making concessions	Small concessions made early to establish a relationship	Concessions made throughout as a part of the bargaining process	Few, if any, small concessions made
Response to opponent's concessions	Usually reciprocate opponent's concessions	Almost always reciprocate opponent's concessions	Opponent's concessions viewed as weakness and almost never reciprocated
Relationship	Short term	Long term	No continuing relationship
Authority	Broad	Broad	Limited
Initial position	Moderate	Extreme	Extreme
Deadline	Very important	Casual	Ignored

SOURCE: Reprinted with permission from *International Journal of Intercultural Relations*, vol. 1, E. S. Glenn, D. Witmeyer, and K. A. Stevenson, "Cultural Styles of Persuasion." Copyright © 1984, Pergamon Press, Ltd.

Table 9–8   **A Cross-Cultural Perspective of Negotiation Styles**

Japanese	North American	Latin American
Emotional sensitivity highly valued.	Emotional sensitivity not highly valued.	Emotional sensitivity valued.
Hiding of emotions.	Dealing straightforwardly or impersonally.	Emotionally passionate.
Subtle power plays; conciliation.	Litigation not as much as conciliation.	Great power plays: use of weakness.
Loyalty to employer. Employer takes care of its employees.	Lack of commitment to employer. Breaking of ties by either if necessary.	Loyalty to employer (who is often family).
Group decision-making consensus.	Teamwork provides input to a decision maker.	Decisions come down from one individual.
Face-saving crucial. Decisions often made on basis of saving someone from embarrassment.	Decisions made on a cost-benefit basis. Face-saving does not always matter.	Face-saving crucial in decision making to preserve honor, dignity.
Decision makers openly influenced by special interests.	Decision makers influenced by special interests but often not considered ethical.	Execution of special interests of decision maker expected, condoned.
Not argumentative. Quiet when right.	Argumentative when right or wrong, but impersonal.	Argumentative when right or wrong; passionate.
What is down in writing must be accurate, valid.	Great importance given to documentation as evidential proof.	Impatient with documentation as obstacle to understanding general principles.
Step-by-step approach to decision making.	Methodically organized decision making.	Impulsive, spontaneous decision making.
Good of group is the ultimate aim.	Profit motive or good of individual ultimate aim.	What is good for group is good for the individual.
Cultivate a good emotional social setting for decision making. Get to know decision makers.	Decision making impersonal. Avoid involvements, conflict of interest.	Personalism necessary for good decision making.

SOURCE: Reprinted with permission from P. Casse, *Training for the Multicultural Manager: A Practical and Cross-Cultural Approach to the Management of People* (Washington, D.C.: Society of Intercultural Education, Training, and Research, 1982).

In sum, American negotiators involved in cross-cultural negotiations should be aware of the way negotiators view the process itself, watch the use of a "middle man," make the assumption the other party can be trusted, consider the process as a problem-solving exercise, recognize the importance of protocol, carefully select the negotiating team, and understand the nature of decision making.[64] Even in using such a process, individuals may face serious ethical dilemmas because conflicts often exist between the laws of the home and host countries as well as with the negotiator's own moral standards. They might use a process similar to that shown in Figure 9–14.

Figure 9–13 **Advice for Americans Who Negotiate with Chinese**

Preparation

Choose interpreters familiar with both cultures.

Include negotiating style in the training agenda.

Enter negotiations even when no immediate benefit is apparent.

Select negotiators with a more restrained style.

Carrying Out the Negotiation

Emphasize the similarities rather than the differences in positions.

Emphasize the strategic, long-range process of negotiation and the gradual accumulation of mutual trust.

Plan for long negotiation sessions.

Allow frequent recesses for private consultations by the teams.

Avoid aggressive behavior, and practice patience.

Be politely formal, and minimize expressions of emotions.

Remember that behavior outside negotiations is as important as behavior during the negotiating sessions.

Assess nonverbal responses, and do not interpret silence as an expression of either approval or disapproval.

Address the group as a whole rather than individuals.

Concluding

Weigh the short-term benefits versus long-term costs of possible concessions.

Be willing to exchange some advantages for a lasting mutual attraction.

Allow for a short delay in the final stages before concluding the negotiations.

Thank the Chinese team for concluding the negotiations to the satisfaction of both sides.

SOURCE: Based on O. Shenkar and S. Ronan, The cultural context of negotiations: The implications of Chinese interpersonal norms, *The Journal of Applied Behavioral Science* 23(2) (1987): 272–273. Reprinted with permission of NTL.

SUMMARY Power may be one of the least understood, but most important, areas of organizational behavior. Individuals exert power to overcome job-related dependencies; social exchanges may create power; or individuals may have a need for power. This chapter has described the sources and uses of power in organizations. We identified position power, personal power, and resource- and information-based power. We analyzed the use of informal networks, alliances, and trade relations in securing power.

We continued the chapter by looking at negotiation as the ritualized use of power in organizations. Two bargaining paradigms—distributive and integrative—

Figure 9–14 **Synergistic Approach (Collaborative/Cultural)**

Preparation	Cross-cultural training.
	Define interests.
Relationship Building	Separate the people from the problem.
	Adjust to their style and pace.
Information Exchange	Exchange task- and participant-related information.
	Clarify interests.
	Clarify customary approaches.
Inventing Options for Mutual Gain Appropriate to Both Cultures	
Choice of Best Option	Insist on using criteria appropriate to both cultures.
Agreement	Translate and back-translate agreement; if necessary, renegotiate.

SOURCE: Based on N. J. Adler, *International Dimensions of Organizational Behavior,* 2nd ed. (Boston: PWS-Kent, 1991), p. 194.

Table 9–9 Diagnostic Questions for Power and Negotiation

- Who has power in the organization?
- How is powerlessness overcome in the organization?
- From what sources does this power stem?
- Is power properly placed?
- Are alliances, informal networks, or trade relations used to develop power?
- What types of negotiations occur in the organization?
- Do the negotiations tend to be distributive or integrative?
- What types of preparations for negotiations occur?
- Are interests identified, the best alternative to a negotiated agreement determined, and bargaining range identified?
- How effective are intercultural negotiations?

were described and compared. Then the process of negotiation was outlined; the steps include preparation, evaluation of alternatives, identifying interests and making trade-offs, and creating joint gains. We also examined a set of negotiation strategies and tactics. Competition, collaboration, and subordination were among the possibilities examined. We concluded the chapter by considering the cross-cultural issues in negotiation. Table 9–9 provides a list of diagnostic questions for assessing the effective use of power and negotiations in organizations.

Reading 9–1

Leadership: The Art of Empowering Others
Jay A. Conger

One ought to be both feared and loved, but as it is difficult for the two to go together, it is much safer to be feared than loved . . . for love is held by a chain of obligation which, men being selfish, is broken whenever it serves their purpose; but fear is maintained by a dread of punishment which never fails.

The Prince, Niccolo Machiavelli

In his handbook, *The Prince,* Machiavelli assures his readers—some being aspiring leaders, no doubt—that only by carefully amassing power and building a fearsome respect could one become a great leader. While the shadowy court life of 16th-century Italy demanded such treachery to ensure one's power, it seems hard to imagine Machiavelli's advice today as anything but a historical curiosity. Yet, interestingly, much of the management literature has focused on the strategies and tactics that managers can use to increase their own power and influence.[1] As such, a Machiavellian quality often pervades the literature, encouraging managers to ensure that their power base is strong and growing. At the same time a small but increasing number of management theorists have begun to explore the idea that organizational effectiveness also depends on the sharing of power—that the distribution of power is more important than the hoarding of power.[2]

While the idea of making others feel more powerful contradicts the stereotype of the all-powerful executive, research suggests that the traditional ways of explaining a leader's influence may not be entirely correct. For example, recent leadership studies argue that the practice of empowering—or instilling a sense of power—is at the root of organizational effectiveness, especially during times of transition and transformation.[3] In addition, studies of power and control within organizations indicate that the more productive forms of organizational power increase with superiors' sharing of power and responsibility with subordinates.[4] And while there is an increasing awareness of this need for more empowering leadership, we have only recently started to see documentation about the actual practices that leaders employ to effectively build a sense of power among organizational members as well as the contexts most suited for empowerment practices.[5]

In this article, I will explore these practices further by drawing upon a recent study of senior executives who proved themselves highly effective leaders. They were selected by a panel of professors at the Harvard Business School and management consultants who were well acquainted with them and their companies. The study included eight chief executive officers and executive vice-presidents of *Fortune* 500 companies and successful entrepreneurial firms, representing industries as diverse as telecommunications, office automation, retail banking, beverages, packaged foods, and management consulting. In each case, these individuals were responsible for either the creation of highly successful companies or for performing what were described as remarkable turnarounds. During my study of these executives, I conducted extensive interviews, observed them on the job, read company and other documents, and talked with their colleagues and subordinates. While the study focused on the broader issue of leadership styles, intensive interviews with these executives and their subordinates revealed that many were characterized as empowering leaders. Their actions were perceived as building confidence during difficult organizational transitions. From this study, I identified certain organizational contexts of powerlessness and management practices derived to remedy them.

In this article I will also illustrate several of these practices through a series of vignettes. While the reader may recognize some of the basic ideas behind these practices (such as providing greater opportunities for initiative), it is often the creative manner in which the leader deploys the particular practice that distinguishes them. The reader will discover how they have been carefully tailored to fit the context at hand. I might add, however, that these practices represent just a few of the broad repertoire of actions that leaders can take to make an empowering difference in their organizations.

A WORD ABOUT EMPOWERMENT

We can think of empowerment as the act of strengthening an individual's beliefs in his or her sense of effectiveness. In essence, then, empowerment is not simply a set of external actions; it is a process of changing the internal beliefs of people.[6] We know from psychology that individuals believe themselves powerful when they feel they can adequately cope with environmental demands—that is, situations, events, and people they confront. They feel powerless when they are unable to cope with these demands. Any management practice that increases an individual's sense of self-determination will tend to make that individual feel more powerful. The theory behind these ideas can be traced to the work of Alfred Bandura, who conceptualized the notion of self-efficacy beliefs and their role in an individual's sense of personal power in the world.[7]

From his research in psychology, Bandura identified four means of providing empowering information to others: (1) through positive emotional support during experiences associated with stress and anxiety, (2) through words of encouragement and positive persuasion, (3) by observing others' effectiveness—in other words, having models of success with whom people identified—and (4) by actually experiencing the mastering of a task with success (the most effective source). Each of these sources of empowerment was used by the study executives and will be identified in the practice examples, as will other sources identified by organizational researchers.

Several Empowering Management Practices

Before describing the actual practices, it is important to first draw attention to an underlying attitude of the study participants. These empowering leaders shared a strong underlying belief in their subordinates' abilities. It is essentially the Theory Y argument;[8] if you believe in people's abilities, they will come to believe in them. All the executives in the study believed that their subordinates were capable of managing their current situations. They did not employ wholesale firings as a means of transforming their organizations. Rather, they retained the majority of their staff and moved those who could not perform up to standard to positions where they could. The essential lesson is that an assessment of staff skills is imperative before embarking on a program of empowerment. This basic belief in employee's abilities underlies the following examples of management practices designed to empower. We will begin with the practice of providing positive emotional support.

1. *The Squirt-gun Shootouts: Providing a Positive Emotional Atmosphere.* An empowering practice that emerged from the study was that of providing positive emotional support, especially through play or drama. For example, every few months, several executives would stage dramatic "up sessions" to sustain the motivation and excitement of their staff. They would host an afternoon-long, or a one- or two-day event devoted solely to confidence building. The event would open with an uplifting speech about the future, followed by a special, inspirational speaker. At these events there would often be films meant to build excitement or confidence—for example, a film depicting a mountain climber ascending a difficult peak. The message being conveyed is that this person is finding satisfaction in the work he or she does at an extraordinary level of competence. There would also be rewards for exceptional achievements. These sessions acted as ceremonies to enhance the personal status and identity of employees and revive the common feelings that bound them together.[9]

An element of play appears to be especially liberating in situations of great stress and demoralization. In the study's examples, play allowed for the venting of frustrations and in turn permitted individuals to regain a sense of control by stepping back from their pressures for a moment. As Bandura suggests, the positive emotional support provided by something like play alleviates, to some extent, concerns about personal efficacy.[10]

For example, one of the subjects of the study, Bill Jackson, was appointed the head of a troubled division. Demand had outstripped the division's ability to maintain adequate inventories, and product quality had slipped. Jackson's predecessors were authoritarian managers, and subordinates were demoralized as well as paranoid about keeping their jobs. As one told me, "You never knew who would be shot next." Jackson felt that he had to break the tension in a way that would allow his staff to regain their sense of control and power. He wanted to remove the stiffness and paranoia and turn what subordinates perceived as an impossible task into something more fun and manageable.

So, I was told, at the end of his first staff meeting, Jackson quietly pulled out a squirt-gun and blasted one of his managers with water. At first, there was a moment of stunned silence, and then suddenly the room was flooded with laughter. He remarked with a smile, "You gotta have fun in this business. It's not worth having your stomach in ulcers." This began a month of squirt-gun fights between Jackson and his managers.

The end result? A senior manager's comment is representative: "He wanted people to feel comfortable, to feel in control. He used waterguns to do that. It was a game. It took the stiffness out of the business, allowed people to play in a safe environment—as the boss says, 'to have fun.'" This play restored rapport and morale. But Jackson also knew when to stop. A senior manager told me, "We haven't used waterguns in nine months. It has served its purpose. . . . The waterfights were like being accepted into a club. Once it achieved its purpose, it would have been overdone."

Interview after interview with subordinates confirmed the effectiveness of the squirt-gun incident. It had been experienced as an empowering ritual. In most contexts, this behavior would have been abusive. Why did it work? Because it is a management practice that fit the needs of subordinates at the appropriate time.

The executive's staff consisted largely of young men, "rough and ready" individuals who could be described as fun-loving and playful. They were accustomed to an informal atmosphere and operated in a very down-to-earth style. Jackson's predecessor, on the other hand, had been stiff and formal.

Jackson preferred to manage more informally. He wanted to convey, quickly and powerfully, his intentions of managing in a style distinct from his predecessor's. He was concerned, however, that his size—he is a very tall, energetic, barrel-chested man—as well as his extensive background in manufacturing would be perceived as intimidating by his young staff and increase their reluctance to assume initiative and control. Through the squirt-gun fights, however, he was able to (1) relieve a high level of tension and restore some sense of control, (2) emphasize the importance of having fun in an otherwise trying work environment, and (3) direct subordinates' concerns away from his skills and other qualities that intimidated them. It was an effective management practice because he understood the context. In another setting, it might have been counter-productive.

2. The "I Make a Difference" Club: Rewarding and Encouraging in Visible and Personal Ways. The majority of executives in the study rewarded the achievements of their staffs by expressing personal praise and rewarding in highly visible and confidence-building ways. They believed that people appreciated recognition of their hard work and success. Rewards of high incentive value were particularly important, especially those of personal recognition from the leader. As Rosabeth Kanter notes, a sense of power comes ". . . when one has relatively close contact with sponsors (higher level people who confer approval, prestige, or backing.)"[11] Combined with words of praise and positive encouragement, such experiences become important sources of empowerment.

The executives in the study took several approaches to rewards. To reward exceptional performance, one executive established the "I Make a Difference Club." Each year, he selects two or three staff members to be recognized for their excellence on the job. It is a very exclusive club, and only the executive knows the eligibility rules, which are based on outstanding performance. Inductees are invited to dinner in New York City but are not told beforehand that they are about to join the "I Make a Difference Club." They arrive and meet with other staff members whom they believe are there for a staff dinner. During dinner, everyone is asked to speak about what is going on in his or her part of the company. The old-timers speak first, followed by the inductees (who are still unaware of their coming induction). Only after they have given their speeches are they informed that they have just joined the club. As one manager said, "It's one of the most wonderful moments in life."

This executive and others also make extensive use of personal letters to individuals thanking them for their efforts and projects. A typical letter might read, "Fred, I would personally like to thank you for your contribution to _____, and I want you to know that I appreciate it." Lunches and dinners are hosted for special task accomplishments.

Public recognition is also employed as a means of rewarding. As one subordinate commented about his boss,

> He will make sure that people know that so and so did an excellent job on something. He's superb on giving people credit. If the person has done an exceptional job on a task or project, he will be given the opportunity to present his or her findings all the way to the board. Six months later, you'll get a call from a friend and learn that he has dropped your name in a speech that you did well. It makes you want to do it again.

I found that the investment in rewards and recognition made by many of these executives is unusually high, consuming a significant portion of their otherwise busy day. Yet the payoff appeared high. In interviews, subordinates described these rewards as having an empowering impact on them.

To understand why some of these rewards proved to be so successful, one must understand their organizational contexts. In some cases, the organizations studied were quite large, if not enormous. The size of these organizations did little to develop in employees a sense of an "I"—let alone an "I" that makes a difference. It was easy for organization members to feel lost in the hierarchy and for their achievements to be invisible, for recognition not to be received for personal contributions. The study's executives countered this tendency by institutionalizing a reward system that provided visibility and recognition—for example, the "I Make a Difference Club," presentations to the Board, and names dropped in speeches. Suddenly, you as a member of a large organization stood out—you were special.

Outstanding performances from each of the executives' perspectives was also something of a necessity. All the executives had demanding goals to achieve. As such, they had to tend to subordinates' sense of importance and contribution. They had to structure reward systems that would keep people "pumped up"—that would ensure that their confidence and commitment would not be eroded by the pressures placed on them.

3. *"Praising the Troops": Expressing Confidence.* The empowering leaders in the study spent significant amounts of time expressing their confidence in subordinates' abilities. Moreover, they expressed their confidence throughout each day—in speeches, in meetings, and casually in office hallways. Bandura comments that "people who are persuaded verbally that they possess the capabilities to master given tasks are likely to mobilize greater sustained effort than if they harbor self-doubts and dwell on personal deficiencies when difficulties arise."[12]

A quote from Irwin Federman, CEO of Monolithic Memories, a highly successful high-tech company, captures the essence and power of a management that builds on this process:

> If you think about it, we love others not for who they are, but for how they make us feel. In order to willingly accept the direction of another individual, it must make you feel good to do so. . . . If you believe what I'm saying, you cannot help but come to the conclusion that those you have followed passionately, gladly, zealously—have made you feel like somebody. . . . This business of making another person feel good in the unspectacular course of his daily comings and goings is, in my view, the very essence of leadership.[13]

This proactive attitude is exemplified by Bob Jensen. Bob assumed control of his bank's retail operations after a reorganization that transferred away the division's responsibility for large corporate clients. Demoralized by a perceived loss in status and responsibility, branch managers were soon asking, "Where's our recognition?" Bob, however, developed an inspiring strategic vision to transform the operation. He then spent much of his time championing his strategy and expressing his confidence in employees' ability to carry it out. Most impressive was his personal canvass of some 175 retail branches.

As he explained,

> I saw that the branch system was very down, morale was low. They felt like they'd lost a lot of their power. There were serious problems and a lot of staff were just hiding. What I saw was that we really wanted to create a small community for each branch where customers would feel known. To do that, I needed to create an attitude change. I saw that the attitudes of the branch staff were a reflection of the branch manager. The approach then was a manageable job—now I had to focus on only 250 people, the branch managers, rather than the 3,000 staff employees out there. I knew I had to change their mentality from being lost in a bureaucracy to feeling like the president of their own bank. I had to convince them they were special—that they had the power to transform the organization. . . . All I did was talk it up. I was up every night. In one morning, I hit 17 branches. My goal was to sell a new attitude. To encourage people to "pump iron." I'd say, "Hi, how's business?", encourage them. I'd arrange tours of the branches for the chairman on down. I just spent a lot of time talking to these people—explaining that they were the ones who could transform the organization.

It was an important tactic—one that made the branch managers feel special and important. It was also countercultural. As one executive told me, "Bob would go out into the field to visit the operations, which was very unusual for senior people in the industry." His visits heightened the specialness that branch managers felt. In addition, Bob modeled self-confidence and personal success—an important tactic to build a sense of personal effectiveness among subordinates.[14]

I also watched Jack Eaton, president of a regional telephone company, praise his employees in large corporate gatherings, in executive council meetings, and in casual encounters. He explained his philosophy:

> I have a fundamental belief and trust in the ability and conscientiousness of others. I have a lot of good people. You can turn them loose, let them feel good about their accomplishments. . . . You ought to recognize accomplishment as well as build confidence. I generally do it in small ways. If someone is doing well, it's important to express your confidence to that person—especially among his peers. I tend to do it personally. I try to be genuine. I don't throw around a lot of b.s.

This practice proved especially important during the transition of the regional phone companies away from the parent organization.

4. *"President of My Own Bank": Fostering Initiative and Responsibility.* Discretion is a critical power component of any job.[15] By simply fostering greater initiative and responsibility in subordinates' tasks, a leader can empower organizational members. Bob Jensen, the bank executive, is an excellent example of how one leader created opportunities for greater initiative despite the confines of his subordinates' positions. He transformed what had been a highly

constricted branch manager's job into a branch "president" concept. The idea was simple—every manager was made to feel like the president of his own community bank, and not just in title. Goals, compensation, and responsibilities were all changed to foster this attitude. Existing measurement systems were completely restructured. The value-of-funds-generated had been the principal yardstick—something over which branch managers had only very limited control because of interest rate fluctuations. Managers were now evaluated on what they could control—that is, deposits. Before, branch managers had rotated every couple of years. Now they stayed put. "If I'm moving around, then I'm not the president of my own bank, so we didn't move them anymore," Jensen explained. He also decentralized responsibilities that had resided higher in the hierarchy—allowing the branch manager to hire, give money to charities, and so on. In addition, a new ad agency was hired to mark the occasion, and TV ads were made showing the branch managers being in charge, rendering personal services themselves. The branch managers even thought up the ad lines.

What Jensen did so skillfully was recognize that his existing managers had the talent and energy to turn their operations around successfully, but that their sense of power was missing. He recognized their pride had been hurt and that he needed to restore a sense of ownership and self-importance. He had to convince his managers through increased authority that they were no longer "pawns" of the system—that they were indeed "presidents" of their own banks.

Another example—this one demonstrating a more informal delegation of initiative—was quite surprising. The setting was a highly successful and rapidly growing computer firm, and the study participant was the vice-president of manufacturing. The vice-president had recently been hired away from another firm and was in the process of revamping manufacturing. During the process, he discovered that his company's costs on its terminal video monitors were quite high. However, he wanted his staff to discover the problem for themselves and to "own" the solution. So one day, he placed behind his desk a black-and-white Sony TV with a placard on top saying $69.95. Next to it he placed a stripped-down version of the company's monitor with a placard of $125.95. Both placards reflected the actual costs of the two products. He never said a word. But during the day as staff and department managers entered their boss's office, they couldn't help but notice the two sets. They quickly got the message that their monitor was costing twice as much as a finished TV set. Within a month, the manufacturing team had lowered the monitor's costs by 40%.

My first impression on hearing this story was that, as a subordinate, I would be hard pressed not to get the point and, more important, I would wonder why the boss was not more direct. Ironically, the boss appears to be hitting subordinates over the head with the problem. Out of con-

text, then, this example hardly seems to make others feel more competent and powerful. Yet staff described themselves as "turned on" and motivated by this behavior. Why, I wondered? A little history will illustrate the effectiveness of this action.

The vice-president's predecessor had been a highly dictatorial individual. He tightly controlled his staff's actions and stifled any sense of discretion. Implicitly, his behavior said to subordinates, "You have no ideas of your own." He fired freely, leaving staff to feel that they had little choice in whether to accept his orders or not. By his actions, he essentially transformed his managers into powerless order-takers.

When the new vice-president arrived, he found a group of demoralized subordinates whom he felt were nonetheless quite talented. To restore initiative, he began to demonstrate the seriousness of his intentions in highly visible and symbolic ways. For example, rather than tell his subordinates what to do, he started by seeding ideas and suggestions in humorous and indirect ways. The TV monitor is only one of many examples. Through these actions, he was able eventually to restore a sense of initiative and personal competence to his staff. While these examples are illustrative of effective changes in job design, managers contemplating job enrichment would be well advised to consult the existing literature and research before undertaking major projects.[16]

5. *Early Victories: Building on Success.* Many of the executives in the study reported that they often introduced organizational change through pilot or otherwise small and manageable projects. They designed these projects to ensure early success for their organizations. For example, instead of introducing a new sales structure nationwide, they would institute the change in one region; a new technology would have a pilot introduction at a single plant rather than systemwide. Subordinates described these early success experiences as strongly reinforcing their sense of power and efficacy. As Mike Beer argues:

> In order for change to spread throughout an organization and become a permanent fixture, it appears that early successes are needed. . . . When individuals, groups, and whole organizations feel more competent than they did before the change, this increased sense of competence reinforces the new behavior and solidifies learning associated with change.[17]

An individual's sense of mastery through actual experience is the most effective means of increasing self-efficacy.[18] When subordinates are given more complex and difficult tasks, they are presented with opportunities to test their competence. Initial success experiences will make them feel more capable and, in turn, empowered. Structuring organizational changes to ensure initial successes builds on this principle.

CONTEXTS OF POWERLESSNESS

The need to empower organizational members becomes more important in certain contexts. Thus, it is important to identify conditions within organizations that might foster a sense of powerlessness. Certain circumstances, for instance, appear to lower feelings of self-efficacy. In these cases, subordinates typically perceive themselves as lacking control over their immediate situation (e.g., a major reorganization threatens to displace responsibility and involves limited or no subordinate participation),[19] or lacking the required capability, resources, or discretion needed to accomplish a task (e.g., the development of new and difficult-to-learn skills for the introduction of a new technological process).[20] In either case, these experiences maximize feelings of inadequacy and lower self-confidence. They, in turn, appear to lessen motivation and effectiveness.

Figure 9–15 identifies the more common organizational factors that affect these self-efficacy or personal power beliefs and contribute to feelings of powerlessness. They include organizational factors, supervisory styles, reward systems, and job design.

For example, during a major organizational change, goals may change—often dramatically—to respond to the organization's new direction. Rules may no longer be clearly defined as the firm seeks new guidelines for action. Responsibilities may be dramatically altered. Power alliances may shift, leaving parts of the organization with a perceived loss of power or increasing political activity. Certain functional areas, divisions, or acquired companies may experience disenfranchisement as their responsibilities are felt to be diminished or made subordinate to others. As a result, employees' sense of competence may be seriously challenged as they face having to accept and acquire new responsibilities, skills, and management practices as well as deal with the uncertainty of their future.

In new venture situations, uncertainty often appears around the ultimate success of the company's strategy. A major role for leaders is to build an inspiring picture of the firm's future and convince organizational members of their ability to achieve that future. Yet, market lead times are often long, and tangible results may be slow in coming. Long work hours with few immediate rewards can diminish confidence. Frustration can build, and questions about the organization's future can arise. In addition, the start-up's success and responses to growth can mean constant change in responsibility, pushing managers into responsibilities where they have had little prior experience; thus, failure may be experienced initially as new responsibilities are learned. Entrepreneurial executives may be reluctant to relinquish their control as expansion continues.

Bureaucratic environments are especially conducive to creating conditions of powerlessness. As Peter Block points out, bureaucracy encourages dependency and submission because of its top-down contract between the organization

Figure 9–15 **Context Factors Leading to Potential State of Powerlessness**

Organizational Factors

Significant organizational changes/transitions
Start-up ventures
Excessive, competitive pressures
Impersonal bureaucratic climate
Poor communications and limited network-forming systems
Highly centralized organizational resources

Supervisory Style

Authoritarian (high control)
Negativism (emphasis on failures)
Lack of reason for actions/consequences

Reward Systems

Noncontingency (arbitrary reward allocations)
Low incentive value of rewards
Lack of competence-based rewards
Lack of innovation-based rewards

Job Design

Lack of role clarity
Lack of training and technical support
Unrealistic goals
Lack of appropriate authority/discretion
Low task variety
Limited participation in programs, meetings, and decisions that have a direct impact on job performance
Lack of appropriate/necessary resources
Lack of network-forming opportunities
Highly established work routines
Too many rules and guidelines
Low advancement opportunities
Lack of meaningful goals/tasks
Limited contact with senior management

SOURCE: Adapted from J. A. Conger and R. N. Kanungo, The empowerment process: Integrating theory and practice, *Academy of Management Review* (July 1988).

and employees.[21] Rules, routines, and traditions define what can and cannot be done, allowing little room for initiative and discretion to develop. Employees' behavior is often guided by rules over which they have no say and which may no longer be effective, given the present-day context.

From the standpoint of supervision, authoritarian management styles can strip away subordinates' discretion and, in turn, a sense of power. Under an authoritarian manager, subordinates inevitably come to believe that they have little control—that they and their careers are subject to the whims or demands of their boss. The problem becomes acute when capable subordinates begin to attribute their powerlessness to internal factors, such as their own personal competence, rather than to external factors, such as the nature of the boss's temperament.

Rewards are another critical area for empowerment. Organizations that do not provide valued rewards or simply do not reward employees for initiative, competence, and innovation are creating conditions of powerlessness. Finally, jobs with little meaningful challenge, or jobs where the task is unclear, conflicting, or excessively demanding can lower employees' sense of self-efficacy.

IMPLICATIONS FOR MANAGERS

Managers can think of the empowerment process as involving several stages, as shown in Figure 9–16.[22] Managers might want to begin by identifying for themselves whether any of the organizational problems and characteristics described in this article are present in their own firms. In addition, managers assuming new responsibilities should conduct an organizational diagnosis that clearly identifies their current situation, and possible problems and their causes. Attention should be aimed at understanding the recent history of the organization. Important questions to ask would be: What was my predecessor's supervisory role? Has there been a recent organizational change that negatively affected my subordinates? How is my operation perceived by the rest of the corporation? Is there a sense of disenfranchisement? Am I planning to change significantly the outlook of this operation that would challenge traditional ways of doing things? How are people rewarded? Are jobs designed to be motivating?

Once conditions contributing to feelings of powerlessness are identified, the managerial practices identified in this article and in the management literature can be used to provide self-efficacy information to subordinates. This in-

formation can result in an empowering experience for subordinates and may ultimately lead to greater initiative, motivation, and persistence.

However, in applying these practices, it is imperative that managers tailor their actions to fit the context at hand. For example, in the case of an authoritarian predecessor, you are more likely to need praise and confidence-building measures and greater opportunities for job discretion. With demanding organizational goals and tasks, the practices of confidence building and active rewarding, an element of play, and a supportive environment are perhaps most appropriate. The specific character of each practice must necessarily vary somewhat to fit your particular situation. For instance, what makes many of the previous examples so important is that the executives responded with practices that organizational members could relate to or that fit their character—for instance, the television and squirt-gun examples. Unfortunately, much of today's popular management literature provides managers with tools to manage their subordinates, yet few highlight the importance of matching the practice to the appropriate context. Empowering is not a pill; it is not simply a technique, as many workshops and articles would lead us to believe. Rather, to be truly effective it requires an understanding of subordinates and one's organizational context.

Finally, although it is not as apparent in the examples themselves, each of the study executives set challenging and appealing goals for their organizations. This is a necessary component of effective and empowering leadership. If goals are not perceived as appealing, it is difficult to empower managers in a larger sense. As Warren Bennis and Burt Nanus argue: "Great leaders often inspire their followers to high levels of achievement by showing them how their work contributes to worthwhile ends. It is an emotional appeal to some of the most fundamental needs—the need to be important, to make a difference, to feel useful, to be part of a successful and worthwhile enterprise."[23] Such goals go

Figure 9–16   **Stages of the Empowerment Process**

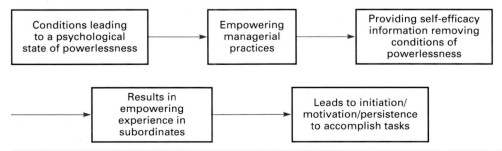

SOURCE: Adapted from J. A. Conger and R. N. Kanungo, The empowerment process: Integrating theory and practice, *Academy of Management Review* (July 1988).

hand in hand with empowering management practices. They were and are an integral part of the empowerment process I observed in the companies I studied.

A WORD OF CAUTION
In closing, it is important to add a note of caution. First of all, empowerment is not the complete or always the appropriate answer to building the confidence of managers. It can lead to overconfidence. A false sense of confidence in positive outcomes may lead employees and organizations to persist in what may, in actuality, prove to be tactical errors. Thus, a system of checks and balances is needed. Managers must constantly test reality and be alert to signs of "groupthink."

Some managers may be incapable of empowering others. Their own insecurities may prevent them from instilling a sense of power in subordinates. This is ironic, since often these are the individuals who need to develop such skills. Yet, as Kanter argues, "Only those leaders who feel secure about their own power outward . . . can see empowering subordinates as a gain rather than a loss."[24]

Certain situations may not warrant empowerment. For example, there are contexts where opportunities for greater initiative or responsibility simply do not exist and, in some cases, subordinates may be unwilling or unable to assume greater ownership or responsibility. As Lyman Porter, Edward Lawler, and Richard Hackman point out, research "strongly suggests that only workers with reasonably high strength of desire for higher-order need satisfaction . . . will respond positively and productively to the opportunities present in jobs which are high in meaning, autonomy, complexity, and feedback."[25] Others may not have the requisite experience or knowledge to succeed. And those given more than they are capable of handling may fail. The end result will be the opposite of what you are seeking—a sense of powerlessness. It is imperative that managers assess as accurately as possible their subordinates' capabilities before undertaking difficult goals and empowering them to achieve.

Second, certain of the empowerment practices described in this article are not appropriate for all situations. For example, managers of subordinates who require structure and direction are likely to find the example of the manager "seeding" ideas with the television set an ineffective practice. In the case of pressing deadline or crisis, such seeding is inappropriate, given its longer time horizons.

When staging playful or unconventional events, the context must be considered quite carefully. What signals are you sending about yourself and your management philosophy? Like rewards, these events can be used to excess and lose their meaning. It is imperative to determine the appropriateness and receptivity of such practices. You may inadvertently mock or insult subordinates, peers, or superiors.

In terms of expressing confidence and rewarding, both must be done sincerely and not to excess. Praising for non-accomplishments can make rewards meaningless. Subordi-

nates may suspect that the boss is simply flattering them into working harder.

In general, however, empowerment practices are an important tool for leaders in setting and achieving higher goals and in moving an organization past difficult transitions.[26] But remember that they do demand time, confidence, an element of creativity, and a sensitivity to one's context to be effective.

ENDNOTES
1. See, for example, J. P. Kotter, *Power in Management,* New York: AMACOM, 1979, and J. Pfeffer, *Power in Organizations,* Marshfield, MA: Pitman, 1981.
2. See P. Block, *The Empowered Manager,* San Francisco: Jossey-Bass, 1987; W. W. Burke, "Leadership as Empowering Others," In S. Srivastva (Ed.), *Executive Power,* San Francisco: Jossey-Bass, 1986, pp. 51–77; and R. M. Kanter, *The Change Masters,* New York: Simon & Schuster, 1983.
3. W. Bennis and B. Nanus, *Leaders,* New York: Harper & Row, 1985; and R. M. Kanter, "Power Failure in Management Circuits," *Harvard Business Review,* July–August 1979, pp. 65–75.
4. See Kanter, Endnote 3; and A. S. Tannenbaum, *Control in Organizations,* New York: McGraw-Hill, 1968.
5. See J. A. Conger and R. N. Kanungo, "The Empowerment Process: Integrating Theory and Practice," *Academy of Management Review,* July 1988; and R. J. House, "Power and Personality in Complex Organizations," in L. L. Cummings and B. M. Staw (Eds.), *Research in Organizational Behavior: An Annual Review of Critical Essays and Reviews,* Vol. 10, Greenwich, CT: JAI Press, 1988. The author is grateful to Rabindra N. Kanungo for his insights and help in conceptualizing the empowerment process.
6. See Conger and Kanungo, Endnote 5.
7. A. Bandura, "Self-Efficacy: Toward a Unifying Theory of Behavioral Change," *Psychological Review,* 1977, 84 (2), pp. 191–215.
8. D. McGregor, *The Human Side of Enterprise,* New York: McGraw-Hill, 1960.
9. See J. M. Beyer and H. M. Trice, "How an Organization's Rites Reveal Its Culture," *Organizational Dynamics,* Spring 1987, pp. 4–25.
10. A. Bandura, *Social Foundations of Thought and Action: A Social Cognitive View,* Englewood Cliffs, NJ: Prentice-Hall, 1986.
11. See Kanter, Endnote 3, p. 66.
12. See Bandura, Endnote 10, p. 400.
13. W. Bennis and B. Nanus, *Leaders,* New York: Harper & Row, 1985, pp. 64–65.
14. See Bandura, Endnote 10.
15. See Kanter, Endnote 3.
16. See J. R. Hackman, "The Design of Work in the 1980s,"

Organizational Dynamics, Summer 1978, pp. 3–17.

17. M. Beer, *Organizational Change and Development,* Santa Monica, CA: Goodyear, 1980, p. 64.

18. See Bandura, Endnote 10.

19. F. M. Rothbaum, J. R. Weisz, and S. S. Snyder, "Changing the World and Changing Self: A Two Process Model of Perceived Control," *Journal of Personality and Social Psychology,* 1982, 42, pp. 5–37; and L. Y. Abramson, J. Garber, and M. E. P. Seligman, "Learned Helplessness in Humans: An Attributional Analysis," in J. Garber and M. E. P. Seligman (Eds.), *Human Helplessness: Theory and Application,* New York: Academic Press, 1980, pp 3–34.

20. See Kanter, Endnote 2.

21. See Block, Endnote 2.

22. See Conger and Kanungo, Endnote 5.

23. Bennis and Nanus, Endnote 13, p. 93.

24. See Kanter, Endnote 3, p. 73.

25. L. W. Porter, E. E. Lawler, and J. R. Hackman, *Behavior in Organizations,* New York: McGraw-Hill, 1975, p. 306.

26. See N. M. Tichy and M. A. Devanna, *The Transformational Leader,* New York: John Wiley, 1986.

DISCUSSION QUESTIONS

1. Under what circumstances are organizational members likely to experience powerlessness?

2. In what ways can a leader provide empowering information to others?

3. Describe four empowering leadership practices. In what situations would each be appropriate?

Reprinted with permission from *Academy of Management Executive,* 1989, 3(1): 17–24.

Activity 9–1

Catherine Devereaux

Step 1:   Read the Catherine Devereaux case.

Dr. Catherine Devereaux, a specialist in cross-cultural communication, was an associate director of the Center for American/Asian Relations at Stanford University. The Center (CAAR), a research and teaching project dedicated to improving the quality of communication between American and Asian business leaders, was administered and staffed by a consortium of faculty from several area universities. Although CAAR originally was funded by a grant from a major oil company, the Center also raised a portion of its income from fees paid by business executives who attended short training programs taught at Stanford by Center faculty.

In late 1987, the directors of CAAR began to consider other ways to generate more income for the Center. The original funding was running out and remaining research grants were not adequate to support the Center's activities. In addition to supporting research projects, CAAR offered numerous courses and workshops; published the bi-monthly *Journal of Cultural Communication;* and developed and distributed teaching materials. The total annual budget for CAAR was roughly $400,000.

CAAR had begun offering seminars for executives in 1987. Called "Cultural Communications," these seminars were generally two-day sessions for which participants from industry paid $1100 each to attend. With the support of an outside marketing and conference firm, Conference Promotions (CP), CAAR ran five of these seminars a year. Under the agreement with Conference Promotions, CAAR was guaranteed $40,000 for each seminar. In 1988, these seminars generated approximately $200,000 in income—half the center's operating budget.

In early 1988, Dr. Devereaux became involved in discussions about future fundraising activities. She and another staff member, Dr. Walter Barnes, had developed two workshops which they believed could become new executive seminars. After a meeting with the Center's advisory board, it was agreed to add the new programs, again with Conference Promotions doing the marketing and organizing. As she proceeded to work up budgets and fees for the new seminars, Dr. Devereaux was mindful of the fact that she had not been very successful in generating research grants. Thus, she hoped to make the new ventures profitable for CAAR.

HISTORY OF CAAR AND THE CULTURAL COMMUNICATIONS SEMINARS

The Center for Asian/American Relations (CAAR) operated under the aegis of Stanford University, but was actually run by a consortium of faculty, graduate students, and staff from several area institutions: the University of California at Berkeley, San Francisco State College, and San Jose State University. The Center had evolved from a series of faculty seminars begun at Stanford in 1980. The seminars, which brought together faculty from a range of disciplines, were regarded as an opportunity for academics to investigate means to further the quality of communication between Asian and American business and government organizations. The Center was housed on the Stanford

Business School Campus; faculty associated with CAAR administered their own research projects and taught in the various courses offered.

In 1983, an umbrella organization was formed for the purpose of providing an administrative infrastructure to support the various activities. A three-year grant was obtained from a major oil company, and subsequently renewed, that paid for support staff and services. At the time, CAAR had five separate research programs (later expanded to seven); published a bi-monthly journal; offered several graduate level courses; and distributed a range of printed and audio-visual teaching materials through the CAAR Case Institute.

Dr. Walter Barnes, an associate professor in the political science department at Berkeley, was the Center's first executive director. Under Dr. Barnes, the Center greatly expanded its educational and curriculum development activities and also fostered links with the local Asian business community. At the end of Dr. Barnes' three-year term, Dr. George Stewart, editor of the *Journal of Cultural Communication* and a professor of anthropology at San Francisco State, became executive director.

By this time, 1986, the scope of CAAR activity was such that grant money was not adequate to meet operating expenses. In 1987, the Center began to offer "Cultural Communication" seminars to American and Asian business executives.

When he became executive director in 1987, Dr. Stewart asked Dr. Catherine Devereaux to join CAAR as an associate director. She became the first woman to join the Center in an administrative capacity. (Of the fifteen faculty associated with the Center, two are women.) Dr. Barnes stayed on as an associate director but devoted only a fraction of his time to Center activities. Despite the reduction in time commitment, Barnes continued to have a large impact on the Center. He supervised several research projects and periodically organized multi-disciplinary conferences, which in turn attracted additional support—usually in the form of corporate gifts to the Center.

Dr. Devereaux, who knew Dr. Barnes prior to joining the Center, characterized her colleague as follows:

> Walt is important to the organization. He is very committed to CAAR. He's got boundless energy and is a brilliant teacher. The Case Institute is filled with the cases and exercises that he has developed.
>
> When Walt was executive director, a lot of things happened. New programs were developed and new staff and faculty became involved. I think that it's been hard for him to make a transition to associate director. Sometimes he still thinks he runs the show.
>
> He's a real innovator but he also can exaggerate. Walt is a super salesman; he can convince you of almost anything. One of my colleagues says that when Walt walks by, he always checks to see that his wallet is in his pocket. I think that you have to be careful

when you deal with him; he can be very persuasive. Generally, I try to stay on his good side.

Prior to joining CAAR, Dr. Devereaux knew Dr. Stewart only slightly. They had been on several panels together at academic conferences on the subject of cross-cultural communication. After working with him for several months, Dr. Devereaux described her impressions of Stewart in the following manner:

> George is a respected academic. He writes a lot and frequently presents papers at professional conferences around the world. Administration is not his strong suit. I don't think he's that interested. He rarely pays attention to the finances and has had only a fleeting interest in the new fund-raising activities under consideration. He teaches in the executive conference, and for awhile he tried to interest some multi-national corporations in becoming associates. I guess I would characterize his style as "hands-off."

Devereaux explained that the Center was not hierarchically structured for the professional staff. It was an association of independent professionals who collaborated on certain research and teaching activities but were otherwise independent.

Catherine Devereaux was a professor in the Communications Department at San Francisco State. She was a graduate of Pomona College and received her Ph.D. from the Kellogg School of Management at Northwestern University. In addition to teaching, she was the author of a textbook on organizational behavior and was considered an authority on cross-cultural communication. Dr. Devereaux devoted approximately 50% of her time to research, teaching, and administration at the Center.

HISTORY OF THE EXECUTIVE SEMINARS

CAAR began offering executive seminars at about the time Dr. Devereaux joined the Center. These seminars dealt with aspects of culture and communications as they related to business dealings in the Far East. Early on CAAR had entered into a relationship with Sam Gallagher, the president of a for-profit firm called Conference Promotions. Conference Promotions (CP) both marketed and administered the executive seminars. Gallagher used direct mail as well as professional contacts to recruit participants; his firm also arranged for facilities to be used and managed all of the logistical aspects of the sessions, such as providing for participants' meals and writing materials. According to Dr. Devereaux, "All we do is come in and teach." Further,

> There is no limit on the number of persons who can attend the seminar, and usually between 160–180 pay the $1100 for the one and one-half days of instruction and workshops. The arrangement between CAAR and CP for these seminars is that no matter what the enrollment, CP will pay CAAR a flat fee. The first year

that fee was $25,000 but has been revised upward to $40,000. The advantage to CAAR from this arrangement is that the Center incurs no costs or risk.

The idea to add two new seminars originated with Dr. Barnes. During early discussions about how to increase funding, Barnes said, "We should do what we do well, which is running seminars." He had been working on a new workshop for a program at Berkeley called "U.S.-Japan Trade Relations," which was intended to bring leaders from Japan and the United States together to develop a framework for trade. His suggestion was that he try it out at Berkeley, and, if it proved successful, it could become the model for another executive seminar.

Simultaneously, Dr. Devereaux and he had developed a communications program for Spartan Laboratories, a corporate associate of the Center. Devereaux explained that this program, "Managing Diversity in the Workplace," also had potential as a seminar:

> We ran the Managing Diversity seminar last April at Spartan, and it was great. My idea was always that we would sell the cases and videos we developed for Spartan as a package, and generate funds for the Center that way. But I also saw that it could become an executive program aimed at helping managers deal with the diverse workforce of the future.

The two new programs would be longer than the executive program. Barnes would oversee the U.S.-Japan program and Devereaux, the Managing Diversity seminar.

PLANNING THE SEMINARS

In June, 1988, staff members from both CAAR and CP met to discuss the new executive programs. Present from CAAR were George Stewart, Walt Barnes, Catherine Devereaux and the administrative director of CAAR, Jane Stuart. CP personnel attending were Sam Gallagher and the vice president for marketing, Pete Larson. Catherine described the meeting as follows:

> It was a breakfast meeting, but it was not a formal planning session in any sense. Walt's U.S.-Japan course had just concluded and so people had a sense of what the program was like. We spent some time describing the "Managing Diversity" Project, its translation into an executive program and the distribution of the training materials.
>
> We all agreed that the "Managing Diversity" program would conform to the basic model of the "Cultural Communications" seminar. That is, CP would market and administer it and CAAR faculty would do the teaching. We agreed that in these programs, unlike the Cultural Communications seminars, faculty should be compensated. After all, we were asking for more commitment of time and effort in these programs than in Cultural Communications. Thus, in addition to ne-

gotiating about the relative shares of net revenue that would go to CP and CAAR, we would also have to consider how the faculty would be compensated. Would it be a fixed cost, or would it come out of CAAR's share of the revenues? We agreed that Sam Gallagher of CP and I would meet in a few weeks to discuss these issues.

> Marketing and distributing the Managing Diversity curriculum materials put us into a new arena. We had developed the materials to be sold to the corporate market as a package. Our idea had been that the Case Institute at CAAR would distribute and sell the materials at a standard price based on the size of a training program a firm might run. For planning purposes, we estimated that the materials (three cases, two videos, hand-outs and teaching notes) required for a class size of 10 should be priced at $1800. In our discussions with CP, Sam felt (and we agreed) that he could probably do a better job marketing the package and producing it at lower cost than our Case Institute. We would need to work out these terms and also some agreement on the copyright of the materials.

> The final issue that came up at the meeting was a real surprise. We later called it the "talent agency concept." Walt introduced the issue by saying, "Sam has a problem: CP only makes money if people enroll in the Cultural Communications seminar on site at Stanford. However, he often gets calls from potential attendees who would rather arrange for in-house training. Sam would like to accommodate them. That is, he would like to arrange for one of our faculty to go on-site and offer the Cultural Communications seminar to a corporate group. In return for finding the client and arranging the on-site Sam would like a share of the fee." I knew that currently when Sam gets these calls he frequently refers them to Walt and George and some of the other faculty.

After the meeting, it was agreed that Barnes and Devereaux would meet with Sam Gallagher separately to work out the arrangements for the U.S.-Japan and Managing Diversity programs respectively. The feeling was that there was no reason that the programs should have the same contract, since they were targeting two different markets and because of the materials component of Managing Diversity.

Catherine and Sam Gallagher met in mid-July. They discussed both the size and the length of the Managing Diversity program. Catherine told Gallagher that the curriculum warranted a three-day program and that the size needed to be limited. Pricing was Sam's expertise.

Gallagher proposed that CP pay CAAR a guaranteed rate based on the number of participants. This was a different structure from the Cultural Communications seminars where CAAR was guaranteed a fixed amount for each seminar. Gallagher explained that Managing Diversity was directed at human resource officers and trainers rather than operating managers. This was a new market, one with less discretionary power to spend company funds than the executive seminar market; therefore, the marketing effort to fill a class would be costly. He would have to do a big mailing with a probable yield of no more than two persons per thousand; he estimated that it would cost him $25,000 to market Managing Diversity. He proposed that CAAR price the program at $2450 and that CAAR would receive the following share of the revenues:

> At 50 attendees, CAAR's share would be $25,000.
>   Above 50 attendees, CAAR and CP would split net revenue, 50/50.

Gallagher's proposal also included a provision for the "talent agency" concept: he proposed that CP get one-third of the fees. On the materials, CP proposed a 50/50 split on the net revenues from their sale. Gallagher ended his presentation by saying, "You realize that these are bargaining positions." (See Figure 9–17 for Gallagher's proposal.)

Because it was summer, Devereaux knew that no one would be around to discuss Gallagher's contract proposals. She was on her own in developing a counter proposal. She sent a memo to Barnes and Stewart outlining what she proposed to do. In it, she outlined some of her concerns:

1. The CAAR/CP split at 50 attendees (30% of the net revenues to CAAR) seemed very generous to

Figure 9–17   General Contract Revisions for Discussion (Draft 7/13/88)

1. CP Responsibilities: Same as Cultural Communications Seminar (create, produce, mail, register, on-site preparation and administration).
2. CAAR Responsibilities: Prepare/select program materials on a timely basis. Submit masters to CP and all instructors. Teach program.
3. Financial Arrangements: See attached.
4. In House: All requests for in-house presentations of this program will be routed through CP. CP will receive 35% and CAAR 65% of all revenues subsequently generated. Faculty consulting fees for in-house presentations will be paid from CAAR's share.
5. Marketing and Resale of Program and Related Instructional Materials: CP will develop a marketing plan for CAAR approval and then be responsible for marketing of program materials. This activity will be at CP's expense. CP will receive 50% of gross revenues and CAAR 50%. CP will either reimburse CAAR for materials at CAAR's cost or produce similar materials at its expense.
6. No complimentary guests.
7. If session is cancelled, no payments made to CAAR.
8. If participants less than 35, 75% gross operating profit to CAAR.

Figure 9–17   (Continued)

Program on Managing Diversity (Draft)

Assumptions Used for Business Plan

- Three-day program length
- 50 minimum and 100 maximum attendees
- Audience profile
    Human resource executives and trainers
    Teams desirable
    Medium to large organizations.
- Price/registration Fee: $2450
- Variable Cost per attendee: 200 (includes meals and materials)
- Session Expenses

Room rental	$1000–2000
Transportation	$1000–1750
Contract Labor	$500
Total	$2500–4250

- Promotion: Net 1.75–2.0 per 1000
- Timing: 2–4 sessions per year

Financial Estimates (Based on 50 attendees)

Price	$ 2,450
Gross Revenue	122,500
Direct Expense	
Promotion	25,000
Variable	10,000
Session	4,000
CAAR Flat Rate at 50	25,000
Over 50, CAAR Rate is 50% of revenues:	
at 75 attendees	$43,375
at 100 attendees	$61,750

CP especially since it would yield only $25,000 to CAAR for three days worth of faculty time investment.

2. CAAR would do better financially under Gallagher's plan as the number of attendees increased. There were two problems here: If Gallagher's marketing efforts faltered and we had only 50 attendees, the income to CAAR might not be worth the effort. Secondly, the structure of the deal was such that it was in both our interests financially to have a lot of people, but what about pedagogically? The attendees were going to be paying top dollar to attend, and would expect faculty attention. As the numbers of attendees increased, so might the time commitment of faculty and the number of faculty who would have to participate.

3. The "talent agency" concept is a problem. As Gallagher proposed it, the revenues from an in-house program would be allocated in the following way: the faculty would charge his/her per diem, CP would take 33%, and CAAR would get the balance to put into general funds. Devereaux wondered why the faculty would agree to such an arrangement.

4. The proposal on the materials seemed okay in its structure. However, given the up-front costs that CAAR incurred in their development, a more reasonable split seemed warranted.

5. There was no mention of faculty salaries in Gallagher's proposal, the presumption being that they would come out of CAAR's revenues.

After receiving her memo, Walt Barnes called Devereaux. He commented, "the split on the seminar is too good a deal for Sam." Barnes suggested that the proposal should be rewritten to make the remuneration very attractive to CAAR at 50 participants. Further, he felt that as part of the agreement, Gallagher should bear the cost of faculty compensation, estimated at $10,000, as a fixed cost. He also felt that the split on the materials should benefit CAAR, as it had undertaken the cost of development.

Devereaux continued to feel uncomfortable with the proposal, particularly since she was the one charged with negotiating the terms. She was not a member of the Stanford Business School faculty and knew that Stanford was sensitive about the use of its name for revenue-producing activities, especially if the instructors involved were not Stanford faculty. The "talent agency" concept, the compensation for program faculty, and joint sales of curricular materials were potentially sticky issues. She decided to consult Richard Warren, a member of CAAR's advisory committee and a well-respected member of the business school faculty.

Warren saw no problem with the materials agreement but suggested that the issues of faculty salaries and referral fees to CP be raised at the next advisory committee meeting. Devereaux described what happened when it was brought up at the meeting:

> Walt was amazing. Remember, he was the one who introduced the talent agency concept at our initial meeting with CP. When we started to discuss it, he diverted attention by linking it with other potentially sticky ethical issues such as the consulting business faculty got from the Cultural Communications conferences. Walt backed off from the talent agency idea when he saw the resistance. On the issue of compensation for teaching in the programs, Warren said that faculty could not be paid extra salary, but that they could be compensated in the form of research funds set aside for their use.

After the meeting, Devereaux prepared her counter-proposal to Gallagher. She met with Stewart to review it.

> I told George that I was going to propose a 50/50 split on the program, with faculty salaries as a fixed cost, and based on attendance of 50. On the materials, I felt that a 65/35 split was fair, the larger share reflecting our development costs. I planned to reject the referral fee proposal based on the consensus of the advisory committee. George agreed with my plan. (See Figure 9–18 for the Devereaux's counterproposal).

After reviewing the proposal with Stewart, Devereaux set up a breakfast meeting with Sam Gallagher. She described his reaction to her revisions:

> Sam didn't like it. He claimed that a 50/50 split would mean that he would have to provide us with a complete accounting of his expenses. I admit I hadn't thought about the need to monitor his costs for such an agreement. He also was not pleased about the rejection of the talent agency fees and our proposal for the materials. He claimed he required the larger share of the materials income because his costs would be higher. He wanted to back off his initial 50/50 split and change it to 65/35 in his favor. The discussion was quite tense.

Between the time Devereaux left Gallagher and returned to her office, Gallagher had telephoned George Stewart to discuss the meeting.

> George told me that Sam had called and that he was afraid that he had offended me. He wanted to arrange a meeting with the three of us. I said to George, "I can't believe that you took this phone call. If he had something to say about our meeting, he should have called me." George reassured me that Sam was not going behind my back. "Oh no, Sam thinks the world of you. He wants to give you some consulting." I said, "Listen George, Sam has just done an end run." I was pissed.

George scheduled an informal meeting soon after that with Catherine and Walt. In the meantime, Catherine made an attempt to locate another vendor of the services Sam Gallagher offered. She was concerned that the marketing costs he was quoting were very high and that, without other bids, CAAR was in a weak bargaining position. When she discussed the idea of another vendor, Walt vetoed the idea, saying that they would not be able to obtain such a detailed proposal from another firm.

At the meeting, Barnes proposed that CAAR go with Gallagher's original proposal with the modification that faculty salary be part of the expenses and not taken out of CAAR's share of the revenues. "As usual Walt dominated the meeting," said Devereaux. "George was not that involved. I knew that Sam was getting a great deal from us, but didn't feel that I had support from George to challenge Walt. So I said, sure, go ahead, as long as the salary issue

Figure 9–18 **Response to CP from CAAR Regarding Contract Proposal (September 10, 1988)**

1. CP Responsibilities: Same as Cultural Communications Seminar (create, produce, mail, register, on-site preparation and administration).
2. CAAR Responsibilities: Prepare/select program materials on a timely basis. Submit masters to CP and all instructors. Teach program.
3. Financial Arrangements: See attached.*
4. In House: This provision is not acceptable to CAAR in any form. Faculty members will continue to make their own arrangements for consulting and in-house training resulting from this program. This is the subject of a Task Force at CAAR.*
5. Marketing and Resale of Program and Related Instructional Materials: This provision is fine in concept, with the following conditions. 1) CAAR will receive 65% of gross revenues, reflecting the development of them, or 2) CAAR will receive a flat rate of $1800 for each set of materials sold.*
6. CAAR and CP will work out an agreement for low fee attendees.
7. If session is cancelled, no payments made to CAAR.
8. If participants less than 35, 75% gross operating profit to CAAR.

Financial Arrangements

Estimated Budget with 50 Participants for a Three Day Program

Price	$ 2,450
Gross Revenue	122,500
Direct Expense	
Promotion	25,000
Variable	10,000
Session	4,000
	39,000
Faculty Salaries	10,000
	$49,000
Net Revenue	$73,500
50/50 Share to CAAR	$36,750
at 75 attendees with 50/50 split	$56,725

*Changes made by CAAR in these items.

is treated as an expense. With 50 attendees, we would get the $25,000 plus the $10,000 for salaries. We discussed the materials and they went along with my proposal to sell them to CP and then CP could price in such a way that they realized a return on the marketing and production. We agreed that $700 was a reasonable price for CAAR to charge CP given our cost calculations."

A meeting was set with Gallagher for the following week to discuss contracts for the US-Japan and Managing Diversity Programs. In the interim, Devereaux and Barnes had a brief conversation at the monthly Faculty Roundtable. She described their conversation and her reactions to it:

Walt said, "I saw Sam on Sunday; he was over at our house for lunch. He's a good guy who wants to be a partner with us in these seminars and other ventures." I knew that Sam and Walt had other dealings. Sam refers consulting opportunities to Walt, and Walt has used Sam to organize other seminars conducted under private auspices.

I responded to Walt, "Sam is a nice guy but he is in business, and we are a non-profit group. I just want to make sure that these seminars pay off for CAAR as well as for Sam." Walt said that Sam was interested in helping us raise money and in doing the fair thing.

From my perspective, it was important that the Center get a substantial share of the funds. But it seemed that bringing in funds was secondary to some of the others. As I think about it, I think it was important to me personally because I saw it as a way for me to bring money into the Center and compensate for my failure to raise substantial research funds.

In November, a breakfast meeting was held at the Hyatt Suburban. The purpose was to establish the contract terms for the two new programs. Present were George Stewart, Walter Barnes, Catherine Devereaux, Sam Gallagher and Pete Larson. Barnes led the discussion.

It soon became evident to Devereaux that "her" program—Managing Diversity—was going to be less profitable than the US-Japan Program that Walt was coordinating. CAAR would be guaranteed $25,000 for US-Japan at 40 participants; it would take 50 attendees before CAAR would receive this amount for Managing Diversity. "Why the discrepancy?" asked Catherine. Gallagher said that it "would be easier to market US-Japan because the Cultural Communications seminar was a direct feeder into it. A special marketing effort would have to be mounted for Managing Diversity because it was a different target audience, thus expenses would be higher." Since we had no way to verify this argument, Catherine accepted it. No one else was interested.

On the sale of materials, CP's proposal was based on the principle of a guaranteed amount. There were problems with this principle in terms of copyrights and the relationship between production costs and price. Devereaux proposed that they agree on a price at which CAAR would sell the materials to CP. Without mentioning numbers, they agreed to meet later to work out a transfer price.

After some additional discussion about the two new

programs, Walt produced the new contract proposal. It was supposed to be identical to Gallagher's original proposal with the addition of $10,000 for faculty time as a program expense. After all those present looked over the document, the following discussion took place:

Walt (to Catherine): Are these numbers OK with you?

Catherine: Yes, as far as they go. But I don't see an item for faculty compensation.

Walt: Sam, how do you think we should manage this, the $10,000 for faculty time?

Sam: Well, I could send CAAR's share of the revenues in two checks, and break out the $10,000 that way.

Walt: You mean one check for $15,000 which is our share of the revenues and $10,000 for the faculty salaries?

Sam: Yeah.

Devereaux was speechless at first. Then she said, "My understanding was that faculty compensation was to be regarded as an expense. I understood that this program would raise at least $25,000 for CAAR's general funds if we had 50 people enroll. Now you're telling me that only $15,000 will go into the general funds and CAAR will totally absorb the faculty salaries." Walt told Catherine that she had misunderstood; they had never agreed to treat faculty salaries as an expense. Stewart was silent: Devereaux later reflected on the meeting:

> Clearly this had been intentional. It was a performance to coopt me. Basically what we ended up accepting from Sam was his opening offer, an offer that he had called a "bargaining position." We accepted it.
>
> Later I said to George: "I can't believe we accepted his opening offer! All our estimates about the funds these programs could generate were inflated. We need to cut the estimates by at least a third in order to pay the faculty salaries." George told me that I get too excited.

The next day Sam called Catherine to report that he had gone over the numbers and found that his costs were not as high as he thought. Thus, at an enrollment of 40,

CAAR would get $25,000 and $32,000 at 50 people and $1000 per registrant over 50. This was certainly an improvement over his original proposal (Figure 9–17), and came close to my proposal with the exception of the faculty salaries (Figure 9–18).

Step 2: Prepare the case for class discussion.

Step 3: Individually, in small groups, or with the entire class, as directed by your instructor, answer the following questions:

Description
1. Describe the interactions between Catherine Devereaux, Walter Barnes, and George Stewart.
2. What types of negotiations did they conduct?

Diagnosis
3. What bases of power did Catherine use?
4. Did she use power effectively?
5. Did she build informal networks, alliances, or trade relations?
6. How effectively did she conduct negotiations inside and outside the organization?
7. What problems arose?

Prescription
8. How should she have handled the negotiations more effectively?
9. What additional sources of power should she use?

Action
10. What likely would have been the consequences?

Step 4: Discussion. In small groups, with the entire class, or in written form, share your answers to the questions above. Then answer the following questions:

1. What symptoms suggest a problem exists?
2. What problems exist in the case?
3. What theories and concepts help explain the problems?
4. What should have been done differently?
5. How effective would such actions likely be?

This case was prepared by Jeanne Stanton and Deborah M. Kolb for the Institute for Case Development and Research, Simmons Graduate School of Management, Boston, MA. Copyright © 1989 by the President and Trustees of Simmons College. Reprinted by permission.

Activity 9–2

Empowerment Profile

Step 1: Complete the following questionnaire.

For each of the following items, select the alternative with which you feel more comfortable. While for some items you may feel that both a and b describe you or neither is ever applicable you should select the alternative that better describes you most of the time.

1. When I have to give a talk or write a paper, I . . .
_____ a. Base the content of my talk or paper on my own ideas.
_____ b. Do a lot of research, and present the findings of others in my paper or talk.

2. When I read something I disagree with, I . . .
_____ a. Assume my position is correct.
_____ b. Assume what's presented in the written word is correct.

3. When someone makes me extremely angry, I . . .
_____ a. Ask the other person to stop the behavior that is offensive to me.
_____ b. Say little, not quite knowing how to state my position.

4. When I do a good job, it is important to me that . . .
_____ a. The job represents the best I can do.
_____ b. Others take notice of the job I've done.

5. When I buy new clothes, I . . .
_____ a. Buy what looks best on me.
_____ b. Try to dress in accordance with the latest fashion.

6. When something goes wrong, I . . .
_____ a. Try to solve the problem.
_____ b. Try to find out who's at fault.

7. As I anticipate my future, I . . .
_____ a. Am confident I will be able to lead the kind of life I want to lead.
_____ b. Worry about being able to live up to my obligations.

8. When examining my own resources and capacities, I . . .
_____ a. Like what I find.
_____ b. Find all kinds of things I wish were different.

9. When someone treats me unfairly, I . . .
_____ a. Put my energies into getting what I want.
_____ b. Tell others about the injustice.

10. When someone criticizes my efforts, I . . .
_____ a. Ask questions in order to understand the basis for the criticism.
_____ b. Defend my actions or decisions, trying to make my critic understand why I did what I did.

11. When I engage in an activity, it is very important to me that . . .
_____ a. I live up to my own expectations.
_____ b. I live up to the expectations of others.

12. When I let someone else down or disappoint them, I . . .
_____ a. Resolve to do things differently next time.
_____ b. Feel guilty, and wish I had done things differently.

13. I try to surround myself with people . . .
_____ a. Whom I respect.
_____ b. Who respect me.

14. I try to develop friendships with people who . . .
_____ a. Are challenging and exciting.
_____ b. Can make me feel a little safer and a little more secure.

15. I make my best efforts when . . .
_____ a. I do something I want to do when I want to do it.
_____ b. Someone else gives me an assignment, a deadline, and a reward for performing.

16. When I love a person, I . . .
_____ a. Encourage him or her to be free and choose for himself or herself.
_____ b. Encourage him or her to do the same thing I do and to make choices similar to mine.

17. When I play a competitive game, it is important to me that I . . .
_____ a. Do the best I can.
_____ b. Win.

18. I really like being around people who . . .
_____ a. Can broaden my horizons and teach me something.
_____ b. Can and want to learn from me.

19. My best days are those that . . .
_____ a. Present unexpected opportunities.
_____ b. Go according to plan.

20. When I get behind in my work, I . . .
_____ a. Do the best I can and don't worry.
_____ b. Worry or push myself harder than I should.

Step 2: Score your responses as follows:

Total your a responses: _____
Total your b responses: _____

(Your instructor will help you interpret these scores.)

Step 3:   Discussion. In small groups or with the entire class, answer the following questions:

Description

1. Look at the two totals. Which score is highest? Which is lowest?
2. Do your scores describe you well? Why or why not?

Diagnosis

3. Think of some experiences you have had that confirm your score.
4. Think of some experiences you have had that disconfirm your score.
5. How does this information help you to act more effectively in organizations?

_____

"The Empowerment Profile" from *The Power Handbook* by Pamela Cuming. Copyright © 1980 by CBI Publishing. Reprinted by permission of Van Nostrand Reinhold Co., Inc.

Activity 9–3   **CNN** Video: **A Case about Sexual Harassment**

Step 1:   View the CNN "Inside Business" video on sexual harassment.

Step 2:   Consider the following situation:

You are the vice president of human resources. A female employee of your organization has just met with you to discuss what she considered to be an incident of sexual harassment by her boss. According to her, he said that he would deny her a well-deserved promotion unless she met him at a secluded restaurant for drinks and dinner.

In small groups or with the entire class, answer the following questions:

1. You are the vice president of human resources. How would you respond to the complaint?

2. You want to conduct an audit of your organization's policies for dealing with such a situation. How would you proceed?

Step 3:   Discussion. In small groups or with the class as a whole, discuss the following:

1. What issues of power are inherent in cases of sexual harassment?
2. How common is sexual harassment in the workplace?
3. What responsibilities do employees have in cases of possible sexual harassment?
4. What responsibilities do employers have in cases of possible sexual harassment?

Activity 9–4   **Contract Negotiations in Western Africa: A Case of Mistaken Identity**

Step 1:   Read the case "Contract Negotiations in Western Africa: A Case of Mistaken Identity."

Peter Janes, a young member of Eurojet's Contracts Department, was on his way to Saheli in French-speaking West Africa to work on the complicated negotiations involved in selling a jet airliner to the Saheli government. He was not altogether thrilled with the assignment, and hoped it would be a quick deal, since financing seemed to be available for it. He had experience in contract negotiation in India, the Philippines, and Saudi Arabia, and most recently, Australia. At 27, he was one of the younger members of the department, but was seen as trustworthy with a high degree of

motivation. If he succeeded, it would be the first deal he brought to closure on his own. But he had serious doubts about the project's feasibility or desirability. In addition, he had left behind what seemed to be the beginning of a great relationship in Australia, and he wanted to get back to his girlfriend. Furthermore, Janes had no desire to become a Francophone Africa expert within the company.

THE COMPANY

Eurojet was one of the larger diversified aircraft manufacturers. It had developed a particular jet for Third World operations, able to operate from hot and high airfields, including unprepared strips. Orders, however, were hard to come by because of the difficulties of Third World financing and the poor financial condition of regional airlines. The company was therefore delighted to learn that its regional sales executive in Saheli, Mr. Ali Osaju, had found a potential sale in the country's desire for a presidential aircraft, along with its need for reliable regional air transport.

The sale looked even more possible when it was discovered that the government Export Import Bank had a substantial budget available for Saheli, making financing of the multimillion dollar aircraft feasible. It would be necessary to arrange an international commercial bank loan for Saheli as well. The potential of the airliner to earn revenue through regional transport was considered important in securing the loan.

THE NEGOTIATING TEAM

In December 1987, the Saheli government announced that they were ready to begin detailed negotiations. According to company policy, negotiations were conducted by the Contracts Department in close cooperation with sales and internal specialist functions. Mr. Janes, having just spent a hard-working three months—he had had four days off in the last six months—based in Australia and working across southeast Asia on specialist leasing packages, was assigned to the team because of his Third World experience, and his ability to speak French. He had been with the company for about two years. He had no experience in Africa.

Mr. Osaju was a highly placed African of Middle Eastern origin, educated in Europe, with a background in aviation. He had joined the company at about the same time as Mr. Janes. He had no previous experience in selling high-tech capital goods, but had many good connections, and was seen as invaluable to the company because of his African cultural background, combined with his European education. He had been developing local contacts in Saheli by spending a week there every two or three months over the past two years.

THE NEGOTIATING POLICY

The company's negotiating policy inevitably led to what was referred to as the "two-headed monster approach." The sales representative was responsible for initial discussions and for overall relations with the customer. The contracts representative was responsible for negotiating concrete offers and signing contracts and finance agreements on behalf of the company. This double approach led to varying degrees of tension between the members of particular teams as well as between the departments in general. Sales were particularly aggrieved that contracts operated on a world-wide rather than a regional basis.

Working in a team where both have important roles to play required considerable sensitivity. In his two years of working at Eurojet, Peter Janes was looked on by the sales people as a considerate and skilled negotiating partner. He was not likely to lose a contract which they had spent years developing because of cultural clumsiness. Nevertheless, he walked a very narrow line, as it was his role to say no to all the wishes of the customer which were not feasible from the company's perspective. As this was to be his first solo contract negotiation, and Ali Osaju's first sale with the company, they shared a certain personal enthusiasm for closing the deal.

THE NEGOTIATION: THE EARLY DAYS

Eurojet was not the only company trying to sell a jetliner to Saheli. The Russians, who had had considerable influence over the country since its independence twenty years earlier, were very present, trying to sell their aircraft and to sabotage the deal with Eurojet. Mr. Janes and Mr. Osaju frequently received strange phone calls in their hotel rooms, and were aware that all their telephone calls were bugged. Once, Mr. Janes returned to his room to find that his briefcase had been tampered with. In addition, another European company with a number of contracts in surrounding countries was trying to arrange a deal.

The main negotiating point of the team to begin with was to have the Sahelis accept one airplane that could be converted from a regional airliner to a VIP presidential jet. The Sahelis originally wanted a specially designed VIP jet, which would have cost an extra ten million dollars and would never have been used other than for the president. The negotiations moved extremely slowly. Mr. Janes and Mr. Osaju spent hours waiting to see officials, chasing papers from one office to another. They became aware that no one official wanted to be responsible for making the decision, in case he would be blamed for it should things go wrong.

They spent many hours debating strategy in the bar of the hotel. Mr. Janes objected to Mr. Osaju telling him what to do. Mr. Osaju objected to Mr. Janes making issues too complicated for the client. The relationship was a very tense one. They both felt they were getting little support from the head office and that the circumstances they were working in were very difficult.

Mr. Janes began to feel he was in a no-win situation. He realized that the negotiating process could go on for months, and he knew that his colleague had already begun to take over his activities with multi-order prospects in Australia. Conditions at the hotel were not that comfortable, and both he and Mr. Osaju were paid on a salary only basis. There were no overseas allowances.

The lack of support from headquarters was a problem for both the negotiators. Communications were difficult, as they felt they could not talk freely over the telephone because of its being bugged. Furthermore, they did not feel their contacts at headquarters would begin to understand the finer points of the negotiation difficulties. They did learn from headquarters that they were considered to be moving too slowly in making the deal.

There were constant discussions on finance, spares, configuration, certification, and training. All the legal and technical documents had to be translated from English to

French, causing many minor but significant misunderstandings. In one case, the standard contract at home called for the Saheli government to waive its "sovereign immunity" and "contract in its private rather than its public capacity." Saheli had adopted the Napoleonic Code from France, and had no equivalent legal concepts. The courts in the home country have a very limited right to hear actions against the Crown, and they assume this element of the law holds true for all countries. The Saheli negotiators listened with polite disbelief to these explanations and sent a telegram to the president saying, "Sahelian sovereignty is being threatened."

Mr. Janes and Mr. Osaju decided on a very basic strategy of patience and a friendly, open manner. Establishing trust and preserving individual and corporate credibility were recognized as being vital. They placed great emphasis on simplifying the bureaucratic process. Two months of negotiating passed with no commitment in sight.

Eurojet management were beginning to show their lack of confidence in the deal. Peter Janes had committed them to one million dollars of expenditure on completing an airliner to the Sahelis' expectations, so that it could be delivered on time, yet they saw no formalization of the contract, nor had they received any of the loan money. On the Saheli side, there was considerable nervousness about the commercial sovereign loans from the international banks.

Mr. Janes continued to make his daily round of visits to offices and homes, establishing himself as open and trustworthy and using his skill in expressing complex legal and technical terms in a simple way. He began to be aware of a warming of perceptions toward him. Up until then he had felt that the Sahelian officials were always guarded, on the defense in the presence of Eurojet's legal commercial representative. He thought that this was because it was his role to say "no" in the negotiations. In the third month of the negotiations, he received an extremely encouraging sign. A source close to the president had recently been quoted as saying, "He (Janes) doesn't say 'yes' very often, but when he says 'yes,' he means 'yes.' " This was the sign that they had been waiting for, that his credibility had been established and they could now begin to deal with some of the more sensitive issues in the negotiation.

Mr. Janes had adapted himself to local culture as much as he could. Although his natural inclination would have been to get things done quickly, deal with business first and make friends later, he was aware that this was not how business deals were made in Saheli. So he spent many hours making friends, going to people's houses, walking around their businesses and factories. On one such occasion, he was walking around a factory with one of his friends, holding his hand as was the custom for Sahelian male friends. To his horror, a group of foreign diplomats came toward them on their tour of the factory. Mr. Janes was aware of an almost superhuman effort on his part not to let go of his friend's hand and keep it relaxed, even as he felt the rest of his body stiffen with tension.

He was unwilling to embarrass people by saying they were wrong, but was equally uncomfortable not striking down the myth. Perhaps it served some purpose. His status as an international soccer player was apparently much greater than that of a young lawyer; perhaps he needed a little extra to justify his power in negotiating and signing the contract. It was relatively easy to give indirect answers to questions, thus saving his conscience and protecting his strangely acquired status. Nonetheless, alluding to his legal training, Mr. Janes had said to Mr. Osaju at this time, "I can put my hand on my heart and say, 'I have not told a lie,' but I don't feel comfortable. We have worked so hard for credibility I would hate a silly issue like this to backfire on us." At the time, they agreed to laugh off the issue, because so far the people involved were not main players in the negotiations.

The issue came to a head one day when he had a chance meeting in the lobby of the hotel with an important Saheli minister and his counterpart from a neighboring country, with whom Eurojet was very keen on doing business. To Mr. Janes' horror, the two launched into an enthusiastic and evidently serious discussion about potential dates for a tour of West Africa by CEDEX. Maybe now, he thought, he had better set the record straight.

EPILOGUE

Mr. Janes continued to make noncommittal replies and managed to avoid any further serious problems. Although greatly disturbing to him personally, it was a nonissue in terms of the negotiations. Fortunately for Peter Janes, he could discuss his feelings about the situation with Ali Osaju, and so relieve some of his own tension by laughing about the absurdity of it.

After ten months of intense negotiations, the deal was almost called off by the negotiating team at the last minute. They had spent days retranslating the French contract back into English, and then sitting by a Sahelian typist who did not speak English saying each word to her phonetically so that she could type it. They both had had very little sleep in order to get the contract finished on time. When they finally went with the attorney general to the president's office to sign the contract, they were as usual kept waiting for a few hours. During that time, the attorney general reread the French contract and discovered numerous spelling mistakes in it. He then declared that he could not give it to the president in its present condition, and that the signing would have to be delayed for another week.

Ali and Peter both hit the walls—literally. It was the last straw. While Ali threw books and papers at the walls, Peter strode around the room shouting that unless they signed immediately, he was withdrawing Eurojet's approval of the contract. The attorney general stood his ground, and Ali and Peter stormed off to the hotel. They could scarcely believe what they had done after almost a year's worth of friendly and meticulous negotiating. Peter went to sleep, exhausted after the last ten days of work and the loss of the contract.

He was woken four hours later to be informed that the attorney general was waiting to see him. He was escorted to an office across the road, where he found the attorney general in his shirtsleeves, sitting at a typewriter, carefully changing all the spelling mistakes himself. He wanted Peter to initial all the changes so that he would feel confident that no substantial changes were being made in the contract. The contract was signed the next day.

Despite Eurojet's advice, the aircraft was not handled by the national airlines but kept under the president's control, and so, rarely used. Debt servicing soon became a problem, and one year later, the aircraft was quietly and informally repossessed. Eurojet has offered to resell the aircraft, but the Saheli government balked at authorizing the sale.

Mr. Osaju spent one more year in Africa, and then was promoted to the Far East where he was made regional sales director. Mr. Janes was promoted to another program in early 1983, where he continued to work for the next four years.

Step 2:   Prepare the case for class discussion.

Step 3:   Individually, in small groups, or with the entire class, as directed by your instructor, answer the following questions:

Description

1. Describe the steps that occurred in the negotiation regarding the sale of the jet airliner to the Saheli government.

Diagnosis

2. How effectively were the negotiations conducted?
3. Did Janes successfully prepare, identify interests, propose alternatives, and recommend trade-offs?
4. To what extent did Peter Janes consider cross-cultural issues in negotiations?
5. What problems have arisen?

Prescription

6. What should Janes have done differently?

Action

7. Would the outcomes likely have been positive?

Step 4:   Discussion. In small groups, with the entire class, or in written form, share your answers to the questions above. Then answer the following questions:

1. What symptoms suggest that a problem exists?
2. What problems exist in the case?
3. What theories and concepts help explain the problems?
4. What should have been done differently?
5. How effective would such actions likely be?

This case was prepared by Gordon Anderson and Christine Mead, Research Assistants, under the supervision of Susan Schneider, associate professor at INSEAD. It is intended to be used as a basis for class discussion rather than to illustrate either effective or ineffective handling of an administrative situation. Copyright © 1988, INSEAD-CEDEP, Fontainebleau, France.

Activity 9–5 — The Used Car Role Play

Step 1:   Read the following background information:

You are about to negotiate the purchase/sale of an automobile. The seller advertised the car in the local newspaper. (Note: Both role players should interpret "local" as the town in which the role play is occurring.) Before advertising it, the seller took the car to the local Volkswagen dealer, who has provided the following information:

1986 VW Jetta diesel, standard shift.
White with red upholstery, tinted glass.
AM/FM radio.
30,450 miles; steel belted radial tires expected to last 65,000.
45 miles per gallon on diesel fuel at current prices (usually about 10 percent less than regular gasoline).
No rust; dent on passenger door barely noticeable.

Mechanically perfect except exhaust system, which may or may not last another 10,000 miles (costs $300 to replace.)
"Blue book" retail value, $5,000; wholesale, $4,400 (local 1988 prices).
Car has spent its entire life in the local area; it is the only used diesel Jetta within a 60-mile radius.

Step 2:   Your instructor will divide the class into groups of two—the buyer and the seller of the used car. Your instructor will then distribute the roles to each group. After assigning one role to each group member, read the role description. Then spend five minutes "getting into your role." As part of your preparation, answer the three questions at the end of your role description.

Step 3: After you have read about and prepared your roles, negotiate with the other party. Spend about fifteen to twenty-five minutes meeting with the other person and decide on a course of action. When you have reached an agreement complete the following information:

Price:
Manner of Payment:
Special Terms and Conditions:
Signed by:
Seller: _____
Buyer: _____

Step 4: The instructor will ask each pair to report its agreement. Then describe the process used in your negotiation.

Step 5: Answer the following questions with the entire class:

Description
1. What solution did each group reach?

Diagnosis
2. What are some key features of the bargaining situation?
3. What influenced the effectiveness of negotiations?
4. What effect did the bargaining range have on the negotiations?
5. What effect did each party's interests and best alternative to a negotiated agreement (BATNA) have on the negotiations?

Prescription
6. How could the effectiveness of the negotiations be improved?

_____

Based on the role play developed by Professor Leonard Greenhalgh of Dartmouth College and used with his permission.

Activity 9–6   The Colortek Job

Step 1: The instructor will divide the class into groups of three. In each group one person will play J. B. Daniels, one will play Chris Dawson, and one will be an observer. The instructor will then distribute the roles to each group. After the group members have received their role assignments, they should read the role descriptions. Then each person should spend five minutes "getting into" his or her role.

Step 2: After you have read about and prepared your roles, negotiate with the other party. Spend about fifteen to twenty-five minutes meeting with the other person and decide on a course of action.

Step 3: The instructor will ask each pair to report its agreement. Then describe the process used in your negotiation.

Step 4: Discussion. Answer the following questions with the entire class:

Description
1. What solution did each group reach?

Diagnosis
2. What are some key features of the bargaining situation?
3. What influenced the effectiveness of negotiations?
4. What creative alternatives were offered?

Prescription
5. How could the effectiveness of the negotiations be improved?

_____

This case was written by Deborah M. Kolb in collaboration with J. William Breslin, Connie Ozawa, and Elaine Landry of the Program on Negotiation at Harvard Law School. Copyright © 1991 by the President and Fellows of Harvard College.

CONCLUDING COMMENTS To become an influential manager, an individual must accumulate power for future use in five ways:

- Develop a reputation as a knowledgeable person or an expert.
- Balance the time spent in each critical relationship according to the needs of the work rather than on the basis of habit or social preference.
- Develop a network of resource persons who can be called upon for assistance.
- Choose the correct combination of influence tactics for the objective and for the target to be influenced.
- Implement influence tactics with sensitivity, flexibility, and adequate levels of communication.[65]

The Empowerment Profile provided data about personal power experiences. The CNN video about sexual harassment allowed you to consider another side of power. In the case of Catherine Devereaux you saw how an individual used diverse sources of power. In "Contract Negotiations in Western Africa" you examined cross-cultural issues in negotiation. The Used Car and Colortek Job role plays gave you the opportunity to practice your negotiating skills.

ENDNOTES

[1] See, for example, I. Cohen and R. Lachman, The generality of the strategic contingencies approach to sub-unit power, *Organization Studies* 9(3) (1988): 371–391; D. C. Hambrick, Environment, strategy and power within top management teams, *Administrative Science Quarterly* 26 (1981): 253–275.

[2] J. P. Kotter, Why power and influence issues are at the very core of executive work. In S. Srivastva and Associates, *Executive Power* (San Francisco: Jossey-Bass, 1986).

[3] A. Kaplan, Power in perspective. In *Power and Conflict in Organizations,* ed. R. L. Kahn and E. Boulding (London: Tavistock, 1964); M. Weber, *The Theory of Social and Economic Organization* (Glencoe, Ill.: Free Press, 1947).

[4] H. Mintzberg, *Power in and around Organizations* (Englewood Cliffs, N.J.: Prentice-Hall, 1983).

[5] *Ibid.*

[6] This discussion of dependence is based in large part on J. P. Kotter, Power, dependence, and effective management, *Harvard Business Review* 55 (1977): 125–136; and J. P. Kotter, Power, success, and organizational effectiveness, *Organizational Dynamics* 6 (1978): 27–40.

[7] P. M. Blau, *Exchange and Power in Social Life* (New York: Wiley, 1964).

[8] R. M. Emerson, Power-dependence relations, *American Sociological Review* 27 (1962): 31–41.

[9] B. Markovsky, D. Weller, and T. Patton, Power relations in exchange networks, *American Sociological Review* 53 (1988): 220–236.

[10] R. M. Kanter, The new managerial work, *Harvard Business Review* (November-December 1989): 85–92.

[11] D. McClelland and D. H. Burnham, Power driven managers: Good guys make bum bosses, *Psychology Today* (December 1975): 69–71; D. McClelland, *Power: The Inner Experience* (New York: Irvington, 1975).

[12] W. C. Grams and R. W. Rogers, Power and personality: Effects of Machiavellianism, need for approval, and motivation on use of tactics, *Journal of General Psychology* 117 (1990): 71–82.

[13] J. Gabarro and J. Kotter, Managing your boss, *Harvard Business Review* 58 (1980): 92–100.

[14] W. F. G. Mastenbroek, *Conflict Management and Organization Development* (Chichester, England: Wiley, 1987).

[15] J. A. Conger and R. N. Kanungo, The empowerment process: Integrating theory and practice, *Academy of Management Review* 13 (1988): 471–482.

[16] R. M. Kanter, Power failures in management circuits, *Harvard Business Review* 57 (1979): 65–75.

[17] R. E. Spekman, Influence and information: An exploratory investigation of the boundary person's bases of power, *Academy of Management Journal* 22 (1979): 104–117.

[18] L. A. Mainiero, Coping with powerlessness: The relationship of gender and job dependency to empowerment-strategy usage, *Administrative Science Quarterly* 31 (1986): 633–653.

[19] See, for example, R. M. Kanter, *The Change Masters* (New York: Simon and Schuster, 1983); and W. W. Burke, Leadership as empowering others. In S. Srivastva and Associates, *Executive Power* (San Francisco: Jossey-Bass, 1986); J. A. Conger and R. N. Kanungo, The empowerment process: Integrating theory and practice.

[20] A. Bandura, Self-efficacy: Toward a unifying theory of behavioral change, *Psychological Review* 84 (1977): 191–215.

[21] J. A. Conger, Leadership: The art of empowering others, *Academy of Management Executive* 3(1) (1989): 17–24.

[22] T. A. Stewart, GE keeps those ideas coming, *Fortune* (August 12, 1991): 41–49.

[23] *Ibid.,* p. 42.

[24] M. A. Rahim, Relationships of leader power to compliance and satisfaction with supervision: Evidence from a national sample of managers, *Journal of Management* 15(4) (1989): 545–556.

[25] See W. G. Astley and P. S. Sachdeva, Structural sources of intraorganizational power: A theoretical synthesis, *Academy of Management Review* 9 (1984): 104–113; Cohen and Lachman, Strategic contingencies approach, provide recent empirical support for the strategic contingencies theory of organizational behavior originally described in D. J. Hickson, C. R. Hinings, C. A. Lee, R. E. Schneck, and J. M. Pennings, A strategic contingencies' theory of intraorganizational power, *Administrative Science Quarterly* 16 (1971): 216–227.

[26] S. J. Pfeffer and G. R. Salancik, *The External Control of Organizations* (New York: Harper & Row, 1978).

[27] J. D. Hackman, Power and centrality in the allocation of resources in colleges and universities, *Administrative Science Quarterly* 20 (1985): 61–77.

[28] D. Farrell and J. C. Petersen, Patterns of political behavior in organizations, *Academy of Management Review* 7 (1982): 403–412.

[29] R. E. Kaplan, Trade routes: The manager's network of relationships, *Organizational Dynamics* (Spring 1984).

[30] *Ibid.*

[31] A. R. Cohen and D. L. Bradford, Influence without authority: The use of alliances, reciprocity, and exchange to accomplish work, *Organizational Dynamics* (1988): 5–16.

[32] Kanter, Power failures.

[33] Cohen and Bradford, Influence without authority.

[34] W. B. Stevenson, J. L. Pearce, and L. W. Porter, The concept of "coalition" in organization theory and research, *Academy of Management Review* 10 (1985): 256–268.

[35] G. Hofstede, Motivation, leadership, and organization: Do American theories apply abroad? *Organizational Dynamics* (Summer 1980): 42–63; G. Hofstede, *Culture's Consequences: International Differences in Work-Related Values* (Beverly Hills, Calif.: Sage, 1980).

[36] By Jennifer Oakes, MBA McGill University, 1984. In N. J. Adler, *International Dimensions of Organizational Behavior*, 2nd ed. (Boston: PWS-Kent, 1991), p. 51.

[37] D. E. Frost, A test of situational engineering for training leaders, *Psychological Reports* 59 (1986): 771–782.

[38] D. A. Lax and J. K. Sebenius, *The Manager as Negotiator* (New York: Free Press, 1986).

[39] D. H. Fenn, Jr., Finding where the power lies in government, *Harvard Business Review* 57 (1979): 144–153.

[40] D. G. Pruitt, Strategic choice in negotiation, *American Behavioral Scientist* 27 (November-December 1983): 167–194.

[41] Lax and Sebenius, *Manager as Negotiator.*

[42] R. Fisher and W. Ury, *Getting to Yes: Negotiating without Giving In* (Boston: Houghton Mifflin, 1981) was an early call for this approach.

[43] M. A. Neale and M. H. Bazerman, *Cognition and Rationality in Negotiation* (New York: Free Press, 1991).

[44] J. S. Carroll and M. H. Bazerman, Negotiator cognitions: A descriptive approach to negotiators' understanding of their opponents, *Organizational Behavior and Human Decision Processes* 41 (1988): 352–370.

[45] Lax and Sebenius, *Manager as Negotiator.*

[46] *Ibid.*

[47] Neale and Bazerman, *Cognition and Rationality.*

[48] R. Fisher and S. Brown, *Getting Together* (Boston: Houghton-Mifflin, 1988).

[49] G. T. Savage, J. D. Blair, and R. L. Sorenson, Consider both relationships and substance when negotiating strategically, *Academy of Management Executive* 3(1) (1989): 37–48.

[50] *Ibid.*

[51] J. Nierenberg and I. S. Ross, *Women and the Art of Negotiating* (New York: Simon and Schuster, 1985).

[52] Lax and Sebenius, *Manager as Negotiator.*

[53] J. L. Graham, The influence of culture on the process of business negotiations, *Journal of International Business Studies* 16(1) (Spring 1985): 81–96.

[54] J. A. Reeder, When West meets East: Cultural aspects of doing business in Asia, *Business Horizons* 30 (1) (1987): 263–275.

[55] Adler, *International Dimensions.*

[56] E. S. Glenn, D. Witmeyer, and K. A. Stevenson, Cultural styles of persuasion, *International Journal of Intercultural Relations,* vol. 1 (New York: Pergamon, 1984).

[57] *Ibid.*

[58] M. Kublin, The Japanese negotiating style: Cultural and historical roots, *Industrial Management* 29 (May-June 1987): 18–23.

[59] O. Shenkar and S. Ronen, The cultural context of negotiations: The implications of Chinese interpersonal norms, *Journal of Applied Behavioral Science* 23 (1987): 263–275.

[60] Adler, *International Dimensions.*

[61] Graham, Influence of culture.

[62] Shenkar and Ronen, Cultural context.

[63] Adler, *International Dimensions.*

[64] P. R. Harris and R. T. Moran, *Managing Cultural Differences,* 3rd ed. (Houston: Gulf, 1991).

[65] B. Keys and T. Case, How to become an influential manager, *Academy of Management Executive* 4(4) (1990): 38–51.

RECOMMENDED READINGS

Bazerman, M. H., and Neale, M. A. *Negotiating Rationally.* New York: Free Press, 1992.

Goldman, A. L. *Settling for More: Mastering Negotiating Strategies and Techniques.* Washington, D.C.: Bureau of National Affairs, 1991.

Gray, B. *Collaborating: Finding Common Ground for Multiparty Problems.* San Francisco: Jossey-Bass, 1989.

Hendon, D. W., and Hendon, R. A. *World Class Negotiating: Dealmaking in the Global Marketplace.* New York: Wiley, 1990.

Srivastva, S., and Associates. *Executive Power.* San Francisco: Jossey-Bass, 1986.

Ury, W. *Getting Past No: Negotiating with Difficult People.* New York: Bantam, 1991.

Chapter Outline

Delineating Conflict and Intergroup Behavior

Learning Objectives

After completing the reading and activities in Chapter 10, students will be able to

1. Discuss the nature of conflict in multinational organizations.

2. Predict the outcomes of conflict in an organization.

3. Diagnose the level and stage of conflict in an organization.

4. Describe four types of interdependent groups and their behavioral and attitudinal consequences.

5. Diagnose examples of perceptual differences among groups and their influence on intergroup relations.

6. Show how the nature of task relations can create conflict.

7. Comment about the way power differences influence intergroup relations.

8. Describe a range of strategies for dealing with conflict and intergroup interactions between groups.

9. Offer a protocol for managing relations between culturally diverse groups.

Boeing Knocks Down the Wall between the Dreamers and the Doers

"Have you hugged an engineer today?" That's the question on Garnet W. Hizzey's door at Boeing Co.'s 777 airplane operation in Renton, Wash. Since Hizzey is the plane's production-engineering manager, that might sound like a forlorn plaint. Actually, it's more a vivid reminder that sweeping changes are afoot.

In big companies, at least, design engineers and manufacturing types hardly ever mix. And until now, Boeing was like most other companies, sorting the dreamers into one fiefdom and the doers into another, with an invisible barrier between. Relations between the two focused on griping about "the other side of the wall"— usually when designers cooked up something that manufacturing considered too expensive or hard to make. With the 777, though, "we won't have the luxury of whining," says Hizzey. His job is to make the widebody transport, which is scheduled to take its maiden flight in mid-1994, easier and cheaper to manufacture than its predecessors. To do that, his 400 engineers are working side by side with designers, an approached called concurrent engineering (CE).

Costly Changes   Hizzey and his crew are at the core of a massive makeover of the way companies develop products. Until recently, designers had a pretty free hand. They would toss the design over the wall to production, then keep on making improvements. Each change, no matter how trivial, typically cost upwards of $10,000. Yet it hasn't been unusual for a complex product to be modified hundreds of times, sometimes even early in production. With the 777, Boeing wants to get the details right before production starts—and weed out all those avoidable costs.

That requires juggling just a few pieces, such as the 132,500 engineered parts in every plane, plus three million rivets, screws, and other fasteners. Boeing can do this because of a huge computer system that runs a European-developed solids-modeling program called Catia. It lets engineers iron out bugs on video screens, where fixes are cheap, instead of on expensive life-size models called mock-ups. The new process brings together representatives from design, production, and Boeing's outside suppliers, with regular input from airline customers, maintenance, and finance. "The magic is, you simulate [assembly] before you actually do it," says Alan R. Mulally, vice-president in charge of 777 design. Boeing hopes this will save as much as 20% of the 777's estimated $4 billion to $5 billion development cost. . . .

Easy Fix   Manufacturing engineers, who wouldn't normally be involved for another year, have already made their mark. For three decades, the skin on Boeing jets has had a bend in it where the top of the wing meets the side of the fuselage. This covers the inside rib of the wing, the structure that attaches the wing to the body. In the assembly process, putting just the right bend in several aluminum body panels that fit side by side has been "like an art form," says Hizzey—difficult, time-consuming, and costly. On the 777, his production engineers suggested redoing the wing-body joint to eliminate the bend. The designers agreed—and solved 30 years of manufacturing headaches by altering one line on a computer screen.

Each design-build team is assigned a part of the plane, such as tail-fin panels or passenger-entry doors. Major suppliers sit on these teams, too, and the biggest contractors—Mitsubishi, Fuji, and Kawasaki Heavy Industries—have real-time tie-ins with Boeing's computers. The teams meet at least every two weeks to review their work with other interested parties, who might range from purchasing officials to airline customers. "I try to think of these teams as little companies," says Stephen R. Johnson, who heads a group of 10 teams designing the wing's training edge. "They each have cost targets and weight targets—and board meetings."

Once the design and manufacturing engineers no longer felt obliged to posture, adds Johnson, they were able to empathize with each other. They even share offices. This has been somewhat traumatic for designers, who now get instant reactions from production engineers. Yet most have bought into the concept. "There were a few agnostics, but they are among the keenest advocates, now," says Hizzey.

Designers used to resent it even more when customers put in their two bits. Gordon A. McKinzie, United's 777 program managers, says he spotted rolling eyes when Boeing engineers learned that United and the No. 2 customer, All Nippon Airways Co., would be snooping around. But later, the designers agree with a United suggestion that the longest wing flap be divided in half to make repairs easier. And they're considering a United request to use more-durable stainless steel bolts and to make door latches so they won't catch fingers as they close. McKinzie says he's amazed at Boeing's candidness: "We feel very privileged to be part of their agony."

Boeing concedes that togetherness has its problems. Some teams lack needed resources or skills, some people were adamantly opposed at the start to sharing data, and some team leaders were inexperienced at running interdepartmental meetings. "Working together is not an esoteric warm and fuzzy thing," says Mulally. "It takes a lot of management and care and nurturing."

Because the process is being refined as it goes on, producing the first 777 will likely take six months more than the usual 48. But if CE brings the project in on schedule and on budget, Boeing will adopt it companywide. So next time, paperless development should be not only cheaper, but smoother and faster, too.[1]

●　●　●　●　●　●　●　●　●　●　●　●　●　●　●　●

The situation at Boeing describes an attempt to resolve a major problem in organizations: the potential conflict and problematic interactions of various groups in an organization. What type of interaction did production and designers traditionally have? What were its consequences? How do they interact now? How have the consequences changed? Do the two groups cooperate or compete? Do they communicate effectively? How would you describe their relationship?

In this chapter we answer these questions by first using a perspective of conflict. We begin by considering the nature of conflict in organizations: its levels, stages, and consequences. We then introduce special issues associated with intergroup relations. We describe the typical ways groups interact as well as the behavioral and attitudinal consequences of these interactions. We examine three influences on these interactions: perceptual differences, task issues, and power differences between groups. We conclude the chapter by examining prescriptions for dealing with conflict and improving the relations between groups.

THE NATURE
OF CONFLICT
IN MULTI-
NATIONAL
AND MULTI-
CULTURAL
ORGANIZATIONS

"Conflict is the result of incongruent or incompatible potential influence relationships" between and within individuals, groups, or organizations.[2] Conflict can be public (overt, visible, and authorized) or private (covert, hidden, and unauthorized), formal or informal, rational (premeditated or logical) or nonrational (spontaneous, impulsive, and emotional).[3] The likelihood of conflict increases when parties have the chance to interact, when the parties see their differences as incompatible, and when one or both parties see some utility in engaging in conflict (and potential gains outweigh potential losses) to resolve incompatibility.[4] Some individuals may be more likely to engage in conflict than others. In one study, for example, individuals with a Type A behavior pattern (see Chapter 3) had a higher frequency of conflict than those with a Type B pattern; women reported a lower frequency of conflict than men.[5]

Conflict most commonly results in four circumstances.[6] First, when mutually exclusive goals or values actually exist or are perceived to exist by the groups involved, conflict can occur. In the opening scenario, for example, production and design departments may not have compatible values. Production engineers may settle for a less-than-satisfactory product, whereas designers may continue to make improvements; these differences could result in disagreement and some degree of conflict. Second, behavior designed to defeat, reduce, or suppress the opponent may cause conflict. Union and management have historically experienced conflict for this reason. If design created unattainable demands, they would contribute to conflict. Third, groups that face each other with mutually opposing actions and counteractions cause conflict. For example, if engineers choose to ignore designers' specifications but the designers still promise a certain product to customers, then conflict will occur. Finally, if each group attempts to create a relatively favored position vis-à-vis the other, conflict may ensue. If both design and production attempt to show top management they are superior to the other group by demonstrating the other's ineptness, conflict occurs.

Conflict can easily occur in multinational or multicultural situations. Here basic differences in language, norms, personal styles, and other cultural characteristics hinder effective communication and set the stage for conflict. Cross-cultural sensitivity and understanding are key ingredients for minimizing dysfunctional conflict.

OUTCOMES OF
CONFLICT

Conflict can have functional or dysfunctional—positive or negative—outcomes. Whether conflict takes a constructive or destructive course is influenced by the sociocultural context in which the conflict occurs, because differences tend to exaggerate barriers and reduce the likelihood of conflict resolution.[7] The issues involved will also affect the likely outcomes. Whether the parties have cooperative, individualistic, or competitive orientations toward conflict will affect the outcomes as well. Obviously, those with cooperative attitudes are more likely to seek a functional outcome. Characteristics of the conflicting parties also affect conflict behavior. Finally, misjudgments and misperceptions contribute to dysfunctional conflict.

Effective managers learn how to create functional conflict and manage dysfunctional conflict. They develop and practice techniques for diagnosing the causes and nature of conflict and transforming it into a productive force in the organization. At Boeing, for example, top management instituted a closer interaction between the design and manufacturing engineers to improve performance.

*Functional
Consequences*

Some conflict is beneficial; it can encourage organizational innovation, creativity, and adaptation. Conflict also can result in more worker enthusiasm or better decisions. Can you think of a situation where such positive outcomes occurred? Perhaps during a disagreement with a friend or coworker you came to hold a different perspective on an issue or learned that your own perceptions or information had been inaccurate. Perhaps a group to which you belonged formed a new partnership as a way of handling competition for limited resources.

Improved ideas through the exchange and clarification of individual thoughts can also result. Sometimes conflict leads to a search for new approaches as a way of resolving disagreements or long-standing problems. It can also simply energize participants and result in greater productivity.

Dysfunctional Consequences

But conflict can also be viewed as dysfunctional for organizations. It can reduce productivity, decrease morale, cause overwhelming dissatisfaction, and increase tension and stress in the organization. It can arouse anxiety in individuals, increase the tension in an organizational system and its subsystems, lower satisfaction, and decrease productivity. In addition, some people, often the losers in a competitive situation, feel defeated and demeaned. As the distance between people increases, a climate of mistrust and suspicion may arise. Individuals or groups may focus more narrowly on their own interests, preventing the development of teamwork. Production and satisfaction may decline; turnover and absenteeism may increase. Diagnosing the location and type of conflict, as described in the next sections, is a first step in managing conflict so that it results in functional outcomes.

LEVELS OF CONFLICT

To manage conflict effectively, managers must pinpoint precisely where it exists so they can choose appropriate management strategies. We can describe six levels of conflict: (1) intrapersonal, (2) interpersonal, (3) intragroup, (4) intergroup, (5) intraorganizational, and (6) interorganizational, as shown in Figure 10–1.[8]

Intrapersonal Conflict

An individual may experience internal conflict in choosing between incompatible goals. Or, he or she may experience role conflict as described in Chapter 3. A designer at Boeing may want to contribute to on-time delivery and improved produc-

Figure 10–1 **Levels of Conflict**

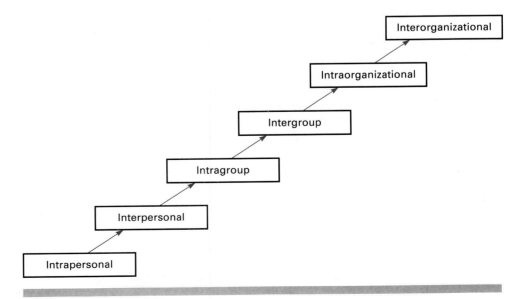

tivity, but he or she may be unwilling to sacrifice design quality. In making such choices, the design engineer may experience cognitive or affective conflict.

Cognitive conflict describes the intellectual discomfort created by incompatible goals. The design engineer may be forced to sacrifice the quality of a proposed change in an airplane to meet an imposed deadline. Such conflict may have productive consequences: The person involved may secure more and better information before acting. Alternatively, such conflict may paralyze the individual's ability to act.

Affective conflict occurs when *competing emotions* accompany the incompatible goals and result in increased stress, decreased productivity, or decreased satisfaction for the individual. The design engineer may experience both frustration and excitement in working with the manufacturing engineers.

Interpersonal Conflict   When two individuals disagree about issues, actions, or goals, and where joint outcomes become important, there is interpersonal conflict. A disagreement between a design engineer and a manufacturing engineer about the specifications for a new system may result in this level of conflict. Interpersonal conflict often arises from differences in individuals' perceptions, orientations, or status. It may motivate individuals to surface additional relevant issues, or it may prevent any further communication.

Intragroup Conflict   A group may also experience either substantive (similar to cognitive) or affective conflict. *Substantive* conflict is based on intellectual disagreement; for example, when various members of the production team draw different conclusions about the nature of design specifications, they may experience substantive conflict. Such conflict often results in better information exchange and decision making. *Affective* conflict is based on the emotional responses to a situation. For example, the design engineers may feel passionate (and even irrational) about the importance of certain specifications as opposed to others; the technical staff may experience different and conflicting emotions about the same specifications. Affective conflict may also result when interacting individuals have incompatible styles or personalities, as described in Chapter 3.

Intergroup Conflict   Intergroup conflict exists between or among groups, such as a marketing department and technical services. It also can exist between groups primarily responsible for planning versus those responsible for operations, such as between the design and manufacturing engineers at Boeing.

Union workers and their nonunion managers, or union leadership and top management, can also be viewed as separate but interacting groups, although some view union-management interactions as examples of interorganizational rather than intergroup conflict. Union and management groups may have different interests that affect their interactions. Workers join unions to obtain greater compensation, achieve more rights on the job, and meet social or self-esteem needs. The backdrop for their interaction in the United States is mandated by the formal labor contract, or the collective bargaining agreement; this specifies the rules of the workplace, amounts of compensation, and methods for settling disputes between labor and management. Representatives of union and management negotiate a contract acceptable to both sides. The ease or rancor involved in reaching and then implementing this agreement often determines whether labor-management relations are congenial or hostile. The existence of conflict between union and management varies in different countries: In Sweden and Germany little manifest conflict exists; in Italy and Canada, manifest conflict is more common.

Intraorganizational Conflict

Though in one sense it encompasses all of the previous levels, typically intraorganizational conflict is diagnosed when conflict characterizes overall organizational functioning. *Vertical conflict* is that between supervisor and subordinates. Managers and subordinates, for example, may disagree about the best ways to accomplish their tasks or the organizational goals; union representatives and plant managers may argue about work rules throughout the organization. *Horizontal conflict* exists between employees or departments at the same level. At Boeing, designers and production engineers have traditionally experienced conflict over the manufacturing, installation, and testing of airplane parts and systems. *Diagonal conflict* often occurs over the allocation of resources throughout the organization—to product development or product sales, for example—or over the involvement of staff people in line decisions. Finally, role conflict, as described in Chapter 3, can be pervasive in the organization. CEOs can ask the following diagnostic questions to determine whether organizational conflict poses a major problem:

1. Am I constantly being confronted with interdepartmental arguments that seem trivial and not really worthy of my time?
2. Is there considerable doubt about who would take over if I left?
3. Is there an undercurrent of hostility between departments?
4. Am I hearing many customer or employee complaints that seem to stem from our own internal communication problems?[9]

Such conflict throughout the organization can energize workers and inspire innovation; but uncontrolled and unmanaged it can also demoralize workers and cause performance to deteriorate.

Interorganizational Conflict

Conflict can also exist between organizations. The amount of conflict may depend on the extent to which the organizations create uncertain conditions for competitors, suppliers, or customers; attempt to access or control the same resources; encourage communication; attempt to balance power in the marketplace; and develop procedures for resolving existing conflict.[10] Recent attempts to manage such conflict and ensure that it has a positive impact on organizational performance have emphasized the formation of strategic alliances and partnerships. Identifying the level of conflict is a prerequisite to selecting appropriate strategies for managing it. Accurate diagnosis also involves specifying the stage of conflict, as described in the next section, since not all conflict is overt warfare.

STAGES OF CONFLICT

The nature of conflict changes over time. When a group cannot accomplish a goal or complete a task, the group's members experience frustration. Then those involved may perceive that conflict exists and formulate ideas about the conflict issue. They gather information and consider multiple points of view to gain a better understanding of the conflict issue. Those affected respond, resolving the conflict or igniting more conflict.[11] Diagnosing the nature of conflict is aided by considering it as a sequence of conflict episodes. Regardless of the level of conflict, a historical but still useful view of the progression of conflict suggests that each episode proceeds through one or more of five possible stages, as shown in Figure 10–2: (1) latent, (2) perceived, (3) felt, and (4) manifest conflict, and (5) conflict aftermath.[12] By specifying the stage of conflict a manager can determine its intensity and select the best strategies for managing it. In the next sections we examine these stages in turn.

Figure 10–2 **Stages of Conflict**

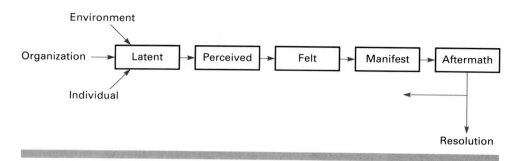

Latent Conflict   Conflict begins when the conditions for conflict exist. Individuals or groups may have power differences, compete for scarce resources, strive for autonomy, have different goals, or experience diverse role pressures. These differences provide the foundation for disagreement and ultimately conflict. Departments such as marketing and technical services frequently experience latent conflict. Inherent differences in perceptions and attitudes contribute to their relationship. Can you think of other situations where latent conflict exists—or where you have experienced latent conflict?

Perceived Conflict   In the next stage individuals or group members know that conflict exists. They recognize differences of opinion, incompatible goals or values, efforts to demean the other party, or the implementation of opposing actions. At Boeing, if a designer misunderstands or disagrees with a production engineer's requirements, perceived conflict may exist.

Felt Conflict   When one or more parties feels tense or anxious as a result of such disagreements or misunderstandings, conflict has moved beyond the perceived to the felt stage. Typically there is a time lag between intellectually perceiving that conflict exists and then feeling it "in the pit of your stomach." Here the conflict becomes personalized to the individuals or groups involved. Have you experienced felt conflict? Do you think any of the designers experiences felt conflict?

Manifest Conflict   Observable behavior designed to frustrate another's attempts to pursue his or her goals is the most overt form of conflict. Both open aggression and withdrawal of support illustrate manifest conflict. At this stage conflict must be used constructively or resolved for effective organizational performance to occur. If a production engineer confronts a designer about his frustration and dissatisfaction with their interactions, manifest conflict may ensue. Demonstrated anger and refusal to support the designer's requirements would further reflect this stage of conflict; so would a high level of creative tension or more positive vocalizations.

Conflict Aftermath   The conflict episode ends with its aftermath, after the conflict has been managed and the resulting energy has been heightened, resolved, or suppressed. The episode results in a new reality, as shown in Figure 10–3. Unresolved conflict, which exists everywhere, simply sows the seeds for manifest conflict later. The process continues and is a normal part of organizational life. The fact that organizations are composed of large numbers of interacting individuals and interacting groups, as described in the next section, increases the likelihood of conflict.

Figure 10–3 Instituting the New Reality

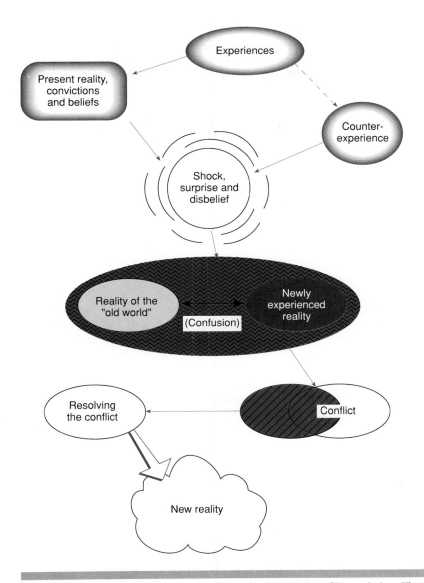

SOURCE: From M. Egberts and J. Van der Vurst, Interpersonal conflict resolution: The unconscious ally, *Leadership and Organization Development Journal (LODJ)* 7(5) (1986): iii. Reprinted with permission of MCB University Press Limited.

INTERACTING GROUPS

No two groups in an organization can exist truly independently. Rather, one group may depend on another for raw materials, other resources, information, or assistance in performing a task. We can describe this interdependence in transactional terms, referring to the exchange of resources, such as budgeted funds, support services, products, and information, between two work units.[13] Work units are perceived as increasingly interdependent in several circumstances. As more resources are exchanged in a given amount of time or more exchanges occur in a given amount of time, interdependence increases. As a greater variety of resources is exchanged, interdependence increases. The extent to which the resource flows both ways between the units will also increase interdependence.

Managers should assess the nature and extent of interdependence in an organization so they understand the potential for conflict and the impact on action one part of the organization will have on another part. Assessment occurs through interviewing and observing key organizational members, such as top and middle managers. Data about the nature of the work flow, the people with whom group and organizational members interact most frequently, and the types of decisions made by various individuals or groups illuminate the nature of interdependence experienced by various groups in the organization.

Interdependence occurs in one of four ways: pooled, sequential, reciprocal, and team, as shown in Figure 10–4.[14] The letters A through D in the figure refer to four separate groups; the arrows show whether the groups interact directly and the direction of the interaction. In pooled interdependence, for example, groups A, B, C, and D have no direct interactions; in team interdependence groups all interact in both directions with every other group. Although any group may demonstrate any of these types of interdependence at specific times, one type will predominate in a group's relationship with other groups. In the next sections we examine each of these types.

Pooled
Interdependence

Groups that rely on each other only because they belong to the same parent organization show *pooled* interdependence. Two restaurants in a fast-food chain show pooled interdependence because their reputations depend on their identification with the parent organization. Two subsidiaries in a conglomerate, such as two department stores in a national chain, may show pooled interdependence because they share a common advertising agency or benefit from mass buying power. The maintenance workers and the cafeteria workers in a single organization are two departments that,

Figure 10–4   **Types of Interdependence**

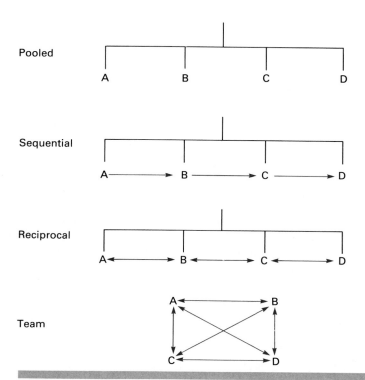

for the most part, demonstrate pooled interdependence. Groups with pooled interdependence may obtain their reputation, staff resources, financing, or other services from corporate headquarters. Basically, however, they operate as separate groups or organizations.

Because these groups have limited interactions, pooled interdependence has few potentially dysfunctional consequences for groups until their representatives need to work together. Such groups may be required to compete for resources, but such interactions are limited. The designers and manufacturing engineers demonstrate more than pooled interdependence. They share more than common resources, reputation, or services.

Sequential Interdependence

Sequential interdependence occurs when one group's operations precede and act as prerequisites for the second group's. In a manufacturing plant, the assembly group and the packing group exhibit sequential interdependence. In the post office, the postal workers at the central post office demonstrate sequential interdependence with the letter carriers in the local post offices; the postal workers in the central office must sort the mail before the local letter carriers can sort and deliver it. In a hospital, the nurses have sequential interdependence with the purchasing department; the purchasing department buys supplies that the nurses then use. But the nurses have more than sequential interdependence with the physicians because the interaction does not stop when nurses receive directions from physicians; they also provide input to the physician's decisions about patient care.

The second group in the sequence may experience difficulty in accomplishing its tasks if its members do not interact effectively with its predecessor. If the first group does not complete its job on time, for example, the performance of the second group is jeopardized. As a result, the members of the second group may resent the first group and limit their interactions with it. Where collaborative relations do not exist between these groups, even sabotage may occur at the extreme. At Boeing, the designers and manufacturing engineers originally had sequential interdependence: The designers offered their prototypes, which the manufacturing engineers then revised. The new relationship, however, changes the nature of the interdependence between designers and manufacturing engineers.

Reciprocal Interdependence

At Boeing, the designers and production engineers now demonstrate reciprocal interdependence; the two groups must repeatedly interact to perform their jobs effectively. Two groups whose operations precede and act as prerequisites to the other's have reciprocal interdependence. Sales and support staff typically have this type of interdependence. A salesperson selling computer hardware relies on technical support staff to handle installation problems; the support staff requires the sales staff's input in identifying customer problems.

As the extent of group interdependence increases, the potential for conflict and dysfunctional behavior increases correspondingly. Reciprocal interdependence easily results in dysfunctional behaviors and attitudes. Because each group relies on the other to perform its own job effectively, any problems between them may result in reduced productivity or decreased worker satisfaction. Conflict is common when there is reciprocal interdependence.

Team Interdependence

Where multiple groups interact, reciprocal interdependences may be multiplied. In such cases we can characterize the interdependence as parallel to the completely connected communication network (described in Chapter 7).[15] In this case, each group's operations precede and act as prerequisites for every other group's operations when their functioning is considered over time. For example, the various departments supervised by a vice president of marketing—sales, support, advertising, and research—may exhibit this type of interdependence. Or we might characterize the overall interdependence of nurses, physicians, and hospital administration in this way. Groups with team interdependence have the greatest potential for conflict and the highest requirements for effective communication. Table 10–1 summarizes the types of interdependence and their potential for conflict.

Intergroup relations also have significant consequences for individual behavior. The interplay of group interactions affects the way a person constructs his or her reality. For example, the relative position of an individual as upper, middle, or lower in the organizational structures of which he or she is a part will determine that person's perception of events.[16] Intergroup issues, as described in the next section, are part of the relationship between subgroups within a group and between groups.

PERCEPTUAL DIFFERENCES AMONG GROUPS

We noted earlier in this book that the perception of events and the attributions of their causes are subjective (see Chapter 2). Perceptual differences, as shown in Figure 10–5, influence group and intergroup interactions. A particular role an individual holds or a group to which he or she belongs influences these perceptions, primarily because of the strong group identity that occurs for most members (see Chapter 5). Differences in personal concerns also may influence the way one group views another's actions. The designers' and production engineers' perceptions of the tasks and collaboration needed to produce the Boeing 777 may differ; each group's perceptions of its own and the other's expertise and time constraints may differ too. Perceptual differences between the groups can create role conflict, as discussed in Chapter 3.

Orientations

All groups evaluate events in terms of their own orientations. Their goal, time, and social orientations may differ. Managers should understand the differences in groups' orientation to help them predict and handle issues that might arise in the groups' interactions.

Goal Orientation Differences in personal concerns and orientations often accompany differences in goals. Marketing departments typically concern themselves with the attractiveness of a product to consumers. Research and development groups focus on the product's innovative characteristics and its value to the advancement of

Table 10–1 **Types of Interdependence and Their Potential for Conflict**

Type of Interdependence	Definition	Potential for Conflict
Pooled	Two groups that have the same parent organization	Low
Sequential	Two groups where one group's operations precede and act as prerequisites for the second group's	Moderate
Reciprocal	Two groups whose operations precede and act as prerequisites to the other's	High
Team	Multiple groups, all of whose operations precede and act as prerequisites to the others'	High

Figure 10–5 **Nature of Perceptual Differences**

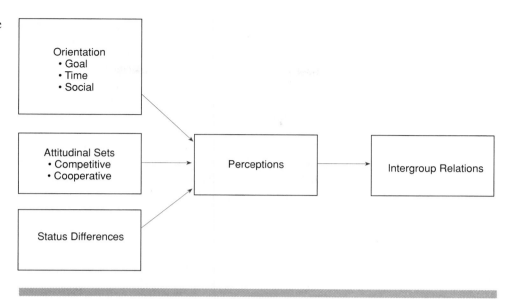

scientific knowledge. Production departments emphasize a product's ease of production and susceptibility to cost controls. How might goal differences between the designers and production engineers at Boeing create perceptual differences? These groups may differ in their attitudes toward introducing state-of-the-art products within a given time and cost constraint. Or they may differ in the priorities they attach to specific product features.

Time Orientation Groups also differ in the extent to which they focus on events now and in the future. A research and development department, for example, has a long-term orientation because new product formulation takes long periods of time. In contrast, a production department has a short-term orientation because its goals emphasize meeting immediate inventory needs. The marketing department may reflect a short-term orientation in its concern for selling the product now, whereas the technical services staff may have a different time orientation in its concern for keeping the product functional over the medium or long term.

Social Orientation The social or extra-work orientations of the groups might also differ. Consider a group of unionized nurses and the nonunionized physicians. The nurses would be more involved with union activities and would probably choose their friends from other nurses or union members. The physicians would be oriented toward their professional group—other physicians. What are the implications of these different orientations? Even when groups such as nurses and other health care professionals are not unionized, their professional allegiances and consequently social interactions probably differ. Or, they may differ in their stages of personal or career development (see Chapter 3) and their professional training: Their social orientations and consequently their perceptions might differ. Can you think of a scenario where the groups might experience problems because of such social differences?

Attitudinal Sets Attitudinal sets held by different groups also contribute to perceptual differences evidenced by interacting groups. Diagnosing the differences in attitudinal sets among groups can help managers and other group members plan for possible conflicts. One such set reflects the extent to which a group has a competitive or cooperative attitude.[17] A group with a competitive attitude toward other groups may encourage its members to have negative attitudes toward the task, distrust other group members, dislike other group members, and act without considering others. A group with a cooperative attitude toward other groups, in contrast, may encourage trust, mutual influence, coordination of effort, and acceptance of differences within the group itself and between its members and the other group's members.

A second attitudinal set is the extent to which a group (because of the individuals in it) has a *cosmopolitan* versus *local* orientation. Cosmopolitans are "those low on loyalty to the employing organization, high on commitment to specialized role skills, and likely to use an outer (professional) reference group orientation"; locals are "those high on loyalty to the employing organization, low on commitment to specialized role skills, and likely to use an inner (organizational) reference group orientation."[18] We might hypothesize, for example, that the production engineers have a local orientation, whereas the designers have a cosmopolitan one. If this theory is true, their perceptions would differ, and overcoming such differences would be a major challenge in building them into a strong team.

Status Differences   Individuals' perceptions frequently influence their view of their own roles and status—rank and standing relative to others—in an organization.[19] Often these perceptions lack clarity and validity. A group of nurses may perceive they have relatively low status compared to a group of physicians and hence make few demands on the physicians, allowing them to direct and organize the nursing staff's work. For effective performance, however, each interacting group must understand clearly what the organization and other groups expect of it. Each group must also assess whether these expectations fit with its own perceptions of its members' jobs and its members' positions in the organization's hierarchy.

Differences in education, experience, or background may influence perceptions of status. Such differences may be reinforced by the rewards assigned in the organization. Real or perceived differences about the relative status of two groups influences their interactions. Differences in identity due to race, gender, ethnicity, and religion unfortunately also affect perceptions of status. In managing a multicultural work force, managers must ensure that differences are confronted and that distinctions based on these factors do not play a dysfunctional role in intergroup interactions.

THE NATURE OF TASK RELATIONS   The activities or processes that interdependent groups perform and the way these activities interrelate play a significant role in intergroup relations. Both the sequencing of task activities and the clarity and certainty of the tasks themselves have consequences for intergroup relations.

Task Interaction   Tasks performed by group members can be independent, dependent, or interdependent of tasks performed by members of the same or different groups, as shown in Figure 10–6. Often there is a correlation between the nature of task interactions and the relationships between interdependent groups.

Where one group's task can be done without any relationship to another group's, the task relations are *independent*. A machine operator and an accountant can each perform his or her task without any assistance from the other. Where one group's task follows another group's task that is a prerequisite to it, the second group has a task that is *dependent* on the first group's. Company recruiters depend on line managers to identify the types of personnel required. Where each group's task follows

Figure 10–6 **Nature of Task Interdependence**

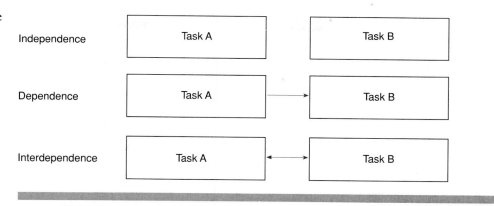

the other's and is prerequisite to it at some time, their tasks are *interdependent*. The copy editor of a publishing firm works on a manuscript provided by an author, who then checks the changes made by the editor.

The nature of task relations generally resembles the nature of interdependence among groups described earlier. Groups showing pooled interdependence most often have independent task relations; groups showing sequential interdependence most often have dependent task relations; groups showing reciprocal or team interdependence most frequently have interdependent task relations.

Groups with independent tasks have much less potential for problematic relations with other groups than those with dependent or interdependent task relations because the independent task groups have less interaction. Interdependent tasks most frequently contribute to problematic relations between interacting groups.

Task Ambiguity The ambiguity or certainty of the task relationships describes whether the interacting groups have clear, predetermined processes of activity. Ambiguity in the task often contributes to difficulty in the groups' interactions. Often a particular group does not understand its responsibilities and the requirements of its task. This situation also results in more task uncertainty. The design engineers may not understand their responsibilities vis-à-vis the production engineers. If this is the case, conflict may arise and contribute to dysfunctional interactions between these two groups. At Boeing, however, they seem to understand their responsibilities, hence minimizing potential and actual conflict.

POWER DIFFERENCES Interacting groups often experience performance difficulties when they differ in the power, or amount of influence and control over others, they have. We have discussed power in Chapter 9, but this section highlights three ways in which power differences affect intergroup relations.

Perceptions of Substitutability If the activities of a group are viewed as replaceable, or if another group can perform the same work, the group is considered substitutable. If a manufacturing group, for example, is perceived to be able to perform development activities, then manufacturing considers the research and development group substitutable, diminishing its power. The more a group performs unsubstitutable tasks, the more power it possesses.

At Boeing, which group might be perceived as more substitutable relative to the other—the designers or the production engineers? Of course, there is no objective answer based on the information provided. But the perceptions of substitutability will influence the relations between these two groups.

Ability to Cope with Uncertainty

How well a group can deal with and compensate for a rapidly changing environment also influences its power.[20] Typically, engineers can cope with uncertainty better than technicians because of their broader professional training and more diverse experiences; hence, they have greater power from this source. In some organizations the marketing department can cope with uncertainty better than production because marketing employees can more easily make adjustments for the client; in other organizations the reverse is true. Any difference would contribute to power differences between the two groups and potentially to dysfunctional intergroup relations.

Control of and Access to Resources

The amount of money, people, and time a group controls also influences its power. The greater the amount of resources it controls, the more power the group has. Managers who control budgets often have greater power than those who do not. Further, when two groups must divide resources, disagreements often arise about their optimal allocation, creating conflict between them. In hospitals, physicians typically have greater access to resources and more influence over their allocation than do nurses; this disparity may further contribute to differences in power between the two groups.

STRATEGIES FOR MANAGING CONFLICT AND INTERGROUP RELATIONS

When diagnosis indicates that a manager must deal with conflict or intergroup relations, he or she may want to help others recognize the nature of the interdependences, agree to appropriate degrees and mechanisms of control and coordination, and then implement strategies for collaboration.[21] In this section we look at conflict-handling behaviors and activities, conflict-resolution processes, and structural mechanisms for managing conflict. Reading 10–1, "Managing Conflict among Groups," extends this discussion of conflict management.

The ease of resolving conflict can vary greatly.[22] For example, conflict that is a matter of principle, has large stakes, and involves a single transaction tends to be more difficult to manage than conflict around divisible issues where neither side must completely give in to the other, has small stakes, and involves a long-term relationship. Similarly, if one party is viewed as gaining at the expense of the other, is incohesive, has weak leadership, feels harmed, and has no neutral third party available as an intermediary, conflict is difficult to manage productively or resolve.

Intervention Styles

Individuals can use at least five behaviors for dealing with conflict: avoidance, accommodation, compromise, forcing, and collaborating.[23] As shown in Figure 10–7, these differ in the extent to which they satisfy a party's own concerns and the other party's concerns. For example, a person or group that uses an *avoiding* mode is unassertive in satisfying its own concerns and uncooperative in satisfying others' concerns. In contrast, a person or group that uses a *collaborating* mode is assertive and cooperative.

Each style is appropriate to different situations that individuals or groups face in organizations. Table 10–2 summarizes the use of these five modes by a group of chief executives. The behavior an individual or group chooses depends on that party's experiences in dealing with conflict, his or her own personal dispositions in interpersonal relations, and the specific elements of a particular conflict episode.

Avoidance Individuals or groups may withdraw from the conflict situation. They act to satisfy neither their own nor the other party's concerns. Avoidance works best

Figure 10–7 **Model of Conflict-Handling Modes**

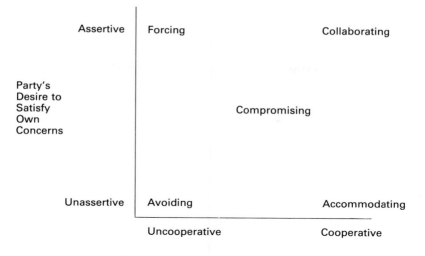

SOURCE: Adapted from K. W. Thomas, Conflict and conflict management. In M. D. Dunnette, ed., *Handbook of Industrial and Organizational Psychology* (New York: Rand McNally, 1976). Used by permission of Houghton Mifflin Company.

when individuals or groups face trivial or tangential issues, when they have little chance of satisfying their personal concerns, when conflict resolution will likely result in significant disruption, or when others can resolve conflict more effectively.

Accommodation Individuals or groups who use accommodation demonstrate a willingness to cooperate in satisfying others' concerns, while at the same time acting unassertively in meeting their own. Accommodating individuals often smooth over conflict. This mode builds social credits for later issues, results in harmony and stability, and satisfies others.

Compromise The compromise mode represents an intermediate behavior on both the assertiveness and cooperation dimensions. It can include sharing of positions, but not moving to the extremes of assertiveness or cooperation. Hence, it often does not maximize satisfaction of both parties. In one study, compromisers had a different communication style from avoiders; they were more likely to focus on communicating information about the job product or plan than messages about rules, regulations, or policies.[24] This style works well when goals are important but not sufficiently important for the individual or group to be more assertive, when the two parties have equal power, or when significant time pressure exists.

Forcing Using the forcing mode, a party tries to satisfy its own concerns while showing an unwillingness to satisfy the other's concerns to even a minimal degree. This strategy works well in emergencies, on issues calling for unpopular actions, and in cases where one party is correct in its position or where one party has much greater power.

Collaborating The collaboration mode emphasizes problem solving with a goal of maximizing satisfaction for both parties. It means seeing conflict as natural, showing

Table 10–2 **Uses of the Five Conflict Modes, as Reported by a Group of Chief Executives**

Conflict-Handling Modes	Appropriate Situations
Competing	1. When quick, decisive action is vital—e.g., emergencies.
	2. On important issues where unpopular actions need implementing—e.g., cost cutting, enforcing unpopular rules, discipline.
	3. On issues vital to company welfare when you know you're right.
	4. Against people who take advantage of noncompetitive behavior.
Collaborating	1. To find an integrative solution when both sets of concerns are too important to be compromised.
	2. When your objective is to learn.
	3. To merge insights from people with different perspectives.
	4. To gain commitment by incorporating concerns into a consensus.
	5. To work through feelings which have interfered with a relationship.
Compromising	1. When goals are important, but not worth the effort or potential disruption of more assertive modes.
	2. When opponents with equal power are committed to mutually exclusive goals.
	3. To achieve temporary settlements to complex issues.
	4. To arrive at expedient solutions under time pressure.
	5. As a backup when collaboration or competition is unsuccessful.
Avoiding	1. When an issue is trivial, or more important issues are pressing.
	2. When you perceive no chance of satisfying your concerns.
	3. When potential disruption outweighs the benefits of resolution.
	4. To let people cool down and regain perspective.
	5. When gathering information supersedes immediate decision.
	6. When others can resolve the conflict more effectively.
	7. When issues seem tangential or symptomatic of other issues.
Accommodating	1. When you find you are wrong—to allow a better position to be heard, to learn, and to show your reasonableness.
	2. When issues are more important to others than yourself—to satisfy others and maintain cooperation.
	3. To build social credits for later issues.
	4. To minimize loss when you are outmatched and losing.
	5. When harmony and stability are especially important.
	6. To allow subordinates to develop by learning from mistakes.

SOURCE: Kenneth W. Thomas, Toward multi-dimensional values in teaching: The example of conflict behaviors, *Academy of Management Review,* 1977, 2, Table 1, p. 487. Reprinted by permission.

trust and honesty toward others, and encouraging the airing of every person's attitudes and feelings. Each party exerts both assertive and cooperative behavior. Parties can use it when their objectives are to learn, to use information from diverse sources, and to find an integrative solution. If the designers and production engineers establish a mutually satisfactory way of working together, they are taking a collaborative or problem-solving approach (see Chapter 9 for further discussion).

Conflict-Handling Certain types of conflict, such as disagreements about goals or values, may call for
Activities the parties to *control the differences* by acknowledging their existence and then acting

without attempting to resolve them. Such differences may be so ingrained in the conflicting parties that effectively managing those involved may preclude resolution of the differences within any reasonable period of time or without changing underlying value systems.

Occasionally, in small group situations, individuals escalate the conflict as a way of ultimately resolving it.[25] An outsider purposely seeks to increase the frustration of the parties as a way of redirecting the conflict's course, increasing participants' understanding of the situation, or leading to a search for adequate behaviors. Three specific intervention techniques typify the strategies that focus on improving the process of interactions between two or more groups: confrontation meeting, organizational mirror, and other third-party interventions.

Confrontation Meeting A confrontation meeting addresses problems experienced by interacting groups that result in dysfunctional organizational performance. It is a one-day meeting where two interacting groups share the problems they face and offer solutions for resolving them.

The one-day meeting occurs as shown in Figure 10–8.[26] First, a top manager introduces the issues and goals that are the focus of discussion during the day and on which the two groups experience problems; the manager may have identified these issues on the basis of prior discussions with group members. Then, in small subgroups from the various interacting groups, the participants gather more detailed information about the problems they face. Next, representatives from each subgroup report on their list of items to the entire group. In natural work groups, participants set priorities for the problems and determine early action steps; they set a concrete

Figure 10–8 **Steps in Confrontation Meeting**

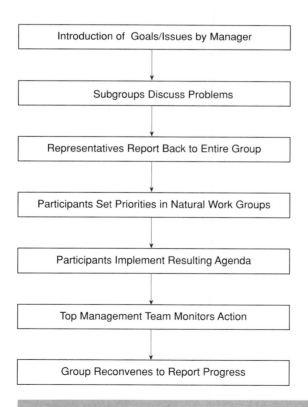

Introduction of Goals/Issues by Manager

Subgroups Discuss Problems

Representatives Report Back to Entire Group

Participants Set Priorities in Natural Work Groups

Participants Implement Resulting Agenda

Top Management Team Monitors Action

Group Reconvenes to Report Progress

agenda about the steps they will take to resolve their problems. Implementation of the plan follows. A top management team continues to meet to plan and monitor follow-up action. Four to six weeks later the group reconvenes to report its progress. The confrontation meeting is most effective in dealing with intergroup problems when the following conditions exist: There is a need for the total management group to examine its own workings; very limited time is available for the activity; top management wishes to improve the conditions quickly; there is enough cohesion in the top team to ensure follow-up; there is real commitment to resolving the issues on the part of top management; and the organization is experiencing or has recently experienced some major change.

Organizational Mirror The organizational mirror is a set of activities that structures the provision of feedback from representatives of various organization groups to a host group about the way the host group is perceived.[27] A consultant begins by conducting preliminary interviews with all members of the groups. Then the consultant reports data from these interviews to the invited and host groups. The groups then discuss the data presented. Small, heterogeneous groups with representatives from the diverse groups meet, discuss the data further (if appropriate), and develop action plans for the problems identified. Implementation of the action plans should follow. Like the confrontation meeting, the organizational mirror requires top management commitment and follow-up for effective action to result.

Third-Party Interventions Third parties frequently intervene to resolve intergroup conflict that occurs in labor-management interactions. As described in the next section, the third party can act as a mediator, arbitrator, or fact finder, as well as provide confrontational or procedural consultation.[28] A third party may escalate the conflict as a way of increasing creativity or surfacing the issues to ultimately defuse the conflict.[29] The third party may stimulate the conflict by changing its antecedent conditions, such as leadership style or organizational structure. He or she may extend the conflict issues, by stressing differences or introducing new facets of existing issues. Adding to the parties involved, possibly resulting in coalition formation, can also augment the conflict. Third parties can also stimulate escalative behaviors, such as by teaching the parties to fight fair or showing them effective ways to prove their point. Finally, third parties can identify consequences that encourage escalation, such as convincing one party it will lose face if it does not fight for its beliefs. Because of potential side effects and lack of qualified change agents, few individuals and groups request escalative interventions.

The third party can also assume one of two roles: interpersonal facilitator or interface conflict solver.[30] As an *interpersonal facilitator,* the third party assumes an active role of identifying areas of agreement and disagreement between the parties. Contact between parties occurs primarily through the facilitator, who acts as a go-between, a message carrier, a spokesperson for one or both groups, or a solution proposer. The facilitator deals with the leaders or key members of disputing parties who meet to exchange positions and formulate proposals or counterproposals. This model works best when two people are involved and personal chemistry prevents quality discussion.

As an *interface conflict solver,* the third party leads key members of opposing groups through a series of meetings and activities that identify and resolve differences. He or she sets expectations, establishes group rules, determines the sequence of speaking, ensures candor, curbs the expression of hostility, avoids evaluations, introduces procedures to reduce disagreements, ensures understanding of positions or statements, and checks implementation of agreed-upon changes. Each group first meets separately to prepare a description of the ideal relationship between the groups and then selects a spokesperson who presents the conclusions at a general meeting of the groups. After the large group meeting, each participant identifies similarities and differences in the two descriptions to develop an integrated model that can direct the functioning of both groups. Next, each group characterizes the actual conditions at that time. The groups then jointly formulate a statement of problems. Together they propose steps for improving the situation. This approach works best when support of group members is key to change, when leaders do not know the entire problem, or when the problem is inherent to the culture of the groups involved.

Third parties can also assume peacemaking roles, and women may be particularly skilled and comfortable in performing such roles.[31] These include "(a) providing *support* by giving people the opportunity to tell their story, (b) *reframing* people's understandings of a situation by providing alternative explanations and choices, (c) *translating* people's perceptions of each other either directly through message carrying or indirectly through responding, and (d) *orchestrating* occasions for private conflicts to be made public."[32]

Conflict-Resolution Processes — Three types of formal processes can address conflicts in organizations and attempt to resolve them: grievance procedures, mediation and arbitration, and negotiation.[33] This "disputing perspective shifts the focus of inquiring from *structures* and formal *rules* to the process of conflict expression and action."[34]

Grievance Procedures Grievance procedures provide a formal process by which workers complain to management if they feel they have not been treated properly or if their rights have been violated. A formal grievance procedure provides a mechanism for responding to workers complaints or clarifying a worker's and employer's rights and obligations; formally brings the matter to the attention of the proper officials (union and management); defines the nature of the complaint; and provides a structure for meetings between the parties involved.[35] Workers typically file grievances to protest unfair treatment or contractual violations, draw attention to a problem in the plant, such as a safety hazard, or exercise power as a test of worker prerogatives.

In a unionized situation, the aggrieved employee presents the complaint orally to the first-line supervisor and union steward. Unresolved grievances then can proceed through the following steps until they are satisfactorily resolved. The supervisor and steward forward the grievance in writing to the plant manager and union grievance committee or business agent. The plant manager and union representative refer the grievance higher in their respective hierarchies, to the company's president, vice president of labor relations, or legal counsel, and to the president of the local union. Management and union submit the grievance to arbitration. The arbitrator, as described in the next section, hears the case and renders a decision.

In a nonunionized situation, the grievance procedure may be less formal. Alternatively, the organization may appoint an ombudsperson who facilitates the grievance resolution process or represents the worker in dealing with management.

Mediation and Arbitration Mediation and arbitration are third-party interventions that use trained individuals to help resolve conflict in organizations. In mediation a neutral party tries to help disputing parties reach a settlement of the issues that divide them. The mediator focuses on bringing the parties to agreement by making procedural suggestions, keeping channels of communication between the parties open, helping establish priorities, and offering creative solutions. A good mediator tries to determine the true intentions of each party and communicate them to the other.

An arbitrator, in contrast to a mediator, acts as a judge in a dispute. Arbitration is a quasi-legal proceeding that resembles a formal judicial procedure but does not take place in a court of law. In arbitration each party presents its position on disputed matters to the arbitrator, who then judges the situation and decides on the disposition of each issue. For example, if a worker files a grievance against his or her employer claiming to have been unfairly discharged, an arbitrator will listen to evidence about the matter from both sides and reach a judgment about the fairness and appropriateness of the discharge.

Negotiation   We examined the negotiation process in detail in Chapter 9. Recall that we characterized the major processes as distributive bargaining and integrative bargaining and proposed a process for effective negotiation in organizations.

Structural Mechanisms   Redesigning formal reporting relationships, adding special managerial roles, or using standard operating procedures more extensively and effectively can improve the management of conflict and intergroup relations. Altering the nature of task relations between two groups may also improve intergroup behavior or reduce conflict. We examine such job redesign strategies in great detail in Chapter 13. In concert with job redesign, the organization must assign rewards (see Chapter 4) that encourage collaborative and functional interdependences and interactions between groups.

Hierarchy   A common superior is assigned to coordinate the work of two interacting groups. This position acts as a conduit for information, often setting priorities for interacting groups or individuals and resolving disputes between them. At Boeing, for example, a senior vice president of operations who supervises both engineers and manufacturing staff might act as a common superior. This approach works best when interacting groups are reasonably close in function or work on similar projects.

Plans and Goals   Plans and goals direct the activities of interacting groups while minimizing their interaction. When plans are used, even the integration of groups geographically distant can be effective. The use of common, or superordinate, goals can have an influence similar to plans because they create a common focus for the groups' activities. A specification of rules and regulations that govern the activities of the designers vis-à-vis the production engineers might limit the amount of conflict between the two groups. The joint use of the available computer technology facilitates the implementation of shared goals and plans. At Boeing, the computer modeling program and resulting collaboration between design engineers and manufacturing occurs within a context of agreed-upon plans and goals.

Linking Roles   Individuals are temporarily placed in positions to act as conduits between interacting groups. They expedite communication by resolving issues through a person at the same level in the organization, rather than by using a common supervisor to solve them.[36] A designated designer serving as a liaison who facilitates communication between the design engineers and production departments acts in a linking role; alternatively, a representative of the production staff may fulfill this role. Sometimes linking roles can distort communication and even contribute to conflict if they inaccurately or inappropriately alter information passed between groups.

Task Forces Special groups of representatives from all parties can be convened to work on problems faced by the interacting groups. Task forces integrate by presenting the ideas of their group to the others' representatives. Task forces typically include one representative from each group affected by or involved in a particular problem or task.

Integrating Roles or Units Analogous to the typically more informal linking roles, a permanent coordinating individual or group of people can be appointed to act as an interface between interacting groups. A project or product manager, for example, coordinates the decisions of such interdependent groups as sales representatives, R&D engineers, and the production line. A unit manager in a hospital, who may be either a medical or nonmedical person, may fulfill the role of coordinating all activities on a particular medical service, such as outpatient, emergency, or obstetrics.

Project or Product Structure Individuals who work on the same product or project can be grouped together. In the case of a hospital, medical teams that include a nurse, physician, social worker, and other support personnel may service a small group of patients with similar illnesses, in the same ward, or with the same primary care physician. At Boeing, designers and production engineers work on the same project teams, thereby forming a close working relationship and sharing a common focus on developing and marketing of specific computer systems. Chapter 11 describes this structure in greater detail.

Matrix Organization Matrix organization is a highly sophisticated organizational design that integrates both functional departments and project groups through a dual authority and reporting system. In a matrix organization, each individual has two superiors. For example, Boeing designers might report to the 777 project manager and the vice president of research and development. But this structure itself is inherently conflict-ridden because of the duality of command. In the past, however, a matrix structure has been used to help organizations cope effectively with very complex, uncertain, and dynamic environments.

MANAGING RELATIONS BETWEEN CULTURALLY DIVERSE GROUPS

Managing culturally diverse groups poses special challenges depending on the extent of the differences. For example, recall the interaction between the designers and manufacturing staff at Boeing. Computerization of the design process facilitated their interaction. Or remember the other interpersonal, process, and structural ways of resolving potential conflict and dealing with intergroup relations described in this chapter. Do these approaches work with culturally diverse groups?

Cultural diversity exaggerates differences between groups and may call for additional strategies and techniques. Managers must be trained to identify cultural differences and then use them for the organization's benefit. In addition, managers need to emphasize a vision or superordinate goal, equalize power, develop mutual respect between groups, and facilitate feedback on process and outcomes between the groups.[37] Objectifying and sharing perceptions about the groups involved and reducing task interdependence may also help alleviate potential dysfunctions between culturally diverse groups.

Table 10–3 **Diagnostic Questions for Managing Conflict and Intergroup Relations**

- Is there conflict in the organization?
- Is the conflict functional or dysfunctional?
- What level of conflict exists?
- What stage of conflict exists?
- What causes the conflict in the organization?
- What is the nature of the relationship between groups in the organization?
- What factors contribute to these relationships?
- How effective are intergroup relationships?
- Are there mechanisms for effectively managing conflict and intergroup relations?

SUMMARY

Conflict frequently characterizes individuals and groups in organizations. It can exist at the intrapersonal, interpersonal, intragroup, intergroup, intraorganizational, and interorganizational levels. As a dynamic force, conflict progresses from latent to perceived, felt, and manifest stages, and finally to a conflict aftermath. Its consequences can be functional, such as increased creativity and exchange of ideas, or dysfunctional, such as increased stress, absenteeism, and turnover or decreased satisfaction and performance.

Interacting groups are especially prone to conflict. Effective intergroup relations require managers and other organizational members to diagnose the extent and causes of their interdependence. Groups can demonstrate pooled, sequential, reciprocal, or team interdependence. Groups experiencing reciprocal or team interdependence more often experience dysfunctional conflict and other problems than those showing pooled or sequential interdependence.

Perceptual differences—including time, goal, and social orientations, attitudinal set, and status differences—create differences between groups. Task relations reflect the nature of group interdependence and can reinforce problematic interactions. Power differences—including the extent of a group's substitutability, its ability to cope with uncertainty, and its access to resources—influence the effectiveness of its interactions with other individuals or groups.

Table 10–3 presents a list of questions for diagnosing conflict and intergroup relations in organizations. Prescriptions for managing conflict and improving intergroup relations include the use of process strategies and introduction of structural mechanisms. Their effectiveness depends on the parties involved and the nature of the situation. In the next part of the book we look at multiple interactions among groups by studying behavior at an organizational level.

Reading 10–1

Managing Conflict among Groups
L. Dave Brown

Conflict among groups is extremely common in organizations, although it often goes unrecognized. Managing conflict among groups is a crucial skill for those who would lead modern organizations. To illustrate:

Maintenance workers brought in to repair a production facility criticize production workers for overworking the machinery and neglecting routine maintenance tasks. The production workers countercharge that the last maintenance work was improperly done and caused the present breakdown. The argument results in little cooperation between the two groups to repair the breakdown, and the resulting delays and misunderstandings ultimately inflate organization-wide production costs.

A large manufacturing concern has unsuccessful negotiations with a small independent union, culminating in a bitter strike characterized by fights, bombings, and sabotage. The angry workers, aware that the independent union has too few resources to back a protracted battle with management, vote in a powerful international union for the next round of negotiations. Management prepares for an even worse strike, but comparatively peaceful and productive negotiations ensue.

Top management of a large bank in a racially mixed urban area commits the organization to system-wide integration. Recruiters find several superbly qualified young black managers, after a long and highly competitive search, to join the bank's prestigious but all-white trust division and yet, subsequently, several leave the organization. Since virtually all the managers in the trust division are explicitly willing to integrate, top management is mystified by the total failure of the integration effort.

These cases are all examples of conflict or potential conflict among organizational groups that influence the performance and goal attainment of the organization as a whole. The cases differ in two important ways.

First, the extent to which the potential conflict among groups is *overt* varies across cases: conflict is all too obvious in the labor-management situation; it is subtle but still evident in the production-maintenance relations; it is never explicit in the attempt to integrate the bank's trust division. It is clear that *too much* conflict can be destructive, and much attention has been paid to strategies and tactics for reducing escalated conflict. Much less attention has been paid to situations in which organizational performance suffers because of *too little* conflict, or strategies and tactics for making potential conflict more overt.

Second, the cases also differ in the *defining characteristics* of the parties: the production and maintenance groups are functionally defined; the distribution of power is critical to the labor and management conflict; the society's history of race relations is important to the black-white relations in the bank. Although there has been much examination of organizational conflict among groups defined by function, there has been comparatively little attention to organizational conflicts among' groups defined by *power differences* (e.g., headquarters-branch relations, some labor-management relations) or by *societal history* (e.g., religious group relations, black-white relations, male-female relations).

It is increasingly clear that effective management of modern organizations calls for dealing with various forms

of intergroup conflict: too little as well as too much conflict, and history-based and power-based as well as function-based conflicts. This paper offers a framework for understanding conflict among groups in the next section, and suggests strategies and tactics for diagnosing and managing different conflict situations.

CONFLICT AND INTERGROUP RELATIONS

Conflict: Too Much or Too Little?

Conflict is a form of interaction among parties that differ in interests, perceptions, and preferences. Overt conflict involves adversarial interaction that ranges from mild disagreements through various degrees of fighting. But it is also possible for parties with substantial differences to act as if those differences did not exist, and so keep potential conflict from becoming overt.

It is only too clear that it is possible to have *too much* conflict between or among groups. Too much conflict produces strong negative feelings, blindness to interdependencies, and uncontrolled escalation of aggressive action and counteraction. The obvious costs of uncontrolled conflict have sparked a good deal of interest in strategies for conflict reduction and resolution.

Is less obvious (but increasingly clear) that it is possible to have *too little* conflict. Complex and novel decisions, for example, may require pulling together perspectives and information from many different groups. If group representatives are unwilling to present and argue for their perspectives, the resulting decision may not take into account all the available information. The Bay of Pigs disaster during the Kennedy Administration may have been a consequence of too little conflict in the National Security Council, where critical information possessed by representatives of different agencies was suppressed to preserve harmonious relations among them (Janis, 1972).

In short, moderate levels of conflict—in which differences are recognized and extensively argued—are often associated with high levels of energy and involvement, high degrees of information exchange, and better decisions (Robbins, 1974). Managers should be concerned, in this view, with achieving levels of conflict that are *appropriate* to the task before them, rather than concerned about preventing or resolving immediately all intergroup disagreements.

Conflict among Groups

Conflict in organizations takes many forms. A disagreement between two individuals, for example, may be related to their personal differences, their job definitions, their group memberships, or all three. One of the most common ways that managers misunderstand organizational conflict, for example, is to attribute difficulties to "personality" factors, when it is, in fact, rooted in group memberships and organizational structure. Attributing conflict between production and maintenance workers to their personalities, for example, implies that the conflict can be reduced by replacing the individuals. But if the conflict is, in fact, related to the differing goals of the two groups, *any* individual will be under pressure to fight with members of the other group, regardless of their personal preferences. Replacing individuals in such situations without taking account of intergroup differences will *not* improve relations.

Groups are defined in organizations for a variety of reasons. Most organizations are differentiated horizontally, for example, into functional departments or product divisions for task purposes. Most organizations also are differentiated vertically into levels or into headquarters and plant groups. Many organizations also incorporate in some degree group definitions significant in the larger society, such as racial and religious distinctions.

A good deal of attention has been paid to the relations among groups of relatively equal power, such as functional departments in organizations. Much less is known about effective management of relations between groups of unequal power or those having different societal histories. But many of the most perplexing intergroup conflicts in organizations include all three elements—functional differences, power differences, and historical differences. Effective management of the differences between a white executive from marketing and a black hourly worker from production is

difficult indeed, because so many issues are likely to contribute to the problem.

Intergroup relations, left to themselves, tend to have a regenerative, self-fulfilling quality that makes them extremely susceptible to rapid escalation. The dynamics of escalating conflict, for example, have impacts within and between the groups involved. *Within* a group (i.e., within the small circles in Figure 10–9), conflict with another group tends to increase cohesion and conformity to group norms (Sherif, 1966; Coser, 1956) and to encourage a world view that favors "us" over "them" (Janis, 1972; Deutsch, 1973). Simultaneously, *between*-groups (i.e., the relations between the circles in Figure 10–9) conflict promotes negative stereotyping and distrust (Sherif, 1966), increased emphasis on differences (Deutsch, 1973), decreased communications (Sherif, 1966) and increased distortion of communications that do take place (Blake and Mouton, 1961). The *combination* of negative stereotypes, distrust, internal militance, and aggressive action creates a vicious cycle: "defensive" aggression by one group validates suspicion and "defensive" counteraggression by the other, and the conflict escalates (Deutsch, 1973) unless it is counteracted by external factors. A less well understood pattern, in which positive stereotypes, trust, and cooperative action generate a benevolent cycle of increasing cooperation, may also exist (Deutsch, 1973).

Figure 10–9   **Varieties of Intergroup Conflict**

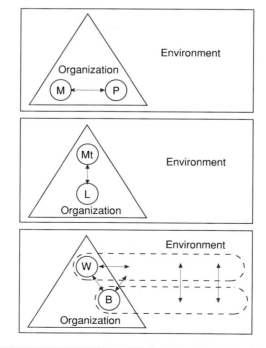

A. Functional Differences:
   Maintenance and Production

   M = Maintenance
   P = Production
   ◄—►= Overt Conflict

B. Power Differences:
   Managment and Labor

   Mt = Management
   L = Labor
   ◄—► = Escalated
        conflict

C. Societal Differences:
   Black and White Managers

   W = Whites
   B = Blacks
   ◄—► = Convert
        conflict

To return to one of the initial examples, both the maintenance concern with keeping the machines clean and the production concern with maximizing output were organizationally desirable. But those concerns promoted a negative maintenance stereotype of production ("too lazy to clean machines") and a production stereotype of maintenance ("want us to polish the machine, not use it") that encouraged them to fight. Part A of Figure 10–9 illustrates the overt but not escalated conflict between the parties.

Introducing power differences into intergroup relations further suppresses communications among the groups. The low-power group is vulnerable, and so must censor communication—such as dissatisfaction—that might elicit retaliation from the high-power group. In consequence, the high-power group remains ignorant of information considered sensitive by the low-power group. The long-term consequences of this mutually reinforcing fear and ignorance can be either escalating oppression—a peculiarly destructive form of too little conflict—or sporadic eruptions of intense and unexpected fighting (Brown, 1978).

The fight between the small independent union and the large corporation described at the outset illustrates the potential for outbursts of violent conflict when the parties are separated by large differences in power. The small union felt unable to influence the corporation at the bargaining table, and so used violence and guerrilla tactics to express its frustration and to influence management without exposing the union to retaliation. Part B of Figure 10–9 illustrates the positions of the parties and the quality of their conflict.

Conflicts among groups that involve societal differences may be even more complicated. Differences rooted in societal history are likely to be expressed in a network of mutually reinforcing social mechanisms—political, economic, geographic, educational—that serve to *institutionalize* the differences. Societal differences do not necessarily imply power differences between the groups, but very frequently the effect of institutionalization is to enshrine the dominance of one party over another. Relations among such groups within organizations are strongly influenced by the larger society. Organizational tensions may be the result of environmental developments that the organization cannot control. In addition, differences associated with histories of discrimination or oppression may involve strong feelings and entrenched stereotypes that can lead to explosive conflict. Societal differences in organizations call for careful management that permits enough overt conflict so the differences are understood, but not so much that they are exacerbated.

The failure to integrate the trust division illustrates the problem of managing institutionalized racism. The black recruits had all the technical skills for success, but they could not join the all-white clubs or buy a house in the all-white suburbs where their colleagues lived, played, and learned the social ropes of the trust business. Nor could they challenge top-level decisions to keep them away from the oldest (and richest) clients ("who might be racist and so take their business elsewhere"). But the failure to face the potential conflicts—among members of the organization and between the organization and its clients—in essence made it impossible for the black managers to become full members. This situation is diagrammed in Part C of Figure 10–9.

Diagnosing the Conflict

Diagnosis is a crucially important and often-neglected phase of conflict management. Since conflict problems are often not recognized until after they have become acute, the need for immediate relief may be intense. But intervention in a poorly understood situation is not likely to produce instant successes. On the contrary, it may make the situation worse.

The manager of conflict should at the outset answer three questions about the situation:

1. At what level or levels is the conflict rooted (e.g., personal, interpersonal, intergroup, etc.)?
2. What role does s/he play in the relations among the parties?
3. What is a desirable state of relations among the parties?

A conflict may be the result of an individual, an interpersonal relationship, an intergroup relationship, or a combination of the three. If the manager understands the contributions of different levels, s/he can respond appropriately. It is generally worthwhile to examine the conflict from *each* of these perspectives early in the diagnosis.

The position of the manager vis-à-vis the parties is also important. Managers who are themselves parties to the dispute are likely to be biased, and almost certainly will be perceived by their opponents as biased. Actual bias requires that the manager be suspicious of his/her own perceptions and strive to empathize with the other party; perceived bias may limit the manager's ability to intervene credibly with the other party until the perception is dealt with. Conflict managers who are organizationally superior to the parties may not be biased in favor of either, but they are likely to have poor access to information about the conflict. For such persons special effort to understand the parties' positions may be necessary. Third parties that are respected and seen as neutral by both sides are in perhaps the best position to intervene, but they are a rare luxury for most situations. In any case, awareness of one's position vis-à-vis the parties can help the manager avoid pitfalls.

Finally, a conflict manager needs to develop a sense of what is too much and what is too little conflict among the parties—when is intervention merited, and should it increase or decrease the level of conflict? Relations among groups may be diagnosed in terms of attitudes, behavior, and structure, and each of those categories have characteristic patterns associated with too much and too little conflict.

Attitudes include the orientations of groups and group

members to their own and other groups—the extent to which they are aware of group interdependencies, the sophistication of group representatives about intergroup relations, and the quality of feelings and stereotypes within groups. Too much conflict is characterized by blindness to interdependencies, naiveté about the dynamics and costs of conflict, and strong negative feelings and stereotypes. Too little conflict, in contrast, is marked by blindness to conflicts of interests, naiveté about the dynamics and costs of collusion, and little awareness of group differences.

Behaviors include the ways in which groups and their members act—the levels of cohesion and conformity within groups, the action strategies of group representatives, the extent to which interaction between the groups is marked by escalating conflict or cooperation. Too much conflict often involves monolithically conforming groups, rigidly competitive action strategies, and escalating aggression among the groups. Too little conflict is associated with undefined or fragmented groups, unswervingly cooperative action strategies, and collusive harmony and agreement in place of examination of differences.

Structures are underlying factors that influence interaction in the long term—the larger systems in which parties are embedded, structural mechanisms that connect the parties, group boundaries and long-term interests, and regulatory contexts that influence interaction. Too much conflict is promoted by undefined or differentiated larger systems, lack of integrative mechanisms that link the groups, clearly defined and conflicting group interests and identities, and few rules or regulations to limit conflict. Too little conflict is encouraged by a shared larger system that suppresses conflict, no mechanisms to promote examination of differences, vague definitions of conflicting group interests and identities, and regulations that discourage overt conflict.

These diagnostic categories and the earmarks of too much and too little conflict are summarized in Table 10–4. Attitudinal, behavioral, and structural aspects of intergroup relations tend to interact with and support one another. The result is a tendency to escalate either the conflict or the collusion until some external force exerts a moderating effect. Thus, intergroup relations are volatile and capable of rapid escalatory cycles, but they also offer a variety of leverage points at which their self-fulfilling cycles may be interrupted by perceptive managers.

Intervention

Intervention to promote constructive conflict may involve *reducing* conflict in relations with too much or *inducing* conflict in relations with too little. In both cases, intervention involves efforts to disrupt a cyclical process produced

Table 10–4 **Diagnosing Conflict among Groups**

Area of Concern	General Issue	Symptoms of Too Much Conflict	Symptoms of Too Little Conflict
Attitudes	Awareness of similarities and differences	Blind to interdependence	Blind to conflicts of interest
	Sophistication about intergroup relations	Unaware of dynamics and costs of conflict	Unaware of dynamics and costs of collusion
	Feelings and perceptions of own and other group	Elaborated stereotypes favorable to own and unfavorable to other group	Lack of consciousness of own group and differences from other group
Behavior	Behavior within groups	High cohesion and conformity; high mobilization	Fragmentization; mobilization
	Conflict management style of groups	Overcompetitive style	Overcooperative style
	Behavior between groups	Aggressive, exploitative behavior; preemptive attack	Avoidance of conflict; appeasement
Structure	Nature of larger system	Separate or underdefined common larger system	Shared larger system that discourages conflict
	Regulatory context for interaction	Few rules to limit escalation	Many rules that stifle differences
	Relevant structural mechanisms	No inhibiting third parties available	No third parties to press differences
	Definition of groups and their goals	Impermeably bounded groups obsessed with own interests	Unbounded groups aware of own interests

by the interaction of attitudes, behavior, and structure. Interventions may start with any aspect of the groups' interaction, although long-term change will probably involve effects in all of them. More work has been done on the problem of reducing conflict than on inducing it—but conflict-reduction strategies often have the seeds of conflict induction within them.

Changing *attitudes* involves influencing the ways in which the parties construe events. Thus *altering group perceptions of their differences or similarities* may influence their interaction. Sherif (1966), for example, reports reduction in intergroup conflicts as a consequence of introducing superordinate goals that both groups desired but whose achievement required cooperation; emphasizing interdependencies may reduce escalated conflict. On the other hand, inducing conflict may require deemphasizing interdependencies and emphasizing conflicts of interest. Attitudes may also be changed by *changing the parties' understanding of their relations.* Increased understanding of the dynamics of intergroup conflict and its costs, for example, may help participants reduce their unintentional contributions to escalation (e.g., Burton, 1969). By the same token, increased understanding may help parties control the development of collusion (Janis, 1972). *Feelings and stereotypes may also be changed* by appropriate interventions. Sharing discrepant perceptions of each other has helped depolarize negative stereotypes and reduce conflict in a number of intergroup conflicts (e.g., Blake, Shepard, and Mouton, 1964), and consciousness raising to clarify self and other perceptions may help to increase conflict in situations where there is too little. Attitude-change interventions, in short, operate on the ways in which the parties understand and interpret the relations among the groups.

Changing *behaviors* requires modifying ways in which group members act. *Altering within-group behavior,* for example, may have a substantial impact on the ways in which the groups deal with each other. When members of a highly cohesive group confront explicitly differences that exist *within* the group, their enthusiasm for fighting with outside groups may be reduced. Similarly, an internally fragmented group that becomes more cohesive may develop an increased appetite for conflict with other groups (Brown, 1977). A second behavior-changing strategy is to *train group representatives to manage conflict more effectively.* Where too much conflict exists, representatives can be trained in conflict-reduction strategies, such as cooperation induction (Deutsch, 1973) or problem solving (Filley, 1975). Where the problem is too little conflict, the parties might benefit from training in assertiveness or bargaining skills. A third alternative is to *monitor between-group behavior,* and so influence escalations. Third parties trusted by both sides can control escalative tendencies or lend credibility to reduction initiatives by the parties that might otherwise be distrusted (Walton, 1969). Similarly, conflict induction may be an outcome of third-party "process consultation" that raises questions

about collusion (Schein, 1969). Behavior-change strategies, in summary, focus on present activities as an influence on levels of conflict, and seek to move those actions into more constructive patterns.

Changing structures involves altering the underlying factors that influence long-term relations among groups. A common alternative is to *invoke larger system interventions.* Conflict between groups in the same larger system is often reduced through referring the question at issue to a higher hierarchical level (Galbraith, 1971). A similar press for conflict induction may be created when too little conflict results in lowered performance that catches the attention of higher levels. A related strategy for managing conflict is to *develop regulatory contexts* that specify appropriate behaviors. Such regulatory structures can limit conflict by imposing rules on potential fights, as collective bargaining legislation does on labor-management relations. Changes in regulatory structures can also loosen rules that stifle desirable conflict. A third strategy is the *development of new interface mechanisms* that mediate intergroup relations. Integrative roles and departments may help to reduce conflict among organizational departments (Galbraith, 1971), while the creation of ombudsmen or "devil's advocates" can help surface conflict that might otherwise not become explicit (Janis, 1972). Another possibility is *redefinition of group boundaries and goals,* so the nature of the parties themselves is reorganized. Redesigning organizations into a matrix structure, for example, in effect locates the conflicted interface within an individual to ensure that effective management efforts are made (Galbraith, 1971). Alternatively, too little conflict may call for clarifying group boundaries and goals so the differences among them become more apparent and more likely to produce conflict. Structural interventions typically demand heavier initial investments of time and energy, and they may take longer to bear fruit than attitudinal and behavioral interventions. But they are also more likely to produce long-term changes.

These strategies for intervention are summarized in Table 10–5. This sample of strategies is not exhaustive, but it is intended to be representative of interventions that have worked with groups that are relatively equal in power and whose differences are primarily related to the organization's task. The introduction of power differences and societal differences raised other issues.

Power Differences

Relations between high-power and low-power groups are worth special examination because of the potential for extremely negative outcomes. The poor communications that result from fear on the part of the low-power group and ignorance on the part of the high-power group can result in either extreme oppression (too little conflict) or unexpected explosions of violence (too much).

It is understandable that high-power groups prefer too little conflict to too much, and that low-power groups are

Table 10–5   **Intervening in Conflict among Groups**

Area of Concern	General Issue	Strategies for Too Much Conflict	Strategies for Too Little Conflict
Attitudes	Clarify differences and similarities	Emphasize interdependencies	Emphasize conflict of interest
	Increased sophistication about intergroup relations	Clarify dynamics and costs of escalation	Clarify costs and dynamics of collusion
	Change feelings and perceptions	Share perceptions to depolarize stereotypes	Consciousness raising about group and others
Behavior	Modify within-group behavior	Increase expression of within-group differences	Increase within-group cohesion and consensus
	Train group representatives to be more effective	Expand skills to include cooperative strategies	Expand skills to include assertive, confrontive strategies
	Monitor between-group behavior	Third-party peacemaking	Third-party process consultation
Structure	Invoke larger system interventions	Refer to common hierarchy	Hierarchical pressure for better performance
	Develop regulatory contexts	Impose rules on interaction that limit conflict	Deemphasize rules that stifle conflict
	Create new interface mechanisms	Develop integrating roles of groups	Create "devil's advocates" or ombudsmen
	Redefine group boundaries and goals	Redesign organization to emphasize task	Clarify group boundaries and goals to increase differentiation

anxious about the risks of provoking conflict with a more powerful adversary. But organizations that in the short run have too little conflict often have too much in the long term. Inattention to the problems of low-power groups requires that they adopt highly intrusive influence strategies in order to be heard (e.g., Swingle, 1967). So the comfort of avoiding conflict between high- and low-power groups may have high costs in the long run.

Managing conflict between high- and low-power groups requires dealing in some fashion with their power differences, since those differences drastically affect the flow of information and influence among the parties. A prerequisite to conflict management interventions may well be *evening the psychological odds,* so that both groups feel able to discuss the situation without too much risk. Evening the odds does not necessarily mean power equalization, but it does require trustworthy protection (to reduce the fear of low-power groups) and effective education (to reduce the ignorance of high-power groups). Given psychological equality, interventions related to attitudes, behavior, and structure that have already been discussed may be employed to promote constructive levels of conflict (e.g., Brown, 1977). It should be noted that for differently powerful groups the boundary between too much and too little conflict is easily crossed. Managers may find themselves oscillating rapidly between

interventions to induce and interventions to reduce conflict between such groups.

To return once again to an initial example, the history of fighting and violence between the small union and the corporation led the latter's managers to expect even worse conflict when faced by the international union. But voting in the international in effect evened the odds between labor and management. Violent tactics considered necessary by the small union were not necessary for the international, and the regulatory structure of collective bargaining proved adequate to manage the conflict subsequently.

Societal Differences

Organizations are increasingly forced to grapple with societal differences. These differences are typically not entirely task-related; rather, they are a result of systematic discrimination in the larger society. Group members enter the organization with sets toward each other with which the organization must cope to achieve its goals. Societal differences are most problematic when they involve histories of exploitation (e.g., blacks by whites, women by men), and successful conflict management of such differences requires more than good intentions.

Managing societal differences in organizations may call for evening the odds, as in managing power differences, since societal differences so often include an element of power asymmetry. But coping with societal differences may also require more, since the effect of institutionalization is to ensure that the differences are preserved. *Invoking pressures from the environment* may be required even to get members of some groups into the organization at all. External forces such as federal pressure for "equal opportunity" and expanding educational opportunities for minorities can be used to press for more attention to societally based conflicts within organizations. Organizations may also develop *internal counterinstitutions* that act as checks and balances to systemic discrimination. A carefully designed and protected "communications group," which includes members from many groups and levels, can operate as an early warning system and as a respected third party for managing societal intergroup tensions in an organization (Alderfer, 1977).

The bank's failure to integrate the trust department turned largely on institutionalized racism. The decision to hire black managers was made partly in response to environmental pressure, and so overcame the initial barrier to letting blacks into the division at all. But once [they were] into the division, no mechanisms existed to press for overt discussion of differences. Without that discussion, no ways could be developed for the black managers to scale the insurmountable barriers facing them. The bank colluded with its supposedly racist clients by protecting them from contact with the new recruits. Although the first step—recruiting the black managers—was promising, trust division managers were unable to make the differences discussable or to develop the mechanisms required for effective management of the black-white differences in the division.

CONCLUSION

It may be helpful to the reader to summarize the major points of this argument and their implications. It has been argued that relations among groups in organizations can be characterized by too much or too little conflict, depending on their task, the nature of their differences, and the degree to which they are interdependent. This proposition suggests that *conflict managers should strive to maintain some appropriate level of conflict,* rather than automatically trying to reduce or resolve all disagreements. Effective management of intergroup conflict requires both understanding and appropriate action. Understanding intergroup conflict involves diagnosis of attitudes, behaviors, structures, and their interaction. *Effective intervention to increase or decrease conflict requires action to influence attitudes, behaviors, and structures grounded in accurate diagnosis.*

Power differences between groups promote fear and ignorance that result in reduced exchange of information between groups and the potential for either explosive outbursts of escalated conflict or escalating oppression. Evening the odds, at least in psychological terms, may be a prerequisite to effective intervention in such situations. *Managers must cope with fear, ignorance, and their conse-quences to effectively manage conflicts between unequally powerful groups.*

Societal differences institutionalized in the larger society may further complicate relations among groups in organizations by introducing environmental events and long histories of tension. Managing such differences may require invocation of environmental pressures and the development of counterinstitutions that help the organization deal with the effects of systemic discrimination in the larger society. *Environmental developments produce the seeds for organizational conflicts, but they also offer clues to their management.*

The importance of effective conflict management in organizations is increasing, and that development is symptomatic of global changes. We live in a rapidly shrinking, enormously heterogeneous, increasingly interdependent world. The number of interfaces at which conflict may occur is increasing astronomically, and so are the stakes of too much or too little conflict at those points. If we are to survive—let alone prosper—in our onrushing future, we desperately need skilled managers of conflict among groups.

REFERENCES

Alderfer, C. P. Improving Organizational Communication Through Long-Term Intergroup Intervention. *Journal of Applied Behavioral Science, 13,* 1977, 193–210.

Blake, R. R., and Mouton, J. S. Reactions to Intergroup Competition under Win-Lose Conditions. *Management Science, 4,* 1961.

Blake, R. R., Shepard, H. A., and Mouton, J. S. *Managing Intergroup Conflict in Industry.* Ann Arbor, Mich.: Foundation for Research on Human Behavior, 1964.

Brown, L. D. Can Haves and Have-Nots Cooperate? Two Efforts to Bridge a Social Gap. *Journal of Applied Behavioral Science, 13,* 1977, 211–224.

Brown, L. D. Toward a Theory of Power and Intergroup Relations, in *Advances in Experiential Social Process,* edited by C. A. Cooper and C. P. Alderfer. London: Wiley, 1978.

Burton, J. W. *Conflict and Communication: The Use of Controlled Communication in International Relations.* London: Macmillan, 1969.

Coser, L. A. *The Functions of Social Conflict.* New York: Free Press, 1973.

Deutsch, M. *The Resolution of Conflict.* New Haven, Conn.: Yale University Press, 1973.

Filley, A. C. *Interpersonal Conflict Resolution.* Glenview, Ill.: Scott, Foresman, 1975.

Galbraith, J. R. *Designing Complex Organizations.* Reading, Mass.: Addison-Wesley, 1971.

Janis, I. *Victims of Groupthink.* Boston: Houghton-Mifflin, 1972.

Lawrence, P. R., and Lorsch, J. W. *Organization and Environment.* Boston: Harvard Business School, 1967.

Robbins, S. P. *Managing Organizational Conflict.* Englewood Cliffs, N.J.: Prentice Hall, 1974.

Schein, E. H., *Process Consultation*. Reading, Mass.: Addison-Wesley, 1969.

Sherif, M. *In Common Predicament*. Boston: Houghton-Mifflin, 1966.

Swingle, P. G. *The Management of Power*. Hillsdale, N.J.: Erlbaum Associates, 1976.

Walton, R. *Interpersonal Peacemaking*. Reading, Mass.: Addison-Wesley, 1969.

DISCUSSION QUESTIONS

1. What types of conflict can exist among groups?

2. Offer a protocol for diagnosing conflict in an organization.

3. Suggest a range of strategies for intervening in conflict among groups.

From D. A. Kolb, I. M. Rubin, and I. N. McIntyre, eds., *Organizational Psychology: Readings on Human Behavior in Organizations*, 4th ed. (Englewood Cliffs, N.J.: Prentice Hall, 1984), pp. 225–236. Copyright © 1984. Reprinted by permission of Prentice Hall.

Activity 10–1

Pharmatech N.V.: Managing Innovation and Production

Step 1: Read the Pharmatech N.V. case.

It was July 12, 1988. Paul Richburg, management consultant, had just spent the day in Amsterdam at Pharmatech N.V. Now back in London, he was starting to review what he had said earlier to Pharmatech's top management.

The company was experiencing a serious problem with the interaction between research and production, which had to be solved as rapidly as possible. The Research and Production divisions needed to work together, and yet the tension and conflicts had been worsening steadily. Realizing that it was essential to improve the interface between these two divisions, top management had made a diagnosis and put forward some suggestions. They had told Paul Richburg that they intended to place a team of development people into the Production Division to ease the innovation process.

Paul had reacted to all the ideas presented to him. Taking stock of his behavior, he was now wondering: "Did I say the right thing?"

PHARMATECH N.V.

Created in 1960, Pharmatech N.V. was a chemical-pharmaceutical company producing OTC (over the counter) products and intermediate products for the pharmaceutical industry. In the early '70s, Pharmatech N.V. had decided to enlarge its scope of activities by specializing in the production of delivery systems such as adapted capsules and coatings for the new generation of biotechnological pharmaceutical products. By 1988, the company had succeeded in getting the final formulations of a considerable number of these modern drugs and was producing a large variety of capsules, pills and sprays. Pharmatech's Research had progressively acquired an in-depth understanding of all the problems related to biotechnological production and had

made a number of interesting and valuable inventions. "Biopolymer coatings" was one of its latest inventions, representing a significant breakthrough for the company.

Headquarters and plants were located approximately 5 km outside Amsterdam. The company included six divisions: Marketing, Research, Development, Production, Administration and Personnel. (See Figure 10–10 for the company organization chart.)

INNOVATION AND PRODUCTION AT PHARMATECH N.V.

The interaction between research and production was as follows:

Innovation started in the Research Division. A team of researchers was permanently trying to discover new processes or products, either requested by the Marketing Division in response to external demand or on their own initiative. After a new product or process had been discovered, analyzed and tested in the laboratories, it was transmitted to the Development Division. The role of the Development Division was to evaluate the potential applications of the new product/process and to develop it from an experiment to a more advanced stage. Three pilot runs would be organized in the Production Division under the supervision of the Research Division. If nothing went wrong during these procedures, then mass production could be launched. The product finally went to the Quality Control Department before being packaged and shipped.

MEETING WITH TOP MANAGEMENT

The relationship between Research and Production had become so strained and the effects of this tension on the company's performance so serious, that top management decided in May 1988 to recruit a consultant who would analyze the

Figure 10-10   **Pharmatech N.V. Organization Chart**

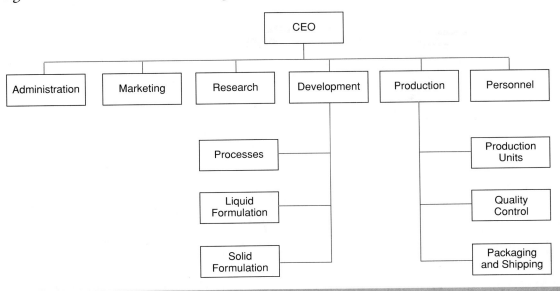

situation and help the company find a solution. They contacted a well-known consulting group, Ransome & Co. Two months later, Paul Richburg, who had been with Ransome more than 10 years, was sent to Amsterdam.

A first meeting was organized with the Research Division director, Dr. Alfons Lambrechts, and the head of the Biotechnology Department, Dr. Rik Dewinter. (See Figure 10–11 for the Research Division organization chart.) During this meeting, Paul Richburg learned a lot about innovation and production at Pharmatech N.V., how Research perceived the problem and its causes, as well as various measures they felt could improve the situation.

CONFLICTS BETWEEN RESEARCH AND PRODUCTION

Both managers agreed that there were several factors creating the interface problem between Research and Production.

First, there was the influx of new technologies into the company. The production methods as well as the products themselves were constantly changing, becoming more sophisticated and requiring increased know-how. From a more classical type of production using chemical reactions, the company was moving toward high-tech production involving biotechnology.

Lambrechts explained that this move presented a problem for many production people who had not had an educational background sufficient to cope with these new sophisticated technologies. Consequently, they would often adopt an attitude of resistance toward new technologies.

"Today, what we need in Production," Lambrechts explained, "is professional people, i.e., with university de-

grees, who act as partners with researchers. Production does not have enough such people, which is a problem when high-tech innovation is increasing at such a rapid pace."

"For example," Dewinter added, "since many Production people do not have a sufficient technical and technological background, they have difficulty preparing the biopolymer coatings obtained by fermentation, which is a biotechnological process."

Dewinter then described other situations where there seemed to be mistrust of new technologies; each illustration revealed professional weakness among some of the production people.

According to Lambrechts, besides the problem of education and technical background within Production, there was also a lack of communication and understanding between researchers and production people. The researchers were not receiving positive reaction from Production and, therefore, were frustrated. Their natural response was, "If nobody is interested in our inventions, why should we innovate?"

Moreover, when the researchers explained to the production people why things had gone wrong and tried to help them, their intervention was not appreciated. "Production people resent researchers interfering in their work," Dewinter explained, "even though all we want is to improve the situation." However, according to the production people, the researchers would only point out what they were doing wrong. At the same time, the researchers believed that the production people were always automatically against their projects and ideas. This attitude resulted in even poorer communication and stronger resistance from Production toward new projects.

Figure 10-11 **Research Management Division Organization Chart**

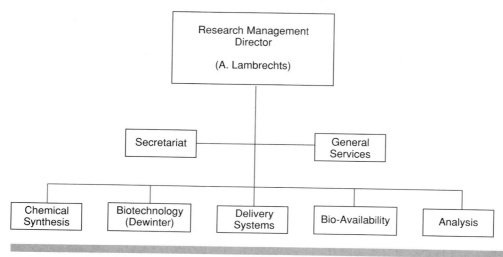

There were a lot of preconceived ideas both within Research and Production. Researchers were seen by production people as being too idealistic, far away from reality. On the other side, research people were convinced that production people did not respect their research work and were against major changes and progress.

The motivation and views of their respective jobs were also considerably different. Researchers were more motivated by a successful idea than by selling and making money. Production people tended to assess success in terms of tons per year. Another difference was that production people were used to processes that ran without problems, whereas researchers expected to work on a trial and error basis in their laboratories.

According to Lambrechts, another matter which concerned Research was the quality control level. The Quality Control Department, which reported to the head of Production, also needed to improve its effectiveness. The people were still handling the new products as if they were classical products with only minor microbiological quality control problems. "The technical responsibility of the Quality Control Department is critical," Dewinter explained. "Biotechnological products have to be handled correctly or a catastrophe could happen."

Apparently the quality control personnel lacked the necessary technical background to cope with the new dimension of their work. Sometimes they made an analysis and sent the results to the customer without checking first with Research whether or not the results were sound. Dewinter commented, "Most of our customers have an excellent technological background and could easily notice such a mistake. Pharmatech N.V. could lose its credibility because of the Quality Control Department's callous attitude."

SOLVING THE PROBLEM

Lambrechts and Dewinter had some ideas for improving the situation, but wondered if they were on the right track and if there might be other solutions. They presented their ideas to Paul Richburg:

1. The role of production people in the innovation process should be enhanced through adequate training.
2. Production's key role in a product's success on the market should also be emphasized.
3. Researchers should go beyond lab research and extend their activities into Development and Production. At the same time, Production should become more involved in Development and Research. In this regard, top management was recommending that a task force be set up where Research and Production would meet to discuss and collaborate at the first phase of any new project. Production people would be exposed to the researchers' style of work, while Research would be able to foresee problems that Production might encounter during the mass production phase.
4. Production people should receive adequate training to acquire a better knowledge of the biotechnological industry.
5. The company should recruit people with the latest technical background.
6. An effort should be made to enhance communication and build up confidence between Research and Development, and Production. This could be achieved through an exchange of people, ideas and experiences.
7. A team from the Development Division could be

integrated into the Production Division. This team would act as a facilitator between Research and Production by playing the role of go-between.

Richburg, especially interested in this last suggestion, asked for more information about it. Lambrechts explained that they had already started this idea. The team had been set up and had received a clear job description (see Figure 10–12). The team had also been introduced to the production people. However, the team was still not operational. Lambrechts had preferred to wait for Richburg's advice before proceeding further.

Paul asked to meet the team or at least one of its members. Thus Lambrechts arranged for him to meet a team member, Mr. Vanderlinden, immediately after the company tour that same day.

VISITING THE COMPANY

Paul then visited the company with Dr. Dewinter as his guide. They walked through the various research laboratories where Paul could see very sophisticated equipment in the various labs. From there they went to the production plant. During the tour, Dewinter explained the roles of the different machines and the various phases from production to packaging and shipping.

Figure 10–12 **Job Description for the Team**

General objectives of the function:
- To introduce new processes and equipment into Production
- To improve existing processes and equipment

Description of the function:
- To upscale and introduce Production to all components and processes from R&D
- To evaluate suitable equipment
- To review and optimize existing processes and methods (quality, yield, efficiency), working together closely with relevant supervisors
- To assist with troubleshooting
- To keep up-to-date information on new technologies and methods
- To evaluate the technical feasibility of alternative production places
- To establish and control a budget for its sector
- To report quarterly on its activities to head of Production

Authority:
- Financial limit to be in accordance with company rules and budget
- May not alter manufacturing processes, formulas or installations without authorization from Production management

Paul was fascinated by the contrast between Research and Production. The environments were so different; noisy in the production units, quiet in the labs. Turbulence versus concentration. Somehow both cultures had to understand the other's job and collaborate.

INTERVIEWING MR. VANDERLINDEN

Following the tour of the company, Paul Richburg was taken to Mr. Vanderlinden's office. After stating the purpose of his visit, Paul asked Mr. Vanderlinden about the job his team would do and its expectations.

"The idea is to use a team of people from the Development Division, who can understand and cope with the concerns of the production people," Vanderlinden said. He then went on to explain that the team's role was to guarantee that innovation would permeate Production smoothly. All the team members were technical people with university degrees. They would report to Production, but would be receptive toward innovation and research. Their objective was to make new research activities and techniques acceptable to production people and ease the transfer of technologies from Research to Production.

"The problem we experience in Research and Development," Vanderlinden lamented, "is that many efforts are made to develop new products and, yet too often, after they leave these departments, we never hear about them again. There are many products in the pipeline, but many of them never reach the other end." Vanderlinden's opinion on this problem was that, until now, no one would dare to kill a project if it were not good. Yet, on the other hand, no one was really pushing its implementation.

According to the job description, the team's role was to coordinate all the practical details regarding the transfer of new technologies, i.e., how to do the transfer, how to get operators when necessary, etc. The team's strategy was to select one of the latest products from the Research Division as a pilot project, then look for ways that this new product could be manufactured in the Production Division without having what Vanderlinden called "the Ping-Pong syndrome" between Research and Production.

"The Ping-Pong syndrome," explained Vanderlinden, "is when a project moves backward and forward between Production and Research. Production receives a new product or process. Then, each time the production people encounter any technical difficulty in manufacturing or using this product or process, they send it back to Research, arguing that the project is not ready for Production. This can happen several times with each project, resulting in a waste of time, money and motivation."

"The problem with researchers," Vanderlinden added, "is that they don't consider the manufacturing of their projects. They assume that any idea can be transferred immediately to Production. However, production people expect easy clear production procedures. They feel that it's not their job to elaborate on those procedures."

In order to avoid this situation, the team intended to analyze thoroughly the feasibility of the pilot project and implement it step by step, slowly but surely. The team would establish the production processes which did not exist. They would help the researchers think about production processes, forcing them to be more systematic, thorough and helpful. They would make researchers sensitive to the technical implementation problems Production might encounter. "Some technical problems may be easy to handle at the lab level but impossible to overcome at a mass production level because of inadequate equipment or procedures," Vanderlinden explained.

Vanderlinden felt that the team's role would be a success if the product could be commercialized without any major problem or conflict during manufacturing. If it appeared that the product could not be commercialized for any reason, the project would immediately be abandoned and no longer prepared for sale, as in the past. "The project must be pushed or killed," said Vanderlinden with determination.

The long-term objective was to promote a new way to facilitate the transfer of innovations within the company.

When asked if the team would get any support, Vanderlinden declared that they had the support of everybody, including top management. There had been positive reaction from both sides, except for some confusion in the Production Division at first, before they clearly understood the team's exact function.

As to immediate concerns, Vanderlinden's main worry was that if the team decided the project should be abandoned, its researchers might react negatively and consider that the team had not been of any help.

Vanderlinden concluded by expressing his personal opinion about innovation and production at Pharmatech N.V. Innovation definitely existed. The difficulty was in the transfer of this innovation to Production. According to him, the company was perhaps too "research-oriented" and did not take the production aspects and concerns seriously enough into account. Vanderlinden also believed that Research should concentrate on one or two priority projects at a time and push them on to Production. This would facilitate the transfer, reassure the production people and give more satisfaction to researchers.

WRAPPING UP THE CONSULTING

At the end of the day, Paul Richburg presented his first findings and comments to Lambrechts and Dewinter. Paul believed that the idea of building a team to go between Research and Production was sound. Paul also supported the idea that a pilot program with one project was the best way to prove the team's effectiveness. Paul agreed that it would probably be more difficult to convince the production people that the team could help them.

Paul felt strongly that Production and Research should remain two different corporate cultures, where researchers worked with ideas in a relatively free way and production people continued to operate systematically and pragmatically, thinking in terms of tons and outputs.

"After all," Paul added, "Research spends the money, but it's Production that brings the money in. Top management has to take these cultural differences into account if they want to manage the innovation process more effectively."

Paul had also already spotted some potential problems which he shared with Lambrechts and Dewinter. He sensed a feeling of ambiguity within Production and Research that might lead to resistance; he was not sure that they felt any need for the team's intervention. Paul was also concerned that the team had not really developed an action plan, with checkpoints enabling them to take stock, to learn from the experience and, if necessary, take another direction. There was also the risk that after a while, having milestones, the team would withdraw. It seemed to Paul that the team was not sufficiently aware of their role as change agents, trying to make a company move to a more integrated cooperative culture. "Maybe they need some training on how to act as internal mediators," he suggested to the managers.

"My biggest concern, however," Paul concluded, "is that Production's perception of the situation is missing. It's necessary to have the opinion of production people regarding the problems as well as their suggestions for solving them before any action be taken."

* * *

Two days after his visit to Pharmatech N.V., Paul Richburg was still wondering if he had said and done the right thing. Was the idea of the team the best way to solve the interaction problem between Research and Production?

He was supposed to return in 10 days, and he wondered what the company's next move should be. "How shall we proceed?" Paul asked himself.

Step 2: Prepare the case for class discussion.

Step 3: Answer the following questions, individually, in small groups, or with the entire class, as directed by your instructor:

Description
1. Describe the interaction between research and production at Pharmatech.

Diagnosis
2. Is there functional or dysfunctional conflict between the two groups?
3. What level of conflict exists?
4. At what stage is the conflict?
5. What causes the conflict?
6. How do intergroup relations contribute to the conflict?

Prescription
7. What options are available to improve the situation?

Action

8. How effective will building a team that incorporates research and production be?
9. What costs and benefits probably will result from implementing the prescription?

Step 4: Discussion. In small groups, with the entire class, or in written form, share your answers to the questions above. Then answer the following questions:

1. What symptoms suggest that a problem exists?
2. What problems exist in the case?

3. What theories and concepts help explain the problems?
4. How can the problems be corrected?
5. Are the actions likely to be effective?

This case was written by Professor Pierre Casse, with the assistance of Béatrice Balthazart, as the basis for class discussion rather than to illustrate either effective or ineffective handling of an administrative situation. Copyright © 1988, IMEDE, Lausanne, Switzerland. The International Institute for Management Development (IMD), resulting from the merger between IMEDE, Lausanne, and IMI, Geneva, acquires and retains all rights. Reproduced by permission.

Activity 10–2 Behavior Description Questionnaire

Step 1: Complete the following questionnaire:

Consider situations in which you find that your wishes differ from the wishes of another person. How do you usually respond to such situations?

On the following pages are several pairs of statements describing possible behavioral responses. For each pair, please circle the "A" or "B" statement, depending on which is most characteristic of your own behavior. That is, please indicate which of these two responses is more typical of your behavior in situations where you find that your wishes differ from someone else's wishes.

In many cases, neither the "A" nor the "B" statement may be very typical of your behavior; but please select the response which you would be more likely to use.

1. A. There are times when I let others take responsibility for solving the problem.
   B. Rather than negotiate the things on which we disagree, I try to stress those things upon which we both agree.
2. A. I try to find a compromise solution.
   B. I attempt to deal with all of his and my concerns.
3. A. I am usually firm in pursuing my goals.
   B. I might try to soothe the other's feelings and preserve our relationship.
4. A. I try to find a compromise solution.
   B. I sometimes sacrifice my own wishes for the wishes of the other person.
5. A. I consistently seek the other's help in working out a solution.
   B. I try to do what is necessary to avoid useless tensions.
6. A. I try to avoid creating unpleasantness for myself.
   B. I try to win my position.
7. A. I try to postpone the issue until I have had some time to think it over.

   B. I give up some points in exchange for others.
8. A. I am usually firm in pursuing my goals.
   B. I attempt to get all concerns and issues immediately out in the open.
9. A. I feel that differences are not always worth worrying about.
   B. I make some effort to get my way.
10. A. I am firm in pursuing my goals.
    B. I try to find a compromise solution.
11. A. I attempt to get all concerns and issues immediately in the open.
    B. I might try to smooth the other's feelings and preserve our relationship.
12. A. I sometimes avoid taking positions which would create controversy.
    B. I will let him have some of his positions if he lets me have some of mine.
13. A. I propose a middle ground.
    B. I press to get my points made.
14. A. I tell him my ideas and ask him for his.
    B. I try to show him the logic and benefits of my position.
15. A. I might try to soothe the other's feelings and preserve our relationship.
    B. I try to do what is necessary to avoid tensions.
16. A. I try not to hurt the other's feelings.
    B. I try to convince the other person of the merits of my position.
17. A. I am usually firm in pursuing my goals.
    B. I try to do what is necessary to avoid useless tensions.
18. A. If it makes the other person happy, I might let him maintain his views.
    B. I will let him have some of his positions if he lets me have some of mine.

19. A. I attempt to get all concerns and issues immediately out in the open.
    B. I try to postpone the issue until I have had time to think it over.
20. A. I attempt to immediately work through our differences.
    B. I try to find a fair combination of gains and losses for both of us.
21. A. In approaching negotiations, I try to be considerate of the other person's wishes.
    B. I always lean toward a direct discussion of the problem.
22. A. I try to find a position that is intermediate between his and mine.
    B. I assert my wishes.
23. A. I am very often concerned with satisfying all our wishes.
    B. There are times when I let others take responsibility for solving the problem.
24. A. If the other's position seems very important to him, I would try to meet his wishes.
    B. I am concerned to work out the best agreed course of action.
25. A. I try to show him the logic and benefits of my position.

B. In approaching negotiations, I try to be considerate of the other person's wishes.
26. A. I propose a middle ground.
    B. I am nearly always concerned with satisfying all our wishes.
27. A. I sometimes avoid taking positions which would create controversy.
    B. If it makes the other person happy, I might let him maintain his views.
28. A. I am usually firm in pursuing my goals.
    B. I feel that differences are not always worth worrying about.
29. A. I propose a middle ground.
    B. I feel that differences are not always worth worrying about.
30. A. I try not to hurt the other's feelings.
    B. I always share the problem with the other person so that we can work it out.

SCORING THE "BEHAVIOR DESCRIPTION QUESTIONNAIRE"

Circle the letters below which you circled on each item of the questionnaire:

Item No.	Competition (Forcing)	Collaboration (Problem Solving)	Sharing (Compromise)	Avoiding (Withdrawal)	Accommodation (Smoothing)
1.				A	B
2.		B	A		
3.	A				B
4.			A		B
5.		A		B	
6.	B			A	
7.			B	A	
8.	A	B			
9.	B			A	
10.	A		B		
11.		A			B
12.			B	A	
13.	B		A		
14.	B	A			
15.				B	A
16.	B				A
17.	A			B	
18.			B		A
19.		A		B	
20.		A	B		
21.		B			A
22.	B		A		
23.		A		B	

Item No.	Competition (Forcing)	Collaboration (Problem Solving)	Sharing (Compromise)	Avoiding (Withdrawal)	Accommodation (Smoothing)
24.			B		A
25.	A				B
26.		B	A		
27.				A	B
28.	A	B			
29.			A	B	
30.		B			A

Total number of items circled in each column:

Competition	Collaboration	Sharing	Avoiding	Accommodation
_____	_____	_____	_____	_____

Step 2: Discussion. In small groups or with the class as a whole, answer the following questions:

1. What did your score pattern look like?
2. Do any patterns emerge among groups in the class?
3. Which modes have you found to be most commonly used? least commonly used?
4. Which modes have you found to be most effective? least effective?
5. In what situations has each mode been most effective?

Reprinted with permission from "Conflict Management" by Randolph Flynn and David Elloy, National Institute for Dispute Resolution (Washington, D.C.), Working Paper, 1987.

Activity 10–3   King Electronics

Step 1: Divide the class into groups of four people. Read the following general description of the situation. The instructor will distribute four roles to each group. Each person in the group should then prepare one role. In preparing for the role play, try to put yourself in the position of the person whose role you are playing.

GENERAL BACKGROUND

King Electronics Company, located in the San Fernando Valley outside Los Angeles, manufactures special government orders on precision instruments. The company has no major product but applies its specialized skills to very complex projects and has done this successfully. Its flexibility in moving from project to project has built a reputation for high quality, for the ability to manufacture precise instruments, and for quick production and delivery.

Many jobs require that proposals with technical and cost information be hand carried to Washington, D.C., by a specific deadline. While management realizes that the nature of its business necessitates rigid time constraints and short time frames, it has been successful because of this opportunistic reaction time. As a result, King Electronics has been rewarded appropriately for its efforts in meeting its customers' demands. See the accompanying organization chart of the Cost Proposal Section (Figure 10–13).

Step 2: Each group of four participants should convene the group meeting in part of the room. Your instructor will tell you how much time you have to reach a solution.

Step 3: Report your group's solution to your instructor.

Step 4: Discussion. Answer the following questions, in small groups or with the entire class:

Description
1. Characterize each participant's behavior. What style did they use?

Figure 10–13 **Organization Chart for King Electronics**

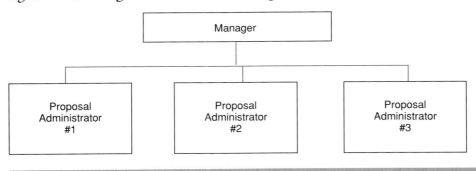

Diagnosis

2. What problems did you encounter in reaching an agreement? Why?

3. Evaluate the effectiveness of conflict resolution in this situation.

Reprinted with permission from "Conflict Management" by Randolph Flynn and David Elloy, National Institute for Dispute Resolution (Washington, D.C.), Working Paper, 1987.

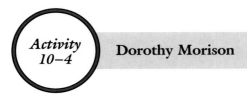

Dorothy Morison

Step 1: Read the Dorothy Morison case.

Dorothy Morison, a manager in the Information Services Division of the Ace Aerospace Company, had experienced little success in her efforts to guide and coordinate division projects. As manager of Systems Engineering, Dorothy's job was to work with personnel in other departments on the planning and implementation of certain programs. Managers from these departments had made it clear, however, that they regarded her attempts at teamwork as interference. Dorothy and her boss, Bill McNulty, found that the only plans accepted were those which were in the "blue sky" area. As McNulty put it, "As soon as we get anywhere close to today's operation or even next year's operation, we are stepping on their turf."

Dorothy's most pressing problem was a project with the acronym ISAC. This project, which involved the development of a new control system, was regarded by the director of Information Services as an opportunity to develop a new product with company-wide application. Hence Dorothy was directed to form a team of analysts from other departments who would do the actual technical work, while she and her staff monitored their progress.

From the beginning other division managers had been reluctant to let their technicians work on the project. As a result project ISAC, which was originally envisioned as a short-term operation, had taken two years and cost several

million dollars. As of early 1985, moreover, ISAC was estimated to be at least two years from completion.

ACE AEROSPACE AND THE INFORMATION SERVICES DIVISION

Ace Aerospace Corporation was one of the top fifty industrial companies in the United States. The corporation, which had existed since the 1920's, designed and built spacecraft, aircrafts, and ships, as well as various specialized electronic systems used for both defense and industrial purposes. Approximately 20,000 of Ace's 80,000 employees were either scientists or engineers.

With the exception of the Information Services Division (ISD) all Ace divisions existed to produce a particular product—a new space telescope, for example. ISD was a support organization providing a number of computer services for other Ace divisions. Each of the ISD departments was responsible for an area of computer support, such as administrative programming or computer graphics. Typically managers and technicians from Information Services worked in a matrix structure with their counterparts in a product division to develop the kinds of programs and services required. For example, a division working on the development of a new ballistic missile would engage Information Services people to design the attendant financial control system. (Because so much of Ace's business was government-sponsored, and hence subject to rigorous reporting requirements, the design of such in-house control systems was an integral part of new product development.)

The five ISD departments were Information Systems Applications, Information Systems Services, Technical Computing, Office and Reprographics Services, and Systems Technology. The last department, within which Dorothy worked, differed from the other four in that it was designed to provide support services within the division. The Systems Engineering segment, of which Dorothy was manager, was intended to serve as a planning and integrating mechanism for projects underway in the other product-oriented departments.

HISTORY OF SYSTEMS ENGINEERING

The director of the Information Services division, Mr. William James, had taken over as division manager six years earlier. Bill James, Dorothy's boss Bill McNulty, Dorothy, and several other managers had come to Information Services from an Ace product division. As the volume and pace of product development increased over the years Ace management had recognized the need for a more company-wide perspective with regard to information services. The new ISD team had been charged with creating systems that would integrate every facet of product development, and do so in such a way as to have company-wide applicability. Personnel in ISD, however, tended to work on a project-by-project basis, tailoring systems to fit a particular situation. James' strategy was to introduce the more generalized approach, called "systems engineering," to the Information Services division.

As part of this effort James formed the Systems Engineering department. He described his intentions for this new department as follows:

> In Information Services we need to be moving toward the future. That's what the Systems Engineering group is supposed to do. Its job is to coordinate and play a liaison role on new projects that involve other groups in ISD and to represent a planning and systems orientation on these projects.

Dorothy, who was the third person to manage Systems Engineering, elaborated on the systems engineering concept:

> Systems engineering is a concept of overview design, setting the direction, setting the parameters within which a project will be conducted. It requires monitoring of the project, giving guidance and technical direction.
>
> This is a system which is used extensively in other Ace divisions. But within ISD it is something new and different.

According to Dorothy her responsibilities were the following: "To perform top-level strategic planning and other staff work for the director (James), to act as project coordinator, and to assist in planning on new projects." Figure 10–14 is a more detailed statement of these duties.

The concept of systems engineering, then, implied that Dorothy and other ISD personnel would work together, frequently in teams, to bring a more global perspective to division activities. In attempting to fulfill the necessary planning and integrating functions, Dorothy came into conflict with the existing management system. For a variety of reasons ISD managers proceeded to resist Dorothy's efforts to work with them and their supervisors and technicians. The managers of two areas in particular—the Applications department and the Services department—were opposed to any outside intervention.

SYSTEMS ENGINEERING AND ISAC PROJECT

The project that best exemplified Dorothy's management problems was the ISAC project. ISAC, which was the acronym for "Information Services Asset Control," was a project begun in the fall of 1982. The objective for this project was to implement a computer hardware inventory control system for the entire Information Services Division. Dorothy provided the following rationale for this project:

> The Information Services Division is responsible for managing certain company assets: computing hardware, the big IBM systems, the terminals, the printers, and the peripheral equipment. There are leases, purchases, buy options and lease option credits. Because we are a government contractor, the way we manage these assets is monitored. It is significant business problem and the ISAC project involves a data processing system that will help us manage and control this asset base.

A team was assembled for the ISAC project that had personnel from Dorothy's area to oversee it and technical people from the ISD and Applications department to do systems analysis. The ISAC project called for technical assistance from all six disciplines within the Applications department. According to Dorothy problems in forming the ISAC team began right at the start:

> Management (from Applications) would not sign up to working as a team. Mr. James had to direct that the people working on the project be allowed to attend meetings in our area. The Applications managers were willing to do what was needed to be done as long as the requirements were spelled out in black and white and "thrown over the transom." These managers claimed that their people got in trouble when anybody but their managers or supervisor directed them. They would work on the project only if *they* were the ones supervising their project.

OTHER MANAGERS' VIEW OF ISAC PROBLEMS

Jim Gardner was the director of the ISD Applications department. Jim was relatively new to the directors' job; however, he had served as a supervisor and then as a manager

Figure 10-14 **Job Description**

Basic Objective

Provide a systems engineering discipline to the planning, coordination, and implementation of computer-based information systems.

Functions and Responsibilities

1. Develop, prepare, and maintain the Information Services Strategic Plan and the ACE Office Automation Strategic Plan. Integrate the plans of the Information Services service centers.
2. Analyze the requirements, coordinate implementation planning, and provide status for system level activities that involve more than one directorate within Information Services. Specify systems requirements for Information Services.
3. Develop, maintain, and/or integrate architectural models as flexible tools for analyzing, planning, and integrating information systems. Conduct the Preliminary Design Review/Critical Design Review for the planning and implementation of architectural changes.
4. Perform systems assurance assessment of the quality of service provided by Information Services. Maintain standards for business systems development and conduct system assurance reviews for compliance.
5. Analyze new information technologies that could be a major enhancement to services provided by Information Services.
6. Evaluate, plan, and coordinate advanced technologies and standards for ACE's automated office systems. Participate in Corporate automated office system activities and obtain approval of any ACE deviations to standards.
7. Apply systems engineering disciplines in formulating recommendations regarding the technical aspects of accessibility, internal accounting, and controls for information systems as requested by the Director of Information Services.

W. E. McNulty, Director
Systems Technology

Approved: W. A. James
Director of Information Services Division

---

in the business applications area for over twenty years. Most of the managers who reported to him had been in their jobs four years or less, having worked for Jim previously as supervisors and technical contributors. Jim believed that relationships within his organization were good. His management philosophy was to hold his managers accountable for their own work and the supervision of their people, not telling them *how* to go about it, but only looking at results. Jim described Applications as a very structured organization, where all layers were held accountable. Boundaries were respected, and for this reason Systems Engineering presented a problem. In his words, "System Engineering gets involved in things that supposedly cut across area lines. They step in to coordinate things between two organizations that feel no need for their coordination."

Jim Gardner claimed that his people did not like to work with Dorothy, not only because she spelled out solutions, but because people felt that if they didn't agree with her, she would immediately refer the problem to Bill James. He expanded on this perception as follows:

To my knowledge she has never influenced Bill to make a policy decision contrary to what I've advocated. She and I have differed, but I have never lost on a single item of importance. I am constantly trying to put a lid on the perception that she runs to Bill to get what she can't do herself. But when a secretary gets a call ordering her manager to attend a meeting with Dorothy's people and she says that Mr. James ordered it, well, it doesn't do a great deal to improve relationships.

Jim Gardner also explained that Dorothy Morison wanted to be assured of staffing in ISAC. She wanted to know who, by name, would be assigned to the project, and who would work on it for its duration. This was not the way Jim wanted his area to operate:

Our responsibility is for the work. It is our management's responsibility to assign the people to do the work. You will tell us what the job is, and we will complete it. Whom we use is not your business. They want meetings with workers. My managers say no, you work through us.

Tom Boone, Jim's manager for Systems Analysis, had been directly involved in the ISAC project. The lack of success on the project stemmed, Boone felt, from the objectives set for it:

Systems Engineering views ISAC as an exercise in developing a whole new system of inventory control. If you give me a technical assignment like this new control system, we have a pretty good method for doing it for at least two years; we've put a couple of hundred programs up. Now, if I'm on schedule, I don't feel I should have to explain or conduct an orientation program about why I did something just so they can document it. When they put out a schedule and I'm committed to meeting it, I'll use the methodology I know best.

People from Systems Engineering don't seem to have the same commitment to schedule that we do. In Applications we in management instill in our personnel a commitment to schedules. Schedules are a must for applications development, because there is no value to the end user unless the application is functional and making data available. That's what we get paid for.

Tom also said that Systems Engineering interfered with the way he and his people did the technical work. He felt that they should be monitoring the schedule and the budget. Instead, he protested:

They come in and ask methodological questions, like, "Why are your people doing logical access maps for the screen view?" Why are they asking me that? How to do the technical work is my job. If I'm not capable of it, fire me.

These problems were common in all project work, Tom explained, but were exacerbated with ISAC because they were taking place within the ISD family. Tom believed that that made resolution of conflicts more difficult.

If I have these kinds of differences between myself and the manager in a user division, I'll get resolution. If I can't do it by negotiation or by force of personality, *then* we'll elevate it to the director. Within Information Services, however, what happens is that it gets elevated to Mr. James immediately. He's a busy man and he doesn't have all the information, so he can't pay much attention to it. So there isn't much follow-through and differences never get resolved.

Paul Martin, the director of Central Data Systems, made the following observation:

When the situation escalates to James, he sometimes circumvents the layers of management and orders people to comply with Systems Engineering requirements.

This leads to perceptions that Systems Engineering has an inordinate amount of influence with top management, and in turn creates mistrust between our technical people and personnel from Systems Engineering.

SYSTEMS ENGINEERING AND THE SERVICES DEPARTMENT

Dorothy Morison had also worked with the ISD Technical Services departments on certain projects. One recent project involved efforts to standardize computer user identification codes within the Ace Corporation. Dorothy's department was to play a liaison role between ISD and Ace corporate headquarters. One manager with whom she was supposed to work, Chuck Dinsmore, had informed Systems Engineering that such standardization was not feasible in his department. He had provided written documentation for this position but said later he believed that his views would be disregarded: "That standard is going to come out as directed by Dorothy. All the comments we made were ignored by her. She will solicit our input and then ignore it."

Chuck Dinsmore also expressed resentment at Dorothy's wish to be involved in technical matters, such as was implied in a recent letter that he had received stating that Systems Engineering planned to review for approval all new business software. Although Chuck's group had always tested and introduced new business software, the recent concern with organization-wide compatibility prompted the directive that new software be cleared with Dorothy's office. Chuck proceeded to ignore this clearance procedure, introducing a new office automation package without notifying Systems Engineering. He expressed his views on this subject as follows: "To coordinate with corporate headquarters and to approve software are two very different matters."

Dorothy expressed her own frustrations with regard to the issue of the standardized user identification codes. She responded as follows to Chuck's claim that she ignored his position:

We don't ignore their input, but it is generally so negative that when you consider all the ramifications you proceed with the best recommendation a composite of all the information. All their reasons for rejecting the plans were in terms of their own convenience. It wasn't as if they proposed an alternative.

From Chuck's perspective standardization will not benefit his department. Therefore, to him it is not a good idea. His attitude is short-range operational, get the job done today, spread my limited resources in the most effective way. The nice thing about Chuck is that he is consistent. We wind up agreeing to disagree.

While all of the above quoted managers concurred that the Information Services Division was generally a positive place to work, they agreed that problems of coordination with Systems Engineering persisted. Dorothy summed up her own perspective on the various areas of disagreement as follows:

> They—the managers in Applications and Technical Services—manage for today. That's their job. But if we follow their line, I fear that we sacrifice tomorrow. And, although Mr. James accepts our planning and future-oriented role in theory, we don't get his backing on a day-to-day basis. Even when the planning position should win out, it doesn't. Ideally we should be able to make a trade-off between today and tomorrow, and get the optimum decisions given all the factors. What generally happens, however, is that today is the winner.

DOROTHY MORISON AND MANAGEMENT STYLE AT ACE

A manager who had worked with Dorothy in the past and who had since moved to another division was interviewed on the subject of management style within the company. He gave the following overview:

> I can't speak for an awful lot of companies, so maybe Ace is somewhat unique, but I would think not. I don't see an awful lot of backstabbing mentality at Ace. But, on the other hand, I don't see alot of cooperation either. One of my managers describes us as a bunch of feudal fiefdoms. I've heard managers say, "Let them go ahead and pass that standard, I'm not going to follow it anyway."
>
> So with that environment, if you are supposed to come up with some standards or integrate across divisional lines, this fiefdom attitude makes your job extremely difficult. Twenty-year managers are strong willed, and if they want to be an adversary, they make a strong adversary.

What did this manager think was the particular source of Dorothy's problems?

> I think the problem is mainly Dorothy's background. She is out of the scientific and engineering area of the company, which means that most of the Information Services people think that she doesn't know what they are about. Dorothy is in a rather difficult position. She has a relationship with McNulty and James that causes her some problems. People feel that she has a pipeline to the top. And they feel that she uses it, whether she does or not. So that's a problem, added to the fact that she's in a very difficult assignment. Nobody understands what her assignment is. Including me. . . . It's James' pet organization in that it was put there to do special things for him. But I wouldn't be surprised if he ignores it. So Dorothy doesn't seem to have the authority or back up she needs.

Alluded to were certain aspects of Dorothy's own management style which exacerbated current problems:

> She is willing to see something that needs to be done and then go out and try to do it. That often runs counter to something that someone else is working on.
>
> (Another manager, Jim Gardner, had described this tendency differently: "She's a perfectionist. She wants things done the way *she* thinks they should be done. So she gives her own opinion on *how* problems should be solved rather than seeing that they *are* solved.")

PROSPECTS FOR THE ISAC PROJECT

Originally Dorothy Morison and Bill McNulty had viewed ISAC as a simple project. But in late 1984 ISAC had been running two years and was, they estimated, at least two years from completion. Other managers felt, however, that if coordination issues were resolved, ISAC could be implemented in less than a year.

SUPPORT FROM THE IS DIRECTOR

Both Bill and Dorothy agreed that they had not received adequate support from Bill James. The responsibilities of Systems Engineering had not been communicated effectively to other ISD managers. Dorothy gave the following example of a situation in which she felt stymied by behavior and attitudes resulting from this failure to make others aware of the scope of her department's responsibilities. (This situation was referred to earlier. It concerned the new procedure for clearance of new software, a procedure with which the manager involved declined to comply.) In mid-1984 Dorothy's department had assimilated planning for systems software, while the actual design of training, counselling, and evaluation programs for software remained under Chuck Dinsmore. Bill James had issued a memo detailing the responsibilities for each department. Dorothy felt that this directive was not sufficiently clear, and so she prepared a written description of how the two organizations should work together. According to Dorothy her efforts at clarification were futile:

> What I did was describe how I thought it ought to work. My first opinion was that all of it—systems software, counseling, and everything to do with office automation—should be put in Systems Engineering. It's too immature a technology, the culture is not right here at Ace; we can't have this territorial rights issue within the organization and do anything decent for the user community. You really need to consolidate it, and that's still my opinion.
>
> But, given that that was not going to be done, I recommended how it should work. Bill James gave the department manager and Chuck two weeks to analyze it and come back with a rebuttal. They didn't even look at it. They came to the meeting with Bill James and mumbled some words and waved their arms. They had done nothing to assess it. So Bill James said, "OK, this is in effect." In a way he slapped their hands for not doing their homework. I talked with him later, and I

Figure 10–15   **Memorandum**

TO: Dorothy Morison
FROM: Diane Petrocelli
SUBJECT: ISAC Team Meetings

Yesterday afternoon, Phyllis told me that Dick was directed by Jim to tell Phyllis not to attend any more of the ISAC Team working meetings. She objected to this saying that meetings like these are how we share and discuss things. She intends to talk to Jim about this. At the next team meeting, it would seem that only team personnel will be able to attend. The other five will not be there. Dorothy, I don't see how we can hold this together and meet our objectives in this continuing environment of conflict. You will remember that things turned to hell in about March. There appears to be no way to shelter the troops, let alone direct my planning efforts and leadership towards an ISAC product. Most of my time is spent in underground one-on-one meetings on approved subjects with precise and limiting boundaries. Coordination and cooperation can only be achieved on a skirmish by skirmish basis. Let's step back and examine the ISAC project impact. It has to be enormous. Each week there is more lost time, increased embittered attitudes, and new petty prerogatives that undermine our ability to work together to produce an ISAC system—one that some of us believe is in the best interest of our division and company.

said, "Bill, if I had come to a meeting as prepared as those guys were, you would have had my hide." And he said, "I did, didn't you notice?" And I said, "They didn't."

So Bill had to write a letter. He had me write the letter. It went to Chuck's manager, but Chuck didn't get a copy directly. So he's just ignoring it. Two weeks ago a new version of the software arrived, and Chuck wrote a highlight report and said we are going to implement it on the first of April. That was the first I heard of it. What do I do about this? I pretend that it is working. I send out notes to the people in other companies saying I'm coordinating this new release of the software. I send copies of that to Chuck so he knows what I am doing.

Day-to-day problems continued to cause delay in the ISAC project. Dorothy described the most recent example:

Last week we had an ISAC working meeting and the people from Systems Analysis were directed not to come. I learned today that one person on loan from Support Data Systems, who had been working on ISAC for two years, was told not to attend any more meetings. This is a perfect example of their attitude, which is, "Don't you dare direct our people."

Figure 10–15 is a copy of a memo from one of Dorothy's subordinates on the subject of this most recent incident.

Step 2:   Prepare the case for class discussion.

Step 3:   Answer the following questions, individually, in small groups, or with the entire class, as directed by your instructor:

Description
1. Describe the interaction among the groups working on the ISAC project.

Diagnosis
2. Is there functional or dysfunctional conflict between the groups?
3. What level of conflict exists?
4. At what stage is the conflict?
5. What causes the conflict?
6. How do intergroup relations contribute to the conflict?

Prescription
7. What options are available to improve the situation?

Action
8. What costs and benefits probably will result from implementing the prescription?

Step 4:   Discussion. In small groups, with the entire class, or in written form, share your answers to the questions above. Then answer the following questions:

1. What symptoms suggest that a problem exists?
2. What problems exist in the case?
3. What theories and concepts help explain the problems?
4. How can the problems be corrected?
5. Are the actions likely to be effective?

This case was prepared by Jeanne Stanton and Deborah Kolb for the Institute for Case Development and Research, Simmons Graduate School of Management, Boston, MA. Copyright © 1986 by the President & Trustees of Simmons College. Reprinted by permission.

Activity 10–5   Windsock, Inc.

Step 1: The class is divided into four groups: Central Office, Product Design, Marketing/Sales, and Production. Central Office is a slightly smaller group. If groups are large enough, assign observers to each one. Central Office is given 500 straws and 750 pins. Each person reads only the role description relevant to his or her group.

Step 2: Groups perform functions and prepare a two-minute report for stockholders.

Step 3: Each group gives a two-minute presentation to stockholders.

Step 4: Observers share insights with subgroups.

Step 5: Discussion. In small groups or with the entire class, answer the following questions:

Description
1. What occurred during the exercise?

Diagnosis
2. Was there conflict?
3. What contributed to the relationships among groups?
4. Evaluate communication and leadership in the groups.

Prescription
5. How could the relationships have been more effective?

Adapted with permission from Christopher Taylor and Saundra Taylor in "Teaching Organizational Team Building through Simulation," *Organizational Behavior Teaching Review* 11(3) (1986–1987): 136–138.

Activity 10–6   World Bank: An Intergroup Negotiation

This is an intergroup activity. You and your team are going to engage in a task in which money will be won or lost. *The objective is to win as much as you can.* There are two teams involved in this activity, and both teams receive identical instructions. After reading these instructions, your team has 15 minutes to organize itself and to plan its strategy.

Step 1: The class is divided into two groups. The size of each of the groups should be no more than ten. Those not in one of the two groups are designated as observers. However, groups should not have less than six members each. The instructor will play the role of the referee/banker for the World Bank.

Step 2: Read the World Bank Instruction Sheet that follows:

WORLD BANK GENERAL INSTRUCTION SHEET

Each team represents a country. Each country has financial dealings with the World Bank. Initially, each country contributed $100 million to the World Bank. Countries may have to pay further monies or may receive money from the

World Bank in accordance with regulations and procedures described below under sections headed Finance and Payoffs.

Each team is given twenty cards. These are your *weapons.* Each card has a marked side (*X*) and an unmarked side. The marked side of the card signifies that the weapon is armed. Conversely, the blank side shows the weapon to be unarmed.

At the beginning, each team will place ten of its twenty weapons in their armed positions (marked side up) and the remaining ten in their unarmed positions (marked side down). These weapons will remain in your possession and out of sight of the other team at all times.

There will be *rounds* and *moves.* Each round consists of seven moves by each team. There will be two or more rounds in this simulation. The number of rounds depends on the time available. Payoffs are determined and recorded after each round.

1. A move consists of turning two, one, or none of the team's weapons from armed to unarmed status, or vice versa.
2. Each team has 2 minutes for each move. There are 30-second periods between moves. At the end of 2

minutes, the team must have turned two, one, or none of its weapons from armed to unarmed status, or from unarmed to armed status. If the team fails to move in the allotted time, no change can be made in weapon status until the next move.

3. The length of the 2½-minute periods between the beginning of one move and the beginning of the next is fixed and unalterable.

Each new round of the experiment begins with all weapons returned to their original positions, ten armed and ten unarmed.

Finances
The funds you have contributed to the World Bank are to be allocated in the following manner:

$60 million will be returned to each team to be used as your team's treasury during the course of the decision-making activities.

$80 million will be retained for the operation of the World Bank.

Payoffs
1. If there is an attack:
   a. Each team may announce an attack on the other team by notifying the referee/banker during the 30 seconds following *any* 2-minute period used to decide upon the move (including the seventh, or final, decision period in any round). The choice of each team during the decision period just ended counts as a move. An attack may not be made during negotiations.
   b. If there is an attack (by one or both teams), two things happen: (1) the round ends, and (2) the World Bank levies a penalty of $5 million for each team.
   c. The team with the greater number of armed weapons wins $3 million for each armed weapon it has over and above the number of armed weapons of the other team. These funds are paid directly from the treasury of the losing team to the treasury of the winning team. The referee/bankers will manage this transfer of funds.
2. If there is no attack:
   At the end of each round (seven moves), each team's treasury receives from the World Bank $2 million for each of its weapons that is at that point unarmed, and each team's treasury pays to the World Bank $2 million for each of its weapons remaining armed.

Negotiations
Between moves each team has the opportunity to communicate with the other team through its negotiators.

Either team may call for negotiations by notifying the referee/bankers during any of the 30-second periods be-

tween decisions. A team is free to accept or reject any invitations to negotiate.

Negotiators from both teams are *required* to meet after the third and sixth moves (after the 30-second period following that move, if there is no attack).

Negotiations can last no longer than 3 minutes. When the two negotiators return to their teams, the 2-minute decision period for the next move begins once again.

Negotiators are bound only by: (a) the 3-minute time limit for negotiations, and (b) their required appearance after the third and sixth moves. They are otherwise free to say whatever is necessary to benefit themselves or their teams. The teams similarly are not bound by agreements made by their negotiators, even when those agreements are made in good faith.

Special Roles
Each team has 15 minutes to organize itself to plan team strategy. During this period before the first round begins, each team must choose persons to fill the following roles. (Each team must have each of the following roles, which can be changed at any time by a decision of the team.)

- *Negotiators*—activities stated above.
- A *representative*—to communicate team decisions to the referee/bankers.
- A *recorder*—to record the moves of the team and to keep a running balance of the team's treasury.
- A *treasurer*—to execute all financial transactions with the referee/bankers.

Step 3: Each group or team will have 15 minutes to organize itself and plan strategy before beginning. Before the first round each team must choose (a) two negotiators, (b) a representative, (c) a team recorder, (d) a treasurer.

Step 4: The referee/banker will signal the beginning of round one and each following round and also end the exercise in about one hour.

Step 5: Discussion. In small groups or with the entire class, answer the following questions:

Description
1. What occurred during the exercise?

Diagnosis
2. Was there conflict? What type, level, or stage?
3. What contributed to the relationships among groups?
4. Evaluate the power, leadership, motivation, and communication among groups.

Prescription
5. How could the relationships have been more effective?

Adapted from J. William Pfeiffer and John E. Jones, eds., *The 1975 Annual Handbook for Group Facilitators,* San Diego, CA: Pfeiffer & Company, 1975. Used with permission.

CONCLUDING COMMENTS

Conflict by itself is neither good nor bad. It must be assessed in the context of the individuals, groups, and organizations involved. The effective organizational member may endure or consciously create conflict. Diagnosing its causes should aid in controlling its dysfunctions and encouraging functional ties. The Behavior Description Questionnaire provided an assessment of personal predispositions for experiencing and abilities for managing conflict in organizations. The King Electronics case allowed you to practice handling conflict.

Conflict often arises because organizations comprise numerous sets of interacting individuals and groups. In this chapter we examined the special issues of interacting groups. Perceptual differences, the nature of task relations, and power differences influence both group interaction and effectiveness. At Pharmatech N.V. and in the case of Dorothy Morison, problems in these areas decreased productivity and worker satisfaction. Windsock, Inc., and the World Bank exercises further exemplified the impact of competitive behavior. Effective performance called for open and honest communication, shared perceptions of organizational situations, and identification with more than one group as a means of increasing the effectiveness of interaction. The nature of the organization's structure, as discussed in the next part of the book, can facilitate such performance.

ENDNOTES

[1] D. J. Yang, Boeing knocks down the wall between the dreamers and the doers, *Business Week* (October 28, 1991): 120–121.

[2] B. Kabanoff, Potential influence structures as sources of interpersonal conflict in groups and organizations, *Organizational Behavior and Human Decision Processes* 36 (1985): 115.

[3] D. M. Kolb and L. L. Putnam, The dialectics of disputing. In D. M. Kolb and J. M. Bartunek, eds., *Hidden Conflict in Organizations* (Newbury Park, Calif.: Sage, 1992), p. 18.

[4] M. Deutsch, Subjective features of conflict resolution: Psychological, social, and cultural influences. In R. Vayrynen, *New Directions in Conflict Theory: Conflict Resolution and Conflict Transformation* (London: Sage, 1991).

[5] R. A. Baron, Personality and organizational conflict: Effects of the Type A behavior pattern and self-monitoring, *Organizational Behavior and Human Decision Processes* 44 (1989): 281–296.

[6] A. C. Filley, *Interpersonal Conflict Resolution* (Glenview, Ill.: Scott, Foresman, 1975).

[7] This discussion is drawn from Deutsch, Subjective features.

[8] C. H. Coombs, The structure of conflict, *American Psychologist* 42(4) (1987): 355–363.

[9] G. Cliff, Managing organizational conflict, *Management Review* 76(5) (May 1987): 53.

[10] J. Pfeiffer, Beyond management and the workers: The institutional function of management, *Academy of Management Review* 1 (1976): 26–46; H. Assael, Constructive roles of interorganizational conflict, *Administrative Science Quarterly* 14 (1968): 573–581.

[11] K. W. Thomas, Organizational conflict. In *Organizational Behavior,* ed. S. Kerr (Columbus, Ohio: Grid, 1979).

[12] L. R. Pondy, Organizational conflict: Concepts and models, *Administrative Science Quarterly* 12 (1967): 296–320.

[13] J. E. McCann and D. L. Ferry, An approach for assessing and managing interunit interdependence, *Academy of Management Review* 4 (1979): 113–119.

[14] J. D. Thompson, *Organizations in Action* (New York: McGraw-Hill, 1967); A. H. Van de Ven, A. L. Delbecq, and R. Koenig, Jr., Determinants of coordination modes within organizations, *American Sociological Review* 41 (1976): 322–338.

[15] Van de Ven et al., Determinants of coordination modes.

[16] K. K. Smith, An intergroup perspective on individual behavior. In H. J. Leavitt, L. R. Pondy, and D. M. Boje, eds., *Readings in Managerial Psychology,* 4th ed. (Chicago: University of Chicago Press, 1989).

[17] D. W. Johnson and F. P. Johnson, *Cooperation and Competition: Theory and Research* (Edina, Minn.: Interaction, 1989).

[18] A. W. Gouldner, Cosmopolitans and locals: Toward an analysis of latent social roles, *Administrative Science Quarterly* 2 (1958): 290.

[19] R. L. Kahn, D. M. Wolfe, R. P. Quinn, and J. D. Snoek, *Organizational Stress: Studies in Role Conflict and Ambiguity* (New York: Wiley, 1964).

[20] D. Hickson, C. Hinings, C. Lee, R. Schneck, and J. A. Pennings, A strategic contingencies theory of intraorganizational power, *Administrative Science Quarterly* 23 (1978): 65–90.

[21] J. McCann and J. R. Galbraith, Interdepartmental relations. In P. C. Nystrom and W. H. Starbuck, eds., *Handbook of Organizational Design,* vol. 2 (New York: Oxford University Press, 1981).

[22] L. Greenhalgh, Managing conflict, *Sloan Management Review* (Summer 1986): 45–51.

[23] Thomas, Conflict and conflict management. In M. D. Dunnette, ed., *Handbook of Industrial and Organizational Psychology* (Chicago: Rand McNally, 1976), pp. 889–935.

[24] D. D. Morley and P. Shockley-Zalabak, Conflict avoiders and compromisers: Toward an understanding of their organizational communication style, *Group and Organization Studies* 11 (December 1986): 387–402.

[25] E. Van de Vliert, Escalative intervention in small-group conflicts, *Journal of Applied Behavioral Science* 21 (1985): 19–36.

[26] R. Beckhard, The confrontation meeting, *Harvard Business Review* 45 (1967): 154, presents an early description of this intervention.

[27] W. L. French and C. H. Bell, Jr., *Organization Development: Behavioral Science Interventions for Organization Improvement,* 2nd ed. (Englewood Cliffs, N.J.: Prentice-Hall, 1978).

[28] H. Prien, Strategies for third-party intervention, *Human Relations* 40 (1987): 699–720.

[29] Van de Vliert, Escalative intervention.

[30] R. R. Blake and J. S. Mouton, Overcoming group warfare, *Harvard Business Review* 62(6) (1984): 98–108.

[31] See D. Kolb, Women's work: Peacemaking in organizations. In D. M. Kolb and J. M. Bartunek, eds., *Hidden Conflict in Organizations* (Newbury Park, Calif.: Sage, 1992); D. M. Kolb, *The Mediators* (Cambridge, Mass.: MIT Press, 1983).

[32] Kolb, Women's work, p. 80.

[33] This grouping with the exception of arbitration is presented by J. Stockard and D. Lach, Conflict resolution: Sex and gender roles. In J. B. Gittler, *The Annual Review of Conflict Knowledge and Conflict Resolution,* vol. 1 (New York: Garland, 1989): 69–91.

[34] Kolb and Putnam, Dialectics of disputing, p. 11.

[35] D. Q. Mills, *Labor-Management Relations* (New York: McGraw-Hill, 1978).

[36] R. Likert and J. Likert, *New Ways of Managing Conflict* (New York: McGraw-Hill, 1976).

[37] N. J. Adler, Organizational development in a multicultural environment, *Journal of Applied Behavioral Sciences* 19(3) (1983): 349–365.

RECOMMENDED READINGS

Gittler, J. B., ed. *The Annual Review of Conflict Knowledge and Conflict Resolution,* vol. 1. New York: Garland, 1989.

Kolb, D. M., and Bartunek, J. M., eds. *Hidden Conflict in Organizations*. Newbury Park, Calif.: Sage, 1992.

Mastenbroek, W. F. G. *Conflict Management and Organization Development*. Chichester, England: Wiley, 1987.

Stroebe, W., et al., eds. *The Social Psychology of Intergroup Conflict: Theory, Research and Applications*. Berlin: Springer-Verlag, 1988.

Vayrynen, R., ed. *New Directions in Conflict Theory: Conflict Resolution and Conflict Transformation*. London: Sage, 1991.

Walton, R. *Managing Conflict*. Reading, Mass.: Addison-Wesley, 1987.

Chapter Outline

- **OPENING CASE** *Structuring the Worldwide Travel Agency*

  The Multinational Corporation

  Types of Division of Labor

  Options for Coordination

  Information-Processing Structures

  Bases of Departmentation

  Configurations According to Means of Coordination

  Structures for Increasing Global Competitiveness

  The Informal Organization

  Diagnosing and Designing Organizational Structures

- **READING 11–1** *Managing 21st Century Network Organizations*
  Charles C. Snow, Raymond E. Miles, and Henry J. Coleman, Jr.

- **ACTIVITIES**

  11–1   Reorganization at Jackson Company

  11–2   Apex College

  11–3   Analysis of Organization Charts

  11–4   Jane Sanderson

  11–5   Magnacomp, Inc.

  11–6   Restructuring for Increased Performance

Evaluating and Selecting Organizational Structures

Learning Objectives

After completing the reading and activities in Chapter 11, students will be able to

1. Identify the issues in structuring an organization that functions in more than one country.

2. Represent an organization's formal structure with an organizational chart.

3. Recognize situations in which various types of differentiation do and should exist in an organization.

4. Assess the nature of coordinating mechanisms in an organization.

5. Describe organic and mechanistic structures.

6. Choose between high and low information-processing capacity structures.

7. Analyze and design an organization according to each of four bases of departmentation.

8. Compare and contrast five structural configurations based on coordinating mechanisms.

9. Comment on the applicability of network-based forms of structure.

10. Discuss the ways the informal organization differs from the formal organization and the implications for effectiveness.

11. Offer a protocol for diagnosing and designing an organizational structure.

Structuring the Worldwide Travel Agency

Worldwide Travel was recently formed as a merger of five travel agencies, three based in the United States and two based in the United Kingdom. The three agencies in the United States ranged in size from 50 to 500 employees; each had an extensive network of offices, as well as its own corporate support staff. The two agencies in the United Kingdom had 200 and 400 employees; each also had numerous branch offices spread throughout Europe, as well as several in strategic locations in the Orient. Figure 11–1 shows the structure of the largest agency that became part of Worldwide Travel. The other organizations had similar structures, varying somewhat in size and complexity.

Marie Fahey had been employed as the director of the Human Resources Department of the largest U.S. agency joining the merger. She had reported directly to the president of the agency, who had recently been named president of the newly created Worldwide Travel. After the merger she was promoted to a new position as special assistant to the president. One of her first responsibilities was to advise the executive management committee about the way the new organization should be structured. She tried to review what she knew about various structural options; she had recently read about some new structural innovations that she might want the management to consider.

*S*tructure refers to the delineation of jobs and reporting relationships in an organization. Its principal function is to influence and coordinate the work behavior of the organization's members in accomplishing the organization's goals. The organization chart shown in Figure 11–1 reflects the formal interactions at Nationwide. It shows the grouping of individuals into departments, the formal reporting relationships, and the way the activities of various organizational members are coordinated. How effective would Nationwide's structure be for the larger Worldwide Travel Company? Do you think such a structure would facilitate or impede communication, decision making, leadership, group and intergroup relations, employee motivation, and other aspects of organizational behavior? Would it likely result in a high-quality product, innovative performance, and high employee productivity?

In this chapter we consider the options available for the structuring of Worldwide Travel. First we discuss the structural issues a multinational firm must consider. Then we examine the building blocks of organization structure. We next look at their combination into a variety of structural models and consider their significance for organizational performance. We also discuss the nature of the informal organization. We conclude by offering a protocol for the diagnosis and design of organization structures.

THE MULTINATIONAL CORPORATION

Organizations that operate in more than one country face unique problems in developing an effective organization design. They attempt to achieve economies of scale, market penetration, technological innovation, and customer service globally, throughout the organization. European companies have a long history of multinational functioning as a way of overcoming the small European market; prior to 1960 they created facsimiles of the parent in individual countries throughout the world, and then in the late 1960s and 1970s moved to worldwide product-line organiza-

Figure 11–1 **Partial Organization Chart for Nationwide**

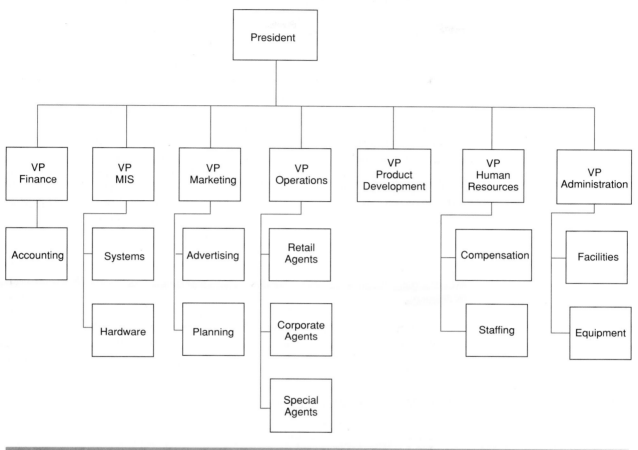

tions that spanned country boundaries.[1] Many multinational organizations, such as Exxon or Ford Motor Company, began in the United States and then expanded into Europe or Asia. Others, such as Honda or Nissan, began abroad and then added divisions in the United States. Alternatively, the major part of an organization can reside in a single country, but such a company may have marketing or other facilities outside the home country, or it may just do business abroad. The array of options for dealing globally is immense, and these are only a few of the possibilities. Such companies often develop in a way that allows them to take advantage of low-cost production opportunities in other countries, to diversify and expand their market, or to localize research and development near to high-technology centers across the world.

The multinational corporation has some unique characteristics. Its structure must respond to variations in values and attitudes in the different countries it inhabits. It also must recognize differences in the importance of egalitarianism, individualism, and other cultural characteristics. Consider a multinational corporation with divisions in France, Italy, and Germany. French and Italian managers like highly centralized and formalized structures; Germans like decentralized structures with high formalization.[2] Or, consider how Japanese and American firms differ, as shown in

Table 11–1. Japanese prefer less specialization, taller hierarchies, and greater formal centralization but less operational centralization than United States firms.[3] The multinational firm that operates in the United States and Japan must somehow reconcile these differences.

The impact of culture on structure is not clear. Multinational corporations may call for a more hybrid structure, or they may not. In studies of multinational banks in Hong Kong, organizations in prerevolutionary Iran, and some Japanese organizations, the multinational corporations had the structures of their home countries rather than host countries.[4] Other studies suggest that organizational structures differ in different countries.[5]

Issues of communication and control are key in multinational firms. Keeping subsidiaries in line with each other and with headquarters personnel poses one such challenge. Ensuring that each part of the organization receives complete, necessary, and relevant information also requires significant coordination. The structure needs to reflect and support the organization's strategy, mission, and goals. A multinational corporation or even an organization that deals globally typically needs a structure that responds and can react to environmental complexity.

TYPES OF DIVISION OF LABOR

Organizations differ in the titles, duties, and responsibilities they assign to the jobs they create. Review the organization chart of Nationwide. It is a pictorial representation of the formal lines of authority and communication in an organization. Each box represents either a particular department or job. The box called Corporate Agents represents a sales and customer service staff that deals with corporate clients. It might include a group of branch officers with their managers and staff, a special programs group, and a customer support group. The blocks in Figure 11–1 labeled President, VP Finance, VP MIS (Management Information Systems), VP Marketing, VP Operations, VP Product Development, VP Human Resources, and VP Administration represent single jobs. The solid lines that connect a subunit to a position or department on a level above or below the subunit represent reporting relationships; for example, the vice president of marketing reports to the president.

Division of labor refers to the way organizations allocate work tasks and responsibilities along with the accompanying authority; it reflects the extent to which organizations have specialization of tasks and roles. An accounts receivable clerk has a relatively specialized job; he or she repeatedly does a limited number of tasks and fulfills a single formal role. The vice president for operations has a less specialized job. Two technical people might have equally specialized jobs: One employee per-

Table 11–1 Comparison of Organizations in Japan and the United States

American	Japanese
Short-term employment	Life-time employment
Individual decision making	Consensual decision making
Individual responsibility	Collective responsibility
Rapid evaluation and promotion	Slow evaluation and promotion
Explicit, formalized control	Implicit, informal control
Specialized career path	Nonspecialized career path
Segmented concern	Holistic concern

SOURCE: Based on W. Ouchi, *Theory Z* (Reading, Mass.: Addison-Wesley, 1978).

forms cost analyses for new products; a second employee develops recruitment plans for new employees.

Typically, the lower in the organizational chart we look, the more often we see positions with more extensive specialization. Office travel agents perform more specialized activities than the office manager; assembly line workers have more specialized tasks than their supervisors or the plant foreman. Differentiation, which is in effect another name for division of labor, occurs in four different ways (as shown in Figure 11–2): horizontal, vertical, personal, and spatial.[6]

Horizontal Differentiation
The division of work at the same level in the hierarchy can occur by function, customer, product, process, or even geographical area. In determining the new structure for Worldwide Travel, what type of horizontal differentiation might Marie Fahey consider? She might recommend, that it be divided into functional areas, such as finance/MIS, marketing/sales, operations, and human resources. Then within each

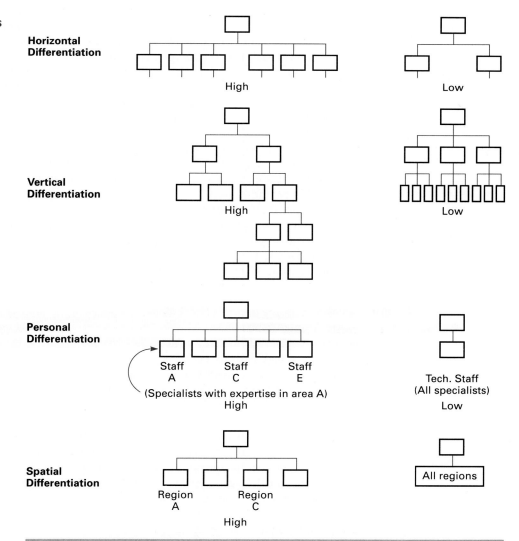

Figure 11–2 Types and Degrees of Differentiation

functional area, additional functional departments would exist—for example, compensation, organization development, staffing, and training in the human resources department.

The extent of horizontal differentiation can vary extensively, depending on such factors as the manager's preference and the size, age, goals, and product or service of the organization. As horizontal differentiation increases, potential barriers to communication are increased. Because communication occurs more easily within a unit than across units, horizontal differentiation may limit the expertise used in making decisions unless there is extensive coordination and communication between and among groups.

Vertical Differentiation

Specialization as a result of differences in levels in the organization's hierarchy creates the vertical type of division of labor. Tall organizations, such as Citibank, AT&T, and Mobil Oil Company, have relatively high vertical differentiation. Flat organizations, such as professional organizations (e.g., law firms, consulting firms), many social service agencies, and scientific or technical organizations have lower vertical differentiation. The five agencies that comprise Worldwide Travel each had relatively flat organizations, that is, relatively low vertical differentiation. How extensive should the differentiation be at the merged company?

Increasing vertical differentiation increases the checks and balances that limit the number of mistakes made in action. Where there is an extensive hierarchy, decisions made by lower-level employees are more often checked by higher-level employees than in flatter organizations. Tall structures offer the second advantage of providing more avenues for advancement within the organization. This may explain the taller hierarchies found in Japanese plants.[7] Blocking of employees because of nonpromotability of other employees is less frequent (see Chapter 3). Also, closer fitting of individuals' personal needs and abilities with jobs is possible because of the diversity of available positions.

But tall structures often slow decision making if multiple levels of the hierarchy are involved in the process. If centralization of decision making accompanies vertical differentiation, workers low in the hierarchy may experience decreased motivation as a result of a lack of autonomy and involvement. Of course, even in a tall structure, decentralization of decision making is possible.

Personal Differentiation

Division of labor can also occur according to individual expertise or training. A medical outpatient clinic served by physicians with such specialties as gerontology, dermatology, and pediatric ophthalmology has relatively high personal specialization. So does a research "think tank," where individual faculty members have subject area expertise and more specialized knowledge in their area of research. Various departments within an organization can also vary in their degree of personal differentiation. Extensive personal differentiation takes advantage of unique capabilities in the work force.

Where at Worldwide is personal differentiation likely to be highest? Where is it the lowest? Areas in a travel agency that require unique knowledge or advanced training, such as cruise planning, development of travel packages, or servicing customers who travel to a relatively untraveled country, may have greater personal differentiation in their members. At the same time, however, a certain level of specialized training is required for all travel agents, thus equalizing the personal differentiation across various parts of the agency.

Spatial Differentiation
Some organizations have division of labor by geographical location. Organizations with multiple operating sites illustrate spatial differentiation. A retail department store with numerous suburban stores, a fast-food chain such as McDonald's or Burger King, a bank, and a large accounting firm show this type of differentiation. Look again at Worldwide. Where does it have spatial differentiation? Clearly its branch structure exemplifies this type of division of labor.

Now imagine that you are Marie Fahey, who will be recommending a structure for Worldwide. How could she incorporate each type of division of labor into the new structure? What types are most important? How would an organization chart that reflects each type look? Which do you think would be most effective? We provide a more conclusive answer to that question in Chapter 12.

OPTIONS FOR COORDINATION

Once an organization has differentiated into positions and departments in a hierarchy, some mechanisms for ensuring communication and integrated decision making among these groups must be instituted for the organization to function effectively. These mechanisms must be introduced at all levels of the organization and may differ in various subunits. Typically, the more differentiation exists in an organization, the more it requires coordination, or integration, for effective performance.

Coordination refers to the extent and means by which an organization integrates or holds together its various parts and facilitates their working together to accomplish a common goal or activity. It occurs through (1) mutual adjustment, (2) direct supervision, (3) standardization of work processes, (4) standardization of outputs, and (5) standardization of skills.[8]

Mutual Adjustment

The simplest form of coordination occurs through informal communication, where two or more people speak directly to one another as needed. When you speak with a coworker about scheduling your vacation, you are using mutual adjustment. When a salesperson checks with an inventory clerk by telephone about the availability of a certain product, he or she coordinates by mutual adjustment. Very simple or very complex organizations generally must rely heavily on mutual adjustment. In the first situation, mutual adjustment sufficiently coordinates the work. In the second, mutual adjustment reduces ambiguity in communication and task performance. Using this type of coordination effectively requires high-quality communication, as described in Chapter 7.

Direct Supervision

More formalized control exists where one individual takes responsibility for the work of others. As groups or organizations increase in size, mutual adjustment becomes insufficient as a coordinating mechanism; here management might add supervision as a means of coordination. The vice president of operations for Worldwide might oversee the work of numerous branch managers who in turn have responsibility for the work of numerous travel agents. In addition to direct supervision, these supervisors may also use other means of coordination, such as mutual adjustment and standardization of work processes.

Direct supervision as a means of coordination has probably received the greatest attention in the organizational literature. It involves coordination through the *chain of command*. At Worldwide one chain might include the president, the vice president of operations, and his or her subordinates; another chain includes the president, the VP of finance, and his or her subordinates. At Worldwide, the workers might experience *unity of command;* that is, each employee will have only one supervisor. In some integrated structures, discussed later in this chapter, unity of command does not always exist.

Span of Control Direct supervision also occurs over a certain number of employees whose activities a manager directs and supervises. Known as the *span of control,* the number of immediate subordinates can vary extensively, from one to one hundred or more. For example, if the vice presidents of operations, finance, MIS, and human resources report to the president of Worldwide, he or she will have a span of control of four; if these vice presidents report instead to an executive vice president, the president will then have a span of control of one.

While research once specified an optimal span of control (five to ten people for middle management and slightly more for top management), a contingency approach now prevails.[9] The ability and expertise of the manager and subordinates will influence an effective span of control. The greater the manager's expertise, the broader an effective span of control can be. A manager who lacks ability must devote more time to supervising subordinates and thus can operate effectively only with a smaller span of control. Those subordinates with greater expertise require less supervisory time from their superiors. In these situations the span of control can be larger.

The nature of the tasks can also influence effective supervision. The more interrelated the tasks that are performed in subordinate positions or the more similar the tasks of subordinates, the more individuals a manager can supervise. Further, if the supervisor can duplicate instructions for more than one subordinate, the span of control can increase. The stability of the tasks that are performed by those in subordinate positions also is significant. As the tasks remain the same over time, subordinates require less supervision, and hence the span of control can increase.

The degree of geographic dispersion of subordinates is associated with the appropriate span of control. The nearer to each other and to their supervisor subordinates are located, the less time a manager must spend in physically moving among them to give them directions. The widespread availability of electronic communications has facilitated such communication even at a geographical distance and should allow larger spans of control.

Finally, the amount and type of interaction required between the superior and those in even higher positions will affect the span of control. A supervisor who must spend extensive time interacting with his or her supervisors has less time available for supervising others; this situation calls for a smaller span of control or greater decentralization of decision making.

Standardization of Work Processes A specification of the procedures or content of work also coordinates the activities of different jobholders. In a restaurant chain, for example, the procedure for baking pizzas may be specified and even written down, or formalized, in a company procedures manual. In a bank, the steps in reconciling cash at the end of the day may be specified for a teller. Lawyers may follow a specified set of procedures in filing a brief. Standardization of work processes is typically useful for coordinating highly specialized or relatively unskilled jobs, for specifying repetitive tasks, or for simplifying parts of very complex jobs. Specifying the steps required to perform a job reduces the need for mutual adjustment or direct supervision.

Standardization of Outputs The specification of the results and outcomes of work, as well as standards of performance at the output stage, also provides direction and coordination for workers. Managers judged on their group's profit may demonstrate coordination by standardization of outputs. So do salespersons who must meet a certain quota. These employees have relatively great discretion in the processes they use to accomplish the outputs. Frequently they use additional coordinating mechanisms, specifically mutual adjustment, to facilitate meeting the performance standards.

Standardization of Skills The final type of coordination specifies the training, expertise, or credentials required to perform the work. The work of medical practitioners, teachers, lawyers, and other professionals is coordinated in this way; they apply specialized knowledge and skills in approaching particular problems and tasks. Accounting and engineering departments often use mutual adjustment with standardization of skills.

Which of these coordinating mechanisms should Worldwide use? Worldwide probably will use all five coordinating mechanisms. The primary mode of coordination often differs in various parts of the organization: coordination of travel agents might rely on standardization of work processes, standardization of skills, direct supervision, or mutual adjustment; middle managers in staff or support departments use direct supervision and mutual adjustment; the MIS department might rely on standardization of skills; the marketing staff may depend on standardization of outputs; top management relies on mutual adjustment. Additional coordinating mechanisms include the use of plans, linking pins, and integrating roles, as described in Chapter 10.

We must also evaluate whether these mechanisms coordinate adequately. Is additional formal coordination required? Would mechanisms different from those currently used coordinate more effectively? Diagnosis of an organization's structure requires a response to such questions.

INFORMATION-PROCESSING STRUCTURES

In selecting a structure, organizations also need to identify the information-processing needs of the particular work group, hierarchical level, or other subunit. The particular structure chosen then reflects the information-processing needs of that level or subunit: Discrete subunits form to meet different needs and are linked. For example, in selecting a structure for Worldwide we can hypothesize that top management might identify different information-processing needs for each functional area, form subunits around these needs, and then link the subunits with direct supervision, standardization of work processes, and standardization of skills for necessary coordination.

Mechanistic versus Organic Organizations Structures organized around information-processing needs can be categorized in one way as either mechanistic or organic.[10] This classification originated in an early study of Scottish electronics firms that linked structure to the nature of the technological environment.[11] As the environment became less stable and more dynamic, the organizations in that study tended to evolve from mechanistic to organic.

Mechanistic Structure Functional and bureaucratic organizations typically have the stability and relative inflexibility of a *mechanistic* structure. Activities are specialized into clearly defined jobs and tasks. A manufacturing organization with a single assembly line divided into innumerable specialized activities is a mechanistic structure. So is a hospital with clearly established protocols for providing care. In a mechanistic organization, persons of higher rank have greater knowledge of the problems facing the organization than those at lower levels. Unresolved problems are thus passed up the hierarchy. Rewards are chiefly obtained through obedience to instructions from supervisors. Mechanistic organizations encourage conformity and discourage innovation because innovation often accompanies disobedience of company regulations.

Standardized policies, procedures, and rules guide much of the decision making in the mechanistic organization. Such organizations often have detailed manuals of organizational policies. Supervisors frequently answer questions or solve problems by referring the employee to the correct section of the written procedures manual. Where such organizations are unionized, the extent of standardization and formalization typically increases; the union contract may list a majority of the organization's employment policies.

Organic Structure   Characterized by flexible organizational designs and the ability to adjust rapidly to change, many of the structures described later in this chapter are *organic*. An organic structure deemphasizes job descriptions and specialization. Persons become involved in problem solving when they have the knowledge or skills that will help solve the problem. A marketing analyst, rather than the vice president of marketing, may be asked to contribute to the organization's strategic plan if he or she has the required knowledge. An engineer with unique expertise in new product design might join a marketing task force.

People holding higher positions are not necessarily assumed to be better informed than employees at lower levels. Organic organizations emphasize decentralization of decision making, where responsibility and accountability are pushed as low in the organization as is possible and effective. These organizations frequently include large numbers of professional employees, for whom involvement in decision making is natural. Structures that bring together individuals with diverse functional expertise are frequently introduced. Such structures may include project teams, matrix structures, integrating or liaison roles, or task forces.

Organic organizations rely more on ad hoc problem solving than existing regulations, policies, or procedures to deal with problems. Supervisors might answer questions by referring an employee to a coworker with knowledge in the problem area. If the problem is sufficiently large or puzzling, the supervisor might convene a task force of workers to address the issues. Hence, organic organizations encourage innovation and problem-solving behavior. Management allocates rewards to individuals who demonstrate initiative and knowledge. Position in the hierarchy and seniority have relatively little importance unless they are associated with special expertise.

In designing Worldwide, Marie Fahey must recommend whether to create a mechanistic or organic structure. Various prototypes of such structures are discussed later in this chapter.

Information-Processing Capability   How do organizations differ in the extent to which their structures facilitate the collection and processing of information?[12] Structures with a *low information-processing capacity* have mechanisms that process information more slowly, in a way similar to mechanistic organizations. In particular, they rely on the hierarchy for communication and problem solving. Significant barriers to lateral communication exist, thereby slowing the processing of information. Low-capacity structures include departmentation by function and geographical location, machine bureaucracies, professional bureaucracies, and divisionalized structures, as described later in this chapter.

Structures with a *high information-processing capacity* have mechanisms that process information quickly and accurately. Top management of these organic organizations might regularly convene task forces to address special organizational problems. Liaison roles that facilitate lateral communication and break down barriers between departments are also common. Increasingly, electronic media, such as fax machines, BITNET, or electronic mail, can increase an organization's information-processing capacity. These information technologies should facilitate coordination of and control across interdependent specialties, such as product development and quality control.[13] A recent study suggests that advanced information technology will lead to organization design changes that include more individuals acting as sources of information but fewer individuals formally involved in an organizational subunit, fewer organizational levels involved in processing information and authorizing action, more even involvement of units across organization levels in decision making, less time spent on decision-making meetings, and more rapid decision making.[14] High-capacity organizations include departmentation by product, project, or client, or along multiple bases, simple structures, or adhocracies.

BASES OF DEPARTMEN-TATION

So far, we have identified division of labor, coordinating mechanisms, and information-processing requirements as key structural elements of organizations. Now we consider some typical methods of organizing these elements into structural configurations at specific levels in the organization. Note that structuring occurs separately at each hierarchical level and in each subunit of the organization. The structural pattern for top management may differ from that of middle management. Groupings of nonmanagerial employees may look very different as well. In this section we examine the following ways of grouping subunits in the organization: (1) by function, (2) by product or project, (3) by customer or client, (4) by geographical location, and (5) along multiple bases.

Function

Departmentation by function describes the structure of many manufacturing and service organizations. It refers to grouping employees according to the major category of organizational work activity. For example, a manufacturing organization might have research and development, human resources, management, engineering, production, marketing, and finance divisions. Within the human resources management division, we might find a further functional grouping of work into training, recruitment, compensation, planning, and organization development departments. Within the marketing division, we might find yet more functional groups, such as market research, advertising, sales, and sales support departments.

Consider the organization shown in Figure 11–3. This chart might represent a toy manufacturer, an advertising agency, or a paper mill. Different vice presidents supervise departments of finance, operations, research and development, and so on; each of these areas may have departments specialized further by function or by other

Figure 11–3 **Functional Structure**

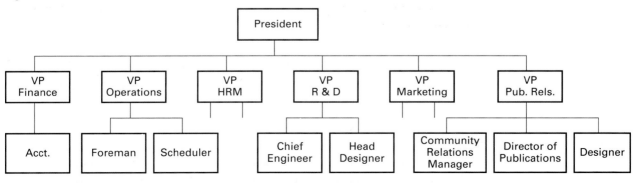

bases. Now look at a possible organizational chart for Worldwide in Figure 11–4; this structure groups workers into functional departments at various levels in the organization.

What advantages does a functional structure offer? It reinforces professional identities because it groups individuals according to their functional specialties and encourages them to work primarily with individuals with related training and expertise. Look at the Marketing Department at Worldwide. Here the human resources professionals work together, sharing ideas and collaborating on special projects. Promotions tend to occur within a functional area, enhancing professional development. The functional structure also avoids duplication of effort. There is only one R&D department and one sales department. These serve the entire organization, not selected divisions or departments.

The functional structure has several limitations. First, it often suffers from coordination and control problems. Barriers arise between departments because of basic differences in expertise, goals, and operating procedures of different functions. Because communication among departments may be limited, and because this structure emphasizes using the hierarchy to make decisions and handle exceptions, organizational problems may receive a slow response. In the functional structure, some individuals may become overly identified with their functional area and lose sight of overall organizational goals. Competition may arise between departments for resources, resulting in conflict within the organization. Two departments, for example, may argue over the adequacy of their staffing budget.

The functional structure works most effectively under four conditions. First, if the organization has a well-developed product or service, then procedures that are standardized, or at least well known and regularly implemented as part of the functional structure, act as coordinating mechanisms and reduce barriers between functions. Second, if the organization operates in a stable environment, it has less need to respond quickly to environmental changes; the slower decision making that characterizes this structure is appropriate. Third, if the roles in the organization group easily into functional areas, then coordination is expedited by a structure that builds

Figure 11–4 **Worldwide as a Functional Structure**

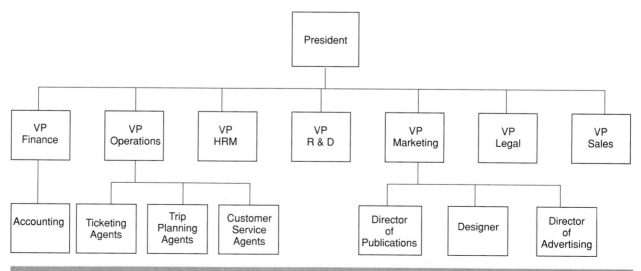

on these relationships. Finally, if the organization is small- to medium-sized, lateral communication throughout the organization is easier than if the organization is large. Does Worldwide have these characteristics? We examine the characteristics that call for a functional structure in more detail in Chapter 12.

Project or Product Rather than grouping employees according to their functional area, grouping can be done according to the product or project on which they work. Subunits with different functional expertise working on the same product or project are grouped together. NASA popularized project management in the 1960s by using it for managing its various space projects; the Apollo, Saturn, and Space Shuttle projects have become household words. More recently some high-technology firms have turned to a project structure. Figures 11–5 and 11–6 show examples of this type of departmentation.

The organization shown in the top of Figure 11–5 has project categories at the director level, but they supervise functional managers of marketing, manufacturing, and research and development. The organization shown in the bottom of Figure 11–5 has project responsibility at two levels. Sometimes project responsibility occurs only at the middle or even lower levels of the organization; for example, the VP of manufacturing might supervise directors of various projects, or the director of quality might supervise various project leaders.

In a product structure, the organization is organized at one or more levels of the hierarchy by product. Or, as shown in Figure 11–6, the product managers can supervise various functional groups instead. In product or project management the structure lasts only for the life of the project. When the project ends, employees

Figure 11–5 Departmentation by Project

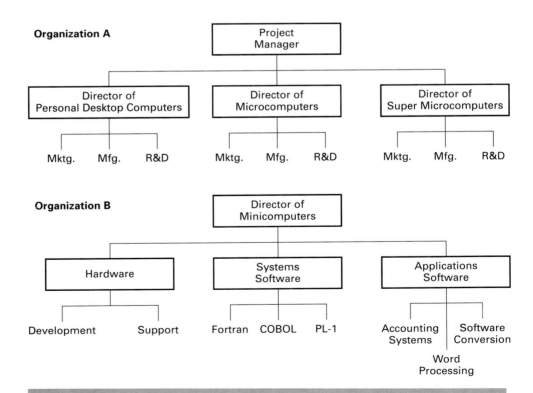

Figure 11–6 **De-
partmentation by
Product**

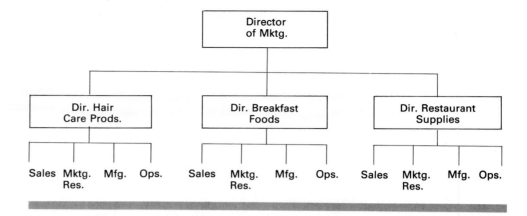

receive new assignments. Manufacturers, such as Procter & Gamble or General Mills, may use product management for most of their marketing efforts.

This structure encourages organizations to differentiate among products or projects and focus on their unique assets and problems in production and sales. For example, the development, production, sales, and distribution of a new cereal must face different issues than does the development of a new hair care product. Similarly, introducing new scheduling software to the marketplace creates some problems that are similar to, but many that are different from those encountered in introducing a new microcomputer. Thus, project or product management allows organizations to focus on problems and opportunities unique to a particular product.

This organization structure also allows organizations to respond more quickly to changes affecting the project or product. Because work efforts are narrowly focused on product or project concerns, team members have common goals, and this narrow focus increases their ability to function effectively. Because of their close involvement in the product or project, they have a better understanding of the specific needs of the situation and can respond to new requirements imposed by the environment or customer more quickly and more effectively. In addition, this structure encourages personnel with different expertise and professional loyalty to focus on a common goal. Bringing diverse expertise to a single problem also allows a more speedy resolution of it.

Some duplication of expertise generally exists on different project teams. Thus, project or product management may cost more than functional departmentation. In addition, because of the lack of professional identity, individuals may fail to keep pace with developments in their own area of expertise, focusing instead on product or project developments. A human resources professional, for example, who provides training for a single product division, may lose touch with more general advances in training. Reorganizing into a product structure focuses employee efforts on dealing with the unique issues involved in developing and distributing a diverse product mix. It allows a relatively fast response to increased competition and other environmental changes.

Consider Worldwide. What would its organizational chart look like if departmentation were by product? Figure 11–7 offers one possible chart. What advantages does this arrangement offer over the functional structure shown in Figure 11–4? What disadvantages does it have?

Figure 11–7 **Worldwide as a Product Structure**

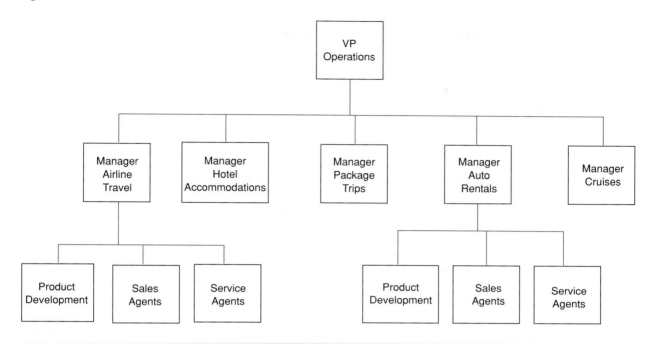

Customer or Client Organization by customer or client parallels departmentation by product or project because it addresses the unique needs of specific customer or client groups. Figure 11–8 offers a prototype of such a structure, which groups employees according to the client they serve. Incorporating a client-oriented structure allows the company to structure product markets to match the needs of different clients—young urban professionals, senior citizens, families with one or more school-age children.

This structure shares the advantages of a product or project structure. It has the ability to differentiate among clients and focus on their unique concerns. It also allows a fast response to changes in client needs and brings diverse expertise to solving a single client's problems.

Departmentation by client also suffers from the same disadvantages as the product or project structure. It can be costly because of the provision of redundant services. It can also distract individuals from maintaining state-of-the-art knowledge in their own fields because they may pay more attention to client needs than to their personal professional development.

Geographical Location Specifying a structure that includes geographical location lets an organization take advantage of regional differences in preferences and costs. Departmentation by geographical location, illustrated in Figure 11–9, describes this type of structure. Workers are grouped according to their own geographical location or the geographical location of the clients they serve. Multinational firms often use this structure, as shown in Figure 11–10. Sales groups within a company frequently use a regional structure. How could Marie Fahey recommend that Worldwide be structured to

Figure 11–8 **Departmentation by Client**

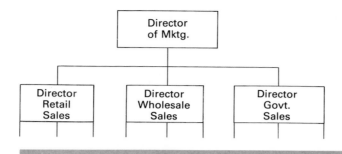

explicitly consider geographical location? She could recommend regional or national offices, as indicated in Figure 11–11.

The advantages of this structure parallel those of departmentation by product, project, or client: the ability to focus on issues unique to geographical areas, the opportunity to focus expertise on special geographical problems, and cost savings or profit opportunities associated with geographical diversity. The disadvantages are also similar: potentially redundant services and failure to develop professionally in areas of functional expertise.

Multiple Bases: The Integrated Structure

The integrated structure is a hybrid structure that incorporates different bases of departmentation. It responds to the needs of a changing and complex environment. The specific integrated form chosen must help organizational members focus both on client needs and the marketing of the organization's product and services.

Characteristics of an Integrated Structure The integrated structure has four major characteristics. First, flexible groupings of individuals allow the organization to take a functional, product, project, geographical, or client orientation. These groupings change as organizational needs change. For example, task forces may be organized or disbanded as the organization introduces new products or withdraws obsolete ones. A project team may form, perform its assigned tasks, and then return its mem-

Figure 11–9 **Departmentation by Geographical Location**

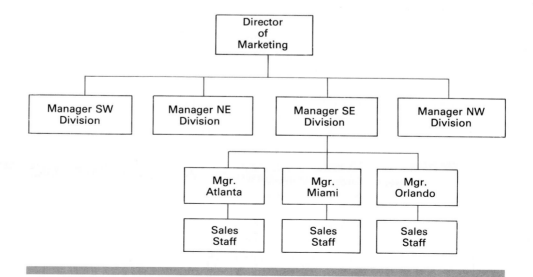

Figure 11–10 **A Multinational Firm with Departmentation by Geographical Location: AEG U.S. Country Organization**

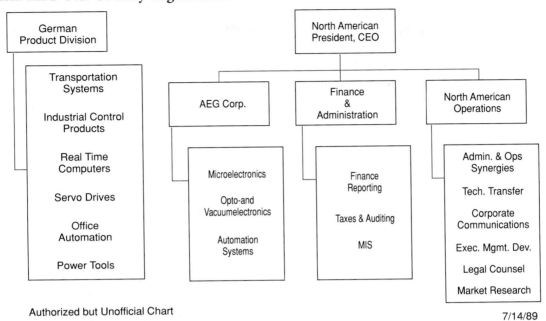

Authorized but Unofficial Chart

7/14/89

SOURCE: Reprinted with permission from A. R. Janger, *How European Countries Organize in the United States* (New York: Conference Board, 1990), p. 9.

bers to their original functional areas. Second, the grouping of individuals emphasizes a market focus. A bank may organize temporary or permanent work teams to service small business, institutional, or other special interest group accounts. In addition, the integrated structure also emphasizes the identification of the market for the organization's product or service. Third, the integrated structure calls for decentralized decision making—that is, increasing the autonomy, responsibility, and accountability of middle managers and professional staff. Finally, grouping of employees occurs across functional divisions, as in the project structure. This structure encompasses a variety of organizational configurations, including task forces, permanent committees, project teams, or a matrix structure.

One study of public accounting firms concluded that four factors influence the type and degree of integration in the structure.[15] First, the firm's strategy about developing specializations in given industries, segmenting the market, or developing unique technical expertise was associated with integration. The greater the emphasis on specialization, segmentation, and expertise, the more prevalent the integrated structure as a way of providing services across divisions. Second, the partner in charge or the top management of the firm clearly influenced the extent of integration. The chief executive needed to be committed to a marketing, integrative focus. Third, office or organizational size affected integration. The smaller the office or organization, the greater the need for the flexibility inherent in an integrated structure. Finally, client requirements, particularly their demands for a variety of services, mandated an integrated structure.

Figure 11–11 **Worldwide with Geographical Departmentation**

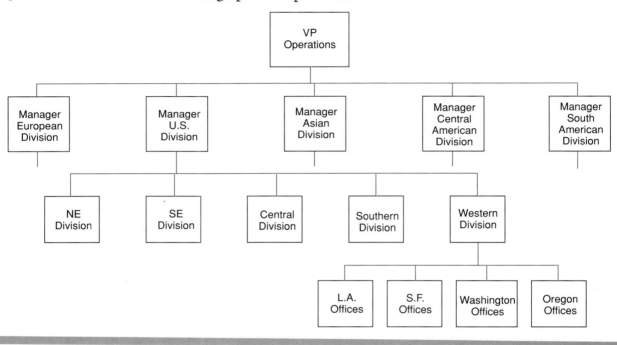

Matrix—A Prototype of an Integrated Structure The matrix structure, as shown in Figure 11–12, incorporates departmentation along multiple dimensions. This structure responds to the need for greater flexibility by an organization.[16]

As high technology forced organizations to deal with extreme ambiguity and volatility in the environment, many organizations found that more traditional structures—departmentation by function, project/product, location, or clientele—were inadequate and ineffective. Such companies as Boeing, TRW, Texas Instruments, and Corning Glass instituted the matrix structure as a way of responding to their environment.[17] Such a structure can respond well to an organization's strategies of diversification and globalization, such as by adding worldwide product managers to geographical profit centers. It offers the advantages of more efficient use of resources through sharing across many projects, increased integration of functional areas for project performance, improved flexibility and adaptability, enhanced vertical and lateral information flow, and a high degree of involvement in decision making.[18] But, the matrix organization violates the unity-of-command principle because most employees have at least two superiors—one in the project or product line, the second in the functional domain. A member of the marketing staff on Project 1 reports to both the vice president of marketing and the director of Microcomputer Project 1. As in departmentation by function, the matrix reinforces professional identities and development.

The matrix structure poses a number of problems.[19] First, extensive overhead costs are incurred as a result of the dual-authority systems that increase the number of managerial personnel beyond normal limits. Second, potential conflict exists when two managers have responsibility for evaluation and allocation of a single employee's time. The product manager for partnership banking and the vice president of lending may perceive that they compete for the time of a loan officer who works on the

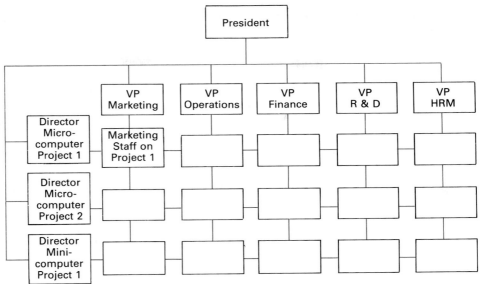

Figure 11–12 Matrix Structure

Each cell represents one or many employees who serve on the project listed for that row and are part of the staff listed in that column.

partnership banking project. This competition can lead to power struggles between functional and product managers, as well as problems in monitoring and controlling work. One researcher has argued that top management must clearly delegate authority to the project manager, and the functional manager must agree to accept the role of a subordinate to him or her.[20] Third, potential ambiguity exists in the reporting relationships. This same loan officer may be confused about who has final authority when his or her two bosses disagree. Fourth, shared decision making may result in lengthened response time because of the time necessary to reach an agreement. Finally, stress experienced by individuals participating in a matrix may increase.

Making a matrix work requires ensuring that the roles of the project and functional managers are clear; there should be a policy and procedures for surfacing problems quickly, and the project manager should have enough power to negotiate with the functional manager.[21] Many organizations have determined that these costs did not outweigh the benefits offered by the increase in coordination provided by the matrix structure. Because the matrix is inherently unstable and must be managed, executives look to other structures for some of the advantages offered by the matrix. Many have combined variations of the matrix with the other structural forms to magnify the assets of the matrix and reduce its liabilities.

How would Worldwide look as a matrix structure? Figure 11–13 offers a possible organization chart.

CONFIGURATIONS ACCORDING TO MEANS OF COORDINATION

A complementary system offers a more comprehensive classification of organizational structures by grouping them according to their mechanisms of coordination (mutual adjustment, direct supervision, standardization of work processes, standardization of outputs, and standardization of skills).[22] Five structural paradigms result. Table 11–2 shows each type, its basic means of coordination, and the bases of departmentation it likely includes. A simple structure, for example, relies on mutual adjustment and direct supervision for coordination and often includes functional

Figure 11–13 **Worldwide with a Matrix Structure**

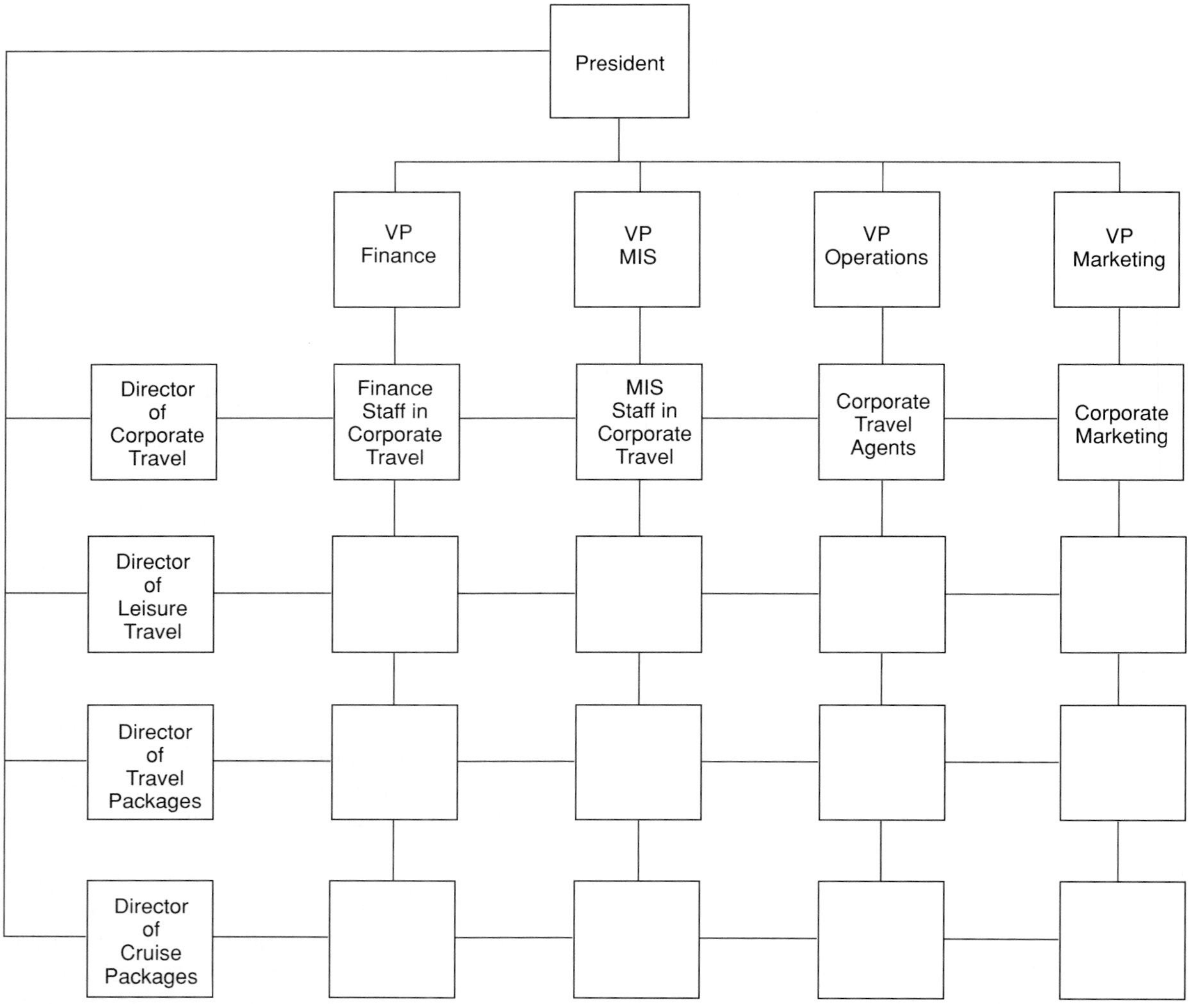

departmentation. The machine and professional bureaucracies also include functional departmentation but rely on standardization of processes and skills, respectively. The divisionalized form uses standardization of outputs and often incorporates departmentation by product, project, client, or geographical location. The adhocracy relies on mutual adjustment for coordination and often includes features of the integrated structure.

Simple Structure   This type of organization relies on mutual dependence and direct supervision as the major coordinating mechanisms. A men's clothing store, a family restaurant, and a small consulting firm probably have this structure. It often exists in relatively young and small organizations because they can tolerate the lack of sophistication inherent in this structure. We might also view such organizations as having a functional structure with few departments.

Table 11–2 Types of Structure According to Means of Coordination

Structure	Means of Coordination	Types of Departmentation Typically Included
Simple structure	Mutual adjustment, direct supervision	Functional
Machine bureaucracy	Direct supervision, standardization of work processes	Functional
Professional bureaucracy	Standardization of skills	Functional
Divisionalized form	Standardization of outputs	Product, project, clientele, geographical location
Adhocracy	Mutual adjustment	Integrated (matrix or other forms)

In the simple structure, the top manager has significant control. Thus entrepreneurs frequently organize their firms along these lines. As the organization grows, the simple structure will frequently departmentalize further by function. As it becomes increasingly large, it will move to a more complex structural form that relies on other means of coordination.

Nationwide, one of the organizations that merged to form Worldwide Travel, likely began as a simple structure, possibly as shown in Figure 11–14. A single product was developed and manufactured by the company under the supervision of the owner and founder. There was relative flexibility and minimal departmentation. As the organization developed more products, it became too complex to remain a simple structure.

Machine Bureaucracy As some organizations increase in size, horizontal and vertical differentiation (into departments and a hierarchy) increases. Frequently accompanied by standardization

Figure 11–14 Nationwide as a Simple Structure

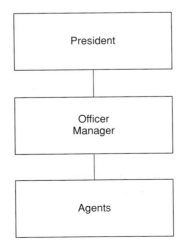

and formalization of behavior, specialization characterizes the machine bureaucracy. Direct supervision and standardization of work processes provide the key coordinating mechanisms. Relatively large operating units prevail in the machine bureaucracy. Large-scale manufacturing organizations, such as automobile, steel, equipment, and consumer goods manufacturers typically organize in this way.

It is unlikely that Worldwide would function as a machine bureaucracy. Because of the extensive knowledge required for performing the job of travel agent, standardized procedures would likely be insufficient for coordinating the work. As more expert computer systems become available, however, some of the operating functions may become more standardized, thereby moving the organization more toward a machine bureaucracy.

Professional Bureaucracy   The professional bureaucracy shares some of the formalization inherent in the machine bureaucracy. Instead of standardization of work processes, however, this structure emphasizes standardization of skills for coordination. Typically, a professional bureaucracy has little vertical or horizontal differentiation, but extensive personal differentiation. Look at the excerpt of an organization chart of a family services agency in Figure 11–15. The organization chart appears to be relatively flat, but extensive differentiation according to specialty exists.

Organizations of this type generally have large numbers of professionals, such as engineers, teachers, physicians, or social workers. Schools, hospitals, and universities frequently take the form of the professional bureaucracy. Parts of Worldwide might be characterized as a professional bureaucracy, particularly if the agents are considered to be professionals.

Divisionalized Form   Think for a minute of IBM, Ford Motor Company, Exxon, General Foods, AT&T, or Shearson/American Express. Since these companies deal with diversified products, each creates units by market or product. The divisionalized structure may include aspects of departmentation by project or product design, as shown in Figure 11–16, or it may represent a conglomerate—a collection of relatively autonomous companies owned by a single parent. A large bank frequently takes a divisionalized structure with separate lending, commercial, and international divisions. Divisions can also be regionally based—some international firms have United States, United Kingdom, Far Eastern, and South American divisions. Each division generally has its own functional or project/product structure.

Figure 11–15   **Family Services Agency**

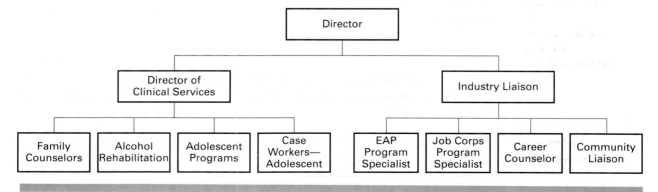

Figure 11–16 **Divisionalized Structure**

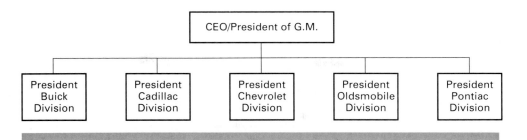

The divisionalized organization emphasizes standardization by outputs: Each manager has bottom-line responsibility. Both the manager's and the organization's performance are judged by these outputs. This divisionalized structure allows organizations to respond to a heterogeneous environment, particularly to diverse cultures. The organization can set up miniorganizations that meet the unique needs of various countries and cultures. This structure also allows increased control over large organizations. By breaking the organization into profit-oriented units, managers are held more accountable. Finally, this structure takes advantage of and reduces the liabilities of a diverse product mix by emphasizing rather than ignoring it.

Divisionalized organizations tend to be older and larger than other forms. Worldwide might move into this structure if it wishes to keep its components intact. As it expands or consolidates its product lines, it might also divisionalize into product, market, or geographical divisions.

Adhocracy The adhocracy form uses a variety of *ad hoc,* or temporary, liaison devices (task forces, integrating roles, project teams, matrix structures) to encourage mutual adjustment among organizational members. Adhocracy calls for a flexible structure that responds to a complex, changing environment. It tends to operate best in such environments with sophisticated technologies. Information technologies, such as electronic mail and video conferencing, can facilitate the teamwork required in such structures. Most integrating structures can be classified as forms of adhocracy.

Worldwide could also be designed to fall into this category. Particularly as the company expands further and faces a more diverse and dynamic environment, and as the technologies become even more sophisticated, it might move toward adopting an adhocracy.

STRUCTURES FOR INCREASING GLOBAL COMPETITIVENESS Executives design organizations to respond to the continuing challenges of a global marketplace. The structures described so far vary in their ability to respond quickly, flexibly, and adaptively to the changing demands of this arena. In this section we consider two types of structures that evolved specifically to increase the ability of organizations to compete globally: (1) the dynamic network structure and (2) loosely and tightly coupled alliances. The interorganizational linkages in these structures buffer organizations from failure and help them transform into more effective and productive organizations.[23]

The Dynamic Network Model The *dynamic network* form of organizational structure extends beyond the boundaries of a single organization, as shown in Figure 11–17.[24] Responding to the competitive environment they face, organizations are increasingly relying on joint ventures, subcontracting, licensing activities, and new business ventures. In its simplest form, a

Figure 11–17 **Example of a Dynamic Network**

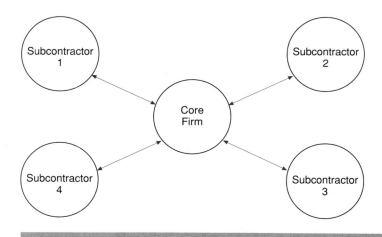

dynamic network has a small staff that develops strategy, subcontracts the work to others, and then monitors the interface of the various subcontractors.[25] The core firm may "sell" personal computers, but parcel out their design, manufacturing, sales, and distribution to subcontractors. By changing the subcontractors, the core organization can remain flexible and responsive to a changing environment.

The dynamic network takes a variety of forms.[26] For example, individual firms may join together into a partnership to work on international projects. In construction, the general contractor and its subcontractors form a stable and continuous network over time. In the German textile industry, associations of specialists, each with unique expertise, form. Strategic partnering in high technology firms also illustrates such network organizations. RCA and Sharp, for example, formed a joint venture to supply both companies with semiconductors.[27] Figure 11–18 shows Worldwide Travel as a dynamic network organization.

These networks have four characteristics.[28] First, independent organizations within the network perform the business functions. Such *vertical disaggregation* occurs for product design, marketing, manufacturing, and other functions. Second, *brokers* assemble the business groups by subcontracting for required services, creating linkages among partners, or locating such functions as design, supply, production, and distribution. Third, *market mechanisms,* such as contracts or payment for results, rather than plans, controls, or supervision, hold the functions together. Finally, *full-disclosure information systems* link the various network components.

The interdependence of firms as a result of their being part of the network creates an industry synergy. Together, by pursuing different strategies yet complementing each other as part of the network, they meet the need for innovation and efficiency. The dynamic network model can also be applied within an organization to foster innovation through a new organization structure that parallels the formal structure. Reading 11–1, "Managing 21st Century Network Organizations," discusses the use and implications of the dynamic network structure in greater detail.

Loosely Coupled Alliances Multinational partnerships offer another way to deal with global competition. Merck, Eli Lilly, Fujisawa, and Bayer shared the license on new drugs as a way of reducing development and distribution costs for the individual companies.[29] Numerous alliances also exist in the computer industry, based on technology sharing, equity partnerships, and joint ventures,[30] as shown in Figure 11–19. Ford Motor Company

Figure 11–18
Worldwide as a Dynamic Network Organization

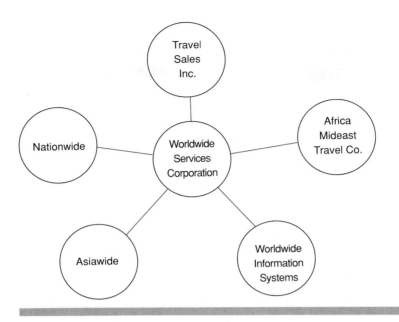

and Mazda Motors Corporation formed a joint venture in 1979 in which they share Ford's skills in international marketing and finance with Mazda's in manufacturing and product development to increase both companies' performance worldwide. "In all, one of every four Ford cars sold in the U.S. last year benefited from some degree of Mazda involvement—in everything from manufacturing methods to steering design—while two of every five Mazdas had some Ford influence."[31] Table 11–3 offers the secrets to the Ford-Mazda success. Other partnerships and joint ventures, such as General Motors and Korea's Daewoo Motor Company (Isuzu) have experienced less success.[32]

Figure 11–20 lists the types of strategic alliances, as well as their prototypic design, benefits, costs, success factors, and human resources issues. Human resources issues revolve around the need to blend different cultures and management styles; reconcile variations in job design; develop compatible staffing, training, performance evaluation, and compensation strategies; address career issues such as promotions; and ensure congruent industrial relations systems in the allied organization.[33]

One interesting alliance is Japan's *keiretsu,* a family of companies joined under various financial agreements, with interlocking directorates, or based on informal social relationships.[34] Ranging in size from ten to hundreds of companies, the keiretsu can be either supplier oriented or bank centered. In a supplier-oriented alliance, companies such as Sony or Honda integrate vertically. In a bank-centered keiretsu, companies such as Mitsubishi integrate vertically and horizontally and have 20 to 40 percent of their stock owned by other members of the alliance. Figure 11–21 shows the Mitsubishi keiretsu and the percentage of each company owned by other members of the alliance. A keiretsu tends to have long-term financial stability because other members can help sustain each company; this stability allows the member companies to focus on long-term development and profitability.

Even small business can use a variety of strategic alliances to develop and sustain technological leadership. These include joint ventures, equity investment in the small company, client-sponsored research contracts, marketing-distribution agreements,

Figure 11–19 **Alliances in the Computer Industry**

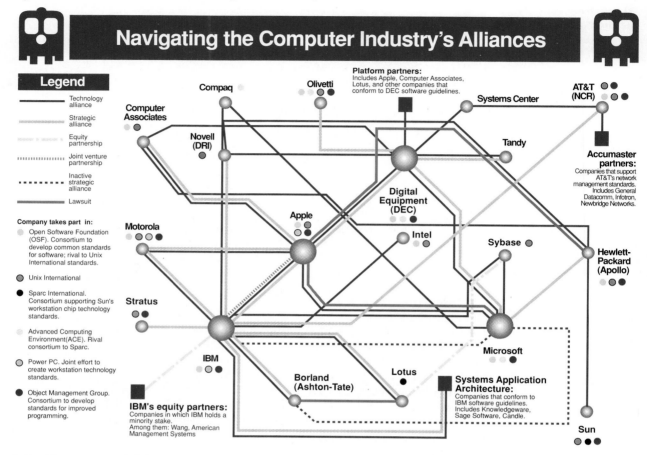

Colored lines represent individual alliances. Compaq, for example, shares some technology with Novell, and Novell has a separate arrangement with IBM.

SOURCE: Reprinted with permission from A. J. Michels, Customers drive company tie-ups, *Fortune,* January 27, 1992, p. 12. Copyright 1992 by CW Publishing, Inc., Framingham, MA 01701. Reprinted from Computerworld.

manufacturing agreements, agreements with universities or research institutes, research and development limited partnerships, and licensing of a company's own technology to another company.[35]

THE INFORMAL ORGANIZATION

So far we have focused our discussion on the formal organization, which describes the prescribed lines of communication, authority, and reporting relationships. The informal organization, in contrast, describes the behavior that complies with and supports the formal structure in an organization. Sometimes these operating relationships and patterned interactions differ from those described in the organizational chart. For example, a quality control manager may formally report to the chief engineer, but informally interact almost exclusively with the plant general manager. Or a chief financial officer may officially report to a company's executive vice president, but actually deal exclusively with the president of the firm.

Table 11–3 **Advice from the Ford-Mazda Alliance**

1. Keep top management involved: The boss must set a tone for the relationship. Otherwise middle managers will resist ceding partial control of a project to a partner.
2. Meet often, and often informally: Meetings should be at all levels and should include time for socializing. Trust can't be built solely around a boardroom table.
3. Use a matchmaker: A third party can mediate disputes, suggest new ways of approaching the partner, and offer an independent sounding board.
4. Maintain your independence: Independence helps both parties hone the areas of expertise that made them desirable partners in the first place.
5. Allow no "sacrifice" deals: Every project must be viable for each partner. It is up to senior management to see that an overall balance is maintained.
6. Appoint a monitor: Someone must take primary responsibility for monitoring all aspects of the alliance.
7. Anticipate cultural differences: They may be corporate or national. Stay flexible, and try to place culturally sensitive executives in key posts.

SOURCE: From The partners, *Business Week,* February 10, 1992, p. 104. Reprinted by special permission. Copyright © 1992 by McGraw-Hill, Inc.

Figure 11–20 **Types of Global Strategic Alliances**

Strategy	Organization Design	Benefits	Costs	Critical Success Factors	Strategic Human Resources Management
Licensing— Manufacturing Industries	Technologies	• Early standardization of design • Ability to capitalize on innovations • Access to new technologies • Ability to control pace of industry evolution	• New competitors created • Possible eventual exit from industry • Possible dependence on licensee	• Selection of licensee that is unlikely to become competitor • Enforcement of patents and licensing agreements	• Technical knowledge • Training of local managers on-site
Licensing— Servicing and Franchises	Geography	• Fast market entry • Low capital cost	• Quality control • Trademark protection	• Partners compatible in philosophies/values • Tight performance standards	• Socialization of franchisees and licensees with core values
Joint Ventures— Specialization Across Partners	Function	• Learning a partner's skills • Economies of scale • Quasi-vertical integration • Faster learning	• Excessive dependence on partner for skills • Deterrent to internal investment	• Tight and specific performance criteria • Entering a venture as "student" rather than "teacher" to learn skills from partner	• Management development and training • Negotiation skills • Managerial rotation

Figure 11–20 (Continued)

Strategy	Organization Design	Benefits	Costs	Critical Success Factors	Strategic Human Resources Management
				• Recognizing that collaboration is another form of competition to learn new skills	
Joint Ventures— Shared Value-Adding	Product or line of business	• Strengths of both partners pooled • Faster learning along value chain • Fast upgrading of technological skills	• High switching costs • Inability to limit partner's access to information	• Decentralization and autonomy from corporate parents • Long "courtship" period • Harmonization of management styles	• Team-building • Acculturation • Flexible skills for implicit communication
Consortia, Keiretsus, and Chaebols	Firm and industry	• Shared risks and costs • Building a critical mass in process technologies • Fast resource flows and skill transfers	• Skills and technologies that have no real market worth • Bureaucracy • Hierarchy	• Government encouragement • Shared values among managers • Personal relationships to ensure coordination and priorities • Close monitoring of member-company performance	• "Clan" cultures • Fraternal relationships • Extensive mentoring to provide a common vision and mission across member companies

Comparison to the Formal Organization We can compare a possible representation of the informal organization of Worldwide, shown in Figure 11–22, to each proposal for a formal chart, shown in Figures 11–4, 11–7, 11–11, and 11–13. Differences between the informal and formal charts arise for four major reasons. First, employees may lack knowledge about the official channels of communication and so use others. Some lower-level employees, for example, may rely on former supervisors for information, rather than going to their current superiors with questions and problems. Technical employees with a problem may go directly to the person they feel has greatest expertise in a particular area, rather than referring it to their boss. The manager of quality engineering may recently have relocated into the quality area from engineering.

Second, interpersonal obstacles may prevent workers from using the formal reporting channels. Some workers may experience personality clashes with their bosses

Figure 11–21   **The Mitsubishi Keiretsu**

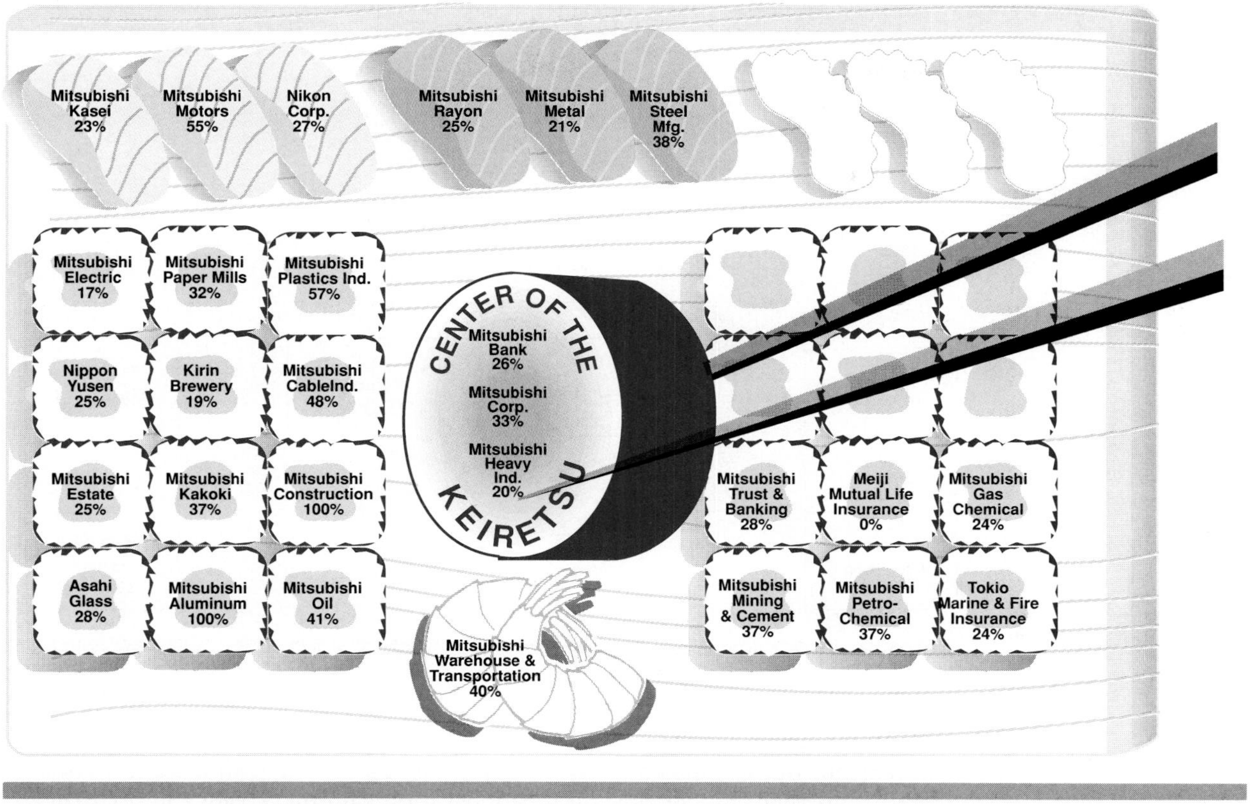

| Mitsubishi Kasei 23% | Mitsubishi Motors 55% | Nikon Corp. 27% | Mitsubishi Rayon 25% | Mitsubishi Metal 21% | Mitsubishi Steel Mfg. 38% |

CENTER OF THE KEIRETSU

Mitsubishi Bank 26%
Mitsubishi Corp. 33%
Mitsubishi Heavy Ind. 20%

Mitsubishi Electric 17%	Mitsubishi Paper Mills 32%	Mitsubishi Plastics Ind. 57%
Nippon Yusen 25%	Kirin Brewery 19%	Mitsubishi CableInd. 48%
Mitsubishi Estate 25%	Mitsubishi Kakoki 37%	Mitsubishi Construction 100%
Asahi Glass 28%	Mitsubishi Aluminum 100%	Mitsubishi Oil 41%

Mitsubishi Warehouse & Transportation 40%

| Mitsubishi Trust & Banking 28% | Meiji Mutual Life Insurance 0% | Mitsubishi Gas Chemical 24% |
| Mitsubishi Mining & Cement 37% | Mitsubishi Petro-Chemical 37% | Tokio Marine & Fire Insurance 24% |

SOURCE: The mighty keiretsu, *Industry Week,* January 20, 1992, p. 52. Reprinted by permission of Eliot Bergman.

and seek assistance from other managers. The head of MIS may work more effectively with the executive vice president than with the vice president of finance/MIS. Other workers may have difficulty communicating with managers because of different personal styles, experiences, or perceptions of job requirements.

Third, workers may be able to obtain a faster response if they bypass certain channels. If a worker has difficulty obtaining needed supplies, he or she may request them directly from the purchasing agent, rather than relying on his or her boss to obtain them or waiting for the required paperwork to be processed through channels. Going to the president of a company for an answer may speed a middle manager's ability to respond to a competitor's introduction of a new product.

Fourth and finally, in some organizations unofficial relationships become legitimized and substitute for the formal ones. Top management may redesign the official reporting relationships to reflect the informal ones that facilitate employee performance and the accomplishment of organizational goals.

Functions of the Informal Organization   The informal organization meets employee needs by serving diverse functions.[36] It may provide employees with a sense of belonging, security, social interaction, self-respect, and recognition. It also eases formal communication by offering informal communication links and a source of practical information for employee decision

Figure 11–22 **The Informal Structure of Worldwide**

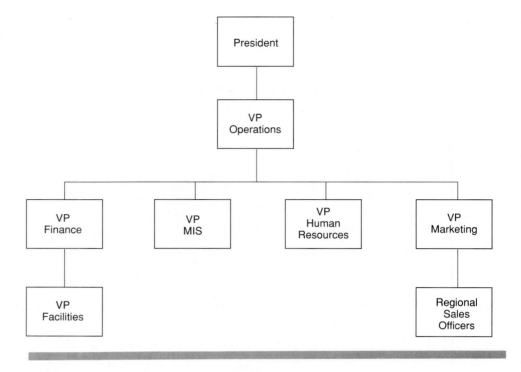

making. Some employees may also use the informal organization to express stress and tension. But the informal organization may also create conflicting loyalties, restrict productivity by creating dysfunctional group norms, create rumors that lead to false information, and resist organizational changes.[37]

Comparing the possible formal and informal organizations of Worldwide suggests significant differences in the intended and actual operation of the company. In diagnosing the structure of an organization, the analyst must check for such discrepancies and attempt to assess the causes. Viewing the informal organization may provide the analyst with a partial prescription for an improved organizational design. The informal organization can either aid or hinder the work specified by the formal structure. Diagnosis of organizational structure should pinpoint dysfunctional differences.

Social Network Analysis   Social networks, or the pattern of interactions between organizational members, describe the emergent structure in organizations which functions simultaneously with but somewhat independently of the formal structure.[38] Network analysis identifies the nature of the links, the roles individuals play, and individuals' positions in the network, as well as its content and other properties, such as connectedness, reachability, and openness to the outside.[39] This network structure can complement or circumvent the formal structure. In one study of patient complaints in a hospital, for example, employees sent complaints to managers who kept passing them to other managers until they were resolved; use of this network superseded the formal procedure for dealing with problems.[40] One recent study even described a multinational organization as an interorganizational network that varies in the dispersal of resources throughout the network and the resulting centrality and power.[41]

**DIAGNOSING
AND DESIGNING
ORGANIZA-
TIONAL
STRUCTURES**

Organizations frequently evolve through several structures as they grow, change their product or market, or experience increased competition. They may have, in turn, functional, product or project, product/matrix, and matrix structures, for example.[42] Effective organization design is dynamic. Implementation of an appropriate structure influences employee behaviors and attitudes.

Some organizations now legitimize the informal organization as part of a new, more adaptive structure. Breaking down the walls of formal structures spurs individual creativity and initiative.[43] So does the frequent realignment of workers into new or different teams. Empowering workers, as described in Chapter 9, is an essential component of this approach to organization design.

Organizational forms will need to become even more flexible and adaptive to keep pace with the pressures of competition. Organizations must create structures that facilitate economic recovery, management productivity, global expansion, and business development.[44] Organizations may increasingly rely on information technology to integrate various functions, products, and even organizations.[45]

SUMMARY

This chapter described a variety of organizational structures and their components. It began by considering some of the issues involved in managing a multinational corporation and designing structures for companies that function globally. Next it examined the division of labor, coordinating mechanisms, and information-processing structures. It considered the ways these basic characteristics determined various paradigms of structure. Table 11–4 summarizes the basic paradigms of organizational structure in four classification schemes.

We first looked at structures where departmentation occurred according to function, product or project, client, or geographical location, or along multiple dimensions. We compared and contrasted these structures and noted the conditions in which each structure was most effective. Then we considered structures that differed in their primary coordinating mechanisms. We discussed the characteristics of the

Table 11–4 Comparison of Paradigms of Organizational Structure

Organization by Departmentation	Classification by Means of Coordination	Mechanistic versus Organic	Information-Processing Capacity
Departmentation by function	Simple structure Machine bureaucracy Professional bureaucracy	Mechanistic	Low capacity
Departmentation by product or project	Adhocracy	Organic	High capacity
Departmentation by geography or client	Divisionalized structure	Mechanistic or organic	Moderate capacity
Departmentation along multiple dimensions	Adhocracy	Organic	High capacity

Table 11–5 **Questions for Diagnosing Organizational Structure**

- What division of labor is there?
- What coordinating mechanisms are there?
- How would you describe information processing in the organization?
- What bases of departmentation exist?
- What structural configuration would describe the organization?
- Does the organization function globally?
- How does its structure respond to the requirements of global competitiveness?
- Does the informal organization reinforce or contradict the formal organization structure?

simple structure, machine bureaucracy, professional bureaucracy, divisionalized form, and adhocracy. The chapter also examined the move toward network structures and alliances in a global environment. It then looked at the nature of the informal organization vis-à-vis the formal structure. It concluded with a discussion of the issues to consider in diagnosing and designing organizational structures. Table 11–5 offers a list of diagnostic questions. Chapter 12 examines the contingencies that affect the choice of an effective structure at any given time.

Reading 11–1

Managing 21st Century Network Organizations
Charles C. Snow, Raymond E. Miles, and Henry J. Coleman, Jr.

What began, quietly, more than a decade ago, has become a revolution. In industry after industry, multilevel hierarchies have given way to clusters of business units coordinated by market mechanisms rather than by layers of middle-management planners and schedulers.

These market-guided entities are now commonly called "network organizations," and their displacement of centrally managed hierarchies has been relentless, though hardly painless—particularly to the million or so managers whose positions have been abolished. Our descriptions of emerging network structures in the late 1970s helped identify this organizational form. Since then, awareness and acceptance have spread rapidly throughout the business community, and recent authors have heralded the network as the organizational form of the future.

The widespread changeover is producing a new agenda for both managers and scholars. To this point, there is growing agreement about the basic characteristics of the network organization, the forces that have shaped it, and some of the arenas for which the network organization appears to be ideally suited and in which it has achieved major success. What is much less clear, however, is how networks are designed and operated, and where their future applications lie. Most troublesome, perhaps, is the question of how the managers of tomorrow's network organizations should be selected and trained.

In this article, we first review the progress of the network form and the factors affecting its deployment across the developed and newly industrializing countries of the world. Next, we discuss the major varieties of the network organization, describing and illustrating three specific types of networks: stable, dynamic, and internal. Finally, we identify three managerial roles (architect, lead operator, and caretaker) critical to the success of every network, and we speculate on how managers may be educated to carry out these roles.

NETWORK STRUCTURES—CAUSES AND EFFECTS

The large, vertically integrated companies that dominated the U.S. economy during the first three quarters of this century arose to serve a growing domestic market for efficiently produced goods. These companies then used their advantages of scale and experience to expand into overseas markets served by less efficient or war-damaged competitors.

Then, during the 1980s in particular, markets around the world changed dramatically, as did the technologies available to serve those markets. Today, competitive pressures demand both efficiency *and* effectiveness. Firms must adapt with increasing speed to market pressures and competitors' innovations, simultaneously controlling and even lowering product or service costs.

Confronted by these demands, the large enterprises designed for the business environment of the 1950s and 1960s—firms that typically sought scale economies through central planning and control mechanisms—understandably faltered. The declining effectiveness of traditionally organized firms produced a new business equation. Instead of advocating resource accumulation and control, this equation linked competitive success to doing fewer things better, with less. Specifically, managers who want their companies to be strong competitors in the 21st century are urged to:

- Search globally for opportunities and resources.
- Maximize returns on all the assets dedicated to a business—whether owned by the managers' firm or by other firms.
- Perform only those functions for which the company has, or can develop, expert skill.
- Outsource those activities that can be performed quicker, more effectively, or at lower cost, by others.

Not surprisingly, firms following these prescriptions frequently find themselves organizing into networks. One firm in the network may research and design a product, another may engineer and manufacture it, a third may handle distribution, and so on. (See Figure 11–23.) When numerous designers, producers, and distributors interact, they bring competitive forces to bear on each element of the product or service value chain, and market factors heavily influence resource-allocation decisions. By using a network structure, a firm can operate an ongoing business both efficiently and innovatively, focusing on those things it does well and contracting with other firms for the remaining resources. Alternatively, it can enter new businesses with minimal financial exposure and at an optimal size, given its unique competencies.

Figure 11–24 summarizes both the competitive realities facing today's firms and the organizational imperatives these realities produce. The benefits of the network structure in meeting these imperatives, as well as some of the possible costs associated with networks, are discussed below.

Globalization and Technological Change

Globalization today is a compelling reality, with at least 70 to 85 percent of the U.S. economy feeling the impact of foreign competition. In growing strength and numbers,

foreign competitors reduce profit margins on low-end goods to the barest minimum, and they innovate across high-end products and services at ever-increasing rates.

Moreover, foreign competitors are technologically sophisticated. Around the world, technology is changing at a faster rate than ever before. Perhaps more important, technological innovations are transferring from one industry to another and across international borders at increasing speed. Firms thus find it difficult to build barriers of either technology or location around their businesses.

As a response to increasing globalization and the ease of technology transfer, many U.S. firms are focusing on only those things they do especially well, outsourcing a growing roster of goods and services and ridding themselves of minimally productive assets. Such delayered companies are not only less costly to operate, they are also more agile. By limiting operations and performing them expertly, firms require less planning and coordination, and they can accelerate product and service innovations to keep pace with marketplace changes.

For these smaller, more adaptive companies, the global economy contains not only an increasing number of competitors but also more candidates for outsourcing and partnering relationships. Indeed, alliances of various kinds have given rise to the "stateless" corporation in which people, assets, and transactions move freely across international borders. As the world economy continues to concentrate into three regional centers (Europe, North America, and the Pacific Rim), companies scramble for presence in each of these huge markets—something most cannot do single-handedly.

Thus, whether the objective is to extend distribution reach, increase manufacturing efficiency and adaptability, add design capability, or whatever, the global economy is full of opportunities for networking. Of course, the opportunities available to one firm are probably equally accessible to others, raising concern that the outsourcing firm may not find a manufacturer, supplier, distributor, or designer when one is needed. Further, there are oft-expressed concerns about quality assurance in geographically far-flung networks and worries that extensive outsourcing will increase the likelihood of innovative products being copied (and improved) as technological competence spreads.

Deregulation

Changing regulatory processes in the U.S. and abroad are a corollary of more sophisticated global competition. Financial deregulation, in particular, has caused an explosion of international profit-seeking activity. For example, the development of overseas capital markets has vaulted formerly minor functions, such as cash management, into the strategic limelight. Many U.S. companies now sweep excess cash from their accounts every afternoon and deposit the funds in overnight money market accounts somewhere in the world.

Figure 11–23 **Network Organization Structure**

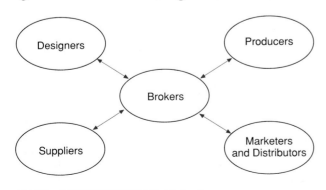

Figure 11-24 **Organizational Responses to the New Business Environment**

The New Competitive Reality

Driving Forces	Interactive Forces	Facilitating Forces

Globalization
  Strong new players at every stage of the value chain (upstream and downstream)
  Competition has reduced all margins—no slack left in most economic systems
 	
Technological Change and Technology Transfer
  Shorter product life cycles
  Lower barriers to entry
  Economies of scope as well as scale
	Deregulation
	  Legal and policy changes produce uncertainty and increase competition
	  Public services are being privatized
	
	Changing Workforce Demographics
	  Domestic workforce is becoming more mature, diverse, and less well trained and educated
	  Global workforce is becoming more mobile
		CAD/CAM and other manufacturing advances
		Faster, lower cost communications and computer technologies
		More social and political freedom

Organizational Imperatives

Product and Service Demands	Managerial Requirements
Focus on distinctive competence Reduce costs and accelerate innovation Hold only productive assets Reduce overall cycle time	Build smaller, better trained permanent workforces Develop and use links to part-time and temporary human resources Develop and use links to global technological resources

Frequently, firms find the rules of the game being rewritten after they have placed their bets. Cross-national differences and changes in tax laws, investment credits, and currency exchange rates force companies to constantly re-evaluate how they report profits and invest excess cash.

Essentially, deregulation unleashes entrepreneurial behavior, which in turn raises the level of competition. Often deregulation creates new outsourcing opportunities—as seen, for example, in the increased privatization of public corporations and agencies in many countries. Most important, deregulation reduces margins, and this requires companies to maximize returns on all assets—those they control as well as those their vendors and partners control.

Work Force Demographics

Changes in the composition of the U.S. work force are also driving companies to abandon the old business equation. Our work force is becoming older, and its growth is slowing. Seventy-five percent of the people who will be in the work force in the year 2000 are already working. As the work force matures, human resource costs will rise, in part because older employees draw more heavily on their companies' health-care and pension benefits. Because older workers are less inclined to move or to be retrained, flexibility and mobility for this segment of the work force will decline. Rising costs and decreasing flexibility are stimulating U.S. companies to search globally for new human resources and to develop empowerment schemes that generate greater returns from their current stock of human capital. Increasingly, so-called minorities will become a larger majority. Women already form a sizable and growing segment of the work force. Immigration from non-English-speaking countries will likely continue (and perhaps expand), adding to training requirements at a time when U.S. public education is in a troubled state.

Given these demographic trends, the network structure and its operating mechanisms offer some distinct advantages. First, as older workers and some women with small children seek shorter working hours, firms already skilled in outsourcing will invent new means of accommodating these employees' requests for part-time and telecommuting work. Second, firms retain as small a permanent work force as possible, turning more frequently to consulting firms and other resources for temporary employees. Third, more and more firms will allow their employees to make their services available to other firms on a contractual basis.

Although the network form allows for a smaller permanent work force, it requires that work force to be highly trained. In fact, it is the ability of the various network components to apply their expertise to a wide range of related activities that provides the overall network with agility and cost efficiency. For their permanent employees, network firms must be prepared to make large and continuing investments in training and development. Most employees in these companies will need to know how to perform numerous operations, and demonstrate an in-depth understanding of the firm's technologies.

Communications and Computer Technologies

Network organizations cannot operate effectively unless member firms have the ability to communicate quickly, accurately, and over great distances. Advances in fiber optics, satellite communications, and facsimile machines have made it much easier for managers to communicate within international network organizations. In addition, microcomputers now offer managers and employees all the computational capacity they need, 24 hours a day. And the micros can follow their users wherever they go. Moreover, the cost of data transmission has been declining consistently since the early 1970s, and the decline shows no signs of slowing down. In short, information-processing capacity and geographic distance are no longer major constraints in designing an organization.

Even more important in the long run, computers are changing the traditional concept of product design and production. Today's computer-aided product engineer can quickly produce a multitude of designs or modifications, each complete with parts and components specifications. To evaluate the design of smaller components, an engineer can use stereo lithography, a computer-aided design/laser hookup that "grows" a prototype in a vat, thus achieving a first stage of "desktop manufacturing." Moreover, computer-controlled, general-purpose plant equipment can manufacture directly from computer-stored specifications. Thus, a single manufacturing site can serve several product designers, using their instructions to guide expensive, but usually fully loaded, equipment. Organizationally speaking, we are at the point where capital investments in complex general-purpose machinery can provide a manufacturing component with the ability to serve numerous partners in a network arrangement.

To summarize, globalization and technological change, coupled with deregulation and changing work force demographics, have created a new competitive reality. Taken together, these forces are placing heavy demands on firms to be simultaneously efficient and adaptive. Global competition and deregulation have squeezed most of the slack out of the U.S. economy, and firms can afford to hold only fully employed, flexible resources. Fortunately, however, network structures permit both high utilization and flexibility. Relying on computer-aided communications, product design, and manufacturing, companies can now forge sophisticated linkages—quickly.

TYPES OF NETWORK ORGANIZATIONS

As firms turned to some form of network organization to meet competitive challenges, three types of structures became prominent: internal, stable, and dynamic. Though similar in purpose, each type is distinctly suited to a particular competitive environment. (See Figure 11–25.)

Internal Network

An internal network typically arises to capture entrepreneurial and market benefits without having the company engage in much outsourcing. The internal-network firm owns most or all of the assets associated with a particular business. Managers who control these assets are encouraged (if not required) to expose them to the discipline of the market. The basic logic of the internal network is that if internal units have to operate with prices set by the market (instead of artificial transfer prices), then they will constantly seek innovations that improve their performance.

The General Motors' components business provides a good example of an internal network.[1] Through a series of reorganizations and consolidations (mostly in the 1980s), GM reduced the number of its components divisions to eight. Each of the eight divisions pursues its own specialty; together, they create what has been called a "specialization consortium."

Turning GM's formerly rigid and inefficient components divisions into a group of coordinated and flexible subcontractors required two major actions. First, the parent corporation established clear performance measures for each of the divisions so that their behavior could be legitimately compared to that of external suppliers. Usually, this meant converting each components facility into a business unit that was encouraged to sell its products on the open market. Second, each division was assigned (or retained) an area of expertise related to a particular automotive system or subassembly. Each division was to be *the* expert at providing its product and to cooperate with other divisions in the consortium whenever appropriate.

To cite a specific example, the AC-Rochester Division was formed in 1988 by merging the former AC Spark Plugs Division and the Rochester Products Division. The combined division specializes in products that govern the flow of air and fluids into and out of the automobile (filters, fuel and exhaust systems, and so forth). The division is organized into several business units, each a specialist, just as AC-Rochester itself is a specialist within the consortium of components divisions. The various business units of AC-Rochester sell their products to GM, of course, but they also sell to Mitsubishi Motors (Japan), Daewoo (Korea), Opel (Europe), and other manufacturers.

Figure 11–25   **Common Network Types**

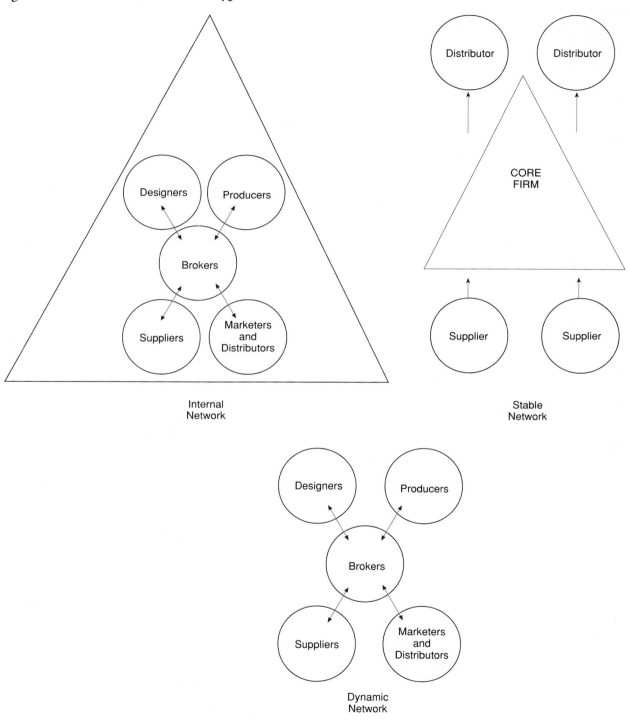

Internal
Network

Stable
Network

Dynamic
Network

If this organizational arrangement were to be extended throughout General Motors, then the parent corporation would eventually evolve toward the brokering function shown in Figure 11–23. That is, corporate headquarters would become a holding company that maintained an interest in a broad array of specialization consortia, each of which possessed the ability to compete favorably in international markets. It would seek, through subsidies, taxes, loans, and investments, to keep the "internal economy" healthy, focused, and renewing.

Multinational resource-based companies also gravitate toward internal networks. For example, an international oil company would likely find it too costly to hold resources for exploration, extraction, refining, and distribution in every country in which it operates. Nor is deployment from a central location very practical. No matter where its resources were concentrated, the firm could not allocate them quickly and efficiently with a central planning mechanism. Instead, an internal network is constructed. For the network to operate properly, each of its nodes must interact regularly with outsiders—trading, buying, or selling products and raw materials to other firms in order to bring real prices to bear on internal transactions. Thus, inside the company, clusters of business units, grouped by region and product category, can be seen buying and selling from one another as well as from outside firms.

A well-conceived internal network can reduce resource redundancy and decrease response time to market opportunities. Such a network achieves total resource utilization. But there are pitfalls. Internal networks may sometimes fall victim to corporate politics. Instead of exchanging goods or services at verifiable market prices, divisions transfer goods at administered prices that do not reflect external realities—and bad decisions result.

Stable Network

The stable network typically employs partial outsourcing and is a way of injecting flexibility into the overall value chain. In the stable network, assets are owned by several firms, but dedicated to a particular business. Often, a set of vendors is nestled around a large "core" firm, either providing inputs to the firm or distributing its outputs. (Again, see Figure 11–25.)

BMW, for example, is organized as a stable network. In principle, any part of a BMW is a candidate for outsourcing, and somewhere between 55 and 75 percent of total production costs at BMW come from outsourced parts. As at GM, various internal BMW operating units are obligated to prove their competence according to market standards. Beyond this, however, BMW keeps pace with developments in a variety of relevant product and process technologies through its own subsidiaries, and by partnering with other firms. Three subsidiaries concentrate on technologically advanced forms of automobile development and production: BMW Motor Sports Group, Advanced

Engineering Group, and the Motorcycle Group. Each of these subsidiaries, especially Motor Sports and Advanced Engineering, focuses on extending the boundaries of knowledge related to automobile engineering and design. The basic objective of these research groups is to understand enough about a particular technology to know who among potential outside vendors would be the best provider. Further, BMW engages in joint ventures and uses its own venture capital fund to participate financially in the operations of other firms. Currently, four areas are closely monitored: new product materials, new production technologies (e.g., with Cecigram in France), electronics (with Leowe Opta), and basic research in several related fields.

Thus, we can see different forms of network operating within the same industry. In its components business, GM is almost entirely an internal network, whereas BMW relies to a greater extent on outsourcing and partnering.

A stable network spreads asset ownership and risk across independent firms. In bad times, however, the "parent" firm may have to protect the health of smaller "family members." The benefits of stability are the dependability of supply or distribution, as well as close cooperation on scheduling and quality requirements. The "costs" of stability are mutual dependence and some loss of flexibility.

Dynamic Network

In faster-paced or discontinuous competitive environments, some firms have pushed the network form to the apparent limits of its capabilities. Businesses such as fashion, toys, publishing, motion pictures, and biotechnology may require or allow firms to outsource extensively. (See Figure 11–25.) In such circumstances, the lead firm identifies and assembles assets owned largely (or entirely) by other companies. Lead firms typically rely on a core skill such as manufacturing (e.g., Motorola), R&D/design (e.g., Reebok), design/assembly (e.g., Dell Computer), or, in some cases, pure brokering.

An example of a broker-led dynamic network is Lewis Galoob Toys. Only a hundred or so employees run the entire operation. Independent inventors and entertainment companies conceive most of Galoob's products, while outside specialists do most of the design and engineering. Galoob contracts for manufacturing and packaging with a dozen or so vendors in Hong Kong, and they, in turn, pass on the most labor-intensive work to factories in China. When the toys arrive in the U.S., Galoob distributes through commissioned manufacturers' representatives. Galoob does not even collect its accounts. It sells its receivables to Commercial Credit Corporation, a factoring company that also sets Galoob's credit policy. In short, Galoob is the chief broker among all of these independent specialists.

Dynamic networks can provide both specialization and flexibility. Each network node practices its particular expertise, and, if brokers are able to package resources quickly, the company achieves maximum responsiveness. However, dynamic networks run the risk of quality variation across firms, of needed expertise being temporarily unavailable, and of possible exploitation of proprietary knowledge or technology. The dynamic network operates best in competitive situations where there are myriad players, each guided by market pressures to be reliable and to stay at the leading edge of its specialty. The dynamic network is also appropriate in settings where design and production cycles are short enough to prevent knockoffs or where proprietary rights can be protected by law or by outsourcing only standard parts and assemblies.

THE BROKER'S ROLE

In hierarchically organized firms, the fundamental role of management is to plan, organize, and control resources that are held in-house. In many network firms, however, certain key managers operate *across* rather than *within* hierarchies, creating and assembling resources controlled by outside parties. These managers, therefore, can be thought of as brokers. Three broker roles are especially important to the success of network organizations: architect, lead operator, and caretaker.

Architect

Managers who act as architects facilitate the emergence of specific operating networks. Entrepreneurial behavior of this sort has been going on for centuries. For example, beginning in the 13th century, some early network architects fueled the rapid growth of the European cottage textile industry by designing a "putting out" system that organized an army of rural workers who spun thread and wove cloth in their homes. The architects of this system financed the network by providing workers with raw materials to be paid for when the finished goods were delivered. In some cases, brokers also supplied product designs and special equipment suitable for cottage production.

A network architect seldom has a clear or complete vision of all the specific operating networks that may ultimately emerge from his or her efforts. Frequently, the architect has in mind only a vague concept of the product and of the value chain required to offer it. This business concept is then brought into clearer focus as the broker seeks out firms with desirable expertise, takes an equity position in a firm to coax it into the value chain, helps create new groups that are needed in specialized support roles, and so on.

In designing an internal network, it may be relatively easy to identify the appropriate organizational units for each stage of the value chain. In the early years at General Motors, for example, Alfred Sloan envisioned an internal network of automotive suppliers, assemblers, producers, and distributors that could be assembled from among the various firms that William Durant had acquired. The internal network that GM uses today is the modern-day result of a similar process.

In both stable and dynamic networks, the architect's role is likely to be more complicated, because the resources that must be organized are not contained entirely within the firm. The managers who designed BMW's stable network, for example, had to identify several outside firms who would be suitable partners for long-term R&D relationships. When partners and relationships change frequently, as in dynamic networks, certain managers must devote ongoing effort to the architect's role.

The overall result of the architect's efforts can be portrayed as a grid of firms and value-chain elements, such as that shown in Figure 11–26. A grid can be developed entirely within an industry, or it can cut across established industry boundaries. The critical factor is that all firms recognize that they are part of the grid and are at least minimally committed to supporting it. Under these conditions, a number of specific operating networks may emerge.

The personal computer business, for example, is organized in large part around three types of operating networks. One type, perhaps best represented by Tandy Corporation (Radio Shack) offers a product that is mostly designed, manufactured, and sold in-house. Thus, Tandy by itself performs all of the major functions along the value chain. A second network type, represented by Apple Computer, looks much like the Tandy network at the upstream (manufacturing) end, but it contains more distributors and retailers downstream. The third type of network, of which there are many examples, has as its center of gravity the distribution and retailing portion of the value chain. Here distributor-retailers buy off-the-shelf components from various manufacturers, then assemble and sell customized packages of computer hardware and software to specialized market segments.

Lead Operator

As the grid of firms clustered around a particular business evolves, emphasis shifts from design to decisions about operation. Managers who act primarily as lead operators take advantage of the groundwork laid by manager-architects (although the two roles may overlap considerably and may be played by the same person or group). Essentially, this means that the lead operator formally connects specific firms together into an operating network. At Galoob Toys, for example, a handful of key executives perform this role. They select from a known set of potential partners those individuals and firms needed to design, manufacture, and sell children's toys. The firm outsources virtually every operating activity, choosing to perform only the brokering role in-house.

The lead-operator role is often played by a firm positioned downstream in the value chain. Brokers in the lead firm rely on their negotiating and contracting skills to hook together firms into more-or-less permanent alliances. Nike, an R&D and marketing company, operates this way. However, the lead-operator role is not limited to downstream

Figure 11–26   **A Value Chain Grid of Firms and Three Operating Networks**

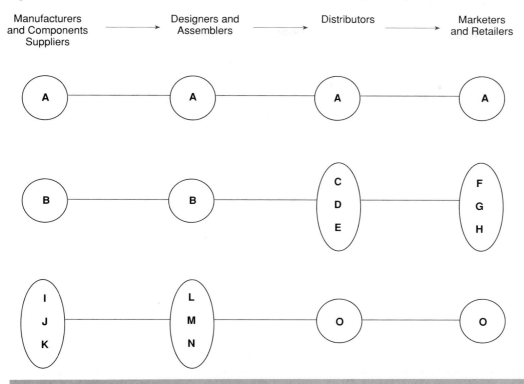

firms. For example, some large semiconductor manufacturers, such as Intel, have formed alliances with particular assemblers and distributors to promote the sale of new memory and operating chips. These firms advertise their new designs to potential end-users, and major exhibitions are staged to showcase the latest hardware and software developments.

Caretaker

Networks require continual enhancement if they are to operate smoothly and effectively. Thus, the process of network development is ongoing. Managers who focus on enhancement activity could be called caretakers. The caretaker role is multifaceted and may be just as important as the architect and lead-operator roles to the ultimate success of a network.

A caretaker may have to monitor a large number of relationships with respect to the specific operating network as well as to the larger grid of firms from which it came. In the operating network, this means sharing information among firms about how the network runs, as well as information on recent technological and marketing developments, schedules, and so on. Downstream firms in the value chain need to be kept abreast of new manufacturing capabilities, and upstream firms need an awareness and understanding of coming changes in the marketplace. Thus, the

caretaker does more than help the network plan; managers who play this role also help the network learn.

With regard to the grid of potential network firms, the caretaker may engage in nurturing and disciplinary behavior. For example, a caretaker may notice that a particular firm appears to be falling behind technologically, or in some other way devaluing its usefulness to the grid. Appropriate actions could be taken to rectify the situation. An even more troublesome case occurs when a firm exploits its position in the grid—for example, by obtaining some short-run gain at the expense of its actual or potential partners. Here the caretaker's challenge is to point out the dysfunctional effects of such behavior on the overall system and teach the offending firm how to behave more appropriately for the common good.

**IMPLICATIONS FOR BROKER
SELECTION AND DEVELOPMENT**

If, as seems likely, network organizations continue to spread, it is important to consider how managers with broker skills will be selected and developed. Positions labeled network architect, operator, or caretaker are not commonly found on organization charts, and no career paths are obvious. Nevertheless, it seems that many corporate experiences, and even some university courses, may be vehicles for developing needed skills. Some examples are discussed below.

Network Design

Many business experiences have characteristics related to network design. For example, in consumer packaged goods firms, product and brand managers learn to build informal networks among the various designers, producers, distributors, and marketers involved in the offering of their product. Similarly, project managers in matrix organizations develop network-building skills as they work across the functional boundaries of their firms and with outside contractors.

Network designers are essentially entrepreneurs, not only pulling together the skills and equipment needed to produce a new product or service, but also, on occasion, arranging the financing. Indeed, many of the network organizations found today in the personal computer, biotechnology, fashion, and entertainment businesses are the joint product of numerous entrepreneurs who originally created a piece of the overall value-chain grid.

However, in most corporations only a limited number of managers are individuals with direct entrepreneurial experience that can be drawn on as a resource. Therefore, firms like 3M and Texas Instruments practice "intrapreneuring"—rewarding their employees for turning ideas into prototype products or services, frequently with limited resources. In fact, one Swedish consulting firm (the Foresight Group) helps firms select and develop intrapreneurs. Interestingly, these consultants accept only volunteers, and they require them to work on their chosen projects while carrying out their regular duties (some limited financial support is also provided). Volunteers are encouraged to "scrounge" for needed resources—both inside and outside the organization. This process has developed many new products, complete with their own internal or external network already in place. The characteristics of intrapreneuring—individual initiative, cross-functional team building, resource acquisition, and so on—are very consistent with the development of successful networks.

Many business schools now offer courses or workshops in entrepreneurship, and most of these cover product and project management, intrapreneuring, and the writing of business plans. While coursework is not a direct substitute for hands-on experience, these courses, often relying on guest lecturers, give students opportunity to explore many aspects of network design and operation.

Network Operation

The task of putting a network into operation by linking all the value-chain components needed for a given product or service involves not only conceptual and organizational skills but also the skill to negotiate mutually beneficial returns for the contributions of all participants. Here one might look to purchasing or sales as a likely breeding ground for ne-

gotiations knowledge and skill. However, experience in such arenas as construction or engineering management may be even more relevant, in that the process of subcontracting is closely akin to network operation. "Partnering" is now common in the construction industry, a process whereby the various parties involved in a project meet in a team-building session to uncover mutual interests and to create the mechanisms and build the trust necessary for resolving the inevitable disputes and inequities.

Again, many business schools now offer courses in negotiation strategies and skills, with emphasis on collaboration and ethical behavior. Understanding the processes of (and the responsibilities involved in) collaborative negotiation is an essential characteristic of the lead operator. The quest is not for an airtight legal contract guaranteeing one's own rights, but for an objective, clearly understood relationship that protects all parties' interests.

Increasingly, as networks extend across international borders, both the network architect and lead operator will require extensive international knowledge and experience. Architects must keep abreast of available skills and resources around the world, and operators must understand how cross-cultural relationships are forged and maintained. It seems likely that courses exploring general international similarities and differences will be helpful, as will courses focused on specific skills, such as those involved in countertrade. Japanese companies are noted for both their ability to build lasting relationships and for their extensive programs for assuring that managers gain hands-on experience across their organizations and various operating regions. Few U.S. firms appear to be as dedicated to such cross-training and experience, and few are as adept at building effective internal and external relationships.

Network Caretaking

In some ways, the function of caretaking—maintaining and enhancing an existing network—is both the least understood and the most challenging of the three broker roles. One aspect of caretaking is simply taking care of one's self—for example, by being an active member of a trade association. A more important purpose of the caretaking function is to develop a sense of community among the members of a network. Networks operate effectively when member firms voluntarily behave as if they are all part of a broader organization sharing common objectives and rewards. This sense of community may be easier to instill in an internal network, where assets are held by a single firm, than in a dynamic network, where assets are spread across changeable combinations of designers, manufacturers, suppliers, and so on. Nevertheless, in either case, the network somehow must create an organization "culture" that transcends ownership and national borders.

Clearly, brokers involved in the task of nurturing networks will benefit from team-building skills. General Electric's Workout Program, for example, is designed in part to bring GE's managers, customers, and vendors together to form effective working relationships. Once more, business school courses may be helpful in this area, but theory lags practice. That is, courses in organization development and change contain many useful concepts, but most are oriented toward developing the single firm, not the set of firms that constitutes a network.

In sum, the job of broker, with its attendant roles of architect, lead operator, and caretaker, is unlikely to be filled by managers from any particular part of today's corporation. Individuals from product management, sales, and purchasing may possess some of the knowledge and skills required by the effective network broker. However, none of these functions appears to be the sole source of future brokers. Further, the broker's job is far too complex to lend itself to the use of any available selection instruments. Consequently, as is often the case, a manager's track record may be the best selection and placement device. In any case, however they are chosen, managers must be found for an increasing number of broker positions in the next century.

THE FUTURE

The forces currently pushing many American companies toward network forms of organization are likely to continue unabated. In fact, the recent emergence of Eastern Europe as a significant factor in the global economy will add to the turbulence currently found in many industries. New foreign producers will add to competitive pressures, and emerging foreign markets will offer opportunities for flexible first movers. In short, it is difficult to imagine any industry ever returning to a form of competition in which traditional pyramidical organizations can survive.

In the future, network organizations will emerge in a variety of circumstances. Dynamic networks, for example, will appear on the fringes of those mature industries that are in danger of stagnation. The ability of networks to generate new products with lower levels of investment will help to invigorate these industry segments. Also, dynamic networks will continue to operate in emerging industries where the pace of new product development and overall market demand cannot be accurately predicted. Alternatively, the efficiency-oriented stable network will become the dominant organizational form in mature, healthy industries. Lastly, an internal network will develop in situations where firms find it is difficult to create a new set of suppliers, but are unwilling to risk the potential inflexibility associated with wholly self-contained units.

Global competition in the 21st century will force every firm to become, at least to some extent, a network designer, operator, and caretaker. And as competition intensifies, companies will find themselves constantly subjecting virtually every internal asset to market tests in order to justify its ownership. However, the most successful firms will not only maximize the utilization of their assets, they will also learn how to market and deploy those assets to other firms. For example, firms will share or lease physical assets (e.g., more than one firm will use the same plant), their skilled staff groups (e.g., logistics units will sell services to other firms), and even their line work teams (e.g., autonomous work groups will be loaned on credit to other firms during slack periods).

Ultimately, every firm may have to decide whether it should create (or join) a cost-based or investment-based network. Eventually, cost-based global networks, which rely on inexpensive labor (or base plants in locales where there is minimal concern for ecological conditions, thus lowering environmental costs) will approach an equilibrium from which it will be difficult to extract further competitive advantages. Investment-driven networks, on the other hand, can be self-renewing. These networks will be constructed around those firms that are prepared to make continual capital expenditures—either for the most-advanced technology or for additional training and development of top-quality people.

DISCUSSION QUESTIONS

1. Briefly identify the forces that call for network structures.
2. What types of network organizations exist?
3. What roles exist in network structures?
4. What training is required for individuals who fill these roles?

ENDNOTE

1. The General Motors and BMW examples used in this article to illustrate internal and stable networks, respectively, were drawn from Charles Sabel, Horst Kern, and Gary Herrigel, "Collaborative Manufacturing: New Supplier Relations in the Automobile Industry and the Redefinition of the Industrial Corporation" (Working Paper, Massachusetts Institute of Technology, 1989).

Activity 11–1

Reorganization at Jackson Company

Step 1: Read the Reorganization at Jackson Company case.

PART I

Jackson Company is a major snack foods and beverage manufacturing corporation formed by a merger between Snack Fo—a snack foods company—and Jackco Company—which manufactured a wide line of carbonated beverage flavors.

After the merger, Snack Fo became the snack foods division and continued to operate as an independent profit center. This division handled the Research and Development, Manufacturing and Marketing functions under a President who reported to the Chief Executive Officer (CEO) of Jackson Company. Snack Fo had one large technical facility which centralized all technical functions under a Vice President who reported to the President. Snack Fo was recognized as a leader and innovator in the snack foods business and top management felt the centralized technical function was a major contributor to their leadership position.

Jackco had three divisions prior to the merger: Bevman, Jackco Domestic and Jackco International. Bevman was the manufacturing division, and was organized as a cost center. Bevman transferred the products it manufactured to Jackco Domestic and Jackco International which were organized as profit centers and handled the marketing and sales of products. Bevman was handled by a Vice President, who reported to an Executive Vice President of Jackson Company. Jackco Domestic and Jackco International were headed by Presidents who reported to the CEO of Jackson Company. These three divisions covered the beverage business.

Prior to 1976 the technical functions—Research and Development, Quality Assurance,[1] and Quality Control[2]—for the beverage business were dispersed among all three divisions, but the major part of the effort was located within Bevman Division. A staff of thirty people reported to a Director of Research, and were physically located in the largest domestic manufacturing facility. The Director of Research reported to the Vice President of Bevman, and was responsible for New Product Development and Quality Assurance. Quality Control was handled by Plant Chemists assigned to each of the 15 plus separate manufacturing plants located at strategic locations around the world. The Plant Chemists reported to the Plant Managers of their respective plants. (See Figure 11–27.)

There was some degree of overlap between the central group and the Plant Chemists particularly in the area of ingredient approval. In their Quality Assurance role, the central group had overall responsibility for approving all ingredients and all finished products. A portion of this responsibility was delegated to the Plant Chemists who were responsible for approving certain locally available ingredients as well as all of the finished product prior to shipment. Copies of the analytical results plus samples of locally approved ingredients and finished products were sent to the Central Laboratory for recheck. Often the results of the Plant Chemist would not agree with the results of the Central Laboratory, thus necessitating decisions to either redo the product or leave it in the marketplace. This decision was made by the Vice President of Bevman with advice from the Director of Research.

PART II

In 1976 Jackson Company decided to centralize the technical functions for the beverage business. The centralization within Snack Fo served as a model for the new organization which would cover all of the technical service activities within Bevman and some of the activities within Jackco Domestic and Jackco International. Since this new function would consolidate some technical activities from all three beverage divisions, the management of Jackson Company decided to create a new position, Vice President of Technical Services (VP-TS) who would report directly to the Jackson Company CEO.

The management decided that no one within the present technical organization was capable of handling this new position, and that it would be filled from outside the company. No announcement of the position was made to the existing staff.

In the fall of 1976, an experienced manager from a food company was recruited and assigned the position of VP-TS. The new manager, Dr. Brower, was just finishing work toward his Ph.D. degree on a part-time basis. He had no previous experience on a top team. Dr. Brower was told that he would report to the CEO and that his broad assignment was to centralize the Research and Development, Quality Control, and Quality Assurance functions for the beverage business. He was in his new assignment for four weeks before any general announcement was made concerning his appointment. A copy of the announcement follows.

Figure 11–27 **Organizational Relationship before the Change, Jackson Co.**

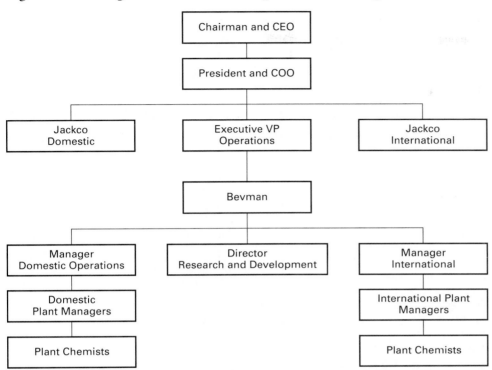

November 26, 1976

TO: All Vice Presidents, Department Heads &
        Managers
FROM: Vice President Personnel

It gives me great pleasure to announce the appointment of Dr. H. A. Brower to the position of Vice President of Research and Technical Services.

Dr. Brower has previous experience with Peptona, USA. In his new position he will report to the office of the CEO.

Please join me in welcoming Dr. Brower and his wife Sarah to the Jackson family.

Dr. Brower was told by the CEO that the people in the present organization were poorly organized and motivated. With respect to this problem, the CEO gave him the charge to develop the appropriate facilities and organization to handle the centralized technical service function. He was given the authority of a Division Vice President with the guidance that expenditures over $100,000 would require the CEO's approval.

Dr. Brower's first step was to recruit from his previous company several people whom he had recognized as quality performers. One of these people, Mr. French, was given the assignment of managing the Quality Control (QC) function. Mr. French had been responsible for the Quality Control Laboratory in one of the plants belonging to Dr. Brower's previous employer.

Dr. Brower and Mr. French had long discussions about methods to organize the Quality Control Department. A specific problem that concerned Dr. Brower was the present structure in which a Plant Chemist reported to each Plant Manager. He felt that the Plant Manager had too much vested interest in assuring that products from his plant were approved by the QC Laboratory, and thus might direct Plant Chemists to approve non-specification products. He also was concerned about the unclear authority in ingredient approval. Finally, Dr. Brower felt it was within his "centralization assignment" to have the Plant Chemists report to the new Technical Services Division.

In late 1977 Mr. French proposed a new organization structure in which the domestic plant chemists would report to him and the international plant chemists to a long-time company employee, Mr. Samson. (See Figure 11–28.) Mr. Samson was well respected for his knowledge of the ingredients and processes required to produce quality products. The proposed organization, particularly with respect

Figure 11–28 **Proposed Changes in Structure at Jackson Company**

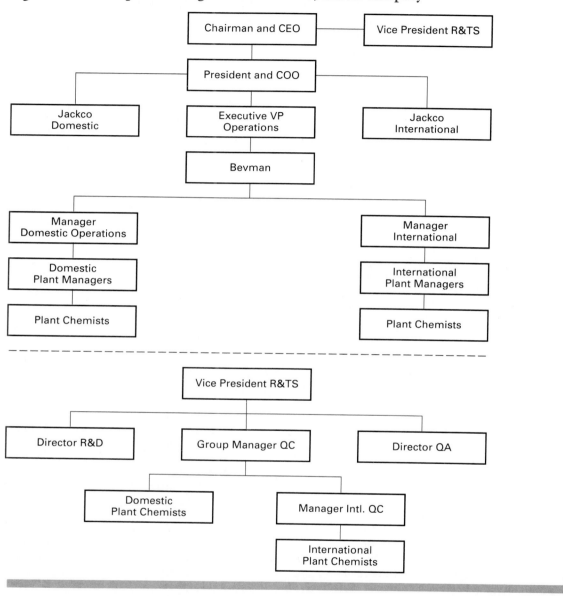

to Mr. Samson, was discussed in detail by Dr. Brower and Mr. French.

Prior to Dr. Brower's arrival, Mr. Samson had responsibility for the total Quality Control program and had served as an advisor to the Plant Chemists. In that position he had supervised two chemists and two technicians in the Central Laboratory. The new position involved less overall responsibility but more supervisory responsibility.

The discussion centered about how Mr. Samson would view this new position and whether he could handle the responsibility. Ultimately, the structure was approved; Mr. Samson agreed to the move, and a plan was developed to implement the structural change.

Prior to any further action, Dr. Brower met with the CEO and obtained his agreement with the changes. Dr. Brower then met with the Vice President of Bevman, Mr. Roberts, told him of the proposed change and stated that it had the approval of the CEO. Mr. Roberts pledged his full support to the change.

The action plan for the reorganization involved two

steps. First, a letter describing the change was to be sent to each Plant Manager by Mr. Roberts. After this activity was completed, Mr. French and Mr. Samson were to personally take a second letter to each Plant Chemist. This second letter described the change and was signed by both Mr. Roberts and Dr. Brower. It was decided not to change the reporting relationships unilaterally, but to work on a plant-by-plant basis until the conversion was complete.

PART III
The program progressed slowly, because the international travel required significant time commitments from Mr. French and Mr. Samson. The program was also delayed by dissension within the Plant Manager group. The dissent primarily centered in the international area. Letters from Mr. Roberts were all mailed the same day, but problems in the international mail system caused the letters to reach the Plant Managers over a two-week period. Two Plant Managers, Mr. O'Leary in Ireland and Mr. Valdez in Uruguay, did not even receive their copies of the letter. Once the letters began arriving, the Plant Managers were rapidly in telephone communication with each other and with the International Operations Manager. The conversion program was placed on hold in the international area until Mr. Roberts was satisfied that communications were complete. The changeover was finally accomplished in June, 1978.

Certain Plant Managers were unhappy with the new organization. This was particularly noticeable in the Brazil and Ireland plants where the Plant Manager routinely told the Plant Chemist that the change was temporary and that things would revert back to "normal."

In August, 1978, the Argentina Plant Manager decided that the Plant Chemist assigned to his plant should be discharged, and he gave the Plant Chemist a written discharge letter. Upon review, Dr. Brower, Mr. French, and Mr. Samson concurred with the dismissal. Word of this incident spread to all of the plants but no official description of the situation leading to the dismissal was ever circulated. A few Plant Chemists asked Mr. Samson about the incident, and in each case he answered their questions fully, stating that the problem involved dishonesty on the part of the chemist. Although he upheld the decision, Dr. Brower felt that the Argentina Plant Manager had overstepped his authority and discussed this problem at length with Mr. Roberts. Ultimately, they decided that potential delays in international communication required delegation of certain authority over the Plant Chemists to the Plant Managers, but that discharge was outside that authority. Mr. Roberts communicated this decision by letter to the Argentina Plant Manager with copies to the International Operations Manager and Dr. Brower.

One major goal of Dr. Brower was to insure that no products contained unapproved ingredients. During the Fall of 1978 and the Winter and Spring of 1979, a number of times at various plants, products were manufactured with materials that had not been approved by the Central Laboratory. These situations were identified only when an ingredient was disapproved after the product had been shipped to customers. In each of these cases Mr. French wrote a letter to the Plant Chemist associated with the problem and reiterated the Division goal. Copies of the letter were sent to Mr. Samson and to the Plant Manager involved.

In early August, 1978, a large shipment of orange flavor was made from the Ireland Plant. One week after the shipment, the Central Laboratory sent a telex disapproving the Orange Oil used in the August orange flavor shipment.

ENDNOTES
1. Quality Assurance is defined as overall responsibility for product quality.
2. Quality Control, in this firm, is defined as the day-to-day checking of product quality.

Step 2:   Prepare the case for class discussion.

Step 3:   Answer the following questions, individually, in small groups, or with the entire class, as directed by your instructor:

Description
1. Describe the original organization at Jackson Company in terms of division of labor and coordinating mechanisms.
2. Classify the organization using (a) form of departmentation, (b) means of coordination, (c) organic versus mechanistic classifications, and (d) information-processing capacity.
3. Describe the organization at Jackson after the reorganization plan was implemented in terms of division of labor and coordinating mechanisms.
4. Classify the new organization by (a) form of departmentation, (b) means of coordination, (c) organic versus mechanistic classification, and (d) information-processing capacity.

Diagnosis
5. Evaluate the appropriateness of both the original and new structures.
6. How does the new structure respond to information-processing needs?
7. Do you think the reorganization was justified? Why or why not?
8. Given the reactions of some of the employees to the changes in organization, how much did the new structure consider worker needs?
9. Were the proposed changes communicated effectively?
10. What changes in the formal organization resulted in shifts in the informal organization?

Prescription
11. What additional changes are required?

Action

12. Was the process used to redesign the organization and then implement the changes effective? What costs and benefits resulted?

Step 4:   Discussion. Answer the following questions, individually, in small groups, or with the entire class, as directed by your instructor:

1. Describe the changes instituted at the Jackson Company.
2. To what problems did the reorganization respond?

3. What other problems exist?
4. What theories and concepts help explain the problems?
5. Did the reorganization help? Why or why not?
6. What other changes are needed?

―――――――

Copyright © 1983 by B. Man Yoon.

Activity 11–2   Apex College

Step 1:   Read the following information about Apex College:

Apex College clears its students for promotion or graduation each term. Currently it has the organizational structure shown in Figure 11–29. The student-record clerks record all grades received. The transcript-approval clerks compare student transcripts to course and credit requirements for each grade. Billing clerks check the arithmetic on the students' bills and enter correct charges and credits on the students' accounts. Loan clerks check to ensure that all loan requirements are met. Cashier clerks examine the students' financial status to authorize promotion.

Step 2:   Answer the following questions, individually, in small groups, or with the entire class, as directed by your instructor:

Description
1. Describe the division of labor.
2. Describe the coordinating mechanisms used.
3. What method of organizing is used?

Diagnosis
4. What kinds of problems does this type of organization solve? create?
5. Is this the most effective kind of organization?

Figure 11–29   **Organization Chart for Apex College**

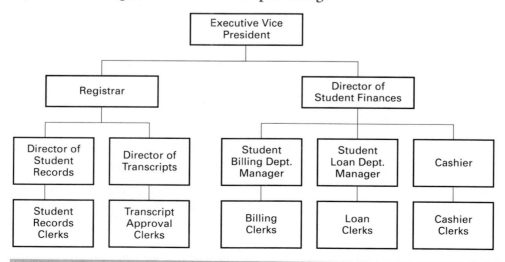

Prescription
6. What changes would you recommend?

Step 3: Discussion. In small groups or with the class as a whole, share your answers to the above questions. Then answer the following:

1. What symptoms suggest a problem exists?
2. What problems exist in the case?
3. What theories and concepts help explain the problems?
4. How can the problems be corrected?
5. Are the actions likely to be effective?

Activity 11–3 **Analysis of Organization Charts**

Step 1: Study the organization charts of three organizations presented in Figures 11–30 through 11–32. Compare and contrast them.

Step 2: Answer the following questions individually, in small groups, or with the entire class, as directed by your instructor:

Figure 11–30 **Organization Chart of a Library**

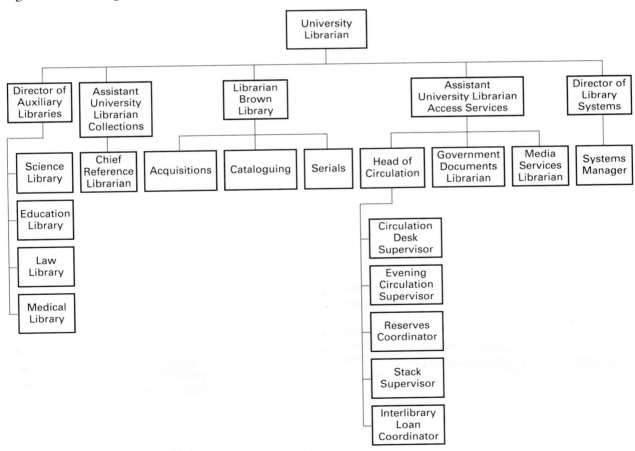

Figure 11–31 **Organization Chart of a Computer Software Company**

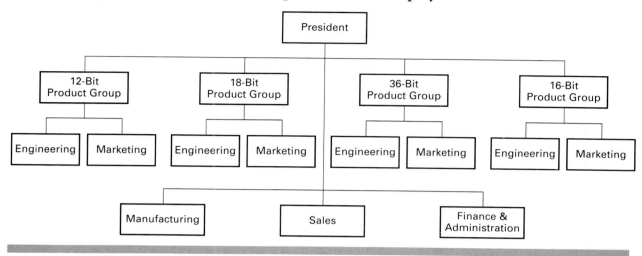

Description

1. Describe the division of labor and coordinating mechanisms for each.

Diagnosis

2. Analyze the method of organizing for each organization.
3. Compare and contrast these designs.

4. What kind of organization does each chart probably represent?
5. What employee attitudes and performance probably occur in each organization?

Prescription

6. What structural changes, if any, might benefit each organization?

Activity 11–4   **Jane Sanderson**

Step 1:   Read the Jane Sanderson case.

JANE SANDERSON (A)

Jane Sanderson was Director of Operations, Southeast, at the Metropolitan Telecommunications Company (MTC). In October 1990, she was confronted with an unexpected change in her responsibilities. The change involved a group of technicians in trucks who reported to one of Jane's subordinates. The group was one of three groups that was being transferred to the Marketing department. Marketing was undergoing a restructuring in order to make itself more sensitive to customer service needs. Sanderson knew that the change would greatly affect her own job objectives.

Sanderson had been with the company for twenty-one years, having started at MTC as a customer service assistant straight out of high school. She had been promoted six times and had made lateral moves ten times, moving from a salary of $77.50 per week to her present salary in the low seventies. As director of Operations, Sanderson was now at

level 3 in the company's six levels of field management, and she supervised three managers (level 2) and a secretary (see organization chart in Figure 11–33). The three managers were responsible for the supply and maintenance of state-of-the-art digital and analog telecommunications circuitry for large-volume customers. One manager was responsible for dispatching the technicians in trucks who called on all customers needing service. One manager supervised the work inside of 80 wiring centers. The third manager was responsible for the largest remote test center (RTC) in the company. Total force in Sanderson's district was 350. Sanderson's performance was evaluated on the basis of customer satisfaction, reduction of costs in her district, meeting her budget, and personal development.

In 1987, after carefully assessing the impact of her lack of formal educational credentials on the career future she was determined to achieve, Sanderson applied to the Simmons College Graduate School of Management. She entered the MBA program as a three-year student in 1988

Figure 11–32 **Organization Chart of a Medical Products Company**

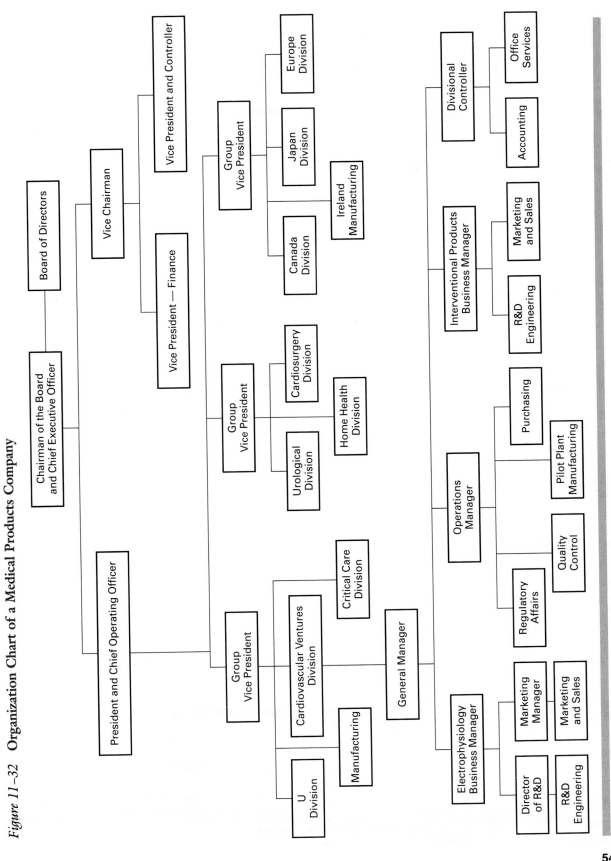

Figure 11–33 **MTC Operations Dept. before Reorganization (Partial Chart)**

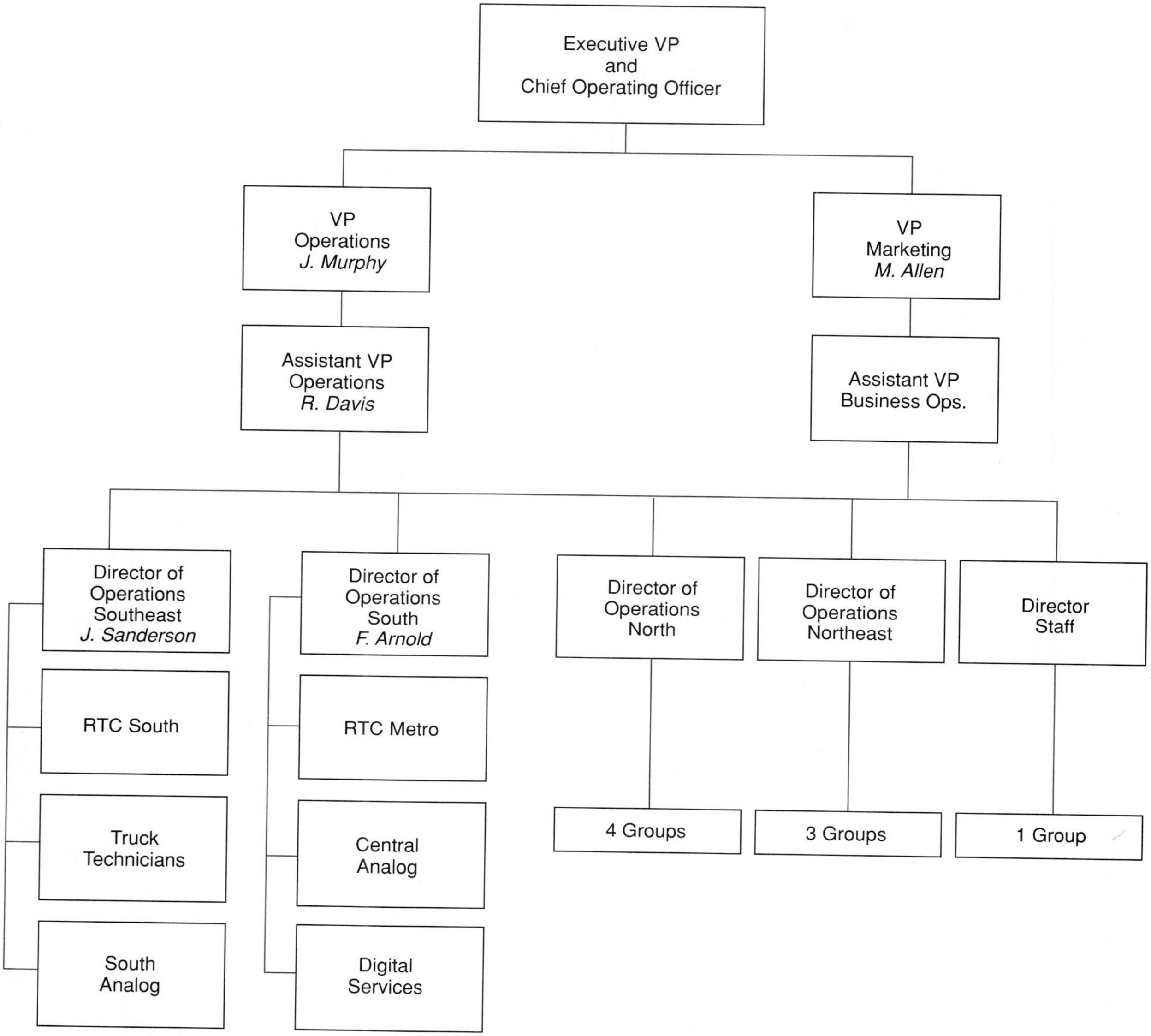

determined to do two things: complete her education and continue to be at her best on the job. Her determination was respected by her boss as well as by her peers and subordinates. To make classes in the evenings during busy periods, she often arrived at work at 4:30 a.m., and she tended to work longer hours than many of her peers and about the same as her bosses—anywhere from 50 to 60 hours a week.

Sanderson's promotion to director level came in June 1989. Her salary was increased 15%, and she was told that she was expected to be a leader among her peers, who were both men and women. Sanderson plunged into her new job as Director of Operations, Southeast, with enthusiasm.

Over the years, as she moved up at MTC, Sanderson had reported to dozens of bosses, all but one of them male. She had learned a great deal from careful observation of others' behavior, and had made many mistakes—and learned from each of them. Her technical skills had been learned on the job, and she had achieved a level of considerable complexity. As Director of Operations, Southeast, she reported directly to Ralph Davis, Assistant Vice President—Operations and on occasion to his boss, Joe Murphy, Vice President—Operations. Davis had been in his position since the fall of 1989. In June 1990, he had acquired Sanderson's department and become her immediate supervisor. Murphy had also moved into his position in the fall of 1989 and he, like Davis, had come from corporate headquarters in Washington, D.C. For both men, these moves represented promotions. Murphy was one of the twelve most senior vice presidents in a company that employed 25,000 people.

The large-volume customers that Sanderson's district served could be divided into two categories, which for simplicity she referred to as megacustomers and large business customers. The megacustomers were very large national telecommunications companies, and they made up about 50% of Metropolitan's revenues. The most challenging mandate of Sanderson's new job was to change the megacustomers' perception that they received substandard service from MTC. The large business customers were large companies that represented 25% of Metropolitan's revenues. The remaining 25% came from residential customers and small businesses.

Reorganization of the Marketing Department

In late September 1990, Sanderson ran into the vice president of Marketing, Mike Allen, at a company fundraiser. He asked if he could visit Sanderson's organization "just to look around." This was not an unusual request. Many people came to visit the remote test center (RTC) in her district. It was an impressive facility, the size of a couple of football fields, and the company's most extensive. Allen did not set a specific date, but said that he would contact Sanderson later with a date and time. Sanderson said she would look forward to his call.

On October 18, 1990, Joe Murphy held a director-level staff meeting to discuss 1990 accomplishments to date and to project what 1991 was going to bring. In addition to Murphy were the directors of Operations and Ralph Davis, the assistant vice president. After the group had dealt with several items of business, Murphy informed those present that he had recently assigned three Operations segments—the technicians in trucks, digital services, and central analog—to the Marketing department to speed along a restructuring that Marketing had undertaken. This was the first time that Sanderson and the other directors heard about this aspect of the restructuring.

The restructuring was undertaken in order to respond to complaints received by the Marketing department from large business customers—which were responsible for 25% of MTC's revenues—about the service they received. Sanderson's district depended very heavily on the technicians in trucks to meet both megacustomers' and large business customers' needs. Of the other two Operations groups now to be assigned to the Marketing department, digital services mainly served megacustomers and central analog mainly served large business customers' accounts. Sanderson saw immediately that her district would have difficulty maintaining a high level of service for the megacustomers if the trucks were dispatched through the Marketing department.

When Murphy asked the group for comments about this change, Sanderson told him in no uncertain terms that the move should not have been made and that it was a bad decision. Murphy seemed taken aback by Sanderson's objections. With no further comment, he called for a break and walked out of the room. "I felt very nervous," Sanderson said thinking back to that meeting.

During the break, Sanderson's boss, Ralph Davis, told her that he agreed with her comments, and he encouraged her to continue this line of discussion after the break was over. When Murphy returned to the room and resumed the meeting, he asked Sanderson to elaborate on her concerns. Although nervous, Sanderson was able to articulate her concerns about maintaining service levels for megacustomers. Murphy ended the discussion by stating that he would take Sanderson's comments under advisement.

A few days after this meeting, Mike Allen, the Marketing vice president, called Sanderson and set up a date to visit her office and the RTC on 6 November. Since this call came in only days after Murphy's meeting, Sanderson was sure that Allen had learned of her disapproval of the recent Operations changes and that he was ready to show her who was in charge. Sanderson called Ralph Davis and invited him to the meeting. He said he would attend.

JANE SANDERSON (B)

The meeting on November 6 was scheduled to begin at 9:00 a.m. Davis called Sanderson and said he would be late. At exactly 9:00 a.m., Allen arrived. He greeted Sanderson and her RTC manager, Peter Smith, in his usual cheerful, friendly manner. He told her that it was great to be back in Operations even if it was only for a few hours. Sanderson picked up on his comment and asked him when he had been in Operations. He looked her straight in the eye and said, "Oh, I had your job more than ten years ago."

The introductions over, Peter Smith made a formal presentation about the RTC, describing how its 100 technicians and 8 supervisors served megacustomers. Allen said he would like to talk to as many of the supervisors and technicians as he could after the presentation.

About halfway through Smith's presentation, Ralph Davis arrived but sat at the back of the conference room and remained quiet. At one point, talking about how the company used to do business, Allen turned to Davis and said, "I have been in this business since before you were born!" There was tension in the room, but Smith ended his presentation gracefully and Sanderson led the way out to the technicians' area. Allen talked to supervisors and technicians for the next hour and a half in a friendly, animated manner while Davis followed behind.

When it was time to leave, Allen pulled Sanderson aside and told her he was very impressed with her and with her operation. He also said that he had wanted to see her operation because he wanted to start a similar set-up in the

Marketing department for large business customers. He added that he would like to call on Sanderson in the future for assistance.

After Allen and Davis left, Sanderson sat at her desk for a few minutes thinking about what she should do now, if anything.

JANE SANDERSON (C)

Jane Sanderson, after some thought, decided that she would write a memo to her boss, Ralph Davis, detailing the events of Mike Allen's visit to the RTC. She drafted the memorandum shown in Figure 11–34. Before sending it, she gave copies of the memo to her Simmons study group and asked them what they thought of it.

JANE SANDERSON (D)

After discussion with her group, Sanderson agreed that she ought to revise the memo, and she wrote the version that appears in Figure 11–34. Sanderson sent the revised memo to Davis, with a copy (and short note) to Mike Allen, vice president of Marketing. In the meantime, she received the memo from Mike Allen shown in Figure 11–35 thanking her for his recent visit to the remote test center (RTC) in Sanderson's district.

JANE SANDERSON (E)

Effective February 1, 1991, Jane Sanderson was named the Operations liaison to the Marketing department for the restructuring effort. In addition, as of the same date, Sanderson's area of responsibility doubled both in geographic terms and in the number of people working in her district. Figure 11–36 (on page 548) shows an organization chart that includes the changes. Sanderson's district continued to rely on the group of technicians in trucks that shifted out of her area to serve both megacustomers and large business customers. The digital services group, which had also been assigned to the Marketing department, was more likely to serve the megacustomers than the large business customers,

Figure 11–34 **Jane Sanderson's Memorandum to Ralph Davis**

MEMORANDUM

TO: Ralph Davis
FROM: Jane Sanderson
DATE: November 7, 1990

My meeting yesterday with Mike Allen, Vice President of Marketing, turned out to be a great success. Mike provided me with an in-depth view of his Department's rationale for absorbing certain portions of the Network Operations Organization. We certainly didn't agree on all issues regarding the structural changes, but both Mike and I left the meeting with a good appreciation of the future needs of our customers and interesting options on how to serve them.

The fact that our 300 largest business accounts are demanding improved service from MTC appears to be the catalyst for the recent changes initiated by Marketing. Mr. Allen has the responsibility of meeting our customers' demands, and our organization is in the best position to offer assistance.

To ensure a proper understanding of critical issues regarding reorganization and to minimize the possibility of "restructuring prior to understanding," I suggested the establishment of a Quality Team. Mike agreed and told me he had been thinking along the same lines.

I readily accepted the responsibility of co-chairing this committee for the Network Department along with a co-chair from Marketing. The objective of the group is not to second guess the organizational changes that have already occurred but to "ensure that the transfer of responsibility from Operations to Marketing is as smooth as possible for our employees thereby making it transparent to our customers." I strongly believe we can only succeed as a Corporation by working together. If we cannot be successful at this, the customer suffers and ultimately our market share of the communications business will decline. I view this committee as a positive step toward normalizing relations with our new partners.

It is important that you and I get together to review our Departmental strategies in order to provide maximum input to the Quality Team. I am available to discuss this with you in greater detail at your convenience.

Thank you for your support.

Figure 11–35   **Memo from Mike Allen, VP of Marketing, to Jane Sanderson**

November 6, 1990

Ms. Sanderson
Mr. Davis

I would like to take this opportunity to thank you both and all the people involved in what was a delightful tour of the . . . Remote Test Center. I was very impressed by your operation but most of all by the people. They were upbeat, enjoying what they were doing and were justifiably proud of the service levels they were giving to some of our most important customers.

I would like to pass along, not only my thanks, but the thanks of the Officer team for the quality service you have given to all our customers, particularly [one of the megacustomers], which is our largest customer.

Once again, give my thanks to all involved.

Michael D. Allen

cc: Joseph T. Murphy

---

but the technicians in trucks were critical for providing good service to both customer groups. Frank Arnold was the director of Operations now assigned to the Marketing department.

During February and early March 1991, both Joe Murphy and Mike Allen were hearing complaints from megacustomers that response time to all problems was slow. Sanderson found that the Marketing department, which now dispatched technicians in trucks for all customers, was responding first to large business customers and second to megacustomers.

Step 2: Prepare the case for class discussion.

Step 3: Answer the following questions individually, in small groups, or with the entire class, as directed by your instructor:

Description
1. Describe the original organization at MTC in terms of division of labor and coordinating mechanisms.
2. Classify the organization using (a) form of departmentation, (b) means of coordination, (c) information-processing capacity.
3. Describe the new organization at MTC.
4. Classify the new organization by (a) form of departmentation, (b) means of coordination, (c) information-processing capacity.

Diagnosis
5. Evaluate the appropriateness of both the original and new structures.

6. What role did Jane Sanderson play in the reorganization? Was she effective?
7. How does the new structure respond to information-processing, division of labor, and coordination needs?
8. What changes in the informal organization likely accompany the changes in the formal structure?

Prescription
9. What additional changes are required?

Action
10. Was the process used to redesign the organization and then implement the changes effective?

Step 4: Discussion. Answer the following questions, individually, in small groups, or with the entire class, as directed by your instructor:

1. Describe the changes instituted at MTC.
2. To what problems did the reorganization respond?
3. What other problems exist?
4. What theories and concepts help explain the problems?
5. Will the reorganization help? Why or why not?
6. What other changes are needed?

This case was prepared by Cinny Little for the Institute for Case Development and Research, Simmons Graduate School of Management, Boston, MA 02215. Copyright © 1991 by the President and Trustees of Simmons College. Reprinted by permission.

Figure 11–36 MTC Operations Dept. after Reorganization (Partial Chart)

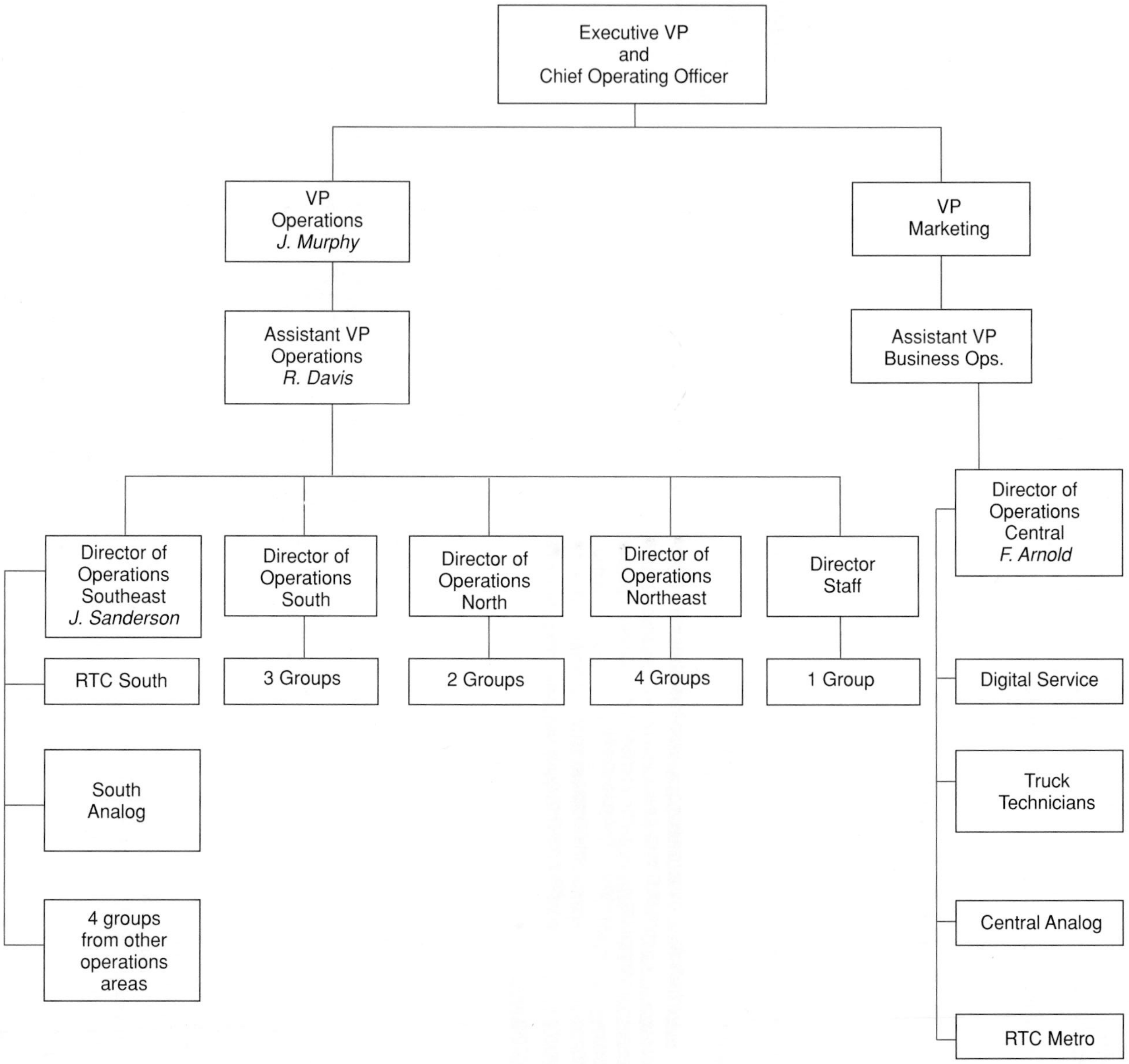

Executive VP and Chief Operating Officer

VP Marketing

Assistant VP Business Ops.

Director of Operations Central
F. Arnold

Digital Service

Truck Technicians

Central Analog

RTC Metro

VP Operations
J. Murphy

Assistant VP Operations
R. Davis

Director of Operations Southeast
J. Sanderson

RTC South

South Analog

4 groups from other operations areas

Director of Operations South

3 Groups

Director of Operations North

2 Groups

Director of Operations Northeast

4 Groups

Director Staff

1 Group

Activity 11–5   Magnacomp, Inc.

Step 1:   Read the following description of Magnacomp, Inc.:

In this exercise you are operating as members of a work team producing Magnaunits. These are assembled from subassemblies and these subassemblies have to be built from smaller units.

   The job of your team is to work together to assemble the final product "Z" at the lowest cost and with acceptable quality. Product cost is measured by the total employee-minutes required to produce the product. The following labor cost schedule is the basis for computing the total cost for a team completing the exercise with an acceptable quality answer.

Number of Members	Cost in $/employee/minute
3	100
4	125
5	150
6	175
7	200
8	225
9	265
10	305

Figure 11–37   **Magnacomp, Inc., Project 1, Flow Chart for Manufacturing**

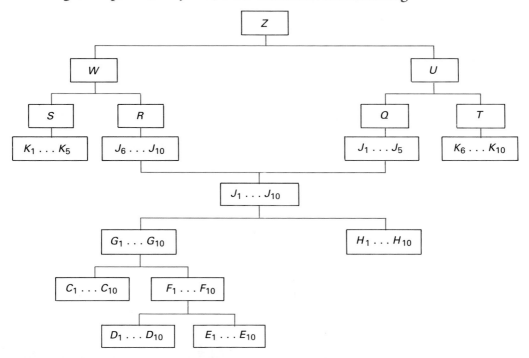

Figure 11–38 Magnacomp, Inc., Project 2, Flow Chart for Manufacturing

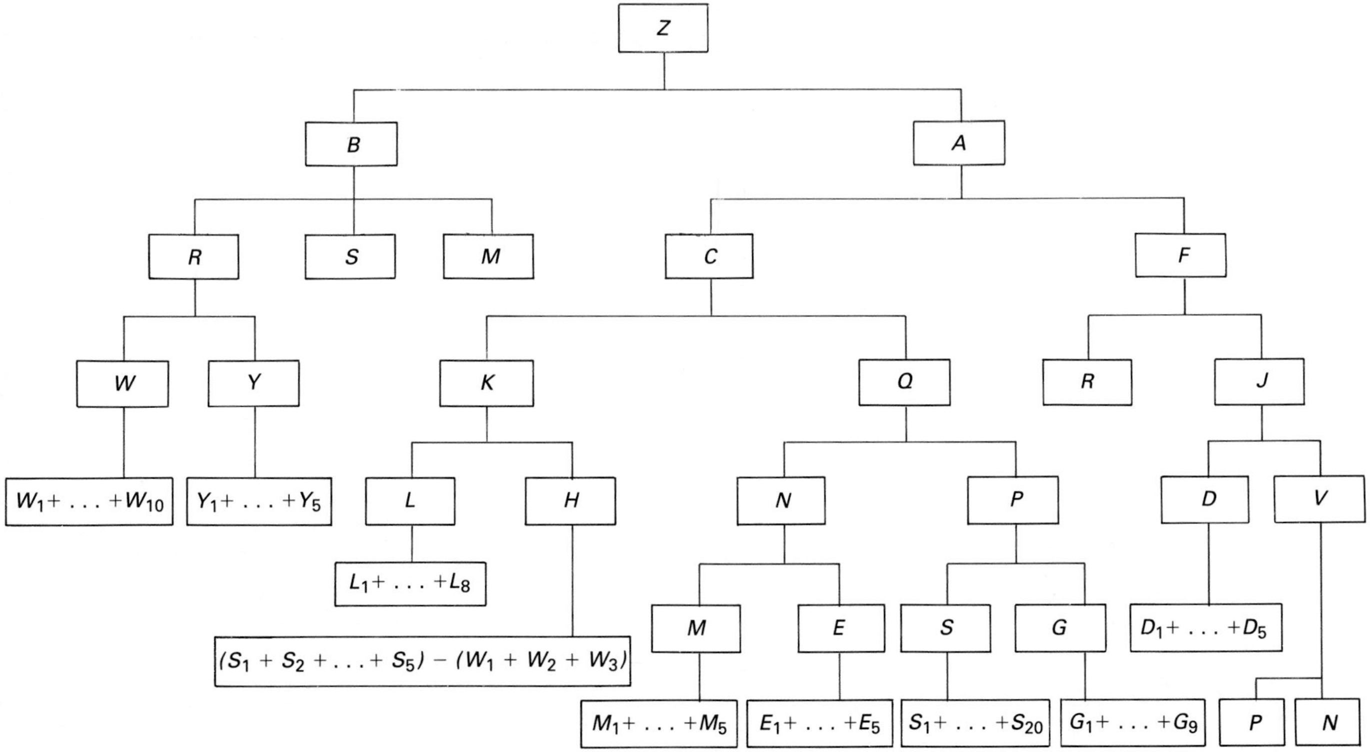

Thus a team completing the task successfully in 15 minutes with five members would have a total cost of $150 × 5 × 15 = $11,250.

Quality is determined by the accuracy of the answer. Deviations greater than ±10 percent will not be acceptable, and a new answer must be computed.

The assembly process is straightforward and there are no tricks in the method.

A deck of cards corresponding to individual parts will be distributed to each company by the instructor. They are identical for each company. These cards, representing raw materials coming into the plant, are in a random order. Operation cards also accompany the individual parts cards. Each part is coded by a letter-number combination. Before the parts can be assembled, various indicated computations must be performed. The parts can then be assembled into subassemblies by performing the appropriate operations.

Work flow is indicated by flow charts, Figures 11–37 and 11–38, which show how assemblies are formed. They do not show the combining operations. The operations necessary to combine subassemblies are indicated on the operations cards included with the parts, and in the description of operations in the tables for Project 1 and Project 2 on this page.

Magnacomp, Inc., Project 1

Operations

1. $Z = W + U$
2. $U = Q \div T$
3. $W = S \div R$
4. $S = K_1 + \ldots + K_5$
5. $R = J_6 + \ldots + J_{10}$
6. $Q = J_1 + \ldots + J_5$
7. $T = K_6 + \ldots + K_{10}$
8. $J_1 \ldots J_{10} = G_1 - H_1, G_2 - H_2, \ldots G_{10} - H_{10}$
9. $G_1 \ldots G_{10} = F_1 \times C_1, F_2 \times C_2, \ldots F_{10} \times C_{10}$
10. $F_1 \ldots F_{10} = D_1 - E_1, D_2 - E_2, \ldots D_{10} - E_{10}$
11. Where $C_1 \ldots C_{10}; E_1 \ldots E_{10}, D_1 \ldots D_{10}; H_1 \ldots H_{10}$ and $K_1 \ldots K_{10}$ are numerical values.

The team determining the value of "Z" within ±10 percent at the lowest cost will be declared the winner. If ties in cost occur, the team with the most accurate answer will win.

Two trials will be run: Project 1 and Project 2.

Magnacomp, Inc., Project 2

Operations

1. $Z = A + B$
2. $B = R - S + M$
3. $R = W \times \Upsilon$
4. $W = W_1 + \ldots + W_{10}$
5. $\Upsilon = \Upsilon_1 + \ldots + \Upsilon_5$
6. $A = C \div F$
7. $C = Q \times K$
8. $K = L \div H$
9. $L = L_1 + \ldots + L_8$
10. $H = (S_1 + \ldots + S_5) - (W_1 + W_2 + W_3)$
11. $Q = P \div N$
12. $N = M - E$
13. $P = S + G$
14. $M = M_1 + \ldots + M_5$
15. $E = E_1 + \ldots + E_5$
16. $S = S_1 + \ldots + S_{20}$
17. $G = G_1 + \ldots + G_9$
18. $F = R \div J$
19. $J = D - V$
20. $D = D_1 + \ldots + D_5$
21. $V = P - N$
22. Where $G_1 \ldots G_9; S_1 \ldots S_{20}; M_1 \ldots M_5; E_1 \ldots E_5; L_1 \ldots L_8; W_1 \ldots W_{10}; \Upsilon_1 \ldots \Upsilon_5;$ and $D_1 \ldots D_5$ are numerical values.

Step 2: Team leaders will be selected. There will be three to five teams depending on class size. Each leader in turn will select two assistants from the class. Each team will then have 10 minutes for a private preliminary planning session. During this time decisions should be made as to an initial organization structure, and an operations plan should be formulated. At this time each team should estimate its manpower needs for the simulation. Each team will be allowed to select additional persons for the simulation, and they will be selected at the end of this planning period. Care should be taken in selecting additional personnel, since the evaluation of performance of the group will be affected by the size of the team. If the team is understaffed it may not be competitive with the other teams in the exercise, and if it is overstaffed the cost of additional personnel will reduce the efficiency measure of the team.

Step 3: The selection of additional team personnel will occur. Those class members not selected will act as observers and report to the class during the discussion period.

Step 4: A second planning session will now be conducted with the complete team. You will have ten minutes.

Step 5: Begin the exercise. Complete the Project 1 phase of the Magnacomp, Inc., simulation. You will have twenty minutes.

Step 6: At the conclusion of Project 1 a ten-minute period will be provided to allow each team to analyze its mode of operations and make changes if necessary.

Step 7: Complete the Project 2 phase of the exercise. You will have twenty minutes.

Step 8: Discussion. After the exercise each team should analyze its mode of operation, its effectiveness, the organization structure developed, the communication channels, and the advantages and disadvantages of the system employed.

Description

1. Prepare an organization chart of your company.
2. Is this the initial form of organization you used? If you modified your initial structure, when, how, and why?

3. How did each member feel about his or her role in the simulation? Why?
4. Do differences exist between the various teams in the exercise with respect to these questions?
5. How was the team's performance? How does it compare with the other teams'?

Diagnosis

6. Can differences be explained in terms of organization structure?
7. How was the division of labor, coordination, and communication handled in the organization?

Prescription

8. What changes would have improved the organization's functioning?

Reprinted by permission from *Managing for Organizational Effectiveness: An Experiential Approach,* by F. E. Finch, H. R. Jones, and J. A. Letterer. New York: McGraw-Hill, 1976, pp. 82–84.

Activity 11–6   **Restructuring for Increased Performance**

Step 1: Review the structure of the School of Management shown in Figure 11–39.

Step 2: Individually, in small groups, or with the entire class, as directed by your instructor, redesign the organization using (1) functional structure, (2) project/product structure, (3) integrated structure, (4) dynamic network structure, and (5) loosely coupled alliance.

Step 3: Select another organization and learn about its structure by reviewing its organizational mission and interviewing key organizational members.

Step 4: Draw the organization's chart.

Step 5: Individually, in small groups, or with the entire class, as directed by your instructor, redesign the organization using (1) functional structure, (2) project/product structure, (3) integrated structure, (4) dynamic network structure, and (5) loosely coupled alliance.

Step 6: Discussion. In small groups or with the entire class, compare and contrast the two organizations. Then answer the following questions:

1. Describe and evaluate the division of labor.
2. Describe and evaluate the coordinating mechanisms.
3. Describe and evaluate the methods of organizing.
4. Compare and contrast the formal and informal structure.

CONCLUDING COMMENTS   As organizations have faced more complex problems, new structures have emerged to respond to the need to process more information more quickly. First project/product management, later matrix organizations, and then integrated structures were developed as new structures. More recently, organizations have turned to more loosely coupled forms, such as the dynamic network structure and various alliances, to allow a more timely response to a changing and competitive environment.

Organizations have moved from mechanistic structures—functional departmentation, simple structures, machine and professional bureaucracies—to more organic ones—adhocracies, product/project management, and integrated structures. They moved from structures with low information-processing capacity to ones with a high capacity. In analyzing various types of organizations by looking at their organization charts, you identified the components of structure and saw their contribution to the

Figure 11–39 **Structure of a School of Management**

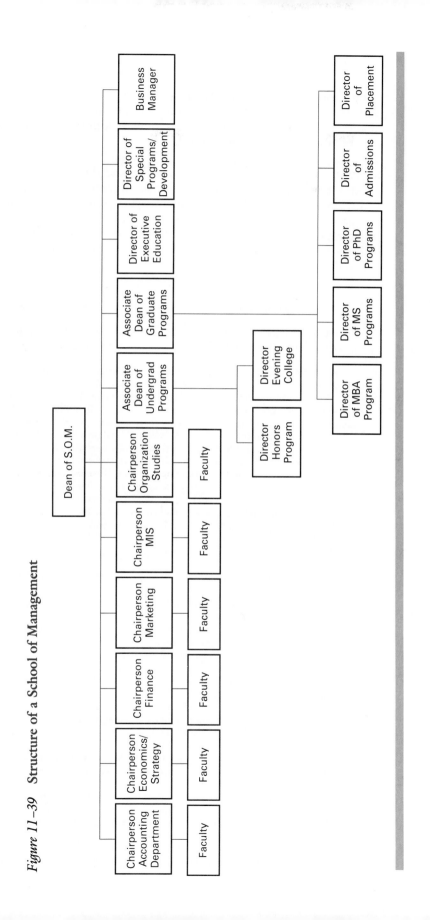

design configuration used in the organization. Working with Magnacomp, Inc., let you develop and experience additional organization structures. You also practiced altering the structures of two organizations as a prerequisite for designing them to meet various contingencies they face.

Analysis of the Reorganization at Jackson Company and Jane Sanderson cases identified different structural configurations and their implications for effectiveness. Often the informal, rather than the formal, organization transacts much of the work of organizations. Social network analysis has increased in popularity as a tool for comparing the formal and informal structures. Chapter 12 extends this analysis of organizational issues by providing a framework for predicting the effectiveness and efficiency of each organizational structure under various environmental and organizational conditions.

ENDNOTES

[1] A. R. Janger, *How European Companies Organize in the United States* (New York: Conference Board, 1990).

[2] G. Hofstede, Motivation, leadership and organization: Do American theories apply abroad? *Organizational Dynamics* (Summer 1980): 42–63; Europe's new managers, *Business Week* (May 24, 1982): 116.

[3] J. R. Lincoln, M. Harrada, and K. McBride, Organizational structures in Japanese and U.S. manufacturing, *Administrative Science Quarterly* 31 (1986): 338–364.

[4] See P. H. Birnbaum and G. Y. Y. Wong, Organizational structure of multinational banks from a culture-free perspective, *Administrative Science Quarterly* 30 (1985): 162–177; R. M. Marsh and H. Mannar, Technological implications theory: A Japanese test, *Organization Studies* 1(2) (1980): 161–183; J. Conaty, H. Mahmoude, and G. A. Miller, Social structure and hierarchy: A comparison of organizations in the U.S. and prerevolutionary Iran, *Organization Studies* 4(2) (1983): 105–128.

[5] M. Maurice, A. Soye, and M. Warner, Society differences in organizing manufacturing units: A comparison of France, West Germany, and Great Britain, *Organization Studies* 1 (1980): 59–86.

[6] P. R. Lawrence and J. W. Lorsch, Differentiation and integration in complex organizations, *Administrative Science Quarterly* 12 (1967): 1–47; P. R. Lawrence and J. W. Lorsch, *Organization and Environment* (Boston: Harvard University Graduate School of Business, Division of Research, 1967).

[7] J. R. Lincoln and K. McBride, Japanese industrial organizations in comparative perspective, *Annual Review of Sociology* 13 (1987): 289–312.

[8] H. Mintzberg, *Structure in Fives: Designing Effective Organizations* (Englewood Cliffs, N.J.: Prentice-Hall, 1983).

[9] S. P. Robbins, *Organization Theory: Structure, Design, and Applications,* 2nd ed. (Englewood Cliffs, N.J.: Prentice Hall, 1983).

[10] C. R. Gullett, Mechanistic vs. organic organizations: What does the future hold? *The Personnel Administrator* 29 (1975): 17.

[11] T. Burns and G. M. Stalker, *The Management of Innovation* (London: Tavistock, 1966).

[12] M. L. Tushman and D. A. Nadler, Information processing as an integrating concept in organizational design, *Academy of Management Review* 3 (1978): 613–625.

[13] T. J. Hallen and O. Hauptman, The substitution of communication technologies for organizational structure on research and development. In J. Fulk and C. Steinfeld, eds., *Organizations and Communication Technology* (Newbury Park, Calif.: Sage, 1990).

[14] G. P. Huber, A theory of the effects of advanced information technologies on organizational design, intelligence, and decision-making, *Academy of Management Review* 15 (1990): 47–71.

[15] J. R. Gordon, L. S. Corsini, and M. L. Fetters, Restructuring accounting firms for better client service, *Sloan Management Review* 26 (Spring 1985): 43–55.

[16] J. R. Galbraith, *Organization Design* (Reading, Mass.: Addison-Wesley, 1977); J. L. Brown and N. M. Agnew, The balance of power in a matrix structure, *Business Horizons* 25 (November-December 1982): 51–54.

[17] J. R. Galbraith and R. K. Kazanjian, Organizing to implement strategies of diversity and globalization: The role of matrix design, *Human Resource Management* 25 (Spring 1986): 37–54.

[18] E. W. Larson and D. H. Gobeli, Matrix management: Contradictions and insight, *California Management Review* 29 (Summer 1987): 126–138.

[19] *Ibid.*

[20] J. M. Sinclair, Is the matrix really necessary? *Project Management Journal* 15 (March 1984): 49–55.

[21] W. F. Joyce, Matrix organization: A social experiment, *Academy of Management Journal* 29 (1986): 536–541; D. H. Hamburger, Making matrix management work, *Project Management Journal* 16 (December 1985): 82–89.

[22] Mintzberg, *Structure in Fives.*

[23] A. S. Miner, T. L. Amburgey, and T. M. Stearns, Interorganizational linkages and population dynamics: Buffering and transformational shields, *Administrative Science Quarterly* 35 (1990): 689–713.

[24] R. E. Miles and C. C. Snow, Organizations: New concepts for new forms, *California Management Review* 28 (Spring 1986): 62–73.

[25] G. Morgan, *Creative Organization Theory: A Resourcebook* (Newbury Park, Calif.: Sage, 1989).

[26] W. W. Powell, Hybrid organizational arrangements: New form or transitional development? *California Management Review* 30 (Fall 1987): 67–87; see also W. W. Powell, Neither market nor hierarchy: Network forms of organization. In B. M. Staw and L. L. Cummings, *Research in Organizational Behavior* 12 (1990): 295–336.

[27] Galbraith and Kazanjian, Organizing to implement strategies.

[28] Miles and Snow, Organizations.

[29] D. Lei and J. W. Slocum, Jr., Global strategic alliances: Payoffs and pitfalls, *Organizational Dynamics* (Winter 1991): 44–62.

[30] Customers drive company tie-ups, *Fortune,* January 27, 1992, p. 12.

[31] K. L. Miller, The partners, *Business Week,* February 10, 1992, p. 103.

[32] D. Darlin and J. B. White, GM venture in Korea nears end, betraying firm's fond hopes, *Wall Street Journal,* January 16, 1992, p. A–1.

[33] W. F. Cascio and M. G. Serapio, Jr., Human resources systems in an international alliance: The undoing of a done deal, *Organizational Dynamics* 19(3) (Winter 1991): 63–74.

[34] The discussion here is based on The mighty keiretsu, *Industry Week* (January 20, 1992): 52–54; Why Japan keeps on winning, *Fortune* (July 15, 1991): 76–85.

[35] J. E. Forrest, Strategic alliances and the small technology-based firm, *Journal of Small Business Management* 28(3) (1990): 37.

[36] P. E. Han, The informal organization you've got to live with, *Supervisory Management* 28 (October 1983): 25–28.

[37] *Ibid.*

[38] W. B. Stevenson, Organization design. In R. Golembiewski, ed., *The Handbook of Organizational Behavior* (New York: Marcel Dekker, in press).

[39] J. Fulk and B. Boyd, Emerging theories of communication in organizations, *Journal of Management* 17 (1991): 407–446.

[40] W. B. Stevenson and M. C. Gilly, Information processing and problem solving: The migration of problems through formal positions and networks of ties, *Academy of Management Journal* 34 (1991): 918–928.

[41] S. Ghoshal and C. A. Bartlett, The multinational corporation as an interorganizational network, *Academy of Management Review* 15 (1990): 603–625.

[42] H. F. Kolodney, Evolution to a matrix organization, *Academy of Management Review* 4 (1979): 543–553.

[43] B. Dumaine, The bureaucracy busters, *Fortune* (June 17, 1991): 35–50.

[44] J. R. Galbraith, Structural responses to competitive strategies. In R. H. Kilmann, I. Kilmann, and Associates, *Making Organizations Competitive: Enhancing Networks and Relationships across Traditional Boundaries* (San Francisco: Jossey-Bass, 1991).

[45] T. G. Gunn, Increasing competitiveness through world-class manufacturing. In Kilmann et al., *Making Organizations Competitive.*

RECOMMENDED READINGS

Hall, R. H. *Organizations, Structures, Processes, and Outcomes,* 5th ed. Englewood Cliffs, N.J.: Prentice Hall, 1991.

Janger, A. R. *How European Companies Organize in the United States.* New York: Conference Board, 1990.

Jelinek, M., Litterer, J. A., and Miles, R. E., eds. *Organizations by Design: Theory and Practice,* 2nd ed. Dallas: Business Publications, 1986.

Kilmann, R. H., Kilmann, I., and Associates. *Making Organizations Competitive: Enhancing Networks and Relationships across Traditional Boundaries.* San Francisco: Jossey-Bass, 1991.

Morgan, G. *Organization Theory: A Resourcebook.* Newbury Park, Calif.: Sage, 1989.

Scott, W. R. *Organizations: Rational, Natural and Open Systems,* 2nd ed. Englewood Cliffs, N.J.: Prentice Hall, 1987.

Chapter Outline

Creating Effective Organizational Designs

Learning Objectives

After completing the reading and activities in Chapter 12, students will be able to

1. Discuss the relevance to organizational design of a multicultural and multinational environment.

2. Identify the components and dimensions of the environment and evaluate the appropriateness of an organization's structure for its environment.

3. Offer several typologies of technology and discuss their implications for organizational design.

4. Describe the nature, formation, and types of organizational goals and show ways in which organization design can consider organizational goals.

5. Discuss the relationship of an organization's strategy to its structure.

6. Describe an organization's work force and show its significance to the organization's structure.

7. Show how an organization's age and size influence its structure.

8. Trace the stages in an organization's development and show their relationship to the organization's structure.

9. Design an organizational structure that most effectively considers the organization's environment, technology, goals, work force, age, size, and stage of growth.

Redesigning Alcoa

Paul H. O'Neill recently became the chairman of the Aluminum Company of America, "becoming the first outsider in the company's 103-year history to call the shots. Although O'Neill knew precious little about the aluminum game, he quickly refocused Alcoa on its notoriously cyclical aluminum businesses, while reassuring investors that there would be no more wild earnings gyrations on his watch. Critics figured that O'Neill was in for a few unpleasant surprises. But Alcoa's return on equity has averaged 15% since he arrived on the scene, 50% above the average of the previous decade."

O'Neill has initiated major changes in the organization. On September 2, 1991, he began "a massive overhaul of management meant to refashion Alcoa into a highly decentralized outfit. At a management powwow in Pittsburgh in early August, some 50 worldwide senior executives were stunned to learn that O'Neill planned to give Alcoa's 25 business-unit managers unprecedented leeway to run their businesses. Also, two levels of top management would be wiped out. Says Australian business-unit manager Robert F. Slagle, one of the fortunate 25: 'We felt liberated.' "

O'Neill chose to eliminate Alcoa's hierarchical chain of command. "Frontline managers will get plenty of decision-making authority—but also the accountability that goes with it. O'Neill expects all of Alcoa's various business lines—it makes everything from aluminum sheet for beverage cans to aerospace parts—to score significant gains over their rivals within two years."

O'Neill also initiated additional changes. "To extend Alcoa's reach in the faster-growing European and Asian markets, he has set up joint ventures with foreign partners. And to smooth out Alcoa's earnings performance, O'Neill and his team are negotiating longer-term metals contracts. They also have set up an innovative variable-rate dividend plan to reward investors who stay with the company during economic downturns. The payoff from all of this: O'Neill believes Alcoa may be able to deliver $1 billion more in annual operating profits by 1995."

These changes pose unusual challenges. "O'Neill's gambit, inspired by his own often-unconventional thinking about management, is hardly risk-free. He's counting on untested line executives to muster the managerial skill and know-how to quickly ratchet up quality and efficiency to world standards. And he's pouring on the demands at a time when aluminum prices are at a five-year low, after plunging over 30% this past year."[1]

W hat factors influenced O'Neill's decision to decentralize decision making to Alcoa's business-unit managers? How effective will this new structure likely be? What contingencies should influence management's choice of the most appropriate and effective structure for an organization?

In this chapter we address these questions by providing a comprehensive framework for evaluating the contingencies that managers must consider in designing an organization's structure. We evaluate Alcoa's decision to change its structure by diagnosing the impact of an organization's (1) environment, (2) technology, (3) goals, (4) strategy, (5) work force, (6) age and size, and (7) life-cycle stage on its structure. We examine changes in these contingencies and organizational structures as organizations grow and change over time. We conclude the chapter by prescribing a methodology for redesigning organizational structures.

ORGANIZA-TIONAL FUNCTIONING IN A MULTINATIONAL AND MULTI-CULTURAL ENVIRONMENT

Organizations that function in a global environment face two major environmental pressures.[2] First, they must be responsive to the local country and culture. Multinational organizations face challenges in the United States that are very different from those in Eastern Europe, Japan, or other parts of Asia. Second, they must react to the forces pushing toward globalization. These include the elimination of economic borders between countries, the increasing similarity of consumer demands and hence products across countries, and the impact of improved communication technologies.[3]

A range of options as described in Chapter 11 exists for the organization that functions multinationally. Executives of such organizations can choose function, product, project, geographical, divisionalized, or integrated structures; they can select a network form or loosely coupled alliance. In addition, firms can develop manufacturing or production operations in other countries; they can enter joint ventures; they can license foreign companies to produce or sell their products; or they can create wholly owned subsidiaries.[4]

Managers may choose one of four strategic approaches.[5] Using *global management,* typical of many oil companies, an organization tends to have similar products in all regional markets. These organizations compete worldwide by creating few or no distinctions between markets, and developing global economies of scale in manufacturing, distribution, and sales. A company that uses *multinational management* emphasizes differences in its product and service for each country. Consumer product companies in the food or electronics industries, for example, design marketing, sales, and even the product itself to meet specific country or regional requirements. *International management* describes an organization between global and multinational management. Organizations such as pharmaceutical companies sell similar products in all countries but tailor them somewhat to meet local regulations. *Transnational management* combines elements of each of these approaches. Beginning with either global, multinational, or international management, transnational management adds elements from the others to meet special market needs, a changing environment, or cost-reduction pressures. In IBM Europe, for example, which has historically served European countries individually, managers are now encouraged to take a pan-European perspective and assume responsibilities for a single product line across national boundaries.[6]

Cultural differences often exist in the structures managers prefer and implement. For example, one study suggested that U.S. managers held an instrumental conception of structure, whereas French managers held a social one, as shown in Table 12–1.[7] The organization's structure must obviously consider these cultural differences for maximum effectiveness. Reading 12–1, "Developing Leaders for the Global Enterprise," describes some additional challenges faced by the leaders of organizations that compete in a global environment.

COMPONENTS OF THE ENVIRONMENT

Economic and market circumstances; technological innovations; federal, state, and local legislation; and political, social, and cultural conditions external to the organization comprise its environment and influence an organization's functioning. Organizational management must select structures that most effectively respond to their

Table 12–1 **American versus French Views of Organization**

Instrumental	Social
1. Positions are defined in terms of tasks.	Positions are defined in terms of social status and authority.
2. Relationships between positions are defined as being ordered in any way instrumental to achieving organizational objectives.	Relationships defined as being ordered by a hierarchy.
3. Authority is impersonal, rational, and comes from role or function. It can be challenged for rational reasons.	Authority comes from status. It can extend beyond the function and cannot be challenged on rational grounds.
4. Superior-subordinate relationships are defined as impersonal and implying equality of persons involved. Subordination is the acceptance of the impersonal, rational, and legal order of the organization.	Superior-subordinate relationships are personal, implying superiority of one person over the other. Subordination is loyalty and deference to the superior.
5. Goal attainment has primacy over power acquisition.	Achievement of objectives is secondary to the acquisition of power.

SOURCE: Reprinted with permission from H. W. Lane and J. J. DiStefano, *International Management Behavior: From Policy to Practice,* 2nd ed. (Boston: PWS-Kent, 1992), p. 197. The material was adapted from Giorgio Inzerilli and Andre Laurent, Managerial views of organization structure in France and the USA, *International Studies of Management & Organization,* 13 (1–2) (1983): 97–118.

environment. Because most organizations face a demanding, intrusive, and somewhat uncontrollable environment, managers can use organization design as one way of increasing the effectiveness of interactions with the environment.

Economic Environment   Organizations typically confront an unpredictable economic environment. In a few years inflation can move from double to single digits and back again. Recession in the early 1990s sent business into a tailspin. The prime rate—which influences an organization's ability to borrow more and hence to function in the marketplace—can also fluctuate widely. As businesses deal more globally, the stability of a variety of monetary currencies becomes significant for an organization's functioning. Organizations must be able to respond efficiently and adaptively to the changing economic situation in several countries at once. They must be able to reduce costs as necessary or use the increased availability of money as an opportunity for innovation or expansion.

National and international competitors, as well as suppliers and customers, comprise the market aspect of the economic environment. For example, the reorganization at Alcoa, with its focus on business units, emphasizes the diversity of markets and the importance of meeting unique market needs. The decentralization was intended to allow Alcoa to identify potential markets and develop new products rapidly.

The internationalization of business has compounded the complexity and unpredictability of the environment. Organizations must learn to function in a worldwide economy with diverse economic conditions in various locales. In many industries competition became more heated in the late 1980s, forcing organizations to restructure as one way of coping more effectively.

Technological Environment Alcoa faces a constantly changing technological environment. Frequent advances in technology require continued emphasis on research and development. In addition, automation and computerization speed the dissemination of information and can increase competitors' productivity. The organization structure thus must facilitate the acquisition, development, and introduction of new technology.

Political/Legal Environment Increased government regulations have constrained management's actions in its production and employment practices. Occupational safety and health guidelines, equal employment opportunity regulations, and foreign trade tariffs and policies influence the way Alcoa and other organizations can do business. In addition, the current political climate—for or against business—will influence Alcoa's ability to compete in the United States and abroad.

Sociocultural Environment Demographic changes have occurred as the population has shifted geographically, the relative age distribution of workers and customers has changed, and the educational level and expectations of organizational members have increased. In the United States many workers have moved from the industrial Northeast and Midwest to the South and West, reducing the pool of skilled workers available to companies such as Alcoa in some of its locations. Large numbers of immigrants in many industrialized countries have altered the available labor pool. As the general population has aged and mandatory retirement has been eliminated, companies such as Polaroid or Digital Equipment Corporation have used early retirement incentives to reduce the number of older workers. Organizational members overall are also better educated than their predecessors, and they have higher expectations about the kind of jobs they want to hold. Extending the company's reach into European and Asian markets calls for more international employees. Alcoa and similar companies must deal with the diversity of cultures in countries outside the United States as well. These countries may have labor patterns and behavioral norms that differ from those in the United States and thus require special human resources policies.

Organizations seek creative ways of attracting new customers or clients and meeting workers' needs. Attempts to unionize white-collar workers and workers in high-technology organizations in the United States have made top management more committed to managing workers effectively and have encouraged executives to increase worker participation in decision making. Countries such as Sweden and West Germany (now part of a united Germany) have succeeded in giving employees more autonomy and decision-making opportunities. Responding to these aspects of the environment has called for more flexible structures, such as Alcoa's decentralization of decision making.

Choose an organization, such as a discount supermarket, a large university, a chain of specialty stores, or an oil refinery. How would you describe each of its environments, and what impact might each environment have on the organization's structure?

ENVIRON-MENTAL DIMENSIONS We can further evaluate the components of the environment along three dimensions: complexity, dynamism, and hostility/munificence.[8] Managers must fit the organization structures described in Chapter 11 to the aspects of the environment described in the next sections.

Complexity The number and variety of environmental elements that affect an organization vary considerably. A branch bank must deal with the environmental components described in the previous section, whereas a local pizza parlor must respond primarily to the economic environment and secondarily to the sociocultural environment. The branch bank has a more complex environment than does the pizza parlor. A multinational firm, such as Alcoa, which must deal with the unique characteristics of numerous cultures and countries, also experiences greater environmental complexity than does a similar organization that operates only in the United States or in any single country. An organization that serves retail and wholesale markets faces a more complex environment than a comparable organization that only markets its product through retail outlets.

The greater the complexity of the environment faced by the organization, the greater should be the decentralization of its decision making. The president of IBM, for example, has recently proposed decentralizing decision-making responsibility to heads of business units, and even lower in the organization, making the "new IBM" a vertical holding company.[9] The ability to decentralize effectively assumes, of course, that qualified and dedicated people exist in sufficient numbers at the lower levels. Top management of the branch bank should decentralize decision making more than the owners of a pizza parlor; partners of a public accounting firm should encourage decentralization more than the director of a one-office accounting firm. Decentralization should also accompany increased differentiation that occurs when divergent or heterogeneous expertise, goals, or personal orientations exist in an organization.[10] Thinking about Alcoa in terms of the complexity of its environment suggests that the decision to decentralize decision making is an appropriate one. Decentralizing decision making places expertise and authority in direct contact with the essential information in the environment. Putting Alcoa's decision making into the hands of the business-unit managers facilitates a faster response to new market trends and demand for new products. Alcoa can then meet the introduction of new products by competitors with a faster introduction of its own products.

But decentralization must be done only to the extent that adequate control can be maintained. As a result of decentralization, the organization can deal with new or sophisticated information more quickly, directly, and effectively; but it can also fail to coordinate activities of its various parts and in an extreme case even send conflicting messages into the marketplace. As the environment becomes increasingly complex, organizations may divisionalize as one way of dealing with diverse environmental elements. The divisionalized structure works best in larger, relatively older companies with complex economic, technological, political/legal, and sociocultural environments.

Dynamism   The degree to which environmental elements experienced by an organization change predictably over time also influences the most effective organizational structure. Changes in the prime rate, for example, affect the availability of funds to organizations. Ongoing technological advancements demand reactions from organizations. New federal legislation may require policy changes in banks, hospitals, or other organizations in regulated industries. Using historical and other data in sophisticated mathematical models, some organizations can predict the nature of environmental changes. But technological change can also occur so rapidly and unpredictably that it may make products obsolete within six to twelve months of their introduction. Manufacturers of computer chips, for example, face a highly uncertain environment for this reason. Although the recession in the early 1990s initially hindered the housing market, the dropping of mortgage rates spurred home buying of certain types of houses. This type of volatility hinders the ability of manufacturers of goods related to the housing industry to predict accurately the demand for their products.

The more frequently and unpredictably the environment changes, the more organic the organization's structure should be. Recall that organic structures, such as project management, integrated, or adhocratic forms, are relatively impermanent, emphasize lateral relationships, decentralize decision making, and deemphasize status and rank differences. They contrast with mechanistic structures, such as functional or bureaucratic forms, which use standardized policies and procedures to guide decision making, specialize activities into clearly defined tasks, use the hierarchy to resolve problems, and reward conformity. Meeting the challenges of a dynamic environment calls for a skilled and experienced work force that can function effectively in an organic structure.

Alcoa faces a very dynamic environment. Does the proposed reorganization respond to a dynamic environment? Clearly the decentralization of decision making and the forming of business units contribute to the creation of a more organic structure than existed before. Though Alcoa does not plan on reducing the size of its organization, simplifying the structure can be another response to a dynamic environment. Recent research indicated that divisionalized firms facing instability reduced the uncertainty by divesting businesses because the divisions that were kept could then better understand the remaining markets.[11]

As the environment becomes more uncertain and unpredictable, the organization requires increased flexibility. Top management can respond to the environment by changing structure, procedures, personnel, processes, or strategy.[12] Although Alcoa is emphasizing a change in structure as a way of dealing with its dynamic environment, it also is altering personnel requirements by giving the business-unit managers more autonomy. Alterations in procedures, processes, and strategy likely will follow.

Linking Roles Lateral linkages help organizations respond to environmental needs by increasing the flow of information in the organization or between the organization and its environment. Organizations can use *integrators* to help coordinate activities across departments or other organizational subgroups. Such individuals should have four primary characteristics.[13] First, they should be seen as having the competence and knowledge to contribute to important decisions without relying on authority associated with the position they hold as the basis for such contributions. Second, they must have balanced orientation and behavior patterns so they can communicate well with diverse types of employees. Third, integrators need to feel they are rewarded for total product responsibility, as well as the performance of their coworkers. Fourth, integrators must have a capacity for resolving interdepartmental conflicts and disputes; they must be able to diagnose the causes and consequences of conflicts and offer constructive ways of resolving them. *Boundary spanners* (as described in Chapter 7) fulfill a similar role but differ from integrators (who facilitate internal coordination, communication, and action) because they process information and represent an organization or its subunits to others *outside* the unit's boundary.

Hostility/Munificence The degree to which the environment creates conflict, threat, or unexpected or overwhelming competition for an organization reflects its hostility or munificence. An organization that has limited competition in its service area may experience a relatively munificent environment. In contrast, an organization faces a hostile environment if its product is threatened with obsolescence because of a technological breakthrough in the marketplace, if it experiences overwhelming and debilitating price competition, or if it is the focus of governmental investigation or unexpected regulation. An organization that faces a takeover attempt or possible bankruptcy also experiences a hostile environment. So does an organization that experiences strong questions about its failure to demonstrate social responsibility; those organizations that pollute the environment or ignore community needs in their operations may experience strong pressure to be more socially responsible.

Organizations with highly hostile environments require high centralization of decision making. Centralization allows the fastest and most controlled means of responding to competition or other threatening events. Organizations typically use this design strategy in the short run, and for a brief period of time it takes priority over other strategies. Organizations have difficulty coping with a hostile environment over a prolonged period of time because it detracts from doing business effectively. In a munificent environment, organizations that experience unexpected environmental pressures respond by increasing their specialization and the deployment of professionals to specialized areas.[14]

Would you describe the environment of Alcoa as hostile or munificent? While Alcoa clearly does not face a munificent environment, neither does it face an extremely hostile one at the time of the reorganization. No unexpected competition or takeover attempts threaten the company. Thus, no urgent need to centralize decision making exists.

Summary of Responses   Table 12–2 shows one assessment of Alcoa's environment, along with those of a public accounting firm, a fast-food restaurant franchise, a university, and a steel manufacturer. Note that differences in their environment call for different organization structures. An organization manages its interaction with the environment through the selection of base of departmentation—functional, project, or integrated, for example—and organizational configuration—simple structure, machine bureaucracy, professional bureaucracy, divisionalized structure, or adhocracy, as described in Chapter 11.

What types of structural configuration fit best with different environments? Table 12–3 summarizes the way an organization's structure relates to the three dimensions of environment. Table 12–4 shows the design top management should select for the organizations shown in Table 12–2. Note, for example, that Alcoa should have an organic structure with decentralized decision making and with some top management control; a neighborhood restaurant, in contrast, would have a mechanistic structure with centralized decision making.

Design dilemmas arise when an organization's environment has competing forces, ones that call for opposite strategies. Top management of Alcoa, for example, may at times face a complex and hostile environment. How does management reconcile the decentralized structure with the centralization required to deal effectively with a hostile environment? Resolving this dilemma generally results in the creation of diverse structures within the same organization: The marketing and research and

Table 12–2   **Typical Environments of Selected Organizations**

Environmental Dimension	Alcoa	Public Accounting Firm	Fast-Food Franchise	University	Steel Manufacturer
Complexity	High	High	Low	High	Moderate
Dynamism	High	Moderate	Low	Moderate	Moderate
Hostility	Moderate	Low	Low	Low	Moderate

Table 12-3 Design Responses to the Environment

Dimension	Response
Complexity	As environmental complexity increases, decentralization of decision making should increase; ultimately divisionalization may be appropriate.
Dynamism	As the environment becomes more dynamic or unpredictable, organization structure should become more organic.
Hostility	When an organization faces a hostile environment, centralization of decision making should occur, at least temporarily.

development departments may form project structures, whereas manufacturing may use functional ones. Alternatively, work units can change their structures as task and environmental demands change.[15] Another approach calls for creating temporary structures in times of crisis. An organization, for example, may have a management council that convenes only in response to hostile environmental events, such as a takeover attempt or unexpected product introductions by a competitor. At all other times, a decentralized structure would exist.

TYPOLOGIES OF TECHNOLOGY

At the same time as most organizations face an increasingly dynamic and unpredictable environment, they also must deal with changing and complicated technologies. Some organizations use technology as a way of dealing with environmental uncertainty. Managers must therefore select the appropriate structure for the technology used in each part of the organization. By selecting nonroutine or innovative technologies they can respond more effectively to the unique and unpredictable demands made by the environment.[16]

Definition of Technology

Technology includes the process that converts raw materials into a product, as well as the delivery of services. Thus technology can refer to the machinery used to alter

Table 12-4 Design Responses to the Environment by Selected Organizations

Environmental Dimension	Alcoa	Public Accounting Firm	Fast-Food Franchise	University	Steel Manufacturer
Complexity	Decentralized decision making	Decentralized decision making	Centralized decision making	Decentralized decision making	Moderately decentralized decision making
Dynamism	Organic	Hybrid	Mechanistic	Hybrid	Hybrid
Hostility/ munificence	Some top management control	Little top management control	Little additional top management control	Little top management control	Some top management control

raw materials into a finished product or the intellectual or analytical processes used to transform information into a product idea. The technical system used by an organization in producing and delivering its product or service significantly influences the nature of effective organizational structures. Historically, three researchers—Joan Woodward, James Thompson, and Charles Perrow—have laid the foundation for the diagnosis and analysis of technology and its impact on organizational structure.

Production Processes   Joan Woodward classified technology in three ways. A *unit* technology describes craft processes that produce custom-made products, such as housewares, clothing, or artwork, or even services such as legal and medical ones. *Mass production,* such as automobile or heavy equipment manufacturing, refers to assembly line operations to produce standardized consumer goods. *Continuous flow* technology, such as chemical or oil refiners, describes an unsegmented, ongoing production process.[17]

How would you classify the manufacturing of aluminum products? Is the technology the same as for their design and development? Manufacturing uses a mass production technology, whereas design and development relies more on a unit process. A recent reformulation proposed the addition of a fourth type: technical batch (or unit) processing, such as aircraft production. Like the traditional unit processing, this technology has a small scale of operations. Unlike the traditional batch processing, the required knowledge complexity is high.

Task Performance   James Thompson describes technology in terms of the tasks performed by an organizational unit.[18] A *long-linked* technology involves the repetitive application of one technology to a standardized raw material. Mass-production assembly lines, such as the post office or steel manufacturing—use this technology. A *mediating* technology repeatedly applies a standardized method to unique raw materials. A social service agency imparts standardized counseling techniques to diverse clients to allow them to act functionally. *Intensive* technology applies diverse techniques and knowledge to various raw materials; the particular techniques used vary according to the problem or situation. Hospital patients receive different treatments depending on their symptoms and diagnosed problems.

Consider the technology used by Alcoa. Long-linked, mass production, and intensive technologies are used by different units in the organization. Manufacturing uses a long-linked technology; human resources management uses a mediating one; and technical support uses an intensive one. Now consider an organization in which you worked. What type of technology did you use?

Knowledge Technology   In a third classification scheme, Charles Perrow focuses specifically on knowledge technology.[19] *Task variability* refers to the number of exceptions that a jobholder encounters. An assembly line worker encounters relatively low task variability, whereas a physician in family medicine encounters high task variability. *Problem analyzability* addresses the extent to which the technology is well understood by those who use it. A salesperson's job has relatively low problem analyzability, whereas a quality control engineer's job is high on this dimension.

Combining these two dimensions results in four types of technology, as shown in Figure 12–1. *Routine* technology, such as that used by many government agencies or manufacturing companies, involves few exceptions and is well defined, understood, and analyzable. A *craft* technology, such as that used by a potter, also has few exceptions but is ill defined and unanalyzable. Organizations such as bridge builders have an *engineering* technology, which has many exceptions but is well understood. A *nonroutine* technology, such as that used by a psychiatrist, has many exceptions and is not well understood.

Figure 12–1 Perrow's Classification of Technology

		Task Variability	
		Routine with Few Exceptions	High Variety with Many Exceptions
Problem Analyzability	Well defined and analyzable	Routine	Engineering
	Ill defined and unanalyzable	Craft	Nonroutine

SOURCE: Based on C. Perrow, A framework for the comparative analysis of organizations, *American Sociological Review* 32 (April 1967): 194–208.

TECHNOLOGY'S IMPACT ON ORGANIZATIONAL DESIGN

Henry Mintzberg integrates these three typologies and identifies two dimensions on which effective structure depends—regulation and sophistication.[20]

Regulation

Regulation refers to the extent to which machinery and equipment control the employee's work. A regulating technology includes Woodward's mass production and continuous flow technologies, Thompson's long-linked and mediating technologies, and Perrow's routine and engineering technologies. Mintzberg suggests that a more regulating technology calls for a more bureaucratized structure. The more routine the technology, the less the need for flexibility, because responses to it can be predetermined and nonvariant. A nonregulating technology includes Woodward's unit technology, Thompson's intensive technology, and Perrow's craft and nonroutine technologies. Less regulating systems such as these call for an organic structure.[21] The less routine the technology, the greater the need for flexibility.

Sophistication

Sophistication describes the complexity or intricacy of the technology. As the technical system increases in sophistication, the organization requires an increasingly elaborate administrative structure, more support staff who have decision-making responsibilities, and more integrating and linking devices.

Table 12–5 summarizes the types of technology and preferred design response for each type under most situations. As noted earlier, the technology varies in different departments. Thus manufacturing has a regulating, sophisticated technology and therefore calls for a mechanistic structure with extensive support staff. Marketing has a nonregulating, sophisticated technology and therefore requires a more organic structure with extensive support staff. Once again, think of a job you have held. How would you describe its technology? What structure would respond most effectively to this type of technology?

Effective organization structures buffer or protect the technology from environmental influences or disturbances.[22] The more specific the technology, such as that of a mechanized bottle capper, the less tolerance the process has for disturbances, and the more the organization must elaborate its structure and administration to protect the operation from disturbances by the environment. Alcoa faces a moderately turbulent environment and must protect the integrity of the technology; therefore, it requires a moderately elaborated structure. As organizations become more

Table 12–5 **Design Responses to Various Types of Technology**

Mintzberg's Classification	Woodward's Classification	Thompson's Classification	Perrow's Classification	Design Response
Regulating	Mass production Continuous flow	Long-linked Mediating	Routine Engineering	Bureaucratized (mechanistic) structure
Nonregulating	Unit	Intensive	Craft Nonroutine	Organic structure
Sophisticated				Extensive support staff Elaborate administrative structure Linking devices
Unsophisticated				Little support staff Simple administrative structure

automated, they require increasing rules and regulations, centralized control, and support staff as a way of buffering the technology.

Most large organizations should have unique structures for the various parts of the organization. Among other contingencies, the specific structures should respond to the technology used by that part of the organization. As the technology changes, the structures may change as well. Such change, however, may be unique to certain countries such as the United States. In Japan, for example, the technological imperative for design is less significant than worker-centered contingencies such as career development and employee welfare.[23] New technologies also change how the job is done and ultimately affect the division of labor, issues of control and coordination, and the organization-environment fit.[24] Organizational design must respond to the complexities created by new technologies.

ORGANIZA-TIONAL GOALS

Organizations such as Alcoa, a large department store chain, a law office, or a hospital have diverse goals that might relate to market share, profitability, product innovation, or quality of working life. What other goals might these organizations have? Currently, at Alcoa, Paul O'Neill wishes to score significant gains over rival companies, smooth Alcoa's earnings performance, and increase annual operating profits. Consider now other organizations you have observed: a small retail store, your local government, a library, an elementary school, or a brokerage house. Can you identify the goals of these organizations? How do they change over time? Managers must identify the goals of all parts of the organization first, and then choose the design most likely to facilitate their accomplishments.

Definition

Goals are the desired outcomes of individual or organizational activities and behaviors. They focus attention, provide a rationale for organizing activities, offer a standard of assessment of performance, legitimize individual and organizational behavior, and provide an identity for the individual.[25] They communicate higher management's philosophy and intentions, and motivate people to achieve.

Goal formation, according to early discussion, occurs in three steps.[26] First, coalitions bargain about goals. Competing groups provide other groups with inducements so that their own goals will predominate. Second, the coalition leaders attempt to strengthen and clarify the goal by trying to satisfy, at least minimally, goals of all coalition members. Third, the group leaders and members adjust the goal to fit with experience.

Top management at Alcoa has a goal of $1 billion more in increased annual operating profits by 1995. According to the coalition approach to goal development, members of the top management team and business units attempt to reach agreement about this goal and how they will jointly attain it. Modifications in process and outcome occur that increase the compatibility of the group goal with those of subgroups in the organization, such as the various business units or even their component departments, and their members. Finally, they agree to an adjusted level of expected profits based on their past experiences. Organizations develop goals through negotiations among various interest groups.[27]

Other organizational theorists have historically viewed the process of goal formation as identifying constraints on an organization's operation,[28] such as specifying the resource pool or research expertise available, and then determining what the organization can and should accomplish given these limitations. The amount of revenues desired, for example, may evolve from the available human resource pool or current market share. Neither goal formation process is straightforward. Organizations continually experience difficulty in specifying clear, responsive, and responsible goals.

Diversity of Goals

The nature of an organization's goals can vary significantly. One clothing manufacturer, for example, may focus on high output regardless of product quality as its goal; another manufacturer may consider producing only high-quality clothing, even in small quantities, as its major goal. In contrast, a public health agency may have frequency-of-service goals; a volunteer organization, such as the PTA, may have a high rate of participation as one of its goals. Some organizations change their goals over time; they may switch from a target market share to a return-on-investment objective.

Table 12–6 reflects the diversity of goals that organizations might have. It shows three typologies, each of which spans a range of possible goals. Not surprisingly, some similarities exist between them: output goals and management goals, for example. Together, these typologies list most of the types of goals organizations choose. Using these typologies, which types of goals does Alcoa or similar organizations likely have? Can you give an example of each type of goal? Table 12–6 provides such examples in the right-hand column.

Goal Incompatibility

Organizations frequently have multiple goals, and these may conflict. For example, goals in the area of public responsibility may require costs that detract from profitability. A goal of providing highest quality service may conflict with a goal of minimizing costs. These conflicts frequently arise from an incongruence between different goal types, such as innovation and productivity goals or societal and output goals. Or, a misfit between the goals of influential individuals, groups, or departments in the organization may prevent diverse constituencies from agreeing on the organization's goals. At some companies return on investment for stockholders may seemingly conflict with improved compensation and quality of work life for employees. At others, a refocusing on new product development may interfere with a goal of manufacturing efficiency. Thus, defining an organization's goals requires significant and complex action to reconcile conflicting and incompatible goals. Dysfunctional *goal displacement*—where individuals or groups divert their energies from the organ-

Table 12–6   **Three Typologies of Organizational Goals and Examples**

Perrow's Classification

Type of Goal	Definition	Example
Societal	Creation and maintenance of cultural values through production of goods or services	To increase the number of managers on boards of charitable organizations
Output	Kinds and quantities of outputs produced	To increase production by 15%
System	The functioning of an organization's system independent of its production of goods or services	To introduce a project structure
Product	Specific characteristics of goods or services	To develop a line of men's cologne
Derived	Organization's use of power in areas apart from production of goods and services	To introduce a mentoring program

Drucker's Classification

Type of Goal	Definition	Example
Market standing	The organization's position in the market; quality and share of the market	To become the sales leader in portable typewriters
Innovation	The value of new product development	To develop two new products
Productivity	The level of output organization-wide	To increase production of shoes by 35%
Physical and financial resources	The nature and extent of resources used in product development and production	To reduce the cost of raw materials by 10%
Profitability	Profit and return on investment	To increase profit by 5%
Manager performance and development	Managerial output, growth, activities, and style	To send all managers to at least one training course
Worker performance and attitudes	Individual output, turnover, absenteeism, satisfaction, and morale	To reduce turnover to less than 10% a year
Public responsibility	The organization's use of natural resources and contribution to the public good	To seek alternative sources of raw materials

Gross's Classification

Type of Goal	Definition	Example
Output	Kinds and levels of output	To add three products to the product line
Adaptation	Those that contribute to the ability to respond to environmental changes; emphasis on research and development, for example	To double the R&D staff
Management	Managerial output, activities, and style	To increase the amount of time managers spend in planning activities

Table 12–6 *(Continued)*

Gross's Classification		
Type of Goal	Definition	Example
Motivation	Encouraging employee motivation	To introduce an incentive program
Position	Those associated with each job in the organization	To increase the autonomy associated with each job

SOURCES: Adapted from C. Perrow, *Organizational Analysis: A Sociological View* (Belmont, Calif.: Wadsworth, 1970); P. Drucker, *The Practice of Management* (New York: Harper, 1954); E. Gross, The definition of organizational goals, *British Journal of Sociology* 20 (1969): 277–294.

ization's original goals to different ones—must be avoided as the solution to incompatible goals.

Organization structures should facilitate goal accomplishment. The restructuring at Alcoa, for example, is intended to refocus on business-unit outcomes. This emphasis should encourage the development of new products and exploitation of market niches. Typically, the more extensive and heterogeneous the goals, the more complex the structure needed to respond to them.[29]

THE ORGANIZA-TION'S STRATEGY

The organization's strategy, or its basic mission, purpose, or niche, also influences its structure. One schema classifies organizations into four strategic types.[30] *Defenders* are organizations that produce a small number of products for a small segment of the market. Cray Computer Company, which produces a high-speed, high-capacity, very expensive computer, likely has this strategy. They emphasize planning and cost control rather than a search for new products. The resulting structure tends to be relatively bureaucratic, emphasizing high horizontal differentiation, centralized control, an elaborate hierarchy, and extensive formalization. *Prospectors,* in contrast, find and develop new products and markets; they emphasize innovation and rapid introduction of new products. Minnesota Mining and Manufacturing Company (3M) likely has this strategy. These organizations call for a more organic structure, with less division of labor, greater flexibility, and more decentralized decision making and control. Frequently 3M purchases small companies and adds them intact into its organization. *Analyzers* combine characteristics of defenders and prospectors. Many banks act as analyzers. They enter new markets or introduce new products after the prospectors. They also maintain efficiency like the defenders. This strategy calls for a hybrid structure, one that has moderately centralized control and encourages both flexibility and stability. Many banks combine elements of product and functional structures. The organization structure has some parts, such as operations, with bureaucratic characteristics, and other parts, such as R&D or marketing, with organic characteristics. *Reactors* design their strategies based on what others in the market have done; they lack a structural imperative. They may pursue one of the other three strategies incidentally, but often do so improperly and hence perform ineffectively.

How would you characterize Alcoa? It can be viewed as a prospector, because it wishes to emphasize innovation and new products. Or it can be viewed as an analyzer, because it offers some of its products after competitors have introduced similar ones. Its introduction of a more organic structure with decentralized decision making fits with either strategy. The dynamic network structure also would respond to these strategic considerations.[31] Alcoa may eventually consider creating a network of suppliers or some strategic partnering as a way of thriving in the global marketplace. Executives in organizations such as Alcoa must identify the organization's strategy and then select the design that best responds to it.

WORK FORCE DIVERSITY

What types of employees comprise the work force at Alcoa? Given its size, its product line, and its location in a large number of countries, Alcoa is likely to have extensive work force diversity. The structure must respond to the particular types of employees in various positions and locations.

Worker Characteristics

Typically, organization structures depend to some extent on the professionalism, expertise, and group memberships (such as union affiliation) of employees. Other employee characteristics that can influence organization structure include education, work experience, demographic characteristics such as age, work values, life and career stages, commitment and other attitudes, and personality variables, as described in Chapter 3. These attributes may affect the extent of involvement in decision making preferred by various organizational members. For example, we might hypothesize that individuals who value internal control and who are beyond the entry stage of their career may function more effectively in decentralized structures than those who value external control and lack work experience.

Employees in a Multinational Organization

Organizations that function in numerous countries likely have employees with different cultural backgrounds, together with accompanying differences in experience, values, and education. In addition, within a given country, an organization's members may come from both its home country and host country. Reconciling differences in perspectives, as well as taking advantage of the different views becomes a major challenge in designing organizations. Establishing structures that allow for the fluid exchange of employees at various sites across the world also may be important for some countries. Facilitating the transfer of skills and the translation of knowledge among locations occurs more easily in product or project structures, where individuals are used to working with diverse groups, than in functional structures that tend to perpetuate a more holistic viewpoint. Network structures provide the greatest opportunity for taking advantage of synergy from diverse countries and using it to make the parent organization more competitive.

Professional and Nonprofessional Employees

Organizations might consider the work force in a particular department, division, or other unit when designing an organization's structure. Professionals generally prefer more decentralized, organic structures, although in some organizations the professional bureaucratic model is used. Less skilled workers seem more able to perform effectively with centralization of authority and more rules and procedures; increasingly, however, even many of these workers desire greater autonomy and involvement in decision making.

SIZE AND AGE OF THE ORGANIZATION

The growth and aging of an organization also determine the most effective structure.

Size

As organizations increase in size, they typically become more heterogeneous in their orientations as well as in the products and services they provide. This change necessitates increased differentiation. Depending on the environment and the technology faced by the organization, this differentiation may result in a move from a simpler functional structure to any of the more complex ones. Figure 12–2 illustrates a typical progression as an organization, such as a restaurant, increases in size.

Figure 12–2   **Changes in Organization Structure with Increases in Size**

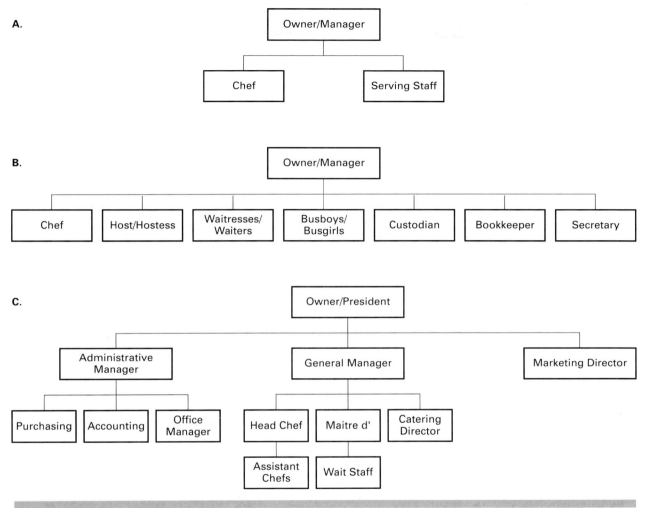

A group of researchers in Aston, England, who studied organizations believe that size dictates certain structural dimensions, specifically the structuring of activities, specialization, standardization, formalization, span of control, and centralization.[32] Other researchers who studied the same organizations found that organizational size also modifies the influence of technology on structure.[33] Though the results suggest the importance of knowing an organization's size in diagnosing the effectiveness of its structure, the impact of size should not preclude the consideration of other contingencies.

Age   The age of an organization, not surprisingly, often correlates with its size. As an organization ages, its behavior tends to become more standardized and formalized. The aging of the United States government illustrates this relationship quite well. Early communication occurred primarily through mutual adjustment. As the government got older, more procedures became standardized, and its structure became more mechanized and bureaucratic. Because age and size often correlate, separating the influences of each contingency on organizational structure poses difficulties for organizational analysts. In redesigning organizations, managers must consider the implications of both contingencies.

ORGANIZA-
TIONAL
LIFE CYCLE

As we noted earlier, some organizations evolve through various organizational structures, such as from functional to project to matrix to project again. At the same time, most organizations also evolve through a life cycle or a series of developmental stages, akin to those described for individuals in Chapter 3. Researchers have noted that these stages occur in a predictable sequence that is not easily reversed.[34] Of course, not every organization passes through every stage described.

Stages in
Organizational
Growth

Organizational growth can be described as progressing through four stages, as shown in Table 12–7: entrepreneurial, collectivity, formalization, and elaboration.[35]

Entrepreneurial Stage   Organizational creation is "a network building enterprise that centers on the inception, diffusion, and adaptation of a set of ideas among a group of people"; they commit to these ideas and enact them.[36] They move from *first ideas* about the organization, to *commitments* and initial planning, to *implementation,* or making the new organization operational.[37] The entrepreneurial stage incorporates two stages of small business growth—existence and survival.[38] *Existence* concerns the development of a customer base, the reliable delivery of the product, and the building of a sufficient cash flow to support the company's activities. In the *survival* stage the company becomes concerned with generating a profit. There is little formal planning and few formal systems. Growth occurs through supervision provided by the leader to a growing number of employees.

Collectivity Stage   Organizations typically experience rapid growth at the collectivity stage, also known as the *success* stage. While innovation and expansion continue, some attempts to stabilize and routinize the organization begin.[39] The owner decides whether to stabilize the company at its present size or strive for more growth.[40] The owner can consolidate the company, professionalize its functional management, and remove himself or herself from an active management role; or the owner can reinvest

Table 12–7   **Summary Model of the Organizational Life Cycle**

Entrepreneurial Stage	Collectivity Stage	Formalization and Control Stage	Elaboration of Structure Stage
Marshalling of resources	Informal communication and structure	Formalization of rules	Elaboration of structure
Lots of ideas		Stable structure	Decentralization
Entrepreneurial activities	Sense of collectivity	Emphasis on efficiency and maintenance	Domain expansion
Little planning and coordination	Long hours spent		Adaptation
	Sense of mission	Conservatism	Renewal
Formation of a "niche"	Innovation continues	Institutional procedures	
"Prime mover" has power	High commitment		

SOURCE: Reprinted by permission of R. E. Quinn and K. Cameron, Organizational life cycles and shifting criteria of effectiveness: Some preliminary evidence, *Management Science* 29 (January 1983), Copyright 1983 The Institute of Management Sciences.

the profits in growth and retain control. Although the founding and early members of the organization remain committed to it, their involvement increasingly becomes a function of the incentives offered. For example, tasks must offer challenge and variety; the organization must provide growth opportunities; and employees require frequent, quality communication.[41]

Formalization Stage Called "the transition [that] represents the most dramatic change in the early evolution of organizations,"[42] the formalization stage signals the maturation of an organization from entrepreneurial to professional.[43] Apple Computer's replacing of Steven Jobs with John Scully in the mid-1980s illustrates this transition. In this *takeoff* stage the owner must address issues of delegation of responsibility and sufficiency of cash to finance growth.[44] As the company matures, ownership and management diverge, although the owner maintains stock control. The transition from owner-manager to a hired manager frequently signals the beginning of this stage in small businesses. In larger organizations, the emphasis on structural elaboration through functional specialization, the development of systematic reward and evaluation systems, and the emphasis on formal planning and goal setting reflect this stage. This change in focus may motivate the more entrepreneurial, innovative workers to leave the organization to seek new outlets for their creativity. Individuals whose goals and orientations are more compatible with the stabilization and formalization processes replace them.

Elaboration Stage In the elaboration stage, the mature organization strives to adapt to changing conditions, renew itself, and seek continued growth opportunities. Developing resource maturity, the company must consolidate its growth, expand its management staff and capabilities, elaborate into line and staff positions, and ensure a return on investment.[45] Some organizations will diversify their product markets as a way of ensuring their continued growth, or they will search for new products and growth opportunities. Either they emphasize decentralization of decision making and team efforts as ways of adapting, or they institutionalize formal controls and procedures. When the mature organization fails to adapt, decline may result.[46]

The politics and power associated with each stage likely differ.[47] The early stages (e.g., entrepreneurial or existence) are characterized by the entrepreneur's exertion of power to shape the organization in his or her image. He or she exerts this power by making or controlling all decisions and creating meaning in the firm. Power in the later stages (e.g., formalization, collectivity, success, takeoff, or resource maturity) involves developing policies and procedures that support the managers' self-interests and also maintain their power. Acquiring political support for managerial decisions becomes increasingly important in the latter stages.[48] In the decline or redevelopment stages, managers compete for scarce resources and to maintain a stake in the organization.

Organizational
Decline

Rather than growing and stabilizing, some organizations experience decline. Such organizations "fail to anticipate, recognize, avoid, neutralize, or adapt to external or internal pressures that threaten the organization's long-term survival."[49] A declining organization generally passes through a series of stages during which the organization is potentially salvageable.[50] First, it is blind to early warning signs; receiving and using good information could halt the decline at this time. Next, management recognizes the need to change but takes no action; prompt action at this stage would stem the decline. In the third stage it takes action but selects an inappropriate one; correct action here, determined by the particular situation, would reverse the decline.

In the fourth stage the organization reaches the point of crisis and faces the last chance for reversing the decline; in some cases an effective reorganization (often after declaring legal bankruptcy) can facilitate this reversal. If the organization reaches the fifth and final stage, it will be forced to dissolve. The speed of its dissolution will depend on how forgiving an environment it faces. Figure 12–3 shows organizational decline as a downward spiral.

Figure 12–3 **Organizational Decline as a Downward Spiral**

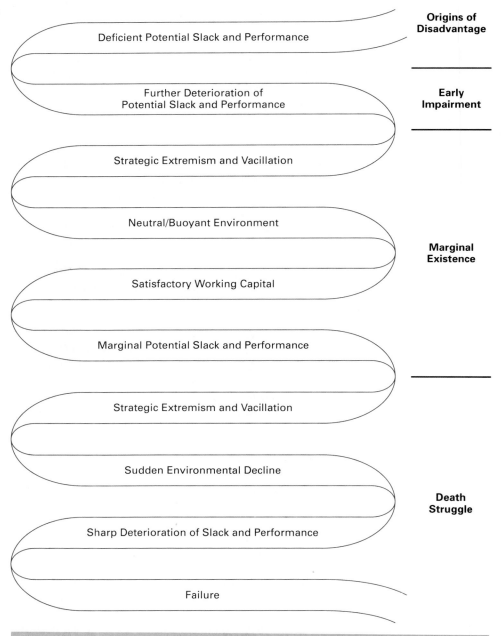

SOURCE: Reprinted from Large corporate failures as downward spirals, by D. C. Hambrick and R. A. D'Aveni, published in *Administrative Science Quarterly* 33 (1) (1988), page 14, by permission of *Administrative Science Quarterly.*

Some organizations find that rather than stabilizing at their present size or growing, they must reduce their work force as a way of responding to environmental or technological changes. IBM, Digital, and Polaroid, among other companies, for example, encouraged workers to take early retirement in response to competitive pressures as a way of reducing salary costs. Declining economic conditions or shifts in demand for a product or service may mandate downsizing. Downsizing can also accompany increasing automation if it reduces the total number of employees necessary to do the same job as previously. Restructuring to increase efficiencies or economies of scale often occurs.

In the initial crisis stage, management centralizes decision making temporarily and simplifies the organization structure. But to ensure that the best employees do not leave the organization, management must share decision making and control. Thus the organization moves from centralization in the short term to decentralization in the longer run.[51] In fact, as part of the decline, top management often witnesses a strong work effort by employees due to ongoing role expectations, a lingering hope of saving the company, the availability of more motivating tasks, and the need to make positive impressions on future employers.[52]

Ethical Development

Table 12–8 provides an interesting companion to the model of development presented here. It lists the five stages in the moral development of an organization.[53] The least morally developed organization is an *amoral organization,* for example Film Recovery Systems, whose use of cyanide jeopardized the health of its workers. The most morally developed organization has total acceptance of a common set of ethical values.

Implications for Organizational Design

Diagnosing an organization's position in its life cycle should provide managers with additional data to use in designing an effective structure. Executives can also focus on finding solutions to the dominant problems associated with each stage of growth.[54] Young organizations require structures that can accommodate innovation and respond to uncertainty. As the organization moves into the collective or success stage, some formal procedures and policies can be introduced, but overall the organization likely has relatively informal communication and structure. As the organization formalizes, top management typically introduces formal planning, evaluation, and reward systems. Functional structures with centralized decision making often fit with the control, specialization of tasks, and authority required at this stage. Such mechanistic structures facilitate stability in the organization. Ultimate survival, however, may require an organization to demonstrate adaptability and flexibility. Organic structures typically allow the decentralized decision making and team action that facilitate organizational effectiveness at this stage.

REDESIGNING THE ORGANIZATION

Where the organization does not function effectively owing to a misfit between these contingencies and its structure, a prescription for change should specify organizational redesign. In particular, organizational redesign is likely to improve such organizational problems as failure to innovate, low productivity, redundant work efforts, ineffective communication, extensive red tape, failure to respond quickly to the environment, and inability to use the skills of workers effectively.

The process of redesigning an organization may look like the one shown in Table 12–9. It involves periodically and repeatedly fitting the pieces of the organizational chart together in a new way. This rearrangement must follow an assessment of the nature of the task, the people, and the existing organizational structure for compatibility and changeability. Alcoa made such a reassessment and decided to

Table 12–8 **A Summary of the Moral Development of Corporations**

Stage in Moral Development	Management Attitude and Approach	Ethical Aspects of Corporate Culture	Corporate Ethics Artifacts	Defining Corporate Behavior
Stage I— the amoral organization	Get away with all you can; it's ethical as long as we're not caught; ethical violations, when caught, are a cost of doing business	Outlaw culture; live hard and fast; damn the risks; get what you can and get out	No meaningful code of ethics or other documentation; no set of values other than greed	Film Recovery System Numerous penny stock companies
Stage II— the legalistic organization	Play within the legal rules; fight changes that effect your economic outcome; use damage control through public relations when social problems occur; a reactive concern for damage to organizations from social problems	If it's legal, it's OK; work the gray areas; protect loopholes and don't give ground without a fight; economic performance dominates evaluations and rewards	The code of ethics, if it exists, is an internal document; "Don't do anything to harm the organization"; "Be a good corporate citizen"	Ford Pinto Firestone 500 Nestle Infant Formula R. J. Reynolds Philip Morris
Stage III— the responsive organization	Management understands the value of not acting solely on a legal basis, even though they believe they could win; management still has a reactive mentality; a growing balance between profits and ethics, although a basic premise still may be a cynical "ethics pays"; management begins to test and learn from more responsive actions	There is a growing concern for other corporate stakeholders other than owners; culture begins to embrace a more "responsible citizen" attitude	Codes are more externally oriented and reflect a concern for other publics; other ethics vehicles are undeveloped	Procter & Gamble (Rely Tampons) Abbott Labs Borden
Stage IV— the emerging ethical organization	First stage to exhibit an active concern for ethical outcomes; "We want to do the 'right' thing"; top management values become organizational values; ethical perception has focus but lacks organization and long-term planning; ethics management is characterized by successes and failures	Ethical values become part of culture; these core values provide guidance in some situations but questions exist in others; a culture that is less reactive and more proactive to social problems when they occur	Codes of ethics become action documents; code items reflect the core values of the organization; handbooks, policy statements, committees, ombudsmen are sometimes used	Boeing General Mills Johnson & Johnson (Tylenol) General Dynamics Caterpillar Levi Strauss

Table 12–8 (Continued)

Stage in Moral Development	Management Attitude and Approach	Ethical Aspects of Corporate Culture	Corporate Ethics Artifacts	Defining Corporate Behavior
Stage V— the ethical organization	A balanced concern for ethical and economic outcomes; ethical analysis is a fully integrated partner in developing both the mission and strategic plan; SWOT (Strengths, Weaknesses, Opportunities, Threats) analysis is used to *anticipate* problems and analyze alternative outcomes	A total ethical profile, with carefully selected core values which reflect that profile, directs the culture; corporate culture is planned and managed to be ethical; hiring, training, firing, and rewarding all reflect the ethical profile	Documents focus on the ethical profile and core values; all phases of organizational documents reflect them	??????

SOURCE: Reprinted with permission from R. E. Reidenbach and D. P. Robin, A conceptual model of corporate moral development, *Journal of Business Ethics* 10 (1991): 282.

Table 12–9 **An Eclectic Design Process**

Step 1. Preliminary Project Planning
- Determine client's hopes and goals for program.
- Establish program scope.
- Assess special needs of target population.
- Choose design model.
- Select top-down vs. bottom-up process.
- Determine appropriate depth of investigation.
- Consider resource/budget factors.

Step 2. Project Start-up
- Create parallel organization/steering committee/task force.
- Present leadership with rationale for program.
- Establish program parameters.
- Establish program goals, phases, time frames.
- Agree on steering-group processes.
- Decide on outward and upward communication channels during project.

Step 3. Project Study/Analysis
- Review/update general organization diagnosis.
- Scan and collect data in line with design model.
- Determine alternative tasks and task processes.
- Test task processes against company mission and operative goals.

- Involve affected employees in review of work context and task processes.
- Project outcomes.
- Critique optimal design using design-model principles, standards, project goals, and organization experience.

Step 4. Implementation Planning
- Develop and test prototypes.
- Determine implementation process.
- Match task processes and people.
- Create support systems.

Step 5. Implementation
- Foster climate conducive to change.
- Form work groups.
- Begin team building/training/management development.
- Institutionalize changes.

Step 6. Implementation Monitoring
- Hold status-review meetings, fine-tune design.
- Conduct independent program evaluation.
- Establish ongoing organization learning mechanism.

SOURCE: Reprinted by permission of publisher, from M. W. Stebbins and A. B. Shani, Organization design: Beyond the "Mafia" model, *Organizational Dynamics* 17(3) © 1989. American Management Association, New York. All rights reserved.

reorganize. The process of redesign must also recognize that change is more than a technical or analytical activity. The redesign must explicitly consider managers' and other employees' abilities to function effectively in the new structure and deal with resistances they likely will create (see Chapter 14).

Such an assessment should address a series of questions. What contingencies have changed? How should the organization's design respond to the changes? Do dysfunctions exist in the present structure? What are the dysfunctions? How can they be corrected? What impact will the changes have on other aspects of organizational functioning, such as motivation, communication, leadership, group dynamics, and individual development? O'Neill at Alcoa decided that increased competitive pressures and a dynamic environment called for increased efficiencies. He restructured the organization to allow faster product development and identification of market niches.

SUMMARY   The redesign of organizations offers an additional framework for understanding organizational functioning and a different type of prescription for responding to many organizational problems discussed earlier. Management must view design as an ongoing process in an organization and make adjustments when necessary. As both a complement and an alternative to interpersonal prescriptions, structural changes can profoundly affect organizational functioning.

In this chapter, we have examined the influence of an array of contingencies on organizational structure, summarized in Table 12–10. We examined the significance of the environment, technology, goals, strategy, organizational demographics, and organizational life cycle on organizational structure and design. Using the case of Alcoa, we considered the implications of these contingencies for restructuring plans.

Table 12–10 **The Impact of Contingencies on Organizational Structure**

Contingency	Impact on Structure
Goals	Extent of specialization
Strategy	Organic versus mechanistic structure
Environment	
complexity	Simple versus bureaucratized structure
change	Organic versus mechanistic structure
hostility	Centralization versus decentralization
uncertainty	Nature of information-processing mechanisms
Technology	
regulation	Organic versus mechanistic structure
sophistication	Extent of support staff development
Work Force	Extent of specialization
professionalism	
expertise	
group membership	
values	
Size	Simple versus elaborated structures
Age	Simple versus elaborated structures

Table 12–11 Diagnostic Questions for Redesigning Organizations

- Are job groups relatively homogeneous and meaningful?
- Are unit groupings of manageable size?
- Is there sufficient coordination among the groupings?
- Have groupings considered the impact of the organization's environment?
- How complex is the environment—is decision making sufficiently decentralized?
- How unpredictable is the environment—is the structure sufficiently organic, and are the information-processing mechanisms sufficient?
- How hostile is the environment—is the structure temporarily centralized?
- Have groupings considered the impact of the organization's technology?
- How regulated is the technology—is the structure sufficiently organic?
- How sophisticated is the technology—is there sufficient support staff?
- Is the technology sufficiently buffered from the environment?
- Have groupings been designed to accomplish the organization's goals—is the division of labor sufficiently specialized?
- Are there linkages among groups that might have different goals?
- Have groupings been designed to meet the needs and abilities of the work force—is the structure sufficiently specialized to respond to differences in employee professionalism? expertise? group membership? values?
- Does the structure make sense for the organization's size—is the structure sufficiently elaborated?
- Does the structure make sense for the organization's age? How old is the organization— is the structure sufficiently elaborated?
- Does the structure make sense for the organization's stage of development?
- Do organizations at the entrepreneurial, collective, and elaborated stages have relatively organic designs?
- Do organizations at the formalization stage have more mechanistic structures?

Organizational design must include a regular, systematic diagnosis of current organizational structure, the contingencies affecting it, and the fit between the structure and these contingencies. Table 12–11 offers a set of diagnostic questions for redesigning organizations.

Reading 12–1

Developing Leaders for the Global Enterprise
Steven H. Rhinesmith, John N. Williamson, David M. Ehlen, and Denise S. Maxwell

A major new organizational form has emerged in the 1980s. The "Global Enterprise" is rapidly coming to dominate competitive behavior in many industries around the world. It operates basically without the constraints or traditions of national boundaries and seeks to compete in any high-potential marketplace on earth.

The Global Enterprise is a consequence of several new and sophisticated forces that have come to shape the world economy over the last decade, including

- aggressive and massive financial accumulation and relatively free-flowing resource transfer;
- well-defined and highly efficient communication channels and information transfer and control systems;
- technology development and application that seek both leading-edge and low-cost positions in product creation and production;
- clear recognition of the potential for mass markets, mass customization, and global brands.

EVOLUTION OF THE GLOBAL ORGANIZATION
A business goes through four conceptually distinct and progressively more complex stages as it evolves from a successful domestic organization to a global corporation:

- **Domestic enterprise.** This business operates solely within its own country—using domestic suppliers and producing and marketing its services and products to customers at home.
- **Exporter.** This is a successful national business that sells or markets its products and services in foreign countries, but operates primarily from its sense of domestic competitiveness and advantage. This firm has little information about marketplace conditions outside its national boundaries and will most often operate through independent agents or distributors. The exporter tends to be opportunistic and transitional in form, as trends and events that it does not anticipate or understand affect its success.
- **International or multinational corporation.** This organization supplements its international sales and distribution capability with localized manufacturing. Such organizations often turn over their foreign operations to locals. Import/export activities move freely within the infrastructure of the multinational corporation; technology and manufacturing may be as equally distributed as sales and logistics. The parent company operates with a centralized view of strategy, technology, and resource allocation, but decision making and customer service shift to the local or national level for marketing, selling, manufacturing, and competitive tactics. Many multinational firms are more accurately characterized as multidomestic, because each national or regional operation acts quite independently of the enterprise's other operations.
- **Global enterprise.** This organization is an extension of the international or multinational corporation. It is constantly scanning, organizing, and reorganizing its resources and capabilities so that national or regional boundaries are not barriers to potential products, business opportunities, and manufacturing locations.

Such an organization is always looking for potential products or businesses. It delivers them in the best markets from the lowest cost positions and with the most appropriate management resources, largely without regard to where dollars, people, resources, and technology reside. The mindset of the Global Enterprise is to reach and penetrate marketplaces before local or international competitors are equipped to exploit the opportunities.

When an organization moves from an international to a global perspective, an essential shift takes place—a shift from the tight control of a bureaucracy to an entrepreneurial, flexible, rapid-response capability that is totally comfortable with cross-cultural influences and conditions.

The Global Enterprise, as Kenichi Ohmae describes it in his book, *Triad Power,* is one that becomes an "insider" in any market or nation where it operates, much as a domestic enterprise operates in a local market. The difference is a global strategic perspective, with cross-cultural integra-

tion and a highly localized sense of customers and competitors.

For many international organizations, one of the central executive-suite issues of the late '80s and into the '90s is how to organize, integrate, and manage their activities to become global players. That will become particularly true for the large U.S. firms that are just now beginning to understand that an export mentality—or having offshore divisions or businesses—does not necessarily mean they are equipped to compete effectively on a global basis.

Increasingly, the issue of global strategy deals with a series of differentiation and integration decisions. On one hand, companies have a clear need for a sense of global strategic intent, or for broad-based resource, technology, and market allocation schemes. At the same time, they need a sense of localized customer focus and competitiveness that deals with regional or local conditions as well as culture, behavior, and values.

Interestingly, most of the current writing and thinking about global organizations focuses on marketing, resource allocation, technology transfer, and organizational configuration as they relate primarily to information-flow, strategy, and control requirements. Little attention is given to the management and human-development needs that arise in the evolution from a domestically postured business to one that operates from a true global perspective.

GLOBAL LEADERSHIP-DEVELOPMENT AGENDA

What are the leadership-development requirements of an organization that is moving through those phases to a global outlook? How can it successfully develop its human resources to meet the changing, emerging, and increasingly complex conditions?

The "Leadership Agenda" (Figure 12–4) shows the leadership-development requirements that face a company as it evolves toward a global perspective. Several premises lie behind the agenda:

The customer is the center or focus of development and training. In other words, the primary focus of training and development is serving customers increasingly well and with competitive advantage.

The company's global strategy "wraps around" the training and development approaches; the organization's essential sense of competitiveness and strategic intent is embedded in all training programs and interventions.

The six leadership-development clusters have a contemporary management viewpoint. The clusters are organized around requirements for global competitive success rather than traditional skill or behavior sets.

Let us define briefly what each of the leadership-clusters comprises and then seek to organize them against the framework of the evolving enterprise.

Figure 12–4 The
Leadership Agenda

Managing the Environmental Scan

This cluster represents the systematic process of assessing and understanding the major internal and external influences on the enterprise's ability to achieve competitive advantage. In a larger sense, the cluster focuses on changing the frame of reference from a local or national orientation to a truly global perspective. It involves understanding influences, trends, and directions in technology, financial resources, marketing and distribution practices, political and cultural influences, and international economics.

Operationally, information systems and data-collection processes need to be reframed and revised to enable the organization to collect and utilize, in a timely and strategic way, the information required to proactively manage the business. That often requires an extensive reorganization of the company's data- and information-collection capacities. The process must ensure that the information to be collected is useful, and that the necessary systems, analytical processes, and human-resource-development schemes are in place to support the business's strategic information requirements.

For many organizations, that task appears complex. For others, it simply means augmenting and enhancing the systems already in place, or taking a new look at the company's strategic intent and articulating the information that is necessary to support the current strategy.

Whatever the degree of revision, it requires an understanding of today's critical success factors—those few things that must go right for the business to prosper—and the appropriate data about them. That often means narrowing, not enlarging, the information agenda and being careful about specifying information and data sets that are crucial to the firm's success.

Managing the Competitive Strategy

The focus of this cluster is understanding and developing competitive strategies, plans, and tactics that operate outside the confines of a domestic marketplace orientation. Again, much of the requirement deals with changing the basic frame of reference or point of view from which competitive activities and strategies are addressed. Several new dimensions need to be addressed and internalized.

One of the first "new understandings" is that the competitive environment operates in a greatly expanded and increasingly complex manner. Market strategy can be complicated by new issues and problems arising from unknown new competitors, the possibility of new entrants or players, and the implications of legislation such as tariffs and quotas.

In another sense, the resources and assets of the enterprise need to be looked at in dramatically expanded ways. For instance, the role of the enterprise's brand positioning has to be considered in terms of global strategic presence, as well as local marketing and competitive conditions.

The internationalization of taste, modified by local culture and values, supports the practice of mass customization and segmentation, but always from the perspective of the global brand, product offering, or business franchise. The issues of quality, resource efficiency, and cost leadership are becoming elements of marketing as well as financial strategy. And innovation and creativity have strong strategic implications as the organization confronts different competitors in virtually every local marketplace.

A customer-back business definition—with the organizational responsiveness and value-adding activities that support changing tastes and needs—still must be the fundamental driving force behind the organization's sense of competitiveness. Being close to customers remains a crucial element of success in the global model.

Such marketing tactics as pricing and promotional plans, which historically have operated on a local basis, must have a strategic or global coherence, as well as a localized sense of advantage and competition.

Managing Organizational Versatility

The advent of the global organization will bring dramatic new changes and learning requirements for individuals; other changes will be reflected in the architecture of the organizational models for tomorrow's successful global enterprises.

The most basic shift will take place as an organization moves from the classical, bureaucratic-control model to one that is characterized by flexible and responsive structures, adaptive and sometimes temporary operating systems, control mechanisms driven by information networks, and decision-making and behavior processes that are entrepreneurial, rapid-response, and risk-oriented.

Unstable business environments and irregular competitive and customer changes will contribute to a state of continuous organization and reorganization of resources, technologies, marketing and distribution systems, and human networks. Such changes will be necessary for adapting to the new success factors that will be critical for the business.

The underlying issue and challenge will be one of rapid and continuous response to opportunities and threats in terms of resource allocation, strategies, and human behavior. Certainly those needs seem straightforward, but the new approaches and systems may seem foreign to the conventional thinking that characterizes management practice in today's successful international enterprises.

Managing Teams and Alliances

The central operating mode for the Global Enterprise will be the creation, organization, and management of multinational teams and alliances—groups that represent diversity in functional capabilities, experience levels, and cultural values.

The effective global manager will need to understand how to organize and lead multinational teams; deal with issues of collaboration and cross-cultural variances; and develop processes for coaching, mentoring, and assessing performance across a variety of attitudes, beliefs, and standards. That requires the ability to effectively lead and direct a diverse group of people, most of whom will have values, beliefs, behaviors, business-practice standards, and traditions that are likely to be culturally different from those of the manager or leader.

Success in the global model will also come from the ability to create links across traditional organizational and national boundaries. Strategic partnerships will be formed to "achieve higher performance and/or lower costs through joint, mutually-dependent action of independent organizations or individuals," according to John Henderson of MIT. The basis for such alliances will be a mutually-shared purpose that transcends cultural differences.

In that sense, the requirements of global leadership extend well beyond traditional management practices, to reflect sensitivity to cultural diversity and perspective, and understanding of different—and sometimes conflicting—social forces without prejudice. Often, a manager will be required to operate in an unfamiliar and uncomfortable organizational setting.

Within the architecture of cross-cultural teams, managers need to recognize and focus on the subtle requirements for organizational loyalty and commitment, despite the presence of different cultural values and beliefs. At the same time, they must manage in the context of continuous change and diversity.

Managing Change and Chaos

Continuous change—not stability—is the dominant influence in global business activities today. That demands not only new skills, but also new realities, and even new comfort zones for global managers, who must realize and understand that global management will operate largely in the face of continuous change. The traditional role of making order out of chaos will shift to one of continuously managing change and chaos in ways that are responsive to customers and competitive conditions.

The idea that change—not stability—will be the regular and understood frame of reference for global management underlies the need for training, development, and understanding for managers who operate in international or global enterprises.

Only recently has the subject of change been given legitimate status in managerial training and learning activities. The real nature of the training and development need remains vague and largely undefined.

The concepts and metaphors that describe the management of change are increasingly visual. Peter Vaill of George Washington University describes it as learning how to "navigate in perpetual whitewater." Others see it as the process of continuous learning and improvement, of dealing with the personal requirements of constantly changing environments, and of viewing success as the process of improving (changing) faster than competitors—learning more quickly about opportunities and responding more completely when information and strategy point the way.

A significant learning opportunity in the domain of managing change is contextual: creating the mindsets, metaphors, beliefs, and attitudes that support and define the impact of irregular and chaotic change at a personal level. That means developing self-management and personal growth practices that can provide the stability, energy, and managerial confidence that are crucial to effectively handling such conditions.

Managing Personal Effectiveness

The personal growth and adaptation requirements for many U.S. managers, as they move toward operating in Global Enterprises, will be far-reaching, primarily because U.S.-based managers generally lack the experience, diversity, and globe-trotting skills of so many of their offshore counterparts.

Personal adaptation to the changing conditions, cultures, and operating requirements of the Global Enterprise represents a significant and largely unfunded training need. Development of global managers in most businesses is done ad hoc, rather than as a systematic and orderly movement toward the skills, perceptions, and attitudes of effective global management.

In many respects, the global leader will need to have a cosmopolitan perspective new to many U.S. firms. A working knowledge of international relations and foreign affairs will be required, as well as a careful and complete sensitivity to the diversity of cultures, beliefs, social forces, and values, and a commitment to treating that diversity largely without prejudice.

Global managers will also have to manage accelerated change in their own lives, family relations, living conditions, and perhaps even economic constraints. A true world view and sense of world citizenship will be a valuable frame of reference.

At the same time, managers must remain grounded in their skills, capacities, and personal sense of energy and balance, often under the continuing impact of destabilizing organizational and personal influences. That will be particularly true as they move across cultures. Even aspects of their life as mundane as personal living requirements will be challenging and at times difficult.

We believe the effective manager will emerge as a kind of global citizen, always anchored in a nationalistic framework, but embodying the openness, adaptability, and personal versatility necessary to live under new and often unpredictable conditions.

Many of the attitudes, skills, and perceptions of global adaptation can be provided in well-structured learning and training experiences. But complete growth will come only when training and personal on-the-job experiences are integrated to reflect a thoughtful, institutionalized development process. For most global managers, that process can and will be a lifelong journey.

The six development clusters represent the essence and focus of the leadership development and training necessary to support the Global Enterprise. They may lack definitive

clarity in today's operating climate, but they point to the direction in which attention and resources must be applied if the successful international organization of today is to make the transition to Global Enterprise.

The "Global Management Matrix" (Figure 12–5) summarizes the focus of leadership attention as an organization increases in complexity from a domestic to a global entity.

THE AMERICAN LEADERSHIP CHALLENGE

It is somewhat ironic that conventional wisdom about the inability of U.S. firms to compete effectively in the global marketplace usually focuses on inadequate spending in technology, plants, and equipment. The real vulnerability may lie in the lack of attention to training and developing key managers in the approaches, concepts, and experiences required to be effective global managers and leaders.

It is equally ironic that the presumed strength of U.S. firms is the level and quality of management and leadership training—either in academic or corporate settings. Our managers are believed to be better trained than their offshore counterparts. The reality as it relates to the global organization may be just the opposite.

U.S. businesses increasingly recognize the need for achieving a global-marketplace perspective. However, they do not have the training and experience needed for developed and seasoned management teams capable of operating at the same skill level as companies from such countries as Japan and Germany. Such nations have been forced by the nature of their competitive positions to compete nationally—and even globally—over the last 10, 20, or more years. Until recently, the United States has had the luxury of being able to remain domestic.

We in the United States are an insular society. That quality is present in our schools, our government, our corporations, and our values and beliefs. To change the pattern in a fundamental way may take years, if not a generation. During that process, we may well be managerially unprepared to meet the requirements for global competitiveness.

What will it take to change and effectively compete?

First, we need to recognize that the new game will not be played or driven by the U.S. business model. To cling to traditional U.S. views of competitiveness and marketplace success will increasingly threaten an organization's ability to compete in the years ahead.

That shift in thinking will be particularly difficult for those American enterprises that have done little in the last 30 or 40 years to educate and train their managers to organize and manage the firm's resources from a multicultural or international perspective. Feeding that deficiency is the failure of the American educational system to provide students with international business skills and cross-cultural knowledge to bring to organizations.

We also need to modify certain barriers, misconceptions, and beliefs, if American enterprise is going to grapple

Figure 12–5 **The Global Management Matrix**

Leadership Development Clusters / Corporate Type	**Managing the environmental scan**—*How do we determine what must go right?*	**Managing the competitive strategy**—*How do we allocate and align resources?*	**Managing organizational versatility**—*How do we organize for success today and tomorrow?*	**Managing teams and alliances**—*How do we connect with others for advantage?*	**Managing change and chaos**—*How do we thrive in times of unpredictable change?*	**Managing personal effectiveness**—*How do we change and grow successfully as individuals?*
Global Enterprise	Global trends, conditions, and resources.	Integrate wholistic strategies.	Create free-flowing resource-allocation schemes.	Create global strategic partnerships—inter- and intraorganizational links.	Proactively create destabilized conditions for advantage.	Transcend cultural differences.
International or Multinational Corporation	Multidomestic trends, environmental conditions, and strategic resources.	Proliferate successful domestic market model with cultural adaptation.	Adapt systems and processes to international competitive conditions.	Develop multinational alliances and ventures; manage cross-cultural work teams.	Respond and adapt to destabilizing change by flexibly relocating resources across national markets.	Work effectively in cross-cultural situations.
Exporter	Offshore market trends and conditions; domestic strategic resources.	Extend domestic success to offshore markets.	Respond to emerging foreign-market opportunities.	Manage cross-cultural distribution links.	Adapt to destabilizing change by flexibly entering or withdrawing from foreign markets.	Understand cross-cultural needs.
Domestic Enterprise	Domestic market trends, resources, and environmental conditions.	Penetrate and segment markets.	Respond to local competitive and market changes.	Manage cross-functional teams.	Flexibly protect ourselves against unpredictable change.	Understand self and associates.

© 1989, Wilson Learning Corporation and Rhinesmith and Associates Inc.

with the question of managerial competitiveness. Some of the barriers appear in research by Andre Laurent, who has studied multinational corporations and has made several key observations:

- Multinational companies do not and cannot submerge the individuality of different cultures. As strong as corporate culture is, people never give up their own backgrounds and preferences. People can adapt, but in periods of crisis or uncertainty, they will retreat to their own sets of beliefs and cultural values.
- Contact with other nationality groups can even promote determination to be different. It is interesting that many people withdraw when confronted with cultural differences, and reinforce their determination not to adjust and not to give up their own values.

- It is useless to present new kinds of management theory and practice to individuals who are culturally unable or unwilling to accept it. For example, performance reviews are difficult in most multinational corporations because of differences in personal style. Americans tend to be open, direct, and blunt; Asians tend to be much more indirect, oblique, and subtle in giving feedback. Thus, something as apparently basic and common as a performance-appraisal system probably cannot be implemented uniformly on a global basis.

Several other key paradigms about cross-cultural awareness that affect our ability to rethink the new game are worth observing:

- The "we are all alike" syndrome is one that many of us have experienced when we have visited a foreign land and come back with the initial perception that all people are very much alike—we are just one, big human race.
- The second stage of understanding comes when we begin to uncover differences—some subtle, some specific. Then we realize that although people have some significant similarities, we can also have strong differences.
- Third comes the realization that we are really both different and similar, and that in an organization, a leadership and management model must address both common and uncommon threads, as well as diverse behaviors and beliefs.

The prevailing attitude of senior executives in American companies seems to be a point of view that suggests, "If we can get our enterprise's corporate culture and values right—no matter where it operates around the globe—then the issue of strategy and local behavior will be predictable and appropriate."

They are saying that the template for values, beliefs, and behaviors of the enterprise must necessarily come from the values, beliefs, behaviors, and attitudes of the parent corporation. We believe that holding on to that viewpoint means starting from the wrong place.

The difficult task for senior management today is to flip-flop the traditional thinking that suggests that values, beliefs, and behaviors need to be highly standardized from a central, corporate perspective, and that strategies and resource-allocation schemes can be played out from a local point of view. We believe the opposite reflects today's reality and is the fundamental operating condition for an organization that wants to achieve true global status.

We believe that in the '90s the challenge for most enterprises as they move toward the global model will lie in successfully managing international teams. And U.S. corporations have done little in the last 30 or 40 years to educate, train, and provide experience for managers to manage a multicultural workforce.

Meeting that challenge will be expensive in terms of both resources and time. U.S. firms need to get on with the task of building a new model for leadership development in a global community—a model that derives not from the traditional management skill base of planning, staffing, and control, but rather from a recognition of a whole new array of leadership requirements:

- The capacity to manage, live with, and operate under conditions of continuous change and turmoil.
- The recognition that global advantage is transitory and that the role of managers and global leaders will be to continuously assess and adjust resources, technologies, organizational structure, and human

beings to reflect simultaneously a centralized view of strategy and a localized view of customers and cultures.
- An acknowledgement that the U.S. business model is not necessarily the best point of departure for evaluating the implications and meaning of global-marketplace trends and opportunities. A fundamental shift in thinking needs to take place in setting assumptions and beliefs about the role enterprises can play in the global marketplace. U.S. businesses have to move from a perspective that considers the rest of the world from a U.S. viewpoint, to a more global outlook that views the home country in the context of the world marketplace.
- A heightened awareness of strategic marketing and global competitiveness. On one hand, brands, technologies, and franchises need to be played out from the advantage of scale and clout that only a global point of view can provide. At the same time, businesses need to recognize and acknowledge the "close to the customer" conditions that operate locally or inside major national marketplaces.
- The development of skills and capabilities to lead multinational teams in flexible and responsive ways. Human resources need to reflect the same capacity for adaptation and flexibility as technology and financial resources. The new organizational model that emerges will shift from the traditional bureaucratic control scheme that drives so many large enterprises today to a contemporary entrepreneurialism characterized by flexibility, resource fluidity, and continuously changing beliefs and attitudes about competitiveness. It will embody a willingness to shed old assumptions and beliefs quickly, and a recognition that home base is really the globe.
- The understanding that managers, particularly in the United States, need cross-cultural and expatriate experiences early on and continually throughout their careers.

The challenge for all of us involved in both management and the development of management is to begin to change the context in which we think about our human-development responsibilities. We clearly need to discard traditional models and views and begin to think from a global rather than a domestic paradigm. In the process, we must challenge and change many of our views about hiring, training, controlling, offering incentives, and measuring our managers.

It is a long-term assignment, probably three to five years for most large enterprises simply to get moving; in all likelihood, it will take a full generation to implement the approach.

By that time, we will have a whole new game to worry about.

DISCUSSION QUESTIONS

1. Describe a global enterprise and an organization's evolution into one.
2. What are the leadership requirements for a global enterprise?
3. What challenges do U.S. corporations face in meeting the global challenge?

Activity 12–1

Words in Sentences Company

Step 1: Form companies and assign workplaces. Each group should include between seven and twelve people and should consider itself a company. In this exercise you will form a "miniorganization" with several other people. You will be competing with other companies in your industry. The success of your company will depend on (a) your objectives, (b) planning, (c) organization structure, and (d) quality control. It is important, therefore, that you spend some time thinking about the best design for your organization.

Step 2: Read the following directions and ask your instructor about any points that need clarification:

DIRECTIONS

You are a small company that manufactures words and then packages them in meaningful English-language sentences. Market research has established that sentences of at least three words but not more than six words are in demand. Therefore, packaging, distribution, and sales should be set up for three- to six-word sentences.

The words-in-sentences industry is highly competitive; several new firms have recently entered what appears to be an expanding market. Since raw materials, technology, and pricing are all standard for the industry, your ability to compete depends on two factors: (1) volume and (2) quality.

GROUP TASK

Your group must design and participate in running a WIS company. You should design your organization to be as efficient as possible during each ten-minute production run. After the first production run, you will have an opportunity to reorganize your company if you want.

RAW MATERIALS

For each production run you will be given a "raw material word or phrase." The letters found in the word or phrase serve as the raw materials available to produce new words in sentences. For example, if the raw material word is "organization," you could produce the words and sentence: "Nat ran to a zoo."

PRODUCTION STANDARDS

There are several rules that have to be followed in producing "words in sentences." If these rules are not followed, your output will not meet production specifications and will not pass quality-control inspection.

1. The same letter may appear only as often in a manufactured word as it appears in the raw material word or phrase; for example, "organization" has two o's. Thus "zoo" is legitimate, but not "zoonosis." It has too many o's and s's.
2. Raw material letters can be used again in different manufactured words.
3. A manufactured word may be used only once in a sentence and in only one sentence during a production run; if a word—for example, "a"—is used once in a sentence, it is out of stock.
4. A new word may not be made by adding "s" to form the plural of an already used manufactured word.
5. A word is defined by its spelling, not its meaning.
6. Nonsense words or nonsense sentences are unacceptable.
7. All words must be in the English language.
8. Names and places are acceptable.
9. Slang is not acceptable.

MEASURING PERFORMANCE

The output of your WIS company is measured by the total number of acceptable words that are packaged in sentences. The sentences must be legible, listed on no more than two sheets of paper, and handed to the Quality Control Review Board at the completion of each production run.

DELIVERY

Delivery must be made to the Quality Control Review Board thirty seconds after the end of each production run.

QUALITY CONTROL

If any word in a sentence does not meet the standards set forth above, all the words in the sentence will be rejected.

The Quality Control Review Board (composed of one member from each company) is the final arbiter of acceptability. In the event of a tie vote on the Review Board, a coin toss will determine the outcome.

Step 3: Design your organization using as many group members as you see fit to produce your words in sentences.

Step 4: Production Run 1. The group leader will hand each WIS company a sheet with a raw material word or phrase. When the instructor announces "Begin production," you are to manufacture as many words as possible and package them in sentences for delivery to the Quality Control Review Board. You will have ten minutes. When the instructor announces "Stop production," you will have thirty seconds to deliver your output to the Quality Control Review Board. Output received after thirty seconds does not meet the delivery schedule and will not be counted.

Step 5: While the output is being evaluated, you may reorganize for the second production run.

Step 6: Production Run 2.

Step 7: The results are presented.

Step 8: Discussion. In small groups, and then with the entire class, answer the following questions:

Description
1. Draw the organizational chart for your WIS company.

Diagnosis
2. Analyze its structure: describe (a) division of labor, (b) mechanisms of coordination, and (c) structural configurations.
3. Using your knowledge of organization design and the contingencies that influence it, evaluate your WIS company's structure.

Prescription
4. How could you have designed a more effective organizational structure?

The origin of this exercise is unknown.

Activity 12–2 Fergusonchemical Europe

Step 1: Read the Fergusonchemical Europe case.

On a gray day in February 1985, Ian Robertson, Land Transportation Manager for Fergusonchemical Europe, sat in his office reviewing a recent organization survey. The results confirmed his worst fears. The survey, which had used scientific sampling procedures, showed that Fergusonchemical Europe's customers were receiving their products when promised only 75 percent of the time. The table on pages 590–591 presents a summary of the survey findings.

These recent findings alone gave management adequate grounds for concern and, combined with information acquired from previous reports, it was clear that Fergusonchemical Europe's customer service was unsatisfactory. The earlier surveys, two in particular, had disturbed the regional distribution management team and had motivated Regional Distribution Manager Philippe Magistretti, Marine Manager Peter Gordon, and Ian Robertson to initiate the recently completed survey.

In 1983, a survey of sales personnel showed that the sales personnel of Fergusonchemical Europe did not consider their organization competitive in areas important to customers. In addition, a 1984 survey of plastics users in the United Kingdom found that Fergusonchemical was not viewed as competitive as British Petroleum, Shell, or DSM

in significant areas of customer service. The same two issues were cited repeatedly by Fergusonchemical customers as sources of frustration. First, Fergusonchemical frequently did not deliver on time. Second, when deliveries were delayed, Fergusonchemical often failed to inform the customers. Given the environment facing the chemical industry in Europe in general, and strategic decisions recently made by Fergusonchemical Europe in particular, distribution management realized, as did senior management, that the existing level of customer service had to be considerably improved.

FERGUSONCHEMICAL EUROPE AND THE INDUSTRY

Fergusonchemical Europe, a wholly-owned subsidiary of Ferguson Corporation, was the ninth largest chemical company in Europe with revenues in 1984 of approximately 2.5 billion dollars. Fergusonchemical's products were classified into seven different chemical product lines. These product lines included: elastomers, plastics, solvents, plasticizers and intermediates, specialties, paramins, and olefins. Each product line was managed by a vice president based at company headquarters in Munich.

In addition to seven product segments, Fergusonchem-

Statistical Check, Last Week of January 1985, Customer Delivery Reliability

	Sweden			U.K.			Netherlands		
	Before	Onday	After	Before	Onday	After	Before	Onday	After
P&I		3			8			1	
Specialties		2			2	3		2	
Elastomers		4		1	12	1		1	
Paramins		2		1	12	2		2	
Plastics		3			9	4		2	
Solvents		2	1		13			3	
Total		16	1	2	67	10		11	
Total %*		94	6	2	85	13		100	

	Raw Data (total)			Total	Weighted Percentages (total %)		
	Before	Onday	After		Before	Onday	After
P&I	3	40	1	44	7	91	2
Specialties	3	22	11	36	8	61	31
Elastomers	4	33	12	49	8	67	25
Paramins	6	28	14	48	13	58	29
Plastics	2	30	18	50	4	60	36
Solvents	—	52	5	57	—	91	9
Total	18	205	61	284		Weighted	
Total %	6	72	22		5	75	20

*Raw data numbers of deliveries checked. Not statistically weighted.
Weather: The last week of January 1985 was affected by the thaw restrictions of truck movement in France. This particularly affected resins and elastomers.

ical Europe was also divided into nine wholly-owned subsidiaries, each one serving one or more Western European countries: the United Kingdom, France, Belgium, West Germany, Netherlands, Italy, Spain, Portugal, and Sweden. Each affiliate had a managing director as well as a marketing manager who coordinated sales within each product line. Salespeople reported to their respective marketing managers who, in turn, reported to both the affiliate managing director and a product vice president located in Munich. Because of this dual reporting relationship, Fergusonchemical Europe had a matrix organization design. Figure 12–6 presents an organization chart for Fergusonchemical Europe. Figure 12–7 presents a partial organization chart which includes regional distribution personnel.

During the 1980's, a number of factors contributed to an increasingly competitive environment for European chemical companies. A key development was the creation of overcapacity, especially in the area of commodity chemicals. In response to strong demand and high earnings during the 1970's, a number of chemical companies expanded their production facilities. Favorable market opportunities during the 1970's also attracted a number of new competitors, primarily from the Gulf oil countries. Their access to large inexpensive oil reserves and relatively low labor costs posed a significant challenge to existing European chemical companies. Projections indicated that chemical companies based in the Middle East would continue to offer increasing competition in the future.

In addition to excess capacity and growing competition, European chemical companies in 1985 were still recovering from the devastating effects of the economic recession of the early 1980's. A number of European chemical companies, including German-based BASF and Hoechst and Dutch-based DSM, initiated strategic diversification programs in response to an increasingly competitive business environment.

Fergusonchemical Europe, however, opted not to concentrate on diversification. Instead, the organization adopted what it termed a "value-added strategy," which influenced product decisions as well as customer relationships. With

Germany			France			Italy			Belgium		
Before	Onday	After	Before	Onday	After	Before	Onday	After	Before	Onday	After
2	13			12	1	No Deliveries			1	3	
1	5	3	1	8	1	1	3	3			1
3	4	3		5	5		2	3		4	
1	2	6		6	2	4	3	3		1	1
1	9	5		2	2	1	3	3		2	4
	10	1		6	1		6	2		2	
8	43	18	1	39	12	6	17	14	1	12	14
12	62	26	2	75	23	16	46	38	4	44	52

Weighing Calculation			
Region Weight	Before	Onday	After
0.06	0.42	5.46	0.12
0.07	0.56	4.27	2.17
0.12	0.96	8.04	3.00
0.15	1.95	8.70	4.35
0.20	0.80	12.00	7.20
0.40	—	36.40	3.60
1	4.69	74.87	20.44	100

the existing industry overcapacity in commodity chemicals, Fergusonchemical Europe decided to focus on the production and sale of specialty chemicals. As specialty chemicals require a more lengthy complex production process, they can command higher prices and therefore offer greater profit potential. Fergusonchemical Europe believed that its technical expertise, production facilities, and resource base gave it a competitive advantage in this market segment.

In addition, the organization made a commitment to value-added customer service, using technical expertise, product knowledge, resource availability and dedicated effort. Fergusonchemical Europe promised to provide a level of customer service superior to that offered by the competition. Executives described this new strategy as a change from production orientation to market orientation. The need for increased sensitivity to customer requirements was stressed throughout the organization.

Paul Stinson, President of Fergusonchemical Europe, was responsible for the development, articulation and selling of the new value-added strategy to both internal and external constituencies. This strategy was summarized by Paul Stinson in a document entitled *Our Future Vision* which was published and widely distributed to company personnel.

SALES, DISTRIBUTION, AND CUSTOMER SERVICE OPERATIONS

In order to implement Fergusonchemical's goal of providing superior customer service, the existing structure needed reassessment. Each affiliate marketing manager served as the link between salespeople, the affiliate managing director and the relevant product vice president at headquarters.

Affiliate marketing managers were assisted with their responsibilities by a secretary and a customer service coordinator. Customer service coordinators were responsible for ensuring that orders generated by sales personnel were smoothly executed. Activities frequently performed by customer service coordinators included processing orders, securing warehouse space, arranging for transportation needs, and answering customers' questions. Customer service coordinators usually reported to a single marketing manager and were considered members of the product team within each affiliate. In cases where product lines were small, a customer service coordinator would work with several marketing managers. In addition to expediting customers' orders, customer service coordinators occasionally assisted marketing managers with other administrative responsibilities. Fergusonchemical Europe employed approximately 120

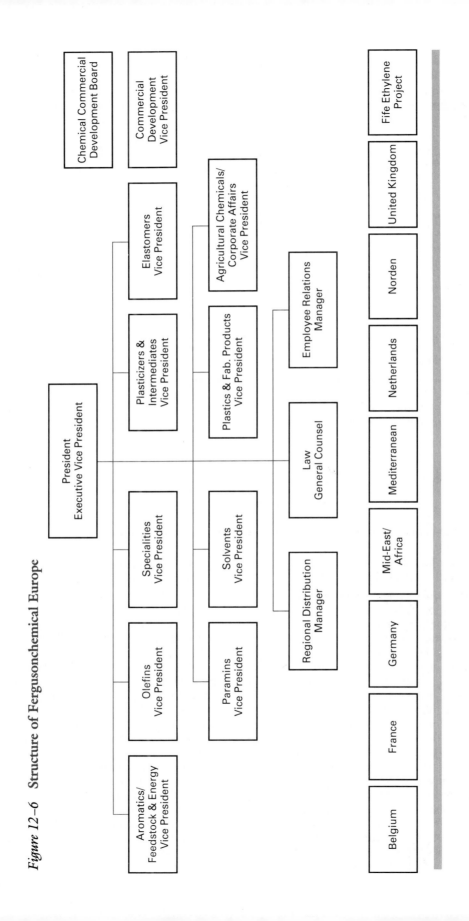

Figure 12–6 **Structure of Fergusonchemical Europe**

592

Figure 12–7 **Partial Organization Chart, Fergusonchemical Europe**

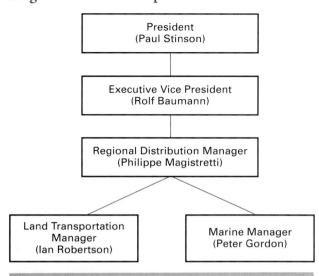

it was difficult for customer service coordinators to assist or learn from one another. Opportunities for career growth and advancement were also restricted because customer service coordinators were isolated within individual product groups. The regional distribution team realized that the present system was inhibiting economies of scale with respect to customer service operations.

Studies indicated that optimum economies of scale could be reached only if a minimum of five customer service coordinators were centrally situated. A recent phone survey supported the team's case for reorganization. The survey showed that customer service coordinators took an average of 70 seconds to answer an inquiry. Regional distribution management believed that all customer inquiries should be answered within 30 seconds. Figure 12–9 presents the results of the telephone survey.

customer service coordinators within their nine affiliate organizations. Figure 12–8 presents a demographic profile of customer service coordinators.

It was apparent from the findings of the recent corporate surveys that the existing organization of the distribution function was unsatisfactory. The regional distribution team (Philippe Magistretti, Ian Robertson and Peter Gordon) was seriously concerned and began a reappraisal of Fergusonchemical Europe's distribution system.

The team felt strongly that distribution activities must be able to meet the dual objective of performing value-added customer service in a cost effective manner. In their discussions, regional distribution management personnel frequently referred to recent management books which stressed the importance of quality in all business activities.

Regional distribution management was particularly concerned about the assignment of customer service coordinators to individual product groups within affiliate organizations. The team was convinced that this structure was both inefficient and ineffective. In most cases, a single customer service coordinator worked within a product group. Therefore, when this person was unavailable because of illness, vacation, or other job responsibilities, customer inquiries frequently went unanswered. Philippe Magistretti and his colleagues maintained that the existing arrangement put customer service "at risk."

Although regional distribution management was willing to acknowledge differences among productive groups, there were many similarities in the activities performed by customer service coordinators. With the current structure,

PROPOSED REORGANIZATION

The recent survey on delivery time delays convinced the regional distribution management team that it must prepare and implement a reorganization plan. The proposed reorganization would remove customer service coordinators from the individual product groups and consolidate them in a central location within each affiliate organization. Instead of each customer service coordinator reporting to an individual affiliate marketing manager, all customer service coordinators would report to an affiliate distribution manager.

The regional distribution team realized that the reorganization plan alone could not rectify the problem of late deliveries. Recent studies had shown that delivery times being quoted to customers were clearly unrealistic for some products. In addition, certain job descriptions needed rewriting in order to give better customer service. However, their analysis showed that a majority of late deliveries were attributable to an inappropriately organized customer service function.

Philippe Magistretti, Ian Robertson, and Peter Gordon were aware that their proposed reorganization would encounter stiff opposition. Affiliate marketing managers in particular would strongly resist the proposed reorganization. On numerous occasions affiliate marketing managers had stressed that the customer service coordinator was the cornerstone of the product team, serving as a vital communications link to the market. Placing the customer service coordinators on the product teams also enhanced their accessibility and commitment to product team members. Marketing managers feared that these benefits would be lost after the reorganization. Finally, affiliate marketing managers questioned whether customer service coordinators were qualified to assume the new responsibilities which the proposed reorganization would entail.

Customer service coordinators also expressed concern regarding the reorganization. Fergusonchemical Europe was described by numerous customer service coordinators as a product driven company where the jobs considered most

Figure 12–8 **Regional Customer Service Coordinator Profiles, Fergusonchemical Europe**

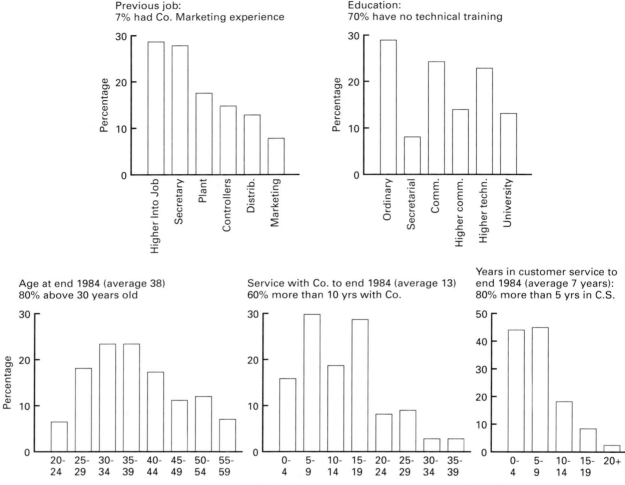

attractive were associated with the product lines. Functional jobs, on the other hand, were viewed by many as "a necessary evil," a concept fostered by some affiliate marketing managers. Customer service coordinators therefore feared loss of both status and identification with a product team with the proposed reorganization.

Richard Elsner, customer service coordinator for the United Kingdom affiliate, voiced the concern of many customer service coordinators. "My biggest source of job satisfaction is helping the customer, particularly when it requires a little bit extra. To help your customers you need rapport and influence within the product team. My fear is that if I am isolated from my product team, I will lose the rapport and influence necessary to help my customers."

Customer service coordinators also worried about possible conflicts of interest between customer service and cost.

As members of a product team, customer service coordinators generally tried to maximize customer service even if it meant costs would be higher. Would a central affiliate distribution center sacrifice customer service in order to reduce costs?

In addition to the above obstacles, the regional distribution management team realized that it operated within a matrix organization of product lines, affiliates, and functions. However, Philippe Magistretti, Ian Robertson and Peter Gordon felt no doubt that the reorganization was necessary. Furthermore, the Executive Vice President of Fergusonchemical Europe, Rolf Baumann, had publicly stated that he supported the establishment of centralized customer service groups within the affiliate organizations. Failure to improve the current level of customer service might well endanger Fergusonchemical Europe's recently

Figure 12–9   **Telephone Survey, Fergusonchemical Europe (Regional Average/High/Low versus Aff's)**

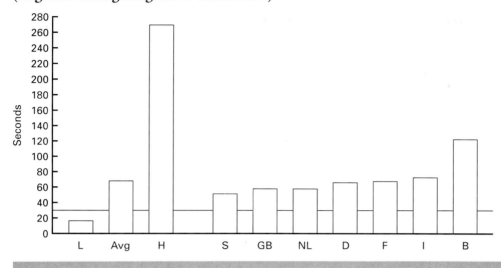

adopted business strategy. The question now facing regional distribution management was how to achieve acceptance and implement the proposed reorganization plan.

Step 2:   Prepare the case for class discussion.

Step 3:   Answer the following questions, individually, in small groups, or with the entire class, as directed by your instructor:

Description
1. Describe the original organization at Fergusonchemical Europe in terms of division of labor and coordinating mechanisms.
2. Classify the original organization using (a) form of departmentation, (b) means of coordination, (c) organic versus mechanistic classifications, and (d) information-processing capacity.
3. Describe the proposed reorganization in terms of division of labor and coordinating mechanisms.
4. Classify the proposed reorganization using (a) form of departmentation, (b) means of coordination, (c) organic versus mechanistic classifications, and (d) information-processing capacity.

Diagnosis
5. Compare and contrast the original and proposed organizations.
6. How do the structures respond to changing information-processing needs?

7. How do the structures respond to the employees' needs?
8. Comment on differences in communication, span of control, unity of command, and decentralization in the structures.
9. What problems does each structure solve? create?

Prescription
10. What changes were required in the original structure?
11. Does the reorganization provide the needed changes?

Action
12. Was the process used to redesign the organization and then implement the changes effective? What costs and benefits resulted?

Step 4:   Discussion. In small groups or with the entire class, share your answers to the questions above. Then answer the following questions:

1. What symptoms suggested that problems existed?
2. What problems exist in the case?
3. What theories and concepts help explain the problems?
4. How were the problems corrected? How should they have been corrected?
5. Will the proposed changes likely be effective?

City of Brookside Redesign

Step 1:   Review the organization structure of the City of Brookside shown in Figure 12–10.

Step 2:   Answer the following questions, individually, in small groups, or with the entire class:

Description
1. Describe the organization's structure: its division of labor and coordinating mechanisms.
2. What structural paradigms best describe the organization?

Diagnosis
3. Describe the nature of the following contingencies: (a) goals, (b) environment, (c) technology, (d) work force, (e) size, and (f) age.
4. How does the organization's structure fit with these contingencies?
5. Is the current design appropriate? effective?

Prescription
6. What changes should be made?

Figure 12–10   **City of Brookside, Existing Organization**

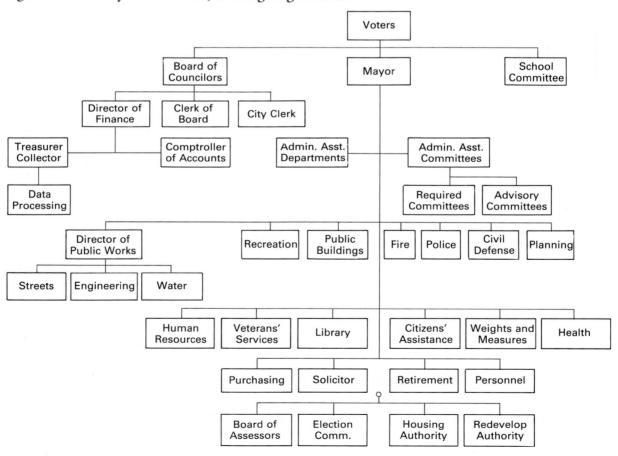

Activity 12–4

Luxor S.A.

Step 1: Read the Luxor S.A. case.

FROM PROFESSIONAL TO MANAGERIAL LEADERSHIP

"It is always painful to make a decision like this, but for the company's sake, we have no choice; we must find a solution to this problem and find it now!" These words, spoken by Mr. Johnson, Direct Sales Department Director, referred to the difficult task of making a decision about George Helmer, Area Sales Manager.

It was April 20, 1988, and Mr. Johnson had asked the Personnel Director, the Group Marketing Director, and a few other colleagues of Luxor S.A. to meet with him to discuss this case in particular as well as the issue in general.

COMPANY BACKGROUND

Luxor S.A., with administrative headquarters and research laboratories located in Luxembourg, had been established in 1973. It had been one of the first companies to manufacture and sell computers to retailers, using a network of subsidiaries and agents in over 80 countries. The company was organized around some key functions such as R&D, Production, Finance, Human Resources, and Sales. (See Figure 12–11 for the Overall Organization Chart.)

In this highly competitive business environment, growth depended on intensive, innovative research and development. Thus the company had always had a policy of investing a significant percentage of its revenue on modernizing its facilities, in research and development activities, and in expanding its worldwide network.

PROFILE OF A SALES PROFESSIONAL

George Helmer, 56 years old, had joined Luxor S.A. in 1975 as a sales representative in the District Sales Division of the company, i.e., the division in charge of all the countries where Luxor had no subsidiaries.

George had had the necessary characteristics to be an outstanding salesman—tenacity, persuasion and verbal skills, excellent contacts with clients. His sales technique was simple but highly efficient, "Meet the potential client, win his trust with informal conversation, let him talk about his business concerns, and then convince him you have the right product for him." Once the client had placed an order, George would keep in touch, become familiar with him through regular visits and small presents. This strategy, based on creating a friendship with the client, often would take a lot of George's time, but the results had been significant. Clients had become faithful and regular customers of the company, and George had soon become one of the best salesmen in his sector, highly appreciated both by the clients and his superiors.

In 1980, he was promoted to Country Sales Manager, responsible for Holland. (See Figure 12–12 for the Direct Sales Division Organization Chart.) George had been pleased

Figure 12–11 **Luxor S.A. Overall Organization Chart (1975)**

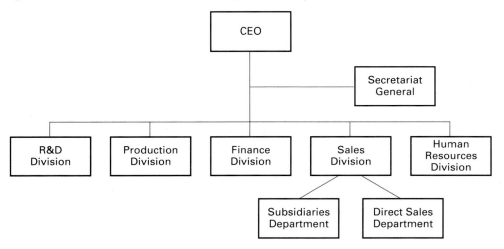

Figure 12–12 **Luxor S.A.—Luxembourg Direct Sales Department (1975)**

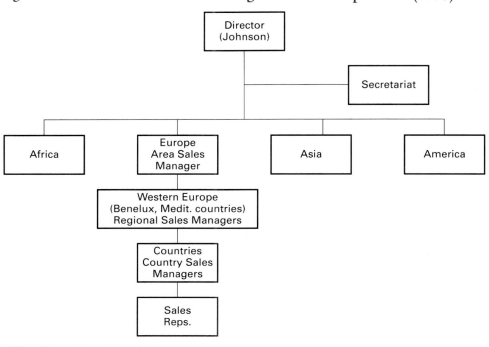

to accept this promotion, as it gave him the opportunity to enlarge his range of customers and improve his sales performance. And indeed, the Holland sector soon registered one of the best sales records in Europe.

Two years later in 1982, George Helmer was promoted again for good services to become Regional Sales Manager for the Western Europe region, in charge of the Benelux countries. George felt honored by this promotion, though sometimes he did miss his former position. Being responsible for three countries meant having to supervise a team of sales representatives and, therefore, fewer opportunities to be in direct contact with clients.

In 1985, George was made Area Sales Manager for Europe, when the position became available. He was then in charge of 12 countries, and George admitted that he had had some difficulties at first. He had sometimes felt snowed under with work but, all in all, considered that he had come through rather well.

He was perceived by his subordinates as an easy-going manager, as having a "laissez-faire" management style. Actually, his subordinates were often on their own, since George was still trying to work in the field visiting clients as much as possible. Concerned mainly with clients and sales performance, he was pragmatic about operational matters. As long as sales records were good in his department, he considered that the other aspects of being a manager, i.e., regarding his team and the company, were minor.

On the whole, George was fully satisfied with his career development, especially as his education had been merely trade school and some crash courses in electronics and computer science. "I owe my position to hard work, loyalty and expertise in the sales field," he would often say to his children, proudly showing them the awards "for excellent sales performance" which he had received in 1979 and 1981.

Everything seemed to be going well until 1986. Then, George Helmer started to encounter some serious difficulties which Mr. Johnson felt were caused by the market and company changes made by Luxor S.A. at that time.

MARKET CHANGES

The company occupied a strong position in the international market and was justifiably proud of its development since the 1973 founding. However, during the late '70s, basic changes occurred in the international computer market which Luxor S.A. had to take into account. The major changes were:

- Competition had become tougher, especially from the United States and Japan which had attacked the European market in force.
- Computer retailers had also become more demanding regarding the product and its business potential. They were expecting original, highly professional customized products which would give them an edge

in the market. They also wanted a comprehensive product line with a good range of software.

- Knowing the clients' markets and the latest concepts in marketing had become essential to establish successful business relations with clients and to penetrate new markets.

Increased market pressure and a more demanding clientele drastically changed the role of salespeople; instead of selling ready-made products, they began working *with* the clients, identifying their specific product needs as well as advising them on appropriate market strategies. In other words, from purely salespeople, they were becoming consultants, seeking solutions to specific problems relating to existing and future markets, providing clients with marketing support, i.e., doing research to develop the products required by the retailers' own customers (end users such as companies, schools, etc.). Salespeople had to have higher technical and scientific competence, financial and marketing knowledge, and negotiation skills. Handling clients and preparing projects had to be highly professional.

COMPANY CHANGES

In late 1986, the new CEO decided that Luxor S.A. needed a structural reorganization and policy revision to maintain a viable position in the global market. Keeping in mind the external changes in the business, the company intended to take the necessary steps to become an innovative, trendsetting, marketing-driven organization. Under the new philosophy, a company would need to work in close partnership with its retailers. Luxor S.A. also recruited a consultant, a management specialist to advise the CEO on reorganization and managerial issues. The new marketing orientation implied a different way of working, i.e.:

- Creating new functions (marketing)
- Redefining roles (managerial instead of professional)
- Introducing marketing people into the sales sector (combining both departments)
- Coordinating all the departments more efficiently (teamwork)
- Using new technology and equipment
- Using specialists in each position, i.e., MBAs, software specialists, etc., instead of generalists

At the beginning of 1987, the CEO sent the following memo along with the new decisions to all the company's executives:

Luxor S.A. is a medium-sized company which, because of its geographical spread and the diversity of its markets, experiences all the logistic problems of a multinational. As a consequence, we must solve, with limited human resources and systems, complex problems due to ever-increasing pressures from our environment. Clear and efficient structures, supported by good management of human resources, are the essential conditions for success and constitute the first priority. I rely on you all to help our Group with the progressive implementation of our new organization.

Business priorities were set on actions that would have a high impact on improving sales and financial results. In the first phase, the company especially wanted:

- to have better control of the Group's margin and pricing guidelines;
- to put all its efforts on the European and North American markets;
- to establish a detailed analysis of the customers' most important needs and Luxor's position vis-à-vis those needs;
- to prepare a detailed analysis of specific needs in each product segment;
- to design operating plans for all subsidiaries.

A new recruitment strategy was implemented and an international trainee program established to prepare new managers. Good professionals and managers were defined as follows:

- Professionals should be creative, relationship oriented, respected, have a strong personality and be known outside the company. They were also expected to have the latest technical expertise in hardware and software.
- Managers should have good planning capability, be able to lead a team, be fair and impartial, be problem-solvers, decision-makers and good coordinators.
- Luxor S.A. should encourage initiative, entrepreneurship and the delegation of responsibility.

THE NEW STRUCTURE

For the first time in the company's history, a Group Marketing structure was set up, combining four divisions: Research, Marketing Services, Product Management, and Sales. (See the New Overall Organization Chart in Figure 12–13 and the Group Marketing Division Organization Chart in Figure 12–14.) The new marketing policy was intended for direct sales as well as the subsidiaries. Thus, instead of functioning rather independently, sales became directly linked to the new Group Marketing structure.

In order to achieve better coordination among all the departments, National and International Project Handling procedures were established. Briefing sessions were held with the salesmen and retailers to identify their needs and prepare project checklists with all the necessary commercial and technical information details required by Product Management to handle a project more efficiently and professionally. They selected 11 clients as a sample to study and learn in more depth about their needs and their own clientele. With this reorganization, Luxor management switched from a "family" and "artisanal" orientation to a more sophisticated (high tech) professional management style. The new emphasis was on communication and coordination.

Figure 12–13 **Luxor S.A. New Overall Organization Chart (1987)**

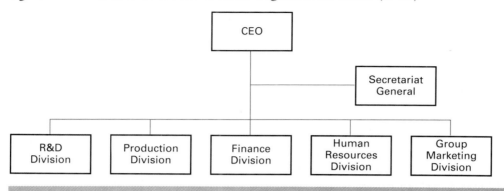

CAUGHT IN THE MIDDLE

The new strategy for the Direct Sales Division and the formerly neglected subsidiaries was to recruit bright young academics with a background in computers for key managerial positions. Traditional executives were not happy with this decision, preferring to hire people from apprenticeships or trade schools as the company had always done. But management continued this policy, convinced that the Direct Sales Division was providing a good preparation for other functions (marketing, subsidiaries, . . .) and was an ideal place to train newcomers and prepare them for playing key roles within the company.

All the executives of the Direct Sales Division were visited personally by the Group Marketing Director and asked to practice the new company strategy and structure. George Helmer, as Area Sales Manager of Europe, held a key position with regard to the function's responsibilities and tasks, e.g.:

- Organization of the department
- Planning
- Leadership and motivation of his team
- Preparation of sales budget
- Analysis of market potential

George, who had not been used to having so many different new tasks and responsibilities, felt a bit overloaded and bewildered. The sales planning and budget, which would have to be established on a much longer term, had to be submitted to Production, Marketing and Accounting before any action could take place. He had always found it easier just to do the work himself. He could not adjust to the new management approach which implied the staff's active participation in decision-making. "Motivation, delegation, entrepreneurship, communication," . . . were only buzzwords to him. He considered the old system to be most efficient, i.e., the manager makes the decisions and his subordinates implement them, and he felt it should so remain.

He had difficulty accepting the new marketing orientation. "My role has always been to sell products to the clients," he said, "clients are not markets. Markets do not concern salespeople. We have always done it well without market researchers, marketing analysis and the like. I don't see why the company tries to modify something that works well! Those sophisticated complications are not necessary."

Moreover, George Helmer now had highly qualified colleagues; they were bright, young and dynamic. He and they did not share many similar interests. Their language, attitudes and views of the work were also different from his. He did not really understand them and felt somewhat threatened by them. Almost immediately, the old executives and staff members in the department formed a sort of "club." Among this group, George was nearly the only one to believe that it was possible to collaborate with the new generation. Confident in his powers of persuasion, he intended to get on well with them, win their trust, and then give them his views on sales.

George had fairly positive results, until it came to discussing details. George was still describing his sales technique, his team, his department and its previous performances, whereas his young colleagues were talking about new approaches to sales, new computer technologies and software, market potentials, the Group's evolution and growth projections for the company.

While the newcomers were trying to carry George along with them in this new business world, his old colleagues were pulling him back to them. "You see!" they were telling him, "we don't share the views of these new recruits. They are nothing like the colleagues we had before. These young people are ambitious. They want to know about everything, to contribute and be involved in everything, even in business management issues and decisions. Our old colleagues were excellent salespeople, because sales were their only objective and preoccupation. We feel sure that they will soon be wanting us and the old system back, simply because the one important thing those technocrats don't have is experience! We are the ones who know what sales are about."

Figure 12–14 **Luxor S.A. Group Marketing Division Organization Chart (1987)**

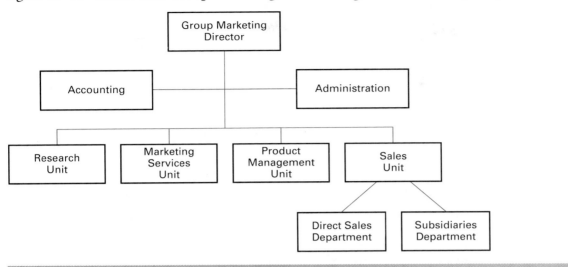

George, who did not want any conflict, decided to keep quiet, do his work and wait. He had always found that to be the best way to avoid making a blunder and running into trouble. One thing he was discovering was that the skills he had used as a salesman did not help him face his new responsibilities and he did not know how to cope with them.

George's passive behavior soon irritated his young subordinates and new colleagues; they reproached him for not being a decision-maker. The more they tried to carry him along, the more George withdrew inside himself. The atmosphere was becoming heavy, and tensions increased. George was losing all credibility among his subordinates, who began to go directly to the Department Director, Mr. Johnson, each time there was an important issue to be discussed. "There's no use going to see Mr. Helmer," one of his young colleagues reported, "he won't make a decision. We don't receive any support from him."

Even his old colleagues and friends no longer came to tease him or ask for his personal advice as they used to do. George was feeling more and more isolated from the others.

ADAPTING OR REGRESSING

In October 1987, Mr. Johnson, the Division Director, invited George to his office to discuss his performance as a manager. He wondered why George was being so inactive; he was expecting George, as Area Sales Manager, to present proposals and decisions to change the atmosphere in his department. George said that he was reflecting on the problem and was trying to find a solution that would satisfy everybody.

So Mr. Johnson waited a few more weeks. When those decisions were still not received and George did not seem to be making any moves, Mr. Johnson began systematically discussing the business issues directly with the Regional and Country Sales Managers.

George felt rejected both by the hierarchy and by his subordinates. He was suffering but did not know how to handle it. He applied himself to keeping a friendly contact with his subordinates. Each time they came to present an idea or a decision, he showed interest in their work, encouraged them and told them he trusted their decisions. But deep inside, he was frustrated that the new colleagues were being given more importance than he was, and that he had lost his power and authority with his people. He felt that he deserved better after so many years of good and faithful service to the company.

The Country Sales Manager commented, "Although Mr. Helmer formally accepted the new organization, I think he is still refusing it, perhaps unconsciously, by behaving passively. He avoids meeting people and talking to anyone in the department, unless he is obliged to."

A few months later, George was still in a state of depression and began to "regress," as one of his colleagues put it. "Mr. Helmer is constantly talking about his 'glorious past,' one of his subordinates reported, "he minimizes our capacities and criticizes the new marketing structure. He keeps giving us the details of his sales performance 10 years ago, telling us that his former colleagues were real sales experts, that we are inexperienced and still have to learn the job and prove ourselves as he did. As to the new marketing structure, he sees it as an obstacle, a useless burden on the system. For him, the client will always remain king, and he believes that all the other company departments should take their lead from and depend on the sales." In his work, George became inefficient, a matter of concern for his superiors. The Direct Sales Department needed efficiently performing people, especially in key managerial positions.

George's attitude towards the younger people and his glorification of the past were creating more and more tensions in the department. Some people could no longer tolerate it and either asked for a transfer or left the company. Rapid turnover among the administrative staff caused numerous administrative mistakes. George Helmer was unable to control what was happening in his department, so he retreated more and more into his ivory tower.

The situation had become so critical that management, concerned with the poor performance of this key department, again tried to discuss the matter with George and help him overcome his problems. Once again, the new structure and strategy and his own key managerial role in the new system were explained to him. George replied calmly, "I don't have any serious objections to the new marketing-oriented structure, but I want to see concrete evidence that it is really necessary, and that the business has improved since it was established."

In February 1988, Mr. Johnson proposed to transfer a Country Sales Manager from another regional department to help George with his job. George agreed to this idea.

Three months later, with the same problem still not solved, Mr. Johnson arranged a meeting with the Personnel Director, the Group Marketing Director and some other colleagues.

After his opening remark, Mr. Johnson stated, "I think you all know the situation; my first question is, 'What do we do about Mr. Helmer?' But, before you react to that question, I want to bring another matter of concern to your attention which is at least as important, if not more, than the first issue."

He then went on, "This is not the first time we have experienced such problems with our staff, and it is probably not the last case. There are other 'Helmers' around. What do we do about them? How can we solve this problem now? George's case is an important issue, but I believe that we should also consider the general problem of adapting to new functions and environments in the future. Keep in mind that the present sales representatives and managers could go through the same problems in 10 or 15 years from now. Things change rapidly in today's business world. The people who fit perfectly in the present environment and in their present functions will not necessarily fit in other future cir-

cumstances. If we do not design a program to prepare and help people progressively handle organization and market changes, we will inevitably experience other leadership shocks and conflicts. What we need is a management perspective that will help people change and adapt as circumstances demand. How do we do that? Where should we start?"

Step 2: Prepare the case for class discussion.

Step 3: Answer the following questions, individually, in small groups, or with the entire class, as directed by your instructor:

Description
1. Describe the 1975 organization of Luxor S.A.
2. Describe the reorganization of international operations.
3. Classify each organization using (a) base of departmentation, (b) means of coordination, and (c) information-processing capacity.

Diagnosis
4. What contingencies influence the reorganization?
5. What type of structure does each contingency call for?
6. How does this structure fit with the actual reorganization of Luxor S.A.?

Prescription
7. What changes are required now?

Action
8. How effective is the change process?

Step 4: Discussion. In small groups, with the entire class, or in written form, share your answers to the above questions. Then answer the following questions:

1. What symptoms suggest a problem exists at Luxor S.A.?
2. What problems exist in the case?
3. What theories and concepts help explain the problems?
4. How can the problems be corrected?
5. Are the actions likely to be effective?

Case written by Professor Pierre Casse. Copyright © 1988 by IMEDE, Lausanne, Switzerland. The International Institute for Management Development (IMI), resulting from the merger between IMEDE, Lausanne, and IMI, Geneva, acquires and retains all rights. Reproduced by permission.

Activity 12–5   Century Supermarket Redesign

Step 1: Review the organizational structure of the regional operations and sales divisions of Century Supermarket shown in Figure 12–15 (on page 604).

Step 2: Answer the following questions, individually, in small groups, or with the entire class:

Description
1. Describe the organization's structure: its division of labor and coordinating mechanisms.
2. What structural paradigms best describe the organization?

Diagnosis
3. Describe the nature of the following contingencies: (a) goals, (b) strategy, (c) environment, (d) technology, (e) work force, (f) size, and (g) age.
4. How does the organization's structure fit with these contingencies?
5. Is the current design appropriate? effective?

Prescription
6. What changes should be made?

Activity 12–6   Organizational Redesign Problem

Step 1: Choose an organization and become familiar with its structure and operation by reviewing organization documents, interviewing members, and observing operations.

Step 2: Describe the organization's operation.

Step 3: Diagnose the organization's structure. Consider division of labor, coordinating mechanisms, structural par-

adigms, and the contingencies that influence its structure. Evaluate its effectiveness.

Step 4: Prescribe a redesign of the organization based on your analysis in Step 3.

CONCLUDING COMMENTS   Organizational design must first include a systematic diagnosis of the current organizational structure. Next, managers or analysts must identify the nature of the contingencies that affect the structure. They must first specify the nature of the environment along the dimensions of complexity, change, and hostility. Second, they should consider the nature of technology—the extent to which it is regulated and sophisticated. Third, they should examine the nature of organizational goals and strategy. Fourth, they should investigate the nature of the organization's work force, its size, and its age. Finally, the managers or analysts should trace the organization's growth and development, specifying its stage in its life cycle. Based on the nature of these contingencies, managers can improve the odds of having a more effective structure through a more scientific, better informed approach.

The activities of this chapter provided practice in such diagnosis and prescription. They offered the opportunity to evaluate the current structure and redesign the structure of Fergusonchemical Europe, Luxor S.A., the City of Brookside, and Century Supermarket. They offered a chance to design a Words in Sentence Company and to redesign another organization.

Figure 12–15 Organizational Chart for the Regional Operations and Sales Divisions of Century Supermarket

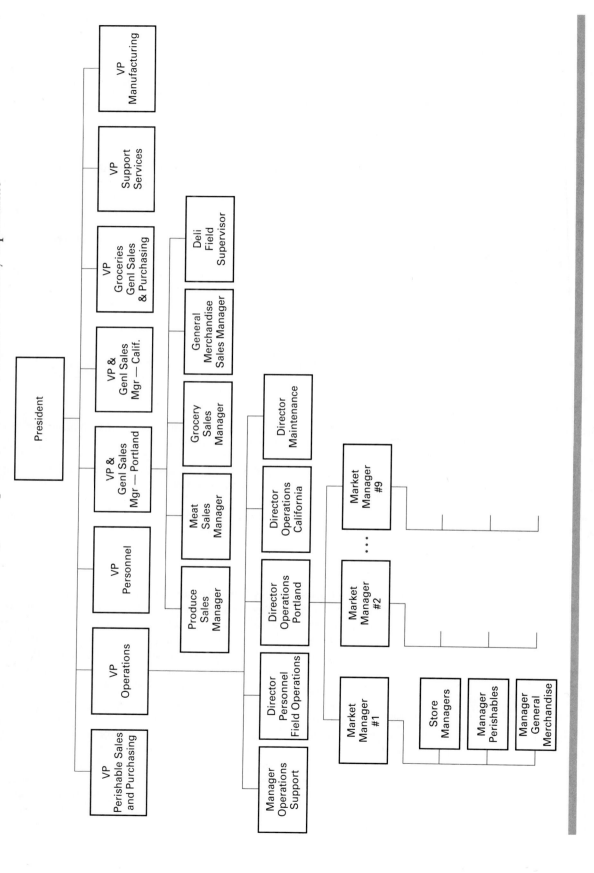

ENDNOTES
[1] Excerpted with permission from "The Recasting of Alcoa," *Business Week,* September 9, 1991, pp. 62, 64. Copyright © 1991 by McGraw-Hill.

[2] H. W. Lane and J. D. DiStefano, *International Management Behavior: From Policy to Practice* (Boston: PWS-Kent, 1992).

[3] H. Crookell, Organization structure for global operations. In P. W. Blanush, J. P. Killing, D. J. Lecraw, and H. Crookell, *International Management: Text and Cases* (Homewood, Ill.: Irwin, 1991).

[4] Lane and DiStefano, *International Management Behavior.*

[5] C. A. Bartlett and S. Ghosal, *Managing across Borders: The Transnational Solution* (Boston: Harvard Business School Press, 1989).

[6] J. B. Levine, IBM Europe starts swinging back, *Business Week* (May 6, 1991): 52–53.

[7] G. Inzerilli and A. Laurent, Managerial views of the organization structure in France and the U.S.A., *International Studies of Management and Organization* 13 (1–2) (1983): 97–118.

[8] See G. G. Dess and D. W. Beard, Objective measurement of organizational environments, *Academy of Management Proceedings* (1982): 345–349; and D. D. Dess and D. W. Beard, Dimensions of organizational task environments, *Administrative Science Quarterly* 29 (1984): 52–73. See also S. M. Shortell, The role of environment in a configurational theory of organizations, *Human Relations* 30 (1977): 275–302; R. B. Duncan, Characteristics of organizational environments and perceived environmental uncertainty, *Administrative Science Quarterly* 17 (1972): 313–327; and H. Mintzberg, *The Structuring of Organizations* (Englewood Cliffs, N.J.: Prentice-Hall, 1979). H. Mintzberg, *Structure in Fives: Designing Effective Organizations* (Englewood Cliffs, N.J.: Prentice-Hall, 1983) specifies five dimensions: complexity, diversity, change, hostility, and uncertainty.

[9] D. A. Depke, The new IBM, *Business Week* (December 16, 1991): 112–118.

[10] P. R. Lawrence and J. W. Lorsch, Differentiation and integration in complex organizations, *Administrative Science Quarterly* 12 (1967): 1–47.

[11] B. W. Keats and M. A. Hitt, A causal model of linkages among environmental dimensions, macro-organizational characteristics, and performance, *Academy of Management Journal* 31 (1988): 570–598.

[12] C. S. Koberg, Resource scarcity, environmental uncertainty, and adaptive organizational behavior, *Academy of Management Journal* 30 (1987): 798–807.

[13] P. R. Lawrence and J. W. Lorsch, New management job: The integrator, *Harvard Business Review* (November-December, 1967).

[14] See the study by M. Yasai-Ardekani, Effects of environmental scarcity and munificence on the relationship of context to organizational structure, *Academy of Management Journal* 32 (1989): 131–156.

[15] R. B. Duncan, Multiple decision-making structures in adapting to environmental uncertainty, *Human Relations* 26 (1973): 273–291; H. R. Johnson, Interactions between individual predispositions, environmental factors, and organizational design. In R. H. Kilmann, L. R. Pondy, and D. P. Slevin, eds., *The Management of Organizational Design,* vol. 2 (New York: North-Holland, 1976), pp. 31–58.

[16] J. R. Montanari, Managerial discretion: An expanded model of organization choices, *Academy of Management Review* 3 (1978): 231–241; W. A. Randolph and G. G. Dess, The congruence perspective of organization design: A conceptual model and multivariate research approach, *Academy of Management Review* 9 (1984): 114–127.

[17] J. Woodward, *Industrial Organizations: Theory and Practice* (London: Oxford University Press, 1965).

[18] J. Thompson, *Organizations in Action* (New York: McGraw-Hill, 1967).

[19] C. Perrow, A framework for comparative analysis of organizations, *American Sociological Review* 32 (April 1967): 196.

[20] Mintzberg, *Structuring of Organizations.*

[21] J. D. Ford and J. W. Slocum, Jr., Size, technology, environment, and the structure of organizations, *Academy of Management Review* 2 (1977): 561–575; L. W. Fry, Technology structure research: Three critical issues, *Academy of Management Journal* 25 (1982): 532–552.

[22] M. Jelinek, Technology, organizations, and contingency, *Academy of Management Review* 2 (1977): 17–26.

[23] J. R. Lincoln, M. Handa, and K. McBride, Organizational structures in Japanese and United States manufacturing, *Administrative Science Quarterly* 31 (1986): 338–364.

[24] M. Liu, H. Denis, H. Kolodny, and B. Stymne, Organization design for technological change. In R. R. Sims, D. D. White, and D. A. Bednar, eds., *Readings in Organizational Behavior* (Boston: Allyn and Bacon, 1992).

[25] R. M. Steers, *Organizational Effectiveness: A Behavioral View* (Santa Monica, Calif.: Goodyear, 1977), p. 21.

[26] R. M. Cyert and J. G. March, *A Behavioral Theory of the Firm* (Englewood Cliffs, N.J.: Prentice-Hall, 1963).

[27] W. R. Scott, *Organizations: Rational, Natural and Open Systems,* 2nd ed. (Englewood Cliffs, N.J.: Prentice-Hall, 1987).

[28] H. Simon, *The New Science of Management Decision* (New York: Harper & Row, 1960).

[29] P. E. Connor, *Organizations: Theory and Design* (Chicago: Science Research Associates, 1980).

[30] R. E. Miles and C. C. Snow, *Organizational Strategy, Structure, and Process* (New York: McGraw-Hill, 1978).

[31] R. E. Miles and C. C. Snow, Organizations: New concepts for new forms, *California Management Review* 28 (Spring 1986): 62–73.

[32] See J. Child, Organizational structure, environment and performance: The role of strategic choice, *Sociology* 6 (1972): 1–22; D. S. Pugh, D. J. Hickson, C. R. Hinings, and C. Turner, The context of organizational structures, *Administrative Science Quarterly* 14 (1969): 91–114.

[33] D. J. Hickson, D. S. Pugh, and D. Pheysey, Operations technology and organization structure: An empirical reappraisal, *Administrative Science Quarterly* 14 (1969): 378–398.

[34] See, for example, D. Lavoie and S. A. Culbert, Stages in organization and development, *Human Relations* 31 (1978): 417–438; I. Adizes, Organizational passages: Diagnosing and treating life cycle problems in organizations, *Organizational Dynamics* (Summer 1979): 3–24; L. Greiner, Evolution and revolution as organizations grow, *Harvard Business Review* (July-August 1972): 37–46.

[35] These steps parallel the four-stage business cycle: startup, growth, maturity, and decline.

[36] A. S. Van de Ven, Early planning, implementation, and performance in organizations. In J. R. Kimberly and R. H. Miles, eds., *The Organizational Life Cycle* (San Francisco: Jossey-Bass, 1980), pp. 83–133.

[37] J. M. Bartunek and B. M. Betters-Reed, The stages of organizational creation, *Journal of Community Psychology* 15(3) (1987): 287–303.

[38] N. C. Churchill and V. L. Lewis, The five stages of small business growth, *Harvard Business Review* (May-June, 1983).

[39] Greiner, Evolution and revolution; Adizes, Organizational passages.

[40] Churchill and Lewis, Five stages.

[41] R. Walton, Establishing and maintaining high commitment work systems. In Kimberly and Miles, *Organizational Life Cycle,* pp. 208–291.

[42] J. R. Kimberly and R. E. Quinn, *Managing Organizational Transitions* (Homewood, Ill.: Irwin, 1984), p. 15.

[43] D. Miller and P. Friesen, Archetypes of organizational transition, *Administrative Science Quarterly* 25 (1980): 269–299; D. Miller and P. Friesen, The longitudinal analysis of organizations: A methodological perspective, *Management Science* 28 (1982): 1013–1034; E. H. Schein, The role of the founder in creating organizational culture, *Organizational Dynamics* 12 (1983): 1–12.

[44] Churchill and Lewis, Five stages.

[45] *Ibid.*

[46] See D. A. Whetten, Sources, responses, and effects of organizational decline. In Kimberly and Miles, *Organizational Life Cycle,* pp. 342–372.

[47] B. Gray and S. S. Ariss, Politics and strategic change across organizational life cycles, *Academy of Management Review* 10 (1985): 707–723.

[48] K. G. Smith, T. R. Mitchell, and C. E. Summer, Top-level management priorities in different stages of the organization's life cycle, *Academy of Management Journal* 29 (1985): 799–820.

[49] W. Weitzel and E. Johnson, Decline in organizations: A literature integration and extension, *Administrative Science Quarterly* 34 (1989): 91–109.

[50] *Ibid.*

[51] S. P. Robbins, *Organization Theory: Structure, Design, and Applications,* 2nd ed. (Englewood Cliffs, N.J.: Prentice-Hall, 1987).

[52] R. I. Sutton, The process of organizational death: Disbanding and reconnecting, *Administrative Science Quarterly* 32 (1987): 542–569.

[53] R. E. Reidenbach and D. P. Robin, A conceptual model of corporate moral development, *Journal of Business Ethics* 10 (1991): 273–284.

[54] See R. K. Kazanjian, Relation of dominant problems to stages of growth in technology-based new ventures, *Academy of Management Journal* 31 (1988): 257–279.

RECOMMENDED READINGS

Bartlett, C. A., and Ghosal, S. *Managing across Borders: The Transnational Solution*. Boston: Harvard Business School Press, 1989.

Hinings, C. R., and Greenwood, R. *The Dynamics of Strategic Change*. New York: Basil Blackwell, 1989.

Pasmore, W. A. *Designing Effective Organizations: The Sociotechnical Systems Perspective*. New York: Wiley, 1988.

Prahalad, C. K., and Doz, Y. L. *The Multinational Mission: Balancing Local Demands and Global Vision*. New York: Free Press, 1987.

Rock, M. L., and Rock, R. H., eds. *Corporate Restructuring: A Guide to Creating the Premium Valued Company*. New York: McGraw-Hill, 1990.

Singh, J. V., ed. *Organizational Evolution: New Directions*. Newbury Park, Calif.: Sage, 1990.

Chapter Outline

Managing Technology and Redesigning Work

Learning Objectives

After completing the reading and activities in Chapter 13, students will be able to

1. Discuss the issues associated with technology in the workplace.

2. Discuss the process of innovation and its relationship to technology in the workplace.

3. Offer strategies for increasing innovation in organizations.

4. Discuss the impact of automation and computerization on work design.

5. Compare and contrast early approaches to work design.

6. Redesign a job using work enrichment.

7. Describe the use of autonomous and self-managing work groups.

8. Cite the options for alternative work arrangements.

9. Discuss the purpose and effectiveness of quality of working life programs and provide examples of them in organizations.

10. Discuss work design outside the United States.

11. Offer a prescription for improving the management of technology and the design of work in given situations.

Work Design and Technology at A.B. Scale Company

The A.B. Scale Company was founded approximately fifteen years ago as a manufacturer of digital scales for industrial use. The company quickly became a leader in the development and introduction of new technology in the industry. Recently, Alan Grant, its president and founder, has been struggling with ways to improve the company's productivity. Attempts to expand the product line of scales and to diversify the business into the distribution of computers and software have been marginally successful. Every time Alan and his technical development staff have created an improvement in the scale technology, the company has experienced great difficulty in translating the idea into success on the shop floor. One improvement resulted in the production employees spending most of their days doing tedious assembly jobs, and caused a significant decline in worker satisfaction and performance. Another improvement included the replacement of some workers with robots. This change also failed to produce a sufficient impact on performance because the plant managers did not know how to manage the increased automation on the shop floor.

Alan has noted that the office staff has successfully automated many of the accounting, order taking, and other clerical functions. He wonders if there are lessons that can be taken from this success and translated to the shop floor. He is also concerned that as the company has grown, the control he once exerted over the quality of the product is being lost. Customer complaints about faulty products have increased markedly over the past two years. Alan feels that his success in the long run will depend on his ability to manage the introduction of new technology in his own workplace as well as at his customers' locations.

How effective is the A.B. Scale Company in managing the development and introduction of new technology? How should the work be designed to create and use technology most effectively? What action should management take to increase worker performance, decrease absenteeism and turnover, and encourage worker and customer satisfaction? How can Alan Grant ensure that his work force is producing a high-quality product as efficiently and effectively as possible?

Technological advances in automation and computerization are dramatically changing the workplace. In the automobile and other manufacturing industries robotics has permeated the production process. Computer-integrated manufacturing (CIM) and computer-aided design and computer-aided manufacturing (CAD/CAM) have computerized production by automating specific operations and tying them together into large systems.[1] The introduction of information technology has revolutionized financial, educational, and other service industries. These changes have motivated efforts in redesigning work, that is, altering the content or context of a job by altering the job's activities, adjusting the interaction between jobs and their holders, changing the conditions of work, modifying the nature and extent of supervisory relations, or changing the scope of individual responsibility.

In this chapter we first consider the issues associated with technology in the workplace. Then we consider the nature of the innovation process and the challenge of ensuring quality on the job. Next we examine diverse ways of designing work in a variety of organizational settings. We suggest work design as a way of dealing with new technologies, as well as motivating individual workers to produce.

TECHNOLOGY IN THE WORKPLACE

First, consider the introduction of computers into the business functions of a university. Whereas various clerks once sent tuition bills, entered payments, credited loans received, and determined an individual's financial status, now integrated software packages allow immediate viewing and updating of any part of a student's financial or academic record. Second, consider the manufacturing of chocolate candy bars. Originally, the process was manually performed and mechanically paced, with workers directly controlling the melting, molding, and wrapping processes. Automating the line and replacing workers with "intelligent" computers significantly streamlined the manufacturing process and increased productivity. Finally, consider the more complicated process of designing and manufacturing circuit boards for computers. How would computer-aided design and manufacturing affect their production? What role would CIM or CAD/CAM play at the A.B. Scale plant? How should the technology used in the design, manufacturing, and support areas be managed? How should the work be designed to respond to such automation?

Managing technology "concerns the process of managing technology development, implementation, and diffusion in industrial and governmental organizations. In addition to managing the innovation process through R&D, it includes managing the introduction and use of technology in products, in manufacturing processes, and in other corporate functions."[2] As effective managers of technology, executives need to integrate technology into the organization's strategic objectives; expedite the use, assessment, transfer, and relinquishing of new technologies; reduce product development time; and manage large, complex technological systems, the organization's use of technology, and technical personnel.[3]

Recent research at MIT about the impact of information technology (IT) suggested that

- IT is enabling fundamental changes in the way work is done; for example, robotics has changed physical production, data processing computers have altered clerical tasks, and CAD/CAM tools have affected new product design.
- IT is enabling the integration of business functions at all levels within and between organizations; for example, just-in-time inventory control places goods where and when they are needed.
- IT is causing shifts in the competitive climate in many industries.
- IT presents new strategic opportunities for organizations that reassess their missions and operations; automation can reduce labor costs, provide additional information for competing, and help transform organizations to more effectively face a turbulent environment.
- Successful application of IT will require changes in management and organizational structures.
- A major challenge for management will be to lead their organizations through the transformation necessary to prosper in a globally competitive environment.[4]

Managers must learn how to harness the power of computers and other new technologies to improve performance. Alan Grant of A.B. Scale Company must seek ways to introduce new, effective technology into the manufacturing and support processes of his firm as a way of ensuring worker performance and product quality. Developing and implementing strategies for managing the technology should then receive a high priority. Executives can also use technology strategically to enhance decision making, improve their sales and marketing capability, and foster adaptability to change.[5] Information technology, for example, can change individual jobs, streamline organizational structures, and provide a competitive advantage. At the same time, organizational leaders must find new ways to manage workers using new technologies. The redesign of jobs, described later in this chapter, is a major response to the new demands placed on workers and organizations.

INNOVATION IN THE WORKPLACE

The management of technology is frequently associated with innovation in organizations. International competition has forced U.S. industry to adopt and implement innovations in the workplace, particularly in updating manufacturing technology. Organizations can use or invent innovation; they can serve as a vehicle for innovation; or organizations themselves, such as business-education collaboratives, can be innovative combinations.[6]

The Innovation Process

How does innovation occur? Figure 13–1 shows that it begins with the recognition that a demand exists for the new product or process, along with the recognition that it is technically feasible. Next the basic idea is formulated, integrating the technical

Figure 13–1 **The Innovation Process**

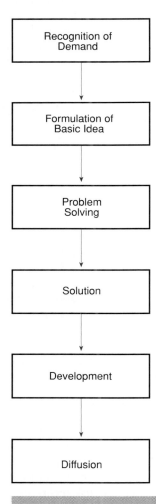

Recognition of Demand

Formulation of Basic Idea

Problem Solving

Solution

Development

Diffusion

SOURCE: Based on D. G. Marquis, The anatomy of successful innovations (November 1969), *Managing Advanced Technology* 1 (1972): 35–48.

and market issues into a design concept. The problem-solving stage follows; here the design is elaborated; resource and technical problems are addressed. False starts may consume time at this stage.[7] A solution, often an invention, moves the design into the prototype of a new product or process. In the development stage, the innovator faces and attempts to solve problems associated with production. Finally, the solution is used and diffused in the workplace.[8] Figure 13–2 complements these steps with a model of the sources of ideas. More recent thinking poses a concurrent interaction model of innovation, as shown in Figure 13–3.[9]

Figure 13–4 offers a compatible view of a technical innovation project. The process, as represented here, has six stages: preproject, project possibilities, project initiation, project execution, project outcome evaluation, and project transfer.[10] Moving through these steps involves idea generation and championing, project leadership, gatekeeping, and coaching, as described in Table 13–1. Building flexibility into work through sociotechnical redesign or flexible arrangements can facilitate the performance of these functions. An organization's ability to innovate also depends on both business unit and corporate resource availability, executive understanding of the technological environment, competitors' innovative strategies, and industry

Figure 13–2 **Flow Model of the Sources of Ideas**

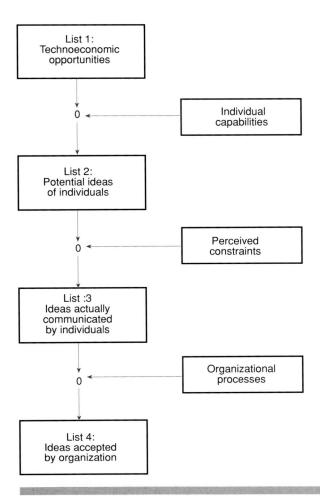

Figure 13–3 **A Concurrent Model of Technological Innovation**

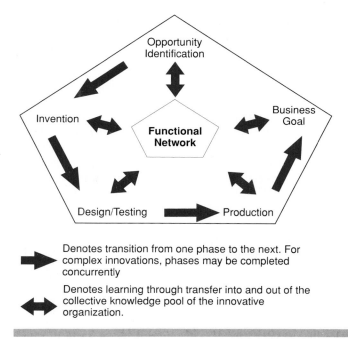

Denotes transition from one phase to the next. For complex innovations, phases may be completed concurrently

Denotes learning through transfer into and out of the collective knowledge pool of the innovative organization.

evolution, as well as the business unit's strategic management capacity and its structural and cultural context.[11] Figure 13–5 offers a format for an audit of these capabilities at the corporate level.

Three major patterns of work on new products and processes are possible. First, they may be centralized into a single R&D facility. Second, they may be decentralized into different units or operating divisions. Third, a combination of corporate and divisional labs or other sites for product development may exist.[12] Figure 13–6 lists some issues that would influence the location and extent of technology development. The general management of the organization or division plays a significant role in developing new technology. So do R&D specialists, sometimes under the leadership of the chief technical officer or chief information officer. Organizations must also have individuals who champion new technology because organizational members and leaders may differ significantly in their commitment to new work products and processes. Reading 13–1, "Innovation Processes in Multinational Corporations," discusses similar issues for organizations operating globally.

The managerial challenges of dealing with innovation can be significant. Managers and employees must adopt a mind-set that encourages the development and presentation of new ideas. They also must willingly expend resources for innovative activities. One study of 51 manufacturing plants showed that general managers and division managers with manufacturing experience were more likely to initiate innovative policy and programs.[13] For example, they were more likely to try out new methods, recruit the best qualified technical workers, emphasize technological forecasting, and tell customers how the organization's modernization would benefit them. The 3M Company, for example, encourages managers to become idea champions, where they push innovations through the organization's hierarchy.[14] The design of work at 3M must facilitate such innovation. Organic forms of organizational design

Figure 13–4 **A Multistage View of a Technical Innovation Project**

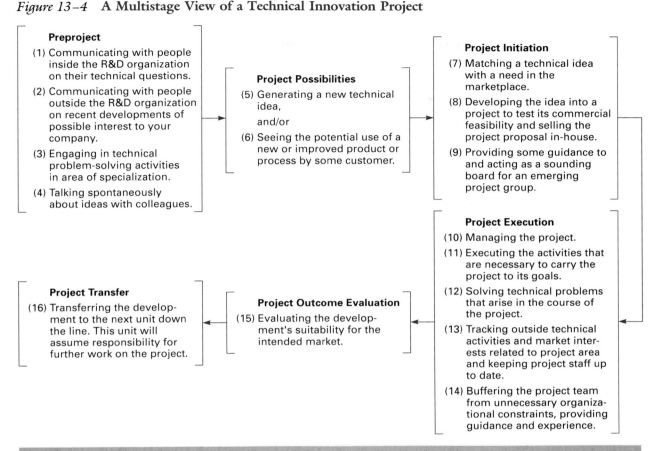

Preproject

(1) Communicating with people inside the R&D organization on their technical questions.

(2) Communicating with people outside the R&D organization on recent developments of possible interest to your company.

(3) Engaging in technical problem-solving activities in area of specialization.

(4) Talking spontaneously about ideas with colleagues.

Project Possibilities

(5) Generating a new technical idea,

and/or

(6) Seeing the potential use of a new or improved product or process by some customer.

Project Initiation

(7) Matching a technical idea with a need in the marketplace.

(8) Developing the idea into a project to test its commercial feasibility and selling the project proposal in-house.

(9) Providing some guidance to and acting as a sounding board for an emerging project group.

Project Execution

(10) Managing the project.

(11) Executing the activities that are necessary to carry the project to its goals.

(12) Solving technical problems that arise in the course of the project.

(13) Tracking outside technical activities and market interests related to project area and keeping project staff up to date.

(14) Buffering the project team from unnecessary organizational constraints, providing guidance and experience.

Project Transfer

(16) Transferring the development to the next unit down the line. This unit will assume responsibility for further work on the project.

Project Outcome Evaluation

(15) Evaluating the development's suitability for the intended market.

SOURCE: Reprinted from Staffing the innovative technology-based organization, by E. B. Roberts and A. R. Fusfeld, *Sloan Management Review,* Spring 1981, pp. 19–34, by permission of the publisher. Copyright © 1981 by the Sloan Management Review Association. All rights reserved.

(see Chapter 11) also aid the innovation process. Collaboration, both among organizational members and through the development of strategic alliances, facilitates innovation.[15]

THE CHALLENGE OF QUALITY

"Quality profitably, promptly and consistently provides the customer with the goods and/or services that meet his/her needs."[16] The concern for quality has its roots in U.S. management principles that were imported into Japan and then well integrated into Japanese management.[17] The International Quality Study reported that today 39 percent of Japanese businesses in the automobile, banking, and computer industries, compared with 16 percent of U.S. businesses, indicated that 75 percent or more of their employees regularly participated in meetings about quality.[18] Often known as *total quality management* (TQM), efforts at continuous organizational, product, and service improvement take a systemwide focus that includes not only the organization but also its customers and suppliers. This approach includes process and product control, as well as attempts to empower the workers with the responsibility and authority for attaining the desired outcomes. Getting and using customer

Table 13-1   Critical Functions in the Innovation Process

Critical Function	Personal Characteristics	Organizational Activities
Idea Generating	Expert in one or two fields. Enjoys conceptualization; comfortable with abstractions. Enjoys doing innovative work. Usually is an individual contributor. Often will work alone.	Generates new ideas and tests their feasibility. Good at problem solving. Sees new and different ways of doing things. Searches for the breakthroughs.
Entrepreneuring or Championing	Strong application interests. Possesses a wide range of interests. Less propensity to contribute to the basic knowledge of a field. Energetic and determined; puts self on the line.	Sells new ideas to others in the organization. Gets resources. Aggressive in championing his or her "cause." Takes risks.
Project Leading	Focus for decision making, information, and questions. Sensitive to the needs of others. Recognizes how to use the organizational structure to get things done. Interested in a broad range of disciplines and in how they fit together (e.g., marketing, finance).	Provides the team leadership and motivation. Plans and organizes the project. Insures that administrative requirements are met. Provides necessary coordination among team members. Sees that the project moves forward effectively. Balances the project goals with organizational needs.
Gatekeeping	Possesses a high level of technical competence. Is approachable and personable. Enjoys the face-to-face contact of helping others.	Keeps informed of related developments that occur outside the organization through journals, conferences, colleagues, other companies. Passes information on to others; finds it easy to talk to colleagues. Serves as an information resource for others in the organization (i.e., authority on who to see or on what has been done). Provides informal coordination among personnel.
Sponsoring or Coaching	Possesses experience in developing new ideas. Is a good listener and helper. Can be relatively objective. Often is a more senior person who knows the organizational ropes.	Helps develop people's talents. Provides encouragement, guidance, and acts as a sounding board for the project leader and others. Provides access to a power base within the organization—a senior person. Buffers the project team from unnecessary organizational constraints. Helps the project team to get what it needs from the other parts of the organization. Provides legitimacy and organizational confidence in the project.

SOURCE: Reprinted from Staffing the innovative technology-based organization, by E. B. Roberts and A. R. Fusfeld, *Sloan Management Review,* Spring 1981, pp. 19–34, by permission of the publisher. Copyright © 1981 by the Sloan Management Review Association. All rights reserved.

Figure 13–5 **Innovative Capabilities Audit Framework at Corporate Level**

1. *Resource Availability and Allocation*
   Corporate R&D funding level and evolution:
   In absolute terms.
   As percentage of sales.
   As compared to average of main competitors.
   As compared to leading competitor.
   Breadth and depth of skills of corporate level personnel in R&D, engineering, market research.
   Distinctive competences in areas of technology relevant to multiple business units.
   Corporate R&D allocation to:
   Exploratory research.
   R&D in support of mainstream business.
   R&D in support of new business definition.
   R&D in support of new business development.

2. *Understanding Competitors' Innovative Strategies and Multi-industry Evolution*
   Intelligence systems and data available.
   Capacity to identify, analyze, and predict competitors' innovative strategies spanning multiple industries.
   Capacity to develop scenarios concerning evolution of interdependencies between multiple industries.
   Capacity to anticipate facilitating/impeding external forces relevant to firm's innovative strategies.

3. *Understanding the Corporate Technological Environment*
   Capacity for technological forecasting in multiple areas.
   Capacity to forecast cross-impacts between areas of technology.
   Capacity to assess technologies in multiple areas.
   Capacity to identify technological opportunities spanning multiple areas.

4. *Corporate Context (Structural and Cultural)*
   Mechanisms to share technologies across business unit boundaries.
   Mechanisms to define new business opportunities across business unit boundaries.
   Internal and external organization designs for managing new ventures.
   Mechanisms to fund unplanned initiatives.
   Evaluation and reward systems for entrepreneurial behavior.
   Movement of personnel between mainstream activities and new ventures.
   Dominant values, corporate mythology, definition of "success."

5. *Strategic Management Capacity to Deal with Entrepreneurial Behavior*
   Top management capacity to define a substantive long-term corporate development strategy.
   Top management capacity to assess strategic importance of entrepreneurial initiatives.
   Top management capacity to assess relatedness of entrepreneurial initiatives to the firm's core capabilities.
   Middle-level management capacity to work with top management to obtain/maintain support for new initiatives (organizational championing).
   Middle-level management capacity to define corporate strategic framework for new initiatives.
   Middle-level management capacity to coach new venture managers.
   New venture managers' capacity to build new organizational capabilities.
   New venture managers' capacity to develop a business strategy for new initiatives.
   Availability of product champions to identify and define new business opportunities outside of mainstream activities.

SOURCE: Reprinted with permission from R. A. Burgelman, T. J. Kosnik, and M. Van den Poel, Toward an innovative capabilities audit framework. In R. A. Burgelman and M. A. Maidique, *Strategic Management of Technology and Innovation* (Homewood, Ill.: Irwin, 1988), p. 111.

Figure 13–6 **Some Issues in Corporate-Divisional R&D Relations**

1. Relative power of corporate versus divisional executives.
2. General divisional reaction against staff overhead and interference.
3. Growth of strategic planning activity in the firm.
4. Lack of R&D inputs into corporate strategy and market planning.
5. High diversification of company product lines, technologies, and markets.
6. Increasing questions about the relevance of corporate R&D.
7. Focus on short-term cost savings for R&D should give corporate R&D a role in long-term R&D, but that is being downplayed.
8. Corporate R&D budgets are generally not growing because they are part of the discretionary budget without powerful constituency.
9. As divisional labs grow stronger, they do not perceive need for corporate lab.
10. Is the vice president of R&D really the chief technical officer of the firm, that is, part of the inner circle of corporate policymakers and decisionmakers?
11. The time lags in getting corporate R&D started and in producing results.
12. The sources and uses of R&D funds in the corporation.
13. Most corporate labs have no mechanisms for going beyond lab scale or semiworks scale of production.
14. Who "owns" the pilot plants and/or access to full-scale production facilities for testing?

SOURCE: From A. Rubenstein, *Managing Technology in the Decentralized Firm* (New York: Wiley, 1989), p. 40. Copyright © 1989 by John Wiley & Sons, Inc. Reprinted by permission.

feedback, assuring vendor and supplier quality, using statistical process control, and designing experiments in quality improvement accompany the changing role of employees.[19]

E. I. Du Pont instituted a TQM effort in response to a survey that suggested that failure costs approximated $400 million annually.[20] The effort required three steps. First, the company provided leadership for process improvements. Second, it offered training in improvement methods. This training included increasing the customer focus; upgrading all networks of interactions between customers, internal Du Pont departments, and suppliers; broadening worker involvement; and upgrading the quality of employee thinking. Third, Du Pont executed projects for continuous improvement that included training sales personnel about how to secure better information from customers and conducting periodic customer services.

Boeing implemented a continuous quality improvement process whose goals were to increase communication, encourage teamwork, and solve quality and productivity problems.[21] Managers and other workers began to collaborate better as a result of increased education about the program, the development and implementation of special training courses, the introduction of a steering council for quality improvement in each division of Boeing, careful team selection, and focus on problem identification and solution.

Quality can be either a top-down or bottom-up effort. For example, workers at General Motors' Saturn plant conducted a work slowdown to protest management's attempt to increase output at the expense of quality.[22]

The Malcolm Baldrige National Quality Award recognizes American manufacturing and service companies that successfully provide high-quality services and products to their customers. The organization is judged on the categories of leadership, information and analysis, strategic quality planning, human resources, quality-assurance products and services, quality results, and customer satisfaction.[23] Table 13–2 lists sample questions in each area from the Self-assessment Questionnaire.

Table 13–2 **Sample Questions from the Malcolm Baldrige National Quality Award Self-assessment Questionnaire**

Leadership

Have all of the executives in your organization received adequate training on quality concepts and tools?

Are all of the executives visibly involved in the development of an effective quality culture?

Information and Analysis

Does the organization collect quantifiable data on all important dimensions of quality of the products and services that are produced?

Are quality data collected and reported on in all functions and departments in the organization, including support functions such as accounting, marketing, et cetera?

Strategic Quality Planning

Does your company collect thorough and appropriate quality-related competitive comparison data and use world-class benchmarks to develop plans?

Are employees, customers, and suppliers involved in the planning process?

Human Resource Utilization

Do you have a corporate plan for the utilization of employees in relation to the quality improvement process?

Does your organization have a structured curriculum for training all levels of employees in quality improvement concepts and tools?

Quality Assurance of Products and Services

Does your organization use a systematic process such as Quality Function Deployment to define customer requirements and expectations?

Is there an auditing process that is used to periodically evaluate the effectiveness of the quality management system?

Quality Results

Is your organization among the top 20 percent in customer satisfaction with your products and services?

Are the data on your level of customer satisfaction collected in a thorough and objective manner?

Customer Satisfaction

Has the trend in customer satisfaction data over the last three years been improving for your organization?

Does your organization have an effective process for handling customer service and complaints?

SOURCE: Reprinted with permission from the Association for Quality and Participation: M. G. Brown, How to determine your quality quotient, *Journal for Quality and Participation* (June 1990): 76–80.

Organizational leaders must define quality, take a customer orientation, focus on the work process, build customer/supplier partnerships, emphasize prevention and an error-free attitude, manage by facts, encourage employee participation and total involvement in quality, and take a continuous improvement focus.[24] Figure 13–7 lists a set of behaviors that should expedite the development of quality, and Figure 13–8 diagrams a set of implementation stages.

Alan Grant might consider implementing a total quality program at A.B. Scale. It should address the problems with faulty products and customer complaints; it should also empower the workers in ways that would reduce their boredom and increase their satisfaction and performance. Still, the costs of such a program are great and must be carefully controlled. Quality is not cheap. The implementation of

Figure 13–7 **Fourteen Steps toward a Quality Goal**

1. Continually improve products and services in order to further the firm's competitive position.
2. Adopt the new philosophy; don't accept delays and mistakes.
3. Don't rely on mass inspection to detect defects; use statistical controls to assure that quality is built into the product.
4. Discontinue the practice of selecting suppliers based on price; reduce the supply base and establish long-term, trusting, single-source partnerships where both buyer and seller can pursue quality improvements.
5. Find problems—whether caused by faulty systems or by production workers—and correct them.
6. Use modern methods of on-the-job training.
7. Improve and modernize methods of supervision.
8. Drive out fear, so that everyone can work productively for the firm.
9. Open up communications between departments.
10. Stop using numerical goals, posters, and slogans as a way to motivate workers without giving them the methods to achieve these goals.
11. Don't depend on work standards that assign numerical quotas.
12. Remove barriers that deprive employees of their pride of workmanship.
13. Establish a dynamic program of education and training.
14. Create an executive management structure that will emphasize the preceding 13 points each day.

SOURCE: Based on H. S. Gitlow and S. J. Gitlow, *The Deming Guide to Quality and Competitive Position* (Englewood Cliffs, N.J.: Prentice-Hall, 1987); K. W. Wilson, 5 Factors in the "quality issue," *Purchasing* (November 5, 1987): 47–48.

total quality typically involves training of managers and employees at all levels, extensive employee time devoted to meeting about and discussing quality improvements, and sometimes costly redesign of work processes.

EARLY WORK REDESIGN APPROACHES

The redesign of work may be a key component of the management of technology and quality improvement efforts. Appropriate work design helps incorporate technical advances into the organization in a way that results in higher worker performance. It helps reinforce the benefits of particular organizational designs by emphasizing or deemphasizing job specialization, introducing new ways of coordinating work, and modifying the chain of command within job sequences. Work redesign can increase worker satisfaction and affect both intrinsic and extrinsic motivation. Inappropriate work design causes workers to complain that their jobs are boring and do not require them to use their skills and knowledge, or, alternatively, that their jobs are too complex and demanding. Productivity may lag, quality may decrease, or schedules may slip. Numerous options for work redesign exist. The earliest focused on changing the horizontal dimension of jobs, that is, the numbers and types of tasks a worker did: Work simplification reduced task performance, and job enlargement increased it.

Work Simplification

How would you characterize the jobs of traditional assembly line workers or employees in a fast-food restaurant? *Work simplification,* which describes these jobs, emphasizes the reduction of a job to its component parts and then a reassembly of these parts into an optimally efficient work process. Table 13–3 lists the six most common features of this type of work redesign. In the manufacturing of lacquer bookcases and storage units, the manufacturing process might be divided into many

Figure 13-8 **Implementing Total Quality**

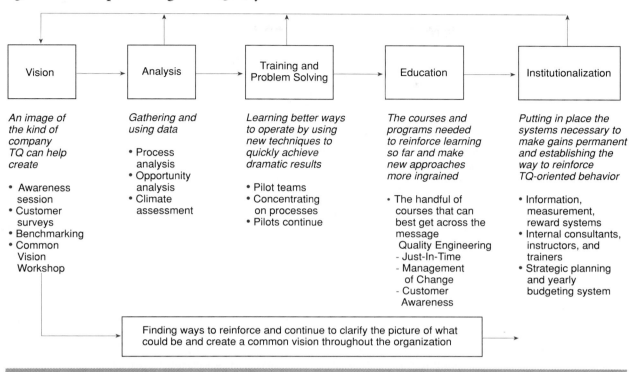

SOURCE: From Dan Ciampa, *Total Quality: A User's Guide to Implementation* (Reading, Mass.: Addison-Wesley, 1992), p. 107. Copyright © 1992 by Addison-Wesley Publishing Company. Reprinted with permission of the publisher.

discrete tasks, each performed by a separate individual. One worker might always cut the backs of the bookcases; another might insert the shelf pegs into the frames; still another might attach the doors for the storage units.

Industrial engineers study the exact series of motions in a job, using detailed observation records and drawing extensive diagrams of the work process. Next, they monitor the time required for each part of the job. Then they identify and attempt to eliminate all false, slow, and useless movements. Finally, they redesign the job by collecting into one series the quickest and best movements. To accomplish the last step, work simplification typically involves a high use of machines, optimum spacing of rest periods, high specialization of work activities, and matching of workers to

Table 13-3 **Characteristics of Work Simplification**

1. Mechanical pacing, or the use of an automated assembly line.
2. Repetitive work.
3. Concentration on a fraction of the product.
4. Specification of the tools and techniques used in production.
5. Limited social interaction among workers.
6. Minimal training.

SOURCE: The description of work simplification is based, in part, on F. W. Taylor's prescriptions in *The Principles of Scientific Management* (New York: Harper, 1911).

jobs best suited to their abilities, experience, and aptitudes. Engineers must design any equipment to fit the mental and physical characteristics of the operators.[25]

Jobs that have become overly complex typically benefit from work simplification. So do jobs that require a precise design of tasks and their interrelationships to increase productivity. Work simplification can also create significant dysfunctions. Workers may become bored or have limited opportunities for individual growth. Top management may automate and mechanize production for its own sake rather than for improving worker performance. An effective work simplification redesign must find ways of ensuring that the process operates smoothly and cost-effectively. Management must find ways of efficiently moving and repositioning items between operations, assembling separate tasks into a more efficient total process, balancing the line to reduce downtime in less time-consuming tasks and encourage effective work pacing, and providing sufficient external supervision.[26]

Should A.B. Scale use work simplification? Jobs that require limited amounts of information processing and decision making by workers and whose workers have low social and growth needs are candidates for work simplification.[27] The increasing number of better-educated workers at A.B. Scale, combined with the introduction of automated processes, reduces the need for work simplification. Instead, those jobs that were the best candidates for simplification can be replaced with robotics or other forms of automation.

Job Enlargement

Job enlargement offers the opposite solution to work simplification for redesigning work. It refers to increasing the scope of the job, to modifying it horizontally by increasing the number of activities or different processes it involves. Rather than encouraging an individual to concentrate on a fraction of the product, job enlargement requires workers to perform numerous, often unrelated, job tasks. A recent experiment that combined clerical jobs, such as coder and keyer of data, resulted in increased employee satisfaction, less mental boredom, greater chances of catching errors, and better customer service.[28]

While the earliest job enlargement programs involved *job extension,*[29] in which workers did more of the same job, *job rotation* is a more common form of job enlargement. The worker performs two or more tasks, but alternates among them in a predefined way over a period of time. A worker, for example, might attach the wheel assembly one week, inspect it the next, and organize the parts for assembly during the third. Job rotation provides a hedge against absenteeism because workers can perform more than a single function. It also can contribute to cross-training workers to facilitate career advancement. Again, A.B. Scale might implement this approach, but it probably will not solve the motivation and performance problems.

WORK ENRICHMENT

Job enrichment is an appropriate response to declining motivation resulting from overly specialized jobs where the worker lacks control of the job process. Declining work motivation, dissatisfaction with growth opportunities and the job in general, and lack of work effectiveness signal a need for job enrichment. In addition, a changing work force that includes more highly educated individuals often requires job redesign; enriching jobs helps meet the needs of such workers.

Instead of altering only the horizontal dimensions of a job, as with work simplification and job enlargement, *job enrichment* involves changing a job both *horizontally* by adding tasks and *vertically* by adding responsibility. Frederick Herzberg's motivation-hygiene model (see Chapter 4) provided the roots for job enrichment programs. He enriched jobs by increasing their motivators, such as challenge, autonomy, and responsibility.[30]

The Job Characteristics Model

The *job characteristics model,* which traces motivation and satisfaction to psychological states experienced by individuals, and then links these states to the characteristics of jobs, replaced the earlier job enrichment model.[31] According to this later model, five core characteristics of the job significantly influence the behaviors and attitudes of workers: (1) skill variety, (2) task identity, (3) task significance, (4) autonomy, and (5) feedback.

1. *Skill variety* describes the degree to which a job requires the worker to perform activities that challenge his or her skills and use diverse abilities. A state police trooper's job requires more skill variety than a crossing guard. A branch manager in a bank uses more diverse skills and abilities than a bank teller.

2. *Task identity* refers to the degree to which a job requires completion of a "whole" and identifiable piece of work—doing a job from beginning to end with a visible outcome. If the workers at A.B. Scale would assemble an entire scale, their job would have high task identity.

3. *Task significance* reflects the degree to which the job is perceived to have a substantial impact on the lives of other people. While task significance depends on individuals' perceptions, and may even vary for a specific job, some jobs inherently seem to have more task significance: classroom teaching has greater task significance than lunchroom monitoring, for example. Assembling an entire scale has more significance than assembling only a circuit board.

4. *Autonomy* means the degree to which the job gives the worker freedom, independence, and discretion in scheduling work and determining how he or she will carry it out. If the workers at the A.B. Scale Company become essentially self-managing and perform the scheduling, quality control, and hiring duties, among others, they will have high autonomy.

5. *Feedback* refers to the degree to which a worker, in carrying out the work activities required by the job, gets information about the effectiveness of his or her efforts. A clerk who receives a list of transcription errors each day receives feedback. Feedback comes from both the supervisor and the work itself, as well as from other sources, such as customers and peers.

Skill variety, task identity, and task significance influence the extent to which an individual jobholder experiences the job as *meaningful.* As workers use their diverse abilities, complete entire tasks, and view their work as having an impact on others' lives, they more likely will *experience the jobs as meaningful.* Autonomy in the job influences the extent to which an individual believes he or she is *responsible for outcomes* of the job. A manager likely feels more responsible for his or her job outcomes than does a person the manager supervises. Feedback in the job increases the individual's *knowledge of the actual results* of the work activities. Increasing the amount of information available to a jobholder increases the individual's ability to know and evaluate his or her effectiveness. These critical psychological states—experienced meaningfulness, experienced responsibility, and knowledge of results—in turn affect such personal and work outcomes as internal work motivation, "growth" satisfaction, general job satisfaction, and work effectiveness. Figure 13–9 summarizes these relationships.

The individual's knowledge and skill, strength of his or her growth needs (needs for learning, personal accomplishment, and development), and satisfaction with the work context moderate the links between the core job characteristics and critical psychological states and between the critical psychological states and outcomes.[32] For example, individuals who have the skills and knowledge to perform enriched jobs will be more satisfied than those who are less competent. Individuals with high

Figure 13–9 **The Job Characteristics Model**

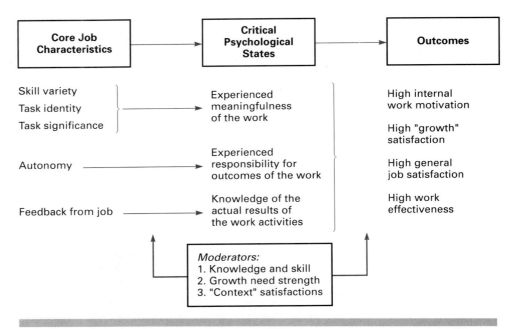

SOURCE: From J. R. Hackman and G. R. Oldham, *Work Redesign*, © 1980, Addison-Wesley Publishing Co., Inc. Reprinted with permission of the publisher.

growth needs typically respond more positively to enriched jobs than those with low growth needs because the latter individuals may not value such opportunities or may be negatively stressed by them. Individuals satisfied with the work context may be more able to take advantage of the opportunities provided by enriched jobs than those dissatisfied with the work context because they are too preoccupied with that aspect of the work.

Strategies of Enrichment

The job characteristics approach calls for enriching a job by increasing one or more of the core dimensions, as shown in Table 13–4.[33] *Combining tasks,* such as by having a typist proofread his or her own work, increases skill variety and task identity. *Forming natural work units* that distribute work in a natural and logical way, such as by giving a nurse the job of doing all nursing tasks for a given patient, increases task identity and task significance. *Establishing client relationships,* such as by having groups of bank loan officers always deal with the same clients, increases skill variety, autonomy, and feedback. *Loading a job vertically* to combine implementation and control, such as by giving production workers responsibility for quality control or meeting schedules, increases autonomy. *Opening feedback channels* by letting the worker know about his or her performance while the job is being done through setting goals and monitoring their accomplishment, increases knowledge of results.

Research has suggested that job characteristics may be related to performance.[34] Figure 13–10 presents a checklist for evaluating the factors that may affect job enrichment. Complete this checklist for a job you have held or have some familiarity with by circling the number that best describes your job on each dimension. Then score your responses. The lower the total score (1 or 2), the more conducive the job is to being enriched; the higher the score (4 or 5), the less effective job enrichment efforts likely will be. Job enrichment programs work better for less complex jobs

Table 13–4 **Ways to Improve Core Job Dimensions**

Job Redesign Activity	Core Dimension Affected
Combine tasks	Skill variety Task identity
Form natural work units	Task identity Task significance
Establish client relationships	Skill variety Autonomy Feedback
Load a job vertically	Task identity Task significance Autonomy
Open feedback channels	Feedback

than inherently richer jobs. Managers can expect enrichment to succeed only if workers want and seek fulfillment in their work and value jobs requiring greater skill and effort. Differences in employer and employee goals may hinder the effectiveness of work enrichment programs. Some managers may want their workers to demonstrate more initiative and autonomy, but the workers want less involvement and learning; or the opposite may be true. In addition, workers' fears and concerns about possible negative consequences of the job redesign effort should be acknowledged and addressed.[35] Thus managers must diagnose the nature of the job itself, the technology, the workers, and management to predict the likely impact and appropriateness of work enrichment. They must also consider the external political environment and its support for redesign efforts.[36]

What elements of the manufacturing job at A.B. Scale Company must Alan Grant change if he chooses to enrich the work? Eliminating a plantwide assembly line and emphasizing performance and control of work by teams will result in jobs that emphasize skill variety, task identity, task significance, autonomy, and feedback. Additional work enrichment would result from combining tasks so that workers assemble most or all of a significant product component, increasing the amount of craftsmanship in the jobs, forming work groups to assemble entire scales, increasing worker involvement in production scheduling and supervision, and increasing feedback on the quality of the finished product through goal-setting activities and worker involvement in some quality-control procedures.

AUTONOMOUS AND SELF-MANAGING WORK GROUPS

Building on job enrichment, recent approaches to redesign emphasize the use of self-managed teams to meet worker needs and increase motivation. Researchers at the Tavistock Institute in England were the first to note the importance of work groups in handling new technology.[37] Scandinavian automobile manufacturers—Saab and Volvo—introduced the concept of *autonomous work groups* for meeting workers' social needs while introducing technological innovation into work.[38] In these self-regulating groups, employees who perform interdependent tasks worked in a common unit, controlled their own task assignments, and performed many roles traditionally assigned to management. Steelcase, a manufacturer of office furniture systems, re-

Figure 13-10 **Job Enrichment Evaluation Form**

The Job Itself

1. Quality is important and attributable to the worker.	/1/2/3/4/5/	Quality is not too important and/or is not controllable by the worker.
2. Flexibility is a major contributor to job efficiency.	/1/2/3/4/5/	Flexibility is not a major consideration.
3. The job requires the coordination of tasks or activities among several workers.	/1/2/3/4/5/	The job is performed by one worker acting independently of others.
4. The benefits of job enrichment will compensate for the efficiencies of task specialization.	/1/2/3/4/5/	Job enrichment will eliminate substantial efficiencies realized from specialization.
5. The conversion and one-time setup costs involved in job enrichment can be recovered in a reasonable period of time.	/1/2/3/4/5/	Training and other costs associated with job enrichment are estimated to be much greater than expected results.
6. The wage payment plan is not based solely on output.	/1/2/3/4/5/	Workers are under a straight piecework wage plan.
7. Due to the workers' ability to affect output, an increase in job satisfaction can be expected to increase productivity.	/1/2/3/4/5/	Due to the dominance of technology, an increase in job satisfaction is unlikely to significantly affect productivity.

Technology

8. Changes in job content would not necessitate a large investment in equipment and technology.	/1/2/3/4/5/	The huge investment in equipment and technology overrides all other considerations.

The Workers

9. Employees are accustomed to change and respond favorably to it.	/1/2/3/4/5/	Employees are set in their ways and prefer the status quo.
10. Employees feel secure in their jobs; employment has been stable.	/1/2/3/4/5/	Layoffs are frequent; many employees are concerned about the permanency of employment.
11. Employees are dissatisfied with their jobs and would welcome changes in job content and work relationships.	/1/2/3/4/5/	Employees are satisfied with their present jobs and general work situation.
12. Employees are highly skilled blue- and white-collar workers, professionals, and supervisors.	/1/2/3/4/5/	Employees are semi- and unskilled blue- and white-collar workers.
13. Employees are well educated with most having college degrees.	/1/2/3/4/5/	The average employee has less than a high school education.
14. Employees are from a small town and rural environment.	/1/2/3/4/5/	The company is located in a large, highly industrialized metropolitan area.
15. The history of union-management (if no union, worker-management) relations has been one of cooperation and mutual support.	/1/2/3/4/5/	Union-management (worker-management) relations are strained, and the two parties are antagonistic to one another.

Figure 13–10 (*Continued*)

	Management	
16. Managers are committed to job enrichment and are anxious to participate in its implementation.	/1/2/3/4/5/	Managers show little interest in job enrichment and even less interest in having it implemented in their department.
17. Managers have attended seminars, workshops, and so forth, are quite knowledgeable of the concept, and have had experience in implementing it.	/1/2/3/4/5/	Managers lack the training and experience necessary to develop and implement job enrichment projects.
18. Management realizes that substantial payoffs from job enrichment usually take one to three years to materialize.	/1/2/3/4/5/	Management expects immediate results (within six months) from job enrichment projects.
Total Score _____	÷ 18 = _____	Job Enrichment Rating

SOURCE: William E. Reif and Ronald C. Tinnell, "A Diagnostic Approach to Job Enrichment," pp. 29–37, *MSU Business Topics*, Autumn 1973. Reprinted by permission of the publisher, Division of Research, Graduate School of Business Administration, Michigan State University.

cently built a state-of-the-art plant designed to let employees run the daily operations. One welder, for example, is now a member of a six-person team that includes assembly, trim, paint, and weld and decides how it will run one of four units in the Casegoods factory.[39] In one recently designed Volvo plant, workers organized into self-managing teams assemble entire automobiles, rather than just smaller components.[40] At its Ayr, Scotland, plant, Digital Equipment Corporation moved from conventional assembly line work in 1984 to what it called high-performance teams. These teams had the characteristics shown in Table 13–5, as well as full responsibility for product assembly, testing, quality evaluation, problem solving, and equipment maintenance.[41] Managers used a supportive style in relating to these teams, and support groups were located near them. The plantwide results included increased productivity, reduced time for product innovations to reach market, reduced inventory, and better decision making. Table 13–6 lists other examples of self-managing teams.

Table 13–5 **Characteristics of Digital's High-Performance Teams**

Self-managing, self-organizing, self-regulating
Front-to-back responsibility for core process
Negotiated production targets
Multiskilling—no job titles
Shared skills, knowledge, experience, and problems
Skills-based pay system
Peer selection, peer review
Open layout, open communications
Support staff on the spot
Commitment to high standards of performance

SOURCE: J. McCalman and D. A. Buchanan, High performance work systems: The need for transition management, *International Journal of Product Management* 10(2): 10–25.

Table 13–6 **Examples of Self-Managing Teams**

General Mills cereal plant in Lodi, California: Teams schedule, operate, and maintain machinery so effectively that the factory runs with no managers present during the night shift.

Federal Express: At a weekly meeting, a team of clerks spotted and eventually solved a billing problem that was costing the company $2.1 million a year.

Chaparral Steel: A team of mill workers traveled the world to evaluate new production machinery. The machines they selected and installed have helped make their mill one of the world's most efficient.

3M: Cross-functional teams tripled the number of new products in one division.

Aetna Life and Casualty: After organizing its home office operations into superteams, Aetna reduced the ratio of middle managers to workers—from 1 to 7 down to 1 to 30—while improving customer service.

Johnsonville Foods of Sheboygan, Wisconsin: Teams of blue-collar workers helped the CEO make the decision to proceed with a major plant expansion. The workers told the CEO they could produce more sausage, faster than he would have ever dared to ask. Since 1986, productivity has risen at least 50 percent.

SOURCE: B. Dumaine, Who needs a boss? *Fortune* (May 7, 1990): 52–53.

Table 13–7 contrasts this new, sociotechnical paradigm to an older view of work design. In the new paradigm autonomous work groups integrate and optimize social and technical systems. Related tasks are joined and performed by self-regulating groups. There are few layers of management, encouraging a collaborative relationship. Ideally employee commitment and performance increase. Self-managing team development proceeds through five stages, as shown in Figure 13–11.[42] The design phase ranges from two to six months and includes the appointment of a steering group to oversee the change and a design team to begin planning for the redesign. Start-up begins with the recommendations of the design team and involves communicating them and related expectations to those affected by the introduction of self-managing teams. Table 13–8 spells out the last three stages in which implementation and expansion of the redesign effort occurs.

Introducing or changing to self-managed teams requires managers to alter their views of power and control. In a case study of a warehouse operation, the early part of the transition was characterized by initial suspicion, uncertainty, and resistance. Gradually the managers realized the positive possibilities inherent in the new work system. They continued to wrestle with the new role of facilitator of these teams; this process eventually resulted in learning a new language and practicing new behaviors.[43]

The introduction of autonomous or self-regulating work groups alleviates the isolation and boredom traditionally felt by manufacturing workers, particularly with increasing automation. Yet, one study of autonomous work groups suggests that in some situations their impact may be limited and accompanied by dysfunctional consequences. A nonunionized British confectionery company that introduced work groups found they affected intrinsic job satisfaction, but not work performance, turnover, job motivation, organizational commitment, or mental health. Both managers and employees liked the system in spite of the personal stress that arose from managing it.[44] Autonomous work groups may have other consequences. Maintenance workers at a mineral-processing plant who worked alongside autonomous

Table 13–7 **Characteristics of Old and New Paradigms of Work Design**

Old Paradigm	New Paradigm
Technology comes first.	Social and technical systems are optimized together.
People are extensions of machines.	People complement machines.
People are expendable spare parts.	People are resources to be developed.
Tasks are narrow and individual; skills are simple.	Related tasks make an optimum grouping; skills are multiple and broad.
Controls—for example, supervisors, staff, procedures books—are external.	Individuals are self-controlled; work groups and departments are self-regulating.
Organization chart has many levels; management style is autocratic.	Organization chart is flat; management is participative.
Atmosphere is competitive and characterized by gamesmanship.	Atmosphere is collaborative and cooperative.
Only the organization's purposes are considered.	Individual and social purposes, as well as the organization's, are considered.
Employees are alienated: "It's only a job."	Employees are committed: "It's my job!"
Organization is characterized by low risk taking.	Organization is innovative: New ideas are encouraged.

SOURCE: M. R. Weisbord, Participative work design: A personal odyssey, *Organizational Dynamics* 13 (Spring 1985): 17. Used by permission. Adapted from E. Trist, The evolution of socio-technical systems—A conceptual framework and an action research program, research paper No. 2, June 1981 (Ontario Ministry of Labor, Ontario Quality of Working Life Center, Toronto).

work groups with skills that overlapped theirs reported lower job satisfaction, organizational commitment, and trust in management than a comparable group who worked in more traditional work settings.[45]

ALTERNATIVE WORK ARRANGEMENTS

In contrast to the previous forms of work design, which focus primarily on the content of the job, alternative work schedules address the context. This approach to redesign can also help meet work needs or provide a context that supports better performance and increased satisfaction by changing the work hours or changing the work location.

Figure 13–11 **Stages in the Development of Self-managing Teams**

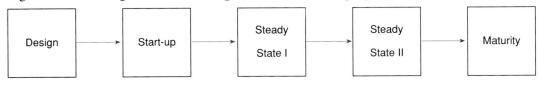

Table 13–8 **Stages in Self-managing Teams**

Steady State I	Steady State II	Maturity
Some team members are skilled in more than one task.	One-third to one-half of team members are skilled in every line function in the team.	Two-thirds or more team members are skilled in every line function in the team.
Zero to one-third of positions in team have trained backup people.	One-third to two-thirds of direct positions have trained backup people.	All line positions have trained backup people.
Less than one-third of their team has mastered a support function.*	Better than one-half of team has mastered a support function.	All team members have mastered at least one support function.
A general plan exists for having backup people.	A detailed plan exists for having backup people, and each knows the next job function.	Detailed plan with each person at least implementing the next function.
Technical problem solving by area coordinators (AC) and support personnel with a few team members invited to give input.	Technical problem solving meetings initiated by AC or support personnel but fully participated in by team.	Technical problem solving meetings initiated by team using support as a resource.
The team maintains the standard way of performing tasks.	With AC encouragement, the team initiates some minor improvements.	The team initiates major improvements and pushes the AC to act on them.
Most new information about the operation or the plant comes to the team from the area coordinator.	The team has some lines of communication—mostly on business-related items.	New information on plant and business as well as team performance comes mostly through team members.
Dealing with individual team members who have performance problems is still left to the area coordinator.	The team tries to resolve individual performance problems, but resolution isn't reached and problems occur.	Team obtains resolution of its people problems.
Decisions made in team meetings are only partially carried out by other team members.	On most decisions, the majority supporting decision tries to carry it out with some people remaining uncommitted.	All team members accept responsibility for carrying out decisions.
One or two team members walk the team through a problem-solving process.	More than one half of team can assist the team using a problem-solving process.	All team members participate in the problem-solving process.
An informal system is in place for pooling resources and helping one another; this usually occurs in high-pressure situations.	A definite plan is in place for pooling resources and helping one another; this occurs when necessary.	A well-developed plan for pooling resources is put to appropriate use routinely.
Regular meetings occur; informal methods of sharing information exist, but communication gaps still exist.	Regular meetings occur and informal communication systems exist with few communication gaps.	Communication gaps are quickly identified and answers sought by team members.
Some cliques within teams are left out and don't feel a part of the team; this causes communication problems within the team.	Team has some cliques but a sense of team identity is developing.	Cliques may exist on a social basis, but the team has a strong sense of identity on work-related matters.

Table 13–8 *(Continued)*

Steady State I	Steady State II	Maturity
Different opinions are heard within the team but are not often dealt with in an effective manner.	Different opinions are seen as natural and discussed in detail prior to any resolution.	Different opinions on work-related issues are actively encouraged by team members and constructively used.
Extra energy and effort are needed to meet even slight variations in production demands.	Extra energy is needed for significant variations in production demands.	Extra energy is given regularly to meet big variations and demands. A lot of the challenges are self-imposed by the team.
Goals for production and efficiency are kept at a conservative level.	Goals are increased to meet customer requirements.	Goals are set by the team to deliberately challenge its capabilities beyond minimum customer requirements.
Problems have to be brought to the attention of the team by the team leader or the area coordinator.	The team recognizes problems when they get to the point of being critical and are affecting overall team effectiveness.	Problems are quickly raised to the surface. Potential problems are foreseen, and plans are made for avoiding them.

*Support functions = Tasks which support production assembly and test.

SOURCE: Reprinted with permission from the Association for Quality and Participation: R. L. Cherry, Stages of work redesign, *Journal of Quality and Participation,* Special Supplement (December 1989), p. 54.

Flexible Hours In programs that offer workers flexible hours, also known as *flextime programs,* employees have some discretion in creating their work schedules. For example, one office clerk at A.B. Scale might work from 7 A.M. to 3 P.M., whereas another clerk might work from 10 A.M. to 6 P.M.

Alternative work schedules take three basic forms: (1) discretionary systems, where the worker chooses the precise days or hours worked; (2) compressed workweek, where the number of hours in a traditional five-day week are worked in four days; and (3) part-time employment.[46] *Discretionary systems* include flexible working hours and staggered starts. Flextime, probably the most common discretionary system, offers workers the choice of starting and ending times so long as they work certain specific hours daily (such as ten to three) and meet the hour requirements (usually thirty-five to forty) of a normal workweek. In a staggered week, another form of flextime, workers alternate between working a four-day thirty-two hour week and a six-day forty-eight hour week.

The compressed workweek has arisen from attempts to shorten the workweek to cut costs and increase worker satisfaction. Compressing means reducing the workweek into fewer days. Four ten-hour working days is a common configuration. The four-day workweek may result in greater employee satisfaction, but this improved attitude may occur at the expense of employee efficiency. Scheduling work in two-week rather than one-week blocks enhances the attractiveness of this option. In this configuration the employee may work four days, have a four-day break, then work four more days, followed by a normal two-day weekend break.

Part-time employment includes jobs done by permanent employees who work less than whole days with predictable or unpredictable hours. Two variations of part-time work became more popular during the 1980s: job sharing and job splitting. In *job sharing,* a whole job is divided into two parts according to time and day of the week. Together the jobholders are responsible for completing the work, and each typically performs all the tasks of the job. One might work mornings and the second afternoons; or one might work the first 2½ days of a five-day week, with the second working the last 2½ days. In *job splitting,* the jobs are divided according to tasks or skills, rather than schedule. In splitting a secretarial job, for example, one person might take all dictation, while the second might do all the manuscript typing. *Contract employment* can also be viewed as a variant of part-time employment. Workers are hired and paid to complete specific projects or tasks. Software development or distribution companies often hire this type of employee because it provides them with maximum flexibility. Workers too retain their personal flexibility and autonomy by having the discretion to develop their own work schedules so long as they complete the project by the specified deadline.

Flexible Location

Increasingly workers perform their jobs at a site away from the organization's physical plant. Computer programmers, in particular, can often perform their jobs remotely, typically from their homes. Workers with family responsibilities may prefer this schedule because it allows home problems to be handled more quickly. Removing traveling time can also increase workers' productivity. Because remote workers typically have less social interaction than on-site workers, this arrangement may not work for everyone.[47]

Effectiveness of Alternative Schedules

Managing alternative work options requires managers to screen candidates carefully and develop a flexible training program. Managers must also establish a viable work plan by setting appropriate performance goals. They must find creative ways to monitor the number of hours worked and to ensure that the organization's needs are met. They must maintain open communication, provide ongoing support, and remain flexible in dealing with employees who take advantage of alternative work options.[48]

A number of studies have documented the benefits of alternative work schedules, including reduced payroll costs, greater corporate flexibility, and successful response to employee needs.[49] Responses to the redesign of the job context have also included an increase in productivity because of reduced use of sick leave; decreased turnover, absenteeism, and overtime; increased employee satisfaction and morale; and decreased transportation demand during peak hours.[50] The major resistance to atypical work schedules stems from the perception that work must be done at the same time by all workers because of the interdependence of the tasks. To overcome this constraint, carefully scheduling tasks and building a small inventory of different product components might be required. Flextime does not work where a company has multiple continuous shifts, machine-paced assembly work, few employees, or highly interdependent operations.[51]

In West Germany and Austria, several companies have even considered introducing a flexyear.[52] In this arrangement workers agree to the number of hours they will work in the following year, but have the freedom to allocate them as desired. They receive equal amounts of pay each month, but may work two or three times as many hours in one month as in another.

QUALITY OF WORKING LIFE PROGRAMS

Quality of work life (QWL) programs incorporate many principles of job enrichment and sociotechnical redesign into comprehensive efforts to improve the quality of the working situation. Such programs were initiated in order to ensure adequate and fair compensation, a safe and healthy working environment, personal growth and development, satisfaction of social needs in the workplace, personal rights, compatibility between work and nonwork activities, and the social relevance of work life.[53] Quality of working life programs typically include participative problem solving, job enrichment, innovative reward systems, and work environment improvements.

Early Program Characteristics QWL programs encourage workers to participate with management in decision making about problems and opportunities in the workplace to increase organizational effectiveness and improve worker satisfaction, commitment, and performance.[54] QWL activities include participative problem solving, restructuring the basic nature of jobs and work systems, fitting rewards to the desired work processes and outcomes, and improving the work environment.

An early and well-known QWL program was initiated at the General Motors assembly plant in Tarrytown, New York, in 1970, at a time when the plant had one of the poorest production and labor records at GM. The plant manager invited workers to participate in the planning and implementation of changes in plant operations, and many of the workers' suggestions were adopted. The plant management next conducted voluntary, joint training of workers and supervisors in problem solving; 95 percent of the work force volunteered to participate in the paid three-day training program. Subsequent evaluations showed that the quality of performance increased, absenteeism dropped, and the number of grievances fell from 2,000 in 1971 to 32 in 1978.[55] Additional early QWL experiments were conducted at the Rushton Mining Company in Pennsylvania, the Harmon Manufacturing Company plant in Bolivar, Tennessee, and the General Foods plant in Topeka, Kansas.[56] They replaced the assembly line with work teams and improved communication between workers and supervisors.

Contemporary Programs Quality of working life programs have become more comprehensive in recent years. In the early 1980s, ten GM plants introduced an operating team system in which a team of ten to fifteen workers received all work assignments and allocated them during regular team meetings. These teams often enriched jobs or operated as quality circles.[57] Later in the decade the Saturn plant of General Motors extended this concept further: Union representatives joined planning groups; work teams were self-managing; team members were responsible for cost and quality control, as well as innovative changes; and status differences were deemphasized in pay and job title.[58] This emphasis on teamwork and employee participation in significant decision making is intended to increase workers' satisfaction and their productivity and decrease their absenteeism and turnover. At Xerox, QWL teams of eight to ten volunteers met weekly to discuss production problems and the status of previously offered recommendations.[59] At Packard Electric, approximately sixty-five committees of hourly workers dealt with health and safety problems, work-related issues, and control limits for defects.[60] In 1987, American Airlines added an extensive employee suggestion program called "Ideas in Action" to its QWL programs.[61] The program's goals included generating profits from employee ideas, promoting workers' sense of involvement, developing an entrepreneurial attitude among employees, and supporting the corporate QWL program. Employees receive cash and prize rewards for good ideas. In 1988 almost one-fourth of the approximately 12,000 suggestions were approved by the program staff of 50, resulting in cost savings of about $31 million.

Other aspects of QWL projects include union support and involvement in the process, voluntary participation by employees, guarantee of job security, training programs in team problem solving, initiation of job redesign efforts, availability of skill training, involvement of workers in planning and forecasting, periodic meetings between workers and management to discuss plant production and operations, and responsiveness to employee concerns.[62] In all unionized organizations, union-management cooperation is key to many QWL efforts.[63]

Table 13–9 compares and contrasts three generations of QWL programs; it indicates how programs have developed from the earliest experiments, as at Tarrytown, to the programs of the 1980s, such as employee involvement groups at Ford and quality circles in many large companies, to the programs of the 1990s.

Quality Circles Some projects have also included *quality circles*—work teams of five to ten members who focused originally on enhancing the quality of production and now recommend all types of improvements to the work process.[64] They are typically trained to identify, analyze, and solve problems and may also monitor ongoing work processes or process improvements.[65] Table 13–10 lists the characteristics of typical quality circles. Table 13–11 shows the phases in a circle's life. Figure 13–12 shows how quality circle ideas lead to productivity and satisfaction. In 1985 more than 90 percent of the *Fortune* 500 companies, including Westinghouse, Hewlett-Packard, Digital Equipment Corporation, Texas Instruments, Xerox, Eastman Kodak, Procter & Gamble, Polaroid, TRW Systems, General Motors, Ford, IBM, and American Airlines, had some form of quality circles.[66]

Most evidence of quality circle success has appeared as anecdotal reports in practitioner literature; little systematic empirical evidence has supported their effectiveness.[67] Employees in some companies that instituted quality circles experienced better health and greater safety on the job.[68] Other benefits have included improved employee satisfaction, morale, job interest, commitment, and involvement; increased opportunity for individual growth; greater sense of ownership and control of the work environment; development of managerial ability for circle leaders; improved communication in the organization; and greater understanding and respect between management and workers.[69]

But quality circles also created many potential problems, such as emphasizing profit to the exclusion of employee growth, failing to keep management and members informed, perceptions of management manipulation of the circle, failure to incorporate suggestions, selecting inappropriate problems, or overestimating the benefits.[70] Table 13–12 cites some advantages and disadvantages of quality circles. The long-run impact of quality circles is also questionable. In one study, performance and attitudes were enhanced initially, and the improvements lasted about two years, but then performance and attitudes returned to previous levels.[71] The problem-solving and personality style of managers will influence their reaction to quality circles and the use of participative management.[72] Managers must adapt any redesign approach to the specific situation to maximize its effectiveness.

Effectiveness of QWL Programs A review of the empirical research provides substantial evidence of the effectiveness of quality of work life programs, although their introduction has not always been smooth.[73] Worker participation in QWL programs affects industrial relations, as reflected in low grievance rates, low absentee rates, fewer disciplinary actions, more positive worker attitudes, and greater participation in suggestion programs.[74] For QWL programs to be effective, the organization's culture must support them. One other factor that may influence success is whether the program creates permanent or temporary structures. One study of 415 middle managers in four manufacturing plants indicated that the managers had more positive attitudes if they participated in permanent rather than temporary problem-solving groups.[75]

Table 13–9   **Three Generations of Quality of Work Life Programs**

	First Generation	Second Generation	Third Generation
Structure			
Integration	QWL outside of/parallel to regular organizational structure; perceived as a program	Some integration of QWL with regular organizational structure	QWL inseparable from regular organizational structure; organizational structure becomes flatter
Adaptation	QWL structure externally imposed by centralized experts/authority	QWL structure shows some adaptations and local variations	Each local QWL structure unique to the particular working environment
Centralization	QWL structure centralized	QWL structure partly centralized, partly decentralized	QWL structure decentralized
Involvement	QWL structure involves only selected employees	QWL structure involves many or most employees	QWL structure involves all employees
Process			
Decision Making	Decision making is management prerogative; QWL provides input to management decisions	Ranges from QWL responsibility for some decisions at discretion of managers to managers being removed from day-to-day work decisions	Roles of management, nonmanagement and union redefined; decisions now made by those closest to impact; organization managed jointly at all levels
Facilitation	Facilitation provided by centralized, external resources	Facilitation moved under decentralized, local control	Each employee acquires skills of facilitator; takes on role as needed
Training and Education	Need for training and education determined and provided by centralized, external sources; focus on orientation for all; skills for facilitators	Groups identify own training needs and arrange as needed; focus on skills needed for QWL process, for all participants	Training locally determined; expands to include any process or work-related skill needed; all acquire skills in QWL process and organization management including financial, etc.
Union-Management Relationship	Formal union-management relationship adversarial; much time spent building up informal communication, respect, trust	Union-management relationship takes on more collaborative, cooperative tone; both sides move back and forth between collaborative and adversarial roles as needed	Collaborative union-management relationship formalized, or roles redefined as traditional distinctions between management and nonmanagement become blurred
Content			
Issues	Issues peripheral to the business; tend to focus on the environmental	Expanded range of issues moves beyond environmental to encompass employee, union, planning, policy, business, and day-to-day work issues; constraints are contract and company policy	No distinction between "QWL issues" and other issues; all ideas considered; contract and company policy built on QWL foundation

SOURCE: M. London, *Change Agents: New Roles and Innovation Strategies for Human Resources Professionals.* San Francisco: Jossey-Bass, 1988, pp. 142–143. Used with permission.

Table 13–10 **Design Characteristics of Quality Circles**

Membership is voluntary.

Members are drawn from a particular work group or department.

The group has the responsibility but not the authority for making suggestions.

The problem-solving domain is limited to quality- and productivity-related issues and cost reduction.

Meetings are usually held on company time.

QC members receive training in group process and problem-solving techniques.

A staff of specially trained facilitators is usually hired to help with training, facilitation of group process at meetings, and performing staff functions associated with the QC process.

No financial rewards for group suggestions are offered.

The group is provided with no systematic information about company performance, costs, long-range plans, and other matters.

The decision to install QCs is usually made at the top of the organization.

SOURCE: G. E. Ledford, Jr., E. E. Lawler III, and S. A. Mohrman, The quality circle and its variations. In J. P. Campbell, R. J. Campbell, and Associates, *Productivity in Organizations: New Perspectives from Industrial and Organizational Psychology* (San Francisco: Jossey-Bass, 1988).

Table 13–11   **Phases of a Circle Program's Life**

Phase	Activity	Destructive Forces
Start-up	Publicize Obtain funds and volunteers Train	Low volunteer rate Inadequate funding Inability to learn group process and problem-solving skills
Initial problem solving	Identify and solve problems	Disagreement on problems Lack of knowledge of operations
Approval of initial suggestions	Present and have initial suggestions accepted	Resistance by staff groups and middle management Poor presentation and suggestions because of limited knowledge
Implementation	Relevant groups act on suggestions	Prohibitive costs Resistance by groups that must implement
Expansion of problem solving	Form new groups Old groups continue	Member-nonmember conflict Raised aspirations Lack of problems Expense of parallel organization Savings not realized Rewards wanted
Decline	Fewer groups meet	Cynicism about program Burnout

SOURCE: Reprinted with permission from E. E. Lawler III and S. A. Mohrman, Quality circles after the fad, *Harvard Business Review* (January-February 1985): 65–71, p. 67. Copyright © 1985 by the President and Fellows of Harvard College; all rights reserved.

Figure 13–12   **The Contribution of Circle Ideas to Productivity and Satisfaction**

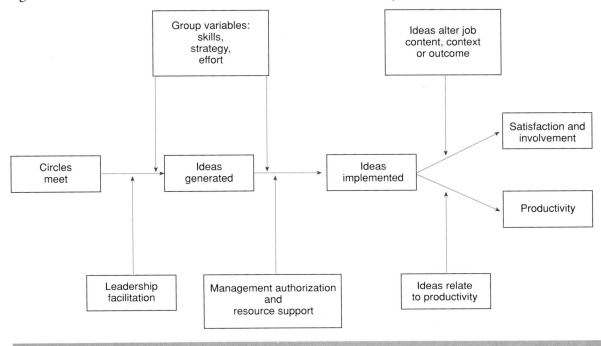

SOURCE: Reprinted with permission from G. E. Ledford, E. E. Lawler III, and S. A. Mohrman, The quality circle and its variations. In J. P. Campbell, R. J. Campbell, and Associates, *Productivity in Organizations: New Perspectives from Industrial and Organizational Psychology* (San Francisco: Jossey-Bass, 1988), p. 262.

WORK DESIGN OUTSIDE THE UNITED STATES   Many of the approaches to work design have their roots outside the United States. West Germany and Japan have focused on continually improving product design and manufacturing, while simultaneously giving workers responsibility for contributing to these improvements. Work enrichment efforts have bloomed in Scandinavia. Volvo and Saab established precedents in the automobile industry with the introduction of autonomous work groups. Worker ownership, a way of salvaging bank-

Table 13–12   **Advantages and Disadvantages of Quality Circles**

Advantages	Disadvantages
Increased emphasis on training and development	Initial drop in productivity
Increased productivity	Large initial investment
Refined measure of productivity	Increased chance of error at first
Consciousness of costs	Disappointment because of unrealistic expectations
Increased satisfaction and pride	Threat to existing authority
Collaborative spirit	Threat to employee status quo
Practice of participative management style	Time loss due to efforts to correct mistrust in motives
Improved planning	Misunderstanding of the nature of QCs
Maximization of use of human resources	Initial confusion
New vehicle for recognition	Threat to existing controls

SOURCE: L. Fitzgerald and J. Murphy, *Installing Quality Circles: A Strategic Approach* (San Diego: University Associates, 1982).

rupt companies or increasing employee motivation, has its model abroad, in such cooperatives as Mondragón in Spain.

U.S. workers resemble the Scandinavian work force: Both include highly educated workers. In part because of this similarity, efforts to apply autonomous work groups in the United States have been relatively successful. The stronger role of the union in the United States has both helped and hindered their introduction because union support has been a prerequisite for their successful implementation.

Japanese management practices also have had a major impact on work design in the United States. These quality circle problem-solving groups were conceived in the United States but developed in Japan to encourage quality control in production. Companies in the United States rediscovered them and modified their use in the 1980s to address a range of productivity issues. Motivation is based on teamwork and a group consciousness.[76] The Japanese also use closely supervised teams in manufacturing and rely on careful control of inventory and production steps to ensure productivity. These design strategies fit with the Japanese emphasis on control, long-term planning and investment, and teamwork. Table 13–13 lists some critical techniques of Japanese-style management. Original attempts to import the Japanese approach intact to the United States led to some problems; adjusting quality circles and Japanese team designs to the United States culture increased their effectiveness. Obviously managers can borrow practices and approaches from other countries, but they must recognize that some translation and adaptation may be necessary to apply them effectively elsewhere.

SUMMARY Technology has had a major impact on the availability and use of information in organizations. Automation has increased productivity and changed the skills required of large numbers of jobholders. Innovation in the workplace now focuses on both products and work processes. Managers must become versatile in developing and introducing new technologies. Ensuring quality challenges managers to improve the design of work.

The choice of work design as a prescription for organizational problems depends on the nature of problems diagnosed. Redesign often offers a good solution to poor motivation, ineffective communication, stress, issues of individual development, and nonproductive group behavior. But it cannot overcome poor selection of personnel. Job redesign must consider job incumbents and their individual qualities just as the selection of employees must consider the design of work in the organization. Figure 13–13 lists a series of diagnostic questions that assess organizational readiness for participation, and Figure 13–14 offers a suggested procedure for large-scale job redesign. Managers should view the management of technology as an ongoing challenge in the workplace. Table 13–14 lists a series of diagnostic questions that focus on this challenge.

Table 13–13 **Critical Techniques of Japanese-Style Management**

Intensive socialization	Nonspecialized career paths
Lifetime employment	Open communication
Competitive education	Consultational decision making
Rotation and slow promotion	Concern for employees
Behavior evaluation	Compensation
Work-group task assignments	

SOURCE: J. B. Cunningham and T. Eberle, A guide to job enrichment and redesign, *Personnel* (February 1990): 56–61.

Figure 13–13 **Questions for Assessing Organizational Readiness for Participation in Work Redesign**

1. To what extent is upper management willing to recognize and reward innovation?
2. To what extent do employees have influence over the physical work environment?
3. To what extent is bottom-up communication—especially of problems—encouraged?
4. To what extent does the prevailing organizational culture place a value on taking responsibility for problems rather than placing blame on others?
5. To what extent is management encouraged to make changes and take risks in striving to reach goals?
6. To what extent is the management philosophy of involving subordinates in problem solving consistent with the philosophy and behavior of top management?
7. To what extent has upper management in the past demonstrated support of projects and needs of middle managers and supervisors?
8. In unionized settings two additional factors deserve consideration: What is the history of union-management collaboration in joint projects? To what extent are the union and management willing to share in the success or failure of joint projects?
9. To what extent does the organization explicitly reward group success? Can this reward system overcome any cultural history of individualism?
10. To what extent do supervisors and managers use a team approach to achieve the work group's objectives?
11. To what extent do company information systems provide timely information on factors over which departments have control?
12. To what extent are the problems in the organization measurable, linear, consistent, and characterized by short time frames?
13. To what extent is the work process and technology such that people work on small, fragmented pieces and thus cannot solve problems in their department or are resisted by other departments when they propose solutions?
14. To what extent does the organization provide a stable working environment through long-term employment and work teams with stable membership?
15. To what extent do potential team leaders have the interpersonal and group skills needed to be effective leaders?
16. To what extent is there a willingness to reallocate resources (time, money, and people) to establish work teams?

SOURCE: Adapted from G. W. Meyer and R. G. Stott, Quality circles: Panacea or Pandora's box? *Organizational Dynamics* 13 (Spring 1985): 47. American Management Association, New York. All rights reserved. Some questions were adapted by the authors from materials developed by the General Motors Education and Training and Organizational Research and Development Departments and the General Motors Department of the United Auto Workers, referenced in *Employee Participation Groups: Reference Manual* (Detroit: G. M. Corporation Managerial Educational Services, 1980).

Figure 13–14 **Steps in Work Redesign**

1. Define the system's goals.
2. Define the relevant tasks and activities.
3. Interview.
4. Define the unique characteristics or constraints.
5. Develop a clustering of tasks.
6. Develop a list of intervention techniques.
7. Relate techniques to requirements and assumptions.
8. Define the appropriate level of implementation.
9. Pull it together in a picture.
10. Screen generalities.
11. Develop a process of implementation.
12. Adapt the job description and process of design.

SOURCE: J. B. Cunningham and T. Eberle, A guide to job enrichment and redesign, *Personnel* (February 1990): 56–61.

Table 13–14 **Diagnostic Questions**

- Are there mechanisms for the effective development and deployment of technology?
- Does innovation occur in the organization?
- Does a good-quality innovation process exist?
- Does a concern for quality exist in the organization?
- Does a total quality management program exist?
- Are the jobs sufficiently specialized?
- Are the jobs sufficiently enriched?
- Do autonomous or self-managing work groups exist? Are they effective?
- Do alternate work arrangements exist? Are they effective?
- Do quality of work life programs exist? Are they effective?
- Do work redesign efforts match the workers' needs and other aspects of the situation?

Reading 13–1

Innovation Processes in Multinational Corporations
Sumantra Ghoshal and Christopher A. Bartlett

INTRODUCTION

It was over twenty years ago that Vernon (1966) proposed the product cycle theory that identified the ability to innovate as the raison d'être for multinational corporations (MNCs). Over the last two decades, many new theories have been proposed to explain why MNCs exist, but innovations have continued to occupy the center stage in all the diverse and eclectic approaches (see Calvet 1981 for a brief review). The strength that allows a firm to invest and manage its affairs in many different countries is its ability to create new knowledge—to innovate—and to appropriate the benefits of such innovations in multiple locations through its own organization more effectively than through market-mediated mechanisms (Buckley and Casson 1976; Rugman 1982).

While theories of the multinational firm highlight the importance of innovations for the existence of such organizations, the emerging phenomenon of global competition (Hout, Porter, and Rudden 1982; Hamel and Prahalad 1985) has made innovations even more important for their survival. While traditionally many MNCs could compete successfully by exploiting scale economies or arbitraging imperfections in the world's goods, labor, and capital markets, such advantages have tended to erode over time. In many industries, MNCs no longer compete primarily with numerous national companies, but with a handful of other giants who tend to be comparable in terms of size, international resource access, and worldwide market position. Under the circumstances, the ability to innovate and to exploit those innovations globally in a rapid and efficient manner has become essential for survival and perhaps the most important source of a multinational's competitive advantage.

In sharp contrast to this practical importance, the topic of innovations in MNCs has received relatively little research attention. Not one of the over 4,000 studies on the topic of innovations (for references, see Gordon et al., 1975; Kelly and Kranzberg 1978; Mohr 1982) has focused specifically on the innovation process in the setting of a multinational corporation. Similarly, in the field of management of MNCs, past research has focussed overwhelmingly on strategy, defined implicitly as the way to enhance efficiency of current operations (see Ghoshal 1986b for a review), or structure, with most attention paid to the determinants of headquarters-subsidiary relations as opposed to their consequences. While some efforts have been made to investigate certain isolated aspects of distributed research and development in MNCs (Ronstadt 1977; Terpstra 1977), the issue of management of innovations has remained peripheral to research on the topic of management of multinational corporations.

THE STUDY

This paper is based on some of the findings of a recently concluded study of innovations in nine large MNCs, viz., Philips, GE, and Matsushita in the consumer electronics industry; L. M. Ericsson, ITT, and NEC in the telecommunications switching industry; and Unilever, Procter and Gamble, and Kao in the soaps and detergents industry. The choice of these industries and companies was based on the logic of maximum variety—the three industries represented very different requirements in terms of local responsiveness and global integration (Prahalad 1975; Porter 1986); within each industry, the selected firms were comparable in terms of size and strategic positions but, because of the differences in their national origins and administrative histories, had very significant differences in their organizational forms and processes (for descriptions and illustrations of these differences, see Bartlett and Ghoshal 1987).[1]

In each of these companies, we tried to identify as many specific cases of innovations as possible and to document their histories in the richest possible detail. To this end, 184 managers of these companies were interviewed, both at the corporate headquarters and also in their national subsidiaries in the United States, the United Kingdom, Germany, Italy, Japan, Singapore, Taiwan, Australia, and Brazil. None of the interviews lasted less than an hour and some took place during multiple meetings involving up to eight hours. We also collected and analyzed relevant internal documents relating to the histories of these innovations. This effort led to identification of thirty-eight cases of innovations for which we could reconstruct fairly extensive histories. While the descriptions possibly suffered from the well-known biases of historical reconstruction, we made all possible efforts to cross-validate the stories through multiple sources and eliminated from the list those cases where different respondents differed significantly in their narration of the sequence of events that led to the innovations. These thirty-eight innovation cases constitute the primary data base for this report.

FOUR DIFFERENT INNOVATION PROCESSES

The innovation process[2] is one of the most complex of all organizational processes, and any stylized representation of this complexity cannot but be guilty of over-simplification. However, past research has suggested a generic stages model, shown in Figure 13–15, that views the innovation process as consisting of three sequential but also interacting subprocesses of sensing, response, and implementation.[3]

To innovate, a firm must sense changes that may demand adaptation or allow exploitation of any internal capability. The acquired stimuli must then be addressed through the firm's response mechanisms: technologies and products must be developed, processes must be improved

Figure 13–15 **A Model of the Innovation Process**

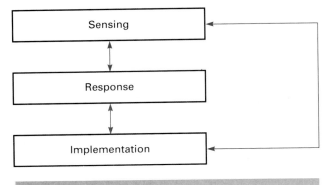

or adapted, or an available capability must be converted into a functional form that satisfies a latent, emerging, or existing demand. Finally, the innovation must be exploited through efficient and effective implementation.

As suggested earlier, this is a highly simplified representation of a complex organizational process. In practice the different stages may be neither as discrete, nor as neatly sequential (Gross et al. 1971; Ginzberg and Reilly 1957). In any specific case, it may be extremely difficult to specify where the sensing process ends and the response process begins, or at what point the implementation phase may be said to have commenced. Similarly, the sequence suggested in the model, while logical, is not an invariant order of events. In reality, the process may be much more iterative, or even circular, with a high degree of interaction among all the three stages (Zaltman et al. 1973).

Despite its simplicity, the model provides a useful starting point for analyzing the administrative tasks of organizing for innovations. To innovate, a firm must develop appropriate capabilities to sense, respond, and implement. But just the capabilities are not enough; the firm must also create appropriate linkages to tie these capabilities together so that they function in an integrative manner. These two dimensions, viz., the configuration of organizational capabilities and the nature of their interlinkages provide, in Roethlisberger's (1977) terms, a "walking stick" for exploring the phenomenon of innovation-organization links.

Table 13–15 summarizes our analysis of the thirty-eight innovation cases in terms of this process model.[4] For each case, we identified the administrative unit or units that carried out the sensing, response, and implementation tasks. This analysis revealed four different patterns in terms of the locations where the three tasks were carried out and, hence, in terms of the interlinkages among organizational units that were required to create and implement the innovation. Each of these patterns represents a different organizational process; collectively they suggest a scheme for classification of innovation processes in multinational corporations.[5] The table represents this classification scheme, and groups the thirty-eight innovation cases according to these categories, each of which is described and illustrated in the following pages.

The Center-for-Global Innovation Process

Center-for-global innovations are those where the center, i.e., the parent company or a central facility such as the corporate R&D laboratory, creates a new product, process, or system for worldwide use.[6] Most instances of center-for-global innovations that we came across in the course of our study were technological innovations, but they were spread around a wide spectrum from minor modifications to substantial reorientations (Normann 1971). Most of the cases involved no participation of the national subsidiaries except for relatively routine tasks such as marketing support or nominal assembly at the implementation stage. In some

Table 13–15   **Innovation Processes in Multinational Corporations**

Innovation Process	Description of Process (locations where different tasks are carried out)			Number of Cases Observed
	Sensing	Response	Implementation	
1. *Center-for-global*	At the center (occasionally, some input may be provided by a particular national subsidiary)	Always at the center	In a number of organizational units worldwide	13
2. *Local-for-local*	In a particular national unit	In the same national unit	In the same national unit	11
3. *Local-for-global*	In a particular national unit	In the same national unit (possibly with some minor help from the center)	Initially in the national unit, subsequently in many units in the worldwide organization of the company	8
4. *Global-for-global*	Many organizational units, including the center and a number of national subsidiaries	Many organizational units, including the center and a number of national subsidiaries	A number of organizational units worldwide	6

others, one or more national organizations also contributed in relatively minor ways in the sensing process, while the response task, in all cases, was entirely carried out at the center. The process by which L. M. Ericsson, the Swedish manufacturer of telecommunications switching and terminal equipments, created the AXE digital switch is one example of this innovation process.

Impetus for the AXE came from early sensing of both shifting market needs and emerging technological changes. The loss of an expected order from the Australian Post Office, combined with the excitement generated by the new digital switch developed by CIT-Alcatel, a small French competitor virtually unknown outside its home country, set in motion a formal review process within Ericsson's headquarters. The review resulted in a proposal for developing a radically new switching system based on new concepts and a new technology. The potential for such a product was high, but the costs and risks were also enormous. The new product was estimated to require over $50 million and about 2,000 man-years of development effort and take at least 5 years before it could be offered in the market. Even if the design turned out to be spectacular, diverting all available development resources during the intervening period could erode the company's competitive position beyond repair.

In sharp contrast to almost all the "principles of innovation" proposed by Drucker (1985), corporate managers of Ericsson decided to place their bet on the proposal for the AXE switch, as the new product came to be called.

The process they adopted was not "incremental" (Quinn 1985), unless the term is so defined as to be all encompassing. A detailed, event-by-event documentation of the history of the switch by a key participant in the development process (Meurling 1985) shows little "controlled chaos" but rather the deliberateness and commitment of a programmed reorientation (Normann 1971). The company provided full authority and all resources so that Ellemtel, the R&D joint venture of Ericsson and the Swedish telecommunications administration, could develop the product as quickly as possible. For over four years, the technological resources of the company were devoted exclusively to this task. The development was carried out entirely in Sweden, and by 1976, the company had the first AXE switch in operation. By 1984 the system was installed in fifty-nine countries around the world.

Not all the cases of center-for-global innovations that we documented were equally effective. NEC, for example, designed the NEAC 61 as a global digital switch and developed it through its traditional centralized development process. However, while the Japanese engineers at the corporate headquarters had excellent technical skills, they were not familiar with the highly sophisticated and complex software requirements of the telephone operating companies in the United States, the principal market at which the product was aimed. As a result, while the switch was appreciated for its hardware capabilities, early sales suffered because the software did not meet some specific end user needs that were significantly different from those of Japanese customers.

The Local-for-Local Innovation Process

Local-for-local innovations are those that are created and implemented by a national subsidiary entirely at the local level. In other words, the sensing, response, and implementation tasks are all carried out within the subsidiary. Most cases of such innovations that we came across tended to be market led rather than technology driven and usually involved only minor modifications of an existing technology, product, or administrative system.

The ability of its local subsidiaries to sense and respond in innovative ways to local needs and opportunities has been an important corporate asset for Unilever. While advanced laundry detergents were not appropriate for markets like India, where much of the laundry was done in streams, a local development that allowed synthetic detergents to be compressed into solid tablet form gave the local subsidiary a product that could capture a significant share of the traditional bar soap market. Similarly, in Turkey, while the company's margarine products did not sell well, an innovative application of Unilever's expertise in edible fats allowed the company to develop a product from vegetable oils that competed with the traditional local clarified butter product, ghee.

As with center-for-global innovations, local-for-local innovations are not always as effective. In Philips, for example, the British subsidiary spent a large amount of resources to create a new TV chassis for its local market that turned out to be indistinguishable from the parent company's standard European model. As a consequence, for years Philips had to operate five instead of four television set factories in Europe.

The Local-for-Global Innovation Process

Local-for-global innovations are those which emerge as local-for-local innovations, are subsequently found to be applicable in multiple locations, and are then diffused to a number of organizational units. Thus, while the initial sensing, response, and implementation tasks are undertaken by a single subsidiary, other subsidiaries participate in the subsequent implementation process, as the innovation is diffused within the company.

Such was the case when Philips' British subsidiary reorganized the structure of its consumer electronics marketing division based on an analysis of changes in its product line and a growing concentration in its distribution channels. The traditional marketing organization, which operated with a standard set of distribution, promotion, and sales policies applied uniformly to all product lines, was proving to be increasingly ineffective in dealing with the large-volume chains that had come to dominate the retail market. Further, Philips' undifferentiated marketing strategies were constraining efforts in the differentiated and rapidly changing markets for its diverse products. To cope with this problem, the U.K. subsidiary abolished this uniform structure for each product line and organized the marketing department into three groups; an advanced system group for dealing with the technologically sophisticated, high-margin, and image-building products like Laservision and compact disc players; a mainstay group for marketing high-volume mature products such as color TV and VCR; and a mass group for mass merchandizing of the older, declining products like portable cassette players and black-and-white TV sets.

This new organization allowed the company to differentiate the nature and intensity of marketing support it provided to different products according to their stages in the product life cycle and to engage various elements of the marketing mix—including promotion, pricing, and distribution—in a more selective and differentiated manner. Within the first year of implementation, the new organization had helped reduce aggregate selling expenses from 18 to 12 percent. During the same period, while overall market demand for consumer electronics products in the United Kingdom had fallen by 5 percent, the subsidiary's sales in this business had risen by 49 percent, including a 400 percent rise in sales to Dixons, the largest reseller chain.

Meanwhile, increasing concentration in the distribution channels and growing necessity for differentiating marketing approaches for different products became manifest Europe-wide. The new model of the marketing organization developed by the British subsidiary was clearly appropriate for many other subsidiaries and, despite some initial resistance, the innovation was transferred to most other national organizations.

Resistance to such transfers, however, is both widespread and strong in MNCs, and it blocked several attempted local-for-global innovations we studied. For example, management of Unilever was unable to transfer a zero phosphate detergent developed by its German subsidiary to other European locations. Insisting that its market needs were different, the French subsidiary insisted on developing its own zero-P project.

The Global-for-Global Innovation Process

Global-for-global innovations are those that are created by pooling the resources and capabilities of many different organizational units of the MNC, including the headquarters and a number of different subsidiaries, so as to arrive at a jointly developed general solution to an emerging global opportunity, instead of finding different local solutions in each environment or a central solution that is imposed on all the units. As an ideal type, this category of innovations involves participation of multiple organizational units in each of the three stages of sensing, response, and implementation. However, the key feature that distinguishes it from the other categories is that the response task is shared, instead of being carried out by a single unit. One of the best examples we observed of this mode of innovation was the way in which Procter and Gamble developed its global liquid detergent.

Despite the success of liquid laundry detergents in the United States, all attempts to create a heavy-duty liquid detergent category in Europe failed due to different washing practices and superior performance of European powder detergents which contained levels of enzymes, bleach, and phosphates not permitted in the United States. But P&G's European scientists were convinced that they could enhance the performance of the liquid to match the local powders. After seven years of work they developed a bleach substitute, a fatty acid with water-softening capabilities equivalent to phosphate, and a means to give enzymes stability in liquid form.

Meanwhile, researchers in the United States had been working on a new liquid better able to deal with the high-clay soil content in dirty clothes in the United States, and this group developed improvements in the builders, the ingredients that prevent redisposition of dirt in the wash. Also during this period, the company's International Technology Coordination Group was working with P&G scientists in Japan to develop a more robust surfactant (the ingredient that removes greasy stains), making the liquid more effective in the cold water washes that were common in Japan. Thus, the units in Europe, the United States, and Japan had each developed effective responses to its local needs, yet none of them had cooperated to share their breakthroughs.

When the company's head of R&D for Europe was promoted to the top corporate research job, one of his primary objectives was to create more coordination and cooperation among the diverse local-for-local development efforts, and the world liquid project became a test case. Plans to launch Omni, the new liquid the U.S group had been working on, was shelved until the innovations from Europe and Japan could be incorporated. Similarly, the Japanese and the Europeans picked up on the new developments from the other laboratories. Joint effort on the part of all these groups ultimately led to the launch of Liquid Tide in the United States, Liquid Cheer in Japan, and Liquid Ariel in Europe. All these products incorporated the best of the developments created in response to European, American, and Japanese market needs.

ASSOCIATIONS BETWEEN INNOVATION PROCESSES AND ORGANIZATIONAL ATTRIBUTES

As we reviewed the key characteristics of the participating organizational components for each of the innovations listed in Table 13–15, four attributes, viz., (1) configuration of organizational assets and slack resources, (2) nature of interunit exchange relationships, (3) socialization processes, and (4) intensity of communication, appeared to have some systematic associations with the organization's ability to create innovations through the different processes we have described. These associations among the organizational factors and innovation processes are schematically represented in Figure 13–16, and are briefly described and illustrated in the following pages.

Configuration of Organizational Assets and Slack Resources

In some companies, such as Matsushita, most key organizational assets and slack resources were centralized at the headquarters. Even though 40 percent of Matsushita's sales were made abroad, only 10 percent of its products were manufactured outside of Japan. The Japanese manufacturing facilities were also the most advanced and well-equipped plants of the company, producing almost all of its sophisticated products. R&D, similarly, was fully centralized in seven research laboratories in Japan. The center-for-global process appeared to contribute most of the significant innovations in companies with such a centralized configuration of organizational assets and resources. In Matsushita, for example, *all* new consumer electronics products introduced between 1983 and 1986 were developed by the parent company in Japan and were subsequently introduced in its different foreign markets.

In companies like Philips, ITT and Unilever, on the other hand, manufacturing, marketing, and even R&D facilities were widely dispersed throughout the organization. The local-for-local (and, to a lesser extent, local-for-global) process contributed a significant number of innovations in these companies. The dispersal of assets and resources was perhaps at its most extreme in the telecommunications business of ITT. The company had practically no central research of manufacturing activity, and each major national subsidiary was fully integrated and self-sufficient in its ability to develop, manufacture, and market new products. Up until the advent of digital switching, all major products including the Metaconta and Pentaconta switches were initially developed in one or the other subsidiary and were subsequently "redeveloped" by other subsidiaries, resulting in many different varieties of the same product being sold in different markets. In Philips, similarly, the list of local-for-local innovations is endless—the first stereo color TV set was developed by the Australian subsidiary, teletext TV sets were created by the British subsidiary, "smart cards" by the French subsidiary, and the programmed word-processing typewriter by North American Philips—to cite but a few examples.

Some of the companies we surveyed were gradually adopting a third system of asset and resource configuration. Instead of either centralization or decentralization, they were developing an interconnected network of specialized assets distributed around the world. Ericsson, NEC, and Procter and Gamble were the most advanced in building such a system, and it is only in these companies that we saw some cases of successful global-for-global innovations (even in these companies, however, most innovations came through the other processes).

In NEC, organizational assets were traditionally cen-

Figure 13–16 **Associations between Innovation Processes and Organizational Attributes**

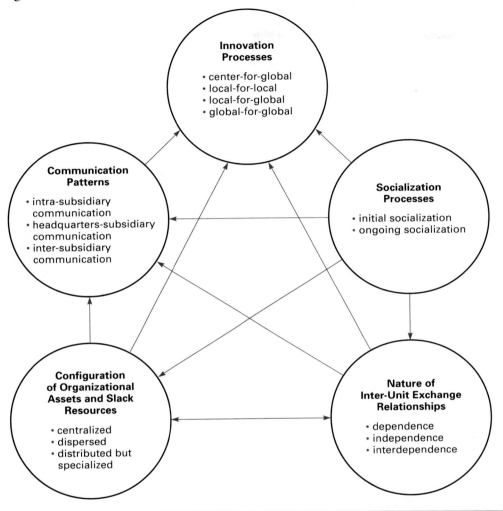

tralized, and most innovations were created through the center-for-global process. The NEAC 61 digital switch, for example, was developed entirely in the company's central facilities in Japan, even though the product was principally aimed at the North American market. Subsequently, however, the company developed specialized software capabilities in the United States, while hardware expertise remained at the center. Such a distribution of resources allowed NEC to approximate the global-for-global process in developing the NEAC 61E auxiliary switch: the headquarters took the lead in building the hardware while the subsidiary participated significantly in designing the software. Similarly, the global liquid project of P&G that we have described earlier in the paper was made possible and necessary because three different research units responsible for product develop-

ment in Japan, Europe, and the United States had each developed specialized capabilities that the others did not possess.

Several researchers have shown how resource configuration constrains all aspects of organizational actions and interactions (Emery and Trist 1965; Aldrich 1976). In the specific context of research on organizational innovations, a number of authors have highlighted the importance of distributed slack resources for creation and innovations (March and Simon 1958; Cyert and March 1963; Mohr 1969; Mansfield 1968; Kanter 1983). It has also been argued that local slack may have opposite effects on creation of innovations and adoption of innovations created elsewhere (Wilson 1966; Sapolsky 1967). Finally, the observation that interdependent, specialized resources might lead to joint innovations is also not new to the literature (Thompson 1967; Kanter 1983). Thus, the innovation process-resource configuration associations we observed are entirely consistent with what would be predicted by existing theory, if applied to the specific context of large, multi-unit organizations.

Nature of Interunit Exchange Relationships

In most of the countries in our sample, interactions among the national subsidiaries were extremely limited, and dyadic relationships between the headquarters and each of the different subsidiaries were the dominant form of interunit exchanges. In some of these companies, such as Kao, the large Japanese manufacturer of soaps and detergents, these dyadic exchange relationships were based primarily on subsidiary dependence on the headquarters. National subsidiaries of this company had neither the competence nor the legitimacy to initiate any new programs or even to modify any product or administrative system developed by the parent company. For example, a particular brand of liquid shampoo that was extremely successful in Japan failed to produce desired effects when introduced in Thailand. The product, aimed to suit the sophisticated needs of the Japanese market, could not compete effectively with simpler but less expensive local products and developed only a marginal 7 percent of market share despite considerable marketing investments. However, the nature of the problem could be identified and some remedial measures taken only after marketing experts from the headquarters visited the subsidiary along with executives from Dentsu, Kao's Japanese advertising agents. The local manager acknowledged that "Japan's expertise, knowledge, and resources made it appropriate for them to make such decisions." In companies where subsidiaries had developed such highly dependent relationships with the headquarters, the center-for-global process was often the exclusive source of innovations. For example, in Kao we did not come across a single case of any other innovation process.

In some other companies, such as ITT and Philips, the subsidiaries had considerable strategic and operational autonomy, though the headquarters exercised varying degrees of administrative control through the budgeting and financial reporting systems. In these companies, where subsidiaries were relatively independent of the headquarters, local-for-local innovations were far more prevalent.

The local-for-global and global-for-global processes essentially require the involvement of multiple organizational units, including a number of different national subsidiaries, and are realizable only when inter-subsidiary exchange relationships are prevalent in the company. However, in all the cases where these innovation processes were effective, such exchange relationships among organizational units appeared to be based on reciprocal interdependence (Thompson 1967), rather than on either dependence or independence.

In Procter and Gamble, for example, teams consisting of representatives from different national organizations in Europe (Euro-brand teams) coordinate regional strategies for different products of the company. For each product group, the team is headed by the general manager of a particular subsidiary and includes brand managers from other major subsidiaries. These teams provide one of the many mechanisms in the company that promote exchange relationships among the different national subsidiaries. Further, by ensuring that general managers from different subsidiaries head the different teams, the company creates reciprocal interdependencies in the relationships, since each general manager recognizes that the level of cooperation he can expect from the brand managers or other subsidiaries in his team is dependent on the level of cooperation his brand managers extend to the other product teams that are headed by the general managers of other subsidiaries.

In contrast, ITT's attempt to develop the System 12 digital switch through a similar global-for-global process floundered because of the absence of such interdependencies. Recognizing that the technical resources required for developing the switch could not be assembled in any one location in its highly decentralized international organization, ITT management decided to adopt the global-for-global process of designing and building the switch through coordinated and joint action involving most of its major national operations. However, conditioned by a long history of local independence, the national subsidiaries resisted joint efforts and common standards leading to constant duplication of efforts, divergence of specifications, delays and an enormous budget overrun.

The effects of centralization and decentralization on innovation has been a topic of considerable debate in the literature. While most authors have argued in favor of a negative correlation between centralization and creation of innovations and a positive correlation between centralization and internal diffusion of innovations (for a review, see Zaltman et al. 1973), it has also been suggested that the relationships may be contingent on the type of innovation as well as the extent to which information and perspectives are shared among members of the organization (Downs and Mohr, 1979). Our findings support the general view that centralization of authority and the resulting dependency relationship between the headquarters and subsidiaries facilitate diffusion of center-for-global innovations but impede creation of local-for-local innovations, while decentralization of authority and the resulting independence of subsidiaries have precisely the opposite effects.

The facilitating influence of reciprocal interdependencies on local-for-global and global-for-global innovations observed by us also finds some support in exchange theory (Emerson 1972). Such interdependencies induce mutual cooperation (March and Simon 1958) and overcome both the bureaucratic and entrepreneurial traps described by Kanter (1983) as impediments to joint problem solving on the part of different organizational members.

Before concluding our discussion on inter-unit exchange relationships, we should note that the configuration of organizational resources tend to have considerable influence on the governance of such exchange, and vice versa. Theoretically, such associations are predicted by the resource dependency perspective (Pfeffer and Salancik 1978). When resources are centralized, as in Matsushita, Kao, and NEC, dyadic relationships of subsidiary dependence on the headquarters can be expected and are also observed. When resources are decentralized, as in Philips and Unilever, the subsidiaries exercise considerable independence and autonomy. Similarly, autonomous and resourceful subsidiaries are able to attract further resources for extension of current activities or creation of new ones, thereby establishing the reverse link between the nature of exchange relationships and the future flow of resources within the organization. Historically, location decisions for new manufacturing capacity in Philips were influenced by the relative power of different subsidiaries almost as much as by the dictates of production and distribution economies. On the other hand, Matsushita captured a very significant research facility in the United States when it acquired Motorola's TV business and senior corporate managers expected this research unit to play a major role in designing components and products for worldwide use. However, this role was inconsistent with the traditional basis of headquarters-subsidiary relationship in the company, and the capability was lost when most research engineers left in response to increasing functional control from the headquarters and the resulting loss of their local independence.

Organizational Socialization Processes

One interesting observation we made in the course of the study is that managers in both Philips and Matsushita were highly socialized into the very strong cultures of their respective organizations, though in very different ways. Further, while collectively, at the center, Matsushita managers continually sought change, individually, as expatriate managers in different national subsidiaries, they were relatively more likely to take a "custodial" stance, resisting change to centrally designed products, processes, and even routine administrative systems. Expatriate managers in Philips, in contrast, were generally more willing to champion local initiatives and thereby foster local-for-local innovations.

Van Maanen and Schein (1979) have argued that the nature of initial and ongoing socialization processes of organizations have some important influences on members' attitudes toward change. Certain socialization processes lead to custodial behavior and resistance to change, while others facilitate both content and role innovations on the part of socialized members. At least in the cases of Philips and Matsushita, the associations between socialization processes and attitude toward change proposed by these authors appear to explain the observed behavioral differences quite remarkably.

Initial postrecruitment training and subsequent career structures are two important constituents of the organizational socialization process, and are both quite different for managers in the two companies. In Matsushita, college graduates are recruited at the center in large batches and are collectively socialized through a common training program that continues for one year or more. Managerial recruits in Philips, on the other hand, are recruited from diverse locations in small numbers, and are quickly posted to different units so as to learn on the job. While cohorts meet infrequently for some classroom sessions, initial socialization tends to be relatively more individually oriented, dependent on the new member establishing personal relationships with existing members, often his or her senior colleagues, on a one-to-one basis.

Before being assigned overseas, Matsushita managers are exposed to another strong dose of formal training. The company's formidable Overseas Training Center (OTC) prepares managers for overseas tours of duty by ensuring that they thoroughly understand Matsushita's practices and values. Expatriate managers are usually posted to a foreign location for relatively long periods, usually five to eight years, after which they return to the headquarters. They may be posted abroad once more, later in their careers, and often to the same location where they had worked earlier, though at more senior levels. In Philips, given the relatively insignificant role of the home country operations in the worldwide business of the company, a large number of managers spend a significant part of their careers abroad continuously, spending between two and three years in a number of different subsidiaries. Many of these managers retire abroad, while some return to take up top-level corporate positions toward the end of their careers.

As suggested by Van Maanen and Schein, collective socialization such as in Matsushita results in relatively stronger conformity to the values that the collectivity is socialized into. Thus, when change is proposed within that collectivity (such as in the headquarters which is seen as the repository of those values), it tends to be supported. However, local changes in national subsidiaries that attempt to modify values, systems, or processes designed by that collectivity tend to be resisted. In contrast, individual socialization, as in Philips, tends to produce less homogeneity of views and greater willingness to change at local levels.

Similarly, the differences in career systems can also be expected to result in very different attitudes to local innovations. In Philips, expatriate managers follow each other into key management and technical positions in the company's national organizations around the world; they perceive themselves as a distinct subgroup within the organization and come to develop and share a distinct subculture. In Matsushita, on the other hand, there is very little interaction among the expatriate managers in different subsidiaries, and they tend to view themselves as part of the parent company on temporary assignment to foreign locations. Consequently, Philips managers tend to identify strongly with the national organization's point of view and to serve as champions of local level changes, while Matsushita managers become more prone to implementing centrally designed products and policies.

Received theory, as well as our own observations in the nine companies, suggests that organizational socialization processes have significant influences on both the basis of internal exchange relations within organizations, and the configuration of assets and slack resources—the two other influencing variables in our model. Institutionalized processes of initial and ongoing socialization of new members lie at the core of organizational cultures and form the administrative routines that govern internal exchange behavior and exercise of choice (Ouchi 1980; Schein 1985; Nelson and Winter 1982). Shared goals and values lead to fluidity in the internal distribution of power, and to flexibility in its use (Pascale and Athos 1981; Kanter 1983). Configuration of organizational resources is a product of organizational goals and internal power structures (Pfeffer and Salancik 1978; Mintzberg 1983) and is thereby indirectly influenced by the socialization processes that affect both these determinants. Illustrations of these influences abound in the organizations we studied. The "ization" program of Unilever—a commitment to "localize" Unilever in each country as well as to "Unileverize" each local operation—is a case in point. This program—backed by extensive ongoing training activities, a planned company-wide transfer policy, and significant commitment of top management time devoted to ensure its reinforcement and salience—has led simultaneously to a gradual reconfiguration of the company's resources from being almost totally decentralized to becoming more specialized and interdependent, and the restructuring of inter-unit interactions from an internal norm of fiercely protected subsidiary autonomy to much greater sharing of influence in which subsidiary initiatives are circumscribed by a significant and substantive role of the center in setting and coordinating strategies, particularly with regard to development and introduction of new products.

Communication Patterns

Almost all studies on innovation-organization linkages have emphasized the central role of communication in facilitating organizational innovations (Allen 1977; Allen, Lee, and Tushman 1980; Burns and Stalker 1961; Kanter 1983; Rogers and Shoemaker 1971). Collectively, this body of theoretical and empirical literature has found consistent support for the proposition that communication is a prerequisite for innovations and, more specifically, that intra-organizational communication is perhaps the most important determinant of an organization's ability to create and institutionalize innovations.

Internal communication patterns in the nine companies we studied could be broadly categorized into three groups. In some companies such as ITT and Philips, internal communication within each subunit (the headquarters or individual national subsidiaries) was intense, but the level of communication among subunits (between the headquarters and each of the subsidiaries as well as among the subsidiaries themselves) was relatively low. In some others, such as Matsushita, communication links between the headquarters and most of the different subsidiaries were especially strong, but internal communication within the subsidiaries as well as communication among the subsidiaries tended to be limited. Finally, the third group consisted of companies like Procter and Gamble and L. M. Ericsson, where both internal communication within subunits and communication among subunits tended to be relatively rich and frequent. Local-for-local innovations were the most common in the first group of companies (although some of them, such as Philips, could also create innovations through the local-for-global process), center-for-global innovations were dominant in the second, and only the third group could create innovations though all the four processes we have described.

By examining internal communication patterns in Philips, one can see how they support local-for-local innovations. Historically, the top management in all national subsidiaries of Philips consisted not of an individual CEO but a committee made up of the heads of the technical, commercial, and finance functions. This system of three-headed management had a long history in Philips, stemming from the functional independence of the two founding Philips brothers, one an engineer and the other a salesman, and has endured as a tradition of intensive intra-unit cross-functional communication and joint decision making within each subsidiary.

In most subsidiaries, these integration mechanisms exist at three organizational levels. At the product management level, article teams prepare annual sales plans and budgets and develop product policies. A second tier of cross-functional coordination takes place through the group management team, which meets once a month to review results, suggest corrective actions, and resolve any inter-functional differences. The highest level cross-functional coordination and communication forum within the subsidiary is the senior management committee (SMC) consisting of the top commercial, technical, and financial managers of the subsidiary. Acting essentially as the local board, the SMC ensures overall unity of effort among the different functional groups within the local unit, and protects the legitimacy and effectiveness of the communication forums at lower levels of the organization. These multilevel cross-functional integrative mechanisms within each subsidiary lie at the heart of Philips' ability to create local innovations in its different operating environments.

If the challenge for improving the efficiency of local-for-local innovations lies in strengthening cross-functional communication within subsidiaries, the key task for enhancing the effectiveness of center-for-global innovations lies in building linkages between the headquarters and the different subsidiaries of the company. The main problem of centrally created innovations is that those developing new products or processes may not understand market needs, or that those required to implement the new product introduction are not committed to it. Matsushita overcomes these problems of center-for-global innovations by creating multilevel and multifunctional linkages between the headquarters and each of the different subsidiaries and these linkages facilitate both the communication of local market demands from the subsidiary to the center, and also central coordination and control over the subsidiary's implementation of the company's strategies and plans, including those of implementing innovations.

The communication links that connect different parts of the Matsushita organization in Japan with the video department of MESA, its U.S. subsidiary, are illustrative of headquarters-subsidiary communication systems in the company. The vice president in charge of this department of MESA has his roots in Matsushita Electric Trading Company (METC), the central organization that has overall responsibility for the company's overseas business. Although formally posted to the United States, he continues to be a member of the senior management committee of METC and spends about a third of his time in Japan. The general manager of this department had worked for fourteen years in the video product division of Matsushita Electric Industries (MEI), the central production and domestic marketing company in Japan. He maintains almost daily communication with the central product division in Japan and acts as its link to the local American market. The assistant manager in the department, the most junior expatriate in the organization, links the local unit to the central factory in Japan. Having spent five years in the factory, he is and acts as its local representative and handles all day-to-day communication with factory personnel.

None of these linkages is accidental. They are deliberately created and maintained and reflect the company's desire to preserve the different perspectives and priorities of its diverse groups worldwide, and ensure that they have linkages to those in the headquarters who can represent and defend their views. Unlike in companies that try to focus headquarters-subsidiary communication through a single channel for the sake of efficiency, Matsushita's multilevel and multifunctional linkages create a broad band of communication through which each central unit involved in creating center-for-global innovations have direct access to local market information, while each local unit involved in implementing those innovations also has the opportunity to influence the innovation process.

Finally, a few companies like P&G and Ericsson are able to create organizational mechanisms that facilitate simultaneously intense intra-unit communication, extensive headquarters-subsidiary communication, and also considerable flow of information among the different subsidiaries. As a result, these companies are able to create innovations through all the four processes.

In Ericsson, for example, intra-subsidiary communication is facilitated both by a culture and tradition of open communication and, more specifically, by extensive use of ad hoc teams and special liaison roles with the express mandate of facilitating intra-unit integration. Headquarters-subsidiary communication is strengthened by mechanisms such as deputing one or more senior corporate managers as members of subsidiary boards. Unlike many companies whose local boards are pro forma bodies aimed at satisfying national legal requirements, Ericsson uses its local boards as legitimate forums for communicating objectives, resolving differences, and making decisions. Intersubsidiary communication is facilitated by a number of processes such as allocating global roles to subsidiaries for specific tasks (for example, Italy is the center for transmission system development, Finland for mobile telephones, and Australia for rural switches) which require them to establish communication links worldwide. However, perhaps the single factor that has the strongest effect on facilitating communication in the dispersed Ericsson organization is its long-standing policy of transferring large numbers of people back and forth between headquarters and subsidiaries.

Executive transfers in Ericsson differ from the more common transfer patterns in multinational corporations in both direction and intensity, as a comparison with NEC's transfer processes will demonstrate. Where NEC may transfer a new technology through one or perhaps a few key managers, Ericsson will send a team of 50 or 100 engineers and managers for a year or two; while NEC's flows are primarily from headquarters to subsidiary, Ericsson's is a balanced, two-way flow with people coming to the parent not only to learn but also to bring their expertise; and while NEC's transfers are predominantly Japanese, Ericsson's multidirectional process involves all nationalities.

Australian technicians seconded to Stockholm in the mid-1970s to bring their experience with digital switching into the development of AXE developed enduring relationships that helped in the subsequent development of a rural switch in Australia through the global-for-global process. Confidences built when an Italian team of forty spent eighteen months in Sweden to learn about electronic switching provided the basis for greater decentralization of AXE software development and a delegated responsibility for developing the switch's central transmission system through a local-for-global process.

Communication may be the final cause (Mohr 1982) that influences innovation processes in organizations, but it is itself a product of different organizational attributes such as the configuration of resources (Pfeffer 1982), internal governance systems (Kaufman 1960), and culture (Schein 1985). Our descriptions of the mechanisms that facilitate communication in some of the companies we surveyed illustrate these linkages, which are part of the model represented in Figure 13–16.

CONCLUSION

In this paper we have identified four organizational attributes that influence the different multinational innovation processes: configuration of organizational assets and slack resources; basis for inter-unit exchange relationships that reflect the distribution of power within the company; training, transfer, and other processes of socializing members; and the nature of intra- and inter-unit communication. Each of these has been identified by earlier researchers as key factors that influence an organization's ability to innovate. Burns and Stalker (1961) emphasized the importance of decentralized authority and intra-unit communication for promoting "grass-roots" innovations (local-for-local, in our terms). Lorsch and Lawrence (1965) highlighted the relevance of cross-functional integration. Quinn (1985) and Peters and Waterman (1982) illustrated the need for fluid power structures and dispersal of organizational resources. And Kanter (1983), in her description of the "integrative organization," identified each of these elements as key requirements for promoting organizational innovations. Thus, our overall findings broadly confirm those of many others who have investigated the effects of different organizational attributes on innovative capability of firms.

At the same time, our findings provide a point of departure and an avenue for incremental extension of existing theory. The source of this extension lies in our explicit focus on multi-unit organizations which necessitates simultaneous consideration of organizational attributes both within individual units and across multiple units. In contrast, most of past research has been limited to organizational subcomponents as the level of analysis, even though conclusions have sometimes been generalized at the level of the total organization. In the case of Burns and Stalker, the level of analysis is stated quite explicitly: "The twenty concerns that were subject of these studies were not all separately constituted business companies. This is why we have used concern as a generic term. . . . [Some of them] were small parts of the parent organization." The other researchers have similarly observed a district sales office of General Electric or a department in the headquarters of 3M, or a divisional data processing office of Polaroid, but not the overall organizational configuration in any one of these physically and goal-dispersed organizations. Given the possibility that there may be trade-offs between integration and differentiation at different levels of the organization (Lawrence and Lorsch 1967), findings at the level of organizational subcomponents can serve as useful hypotheses but not as validated conclusions at the level of multi-unit, complex organizations.

By broadening the focus to include inter-unit interactions, we have identified four different organizational processes through which innovations may be created and institutionalized in multi-unit companies. It is also manifest that the different processes are facilitated by organizational attributes that are not only different but possibly also contradictory. Local-for-local innovations, for example, tend to be incremental (Quinn 1985) and unprogrammed (Drucker 1985) changes that are facilitated by distributed resources

and decentralized authority—attributes of the organic concern described by Burns and Stalker. Some center-for-global innovations, on the other hand, can be reorientations (Normann 1971) that are highly programmed, and they may be facilitated by precisely the opposite characteristics of centralization of organizational resources and authority. Factors that facilitate innovativeness on the part of a subunit may not be those that facilitate their adoption of innovations created elsewhere in the company, nor their participation in joint efforts. By differentiating among the processes, we have taken a step, albeit small, in the direction of a more disaggregated analysis of innovation-organization links advocated by Downs and Mohr (1979).

Our findings of the organizational attributes that facilitate each of these different innovation processes are summarized in Table 13–16. Given the exploratory nature of the study, these findings are, at best, grounded hypotheses that clearly require more systematic and rigorous analysis. These hypothesis, however, have some significant consequences for theory and therefore appear to be deserving of the additional efforts that are necessary to test and validate them.[7]

At a more normative level, the complexity and diversity of technological, competitive, and market environments confronting most worldwide industries may require participating multinationals to create organizational mechanisms that would facilitate simultaneously all the innovation processes we have described. Although a few companies in our sample had begun to achieve this state on a partial and temporary basis, creating such a capability on a more general and permanent basis may be a challenge of considerable magnitude, given the potential contradictions in organizational attributes that facilitate each of these innovation processes. A more systematic study on the topic can lead to reliable suggestions on how these potential contradictions can be overcome. Based on our discussions with a number of MNC managers to whom we have presented our findings, we are convinced that such a study would be of great value to them.

NOTES

1. This study of innovations in MNCs was a part of a larger research project on management of multinational corporations which covered a number of issues other than management of innovations. The overall findings of the project are being reported in our forthcoming book, *Managing Across Borders: The Transnational Solution.*

2. The term *innovation* has been defined in many different ways. However, these definitions can be broadly classified into two categories: those that see innovation as the final event—"the idea, practice, or material artifact that has been invented or that is regarded as novel independent of its adoption or nonadoption" (Zaltman et al. 1973:7), and those who, like Myers and Marquis, see it as a process "which proceeds from the conceptualization

Table 13–16 **Associations between Innovation Processes and Organizational Factors: A Summary**

Innovation Process	Configuration of Assets and Stock Resources	Socialization Processes	Nature of Interunit Exchange Relationships	Communication Patterns
1. *Center-for-global*	Centralized at headquarters	Formal and collective initial training, transfers of few people from headquarters to subsidiaries, infrequently and for long terms	Subsidiaries dependent on headquarters	High density of communication between headquarters and subsidiaries
2. *Local-for-local*	Dispersed to subsidiaries	Informal and individual initial training; subsidiary-to-subsidiary transfers of an international cadre of managers	Subsidiaries independent of headquarters	High density of communication within subsidiaries
3. *Local-for-global*	Dispersed to subsidiaries	Informal but both collective and individual initial training; subsidiary-to-subsidiary transfers of an international cadre of managers	Subsidiaries independent of headquarters but mutually dependent on each other	High density of communication within and among subsidiaries.
4. *Global-for-global*	Distributed, specialized	Both collective and individual initial training, two-way transfers of large numbers of managers among headquarters and the different subsidiaries	Headquarters and subsidiaries mutually dependent on one another	High density of communication within subsidiaries, among subsidiaries, and between the headquarters and the subsidiaries

of a new idea to a solution of the problem and then to the actual utilization of a new item of economic or social value" (1969:1). We adopt the latter definition and, throughout the paper, use the terms innovation and innovation process interchangeably.

3. The sense-response-implement model has an extensive history in multiple fields. It is directly adopted from the unfreeze-change-refreeze framework in the field of organization development proposed by Lewis and subsequently enhanced by Bennis, Schein, Beckhard, and others. For a brief review of this literature, see Lorange et al. (1986). The same model, with different labels, has been adopted in the marketing field to describe the new product introduction process (see, for example, Urban and Hauser 1980), and by many scholars who have studied the organizational innovation process (see Zaltman et al. 1973 for a review).

4. To save space, we do not list the thirty-eight innovation

cases, but interested readers can find such a list in Ghoshal (1986:a).

5. Both the spirit of this analysis and the actual methodology were inspired by the work of Bower (1980). However, given a relatively large number of cases, a more formal case clustering approach was adopted.

6. The terms global and worldwide have been used somewhat loosely in the paper to imply many different national subsidiaries or environments.

7. We have since pursued this research direction and the results tend to support the hypotheses. These findings will be reported in a forthcoming paper.

BIBLIOGRAPHY

Aldrich, H. E. "Resource Dependency and Interorganizational Relations." *Administration and Society* 7 (1976): 419–54.

Allen, T. J. *Managing the Flow of Technology.* Cambridge, MA: MIT Press, 1977.

Allen, T. J., and S. Cohen. "Information Flow in R&D Laboratories." *Administrative Science Quarterly* 14 (1969): 12–19.

Allen, T. J.; D. M. S. Lee; and M. L. Tushman. "R&D performance as a Function of Internal Communication, Project Management, and the Nature of Work." *IEEE Transactions on Engineering Management* EM-27 (1980): 2–12.

Bartlett, C. A., and S. Ghoshal. "Managing Across Borders: New Strategic Requirements." *Sloan Management Review* (Summer 1987): 7–17.

———. *Managing Across Borders: The Transnational Solution.* Boston: Harvard Business School Press, forthcoming.

Bower, J. L. *Managing the Resource Allocation Process.* Boston: Harvard Business School Press, 1980.

Buckley, P. J., and M. C. Casson. *The Future of the Multinational Enterprise.* London: Macmillan Press, 1976.

Burns, T., and G. M. Stalker. *The Management of Innovation.* London: Tavistock, 1961.

Calvet, A. L. "A Synthesis of Foreign Direct Investment Theories and Theories of the Multinational Firm." *Journal of International Business Studies* (Spring-Summer 1981): 43–59.

Cyert, R. M., and J. G. March. *A Behavioral Theory of the Firm.* Englewood Cliffs, NJ: Prentice-Hall, 1963.

Downs, G. W., and L. B. Mohr. "Conceptual Issues in the Study of Innovation." *Administrative Science Quarterly* 21 (1976): 700–14.

———. "Toward a Theory of Innovation." *Administration and Society* 10, no. 4 (1979): 379–407.

Drucker, P. F. *Innovation and Entrepreneurship.* New York: Harper and Row, 1985.

Emerson, R. N. "Exchange Theory, Part II: Exchange Relations, Exchange Networks, and Groups as Exchange Systems." In J. Berger, M. Zelditch, and B. Anderson, eds., *Sociological Theories in Progress,* vol. 2. Boston: Houghton Mifflin, 1972.

Emery, F. E., and F. L. Trist. "The Contextual Texture of Organizational Environments." *Human Relations* 18 (1965): 21–31.

Ghoshal, S. "The Innovative Multinational: A Differentiated Network of Organizational Roles and Management Processes." Ph.D. diss. Graduate School of Business Administration, Harvard University, 1986(a).

———. "Global Strategy: An Organizing Framework." Paper presented to the Annual Conference of the Academy of International Business, London, 1986(b).

Ginzberg, E., and E. Reilly. *Effective Change in Large Organizations.* New York: Columbia University Press, 1957.

Gordon, G.; J. R. Kimberley; and A. MacEachron. "Some Considerations in the Design of Problem Solving Research on the Diffusion of Medical Technology." In W. J. Abernathy, A. Sheldon, and C. K. Prahalad, eds., *The Management of Health Care.* Cambridge, MA: Ballinger, 1975.

Gross, N.; J. B. Giacquinta; and M. Berstein. *Implementing Organizational Innovations: A Sociological Analysis of Planned Educational Change.* New York: Basic Books, 1971.

Hamel, G., and C. K. Prahalad. "Do You Really Have a Global Strategy?" *Harvard Business Review* (July-August 1985): 139–148.

Hout, T.; M. E. Porter; and E. Rudden. "How Global Companies Win Out." *Harvard Business Review* (September-October 1982): 98–108.

Kanter, R. M. *The Change Masters.* New York: Simon and Schuster, 1983.

Kaufman, H. *The Forest Ranger: A Study in Administrative Behavior.* Baltimore: Johns Hopkins University Press, 1960.

Kelly, P., and M. Kranzberg. *Technological Innovations: A Critical Review of Current Knowledge.* San Francisco: San Francisco University Press, 1978.

Lawrence, P. R., and J. W. Lorsch. *Organization and Environment.* Boston: Graduate School of Business Administration, Harvard University, 1967.

Lorange, P.; M. Scott Morton; and S. Ghoshal. *Strategic Control.* St. Paul: West Publishing Co., 1986.

Lorsch, J. W., and P. A. Lawrence. "Organizing for Product Innovation." *Harvard Business Review* (January-February 1965): 109–120.

Mansfield, E. *The Economics of Technological Change.* New York: W. W. Norton, 1968.

March, J. G., and H. A. Simon. *Organizations.* New York: Wiley, 1958.

Meurling, J. *A Switch in Time.* Chicago: Telephony Publishing Corp., 1985.

Mintzberg, H. *Power in and Around Organizations.* Englewood Cliffs, NJ: Prentice-Hall, 1983.

Mohr, L. B. "Determinants of Innovation in Organizations." *American Political Science Review* 63 (1969): 111–26.

———. *Explaining Organizational Behavior.* San Francisco: Jossey-Bass, 1982.

Myers, S., and D. G. Marquis. *Successful Industrial Innovations.* Washington, D.C.: National Science Foundation, NSF 69–17,1969.

Nelson, R. R., and S. G. Winter. *An Economic Theory of Evolutionary Capabilities and Behavior.* Cambridge: Harvard University Press, 1982.

Normann, R. "Organizational Innovativeness: Product Variation and Reorientation." *Administrative Science Quarterly* 16, no. 2 (1971): 203–15.

Ouchi, W. G. "Markets, Bureaucracies, and Clans." *Administrative Science Quarterly* 25 (1980): 129–41.

Pascale, R. T., and A. G. Athos. *The Art of Japanese Management*. New York: Warner Books, 1981.

Peters, T. J., and R. H. Waterman. *In Search of Excellence*. New York: Harper & Row, 1982.

Pfeffer, J. *Power in Organizations*. Boston: Pitman, 1982.

Pfeffer, J., and G. R. Salancik. *The External Control of Organizations: A Resource Dependency Perspective*. New York: Harper and Row, 1978.

Porter, M. E. "Competition in Global Industries: A Conceptual Framework." In M. E. Porter, ed., *Competition in Global Industries*. Boston: Harvard Business School Press, 1986.

Prahalad, C. K. "The Strategic Process in a Multinational Corporation." Ph.D. diss., Graduate School of Business Administration, Harvard University, Boston, 1975.

Quinn, J. B. "Managing Innovations: Controlled Chaos." *Harvard Business Review* (May-June 1985): 73–84.

Roethlisberger, F. J. *The Elusive Phenomenon*. Boston: Division of Research, Graduate School of Business Administration, Harvard University, 1977.

Rogers, E. M., and F. F. Shoemaker. *Communication of Innovations: A Cross-cultural Approach*. New York: Free Press, 1971.

Ronstadt, R. C. *Research and Development Abroad by U.S. Multinationals*. New York: Praeger, 1977.

Rugman, A. M. *New Theories of the Multinational Enterprise*. New York: St. Martin's Press, 1982.

Sapolsky, H. M. "Organizational Structure and Innovation." *Journal of Business* 40 (1967): 497–510.

Schein, E. H. *Organizational Culture and Leadership*. San Francisco: Jossey-Bass, 1985.

Terpstra, V. "International Product Policy: The Role of Foreign R&D." *The Columbia Journal of World Business* (Winter 1977): 24–32.

Thompson, J. D. *Organizations in Action: Social Science Bases of Administrative Theory*. New York: McGraw Hill, 1967.

Urban, G. L., and J. R. Hauser. *Design and Marketing of New Products*. Englewood Cliffs, NJ: Prentice-Hall, 1980.

Van Maanen, J., and E. H. Schein. "Toward a Theory of Organizational Socialization." In B. Shaw, ed., *Research in Organizational Behavior*. JAI Press, 1979.

Vernon, R. "International Investment and International Trade in the Product Cycle." *Quarterly Journal of Economics* (May 1966): 190–207.

Wilson, J. Q. "Innovation in Organization: Notes toward a Theory." In J. D. Thompson, ed., *Approaches to Organization Design*. Pittsburgh: University of Pittsburgh Press, 1966.

Zaltman, G.; R. Duncan; and J. Holbeck. *Innovations and Organizations*. New York: Wiley, 1973.

DISCUSSION QUESTIONS

1. Describe the generic innovation process.
2. Compare and contrast the four different patterns of innovation process.
3. What organizational attributes are associated with an organization's ability to create innovations?
4. How do the attributes differ for the four patterns of the innovation process?

Activity 13–1

Major Life Insurance Company

Step 1: Read the following scenario:

Major Life Insurance is a *Fortune* 500 insurance company located in the midwestern United States. The group life insurance department is typical of the company's many departments. It employs 100 people: 30 actuaries, 30 analysts, and 40 clerks. Together these employees set insurance rates, design and run computer programs to provide information required to set rates, answer questions from other departments about existing policies, and maintain records about the purchase of life insurance by customers.

Recently the department has been experiencing major performance problems from its workers. These include declining productivity, increasing numbers of errors or policies that need to be rewritten, and increasing absenteeism among its workers. Other departments in the company complain that they frequently cannot obtain answers to their questions. Customer complaints to all departments at Major Life have increased dramatically.

Step 2: Individually or in small groups, design a total quality program for Major Life.

Step 3: Discussion. In small groups or with the entire class, share the plans you developed. Then answer the following questions:

1. What elements do these plans have in common?

2. What are the strengths and weaknesses of each plan?
3. What should be the key components of all plans?
4. What problems might arise as a result of the implementation of these plans?

Activity 13–2

(CNN) Video: Planning for Innovation

Step 1: Read the following scenario:

Mason, Inc., is a *Fortune* 500 company that designs, develops, and manufactures personal grooming products. From 1950 to 1980 it was a leader in introducing new, profitable products into the marketplace. Its Research and Development Division grew from 20 to 150 professionals during that time. Since 1980, however, the company has relied on its past successes and has failed to introduce any significant innovative product into the marketplace. Top management wants to reestablish Mason's reputation as the number-one innovator in the industry.

Step 2: Individually or in small groups, offer a plan for encouraging innovation at Mason, Inc. Discuss staffing, rewards, organizational structure, work design, and any other facets of organizational behavior that apply.

Step 3: Discussion. In small groups or with the entire class, share the plans you developed. Then answer the following questions:

1. What elements do these plans have in common?
2. How well do the plans follow the innovation process?
3. Do the plans incorporate provisions for fulfilling the various roles required for innovation?
4. What are the strengths and weaknesses of each plan?
5. What should be the components of an effective plan?

Step 4: View the CNN video about intrapreneurship.

Step 5: Answer the following questions:
1. How would a program like the ones at 3M and Bell Atlantic complement the program you designed for Mason, Inc.?
2. What are the costs and benefits of such a plan?

Activity 13–3

American Optical Company—Soft Contact Lens Division

Step 1: Read the American Optical Co. case.

It is the spring of 1976; Floyd Sundue, director of the fledgling Soft Contact Lens Division of the American Optical Corporation, is faced with a fundamental decision regarding the design of a new production facility. The conventional approach is to design such a facility as a single-flow shop. The specific manufacturing process provides him with a unique opportunity to implement a new concept—autonomous work groups. His past experience with organizations indicates the new facility could benefit from the approach.

As Floyd mulls over his notes, he knows a decision must be made quickly. The market for soft contact lenses has been growing rapidly. It has been dominated by Bausch and Lomb—the first company to obtain FDA approval for their product. Now, five years later, FDA approval for American Optical is imminent. The slow approval process

has given Bausch and Lomb a virtual monopoly of the market. However, the market has continued to grow at a rapid pace. Floyd knows he needs to get his product on the market quickly if he wants to be a major producer of soft contact lenses.

HISTORY OF THE SOFT CONTACT LENS

The hydrophilic (water absorbing) material from which the lenses are produced was first developed by the Czechoslovakians. It was intended for the treatment of eye diseases such as glaucoma or to place drugs under the skin. In theory, the material would absorb the drug to be administered; then, once in place, it would be gradually released over an extended period of time. The purpose was to administer drugs to a patient.

In 1965, the Czechoslovak Academy licensed Flexible Lenses (a subsidiary of National Patent Corporation) to sell the material in Europe and the Americas. The licensee approached American Optical with the material, but no agreement could be reached. Bausch and Lomb was then approached. They recognized the vast potential in using the material for the manufacture of a soft contact lens. Agreement was reached, and, in 1971, Bausch and Lomb placed the first soft contact lens on the market. They were the undisputed market leader[1] in soft contact lens.

In the late sixties, there was another development with far-reaching implications for the industry. The Federal Food and Drug Administration (FDA) reviewed the material and classified it as a drug. This classification means that a prospective manufacturer must meet stringent requirements before receiving FDA approval for marketing the product. Specifically:

1. Intensive clinical studies of the lens material and the procedure for regular cleaning suggested to the user.
2. Implementing procedures for recalling lenses distributed through various marketing channels.
3. The process, facilities, and controls must conform to good manufacturing practices as interpreted by the FDA.

Approval of a New Drug Application or any significant alteration of approved materials or processes required three to four years. The earliest a company could enter the market was 1974, even if it had a new material patented and a manufacturing process developed. Bausch and Lomb had a significant time advantage over their competition; until 1974, they monopolized the market.

HISTORY OF AMERICAN OPTICAL

American Optical, located in Southbridge, Massachusetts, was founded about 1833 and went public about 1869. In 1967, Warner-Lambert purchased American Optical. At the time, American Optical revenues were about $148 million and net income was about $10 million.

In the early 1970s, Warner-Lambert decided to market the soft lens and, in 1973, purchased it from Griffin Laboratory of Buffalo and Toronto. Griffin Laboratory, a subsidiary of Frigitronics, had patent approval and appeared likely to receive FDA approval soon. Griffin's present production was being sold primarily to the Canadian market. American Optical dubbed it the SOFTCON lens.

Approval came in 1974. However, the approval only covered sales to the smaller therapeutic lens segment of the market. Patients requiring protection for an irritated eye could use the lens under close supervision. Examples are irritation due to an infected eyelid or as a "bandage" after eye surgery.

This was a disappointment. The major market segment was for corrective usage. These users would insert the lens in their eyes and be responsible for cleansing it daily without any supervision. The FDA had withheld approval because the daily cleaning and sterilization process was considered inadequate. Patents and the physical characteristics of the Griffin lens material prevented the company from adopting a similar heat-based process.

Dave Inman, president of the Optical Division of Warner-Lambert, initiated a search for another contact lens manufacturer while efforts to improve the SOFTCON cleaning process continued. He located Union Optical Company, which appeared likely to receive FDA approval for corrective use soon. American Optical bought the right to market the lens for corrective use in early 1975. They called this lens AOSOFT.

This purchase reflected the importance which the AO management attached to quickly entering the soft contact lens market. The market had expanded from $8 million sales in 1971 to more than $55 million by 1974. Bausch and Lomb continued to dominate the market. A new competitor, Continuous Curve, was making lenses. The urgency of entering the market seemed evident, especially if AO was to have any significant share.

The responsibility for both manufacturing and marketing was assigned to Floyd Sundue. Floyd had wide exposure to numerous facets of business both as a consultant and as assistant to Inman. He was also experienced in implementing the concept of autonomous work groups.

DESCRIPTION OF THE PHYSICAL PROCESS

The American Optical process for producing soft lenses was based on the following steps (see Figure 13–17). First, raw material was pulled from inventory. The chemicals were mixed and formed into rods. The rods were labeled and held until the Quality Assurance Department had taken samples and had given approval. Then small (approximately ½ inch long) buttons were cut and grouped into lots of approximately 50. The buttons were placed in jars. The buttons in each jar were cut to the same prescription specifications. Typically, two jars formed an order.

The initial step in cutting the lens was performed by a Base Curve Cutter. Here, the button was held securely in a chuck and the lathe cut the concave side of the lens which would be in direct contact with the eyeball. This was a critical operation, and the lathe needed to be set up exactly to the engineering specifications.

The second step was Bevel Grinding. Here the edge of the base curve was beveled. Succeeding stations buffed the edge and polished the bevel. These operations contributed to a better fit on the eye. Then the base curve was polished for optical clarity.

After the beveling and polishing operations, the button was mounted on a chuck. The chuck was a round tube with a convex end. Hot wax was used to fix the concave base curve to this end. The chuck held the base curve while the front curve was out on the lathe.

The Front Curve Cutter cut the button to a specific curvature and thickness. At its thickest, the lens was about

Figure 13–17 **Soft Contact Lens Cutting and Polishing**

"Buttons" or hard disks about 1/4 inch thick with face and diameter trimmed are sent to processing.

The button is lathed on one side to the shape of the eye's cornea (base curve), the edge is beveled. Then, edge and base curve are both polished.

The front side is mounted and lathed to a specific curvature and thickness to fill the prescription of the patient. The original button now has a center thickness of 1/10 millimeter.

The front side is polished for an optically clear prescription lens.

The lens is hydrated in a saline solution to make it soft, and given a final inspection by the module.

The lens is placed in a vial, labeled and is sent to Quality Assurance for audit.

one-tenth of a millimeter. With such tight tolerances, the lathe had to be set up and operated to precisely engineered specifications.

The convex surface was then polished to get an optically clear lens. The lens then went through an ultrasonic vapor degreaser to remove it from the chuck and clean the wax off it. At this point, all the cutting and polishing operations required to make a prescription lens were completed. It was now necessary to soften the hard plastic lens.

Before being sent for softening, all lenses were thoroughly inspected at the Dry Inspection Station. Under a microscope the inspector could spot defects like pits, gouges, and scratches.

Next, the lenses were softened by placing them in a saline solution. The lenses absorbed the moisture until they were completely soft. The hydration process took between ten to twelve days.

During hydration the lens grew larger. Certain material and process defects only became apparent then. So, another

inspection of all lenses was done under a microscope. Defective lenses were discarded.

The remaining lenses were free of any physical defects. However, even though they were all cut to the same prescriptive specifications, the margin of error was so small that a small percentage often differed from the required specifications. A significant fraction of the buttons in an order met the derived specifications. The remaining nondefective lenses were usable but met different prescriptive standards. Each lens had to be correctly labeled for physical characteristics. This labeling required another inspection of all lenses, which was done on a magnified projector. The lenses were each placed in a separate vial and labeled.

The final step was to sterilize the lens. This was done in an autoclave over a one-day period. The lens was then moved to a quarantine area to ensure that the sterilization was effective. After a couple of days in quarantine, it was moved to the finished good inventory racks and was ready for shipping.

PRESENT FACILITIES

American Optical had been waiting for FDA approval for some years. SOFTCON had therapeutic approval since 1974. Now it appeared that AOSOFT would receive approval for corrective use. As yet the demands on manufacturing had been light. While they waited for approval, the emphasis had been on improving productivity.

Processing was presently being done in leased facilities in Framingham, Massachusetts. Three experimental modules had been set up. The module layout is shown in Figure 13–18. Each module could make either AOSOFT or SOFTCON lenses with some changes to the equipment. Switching over required approximately two days.

Each module would operate for two shifts. Each of the six teams had eleven people with tasks broken down as shown below:

Operator Function	Task Breakdown
A	Base Curve Cutting
B	Bevel Grinding, Edge Buffing, Bevel Polishing, Base Curve Polishing
C	Measure, Mount & Inspect for Optical Clarity
D	Front Curve Cutting
E	Front Curve Polishing, Deblocking & Cleaning
F	Dry Inspection
G	Hydrating & Wet Inspection
H	Label Making, Vial Filling & Capping

Figure 13–18 **Module Floor Plan**

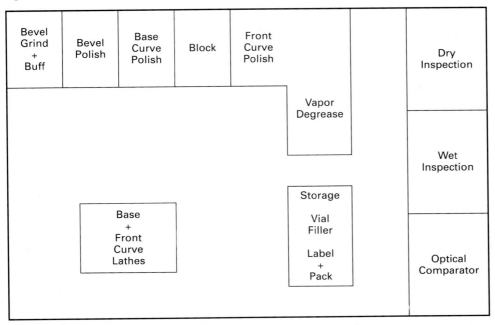

The Rod Casting and Button Making operations were highly automated. Presently, one person was responsible for making all the buttons required. The small teams and their separate physical facilities were dictated by the experimental nature of the work. Floyd had seen an opportunity to implement the autonomous work group concept. He felt the experience gained would help in designing the larger facility which would be required when the corrective lens approval was received.

He organized each work group so it would have the full responsibility for decisions directly affecting their own work—including when to take breaks (e.g., lunch hours); hiring and firing personnel; planning the day's production; and assignment of tasks. Each team was responsible for the work they produced. Furthermore, each team member was responsible for checking the work of team members before them in the process sequence. This checking was in addition to the 100 percent inspections done as part of the process.

Teams were carefully selected to have a blend of experienced and entry-level operators who were compatible with each other. Some operators were interviewed on three separate occasions. Each member of the team went through a fourteen-week training period. Benefits of the product to society were demonstrated, and they were given a great deal of technical information about the process.

The results had been very gratifying; Paul Rivens, his Personnel Manager, had summarized them in a memorandum (Figure 13–19). Floyd placed a lot of emphasis on these results as he thought of the design of the new facility.

Floyd had also obtained estimates of process time and equipment capacity (Figure 13–20). These estimates were based on the performance of the six experimental teams. He noted that manufacturing now assumed a 150 percent increase in standard yield versus the old Griffin Laboratory standard. Although lower than the yields claimed by Rivens in his memorandum, productivity was clearly up.

Floyd had further reason to trust the increased productivity figures. He had organized a Quality Assurance function with one objective. They were to ensure that American Optical complied with every FDA requirement. This meant that in addition to sampling for product quality, adequate documentation was required on each batch as it went through the production process. If the FDA suspected the process was not properly followed, adequate documentation was necessary to convince them it was. If the documentation was unavailable, the FDA could shut down the entire facility. These records also provided an independent check on productivity. They corroborated the figures in Rivens' memorandum.

Another piece of data Floyd had collected was the cost of equipment (Table 13–17). The equipment cost represented about half the total cost of installing a module. The other half was primarily the labor cost of installation.

THE COMPETITION

Other than Bausch and Lomb, there are two major competitors to American Optical for the soft contact lens market. These are Continuous Curve Contact Lenses, Inc., and

Figure 13–19 **Memorandum from Rivens to Sundue**

TO: Floyd Sundue
FROM: Paul Rivens
DATE: February 1976
RE: Autonomous Work Groups

As you requested at our last staff meeting, these are my comments on the viability of the autonomous work group concept for the large-scale production of lenses. I am convinced that (a) this concept will work based on the results achieved with the test groups and (b) it must be implemented if we are to attract a stable well-motivated labor force in the Framingham area.

Test Group Results:
A pilot team with 11 members was formed in Framingham in 1974. Since then, five other teams have been hired and trained. The operating results have been good. After a fourteen-week training period, productivity has tripled and yield almost doubled when compared to the rates achieved at Griffin Labs.

The modules were set up as an easily distinguishable physical facility to reinforce the team's feelings of independence. Work locations were positioned so operators faced each other and could communicate and socialize easily. All efforts were made to provide a well-lighted and pleasant work space.

We found the proximity of the equipment encourages the operators to switch jobs. This reinforces their training. It also helps the team cover for absentees and to work with other operators in order to reach the production targets they set. It also provides the operators with an opportunity to break the routine of a repetitive, boring job.

Detractors at corporate offices say the socializing between team members and the job switching can be counterproductive. The productivity and yield performance figures indicate that this is simply not true. The teams also show a willingness to impose and police standards of behavior. For example, the second shift supervisor asked operators to formulate such standards. They have compiled a code covering clothes, language, break times, etc. Morale and productivity continue to be high.

These tests have also given us greater insight into the functioning of work groups. This experience will enable us to form effective teams on an ongoing basis. For example, we asked our first test teams to select their own team leader. Three teams tried this and, in each case, the leader appeared incapable of leading, perhaps because the teams had chosen leaders they could manipulate. Subsequently, we selected the team leader, trained him in recruiting and supervisory skills, and built the team around him. This has proven to be an effective strategy.

Evidence of high morale is our low rates of absenteeism (5%) and turnover (10%). These rates are particularly significant as our labor is primarily entry-level and unemployment in the Framingham area is only 2.8 percent. As you know, when both factors are present, we would typically have high rates of turnover and absenteeism. This did not happen. Perhaps the pay structure (a base salary 10% above the area average with merit increases in the third, sixth, and ninth months) has contributed to this. I believe, however, that the main reason is the autonomous work group. The team members develop strong relationships as they work in the same module day after day trying to achieve common goals. They are reluctant to leave what has become an enjoyable and stimulating work environment.

The results support the high morale evident in the teams. The teams have identified with, and feel accountable for, the finished lens. So, they evidence considerable pride and satisfaction in meeting production targets with a quality product.

The motivation and stability of the teams must be of prime concern in an era of labor confrontation. The experience of the American industry confirms that conventional organizations cause employee alienation and low morale. The effects are high absenteeism, turnover, and sometimes acts of sabotage, and the election of an unfriendly union. Griffin Labs had set up a conventional flow shop. They had a union. They also had low productivity and yields.

The results of our test groups are extremely encouraging. Productivity is high and the work force appears well satisfied. I feel the concept has proven itself. Our new facility should be designed to house more such modules.

Figure 13–20 **Equipment Capacity**

Base Curve Lathe: 95–105 lenses per day
Base Curve Polish: 175 lenses per day
Measure & Mount: 100–110 lenses per day
Front Curve Cut: 35–45 lenses per day
Front Curve Polish; Deblock & Clean:
    100–110 lenses/day for all 3 lathes
Dry Inspection: 70 lenses/hour
Wet Inspection (Vertexometer): 2 orders*/day
Wet Inspection (J&L): 2 orders/day

---

*An order is 100 lenses at the first work station. As it is processed, defective lenses are discarded. Figures for wet inspection and for packing represent capacity assuming yield standards are met.

Table 13–17 **Equipment Costs/Module**

Item Description	Quantity	Cost/Item
Lathes	4	$5,500.00
Polishers	4	950.00
Bevel Grinder	1	800.00
Vapor Degreaser	1	3,500.00
Ultrasonic Cleaners	4	1,200.00
Radius Gauges and Tools	1	800.00
Microscopes	3	1,100.00
Vertexometer	2	1,500.00
Optical Comparator	1	2,500.00
Oven for hydrating solution	1	1,000.00
Laminar Flow Booth for Packaging	1*	800.00
Vial Filler for Saline Solution	1	7,000.00

*The Laminar Flow Booth can package 1,200 lenses/day.

the Milton Roy Corporation. Continuous Curve succeeded in obtaining the necessary approval in 1974. Milton Roy is due to get approval shortly. Other manufacturers are primarily small laboratories spread around the country. They make special lenses for therapeutic use and are a negligible factor in the corrective lens market.

Table 13–18 shows dollar sales over the past five years, with the 1976, 1977, and 1980 forecast. The present market of $94 million is expected to more than double by 1980. American Optical's target for 1980 is a 20 percent market share.

Bausch and Lomb has the timing advantage and consumer recognition. Their manufacturing process differs from American Optical's. It is a highly automated technique. They spin-cast the liquid monomer (hydrophilic material) in a revolving mold. The amount of plastic injected into the mold, the rotation speed, and the mold's design determine the shape of the lens. The result is a lens with an aspherical base curve. The lens is polished for optical clarity and hydrated to make it soft.

The American Optical management feels it has a superior product on several counts:

- It knows the hydrophilic material it uses has a higher moisture content than Bausch and Lomb's. Bausch and Lomb has a 38.6% moisture content compared to 42.5% for AOSOFT and 55% for SOFTCON. The higher moisture content is more gentle to the cornea. American Optical expects this will help obtain better physician and customer acceptance.
- American Optical cuts a spherical base curve on their lens versus the Bausch and Lomb aspherical base curve. The spherical curve conforms more closely to the spherical contours of the human eye. The AO lens would prove easier to fit.
- American Optical bevels the edge of the lens to provide a less ragged edge than the Bausch and Lomb

Table 13–18 **Sales ($ millions)**

Year	Bausch & Lomb	Continuous Curve	Milton Roy Corporation	American Optical	
				AOSOFT	SOFTCON
1971	8				
1972	18				
1973	33				
1974	54	3.5			0.5
1975	70	5			1
*1976**	85	6	1		2
*1977**	100	11	3	7	2
*1980**	130			50	10

*Forecasted years

lens. This would make it easier to wear, increasing customer acceptance.

Management is also encouraged by results in countries where soft contact lenses are already being sold. Lenses manufactured by both techniques are sold in Canada, France, Germany, and the United Kingdom. Doctors have expressed a definite preference for the lathe-cut lens over the spin-cast lens.

American Optical intends to take an aggressive marketing stance. A program to increase consumer recognition has been developed. The company will offer about 200 different types of AOSOFT lens. A large finished goods inventory will be maintained to satisfy customer orders expeditiously.

Floyd has devoted considerable time to developing the marketing strategy. He now feels he should concentrate on manufacturing. If manufacturing cannot produce enough lenses, the company's growth will be constrained.

EVALUATION OF ALTERNATIVES

The current facilities (3 modules for 6 teams) could produce about $6 million worth of lenses. The leased space provided no room for expansion. It was evident that new facilities would have to be built. With this in mind, American Optical had purchased a tract of land close to the leased facilities. They planned on the new facility starting production in 1977.

The conventional design of such facilities was the approach used by Griffin Laboratory. There would be a Base Curve Cutting Department, followed by a Bevel and Polish Department and so on. Each operation would be done in a specialized area. The present modular facility could continue primarily as a developmental group with the capability to supplement production if necessary.

The approach Floyd was leaning toward was to continue with the autonomous work group concept. Results, so far, had been excellent. True, they had been with experimental teams, but other firms—Volvo, General Foods, etc.—had reported equally good results. If he selected this alternative, a large building could be constructed with separate modules within it. As increasing sales required increased production, more modules could be added.

There were, he recognized, some very tangible benefits associated with the conventional flow shop. Firstly, the capacity of each department could be better balanced. The equipment would be more fully utilized and capital cost would be lower. A rough calculation (Table 13–19) showed that better utilization could be achieved in the modules. But, he knew that two additional people were required to perform certain management tasks, minor maintenance, set up equipment, and handle material.

Secondly, less training time is required when an operator needs to know only one job. One of the strengths of a module was the variety of jobs it offered. The experimental groups had been trained on each job. Training over the

14-week period also showed workers how an autonomous work group operated.

Thirdly, setup time would increase with the modular approach. Each team would set up its work at the beginning of a shift and clean up at the end. This meant an hour of lost production. In a conventional flow shop, the new shift would continue with the work left by the last shift. There would be less setup and cleanup time. Floyd also recognized some very substantial intangible benefits to be obtained by using autonomous work groups.

Results of the experiment had shown, he felt, that the teams identified with and felt accountable for the end product. This was evident by their high morale. Absenteeism and turnover were low. The effects of low morale and employee alienation could be acts of sabotage or unionization with the intent to strike. He was well aware of the present atmosphere of labor confrontations as in the recent bitter strike at General Motors in Lordstown. This attitude could be expected to be widespread amongst the entry-level work force which American Optical was planning to hire. Yet, these workers had been making a quality product and appeared to derive satisfaction and pride from meeting their productivity targets. What is more, these targets were much higher than those achieved by the conventional flow shop of Griffin Laboratory. Though some of the increased productivity could be attributed to process improvements, he felt that the operator's attitude was the biggest contributor.

Another important feature which the work groups provided was manufacturing control. Since the operators were entry-level, they had little prior experience. The module concept made it easy to sequence jobs with each team. Further, if defects appeared on inspection, it would be relatively easy to trace it to a specific machine or operator. A conventional flow shop would require each job to carry considerable documentation to perform the same function.

Table 13–19   **Utilization Percentages**

Task	Capacity	Utilization (percent)
Base Curve	100 lenses/day	100
*Base Curve Polish***	175 lenses/day	57
Measure and Mount	105 lenses/day	95
Front Curve	120 lenses/day	83
Front Curve Polish	105 lenses/day	95
*Dry Inspection***	70 lenses/hour	18
Vertexometer†	2 orders/day	50
J&L†	2 orders/day	50
Label and Pack	1 order/day	100

*One person can perform Base Curve Polish and Dry Inspection.
†One person can perform the Vertexometer and J&L functions.

The rapid identification and accurate tracing of process problems would increase yield substantially.

The modular design would also make it easier to alter manufacturing capacity. Forecasts of the soft contact lens market size had been notoriously inaccurate. For example, in 1974 the total industry sales were expected to peak at $100 million. Sales were already approaching that figure (see Table 13–18) in 1976. A peak of $300 million, sometime in the early eighties, was now projected. Floyd felt this was very optimistic. He felt the $200 million sales in 1980 would be the peak. Given this wide range of potential sales, he felt the modular design offered the most flexibility.

Finally, the modular design made it easier for Quality Assurance because it generated data per the FDA requirements. It would be possible to meet FDA requirements with a conventional flow shop as well. However, a new reporting system would have to be devised and possibly more data collected.

CONCLUSION

As Floyd reviewed the alternatives open to him, he tended to favor the autonomous work group approach. But, he wondered, had he considered all the pros and cons? Was there some way he could quantify the intangible benefits? The experimental work groups had performed well; would the results continue to be as good? He knew the Executive Committee would favor the conventional flow shop approach. Should he supplement his efforts to convince them that the new concept was a preferable alternative with additional data?

NOTE

1. National Patent filed suit in October 1972 seeking further royalty payments and the dissolution of the exclusive licensing agreement. The suit was still being contested.

Step 2: Prepare the case for class discussion.

Step 3: Answer the following questions, individually, in small groups, or with the entire class, as directed by your instructor:

Description
1. Describe the process for producing soft lenses.

Diagnosis
2. Why is American Optical considering the introduction of autonomous work groups?
3. Further explain the advantages and disadvantages of this work redesign using theories or concepts from the following areas: perception, motivation, communication, decision making, group dynamics, intergroup relations, leadership, power, and organization structure.

Prescription
4. Should management institute the new work design?

Action
5. What secondary consequences would the redesign have?
6. Should they renegotiate the contract?

Step 4: Discussion. Share your answers to the above questions, in small groups, with the entire class, or in written form. Then answer the following questions:

1. What symptoms suggest that a problem exists?
2. What problems exist in the case?
3. What theories and concepts help explain the problems?
4. How can the problems be corrected?
5. Are the actions likely to be effective?

Case prepared by Associate Professor Ashok Rao based on research done by Professors Ashok Rao and Herb Graetz. Copyright © by Ashok Rao.

Activity 13–4   Sociotechnical Redesign Exercise

Step 1: Your instructor will organize the class into teams. You will be a member of one of these teams whose job it will be to accomplish a simple production task. This will entail gathering, stapling, and folding three-page packets of paper, then stuffing them into envelopes and sealing them. You will determine the layout and production process you will use. Teams will compete with each other to complete the production task in the shortest time.

Step 2: Read the following directions, and ask your instructor about any points that need clarification:

Four members of your team will be performing a "production" task. Your team's first assignment is to select those four individuals. Remaining team members will participate in the planning process, but once production begins, they will act as observers, filling the roles specified by your instructor.

Your team will receive the following materials: stapler(s), staples, rubber bands, three stacks of colored paper, and envelopes.

Use all of the paper at your workstation to form as many three-page packets as you can. The colors must be in the same sequence for every packet that you complete. Staple each packet of three pages in the upper left-hand corner, then fold the packet to fit an envelope. Stuff each packet into an envelope. Seal each envelope. Count envelopes into stacks of five and put a rubber band around each stack. You will be competing with the other teams to see who can complete the entire task in the shortest time.

The work may be structured in any way your team decides. You will have five to ten minutes to discuss the technique you will employ. Do not begin setting up your process until you have been instructed to do so.

Step 3: Design your team's process using at most four members of your team.

Step 4: Your instructor will indicate when production can begin. Your team's goal is to be the first team to complete the task. Team members who are not participating in the manufacturing process may be assigned special roles by the instructor.

Step 5: Discussion. In small groups or with the entire class, discuss the way individual groups performed by answering the following questions:

1. Which team finished the task first? Why?
2. What did you observe about productivity rates at the beginning of the operation compared with the end?
3. Did the team's initial estimates of subtask times (e.g., stapling, folding) differ from actual task times? If so, how did the teams respond?
4. How did the team members feel as they performed the production task?

This exercise is adapted with permission from K. Brown, Integrating sociotechnical systems into the organizational behavior curriculum: Discussion and class exercise, *Organizational Behavior Teaching Review,* 12(1) (1987–1988): 35–48.

Activity 13–5

Century Park Sheraton Singapore

Step 1: Read the Century Park Sheraton Singapore case.

CENTURY PARK SHERATON SINGAPORE

Chua Soon Lye, Personnel Director at Singapore's Century Park Sheraton had played a central role in the hotel's program to build greater employee commitment. Though Mr. Chua was pleased with the smooth implementation of the work excellence committees in the hotel, he wondered if the base of employee involvement was firm enough to move to even greater employee responsibility in decision making in the future. Over drinks in the hotel's lounge, Mr. Chua elaborated upon his concerns.

The work excellence committee was formed within this organization to achieve the goals of increased organizational effectiveness and improved employee welfare through a process of union-management joint consultation on work-related issues. While we have made significant progress in reaching our goals through improved labor-management relations, we have yet to reach our final objective of an equal sharing of the responsibility in decision making in all aspects of the hotel's operations. Could these aspirations be too demanding of our people? Had the pace of our program for employee participation been too rapid?

On the other hand, I believe that the success of activities like work excellence committees is built upon a momentum. Thus, I feel the need to press forward

to the next level. This "dilemma" is a happy one in fact, because it arose as a consequence of our success.

The Hotel

Century Park Sheraton Singapore (CPSS), a 464-room, luxury hotel, decorated in classical English 19th century style, was officially opened on January 1979. It is a 14-story hotel situated on Nassim Hill, off Tanglin Road, on one end of the Orchard Road tourist belt. It was the first ANA-managed hotel[1] in Singapore.

The hotel, sited on 11,500 sq. metres, offers the following facilities: Hubertus Grill, a western-style grill room; Unkai, a Japanese restaurant; a 250 seat coffee house and cafe terrace, a cocktail lounge, discotheque, a 180-seat function room and a swimming pool.

Under the general manager and the resident manager are the departments of sales, purchasing, front office, accounts, food and beverage, personnel, engineering, housekeeping and security. (See Figure 13–21.) The maximum number of employees had been around 640, but by August 1985 the level had dropped to 504.

The Chinese constituted the majority in the hotel's workforce; Indians, Malays, and Eurasians made up the balance. A small number of expatriate personnel were also employed for their expertise. The General Manager and some chefs were German while the Resident Manager, the Director of Food and Beverage, and the Executive Chef were Swiss.

Figure 13–21   **Simplified Organization Chart Showing Reporting Relationships**

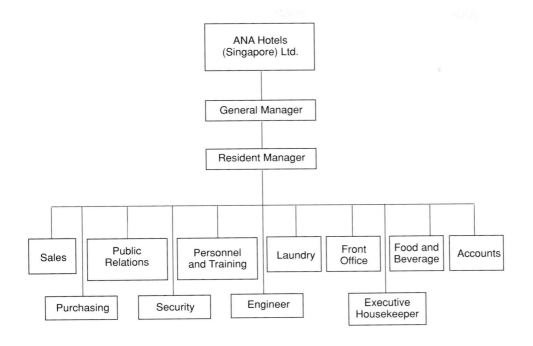

The CPSS, like the other hotels within the industry, provides on-the-job training in various functions. This was because the Singapore population had little experience in the hotel industry. While it was quite common for management personnel to have university or other professional qualifications, rank-and-file personnel were likely to have some secondary education or hold trade certificates. Because the education system offered instruction in the four official languages of the country, some hotel employees were more literate in Chinese, Malay or Tamil than in English. English, however, is the language used for official communication.

A great number of CPSS's employees subscribe to the Food and Drinks Allied Workers' Union, the union for the hotel industry. This union is affiliated to the national federation of unions. But the union's role has to be seen in the context of a country which prides itself on favorable labor-management relations and boasts a record of not having a strike since 1977.

Early Efforts
Mr. Chua, who had worked in the personnel function in both the shipbuilding and aircraft servicing industries, had joined the CPSS Hotel in 1979. Over the years he witnessed the change in labor-management relations. Mr. Chua traced the sequence of events.

We got off to a slow start. Before 1981, the labor-management characteristics in the hotel were more typical of traditional confrontational attitudes between labor and management. This impeded efforts at bringing about change to raise productivity.

We wanted to increase productivity through restructuring jobs. This led to the formation of a 9-person joint union and management committee called the Job Enlargement and Enrichment Committee in May 1982. The original implementation of these changes was to have been around October of that year. Job restructuring in effect would mean a recombination of duties, or more shifts, *e.g.,* the pool attendant, groundsmen and housemen, originally three jobs, were to become one. Cashiers were expected to manage the till at more than one location in the hotel. Despite reassurances that training would be provided and that there were to be no retrenchments, there was more talk than progress.

I am proud of the fact that we began on the productivity effort through human resources management even before the government launched its productivity movement. This is a nationally promoted effort to increase productivity consciousness in the Singapore workforce. By 1982, we had started both the quality circle and the work excellence programs. But I felt that we were making progress only after the labor contract was negotiated, and new union leaders were elected in that year. In retrospect, 1982 was a turning point.

The Work Excellence Program

The concept underlying the work excellence committee was first introduced to Singapore in 1981. It was believed that improved labor-management cooperation would result from regular consultation on work-related issues by committees comprised of labor and management representatives. This concept was the theme of the May Day seminar organized by the National Trade Union Congress (NTUC). The Shangri-la Hotel, which was the first hotel to embark on this program of labor-management cooperation, was heralded as the model for work excellence committees in the hotel industry. It was also at this seminar that the acronym WE committee (WE standing as much for 'us' as for work excellence) was established.

The adoption of WE committees in CPSS took place through a series of steps. Separate meetings at top management, departmental, and union levels were held through the months of July and August 1982 to discuss the feasibility of WE committees. When union and management met jointly, the meetings were conducted with the aid of an official from the National Productivity Board[2] (NPB). The consultant from NPB emphasized that his role would lessen progressively as improvements in labour management cooperation were made. It was only after the preliminary groundwork was laid that a joint formal application was extended to the NPB to organize WE committees in the hotel.

An important part of installing WE activities was the training session organized for 27 persons from both union and management over a period of three days. Activities of the program included games in small group sessions to learn different methods of conflict resolution. One session resulted in both management and union recording two unflattering lists outlining their perceptions of each other. Union members perceived the management to be, among other things, sarcastic, high in flattery, autocratic, and making empty promises. On the other hand, management perceived the union leaders to be revengeful, insincere, and giving lip service. The discrepancy between the desired and actual state of affairs was the starting point for future improvements.

Monthly WE meetings were to follow. Minutes for these meetings were recorded. The early meetings were concerned with the setting up of steering WE committees, and the drawing up of a 'code of conduct.' (See Figures 13–22 and 13–23.) Training of key personnel was completed by

April 1983. Those leading in forming sectional WE committees were the security, accounting, housekeeping, and laundry departments. Other departments seemed to Mr. Chua to be dragging their feet.

Some Results

By July 1983, the stalemated job enlargement exercise was brought under the umbrella of the WE program. Revised job descriptions, made possible by employees taking on a wider range of job duties were submitted by departments.

Progress was also seen in the widening range of topics discussed by the WE steering committee. By October 1983, the meeting agenda had moved beyond the problem of setting up WE committees to issues including incentive schemes, operational hours of the cafe, job training, time cards for middle management, salary adjustments and second-tier wage adjustments (a merit scheme operating in Singapore). Because the NPB consultant felt that the meetings were proceeding well he no longer attended meetings.

CPSS's early efforts did not go unrecognized—it was one of the six recipients of the First Productivity Award given by NPB. (See Figure 13–24 for criteria.) This recognition was to foreshadow other improvements at the hotel.

Dahak Ibrahim, chairman of the branch union at the hotel, noted at a national work excellence convention in mid-1984:

> Improvements in efficiency have not been confined to the hotel operation. Labor-management cooperation have also resulted in improved benefit and welfare schemes. Less time is spent on grievances—we used to have monthly grievance meetings. I have found our colleagues also more open and accepting of changes.

At this same convention, it was reported that there were 7 department WE committees, 21 sectional committees and 197 WE committee members in the Sheraton.

Employee numbers had been decreasing even in years when the occupancy rates were increasing. In August 1985, the staff complement was down to 504 persons. Despite Mr. Chua's attempts to maintain a low profile on CPSS's productivity efforts, there was pressure to share their experiences through talks and conferences. As the word of their successes spread, CPSS also increasingly received visitors anxious to learn about the productivity movement.

Quality Circle Activities

The QC program was started in February 1982, at the suggestion of Mr. Zimmer, then Sheraton's Resident Manager, upon his return from a seminar on quality circles organized by the Singapore National Employers Federation. Workshops were organized for QC facilitators and leaders. By August, Sheraton's pilot circle "The Searcher," was in operation in the Laundry department. After two months of activities, it made its first presentation to management as part of the activities for "Productivity Month." After this

Figure 13–22 **An Abridged Version of the Constitution for Work Excellence Committees**

J. CONSTITUTION FOR WORK EXCELLENCE COMMITTEES

1. Work Excellence Committee
   1.1 It is a committee within an organization, made up of management and employee representatives for joint consultation. Joint consultation, in its simplest form, is an arrangement to enable management and employee representatives to come together to discuss work-related issues to improve the overall effectiveness of the organization as well as the well-being of the workforce at the enterprise level.

2. Purpose of the Work Excellence Committee
   2.1 The primary purpose of WE Committee is to build a harmonious labor-management climate within an organization to achieve the organizational goals.

3. Objectives of the Work Excellence Committee
   3.1 To create a congenial climate throughout the hotel.
   3.2 To encourage labor and management to discuss and cooperate on work-related issues.
   3.3 To foster trust among all employees.
   3.4 To instill a sense of pride, dedication and commitment to work.
   3.5 To promote mutual respect, understanding and team-spirit.
   3.6 To involve employees in planning, problem solving and information sharing.
   3.7 To promote teamwork and advise on small group activities, *e.g.,* QC Circles in the hotel.
   3.8 To provide employees with social, cultural and recreational programs.

4. Functions of Steering Committee
   4.1 To advise other WE Committees and sub-committees.
   4.2 To give guidelines and direction for other WE Committees to operate and function.
   4.3 To have consultation between management and union employee representatives at the highest level.
   4.4 To initiate the setting up of WE Committees in the whole organization and co-ordinate their activities.
   4.5 To monitor the progress of WE Committees and sub-committees.
   4.6 To deal with whatever problems that may arise affecting the whole organization.
   4.7 To initiate programs that affect the whole organization.
   4.8 To monitor the industrial relations climate in the whole organization.
   4.9 To explain to employees the rationale of policies and activities to the companies.

5. Composition of WE Steering Committees
   5.1 The committee comprises of representatives from the management and labor, preferably with equal number from each side.
   5.2 The management representatives are appointed by the General Manager while the Union representatives are appointed by the Union.
   5.3 The Chairman shall be selected by the WEC. The Chairman will appoint a designate who will chair in his absence.
   5.4 The term of office of the Committee members shall be three full years.

6. Secretariat
7. Meetings
8. Duties and Responsibilities
9. Attendance by other persons
10. Code of Behavior
11. Publicity
12. Amendments to Constitution

---

presentation, enthusiasm was high. Other circles formed were "The Adventurer" in Security, "Homemaker" in Housekeeping and "Improve the QCC" in the kitchen. However, by July 1983 Mr. Chua noted that attendance at QC steering committee meetings was falling off.

By then the WE program was also in operation. CPSS also participated in other activities to support government-promoted programs. Among them was the "Use Your Hand Exercise," organized on a fortnightly basis from November 1983. Sheraton also took an active part in the "Courtesy Month," the "Productivity Month," and the "Save Water Campaign."

There were other activities more specific to the hotel—the "Ken Fixit" program (a preventative maintenance pro-

Figure 13-23 **Century Park Sheraton Singapore Work Excellence Organizational Structure**

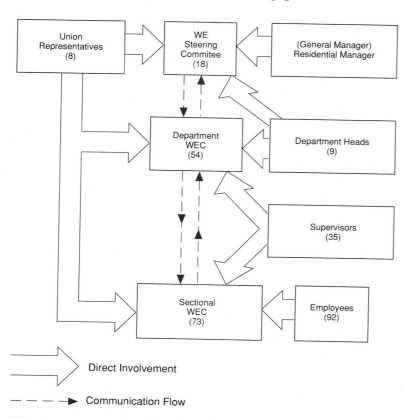

Direct Involvement

Communication Flow

gram specifically for guest rooms), the Preventative Maintenance Program (with a more general focus on all equipment) and the Training and Rewriting Procedures Program (aimed at simplifying procedures and reducing the volume of paper work).

Interest in QC activities continued to fall. One QC leaders' meeting which was to have been held had to be cancelled due to poor response. The problem of low enthusiasm with QCs was discussed at WE meetings and the decision to continue activating interest in QCs was adopted. More QC leaders were trained in April 1984, and a QC workshop was organized to keep the QC effort alive.

Meanwhile, Mr. Alex Kuenzli, a Swiss hotelier whose last posting was in Mauritius, had succeeded Mr. Zimmer as the Resident Manager. He commented in hindsight about QC activities.

It would have been better if we had the organization structure first to support small group participation activities like quality circles. We started the QCs first, which was then followed by the work excellence committees. If we had proceeded the other way round, it is likely that we could have sustained interest in QCs longer.

Some Concerns
The Changing Hotel Industry

While the late seventies and the early eighties saw an increasing number of tourist arrivals and optimistic predictions which led to the overbuilding of new hotels, the tide was beginning to turn by 1984. A sense that the growth momentum was coming to a halt, and that harder times were ahead was already prompting the management at CPSS, more experienced than other newcomers to the industry, to take steps to plan for the change. By mid 1985, their fears were becoming fact. Room occupancy at CPSS fell to an all time low of 63%, a drop from 80% in 1984, and 75% in 1983, and even poorer occupancy rates were forecast for the industry.

In spite of the current uncertain economic situation and competition (which Mr. Kuenzli described as "like a jellyfish"), he had confidence that CPSS had a better chance than many others of surviving the recession. His hotel had adopted the policy of reducing manpower by attrition and of increasing productivity through the programs managed by Mr. Chua.

The improved labor-management relations had enabled the hotel to function with less staff, but with no apparent drop in performance. Mr. Kuenzli noted with pride

Figure 13–24   **National Productivity Awards 1985**

The National Productivity Council will once again be considering nominations for the National Productivity Awards this year. The Awards, introduced in 1983, are presented annually to organizations in recognition of their good productivity practices.

The following guidelines are used in the selection of companies for the Award:

- A company's training tradition or efforts to train and develop staff.
- The state of labor-management relations in the company and the existence of cooperation mechanisms such as Work Excellence Committees.
- A company's management philosophy which draws out the best in their people and includes respect for individual excellence within the context of teamwork as well as respect for work discipline.
- The efforts put in by the company to enhance employee's loyalty and identification with the company through various measures, *e.g.,* company welfarism, promotion programs such as 3Ps, in-house newsletters, etc.
- Worker participation activities of the company, *e.g.,* small group activities like QC Circles.
- Good occupational safety and health record and work environment.
- A company's efforts in quality and in mechanization, automation, computerization and other improvements in technology.

Organizations interested in the Awards can write to or call Miss Judith Choo of the National Productivity Awards Secretariat, National Productivity Board, 55 Cuppage Road #08–16, Cuppage Centre, Singapore 0922, tel. 734-5534 ext. 293.

Published by NPB
Singapore Productivity News
June 1985

that the staff managed the increased occupancy in 1984 well, even though there were 100 fewer people to do more work. Mr. Kuenzli explained:

> The WE committees are now part of the solution to the current situation. We are hoping that the improved understanding of the employees achieved through our efforts in the last few years will help us meet the competition in further lowering costs and providing better service.
>
> No, I am not impatient at what appears to be long discussions over issues in these committees. I can sit through them as well as anybody else.
>
> The difference I see between Singapore and German labor-management cooperative efforts is probably one of degree of commitment. Issues discussed here in Singapore tend not to be as petty. And there is just that much more enthusiasm.
>
> We also try to keep employees informed about the hotel's economic performance. This is done through briefing sessions which I personally conduct, and which are specially scheduled for staff of different departments. All hotel employees are invited to attend. Sometimes members of the audience, not so fluent in English, may not exactly follow all I am saying, but they appreciate the trouble I am taking. Afterwards, they may get an explanation from the others about what I have said.

At the session for the general administration staff held on July 18, 1985, Kuenzli started off the meeting by expressing his confidence that the CPSS would continue to succeed despite heavy competition (which he admitted was reaching a stage where even he was beginning to be somewhat apprehensive). He informed members present about a 14–15% drop in occupancy rates for gazetted hotels,[3] due to the decline in tourist arrivals.

Charts of the hotel's economic performance were presented, as were figures of the planned versus actual gross operating profits. Mr. Kuenzli emphasized that despite the cost savings of S$800,000[4] as a result of declining staff strength, there was a shortfall from loss in the budgeted gross operating profit. He also mentioned the loss leaders in the hotel. Members at the meeting were briefed on the hotel's latest efforts at boosting sales, and given an update on the opening of the new Sheraton Towers and its possible impact on the Century Park Sheraton. Though Sheraton Towers was positioned at the top end of the exclusive range in hotels, its room rates quoted during the opening period were competitive with Century Park Sheraton's rates.

Demands on Middle Management

Mr. Chua, an unassuming man with an infectious enthusiasm, described the pressures on the management of the hotel in the implementation of a participative philosophy.

We try to manage by example. It means that we are tough on keeping manpower costs down within our own departments. For example, the personnel department runs on a staff of three, including myself. We encourage our managers to pitch in whenever necessary. Mr. Moser, our Food and Beverage manager, will help to clear tables; Mr. Kuenzli set an example by even washing toilets—we have that on video! I am glad to see our management staff pitching in spontaneously.

Ironically, an indirect measure of our success is perhaps reflected in the fact that it is becoming increasingly difficult to recruit management people from outside this hotel who can meet the demands of the job. People from within-the-ranks of this hotel seem better suited for management positions. We have tried quite recently to employ a few management personnel from other hotels, but found that these newcomers experienced some difficulties in adjusting to our organization. Our high expectations of management personnel make even our own employees feel somewhat apprehensive about accepting management positions within the hotel.

Mr. Kuenzli echoed this view:

I do not mind admitting that I am rather demanding of my managers, more so than of the rank-and-file. I expect each manager to work at labor-management cooperative efforts even if he meets with little enthusiasm from his department and feels discouraged about his attempts.

Future Directions for Labor-Management Relations

Reflecting on the past few years, Mr. Chua wondered what steps he could take to ensure the continuing success of the programs and to move to a new level of commitment and involvement.

There are increasing challenges ahead. I am a little apprehensive that some among us feel that we have "arrived" at labor-management efforts for the hotel. Winning the productivity award and having many people interested in studying our success may have lulled us into thinking that all is well. We have to push forward in order not to fall behind. Besides we must plan now to be ahead of the competition in labor-management cooperation, which means that we should be pressing towards getting our employees involved in making decisions in the hotel. Are we ready for this next challenge?

I also think our promotion of the WE committees detracted from the quality circle movement, when actually these activities should be complementary. Ideas for improvements can be generated by these circles, and then channelled through the WE committees. I would like to see a revival of interest in quality circles.

While I appreciate the top management's acknowledgements of my efforts, I think it is not quite right that I should be needed to keep enthusiasm high for the program. I noticed upon my return after having been away for a few weeks last year that there was a slight falling off of activities in my absence. This should not be so. A truly successful program should be independent of particular individuals . . . and that should also be part of our next objectives.

Step 2: Prepare the case for class discussion.

Step 3: Answer the following questions, individually, in small groups, or with the entire class, as directed by your instructor:

Description

1. Describe the introduction and use of work excellence committees at the Century Park Sheraton Singapore.

Diagnosis

2. Why were the work excellence committees formed?
3. How did they affect labor-management relations?
4. What other effects did the work excellence committees have on the hotel and its management?
5. Why did the quality circle program deteriorate?
6. Explain the advantages and disadvantages of the work excellence committees using theories or concepts from the following areas: perception, motivation, communication, decision making, group dynamics, leadership, and power.

Prescription

7. What steps should Mr. Chua take to ensure the continuing success of the work excellence committees?
8. Should he reinvigorate the quality circle program?
9. Should Mr. Chua institute any other changes?

Action

10. What consequences would such changes likely have?

Step 4: Discussion. Share your answers to the above questions, in small groups, with the entire class, or in written form. Then answer the following questions:

1. What symptoms suggested that a problem existed?
2. What problems existed at the Century Park Sheraton Singapore?
3. What theories and concepts help explain the problems?
4. How were the problems corrected?
5. Were the actions effective?
6. Are additional actions necessary?

ENDNOTES

1. This is a chain of hotels owned or managed by All Nippon Airways.
2. The National Productivity Board (NPB) is a statutory

body charged with the responsibility of the implementation of productivity efforts. Among its activities were the conducting of extensive training courses for management and supervisors. It also promotes specific productivity programs like Quality Control Circles and joint labor management consultation schemes like the work excellence committees.

3. Hotels which met the evaluation scheme for luxury.
4. C$480,000

Case material of the Western School of Business Administration is prepared as a basis for classroom discussion. This case was prepared by Sing Chee Ling, under the supervision of Professor Joseph J. DiStafano. Copyright © 1986, University of Western Ontario.

Activity 13–6

Fine Furniture, Inc.

Step 1: Read the following scenario:

Fine Furniture, Inc., manufactures Scandinavian-style, high technology European-style, and Formica and lacquer contemporary bookcases and storage units. The company employs approximately 500 workers in its large manufacturing facility in southeastern United States. Many of these employees pride themselves on being craftspeople in various aspects of furniture manufacturing. Currently the company emphasizes high specialization of work functions. The manufacturing process is divided into many discrete tasks, each performed by a separate individual. One worker, for example, may cut the backs of the bookcases; another may insert the shelf pegs into the frames; still another might attach the doors to the storage units. The plant is currently being automated.

Workers often complain that they are not really using their skills in furniture building; and describe their jobs as mechanical and boring. They also complain that they feel as if each is "a small cog in a very large machine." Retailers who distribute Fine Furniture's products have noticed an increase in the number of defective pieces they have received and that production slowdowns have delayed product delivery from three to six months.

Manufacturing employees receive an hourly wage that ranges between ten and twenty dollars per hour, depending on their seniority and special skills. In peak production seasons, employees work overtime and can increase their earning by 25 to 50 percent. Employees are represented by a local of the International Teamsters Union, which has succeeded in negotiating a high-paying contract for its employees. Recently, however, employees have demonstrated some dissatisfaction with the union's lack of attention to ensuring job security. The introduction of automation to the manufacturing process has resulted in approximately 5 percent of the work force receiving layoff notices in the past year.

Top management has informed both the union representatives and the manufacturing work force that it intends to increase the amount of automation in the workplace, even introducing some new robotics that has successfully been used to manufacture furniture abroad.

Step 2: Individually or in small groups, design a QWL program for Fine Furniture.

Step 3: Discussion. In small groups or with the entire class, share the programs you developed. Then answer the following questions:

1. What elements do these programs have in common?
2. How will the programs address the problems at Fine Furniture?
3. What are the strengths and weaknesses of each program?
4. What should be the components of an effective QWL program?
5. What other options are available for improving the situation?

CONCLUDING COMMENTS The increased availability of sophisticated technology and automation in the workplace has created significant management issues. In this chapter we examined the managerial issues associated with the management of technology. We also looked at the role innovation plays in ensuring state-of-the-art organizational practices. Then we described early and contemporary approaches to work design. We examined work simplification and job enlargement, as well as work enrichment. We looked at the organizational trend toward introducing autonomous and self-managing work groups. Alternative work arrangements and quality of working life programs also attempt to increase worker productivity and satisfaction.

The activities of this chapter offered the opportunity to consider issues associated with managing technology, including the impact of innovation and various work redesigns. You redesigned work at the Major Life Insurance Company and Fine Furniture, Inc. You offered ways an organization can be more innovative and viewed a video about intrapreneurship as part of "Planning for Innovation." The "Socio-technical-Redesign Exercise" allowed you to experience the impact of various work design approaches. The cases of American Optical and the Century Park Sheraton Singapore also allowed a comparison of the relative impact of different redesign approaches and issues for managing technology. Managing technology, innovating in the workplace, and redesigning work must consider the nature of the jobs, workers, technology, management, and organizations involved. The process of implementing the proposed changes is also a key to its effectiveness.

ENDNOTES

[1] H. Shaiken, *Work Transformed* (New York: Holt, Rinehart, and Winston, 1984).

[2] J. A. Edosomwan, *Integrating Innovation and Technology Management* (New York: Wiley, 1989), p. 15.

[3] *Ibid.*

[4] M. S. Scott-Morton, *The Corporation of the 1990s: Informational Technology and Organizational Transformation* (New York: Oxford University Press, 1991).

[5] P. S. DeLisi, Lessons from the steel axe: Culture, technology, and organizational change, *Sloan Management Review* (Fall 1990): 83–93.

[6] J. R. Kimberly, The organizational context of technological innovation. In D. D. Davis and Associates, eds., *Managing Technological Innovation* (San Francisco: Jossey-Bass, 1986).

[7] A. Rubenstein, *Managing Technology in the Decentralized Firm* (New York: Wiley, 1989).

[8] See D. G. Marquis, The anatomy of successful innovations (November 1969), by Technology Communications, Inc. Reprinted in *Managing Advanced Technology,* vol. 1 (New York: American Management Association, 1972), pp. 35–48.

[9] J. B. Bush, Jr., and A. L. Frohman, Communication in a "network" organization, *Organizational Dynamics* 20(2) (1991): 23–36.

[10] E. B. Roberts and A. R. Fusfeld, Staffing the innovative technology-based organization, *Sloan Management Review* (Spring 1981): 19–34.

[11] R. A. Burgelman, T. J. Kosnik, and M. Van den Poel, Toward an innovative capabilities audit framework. In R. A. Burgelman and M. A. Maidique, *Strategic Management of Technology and Innovation* (Homewood, Ill.: Irwin, 1988).

[12] Rubenstein, *Managing Technology.*

[13] J. E. Ettlie, What makes a manufacturing firm innovative? *Academy of Management Executive* 4(4) (1990): 7–20.

[14] T. Peters and R. Waterman, *In Search of Excellence* (New York: Harper & Row, 1982).

[15] J. E. McCann, Design principles for an innovating company, *Academy of Management Executive* 5(2) (1991): 76–93.

[16] J. Stitt, *Managing for Excellence* (Milwaukee: Quality Press, 1990).

[17] D. Ciampa, *Total Quality: A User's Guide for Implementation* (Reading, Mass.: Addison-Wesley, 1992).

[18] T. E. Benson, Challenging global myths, *Industry Week* (October 7, 1991): 13–25.

[19] *Profiles in Quality: Blueprints for Action from 50 Leading Companies* (Boston: Allyn and Bacon, 1991).

[20] *Ibid.*

[21] *Ibid.*

[22] D. Woodruff, At Saturn what workers want is . . . fewer defects, *Business Week* (December 2, 1991): 117–118.

[23] M. G. Brown, How to determine your quality quotient, *Journal for Quality and Participation* (June 1990): 76–80.

[24] T. E. Benson, The gestalt of total quality management, *Industry Week* (July 1, 1991): 30–31.

[25] C. Perrow, The organizational context of human factors engineering, *Administrative Science Quarterly* 28 (1983): 521–541.

[26] F. E. Emery, The assembly line—Its logic and our future, *National Labour Institute Bulletin* 1 (1975): 1–19.

[27] T. Cummings, Designing work for productivity and quality of work life, *Outlook* 6 (1982).

[28] M. A. Campion and C. L. McClelland, Interdisciplinary examination of the costs and benefits of enlarged jobs: A job design quasi-experiment, *Journal of Applied Psychology* 76(2) (1991): 186–198.

[29] J. D. Kilbridge, Reduced costs through job enlargement: A case, *Journal of Business* 33 (1960): 357–362.

[30] F. Herzberg and A. Zautra, Orthodox job enrichment: Measuring true quality in job satisfaction, *Personnel* (September-October 1976).

[31] J. R. Hackman and G. Oldham, *Work Design* (Reading, Mass.: Addison-Wesley, 1980).

[32] *Ibid.*

[33] *Ibid.*

[34] L. R. Berlinger, W. H. Glick, and R. C. Rodgers, Job enrichment and performance improvement. In J. P. Campbell, R. J. Campbell, and Associates, *Productivity in Organizations: New Perspectives from Industrial and Organizational Psychology* (San Francisco: Jossey-Bass, 1988).

[35] R. L. Anderson and J. R. Terborg, Employee beliefs and support for a work redesign intervention, *Journal of Management* 4(3) (1988): 493–503.

[36] J. Pontusson, The politics of new technology and job redesign: A comparison of Volvo and British Leyland, *Economic and Industrial Democracy* 11 (1990): 311–336.

[37] J. Woodward, *Industrial Organization: Theory and Practice* (London: Oxford University Press, 1965); E. Trist and K. W. Bamforth, Some social and psychological consequences of the long-wall method of coal getting, *Human Relations* 4 (1951): 3–38; A. K. Rice, *Productivity and Social Organization: The Ahmedabad Experiments* (London: Tavistock, 1958).

[38] T. G. Cummings, Self-regulating work groups: A sociotechnical synthesis, *Academy of Management Review* 3 (1978): 625–634.

[39] Steelcase, *Industry Week* (October 21, 1991): 53–54.

[40] Volvo's radical new plant: "The death of the assembly line?" *Business Week,* August 28, 1989.

[41] J. McCalman and D. A. Buchanan, High performance work systems: The need for transition management, *International Journal of Product Management* 10(2): 10–25.

[42] R. L. Cherry, Stages of work redesign, *Journal of Quality and Participation,* Special Supplement (December 1989): 52–55.

[43] C. C. Manz, D. E. Keating, and A. Donnellon, Preparing for an organizational change to employee self-management: The managerial transition, *Organizational Dynamics* (Autumn 1990): 15–26.

[44] T. D. Wall, N. J. Kemp, P. R. Jackson, and C. W. Clegg, Outcomes of autonomous workgroups: A long-term field experiment, *Academy of Management Journal* 29 (1986): 280–304.

[45] J. L. Cordery, W. S. Mueller, and L. M. Smith, Attitudinal and behavioral effects of autonomous group working: A longitudinal field study, *Academy of Management Journal* 34(2) (1991): 464–476.

[46] J. W. Newstrom and J. L. Pierce, Alternative work schedules: The state of the art, *Personnel Administrator* 24 (1979): 19–23.

[47] B. Shamir and I. Salomon, Work-at-home and the quality of working life, *Academy of Management Review* 10 (1985): 455–464.

[48] S. G. Schroeder, Alternate workstyles: A solution to productivity problems? *Supervisory Management* 28 (July 1983): 24–30; W. Olsten, Effectively managing alternative work options, *Supervisory Management* 29 (April 1984): 10–15.

[49] B. Olmsted, (Flex)time is money, *Management Review* (November 1987): 47–51; C. Scordato and J. Harris, Workplace flexibility, *HR Magazine* (January 1990): 75–78.

[50] Newstrom and Pierce, Alternative work schedules.

[51] J. A. Hollingsworth and F. A. Wrebe, Flextime: An international innovation with limited U.S. acceptance, *Industrial Management* 31 (March-April, 1989): 22–26.

[52] *Ibid.*

[53] R. E. Walton, Quality of working life: What is it? *Sloan Management Review* 15 (1973): 11–21.

[54] D. A. Nadler and E. E. Lawler III, Quality of work life: Perspectives and directions, *Organizational Dynamics* (Winter 1983).

[55] R. H. Guest, Quality of work life—Learning from Tarrytown, *Harvard Business Review* 57 (1979): 76–87.

[56] See R. Zager and M. P. Rosow, eds., *The Innovative Organization: Productivity Programs in Action* (New York: Pergamon, 1982).

[57] H. C. Katz, *Shifting Gears: Changing Relations in the U.S. Automobile Industry* (Cambridge, Mass.: MIT press, 1985).

[58] M. Edid, How power will be balanced on Saturn's shop floor, *Business Week* (August 5, 1985).

[59] T. A. Kochan, H. C. Katz, and N. R. Mower, *Worker Participation and American Unions* (Kalamazoo, Mich.: Upjohn Institute for Employment Research, 1984).

[60] *Ibid.*

[61] M. Gates, Do people make a difference? *Incentive* (May 1989): 16–18, 138–139.

[62] See I. Bluestone, How quality-of-worklife projects work for the United Auto Workers, *Monthly Labor Review* (July 1980); S. H. Fuller, How quality-of-worklife projects work for General Motors, *Monthly Labor Review* (July 1980): 39–41.

[63] J. W. Thacker and M. W. Fields, Union involvement in quality-of-work-life efforts: A longitudinal investigation, *Personnel Psychology* 40 (1987): 97–111.

[64] See S. D. Goldstein, Organizational dualism and quality circles, *Academy of Management Review* 10 (1985): 509–526; G. W. Meyers and R. G. Scott, Quality circles: Panacea or Pandora's Box? *Organizational Dynamics* 13 (Spring 1985): 34–50; L. R. Smeltzer and B. L. Kedia, Knowing the ropes: Organizational requirements for quality circles, *Business Horizons* 28 (July-August 1985): 30–34; G. P. Shea, Quality circles: The danger of bottled change, *Sloan Management Review* 27 (Spring 1986): 33–46; R. P. Steel and R. F. Lloyd, Cognitive, affective, and behavioral outcomes of participation in quality circles: Conceptual and empirical findings, *Journal of Applied Behavioral Science* 24 (1988): 1–17 for further discussion of quality circles.

[65] D. Hutchins, *Quality Circles Handbook* (New York: Nichols, 1985).

[66] T. R. Miller, The quality circle phenomenon: A review and appraisal, *SAM Advanced Management Journal* 54(1) (1989): 4–7, 12; E. E. Lawler III and S. Mohrman, Quality circles after the fad, *Harvard Business Review* (January-February 1985): 65–71.

[67] G. E. Ledford, Jr., E. E. Lawler III, and S. A. Mohrman, The quality circle and its variations. In Campbell et al., *Productivity in Organizations*.

[68] K. Bradley and S. Hill, Quality circles and managerial interests, *Industrial Relations* 26 (Winter 1987): 68–82.

[69] E. R. Ruffner and L. P. Ettkin, When a circle is not a circle, *SAM Advanced Management Journal* 52 (Spring 1987): 9–15.

[70] *Ibid.*

[71] R. W. Griffin, Consequences of quality circles in an industrial setting: A longitudinal assessment, *Academy of Management Journal* 31 (1988): 338–358.

[72] R. E. Alie, The middle-management factor in quality circle programs, *SAM Advanced Management Journal* 51 (Summer 1986): 9–15.

[73] J. Simmons and W. Mares, *Working Together* (New York: Knopf, 1983); J. A. Pearce II and E. C. Ravlin, The design and activation of self-regulating work groups, *Human Relations* 40 (1987): 751–782.

[74] H. C. Katz, T. A. Kochan, and M. R. Weber, Assessing the effects of industrial relations systems and efforts to improve the quality of working life on organizational effectiveness, *Academy of Management Journal* 28 (1985): 509–526.

[75] G. R. Bushe, Temporary or permanent middle-management groups? Correlates with attitudes in QWL change projects, *Group and Organization Studies* 12 (March 1987): 23–27.

[76] J. B. Cunningham and T. Eberle, A guide to job enrichment and redesign, *Personnel* (February 1990): 56–61.

RECOMMENDED READINGS

Ciampa, D. *Total Quality: A User's Guide for Implementation*. Reading, Mass.: Addison-Wesley, 1992.

Edasomwan, J. A. *Integrating Innovation and Technology Management*. New York: Wiley, 1989.

Goodman, P. S., Sproull, L. S., and Associates. *Technology and Organizations*. San Francisco: Jossey-Bass, 1990.

Henry, J. and Walker, D., eds. *Managing Innovation*. London: Sage, 1991.

Rubenstein, A. *Managing Technology in the Decentralized Firm*. New York: Wiley, 1989.

Scott Morton, M. S., ed. *The Corporation of the 1990s: Informational Technology and Organizational Transformation*. New York: Oxford University Press, 1991.

Chapter Outline

- **OPENING CASE** *Introducing School-Based Management at the Roosevelt School*

  Changing Organizations in a Global Environment

  Diagnosing Forces that Influence Change

  Building an Action Plan

  Selecting a Change Agent

  Selecting an Intervention Strategy

  Implementing Organizational Changes

  Making Organizational Transformations

  Responding to Crises

  Evaluating the Change Process

  Institutionalizing Action in Organizations

  Ensuring Organizational Effectiveness

  Managing in a Multinational and Multicultural Context

  A Review of the Diagnostic Approach

- **READING 14–1** *The Multicultural Organization*
  Taylor Cox, Jr.

- **ACTIVITIES**

  14–1 First Canadian Club

  14–2 Bridgeton Temporary Services

  14–3 Managing an Organizational Crisis

  14–4 Managerial Systems Ltd.

  14–5 Case Analysis

  14–6 Organizational Analysis

Changing Organizations through Effective Action

Learning Objectives

After completing the reading and activities in Chapter 14, students will be able to

1. Describe an approach to changing organizations in a global environment.

2. Diagnose the forces that affect change and offer ways of strengthening or weakening them.

3. Identify possible change agents and the advantages and disadvantages of using each type.

4. Describe three types of intervention strategies and possible uses of each one.

5. Offer a protocol for implementing changes in organizations.

6. Identify the key issues in transforming an organization.

7. Offer advice to executives and other organizational members for responding to crisis situations.

8. List the steps in evaluating an organizational change.

9. Define organizational effectiveness and specify criteria of effective organizations.

10. Describe and apply the complete diagnostic approach to an organizational situation.

Introducing School-Based Management at the Roosevelt School

The Roosevelt School recently received a mandate to introduce school-based management. This meant that a team of teachers, support staff, and parents would assist in the administration of the school. Developers of the concept felt that school-based management could be a particularly powerful way of managing the schools in a multicultural environment such as that of the Roosevelt School, where the students and staff represented a diversity of ethnic, racial, and religious backgrounds. The newly formed management committee would have oversight responsibility for the development and implementation of the school's budget, staffing, and program evaluation.

Jenny Blake, one of the teachers elected to serve on the school-based management committee, was very concerned about the school's ability to move to this type of decentralized management. She had worked with Sonya James, the principal of the Roosevelt School, for almost fifteen years and knew that Sonya was highly invested in "doing things her own way." Sonya had successfully run the school in a relatively autocratic manner for a number of years. Recently, however, she seemed to struggle with the new demands placed on her by parents, teachers, and students. Student and faculty performance had both declined over the past few years.

Jenny felt that school-based management was a step toward increasing the staff's ability to deliver quality education. She also knew that Sonya was afraid of the changes it would create, especially the limitations on her control over school matters. Jenny had spoken with many teachers about the proposed changes, and most expressed both enthusiasm about the concept and skepticism about how it would be implemented and then whether it would have a positive impact. Jenny thought the new approach would help not hinder Sonya in coping with the frequent fiscal, personnel, and educational crises her school and its staff seemed to increasingly face. But more importantly, she saw school-based management as giving the staff a voice in the management of the school, one that Jenny and many of her colleagues felt was long overdue.

How will the Roosevelt School move to school-based management? What changes will be required? Who will implement them? What resistances will they face? How will those involved ensure and test the effectiveness of school-based management? In this chapter we consider primarily the *action* step of the diagnostic approach. The chapter begins with a general approach to changing organizations and introduces the technique of force field analysis, which focuses on identifying and modifying the forces that influence change. It continues with the issues associated with selecting a change agent, choosing appropriate intervention strategies, and then implementing the change. We examine the nature of organizational transformations and organizational responses to crises as well. The chapter continues its discussion of change by offering approaches to evaluating and institutionalizing the changes, as well as increasing the effectiveness of organizations. It concludes with an overview of organizational effectiveness and a review of the diagnostic approach.

CHANGING ORGANIZATIONS IN A GLOBAL ENVIRONMENT

What is the first step you would take in ensuring that the new school-based management will be effective? Should Jenny Blake begin by diagnosing the situation, fleshing out a detailed plan for implementing the proposed changes in administration, presenting it to Sonya James with a timetable for implementation, and then appearing the next day ready to begin? Or, should Sonya schedule a meeting with the faculty and parents involved in and affected by the new school-based management, jointly agree on the diagnosis of the situation, brainstorm ways of introducing the required changes effectively, meet repeatedly to detail plans for implementing them, and finally implement each step of the plans in sequence?

The Consulting Model of Change

The model of planned change used here incorporates some elements of each of these approaches, but includes seven steps, shown in Figure 14–1, that reflect a systematic approach to introducing change.[1] Although this model was developed more than two decades ago, it remains a robust and useful approach to introducing change and implementing *action* in organizations. It can be applied in a local setting with a multicultural work force, as described in the opening scenario, or in a global environment with a multinational work force.

Scouting Change begins by obtaining preliminary information about those involved in the change situation. In particular, the person responsible for making the changes or for ensuring that they occur must assess the organization's readiness for change, including a consideration of the environment in which it functions and the nature of its work force. In the case of Roosevelt School, Sonya James, Jenny Blake, and others involved in the school-based management must *scout* the organization before implementing the new form of administration. They might consider, for example, how the multicultural work force will handle the change and the implications of diverse perspectives on the new form of management. Scouting ends with the change agent's decision about whether to proceed with the change effort.

Entry The change agent next attempts to negotiate a written or unwritten *contract* with the organization. The change agent identifies a reasonable point or person of contact in the organization and then must develop an effective working relationship with him or her. Developing an effective point of contact can be particularly difficult in a multinational organization with globally dispersed work sites. In the situation at Roosevelt, however, proponents of school-based management must talk to faculty, staff, administrators, and parents about its implications for the school and ideally secure their approval of and commitment to the change. Organizational members who will serve as the primary implementers of change, such as those on the school-based management committee, must be identified.

Diagnosis The diagnosis step involves problem definition, further goal specification, and an evaluation of the resources available to deal with the problem. The

Figure 14–1 **Model of Planned Change**

Scouting → Entry → Diagnosis → Planning → Action → Evaluation → Termination

activities of this step correspond to the discussion of diagnosis presented throughout this book. An awareness of the elements involved in global performance is key in many organizational settings.

Planning The change agent and client generate alternative strategies for meeting the objectives of the change. They outline the prescription for change, determine the steps in its implementation, and detail the nature, cost, timing, and personnel required for any new system. This step also requires anticipating and planning for all possible consequences of the change effort. Sonya James or other faculty members might take major responsibility for planning action, repeatedly testing support for the proposed action with the rest of the school's faculty, staff, and parents.

Action The change agent—Sonya James, Jenny Blake, other faculty, parents, or top administrators in the school system—implements the best strategy. For example, the change agents would form problem-solving groups or offer training to managers; reallocation of decision making would also occur.

Evaluation The change agent collects data about the nature and effectiveness of the change as it occurs. The results of the evaluation indicate whether the change process is complete, or whether a return to an earlier stage should occur. The criteria for success should be specified in advance of a change effort; these criteria may be culturally linked and varied. If ineffective outcomes result from the introduction of school-based management, the process should return to an earlier stage: for example, scouting (to determine whether the client is really committed to the change), diagnosis (to determine the real nature of the problems), or planning (to determine the best strategy for meeting the change objectives).

Termination Plans for continuing the change into the future or for knowing when it will end should be specified. Ensuring the institutionalization of effective changes should also occur as part of this step. Successful changes should become institutionalized; that is, the changed processes should be established as permanent ways of operating. Failures may terminate the change process or may signal a need for other changes, such as different staffing activities, a new reward system, or new technology.

DIAGNOSING FORCES THAT INFLUENCE CHANGE

Beginning the change process calls for understanding and changing the forces that affect the change. We can use an analytical technique called *force field analysis,* which views a problem as a product of forces working in different, often opposite directions.[2] An organization, or any of its subsystems, will maintain the status quo when the sum of opposing forces is zero. When forces in one direction exceed forces in the opposite one, the organization or subsystem will move in the direction of the greater forces. For example, if the forces for change exceed the forces against change, then change likely will occur.

To move an organization toward a different desired state requires either increasing the forces for change in that direction, decreasing the forces against change in that direction, or both. Generally, reducing resistance forces creates less tension in the system and fewer unanticipated consequences than increasing forces for change. At the Roosevelt School, for example, reducing the resistances to the changes created by the introduction of school-based management increases the likelihood of the changeover. Figure 14–2 shows what happens when a resistance force is eliminated. When the managers no longer resist change, the present state, as shown by the solid

Figure 14–2 Identifying Target Forces

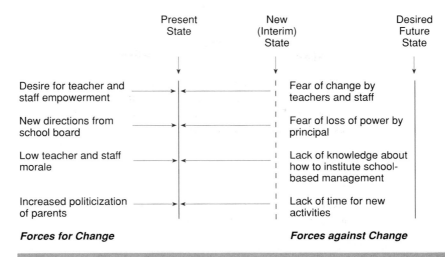

Present State	New (Interim) State	Desired Future State

Desire for teacher and staff empowerment → ← | Fear of change by teachers and staff

New directions from school board → ← | Fear of loss of power by principal

Low teacher and staff morale → ← | Lack of knowledge about how to institute school-based management

Increased politicization of parents → ← | Lack of time for new activities

Forces for Change   **Forces against Change**

vertical line, moves closer to the desired state, as indicated by the broken vertical line. A complete analysis looks at ways to alter all forces—for and against change.

Identifying Forces for Change

Let us consider again the situation at the Roosevelt School. School-based management focused on changing school governance to greater participation by more diverse constituencies; it meant removing some control from the school principal and other top administrators. What forces for change, also known as *driving forces,* exist? Increased demands for parental involvement, an increasingly complex educational situation, and changes in state legislation are among the forces that spurred the change.

Changes in the organization's environment, such as new laws or regulations, rapidly increasing competition, or an unpredictable rate of inflation, may require the organization to implement new structures or reward systems. New product development or product selection resulting from the availability of improved technology, changes in competition in the industry, or unusual requirements of a new client may also affect the organization. Similarly, changes in the work force, such as more educated workers, more women, or more technically trained management may call for new forms of decision making or communication. Finally, reduced productivity, product quality, satisfaction, commitment, or increased turnover or absenteeism may call for changes in intra- or interdepartmental relations. Frequently, one or two specific events external to the organization precipitate the change. Careful description of the organizational system should pinpoint the forces for change. Can you make a complete list of forces for change at the Roosevelt School? Or think about a situation you have faced that calls for change. What forces for change existed in that situation?

Identifying Forces against Change

Forces known as *resistance forces,* as shown in Figure 14–3, counteract the forces for change. Middle managers might resist changes in their routines and supervisory activities; they may also be unwilling to relinquish their decision-making authority. Top management may be unwilling to allocate the resources required to change the culture. Identifying and then reducing resistance forces may be essential to making an individual or group receptive to change.

Forces against change often reside within the organization and stem from rigid organizational structures and rigid individual thinking. Specific forces against change

Figure 14–3
Sources of Resistance to Change

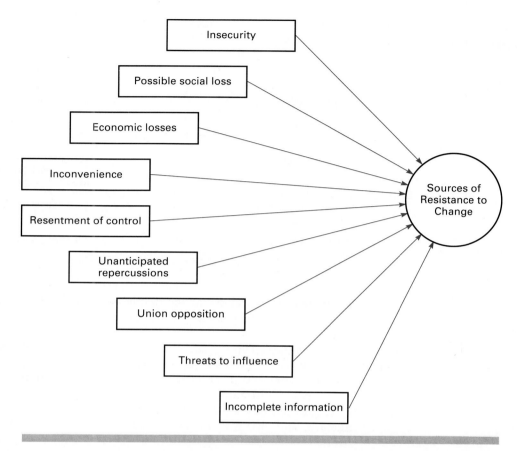

include employees' distrust of the change agent, fear of change, desires for maintaining power, and complacency; lack of resources to support the change; conflicts between individual and organizational goals; and organizational inertia against changing the status quo. These forces frequently combine into significant resistance to change.

Resistance results from a variety of factors. First, it occurs when a change ignores the needs, attitudes, and beliefs of organizational members. If workers have high security needs, they may perceive as threatening the increasing automation of the workplace. Second, individuals resist change when they lack specific information about the change; they may not know when, how, or why it is occurring. Third, individuals may not perceive a need for change; they may feel that their organization is currently operating effectively and profitably. In these cases change often is neither voluntary nor requested by organizational members. Fourth, organizational members frequently have a "we-they" attitude that causes them to view the change agent as their enemy. Particularly when change is imposed by representatives of a distant corporate headquarters or of an outside consulting firm, organizational members may feel inconsequential to the change. Fifth, members may view change as a threat to the prestige and security of their supervisor. They may perceive the change in procedures or policies as a commentary that their supervisor's performance is inadequate. Sixth, employees may perceive the change as threats to their expertise, status, or security. The introduction of a new computer system, for example, may cause employees to feel that they lack sufficient knowledge to perform their jobs; the revision of an organization's structure may challenge their relative status in the organization; the introduction of a new reward system may threaten their feelings of job security. For effective change to occur, the change agent must confront each of these factors and overcome the resulting resistance to change.

Can you think of other forces against change in the situation at the Roosevelt School? Think about another situation that calls for changes. What forces against change exist in that situation? How do change agents deal with these forces?

BUILDING AN ACTION PLAN

Following the identification of the forces for and against change, the person responsible for implementing the change must identify alternative actions for changing each force and then organize them into an action plan. The analytical approach we are describing here must be supplemented with a consideration of individuals' psychological reactions to change and development of appropriate strategies for dealing with them. It can also use action research methodology as a basis of studying and intervening in organizational situations. In action research, as shown in Figure 14–4, the change agent collaborates extensively with the client in gathering and feeding back data. Together they collect and discuss the data, and then use the data for planning.[3]

Consider the possible reluctance of the principal to reduce her involvement in decision making, a force against change in the organization. The following actions could reduce this reluctance: implementing the change slowly, educating the principal about the value of the change, or testing an experimental version of new pro-

Figure 14–4 **Action Research Model**

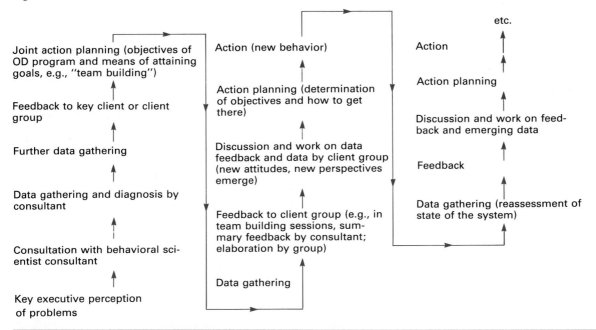

SOURCE: W. French, "Organization Development: Objectives, Assumptions and Strategies." © 1969 by the Regents of the University of California. Reprinted from *California Management Review* 12, no. 2, p. 26 by permission of the Regents.

cedures to increase teacher and staff participation in decision making. Table 14–1 lists these alternatives, as well as alternative actions for changing a second target force. It also cites the feasibility and action priority of each alternative.

Overcoming resistance to change is a key action issue for managers or external change agents. Employees can sabotage change efforts, increasing their cost and decreasing their effectiveness. Resistance to change can result in behavior ranging from lowered productivity, increased absenteeism, and decreased motivation to slow-downs, strikes, or unionization. The change agent must plan ways to overcome resistance to change, as shown in Figure 14–5. Employee participation in task forces, quality circles, and other vehicles that encourage their contribution to decision making should reduce resistance. The agent can also let the clients experience the need for change by highlighting the limitations of the current work circumstances.

The person responsible for change should maintain open and frequent communication with the individuals, groups, or organizations involved; for example, he or she might schedule regular informational meetings for all employees affected by the change. The change agent should also consider the needs of individual employees because responding to needs when possible helps develop in the individuals a vested interest in and ultimately support for the change. Finally, where possible, the change agent should encourage voluntary change. Establishing a climate of innovation and experimentation can reduce the organization's tendency to maintain a status quo. Particularly when change is rewarded, individuals will feel more comfortable in changing. Table 14–2 summarizes the approaches to dealing with resistance to change.

Development of an action plan concludes with a specification of each action in the order it will be performed. You can continue the analysis for the Roosevelt School, or try a similar analysis with an organizational change situation you have faced. Be sure to perform all the steps described above and summarized in Figure 14–6.

Table 14–1 **An Example of an Analysis of Target Forces at the Roosevelt School**

Target Forces	Alternate Actions	Feasibility	Action Priority
Fear of change by the principal, teachers, and staff	Implement change slowly	Moderate; change can occur over a 12-month period	High
	Educate workers about the change	High; easy and relatively low cost	High
	Illustrate the benefits of the new system	High; easy and relatively low cost	High
	Pilot-test the system for small group	Moderate; time-consuming and pilot may be difficult to design	Medium-high
	Involve employees in planning the change	High; time-consuming but important to acceptance	Medium
Lack of knowledge about how to institute new system	Offer training in culture change	High; important to eventual implementation	High
	Provide new policies and procedures	High; important to system implementation	Medium

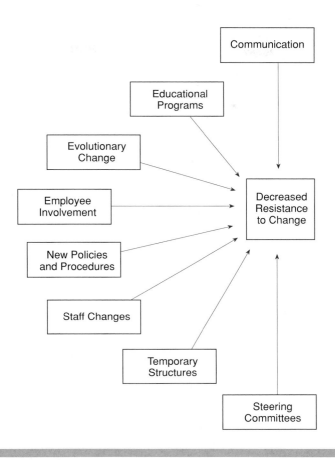

Figure 14–5 Overcoming Resistance to Change

SELECTING A CHANGE AGENT

Who could make the changes inherent in school-based management described in the introductory scenario? Should top administrators of the school department direct the proposed changes? Should the Roosevelt School principal or other members of the school community be responsible? Or, should they use an outside consultant to facilitate the changes? Figure 14–7 offers a typology of change agents. Clearly, the use of *internal* as opposed to *external* change agents presents some trade-offs. Table 14–3 summarizes the advantages and disadvantages of each, and takes into account the costs, knowledge, experiences, and objectivity of potential change agents.

Internal Change Agents

The school principal, faculty, and even some parents have firsthand knowledge of the organization, are known and immediately available to organizational members, and require almost no additional expenditures in fees or additional salary. However, because of their investment in the organization, insiders can be too close to the problem and not objective in looking at it, or they can be viewed as part of the problem. Their services can be costly if measured in time unavailable for other projects.

Most frequently, the manager of the group involved in a change becomes the implementor of the changes. This selection occurs informally, primarily because he or she is closest to the situation, has greatest knowledge of it, and has control over it. Further, the manager is already on board, which can reduce the time required to

Table 14–2 **Approaches to Dealing with Resistance to Change**

Approach	Commonly Used in Situations	Advantages	Drawbacks
Education and communication	Where there is a lack of information or inaccurate information and analysis.	Once persuaded, people will often help with the implementation of change.	Can be very time-consuming if lots of people are involved.
Participation and involvement	Where the initiators do not have all the information they need to design the change and where others have considerable power to resist.	People who participate will be committed to implementing change.	Can be very time-consuming if participators design an inappropriate change.
Facilitation and support	Where people are resisting because of adjustment problems.	No other approach works as well with adjustment problems.	Can be time-consuming, and still fail.
Negotiation and agreement	Where someone or some group will clearly lose out in a change and where that group has considerable power to resist.	Sometimes it is a relatively easy way to avoid major resistance.	Can be too expensive in many cases if it alerts others to negotiate for compliance.
Manipulation and co-optation	Where other tactics will not work or are too expensive.	It can be a relatively quick and inexpensive solution to resistance problems.	Can lead to future problems if people feel manipulated.
Explicit and implicit coercion	Where speed is essential and the change initiators possess considerable power.	It is speedy and can overcome any kind of resistance.	Can be risky if it leaves people mad at the initiators.

SOURCE: Reprinted by permission of *Harvard Business Review*. An exhibit from "Choosing Strategies for Change" by J. P. Kotter and L. A. Schlesinger (March/April 1979). Copyright © 1979 by the President and Fellows of Harvard College; all rights reserved.

begin the change. In addition, other organizational members already know the manager and have clear expectations about actions he or she might take.

Other organizational members can be used as internal consultants, likely reducing resistance to change from coworkers. They can focus on organizational processes—that is, the nature of interactions between managers and subordinates—especially focusing on teaching managers how to develop others and help others conduct problem solving activities.[4] Union Electric used internal consultants to help

Figure 14–6 **Summary of Steps in Change**

1. Identify forces for change.
2. Identify forces against change.
3. Brainstorm actions to reduce forces against change.
4. Brainstorm actions to enhance forces for change.
5. Assess feasibility of each action specified.
6. Prioritize actions.
7. Build an action plan from ranking of actions.
8. Develop timetable and budget for action plan.

Figure 14–7 **Types of Change Agents**

Change Generators

1. *Key change agents.* Those who convert an issue into a felt need. This is usually the role of a charismatic leader. An example is Lee Iacocca, whose methods, style, and values dominated the change process at Chrysler. Iacocca eventually became a symbol of U.S. pride and rebirth.
2. *Demonstrators.* These change agents demonstrate support for the change conceptualized by the key change agent. They are first in the line of confrontation to face those who prefer the status quo. The demonstrator's role is to provide visible, vocal support for the change.
3. *Patrons.* These individuals support the change process, financially or psychologically. For instance, a patron of change may provide the key change agent with a budget, a prestigious title, a promotion, or other symbols of support.
4. *Defenders.* This role entails defending the change at the grass roots—the lower levels of the organization. The manager-defender is caught up by the charisma of the key change agent, by becoming an adherent, and by spreading the word among the troops. Defenders may see how they can benefit from the change, or they may be pushed into defending the change by resisters.

Change Implementors

5. *External change implementors.* These individuals are invited from outside the organization to implement change. They may be consultants for organizational development efforts hired to articulate and implement the key change agent's vision. External change agents have the advantage of a fresh perspective and no vested interest in keeping things the way they are.
6. *External/internal change implementors.* These individuals develop internal implementors. Staff managers from

headquarters, who are alien to the field organizations, may have the task of carrying the word from on high to the masses. They are external in the sense that they appear to come from outside. Yet they are long-standing members of the organization with the traditional supports.
7. *Internal change implementors.* These are managers who assume the responsibility to implement the change in their own organizations. Convinced of the need for change, they model other change agents to move their units in the desired direction, often translating or redefining the change to meet their own needs.

Change Adopters

8. *Early adopters.* These managers practice the new change. The first adopters show the highest commitment and become the prototypes for the change. Going beyond implementation, they maintain the change, making it the norm in their organization.
9. *Maintainers.* These managers are primarily concerned with meeting current business needs, doing their jobs to keep the organization going. However, they are willing to adopt the change in the process, because they see how it contributes to their own work. Their objective is to sustain the organization, and they realize that the change is one of the things that you have to do now and then to assure the organization's survival. An example is how managers readily take on new or added responsibilities in the wake of a reorganization of functions and reporting relationships.
10. *Users.* Managers become users when they make a habit of the change. Initially, they have the least commitment to the change, and they are probably the last adopters. Yet they are likely to benefit the most from the change. Without them, the change would never be successful.

SOURCE: M. London, *Change Agents: New Roles and Innovation Strategies for Human Resource Professionals.* San Francisco: Jossey-Bass, 1988, pp. 58–59. Used with permission of the publisher.

introduce and then influence acceptance of a quality improvement process whose goals were "increasing job satisfaction, building an environment that encourages innovative ideas, improving operational results, improving employee skills and improving communication through teamwork."[5]

External Change Agents Consultants offer the opposite advantages and disadvantages. They tend to have more technical knowledge, diverse competencies, and objectivity. They may lack information about the particular situation, take longer to start implementing the change, and add large out-of-pocket costs.

Table 14–3 **Advantages and Disadvantages of Internal and External Change Agents**

	Internal Agents	External Agents
Advantages	Possess better knowledge of the organization	Have more objective views of the organization
	Are more quickly available	Have more experience in dealing with diverse problems
	Require lower out-of-pocket costs	Can call on more individuals with diverse expertise
	Are a known quantity	Have more technical knowledge, competence, and skills available
	Have more control and authority	
Disadvantages	May be too close to the problem	Have less knowledge of the organization
	May hold biased views	Require higher out-of-pocket costs
	May create additional resistance if viewed as part of the problem	Are an unknown quantity
	Must be reassigned; not available for other work	Have longer start-up time
		Reflect unfavorably on the image of management

One study of the personality of change agents indicated that the most effective organizational development consultants could be described as empathetic, sensitive, open, tolerant, flexible, patient, friendly, cooperative, and imaginative. They developed and used information to understand situations and identify behavior patterns. They acted in a self-reliant fashion, were bold, risk-taking, and initiating. In contrast, the least effective consultants were suspicious, tense, directive, and impersonal. They stayed within bounds of known facts, focused on the practical, secured minimal information, and were more concerned with the how than the why of situations. They also were shy and aversive to risk.[6] Following the steps shown in Figure 14–8 should facilitate the selection of the most appropriate change agent.

SELECTING AN INTERVENTION STRATEGY

In this book we have discussed behavioral, structural, and technological focuses of change in an organization. The behavioral focus deals with changes in the knowledge, skills, interactions, and attitudes of organization members; it can also involve improving their communication, group behavior, intergroup behavior, and leadership skills, as well as their power relations. The structural approach calls for redesigning organizations and jobs or work situations. The technological approach requires changing equipment, methods, materials, or techniques and changing the relationship between the worker and his or her job. The choice of a specific intervention strategy depends on several criteria: (1) the target system, (2) the target group, (3) the depth of intervention desired, (4) the nature of the prescribed change mechanisms, and (5) the expertise of the change agent. In this chapter we offer an overview of these options, rather than an in-depth analysis of each intervention strategy; managers and consultants must use additional sources for becoming expert in specific interventions.

Figure 14–8 **Select-ing a Change Agent**

1. Determine the objectives of the change.
2. Consider the extent of help and involvement desired.
3. Consider the extent of help and involvement available in the organization.
4. Identify individuals with expertise congruent with the objectives.
5. Identify and specify relevant constraints: time, cost, effort, involvement, and other resources.
6. Communicate expectations, including needs, constraints, and personal biases, to the change agent.
7. Establish criteria for evaluating the change plan: cost, time, effort, or other resources needed; technical feasibility; likelihood of success; congruence between consultants' experience and proposed plan; ease of implementation; and likelihood of resistance.
8. Determine the trade-offs in selecting various change agents (cost versus experience, for example).
9. Assess which change agents fit the organization's needs.

The Target System

Intervention strategies can focus on the technical, social, administrative, or strategic systems.[7] Low productivity may signal problems with the technical system. Providing capital improvements and offering workers training can help resolve technical system problems.

Inadequate quality of working life may suggest problems with the organization's social system. Interventions that alter the reward system, integrate organizational values into change efforts, confront organizational power and politics, and improve communication address these problems.

An organization that responds slowly in receiving and distributing information may have an ineffective system for administering the organization. Ensuring that a logical organization structure exists, communicating the structure to organizational members, clarifying policies, procedures, and standards, and maintaining a strong system of collecting and disseminating information can aid the effectiveness of the administrative system.

Management strength and competence reflect the health of the strategic system, which includes top management, planning, and managing information. Choosing appropriate management styles, systematically evaluating the environment, adapting to changing conditions, building executive succession systems, and encouraging innovation are interventions that strengthen the strategic system.

The Target Group

The selection of the appropriate target for change depends on the nature of the diagnosed problem. Interventions can focus on a person, role, dyad or triad, team or group, intergroup interaction, or the entire organization.[8] The analysis of the forces for and against change also helps pinpoint the appropriate target. If, for example, one supervisor refuses to adopt a new policy, the target of change should be the individual. If, on the other hand, the organization lacks effective policies for dealing with unions, then the organization should be the target.

Too often, change agents misfocus interventions by addressing the wrong target. Consider the situation where some employees report late to work. Some organizations try to resolve this problem by instituting earlier official starting times. What is the target of this change? What might be the consequences of such a change? In this situation, the change should focus on the tardy individuals, rather than on the entire organization.

Depth of Intervention Similar assessment of the appropriate *depth* of intervention must occur. One historical view looked at the extent to which strategies ranged from deep to surface, that is, the extent to which they deal with an individual's more central and private aspects rather than the individual's more external and public aspects.[9] Modification of reward systems, which interface with individual performance and motivation, illustrate moderately surface strategies. Processes that attempt to alter individual work style by focusing on feelings, attitudes, and perceptions exemplify deeper strategies. In the deepest level of interventions, which should only be used when more surface strategies cannot produce enduring change, strategies try to increase the individual's knowledge of his or her own attitudes, values, and conflicts as a first step in change.

A second way of looking at the depth of intervention considers the level of the change attempt.[10] First-order changes reinforce present understandings of situations. They include adjustments in structure, reward system, or other organizational behaviors. Second-order changes modify the present understanding in a particular direction. They involve a change in the schemata used to view the situation and may be a response to major environmental shifts or an experience of crisis.[11] A decline in productivity, once viewed as a technical problem, can now be handled as a QWL issue. Third-order changes give organizational members the capacity to change their understanding of the situation. The introduction of school-based management is potentially a third-order change because it requires the school's constituencies to think about the school as an egalitarian system with shared responsibility for its effectiveness rather than a hierarchical system with responsibility localized in the top executive, in this case the school principal. Training organizational members to view a situation through new lenses offers more long-term possibilities for change.

Nature of the Change Mechanisms The nature of the change mechanisms chosen depends on the problem diagnosis and force field analysis. Figure 14–9 offers an array of such mechanisms. Change agents can provide feedback to organizational members about their or others' attitudes and behaviors as a way of spurring change. If a male manager learns, for example, that his subordinates view him as too autocratic, he might modify his leadership style. Change agents can also increase interaction and communication through altering the organization's structure. The introduction of project teams facilitates lateral communication; so does the implementation of QWL programs that encourage team collaboration and problem solving. Change agents might also alert management and workers to changing sociocultural norms. Although the term *organization development* has been used generically to describe a wide range of approaches to organizational change, it more recently has been used to describe a more limited effort that uses behavioral science knowledge, focuses on an organization's problem-solving and renewal processes, emphasizes the collaborative management of organizational culture, introduces work teams, and requires the help of a change agent or catalyst.[12] Some strategies encourage confrontation and resolution of differences; confrontation meetings, process consultation, and third-party facilitation can take this approach to change. Finally, change mechanisms can include education of workers through training and skill practice.

Problems based in individual performance frequently call for the use of feedback and increased interaction as change mechanisms. Problems of conflict generally require confrontation and working for resolution of differences, or creation of an awareness of new norms emphasizing teamwork. Leadership dilemmas may be corrected by education of leaders, including delivery of new knowledge and skill practice. While some change mechanisms respond best to specific types of problems, use of multiple change mechanisms strengthens the action and resulting change.

Figure 14–9 Mechanisms of Change

The change strategies preferred vary in different countries. In Italy, for example, where managers' and consultants' values do not support dealing with emotionally charged issues in a group context, team building and third-party interventions are common, whereas t-groups, confrontation meetings, and process consultation are not.[13]

Expertise of the Change Agent

Of course, the precise change mechanism used depends to some extent on the expertise of the change agent. Organizational members, as well as external consultants, often have training or experience in performing certain types of interventions. Thus selection of the strategy should complement selection of the change agent.

IMPLEMENTING ORGANIZATIONAL CHANGES

Action follows the identification of target forces for change and the selection of the change agent and intervention strategy. Implementation must ensure that the strategies succeed. Although careful preparation for change, including description, diagnosis, and prescription, increases the chances of success, it does not guarantee effective action. Implementation requires an ongoing assessment of the reactions of organizational members to the change. Briefing sessions, special seminars, or other means of information dissemination must permeate the change effort. Implementation must include procedures for keeping all participants informed about change activities and effects.

The use of a broad-based steering committee to oversee the change may increase its likelihood of success.[14] Such a group, composed of representatives of top management, first-line supervisors, and rank-and-file employees, can advise on issues related to program budget as well as on organizational policies and priorities.

Further, the dynamic nature of organizational systems calls for flexibility in action: All efforts must include contingency plans for unanticipated costs, consequences, or resistance. A strong commitment to the change on the part of top management can buffer change efforts for such difficulties and can ensure the transfer of needed resources to the action program.

Managing Large-Scale Change

Managing large-scale organizational change might require a more elaborated approach. The process includes four components—(1) pattern breaking, (2) experimenting, (3) visioning, and (4) bonding and attunement—as shown in Figure 14–10.[15] *Pattern breaking* involves freeing the system from structures, processes, and functions that are no longer useful. An organization can be open to new options if it can relinquish approaches that no longer work, if its managers are rewarded for weeding out unproductive products and processes, and if it is willing to challenge long-held traditions. At the Roosevelt School, replacing some of the structures and processes associated with the former, non-school-based management workplace was a first step in instituting change. *Experimenting* by generating new patterns encourages flexibility and yields new options. Training small groups of supervisors to institute teamwork illustrates this element. To experiment, organizations must have a philosophy and mechanisms in place that encourage innovation and creativity. *Visioning,* the third element, calls for the selection of a new perspective as the basis of the change. Visioning activities, such as building shared meaning throughout the organization and using current mission statements, generates support for and commitment to the planned changes. Schoolwide meetings at Roosevelt to share ideal views about school-based management would help accomplish this step. In the last component, called *bonding and attunement,* management attempts to integrate all facets of the organizational change to move members toward the new way of action by focusing them on important tasks and generating constructive interpersonal relationships.

Ethical Issues in Implementation

Change agents often confront issues of integrity in their interactions with organizations. Five types of ethical dilemmas include misrepresentation and collusion, misuse of data in change efforts, manipulation and coercion, value and goal conflict, and technical ineptness.[16] Some managers may implement their personal change agenda at the expense of solid diagnosis of the organization's needs. Still others may promise more than they can deliver. Some consultants fail to build ways of institutionalizing the change into their process so the organization can continue to rely on (and pay) them. Table 14–4 presents possible ethical dilemmas associated with stages of organization development change. Organizational leaders, as well as internal and external consultants, should ensure that the selection and implementation of change strategies respond to well-documented organizational and individual needs. They must also ensure that the change process respects the rights of individuals in the workplace. Table 14–5 lists fourteen danger signs of unethical behavior.

Figure 14–10 **Steps in Managing Large-Scale Change**

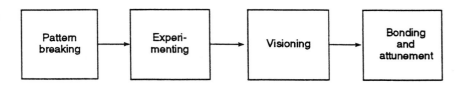

Pattern breaking → Experimenting → Visioning → Bonding and attunement

Table 14–4 **Organization Development Change Stages**

Stage	Purpose	Role of Change Agent	Role of Client System	Dilemmas
Initiation	First information sharing	To provide information on background, expertise, and experience	To provide information on possible needs, relevant problems, interest of management and representative groups	Misrepresentation of the consultant's skill base and background Misrepresentation of organizational interest
Clarification	Further elaboration of initiation stage	To provide details of education, licensure, operative values, optimum working conditions	To provide a detailed history of special problems, personnel, marketplace, internal culture, and organizational politics	Inappropriate determination of who the client is Avoidance of reality testing Inappropriate determination of value orientation
Specification/ agreement	Sufficient elaboration of needs, interest, fees, services, working conditions, arrangements	To specify actual services, fees to be charged, time frame, actual work conditions	To specify whose needs are to be addressed, goals, objectives, and possible evaluative criteria or end-state outcomes	Inappropriate structuring of the relationship Inappropriate definition of change problem Collusion to exclude outside parties
Diagnosis	To obtain an unfiltered and undistorted view of the organization's problems and processes pinpointing change targets and criterion	To collect data concerning organizational problems and processes, and to provide feedback	To assist change agent in data collection	Avoidance of problems Misuse of data Distortion and deletion of data Ownership of data Voluntary consent Confidentiality
Goal setting/ action planning	To establish the specific goals and strategies to be used	To agree mutually with the client system on the goals and strategies to be used	To agree mutually with the change agent on the goals and strategies to be used	Inappropriate choice of intervention goal and targets Inappropriate choice of operative means Inappropriate scope of intervention
Systems intervention	The intervention into on-going behaviors, structures, and processes	To intervene at specific targets, at a specific depth	To invest the energy and resources required by planned intervention	Assimilation into culture Inappropriate depth of intervention Coercion vs. choice, freedom, and consent to participate Environmental manipulation
Evaluation	To determine the effectiveness of the intervention strategies, energy, and resources used, as well as the change agent-client system relationship	To gather data on specified targets and report findings to the client system	To analyze the evaluation data and determine effectiveness of the intervention	Misuse of data Deletion and distortion of data
Alteration	To modify change strategies, depth, level, goals, targets, or resources utilized if necessary	To make alteration to meet original goals, or to develop new mutual goals and strategies with client system	To make known needs and expectations, and to provide the context for a modification of the original agreement, if necessary	Failure to change and lack of flexibility Adoption of inappropriate strategy

(continued)

Table 14–4 *(Continued)*

Stage	Purpose	Role of Change Agent	Role of Client System	Dilemmas
Continuation/ maintenance	To monitor and maintain ongoing strategies, provide periodic checks, and continue intervention based on original or altered plans and strategies	To specify the parameters of the continuation of the maintenance of the relationship	To provide or allocate the resources required to maintain or continue the intervention	Inappropriate reduction of dependency Redundancy of effort Withholding of services
Termination	To have the change agent disenfranchise self from the client system and establish a long-term monitoring system	To fulfill the role agreed on in previous stages and evaluate overall effectiveness from feedback from the client system	To determine the organization's state of health, and whether it has developed the adaptive change process	Inappropriate transition of change effort to internal sources Premature exit Failure to monitor change

Reprinted with permission from L. P. White and K. C. Wooten, Ethical dilemmas in various stages of organizational development, *Academy of Management Review* 8(2) (1983): 690–697, p. 695.

MAKING ORGANIZATIONAL TRANSFORMATIONS

Environmental pressures, global competition, or deregulation spur organizational transformations. Conditions external to the organization, such as a threat posed by the environment or some misfit between the organization and the environment, can precipitate such change. Organizational growth, pressure by specific constituencies, a real or perceived crisis, or atypical performance demands can also pressure the organization to change. Finally, environmental catastrophes, environmental opportunities, managerial crises, or external or internal revolutions are specific events that trigger basic changes in organizations.

Table 14–5 **Danger Signs of Unethical Behavior**

1. Emphasis on short-term revenues over long-term considerations.
2. Routinely ignoring or violating internal or professional codes of ethics.
3. Looking for simple solutions to ethical problems, being satisfied with quick fixes.
4. Unwillingness to take an ethical stand if there is a financial cost.
5. Creation of an internal environment that discourages ethical behavior or encourages unethical behavior.
6. Dispatch of ethical problems to the legal department.
7. View of ethics solely as a public relations tool.
8. Treatment of employees that differs from treatment of customers.
9. Unfair or arbitrary performance appraisal standards.
10. Lack of procedures or policies for handling ethical problems.
11. Lack of mechanisms for internal whistle-blowing.
12. Lack of clear lines of communication.
13. Sensitivity only to shareholder needs and demands.
14. Encouragement of employees to ignore their personal ethical values.

SOURCE: Based on R. A. Cooke, Danger signs of unethical behavior: How to determine if your firm is at ethical risk, *Journal of Business Ethics,* 10 (1991): 249–253.

Transforming Organizations

Even if managers and other organizational members diagnose a situation correctly and select appropriate prescriptions for improving it, the complementary action sometimes does not result in the intended outcomes. Sometimes more basic changes, including transformations of the organization itself, are required. *Transformation* means fundamentally changing organizations to function better in today's competitive world.[17] In the 1980s Jack Welch transformed General Electric to focus on the core business elements by reducing the size of the work force, opening communication, flattening the management hierarchy and changing managers' roles, developing a new shared corporate vision, and altering the organization's value statements.[18] Four types of changes can be called transformational: (1) changes in what drives the organization, such as marketing or production; (2) changes in the relationship between parts of the organization, such as between sales and operations; (3) changes in the way work is done; and (4) basic cultural changes.[19] Major researchers in the area agree with the observations about transformation shown in Table 14–6.

Transformational change, or "frame-breaking" change, differs from the more frequently observed, converging change, which involves fine-tuning in a company or making incremental modifications to minor shifts in the environment.[20] Frame-breaking change involves redefining the organization's mission, changing the distribution of power within the organization, reorganizing, altering patterns of interaction, and hiring new executives.

The *punctuated equilibrium paradigm* describes organization change as an alternation of long periods of stability and short periods of revolutionary change.[21] During the stable or *equilibrium* periods *deep structures* comprise its operating and performance choices. These basic parts and activity patterns of a system make incremental adjustments to adapt to external changes. At times, however, *revolutionary* changes dismantle the deep structure. The organizations or other systems may outgrow their deep structures, lack sufficient resources for dealing with the environment, or face a traumatic external environment. Emotions of participants intensify, and outsiders may play more critical roles during the revolutionary period; ultimately chaos becomes clarity, and new deep structures develop.

Table 14–6 Observations about Organizational Transformation

1. Transformation is a response to environmental and technological change by different types of organizations.
2. Transformation is a new model of the organization for the future.
3. Transformation is based on dissatisfaction with the old and belief in the new.
4. Transformation is a qualitatively different way of perceiving, thinking, and behaving.
5. Transformation is expected to spread throughout the organization at different rates of absorption.
6. Transformation is driven by line management.
7. Transformation is ongoing, endless, and forever.
8. Transformation is orchestrated by inside and outside experts.
9. Transformation represents the leading edge of knowledge about organization change.
10. Transformation generates more open communication and feedback throughout the organization.

SOURCE: Based on R. H. Kilmann, T. J. Covin, and Associates, eds., *Corporate Transformation: Revitalizing Organizations for a Competitive World* (San Francisco: Jossey-Bass, 1988).

Most organizations evolve through relatively long periods of incremental change and adaptation.[22] Periodically, reorientations follow; these periods are relatively short times of discontinuous change where the organization's strategy, power relations, structure, and controls fundamentally transform into a new configuration. At these times, action effectiveness may decline unless significant changes in the organization occur.

Such transitions correspond to significant changes in the primary tasks or goals of an organization and its strategy to achieve them.[23] They often involve structural change, a new kind of leadership, and a network of supporters.[24] Eastman Kodak Company found itself stagnant and overly bureaucratic in the early 1980s. Its leadership responded to the resulting organizational ineffectiveness by changing the organizational structure, creating new alliances with customers, and facilitating new ideas and ventures in the mid-1980s.[25] Top management diversified the company extensively through acquisitions, joint ventures, and new start-ups; they integrated the organization through thinking about issues laterally—across departments and functions; they developed synergies between worldwide R&D and global manufacturing; they made quality a key ingredient of the corporate culture; and they changed the reward system to tie pay to performance.

Transformational leaders (see Chapter 8) play a major role in transforming and revitalizing organizations. They must overcome resistance to change in the organization's technical, political, and cultural systems.[26] Figure 14–11 describes the four stages of transition these leaders direct.

Another model of the transformation process suggests that it is a function of a reframing of the situation by individuals involved.[27] It begins with a challenge to the original frame; typically a crisis motivates such a need for a new understanding. Preparation for reframing occurs next; here different information about the problems lead to new understandings of the situation. Then participants develop new and different frames or understandings. The transformation concludes with members adopting and accepting the new view or understanding. This model applies to all stages of an organization's life cycle. Transformation can also apply to emerging organizations whose survival may depend on their ability to deal with critical issues at a single point in time. Internal conditions, such as a surplus of resources, system readiness, sufficient information linkages within the organization, and a change agent with leadership and power, permit transitions of the organization. Did conditions at the Roosevelt School call for an organizational transformation? Will school-based management result in one?

RESPONDING TO CRISES

Crises in organizations can also precipitate change. Consider the threat posed by a hostile takeover attempt. An organization immediately alters its structure and personnel to prevent such a crisis. Crises can arise from potential bankruptcy, industrial accidents, product defects or tampering, major computer breakdowns, or a myriad of other causes. The Tylenol tampering, the *Challenger* explosion, the Union Carbide explosion in Bhopal, India, and the Chrysler bankruptcy captured the public's attention in the 1980s. Figure 14–12 illustrates the different types of corporate crises. Note that they can be categorized according to severity and along a technical-social dimension and can threaten organization functioning from inside or outside.[28]

Being prepared to deal with crises may call for establishing a multifaceted portfolio of technology, conducting periodic crisis audits to identify the potential for a catastrophe, and building crisis management teams or units that can practice their coping skills far in advance of a disaster.[29] Management should consider crisis man-

Figure 14–11 **Four Stages of Transition in Change**

Stage 1: Shock

People experience impending change as threat. They shut down thinking and as many systems as possible (just as in physiological shock). People need warm blankets and rest, that is, time to recover, emotional support, information, and an opportunity to gather with others. Productivity is low. People cannot think and do not remember.

What to do: Help people look for common ground in shock, build support network, and give information again and again. Managers should give visible support. Do not involve people in planning. Provide safety, that is, clear organization expectations, reward systems, support systems, and available resources.

Stage 2: Defensive Retreat

Holding on, attempting to maintain old ways. A great deal of anger, refusal to let go of past. People and organizations can get stuck here or recycle back to Stage 1 as each element of change is introduced.

What to do: Help people identify what they are holding on to, and then how to maintain it in the new situation or how to let it go. Identify areas of stability: things that are not changing. Give information continually and consistently. Ask "what is risky" and provide safety in response to discomfort with risk taking.

Stage 3: Acknowledgment

Sense of grief and sadness over loss. Letting go, beginning to see the value of what is coming, and looking for ways to make it work by considering the pros and cons. Ability to take risks begins here. It takes the form of risk taking and exploring new ways to look at things and to do things. Can lead to high energy if managed well.

What to do: Involve people in exploring options and planning through use of careful decision-making process as a structure/support. Overtly encourage and support risk taking by pointing out ways that the organization will support it. Emphasize that everyone is learning.

Stage 4: Adaptation and Change

What is coming has arrived. Ready to establish new routines and to help others. Risk taking comes into full bloom at this stage relative to changing methods, products, whatever is called for.

What to do: Implement plans. Encourage and support risk taking using the supports and structures developed in stage 3. Establish feedback loops so that information travels in all directions, new learning occurs, and mid-course corrections can be made when necessary.

SOURCE: M. Moore and P. Gergen, Turning the pain of change into creativity and structure for the new order. In R. H. Kilmann, T. J. Covin, and Associates, *Corporate Transformation: Revitalizing Organizations for a Competitive World*, San Francisco: Jossey-Bass, 1988, p. 376. Used by permission of the publisher.

agement part of their strategic planning so that they do not make short-sighted, inappropriate decisions under pressure.[30]

The effectiveness of an organization's response to a crisis depends on several factors.[31] First, the organization's members must have or be able to secure adequate information and resources to cope with the emergency. Second, they must define emergency work, distinguish it from regular work, but maintain functional roles while doing it. Finally, the organization must demonstrate flexibility in operations and decision making so managers can deal readily with uncertainty and loss of autonomy and control. In addition, organizational members must think creatively and avoid groupthink (see Chapter 5) in a crisis.

Regardless of the mechanisms chosen, managers should conduct crisis management in five phases, as summarized in Figure 14–13.[32] First, managers must be alert to crisis warnings, events that signal the advent of a crisis; repeated memoranda about the same mechanical difficulties experienced by an aircraft might provide such a warning. Second, top management must prepare for and prevent a disaster. A crisis

Figure 14–12 Types of Organizational Crises

Technical/Economic

Cell 1	Cell 2
Major industrial accidents Product injuries Computer breakdown Defective, undisclosed information	Widespread environmental destruction Natural disasters Hostile takeover Societal crises (civil or political) Large scale systems failure

Internal   **External**

Cell 3	Cell 4
Failure to adapt/change Sabotage by insiders Organizational breakdown Communication breakdown On-site product tampering Illegal activities Occupational health diseases	Symbolic projection Sabotage by outsiders Terrorism, executive kidnapping Off-site product tampering Counterfeiting

Human/Organizational/Social

SOURCE: Reprinted with permission from P. Shrivastava and I. I. Mitroff, Strategic management of corporate crises, *Columbia Journal of World Business* 22 (Spring 1987): 7. Copyright 1987 by *Columbia Journal of World Business*. Reprinted with permission.

management team can systematically watch for and respond to early warning signals. Next, management should have contingency plans for containing and limiting damage. Implementation of short- and long-term recovery mechanisms follows. Procedures for dealing with such crises as product tampering, computer breakdowns, or hostile takeover attempts should exist, and management should be able to install them immediately. Finally, learning about ways to improve crisis management should conclude the response.

EVALUATING THE CHANGE PROCESS

Follow-up—both informal and formal—is critical to the success of any organizational improvement and should occur regularly as part of action. Table 14–7 offers a checklist that can be used to assist in such assessment; it evaluates client characteristics, the fit between consulting team and client, and characteristics of the individual. Another way of evaluating the change is to consider it more akin to a training

Figure 14–13 Stages of Crisis Management

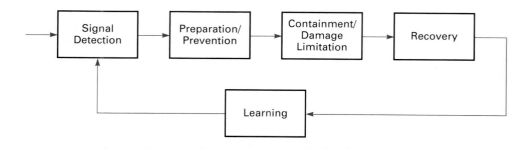

SOURCE: Reprinted from I. I. Mitroff, Crisis management: Cutting through the confusion, *Sloan Management Review* 29 (Winter 1988): 19, by permission of publisher. Copyright 1988 by the Sloan Management Review Association. All rights reserved.

Table 14–7 **Common Behavior Changes in Successful Organizational Change Efforts: Diagnostic Tool for Predicting the Success of Organizational Planned Change**

Client Characteristics	Rating	Consulting Team/Client Characteristics	Rating	Environmental Characteristics	Rating
Commitment of top management		Values fit		External stakeholders' current dissatisfaction	
Capable evangelist		Goals fit		External stakeholders' anticipated future dissatisfaction	
Supportive organization culture		Methodology fit		Common perception among internal stakeholders regarding the environment	
Flexible organization structure		Competence fit		Level of consensus between the consulting team and top management regarding the environment	
Readiness of employee population					

intervention and then to consider the participants' affective reactions, learning, behavioral changes, and performance changes.[33]

Change Outcomes *Affective reactions* refer to participants' attitudes toward the intervention. Change agents or top management frequently use questionnaires or interviews to assess whether organizational members found the intervention useful or effective.

Learning refers to the participants' understanding of new ways of acting and acquisition of new skills as a result of an intervention. Did participants learn how to conduct quality circles or manage autonomous work groups? Did they acquire additional information about other cultures or international business as a result of training programs? Change agents can analyze the differences between scores on pre- and post-tests, follow-up interviews, or open-ended survey responses to evaluate learning.

Behavioral changes include the participants' actions on the job. Do they interact differently with peers and subordinates? Do they use new or different techniques to accomplish their job activities? Figure 14–14 describes common behavior changes in a successful organization development effort; these changes should occur as a result of other change efforts as well.

Performance changes are reflected in objective organizational measures, such as productivity and quality rates, sales volume, profit, absenteeism, and turnover, as well as more subjective performance-appraisal ratings. We can assess, for example, whether the introduction of a new reward system increases worker output or whether a new quality-control system improves product quality.

Figure 14–14 **Common Behavior Changes in Successful Organization Change Efforts (as Reported by Participants)**

Question 1: Common behavior changes for individuals at all organizational levels

Communicating openly. Sharing intentions, motives, needs, feelings, and cognitions relevant to the work situation. Giving feedback that is descriptive rather than evaluative, and specific rather than general. Asking for and accepting feedback. Listening—including paraphrasing, summarizing, restating, asking for clarification, and checking out impressions. Directly confronting differences when they arise. Acting to produce structural and normative changes that lead to increased information sharing, such as loosening implicit or explicit guidelines as to who should talk to whom, and circulating minutes of meetings.

Collaborating. Solving problems as close to where they occur as possible. Discussing, planning, and readjusting organizational actions jointly and cooperatively. Holding more group and intergroup discussions and meetings. Involving critical outsiders to the organization in decisions that pertain to them. Making all the serious and creative decisions—particularly decisions where there are multiple stakeholders—in teams. Expanding influence skills beyond bargaining and authoritative commands to include softer means of influence such as seeding ideas, cajoling, and nudging. Moving away from "oneupmanship" and competition, and toward agreement and cooperation.

Taking responsibility. Figuring out for oneself what is necessary to be effective in one's job and taking initiative for getting whatever information, cooperation, services, or materials are needed from other relevant parties inside or outside of the organization. Asking for and taking responsibility and authority. Persisting in the struggle to make needed changes, especially in the face of frustration and ambiguity. Forming and offering more suggestions. Stating one's own contribution to a problematic situation rather than blaming others. Exhibiting behaviors that demonstrate movement along a continuum from monitoring one's own work to managing and prioritizing it to affecting the design of it to affecting its organizational context (e.g., policies and procedures) to affecting the goals and directions of the organization itself. Taking responsibility is also reflected in expressions of interest and excitement in the work and in *decreased* approval seeking, face saving, indifference, burnout, or "coasting."

Maintaining a shared vision. Developing and communicating written statements of philosophy. Holding meetings to develop clarity of values, purpose, and the means by which the purpose will be achieved. Talking about how organization values translate into daily work behav-

ior. Changing organizational structure, policies, and practices to reflect stated values. Having and telling a "story," a shared history that gives meaning to the organization's activities. Creating rituals and ceremonies to reestablish and remember values. Setting, discussing, and reinforcing high standards.

Solving problems effectively. Defining problems from a win/win perspective, with an open-minded search for solutions that are mutually acceptable instead of pressing for one's own "right" answer. Taking problems out of a personal context and instead working on them vis-à-vis an agreed-upon superordinate goal. Keeping problem definition separate from solution seeking. Generating and simultaneously entertaining multiple explanations for a phenomenon. Generating and discussing multiple alternatives for resolving problems.

Respecting/supporting. Providing recognition for a job well done. Talking about what's going well versus what's deficient. Making use of an individual's assets versus trying to "correct" their shortcomings. Acknowledging people. Encouraging and rewarding people for taking time for themselves and their families. Equalizing status symbols. Helping; standing in for one another. Treating people equitably. Suspending judgment when things go wrong; allowing for goodness in others and not automatically attributing negative motives. An *absence* of disrespectful and nonsupportive behaviors such as racial, ethnic, and sexist jokes, "scapegoating," and stereotyping. An *absence* of discrimination based on race, sex, or ethnicity. An *absence* of aggressive or punitive behavior.

Processing/facilitating interactions. Stopping meetings or one-on-one discussions to examine the process when things are not going well. Assigning (and rotating) the task of observing group process. Reserving time at the end of meetings to critique what was done well/poorly, what facilitated making the decision and/or doing the task, and so on. Clarifying meeting goals and purposes. Rotating the chairperson role. Making group-facilitating rather than group-hindering interventions. Group members changing their roles in the group depending on what is needed for the group to function well. Effectively managing the process of meetings by consensually establishing relevant agendas, holding to them, and recording what is going on so people can understand and follow.

Inquiring. Taking multiple and numerous measures of the discrepancies between the organization's goals and its current state. Taking baselines and using surveys, audits, unobtrusive measures and control groups where possible to gain information about how the organization is func-

Figure 14–14 *(Continued)*

tioning. Experimenting with changes in such a way that the outcome will allow causal inference and useful conclusions. Soliciting information from customers, regulators, and competitors. Looking for new ideas in books, articles, technical studies, speeches, and from one another. Frequently examining and questioning structure, practices, and policies to be sure they maximize achievement of the organization's goals.

Experimenting. Taking risks. Having a "bias for action" and not waiting for the perfect design or plan before trying things out. Allowing time to meet, talk, and try new behaviors. Accepting mistakes. Rewarding good tries. Having fewer restrictions on how things get done. Eliminating symbols of conformity (e.g., three-piece suits) and structures/policies that demand conformity (e.g., timeclocks). Deemphasizing action plans, milestones, and measurable objectives. Acting as umbrellas over experimental programs. Backing/sheltering risk takers, especially when they fail. Defending against intrusions from higher levels. Working with those who are experimenting to demonstrate that experimentation is valued and represents an investment in the organization's future.

Question 2: Common behavior changes for managers

Generating participation. Linking planning and implementation in terms of time and who does it. Involving people when they have the necessary expertise, when the decision must be high quality, and when implementation depends on them. Using meetings, workshops, or a consultant to solicit input from people on proposed changes. *Not* dictating the exact way to accomplish a delegated task. Structuring the work in a way that opens possibilities for self-management by the job incumbent. Providing task and job designs that provide meaningful work, real responsibility for work outcomes, and reliable knowledge of results. Relaxing traditional authoritarian forms of control (e.g., over budgets and allocations of resources and people) and allowing workers to do more. Changing behavior *away from* unilateral edicts and imposing one's will as the basis for power and toward softer influence techniques. Facilitating more than directing.

Leading by vision. Continually articulating the organization's purpose, goals, values, and standards and the means by which they are to be carried out operationally. Setting up feedback mechanisms to find out if the vision is being implemented. Structuring the organization and devising policies to be consistent with stated purpose, values, and goals. Reinforcing behaviors that reflect organizational values. Creating ceremonial occasions to reinforce values and goals. Scheduling their own activities to reflect commitment to values and goals. "Role-modeling" behaviors that exemplify the organization's priorities and values.

Functioning strategically. Talking about underlying causes, interdependencies, and long-range consequences and acting accordingly. *Not* acting based on a single-function view of the organization. Having long time horizons. Resisting giving in to short-term pressures for quick results in order to allow people to learn new behaviors. Deliberately and thoughtfully planning the markets and businesses in which the organization is engaged. Fitting the organizational structure to the organization's key objectives and to the nature of its businesses and markets. Planning for the skills and knowledge required for meeting future objectives. Creating a well-thought-out and well-understood strategic design to guide operating plans and activities.

Promoting information flow. Clearly communicating the elements of the job that need to be accomplished in order to succeed (e.g., communicating standards, goals, tolerances to be worked within, and limits of authority). Being clear about feelings, needs, expectations, commitment, and loyalty issues. Establishing multiple channels for upward, sideways, and downward communication that complement the core chain of command lines (e.g., use of task forces, advisory groups, and unions). Enhancing mechanisms and influencing social norms to promote direct cross-unit communication.

Developing others. Teaching needed skills. Helping subordinates identify needs, interests, skills, aspirations, and talents. Rewarding desired behaviors with "strokes" or whatever rewards the manager controls. Delegating tasks based on subordinates' competencies and according to a developmental plan. *Not* doing subordinates' jobs for them. Relating subordinates to a larger context. Giving people accurate information regarding their performance. Providing personal growth experiences for subordinates. Judging subordinates by their end outputs, not the methods used to produce them. Processing successes and failures with subordinates to help them learn. Helping subordinates take advantage of opportunities and resources offered by the organization.

SOURCE: From *Journal of Applied Behavioral Science,* "Common Behavior Changes in Successful Organization Development Efforts," by J. I. Porras and S. I. Hoffer, 22 (4), 1986, pp. 486–487.

Data Collection Collection of data about organizational changes resembles the description that occurs during the t phase of the diagnostic approach. Data can be collected through the use of interviews, questionnaires, observation, or company records. In general, evaluation should use multiple methods to measure most accurately the impact of the change. It should use the most appropriate methods to compare actual performance or outcomes against objectives, standards, policies, or other plans and then to draw a summary conclusion about action effectiveness.

Figure 14–15 offers a summary checklist for evaluating organizational improvement efforts. These evaluation questions highlight each facet of the diagnostic approach described in this book. Evaluation involves first describing the objectives of the change and its environmental context, including both internal and external factors (see questions 1–9). Evaluation next reviews the diagnosis of the organizational problem by viewing the guiding assumptions and models for the improvement effort (see questions 10 and 11). Third, evaluation includes monitoring the prescription for change by analyzing the early program phases (see questions 12–15). Finally,

Figure 14–15 **Questions for Evaluating Organizational Improvement Efforts**

Factor	Question
Outcomes	
Objectives	1. *What were the intended outcomes of the program and what were the actual outcomes?* It is necessary to determine why the program was initiated and its impact on "bottom line" outcomes such as productivity, turnover, absenteeism and satisfaction.
Environmental Context (External Factors)	
Labor market and characteristics of workforce	2. *How tight was the labor market and what were the characteristics of the available labor pool?* Ascertain unemployment level and characteristics of work force when evaluating an organizational improvement program.
Social and political trends	3. *Were there changes occurring in society affecting workers and the organization?* The success of a program may be affected by how consistent it is with certain societal trends.
Economy and market	4. *What was the general state of the economy at the time of the improvement program?* Certain programs may work only in favorable economic conditions.
Environmental stability	5. *How much is the organization's immediate environment changing—and is the organizational structure appropriately matched?* A program may be greatly affected by the degree of congruence between an organization's structure and degree of environmental uncertainty that exists for the organization.
Internal Factors	
Product technology	6. *What is the product of the organization and the primary technology used to transform inputs into outputs?* Ascertain the match between technology, structure and kind of people involved and whether the program is congruent with them or tries to make them congruent with the program.
Structure	7. *Where on the mechanistic-to-organic structure continuum is the organization?* The program should be consistent with the organization's structure or explicitly attend to changing that structure.
Size	8. *How large is the organization and the plant or division within which the problem is taking place?* Size affects complexity of programs and the organizational resources available.

Figure 14–15 *(Continued)*

Factor	Question
Organizational climate	9. *What are the prevailing norms and values in the organization regarding involvement in organizational improvement efforts?* Programs require changed behavior, thus changed climate—which requires program attention to resistance.
Guiding Assumptions and Models	
	10. *How explicit were the assumptions about organizations and change that guided the organizational improvement program?* Being explicit about assumptions increases the chance that all involved understand the program and that the assumptions are more carefully examined and tested.
	11. *How comprehensive and consistent with current organizational theory were the guiding assumptions and models?* The success of a program can be influenced both by internal logic and by failure to incorporate what we know about organizations and improvement.
Program Phases Initiation phase	12. *What was the reason for starting the program and who was initially involved?* Programs generally require a broadly shared "felt need" and involvement of affected people to succeed.
Entry and start-up phase	13. *What were the initial activities at the start of the program and who was involved?* The pitfall to avoid is premature implementation; moving into a program without adequate diagnosis increases resistance stemming from lack of understanding and support. Prescription without diagnosis leads to malpractice.
Diagnostic phase	14. *What were the explicit diagnostic activities?*
	15. *What aspects of the organization were diagnosed and how?* Pitfalls include the "elephant problem" (sending eight blind men out to touch the organization and try to put the separate "felt" pieces together) and the "expert" problem, caused by outsiders who do a fancy diagnosis that no one understands.
Strategy planning phase	16. *How was the actual program planned and by whom?* The two dimensions to assess are (1) how available resources (internal and external consultants) were used, and (2) how the diagnostic model and data were used.
	17. *How explicit and detailed were the plans?* Lack of planning leads to seat-of-the-pants implementation of a program.
Implementation phase	18. *What was actually done, how, when, and by whom?* Two pitfalls are incomplete, patchwork implementation and *intervention interruptus*, or failing to carry the program through to completion.
Evaluation and corrective action phase	19. *Was there explicit evaluation and monitoring of the program and, if so, what was measured and how?* Political pressure resulting from overadvocacy of programs sets up forces against evaluation. Evaluative measures should be directly related to intended program outcomes.
	20. *What was done with the evaluation—did it result in corrective action or modification of the program?* Corrective action may fail because of lack of top-level organizational commitment and/or postimplementation letdown and regression when the novelty wears off.

SOURCE: Reprinted, by permission of the publisher, from "When Does Work Restructuring Work? Organizational Innovations at Volvo and GM," by Noel Tichy with Jay N. Nisberg, *Organizational Dynamics*, Summer 1976. © 1976 American Management Association.

evaluation focuses on the action itself, assessing strategy, planning, implementation, and follow-up (see questions 16–20).

INSTITUTION-ALIZING ACTION IN ORGANIZATIONS

Action must extend beyond short-run changes for real organizational improvement to result. Getting the change to "stick" must be a significant goal of the change effort. How, for example, does school-based management become a permanent part of governance at the Roosevelt School? Certainly, the way the activities are performed in moving from prescription to action influences the permanency of the change. Accurate targeting of forces influencing change, followed by careful selection of change agents and intervention strategies and concluding with effective action, contributes to long-range improvement.

In addition, mechanisms for continually monitoring the changes must be developed and instituted. Permanent committees or task forces to observe ongoing implementation and outcomes of the change can serve the monitoring function. Formulation of new organizational policies based on the change can encourage its continuation. Most of all, commitment to the change by all organizational members will expedite its institutionalization.

Managers must build *learning organizations,* ones that emphasize ongoing adaptability and generativity, thereby emphasizing coping and creatively looking at the world.[34] "Leaders in learning organizations are responsible for *building organizations* where people are continually expanding their capabilities to shape their future—that is, leaders are responsible for learning."[35]

ENSURING ORGANIZA-TIONAL EFFECTIVENESS

Researchers have argued that effectiveness serves as a central focus in all organizational analysis, acting as the goal of organization design and organization change.[36] Although some researchers suggest that there are limitations in the definition of this concept,[37] many agree that the organizational effectiveness concept reflects and represents a wide range of desirable organizational outcomes.

Organizational effectiveness has been defined and assessed in four major ways: (1) the organization's ability to accomplish its goals; (2) its ability to acquire needed resources from its external environment and thus achieve a competitive advantage; (3) its ability to satisfy, at least minimally, all of its strategic constituencies, including suppliers, consumers, members, and so on; and (4) the relative emphasis the organization's key constituencies place on people over organization, flexibility over control, and means versus ends. Four models result, as shown in Figure 14–16. Choice of the best model may depend on the organization's life cycle: Organizations in the entrepreneurial stage will use the open-systems model; in the collectivity stage, the human-relations model; in the formalization stage, the internal-process and rational-goal models; in the elaboration stage, the open-systems model; and in the decline stage, the open-systems model.[38] Together these models can provide one set of guidelines for evaluating the organization's performance.[39] Table 14–8 provides one listing of effectiveness criteria. Note that an organization will not be judged effective unless many of these criteria are met. Such an effectiveness analysis can be refined and focused by asking six additional questions:

1. What domain (e.g., organization-environment relations, production of organizational outputs, morale, or input acquisition) should be the focus of the analysis of effectiveness?

Figure 14–16 **Four Models of Effectiveness Values**

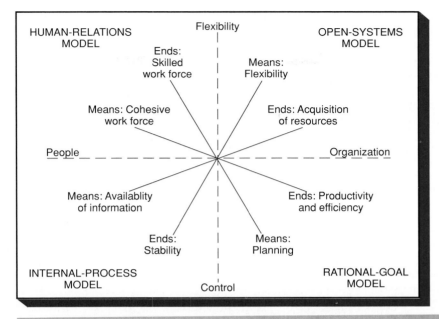

Figure 14–16 **Four Models of Effectiveness Values**

SOURCE: Reprinted with permission from R. E. Quinn and K. S. Cameron, Organizational life cycles and shifting criteria of effectiveness, *Management Science,* 29(1) (1983): 33–51, p. 42.

2. Whose perspective or which constituency's point of view should be considered?
3. What level of analysis (e.g., individual, group, or organizational) should be used?
4. What time frame (short or long term) should be used?
5. What type of data (e.g., individual perceptions or organizational records) should be used?
6. What reference (e.g., comparison organizations, the organization's goals, improvement, or established standards) should be used?[40]

Increased effectiveness results from a recognition of the complexity of organizations, as well as the individuals and groups that compose them.

MANAGING IN A MULTINATIONAL AND MULTICULTURAL CONTEXT

The manager of the twenty-first century must have a global perspective. As a global manager he or she must have the ability to develop and use global strategic skills, manage change and transition, manage cultural diversity, design and function in flexible organization structures, work with others and in teams, communicate, learn, and transfer knowledge in an organization.[41] He or she will lead flatter organizations that must be able to adapt rapidly to a changing environment. Empowering large groups of workers with multicultural backgrounds will be a key skill.

In this book we have looked at the issues related to managing in a wide range of organizations, including those that deal nationally and internationally. We have examined the unique challenges of leading and managing a multicultural work force. Reading 14–1, "The Multicultural Organization," reviews and elaborates on these challenges.

Table 14–8 **Effectiveness Criteria: Partial Listing of Univariate Measures of Organizational Effectiveness**

- Overall effectiveness: The degree to which the organization is accomplishing all its major tasks or achieving all its objectives. A general evaluation that takes in as many single criteria as possible and results in a general judgment about the effectiveness of the organization.
- Quality: The quality of the primary service or product provided by the organization. This may take many operational forms, primarily determined by the *kind* of product or service provided by the organization.
- Productivity: The quantity of or volume of the major product or service that the organization provides. Can be measured at three levels: individual, group, and total organization. This is not a measure of efficiency; no cost/output ratio is computed.
- Readiness: An overall judgment concerning the probability that the organization could successfully perform some specified task if asked to do so.
- Efficiency: A ratio that reflects a comparison of some aspect of unit performance to the costs incurred for that performance. Examples: dollars per single unit of production, amount of downtime, degree to which schedules, standards of performance, or other milestones are met. On occasion, just the total amount of costs (money, material, etc.) a unit has incurred over some period can be used.
- Profit or return: The return on the investment used in running the organization from the owners' point of view. The amount of resources left after all costs and obligations are met, sometimes expressed as a percentage.
- Growth: An increase in such things as manpower, plant facilities, assets, sales, profits, market share, and innovations. A comparison of an organization's present state with its own past state.
- Utilization of environment: The extent to which the organization successfully interacts with its environment, acquiring scarce, valued resources necessary for its effective operation. This is viewed in a long-term, optimizing framework and not in a short-term, maximizing framework. For example, the degree to which it acquires a steady supply of manpower and financial resources.
- Stability: The maintenance of structure, function, and resources through time, and more particularly through periods of stress.
- Turnover or retention: Frequency or amount of voluntary terminations.
- Absenteeism: The frequency of occasions of personnel being absent from the job.
- Accidents: Frequency of on-the-job accidents resulting in down time or recovery time.
- Morale: A predisposition in organization members to put forth extra effort in achieving organizational goals and objectives. Includes feelings of commitment. Morale is a group phenomenon involving extra effort, goals communality, and feelings of belonging. Groups have some degree of morale, while individuals have some degree of motivation (and satisfaction). By implication, morale is inferred from group phenomena.
- Motivation: The strength of the predisposition of an *individual* to engage in goal-directed action or activity on the job. This is not a feeling of relative contentment with various job outcomes as is satisfaction, but more akin to a feeling of readiness or willingness to work at accomplishing the job's goals.
- Satisfaction: The degree of feeling of contentment felt by a person toward his organizational role or job. The degree to which individuals perceive they are equitably rewarded by various aspects of their job situation and the organization to which they belong.
- Internalization of organizational goals: The acceptance of organizational goals by individuals and units within the organization. Their belief that the organization's goals are right and proper.
- Conflict-Cohesion: A bipolar dimension defined at the cohesion end by an organization in which the members like one another, work well together, communicate fully and openly, and coordinate their work efforts. At the other end lies the organization with verbal and physical clashes, poor coordination, and ineffective communication.
- Flexibility-Adaptation: The ability of an organization to change its standard operating procedures in response to environmental changes, to resist becoming rigid in response to environmental stimuli.
- Evaluations by external entities: Evaluations of the organization or organizational unit by those individuals and organizations in its environment with which it interacts. Loyalty to, confidence in, and support given the organization by such groups as suppliers, customers, stockholders, enforcement agencies, and the general public.
- Climate*: The nature of the internal environment of the organization.
- Quality of working life*: The quality of the employee's relationship to his or her working environment.

*These dimensions were added by the author of this book.

SOURCE: Adapted from J. P. Campbell, "Research into the Nature of Organizational Effectiveness: An Endangered Species?" Unpublished manuscript. Minneapolis: University of Minnesota, 1973.

A REVIEW OF THE DIAGNOSTIC APPROACH

This book presents the diagnostic approach as a way of increasing organizational effectiveness and addressing issues of effective global management. You should now be able to apply this approach to the situation at the Roosevelt School, as well as to the other situations described in this book. Description should be followed by diagnosis, prescription, and then action. Figure 14–17 summarizes the diagnostic questions for addressing various aspects of organizational behavior, including organizational change. Prescriptions must be formulated for each problem identified. Then you must consider the actions necessary for implementation of the prescriptions offered.

Managers and other organizational members have significant responsibility for ensuring organizational effectiveness. The leadership style they choose, their ability to communicate with peers, subordinates, and superiors, the quality of their decision making, and their skill in group work, for example, contribute to organizational functioning. Understanding and choosing the appropriate individual and group behaviors are essential for employee productivity, satisfaction, adaptability, and other outcomes. Using the diagnostic approach should help managers and other organizational members improve personal and organizational behavior.

As good diagnosticians, managers must quickly recognize threats to organizational growth and success. If profits and performance drop dramatically, a major alteration of the organization's culture, structure, and management style may be required. While downsizing the organization is one possibility, remaking the organization is another option. Apple Computers, for example, responded to a threat of an industrywide shakeout in the early 1980s by changing from a technical superstar entrepreneurial organization to a market and consumer-oriented one, and in 1990 it faced new product concerns.[42]

Managers must develop new and creative strategies for responding to increasing environmental pressures. The emphasis on teamwork, the movement to a more collaborative culture, and the call for visionary leadership are some of the factors that ultimately will stimulate the development of new organizational forms. The creation of new strategic partnerships, megaorganizations in the service sector resulting from mergers and acquisitions, and intrapreneurial departments within existing organizations should contribute to increased organizational effectiveness.

The challenges for managers to increase and preserve organizational effectiveness never stop. Apparently effective, high-performing organizations can experience unanticipated problems and even decline. Introducing change in multinational and multicultural organizations may be more difficult than in organizations that operate solely in the United States. Managers must be vigilant and use analytical tools such as the diagnostic approach to help ensure organizational effectiveness. They must understand the complexities of managing in a global economy and successfully develop and implement new competitive strategies, as well as manage an increasingly diverse work force. Improving individual, group, and organizational behavior and attitudes plays a major role in building effective organizations.

SUMMARY

Organizational change is the final step of the diagnostic approach, following description, diagnosis, and prescription. Action involves scouting, entry, diagnosis, and planning activities, followed by evaluation and institutionalization of the change. In this chapter we examined each facet of the change process. We focused initially on the steps of planned change, using force field analysis as an analytical technique to diagram the change process.

(text continues on page 710)

Figure 14–17 **The Summary Diagnostic Checklist**

Historical Perspectives

Is there an appropriate division of labor?

Is work done efficiently, and are workers sufficiently trained to do their jobs?

Do employees have specified areas of responsibility?

Is the work defined effectively?

Do work groups operate effectively?

Do managers perform organizing roles and have an appropriate span of control?

Does the group have effective task and social leadership?

Does management work with the correct assumptions about employees?

Is decision making effective?

Is the interface of technology and individual workers effective?

Does the organization's structure respond to the environmental contingencies?

Is there a good fit between inputs and transformations?

Are there good fits between individuals, tasks, organizational arrangements, and the informal organization?

Perception

What factors influence the perceptions of organizational members?

What distortions of perception occur?

Attribution

What factors influence the attributions of organizational members?

What biases exist in these attributions?

Learning

What behaviors are reinforced as part of the learning process?

What cues encourage learning?

What learning themes exist in the organization?

How are these learning themes supported in the organization?

Attitudes

What beliefs and values do individuals hold?

How do these beliefs and values influence the individuals' attitudes?

What functional and dysfunctional behavioral intentions result from the individuals' attitudes?

Personality

Do the personality styles of individuals fit with the situation?

Do the personality styles of participants fit with those of other organizational members?

Individual Development

Do the organizational members experience problems in adult or career development?

How compatible are the adult and career development stages of various organizational members?

How effective are the interactions between work and family?

How does the organization help its members balance work and family responsibilities?

Role Pressures

Do individuals experience role conflict?

Do individuals experience role overload?

Are roles clear or ambiguous?

Do the socialization processes used fit with the situational requirements and help reduce role ambiguity?

How do managers and other organizational members deal with role pressures?

Stress

Is there stress in the situation?

Are there mechanisms for effectively managing stress?

Figure 14–17
(Continued)

Motivation
Do rewards satisfy individuals' needs?
Are rewards applied equitably and consistently after desired behaviors?
Do individuals value the rewards they receive?
Are rewards consistently applied in proportion to performance?
Do individuals perceive that their efforts correlate with performance?
Do individuals set goals that are specific and moderately difficult yet accepted?
Do individuals receive feedback about their goal accomplishment as part of the
   organization's reward system?
What type of reward system exists?
Does it encourage desired outcomes such as innovation, productivity, or attendance?
Are benefits and incentive systems effective in motivating desired outcomes?

Culture
What type of culture exists in the organization?
What components reinforce the culture?
Does the culture reinforce team performance?

Team Effectiveness
Did the team form effectively?
How effectively did the team deal with all stages of development?
What are the team's norms, and are they functional?
What roles did the team perform, and are they functional?
Are individual and team goals congruent?
Is the team's structural configuration appropriate to the task, people, and informational
   processing needs of the team?
Does the team function well in a multinational and multicultural environment?
What strategies does or should the team use to improve its effectiveness?

Decision Making
What type of decision is being made?
What types of information have been collected for making the decision?
Do organizational members make high-quality, accepted, ethical decisions?
Do the decision makers follow the basic process of decision making?
Do ways of dealing with the limitations of the process exist?
Is the group appropriately involved in decision making?
What barriers are there to effective decision making?
What techniques can be used to overcome these barriers?

Communication
What encoding and decoding errors occur in communication?
Do senders use effective language?
Does nonverbal communication reinforce or contradict the message being sent?
What type of listening is occurring?
How effective is listening?
What media are the most appropriate for transmission?
What types of noise exist in the organization?
Does two-way communication exist?
How effective are downward, upward, and lateral communication?
What special roles exist to facilitate communication?
Does the organization's structure help or hinder communication?
Do interpersonal relations help or hinder communication?
Are informal communication mechanisms functional?
Are attitudes of communicating parties compatible?
What types of communication networks exist, and are they functional?
Does communication consider the diversity of the parties?

(continued)

Figure 14–17
(Continued)

Does communication lack cross-cultural sensitivity?
Is the climate supportive or defensive?
Do individuals use assertive, nonassertive, or aggressive communication?
Do individuals practice active listening?

Leadership
Do the managers have the traits necessary for effective leadership?
Do the managers display the behaviors required for effective leadership?
Do managers exhibit balanced managerial roles?
Do the leaders encourage the appropriate amount of participation in decision making?
Does the leadership style fit with the nature of the task, leader-member relations, and position power of the leader?
Is leadership superfluous to the situational features and the followers' needs?
Does it meet their needs?
Does the leadership style fit with the maturity of the followers?
Do followers attribute attitudes to the leaders accurately?
Do transformational leaders exist?
Do superleaders exist?

Power
Who has power in the organization?
How is powerlessness overcome in the organization?
From what sources does the power stem?
Is power properly placed?
Are alliances, informal networks, or trade relations used to develop power?

Negotiation
What types of negotiations occur in the organization?
Do the negotiations tend to be distributive or integrative?
What types of preparations for negotiations occur?
Are interests identified, the best alternative to a negotiated agreement determined, and bargaining range identified?
How effective are intercultural negotiations?

Conflict
Is there conflict in the organization?
Is the conflict functional or dysfunctional?
What level of conflict exists?
What stage of conflict exists?
What causes conflict in the organization?

Intergroup Relations
What is the nature of the relationship between groups in the organization?
What factors contribute to these relationships?
How effective are intergroup relationships?
Are there mechanisms for effectively managing conflict and intergroup relations?

Organizational Structure
What division of labor is there?
What coordinating mechanisms are there?
How would you describe information processing in the organization?
What bases of departmentation exist?
What structural configuration would describe the organization?
Does the organization function globally?
How does its structure respond to the requirements of global competitiveness?
Does the informal organization reinforce or contradict the formal organization structure?

Figure 14–17
(Continued)

Organization Redesign
Are job groups relatively homogeneous and meaningful?
Are unit groupings of manageable size?
Is there sufficient coordination among the groupings?
Have groupings considered the impact of the organization's environment?
How complex is the environment—is decision making sufficiently decentralized?
How unpredictable is the environment—is the structure sufficiently organic, and are the information-processing mechanisms sufficient?
How hostile is the environment—is the structure temporarily centralized?
Have groupings considered the impact of the organization's technology?
How regulated is the technology—is the structure sufficiently organic?
How sophisticated is the technology—is there sufficient support staff?
Is the technology sufficiently buffered from the environment?
Have groupings been designed to accomplish the organization's goals—is the division of labor sufficiently specialized?
Are there linkages among groups that might have different goals?
Have groupings been designed to meet the needs and abilities of the work force—is the structure sufficiently specialized to respond to differences in employee professionalism? expertise? group membership? values?
Does the structure make sense for the organization's size—is the structure sufficiently elaborated?
Does the structure make sense for the organization's age—is the structure sufficiently elaborated?
Does the structure make sense for the organization's stage of development?
Do organizations at the entrepreneurial, collective, and elaborated stages have relatively organic designs?
Do organizations at the formalization stage have more mechanistic structures?

Technology and Innovation
Are there mechanisms for the effective development and deployment of technology?
Does innovation occur in the organization?
Does a good-quality innovation process exist?

Quality
Does a concern for quality exist in the organization?
Does a total quality management program exist?

Work Redesign
Are the jobs sufficiently specialized?
Are the jobs sufficiently enriched?
Do autonomous or self-managing work groups exist? Are they effective?
Do alternate work arrangements exist? Are they effective?
Do quality of work life programs exist? Are they effective?
Do work redesign efforts match the workers' needs and other aspects of the situation?

Change
Are the steps of the change model implemented?
Are forces for and against change identified?
Are appropriate change agents selected?
Do intervention strategies fit with the change situation?
Is a transformational change required, and how can it be implemented?
Are changes evaluated?
Do mechanisms exist for institutionalizing the change?
Does the organization have mechanisms for dealing with crises?

Action begins by identifying the forces for and against change, then seeking ways to overcome resistance to change. Next, selection of a change agent occurs. He or she then chooses the appropriate intervention strategy, considering the target system, target group, depth of intervention, prescribed change mechanisms, and expertise of the change agent. We considered ways of evaluating and then institutionalizing changes. We concluded the book with a discussion of organizational effectiveness, including comments about the multiple ways of assessing it. We once again noted the managerial challenge of leading organizations in a global environment and with a multicultural work force. Finally, we reviewed the diagnostic approach as a major tool to help managers face this challenge.

Reading 14–1

The Multicultural Organization
Taylor Cox, Jr.

As we begin the 1990s, a combination of workforce demographic trends and increasing globalization of business has placed the management of cultural differences on the agenda of most corporate leaders. Organizations' workforces will be increasingly heterogeneous on dimensions such as gender, race, ethnicity and nationality. Potential benefits of this diversity include better decision making, higher creativity and innovation, greater success in marketing to foreign and ethnic minority communities, and a better distribution of economic opportunity. Conversely, cultural differences can also increase costs through higher turnover rates, interpersonal conflict, and communication breakdowns.

To capitalize on the benefits and minimize the costs of worker diversity, organizations of the '90s must be quite different from the typical organization of the past. Specifically, consultants have advised organizations to become "multicultural."[1] The term refers to the degree to which an organization values cultural diversity and is willing to utilize and encourage it.[2]

Leaders are being charged to create the multicultural organization, but what does such an organization look like, and what are the specific ways in which it differs from the traditional organization? Further, what tools and techniques are available to assist organizations in making the transition from the old to the new?

This article addresses these questions. I have used an adaptation of the societal-integration model developed by Milton Gordon, as well as available information on the early experience of American organizations with managing diversity initiatives, to construct a model of the multicultural organization.

CONCEPTUAL FRAMEWORK
In his classic work on assimilation in the United States, Milton Gordon argued that there are seven dimensions along which the integration of persons from different ethnic backgrounds into a host society should be analyzed.[3] I use "integration" to mean the coming together and mixing of people from different cultural identity groups in one organization. A cultural identity group is a group of people who (on average) share certain values and norms distinct from those of other groups. Although the boundaries of these groups may be defined along many dimensions, I am primarily concerned with gender, race, ethnicity, and national origin. Gordon's seven dimensions are:

1. Form of acculturation
2. Degree of structural assimilation
3. Degree of intergroup marriage
4. Degree of prejudice
5. Degree of discrimination
6. Degree of identification with the dominant group of the host society
7. Degree of intergroup conflict (especially over the balance of power)

Although Gordon's interest was in societal-level integration, I believe his model can be easily and usefully adapted for analysis of cultural integration for organizations. Therefore, an adaptation of his seven-point framework is used here as a basis for describing organizational models for integrating culturally divergent groups. Table 14–9 shows my proposed six-dimensional adaptation of the Gordon framework along with definitions of each term.

Acculturation is the method by which cultural differences between the dominant (host) culture and any minority culture groups are resolved or treated. There are several alternatives, the most prominent being (1) a unilateral process by which minority culture members adopt the norms and values of the dominant group in the organization *(assimilation);* (2) a process by which both minority and majority culture members adopt some norms of the other group *(pluralism);* and (3) a situation where there is little adaptation on either side *(cultural separatism).*[4] Pluralism also means that minority culture members are encouraged to

Table 14–9 **Conceptual Framework for Analysis of Organizational Capacity for Effective Integration of Culturally Diverse Personnel**

Dimension	Definition
1. Acculturation	Modes by which two groups adapt to each other and resolve cultural differences
2. Structural Integration	Cultural profiles of organization members including hiring, job-placement, and job status profiles
3. Informal Integration	Inclusion of minority-culture members in informal networks and activities outside of normal working hours
4. Cultural Bias	Prejudice and discrimination
5. Organizational Identification	Feelings of belonging, loyalty and commitment to the organization
6. Intergroup Conflict	Friction, tension and power struggles between cultural groups

enact behaviors from their alternative culture as well as from the majority culture. They are therefore able to retain a sense of identity with their minority-culture group. Acculturation is concerned with the cultural (norms of behavior) aspect of integration of diverse groups, as opposed to simply their physical presence in the same location.

Structural integration refers to the presence of persons from different cultural groups in a single organization. Workforce profile data has typically been monitored under traditional equal opportunity and affirmative action guidelines. However, to get a proper understanding of structural integration it is important to look beyond organization-wide profile data, and examine cultural mix by function, level, and individual work group. This is because it is commonplace in American companies for gaps of fifteen to thirty percentage points to exist between the proportion of minority members in the overall labor force of a firm, and their proportion at middle and higher levels of management.[5]

Even within levels of an organization, individual work groups may still be highly segregated. For example, a senior human resource manager for a *Fortune* 500 firm who is often cited as a leader in managing diversity efforts, recently told me that there are still many "white-male bastions" in his company. As an assistant vice-president with responsibility for equal opportunity, he indicated that breaking down this kind of segregation was a focal point of his current job.

The *informal integration* dimension recognizes that important work-related contacts are often made outside of normal working hours and in various social activities and organizations. This item looks at levels of inclusion of minority-culture members in lunch and dinner meetings, golf and other athletic outings, and social clubs frequented by organization leaders. It also addresses mentoring and other informal developmental relationships in organizations.

Cultural bias has two components. Prejudice refers to negative attitudes toward an organization member based on his/her culture group identity, and discrimination refers to

observable adverse behavior for the same reason. Discrimination, in turn, may be either personal or institutional. The latter refers to ways that organizational culture and management practices may inadvertently disadvantage members of minority groups. An example is the adverse effect that emphasizing aggressiveness and self-promotion has on many Asians. Many managers that I have talked to are sensitive to the fact that prejudice is a cognitive phenomenon and therefore much more difficult than discrimination for organization managers to change. Nevertheless, most acknowledge the importance of reducing prejudice for long-range, sustained change.

Prejudice may occur among minority-culture members as well as among dominant-culture members. Putting the debate over whether rates of prejudice differ for different groups aside, it must be emphasized that the practical impact of prejudice by majority-culture members is far greater than that of minority-culture members because of their far greater decision-making power (except under extraordinary conditions, such as those of South Africa).

Organizational identification refers to the extent to which a person personally identifies with, and tends to define himself or herself as a member in the employing organization. Levels of organizational identification have historically been lower in the United States than in other countries (notably Japan). Indications are that recent changes in organizational design (downsizing and de-layering) have reduced organizational identification even further. Although levels of organizational identification may be low in general in the U.S. workforce, we are concerned here with comparative levels of identification for members of different cultural identity groups.

Finally, *intergroup conflict* refers to levels of culture-group-based tension and interpersonal friction. Research on demographic heterogeneity among group members suggests that communication and cohesiveness may decline as members of groups become dissimilar.[6] Also, in the specific context of integrating minority-group members into organizations, concerns have been raised about backlash from white males who may feel threatened by these developments. It is therefore important to examine levels of intergroup conflict in diverse workgroups.

TYPES OF ORGANIZATIONS

This six-factor framework will now be employed to characterize organizations in terms of stages of development on cultural diversity.[7] Three organization types will be discussed: the monolithic organization, the plural organization and the multicultural organization. The application of the six-factor conceptual framework to describe the three organization types appears in Table 14–10.

Monolithic Organization

The most important single fact about the monolithic organization is that the amount of structural integration is minimal. The organization is highly homogeneous. In the United States, this commonly represents an organization characterized by substantial white male majorities in the overall employee population with few women and minority men in management jobs. In addition, these organizations feature extremely high levels of occupational segregation with women and racioethnic minority men (racially and/or culturally different from the majority) concentrated in low-status jobs such as secretary and maintenance. Thus, the distribution of persons from minority-cultural backgrounds is highly skewed on all three components of function, level, and workgroup.

To a large extent, the specifications on the frameworks'

other five dimensions follow from the structural exclusion of people from different cultural backgrounds. Women, racioethnic minority men, and foreign nationals who do enter the organization must adopt the existing organizational norms, framed by the white male majority, as a matter of organizational survival.

Ethnocentrism and other prejudices cause little, if any, adoption of minority-culture norms by majority group members. Thus, a unilateral acculturation process prevails. The exclusionary practices of the dominant culture also apply to informal activities. The severe limitations on career opportunities for minority-culture members creates alienation, and thus the extent to which they identify with the organization can be expected to be low compared to the more fully enfranchised majority group.

One positive note is that intergroup conflict based on culture-group identity is minimized by the relative homogeneity of the workforce. Finally, because this organization type places little importance on the integration of cultural minority group members, discrimination, as well as prejudice, are prevalent.

While the white-male dominated organization is clearly the prototypical one for the monolithic organization, at least some of its characteristics are likely to occur in organizations where another identity group is dominant. Examples include minority-owned businesses, predominantly Black and predominantly Hispanic colleges, and foreign companies operating in the United States.

Aside from the rather obvious downside implications of the monolithic model in terms of underutilization of human resources and social equality, the monolithic organi-

Table 14–10 **Organizational Types**

Dimension of Integration	Monolithic	Plural	Multicultural
Form of Acculturation	Assimilation	Assimilation	Pluralism
Degree of Structural Integration	Minimal	Partial	Full
Integration into Informal Organization	Virtually none	Limited	Full
Degree of Cultural Bias	Both prejudice and discrimination against minority-culture groups is prevalent	Progress on both prejudice and discrimination but both continue to exist especially institutional discrimination	Both prejudice and discrimination are eliminated
Levels of Organizational Identification*	Large majority-minority gap	Medium to large majority-minority gap	No majority-minority gap
Degree of Intergroup Conflict	Low	High	Low

*Defined as difference between organizational identification levels between minorities and majorities.

zation is not a realistic option for most large employers in the 1990s. To a significant degree, large U.S. organizations made a transition away from this model during the '60s and '70s. This transition was spurred by a number of societal forces, most notably the civil-rights and feminist movements, and the beginnings of changes in workforce demographics, especially in the incidence of career-oriented women. Many organizations responded to these forces by creating the plural organization.

Plural Organization

The plural organization differs from the monolithic organization in several important respects. In general, it has a more heterogeneous membership than the monolithic organization and takes steps to be more inclusive of persons from cultural backgrounds that differ from the dominant group. These steps include hiring and promotion policies that sometimes give preference to persons from minority-culture groups, manager training on equal opportunity issues (such as civil rights law, sexual harassment, and reducing prejudice), and audits of compensation systems to ensure against discrimination against minority group members. As a result, the plural organization achieves a much higher level of structural integration than the monolithic organization.

The problem of skewed integration across functions, levels, and work groups, typical in the monolithic organization, is also present in the plural organization. For example, in many large U.S. organizations racioethnic minorities now make up twenty percent or more of the total workforce. Examples include General Motors, Chrysler, Stroh Brewery, Phillip Morris, Coca-Cola, and Anheuser-Busch. However, the representations of nonwhites in management in these same companies averages less than twelve percent.[8] A similar picture exists in workgroups. For example, while more than twenty percent of the clerical and office staffs at General Motors are minorities, they represent only about twelve percent of technicians and thirteen percent of sales workers. Thus, the plural organization features partial structural integration.

Because of the greater structural integration and the efforts (cited previously) which brought it about, the plural organization is also characterized by some integration of minority-group members into the informal network, substantial reductions in discrimination, and some moderation of prejudicial attitudes. The improvement in employment opportunities should also create greater identification with the organization among minority-group members.

The plural organization represents a marked improvement over the monolithic organization in effective management of employees of different racioethnic, gender, and nationality backgrounds. The plural organization form has been prevalent in the U.S. since the late 1960s, and in my judgment, represents the typical large firm as we enter the 1990s. These organizations emphasize an affirmative action approach to managing diversity. During the 1980s increased evidence of resentment toward this approach among

white males began to surface. They argue that such policies, in effect, discriminate against white males and therefore perpetuate the practice of using racioethnicity, nationality, or gender as a basis for making personnel decisions. In addition, they believe that it is not fair that contemporary whites be disadvantaged to compensate for management errors made in the past. This backlash effect, coupled with the increased number of minorities in the organization, often creates greater intergroup conflict in the plural organization than was present in the monolithic organization.

While the plural organization achieves a measure of structural integration, it continues the assimilation approach to acculturation which is characteristic of the monolithic organization. The failure to address cultural aspects of integration is a major shortcoming of the plural organization form, and is a major point distinguishing it from the multicultural organization.

The Multicultural Organization

In discussing cultural integration aspects of mergers and acquisitions, Sales and Mirvis argued that an organization which simply contains many different cultural groups is a plural organization, but considered to be multicultural only if the organization *values* this diversity.[9] The same labels and definitional distinction is applied here. The meaning of the distinction between *containing* diversity and *valuing* it follows from an understanding of the shortcomings of the plural organization as outlined previously. The multicultural organization has overcome these shortcomings. Referring again to Table 14–10, we see that the multicultural organization is characterized by:

1. Pluralism
2. Full structural integration
3. Full integration of the informal networks
4. An absence of prejudice and discrimination
5. No gap in organizational identification based on cultural identity group
6. Low levels of intergroup conflict

I submit that while few, if any, organizations have achieved these features, it should be the model for organizations in the 1990s and beyond.

CREATING THE MULTICULTURAL ORGANIZATION

As I have discussed issues of managing diversity with senior managers from various industries during the past year, I have observed that their philosophical viewpoints cover all three of the organizational models of Table 14–10. The few who are holding on to the monolithic model often cite geographic or size factors as isolating their organizations from the pressures of change.

Some even maintain that because American white males will continue to be the single largest gender/race identity group in the U.S. workforce for many years, the monolithic organization is still viable today. I think this view is misguided. By understanding the generic implications of managing diversity (that is, skill at managing work groups which include members who are culturally distinct from the organization's dominant group), it becomes clear that virtually all organizations need to improve capabilities to manage diverse workforces.

Further, focusing too much attention on external pressures as impetus for change misses the fact that gross underutilization of human resources and failure to capitalize on the opportunities of workforce diversity represent unaffordable economic costs.

Fortunately, the monolithic defenders, at least among middle and senior managers, seem to represent a minority view. Based on my observations, the majority of managers today are in plural organizations, and many are already convinced that the multicultural model is the way of the future. What these managers want to know is how to transform the plural organization into the multicultural organization. Although progress on such transformations is at an early stage, information on the tools that have been successfully used by pioneering American organizations to make this transformation is beginning to accumulate.

Table 14–11 provides a list of tools that organizations have used to promote organization change toward a multicultural organization. The exhibit is organized to illustrate my analysis of which tools are most helpful for each of the six dimensions specified in Table 14–9.

Creating Pluralism
Table 14–11 identifies seven specific tools for changing organizational acculturation from a unilateral process to a reciprocal one in which both minority-culture and majority-culture members are influential in creating the behavioral norms, values, and policies of the organization. Examples of each tool are given below.

Training and Orientation Programs. The most widely used tool among leading organizations is managing or valuing cultural diversity training. Two types of training are most popular: awareness and skill-building. The former introduces the topic of managing diversity and generally includes information on workforce demographics, the meaning of diversity, and exercises to get participants thinking about relevant issues and raising their own self-awareness. The skill-building training provides more specific information on cultural norms of different groups and how they may affect work behavior. Often, these two types of training are combined. Such training promotes reciprocal learning and acceptance between groups by improving understanding of the cultural mix in the organization.

Among the many companies who have made extensive use of such training are McDonnell Douglas, Hewlett-Packard, and Ortho Pharmaceuticals. McDonnell Douglas has a program ("Woman-Wise and Business Savvy") focusing on gender differences in work-related behaviors. It uses same-gender group meetings and mixed-gender role-plays. At its manufacturing plant in San Diego, Hewlett-Packard conducted training on cultural differences between American-Anglos and Mexican, Indochinese, and Filipinos. Much of the content focused on cultural differences in communication styles. In one of the most thorough training efforts to date, Ortho Pharmaceuticals started its three-day training with small groups (ten to twelve) of senior managers and eventually trained managers at every level of the company.

Specific data on the effectiveness of these training efforts is hard to collect, but a study of seventy-five Canadian consultants found that people exposed to even the most rudimentary form of training on cultural diversity are significantly more likely to recognize the impact of cultural diversity on work behavior and to identify the potential advantages of cultural heterogeneity in organizations.[10]

In addition, anecdotal evidence from managers of many companies indicates that valuing and managing diversity training represents a crucial first step for organization change efforts.

New member orientation programs are basic in the hiring processes of many organizations. Some companies are developing special orientations as part of its managing diversity initiatives. Procter & Gamble's "On Boarding" program, which features special components for women and minority hires and their managers, is one example.

Language training is important for companies hiring American Asians, Hispanics, and foreign nationals. To promote pluralism, it is helpful to offer second-language training to Anglos as well as the minority-culture employees, and take other steps to communicate that languages other than English are valued. Leaders in this area include Esprit De Corp, Economy Color Card, and Pace Foods. For many years, the women's clothier Esprit De Corp has offered courses in Italian and Japanese. At Economy Color Card, work rules are printed in both Spanish and English. Pace Foods, where thirty-five percent of employees are Hispanic, goes a step farther by printing company policies and also conducting staff meetings in Spanish and English. Motorola is a leader in the more traditional training for English as a second language where classes are conducted at company expense and on company time.

Insuring Minority-Group Input and Acceptance. The most direct and effective way to promote influence of minority-culture norms on organizational decision making is to achieve cultural diversity at all organization levels. However, an important supplemental method is through ensuring diversity on key committees. An example is the insistence of *USA Today* President Nancy Woodhull on having gender, racioethnic, educational, and geographic diversity represented in all daily news meetings. She attributes much of the company's success to this action.

Another technique is explicitly mentioning the importance of diversity to the organization in statements of mis-

Table 14–11 **Creating the Multicultural Organization: Tools for Organization Change**

Model Dimension	Tools
I. Pluralism *Objective/s:* —create a two-way socialization process —ensure influence of minority-culture perspectives on core organization norms and values	1. Managing/valuing diversity (MVD) training 2. New member orientation programs 3. Language training 4. Diversity in key committees 5. Explicit treatment of diversity in mission statements 6. Advisory groups to senior management 7. Create flexibility in norm systems
II. Full Structural Integration *Objective/s* —No correlation between culture-group identity and job status	1. Education programs 2. Affirmative action programs 3. Targeted career development programs 4. Changes in manager performance appraisal and reward systems 5. HR policy and benefit changes
III. Integration in Informal Networks *Objective/s* —eliminate barriers to entry and participation	1. Mentoring programs 2. Company-sponsored social events
IV. Cultural Bias *Objective/s* —eliminate discrimination —eliminate prejudice	1. Equal opportunity seminars 2. Focus groups 3. Bias reduction training 4. Research 5. Task forces
V. Organizational Identification —no correlation between identity group and levels of organization identification	1. All items from the other five dimensions apply here
VI. Intergroup Conflict *Objective/s* —minimize interpersonal conflict based on group identity —minimize backlash by dominant-group members	1. Survey feedback 2. Conflict management training 3. MVD training 4. Focus groups

sion and strategy. By doing this, organizations foster the mind-set that increased diversity is an opportunity and not a problem. Examples of organizations that have done this are the University of Michigan and the Careers Division of the National Academy of Management. The latter group has fostered research addressing the impact of diversity on organizations by explicitly citing this as part of its interest.

Another way to increase the influence of minority-group members on organizational culture and policy is by providing specially composed minority advisory groups direct access to the most senior executives of the company. Organizations which have done this include Avon, Equitable Life Assurance, Intel, and U.S. West. At Equitable, committees of women, Blacks and Hispanics (called "Business Resource Groups") meet with the CEO to discuss important group issues and make recommendations on how the organizational environment might be improved. CEO John Carver often assigns a senior manager to be accountable for following up on the recommendations. U.S. West has a thirty-three-member "Pluralism Council" which advises senior management on plans for improving the company's response to increased workforce diversity.

Finally, a more complex, but I believe potentially powerful, tool for promoting change toward pluralism is the development of flexible, highly tolerant climates that encourage diverse approaches to problems among all employees. Such an environment is useful to workers regardless of group identity, but is especially beneficial to people from nontraditional cultural backgrounds because their approaches to problems are more likely to be different from past norms. A company often cited for such a work environment is Hewlett-Packard. Among the operating norms of the company which should promote pluralism are (1) encouragement of informality and unstructured work; (2) flexible work schedules and loose supervision; (3) setting objectives in broad terms with lots of individual employee discretion over how they are achieved; (4) a policy that researchers should spend at least ten percent of company time exploring personal ideas. I would suggest that item 4 be extended to all management and professional employees.

Creating Full Structural Integration

Education Efforts. The objective of creating an organization where there is no correlation between one's culture-identity group and one's job status implies that minority-group members are well represented at all levels, in all functions, and in all work groups. Achievement of this goal requires that skill and education levels be evenly distributed. Education statistics indicate that the most serious problems occur with Blacks and Hispanics.[11]

A number of organizations have become more actively involved in various kinds of education programs. The Aetna Life Insurance Company is a leader. It has initiated a number of programs including jobs in exchange for customized education taught by community agencies and private schools, and its own in-house basic education programs. The company has created an Institute for Corporate Education with a full-time director. Other companies participating in various new education initiatives include PrimAmerica, Quaker Oats, Chase Manhattan Bank, Eastman Kodak, and Digital Equipment. In Minnesota, a project headed by Cray Research and General Mills allows businesses to create schools of its own design. I believe that business community involvement in joint efforts with educational institutions and community leaders to promote equal achievement in education is critical to the future competitiveness of U.S. business. Business leaders should insist that economic support be tied to substantive programs which are jointly planned and evaluated by corporate representatives and educators.

Affirmative Action. In my opinion, the mainstay of efforts to create full structural integration in the foreseeable future, will continue to be affirmative action programs. While most large organizations have some kind of program already, the efforts of Xerox and Pepsico are among the standouts.

The Xerox effort, called "The Balanced Workforce Strategy," is noteworthy for several reasons including: an especially fast timetable for moving minorities up; tracking representation by function and operating unit as well as by level; and national networks for minority-group members (supported by the company) to provide various types of career support. Recently published data indicating that Xerox is well ahead of both national and industry averages in moving minorities into management and professional jobs, suggests that these efforts have paid off (*Wall Street Journal,* November 5, 1989).

Two features of Pepsico's efforts which are somewhat unusual are the use of a "Black Managers Association" as a supplemental source of nominees for promotion to management jobs, and the practice of hiring qualified minorities directly into managerial and professional jobs.

Career Development. A number of companies including Mobil Oil, IBM, and McDonald's have also initiated special career development efforts for minority personnel. IBM's long-standing "Executive Resource System" is designed to identify and develop minority talent for senior management positions. McDonald's "Black Career Development Program" provides career enhancement advice, and fast-track career paths for minorities. Company officials have stated that the program potentially cuts a fifteen-year career path to regional manager by fifty percent.

Revamping Reward Systems. An absolutely essential tool for creating structural integration is to ensure that the organization's performance appraisal and reward systems reinforce the importance of effective diversity management. Companies that have taken steps in this direction include the Federal National Mortgage Association (Fannie Mae), Baxter Health Care, Amtrak, Exxon, Coca-Cola, and Merck. Fannie Mae, Baxter, Coca-Cola, and Merck all tie compensation to manager performance on diversity management efforts. At Amtrak, manager promotion and compensation are tied to performance on affirmative action objectives, and at Exxon, evaluations of division managers must include a review of career development plans for at least ten women and minority men employees.

For this tool to be effective, it needs to go beyond simply including effective management of diversity among the evaluation and reward criteria. Attention must also be given to the amount of weight given to this criterion compared to other dimensions of job performance. How performance is measured is also important. For example, in addition to work-group profile statistics, subordinate evaluations of managers might be useful. When coded by cultural group, differences in perceptions based on group identity can be noted and used in forming performance ratings on this dimension.

Benefits and Work Schedules. Structural integration of women, Hispanics, and Blacks is facilitated by changes in human resource policies and benefit plans that make it easier for employees to balance work and family role demands. Many companies have made such changes in areas like child care, work schedules, and parental leave. North Carolina National Bank, Arthur Andersen, Levi Strauss, and IBM are examples of companies that have gone farther than most. NCNB's "select time" project allows even officers and professionals in the company to work part-time for several years and still be considered for advancement. Arthur Andersen has taken a similar step by allowing part-time accountants to stay "on-track" for partnership promotions. Levi Strauss has one of the most comprehensive work-family programs in the country covering everything from paternity leave to part-time work with preservation of benefits. These companies are leaders in this area because attention is paid to the impact on advancement opportunities and fringe-benefits when employees take advantage of scheduling flexibility and longer leaves of absence. This kind of accommodation will make it easier to hire and retain both men and women in the '90s as parents struggle to balance work and home time demands. It is especially important for women, Hispanics, and Blacks because cultural traditions put great emphasis on family responsibilities. Organization change in this area will promote full structural integration by keeping more racioethnic minorities and white women in the pipeline.

Creating Integration in Informal Networks

Mentoring and Social Events. One tool for including minorities in the informal networks of organizations is company-initiated mentoring programs that target minorities. A recent research project in which a colleague and I surveyed 800 MBAs indicated that racioethnic minorities report significantly less access to mentors than whites. If company-specific research shows a similar pattern, this data can be used to justify and bolster support among majority-group employees for targeted mentoring programs. Examples of companies which have established such targeted mentoring programs are Chemical Bank and General Foods.

A second technique for facilitating informal network integration is company-sponsored social events. In planning such events, multiculturalism is fostered by selecting both activities and locations with a sensitivity to the diversity of the workforce.

Support Groups. In many companies, minority groups have formed their own professional associations and organizations to promote information exchange and social support. There is little question that these groups have provided emotional and career support for members who traditionally have not been welcomed in the majority's informal groups. A somewhat controversial issue is whether these groups hinder the objective of informal-network integration. Many believe that they harm integration by fostering a "we-versus-they" mentality and reducing incentives for minorities to seek inclusion in informal activities of majority-group members. Others deny these effects. I am not aware of any hard evidence on this point. There is a dilemma here in that integration in the informal networks is

at best a long-term process and there is widespread skepticism among minorities as to its eventual achievement. Even if abolishing the minority-group associations would eventually promote full integration, the absence of a support network of any kind in the interim could be a devastating loss to minority-group members. Therefore, my conclusion is that these groups are more helpful than harmful to the overall multiculturalism effort.

Creating a Bias-Free Organization

Equal opportunity seminars, focus groups, bias-reduction training, research, and task forces are methods that organizations have found useful in reducing culture-group bias and discrimination. Unlike prejudice, discrimination is a behavior and therefore more amenable to direct control or influence by the organization. At the same time, the underlying cause of discrimination is prejudice. Ideally, efforts should have at least indirect effects on the thought processes and attitudes of organization members. All of the tools listed, with the possible exception of task forces, should reduce prejudice as well as discrimination.

Most plural organizations have used equal opportunity seminars for many years. These include sexual harassment workshops, training on civil rights legislation, and workshops on sexism and racism.

Focus Groups. More recently, organizations like Digital Equipment have used "focus groups" as an in-house, ongoing mechanism to explicitly examine attitudes, beliefs, and feelings about culture-group differences and their effects on behavior at work. At Digital, the centerpiece of its "valuing differences" effort is the use of small groups (called Core Groups) to discuss four major objectives: (1) stripping away stereotypes; (2) examining underlying assumptions about outgroups; (3) building significant relationships with people one regards as different; (4) raising levels of personal empowerment. Digital's experience suggests that a breakthrough for many organizations will be achieved by the simple mechanism of bringing discussion about group differences out in the open. Progress is made as people become more comfortable directly dealing with the issues.

Bias-Reduction Training. Another technique for reducing bias is through training specifically designed to create attitude change. An example is Northern Telecom's 16-hour program designed to help employees identify and begin to modify negative attitudes toward people from different cultural backgrounds. Eastman Kodak's training conference for its recruiters is designed to eliminate racism and sexism from the hiring process. This type of training often features exercises that expose stereotypes of various groups which are prevalent but rarely made explicit and may be subconscious. Many academics and consultants have also developed bias-reduction training. An example is the "Race Relations Competence Workshop," a program developed by Clay Alderfer and Robert Tucker of Yale University. They have found that participants completing the workshop have more positive attitudes toward Blacks and interrace relations.

Leveraging Internal Research. A very powerful tool for reducing discrimination and (to a smaller extent) prejudice, is to conduct and act on internal research on employment experience by cultural group. Time, Inc., conducts an annual evaluation of men and women in the same jobs to ensure comparable pay and equal treatment. A second example comes from a large utility company which discovered that minority managers were consistently underrepresented in lists submitted by line managers for bonus recommendations. As a result of the research, the company put pressure on the managers to increase the inclusion of minority managers. When that failed, the vice president of human resources announced that he would no longer approve the recommendations unless minorities were adequately represented. The keys to the organization change were, first obtaining the data identifying the problem and then acting on it. My experience suggests that this type of research-based approach is underutilized by organizations.

Task Forces. A final tool for creating bias-free organizations is to form task forces that monitor organizational policy and practices for evidence of unfairness. An example of what I consider to be a well-designed committee is the affirmative action committee used by Philip Morris which is composed of senior managers and minority employees. This composition combines the power of senior executives with the insight into needed changes that the minority representatives can provide. Of course, minority culture-group members who are also senior managers are ideal but, unfortunately, such individuals are rare in most organizations.

Minimizing Intergroup Conflict

Experts on conflict management have noted that a certain amount of interpersonal conflict is inevitable and perhaps even healthy in organizations.[12] However, conflict becomes destructive when it is excessive, not well managed, or rooted in struggles for power rather than the differentiation of ideas. We are concerned here with these more destructive forms of conflict which may be present with diverse workforces due to language barriers, cultural clash, or resentment by majority-group members of what they may perceive as preferential and unwarranted treatment of minority-group members.

Survey Feedback. Probably the most effective tool for avoiding intergroup conflict (especially the backlash form that often accompanies new initiatives targeting minority-groups of the organization) is the use of survey feedback. I will give three examples. As one of the most aggressive affirmative action companies of the past decade, Xerox has found that being very open with all employees about the specific features of the initiative as well the reasons for it, was helpful in diffusing backlash by whites. This strategy is exemplified by the high profile which Chairman David Kearns has taken on the company's diversity efforts.

A second example is Procter & Gamble's use of data on the average time needed for new hires of various culture groups to become fully integrated into the organization. They found that "join-up" time varied by race and gender with white males becoming acclimated most quickly, and black females taking the longest of any group. This research led to the development of their "on-boarding program" referred to earlier.

A final example is Corning Glass Works' strategy of fighting white-male resistance to change with data showing that promotion rates of their group was indeed much higher than that of other groups. This strategy has also been used by U.S. West, which recently reported on a 1987 study showing that promotion rates for white men were seven times higher than white women and sixteen times higher than nonwhite women.

The beauty of this tool is that it provides the double benefit of a knowledge base for planning change, and leverage to win employee commitment to implement the needed changes.

Conflict-Resolution Training. A second tool for minimizing intergroup conflict is management training in conflict resolution techniques. Conflict management experts can assist managers in learning and developing skill in applying alternative conflict management techniques such as mediation and superordinate goals. This is a general management skill which is made more crucial by the greater diversity of workforces in the '90s.

Finally, the managing and valuing diversity training and focus group tools discussed previously are also applicable here. AT&T is among the organizations which have explicitly identified stress and conflict reduction as central objectives of its training and focus group efforts.

CONCLUSION

Increased diversity presents challenges to business leaders who must maximize the opportunities that it presents while minimizing its costs. To accomplish this, organizations must be transformed from monolithic or plural organizations to a multicultural model. The multicultural organization is characterized by pluralism, full integration of minority-culture members both formally and informally, an absence of prejudice and discrimination, and low levels of intergroup conflict; all of which should reduce alienation and build organizational identity among minority group members. The organization that achieves these conditions will create an environment in which all members can contribute to their maximum potential, and in which the "value in diversity" can be fully realized.

1. See, for example, Lennie Copeland, "Valuing Workplace Diversity," *Personnel Administrator,* November 1988; Badi Foster et al., "Workforce Diversity and Business," *Training and Development Journal,* April 1988, 38–42; and R. Roosevelt Thomas, "From Affirmative Action to Affirming Diversity," *Harvard Business Review,* Vol. 2, 1990, 107–117.

2. This definition has been suggested by Afsavch Nahavandi and Ali Malekzadeh, "Acculturation in Mergers and Acquisitions," *Academy of Management Review,* Vol. 13, 83.

3. In his book, *Assimilation in American Life* (New York; Oxford Press, 1964) Gordon uses the term assimilation rather than integration. However, because the term assimilation has been defined in so many different ways, and has come to have very unfavorable connotations in recent years for many minorities, I will employ the term integration here.

4. These definitions are loosely based on J. W. Berry, 1983. "Acculturation: A Comparative Analysis of Alternative Forms," in R. J. Samuda and S. L. Woods: *Perspectives in Immigrant and Minority Education,* 1983, 66–77.

5. This conclusion is based on data from nearly 100 large organizations as cited in "Best Places for Blacks to Work," *Black Enterprise,* February 1986 and February 1989 and in Zeitz and Dusky, *Best Companies for Women,* 1988.

6. Examples of this research include, Harry Triandis, "Some Determinants of Interpersonal Communication," *Human Relations,* Vol. 13, 1960, 279–287 and J. R. Lincoln and J. Miller, "Work and Friendship Ties in Organizations," *Administrative Science Quarterly,* Vol. 24, 1979, 181–199.

7. The concept of stages of development toward the multicultural organization has been suggested in an unpublished paper titled "Toward the Multicultural Organization" written by Dan Reigle and Jarrow Merenivitch of the Procter & Gamble Company. I credit them with helping me to recognize the evolutionary nature of organizational responses to workforce diversity.

8. See note 5.

9. A. L. Sales and P. H. Mirvis, "When Cultures Collide: Issues of Acquisitions," in J. R. Kimberly and R. E. Quinn, *Managing Organizational Transition,* 1984, 107–133.

10. For details on this study see, Nancy J. Adler, *International Dimensions of Organizational Behavior* (Kent Publishing Co., 1986), 77–83.

11. For example, see the book by William Julius Wilson which reviews data on educational achievement by Blacks and Hispanics in Chicago, *The Truly Disadvantaged: Inner City, the Underclass and Public Policy* (The University of Chicago Press, 1987). Among the facts cited is that less than half of all Blacks and Hispanics in inner city schools graduate within four years of high school enrollment and only four in ten of those who do graduate read at the eleventh grade level or above.

12. For example, see *Organization Behavior: Conflict in Organizations,* by Gregory Northcraft and Margaret Neale (The Dryden Press, 1990), 221.

DISCUSSION QUESTIONS

1. Define the six dimensions of cultural integration.
2. Compare and contrast monolithic, plural, and multicultural organizations along six dimensions of integration.
3. Offer a protocol for creating an effective multicultural organization.

Reprinted with permission from the *Academy of Management Executive,* 5(2) (1991): 34–47.

Activity 14–1   **First Canadian Club**

Step 1:   Read the First Canadian Club case.

Miss Sally Newton was the only purchasing officer of First Canadian Club, a fitness club with 20 centers scattered around Canada. In February 1988, she was thinking of how to handle the resistance coming from some center managers, especially the "alliance" of three Toronto centers, to the newly introduced centralized purchasing system designed by her one month earlier.

FIRST CANADIAN CLUB

First Canadian Club was founded in 1979 and owned by Mr. Jim Stewart, a business administration graduate from the University of Western Ontario. At the age of 25, he opened his first fitness center in Toronto, Ontario. Over the past ten years, the club had been growing gradually, and in 1988, it had 20 centers scattered around Canada (see table, p. 720). The head office, however, remained in Waterloo.

Locations of the 20 Fitness Centers of the First Canadian Club

Location	Number of Centers
Kingston, Ontario	1
Jonquière, Quebec	1
Laval, Quebec	2
London, Ontario	2
North Bay, Ontario	1
Ottawa, Ontario	1
Peterborough, Ontario	2
Sarnia, Ontario	1
Sault Ste. Marie, Ontario	1
Sudbury, Ontario	1
Toronto, Ontario	3
Waterloo, Ontario	1 (including head office)
Windsor, Ontario	2
Winnipeg, Manitoba	1
Total	20

SALLY NEWTON

Sally Newton was 24. Right after earning a diploma in psychology from Fanshawe College, London, Ontario, she joined First Canadian Club in January 1988 as the purchasing officer of the club. Her job responsibilities included the administration of purchasing and inventory control. Before her college studies, she had a number of years of work experience in various areas but none of them specifically related to purchasing or inventory control. As she said herself, "This is my first job in this area."

THE PURCHASE SYSTEM IN FIRST CANADIAN CLUB BEFORE SALLY NEWTON

"If there was really a purchasing system in the First Canadian Club before Sally came, I could only say it was a 'very very loose' one," one staff member commented.

First Canadian Club needed many different kinds of items to keep its centers running. They ranged from parts for machines and equipment like bike parts and suntan bulbs to stationery supplies and toiletries. Before Sally joined the club, each center was responsible for its own purchasing. Most centers did not keep any inventory and purchased needed items on an ad hoc basis (i.e., buy when needed at a nearby store). In the head office, there was a part-time employee also doing the purchasing and inventory control job but only for the head office. She did not purchase items for the other 19 centers, but kept records for them.

SALLY NEWTON'S NEW CENTRALIZED PURCHASING SYSTEM

During her first week in the First Canadian Club, Sally examined the two binders which were left by the part-time employee. She was surprised to find that the club was using the center-based ad hoc basis purchasing system and thought that a centralized one might work in this situation. She talked to her boss about this idea, and her boss encouraged her to investigate further.

She then went to do some research work on it and found that a centralized purchasing system could really save a considerable amount of money for the club. For example, she found a supplier that would reduce the cost of toiletry purchases by nearly 50 percent if the club bought in bulk through it. Therefore, along with searching for more suppliers for different items, she spent time on developing the details of the centralized purchasing system.

Basically, the new system that Sally had designed centralized all purchases in the head office. Instead of each center buying its own supplies, the center manager was asked to fill in an order form and fax it to the head office. The deadline was 5 o'clock on Monday every week, and the items requested would be sent to the requesting center on the following Monday. Sally had the authority to disapprove or reduce the amount requested if she thought it was not justified. However, each center was allowed to have petty cash of one hundred dollars for making any urgent purchases.

By the end of January, she finished the plan, which was approved by her boss immediately. She notified all 20 centers with a memo that explained the reasons for the new purchasing system and the procedures for making the change.

RESISTANCE RECEIVED FROM CENTER MANAGERS

After about one month of implementation, Sally was a bit frustrated by the resistance from some of the center managers. Some managers did not use the order form but just called in right away when they needed some items. The most difficult problem was that the three fitness centers in Toronto "joined" together and resisted changing to the new system.

Sally was thinking of how to handle this situation, especially how to tackle the problem of the "alliance" of the three Toronto centers.

Step 2: Prepare the case for class discussion.

Step 3: Answer the following questions, individually, in small groups, or with the entire class, as directed by your instructor:

Description

1. How does the new purchasing system work?
2. How does it compare to the old purchasing system?

Diagnosis

3. How were the new changes implemented?
4. Was the appropriate change agent used?
5. Were resistances to change identified and addressed?
6. What problems remain after the changes?
7. Were the changes evaluated?
8. How should the changes have been implemented?

Prescription

9. What course of action would you propose now?

Action

10. How does your plan of action compare to that actually implemented?

Step 4: Discussion. In small groups, with the entire class, or in written form, share your answers to the above questions. Then answer the following questions:

1. What symptoms suggested that a problem existed?
2. What problems were addressed in the case?
3. What theories and concepts help explain the problems?
4. How were the problems corrected?
5. Analyze the change process.
6. Was the change effective?

This case was written by Patrick Y. K. Chau during the 1989 Case Writing Workshop. Reprinted by permission of Patrick Y. K. Chan, Purchasing Management Association of Canada, Western Business School, the University of Western Ontario. Copyright © 1989.

Activity 14–2 — Bridgeton Temporary Services

Step 1: Your instructor will divide you into groups of four to six people; one group will represent management, and the rest, competing consulting groups.

Step 2: Read the following description:

The Bridgeton Temporary Services provides bookkeeping and accounting services on a contract basis. Employees act as accounts payable clerks, accounts receivable clerks, general bookkeepers, computer programmers, and accountants. The seventy-five employees are each assigned to a supervisor who decides where each person will work. The supervisor also checks with the client for an evaluation of Bridgeton's employees. Employees report each day to the client, but must notify their supervisor at Bridgeton that they have arrived.

Employees have a variety of education, from high school diplomas to masters degrees. The firm also employs a number of working mothers with CPAs who do not want full-time employment. Employees generally stay with Bridgeton ten to twelve months. Then they secure full-time employment elsewhere, decide they do not wish to be employed at all, or obtain part-time employment with one of Bridgeton's clients. In addition to relatively high turnover, Bridgeton also suffers from high absenteeism. When questioned, the employees indicate that no one cares about them, that their pay is low, that their work frequently is uninteresting and below their capabilities, that they are moved among jobs too frequently, and that they frequently are not notified about their work assignment until thirty minutes before they are expected to be at the workplace. Many add that

they feel someone is always looking over their shoulder. The company itself has more requests for temporary help than it can fill, yet it has been unable to secure enough workers. Some clients have complained about poor-quality work from some of the bookkeepers. Also, although revenues are increasing, profits have not kept pace.

Step 3: *The Management Group.* Assume that you are the top management of Bridgeton Temporary Services. You are concerned with the high rate of turnover and absenteeism in your company. You want to hire a group of consultants to diagnose your company's problem and to recommend a plan for solving it. Shortly they will ask for a preliminary meeting to gather information to use in formulating their consulting proposal. You should be prepared to provide them with your requirements and timetables, as well as with any constraints, financial or otherwise, that you see as relevant to their task. You must then develop guidelines for judging the various proposals presented. You expect, at a minimum, that each will include a diagnosis, change strategy, and plans for implementation, as well as the rationales on which these are based.

The Consulting Groups. Your group is interested in being hired as consultants to Bridgeton Temporary Services. The company's president is concerned with the high rate of turnover and absenteeism. The president has asked you to diagnose the company's problems and to recommend a plan for solving them. Specifically, the president wants you to answer the following questions:

1. What do you think the real problem is and why?
2. What solution(s) would you propose and why?
3. How would you implement your plan?
4. What reasons would you give for doing it this way?

You will have the opportunity to meet briefly with the top management of the firm in a short while to get answers to preliminary questions you have about the company. Then, on the date given by your instructor, you will offer your plan. The plan should include diagnosis, change strategy, and implementation.

Step 4: The management and consulting groups meet, independently and then together.

Step 5: The consulting teams present their proposals one at a time.

Step 6: The management team selects the consulting team they would like to hire and then describes its criteria for selection.

Step 7: Discussion. With the entire class, answer the following questions:

1. What group was hired? Why?
2. What symptoms existed?
3. What problems were identified?
4. What intervention strategies were proposed? Would they be effective?
5. What makes an effective consulting proposal?

Activity 14–3   Managing an Organizational Crisis

Step 1: Read the following scenario:

You are the vice president of marketing of a small manufacturing firm that processes baby food from local produce. Your firm sells the food to mothers who wish only the freshest products for their infants. Your products are stored in the refrigerator section of the grocery store and have a relatively short shelf life. Because of the concern about preservatives and healthful living, your company has grown significantly in the past five years.

Yesterday the local newspaper revealed that they had done a chemical analysis of a batch of your food and found traces of a compound that is known to cause cancer in mice. They warned the public to stop buying your product. You know that if you cannot reassure the public about the integrity of your product, the loss of sales will threaten your company's survival.

Step 2: Individually or in small groups, offer a plan for dealing with this crisis.

Step 3: Discussion. In small groups or with the entire class, share the plans you have developed. Then answer the following questions:

1. What were the key elements of the plans?
2. How did the plans differ?
3. How could these differences be reconciled?
4. What are the strengths and weaknesses of each plan?
5. What problems might arise in their implementation?
6. What are the components of an effective plan for dealing with the crisis?

Activity 14–4   Managerial Systems Ltd.

Step 1: Read the Managerial Systems Ltd. case.

INTRODUCTION

It had been a rough week for Managerial Systems Ltd. By Thursday, MSL's president, Ken Long, had received upsetting phone calls from consultants Phil Mercer, Ray Terrell, and Fred Sargent concerning client difficulties. He had also talked at length with Karen Webster about conflicts between her personal and professional lives. Crises always seemed to come in avalanches. Tomorrow's staff meeting promised to last the entire spring day, ruining any plans Ken had for sailing.

MANAGERIAL SYSTEMS LTD.

Managerial Systems Ltd. was a behaviorally based consulting organization focused on helping client companies improve the effectiveness of managerial systems through the application of sophisticated behavioral science technologies. (Figure 14–18 briefly explains the basics of behavioral consulting.) MSL consultants worked with client organizations to help define needs and then identify the proper methods for satisfying those needs. (Figure 14–19 lists the types of services provided in the past.) All MSL consultants had at least a master's degree in the behavioral sciences and most had obtained a doctorate in a related field. Many had worked in the behavioral area in either private practice or with institutions prior to joining MSL. (Figure 14–20 is a selected biography of representative consultants' backgrounds.)

MSL incorporated in 1977 when Ken Long, the president, resigned his professorship at a prominent southern business school in order to devote his full time to the company. In the past four years MSL had expanded to ten consultants, two research assistants, and five support staffers. MSL's primary clients had been in the petrochemical industry. However, attempts to implement a strategy of diversification had begun this year.

The diversification into other industries presented something of a problem for MSL. MSL's consulting expertise had been developed and proven in the petrochemical field. But potential clients questioned how well that expertise would translate to their specific types of problems. To help overcome these questions, Ken had decided to concentrate in three areas related to the prior experience of MSL. These included flow process plants, e.g., petrochemical, energy services and equipment companies, and banking. Ken anticipated no major problems transferring techniques from one industry to the others. This was because MSL tailors its behavioral intervention to a client's particular set of needs.

Ken wanted each consultant to bring in at least one new client by the end of the year. Each consultant was asked to make contacts in new companies and arrange a presentation of MSL's array of services to management. Several of the consultants expressed their feelings of uneasiness in taking on a sales role. They felt they lacked sufficient experience to decide which companies and executives to approach as potential clients. Once they managed to make contact, the consultants were worried about how to make an effective presentation. To alleviate these concerns, Ken had begun training the consultants in sales techniques. The consultants were taught basic sales techniques tailored to MSL's particular marketing needs.

Long felt it was important for MSL's consultants to have divergent backgrounds both academically and professionally. However, he insisted that potential consultants have a fundamental belief in the benefits of a capitalistic society. When hiring consultants he discussed at length how the individual felt about working for major oil companies. If

Figure 14–18   **Description of Organizational Development (OD)**

Organizational Development (OD) is a process by which behavioral science principles and practices are used in an ongoing organization in a planned and systematic way. It is utilized to attain such goals as developing greater organizational competence while improving the quality of work life and the organization's effectiveness. (Effectiveness refers to setting and attaining appropriate goals in a changing environment.) OD differs from other planned change efforts such as the purchases of new equipment or floating a bond issue to build a new plant, in that the focus includes the motivation, utilization, and integration of human resources within the organization and is focused on total system change.

OD is a vehicle for helping organizations adjust to accelerated technological enrichment, group team-building, or management by objectives. OD may use specific techniques, but only after the relevance and utility of a special technique has been clearly demonstrated by careful diagnosis.

Interventions or techniques can be grouped in ten basic classifications:

—Individual consultation (counseling-coaching) usually involving a change agent in a one-on-one helping interaction with a single client.
—Unstructured group training involving individuals in a group lacking specific task purpose except that of understanding individual or group dynamics.
—Structured group training including management and group development courses structured to change participant attitudes, convey knowledge, or develop skills.
—Process consultation involving small groups or work teams identifying and solving common problems.
—Survey-guided development, involving collection of data about client work-group or organizational functioning and feeding back data to work groups to use in problem solving.
—Job redesign involving altering the tasks, responsibilities, interactions patterns, or the technical and physical environment intrinsic to the work itself.
—Personnel systems involving implementation through traditional personnel functions.
—Management information and financial control systems involving tracking and evaluating employee or work-group performance.
—Organizational design involving a structural change in organizational authority and reporting relationships.
—Integrated approaches including more than one of the methods described above.

SOURCE: Edgar F. Huse. *Organization Development and Change* (St. Paul, Minn.: West, 1980).

Figure 14–19 **Consulting Services Rendered to Clients—1980**

Organizational Development initiation, planning, and
  execution
Managerial effectiveness training
Supervisory skills training
Organizational team-building
Organizational diagnostic surveys
  —Organizational climate
  —Employee attitude assessment
  —Specific areas of concern
Managerial expectations clarification
  —Goal setting
  —Organizational dissemination
  —Individual superior-subordinate clarifications
Performance feedback enhancement
  —Establishing organizational systems
  —Expectations setting/feedback skills training
Development of organizational systems
  —Progressive discipline
  —Managerial communications
  —Work system redesign
  —Managerial succession system

Employee Assistance Programs
  —Individual managerial counseling
  —Employee psychological services
  —Alcoholic/drug abuse program
  —Assisting terminated and retiring employees
Effective planning and implementation of organizational
  changes
EEO Audit simulation
EEO Assimilation Programs
Research Studies
  —Attrition problems
  —Employee acceptance/rejection of anticipated change
  —EEO-related employee attitudes
  —Organization-wide training systems
Workshops on special topics
  —Management of stress situations
  —Assimilation of new managers
  —Problems faced by temporary supervisors
  —Successful specific conflict resolution
Facilitating development of overall top management goals

there was a wide gap in the beliefs of MSL and the consultant, Ken would refuse to hire them. He felt the strains of working to improve a system one did not believe in would be detrimental to the consultant's working abilities and effectiveness. Ken encouraged the consultants to come to him to talk about any problems they were having on the job. He felt this minimized the chances of a consultant working him/herself into a corner over an issue.

Ken emphasized the importance of doing a thorough job with a client company. Many times a client company would bring in MSL to solve a specific problem that management had isolated. MSL wanted to gather their own data in order to determine the validity of management's point of view and to find out if there were any additional problems related to the ones indicated. MSL was prepared to walk away from a contract if management refused to allow them to do the necessary research or if management wanted their services for any reason other than to improve working conditions.

THE DILEMMAS
Phil Mercer
Phil had just completed a large project on the reasons for the engineer attrition rate for a major oil company. The report and final recommendations would be ready the following week. Phil was quite pleased with the results. He attributed the success of the project to the agreement of management to release the report and the final recommendations to the engineers. The engineers took this as a sign that management was making a serious effort to correct many of the problems they faced at work. Therefore, they cooperated fully and candidly with Phil in the interviewing process.

Phil called Mr. Spencer, the Vice-President of Personnel, Engineering, to inform him of the date the report would be ready. He also inquired about distributing the report to the engineers. Mr. Spencer said the report would not be released as planned. A two-page summary of it would be made available. The recommendations would be omitted.

This upset Phil. He had given his word to the engineers that they would receive copies of the report and the recommendations. He reminded Mr. Spencer of management's promise to release it. All the positive effects of the promised release would be negated and the engineers' attitudes would sour. Phil questioned the wisdom of such a move. Mr. Spencer blamed the change in plans on MSL's failure to stay within the contracted budget. He said there were insufficient funds available to copy the report. Phil was at a loss on what to reply, so he terminated the conversation, promising to call again in the next few days.

Phil reviewed his alternatives. He could try again to convince Mr. Spencer to release the results regardless of the costs involved. He thought this would be fruitless based on the previous conversation. Phil considered going directly to the engineers and giving them the report and the recommendations without management's approval. After all, they had been promised a copy of the report and he could provide it verbally anyway. He also thought about going to someone higher in the company who could countermand Spencer's decision.

Figure 14-20   Selected Biographies of MSL Consultants

Karen Webster	30, MBA from Tulane University, BA, psychology, had been with MSL for four years. Prior to joining MSL, Karen worked in a managerial capacity in private business. Her consulting expertise was primarily in management and supervisory development.
Fred Sargent	55, had been with the firm for three years, joining MSL upon completion of a doctorate in Adult Education. He spent twenty-five years in the Army and rose to the rank of Colonel. During his military career, Fred held many managerial positions, planning and implementing numerous training programs. He also earned an MBA from Syracuse University while in the Army. His Army experiences carried over easily in behavioral consulting where Fred focused on development and execution of organizational needs analysis and management training programs.
Ray Terrell	32, received his Ph.D. in clinical psychology following a master's degree in counseling. He had joined MSL on a part-time basis one and a half years ago while continuing to teach at a local university. Small group facilitation had been Ray's specialty within MSL.
Phil Mercer	36, had been with MSL on a part-time basis for a year. He continued to teach in the Social Work Department at a local university. His academic credentials included an MSW, an MPH, and a Ph.D. in Human Ecology, a discipline which works against exploitation of the environment. This degree strongly reflected Phil's personal values. He spent many years "throwing rocks at big business from the outside" but had never been a part of that world. He went into consulting to learn more about how big business works and to help improve conditions for people working in the system.

Phil called Ken to talk about the situation. Ken suggested that Phil bring up the issue at tomorrow's staff meeting. Before hanging up Ken mentioned that the company had contacted him about another consulting job. He wanted Phil to think about whether or not MSL should accept the job in light of the situation with Mr. Spencer.

Fred Sargent

Hugh Cavanaugh was the Operations Manager of a medium-sized petrochemical refinery located on the Louisiana coast. The refinery was part of a large, well-known energy concern. Cavanaugh was from the traditional school of management ("seat of the pants" or "we've always done it this way"). At sixty-two, his physical condition was excellent, considering his recovery from open-heart surgery two years earlier. Although every other member of the Management Committee supported the Plant Manager's initiation of MSL's organizational development (OD) efforts within the refinery (which included supervisory training, team-building, and EEO development work), Cavanaugh thought OD was a waste of time. He reportedly said, "Young Turks come in and try to change the organization when they don't even understand its history . . . besides, the refinery was maximizing production capacity way before all this new OD rubbish came up." Cavanaugh constantly refuted the OD effort along with other organizational changes. He was against the massive computerization then under way, and blatantly expressed his feelings throughout the refinery. As Operations Manager with thirty-seven years of experience, Hugh was in a potentially powerful position on the Man-

agement Committee. As a result, his negative attitude hindered the effectiveness of the Management Committee in the change process.

Dennis Kline, the refinery's young, aggressive Plant Manager, was a strong supporter of OD and realized its potential for improving the refinery's productivity. He had been in his present position for one year, and one of his first actions had been to initiate the OD effort with MSL's assistance. This was a good way to revitalize the workforce while improving the bottom line. The OD effort would help him gain the respect of the refinery employees by demonstrating his concern for their working environment. Hugh had been his only obstacle to implementing the OD effort. He had tried to energize Hugh by utilizing him as a leader to work decisions and assume responsibility for part of the OD effort. Kline figured that if Cavanaugh felt ownership of the ideas and participated in them from their inception, he would realize their value and be won over. However, Cavanaugh refused to get involved in any way and stonewalled all of Kline's efforts over the entire year. Kline had tried everything short of firing Hugh.

Fred Sargent, MSL's senior consultant working with the Management Committee, knew that the members of the committee recognized Hugh's biases against OD, but they really did not have the professional insight and objectivity to see that he had no capability for change. Some of the committee members had blinders on due to their longtime friendship and respect for Hugh. As a result, the whole Management Committee was having a difficult time accepting the realities of the situation. But it was quite obvious to Sargent, based on his past consulting experience, that as long as Cavanaugh was a forceful member of the Management Committee, MSL's OD efforts could never reach their full potential.

Should Fred work with the Management Committee to accept the fact that Hugh would never change, he would be the catalyst for Hugh's encouraged early retirement. This would then allow Sargent to facilitate the OD process. But, if Fred was linked to Hugh's encouraged retirement, he might be labeled as a "hit man," which could inhibit his ability to work with the Management Committee and other members of the refinery organization. They might see Fred's actions as part of a conspiracy to do some housecleaning and thus find working through behavioral dilemmas with him quite threatening. In addition, the loss of Cavanaugh could be detrimental to the refinery's operations. His position as Operations Manager was a subtle link in labor negotiations currently under way as a result of a recent wildcat strike. Cavanaugh was well-respected by his subordinates, and quite effective in the technical aspects of his job which gave him influence on the union negotiations. It was Fred's feeling that Cavanaugh's work was his life and crucial to his survival, both psychologically and financially. life and crucial to his survival, both psychologically and financially.

Feeling extremely frustrated, Fred approached George Davenport, Process Division Manager, Management Committee member, and a longtime friend of Hugh Cavanaugh. George was in his early sixties, but, unlike Hugh, had been able to adjust to organizational changes quite well. He was able to see the potential benefits of OD and could look at the situation from a broad perspective.

Fred: George, I'm really concerned about the slow progress of the Management Committee in this recent OD effort concerning EEO and team building. What do you see as the barrier?

George: I seem to be having the same feelings that things are moving rather slowly. If only we could get Hugh on board . . . I think things would take off. I've tried to talk to him about the value of the OD efforts, but I can understand his objections. After all, our past experience with consultants billing themselves as OD experts has not been too good. They cost an arm and a leg and talk in generalities, never touching on our specific problems. However, your company has tailored its efforts to our specific needs. Also, Hugh's knowledge and understanding of company history can't be matched—even by the Plant Manager! He really feels outside consultants aren't qualified to facilitate changes in the organization.

Fred: But, George, everyone else on the committee seems able and ready to accept the OD efforts.

Hugh is living in the past. He's dug in his heels and won't budge.

George: Well, I do know he's too valuable not to have on the Management Committee at this point.

Fred Sargent was in a bind and didn't know what to do. If he didn't take any immediate action and chose to buy time, hoping to either change Hugh Cavanaugh or wait for his scheduled retirement, the entire OD effort might be doomed. Cavanaugh would do everything in his power to stop the effort, if not through the Management Committee, then verbally throughout the refinery. Another option for Sargent was to take on the biggest challenge of his career and spend all his time trying to change Hugh Cavanaugh. If he could somehow work it so Cavanaugh received full credit for part of the OD effort and was recognized by corporate headquarters for this accomplishment, he'd have no choice but to go along with the continuation of the effort.

Other options open to Fred include convincing Dennis Kline to "force" Hugh's early retirement with all the usual fanfare; going to corporate headquarters Human Resources Vice-President or the Vice-President of Refining (who were both strong OD supporters) and explaining the situation; going to Hugh directly and asking him to retire; slowly showing the Management Committee in a calculated way that Hugh was damaging the refinery's effectiveness; or creating a scandal in order to get Hugh fired if he refused to retire.

Fred decided that the next step would be to bring his dilemma to MSL's monthly staff meeting for discussion.

Karen Webster

Karen had several problems at work to think about that night. She usually discussed things with her husband, Jack, in order to put things into a better perspective. The weekly staff meeting was coming up and she wanted to be prepared to present her dilemmas as clearly and concisely as possible to the other consultants to get their opinions.

Karen joined MSL at its inception and had been very active in helping the company to reach its current size and in building its good reputation. She was the only woman consultant for several years. MSL did most of its consulting in flow processing plants, and many of the plant managers were products of the "Good Ole Boy" syndrome. They had grown up in the back country and had been taught that women stayed at home. There were few, if any, women working in the plants because of the rough nature of the work. Karen found that it was difficult to get the managers to accept her as a professional, knowledgeable consultant. She had to prove herself time and again. She found that she couldn't allow her clients to think of her as a woman first and a consultant second. Her professional reputation had been built with these men through much hard work and continuing efforts to educate them.

After working for MSL for five years, Karen and Jack had decided to begin a family. A lot of thought had gone into this decision. Karen had no plans to stop working after the baby was born. This opened several areas of potential conflict between raising the baby and Karen's career. However, after carefully evaluating the situation, she began planning her projects so any traveling would be completed by the end of her seventh month of pregnancy. Back in December she had confirmed plans for an eight-day team-building session at a plant seventy-five miles away. She planned to commute every other day. This session would be the culmination of almost a year of hard work.

Several days ago the client company had contacted Karen and stated that the session would have to be pushed back. The new dates coincided with the end of the eighth month of her pregnancy. She was very concerned about this change. The thought of having to drive to and from the plant every other day was not pleasant. She also disliked the idea of staying at the plant for the entire week. She knew Jack would be upset if she were gone from home so late in her pregnancy. She would tire more easily and would not be as effective as usual. However, she had made a commitment to the client to complete the team-building process. Karen felt very strongly about fulfilling her obligations to MSL and to her career.

Karen considered her options. On some projects it would be possible to bring in another consultant to complete the training. However, this was not the case with team-building. Team-building's purpose was to improve the effectiveness and performance of people who work together closely on a regular basis. Because of the difficulty and time necessary to build a close, trusting relationship between the consultant and the group, it would be impossible for another consultant to take over. She could also go back to the client company and try to convince management to allow the original dates to stand. She could refuse to do the training now and try to complete it after she returned to work.

As Karen talked with Jack she voiced these possibilities and wondered how the other consultants would react to her situation. She was worried about the impact cancellation would have on her career and professional reputation. There was even a possibility that MSL would lose the client if she canceled. How would her decision affect Ken's decision to hire other women consultants? Karen wanted to get some feedback from the other consultants at the staff meeting before making her decision.

Ray Terrell

Back at MSL's New Orleans office on the morning of the monthly staff meeting, Ray Terrell's mind began to wander. Only twenty-four hours ago he had been in Dallas, Texas, in the midst of a tension-filled Management Committee meeting and a potentially explosive discussion with Bill Matthews, Vice-President of Refining–Southwest Region for a major energy concern. Ray had decided that this was an issue to be discussed by the entire MSL professional staff, as it had serious implications for MSL's future. He began to jot down notes in preparation for the meeting. . . .

During the first quarter of this year, Ray had become involved in an OD effort at one of the company's Southwest Region refineries located in Corpus Christi, Texas. Terrell, representing MSL, spent approximately three weeks in the data-gathering phase of the OD process, which included employee-consultant interviews in all refinery divisions. According to MSL's standard practice, prior to conducting the employee interviews, Ray had assured the employees that any information obtained during the interviews would be kept confidential. The Management Committee was aware of this practice but had no explicit confidentiality agreement with MSL. MSL had no formalized written statement on the subject of confidentiality in their signed contracts due to their philosophy of tailoring each OD effort to the particular client. It was strongly believed by all MSL consultants that their current practice was in the best interest of the client organization, the individual, and the consulting firm. This was based on the premise that a consulting organization's ability to connect accurate data about individuals and corporations was critical to successful performance. Effective data-gathering depended on trust that the information would not be used to the possible detriment of the individual unless clearly indicated up front.

Upon completion of the data-gathering phase, Ray compiled his results into a written document and presented it to the refinery's Management Committee which included Bill Matthews as an ex officio member. The report emphasized a heavy concern for race relations as expressed by black wage earners in particular. Ray had stated, in a broad general sense, that blacks felt mistreated given their seniority and the jobs they got in relation to other refinery workers with similar seniority. He supported this racial concern by stating that blacks felt they were not receiving as adequate career counseling and development as white workers were (both in technical areas and otherwise) so that blacks could compete for higher level positions. Ray's report concluded with recommended action steps which specific supervisory training in EEO awareness and counseling skills as the first steps. In addition, Ray would undertake an intensive study and revamping of the company's employee training program and practices.

Following Ray's presentation, Plant Manager Ron Gallagher called for a discussion. The EEO issue was of great concern to the entire committee, given an impending Department of Labor audit within a few months. Negative audit results could cause significant delay in the expected promotions of Ron (to a headquarters divisional V-P position) and Bill Matthews (to President of the corporation's small Chemical Division) at the end of the year. It was obvious to Ray that he had hit one of the company's most vulnerable spots. This meant that chances for successful implementation of his recommendations were even greater than he had expected. As a result, MSL could probably count on at least six months of steady billing. This would definitely please Ken.

The Management Committee discussion did not seem to be accomplishing anything. It was apparent the members were quite uncomfortable with the topic of EEO in addition to being defensive of their own subdivisions' nondiscriminatory posture. Finally Bill Matthews spoke. He congratulated Ray on his effective presentation, reiterated his deep concern for the findings, and stated that he was all for immediate action. However, it would be essential for the Management Committee to find out exactly who had expressed these concerns so that steps could be taken to rectify their situation right away. After all, Ray and MSL were working for management. Of course, his major concern was for the employees, but there was the upcoming audit to consider, since EEO charges or possible lawsuits could easily result in a prolonged audit and bad publicity. Once the situation was under control, the problem as a whole could be tackled.

When Matthews finished there was an awkward silence in the room. Ron Gallagher made an attempt to neutralize the situation by acknowledging the refinery's potential racial problem and admitting that blacks never came to any of the refinery's social gatherings.

Terrell could not believe that Matthews had the nerve to ask for identification of his information sources in front of the entire Management Committee! He was even more enraged that no one had objected to the request. Terrell did not know how to respond. As a management consultant he did have a responsibility to management, but had Matthews overstepped the professional boundary? This company was currently MSL's largest client, having produced the majority of projects and billing days throughout MSL's short history. If this situation got out of control, there was the possibility that the relationship would be severed. This could be devastating to MSL, since their diversification strategy targets for this quarter had not been realized. At this point MSL was relying heavily on its current clients to produce further projects in other areas of their organizations. This vertical penetration marketing strategy had worked very well with almost no specific sales effort on the part of MSL consultants and now seemed crucial to the firm's immediate survival.

Since all refinery divisions were represented on the Management Committee would Ray be putting MSL's immediate financial future on the line if he did not divulge his information sources? Additionally, if Gallagher and Matthews did get those promotions into the upper echelons of the company, would he be jeopardizing MSL's future with the entire corporation and MSL's reputation in the

industry? Finally, one of his goals as an MSL consultant was to improve organizational effectiveness. If he gave the Management Committee the information Matthews wanted, he could be the catalyst needed for the refinery to address the racial concerns affecting the organization's effectiveness.

Ray's mind raced through his confused thoughts. Matthews would be expecting an answer. Ray decided to hold his tongue for the moment and told the Management Committee he'd be in touch with them at their meeting next week.

THE STAFF MEETING

Ken opened the staff meeting with a brief discussion of the various projects in progress. He then asked the consultants if they had any problems they wanted to discuss. Four hands shot up and Karen, Phil, Ray, and Fred then presented the problems confronting them. Once the initial recitals had been made, Ken recommended a fifteen-minute coffee break so everyone could digest the problems they had just heard about. He asked the group to think about possible courses of action for each situation, the pros and cons of each, and what their final recommendations would be.

Step 2: Prepare the case for class discussion.

Step 3: Answer the following questions, individually, in small groups, or with the entire class, as directed by your instructor:

Description
1. Describe the situation. What symptoms of problems exist?

Diagnosis
2. Diagnose the situation. What problems exist? What theories and concepts help explain the problems?

Prescription
3. Prescribe ways of improving the situation.

Action
4. Devise an action plan.

Step 4: Discussion. In small groups, with the entire class, or in written form, share your answers to the above questions.

This case was written by Molly Batson and Nancy Sherman under the supervision of Associate Professor Jeffrey A. Barach, A. B. Freeman School of Business. This case has been prepared as a basis for class discussion rather than to illustrate effective or ineffective administrative practices. Copyright 1982 by the School of Business, Tulane University. Reproduced with permission.

Case Analysis

Step 1: Choose a problematic situation you encountered in an organization of which you were a member.

Step 2: Describe the situation.

Step 3: Diagnose the situation.

Step 4: Prescribe ways of improving the situation.

Step 5: Devise an action plan.

Step 6: Discussion. Share your analysis with the rest of the class, in small groups, with the entire class, or in written form.

Organizational Analysis

Step 1: Choose an organization of which you were a member.

Step 2: Describe the interpersonal processes, organizational structure, and work design that characterized the organization.

Step 3: Diagnose any problems that existed in the organization.

Step 4: Prescribe ways of improving the situation.

Step 5: Devise an action plan.

Step 6: Discussion. Share your analysis with the rest of the class, in small groups, with the entire class, or in written form.

CONCLUDING COMMENTS

Managers and other change agents can use a variety of approaches to implement change in organizations. Action involves identifying forces for and against change, overcoming resistance to change, and selecting the most appropriate change agent. You have performed these steps as a consultant to the Bridgeton Temporary Services, in "Managing an Organizational Crisis," and in analyzing the First Canadian Club case.

Planning for action in an organization of your choice requires an examination of the entire change process as well as proposals for evaluating strategies and methods of institutionalizing the organizational improvements. In addition, the effectiveness of organizational change likely will increase if well-defined boundaries to the change problems exist; employees perceive a set of issues as vital, salient, and important to improve; key parties are involved; participants receive training in problem solving and decision making; strong leadership functions; and rewards support the change. Finally, in this chapter we considered the issue of organizational effectiveness. In studying Managerial Systems Ltd. and both a case situation and an organization of your choice, you used the diagnostic approach to evaluate and increase organizational effectiveness.

ENDNOTES

[1] D. A. Kolb and A. L. Frohman, An organization development approach to consulting, *Sloan Management Review* (Fall 1970): 51–65.

[2] This technique is based on an early work in the field, K. Lewin, *Field Theory in Social Science* (New York: Harper & Row, 1951).

[3] W. French, Organization development—Objectives, assumptions, and strategies, *California Management Review* 12 (1969): 23–34.

[4] W. H. Wagel and H. Z. Levine, HR '90: Challenges and opportunities, *Personnel* (June 1990): 18–42.

[5] *Ibid.,* p. 28.

[6] E. F. Hamilton, An empirical study of factors predicting change agents' effectiveness, *Journal of Applied Behavioral Science* 24(1) (1988): 37–59.

[7] K. Albrecht, *Organization Development: A Total Systems Approach to Positive Change in Any Business Organization* (Englewood Cliffs, N.J.: Prentice-Hall, 1983).

[8] M. B. Miles and R. A. Schmuck, The nature of organization development. In *Organization Development in Schools,* ed. R. A. Schmuck and M. B. Miles (La Jolla, Calif.: University Associates, 1976).

[9] *Ibid.*

[10] J. M. Bartunek and M. Moch, First-order, second-order, and third-order change and organizational development interventions, *Journal of Applied Behavioral Science* 23(4) (1987): 483–500; see also J. M. Bartunek, The multiple cognitions and conflicts associated with second order organizational change. In J. K. Murnigham, ed., *Social Psychology in Organizations: Advances in Theory and Research* (in press).

[11] Bartunek, Multiple cognitions and conflicts.

[12] W. L. French and C. H. Bell, Jr., *Organization Development: Behavioral Science Interventions for Organization Improvement,* 3rd ed. (Englewood Cliffs, N.J.: Prentice-Hall, 1984).

[13] R. W. Bass and M. V. Mariono, Organization development in Italy, *Group and Organization Studies* 12(3) (1987): 245–256.

[14] W. L. French, A checklist for organizing and implementing an OD effort. In *Organization Development: Theory, Practice, and Research,* ed. W. L. French, C. H. Bell, Jr., and R. A. Zawacki (Dallas: Business Publications, 1978).

[15] G. Barczak, C. Smith, and D. Wilemon, Managing large-scale organizational change, *Organizational Dynamics* 16 (Autumn 1987): 22–35.

[16] L. P. White and K. C. Wooten, Ethical dilemmas in various stages of organizational development, *Academy of Management Review* 8(2) (1983): 690–697.

[17] R. H. Kilmann, T. J. Covin, and Associates, eds., *Corporate Transformation: Revitalizing Organizations for a Competitive World* (San Francisco: Jossey-Bass, 1988).

[18] D. K. Hurst, Cautionary tales from the Kalahari: How hunters become herders (and may have trouble changing back again), *Academy of Management Executive* 5(3) (1991): 74–86.

[19] R. Beckhard, The executive management of transformational change. In Kilmann et al., *Corporate Transformation.*

[20] M. L. Tushman, W. H. Newman, and E. Romanelli, Convergence and upheaval: Managing the unsteady pace of organizational evolution. In K. S. Cameron, R. E. Sutton, and D. A. Whetton, eds., *Readings in Organizational Decline: Framework, Research, and Prescriptions* (Cambridge, Mass.: Ballinger, 1988).

[21] See C. J. G. Gersick, Revolutionary change theories: A multilevel exploration of the punctuated equilibrium paradigm, *Academy of Management Review* 16(1) (1991): 10–36.

[22] M. L. Tushman and E. Romanelli, Organizational evolution: A metamorphosis model of convergence and reorientation. In L. L. Cummings and B. M. Staw, eds., *Research in Organizational Behavior,* vol. 7 (Greenwich, Conn.: JAI Press, 1985).

[23] J. R. Hackman, The transition that hasn't happened. In J. R. Kimberly and R. E. Quinn, eds., *Managing Organizational Transitions* (Homewood, Ill.: Irwin, 1984).

[24] M. Beer, The critical path for change: Keys to success and failures in six companies. In Kilmann et al., *Corporate Transformation.*

[25] R. M. Kanter, *When Giants Learn to Dance* (New York: Simon & Schuster, 1989).

[26] N. Tichy and D. Ulrich, Revitalizing organizations: The leadership role. In Kimberly and Quinn, *Managing Organizational Transitions.*

[27] See J. M. Bartunek and M. R. Louis, The interplay of organization development and organizational transformation. In W. A. Pasmore and R. W. Woodman, eds., *Research in Organizational Change and Development,* vol. 2 (Greenwich, Conn.: JAI, 1988); J. M. Bartunek, The dynamics of personal and organizational reframing. In R. Quinn and K. Cameron, eds., *Paradox and Transformation: Towards a Theory of Change in Organizations and Management* (Cambridge, Mass.: Ballinger, 1989).

[28] P. Shrivastava and I. I. Mitroff, Strategic management of corporate crises, *Columbia Journal of World Business* 22 (Spring 1987): 5–12.

[29] *Ibid.*

[30] H. Kuklan, Managing crises: Challenges and complexities, *SAM Advanced Management Journal* 51 (Autumn 1986): 39–44.

[31] D. S. Mileti and J. H. Sorenson, Determinants of organizational effectiveness in responding to low-probability catastrophic events, *Columbia Journal of World Business* 22(1) (1987): 13–21.

[32] I. I. Mitroff, Crisis management: Cutting through the confusion, *Sloan Management Review* 29(2) (1988): 15–20.

[33] This model is drawn from D. L. Kirkpatrick, Four steps to measuring training effectiveness, *Personnel Administrator* 28 (November 1983): 19–25.

[34] P. M. Senge, The leader's new work: Building learning organizations, *Sloan Management Review* (Fall 1990): 7–23.

[35] *Ibid.*, p. 9.

[36] P. S. Goodman and J. M. Pennings, eds., *New Perspectives on Organizational Effectiveness* (San Francisco: Jossey-Bass, 1977); *Organization Development,* ed. French et al.; R. H. Kilmann, L. R. Pondy, and D. P. Slevin, eds., *The Management of Organization Design: Research and Methodology,* vol. 2 (New York: Elsevier North-Holland, 1976).

[37] See, for example, J. P. Campbell, On the nature of organizational effectiveness. In Goodman and Pennings, *New Perspectives;* and R. M. Steers, Problems in the measurement of organizational effectiveness, *Administrative Science Quarterly* 20 (1975): 546–558.

[38] K. S. Cameron and D. A. Whetten, Perceptions of organizational effectiveness over organizational life cycles, *Administrative Science Quarterly* (December 1981): 525–544; R. E. Quinn and J. Rohrbaugh, A spatial model of effectiveness criteria: Towards a competing values approach to organizational analysis, *Management Science* (March 1983): 363–377; R. E. Quinn and K. S. Cameron, Organizational life cycles and shifting criteria of effectiveness: Some preliminary evidence, *Management Science* (January 1983): 33–51.

[39] S. Strasser, J. D. Eveland, G. Cummings, O. L. Deniston, and J. H. Romani, Conceptualizing the goal and system models of organizational effectiveness, *Journal of Management Studies* (July 1981): 323; K. S. Cameron, The effectiveness of ineffectiveness. In B. M. Staw and L. L. Cummings, *Research in Organizational Behavior,* vol. 6 (Greenwich, Conn.: JAI Press, 1984).

[40] K. S. Cameron, Critical questions in assessing organizational effectiveness, *Organizational Dynamics* (Autumn 1980): 66–80.

[41] H. W. Lane and J. J. DiStefano, *International Management Behavior: From Policy to Practice,* 2nd ed. (Boston: PWS-Kent, 1992).

[42] Kanter, *When Giants Learn to Dance;* G. P. Zachary, Apple's Gasee plans to resign as shake-up continues, *Wall Street Journal,* February 7, 1990, p. B1.

RECOMMENDED READINGS

Gellerman, W., Frankel, M. S., and Ladenson, R. F. *Values and Ethics in Organization and Human Systems Development: Responding to Dilemmas in Professional Life.* San Francisco: Jossey-Bass, 1990.

Kilmann, R. H. *Managing Beyond the Quick Fix.* San Francisco: Jossey-Bass, 1988.

Masarik, F. *Advances in Organization Development,* vol. 1. Norwood, N.J.: Ablex, 1990.

Mohrman, A. M., Jr., et al., eds. *Large-Scale Organizational Change.* San Francisco: Jossey-Bass, 1989.

Woodman, R., and Pasmore, W., eds. *Research in Organizational Change and Development,* vol. 4. Greenwich, Conn.: JAI Press, 1990.

Name Index

Subject Index